Florida Constitutional Law

Florida Constitutional Law

Cases in Context

Jon L. Mills

PROFESSOR OF LAW, DEAN EMERITUS AND
DIRECTOR OF THE CENTER FOR GOVERNMENTAL RESPONSIBILITY
UNIVERSITY OF FLORIDA LEVIN COLLEGE OF LAW

Mary E. Adkins

MASTER LEGAL SKILLS PROFESSOR
UNIVERSITY OF FLORIDA LEVIN COLLEGE OF LAW

Timothy McLendon

LEGAL SKILLS PROFESSOR AND ASSISTANT DIRECTOR
OF THE CENTER FOR GOVERNMENTAL RESPONSIBILITY
UNIVERSITY OF FLORIDA LEVIN COLLEGE OF LAW

CAROLINA ACADEMIC PRESS
Durham, North Carolina

ISBN   978-1-5310-1879-5
eISBN   978-1-5310-1880-1
LCCN   2020952156

Carolina Academic Press
700 Kent Street
Durham, North Carolina 27701
Telephone (919) 489-7486
www.cap-press.com

Printed in the United States of America

*To my wife Beth for her wisdom, support, and love and to my daughters
Marguerite and Elizabeth who inspire me and give me faith in the
next generation and in the the future.
— Jon L. Mills*

*To my husband Mitchell Prugh, whose love, good judgement,
and support make everything he touches better.
— Mary E. Adkins*

*To Amy, Hannah & Isaiah in appreciation for their love and support.
— Timothy E. McLendon*

Contents

Table of Cases

Acknowledgments

In memoriam, we thank our friends and mentors the late Justice Ben Overton and the late Judge Robert Mann, each of whom interpreted the constitution as judges and taught it as professors at the University of Florida. They provided the building blocks and inspiration for these materials. And we wish to thank our friend and colleague, Deb Cupples, who taught us all how to use words, interpret constitutions, and live a wonderful life.

The authors would like to acknowledge the contributions of the following people for their help with this book. Thank you to TJ Smithers and the team at Carolina Academic Press for their patience and good advice. We also wish to thank:

Blake Bachman

Caroline Bradley

Joel Brown

Timothy Cerio

Betty Donaldson

Al Hadeed

Clay Henderson

Deborah Kearney

Bre Lamb

Hon. Scott Makar

Karen Miller

Mark Natirboff

Mitchell Prugh

Laura Rosenbury

John Wilcox

We also wish to acknowledge the unique perspective on the Florida Constitution provided to us and our students at the University of Florida Levin College of Law through the Overton Lecture Series. The Overton Lectures have been given each year since 2013 by current and former members of the Florida Supreme Court and constitutional law experts. The series was created through the vision and generosity of Judge Karen Miller in memory of the late Justice Ben Overton. Participants have included Justice Barbara Pariente, Justice Charles Canady, Justice Jorge Labarga, Justice Harry Anstead, Justice John Couriel, Justice Alan Lawson, Justice Fred Lewis, and Justice James Perry.

Introduction:
History and Perspective

A. Florida's Constitution: How We Got Here
B. State Constitutions and the U.S. Constitution
   1. *Michigan v. Long*

A. Florida's Constitution:
How We Got Here

Floridians today are governed by a Constitution forged at a time of great change in this state. In the mid-1960s, Florida was poised between its roots in the segregated South and its new growth in the Space Age. Its Constitution, Florida's fifth as a state, had been adopted in 1885, after Reconstruction ended; that Constitution reflected the reassertion of the values of the vanquished Confederates. Yet by the middle of the twentieth century, Florida was rapidly becoming more urban and diverse than any of the other former Confederate states.

Florida's 1838 Constitution is generally counted as its first, as it was drafted in anticipation of statehood; statehood occurred in 1845. Just sixteen years after becoming a state, however, Florida seceded from the Union and adopted a new constitution that began with an "Ordinance of Secession."[1] After the end of the Civil War, four years later, a constitution was drafted but never adopted; though it revoked the Ordinance of Secession, it limited suffrage to white male citizens, and thus did not meet the requirements of Congress.[2]

When Reconstruction came to Florida, the Congress required Florida to hold a convention to create a new constitution. That constitution would have to conform to the federal Constitution, including the Thirteenth and Fourteenth Amendments, requiring equal treatment of people of all races, including formerly enslaved people. In 1868, opposing forces representing "radical" groups, which contained most of the African American delegates (who numbered 18 of the 48 delegates), and "moderates" argued over the contents of the next constitution. The moderates left the convention; the radicals continued the work of drafting a constitution. However,

---

1. FLA. CONST. OF 1861, Ordinance of Secession.
2. FLA. CONST. OF 1865, art. VI, §1.

the moderates returned, were eventually recognized as a majority, and prevailed. Thus, the resulting Constitution did not provide for as many protections for African Americans as the radicals fought for.[3] The legislative apportionment scheme favored counties with mostly white populations over those with larger African American populations. Almost all offices were appointed, allowing Northern reformers to retain control of government.[4] However, this Constitution did provide for all men, not just white men, to vote.[5] And compared to the Constitution that would come next, it was practically a model of fairness.

This Constitution established some principles that would remain in the next Constitution. For example, it banned lotteries, and curiously did so in the legislative article.[6] So would the 1885 Constitution.[7] The 1868 Constitution provided for a Lieutenant Governor who would also be President of the Senate, a scheme imitating the U.S. Constitution.[8] The 1885 Constitution would eliminate the Lieutenant Governor position, but keep the Senate President as next in line for the Governor's office.[9] The 1868 Constitution gave the Governor broad appointive powers; he not only appointed his cabinet, but also the county-wide officers in every county, and every judge and state attorney in the state.[10]

Additionally, the 1868 Constitution brought forth some issues that, though erased by the 1885 Constitution, would be revived in the 1968 Constitution and amendments to it. Among these was a statement in the Education article that it was "the paramount duty" of the state to provide for the "ample education" of Floridians.[11] In 1998, a Constitution Revision Commission would revive the "paramount duty" language, although slightly diluted: it declared it "a" (not "the") paramount duty of the state to provide an "adequate" education to Floridians.[12]

The 1868 Constitution barred felons from voting,[13] as had—and as would—all Florida Constitutions until a 2018 amendment reinstated the right of most felons to vote.[14] The legislative implementation of that amendment, however, required "completion of sentence" to include payment of financial obligations.

---

3. Talbot D'Alemberte, The Florida State Constitution (2d ed.) (Oxford: Oxford University Press 2017), 10–11.

4. *Id.* at 11.

5. Fla. Const. of 1868, art. XIV, § 1.

6. Fla. Const. of 1868, art. IV, § 20.

7. Fla. Const. of 1885, art. III, § 23.

8. Fla. Const. of 1868, art. V, § 14.

9. Fla. Const. of 1885, art. IV, § 19.

10. Fla. Const. of 1868, art. V, §§ 17, 19; Fla. Const. of 1868, art. VI, §§ 3, 7, 9, 15, 19.

11. Fla. Const. of 1868, art. VIII, § 1.

12. Fla. Const. of 1968, art. IX, § 1 (am. 1998).

13. Fla. Const. of 1868, art. XIV, § 2.

14. Fla. Const. of 1838, art. VI, §§ 4, 13; Fla. Const. of 1861, art. VI, §§ 2, 9; Fla. Const. of 1865, art. VI, §§ 2, 9; Fla. Const. of 1885, art. VI, §§ 4, 5; Fla. Const. of 1968, art. VI, § 4 (am. 2018).

The 1868 Constitution allowed Seminole Indians to have a seat in each house of the Legislature.[15] No other Florida Constitution provided for Seminole representation. In fact, the 1861 Constitution restricted legislative office-holding to white male citizens of the Confederate States of America, and the 1865 Constitution to white male citizens of the United States.[16]

Finally, both the 1868 and 1885 Constitutions could be amended only by constitutional convention or by the Legislature. However, the 1868 document provided that amendments must be approved by two successive Legislatures, making amendment more difficult; the 1885 Constitution provided for only one.[17] In stark contrast, and perhaps in revolt, the 1968 Constitution would provide no fewer than four ways to amend—and later a fifth.[18]

Reconstruction ended and, without the heavy thumb of Northern reformers, the native whites regained control. The Constitution they drafted in 1885 can be seen as a reaction to that of 1868. The 1885 Constitution did somewhat reflect the values of the people, but the only people reflected were white men. The 1885 Constitution mandated that schools be segregated—even though the public school system was only larval at the time.[19] It banned mixed-race marriages "forever."[20] Though it provided for a basic court system, it also allowed the Legislature to create courts on an ad hoc basis, leading to a wildly uneven judicial system in which courts and jurisdictions varied county by county.[21]

Home rule for local governments barely existed; any needs beyond the routine had to be approved by the Legislature, making legislators essentially czars over their districts.[22] But the Legislature met only once every two years, and only for sixty days.[23] As a result, local bills choked the legislative agenda, making significant legislation difficult to squeeze into the sixty days.

Power in the executive branch was diffuse to the point of absurdity. The Governor could not be re-elected, and had no Lieutenant Governor.[24] After all, as some stated, a Lieutenant Governor would have only one job: to wait for the Governor to stop breathing.[25] But the Governor shared governing duties with a "cabinet" of six other officials elected statewide: the Superintendent of Public Instruction, the Attorney

---

15. Fla. Const. of 1868, art. XVI, §7.

16. Fla. Const. of 1861, art. IV, §§5, 6; Fla. Const. of 1865, art. IV, §§4, 5.

17. Fla. Const. of 1868, art. XVII, §§1, 2; Fla. Const. of 1885, art. XVII, §§1, 2.

18. Fla. Const. of 1968, art. XI, (am. 1988).

19. Fla. Const. of 1885, art. XII, §12.

20. Fla. Const. of 1885, art. XVI, §24.

21. Fla. Const. of 1885, art. VI.

22. Mary E. Adkins, Making Modern Florida (Gainesville: University Press of Florida 2016) 7, 95.

23. Fla. Const. of 1885, art. III, §2.

24. Fla. Const. of 1885, art. IV, §§2, 19.

25. Reubin O'D. Askew, interview by Mike Vasilinda, May 9, 2001. Tallahassee: Legislative Research Center & Museum.

General, the Commissioner of Agriculture, the Secretary of State, the Commissioner of Insurance, and the Comptroller; the occupants of these positions could be re-elected indefinitely.[26] Thus, the Governor was actually the least powerful of the seven. These seven elected executives convened as departments overseeing a bewildering and byzantine network of subjects—so many that no one seemed to know exactly how many there were. Most guesses were around 150. The scheme was often referred to as the "plural executive." Wags called it the "seven Governors" plan.

Voting was available, nominally, to all men who had lived in Florida for one year and in the county in which he wished to vote for six months.[27] But the Constitution allowed the Legislature to institute a poll tax, which it did in 1889, keeping most blacks and many poor whites from voting.[28] It also provided that anyone ever convicted of a laundry list of crimes could not vote unless his rights had been specifically restored; that "insane" people similarly could not vote; and that anyone associated with betting or with fighting a duel could not hold public office.[29] At least the 1838 ban from public office of bankers and "ministers of the gospel" had been removed.[30]

Legislative apportionment was accurate for 1885, when most residents lived within fifty miles of Georgia or Alabama. However, as central and southern Florida experienced periods of steep population growth during the twentieth century, the Constitution's strictures on the apportionment provisions made meaningful reapportionment nearly impossible. For example, the Constitution provided that every county have at least one representative, but that no county have more than three. By 1960, when Dade County had more than 900,000 people but, for example, Lafayette County had fewer than 3,000, the apportionment scheme required each of Dade's three representatives to represent 300,000 people while Lafayette's one representative represented 3,000.[31]

By the time World War II was over and soldiers and sailors began returning home, many moved to Florida, creating another population boom. This one never stopped, and nearly all of the growth was in the south and central parts of the state. Yet most of the legislative districts remained in the north, as they had been drawn in 1885.

This sustained, rapid population growth gave rise to a number of problems. First, the Legislature was malapportioned. Because most people resided in South Florida, and most legislative districts were in the north of the state, the residents in the north had more legislators paying attention to their needs than southern residents did. As mentioned above, each district in the southern part of the state contained many more people than each district in the northern part. During much of the period of the

---

26. FLA. CONST. OF 1885, art. IV, §20.
27. FLA. CONST. OF 1885, art. VI, §1.
28. FLA. CONST. OF 1885, art. VI, §8.
29. FLA. CONST. OF 1885, art. VI, §§4, 5.
30. FLA. CONST. OF 1838, art. VI, §§3, 10.
31. Florida Census: 1960, http://fcit.usf.edu/florida/docs/c/census/1960.htm.

1950s and 1960s, less than twenty percent of the population could elect a majority of representatives in either house of the Legislature.[32]

Worse for the growing areas, most legislators representing the northern districts came from rural areas that had not experienced, and did not wish to experience, the rapid growth South Florida had seen. They had no sympathy for the needs the population growth in South Florida had created. Seeing the large population of newcomers—people not from Florida and not from the South—the rural legislators formed a bloc, explicitly promising one another to vote together to preserve the "Southern way of life." A newspaper editor dubbed the group the "Pork Chop Gang," referring to the "pork" the legislators brought to their rural districts.[33] The nickname stuck, and the legislators themselves embraced it.

The Pork Chop Gang exerted complete control over the legislative agenda, and resisted advice and outside attempts to make the apportionment scheme more equitable. After all, a fair apportionment, one that would put most districts in the south, where the people were, would drain the north of districts. The Pork Chop Gang members occupied the districts that would disappear. Were meaningful reapportionment to occur, the Pork Choppers would lose their jobs.

Even if the members of the Pork Chop gang had wanted a more representative apportionment, they would have been hard-pressed to create one under the 1885 Constitution. Remember that it required each county to have at least one representative and no county to have more than three.[34] Under this straitjacket, Dade County, with its million residents, could do no better than three representatives, and Lafayette and the other tiny counties could do no worse than one. To change apportionment significantly, the Constitution would have to change.

The Constitution, though, could be changed only two ways. The first, a full-fledged constitution convention, was unlikely to ever occur. The only other way to amend the Constitution was through the Legislature.[35]

The Pork Choppers were in charge of the barbecue, so there would be no hog turning on the spit.

A second difficulty the 1885 Constitution created was the chaos its crazy-quilt court system caused. It called for a state Supreme Court, Circuit Courts, Criminal Courts, County Courts, County Judges, and Justices of the Peace.[36] Though each county was required to have a county judge, county courts were optional creatures

---

32. Manning J. Dauer, *Florida: The Different State, in* SUSAN A. MacMANUS, ED., REAPPORTIONMENT AND REPRESENTATION IN FLORIDA: A HISTORICAL COLLECTION (Tampa: University of South Florida, 1991).

33. STEPHEN ANSOLABEHERE & JAMES M. SNYDER, JR., THE END OF INEQUALITY: ONE PERSON, ONE VOTE AND THE TRANSFORMATION OF AMERICAN POLITICS (New York: Norton, 2008); ALLEN MORRIS, RECONSIDERATION: SECOND GLANCES AT FLORIDA LEGISLATIVE EVENTS (Tallahassee: Officer of the Clerk, Florida House of Representatives, 1982).

34. FLA. CONST. OF 1885, art. VII, § 3.

35. FLA. CONST. OF 1885, art. XVII.

36. FLA. CONST. OF 1885, art. V, § 1.

of the Legislature and, when created, had a different jurisdiction than county judges did.[37] These optional county courts heard appeals from justice-of-the-peace courts; appellants could demand de novo review.[38] Though the salaries of justices and circuit judges were prescribed in the Constitution, county judges' compensation was "provided by law."[39] Every county also had at least two justices of the peace, whose jurisdiction varied according to whether that county had an optional County Court.[40] Where there was a justice of the peace, there was also a constable.[41] Escambia County and any other county where the Legislature deemed it "expedient" got an additional court, called the Court of Criminal Record.[42] The Legislature could also establish municipal courts, and, of course, any court the Legislature could create it could also abolish.[43]

The variation among courts and jurisdictions from county to county made for confusion among litigants, but served as job security for experienced lawyers, whose knowledge of the ins and outs of jurisdictions gave them an advantage over newer lawyers.

Third, the weakness of the Governor's office did not spring only from the Governor's status as the lone state-level elected officer who could not succeed himself. It also was vulnerable because the Governor had no Lieutenant. Instead, in the event the Governor could not complete his term, the office would fall to the President of the Senate and, failing that, the Speaker of the House.[44]

It took nearly seventy years for the fallacy of this scheme to become apparent. In 1952, Governor Dan McCarty was elected at the healthy young age of forty. Before he had been in office a year, however, he died. The President of the Senate, Charley Johns of Starke, became acting Governor—a man who had been elected to his state senate seat in a rural district which, at its most recent census, had a population of only 11,457, less than one-half of one percent of the state's population.[45] Johns, a Pork Chopper, had very different priorities than McCarty had had, and replaced several of McCarty's appointees with his own. He lost resoundingly in the special midterm election to fill the remaining two years of McCarty's original term. His short tenure, combined with the stark policy differences between him and his predecessor, made clear that the gubernatorial succession scheme was flawed: it allowed a person elected by a tiny percentage of the population to govern the state with no commitment to continuing the policies of his predecessor.

Fourth, the lack of power of municipal government officials to make major decisions concerning their localities meant that localities depended on their legislators

---

37. FLA. CONST. OF 1885, art. V, §§ 16, 17, 18.
38. FLA. CONST. OF 1885, art. V, § 18.
39. FLA. CONST. OF 1885, art. V, § 16.
40. FLA. CONST. OF 1885, art. V, § 22.
41. FLA. CONST. OF 1885, art. V, § 23.
42. FLA. CONST. OF 1885, art. V, § 24.
43. FLA. CONST. OF 1885, art. V, § 32, 34.
44. FLA. CONST. OF 1885, art. IV, § 19.
45. Florida Census: 1950, http://fcit.usf.edu/florida/docs/c/census/1950.htm.

for any positive structural change.[46] But the Constitution provided that the Legislature met for only sixty days every two years. By the time the legislative session started, legislators had armloads of local bills to pass; little time was left to consider the needs of the state as a whole.

Fifth, the Constitution retained its racist provisions. Though *Brown v. Board of Education* had been decided in 1954 and 1955, the provision mandating racially segregated schools remained in the Constitution.[47] And the provision allowing a poll tax remained, although the Legislature had removed the law implementing one in 1938.[48]

By the early 1960s, the world's eyes were on Florida—Cape Canaveral, in Brevard County, in particular—as it led the race to the moon. The space industry led Brevard to experience a population increase of 471 percent between 1950 and 1960, and the county was on track to more than double between 1960 and 1970.[49] In 1965, Walt Disney announced he had bought tens of thousands of acres of swampy land in Central Florida to build what he was then calling Disneyland East.

Yet Florida's government, as constructed by its Constitution, was a backward-facing embarrassment, its legislators mulishly favoring rural interests over urban needs and its court system unable to provide uniform justice throughout the state.

In the years following World War II, groups interested in government had attempted to draft new constitutions, but no effort stuck. The Florida Bar created two drafts, both of which the Legislature ignored; the League of Women Voters published a "yardstick for constitutional revision." The nearly all-male Legislature, still living in an era that dismissed women, paid no attention to it. When LeRoy Collins was Governor, from 1954 through 1960, he tried nearly every year to encourage the formation of a new constitution, from commissions to committees to workshops. The Pork Chop Legislature, displeased with the "urban" Tallahassee reformer who had defeated their rural Bradford County chum Charley Johns in the race for Governor, made it a point not to approve or even encourage Collins's efforts.[50]

Then, in 1962, the U.S. Supreme Court decided *Baker v. Carr*, in which it ruled that federal courts could become involved in state legislative apportionment suits.[51] The same day, a Florida case was filed in the United States District Court for the Southern District of Florida, challenging Florida's apportionment scheme. The case

---

46. FLA. CONST. OF 1885, art. VIII, §8; FLA. CONST. OF 1885, art. III, §§20, 21, 24.

47. 347 U.S. 483 (1954); 349 U.S. 294 (1955); FLA. CONST. OF 1885, art. XII, §12.

48. Florida abolished the poll tax in 1938. U.S. Senator from Florida Spessard Holland led the charge that abolished poll taxes in federal elections in 1964 with the passage of the 24th amendment. Darryl Paulson, *Florida's History of Suppressing Black Votes*, TAMPA BAY TIMES, October 11, 2013.

49. Florida Census: 1950, http://fcit.usf.edu/florida/docs/c/census/1950.htm; Florida Census: 1960, http://fcit.usf.edu/florida/docs/c/census/1960.htm; Florida Census: 1970, http://fcit.usf.edu/florida/docs/c/census/1970.htm.

50. See generally MARY E. ADKINS, MAKING MODERN FLORIDA: HOW THE SPIRIT OF REFORM SHAPED A NEW STATE CONSTITUTION, Chapter 1 (Gainesville, FL: University Press of Florida 2016).

51. *Baker v. Carr*, 369 U.S. 185 (1962).

would become known as *Swann v. Adams*, and, like apportionment cases in many states, would be influenced by evolving federal standards for apportionment. When, in 1964, the Supreme Court decided a group of consolidated cases known as *Reynolds v. Sims*, it established "one person, one vote" as the law of the land.[52] It decided *Swann v. Adams*, part of another group of state apportionment cases, one week after *Reynolds*, holding *Swann* and the other cases to the *Reynolds* standard.[53]

In the meantime, Florida, like other states, had paid attention when *Baker* had been decided. In the two years after *Baker*, most states accomplished some form of reapportionment.[54] In Florida, the Legislature took baby steps toward better apportionment with each decision in the *Swann v. Adams* saga.[55] But it was constrained by its Constitution's apportionment rules.

By 1965, the Pork Chop Gang's hold had loosened just enough that the Legislature was able to pass a joint resolution to establish another constitution revision commission, one with the mission of creating a new constitution.[56] Like the commissions established in the 1950s, its recommendations would have to be approved by the Legislature before they could appear on the ballot. Had the Legislature changed enough to pass a new proposed constitution to the voters for approval?

The commission met throughout 1966. Its chair, Chesterfield Smith, was then known as a forceful and powerful lawyer and lobbyist for the phosphate industry, a notorious polluter. What he was not yet famous for was his reformist streak. That quality would flower during his role leading the Constitution Revision Commission (and would even, eventually, cause him to curb his phosphate clients' excesses).

The commission, led by Smith and peopled with young reformers who would later become well-known (among them Reubin Askew and Lawton Chiles), drafted a new constitution that was devoid of racist language, that strengthened individual rights, and that expanded home rule. It called for the Legislature to meet yearly, as the 1868 Constitution had.[57] It did not appreciably strengthen the office of Governor, however, even though Smith and others argued mightily to eliminate the elected cabinet.

The draft constitution went to the Legislature in January 1967 to await its fate. But that fate changed without notice when, on the opening day of the special session at which the Legislature was to take up constitution reform, the U.S. Supreme Court ruled on the latest apportionment scheme challenged in *Swann v. Adams*.[58] The Court

---

52. *Reynolds v. Sims*, 377 U.S. 533 (1964).

53. *Swann v. Adams (I)*, 378 U.S. 553 (1964).

54. Bernard Schwartz, Super Chief: Earl Warren and His Supreme Court—A Judicial Biography 417 (New York: New York University Press, 1983).

55. *Sobel v. Adams*, 285 F. Supp. 316 (S.D. Fla. 1962); *Sobel v. Adams*, 214 F. Supp. 811 (S.D. Fla. 1963); *Swann v. Adams*, 379 F. 871 (1964); *Swann v. Adams*, 258 F. Supp. 819 (S.D. Fla. 1965).

56. SB 65-977 (1965).

57. Fla. Const. of 1868, art. IV, § 2.

58. 385 U.S. 440 (1967).

once again invalidated the apportionment and told the Legislature that, this time, the Court, and not the Legislature, would create a fair scheme.

It was the Legislature elected under the Court-approved apportionment scheme that finally met to consider the new proposed constitution. Whether the previous Legislature would have approved the revision commission's proposal will never be known, but the new reformed Legislature—the one that finally gave full representation to the population centers in the state—approved the new constitution with just a handful of changes and passed it on to the voters. The voters approved their new Constitution in November of 1968.

Among the changes the Legislature had made to the new Constitution was, perhaps surprisingly, to strengthen the office of the Governor. The new Constitution allowed the Governor to serve two terms, not just one, and provided for a Lieutenant Governor.[59]

The new Constitution did not, however, contain a judicial article. Though the revision commission had passed one to the Legislature, the Legislature could not agree on a version to send to the voters. That part of the Constitution would not pass at the ballot box until four years later, in 1972. It gave Florida the uniformly organized four-tier judicial system we now know: a seven-justice Supreme Court, District Courts of Appeal, multi-county judicial circuits (currently twenty), and county courts.[60]

Several aspects of the 1968 Constitution harked back to the 1868 Reconstruction Constitution: both have a Legislature that meets annually;[61] both have a Lieutenant Governor;[62] the 1968 Constitution was amended in 1998 to eliminate half the elected cabinet, edging closer to the all-appointive cabinet of the 1868 Constitution;[63] both have appellate judges appointed, albeit through different methods;[64] both explicitly value public education.[65]

But one of the more remarkable features of the 1968 Constitution is its malleability. When adopted in 1968, it provided for four amendment methods: by convention and by the Legislature, as before;[66] by citizens' initiative;[67] and by a method unique, then and now, to Florida: an automatically recurring, appointed Constitution Revision Commission able to place proposals directly on the ballot without legislative approval.[68] Since 1968, a fifth method has been adopted: a Taxation and Budget Reform Com-

---

59. FLA. CONST. OF 1968, art. IV, §§ 2, 5.
60. FLA. CONST. art. V (1972).
61. FLA. CONST. OF 1868, art. IV, § 2; FLA. CONST. OF 1968, art. III, § 3(b).
62. FLA. CONST. OF 1868, art. V, § 14; FLA. CONST. OF 1968, art. IV, § 2.
63. FLA. CONST. OF 1868, art. V, § 17; FLA. CONST. OF 1968, art. IV, § 4 (am. 1998).
64. FLA. CONST. OF 1868, art. VI, § 3; FLA. CONST. OF 1972, art. V, § 11.
65. FLA. CONST. OF 1868, art. VIII, § 1; FLA. CONST. OF 1968, art. IX, § 1(a) (am. 1998).
66. FLA. CONST. OF 1968, art. XI, §§ 1, 4.
67. FLA. CONST. OF 1968, art. XI, § 3.
68. FLA. CONST. OF 1968, art. XI, § 2.

mission, also appointed and also with direct-to-ballot authority, but restricted to tax and budget-related issues.[69]

Not surprisingly, since 1968, Florida's Constitution has been amended more than one hundred times. Whether that is good or bad is in the eye of the beholder—or, perhaps, of the scholar.

B. State Constitutions and the U.S. Constitution

Why do states have constitutions when the United States already has one? That is not an embarrassing question; in fact, in a certain light, it is quite reasonable. In England's North American colonies, colonial constitutions already existed. When the States became United, these now-state constitutions remained as the guiding documents for their respective states. Not until 1787 did the United States adopt its own federal constitution, and it was not met with universal approbation. After all, the delegates had traveled to Philadelphia not to write a new document but to reform the Articles of Confederacy. Their work that summer experienced mission creep, and soon they were crafting not just a contract between states, as the Articles had been, but an entire document created "to form a more perfect Union."

The U.S. Constitution describes relatively few abilities and responsibilities of the federal government, and leaves the remaining governing authority with the states. It is that authority that is described in the various state constitutions. So one major function of a state constitution is to describe the nature of a state's authority. For that reason, most state constitutions are considerably longer than the U.S. Constitution: they have more to do.

So why do so many state constitutions contain language that is similar, if not identical, with language in the U.S. Constitution? More to the point, how should a lawyer treat this language? Courts have provided some guidance, coming down firmly in the position that any judicial decision resting primarily on state constitutional grounds—*even if those grounds consist of language identical to that of the U.S. Constitution*—cannot be reviewed by federal courts.[70] The U.S. Supreme Court articulated this principle in *Michigan v. Long*. An excerpt follows.

A few years before *Michigan v. Long*, Justice Brennan wrote an article published in the *Harvard Law Review* urging state courts to consider the U.S. Supreme Court's rulings on rights to be a floor—a minimum standard—for assessing the extent of human rights:

---

69. Fla. Const. of 1968, art. XI, §6 (am. 1988).
70. *Michigan v. Long*, 463 U.S. 1032, 1039 (1983).

[S]tate courts cannot rest when they have afforded their citizens the full protections of the federal Constitution. State constitutions, too, are a font of
individual liberties, their protections often extending beyond those required
by the Supreme Court's interpretation of federal law. The legal revolution
which has brought federal law to the fore must not be allowed to inhibit the
independent protective force of state law—for without it, the full realization
of our liberties cannot be guaranteed.[71]

Michigan v. Long
463 U.S. 1032 (1983)

Opinion

Justice O'CONNOR delivered the opinion of the Court.

In *Terry v. Ohio*, 392 U.S. 1, 88 S.Ct. 1868, 20 L.Ed.2d 889 (1968), we upheld the
validity of a protective search for weapons in the absence of probable cause to arrest
because it is unreasonable to deny a police officer the right "to neutralize the threat
of physical harm," *id.*, at 24, 88 S.Ct., at 1881, when he possesses an articulable suspicion that an individual is armed and dangerous. We did not, however, expressly
address whether such a protective search for weapons could extend to an area beyond
the person in the absence of probable cause to arrest. In the present case, respondent
David Long was convicted for possession of marijuana found by police in the passenger
compartment and trunk of the automobile that he was driving. The police searched
the passenger compartment because they had reason to believe that the vehicle contained weapons potentially dangerous to the officers. We hold that the protective
search of the passenger compartment was reasonable under the principles articulated
in Terry and other decisions of this Court. We also examine Long's argument that
the decision below rests upon an adequate and independent state ground, and we
decide in favor of our jurisdiction.

* * *

We granted certiorari in this case to consider the important question of the authority of a police officer to protect himself by conducting a Terry-type search of the
passenger compartment of a motor vehicle during the lawful investigatory stop of
the occupant of the vehicle. 459 U.S. 904, 103 S.Ct. 205, 74 L.Ed.2d 164 (1982).

II

Before reaching the merits, we must consider Long's argument that we are without
jurisdiction to decide this case because the decision below rests on an adequate and
independent state ground. The court below referred twice to the state constitution

---

71. William J. Brennan, Jr., *State Constitutions and the Protection of Individual Rights*, 90 Harv.
L. Rev. 489,491 (1977).

in its opinion, but otherwise relied exclusively on federal law.[72] Long argues that the Michigan courts have provided greater protection from searches and seizures under the state constitution than is afforded under the Fourth Amendment, and the references to the state constitution therefore establish an adequate and independent ground for the decision below.

It is, of course, "incumbent upon this Court ... to ascertain for itself ... whether the asserted non-federal ground independently and adequately supports the judgment." *Abie State Bank v. Bryan*, 282 U.S. 765, 773, 51 S.Ct. 252, 255, 75 L.Ed. 690 (1931). Although we have announced a number of principles in order to help us determine whether various forms of references to state law constitute adequate and independent state grounds,[73] we openly admit that we have thus far not developed a satisfying and consistent approach for resolving this vexing issue. In some instances, we have taken the strict view that if the ground of decision was at all unclear, we would dismiss the case. [citations omitted] In more recent cases, we have ourselves examined state law to determine whether state courts have used federal law to guide their application of state law or to provide the actual basis for the decision that was reached. *See Texas v. Brown*, ___ U.S. ___, ___, 103 S.Ct. 1535, 1538, 75 L.Ed.2d 502 (1983) (plurality opinion). *Cf. South Dakota v. Neville*, ___ U.S. ___, ___, 103 S.Ct. 916, 925, 74 L.Ed.2d 748 (1983) (Stevens, J., dissenting). In *Oregon v. Kennedy*, 456 U.S. 667, 670–671, 102 S.Ct. 2083, 2086–2087, 72 L.Ed.2d 416 (1982), we rejected an invitation to remand to the state court for clarification even when the decision rested in part on a case from the state court, because we determined that the state case itself rested upon federal grounds. We added that "[e]ven if the case admitted of more doubt as to whether federal and state grounds for decision were intermixed, the fact that the state

---

72. [FN3.] On the first occasion, the court merely cited in a footnote both the state and federal constitutions. See 413 Mich., at 471, n. 4, 320 N.W.2d, at 869, n. 4. On the second occasion, at the conclusion of the opinion, the court state: "We hold, therefore, that the deputies' search of the vehicle was proscribed by the Fourth Amendment to the United States Constitution and art. 1, §11 of the Michigan Constitution." *Id.*, at 472–47, 320 N.W.2d, at 870.

73. [FN4.] For example, we have long recognized that "where the judgment of a state court rests upon two grounds, one of which is federal and the other non-federal in character, our jurisdiction fails if the non-federal ground is independent of the federal ground and adequate to support the judgment." *Fox Film Corp. v. Muller*, 296 U.S. 207, 210, 56 S.Ct. 183, 184, 80 L.Ed. 158 (1935). We may review a state case decided on a federal ground even if it is clear that there was an available state ground for decision on which the state court could properly have relied. *Beecher v. Alabama*, 389 U.S. 35, 37, n. 3, 88 S.Ct. 189, 190, 19 L.Ed.2d 35 (1967). Also, if, in our view, the state court "'felt compelled by what it understood to be federal constitutional considerations to construe ... its own law in the manner that it did,'" then we will not treat a normally adequate state ground as independent, and there will be no question about our jurisdiction. *Delaware v. Prouse*, 440 U.S. 648, 653, 99 S.Ct. 1391, 1395, 59 L.Ed.2d 660 (1979) (quoting *Zacchini v. Scripps-Howard Broadcasting Co.*, 433 U.S. 562, 568, 97 S.Ct. 2849, 2854, 53 L.Ed.2d 965 (1977)). See also *South Dakota v. Neville*, ___ U.S. ___, ___, n. 3, 103 S.Ct. 1535, 1540, n. 3, 75 L.Ed.2d 502 (1983). Finally, "where the non-federal ground is so interwoven with the [federal ground] as not to be an independent matter, or is not of sufficient breadth to sustain the judgment without any decision of the other, our jurisdiction is plain." *Enterprise Irrigation District v. Farmers Mutual Canal Company*, 243 U.S. 157, 164, 37 S.Ct. 318, 321, 61 L.Ed. 644 (1917).

court relied to the extent it did on federal grounds requires us to reach the merits." *Id.*, at 671, 102 S.Ct., at 2087.

This ad hoc method of dealing with cases that involve possible adequate and independent state grounds is antithetical to the doctrinal consistency that is required when sensitive issues of federal-state relations are involved. Moreover, none of the various methods of disposition that we have employed thus far recommends itself as the preferred method that we should apply to the exclusion of others, and we therefore determine that it is appropriate to reexamine our treatment of this jurisdictional issue in order to achieve the consistency that is necessary.

The process of examining state law is unsatisfactory because it requires us to interpret state laws with which we are generally unfamiliar, and which often, as in this case, have not been discussed at length by the parties. Vacation and continuance for clarification have also been unsatisfactory both because of the delay and decrease in efficiency of judicial administration, see *Dixon v. Duffy*, 344 U.S. 143, 73 S.Ct. 193, 97 L.Ed. 153 (1952), and, more important, because these methods of disposition place significant burdens on state courts to demonstrate the presence or absence of our jurisdiction. See *Philadelphia Newspapers, Inc. v. Jerome*, 434 U.S. 241, 244, 98 S.Ct. 546, 548, 54 L.Ed.2d 506 (1978) (Rehnquist, J., dissenting); *Department of Motor Vehicles v. Rios*, 410 U.S. 425, 427, 93 S.Ct. 1019, 1021, 35 L.Ed.2d 398 (1973) (Douglas, J., dissenting). Finally, outright dismissal of cases is clearly not a panacea because it cannot be doubted that there is an important need for uniformity in federal law, and that this need goes unsatisfied when we fail to review an opinion that rests primarily upon federal grounds and where the independence of an alleged state ground is not apparent from the four corners of the opinion. We have long recognized that dismissal is inappropriate "where there is strong indication ... that the federal constitution as judicially construed controlled the decision below." [*Minnesota v.*] *National Tea Co.*, *supra*, 309 U.S., at 556, 60 S.Ct., at 679 (1940).

Respect for the independence of state courts, as well as avoidance of rendering advisory opinions, have been the cornerstones of this Court's refusal to decide cases where there is an adequate and independent state ground. It is precisely because of this respect for state courts, and this desire to avoid advisory opinions, that we do not wish to continue to decide issues of state law that go beyond the opinion that we review, or to require state courts to reconsider cases to clarify the grounds of their decisions. Accordingly, when, as in this case, a state court decision fairly appears to rest primarily on federal law, or to be interwoven with the federal law, and when the adequacy and independence of any possible state law ground is not clear from the face of the opinion, we will accept as the most reasonable explanation that the state court decided the case the way it did because it believed that federal law required it to do so. If a state court chooses merely to rely on federal precedents as it would on the precedents of all other jurisdictions, then it need only make clear by a plain statement in its judgment or opinion that the federal cases are being used only for the purpose of guidance, and do not themselves compel the result that the court has reached. In this way, both justice and judicial administration will be greatly improved. If the state court decision indicates clearly and expressly that it is alternatively based on bona fide separate, adequate, and independent grounds, we, of course, will not undertake to review the decision.

This approach obviates in most instances the need to examine state law in order to decide the nature of the state court decision, and will at the same time avoid the danger of our rendering advisory opinions. It also avoids the unsatisfactory and intrusive practice of requiring state courts to clarify their decisions to the satisfaction of this Court. We believe that such an approach will provide state judges with a clearer opportunity to develop state jurisprudence unimpeded by federal interference, and yet will preserve the integrity of federal law. "It is fundamental that state courts be left free and unfettered by us in interpreting their state constitutions. But it is equally important that ambiguous or obscure adjudications by state courts do not stand as barriers to a determination by this Court of the validity under the federal constitution of state action." *National Tea Co., supra*, 309 U.S., at 557, 60 S.Ct., at 679.

The principle that we will not review judgments of state courts that rest on adequate and independent state grounds is based, in part, on "the limitations of our own jurisdiction." *Herb v. Pitcairn*, 324 U.S. 117, 125, 65 S.Ct. 459, 463, 89 L.Ed. 789 (1945).[74] The jurisdictional concern is that we not "render an advisory opinion, and if the same judgment would be rendered by the state court after we corrected its views of federal laws, our review could amount to nothing more than an advisory opinion." *Id.*, at 126, 65 S.Ct., at 463. Our requirement of a "plain statement" that a decision rests upon adequate and independent state grounds does not in any way authorize the rendering of advisory opinions. Rather, in determining, as we must, whether we have jurisdiction to review a case that is alleged to rest on adequate and independent state grounds, see *Abie State Bank v. Bryan, supra*, 282 U.S., at 773, 51 S.Ct., at 255, we merely assume that there are no such grounds when it is not clear from the opinion itself that the state court relied upon an adequate and independent state ground and when it fairly appears that the state court rested its decision primarily on federal law.

Our review of the decision below under this framework leaves us unconvinced that it rests upon an independent state ground. Apart from its two citations to the state constitution, the court below relied exclusively on its understanding of *Terry* and other federal cases. Not a single state case was cited to support the state court's holding that the search of the passenger compartment was unconstitutional.[75] Indeed,

---

74. [FN7.] In *Herb v. Pitcairn*, 324 U.S. 117, 128, 65 S.Ct. 459, 464, 89 L.Ed. 789 (1945), the Court also wrote that it was desirable that state courts "be asked rather than told what they have intended." It is clear that we have already departed from that view in those cases in which we have examined state law to determine whether a particular result was guided or compelled by federal law. Our decision today departs further from *Herb* insofar as we disfavor further requests to state courts for clarification, and we require a clear and express statement that a decision rests on adequate and independent state grounds. However, the "plain statement" rule protects the integrity of state courts for the reasons discussed above. The preference for clarification expressed in *Herb* has failed to be a completely satisfactory means of protecting the state and federal interests that are involved.

75. [FN9.] At oral argument, Long argued that the state court relied on its decision in *People v. Reed*, 393 Mich. 342, 224 N.W.2d 867, cert. denied, 422 U.S. 1044, 95 S.Ct. 2660, 45 L.Ed.2d 696 (1975). See Tr. of Oral Arg., at 29. However, the court cited that case only in the context of a statement

the court declared that the search in this case was unconstitutional because "[t]he Court of Appeals erroneously applied the principles of *Terry v. Ohio* ... to the search of the interior of the vehicle in this case." 413 Mich., at 471, 320 N.W.2d, at 869. The references to the state constitution in no way indicate that the decision below rested on grounds in any way independent from the state court's interpretation of federal law. Even if we accept that the Michigan Constitution has been interpreted to provide independent protection for certain rights also secured under the Fourth Amendment, it fairly appears in this case that the Michigan Supreme Court rested its decision primarily on federal law.

Rather than dismissing the case, or requiring that the state court reconsider its decision on our behalf solely because of a mere possibility that an adequate and independent ground supports the judgment, we find that we have jurisdiction in the absence of a plain statement that the decision below rested on an adequate and independent state ground. It appears to us that the state court "felt compelled by what it understood to be federal constitutional considerations to construe ... its own law in the manner it did." *Zacchini v. Scripps-Howard Broadcasting Co.*, 433 U.S. 562, 568, 97 S.Ct. 2849, 2854, 53 L.Ed.2d 965 (1977).[76]

* * *

V

The decision of the Michigan Supreme Court is reversed, and the case is remanded for further proceedings not inconsistent with this opinion.

It is so ordered.

Justice BLACKMUN, concurring in part and concurring in the judgment.

I join Parts I, III, IV, and V of the Court's opinion. While I am satisfied that the Court has jurisdiction in this particular case, I do not join the Court, in Part II of its opinion, in fashioning a new presumption of jurisdiction over cases coming here from state courts. Although I agree with the Court that uniformity in federal criminal

---

that the State did not seek to justify the search in this case "by reference to other exceptions to the warrant requirement." 413 Mich., at 472, 320 N.W.2d, at 869–870 (footnote omitted). The court then noted that *Reed* held that "'A warrantless search and seizure is unreasonable per se and violates the Fourth Amendment of the United States Constitution and art. 1, § 11 of the state constitution unless shown to be within one of the exceptions to the rule.'" *Id.*, at 472–473, n. 8, 320 N.W.2d, at 870, n. 8.

76. [FN10.] There is nothing unfair about requiring a plain statement of an independent state ground in this case. Even if we were to rest our decision on an evaluation of the state law relevant to Long's claim, as we have sometimes done in the past, our understanding of Michigan law would also result in our finding that we have jurisdiction to decide this case. Under state search and seizure law, a "higher standard" is imposed under art. 1, § 11 of the 1963 Michigan Constitution. See *People v. Secrest*, 413 Mich. 521, 525, 321 N.W.2d 368, 369 (1982). If, however, the item seized is, *inter alia*, a "narcotic drug ... seized by a peace officer outside the curtilage of any dwelling house in this state," art. 1, § 11 of the 1963 Michigan Constitution, then the seizure is governed by a standard identical to that imposed by the Fourth Amendment. See *People v. Moore*, 391 Mich. 426, 435, 216 N.W.2d 770, 775 (1974)....

law is desirable, I see little efficiency and an increased danger of advisory opinions in the Court's new approach.

Justice BRENNAN, with whom Justice MARSHALL joins, dissenting. [Dissents were entirely on merits and not on jurisdiction. Thus, the dissents are omitted here.]

Justice STEVENS, dissenting.

The jurisprudential questions presented in this case are far more important than the question whether the Michigan police officer's search of respondent's car violated the Fourth Amendment. The case raises profoundly significant questions concerning the relationship between two sovereigns—the State of Michigan and the United States of America.

The Supreme Court of the State of Michigan expressly held "that the deputies' search of the vehicle was proscribed by the Fourth Amendment of the United States Constitution and art. 1, § 11 of the Michigan Constitution." Pet. for Cert. 19.... The state law ground is clearly adequate to support the judgment, but the question whether it is independent of the Michigan Supreme Court's understanding of federal law is more difficult. Four possible ways of resolving that question present themselves: (1) asking the Michigan Supreme Court directly, (2) attempting to infer from all possible sources of state law what the Michigan Supreme Court meant, (3) presuming that adequate state grounds are independent unless it clearly appears otherwise, or (4) presuming that adequate state grounds are not independent unless it clearly appears otherwise. This Court has, on different occasions, employed each of the first three approaches; never until today has it even hinted at the fourth. In order to "achieve the consistency that is necessary," the Court today undertakes a reexamination of all the possibilities. *Ante*, at 3475. It rejects the first approach as inefficient and unduly burdensome for state courts, and rejects the second approach as an inappropriate expenditure of our resources. *Ibid*. Although I find both of those decisions defensible in themselves, I cannot accept the Court's decision to choose the fourth approach over the third—to presume that adequate state grounds are intended to be dependent on federal law unless the record plainly shows otherwise. I must therefore dissent.

If we reject the intermediate approaches, we are left with a choice between two presumptions: one in favor of our taking jurisdiction, and one against it. Historically, the latter presumption has always prevailed. [citations omitted] The rule, as succinctly stated in *Lynch* [*v. New York ex rel. Pierson*, 293 U.S. 52, 55 S. Ct. 16, 79 L. Ed. 191 (1934)], was as follows:

> "Where the judgment of the state court rests on two grounds, one involving a federal question and the other not, or if it does not appear upon which of two grounds the judgment was based, and the ground independent of a federal question is sufficient in itself to sustain it, this Court will not take jurisdiction." [citations omitted]

The Court today points out that in several cases we have weakened the traditional presumption by using the other two intermediate approaches identified above. Since those two approaches are now to be rejected, however, I would think that stare decisis would call for a return to historical principle. Instead, the Court seems to conclude that because some precedents are to be rejected, we must overrule them all.

Even if I agreed with the Court that we are free to consider as a fresh proposition whether we may take presumptive jurisdiction over the decisions of sovereign states, I could not agree that an expansive attitude makes good sense. It appears to be common ground that any rule we adopt should show "respect for state courts, and [a] desire to avoid advisory opinions." *Ante*, at 3475. And I am confident that all members of this Court agree that there is a vital interest in the sound management of scarce federal judicial resources. All of those policies counsel against the exercise of federal jurisdiction. They are fortified by my belief that a policy of judicial restraint—one that allows other decisional bodies to have the last word in legal interpretation until it is truly necessary for this Court to intervene—enables this Court to make its most effective contribution to our federal system of government.

The nature of the case before us hardly compels a departure from tradition. These are not cases in which an American citizen has been deprived of a right secured by the United States Constitution or a federal statute. Rather, they are cases in which a state court has upheld a citizen's assertion of a right, finding the citizen to be protected under both federal and state law. The complaining party is an officer of the state itself, who asks us to rule that the state court interpreted federal rights too broadly and "overprotected" the citizen.

Such cases should not be of inherent concern to this Court. The reason may be illuminated by assuming that the events underlying this case had arisen in another country, perhaps the Republic of Finland. If the Finnish police had arrested a Finnish citizen for possession of marijuana, and the Finnish courts had turned him loose, no American would have standing to object. If instead they had arrested an American citizen and acquitted him, we might have been concerned about the arrest but we surely could not have complained about the acquittal, even if the Finnish Court had based its decision on its understanding of the United States Constitution. That would be true even if we had a treaty with Finland requiring it to respect the rights of American citizens under the United States Constitution. We would only be motivated to intervene if an American citizen were unfairly arrested, tried, and convicted by the foreign tribunal.

In this case the State of Michigan has arrested one of its citizens and the Michigan Supreme Court has decided to turn him loose. The respondent is a United States citizen as well as a Michigan citizen, but since there is no claim that he has been mistreated by the State of Michigan, the final outcome of the state processes offended no federal interest whatever. Michigan simply provided greater protection to one of its citizens than some other State might provide or, indeed, than this Court might require throughout the country.

I believe that in reviewing the decisions of state courts, the primary role of this Court is to make sure that persons who seek to vindicate federal rights have been fairly heard. That belief resonates with statements in many of our prior cases. In *Abie State Bank v. Bryan*, 282 U.S. 765, 51 S.Ct. 252, 75 L.Ed. 690 (1931), the

Supreme Court of Nebraska had rejected a federal constitutional claim, relying in part on the state law doctrine of laches. Writing for the Court in response to the Nebraska Governor's argument that the Court should not accept jurisdiction because laches provided an independent ground for decision, Chief Justice Hughes concluded that this Court must ascertain for itself whether the asserted nonfederal ground independently and adequately supported the judgment "in order that constitutional guarantees may appropriately be enforced." *Id.*, at 773, 51 S.Ct., at 255. He relied on our earlier opinion in *Union Pacific Railroad Co. v. Public Service Commission of Missouri*, 248 U.S. 67, 39 S.Ct. 24, 63 L.Ed. 131 (1918), in which Justice Holmes had made it clear that the Court engaged in such an inquiry so that it would not "be possible for a State to impose an unconstitutional burden" on a private party. *Id.*, at 70, 39 S.Ct., at 25. And both *Abie* and *Union Pacific* rely on *Creswill v. Knights of Pythias*, 225 U.S. 246, 261, 32 S.Ct. 822, 827, 56 L.Ed. 1074 (1912), in which the Court explained its duty to review the findings of fact of a state court "where a Federal right has been denied."

Until recently we had virtually no interest in cases of this type. Thirty years ago, this Court reviewed only one. *Nevada v. Stacher*, 358 U.S. 907, 79 S.Ct. 232, 3 L.Ed.2d 228 (1953). Indeed, that appears to have been the only case during the entire 1952 Term in which a state even sought review of a decision by its own judiciary. Fifteen years ago, we did not review any such cases, although the total number of requests had mounted to three. [FN omitted.] Some time during the past decade, perhaps about the time of the 5-to-4 decision in *Zacchini v. Scripps-Howard Broadcasting Co.*, 433 U.S. 562, 97 S.Ct. 2849, 53 L.Ed.2d 965 (1977), our priorities shifted. The result is a docket swollen with requests by states to reverse judgments that their courts have rendered in favor of their citizens. [FN omitted.] I am confident that a future Court will recognize the error of this allocation of resources. When that day comes, I think it likely that the Court will also reconsider the propriety of today's expansion of our jurisdiction.

The Court offers only one reason for asserting authority over cases such as the one presented today: "an important need for uniformity in federal law [that] goes unsatisfied when we fail to review an opinion that rests primarily upon federal grounds and where the independence of an alleged state ground is not apparent from the four corners of the opinion." *Ante*, at 3475 (emphasis omitted). Of course, the supposed need to "review an opinion" clashes directly with our oft-repeated reminder that "our power is to correct wrong judgments, not to revise opinions." *Herb v. Pitcairn*, 324 U.S. 117, 126, 65 S.Ct. 459, 463, 89 L.Ed. 789 (1945). The clash is not merely one of form: the "need for uniformity in federal law" is truly an ungovernable engine. That same need is no less present when it is perfectly clear that a state ground is both independent and adequate. In fact, it is equally present if a state prosecutor announces that he believes a certain policy of nonenforcement is commanded by federal law. Yet we have never claimed jurisdiction to correct such errors, no matter how egregious they may be, and no matter how much they may thwart the desires of the state electorate. We do not sit to expound our understanding of the Constitution to interested listeners in the legal community; we sit to resolve disputes. If it is not apparent that our views would affect the outcome of a particular case, we cannot presume to interfere. Finally, I am thoroughly baffled by the Court's suggestion that it must stretch its jurisdiction and reverse the judgment of the Michigan Supreme Court in order to show "[r]espect for the independence of state courts." *Ante*, at 3475. Would we show respect for the Republic of Finland by convening a special sitting for the sole purpose of declaring that its decision to release an American citizen was based upon a misunderstanding of American law?

I respectfully dissent.

———————

As you read the cases, commentary, and questions in this book, think of the role Florida's Constitution plays in the federal system. In the interplay between state courts, the state Legislature, the federal courts, and the Congress, how does each entity play its role? How do courts interpret the Florida Constitution? Do federal courts treat it differently than state courts do? Construing a constitution gets even more entertaining once you realize the many ways provisions can be interpreted. More than seventy years ago, the legal scholar Karl Llewellyn wrote an article for the *Vanderbilt Law Review* setting out twenty-eight canons of statutory and constitutional interpretation—and the twenty-eight opposing canons. All, Llewellyn stated, are correct, depending on context.[77]

As a convenience to readers, and because Florida's Constitution changes every two years, we recommend you refer to a regularly updated online version of it. One such link is http://www.leg.state.fl.us/statutes/index.cfm?submenu=3.

We hope you enjoy your journey through Florida's legal world.

———————

77. Karl N. Llewellyn, *Remarks on the Theory of Appellate Decision and the Rules or Canons About How Statutes are to be Construed*, 3 VAND L. REV. 395–406 (1949–50); *see generally Plante v. Smathers*, 372 So. 2d 933 (Fla. 1979); *Gray v. Bryant*, 125 So. 2d 846 (Fla. 1960); *Taylor v. Dorsey*, 19 So. 2d 876 (Fla. 1944).

Florida Constitutional Law

Article I

Declaration of Rights — Cases

A. Article I, Section 23 — Right to Privacy
　　1. *In re T.W., a Minor*, 551 So. 2d 1186 (Fla. 1989).
　　2. *In re Guardianship of Schiavo*, 916 So. 2d 814 (Fla. 2d DCA 2005).
　　3. *State v. Eitel*, 227 So. 2d 449 (Fla. 1969).
　　4. *Florida Board of Bar Examiners re: Applicant*, 443 So. 2d 71 (Fla. 1983).
　　5. *City of North Miami v. Kurtz*, 653 So. 2d 1025 (Fla. 1995).
　　6. *Post-Newsweek Stations Florida, Inc. v. Doe*, 612 So. 2d 549 (Fla. 1992).
　　7. *State v. Rolling*, 22 Media L. Rptr. 2264 (Fla. Cir. Ct. 1994).
　　8. *Krischer v. McIver*, 697 So. 2d 97 (Fla. 1997).

B. Article I, Section 12 — Searches & Seizures
　　9. *Bernie v. State*, 524 So. 2d 988 (Fla. 1988).
　　10. *State v. Wells*, 539 So. 2d 464 (Fla. 1989), *aff'd*, 495 U.S. 1 (1990).
　　11. *State v. Hume*, 512 So. 2d 185 (Fla. 1987).

C. Article I, Section 4 — Freedom of Speech and Press
　　12. *State v. Elder*, 382 So. 2d 687 (Fla. 1980).

D. Article I, Section 5 — Right to Assemble
　　13. *Cate v. Oldham*, 450 So. 2d 224 (1984).

E. Article I, Section 6 — Right to Work
　　14. *Hillsborough County Governmental Employees Association, Inc. v. Hillsborough County Aviation Authority*, 522 So. 2d 358 (Fla. 1988).
　　15. *United Teachers of Dade v. School District of Miami-Dade County*, 68 So. 3d 1003 (Fla. 3d DCA 2011).

F. Article I, Section 8 — Right to Bear Arms
　　16. *Norman v. State*, 215 So. 2d 18 (Fla.), *cert. denied*, 138 S. Ct. 469 (2017).

G. Article I, Section 10 — Prohibited Laws
　　i. *Ex Post Facto* Laws
　　　　17. *Shenfield v. State*, 44 So. 3d 96 (Fla. 2010).
　　ii. Abrogation of Contracts
　　　　18. *Pomponio v. Claridge of Pompano Condominium*, 378 So. 2d 774 (Fla. 1979).

H. Article I, Section 21 — Access to Courts
　　19. *Kluger v. White*, 281 So. 2d 1 (Fla. 1973).
　　20. *Lasky v. State Farm Insurance Co.*, 296 So. 2d 9 (Fla. 1974).
　　21. *Diamond v. Squibb & Sons, Inc.*, 397 So. 2d 671 (Fla. 1981).
　　22. *Damiano v. McDaniel*, 689 So. 2d 1059 (Fla. 1997).

A. Article I—Declaration of Rights

The first article of the Florida Constitution is dedicated to identifying the fundamental rights of Florida citizens. The Declaration of Rights, found in Article I of the Florida Constitution, is the approximate equivalent of the Bill of Rights in the U.S. Constitution. The federal Bill of Rights serves as the baseline for individual rights, while Florida's Declaration of Rights expands upon this foundation. Both Florida's Declaration of Rights and the Federal Bill of Rights attempt to strike a balance between the rights of individuals and the necessary powers of the state. However, unlike the Bill of Rights, which has been subjected only to the varying interpretations of the federal courts over the years, Florida's Declaration of Rights has been redrafted with every new state Constitution, and has been amended several times. In the article referred to in the History and Perspective chapter, Justice Brennan explained how this critical difference between the federal and state Constitutions has worked to expand the civil liberties of Americans.

Chesterfield Smith, the chair of the Constitution Revision Commission that drafted Florida's current Constitution in 1966, furthered this thought in a speech addressing the 1997–98 Constitution Revision Commission. Smith opined: "I thus urge you, foremost and first, to make the great State of Florida a leader, a pioneer, among states, of expanding and protecting human rights. Government structure is important, but in finality, not near so important as human rights...."[1]

His own CRC's committee on human rights took the job seriously, as fellow CRC member and soon-to-be House Speaker Ralph Turlington later remembered: they "were all attorneys who were re-living their law school experiences." Their debates, he recalled, "were always accompanied by some very long philosophical discussions."[2] That committee's work may, in retrospect, be more remarkable for the battles it lost than for those it won. The committee failed, after a long battle, to get equal rights for women in their draft (the only woman on the CRC changed her vote from "yes" to "no"); did not get the entire waiver of sovereign immunity its chair, controversial justice B.K. Roberts, desired; and carried language over from the previous Constitution that prohibited "aliens ineligible for citizenship" from owning land. That language, racist at its inception (it was targeted at Asian farmers coming to the U.S. early in the twentieth century), stayed in the Constitution fifty more years, until it was eliminated by a CRC proposal adopted in 2018.

The cases in this Chapter explore and contrast Florida's privacy provision in Section 23 vis-à-vis the federal right to privacy, and likewise compare Florida's search and seizure provision in Section 12 with the Federal standard under the Fourth Amendment. The search and seizure provision offers the first of the so-called linkage amendments under which the interpretation of a Florida constitutional provision must track that of the U.S. Supreme Court for the equivalent federal provision. A similar linkage now exists with regard to cruel and unusual punishments in Section 17. The following cases involve several provisions entirely absent from the U.S. Constitution, including Florida's right to work provision, the access to the courts provision (which, at the federal level, is deemed incorporated into the Due Process and Equal Protection Clauses), and the right of access to public meetings and records. The cases also address freedom of speech, due process, and equal protection. Although these provisions are phrased differently in Florida's Constitution, the reader should determine whether and to what extent the analysis of these provisions varies from their federal counterparts.

The goal of this Chapter is to highlight the distinct provisions of Florida's Declaration of Rights and to allow the student to develop an ability to analyze these issues. When a point of reference exists within the federal Constitution, attempt to identify the differences between the two Constitutions.

Article I, Section 23 — Right to Privacy

The right to privacy was originally proposed by the 1977–78 Constitution Revision Commission, but that proposal was rejected by voters. However, the 1980 amendment

---

1. Florida Constitution Revision Comm'n, J. of the 1997–98 Constitution Revision Comm'n, June 16, 1997, at 8–9, *available online at:* https://fall.law.fsu.edu/new_crc/pdf/crc1.pdf (last accessed Sept. 4, 2020).

2. Interview of Ralph Turlington by Sid Johnston, Dec. 17, 1986 (Samuel Proctor Oral History Program (SPOHP), University of Florida).

proposed by the Florida Legislature and adopted by the people is substantially the same as the rejected provision. It is notable that the sponsors of the resolution to create the privacy provision, one of whom was co-author Jon L. Mills, represented a bipartisan and politically diverse group. The final legislative vote was 34–2 in the Senate and 98–4 in the House. As will be seen, the fact that the Florida Constitution, unlike the U.S. Constitution, has an explicit right to privacy included in the text of the state constitution is significant in how the Florida Supreme Court interprets the provision. In the cases that follow, we will explore how the Florida Supreme Court interprets this right to privacy in the contexts of laws impacting bodily autonomy, including abortion, physician-assisted suicide and the refusal of medical treatment, as well as the interaction of the right to privacy with the right of access to public records.

In re T.W., a Minor

551 So. 2d 1186 (Fla. 1989)

SHAW, Justice.

We have on appeal *In re T.W.*, 543 So.2d 837 (Fla. 5th DCA 1989), which declared unconstitutional ... the [Parental Consent Statute requiring a pregnant minor to obtain her parent's permission before obtaining an abortion]. We have jurisdiction. Art. V, § 3(b)(1), Fla. Const. We approve the opinion of the district court and hold the statute invalid under the Florida Constitution.

I.

The procedure that a minor must follow to obtain an abortion in Florida is set out in the parental consent statute and related rules. Prior to undergoing an abortion, a minor must obtain parental consent or, alternatively, must convince a court that she is sufficiently mature to make the decision herself or that, if she is immature, the abortion nevertheless is in her best interests. Pursuant to this procedure, T.W., a pregnant, unmarried, fifteen-year-old, petitioned for a waiver of parental consent under the judicial bypass provision on the alternative grounds that (1) she was sufficiently mature to give an informed consent to the abortion, (2) she had a justified fear of physical or emotional abuse if her parents were requested to consent, and (3) her mother was seriously ill and informing her of the pregnancy would be an added burden. The trial court, after appointing counsel for T.W. and separate counsel as guardian ad litem for the fetus, conducted a hearing within twenty-four hours of the filing of the petition.

* * *

Because the questions raised are of great public importance and are likely to recur, we accept jurisdiction despite T.W.'s abortion....

The seminal case in United States abortion law is *Roe v. Wade*, 410 U.S. 113 (1973). There, the Court ruled that a right to privacy implicit in the fourteenth amendment embraces a woman's decision concerning abortion. Autonomy to make this decision constitutes a fundamental right and states may impose restrictions only when narrowly drawn to serve a compelling state interest. The Court recognized two important state interests, protecting the health of the mother and the potentiality of life in the fetus, and ruled that these interests become compelling at the completion of the first trimester of pregnancy, and upon viability of the fetus (approximately at the end of the second trimester), respectively. Thus, during the first trimester, states must leave the abortion decision to the woman and her doctor; during the second trimester, states may impose measures to protect the mother's health; and during the period following viability, states may possibly forbid abortions altogether. Although the workability of the trimester system and the soundness of *Roe* itself have been seriously questioned in *Webster v. Reproductive Health Services*, 492 U.S. 490 (1989), the decision for now remains the federal law. Subsequent to *Roe*, the Court issued several decisions dealing directly with the matter of parental consent for minors seeking abortions. *See Planned Parenthood Ass'n v. Ashcroft*, 462 U.S. 476 (1983); *Bellotti v. Baird*, 443 U.S. 622 (1979) (plurality opinion); *Planned Parenthood v. Danforth*, 428 U.S. 52 (1976).

To be held constitutional, the instant statute must pass muster under both the federal and state constitutions. Were we to examine it solely under the federal Constitution, our analysis necessarily would track the decisions noted above. However, Florida is unusual in that it is one of at least four states having its own express constitutional provision guaranteeing an independent right to privacy, and we opt to examine the statute first under the Florida Constitution. If it fails here, then no further analysis under federal law is required.

As we noted in *Winfield v. Division of Pari-Mutuel Wagering*, 477 So.2d 544 (Fla.1985), the essential concept of privacy is deeply rooted in our nation's political and philosophical heritage. Justice Brandeis in *Olmstead v. United States*, 277 U.S. 438, 478 (1928) (Brandeis, J., dissenting), eloquently expressed the fundamental and wide-ranging "right to be let alone":

> The makers of our Constitution undertook to secure conditions favorable to the pursuit of happiness. They recognized the significance of man's spiritual nature, of his feelings and of his intellect.... They sought to protect Americans in their beliefs, their thoughts, their emotions and their sensations. They conferred, as against the government, the right to be let alone—the most comprehensive of rights and the right most valued by civilized men.

Pursuant to this principle, the United States Supreme Court has recognized a privacy right that shields an individual's autonomy in deciding matters concerning marriage, procreation, contraception, family relationships, and child rearing and education. *Roe*, 410 U.S. at 152–53. It is this general right to privacy that protects against the public disclosure of private matters. *Nixon v. Administrator of General Servs.*, 433 U.S. 425 (1977); *Whalen v. Roe*, 429 U.S. 589 (1977). The Court, however, has made it clear that the states, not the federal government, are the final guarantors of personal privacy: "But the protection of a person's general right to privacy—his right to be let alone by other people—is, like the protection of his property and of his very life, left largely to the law of the individual States." *Katz v. United States*, 389 U.S. 347, 350–51 (1967). While the federal Constitution traditionally shields enumerated and implied individual liberties from encroachment by state or federal government, the federal Court has long held that state constitutions may provide even greater protection. *See, "on its own"*

e.g., *Pruneyard Shopping Center v. Robins*, 447 U.S. 74, 81 (1980) ("Our reasoning … does not *ex proprio vigore* limit the authority of the State to exercise its police power or its sovereign right to adopt in its own Constitution individual liberties more expansive than those conferred by the Federal Constitution.").

> State constitutions, too, are a font of individual liberties, their protections often extending beyond those required by the Supreme Court's interpretation of federal law. The legal revolution which has brought federal law to the fore must not be allowed to inhibit the independent protective force of state law—for without it, the full realization of our liberties cannot be guaranteed.

W. Brennan, *State Constitutions and the Protection of Individual Rights*, 90 Harv.L.Rev. 489, 491 (1977).

In 1980, Florida voters by general election amended our state constitution to provide:

> Section 23. Right of privacy.—Every natural person has the right to be let alone and free from governmental intrusion into his private life except as otherwise provided herein. This section shall not be construed to limit the public's right of access to public records and meetings as provided by law.

Art. I, § 23, Fla. Const. This Court in *Winfield* described the far-reaching impact of the Florida amendment:

> The citizens of Florida opted for more protection from governmental intrusion when they approved article I, section 23, of the Florida Constitution. This amendment is an independent, freestanding constitutional provision which declares the fundamental right to privacy. Article I, section 23, was intentionally phrased in strong terms. The drafters of the amendment rejected the use of the words "unreasonable" or "unwarranted" before the phrase "governmental intrusion" in order to make the privacy right as strong as possible. Since the people of this state exercised their prerogative and enacted an amendment to the Florida Constitution which expressly and succinctly provides for a strong right of privacy not found in the United States Constitution, it can only be concluded that the right is much broader in scope than that of the Federal Constitution.

Winfield, 477 So.2d at 548. In other words, the amendment embraces more privacy interests, and extends more protection to the individual in those interests, than does the federal Constitution.

Consistent with this analysis, we have said that the amendment provides "an explicit textual foundation for those privacy interests inherent in the concept of liberty which may not otherwise be protected by specific constitutional provisions." *Rasmussen v. South Fla. Blood Serv.*, 500 So.2d 533, 536 (Fla.1987). We have found the right implicated in a wide range of activities dealing with the public disclosure of personal matters.... Florida courts have also found the right involved in a number of cases dealing with personal decisionmaking [and health-related decisions]....

The privacy section contains no express standard of review for evaluating the lawfulness of a government intrusion into one's private life, and this Court when called upon, adopted the following standard:

> Since the privacy section as adopted contains no textual standard of review, it is important for us to identify an explicit standard to be applied in order to give proper force and effect to the amendment. The right of privacy is a fundamental right which we believe demands the compelling state interest standard. This test shifts the burden of proof to the state to justify an intrusion on privacy. The burden can be met by demonstrating that the challenged regulation serves a compelling state interest and accomplishes its goal through the use of the least intrusive means.

Winfield, 477 So.2d at 547. When this standard was applied in disclosural cases, government intrusion generally was upheld as sufficiently compelling to overcome the individual's right to privacy. We reaffirm, however, that this is a highly stringent standard, emphasized by the fact that no government intrusion in the personal decision-making cases cited above has survived.

Florida's privacy provision is clearly implicated in a woman's decision of whether or not to continue her pregnancy. We can conceive of few more personal or private decisions concerning one's body that one can make in the course of a lifetime, except perhaps the decision of the terminally ill in their choice of whether to discontinue necessary medical treatment.... The decision whether to obtain an abortion is fraught with specific physical, psychological, and economic implications of a uniquely personal nature for each woman. *See Roe*, 410 U.S. at 153. The Florida Constitution embodies the principle that "[f]ew decisions are more personal and intimate, more properly private, or more basic to individual dignity and autonomy, than a woman's decision ... whether to end her pregnancy. A woman's right to make that choice freely is fundamental." *Thornburgh v. American College of Obstetricians and Gynecologists*, 476 U.S. 747 (1986).

The next question to be addressed is whether this freedom of choice concerning abortion extends to minors. We conclude that it does, based on the unambiguous language of the amendment: The right of privacy extends to "[e]very natural person." Minors are natural persons in the eyes of the law and "[c]onstitutional rights do not mature and come into being magically only when one attains the state-defined age of majority. Minors, as well as adults, ... possess constitutional rights." *Danforth*, 428 U.S. at 74.

II.

Common sense dictates that a minor's rights are not absolute; in order to overcome these constitutional rights, a statute must survive the stringent test announced in *Winfield*: The state must prove that the statute furthers a compelling state interest through the least intrusive means. The *Roe* Court recognized two state interests implicated in the abortion decision: the health of the mother and the potentiality of life in the fetus. Under *Roe*, the health of the mother does not become a compelling state interest until immediately following the end of the first trimester because until that time, "mortality in abortion may be less than mortality in normal childbirth." *Roe*, 410 U.S. at 163. Due to technological developments in second-trimester abortion procedures, the point at which abortions are safer than childbirth may have been extended into the second trimester. *See City of Akron*, 462 U.S. at 429 n. 11. We nevertheless adopt the end of the first trimester as the time at which the state's interest in maternal health becomes compelling under Florida law because it is clear that prior to this point no interest in maternal health could be served by significantly restricting the manner in which abortions are performed by qualified doctors, whereas after this point the matter becomes a genuine concern. Under Florida law, prior to the end of the first trimester, the abortion decision must be left to the woman and may not be significantly restricted by the state. Following this point, the state may impose significant restrictions only in the least intrusive manner designed to safeguard the health of the mother. Insignificant burdens during either period must substantially further important state interests. . . .

Under *Roe*, the potentiality of life in the fetus becomes compelling at the point in time when the fetus becomes viable, which the Court defined as the time at which the fetus becomes capable of meaningful life outside the womb, albeit with artificial aid. *Roe*, 410 U.S. at 160. Under our Florida Constitution, the state's interest becomes compelling upon viability, as defined below. Until this point, the fetus is a highly specialized set of cells that is entirely dependent upon the mother for sustenance. No other member of society can provide this nourishment. The mother and fetus are so inextricably intertwined that their interests can be said to coincide. Upon viability, however, society becomes capable of sustaining the fetus, and its interest in preserving its potential for life thus becomes compelling. Viability under Florida law occurs at that point in time when the fetus becomes capable of meaningful life outside the womb through standard medical measures. Under current standards, this point generally occurs upon completion of the second trimester. . . . Following viability, the state may protect its interest in the potentiality of life by regulating abortion, provided that the mother's health is not jeopardized.

III.

The challenged statute fails because it intrudes upon the privacy of the pregnant minor from conception to birth. Such a substantial invasion of a pregnant female's privacy by the state for the full term of the pregnancy is not necessary for the preservation of maternal health or the potentiality of life. However, where parental rights over a minor child are concerned, society has recognized additional state interests — protection of the immature minor and preservation of the family unit. For reasons set out below, we find that neither of these interests is sufficiently compelling under Florida law to override Florida's privacy amendment.

In evaluating the validity of parental consent and notice statutes, the federal Court has taken into consideration the state's interests in the well-being of the immature minor, *see Ashcroft*; *City of Akron*; *Bellotti*; *Danforth*, and in the integrity of the family, *see Bellotti*. In *Bellotti*, the Court set forth three reasons justifying the conclusion that states can impose more restrictions on the right of minors to obtain abortions than they can impose on the right of adults: "[T]he peculiar vulnerability of children; their inability to make critical decisions in an informed, mature manner; and the importance of the parental role in child rearing." *Bellotti*, 443 U.S. at 634. The Court pointed out that "during the formative years of childhood and adolescence, minors often lack the experience, perspective, and judgment to recognize and avoid choices that could be detrimental to them," and that the role of parents in "teaching, guiding, and inspiring by precept and example is essential to the growth of young people into mature, socially responsible citizens," *id.* at 638. In assessing the validity of parental consent statutes, the federal Court applied a relaxed standard; the state interest need only be "significant," not "compelling," to support the intrusion.[3] *Intermediate scrutiny*

We agree that the state's interests in protecting minors and in preserving family unity are worthy objectives. Unlike the federal Constitution, however, which allows intrusion based on a "significant" state interest, the Florida Constitution requires a "compelling" state interest in all cases where the right to privacy is implicated. *Winfield.* We note that Florida does not recognize these two interests as being sufficiently compelling to justify a parental consent requirement where procedures other than abortion are concerned....

Under [Florida's parental consent statute], a minor may consent, without parental approval, to any medical procedure involving her pregnancy or her existing child—no matter how dire the possible consequences—except abortion. Under In re *Guardianship of Barry*, 445 So.2d 365 (Fla. 2d DCA 1984) (parents permitted to authorize removal of life support system from infant in permanent coma), this could include authority in certain circumstances to order life support discontinued for a comatose child. In light of this wide authority that the state grants an unwed minor to make life-or-death decisions concerning herself or an existing child without parental consent, we are unable to discern a special compelling interest on the part of the state under Florida law in protecting the minor only where abortion is concerned. We fail to see the qualitative difference in terms of impact on the well-being of the minor between allowing the life of an existing child to come to an end and terminating a pregnancy, or between undergoing a highly dangerous medical procedure on oneself and undergoing a far less dangerous procedure to end one's pregnancy. If any qualitative difference exists, it certainly is insufficient in terms of state interest. Although the state does have an interest in protecting minors, "the selective approach employed by the legislature evidences the limited nature of the ... interest being furthered by these provisions." *Ivey v. Bacardi Imports Co.*, 541 So.2d 1129, 1139 (Fla.1989). We note that the state's adoption act similarly contains no requirement that a minor

---

3. [FN 2.] *See City of Akron v. Akron Center for Reproductive Health, Inc.*, 462 U.S. 416, 427 n. 10 (1983) ("[T]he Court has repeatedly recognized that, in view of the unique status of children under the law, the States have a 'significant' interest in certain abortion regulations aimed at protecting children 'that is not present in the case of an adult.'").

obtain parental consent prior to placing a child up for adoption, even though this decision clearly is fraught with intense emotional and societal consequences. See ch. 63, Fla.Stat. (1987).

The parental consent statute also fails the second prong of the Winfield standard, i.e., it is not the least intrusive means of furthering the state interest. Any inquiry under this prong must consider procedural safeguards relative to the intrusion. As pointed out by the district court below, although the instant statute does provide for a judicial bypass procedure, it makes no provision for a lawyer for the minor or for a record hearing. . . . Additionally, we note that the statute fails to make any exception for emergency or therapeutic abortions, procedures clearly no different, in terms of impact upon the minor, from other medical procedures that a minor can unilaterally authorize under section 743.065. Accordingly, we conclude that the statute fails to provide adequate procedural safeguards.

Based on the foregoing analysis of our state law, we hold that section 390.001(4)(a), Florida Statutes violates the Florida Constitution. Accordingly, no further analysis under federal law is required. We expressly decide this case on state law grounds and cite federal precedent only to the extent that it illuminates Florida law. We approve the district court's decision.

It is so ordered.

BARKETT and KOGAN, JJ., concur.

EHRLICH, Chief Justice, concurring specially.

I generally concur with the majority opinion and the result it reaches. I write only to express my disagreement with the definition of "viability" adopted by the majority and to elucidate my views.

I wholeheartedly concur that Florida's express constitutional right of privacy, article I, section 23, Florida Constitution, is implicated in this case. Specifically, I note that the privacy provision was added to the Florida Constitution by amendment in 1980, well after the decision of the United States Supreme Court in *Roe v. Wade*, 410 U.S. 113 (1973). It can therefore be presumed that the public was aware that the right to an abortion was included under the federal constitutional right of privacy and would therefore certainly be covered by the Florida privacy amendment [and] the right of privacy extends to minors.

It is therefore necessary for us to decide whether the state has a compelling interest sufficient to outweigh the minor girl's right of privacy, and if so, whether this statute is the least intrusive means of furthering that compelling interest. *Winfield v. Division of Pari-Mutuel Wagering*, 477 So.2d 544 (Fla.1985). I agree that the state does not have a compelling interest sufficient to support the statute in this case, and even if the state's interest were compelling, I believe this statute is not the least intrusive means of furthering any such interest.

I recognize, as does the majority, that the state has legitimate interests in any restrictions on the ability to obtain an abortion: protecting the health of the mother and protecting the potential life represented by the fetus. As these interests exist throughout pregnancy, see *City of Akron v. Akron Center for Reproductive Health, Inc.*, 462 U.S. 416, 428–30 (1983), the question becomes at what point, if ever, they become compelling so as to outweigh the privacy rights of the individual under article I, section 23.

As to the first state interest, protecting the health of the mother, I agree that we should adopt the United States Supreme Court's analysis: The state's interest in the health of the mother does not become compelling until the point when the abortion procedure becomes equally or more dangerous for the mother than childbirth. *Roe*, 410 U.S. at 149–50. The Court in *Roe* identified this point, based on available medical evidence, as approximately at the end of the first trimester. Because of advances in medical technology, the specific point at which the state's interest in the health of the mother becomes compelling has become less definite, and may have been extended into the second trimester. *City of Akron*, 462 U.S. at 429 n. 11. Once the state's interest in the health of the mother becomes compelling, the state may regulate the abortion procedure in the least restrictive ways that are reasonably related to furthering that state interest.... Examples of regulations permissible during the first trimester are requiring informed consent and the maintenance of certain records. See *Planned Parenthood v. Danforth*, 428 U.S. 52 (1976). Therefore, to the extent that section 390.001(4), Florida Statutes, requires the informed consent of the pregnant woman (adult or minor) it serves a valid purpose. However, I do not believe that this interest can support the [Parental Consent Statute] given the fact that the girl is considered competent to give consent to any other medical procedure related to her pregnancy as though she were an adult.

With regard to the state's interest in potential life, I believe that this Court is not in a position to radically alter the traditional legal view that the unborn are not legal "persons" and decide an issue on which there is no social, religious, philosophical, or scientific consensus, i.e., when life begins. However, the mother's privacy rights cannot be considered in a vacuum. Even though the fetus is not a legal "person," it is a potential life in which the state has an important interest. As the Court noted in *Roe*:

> The pregnant woman cannot be isolated in her privacy. She carries an embryo and, later, a fetus.... The situation therefore is inherently different from marital intimacy, or bedroom possession of obscene material, or marriage, or procreation, or education, with which [other privacy cases] were respectively concerned.... The woman's privacy is no longer sole and any right of privacy she possesses must be measured accordingly.

Roe, 410 U.S. at 159. Therefore, as an essential part of our discussion of the mother's right of privacy guaranteed by the Florida Constitution, we must consider the point at which a line can be drawn separating the time in the pregnancy when the mother's privacy right controls, and the time when the state's interest in the potential life represented by the fetus becomes "compelling" so as to outweigh that privacy right....

I recognize that in cases involving minors, the state has an additional interest in protecting the immature minor and the integrity of the family. I agree, however, that in light of section 743.065 the state's interest in the parental consent statute is not compelling. [The Parental Consent Statute allows the pregnant minor alone to make life-or-death decisions about medical treatment for her unborn child in every case except abortion.] Given this statutory scheme, I must agree that the state has failed to prove that its interest in protecting the immature minor is compelling so as to out-weigh the privacy rights of the minor girl....

I also agree that even if the state had a compelling interest sufficient to support this statute, this statute also fails the second prong of the [strict scrutiny] standard, i.e., it is not the least restrictive means of furthering the state's interest. As the United States Supreme Court noted in *Bellotti v. Baird*, 443 U.S. 622, 644 (1979), "the [judicial alternative] procedure must ensure that the provision requiring parental consent does not in fact amount to the 'absolute, and possibly arbitrary, veto' that was found im-permissible in *Danforth*" but must "provide an effective opportunity for an abortion to be obtained."

Section 390.001(4)(a) provides for neither a record hearing nor the appointment of counsel for the minor....

I agree that section 390.001(4)(a), Florida Statutes (Supp.1988), is violative of article I, section 23, of the Florida Constitution, and I therefore concur.

OVERTON, Justice, concurring in part, dissenting in part.

I concur in parts I and II; however, I must dissent from the majority's holding in part III. While I agree that section 390.001(4)(a), Florida Statutes (Supp.1988), is un-constitutional as it was interpreted and applied by the trial court, I would not declare the statute unconstitutional vel non but would interpret the statute so that it can be applied in accordance with the principles set forth by the United States Supreme Court in *Bellotti v. Baird*, 443 U.S. 622 (1979). In that decision, the United States Supreme Court approved this type of statute and stated: "[T]he [judicial alternative] procedure must ensure that the provision requiring parental consent does not in fact amount to the 'absolute, and possibly arbitrary, veto' that was found impermissible in *Danforth*," but must "provide an effective opportunity for an abortion to be obtained."

As explained by Justice McDonald in his concurring and dissenting opinion, a minor has the disability of nonage, including the inability to contract. The legislature has the power to set forth certain instances where the disability is removed. *See* ch. 743, Fla.Stat. (1987). Our right of privacy provision contained in article I, section 23, of the Florida Constitution, did not absolutely remove a minor's disability of nonage for obtaining an abortion or any other medical procedure, and those parts of the majority opinion in which I have concurred did not, in my view, so hold. The right of privacy provision, adopted by the people of this state in 1980, effectively codified within the Florida Constitution the principles of *Roe v. Wade*, 410 U.S. 113 (1973), as it existed in 1980. As illustrated by the multiple United States Supreme Court cases construing state statutes relating to parental consent, the principles of

Roe did not remove the disability of nonage for a minor to have an abortion. *See Planned Parenthood Ass'n v. Ashcroft*, 462 U.S. 476 (1983); *City of Akron v. Akron Center for Reproductive Health, Inc.*, 462 U.S. 416 (1983); *Bellotti.*

Section 390.001(4)(a) can easily be construed to be within the principles set forth in these cases....

We have a duty to construe this statute as constitutional if at all possible.... Applying this principle of statutory interpretation, the Court would not be changing the intent of the legislature in this case because "[t]he legislature will be presumed to have intended a constitutional result."

... I find that the statute can be interpreted to ensure that parental consent does not amount to an absolute veto and this Court can adopt procedures to provide minors with effective opportunities to obtain abortions. Further, I conclude that the majority has abdicated its responsibility by not so construing the statute, thus leaving the legislature with the problem of redrafting a constitutional statute....

MCDONALD, Justice, dissenting.

I disagree that [the Parental Consent Statute] is unconstitutional.... [I]f this case were on the subject of a legislative intrusion on an adult woman's right to have an abortion, I would concur.

My principal disagreement lies in my conclusion that, absent an enabling statute, a minor does not have the capacity to consent to an abortion. This is because of the common law and long-recognized disability of minors because of nonage. A minor lacks the capacity to contract. When she consents to an abortion she contracts with another person to perform a surgical procedure on her. Absent parental or statutory authorization, she cannot do this. A minor's incapacity was recognized by the legislature when it enacted section 743.065, Florida Statutes (1987), authorizing the power to consent for certain medical procedures. The legislature chose to exclude its grant of consent power to abortion medical procedures. It did the same in [other statutes involving medical procedures.] I do not look upon § 390.001(4)(a) as an invasion of privacy, but rather a method of providing a vehicle to fulfill a pregnant minor's desire to terminate a pregnancy. Viewed in that light, the statute is constitutional.

I do not believe any procedural deficiencies in the statute make it unconstitutional. Procedure is the responsibility of this Court. We have provided a procedural rule to accompany the statute. If additional procedural safeguards are indicated, we can provide those. The statute need not die on this basis.

* * *

Questions

1. According to the Court, what level of state interest does Section 23 mandate before an individual may be subjected to "governmental intrusion"? (NOTE that under federal case law, the standard for minors is less stringent.)

2. What three interests does the state advance in this case?

3. Once the Court has found that the statute implicates a privacy interest, why does the statute fail under the two-prong test?

4. How does "viability" play a role in the majority's opinion? What is Justice Ehrlich's criticism of the majority on this point?

5. How does Justice Grimes's reasoning differ from the majority opinion?

6. Formulate the equal protection challenge to section 390.001(4)(a).

———————

In 1999, the Florida Legislature adopted a statute requiring parental notification and a 48-hour waiting period when a minor sought to obtain an abortion. *See* FLA. STAT. § 390.01115 (1999) ("The Parental Notice Act"). The statute was immediately challenged by women's groups and abortion clinics, and a trial court injunction prevented it from ever taking effect. On appeal, the Florida Supreme Court found that the Parental Notice Act also violated Article I, Section 23. *See North Fla. Women's Health & Counseling Svcs. v. State*, 866 So. 2d 612 (Fla. 2003). The Court found that this statute also interfered with the privacy rights of minors and had no compelling government interest. *Id.* at 632–33. Significantly, the Court rejected the state's argument that Florida should follow the jurisprudence of the United States Supreme Court, which in *Planned Parenthood v. Casey*, 505 U.S. 833, 877 (1992), had substituted an "undue burden" standard for the previous strict scrutiny afforded in abortion cases. Instead, the Florida Supreme Court reaffirmed its holding that the explicit privacy guarantee found in the Florida Constitution required adherence to strict scrutiny. *North Fla. Women's Health*, 866 So. 2d at 635 (also stating that each of the rights mentioned in the Declaration of Rights should be considered a "fundamental right"). Finally, in rejecting the state's argument that it had demonstrated a compelling interest in the health of minors, the Florida Supreme Court noted that, as it had found in *In re T.W.*, and other cases involving minor parents, statutory law gave the mother unrestricted autonomy over decisions involving her pregnancy or born children. *See id.* at 633 (quoting *In re T.W.*, 551 So. 2d at 1195).

In response to this decision, the Florida Legislature proposed a constitutional amendment to allow parental notification, and this was adopted by the voters in November 2004. The new constitutional provision is located in Article X, and provides:

> **§ 22. Parental notice of termination of a minor's pregnancy.** The Legislature shall not limit or deny the privacy right guaranteed to a minor under the United States Constitution as interpreted by the United States Supreme Court. Notwithstanding a minor's right of privacy provided in Section 23 of Article I, the Legislature is authorized to require by general law for notification to a parent or guardian of a minor before the termination of the minor's pregnancy. The Legislature shall provide exceptions to such requirement for notification and shall create a process for judicial waiver of the notification.

FLA. CONST. art. X, § 22. Acting under this authority, the Legislature adopted the current Parental Notice of Abortion Act, Section 390.01114, Florida Statutes. The

Parental Notice Act mandates that a doctor provide actual notice to the parents of a minor seeking abortion.[4] However, the statute also provides an expedited judicial process for waiving the notice.[5] Federal courts subsequently upheld this statute against challenges brought under the U.S. Constitution. *See Womancare of Orlando, Inc. v. Agwunobi*, 448 F. Supp. 2d 1309 (N.D. Fla. 2006).

In re Guardianship of Schiavo

916 So. 2d 814 (Fla. 2d DCA 2005)

ALTENBERND, Chief Judge.

Robert and Mary Schindler, the parents of Theresa Marie Schiavo, appeal the trial court's order denying their motion for relief from judgment filed pursuant to Florida Rule of Civil Procedure 1.540(b)(4). This case has an extensive legal history, and this is not the first motion that the Schindlers have filed seeking relief from the trial court's judgment.

The judgment was entered by the trial court in February 2000 following an extensive trial. The trial court determined, based on clear and convincing evidence, that Theresa Schiavo was in a persistent vegetative state and that she herself would elect to forego further use of a feeding tube. This court affirmed that judgment. *See In re Guardianship of Schiavo*, 780 So.2d 176 (Fla. 2d DCA 2001) (*Schiavo I*).

As a result of an earlier motion for relief from judgment, we required the trial court to reconfirm that medical science offered no meaningful treatment for her condition. *In re Guardianship of Schiavo*, 800 So.2d 640 (Fla. 2d DCA 2001) (*Schiavo III*). The trial court decided not only to reconfirm that issue but also to review its earlier decision that Mrs. Schiavo was in a persistent vegetative state. Following another extensive hearing at which many highly qualified physicians testified, the trial court denied the motion for relief from judgment. This court affirmed that decision. *In re Guardianship of Schiavo*, 851 So.2d 182 (Fla. 2d DCA 2003) (*Schiavo IV*).

The trial court's decision does not give Mrs. Schiavo's legal guardian the option of leaving the life-prolonging procedures in place. No matter who her guardian is, the guardian is required to obey the court order because the court, and not the guardian, has determined the decision that Mrs. Schiavo herself would make.

The legal process utilized by the trial court in this case is not new. Long before Mrs. Schiavo suffered her heart attack in February 1990, the Supreme Court of Florida had already determined that the express right of privacy in article I, section 23, of the Florida Constitution gave both competent and incompetent persons the right to

---

4. *See* FLA. STAT. § 390.01114(3) (2020). The statute provides an exception in cases of medical emergency. *Id.*

5. *See* FLA. STAT. § 390.01114(4) (2020). The statute requires that this waiver process maintain the minor's anonymity, allow her access to counsel, and be completed within three days. *Id.*

forego life-prolonging procedures. *See John F. Kennedy Mem'l Hosp. v. Bludworth,* 452 So.2d 921 (Fla.1984); *see also Corbett v. D'Alessandro,* 487 So.2d 368 (Fla. 2d DCA 1986); *In re Guardianship of Barry,* 445 So.2d 365 (Fla. 2d DCA 1984). In *Corbett,* this court interpreted this constitutional protection to apply not only to persons who have the foresight and resources to prepare a living will, but also to those whose wishes have not been reduced to writing. Earlier, in *Barry,* the right had been recognized by this court for a child who could not have prepared a written directive.

Both the Supreme Court of Florida and this court have concluded that the decision to "terminate artificial life supports is a decision that normally should be made in the patient-doctor-family relationship." *Bludworth,* 452 So.2d at 926; *see also [In re Guardianship of] Browning,* 543 So.2d 258 (Fla. 2d DCA 1989), *approved,* 568 So.2d 4 (Fla.1990). We have, however, emphasized that the courts remain open to make these decisions under the Florida Constitution when family members cannot agree or when a guardian believes that it would be more appropriate for a neutral judge to make the decision. *See, e.g., Bludworth,* 452 So.2d at 926–27; *Browning,* 543 So.2d at 269. As we explained in *Schiavo I,* this is the approach that Mr. Schiavo, in his capacity as legal guardian of his wife, selected in light of the bitter conflict within this family.

Following the exhaustion of all appellate review of both the final judgment that was entered in February 2000 and the order denying the subsequent motion for relief from judgment, the trial court ordered that, on October 15, 2003, the hospice facility must cease supplying nutrition and hydration through Mrs. Schiavo's feeding tube. The hospice facility obeyed this order. On October 21, 2003, the legislature enacted chapter 2003–418, and the Governor signed the act into law. Pursuant to this new act, the Governor ordered a stay, which both this court and the trial court honored. Thus, the hospice facility restored the supply of nutrition and hydration through the feeding tube. Thereafter, the supreme court unanimously held that chapter 2003–418 was unconstitutional as a violation of the separation of powers under the Florida Constitution. *Bush v. Schiavo,* 885 So.2d 321 (Fla.2004).

Before chapter 2003–418 was held unconstitutional, the Governor requested the Chief Judge of the Sixth Judicial Circuit to appoint a special guardian ad litem for Mrs. Schiavo. Chief Judge David Demers honored that request and appointed a guardian ad litem. The guardian, Dr. Jay Wolfson, has degrees in both law and public health. He submitted a lengthy report to both the court and the Governor. In his summary, Dr. Wolfson stated, in part:

> The [guardian ad litem] concludes that the trier of fact and the evidence that served as the basis for the decisions regarding Theresa Schiavo were firmly grounded within Florida statutory and case law, which clearly and unequivocally provide for the removal of artificial nutrition in cases of persistent vegetative states, where there is no advance directive, through substituted/ proxy judgment of the guardian and/or the court as guardian, and with the use of evidence regarding the medical condition and the intent of the parties that was deemed, by the trier of fact to be clear and convincing.

Now, the Schindlers have filed a motion in the trial court, pursuant to Florida Rule of Civil Procedure 1.540(b)(4), for relief from the judgment, claiming that the trial court's February 2000 judgment is void. This is one of the exceptional grounds on which a judgment that is more than one year old may be challenged. This ground, however, is generally limited to circumstances in which the trial court enters a judgment when it lacks jurisdiction over the subject matter of the case or jurisdiction over the parties. *See Curbelo v. Ullman,* 571 So.2d 443, 445 (Fla.1990); *Varnes v. Kirk,* 251 So.2d 324 (Fla. 1st DCA 1971)....

In this case, it is beyond any question that the trial court obtained lawful jurisdiction over the subject matter of this guardianship and the person of Mrs. Schiavo [in] 1990. Thus, it is doubtful that the Schindlers' most recent motion for relief from judgment contains even a facially sufficient claim.

In their brief, the Schindlers first argue that the judgment is void because the trial court, and not a guardian, made the decision as to what Mrs. Schiavo would elect to do in light of her persistent vegetative state. Despite the well-established law authorizing this process as a method to fulfill the patient's right of privacy under the Florida Constitution, the Schindlers argue that this process provides insufficient due process and violates Mrs. Schiavo's right to privacy. The right of the trial judge to make this decision for Mrs. Schiavo, relying on clear and convincing evidence of the decision that she herself would have made, is a matter that the Schindlers raised in the first appeal. This court expressly rejected these arguments several years ago. *See Schiavo I,* 780 So.2d at 179. Thus, these arguments are not only issues that would not render a judgment void, but they are also issues that have long been resolved in this case.

The Schindlers also argue that the judgment is void because Mrs. Schiavo was denied a full and fair opportunity to defend her rights in this case. As we have explained in the past, this is not a case where the trial court validated the guardian's decision for the ward without a full and independent inquiry. Instead, both Mr. Schiavo and the Schindlers were allowed to present evidence to the trial court as if each were her guardian. *Id.* The trial court then made its decision pursuant to law and based upon a heightened standard of proof. That decision has been subject to appeals and postjudgment scrutiny of all varieties, and it remains a valid judgment pursuant to the laws and the constitution of this state. Not only has Mrs. Schiavo's case been given due process, but few, if any, similar cases have ever been afforded this heightened level of process.

We note that the case law generally allows a party to file only one motion for relief under rule 1.540(b). *See* Berman, *supra* ¶ 540.5(b).... Because of the nature of this case, neither the trial court nor this court has enforced these general rules. The Schindlers have filed numerous motions, but they have failed to present any lawful basis for relief from judgment.

For those of us who are not trained physicians and who do not deal on a daily basis with patients in vegetative states, or with the difficult decision to remove life-sustaining treatment, the images of Mrs. Schiavo's face are haunting. But the images do not reveal the full extent of the devastation to her brain and her inability to engage in cognition. Dr. Wolfson, the guardian who was appointed at the request of the Governor, visited Mrs. Schiavo many times in 2003. He was unable to independently observe any "consistent, repetitive, intentional, reproducible interactive and aware activities." His report does not challenge the now well-established medical diagnosis that Mrs. Schiavo's movements are merely reflexive. As he explained: "This is the confusing thing for the lay person about persistent vegetative states."

Our previous statements on the matter apply with undiminished relevancy in this appeal:

> The judges on this panel are called upon to make a collective, objective decision concerning a question of law. Each of us, however, has our own family, our own loved ones, our own children. From our review of the video-tapes of Mrs. Schiavo, despite the irrefutable evidence that her cerebral cortex has sustained the most severe of irreparable injuries, we understand why a parent who had raised and nurtured a child from conception would hold out hope that some level of cognitive function remained. If Mrs. Schiavo were our own daughter, we could not but hold to such a faith.
>
> But in the end, this case is not about the aspirations that loving parents have for their children. It is about Theresa Schiavo's right to make her own decision, independent of her parents and independent of her husband. In circumstances such as these, when families cannot agree, the law has opened the doors of the circuit courts to permit trial judges to serve as surrogates or proxies to make decisions about life-prolonging procedures. It is the trial judge's duty not to make the decision that the judge would make for himself or herself or for a loved one. Instead, the trial judge must make a decision that the clear and convincing evidence shows the ward would have made for herself. It is a thankless task, and one to be undertaken with care, objectivity, and a cautious legal standard designed to promote the value of life.

Schiavo IV, 851 So.2d at 186–87.

We are well aware that many people around the world disagree with the trial court's decision. However, when he became a judge, the trial court judge took an oath, required by the Florida Constitution, to obey the rule of law and the constitution of this state. The trial judge followed and obeyed the law as set out by the precedent of the Supreme Court of Florida and by the general laws adopted by the Legislature. The trial judge made this most difficult decision after fully considering the evidence and applying a heightened standard of proof that is designed to protect society's interest in sustaining life.

It is important for all to understand that the Florida Constitution has long been interpreted to authorize the process used by the trial court in this case. The legislature has passed general laws implementing these constitutional rights. Neither the trial court nor this court can change this established law at this stage of these proceedings. No one who considers the dismal history of countries in which courts and judges have abandoned the rule of law would ask us to abandon the rule of law even in this case.

Accordingly, we affirm the trial court's denial of this motion for relief from judgment, and we deny the motion for stay pending appeal. In light of the trial court's order requiring the removal of life-sustaining procedures effective Friday, March 18, 2005, and given the lack of merit in the issues pursued in this appeal, we issue our mandate in conjunction with this opinion, and we will not entertain any motions for rehearing.

Affirmed; motion for stay denied.

Notes and Questions

1. In both of the previous cases, the courts dealt with individuals who in many situations have diminished legal capacity (i.e., minors and incapacitated individuals) but found that point irrelevant since the right to privacy under the Florida Constitution applies to "every natural person." Similarly, death would not "abolish the constitutional protections for privacy that existed at the moment of death." *Weaver v. Myers*, 229 So. 3d 1118, 1128 (Fla. 2017).

2. Perhaps not surprisingly, courts have not expanded the right to privacy beyond "every natural person." The right to privacy under the Florida Constitution "is a personal one, inuring solely to individuals." *Alterra Healthcare Corp. v. Estate of Francis Shelley*, 827 So. 2d 936, 941 (Fla. 2002); *see, e.g., Florida Ass'n of Prof. Lobbyists v. Div. of Leg.*, 431 F. Supp. 2d 1228, 1236 (N.D. Fla. 2006) (finding that a lobbying firm, as a business entity, was not entitled to privacy rights).

State v. Eitel

227 So. 2d 449 (Fla. 1969)

MANN, ROBERT T., District Court Judge.

Any man's death diminishes me.

John Donne, *Devotions XVII.*

No one pretends that actions
Should be as free as opinions.

John Stuart Mill, *On Liberty.*

Does a motorcyclist have a constitutional right to ride the highways without the protective helmet and goggles or face mask the legislature says he must wear? The trial judge thought so. Michigan and Louisiana courts have agreed. But others have upheld similar statutes, declaring that the danger of flying stones is likely to distract the cyclist and send him hurtling into the path of motorists, or that "it is to the interest of the state to have strong, robust, healthy citizens, capable of self-support, of bearing arms, and of adding to the resources of the country." We approve without hesitation the requirement of protection for the eyes. Any collision between the naked eyeball of the cyclist and the dirt increasingly airborne in our time is likely to pose a menace to others. But we ought to admit frankly that the purpose of the helmet is to preserve the life and health of the cyclist, and for some more divinely ordained and humanely explicable purpose than the service of the state.

The search for precedent is often frustrated, but we believe that society has an interest in the preservation of the life of the individual for his own sake. Suicide, for example, has been a common-law crime for centuries. *Hales v. Petit*, 1 Plowd. 262 (1561). But we find uneasiness in American legislatures and courts when dealing with self-preservation. They are inclined to require *others* to furnish the individual the means for his own protection. Employers are required to furnish safety equipment; automobile manufacturers are required to furnish seat belts. *See* Fla. Stats. § 440.56 (1967), F.S.A.; 15 U.S.C.A. § 1381 et seq. and standards adopted thereunder. Or they incline to emphasize protection of *others* rather than *self*. Those religious cultists who handle snakes were forbidden to do so in the name of public safety, for example. *State v. Massey*, 229 N.C. 734, 51 S.E.2d 179 (1949), *cert. den. sub nom. Bunn v. North Carolina*, 336 U.S. 942 (1949).

We hold that the legislature may impose a minimal inconvenience which affords effective protection against a significant possibility of grave or fatal injury. We have known the pleasure of wind in our faces, but it is relative: death has come with increasing and alarming frequency to motor-cyclists in recent years. Seventy-seven per cent of the motorcycle accident deaths studied by a California physician were caused by craniocerebral injury with no potentially fatal trauma to other parts of the body. Graham, *Fatal Motorcycle Accidents*, 14 J.For.Sci. 79 (1969). A New York legislative report, citing the rapid increase in number of motorcycle accidents, stated that 89.2% Of these accidents resulted in injury or death and that almost all fatalities involved head injuries, most of which could have been avoided or ameliorated by the use of a proper helmet. McKinney's Session Laws of New York 1966, at p. 2961. An orthopedic surgeon testified in this case that he had cared for six persons injured in motorcycle crashes while wearing protective helmets. None had severe head injury. The inconvenience to the person will vary, but the danger is real and the protection reasonably adapted to its avoidance.

These unwilling cyclists must obey this law. We admire John Stuart Mill's *Essay on Liberty*, which their counsel cite to persuade us that the State of Florida has unconstitutionally infringed Eitel's and Thompson's right to be let alone. But Mill said there that "no person is an entirely isolated being; it is impossible for a person to do anything seriously or permanently hurtful to himself, without mischief reaching at least to his near connections, and often far beyond them." If he falls we cannot leave him lying in the road. The legislature may constitutionally conclude that the cyclist's right to be let alone is no more precious than the corresponding right of ambulance drivers, nurses and neurosurgeons.

The statute requires that the protective equipment meet the standards of the highway Safety Act of 1966, 23 U.S.C.A. § 401 et seq. Standard 4.4.3, promulgated after the enactment but before the effective date of the Florida act, leaves the specifications to the state. The Department of Public Safety adopted Chapter 295G of its Rules months before these charges were brought. We find no unconstitutional delegation of power, nor any vagueness here. Indeed, we think it wise for the Legislature, which stated its purpose with sufficient clarity, to leave to administrative officials the specification of impact strength and the like.

Reversed and remanded.

ROBERTS, Acting C.J., and DREW, CARLTON, ADKINS and BOYD, JJ., and MELVIN, Circuit Judge, concur.

Questions

1. What is the "balancing test" enunciated by the Court in this case?

2. Note that this case came before the adoption of Section 23. As you read Section 23 and think about the Court's reasoning in this case:

    a. Which entity is the Court protecting in this case?

    b. Would that entity also be protected under Section 23?

3. Note that in the last paragraph of the case, the Court mentions "delegation of power" by the Legislature to a department of the executive branch. Although this issue will be explored later, for now, make a mental note of why the Court finds that the delegation of power is proper in this instance.

Florida Board of Bar Examiners re: Applicant

443 So. 2d 71 (Fla. 1983)

ALDERMAN, Chief Justice.

Applicant seeks review of a ruling by the Board of Bar Examiners refusing to process his application for admission to The Florida Bar until he answers item 28(b) of the applicant's questionnaire and affidavit and until he executes the authorization and release form required by the Rules of the Supreme Court Relating to Admissions to the Bar. Applicant maintains that the Board's action violates his right of privacy and his right to due process of law guaranteed by the Florida and United States Constitutions, and his rights guaranteed by section 90.503, Florida Statutes (1981), and article I, section 2 of the Florida Constitution. We find no merit to his contentions and approve the decision of the Florida Board of Bar Examiners requiring applicant to complete all portions of the questionnaire, including item 28(b), and to execute an unaltered authorization and release form before the Board will process his application for admission to The Florida Bar.

Applicant applied for admission to The Florida Bar in April 1982 by submitting application for admission form No. 1 and a modified authorization release. On his authorization release, he included a proviso that his release did not apply to his medical records. On his application, he expressly declined to answer question 28(b) on the basis that it violates his constitutional rights. In answering the questionnaire, the applicant disclosed under item 12 that he had served on active duty with the United States Marine Corps and that he had not been discharged, but rather had been transferred to a temporary retired list for medical reasons and later had been retired.

Item 28(b) asks:

Have you ever received REGULAR treatment for amnesia, or any form of insanity, emotional disturbance, nervous or mental disorder?

If yes, please state the names and addresses of the psychologists, psychiatrists, or other medical practitioners who treated you. (Regular treatment shall mean consultation with any such person more than two times within any 12 month period.)

The authorization and release form provided by the Board in compliance with the rules of admission states:

I, _____, having filed an application with the Florida Board of Bar Examiners and fully recognizing the responsibility to the Public, the Bench, and the Bar of this State lodged with the Florida Board of Bar Examiners by the Supreme Court of Florida under the Constitution of the State of Florida to determine that only those of high character and ability are admitted to The Bar of Florida, hereby authorize and request every medical doctor, school official, and every other person, firm, officer, corporation, association, organization or institution having control of any documents, records or other information pertaining to me *relevant to my good moral character and fitness to perform the responsibilities of an attorney*, to furnish the originals or copies of any such documents, records and other information to said Board, or any of its representatives, and to permit said Board, or any of its representatives, to inspect and make copies of any such documents, records and other information including but not limited to any and all medical reports, laboratory reports, X-rays, or clinical abstracts which may have been made or prepared pursuant to, or in connection with, any examination or examinations, consultation or consultations, test or tests, evaluation or evaluations, of the undersigned.

I hereby authorize all such persons as set out above to answer any inquiries, questions, or interrogatories concerning the undersigned which may be submitted to them by the Florida Board of Bar Examiners or its authorized representative, and to appear before said Board, or its authorized representative, and to give full and complete testimony concerning the undersigned, including any information furnished by the undersigned. I hereby relinquish any and all rights to said reports, including but not limited to clinical abstracts, consultations, evaluations, or any other information incident in any way to cooperation with the Florida Board of Bar Examiners, or its authorized representative, and fully understand that I shall not be entitled to have disclosed to me the contents of any of the foregoing.

I hereby release and exonerate every medical doctor, school official, and every other person, firm, officer, corporation, association, organization or institution which shall comply in good faith with the authorization and request made herein from any and all liability of every nature and kind growing out of or in anywise pertaining to the furnishing or inspection of such documents, records and other information or the investigation made by said Florida Board of Bar Examiners. The undersigned further waives absolutely any privilege __he may have *relevant to h____ good moral character and fitness to perform the responsibilities of an attorney* under Sections 90.242 and 490.32, Florida Statutes.

(Emphasis supplied.)

The executive director of the Board, on behalf of the Board, advised the applicant that processing of his application would be withheld for ten days pending receipt of an executed and unaltered authorization and release and a response to question 28(b). More correspondence between the Board and the applicant ensued for several months, concluding in the Board's decision not to process his application until he complied with the requirements of the Board.

Applicant seeks review of the Board's refusal to process his application and initially contends that to require him to answer question 28(b) and to submit an unconditional authorization and waiver violates his constitutional right of privacy under the Florida and United States Constitutions.

Article I, section 23 of the Florida Constitution provides:

Every natural person has the right to be let alone and free from governmental intrusion into his private life except as otherwise provided herein. This section shall not be construed to limit the public's right of access to public records and meetings as provided by law.

Applicant concedes and we agree that this constitutional provision was not intended to provide an absolute guarantee against all governmental intrusion into the private life of an individual.

Preliminarily, we must determine whether the requirement that applicant answer item 28(b) and execute the authorization and release falls within the governmental intrusion as contemplated by article I, section 23, and, if so, we must decide whether this intrusion violates the applicant's constitutional right of privacy. The action of the Board clearly is not within the exception proviso of article I, section 23. It is just as evident that the Board's action does constitute governmental action. The exclusive jurisdiction to regulate admission of persons to the practice of law is vested in this Court. Art. V, § 15, Fla. Const. We established the Florida Board of Bar Examiners as an arm of this Court to assist us in this function.

We also find that the applicant's right of privacy is implicated by item 28(b) and the authorization and release form which allow a limited intrusion into his private life. The extent of his privacy right, however, must be considered in the context in which it is asserted and may not be considered wholly independent of those circumstances. He has chosen to seek admission into The Florida Bar. He has no constitutional right to be admitted to the Bar. Rather, the practice of law in this state is a privilege. *State ex rel. The Florida Bar v. Evans,* 94 So.2d 730 (Fla.1957). In this case, the applicant's right of privacy is circumscribed and limited by the circumstances in which he asserts that right. By making application to the Bar, he has assumed the burden of demonstrating his fitness for admission into the Bar. Fla.Sup.Ct. Bar Admiss. Rule, art. III, § 2. This encompasses mental and emotional fitness as well as character and educational fitness.

Although circumscribed and limited by the context in which it is asserted, the applicant does have a right of privacy, and we must determine whether it has been unconstitutionally intruded upon by the Board's requirements. We have not yet decided a case in which we have had to determine the appropriate standard of review in assessing a claim of unconstitutional governmental intrusion into one's privacy rights under article I, section 23. We need not make that decision in the present case since we find that the Board's action meets even the highest standard of the compelling state interest test.

The compelling state interest or strict scrutiny standard imposes a heavy burden of justification upon the state to show an important societal need and the use of the least intrusive means to achieve that goal. *Carey v. Population Services International*, 431 U.S. 678 (1977); *Roe v. Wade*, 410 U.S. 113 (1973); *In re Estate of Greenberg*, 390 So.2d 40 (Fla.1980).

Applicant concedes and we agree that the state's interest in ensuring that only those fit to practice law are admitted to the Bar is a compelling state interest. He admits that there is a legitimate need for the intrusion. His concern is not with the end sought to be achieved by the Board but is rather with the means employed by the Board to fulfill its responsibilities. He asserts that the authorization and release form and item 28(b) are unnecessarily overbroad and suggests that there should be some time limitation relative to the information sought.

That the state has a compelling state interest in regulating the legal profession has been expressly recognized by the Supreme Court of the United States. *Goldfarb v. Virginia State Bar*, 421 U.S. 773, 792 (1975)....

In charging the Board with the duty to determine the character and fitness of applicants to The Florida Bar, we have required that:

> Prior to recommending an applicant for admission to practice the profession of law in Florida, the Florida Board of Bar Examiners shall conduct an investigation and otherwise inquire into and determine the character, fitness, and general qualifications of every applicant. In every such investigation and inquiry, the Board may obtain such information as bears upon the character, fitness, and general qualifications of the applicant and take and hear testimony, administer oaths and affirmations, and compel, by subpoena, the attendance of witnesses and the production of books, papers and documents. Any member of the Board may administer such oaths and affirmations. Such investigations and inquiries shall be informal, but they shall be thorough, with the object of ascertaining the truth. Technical rules of evidence need not be observed. Any investigative hearing for such purpose may be held by a division of the Board consisting of not less than three members of the

Board. Each division shall record its proceedings and shall report its decisions to the full Board. Formal hearings held in response to Specifications shall be conducted before a quorum of the Board which shall consist of not less than five members.

Fla.Sup.Ct. Bar Admiss. Rule, art. III, § 3(a). It is imperative for the protection of the public that applicants to the Bar be thoroughly screened by the Board. Necessarily, the Board must ask questions in this screening process which are of a personal nature and which would not otherwise be asked of persons not applying for a position of public trust and responsibility. Because of a lawyer's constant interaction with the public, a wide range of factors must be considered which would not customarily be considered in the licensing of tradesmen and businessmen. *The Florida Bar, Petition of Rubin*, 323 So.2d 257 (Fla.1975). The inquiry into an applicant's past history of regular treatment for emotional disturbance or nervous or mental disorder requested by item 28(b) furthers the legitimate state interest since mental fitness and emotional stability are essential to the ability to practice law in a manner not injurious to the public. The pressures placed on an attorney are enormous and his mental and emotional stability should be at such a level that he is able to handle his responsibilities.

We find that the Board has employed the least intrusive means to achieve its compelling state interest. The information sought by item 28(b) is vital to the Board in evaluating an applicant's fitness. To ensure that it has all of the information necessary for its evaluation, the Board rather than the applicant must be the judge of what part of the applicant's past history is relevant.

There is no precise list of medical conditions that may affect a person's fitness to practice law and no uniformity among people who suffer from these conditions. The means employed by the Board cannot be narrowed without impinging on the Board's effectiveness in carrying out its important responsibilities. A time limitation on the information sought could preclude the Board from obtaining vitally relevant information which could impact on its decision as to an applicant's mental and emotional fitness to practice law. The fact that the information obtained in response to the Board's inquiry is held in confidence by the Board and by this Court minimizes the intrusion on an applicant's privacy. Additionally, the authorization and release form, contrary to applicant's assertion, is not a blanket release but rather is expressly limited to information *relevant* to an applicant's "good moral character and fitness to perform the responsibilities of an attorney." We hold that the Board's action does not violate article I, section 23 of the Florida Constitution.

We also hold that the Board's action does not violate applicant's federal constitutional right of privacy....

Even applying the highest standard of review, we have already decided that the Board has demonstrated a compelling state interest and use of the least intrusive means to achieve that interest.

We likewise find no merit to applicant's claim that the Board's challenged action violates his right to due process of law or that it violates his rights guaranteed by article I, section 2 of the Florida Constitution, which provides in pertinent part that no person shall be deprived of any right because of physical handicap.

* * *

Accordingly, we approve the ruling of the Florida Board of Bar Examiners requiring applicant to answer item 28(b) and to file an unaltered authorization and release form. Until that time, the Board is fully warranted in not processing his application.

It is so ordered.

BOYD, OVERTON, McDONALD, EHRLICH and SHAW, JJ., concur.

ADKINS, Justice, dissenting.

As to the petitioner's claim predicated on the Florida Constitution, I agree with the majority that the state's interest in ensuring that only those fit to practice law are admitted to The Florida Bar is a compelling state interest. However, I must agree with the petitioner's assertion that the authorization and release form and item 28(b) are unnecessarily overbroad. I also agree with the majority's conclusion that mental fitness and emotional stability are essential to the ability to practice law in a manner not injurious to the public. However, I do not agree with the assertion that the means employed by the Board cannot be narrowed without impinging on the Board's effectiveness in carrying out its responsibilities. As petitioner argues, it is difficult to conceive of information in which an individual has a greater legitimate expectation of privacy than medical records containing communications and other information between an applicant and a psychiatrist, psychologist, or counselor. Accordingly, information which is irrelevant to an applicant's ability to practice law in this state should not come within the scope of the Board's inquiry. An applicant's past treatment for some emotional disturbance, such as loss of a parent for instance, or treatment for amnesia which occurred, say, as a child ten or fifteen years ago surely is not relevant to the potential of that applicant to be a fit and worthy member of The Florida Bar today. At a minimum I feel there must be some time frame incorporated in question 28(b) and the authorization of the release of medical records relating to treatment for emotional disturbances, etc. In addition, I feel the form of the question seeking information about regular treatment for emotional disturbances, etc., could be phrased in terms which elicit information with regard to problems which, in the judgment of the medical community, impact on one's fitness to practice law. Such an approach would be consistent with the mandate of article I, section 23 of the Florida Constitution.

For these same reasons, I would hold that the Board's action also violates the applicant's federal constitutional right of privacy. I do not believe the least intrusive means have been employed and, if a balancing test were held to be the appropriate standard, the interests served by the question as it exists do not outweigh the privacy interests of the individual hindered.

Notes and Questions

1. What is the two-prong test the majority employs in this case? (Hint: the majority and dissent disagree whether the state met the second prong.)

2. According to the Court, what is the level/standard to which the state's interest must rise in order to uphold state action against a challenge grounded on privacy (part 1 of 2-part test,) and how does the Court justify the validity of question 28(b)?

3. How would the dissent require the Board of Bar Examiners to amend question 28(b)?

City of North Miami v. Kurtz

653 So. 2d 1025 (Fla. 1995)

OVERTON, Justice.

We have for review *Kurtz v. City of North Miami*, 625 So.2d 899 (Fla. 3d DCA 1993). After the district court issued that decision, it certified, in a separate order, the following question as one of great public importance:

> DOES ARTICLE I, SECTION 23 OF THE FLORIDA CONSTITUTION PRO-HIBIT A MUNICIPALITY FROM REQUIRING JOB APPLICANTS TO RE-FRAIN FROM USING TOBACCO OR TOBACCO PRODUCTS FOR ONE YEAR BEFORE APPLYING FOR, AND AS A CONDITION FOR BEING CONSIDERED FOR EMPLOYMENT, EVEN WHERE THE USE OF TO-BACCO IS NOT RELATED TO JOB FUNCTION IN THE POSITION SOUGHT BY THE APPLICANT?

This question involves the issue of whether applicants seeking government employment have a reasonable expectation of privacy under article I, section 23, as to their smoking habits.[6]

We have jurisdiction. Art. I, §3(b)(4), Fla. Const. For the reasons expressed, we answer the certified question in the negative, finding that Florida's constitutional privacy provision does not afford Arlene Kurtz, the job applicant in this case, protection under the circumstances presented.

The record establishes the following unrefuted facts. To reduce costs and to increase productivity, the City of North Miami adopted an employment policy designed to reduce the number of employees who smoke tobacco. In accordance with that policy decision, the City issued Administrative Regulation 1-46, which requires all job applicants to sign an affidavit stating that they have not used tobacco or tobacco products for at least one year immediately preceding their application for employment. The intent of the regulation is to gradually reduce the number of smokers in the City's work force by means of natural attrition. Consequently, the regulation only applies to job applicants and does not affect current employees. Once an applicant has been

---

6. [FN 1.] Notably, because Florida's constitutional privacy provision applies only to government action, the provision would not be implicated if a job applicant was applying for a position with a private employer.

hired, the applicant is free to start or resume smoking at any time. Evidence in the record, however, reflects that a high percentage of smokers who have adhered to the one year cessation requirement are unlikely to resume smoking.

Additional evidence submitted by the City indicates that each smoking employee costs the City as much as $4,611 per year in 1981 dollars over what it incurs for non-smoking employees. The City is a self-insurer and its taxpayers pay for 100% of its employees' medical expenses. In enacting the regulation, the City made a policy decision to reduce costs and increase productivity by eventually eliminating a substantial number of smokers from its work force. Evidence presented to the trial court indicated that the regulation would accomplish these goals.

The respondent in this case, Arlene Kurtz, applied for a clerk-typist position with the City. When she was interviewed for the position, she was informed of Regulation 1-46. She told the interviewer that she was a smoker and could not truthfully sign an affidavit to comply with the regulation. The interviewer then informed Kurtz that she would not be considered for employment until she was smoke-free for one year. Thereafter, Kurtz filed this action seeking to enjoin enforcement of the regulation and asking for a declaratory judgment finding the regulation to be unconstitutional.

In ruling on a motion for summary judgment, the trial judge recognized that Kurtz has a fundamental right of privacy under article I, section 23, of the Florida Constitution. The trial judge noted that Kurtz had presented the issue in the narrow context of whether she has a right to smoke in her own home. While he agreed that such a right existed, he concluded that the true issue to be decided was whether the City, as a governmental entity, could regulate smoking through employment. Because he found that there is no expectation of privacy in employment and that the regulation did not violate any provision of either the Florida or the federal constitutions, summary judgment was granted in favor of the City.

The Third District Court of Appeal reversed. The district court first determined that Kurtz' privacy rights are involved when the City requires her to refrain from smoking for a year prior to being considered to employment. The district court then found that, although the City does have an interest in saving taxpayers money by decreasing insurance costs and increasing productivity, such interest is insufficient to outweigh the intrusion into Kurtz' right of privacy and has no relevance to the performance of the duties involved with a clerk-typist. Consequently, the district court concluded that the regulation violated Kurtz's privacy rights under article I, section 23, of the Florida Constitution. We disagree.

Florida's constitutional privacy provision ... protects Florida's citizens from the government's uninvited observation of or interference in those areas that fall within the ambit of the zone of privacy afforded under this provision. *Shaktman v. State*, 553 So.2d 148 (Fla.1989). Unlike the implicit privacy right of the federal constitution, Florida's privacy provision is, in and of itself, a fundamental one that, once implicated, demands evaluation under a compelling state interest standard. *Winfield v. Division of Pari-Mutuel Wagering*, 477 So.2d 544 (Fla.1985). The federal privacy provision, on the other hand, extends only to such fundamental interests as marriage, procreation, contraception, family relationships, and the rearing and educating of children. *Carey v. Population Serv. Int'l*, 431 U.S. 678 (1977)

Although Florida's privacy right provides greater protection than the federal constitution, it was not intended to be a guarantee against all intrusion into the life of an individual. *Florida Bd. of Bar Examiners re Applicant*, 443 So.2d 71 (Fla.1983). First, the privacy provision applies only to government action, and the right provided under that provision is circumscribed and limited by the circumstances in which it is asserted. *Id.* Further, "[d]etermining 'whether an *individual* has a legitimate expectation of privacy in any given case must be made by considering all the circumstances, especially objective manifestations of that expectation.'" *Stall v. State*, 570 So.2d 257, 260 (Fla.1990) (alteration in original) (quoting *Shaktman*, 553 So.2d at 153 (Fla.1989) (Ehrlich, C.J., concurring)), *cert. denied*, 501 U.S. 1250 (1991). Thus, to determine whether Kurtz, as a job applicant, is entitled to protection under article I, section 23, we must first determine whether a governmental entity is intruding into an aspect of Kurtz's life in which she as a "legitimate expectation of privacy." If we find in the affirmative, we must then look to whether a compelling interest exists to justify that intrusion and, if so, whether the least intrusive means is being used to accomplish the goal.

In this case, we find that the City's action does not intrude into an aspect of Kurtz' life in which she has a legitimate expectation of privacy. In today's society, smokers are constantly required to reveal whether they smoke. When individuals are seated in a restaurant, they are asked whether they want a table in a smoking or non-smoking section. When individuals rent hotel or motel rooms, they are asked if they smoke so that management may ensure that certain rooms remain free from the smell of smoke odors. Likewise, when individuals rent cars, they are asked if they smoke so that rental agencies can make proper accommodations to maintain vehicles for non-smokers. Further, employers generally provide smoke-free areas for non-smokers, and employees are often prohibited from smoking in certain areas. Given that individuals must reveal whether they smoke in almost every aspect of life in today's society, we conclude that individuals have no reasonable expectation of privacy in the disclosure of that information when applying for a government job and, consequently, that Florida's right of privacy is not implicated under these unique circumstances.

In reaching the conclusion that the right to privacy is not implicated in this case, however, we emphasize that our holding is limited to the narrow issue presented. Notably, we are not addressing the issue of whether an applicant, once hired, could be compelled by a government agency to stop smoking. Equally as important, neither are we holding today that a governmental entity can ask any type of information it chooses of prospective job applicants.

… For the reasons expressed, we answer the question in the negative, finding that Florida's constitutional privacy provision does not afford the applicant, Arlene Kurtz, protection because she has no reasonable expectation of privacy under the circumstances of this case. Accordingly, we quash the district court's decision, and we remand this case with directions that the district court of appeal affirm the trial court judgment.

It is so ordered.

GRIMES, C.J., and HARDING, WELLS and ANSTEAD, JJ., concur.

KOGAN, J., dissents with an opinion, in which SHAW, J., concurs.

KOGAN, Justice, dissenting.

As the majority itself notes, job applicants are free to return to tobacco use once hired. I believe this concession reveals the anti-smoking policy to be rather more of a speculative pretense than a rational governmental policy. Therefore I would find it unconstitutional under the right of due process. *See Department of Law Enforcement v. Real Property,* 588 So.2d 957 (Fla.1991).

The privacy issue is more troublesome, to my mind. There is a "slippery-slope" problem here because, if governmental employers can inquire too extensively into off-job-site behavior, a point eventually will be reached at which the right of privacy under article I, section 23 clearly will be breached. An obvious example would be an inquiry into the lawful sexual behavior of job applicants in an effort to identify those with the "most desirable" lifestyles. Such an effort easily could become the pretext for a constitutional violation. The time has not yet fully passed, for example, when women job applicants have been questioned about their plans for procreation in an effort to eliminate those who may be absent on family leave. I cannot conceive that such an act is anything other than a violation of the right of privacy when done by a governmental unit.

Health-based concerns like those expressed by the City also present a definite slippery slope to the courts. The time is fast approaching, for example, when human beings can be genetically tested so thoroughly that susceptibility to particular diseases can be identified years in advance. To my mind, any governmental effort to identify those who might eventually suffer from cancer or heart disease, for instance, itself is a violation of bodily integrity guaranteed by article I, section 23. Moreover, I cannot help but note that any such effort comes perilously close to the discredited practice of eugenics.

The use of tobacco products is more troubling, however. While legal, tobacco use nevertheless is an activity increasingly regulated by the law. If the federal government, for instance, chose to regulate tobacco as a controlled substance, I have no trouble saying that this act alone does not undermine anyone's privacy right. However, regulation is not the issue here because tobacco use today remains legal. The sole question is whether the government may inquire into off-job-site behavior that is legal, however unhealthy it might be. In light of the inherently poor fit between the governmental objective and the ends actually achieved, I am more inclined to agree with the district court that the right of privacy has been violated here. I might reach a different result if the objective were better served by the means chosen.

SHAW, J., concurs.

Notes and Questions

1. What if the employer in the previous case was a private company? In each of the cases so far, we have looked at intrusion by the government—whether by law or by policy—on an individual's privacy. But these cases would have had different outcomes had the intruding party been a private actor. As with many federal constitutional rights, the right to privacy under the Florida Constitution applies only to intrusions by the government.

2. An activity where someone might have a reasonable expectation of privacy in one context might not be the same in another. In *Stall v. State*, 570 So. 2d 257 (Fla. 1990), the Supreme Court upheld Florida's criminal prohibition selling or purchasing obscene materials. The Court noted that the U.S. Supreme Court had, in *Stanley v. Georgia*, 394 U.S. 557 (1969), found that the federal privacy right protected an individual's private possession of obscene materials. However, the Court explained "[a]lthough one may possess obscene material in one's home, there is no legitimate reasonable expectation of privacy in being able to patronize retail establishments for the purpose of purchasing such material." *Stall*, 570 So. 2d at 260.

Post-Newsweek Stations Florida, Inc. v. Doe

612 So. 2d 549 (Fla. 1992)

McDONALD, Justice.

We review *Doe v. State*, 587 So.2d 526, 528–29 (Fla. 4th DCA1991), in which the district court certified the following questions:

> 1. In a criminal proceeding charging a defendant with prostitution, does a non-party who claims a right of privacy in documents held by the state attorney as criminal investigative information have standing to seek an order of the trial court which would deny the public and the press access to evidence revealing names of the defendant's clients when pursuant to the defendant's discovery motion the state is prepared to deliver said evidence to the defendants as required by Florida rule of criminal procedure 3.220 and which upon delivery would otherwise render them "public records" pursuant to *Bludworth v. Palm Beach Newspapers, Inc.*, 476 so.2d 775 (Fla. 4th DCA1985), *rev. denied*, 488 so.2d 67 (Fla. 1986)?
>
> 2. In a criminal proceeding charging a defendant with prostitution, does the trial court abuse its discretion under section 119.011(3)(c)5 of the public records act in denying closure of discovery documents where an unnamed third party claims that release of such information would be defamatory to him and would invade his right of privacy both under the act, article I, section 23 of the Florida Constitution and the federal constitution, and the trial court finds that release of the information will harm the third party?

No right of privacy for John

We have jurisdiction pursuant to article V, section 3(b)(4), Florida Constitution. We answer the first question in the affirmative and under the facts of this case answer the second question in the negative and approve the decision of the district court.

In July 1991, the Broward County Sheriff's Office investigated allegations that Kathy Willets and her husband, Deputy Sheriff Jeffrey Willets, were involved in a criminal prostitution scheme. On July 23, 1991, the police obtained a search warrant and searched the Willets' home. Various pieces of evidence were seized, including cassette tapes containing recorded telephone conversations, business cards of alleged customers of Kathy Willets, a Rolodex containing names and addresses, and other lists stating the names, amounts paid, and sexual notations regarding her customers.

The state charged Kathy Willets with one count of prostitution, Jeffrey Willets with one count of living off the proceeds of prostitution, and charged both with illegal wiretapping. On August 31, 1991, the Willets filed a discovery request under rule 3.220 of the Florida Rules of Criminal Procedure asking the state to turn over all of the material seized from their home, including the documents identifying the John Does. Numerous John Does, styled as interested parties/witnesses, filed a motion in the trial court to deny public access to pretrial discovery materials.[7] The trial court denied the Does' motion and declared that, once the state attorney provided the discovery documents to the Willets, the documents became records available for public inspection. When the state announced that it was prepared to disclose the material in its possession as required by rule 3.220, the Does moved for a stay of release of the discovery materials. The trial judge concluded that people named on the "client list" of a prostitute have no reasonable expectation of privacy as to their identity and ordered the release of the names and addresses contained in the documents. He reserved ruling, subject to an in-camera review, on whether other material or information should be released. The district court subsequently stayed the order, affirmed the trial court's decision, and certified the questions.

Pursuant to rule 3.220(m), the Does have standing to challenge the release of the discovery materials. Rule 3.220(m) provides that "[u]pon request of *any person,* the court may permit any showing of cause for denial or regulation of disclosures, or any portion of such showing to be made in camera." (Emphasis added). In addition, rule 3.220(*l*) allows the court to restrict disclosure to protect a witness from "harassment, unnecessary inconvenience or invasion of privacy." Even though the Does are not parties named in the state's criminal action against the Willets, the broad language of rule 3.220 permits them to show cause for denying the disclosure of the discovery information at issue in the criminal proceeding. Therefore, we answer the first certified question in the affirmative.

Our answer to the second certified question requires us to analyze the discovery information under the rubric of the rules of criminal procedure, the public records

---

7. [FN1.] Five John Does initially submitted sworn affidavits in support of their motions for closure. The affidavits asserted that the affiants were "private" individuals and that release of the information would be defamatory to the Does' personal and professional reputations. All of the affidavits were identical in form and content, except for one which adds a paragraph stating that he sent a letter and his business card to Kathy Willets and spoke to her on the telephone, but claiming that he did not "meet Kathy Willets, travel to her house, or engage or attempt to engage in any illegal activity with her." Affidavit of John Doe, August 19, 1991.

law, and the right to privacy. Rule 3.220 requires the state to disclose to the defendant, upon request, any tangible papers or objects which were obtained from or belonged to the accused. The state, which takes no position on the issue in this case, was prepared to comply with the Willets' discovery request when the Does sought a stay in the trial court. The media contends that the Public Records Act establishes a statutory right of access to the pretrial discovery information. The Does, on the other hand, argue that disclosure of the discovery information will violate their right of privacy and that the information should be exempted from the disclosure requirements of the public records law, chapter 119, Florida Statutes (1989).

Florida law clearly expresses that it is the policy of this state that all government records, with particular exemptions, shall be open for public inspection. § 119.01. Subsection 119.011(3)(c) provides an exemption for criminal investigative information developed for the prosecution of a criminal defendant. Pursuant to the statute, such information will not be accessible to the public until the information is given or required by law or agency rule to be given to the accused. § 119.011(3)(c)(5). Rule 3.220 requires the state to turn over the discovery information to the defendant. In *Florida Freedom Newspapers, Inc. v. McCrary,* 520 So.2d 32 (Fla.1988), we stated that, once the state gives the requested information to the defendant, pretrial discovery information attains the status of a public record. However, *McCrary* qualified the statutory right of access to public records by balancing it against the constitutional rights of a fair trial and due process. *Id.* at 36. Here, we also qualify the public's statutory right of access to pretrial discovery information by balancing it against the Does' constitutional right to privacy.

The Does bear the burden of proving that closure is necessary to prevent an imminent threat to their privacy rights. *Barron v. Florida Freedom Newspapers, Inc.,* 531 So.2d 113 (Fla.1988); *Miami Herald Publishing Co. v. Lewis,* 426 So.2d 1 (Fla.1982). The media argue that the Does have failed to satisfy the three-pronged test articulated in *Lewis,* and, therefore, they have failed to carry their burden to justify closure.... The *Lewis* test balances a criminal defendant's rights to a fair trial against the public's right to disclosure in pretrial proceedings. We conclude, however, that the *Lewis* test is not applicable to the balancing of interests in the instant case. First, the *Lewis* test does not address the impact of public disclosure on a third party's right of privacy. Unlike the defendant in *Lewis,* the John Does have not been charged with any crime. Second, *Lewis* dealt with the closure of a pretrial hearing, not with the closure of pretrial discovery documents that are at issue in this case.

The more appropriate standard that we choose to apply in the instant case was set forth by this Court in *Barron:*

> [C]losure of court proceedings or records should occur only when necessary (a) to comply with established public policy set forth in the constitution, statutes, rules, or case law; (b) to protect trade secrets; (c) to protect a compelling governmental interest [e.g., national security; confidential informants]; (d) to obtain evidence to properly determine legal issues in a case; (e) *to avoid substantial injury to innocent third parties* [e.g. to protect young witnesses from offensive testimony; to protect children in a divorce]; or (f) *to avoid*

> *substantial injury to a party by disclosure of matters protected by a common*
> *law or privacy right not generally inherent in the specific type of civil proceeding*
> *sought to be closed.*

531 So.2d at 118 (emphasis supplied). The media oppose application of the *Barron* test because that case involved a common law right of access to judicial records rather than a statutory right of access. However, whether public access is afforded via a common law right or a statutory right, both the goals of opening government to public scrutiny and simultaneously protecting individuals from unwarranted government intrusion are served by application of the *Barron* standard.

Barron recognized that "it is generally the content of the subject matter" that determines whether a privacy interest exists that might override the public's right to inspect the records. *Id.* The Does assert that the materials at issue include intimate information relating to genital size and sexual performance. Although documents containing such information were seized from the Willets' home, the trial court limited its order to the release of only the names and addresses on the state's witness list. Therefore, the matter we address here is limited strictly to the names and addresses contained on the same list.

According to the Does' reasoning, Florida's constitutional right to privacy protects them from having their names and addresses released to the public. Since its adoption by the voters of Florida in 1980, the privacy amendment has provided the basis for protecting several types of information and activities from public disclosure. *In re T.W.,* 551 So.2d 1186 (Fla.1989) (woman's decision of whether to continue her pregnancy); *Rasmussen v. South Florida Blood Service, Inc.,* 500 So.2d 533 (Fla.1987) (confidential donor information concerning AIDS-tainted blood supply); *Florida Board of Bar Examiners re: Applicant,* 443 So.2d 71 (Fla.1983) (bar application questions concerning disclosure of psychiatric counseling). The privacy amendment has not been interpreted to protect names and addresses contained in public records, and we reject the Does' suggestion that the privacy right should be extended that far based on the facts of this case. The Does in the instant case had their names and addresses associated with a criminal prostitution scheme. Any right of privacy that the Does might have is limited by the circumstances under which they assert that right. *See Florida Board of Bar Examiners,* 443 So.2d at 74. The circumstances here do not afford them such a right. Because the Does' privacy rights are not implicated when they participate in a crime, we find that closure is not justified under *Barron.*

Even though the names and addresses of people on the witness list of a criminal prosecution may be disclosed to the public, we emphasize that the public does not have a universal right to all discovery materials. Depending on the circumstances and the subject matter, discovery may "seriously implicate privacy interests of litigants and third parties." *Seattle Times Co. v. Rhinehart,* 467 U.S. 20, 35 (1984). The purposes of criminal discovery are to narrow the issues of the case, to ascertain facts that will be relevant at trial, and to avail the parties of information that will avoid surprise tactics in the courtroom. *State v. Tascarella,* 580 So.2d 154 (Fla.1991). Discovery is not intended to be a vehicle for the media to use in its search for newsworthy information. This Court is wary of an outcome that will cause victims and witnesses to withhold valuable discovery information because they fear that personal information will be divulged without discretion. However, we also recognize that this state's open government policy requires that information be available for public inspection unless the information fits under a legislatively created exemption. *Wait v. Florida Power & Light Co.*, 372 So.2d 420 (Fla.1979).

We are confident that the in-camera proceeding conducted by the trial judge protects any privacy interests of third parties like the John Does. The purpose of the in-camera inspection is to balance the privacy interests of the parties with the public's need to know the information. *State v. Burns*, 830 P.2d 1318 (Mont.1992). In addition to lending credence to the trial court's decision whether to release the information, the in-camera inspection also "helps dispel any cloud of public suspicion that might otherwise be suspended over governmental efforts to sustain secrecy *sua sponte*." *Tribune Co. v. Public Records*, 493 So.2d 480, 484 (Fla. 2d DCA1986), *review denied*, 503 So.2d 327 (Fla.1987).

We hold that the trial judge did not abuse his discretion in concluding that the Does lacked a privacy interest in their names and addresses. Although the trial judge did not make a finding as to whether release of the information would be defamatory to the good name of a victim or witness, our conclusion that the Does do not have a privacy interest in their names and addresses negates the need for such a factual determination.

For the reasons stated, we find that the Does have failed to show good cause for prohibiting the disclosure of the names and addresses on the witness list. We therefore approve the district court's decision affirming the trial court's order.

It is so ordered.

OVERTON, SHAW, GRIMES and HARDING, JJ., concur.

BARKETT, C.J., concurs with an opinion. [omitted]

KOGAN, Justice, dissenting.

In many years as a trial judge I personally had the opportunity to see a large number of cases in which unfounded innuendo, malicious gossip, and irrelevant speculation about private lives found their way into the State's discovery materials. There may be a case for allowing public access to such materials when they only affect the parties to the proceeding itself, public figures, or persons *actually charged* with a related crime. But the same conclusion is far less supportable when the material affects private persons who are not parties to the proceeding and are not charged with criminal wrongdoing.

The various John Does in this case are not presently charged with any crime. For all we know, any information about them now in the State's possession may be unfounded, distorted, or even contrived. There has been no information or indictment issued against them. That being the case, I cannot conclude that the public records laws ever were meant to subject at least some of these John Does to public scrutiny of their private lives. People have a constitutionally protected interest in their good names. Art. I, §§ 2, 9, Fla. Const.; *see, e.g., Ritter v. Board of Comm'rs*, 96 Wash.2d 503, 637 P.2d 940 (1981).

The Florida Constitution recognizes that people cannot be stripped of such an interest without good and just reason. Art. I, §9, Fla. Const. We have recognized, as the majority notes, that the public records laws themselves allow courts to order that discovery documents be withheld if this is the only way to preserve other constitutional rights. *Florida Freedom Newspapers, Inc. v. McCrary,* 520 So.2d 32 (Fla.1988).

For these reasons, I dissent from the majority's analysis and conclusion. I would remand to the trial court for a determination of whether there is any legitimate public concern in the names, addresses, and other information contained in the State's discovery materials as to each John Doe. I strongly doubt that any legitimate public concern would exist with regard to private individuals not charged with a crime, although there could be a legitimate public interest if any of the material reflects on public figures or persons actually charged with a crime arising from this or a related case.

I am especially troubled by the majority's tacit assumption that people's interest in their good names evaporates merely because of unfounded, unproven, and possibly erroneous information that they have participated in criminal activity. Majority op. at 552–53. At the very least, I believe that private individuals have a right to require the State at least to commence a criminal prosecution against them before it can release scandalous material the State itself has collected alleging criminal wrongdoing. In effect, the majority authorizes the State to brand such persons as criminals without even offering them the procedural protections guaranteed by our Constitution or a forum for vindication. This is a process more reminiscent of Nathaniel Hawthorne's scarlet letter than modern constitutional law.

State v. Rolling

22 Media L. Rptr. 2264 (Fla. Cir. Ct. 1994)

STAN R. MORRIS, Circuit Judge.

The State Attorney, on behalf of the families of the murdered victims, filed a motion requesting non-disclosure of those photographs and videotapes which depict the victims both at the murder scene and the autopsy room of the District III Medical Examiner. The motion was supported by 12 affidavits from the parents and siblings of each murder victim expressing their belief they would suffer future harm by further disclosure of these photographs and their opinion that their rights of privacy would be thereby violated. Attached as exhibits were various demands by the media to see and copy these and other discovery materials. The issue was raised prior to trial and at the penalty phase proceedings subsequent to the entry of the plea of guilty by the defendant.

The record contains hundreds of photographs taken at the scene or at the autopsies, only seventeen of which were admitted into evidence. Prior to trial and again prior to the penalty phase proceedings, the court had held a series of hearings upon motion of the defendant to limit or prohibit the use of the victims photographs at trial or at the penalty phase. The Court, after hearing, excluded some photographs on the basis that they were irrelevant or, on the basis that their relevance was outweighed by the potential for prejudice to the Defendant. The Court required other photographs to be altered or cropped in such a fashion as to reduce undue prejudicial impact. The Court then ordered the State to file all photographs in the record for any future review by an appellate court.

During the penalty phase the Court did not close proceedings or in any way impede the right of the media or public present in the courtroom. Any difficulty in observing the proceedings was the product of the physical design of the courtroom and the positioning of video cameras (located on a stand built by the media at their request) inside the rail and to the back and side of the jury box at an angle, so that the camera might record the proceedings from the jurors' perspective. The Court did prohibit the future disclosure, observation or copying of the photographs of the victims until a full hearing was held. All other physical evidence, including photographs of the crime scenes not depicting the victims, was displayed each evening for the media and public on a table or easel located immediately behind the bar.

A hearing was held on the State's motion on April 12, 1994, at which the Defendant, his counsel, the State Attorney and two counsel representing media organizations were present and presented argument. Media attorneys present represented the Gainesville Sun, the Orlando Sentinel, the Florida Alligator and WESH-TV Orlando. The State presented the motion on behalf of the victims in anticipation of demand on the Clerk of Court and upon other records custodians for review and copying of the photographs and of crime scene videotapes. The videotapes had not been admitted into evidence. The Defendant took no position on these issues. At the hearing, counsel represented that some media representatives could not see the exhibits offered into evidence, although access to such exhibits was needed in order to adequately evaluate government operations. Reporters wished to be able to place themselves in the position of the jurors in order to evaluate independently the impact of the photographs on the proceeding. Media counsel offered a compromise on behalf of their clients to limit themselves to review only those photographs presented to the jury, to do so in the presence of the Clerk and not to reproduce, copy or remove the photographs. In addition, they stated it was not their intention to print or publish the photographs.

The Public Records Issue:

The first question to be answered is whether the photographs of the bodies of the victims are public records under the law of the State of Florida. The court finds that they are public records. The photographs were taken by officers of the State in the course of the investigation and are in the possession of officers of the State in their official capacities. All were created as part of the criminal investigation of this case and all were subject to pretrial discovery pursuant to Florida Rule of Criminal Procedure 3.220. The photographs have been the subject of numerous orders prohibiting pretrial disclosure in order to preserve the fair trial rights of the defendant. The rationale of all previous orders of nondisclosure, that the defendant's right to a fair trial might be compromised by the disclosure, no longer applies. The materials must be disclosed and are subject to inspection and copying unless the law recognizes some exception sufficient to prohibit or in some fashion restrict public access.

The Standing Issue:

The media questioned the standing of the State Attorney to raise the claim that disclosure of the materials would in some way compromise the right to privacy of the victims' families. The court finds that the State Attorney does have standing. First, the material sought by the media is in the possession of the State Attorney in his capacity as records custodian. It is the State Attorney, as well as the Clerk of Court, who is requested to release the material to the media. The State has had standing to contest pretrial motions for nondisclosure in order to protect the defendant's right to a fair trial. Rule 3.220, Fla.R.Crim.P., allows "any person" to raise the issue of nondisclosure. The State Attorney is given statutory duties to notify and inform victims of the progress of the prosecution, as well as to present matters on their behalf such as requests for restitution. The victims themselves, through correspondence to this Court, have raised the issue and have requested that the photographs not be disclosed in order to protect their rights to privacy. The Court finds that the State Attorney has standing to raise this issue and that the issue is one properly addressed to the trial judge as collateral to the issues of guilt, innocence and sentence. The right of the public access to public records, the right to a fair trial and the right to privacy has dominated much of this Court's time and attention for the past two years.

The Existence of a Right to Privacy in the Materials themselves.

It is important to note that this case does not deal with the First Amendment right of the Press to publish material already legitimately in their possession, nor does it involve any action against the Press for improper disclosure of such material. Those issues, should they arise, would be governed by the principles enunciated in *Florida Star v. B.J.F.*, 488 U.S. 887 (1988) and similar cases. Rather, this case deals with the obligation of a government official having custody of public records to disclose those records, when the disclosure would impinge on recognized privacy interests of an individual who is the subject of those records. It is the Public's Right to Know rather than the Media's Right to Publish which is at issue here.

The Supreme Court of Florida has clearly held that the Public's interest in the disclosure of public records pursuant to statute is to be balanced against the privacy rights of the subjects of those records. In *Post-Newsweek Stations, et al. v. John Doe, et al.*, 612 So.2d 549 (1992), the Court stated: "Here, we also qualify the public's *statutory right of access to pretrial discovery information* by balancing it against the Does' constitutional right to privacy." In coming to its decision, the Court relied on *Barron v. Florida Freedom Newspapers*, 531 So.2d 113 (Fla., 1988) to establish the various grounds on the basis of which material statutorily subject to disclosure may be withheld from the public: "Closure of court proceedings or records should occur only when necessary ... (f) to avoid substantial injury to a party by disclosure of matters protected by a common law or privacy right not generally inherent in the specific type of civil proceeding sought to be closed." The Supreme Court in *Barron* had specifically found that "under appropriate circumstances, the constitutional right of privacy established in Florida by the adoption of article I, section 23, could form a constitutional basis for closure under (e) or (f)". *Barron* at 16....

The Court finds that the materials at issue in this case, photographs of the nude and mutilated bodies of the victims as they were found by investigating officers, although they are public records as defined by statute, are materials which would be subject to a right to privacy were the victims still alive.

The existence of a Right to Privacy in the Relatives of the Victims:

Although the victims in this case would have had a Right to Privacy in the materials if they had survived, the Court must now determine whether the close relatives of the victims have a privacy interest which survives the deaths of the victims. The close relatives of the victims might acquire such a right, either derivative from the victims themselves or in their own right.

Most courts considering the issue have held that the close relatives of a victim do not acquire a derivative right to privacy. The victim's right to privacy does not survive the death of the victim. In so doing, the courts have adhered to the common law rule that actions involving libel, defamation and the like do not survive the death of a party. The recent Florida case of *Williams v. City of Mineola*, 575 So.2d 683 (Fla. 5th D.C.A., 1991), apparently follows this policy when a post-death action for damages for wrongful disclosure is brought by the survivors of the victim.

A decision in at least one federal court concluded that a relatives' right of privacy does exist, a right which may, upon balance, be sufficient to prohibit disclosure of materials which would be subject to a right of privacy were the victim alive. *N.Y. Times v. NASA*, 782 F.Supp. 628, 19 Media L.Rep. 1688 (1991). In that case, the families of deceased astronauts did not wish to suffer by hearing the voices of the deceased repeated in the media. The Court found this to be a sufficient basis to deny a federal disclosure demand because the statute specifically excepted this type of material from disclosure under the privacy rights acknowledged as part of federal law. Although the specific legal bases differ, the content analysis directed by the Florida Supreme Court leads to the conclusion that a photograph of a stabbed and mutilated child or sibling should be afforded the same status under our law as would a voice under federal notions of privacy.

In addition, the relatives of the victims may claim a right of privacy in their own right, to prevent the direct trauma, sorrow and humiliation which they might suffer from public display of intimate and potentially embarrassing photographs of the mutilated bodies of their children. The families have sought prohibition of any future disclosure. They claim a right to privacy and they wish to be harmed no further by being confronted in the media with the images of their slain and mutilated loved ones. This Court has reviewed the photographs many times in camera, in hearings and during the penalty phase proceedings. Common sense and experience dictate that no reasonable person could expect these claimants to face these images in a public forum without great emotional distress and trauma.

The *Barron* court noted "it is generally the content of the subject matter rather than the status of the party that determines whether a privacy interest exists and closure should be permitted." The court then went on to hold that one of the bases on which the privacy interest might, on balance, outweigh the public's right to know was "(e) to avoid substantial injury to innocent third parties [e.g., to protect young witnesses from offensive testimony; to protect children in a divorce]." Although the issue arose, in *Barron*, in the context of the closing of a court proceeding to media representatives, the rationale extends to other situations where the right to privacy might require the non-disclosure of otherwise public material. The potential for substantial injury to innocent third parties presumptively applies to the intimate relatives of murdered victims. The content of the subject matter—the photographs of the nude bodies, the stab wounds and mutilations of the victims—can reasonably be expected to cause extreme emotional distress and trauma if encountered in supermarket tabloids, newspapers, magazines, television programs or the like, especially since these involve utilization of the photographs for commercial gain.

Based on all the factors in this case, the Court concludes that there exists a right to privacy for intimate relatives of the victims, whether it is a derivative right which survives the death of the victims, or it is the right of the family members in their own right. The privacy interest of the intimate relative, however, is less than that which would inure to the offended individual, if the offended individual had lived. The relative strength of the privacy interest depends on the intimacy of the relationship between the relative and the victim. In this case, the photographs are intimate, embarrassing and trauma producing photographs of the victims, who are the children of those asserting the right—the closest possible familial relationship. The right is less weighty, however, than would be the right to privacy held by the victims themselves, and is further attenuated by the distance of the relatives from the victims and from the event itself. It is this lesser right which is to be weighed, on balance, against the right of the public to disclosure of public documents.

The Test to be Applied:

The test to be applied, then, is one of a careful balancing of the public's right to know against the residual privacy interest of the victims' relatives. In balancing these interests, the Court looks first to the policy of disclosure of public records—that it permits the public to evaluate the actions of public officials in order to hold them accountable for those actions. The Court is aware that the Court cannot substitute its judgment on the publication value of the materials for that of the members of the media, but can decide whether the information has significant relevance to that function and whether the same information is available from other, less intrusive, sources. The more likely that disclosure of the material will permit the public to oversee and to judge governmental operations, the greater the need for full disclosure.

The public's right to information which permits the public to evaluate the operations of government must be balanced against the intrusion on the right to privacy, a balancing which should include at least four factors:

a. The relevance of disclosure of the material to furthering public evaluation of governmental accountability;

b. The seriousness of the intrusion into the close relatives' right to privacy by disclosure of the material;

c. The availability, from other sources—including other public records—of material which is equally relevant to the evaluation of the same government action but is less intrusive on the right to privacy;

d. The availability of alternatives other than full disclosure which might serve to protect both the interests of the public and the interests of the victims.

In that balance, the less the information tends to open governmental operation to public view and the greater the intrusiveness of disclosure of personal information on this lessened right to privacy, the more the pendulum swings to prohibition of disclosure; conversely, the more the information opens the government operations to scrutiny and the less personal and intrusive it is, the more the pendulum swings to disclosure of the information. If equivalent material is available from other sources, for example, the written description of the crime scene as opposed to more sensationalistic photographs of the bodies, the need for disclosure of the material is lessened.

The Balance:

In balancing these factors, the Court finds:

a. The materials sought to be disclosed facilitate evaluation of public law enforcement officials in carrying out their duties of investigating criminal offenses. The photographs show what public officers found, and permit evaluation of the subsequent investigation. The photographs admitted at trial permit public evaluation of the jury's performance and the actions of the trial judge in admitting or excluding photographs. The public interests involved are weighty interests, and the photographs are relevant to the ability of the public to hold public officials accountable for their actions.

b. Because the photographs depict the nude, mutilated bodies of their children or siblings, public disclosure would be a serious infringement of the right to privacy of the childrens' parents and siblings. This is a factor which weighs heavily with the Court.

c. Information equivalent to that provided by disclosure of the photographs is available to the public through other sources. The actual photographs add but little to what the public can learn through a review of other documents already disclosed, particularly the detailed descriptions of the crime scenes filed by the investigators of those crime scenes and the reports of the autopsies performed on the bodies of the victims.

Although disclosure of the photographs are of little additional value to the information available from other sources, the photographs are not without some value. Photographs are less subjective than are written descriptions of crime scenes and disclosure of the photographs might permit the public to evaluate the impact of the photographs on the jurors and to evaluate the adequacy of the crime scene reports themselves.

d. Having carefully weighed the various factors affecting disclosure in this case, the Court believes that a remedy can be devised which can preserve the rights of both the public and the victims' relatives, a remedy suggested by counsel for the Media. A viable alternative exists, less restrictive than that of nondisclosure of the material.

The Remedy:

Having weighed carefully the relative weight of the interests of the parties, the Court believes that the suggestion of the attorney for the media, made at the hearing on this matter, will adequately protect the right to privacy on the part of the victims' families and, at the same time, will insure the media and interested public access to the photographs adequate for the purpose of insuring accountability of public officials. The remedy suggested by the attorney for the media is adopted by the Court.

At the hearing, it was suggested that the Court allow access by members of the public and the media only to those photographs seen by the jury, but not permit the photographs to be removed from the possession of the records custodian, or to be reproduced. The Court concurs with the suggestion of the attorneys for the media, but feels that it should not be limited only to those photographs seen by the jurors. Under the suggested procedure, the victims' families have no justifiable fear of being confronted with these photographs in a public forum. This remedy permits the public and media to independently evaluate what the jurors saw, close-up as they saw it, and to reach whatever independent conclusion they deem proper. It permits interested members of the public and the media access to the material sufficient to enable them to carry out the oversight function envisioned by Florida's Public Records law. In addition, in the event that, after privately reviewing the material, members of the public or the media conclude that the limited availability of the material is not sufficient to achieve the purpose of disclosure of public records — that of evaluating governmental accountability — they can move for full disclosure, including the copying and photographing of those specific items which they deem necessary, presenting to the Court the reasons why copying and photographing the items promotes the public interest. At a subsequent hearing, the Court would be able to again evaluation the need for more complete disclosure against the interests of the victims' close relatives in nondisclosure.

The State suggests that those statutes prohibiting pornography would justify closure on this instance. The Court doubts that the statute would apply in this case, but finds no need to make such analysis when condition 1 e) of the third factor of *Barron* suffices to justify a limited disclosure.

WHEREFORE, IT IS ORDERED AND ADJUDGED THAT

1. The photographs of the victims and videotapes of the crime scenes produced or acquired by law enforcement officers or by any other government officer in the investigation or prosecution of this case shall be made available, upon reasonable request to the records custodian having possession of such photographs or videotapes, for viewing and inspection by members of the public.

2. The records custodian shall inform any member of the public wishing to view such material of the restrictions on copying or removing such material that have been set out in this order before the record custodian permits access to the material.

3. The records custodian shall take every precaution to ensure that such photographs and videotapes shall not be removed or copied, which may include restrictions on items which may be carried into the room in which the material is to be viewed, restrictions on the number of persons who may be permitted to view the material at the same time, and the requirement that the records custodian maintain possession of the material while it is being viewed.

4. No further access to the materials shall be permitted except upon order of this Court, predicated on a written motion with notice to the State, and after a hearing at which the movant shall bear the burden of showing the necessity for further access.

DONE AND ORDERED.

Questions

1. Why is this case an expansion of the *Barron* standard?

2. In what ways does this case expand Florida's constitutional right of privacy?

3. Could the victims' families have successfully sued in tort for invasion of privacy?

Krischer v. McIver

697 So. 2d 97 (Fla. 1997)

GRIMES, Justice.

We have on appeal a judgment of the trial court certified by the Fourth District Court of Appeal to be of great public importance and to require immediate resolution by this Court. We have jurisdiction under article V, section 3(b)(5) of the Florida Constitution.

Charles E. Hall and his physician, Cecil McIver, M.D., filed suit for a declaratory judgment that section 782.08, Florida Statutes (1995), which prohibits assisted suicide, violated the Privacy Clause of the Florida Constitution and the Due Process and Equal Protection Clauses of the Fourteenth Amendment to the United States Constitution.[8] They sought an injunction against the state attorney from prosecuting the physician for giving deliberate assistance to Mr. Hall in committing suicide. After a six-day bench trial, the trial court issued a final declaratory judgment and injunctive decree responding to the "question of whether a competent adult, who is terminally ill, immediately dying and acting under no undue influence, has a constitutional right to hasten his own death by seeking and obtaining from his physician a fatal dose of prescription drugs and then subsequently administering such drugs to himself." The court concluded that section 782.08 could not be constitutionally enforced against the appellees and enjoined the state attorney from enforcing it against Dr. McIver

---

8. [FN 1.] Three patient-plaintiffs originally joined in the action but two died before the trial.

should he assist Mr. Hall in committing suicide. The court based its conclusion on Florida's privacy provision and the federal Equal Protection Clause but held that there was no federal liberty interest in assisted suicide guaranteed by the federal Due Process Clause.

Mr. Hall is thirty-five years old and suffers from acquired immune deficiency syndrome (AIDS) which he contracted from a blood transfusion. The court found that Mr. Hall was mentally competent and that he was in obviously deteriorating health, clearly suffering, and terminally ill. The court also found that it was Dr. McIver's professional judgment that it was medically appropriate and ethical to provide Mr. Hall with the assistance he requests at some time in the future.

Dr. McIver had testified that he would assist Mr. Hall in committing suicide by intravenous means. In granting the relief sought by the respondents, the court held that "the lethal medication must be self administered only after consultation and determination by both physician and patient that Mr. Hall is (1) competent, (2) imminently dying, and (3) prepared to die." The court explained that Mr. Hall must state that he subjectively believes that his time to die has come because he has no hope for further life of satisfactory quality and would die soon in any event "and that at that time, Dr. McIver must conclude that Mr. Hall's belief—and his chosen option—is objectively reasonable at the time."

The state attorney appealed. The trial court then set aside the automatic stay imposed by Florida Rule of Appellate Procedure 9.310(b)(2). When this Court assumed jurisdiction of the case, we reinstated the stay and provided for expedited review.

At the outset, we note that the United States Supreme Court recently issued two decisions on the subject of whether there is a right to assisted suicide under the United States Constitution. In *Washington v. Glucksberg,* 521 U.S. 702 (1997), the Court reversed a decision of the Ninth Circuit Court of Appeals which had held that the State of Washington's prohibition against assisted suicide violated the Due Process Clause. Like the trial court's decision in the instant case, the Court reasoned that the asserted "right" to assistance in committing suicide was not a fundamental liberty interest protected by the Due Process Clause.

In the second decision, the Court upheld New York's prohibition on assisted suicide against the claim that it violated the Equal Protection Clause. *Vacco v. Quill,* 521 U.S. 793 (1997). In reversing the Second Circuit Court of Appeals, the Court held that there was a logical and recognized distinction between the right to refuse medical treatment and assisted suicide and concluded that there were valid and important public interests which easily satisfied the requirement that a legislative classification bear a rational relation to some legitimate end. Thus, the Court's decision in *Vacco* rejected one of the two bases for the trial court's ruling in the instant case.

The remaining issue is whether Mr. Hall has the right to have Dr. McIver assist him in committing suicide under Florida's guarantee of privacy contained in our constitution's declaration of rights. Art. I, § 23, Fla. Const. Florida has no law against committing suicide.[9] However, Florida imposes criminal responsibility on those who assist others in committing suicide. Section 782.08, Florida Statutes (1995), which was first enacted in 1868, provides in pertinent part that "every person deliberately assisting another in the commission of self murder shall be guilty of manslaughter." *See also* §§ 765.309, 458.326(4), Fla. Stat. (1995) (disapproving mercy killing and euthanasia). Thus, it is clear that the public policy of this state as expressed by the legislature is opposed to assisted suicide.

Florida's position is not unique. Forty-five states that recognize the right to refuse treatment or unwanted life support have expressed disapproval of assisted suicide. Edward R. Grant & Paul Benjamin Linton, *Relief or Reproach?: Euthanasia Rights in the Wake of Measure 16,* 74 Or. L.Rev. 449, 462–63 (1995). As of 1994, thirty-four jurisdictions had statutes which criminalized such conduct. *People v. Kevorkian,* 447 Mich. 436, 527 N.W.2d 714 (1994).[10] Since that date, at least seventeen state legislatures have rejected proposals to legalize assisted suicide. *Washington.*

The only case in the nation in which a court has considered whether assisted suicide is a protected right under the privacy provision of its state's constitution is *Donaldson v. Lungren,* 2 Cal.App.4th 1614, 4 Cal.Rptr.2d 59, 63 (1992), which held: "We cannot expand the nature of Donaldson's right of privacy to provide a protective shield for third persons who end his life." The court reasoned:

> In such a case, the state has a legitimate competing interest in protecting society against abuses. This interest is more significant than merely the abstract interest in preserving life no matter what the quality of that life is. Instead, it is the interest of the state to maintain social order through enforcement of the criminal law and to protect the lives of those who wish to live no matter what their circumstances. This interest overrides any interest Donaldson possesses in ending his life through the assistance of a third person in violation of the state's penal laws.

Id. See Kevorkian v. Arnett, 939 F.Supp. 725 (C.D.Cal.1996) (there is no persuasive authority to believe that the California Supreme Court would hold contrary to *Donaldson* when directly presented with the issue).

* * *

We have previously refused to allow the state to prohibit affirmative medical intervention, such as the case with the right to an abortion before viability of the fetus, only because the state's interests in preventing the intervention were not compelling. *In re T.W.,* 551 So.2d 1186 (Fla.1989) (state's interest in prohibiting abortion is compelling after fetus reaches viability). This is because, under our privacy provision, once a privacy right has been implicated, the state must establish a compelling interest

---

9. [FN 2.] At common law committing suicide was a criminal offense which resulted in the forfeiture of the suicide's goods and chattels. These sanctions were later abolished in recognition of the unfairness of penalizing the suicide's family. *See Washington.*

10. [FN 3.] Iowa and Rhode Island have subsequently enacted statutes against assisted suicide. Iowa Code Ann. §§ 707A.2, 707A.3 (Supp.1997); R.I. Gen. Laws §§ 11-60-1, 11-60-3 (Supp.1996).

to justify intruding into the privacy rights of an individual. *Winfield v. Division of Pari-Mutuel Wagering*, 477 So.2d 544 (Fla.1985).

This Court has also rendered several prior decisions declaring in various contexts that there is a constitutional privacy right to refuse medical treatment. Those cases recognized the state's legitimate interest in (1) the preservation of life, (2) the protection of innocent third parties, (3) the prevention of suicide, and (4) the maintenance of the ethical integrity of the medical profession. However, we held that these interests were not sufficiently compelling to override the patient's right of self-determination to forego life-sustaining medical treatment.

The respondents successfully convinced the trial court that there was no meaningful difference between refusing medical treatment and obtaining a physician's assistance in committing suicide. We cannot agree that there is no distinction between the right to refuse medical treatment and the right to commit physician-assisted suicide through self-administration of a lethal dose of medication. The assistance sought here is not treatment in the traditional sense of that term. It is an affirmative act designed to cause death—no matter how well-grounded the reasoning behind it. Each of our earlier decisions involved the decision to refuse medical treatment and thus allow the natural course of events to occur. *In re Dubreuil*, 629 So.2d 819 (Fla.1993) (due to religious beliefs, individual wanted to refuse blood transfusion); *In re Guardianship of Browning*, 568 So.2d 4 (Fla.1990) (surrogate asserted right of woman who was vegetative but not terminally ill to remove nasogastric feeding tube); *Public Health Trust v. Wons*, 541 So.2d 96 (Fla.1989) (same facts as *Dubreuil*); *Satz v. Perlmutter*, 379 So.2d 359 (Fla.1980) (individual suffering from Lou Gehrig's disease sought to remove artificial respirator needed to keep him alive).

In the instant case, Mr. Hall seeks affirmative medical intervention that will end his life on his timetable and not in the natural course of events. There is a significant difference between these two situations. As explained by the American Medical Association:

> When a life-sustaining treatment is declined, the patient dies primarily because of an underlying disease. The illness is simply allowed to take its natural course. With assisted suicide, however, death is hastened by the taking of a lethal drug or other agent. Although a physician cannot force a patient to accept a treatment against the patient's will, even if the treatment is life-sustaining, it does not follow that a physician ought to provide a lethal agent to the patient. The inability of physicians to prevent death does not imply that physicians are free to help cause death.

AMA Council on Ethical and Judicial Affairs, Report I-93-8, at 2.

Measured by the criteria employed in our cases addressing the right to refuse medical treatment, three of the four recognized state interests are so compelling as to clearly outweigh Mr. Hall's desire for assistance in committing suicide.

First, the state has an unqualified interest in the preservation of life. *Cruzan v. Director, Missouri Department of Health*, 497 U.S. 261 (1990). The opinion we adopted in *Perlmutter* included the caveat that suicide was not at issue because the discontinuation of life support would "merely result in [the patient's] death, if at all, from natural causes." *Satz v. Perlmutter*, 362 So.2d 160, 162 (Fla. 4th DCA 1978); *accord Browning*, 568 So.2d at 14. Although the constitutional privacy provision was not involved, in Mr. Perlmutter's case a sharp distinction was drawn between disconnecting a respirator that would result in his death from "natural causes" (i.e., the inability to breathe on his own) and an "unnatural death by means of a 'death producing agent.'" *Perlmutter*, 362 So.2d at 162. It is the second scenario that we encounter in the instant case. Mr. Hall will not die from the complications of his illness. Rather, a physician will assist him in administering a "death producing agent" with the intent of causing certain death. The state has a compelling interest in preventing such affirmative destructive act and in preserving Mr. Hall's life.

The state also has a compelling interest in preventing suicide. As the United States Supreme Court explained in *Washington:*

> Those who attempt suicide—terminally ill or not—often suffer from depression or other mental disorders. Research indicates, however, that many people who request physician-assisted suicide withdraw that request if their depression and pain are treated. The New York Task Force, however, expressed its concern that, because depression is difficult to diagnose, physicians and medical professionals often fail to respond adequately to seriously ill patients' needs. *Id.*, at 175. Thus, legal physician-assisted suicide could make it more difficult for the State to protect depressed or mentally ill persons, or those who are suffering from untreated pain, from suicidal impulses.

Washington, 521 U.S. at ___, 117 S.Ct. at 2273.

Finally, the state also has a compelling interest in maintaining the integrity of the medical profession. While not all health care providers agree on the issue, the leading health care organizations are unanimous in their opposition to legalizing assisted suicide. The American Medical Association, which represents 290,000 physicians, as late as June of 1996 overwhelmingly endorsed a recommendation to reaffirm the ethical ban on physician-assisted suicide. American Medical Association, Press Release, "AMA Soundly Reaffirms Policy Opposing Physician-Assisted Suicide" (June 24, 1996). The same position is endorsed by the Florida Medical Association, the Florida Society of Internal Medicine, the Florida Society of Thoracic and Cardiovascular Surgeons, the Florida Osteopathic Medical Association, the Florida Hospices, Inc., and the Florida Nurses Association. Who would have more knowledge of the dangers of legalizing assisted suicide than those intimately charged with maintaining the patient's well-being?

In addition, the Code of Medical Ethics, § 2.211, states that physician-assisted suicide is "fundamentally incompatible with the physician's role as healer, would be difficult or impossible to control, and would pose serious societal risks." Even the Hippocratic Oath itself states that a physician "will neither give a deadly drug to anybody if asked for it, nor … make a suggestion to this effect." Physician-assisted suicide directly contradicts these ethical standards and compromises the integrity of the medical profession and the role of hospitals in caring for patients.

We do not hold that a carefully crafted statute authorizing assisted suicide would be unconstitutional. Nor do we discount the sincerity and strength of the respondents' convictions. However, we have concluded that this case should not be decided on the basis of this Court's own assessment of the weight of the competing moral arguments. By broadly construing the privacy amendment to include the right to assisted suicide, we would run the risk of arrogating to ourselves those powers to make social policy that as a constitutional matter belong only to the legislature. *See* art. II, § 3, Fla. Const. (separation of powers).

We reverse the judgment of the trial court and uphold the constitutionality of section 782.08.

It is so ordered.

SHAW and WELLS, JJ., concur.

OVERTON and HARDING, JJ., concur with an opinion.

KOGAN, C.J., dissents with an opinion.

ANSTEAD, J., recused.

OVERTON, Justice, concurring.

I concur with the majority opinion to the extent that it finds the statute at issue to be facially constitutional. I also agree that the statute is not unconstitutional as applied under the circumstances existing in this record. I write separately to emphasize that, under the present circumstances, (1) the absolute right to assisted suicide is not, in my view, protected under our right of privacy contained in article I, section 23, of the Florida Constitution, and (2) court-approved assisted suicide, without authorization and specific legislative directives based on input from the medical and scientific community, could present more problems than it solves.

I recognize that few things could be considered more private than the decision to end one's life. This does not mean, however, that an individual has an absolute right to obtain assistance from a third party to accomplish this task.

Essentially, Mr. Hall is asking that we find the assisted suicide statute to be facially unconstitutional to provide him "carte blanche" authority to end his life *at some point in the future.* This is essentially the same question that was recently presented to the United States Supreme Court in *Vacco v. Quill*, 521 U.S. 793 (1997), and *Washington v. Glucksberg*, 521 U.S. 702 (1997), wherein the Court refused to recognize an open-ended constitutional right to commit suicide under either the Equal Protection Clause or the Due Process Clause. As Justice Stevens stated in his concurrence in *Vacco*, "the value to others of a person's life is far too precious to allow the individual to claim a constitutional entitlement to complete autonomy in making a decision to end that life." ____ U.S.at ____, 117 S.Ct. 2293 (Stevens, J., concurring in the judgment).

The State's policy of preventing suicide has been in existence for over 100 years. Advances in technology now provide efficient methods for enabling assisted suicide but also raise many new issues that must be addressed before such methods are implemented. As set forth in the majority opinion, the risks associated with assisted suicide at this time are overwhelming. Consequently, in my view, the State has clearly established under the circumstances presented that its compelling interests in preventing suicide outweigh any interests Mr. Hall may have in obtaining assistance to end his life at some point in the future.

In sum, I conclude that there is no absolute right to assisted suicide under our privacy provision. Further, I believe the statute, as applied under the facts of this case, is not unconstitutional. In reality, this Court may never be able to find an exception for an as-applied challenge to the statute until extensive evaluation of the problems involved in this issue occurs and the many difficult questions are answered. The public would be much better served if the legislature, with significant input from the medical and scientific community, would craft appropriate exceptions to the general prohibition of assisted suicide, which include suitable standards, definitions, and procedures ensuring that the use of assisted suicide would truly be used to assist only those individuals who suffer unbearable pain in the face of certain death.

KOGAN, Chief Justice, dissenting.

The notion of "dying by natural causes" contrasts neatly with the word "suicide," suggesting two categories readily distinguishable from one another. How nice it would be if today's reality were so simple. No doubt there once was a time when, for all practical purposes, the distinction was clear enough to all. But that was a time before today, before technology had crept into medicine, when dying was a far more inexorable process. Medicine now has pulled the aperture separating life and death far enough apart to expose a limbo unthinkable fifty years ago, for which the law has no easy description. Dying no longer falls into the neat categories our ancestors knew. In today's world, we demean the hard reality of terminal illness to say otherwise.

Once Florida had set itself adrift from the common law definition, the problem that immediately arose—that has vexed our courts ever since—is where to draw the new dividing line between improper "suicide" and the emerging "right of self-determination" without simultaneously authorizing involuntary euthanasia. This is no simple task. And until today, no Florida court had attempted it. The majority tries to fix the mark through scrutinizing the *means* by which dying occurs: Suicide thus is "active" death caused by a "death producing agent," whereas Floridians have a right to choose "passive" death through "natural causes." While language in our prior opinions can be read to support this view, I am not convinced this language can be stretched beyond the differing facts we previously faced. All of these earlier cases dealt with the refusal of medical treatment needed *if life was to continue.* The present case asks a far different question: How must Charles Hall die, given the fact an agonizing death is both imminent and inevitable? Principles developed in these earlier cases were not intended to, and to my mind cannot properly, resolve the very different and very troubling legal issues surrounding an unstoppable, painful death.

To my mind, the right of privacy attaches with unusual force at the death bed. This conclusion arises in part from the privacy our society traditionally has afforded the death bed, but also from the very core of the right of privacy—the right of self-determination even in the face of majoritarian disapproval. *See Shaktman v. State*, 553 So.2d 148, 151 (Fla.1989). What possible interest does society have in saving life when there is nothing of life to save but a final convulsion of agony? The state has no business in this arena. Terminal illness is not a portrait in blacks and whites, but unending shades of gray, involving the most profound of personal, moral, and religious questions. Many people can and do disagree over these questions, but the fact remains that it is the dying person who must resolve them in the particular case. And while we certainly cannot ignore the slippery-slope problem, we previously have established fully adequate standards to police the exercise of privacy rights in this context to ensure against abuse.

Finally, I cannot ignore the majority's statement that the issues in this case must be left to the legislature. Such a statement ignores fundamental tenets of our law. Constitutional rights must be enforced by courts even against the legislature's powers, and privacy in particular must be enforced even against majoritarian sentiment. *Shaktman.* Indeed, the overarching purpose of the Florida Declaration of Rights along with its privacy provision is to "protect each individual within our borders from the unjust encroachment of state authority—from whatever official source—into his or her life." *Traylor v. State*, 596 So.2d 957, 963 (Fla.1992).

There is no doubt that the state has an interest in preserving life. *Id.* at 14. In the vast majority of cases, that interest also is compelling. None of our case law assumes otherwise. But as our cases clearly show, there are rare instances when the state's interest falls below the mark of "compelling." Indeed, the issue before us today as in our earlier cases is the

> "substantial distinction in the State's insistence that human life be saved where the affliction is curable, as opposed to the State interest where, as here, the issue is not whether, but when, for how long and at what cost to the individual [his][or her] life may be briefly extended."

Browning, 568 So.2d at 14 (quoting *Satz v. Perlmutter*, 362 So.2d 160, 162 (Fla. 4th DCA 1978) (quoting *Superintendent of Belchertown State School v. Saikewicz*, 373 Mass. 728, 740–44, 370 N.E.2d 417, 425–26 (1977)), *approved*, 379 So.2d 359 (Fla.1980)). Because Mr. Hall's case involves this same critical distinction, the right of privacy clearly attaches to the decisions he is confronting with the help of his physician. I cannot in good conscience say that the state's interest is compelling, given the fact that Mr. Hall's life no longer can be saved.

I respectfully dissent.

B. Article I, Section 12 — Searches and Seizures

This was the first Florida constitutional provision subject to a so-called "linkage amendment" under which the text of the Florida provision is linked to the analogous federal provision. The 1982 amendment was a response to the Florida Supreme Court's decision in *State v. Sarmiento*, 397 So. 2d 643 (Fla. 1981), where the Court found that the Florida provision provided greater protection than the Fourth Amendment. In the following case, the Court considers the impact of this linkage amendment on its ability to interpret the Constitution.

Bernie v. State

524 So. 2d 988 (Fla. 1988)

PER CURIAM.

This is a petition to review *State v. Bernie*, 472 So.2d 1243 (Fla. 2d DCA 1985), in which the district court expressly construed article I, section 12, Florida Constitution, relating to search and seizure, as amended in 1982. The district court applied the exclusionary rule's "good faith" exception and upheld the search and seizure of cocaine from a residence. We have jurisdiction, article V, section 3(b)(3), Florida Constitution, and approve the result of the district court decision.

On October 13, 1983, Emery Air Freight received an envelope addressed to petitioner Vickie Bernie. The envelope broke open during transit, revealing a suspicious substance. Emery notified a drug enforcement agent, who tested the substance and identified it as cocaine. Emery then notified the Sarasota County sheriff's office. Petitioner Bruce Bernie came to Emery's Tampa office to check on the whereabouts of the package, at which time Emery's employees advised him that the package would be delivered the following day, October 14.

On October 14, based on an affidavit setting forth the preceding facts, police obtained a search warrant for the Bernies' residence relative to the prospective controlled delivery of the cocaine. A few minutes after the controlled delivery, police executed the warrant, arrested the Bernies, and charged them with possession of cocaine.

The Bernies moved to suppress the evidence on the grounds that it was the product of an unreasonable search and seizure, relying on the provisions of section 933.18, Florida Statutes (1983), and *Gerardi v. State*, 307 So.2d 853 (Fla. 4th DCA 1975). Section 933.18, Florida Statutes (1983), concerns the issuance of a search warrant for a private home and provides:

> 933.18 When warrant may be issued for search of private dwelling.—No search warrant shall issue under this chapter or under any other law of this state to search any private dwelling occupied as such unless:

> ....

(5) The law relating to narcotics or drug abuse *is being violated therein;*

. . . .

... No warrant shall be issued for the search of any private dwelling under any of the conditions hereinabove mentioned except on sworn proof by affidavit of some creditable witness that he has reason to believe that one of said conditions exists, which affidavit shall set forth the facts on which such reason for belief is based.

(Emphasis added.) In *Gerardi*, the Fourth District Court of Appeal held that section 933.18 "not only does not authorize issuance of a search warrant for search of a private dwelling for violations of the law relating to narcotics or drug abuse *unless such law is currently being violated therein,* it expressly prohibits such issuance." *Id.* at 855 (emphasis added). On the basis of this authority, the trial judge granted the Bernies' motion to suppress.

On appeal, the Second District Court reversed. The district court recognized that the requirements of section 933.18 were clear: "[A] present or known violation of a narcotics law must exist in the home to be searched prior to the issuance of the warrant for the search of that home." *Bernie*, 472 So.2d at 1245. Since the allegation in the affidavit failed to allege that any narcotics law "was being violated therein," the affidavit was legally inadequate and the warrant should not have been issued. *Id.* at 1246. The district court held that *Gerardi*, which required suppression of the evidence, was inapplicable because of the amendment to article I, section 12, of the Florida Constitution in 1982. The district court applied our recent decision in *State v. Lavazzoli*, 434 So.2d 321 (Fla.1983), interpreting the new constitutional provision as linking Florida's exclusionary rule to the federal exclusionary rule and determined that *United States v. Leon*, 468 U.S. 897 (1984), and *Massachusetts v. Sheppard*, 468 U.S. 981 (1984), were applicable. The district court concluded that the "exclusion of the cocaine would be improper because 'there is no police illegality and thus nothing to deter.'" *Bernie*, 472 So.2d at 1247, quoting *Leon*, 468 U.S. at 921.

Article I, section 12, of the Florida Constitution, relating to search and seizure, as amended in 1982, effective January 3, 1983, states:

Searches and seizures.—The right of the people to be secure in their persons, houses, papers and effects against unreasonable searches and seizures, and against the unreasonable interception of private communications by any means, shall not be violated. No warrant shall be issued except upon probable cause, supported by affidavit, particularly describing the place or places to be searched, the person or persons, thing or things to be seized, the communication to be intercepted, and the nature of evidence to be obtained. This right shall be construed in conformity with the 4th Amendment to the United States Constitution, as interpreted by the United States Supreme Court. Articles or information obtained in violation of this right shall not be admissible in evidence *if such articles or information would be inadmis-*

sible under decisions of the United States Supreme Court construing the 4th Amendment to the United States Constitution.

The underlined portions constitute the 1982 amendment.

Part I. *Prospective Application of the 1982 Amendment*

Prior to passage of this amendment, Florida courts "were free to provide its citizens with a higher standard of protection from governmental intrusion than that afforded by the Federal Constitution," *Lavazzolli*, 434 So.2d at 323. With this amendment, however, we are bound to follow the interpretations of the United States Supreme Court with relation to the fourth amendment, and provide no greater protection than those interpretations. Indeed, an exclusionary rule that was once constitutionally mandated in Florida can now be eliminated by judicial decision of the United States Supreme Court.

We are furthermore bound by prospective decisions of that Court, even though the electors, in considering the 1982 amendment, could not have foreseen, nor ratified, those decisions. The argument has been advanced that this Court could not be bound by future decisions of this country's highest court. Nevertheless, decisions rendered by the United States Supreme Court after adoption of the 1982 amendment must have the same controlling weight as those rendered before. The language of article I, section 12, clearly indicates an intention to apply to all United States Supreme Court decisions regardless of when they are rendered.

Part II. *Validity of the Search Warrant*

The proliferation of illegal drugs has intensified the use of commercial delivery services to transport this type of contraband. Law enforcement personnel are occasionally informed by transportation employees that certain packages contain drugs. This information is utilized to search and seize the package and have it delivered to the addressed premises, where the package is seized in the possession of the addressee. This is characterized as an "anticipatory search," which is defined as one based upon an affidavit showing probable cause that at some future time, but not presently, certain contraband will be at the location set forth in the warrant. *See* 2 W. LaFave, *Search and Seizure* § 3.7(c) (2d ed. 1978). The law is clear that such warrants are not *constitutionally* invalid for lack of a present violation of law at the premises where the contraband will be delivered in the future.

No language in either the Florida Constitution or the United States Constitution prohibits issuance of a warrant for service at a future time. One court found no probable cause defect in an anticipation warrant "as long as the evidence creates substantial probability that the seizable property will be on the premises when searched." *People v. Glen*, 30 N.Y.2d 252, 331 N.Y.S.2d 656, 282 N.E.2d 614 (1972). A number of federal circuit courts of appeals have expressly upheld similar anticipatory searches. In *United States v. Hendricks*, 743 F.2d 653 (9th Cir.1984), *cert. denied*, 470 U.S. 1066 (1985), customs intercepted a box arriving from Brazil, addressed to the defendant at a residence. The box contained a suitcase which held approximately seven pounds of cocaine. Although the court found the search warrant invalid because it failed to establish a sufficient probable cause nexus between the box containing the cocaine and the house, *Leon* applied and the evidence was admissible. In *United States v. Goff,* 681 F.2d 1238 (9th Cir.1982), the court found the informant's information sufficiently corroborated and the search warrant not invalid merely because it anticipated that the defendants would arrive at the airport within a reasonable time. *See also United States v. Foster,* 711 F.2d 871 (9th Cir.1983), *cert. denied,* 465 U.S. 1103 (1984); *United States v. Valenzuela,* 596 F.2d 824 (9th Cir.), *cert. denied,* 441 U.S. 965 (1979). Without question, this type of search is constitutionally permissible with a warrant.

The United States Supreme Court, however, in its recent decision in *Illinois v. Andreas,* 463 U.S. 765 (1983), determined no warrant was necessary under the limited circumstances in that case. In *Andreas,* the United States Supreme Court held that the warrantless reopening of a sealed container, in which contraband drugs had been discovered in an earlier lawful search of the contraband in transit, did not intrude on any legitimate expectation of privacy. Further, the warrantless search did not violate the fourth amendment where there was no substantial likelihood that the container's contents had been changed during a gap in surveillance.

The factual circumstances in *Andreas* and the instant case are similar. The facts in the instant case establish a prior legal search resulting from the fact that the envelope carrying the prohibited drugs broke open during transit and the contents were properly examined and identified as a prohibited drug. Under the principles established in *Andreas,* given this proper prior legal search, the recipients no longer enjoyed any expectation of privacy in the package. Further, the resealed package of cocaine remained in the constructive possession of law enforcement officials for its subsequent controlled delivery to the Bernies. *Andreas* clearly allows this type of warrantless, controlled delivery and subsequent search and reopening where there is no substantial likelihood that the container contents were changed. *See also United States v. DeBerry,* 487 F.2d 448 (2d Cir.1973). The law is now clear that neither the Florida Constitution nor the United States Constitution requires issuance of a warrant for this type of search.

We must, however, consider the effect of section 933.18. Section 933.18 requires issuance of a warrant for the entry into a private dwelling. It provides, in part: "No search warrant shall issue under this chapter or under any other law of this state to search any private dwelling occupied as such unless" ... [t]he law relating to narcotics or drug abuse *is being violated therein.* (Emphasis added.) The drugs involved in the instant case were in the constructive possession of the law enforcement officers because of their prior legal search and seizure. The evidence and supporting affidavit in the instant case show that the Bernies requested delivery of the contraband to their residence and that they knew the contraband was presently in transit and would arrive on a particular day. Since the contraband had already been discovered by a legal search, the Bernies had no expectation of privacy in the contraband package. We find that a reasonable construction of the emphasized words in the statute allows a warrant to be issued when the evidence and supporting affidavit show that the drugs have already been discovered through a legal search and seizure and are presently in the process of being transported to the designated residence which is being used as the drug drop. It is our view that this is not the type of *in futuro* allegation for a warrant that the legislature intended to prohibit by this statute. In this circumstance, the state already knows the drug laws have been violated. Because we hold the warrant valid under our statute, the application of *Leon* is unnecessary. There was clearly probable cause to obtain a warrant, as required by section 933.18, to seize a package already in law enforcement's constructive possession and which law enforcement knew contained contraband drugs.

Conclusion

To summarize, we hold (1) the 1982 amendment to article I, section 12, of the Florida Constitution brings this state's search and seizure laws into conformity with all decisions of the United States Supreme Court rendered before and subsequent to the adoption of that amendment; (2) the anticipatory search warrant issued under the circumstances of this case is valid and does not violate the provisions of the United States Constitution, the Florida Constitution, or section 933.18.

For the reasons expressed, we approve the decision of the district court of appeal.

It is so ordered.

McDONALD, C.J., SHAW, J., and BEN C. WILLIS (Ret.), Associate Justice, concur as to Part I and Part II.

EHRLICH, J., concurs as to Part I and Part II with an opinion, in which McDONALD, C.J., and SHAW, J., concur. [omitted]

OVERTON, J., concurs in the judgment, agrees to Part II, but concurs in result only in Part I, with an opinion.

KOGAN, J., concurs as to Part I, but dissents as to Part II with an opinion.

BARKETT, J., dissents as to Part I and Part II with an opinion.

OVERTON, Justice, concurring in judgment.

I concur in the judgment. I approve in full the part II holding that *Illinois v. Andreas*, 463 U.S. 765 (1983), should be applied to the facts of this case, although I do not find we are mandated to do so.

I disagree with the holding in part I that the amendment to article I, section 12, in 1982, absolutely binds us to prospective decisions of the United States Supreme Court and thereby makes unknown United States Supreme Court decisions part of our Florida Constitution. I believe the 1982 amendment simply requires this Court to interpret the Florida constitutional provision, section 12 of article I, in accordance with the United States Supreme Court decisions existing at the time the amendment was adopted. United States Supreme Court decisions rendered after November, 1982, should be considered only persuasive authority. My reasoning is twofold. First, a constitution, in the American sense, is a written document totally superior to the operations of government. As such, neither our legislature, by statutes, nor our courts, through decisions, can amend the Florida Constitution. The majority compromises this principle by allowing the federal government to amend our constitution by unknown future decisions of the United States Supreme Court. To interpret the new constitutional provision set forth in article I, section 12, to mean that its application depends entirely on the future whims of the United States Supreme Court and its decisions, whatever their result, is contrary to the meaning and purpose of a constitution. I note that if the United States Supreme Court decided to substantially expand the exclusionary rule's scope, justified on the basis of supervising the federal courts, we would be bound by that decision under the majority's opinion. Such a decision is contrary to the purpose of the 1982 amendment because the people of this state clearly intended to reduce the scope of the exclusionary rule—not expand it.

Second, I object to the prospective required tie-in to United States Supreme Court decisions because I subscribe to the principles we set forth for the legislature in *Freimuth v. State*, 272 So.2d 473 (Fla.1972). In that case, we addressed the validity of a criminal statute, section 404.01(3), Florida Statutes (1971), which defined a hallucinogenic drug as "lysergic acid ... and any other drug to which the drug abuse laws of the United States apply." We determined the legislature *could not* define a hallucinogenic drug in accordance with a federal statute enacted after the effective date of the Florida statute. We stated that it is "'an unconstitutional delegation of legislative power for the legislature to adopt in advance any federal act or the ruling of any federal administrative body that Congress or such administrative body might see fit to adopt in the future,'" 272 So.2d at 476, quoting *Florida Industrial Commission v. State*, 155 Fla. 772, 21 So.2d 599, 603 (1945). The principle is clear that new laws should be controlled by representatives of the people, not by a broad designation to a governmental entity outside the state and not responsible to the citizens of the state. I apply the same principle to this constitutional provision. A fair reading of this constitutional provision does not justify a conclusion that the people knew, in ratifying the 1982 amendment to the Florida Constitution, that they were voting to approve future unknown decisions of the United States Supreme Court as part of their constitution. If prospective application had been intended, both the amendment and the ballot would have clearly reflected that intent.

Although I do not believe we are bound by decisions of the United States Supreme Court rendered after November of 1982, I also do not believe we are in any way restricted in applying the principles of those cases. I would consider them as persuasive authority, but not mandated by the constitutional amendment. In this regard, I would approve the principles of *Illinois v. Andreas*.

KOGAN, Justice, concurring in part, dissenting in part.

I concur with part I of the Court's opinion regarding the issue of the prospective application of article I, section 12 of the Florida Constitution. However, I must dissent from the Court's failure to address the issues raised in the second district's opinion, as well as from part II of the Court's opinion applying *Illinois v. Andreas*, 463 U.S. 765 (1983) to the present set of circumstances. This application discards, without comment, both established precedent of this Court, as well as that of the district courts of appeal, and significant statutory law, which must be strictly complied with.

The second district below held that the evidence recovered in the Bernie's home was admissible despite the patent invalidity of the search warrant, *State v. Bernie*, 472 So.2d 1243, 1246 (Fla. 2d DCA 1985). The court reasoned that because the officers allegedly acted in good faith in procuring and executing the warrant, the facial invalidity would not prohibit admission of the evidence, citing *United States v. Leon*, 468 U.S. 897 (1984). In that case, by which Florida courts are bound since the effective date of the 1982 amendment to Article I, section 12 of the Florida Constitution, the United States Supreme Court decided that where police officers act in good faith upon a search warrant that is facially insufficient or defective, the exclusionary rule of the fourth amendment to the United States Constitution would not prevent admission of evidence recovered pursuant to that warrant.

The majority opinion in the present case does not sufficiently address the holding of the district court, or the issues raised thereby. To ignore the work of that court, literally without comment, fails to settle an extremely important issue of search and seizure law which has been directly presented to this Court. The majority's lack of comment on this issue requires me to address it.

We are not bound; however, by those decisions which are not on point, or even analogous to the situations which we face in Florida that are unique to Florida law. The majority relies on the United States Supreme Court's decision in *Illinois v. Andreas*, to hold that there are no constitutional restrictions on the admission of evidence recovered from a citizen's private residence that has been previously legally opened by authorities, and resealed and delivered to that residence.

I am unconvinced by the Court's pronouncement that the facts in that case are similar to those in the present case. I believe that the facts in *Andreas* are sufficiently dissimilar from those in this case to remove the controlling effect of *Andreas*. In *Andreas*, the initial discovery was the result of a proper border search. Here, there was no border search, but rather the package merely broke open in transit. Moreover, the situation in *Andreas* involves a good faith attempt to obtain a warrant. Because the contraband was about to be removed from the premises, police in that case were forced to move quickly, without a warrant. In this case; however, the police obtained a warrant that was patently defective. On its face the warrant was invalid.

Even assuming that the Bernies did not have a reasonable expectation of privacy in the package, which the Court in *Andreas* purports to hold, there is no doubt that they did maintain a reasonable expectation of privacy in their home. In *Andreas*, the police arrested the defendant, while he was physically in possession of the package, outside his residence. *The police never entered Andreas' home.* That case involved only the unwarranted search of a package which had already been properly opened by authorities. In the present case, the *police entered the Bernie's home* with an invalid warrant. It cannot even colorably be argued that *Andreas* allows the unwarranted entrance into a private residence. The Court today goes far beyond the holding of *Andreas* and further beyond what the constitution and the laws of this state will allow.

More fundamentally, the majority ignores statutes regulating the issuance of search warrants and execution. It has been well settled law for over six decades that laws regulating searches and seizures must be strictly complied with. "It is almost axiomatic that statutes and rules authorizing searches and seizures are strictly construed and affidavits and warrants issued pursuant to such authority must meticulously conform to statutory and constitutional provisions." *State v. Tolmie*, 421 So.2d 1087 (Fla. 4th DCA 1982) (citations omitted). The reason for this strict adherence is obvious. Aside from the constitutional ramifications of failure to guard against unreasonable searches, the legislated rules which regulate the issuance of warrants, and the conduct of searches, are intended not only to guarantee those constitutional rights, but to prevent the real and significant spectre of police misconduct. To allow any variance from these express legislative mandates would not only flaunt legislative authority to regulate such conduct, but actually encourage misconduct.

The Court today has allowed the admission of evidence which, according to any reasonable construction of the regulating statute was obtained in violation of that statute. Certainly the second district below recognized this, as did the fourth district in *Gerardi v. State*, 307 So.2d 853 (Fla. 4th DCA 1975). *See State v. Bernie*, 472 So.2d 1243, 1245 (Fla. 2d DCA 1985). The majority, in its haste to discard the plain meaning of the statute, does not expressly overrule *Gerardi*, but attempts to find some other "reasonable construction" of the statute by explaining that because the contraband was discovered by law enforcement officers before it arrived at the Bernies' residence, the cocaine was in the constructive possession of the police. While this may be a "reasonable construction" of the statute, it is by no means a permissible one.

As clarified previously, our statutes regulating search and seizure must be strictly construed. We are bound by this significant precedent the same way we are bound by United States Supreme Court decisions that are on point. To ignore this precedent without expressly overruling it, as the Court has done today, ignores the time-honored principle of *stare decisis*. Whatever the end result of the Court's opinion, I cannot believe that it is worth that.

Even assuming *arguendo* that *Andreas* does control, and that there are no constitutional barriers to the admission of this evidence, it is obvious that the additional statutory requirements bar the admission of this evidence. The Court in *Andreas* did not address any issues of statutory or other legislative regulation of search and seizure because the state of Illinois does not necessarily have a statute such as the one involved in this case. This Court, in its haste to achieve what it believes is the proper result, treads upon the legislature's authority to regulate the issuance of search warrants and searches and seizures in this state. The statutory regulations of search warrant issuance are *in addition to* those requirements specified in the state and federal constitutions. They are not mere reinterpretations of the constitution, but substantive and procedural requirements intended to supplement those constitutional requirements. The judicial reinterpretation of one constitutional requirement does not, as the Court implies today, rescind the legislature's enactments intended to *further* protect the citizens of this state from unreasonable searches and seizures. Again, even though the constitutional barriers to the admission of this evidence may have been torn down (and I do not believe that they have), the statutory ones still stand, until the legislature removes them, or a court of sufficient jurisdiction and power expressly declares them unconstitutional. Until then, they must be given their full force and effect by this Court, and they must also be strictly and meticulously construed, so as to give our citizens the fullest protection intended by our legislature.

For these reasons I must vigorously dissent from that portion of the Court's opinion which holds that the anticipatory search warrant issued, and the ensuing search in this case were valid. Although I concur with the Court's prospective application of United States Supreme Court cases to our search and seizure constitutional law, I would quash the opinion of the district court, because of the reasons stated above.

BARKETT, Justice, dissenting.

I must respectfully dissent. In my view, the evidence was illegally obtained under section 933.18, Florida Statutes, (1985), and therefore should have been excluded. I find the majority's analysis, especially its discussion of *Illinois v. Andreas*, totally inapplicable to the case before us and therefore totally unpersuasive.

The bottom line of the majority's decision is its construction of section 933.18 to permit the issuance of a warrant "when the evidence and supporting affidavit show that the drugs have already been discovered through a legal search and seizure and are presently in the process of being transported to the designated residence which is being used as the drug drop." Majority opinion at 992.

The majority, however, fails to provide any guidance as to how it arrived at its destination. Rather than applying conventional rules of statutory construction to a Florida statute that has been part of our law for over sixty years, the majority appears to somehow premise its conclusion on a case which cannot possibly have any relevance to the issue before us, *Illinois v. Andreas*.

Andreas dealt with a warrantless search. This case involves the validity of a warrant. *Andreas* did not involve rules of statutory construction because no state or federal statute was implicated. The validity of the warrant in this case depends on the construction of a state statute. *Andreas* did not involve the search of a private home. This case does. Without analysis, the majority somehow translates the *Andreas* lack of expectation of privacy in a package delivered outside the home to a lack of expectation of privacy inside a home, and then apparently uses that "analysis" as the basis of construing our Florida statute.

On this issue, I agree totally with Justice Kogan's opinion on the invalidity of the warrant and on his analysis of *United States v. Leon*.

I also believe that article I, section 12 of the Florida Constitution should be construed as an approval only of those decisions of the United States Supreme Court in existence prior to the vote on the amendment and not inconsistent with other provisions of our constitution. If the intent of the amendment was to provide Floridians with *only* the search and seizure protections of the federal constitution, this goal could have been accomplished more easily by simply repealing article I, section 12.

This, however, was not done. On the contrary, the amendment left intact the original provisions of article I, section 12, pertaining to search and seizure, including those provisions that differ from, and are more restrictive than, the fourth amendment.[11] Moreover, in addition to the internal conflicts within article I, section 12, the amendment raises questions of conflict with other specific provisions of our constitution, e.g., article I, section 23 (right to privacy) and article XI (providing means for amending state constitution) of the Florida Constitution. These questions and conflicts require that this unique addition to the Florida Constitution be narrowly construed.

Questions

1. What is the rule of this case (how does the amended Section 12 change the Court's reliance on precedent)?

2. a. When dealing with privacy cases, the Court often relied on the "public's intent" (what privacy was meant to encompass) at the time the privacy amendment was ratified. What does the majority say about the public's intent concerning the 1982 amendment of Section 12?

 b. What is Justice Ehrlich's view?

 c. What is Justice Overton's view on this matter and what is his reasoning?

State v. Wells

539 So. 2d 464 (Fla. 1989)

PER CURIAM.

On motion for rehearing by petitioner, we withdraw our prior opinion in this cause and substitute the following as the opinion of the Court.

We have for review *Wells v. State*, 492 So.2d 1375 (Fla. 5th DCA 1986), based on express and direct conflict with *State v. Wargin*, 418 So.2d 1261 (Fla. 4th DCA 1982). We have jurisdiction. Art. V, § 3(b)(3), Fla. Const. We approve in part and quash in part the decision of the district court below.

While driving a car loaned by a friend, respondent was stopped by the highway patrol for speeding. The trooper noticed the smell of alcohol upon respondent's breath and arrested him for driving under the influence. At this time, respondent agreed to accompany the trooper to the station to take a breathalyzer test.[12] When respondent asked if he could retrieve a coat from the automobile, the trooper agreed, but accompanied respondent to the vehicle. At this point, the trooper saw an amount of cash lying on the car's floorboard. 492 So.2d at 1375–76.

Suspicious of the cash's origin, the trooper asked respondent to open the trunk of the car. Respondent agreed, stating that he did not know what was in the trunk.

---

11. [FN 4.] *E.g.*, article 1, section 12 includes as an express provision the right to be secure "against the unreasonable interception of private communications by any means."

12. [FN 1.] A test later showed that respondent's blood alcohol content was below the legal limit. *Wells v. State*, 492 So.2d 1375, 1476 n. 1 (Fla. 5th DCA 1986).

However, neither respondent nor the trooper were able to manipulate a special locking mechanism that opened the trunk only when the key was pushed in and turned simultaneously. Giving up the effort, the trooper told respondent that the automobile must be impounded and received permission to force the trunk open if necessary and look inside. The trooper did not ask for or receive permission to look in the passenger compartment.

The car subsequently was transported to a facility under contract with the state, where a search was conducted. During this search, two marijuana cigarette butts were found in an ashtray. The trooper, assisted by others, opened the trunk with the key and found a locked suitcase inside. Under the direction of the trooper, employees of the facility attempted to pry open the suitcase with a knife. Some ten minutes later they succeeded, and found a garbage bag inside containing a large amount of marijuana.

Respondent was charged with possession of a controlled substance. After his motion to suppress the contraband was denied at trial, respondent pled nolo contendere, but reserved his right to appeal on the suppression issue. The Fifth District later determined that the trial court had erred, and ordered the contraband suppressed. From this order, the state now seeks review.

The facts of this case raise three distinct questions of search and seizure law: the scope of the consent search conducted in this instance, the propriety of opening the locked container found during the automobile inventory search, and the propriety of the impoundment of respondent's vehicle.

The Consent Search

The state urges us to hold that respondent's general consent to open and look into the trunk of the automobile was sufficient to authorize the opening of any locked or closed containers found there. In support of this argument, the state contends that *Wargin* correctly extended the principles of *United States v. Ross*, 456 U.S. 798 (1982), to the consent-search context. We cannot agree.

Ross clearly stands for the proposition that, so long as probable cause exists to search an automobile, the police lawfully can search any container found inside. Thus, the *Ross* Court upheld the search of an automobile after the police received a tip from a reliable informant that drugs were being sold from the vehicle, stopped it and found a paper bag and a zippered pouch containing contraband and a large amount of cash. 456 U.S. at 800–01. Based on these facts, *Ross* held: "If *probable cause* justifies the search of a lawfully stopped *vehicle*, it justifies the search of every part of the vehicle and its contents that may conceal the object of the search." *Id.* at 825 (emphasis added).

There was no issue of a consent search in *Ross*. Indeed, the principles that apply to probable cause searches are totally incongruous to the freedom of choice inherent in consent.... A consensual search by its very definition is circumscribed by the extent of the permission given, as determined by the totality of the circumstances. *Id.* On the other hand, a probable cause search and its scope are compelled, no matter what might be the wish of the individual. A theory based on consent and one based upon state-sponsored coercion thus are incompatible, and fusing them could lead to absurd results. Under such logic, the search of the trunk of a car would be permitted even if the defendant had said, "You can look in my car but *not* in my trunk."

Thus, we decline to apply *Ross* to consent searches, and, to the extent it conflicts with our opinion today, we disapprove *Wargin*. We cannot agree that the state and its agents, by receiving an ill-defined or limited consent to be searched, suddenly are vested with all the authority conferred by a warrant. Such a holding effectively would vitiate the entire theory upon which the consent search rests.

We also concur with the district court's conclusion that the consent given in this instance did not permit the police to pry open locked luggage with a knife. Respondent's permission merely indicated that the police could look into the automobile trunk. This was an insufficient basis for the police action that followed.

In so holding, we decline to establish a rule that effectively would countenance breaking open a locked or sealed container solely because the police have permission to be in the place where that container is located, as in this instance. This would render the very act of locking or sealing the container meaningless and would utterly ignore a crucial concern underlying fourth amendment jurisprudence: the expectation of privacy reasonably manifested by an individual in his locked luggage, no matter where that luggage is located.

When the police are relying upon consent to conduct a warrantless search, they have no more authority than that reasonably conferred by the terms of the consent. If that consent does not convey permission to break open a locked or sealed container, it is unreasonable for the police to do so unless the search can be justified on some other basis. Our own courts generally have agreed on this principle. *State v. Carney*, 423 So.2d 511 (Fla. 3d DCA 1982) (permission to go aboard boat did not give consent to open hidden compartments and containers therein); *Loftis v. State*, 391 So.2d 219 (Fla. 1st DCA 1980) (defendant's cooperation in opening truck did not give agricultural inspector consent to remove and open taped package), *review denied*, 399 So.2d 1146 (Fla.1981); *Major v. State*, 389 So.2d 1203 (Fla. 3d DCA 1980) (no consent where defendant opened tote bag for airport officer to look in, but where officer spontaneously reached in and grabbed a nasal inhaler containing contraband), *review denied*, 408 So.2d 1095 (Fla.1981); *Rose v. State*, 369 So.2d 447 (Fla. 1st DCA 1979) (no consent when defendant allowed officers to look in camper but apparently denied access to containers); *Raleigh v. State*, 365 So.2d 1048 (Fla. 4th DCA 1978) (no consent where occupants acquiesced to warrantless search of vehicle's trunk where officer opened trunk himself without asking permission).

In the present case, the arresting officer plainly stated that he had no actual consent to open the suitcase found in the automobile trunk.[13] We thus must agree with the

---

13. [FN 3.] The following colloquy with the arresting officer occurred:

   Q. Did [Wells] give you permission to go into the trunk of that car?

   A. Oh, yes, no problem, but he said—I said: "Do you mind if I look in your trunk," and he said, "Sure, go right ahead."

court below that the general consent to look in an automobile trunk in this case did not constitute permission to pry open a locked piece of luggage found inside. *Wells*, 492 So.2d at 1378. The very act of locking such a container constitutes a manifest denial of consent to open it, readily discernible by all the world. It creates a legally recognized zone of privacy inside that container, *Arkansas v. Sanders*, 442 U.S. 753, 765–66 (1979), that is protected under the United States Constitution and Florida's privacy amendment from the kind of governmental intrusion without probable cause that occurred in this case. *See* Art. I, §23, Fla. Const.

As to the marijuana cigarette butts found in the ashtray, we conclude that their seizure is not sustainable under a consent theory, since the trooper neither asked for nor received permission to search the passenger compartment.

The Inventory Search

We must also reject the state's contention that the seizure of the luggage was independently permissible under an inventory search theory. In *Colorado v. Bertine*, 479 U.S. 367 (1987), the United States Supreme Court delineated the requirements for opening sealed containers during a proper inventory search. *Bertine* stated:

> We emphasize that, in this case, the trial court found that the police department's procedures *mandated the opening of closed containers and the listing of their contents.* Our decisions have always adhered to the requirement that inventories be conducted according to standardized criteria.

Id. 107 S.Ct. at 742 n. 6 (emphasis added; citations omitted). As Justice Blackmun noted in his special concurring opinion, joined by two other justices:

> The underlying rationale for allowing an inventory exception to the Fourth Amendment warrant rule is that police officers are not vested with discretion to determine the scope of the inventory search. This absence of discretion ensures that inventory searches will not be used as a purposeful and general means of discovering evidence of crime. Thus, it is permissible for police officers to open closed containers in an inventory search *only if they are following standard police procedures that mandate the opening of such containers in every impounded vehicle.*

Id. at 744 (Blackmun, Powell & O'Connor, JJ., concurring) (emphasis added; citation omitted).

The impermissible discretion to open or not to open containers is evident in this case. Contrary to *Bertine*'s holding, the Florida Highway Patrol ("Patrol"), at least upon this record, operates under no mandatory standardized policy regarding closed containers. Unlike in *Bertine*, this record is devoid of any trial-court finding "that the

----

….

Q. Now, since [Wells] had indicated to you that he did not know what was in the trunk, you clearly did not extend the questioning to say: "Well, whatever I find in the trunk, is it okay if I look in that, too?"
A. No, I didn't.

police department's standard procedures did mandate the opening of closed containers and the listing of their contents." *Id.* Joining this action as *amicus curiae,* the Patrol itself has submitted copies of relevant portions of its Policy Manual, which fail to address the question. Chapter 16 of the Policy Manual, governing the receipt of property and vehicles, speaks in general terms and requires nothing more than an "[i]nventory of all articles in the vehicle ... such as articles of clothing, equipment and tools." Policy Manual, at 16-4. There is no mention of opening closed containers.

In the absence of a policy specifically requiring the opening of closed containers found during a legitimate inventory search, *Bertine* prohibits us from countenancing the procedure followed in this instance. The police under *Bertine* must mandate either that all containers will be opened during an inventory search, or that no containers will be opened. There can be no room for discretion. Since this record reveals no such mandatory policy, we must hold that the opening of the luggage in this instance violated *Bertine.*

The Impoundment Issue

Finally, we find that the impoundment in this instance, and hence the search of the interior of the car that followed was proper under *Bertine.* This conclusion is compelled by the fact that, to the extent of any inconsistency, *Bertine* has superseded *Miller v. State,* 403 So.2d 1307 (Fla.1981), and *Sanders v. State,* 403 So.2d 973 (Fla.1981). Under the analysis in *Bertine,* we believe the Patrol is not compelled to provide an alternative to impoundment, as we held in *Miller* and *Sanders.* Thus, we believe the officer in this instance acted reasonably by choosing to impound an automobile containing several thousand dollars in cash rather than leave it unprotected at the roadside.

For this reason, we conclude that the seizure of the marijuana cigarette butts in this instance was permissible as an incident of a proper impoundment. *See* Art. I, §12, Fla. Const. Since the cigarette butts were not inside any closed or locked container, the suppression of the butts was improper under *Bertine.*

We, thus, approve in part and quash in part the result reached by the district court below, and remand for proceedings consistent with this opinion. No renewed motion for rehearing will be entertained.

It is so ordered.

EHRLICH, C.J., and BARKETT, GRIMES and KOGAN, JJ., concur.

SHAW, J., dissents with an opinion, in which OVERTON and McDONALD, JJ., concur.

SHAW, Justice, dissenting.

Article I, section 12 of the Florida Constitution provides that rights granted therein involving searches and seizures will be construed in conformity with the fourth amendment to the United States Constitution, as interpreted by the United States Supreme Court. Thus, the issue of impoundment and inventory search is controlled by *South Dakota v. Opperman,* 428 U.S. 364 (1976), and its progeny. I agree with the majority that *Colorado v. Bertine,* 479 U.S. 367 (1987), has overruled *Miller v. State,*

403 So.2d 1307 (Fla.1981), and *Sanders v. State*, 403 So.2d 973 (Fla.1981), that the police are not required to provide an alternative to impoundment, and that the marijuana cigarette butts found in the car's ashtray are admissible. For the reasons which follow, I do not agree that *Bertine* mandates exclusion of the eighteen pounds of marijuana found in the locked suitcase.

Wells was stopped for speeding on a rural road between Palatka and St. Augustine in the evening hours. He alighted from his car and produced an expired driver's license and a car title in another's name. After the officer detected alcohol on his breath, Wells failed a roadside sobriety test and was arrested for driving under the influence. Wells asked, however, to retrieve a coat from the car. While doing so, the officer saw a large sum of cash lying on the floorboard in front of the driver's seat. Wells gave conflicting explanations of this money and it was impounded and inventoried. The arresting officer asked Wells to open the car trunk and Wells agreed, saying he did not know what was inside, but neither the officer nor Wells could open the trunk. Wells agreed that the trunk could be forcibly opened, if necessary, after towing. The car was left with a backup officer and later towed. The arresting officer transported Wells to the local police station for a breathalyzer test and proceeded to the storage area to inventory the car. The arresting officer found two marijuana cigarette butts in the car's ashtray. The tow operator then opened the trunk where a locked suitcase was found. The suitcase was forced open and eighteen pounds of marijuana in a trash bag were seized.

The majority holds that the police acted properly in impounding the car. However, relying primarily on *Bertine*, the majority holds that the eighteen pounds of marijuana should be excluded because Florida Highway Patrol standardized procedures do not specifically mandate that locked containers found in impounded cars be opened and inventoried. Although the FHP can easily remedy this perceived deficiency in their operating instructions, I am persuaded that the current instructions effectively mandate the opening and inventorying of such closed containers when a vehicle is impounded and that these instructions are indistinguishable from those in *Bertine*.

The inventorying of the contents of impounded cars is based on three distinct needs: to protect the owner's property; to protect the police against claims over lost or stolen property; and to protect the police from potential dangers, such as explosives. *Opperman*, 428 U.S. at 369. The Florida Highway Patrol, Forms and Procedures Manual, section 16.00.00, ... make clear that an inventory is required for all impounded cars and that the inventory will be comprehensive and detailed, extending down to articles, not merely containers, closed or otherwise. This reading of the instructions is consistent with the testimony of the officer who conducted the arrest and inventory. According to this officer, he consulted with his backup officer and supervisor, and, as in the case of previous arrests, the inventory was performed according to procedures he was supposed to follow. This understanding of the standard instructions by the persons to whom they are addressed is also consistent with the three purposes of the inventory set forth in *Opperman* and reiterated in *Bertine*, none of which would be adequately served if closed containers were not opened and inventoried when vehicles are impounded.

The majority's conclusion that here, unlike *Bertine*, the police operating instructions do not mandate the opening of closed containers is contrary to the facts of *Bertine* as we have them. Neither Chief Justice Rehnquist's opinion for the Court nor Justice Blackmun's concurring opinion actually quotes the police operating instructions which the Court found mandated opening closed containers for inventory. These instructions were, however, quoted by Justice Marshall in dissent where he argued that no standardized criteria limited the police officer's discretion. The operative words are "the Officer shall conduct a detailed vehicle inspection and inventory and record it upon the VEHICLE IMPOUND FORM." *Bertine*, 479 U.S. at 380 n.4. These instructions require a "detailed" inventory but they are certainly no more explicit or definitive than the Patrol instructions quoted above which make the impounding officer responsible for the vehicle, its parts and contents, and require completion of an inventory form listing all articles, such as articles of clothing, equipment, and tools. Chief Justice Rehnquist, for the Court, responded to Justice Marshall's criticism by finding that the instructions not only circumscribed the discretion of individual officers, they also protected the vehicle and its contents and minimized claims of property loss. *Bertine*, 479 U.S. at 376 n.7. The standard Patrol instructions here are even more specific than those which the *Bertine* concurring opinion found "mandate[d] the opening of closed containers and the listing of their contents." 479 U.S. at 377 (Blackmun, J., concurring). In my view, *Bertine* stands for the proposition that when a legitimate impoundment is made and standard police instructions mandate that an inventory be conducted, contraband discovered is constitutionally admissible.

The majority also distinguishes *United States v. Ross*, 456 U.S. 798 (1982), holding that *Ross* addresses probable cause searches only and is not relevant to consent searches. However, in cases cited by petitioner and not distinguished by the majority, federal courts have found *Ross* relevant to the scope of a consent search. *United States v. Kapperman*, 764 F.2d 786, 794 (11th Cir.1985); *United States v. White*, 706 F.2d 806, 808 (7th Cir.1983). Moreover, on the authority of *Bertine*, *Ross* is relevant to inventory searches.

> "When a legitimate search is under way, and when its purpose and its limits have been precisely defined, nice distinctions between closets, drawers, and containers, in the case of a home, or between glove compartments, upholstered seats, trunks, and wrapped packages, in the case of vehicle, must give way to the interest in the prompt and efficient completion of the task at hand." *United States v. Ross, supra*, 456 U.S. at 821.

> We reaffirm these principles here: "'[a] single familiar standard is essential to guide police officers, who have only limited time and expertise to reflect on and balance the social and individual interest involved in the specific circumstances they confront.'" See [*Illinois v.*] *Lafayette, supra*, 462 U.S. [640], at 648 (1983)] (quoting *New York v. Belton*, 453 U.S. 454, 458 (1981)).

Bertine, 479 U.S. at 375. The broad application of these quoted words and the fact that the *Bertine* Court chose to affirm their application to a non-probable cause, inventory search strongly suggests that the Supreme Court does not take the narrow view of *Ross* which the majority adopts here. While *Ross* would not be authority to exceed the specific scope of a restricted consent, as the majority points out, it would appear to be applicable to an unrestricted consent search, or an inventory search, such as here.

In summary, the majority has misapplied *Bertine* which, in my view, is factually and legally indistinguishable from the case at hand. I would quash the decision below and reinstate the conviction.

OVERTON and McDONALD, JJ., concur.

Questions

1. What law (precedent case) did the Court apply to the question of the FHP's ability to open sealed containers based on Wells's consent?

2. Which precedent cases provided the basis for the Court's reasoning in deciding whether the cigarette butts found in the ashtray were legally seized and why?

State v. Hume

512 So. 2d 184 (Fla. 1987)

OVERTON, Justice.

Both the state and Robert William Hume petition this Court to review *State v. Hume*, 463 So.2d 499 (Fla. 1st DCA 1985), in which the district court construed article I, section 12, of the Florida Constitution (the new search-and-seizure section), and applied section 901.19, Florida Statutes (1985) (knock-and-announce statute). We have jurisdiction. Art. V, §3(b)(3), Fla. Const. We hold that it was error to suppress statements transmitted by an electronic eavesdropping device worn by a police undercover agent in Hume's home and to suppress contraband seized immediately following Hume's arrest.

The facts reflect that a police undercover agent knew Hume and had purchased cocaine from him. On January 10, 1983, the police obtained an arrest warrant for Hume based on his narcotics violations. One week later, the police undercover agent equipped himself with a "body bug," a device designed to record and transmit his conversations to fellow officers, and went to Hume's apartment to purchase a larger amount of cocaine. Hume invited the undercover agent to enter and escorted him to the bedroom, where Hume displayed plastic bags containing marijuana and cocaine. After seeing the illegal drugs, the undercover agent used a code word in their conversation to indicate to officers waiting outside that contraband was present. He then proceeded with Hume to the front door of the apartment. As the undercover agent opened the front door, the other officers, who possessed the warrant for Hume's arrest, immediately entered and arrested Hume. The undercover agent returned to the bedroom and seized the drugs and drug paraphernalia. Hume was charged with unlawful sale/delivery of cocaine, trafficking in cocaine, and unlawful possession of marijuana with intent to distribute.

This cause concerns two search and seizure issues: (1) the recorded conversation in Hume's home by the undercover agent and (2) the asserted failure of the arresting officers to comply with the knock-and-announce requirement of section 901.19, Florida Statutes.

Sarmiento: Electronic Eavesdropping in the Home

Hume moved to suppress the evidence of his conversation transmitted by the agent's body bug on the authority of *State v. Sarmiento*, 397 So.2d 643 (Fla.1981), which held that, under the then-existing provisions of article I, section 12, of the Florida Constitution, the interception and simultaneous transmission of personal conversations within a defendant's home violated the defendant's reasonable expectation of privacy and was prohibited by that section of the Florida Constitution. The trial court in the instant case granted the motion to suppress, but the district court reversed, holding that *Sarmiento* was no longer legal precedent because it did not survive the conformity amendment to article I, section 12.

That amendment provides that the right of the people to be secure in their persons, houses, papers and effects against the unreasonable interception of private communications shall be construed in conformity with the fourth amendment to the United States Constitution, as interpreted by the United States Supreme Court.

The district court concluded that, under *United States v. White*, 401 U.S. 745 (1971), the surreptitious interception and transmission of conversations between an undercover agent and a defendant in the defendant's home does not violate the fourth amendment of the United States Constitution.

In this proceeding, Hume contends that the recent amendment to section 12 of article I does not affect our *Sarmiento* precedent. We disagree. In our view, the amendment to section 12 was intended, in part, to overrule our decision in *Sarmiento*. We conclude that, in *United States v. White*, the United States Supreme Court ruled directly on the *Sarmiento* factual situation of an uninvited third party's interception of conversations occurring within the sanctity of the home through electronic equipment. The issue in *White* was set forth as follows:

> The issue before us is whether the Fourth Amendment bars from evidence the testimony of governmental agents who related certain conversations which had occurred between defendant White and a government informant, Harvey Jackson, and which the agents overheard by monitoring the frequency of a radio transmitter carried by Jackson and concealed on his person. On four occasions the conversations took place in Jackson's home.... Four other conversations—*one in respondent's home,* one in a restaurant, and two in Jackson's car—were overheard by the use of radio equipment.

Id. at 746–47 (footnotes omitted; emphasis added). The opinion, written by Justice White, states:

> Concededly a police agent who conceals his police connections may write down for official use his conversations with a defendant and testify concerning them, without a warrant authorizing his encounters with the defendant and

without otherwise violating the latter's Fourth Amendment rights. For constitutional purposes, no different result is required if the agent instead of immediately reporting and transcribing his conversations with defendant, either (1) simultaneously records them with electronic equipment which he is carrying on his person; (2) or carries radio equipment which simultaneously transmits the conversations either to recording equipment located elsewhere or to other agents monitoring the transmitting frequency. If the conduct and revelations of an agent operating without electronic equipment do not invade the defendant's constitutionally justifiable expectations of privacy, neither does a simultaneous recording of the same conversations made by the agent or by others from transmissions received from the agent to whom the defendant is talking and whose trustworthiness the defendant necessarily risks.

... If the law gives no protection to the wrongdoer whose trusted accomplice is or becomes a police agent, neither should it protect him when that same agent has recorded or transmitted the conversations which are later offered in evidence to prove the State's case.

....

Nor should we be too ready to erect constitutional barriers to relevant and probative evidence which is also accurate and reliable. An electronic recording will many times produce a more reliable rendition of what a defendant has said than will the unaided memory of a police agent. It may also be that with the recording in existence it is less likely that the informant will change his mind, less chance that threat or injury will suppress unfavorable evidence and less chance that cross-examination will confound the testimony. Considerations like these obviously do not favor the defendant, but we are not prepared to hold that a defendant who has no constitutional right to exclude the informer's unaided testimony nevertheless has a Fourth Amendment privilege against a more accurate version of the events in question.

It is thus untenable to consider the activities and reports of the police agent himself, though acting without a warrant, to be a "reasonable" investigative effort and lawful under the Fourth Amendment but to view the same agent with a recorder or transmitter as conducting an "unreasonable" and unconstitutional search and seizure.

Id. at 751–53 (citations omitted). Chief Justice Burger and Justices Stewart and Blackmun joined in the opinion with Justice White. Justice Black concurred in result because he would hold, for the reasons he expressed in *Katz v. United States*, 389 U.S. 347, 364 (1967), that eavesdropping carried on by electronic means does not constitute a search or seizure and is thus not violative of the fourth amendment. Further, the United States Supreme Court reaffirmed this holding in *United States v. Caceres*, 440 U.S. 741 (1979). In a seven-to-two majority opinion, the Court cited *White* for the proposition that

"[i]f the conduct and revelations of an agent operating without electronic equipment do not invade the defendant's constitutionally justifiable expectations of privacy, neither does a simultaneous recording of the same conversations made by the agent or by others from transmissions received from the agent to whom the defendant is talking and whose trustworthiness the defendant necessarily risks."

440 U.S. at 751 (quoting 401 U.S. at 751).

We conclude that the *White* and *Caceres* decisions establish clear precedent that the recording of conversations between a defendant and an undercover agent in a defendant's home, such as occurred in the instant case, does not violate the fourth amendment of the United States Constitution and, accordingly, does not violate the newly adopted article I, section 12, of the Florida Constitution. We also agree with the state that our right-of-privacy provision, article I, section 23, of the Florida Constitution, does not modify the applicability of article I, section 12, particularly since the people adopted section 23 prior to the present section 12.

Statutory Knock-and-Announce Requirements

In the second issue, the trial court suppressed the seized contraband observed by the undercover agent in the bedroom because the arresting officers, in entering Hume's apartment with the arrest warrant, failed to comply with Florida's knock-and-announce statute, section 901.19(1), and because the warrantless seizure was not justified by any exception to the warrant requirement. The district court affirmed the trial court in suppressing this evidence. In doing so, the district court noted that neither party had challenged the trial court's finding that the agent, after signalling to the other officers, "on his own initiative opened the front door to allow the outside officers to enter and arrest [Hume]." 463 So.2d at 500 (footnote omitted). The district court recognized a line of cases holding that the knock-and-announce statute does not apply when an undercover officer departs a defendant's residence and then re-enters with other officers who assist in arresting a defendant, but distinguished this line from the instant case on the basis that the agent did not leave and re-enter Hume's apartment prior to accomplishing the arrest: "While it is arguable that this fact constitutes a distinction without a difference ... we are not prepared to so hold as a matter of law, especially given the mandate to strictly construe exceptions to Section 901.19(1)." 463 So.2d at 501–02.

Numerous cases by this Court and other district courts of appeal have determined that the knock-and-announce statute is not applicable when an undercover officer re-enters the premises with assistants after having previously been admitted voluntarily. *See Griffin v. State*, 419 So.2d 320 (Fla.1982); *State v. Cantrell*, 426 So.2d 1035 (Fla. 2d DCA), *review denied*, 434 So.2d 886 (Fla.1983), *cert. denied*, 464 U.S. 1047 (1984); *State v. Steffani*, 398 So.2d 475 (Fla. 3d DCA 1981), *approved*, 419 So.2d 323 (Fla.1982). We find no real factual distinction between this line of cases and the instant case. Therefore, we quash this portion of the district court decision.

Once Hume invited the undercover agent into his apartment and openly engaged in criminal conduct, he relinquished his right to assert a violation of his reasonable expectation of privacy and immediately subjected himself to arrest and the contraband in plain view to seizure. Under these circumstances, we do not find that the statutory provisions require that arresting officers "knock and announce" after the undercover agent within the premises has summoned them to assist in safely arresting a defendant and seizing the contraband. Since the undercover agent had already lawfully intruded into Hume's apartment and since he could have arrested Hume inside the premises at any time, we find that the enlistment of additional officers waiting outside the home did not constitute an intrusion offensive to section 901.19(1) or Hume's claimed expectations of privacy. To rule otherwise would be contrary, in our view, to the intent of section 901.19(1) and would compromise an officer's safety. Thus, under these circumstances, both the arrest of Hume and the seizure of the contraband were valid.

For the reasons expressed, we approve in part and quash in part the opinion of the district court and remand for further proceedings consistent with this opinion.

It is so ordered.

McDONALD, C.J., and EHRLICH and SHAW, JJ., concur.

BARKETT, J., dissents with an opinion.

BARKETT, Justice, dissenting.

I dissent. Article I, section 12, has not been repealed and therefore remains vital to protect Florida citizens against unreasonable searches and seizures in situations which have not yet been, and in some cases could never be, resolved by the United States Supreme Court. Article I, section 12, unlike the fourth amendment, provides an express guarantee "against the unreasonable interception of private communications by any means." This express right was not modified and must continue to be given full force and effect apart from the vagaries of fourth amendment jurisprudence.[14] Thus, application of our exclusionary rule with respect to this right cannot be construed in conformity with United States Supreme Court decisions. Therefore, federal judicial doctrines developed in the electronic surveillance area do not apply when construing article I, section 12, and this Court's decision in *State v. Sarmiento*, 397 So.2d 643 (Fla.1981), is dispositive of the case at bar.

Moreover, in addition to the express rights of article I, section 12, other provisions that protect Florida citizens are implicated in this case. Florida citizens' rights to privacy, particularly in the sanctity of the home, are expressly protected in this state by constitutional and statutory guarantees. *See, e.g.,* art. I, §23, Fla. Const.; §933.18, Fla.Stat. (1985). Because these protections have no counterpart in federal law, whether or not the private conversation that is being transmitted or recorded takes place in the home or elsewhere is not relevant to United States Supreme Court analysis. *See*

---

14. [FN 11.] Any other reading of our amendment could conceivably result in complete nullification of this express protection. For example, the United States Supreme Court could recede from its present position and decide that electronic surveillance is not a search under the fourth amendment. *See Katz v. United States*, 389 U.S. 347 (1967) (Black, J., dissenting).

United States v. White, 401 U.S. 745 (1971). United States Supreme Court decisions are not controlling, therefore, because in determining what privacy expectations are constitutionally justifiable under *Katz v. United States*, 389 U.S. 347 (1967), we cannot ignore these specific expressions of the will of the people of Florida.

There is no bright line between the privacy protections afforded under article I, section 12, and the privacy interests protected by article I, section 23. Section 23 comes into play in cases involving electronic surveillance because this aspect of governmental activity infringing on privacy is one that section 23 was particularly designed to check. The people have recognized and acted to protect themselves against the dangers inherent in unauthorized use of electronic surveillance. We cannot interpret the conformity amendment as negating, by implication, rights that the voters of this state have designated to be of constitutional stature.

Even if we were bound in the area of electronic surveillance by United States Supreme Court decisions existing at the time of our article I, section 12 amendment, I do not believe that any of that Court's decisions are controlling here. *White* is the closest case factually; however, it was only a plurality decision.[15] I agree with Judge Hubbart that "the authority of the *White* Court's equivocal ruling is itself doubtful as it ... did not muster a majority of the Court. We are thus left, at best, with federal support for both sides of the constitutional issue stated herein." *State v. Shaktman*, 389 So.2d 1045, 1049 (Fla. 3d DCA 1980) (Hubbart, J., dissenting), *review denied*, 397 So.2d 779 (Fla.1981). *See also Marks v. United States*, 430 U.S. 188, 193 (1977); *Gregg v. Georgia*, 428 U.S. 153, 169 n. 15 (1976) (holding of court limited to position subscribed to by members who concurred on narrowest grounds).

Accordingly, I dissent.

Questions

1. a. According to the Court, what is the interaction between Section 12 and Section 23?

   b. Do you agree with the Court on this point and why?

2. Is the Court's statement about the interaction of the two cases dispositive of future cases?

3. What is dissenting Justice Barkett's two-step argument?

---

15. [FN 12.] In a sharply divided opinion, five justices concurred in the result, Justice Black joining the majority based on the view that eavesdropping by electronic means in any situation is not covered by the fourth amendment. *See United States v. White*, 401 U.S. 745, 754 (1971) (Black, J., concurring) (citing his dissent in Katz, 389 U.S. at 349–364).

C. Article I, Section 4—
Freedom of Speech and Press

State v. Elder

382 So. 2d 687 (Fla. 1980)

SUNDBERG, Justice.

This is an appeal from an order of the County Court for Duval County, Florida, which initially and directly passed upon the validity of section 365.16(1)(b), Florida Statutes (1977). The issue presented is whether section 365.16(1)(b), which forbids the making of an anonymous telephone call with the intent to annoy, abuse, threaten, or harass the recipient of the call, is unconstitutionally overbroad on its face. We have jurisdiction pursuant to article V, section 3(b)(1), Florida Constitution.

Appellee, Arlene Elder, was charged by amended information with making a telephone call, without disclosing her identity, to one Victoria Elaine Elder solely to annoy, abuse, threaten or harass her contrary to section 365.16(1)(b), Florida Statutes (1977).[16] Appellee moved to dismiss the information on the grounds that the statutory provision was facially overbroad in violation of article I, sections 4 and 9 of the Florida Constitution, and the first and fourteenth amendments to the United States Constitution. The county court found that subsection (1)(b) proscribed "pure speech" contrary to the case law which the court said admits of only two classes of unprotected speech language posing a clear and present danger of breach of the peace ("fighting words") and obscenity. The court stated that because neither the statutory language nor any judicial gloss had limited the statute's application to fighting words or obscenity, the statute was overbroad without regard to the particular facts of the case. To support its conclusion that the statute was overbroad, the court cited several examples of constitutionally protected speech which would purportedly come within the statute's proscription: a phone call made with specific intent to "annoy" a person by telling him that he had bad manners; a phoned "threat" to a friend telling him

---

16. [FN1.] Although we are here concerned only with subsection (1)(b), the provision under which appellee is charged, we state the substance of subsection (1) in full because of close interrelation of their provisions:

(1) Whoever by means of telephone communication:

(a) Makes any comment, request, suggestion, or proposal which is obscene, lewd, lascivious, filthy, or indecent; or

(b) Makes a telephone call, whether or not conversation ensues, without disclosing his identity and with intent to annoy, abuse, threaten, or harass any person at the called number; or

(c) Makes or causes the telephone of another repeatedly or continuously to ring, with intent to harass any person at the called number; or

(d) Makes repeated telephone calls, during which conversation ensues, solely to harass any person at the called number,

shall be guilty of a misdemeanor of the second degree.

that if he does not pay off a small debt he will never be spoken to again; one businessman calling another intending to "abuse" and "annoy" the latter by calling him dishonest. Finally, the court rejected any limiting construction of section 365.16(1)(b) on the basis that to so limit the statute and at the same time apply it to the defendant would deny him due process of law because of the lack of prior notice of the conduct proscribed. For the following reasons, we believe that the county court erred in finding section 365.16(1)(b) facially unconstitutional.[17]

We begin with the proposition that because of the transcendent value of constitutionally protected expression, statutes regulating expression must be narrowly tailored to further the legitimate state interest involved, *Grayned v. City of Rockford*, 408 U.S. 104 (1972); *McCall v. State*, 354 So.2d 869 (Fla.1978); so that the first amendment freedoms are given the breathing room needed to survive. *NAACP v. Button*, 371 U.S. 415 (1963); *Brown v. State*, 358 So.2d 16 (Fla.1978). Where a statute punishes only spoken words it is facially constitutional under the overbreadth doctrine only if, as construed by the state courts, it is not susceptible of application to constitutionally protected speech. *Gooding v. Wilson*, 405 U.S. 518 (1972); *Spears v. State*, 337 So.2d 977 (Fla.1976). We note in passing that the trial court, in ruling that section 365.16(1)(b) was unconstitutionally overbroad because it was not limited to the proscription of fighting words or obscenity, overlooks the fact that the constitutional right of free speech does not absolutely protect libelous or slanderous speech, nor does free speech absolutely insulate a person from tort liability for invasion of privacy or intentional infliction of emotional distress, nor from criminal liability for certain forms of "pure speech."[18] Such expression belongs to "that category of utterances which 'are no essential part of any exposition of ideas, and are of such slight social value as a step to truth that any benefit that may be derived from them is clearly outweighed by the social interest in order and morality.'" *Gertz v. Robert Welch, Inc.*, 418 U.S. 323, 340 (1974), quoting *Chaplinsky v. New Hampshire*, 315 U.S. 568, 572 (1942).

We need not, however, pass on whether section 365.16(1)(b) validly proscribes pure speech. Rather, we disagree with the trial court's characterization of the section as a proscription of pure speech. This statutory provision is not directed at the communication of opinions or ideas, but at conduct, that is, the act of making a telephone call or a series of telephone calls, without disclosing identity and whether or not conversation ensues, with the intent to annoy, abuse, threaten or harass the recipient of the call. *Accord, Baker v. State*, 16 Ariz.App. 463, 494 P.2d 68 (1972). *Cf. S.H.B. v. State*, 355 So.2d 1176 (Fla.1978) That this conduct may be effected in part by verbal means does not necessarily invalidate the statute on freedom of speech grounds. At

17. [FN2.] We do agree, however, with the county court's threshold finding that a defendant may challenge a statute's validity on overbreadth grounds without first demonstrating that his own conduct could not be regulated by a statute drawn with the requisite narrow specificity. *Lewis v. City of New Orleans*, 415 U.S. 130 (1974); *State v. Keaton*, 371 So.2d 86 (Fla.1979).

18. [FN3.] *E.g., Watts v. United States*, 394 U.S. 705 (1969) (threatening the President with bodily harm); *State v. Saunders*, 339 So.2d 641 (Fla.1976) (falsely reporting some physical hazard in circumstances where such a report creates a clear and present danger of bodily harm to others, such as yelling "fire" in a crowded theater); *State v. Beasley*, 317 So.2d 750 (Fla.1975) (speech inciting a riot).

most, the use of words as the method with which to harass the recipient of the call involves conduct mixed with speech, to which the controlling constitutional considerations differ somewhat from those applied to pure speech. Specifically, with regard to overbreadth, the applicable test is stated in *Broadrick v. Oklahoma*, 413 U.S. 601, 615 (1973): "(W)here conduct and not merely speech is involved, we believe that the overbreadth of a statute must not only be real, but substantial as well, judged in relation to the statute's plainly legitimate sweep." As construed below, section 365.16(1)(b) is clearly applicable to a whole range of activity which is easily identifiable and which constitutionally may be proscribed. *See Parker v. Levy*, 417 U.S. 733 (1974). We hold, therefore, that the asserted overbreadth of section 365.16(1)(b) is not real and substantial judged in relation to the statute's plainly legitimate sweep.

In construing section 365.16(1)(b), we are mindful of our responsibility to resolve all doubts as to the validity of a statute in favor of its constitutionality, provided the statute may be given a fair construction that is consistent with the federal and state constitutions as well as with the legislative intent. *State v. Keaton*, 371 So.2d 86 (Fla.1979); *White v. State*, 330 So.2d 3 (Fla.1976). The Court will not, however, abandon judicial restraint and invade the province of the legislature by rewriting its terms. *State v. Keaton*; *Brown v. State*, 358 So.2d 16 (Fla.1978). In dealing with statutory regulation of first amendment activity, this Court has in the past strictly construed a challenged statute to uphold it against vagueness or overbreadth attacks. *See, e.g., State v. Saunders*, 339 So.2d 641 (Fla.1976); *White v. State, supra*. After careful consideration we, likewise, here conclude that the language of section 365.16(1)(b) is fairly susceptible to a constitutional construction that is consistent with the legislative intent.

The closely related provisions of subsections (1)(b) through (1)(d) of section 365.16 evince a legislative intent to proscribe an act or a course of conduct that serves little, if any, informative or legitimate communicative function. The statute is carefully worded as to the specific conduct proscribed and is carefully limited with preconditions so as not to infringe on legitimate free speech rights.[19] First of all, the statutory proscription of subsection 365.16(1)(b) through (1)(d) is applicable only against the person performing the act of telephoning someone. This in itself shows a legislative concern not with the content of what was said but with the act of intruding upon another's privacy. Specifically, under subsection (1)(b), this legislative concern is further highlighted by the lack of any requirement that conversation ensue. Next, for conviction under subsection (1)(b), the caller must make the call without disclosing his identity. We wholly agree with the analysis of the United States District Court in *United States v. Dorsey*, 342 F.Supp. 311 (E.D.Pa.1972), that the "anonymity of the caller is in itself a circumstance raising discomfort and fear in the receiver of the call." *Id.* at 313 (construing federal statutory counterpart to Florida subsection 365.16(1)(b)). This anonymity is also a factor militating against any legitimate free speech

---

19. [FN5.] Indeed, subsection 365.16(1)(c), causing the telephone of another to ring repeatedly with intent to harass, does not even purport to regulate free speech activity.

communicative function. In addition, it must be shown that when the telephone call was made it was the caller's intent to annoy, abuse, threaten or harass. This improper intent must be the motivating factor in the caller's telephoning another person and the call must not serve a legitimate communicative or informative function.[20] Thus, the caller may not circumvent the salutary proscription of the statute merely by using words as the means with which to annoy, abuse, threaten or harass." "(I)t has never been deemed an abridgement of freedom of speech or press to make a course of conduct illegal merely because the conduct was in part initiated, evidenced, or carried out by means of language, either spoken, written, or printed." *Cox v. Louisiana*, 379 U.S. 559, 563 (1963).

Finally, the statutory language of subsection (1)(b), "to annoy, abuse, threaten or harass" presupposes that the telephone call is uninvited. It is this nonconsensual element of the telephone call which distinguishes the situation here from that in *State v. Keaton*, 371 So.2d 86 (Fla.1979), where we held that subsection (1)(a) of section 365.16 (barring obscene or indecent comments or suggestions over the telephone) was unconstitutionally overbroad. In that decision we stated:

> We do not hold that the state may not proscribe obscene telephone communications regardless of the circumstances. Were section 365.16(1)(a) limited to obscene calls to a listener at a location where he enjoys a reasonable expectation of privacy (such as the home) which calls are intended to harass the listener, the enactment would pass constitutional muster. Because such a statute would assume the existence of a listener who is unwillingly subjected to vulgar or obscene epithets, it would constitute a valid legislative attempt to protect the substantial privacy interests of the listener.

Id. at 92. What was broadly proscribed under subsection (1)(a), then, was not simply the act of making an uninvited obscene telephone call, but also the content of pure speech consensually communicated through a telephone.[21] We declined in *Keaton* to uphold section 365.16(1)(a) by narrowly construing it to proscribe only "obscenity" as defined under *Miller v. California*, 413 U.S. 15 (1973), a form of expression unprotected in the public form, because the statute could nevertheless contravene the first amendment in failing to contain the essential qualifying element of an unwilling listener.

In contrast to the statutory provision involved in *Keaton*, section 365.16(1) (b) does assume the existence of an unwilling listener. While it is true that a person may often be a "captive" outside the sanctuary of the home and subject to objectionable forms of expression, the United States Supreme Court, as well as this Court, have recognized that government may properly act in many situations to

---

20. [FN6.] At least one legitimate communicative or informative function is stated in section 365.16 itself. Subsection (5) of section 365.16 provides: "Nothing contained in this section shall apply to telephone calls made in good faith in the ordinary course of business or commerce."

21. [FN7.] The statute would purport to criminalize the "telling (of) an 'off color joke' to a willing listener or ... a sexually oriented conversation between lovers." *State v. Keaton*, 371 So.2d at 90.

prohibit intrusion into the privacy of the home of unwelcome views and ideas which cannot be totally banned from the public dialogue. Compare *Erznoznik v. City of Jacksonville*, 422 U.S. 205 (1975); *Gooding v. Wilson*, 405 U.S. 518 (1972); *Cohen v. California*, 403 U.S. 15 (1971); *Brown v. State*, 358 So.2d 16 (Fla.1978); and *Spears v. State*, 337 So.2d 977 (Fla.1976), with *FCC v. Pacifica Foundation*, 438 U.S. 726 (1978); *Rowan v. United States Post Office Dept.*, 397 U.S. 728 (1970); *Breard v. Alexandria*, 341 U.S. 622 (1951); *Kovacs v. Cooper*, 336 U.S. 77 (1949); and *State v. Keaton, supra*.[22]

The United States Supreme Court has thus clearly established that the privacy interest of a person may be accorded greater protection within the sanctum of the home or other private place than it may be accorded in the public forum. *Rowan v. United States Post Office Dept., supra*; *Stanley v. Georgia*, 394 U.S. 557 (1969). As a result, the federal and state constitutions will tolerate greater limits upon the dialogue of a speaker in order to prevent a nonconsensual intrusion upon those privacy interests. *State v. Keaton*, 371 So.2d at 92–93. We conclude that whatever minimal free speech value may be associated with an unwanted, anonymous, abusive telephone call simply because it is effected through verbal means under section 365.16(1)(b),[23] such value is clearly outweighed by the substantial privacy interests of the listener. These privacy interests constitutionally entitle the state to protect him from unwilling subjection to verbal or nonverbal abuse.

Accordingly, we hold that section 365.16(1)(b), as construed in this opinion, is constitutional. We, therefore, reverse the County Court for Duval County and remand this cause to that court for proceedings not inconsistent with this decision.

It is so ordered.

ENGLAND, C.J., and ADKINS, BOYD, OVERTON, ALDERMAN and McDONALD, JJ., concur.

Questions

1. Compare the federal and Florida constitutional provisions relating to free speech. Do you think that the language of the Florida constitutional provision is more extensive than the First Amendment?

2. According to the Court, why does the statute not regulate "pure speech"?

---

22. [FN8.] This is not to say that reasonable "time, place and manner" limitations, which are neutral as to content and which further significant governmental interests, may not be placed upon the exercise of first amendment expression in the public forum, particularly where conduct is mixed with speech. *See, e.g., Grayned v. City of Rockford*, 408 U.S. 104 (1972); *Cox v. Louisiana*, 379 U.S. 536 (1963); *Kovacs v. Cooper*, 336 U.S. 77 (1949); *Cantwell v. Connecticut*, 310 U.S. 296 (1940); *McCall v. State*, 354 So.2d 869 (Fla.1978); *White v. State*, 330 So.2d 3 (Fla.1976). *See also Erznoznik v. City of Jacksonville*, 422 U.S. 205 (1975), and *Lehman v. City of Shaker Heights*, 418 U.S. 298 (1974).

23. [FN9.] "Resort to epithets or personal abuse is not in any proper sense communication of information or opinion safeguarded by the Constitution, and its punishment as a criminal act would raise no question under that instrument." *Cantwell v. Connecticut*, 310 U.S. 296, 309–10 (1940).

3. If this were a "pure speech" case, how would the Court determine whether the statute is unconstitutional?

D. Article I, Section 5 —
Right to Assemble [and Petition]

Cate v. Oldham
450 So. 2d 224 (1984)

ADKINS, Justice.

This cause is before us on discretionary review of two questions certified to this Court by the Eleventh Circuit Court of Appeals. We have jurisdiction. Art. V, § 3(b)(6), Fla.Const. The questions certified by the federal appellate court are:

> 1) Under the common law of Florida, may a state official who has been sued in his official capacity for alleged negligence in the exercise of his official duties, maintain an action for malicious prosecution against plaintiffs in the negligence action?

> 2) If the answer is "yes", what is the standard of malice that the state official/plaintiff must prove in order to prevail on the merits of the malicious prosecution action? How does this standard compare with the level of malice that must be proved in malicious prosecution actions where private parties are the plaintiffs?

Cate v. Oldham, 707 F.2d 1176, 1185 (11th Cir.1983).

The facts leading up to this suit are somewhat complex. Petitioner Kenneth Cate was retained by the estate of Mary Bradham to investigate the possibilities for suit on behalf of the estate against the state and respondent Gordon Oldham. Mary Bradham had died as a result of a battery committed by her estranged husband, Ernest Bradham. Cate did file a wrongful death action in the circuit court alleging that Oldham, as state attorney, had breached his duty to prosecute Ernest Bradham because he knew of Bradham's dangerous propensities but had, nevertheless, failed to adequately prosecute and investigate Bradham. The wrongful death action resulted in a summary judgment for the state and Oldham. The result was affirmed, per curiam without opinion, by the Fifth District Court of Appeal. *Russell v. State,* 392 So.2d 91 (Fla. 5th DCA 1980). Attorney's fees were then sought by the state under section 57.105, Florida Statutes (1979). The trial court awarded attorney's fees but the district court reversed the award.

Thereafter, Oldham individually filed suit against Cate, Cate's law firm, and Bradham's estate alleging that the wrongful death action brought by those parties was a malicious prosecution action and seeking both compensatory and punitive damages. Subsequently, a suit for malicious prosecution was also filed by the state and Oldham in his capacity as state attorney, denominated as "State *ex rel.* Gordon G. Oldham, Jr., Plaintiff."

Petitioners' motions to dismiss the individual action brought by Oldham were denied by the trial court. Petitioners then filed a petition for injunctive and declaratory relief, pursuant to 42 U.S.C. § 1983, in federal district court asserting that the malicious prosecution action filed against them was a violation of their first amendment rights. On the same date petitioners also filed a petition for writ of certiorari in Florida's Fifth District Court of Appeal from the denial of their motion to dismiss. The district court of appeal denied interlocutory relief citing *Hawaiian Inn of Daytona Beach, Inc. v. Snead Construction Corp.*, 393 So.2d 1201 (Fla. 5th DCA 1981). In the same order the district court of appeal denied petitioners' motion to certify the issue to this Court.

In conjunction with the petition for injunctive and declaratory relief in the federal court the petitioners requested a temporary restraining order and applied for a preliminary injunction. The court denied both requests. The federal district court also dismissed with prejudice the petition for injunction to prevent the suit by the state and Oldham in his official capacity on the basis that the state was not a "person" within the meaning of 42 U.S.C. § 1983. Petitioners then took an appeal to the United States Eleventh Circuit Court of Appeal.

On June 2, 1983, the Eleventh Circuit Court of Appeals affirmed the dismissal of the petitioner's section 1983 action under the broad immunity provided the states by the eleventh amendment to the United States Constitution rejecting the application of either the *Younger* or *Pullman* abstention doctrines to this case. The court also certified the questions being presented to this Court.

We answer the first question certified in the negative.

Section 2.01 of the Florida Statutes (1981) declares that the common and statute laws of England which are of a general nature, down to July 4, 1776, are in force in this state. The only exception provided is if the statute or common law is inconsistent with the United States Constitution or laws of the United States or Florida. Since there is an absence of any statutory law on the point addressed in this question, it is therefore proper that we examine the common law cause of action for malicious prosecution.

The common law required a showing of special damage before the action for malicious prosecution could lie. The policy behind this determination was an Englishman's right to petition his fellow citizens for redress of grievances against individuals generally. *Parker v. Langley*, 93 Eng.Rep. 293, 294–97 (K.B.1714). In *Parker v. Langley* the court stated:

> The applying in a civil action to a Court of Justice for satisfaction or redress has been so much favoured, that no action has ever been allowed against a plaintiff for such suit singly and directly, on pretence of its being false and malicious.

Id. at 294.

The fact that pre-revolutionary judges based their disfavor of malicious prosecution on the right to petition generally is of dispositive significance in this proceeding. The right to petition government specifically, for redress of grievances against government, was separately and expressly protected by Parliament. By statute, except for the crimes of riot and unlawful assembly, no other criminal sanction and no form of action could ever be imposed or brought because of a previous petition to the government for redress of a grievance against any part of government. *See* 1 W. Blackstone, *Commentaries* 138–39. The right to petition was so important a part of the constitutional scheme that the royal charters of each of the American colonies guaranteed this right. R. Bailey, *Popular Influence Upon Public Policy: Petitioning in Eighteenth-Century Virginia* 13 (1979). So strongly protected was the exercise of this right that judges in colonial times were reprimanded and fined for inquiring into the contents of petitions against government and for rejecting those they deemed to be false. *Id.* at 39–41.

At the time the American Bill of Rights was adopted the English constitution permitted only two governmental restrictions on the right to petition. The first restriction was a "time, place and manner" limitation by Parliament on the number of persons permitted to subscribe to a given petition. The only other permissible governmental restriction was by prosecution for the offenses of riot or tumult when great numbers of persons rioted after presenting a petition to the king or Parliament.

The presentation of a complaint to government concerning its conduct is now expressly held central to the right to petition that government for the redress of grievances against it. *See, e.g., California Motor Transport Co. v. Trucking Unlimited,* 404 U.S. 508 (1972); *Mid-Texas Communications Systems, Inc. v. American Telephone & Telegraph Co.,* 615 F.2d 1372, 1382 (5th Cir.), *cert. denied,* 449 U.S. 912 (1980). No Anglo-Commonwealth case has been cited by either party in this case in which government has been permitted, or even attempted, to sue its subjects for malicious prosecution. We find only two United States cases which have directly addressed this issue.

In *City of Long Beach v. Bozek,* 31 Cal.3d 527, 645 P.2d 137, 183 Cal.Rptr. 86 (1982), *vacated,* 459 U.S. 1095 (1983), *on remand,* 33 Cal.3d 727, 661 P.2d 1072, 190 Cal.Rptr. 918 (1983) (prior opinion reiterated in its entirety), the Supreme Court of California held that governmental entities may not maintain actions for malicious prosecution against those who have previously sued such entities without success. First, the court concluded in *Bozek* that the plaintiff's suit against the City of Long Beach and two city police officers for false imprisonment, false arrest, negligent hiring, assault and battery was a protected exercise of the right of petition. The court also found that the bringing of suits against the government is absolutely privileged. The court rejected the city's "most persuasive argument" that malicious prosecution actions must be allowed in order to compensate municipalities for expenses incurred in defending against baseless suits and to deter the proliferation of such suits and concluded that new statutes allowing award of attorney's fees as costs was a preferable remedy.

The only other case which faced this issue was *Board of Education v. Marting,* 7 Ohio Misc. 64, 217 N.E.2d 712 (Ct.C.P. Madison County 1966). In *Marting* a three-judge panel of the Court of Common Pleas held that a board of education lacked the legal capacity, power, and authority to sue citizens for malicious prosecution.

The judges' unanimous holding was based in part on constitutional considerations and in part on historical analysis.

There simply is no historical basis for a state officer to retaliate with a malicious prosecution action when he has been sued in his official capacity. Malicious prosecution is considered a personal tort. *Tatum Brothers Real Estate & Investment Co. v. Watson*, 92 Fla. 278, 109 So. 623 (1926). The gravamen of the action is injury to character. *Tidwell v. Witherspoon*, 21 Fla. 359, 360–61 (1885).

At common law successful defendants could either tax costs and fees in the original action, or they could sue for malicious prosecution upon the basis of those losses; they could not do both. *Parker v. Langley*, 93 Eng.Rep. at 297. There being no Florida decision or statute to the contrary, the common law rule precludes such an attempt at double recovery here. A government official sued only in his or her official capacity, and from whom no relief is sought which would run against his or her personal, as opposed to governmental behavior or finances, can claim no greater right to seek greater sanctions. He or she has personally suffered no loss which is not redressable through his or her application for redress in the suit in which he or she is originally sued. It is reasonable to compel such officials to seek such redress in the suit in which they are named defendants in their official capacity.

We have concluded that the common law of Florida does not allow a state official who has been sued in his official capacity to maintain an action for malicious prosecution. Since we have responded in the negative it is unnecessary for us to answer the second question certified to us.

It is so ordered.

ALDERMAN, C.J., and BOYD, OVERTON, McDONALD, EHRLICH and SHAW, JJ., concur.

Questions

1. Why would allowing a state official to file a malicious prosecution suit against an "angry taxpayer" who previously sued him, unsuccessfully, offend Florida's Constitution?

E. Article I, Section 6 — Right to Work

This provision of the Florida Constitution is based on a 1944 amendment to the 1885 Constitution. Note that the provision forbids both mandatory union membership and any restrictions on the right to collectively bargain. Though the framers of the 1968 Constitution left the right-to-work provision in, they added a provision that public employees may not strike. This provision may have been added in response to the Spring 1968 teachers' strike in Florida, in which teachers who were members of the Florida Education Association, a union, struck for higher wages and better conditions. The following cases explore the impact of this provision on public employees.

Hillsborough County Governmental Employees Association, Inc. v. Hillsborough County Aviation Authority

522 So. 2d 358 (Fla. 1988)

KOGAN, Justice.

This case is before the Court on petition to review a decision of the Second District Court of Appeal, *Hillsborough County Aviation Authority v. Hillsborough County Governmental Employees Association,* 482 So.2d 505 (Fla. 2d DCA 1986). Because that court certified to us a question of great public importance, we have jurisdiction. Art. V, § 3(b)(4), Fla. Const.

The petitioners, Hillsborough County Governmental Employees Association (GEA) and the Hillsborough County Police Benevolent Association (PBA), as certified negotiators for their respective groups of public employees, bargained collectively for, and reached an agreement with, the respondents, the Hillsborough County Aviation Authority (Authority). The agreements were ratified by the employees and, pursuant to section 447.309(3), Florida Statutes (1985), the Authority requested the Hillsborough County Civil Service Board (Board) to amend its rules to comport with the new provisions of the agreement. The Board refused to amend its rules concerning personal holidays, funeral leave, and seniority, at which time the Authority notified the employees that it would not implement the new contractual provisions. The PBA and the GEA filed unfair labor practice charges with the Public Employees Relations Commission (PERC). The PERC determined that the Authority had committed an unfair labor practice by refusing to implement the new provisions.

The Board and the Authority appealed to the second district, arguing that the Authority had not committed an unfair labor practice since it was following the law expressed in section 447.309(3), Florida Statutes (1985), and that court's decision in *Pinellas County Police Benevolent Association v. Hillsborough County Aviation Authority,* 347 So.2d 801 (Fla. 2d DCA 1977). PBA and GEA argued that if section 447.309(3) were given the construction urged by the Board and the Authority, it would unconstitutionally abridge the right to bargain collectively, as enunciated in Article I, section 6 of the Florida Constitution, citing *Hotel, Motel, Restaurant Employees & Bartenders Union v. Escambia County School Board,* 426 So.2d 1017 (Fla. 1st DCA 1983). The court, rather than addressing the constitutionality of section 447.309(3), reversed PERC's decision on the ground that the Authority could not have violated its duty to bargain in good faith if it was simply following statutory and case law. The district court then certified to this Court the following question of great public importance:

> When provisions of a collective bargaining agreement which has been entered into by a public employer conflict with civil service rules and regulations and the governmental body having amendatory power over the civil service rules and regulations refuses to amend those rules and regulations in such a manner as to eliminate the conflict, does section 447.309(3) apply to civil

service rules and regulations and therefore govern the effectiveness of the collective bargaining agreement?

482 So.2d at 509. For the reasons which follow we must answer the certified question in the negative and quash that portion of the decision of the district court of appeal which conflicts with this opinion.

Before analyzing these issues it is necessary to set out all the relevant statutory and constitutional provisions. Section 447.309(3) provides:

> If any provision of a collective bargaining agreement is in conflict with any law, ordinance, rule, or regulation over which the chief executive officer has no amendatory power, the chief executive officer shall submit to the appropriate governmental body having amendatory power a proposed amendment to such law, ordinance, rule, or regulation. *Unless and until* such amendment is enacted or adopted and becomes effective, the conflicting provision of the collective bargaining agreement shall not become effective (Emphasis added).

This statute clearly provides that collective bargaining agreements do not become effective unless and until the appropriate governmental body makes the necessary amendments. It is upon this statute that the Board and the Authority heavily rely.

Taking the contrary position GEA, PBA, and PERC argue that section 447.601, Florida Statutes (1985), resolves any conflict between the agreement and civil service rules. That statute provides:

> The provisions of this part ["Public Employees"] shall not be construed to repeal, amend, or modify the provisions of any law or ordinance establishing a merit or civil service system for public employees or the rules and regulations adopted pursuant thereto or to prohibit or hinder the establishment of other such personnel systems *unless the provisions of such merit or civil service system laws or ordinances or rules and regulations adopted pursuant thereto are in conflict with the provisions of this part, in which event such laws, ordinances, or rules and regulations shall not apply,* except as provided in § 447.301(4) ["Public Employee Grievances"] (Emphasis added).

It is somewhat less clear what conflict this resolves. PERC, GEA and PBA argue that this provision mandates that when collective bargaining provisions conflict with civil service laws, ordinances, or rules, the bargaining contract must prevail. The result obtained under their interpretation of section 447.309(3) is opposite the result urged by the Authority, the Board, and the second district under their interpretation of this section. Because section 447.601 is ambiguous the conflict addressed is unclear. Certainly PERC's interpretation is one viable alternative, but it is by no means the only reasonable interpretation of the statute.

Against these statutory provisions there exists a backdrop of two seemingly contradictory constitutional provisions. The first, as part of the Florida Constitution's "Declaration of Rights," guarantees all persons the right to bargain collectively with their employers. This right has been held to apply to public employees as well as those working in the private sector. *Dade County Classroom Teachers Association v. Ryan,*

225 So.2d 903 (Fla.1969). Article III, section 14 authorizes the legislature to create local civil service systems for state, county, district, or municipal employees. Pursuant to this constitutional provision, the legislature has set up numerous civil service boards around the state, including the Hillsborough County Civil Service Board.

It is with these constitutional and statutory provisions in mind that we examine the contentions of the parties. The Board argues that under section 447.309(3), it has the power to reject any application to amend its rules to conform with the collective bargaining agreement. The primary purpose of the civil service system, the Board further contends, is to maintain uniformity of pay and benefits throughout the local government. The Board's interpretation of the statute, the same interpretation given to it by the first district in *Escambia County,* would defeat the purpose of the civil service system because there would no longer be uniformity among the several collective bargaining units to which its rules apply.

The Authority argues, as it did in the second district below, that it could not have committed an unfair labor practice because it was merely following established statutory and case law. Their contention centers on an interpretation that the fair labor practices laws are punitive in nature rather than remedial.

GEA, PBA, and PERC contend that the interpretation of section 447.309(3) by the second district and the Board would render the statute unconstitutional as an impermissible abridgement of the right to bargain collectively. The employees argue that so long as the Board has the unilateral right to strike down any portion of the collective bargaining agreement, the right to enter into an effective collective bargaining agreement is nullified, thus violating Article I, section 6 of the Florida Constitution. The employees further contend that this Court should adopt the first district's interpretation of section 477.601 in *Escambia County.* The first district stated that when there is a conflict between the civil service rules and the collective bargaining agreement, the agreement controls.

Civil service boards began as a means of maintaining uniformity in wages, hours, and terms and conditions of employment among all public employees within the board's jurisdiction. The purpose was to insure that some public employees did not receive more or less benefits than other public employees for doing essentially the same job. The civil service system has evolved to the point where it is not necessary for each public employee doing the same job to rely on the civil service board to insure that terms and conditions of employment are uniform. Within each profession or type of employment in the civil service system, a union has evolved to help maintain fair and uniform working conditions. For example, police officers have the PBA to insure that they are treated in a fair and uniform manner just as government workers have the GEA to do the same for them.

The civil service board does not function to insure that police officers and government workers are treated uniformly with respect to each other and to the remaining public employees within the board's jurisdiction. Rather, due to the advent of public employee unions and collective bargaining, as guaranteed by our state constitution, the purpose of the civil service board has evolved to insure that public employees not represented by a union are treated in a uniform manner with respect to wages, hours, and terms and conditions of employment.

Our analysis must begin with a determination of which statute applies to the present set of circumstances. It is clear and unambiguous that section 447.309(3) must apply. The plain language of section 447.309(3) provides that the governmental body possessing amendatory power over the civil service rules and regulations may exercise discretion over whether the rules will be amended. While this discretion is not express, it is clear from the words "unless and until" that the Board has the power to decline proposed amendment changes.

While section 447.309(3) clearly applies, it is unclear whether section 447.601 applies to this case. The language of that statute does not clarify whether it was intended to control conflicts between collective bargaining agreements and civil service rules. The legislative history of this statute is equally ambiguous on the question of whether it should apply to this particular type of conflict. Accordingly, we must reject the argument that section 447.601 controls this conflict. Section 447.309(3) is the statute intended by the legislature to control conflicts between the civil service laws, ordinances, and rules or regulations. The question of whether such application unconstitutionally abridges the right to bargain collectively must be addressed. For the reasons which follow, we hold that it does.

To fully understand the effect of the Florida Constitution on these statutory provisions, it is first essential to examine the purpose behind them. There is little question that Article I, section 6 was intended to, and does, benefit all employees, public or private. This Court has held that this provision grants public employees the same right to bargain collectively with their employers as that granted to private employees. *City of Tallahassee v. Public Employees Relations Commission,* 410 So.2d 487 (Fla.1981); *Dade County Classroom Teachers Association v. Ryan,* 225 So.2d 903 (Fla.1969). In comparison Article III, section 14 is also intended to benefit public employees. This benefit is accomplished through the regulation and rule-making power of the several local civil service boards that are charged with ensuring personnel systems are uniformly administered and that equal pay is given for equal work. Thus on the face of these two constitutional provisions, there is no real conflict since both are clearly intended to benefit public employees.

At the point in which the civil service system is implemented, problems have arisen. As applied section 447.309(3), Florida Statutes (1985), abridges the right of public employees to bargain collectively. Giving a local civil service board absolute veto power over the provisions of a collective bargaining agreement renders that agreement a nullity. It is presumed that the intent of the constitution is to grant the right of *effective* collective bargaining. Any restriction on the right to bargain collectively must necessarily violate article I, section 6 of the Florida Constitution.

We must note at this point that our holding does not apply to conflicts arising between collective bargaining agreements and statutes or ordinances. Rather, we object to the unbridled discretion of civil service boards to strike down collective bargaining agreements through their rule making and amendatory power. Thus, section 447.309(3) stands as it applies to conflicts between statutes or ordinances and agreements reached between public employers and employees through the art of collective bargaining.

The right to bargain collectively is, as a part of the state constitution's declaration of rights, a fundamental right. As such it is subject to official abridgement only upon a showing of a compelling state interest. This strict-scrutiny standard is one that is difficult to meet under any circumstance; it is especially difficult when there is seemingly no check on a board's discretion. There may be some instances when the state can meet this standard, but in this case no compelling state interest has been shown. The Board and the Authority argue that the goals of uniformity and equal pay for equal work constitute the compelling state interest necessary to override a fundamental right. Initially there is some doubt as to whether the civil service rules actually accomplish these goals. However, even if they do, uniform personnel administration is not so compelling an interest as to warrant the abridgement of an express fundamental right. The goal of equal pay for equal work is a noble one, and one that should be maintained whenever possible. However, there must exist some less intrusive means of accomplishing that goal without impeding so dramatically on the right to bargain collectively. Moreover, the right to collectively bargain is not necessarily inconsistent with the goals of uniformity and equal pay for equal work. The parties to a negotiation are not prevented from discussing these issues. Since these goals benefit both employer and employee, it would seem likely that such discussions would be a necessity in any collective bargaining session.

The art of collective bargaining is one of give and take. It is probable that through the process of negotiation the employees were required to forfeit some benefit to which they were otherwise entitled in order to gain the personal holidays, funeral leave, and seniority benefits which they did receive, and which the Board eventually refused. Were an entity such as a civil service board allowed to strike provisions at will, the entire collective bargaining agreement would be of no value. We believe that this is far too great a price to pay for so-called uniform personnel administration.

The Florida Constitution guarantees public employees the right of effective collective bargaining. This is not an empty or hollow right subject to unilateral denial. Rather it is one which may not be abridged except upon the showing of a compelling state interest. No such showing has been made here, so this impediment upon a fundamental right cannot be sustained. Accordingly, we answer the certified question in the negative. While it is clear that section 447.309(3) does apply to this conflict, it is equally clear that the statute, as applied, unconstitutionally abridges the fundamental right of public employees to bargain collectively.

Therefore, we hold that a public employer must implement a ratified collective bargaining agreement with respect to wages, hours, or terms and conditions of employment, despite the fact that such implementation may conflict with applicable civil service board rules.... Accordingly, we remand this case for disposition consistent with this opinion.

It is so ordered.

EHRLICH, SHAW, BARKETT and GRIMES, JJ., concur.

OVERTON, J., dissents with an opinion, in which McDONALD, C.J., concurs.

OVERTON, Justice, dissenting.

I dissent. I totally disagree with the conclusion that section 447.309(3), Florida Statutes (1985), is unconstitutional as applied. The majority, by its action, has effectively eliminated civil service systems in the state of Florida whenever a labor union has negotiated a collective bargaining agreement for governmental employees. Civil service systems are not just creatures of the legislature, but are expressly authorized under article III, section 14, of the Florida Constitution. The majority opinion has rendered this provision a nullity in situations where a collective bargaining agreement exists.

This majority fails to properly consider that civil service systems in most governmental entities regularly cover multiple employee groups. Civil service was instituted to protect public employees from the vagaries of political change and resulting political cronyism by the establishment and maintenance of a uniform personnel system. This opinion eliminates a large part of that goal and purpose. Now, employees with the same governmental entity, because they belong to different employee groups for collective bargaining purposes, can have different holidays, leave, and grievance procedures and no uniform personnel processes. In my view, this will clearly cause dissatisfaction and animosity between the various employee groups within one governmental entity. Politics will again be substantially involved because one employee group will invariably have more political clout than another.

This decision is a death knell for civil service systems. Eventually, public employees will have only the collective bargaining agreements to look to for their protection because civil service systems will have been phased out in view of the fact that the prime purpose for their existence has been eliminated by this judicial legislation.

Article III, section 14, authorizing the legislature to create civil service systems, and article I, section 6, providing a general right-to-work provision and a right for employees to collectively bargain, are both constitutional provisions established to protect the interests of public employees. They should be construed together in a manner that benefits public employees and not in a way that makes one superior to the other.

I find the legislature, in enacting section 447.309(3), did so to make sure that public employees of one entity would be treated uniformly. This is a rational legislative justification for the statute. The act, in my view, is in accordance with the legislature's constitutional authority and has the clear intent of furthering the purpose of the civil service system. I would approve the full opinion of the Second District Court of Appeal.

McDONALD, C.J., concurs.

Questions

1. a. Why does the Court find § 447.309(3) to be unconstitutional?

b. Why is the Court so concerned about the workers' position in such a situation?

2. Who is protected by Section 6?

United Teachers of Dade v. School District of Miami-Dade County

68 So. 3d 1003 (Fla. 3d DCA 2011)

SHEPHERD, J.

This case arises out of a refusal by the School District of Miami-Dade County (the District) to permit a non-union teacher from having representation at a performance review proceeding. If the teacher had been a union member, he would have been permitted to have representation. The appellant, United Teachers of Dade (UTD), insists the District acted alone. The teacher appellee, Shawn Beightol, argues the District did not act alone, but rather UTD "caused" the District's action, and UTD's actions were unlawful within the meaning of sections 447.501(2)(a) and (b), Florida Statutes (2010). After taking testimony, a Commission-designated hearing officer agreed with Beightol. The Florida Public Employees Relations Commission (PERC) found competent substantial evidence to support the recommendation of the hearing officer and entered a final order adopting the recommendation. We affirm this order. We disagree with the hearing officer and PERC only in their decision not to award attorney fees to Beightol for his trouble.

A brief summary of the procedural background and history of this case is necessary to explain our decision.

Procedural Background and History

UTD is the exclusive bargaining agent for all teachers employed by the District, including non-union members. The District and UTD were signatories to a collective bargaining agreement (CBA) from July 1, 2006, to June 30, 2009, and are signatories to a successor CBA in effect from July 1, 2009, to June 30, 2012. Both the predecessor and successor contracts provide for conferences-for-the-record (CFRs), which are formal meetings between an employee and his or her worksite administrator or representative from the Office of Professional Standards (OPS) to address performance standards or the results of an investigation. Article XXI, "Employee Rights and Due Process, Subsection 1A., Conference-for-the-Record," states, in pertinent part:

2. Any employee summoned ... for a Conference-for-the-Record which may lead to disciplinary action or reprimand, shall have the right to request Union representation and shall be informed of this right. If Union representation is provided, the employee shall have the right to be accompanied at the Conference-for-the-Record by up to two representatives of the Union and shall be informed of this right.

3. Employees shall be given two days' notice and a statement of the reason for the conference, except in cases deemed to be an emergency. When Union representation is requested, and the employee is to be represented by the Union, the Conference-for-the-Record must be scheduled at a time when Union representation (building steward, where appropriate) can be present.

. . . .

5. Where Union representation is provided herein, the employee shall be represented by the bargaining agent. The bargaining agent shall have the right to refuse representation in accordance with its own internal, nondiscriminatory rules. An employee may not be represented by an attorney in a conference-for-the-record.

On September 29, 2009, Beightol received a notice summoning him to a CFR scheduled for October 7, 2009. Upon receiving the notice, Beightol requested representation by Professional Educators Network (PEN), a professional organization of which Beightol was a member. Beightol also requested representation from UTD, but UTD's Deputy Chief of Staff denied representation because Beightol was not a dues-paying member of the union. OPS also denied Beightol's request to have a PEN representative, stating he had a right to request union representation, but that any non-union representative would have to sit in the waiting area and could periodically consult with Beightol outside the hearing room. At the CFR on October 7, Beightol's non-attorney PEN representative was refused entry to the hearing room. Beightol's unfair labor practice charges followed.

Analysis

The charges in this case were brought pursuant to sections 447.501(2)(a) and (b) of the Florida Public Relations Act, Chapter 447, Part II, of the Florida Statutes. These sections of the Act prohibit a public employee organization from:

(a) Interfering with, restraining, or coercing public employees in the exercise of any of their rights guaranteed them under [Chapter 447, Part II, of the Florida Statutes]. . . .

(b) Causing or attempting to cause a public employer to discriminate against an employee because of the employee's membership or non-membership in an employee organization. . . .

§ 447.501(2).

The issue on appeal is whether substantial competent evidence supports the findings of the hearing officer. If the record contains substantial competent evidence in support of the findings, neither PERC nor an appellate court can overturn the hearing officer's findings based upon disputed issues of fact. *Boyd v. Dep't of Revenue*, 682 So.2d 1117, 1118 (Fla. 4th DCA 1996).

UTD first seeks refuge in the agreement itself, emphasizing that the provision it negotiated does not require the District's policy of excluding non-union representatives from CFRs. Here, UTD fails to appreciate its legal obligation to the bargaining unit.

UTD is the bargaining agent for **all** employees in the bargaining unit, union members and non-union members alike.[24] UTD may not prefer its dues-paying members over non-dues-paying members in its representation and negotiations. *See* § 447.501(2)(b). By the same token, it cannot in good faith negotiate, maintain or condone a contract provision which it knows to create and perpetuate a system which requires employees to become UTD members to obtain a benefit. *See* § 447.501(2)(b); *Spiegel v. Dade Cnty. Police Benevolent Ass'n,* 14 FPER ¶ 19092 (1988). Article XXI, section 1A, subsections 2, 3, and 5 of the collective bargaining agreement provide a benefit available only to UTD dues-paying members in that only dues-paying UTD members are entitled to have up to two UTD representatives at a CFR. UTD neglected to negotiate a comparable contractual right for bargaining unit employees who are not dues-paying UTD members. The hearing officer found, and PERC agreed, that UTD's motivation in negotiating, administering, and maintaining Article XXI, section 1(A) of the CBA was "to create and perpetuate a system which requires employees to become UTD members to obtain the right of representation at a CFR." Competent substantial evidence supports the hearing officer's findings.

The contract provision at issue in this case has been part of the CBA since some time prior to 1995. UTD Deputy Chief of Staff, Michael Molnar, testified it has long been UTD policy to refuse union representation to non-union members who are summoned to a CFR. Joyce Castro, a district director of OPS, testified that the District prohibits non-union employees from having representation at a CFR.[25] Deputy Chief of Staff Molnar confirmed that UTD is well aware the District's policy of refusing representation to non-union members of the bargaining unit results in a lack of representation for non-union members at a CFR. Furthermore, Beightol's own testimony confirms this practice has long existed and been condoned by UTD. In February 2008, Beightol, then a UTD steward, attempted to represent a non-UTD member at a CFR. UTD would not allow him to represent the non-member during the conference-for-the-record and neither would the District.

UTD next argues it had nothing to do with the District's policy of not allowing employees who are not union members to have a non-union representative at their CFRs. UTD relies on the fact that no evidence has been found of specific discussions between UTD and the District relating to the implementation of the discriminatory provision. However, as UTD must know, "unless the employer is a latter day George Washington, [direct evidence of] discrimination is as difficult of proof as who chopped down the cherry tree." *Thornbrough v. Columbus & Greenville R.R. Co.,* 760 F.2d 633, 638 (5th Cir.1985); *see also Sch. Bd. of Leon Cnty. v. Hargis,* 400 So.2d 103, 107 (Fla. 1st DCA 1981) (finding direct evidence of discriminatory intent is "seldom present").

---

24. [FN 1.] The UTD bargaining unit—the employees it claims to represent—includes all instructional staff, paraprofessionals, and office staff employed by the District. Sixteen thousand of these employees have elected not to join the union.

25. [FN 2.] However, a non-union member's representative is allowed to sit in the reception area, and the employee may consult with his or her representative in the reception area as often as the employee desires.

For this reason, it is well established in the field of discrimination that circumstantial evidence evaluated in the light of common experience may be relied upon to establish discriminatory motive. *See Grigsby v. Reynolds Metals Co.*, 821 F.2d 590, 594 (11th Cir.1987) (noting that "[t]he McDonnell Douglas-Burdine proof structure 'was never intended to be rigid, mechanized, or ritualistic. Rather, it is merely a sensible, orderly way to evaluate the evidence in light of common experience as it bears on the critical question of discrimination'").

In this case, the plain language of the CBA, in tandem with evidence of the District's and UTD's implementation of that language, results in the discriminatory conferral of a benefit on union members. OPS District Director Joyce Castro testified she understood the Article XXI "Employee Rights and Due Process" subsections at issue in this case only allow for UTD representation at CFRs, and during the years she has been a District Director, UTD had never appeared on behalf of a non-union member at a CFR. UTD Deputy Chief of Staff Michael Molnar testified that as long as he has been employed by UTD, since 1995, it has been UTD policy to refuse union representation to non-union members at a CFR, with full knowledge non-union members would have no representation at CFRs. During these years, UTD negotiated at least five successor contracts with the District. It never sought to rectify the discriminatory effect of Article XXI, section 1A on non-union members. Our task on review of the final order before us is directed to whether there is competent substantial evidence in the record to support the hearing officer's finding of intent, approved by PERC in its Final Order, not whether there is substantial competent evidence to support a different or contrary finding. *See Tamiami Trail Tours, Inc. v. King,* 143 So.2d 313, 316 (Fla.1962). Based upon the record before us, we find there is substantial competent evidence in the record to support the decision of the hearing officer in this case. Only a willing suspension of belief would liberate us to accept UTD's urging of a different or contrary finding.

Although PERC correctly determined UTD committed an unfair labor practice, it erred in denying Beightol an award of attorney fees and costs. Under section 447.503(6)(c), Florida Statutes (2010), "the commission may award to the prevailing party all or part of the costs of litigation, reasonable attorney fees, and expert witness fees whenever the commission determines that such an award is appropriate." Such an award is appropriate where the party in violation knew or should have known that its conduct violated established law. *City of Delray Beach v. Prof'l Firefighters of Delray Beach,* 636 So.2d 157, 163 (Fla. 4th DCA 1994). UTD knew or should have known that its conduct in this case violated established law. Florida is a right-to-work state. Those who work in this state have a constitutionally protected right to refrain from joining a labor organization. *See* art. I, §6, Fla. Const.; *see also* §447.301, Fla. Stat. (2010). The Florida legislature has enacted laws expressly designed to protect public employees from interference and coercion in the exercise of this right. *See* §447.501(2)(a). PERC also has been vigilant in protecting non-union members of a bargaining unit from being treated differently by their bargaining agent.

The seminal PERC decision in this area is *Spiegel v. Dade County Police Benevolent Ass'n,* 14 FPER ¶ 19092 (1988). In *Spiegel*, the Dade County Police Benevolent Association (Dade PBA) and the City of Hialeah entered into a collective bargaining agreement which allowed employees to select from one of two health insurance programs: Option A was available to any member of the bargaining unit, while Option B was available only to Dade PBA members. Option B provided benefits which were superior to those provided in Option A. In a fashion uncannily parallel to the case before us, the hearing officer in *Spiegel* described the central issue in the case to be

> whether it is an unlawful encouragement to join the union and an act of interference, restraint or coercion of public employees' right to 'refrain from forming, joining or participating in an employee organization for a certified union to maintain and administer a contractual provision providing for optional health insurance exclusively for its members.'

14 FPER ¶ 109092, at 228. Applying case law rising under the National Labor Relations Act, 29 USCA sections 158(a)(1), (2), (3), and (b)(1)(A) and (2), both the hearing officer and PERC "[found] the Dade PBA guilty of committing an unfair labor practice by administering and maintaining a contract provision which provided benefits to its members which are not available to non-members." 14 FPER ¶ 109092, at 223. *Spiegel* is distinguishable from our case only in that the discrimination there was apparent on the face of the collective bargaining agreement. However, as we have demonstrated, a party cannot escape judgment simply because no direct evidence is available to the party seeking relief. The evidence before the hearing officer in our case included not only a provision of the collective bargaining agreement, but also competent substantial evidence of the District's and UTD's implementation of the provision. Both the hearing officer and PERC correctly relied upon *Spiegel* in reaching their respective decisions. The logic and reasoning found in *Spiegel* are directly applicable to the facts of our case.

UTD argues that *Spiegel* is inapplicable to the knowledge element of the attorney fee and cost issue because it was decided twenty-three years ago and has not been cited by a court. However, as counsel for UTD agreed in oral argument, *Spiegel* is readily discoverable through computer assisted research commonly available to lawyers and law firms. We are unaware of any statute of limitations applicable to PERC decisions and opinions.

In approving the hearing officer's decision not to award attorney fees and costs to Beightol, PERC mistakenly thought Beightol did not bring *Spiegel* to the attention of the hearing officer. That is not so. Beightol brought *Spiegel* to the attention of the hearing officer both during the proceedings and in his proposed final order. This oversight formed the substantial basis for PERC's denial of an award of attorney fees and costs to Beightol in this proceeding. As we have shown, *Spiegel* is the seminal case prohibiting labor organizations from encouraging membership in a union by providing union members with superior contractual privileges. The prohibition is an intuitively obvious one, about which UTD should need little formal guidance. However, *Spiegel*, in the books now for twenty-three years, resolves all doubt concerning whether UTD knew or should have known it violated established law. Beightol is entitled to an award of his attorney fees and costs in this case.

Accordingly, we affirm that portion of the final order finding that UTD committed an unfair labor practice, but reverse that portion of the final order denying Beightol his attorney fees and costs.

Affirmed in part, reversed in part and case remanded with directions.

F. Article I, Section 8 — Right to Bear Arms

Some version of this amendment has been a part of the Florida Constitution since 1868. The current provision was taken from the 1885 Constitution. In 1990, an amendment provided for a three-day waiting period. The current provision must be read in conjunction with Article VIII, Section 5(b), which provides that counties have the option of requiring three-to-five-day waiting periods and criminal background checks for the purchase of firearms, a provision proposed by the 1998 Constitution Revision Commission and adopted in 1998.

Norman v. State

215 So. 3d 18 (Fla.), *cert. denied*, 138 S. Ct. 469 (2017)

PARIENTE, J.

In this case, we determine the constitutionality of section 790.053, Florida Statutes (2012) ("Florida's Open Carry Law"), first passed by the Legislature in 1987 and challenged by Norman as a violation of his right to bear arms for self-defense outside the home under both the United States and Florida Constitutions. The Fourth District Court of Appeal concluded that Florida's Open Carry Law does not violate the Second Amendment to the United States Constitution or article I, section 8, of the Florida Constitution. *Norman v. State*, 159 So.3d 205 (Fla. 4th DCA 2015). We accepted jurisdiction on the basis that the Fourth District expressly construed the United States and Florida Constitutions and expressly declared valid a state statute. See art. V, §3(b)(3), Fla. Const.

Florida's Open Carry Law is a provision within Florida's overall scheme regulating the use of firearms (codified in chapter 790, Florida Statutes), but still allowing the possession of firearms in most instances. *See* §790.06, Fla. Stat. (2012). Chapter 790 permits individuals to carry firearms in public, so long as the firearm is carried in a concealed manner. Pursuant to section 790.06, Florida employs a "shall issue" scheme for issuing licenses to carry concealed firearms in public. *See id.* Under this licensing scheme, which leaves no discretion to the licensing authority, the licensing authority must issue an applicant a concealed carry license, provided the applicant meets objective, statutory criteria. *Id.* Accordingly, as the Fourth District observed in explaining the breadth of Florida's "shall issue" licensing scheme, the right of Floridians to bear arms for self-defense outside of the home is not illusory:

Florida's licensing statute does not effectively act as an exclusionary bar to the right to bear arms in lawful self-defense outside the home.... [In] over two decades from 1987 to 2014, Florida issued concealed weapons permits to more than 2.7 million people. As of December 2014 there were 1,535,030 active permits issued in a population of over 19 million. No empirical evidence suggests in any way that Florida concealed carry permits are unduly restricted to only a few people, such that a citizen's right to lawfully carry a firearm is illusory.

Norman, 159 So.3d at 219 (footnotes omitted). Further, pursuant to chapter 790, Florida law provides sixteen exceptions to Florida's Open Carry Law, including a broad exception that applies to persons "engaged in fishing, camping, or lawful hunting or *going to or returning* from a fishing, camping, or lawful hunting expedition." § 790.25(3)(h), Fla. Stat. (2012) (emphasis added); *see also* § 790.25(3), Fla. Stat. (2012) (providing a list of sixteen statutory exceptions to the Open Carry Law). Because of the comprehensive nature of Florida's regulatory scheme of firearms, we review the constitutionality of Florida's Open Carry Law within the context of chapter 790.

As we explain more fully below, we agree with the Fourth District that the State has an important interest in regulating firearms as a matter of public safety, and that Florida's Open Carry Law is substantially related to this interest. *Norman*, 159 So.3d at 222–23. We conclude that Florida's Open Carry Law violates neither the Second Amendment to the United States Constitution, nor article I, section 8, of the Florida Constitution. Accordingly, we affirm the Fourth District's well-reasoned opinion upholding Florida's Open Carry Law under intermediate scrutiny. *See id.* at 209.

FACTS AND PROCEDURAL HISTORY

On February 19, 2012, Dale Lee Norman received by mail a license issued by the Florida Department of Agriculture and Consumer Services authorizing Norman to carry his firearm in public in a concealed manner. He left his Fort Pierce home on foot with a .38 caliber handgun and his new concealed-carry license. A few minutes after he left his home, a bystander observed Norman walking alongside U.S. Highway 1 with his handgun holstered on his hip and not covered by any article of clothing. The bystander alerted the Fort Pierce Police Department, which dispatched officers. Fort Pierce Police Department officers arrived on the scene approximately five minutes later and also "saw [Norman] carrying a firearm in 'plain view' in a holster on his hip. The firearm was on the outside of [Norman's] tight fitting tank top." *Norman*, 159 So.3d at 227. A dashboard camera from a responding officer's patrol car that captured Norman's arrest on video "showed that [Norman's] gun was completely exposed to public view, in its holster, and not covered by [his] shirt." *Id.* at 209.

Norman was charged with Open Carrying of a Weapon (firearm) in violation of section 790.053, Florida Statutes (2012), a second-degree misdemeanor carrying a maximum penalty of a $500 fine and a term of imprisonment not exceeding 60 days. *See id.*; *see also* §§ 775.082, 775.083, Fla. Stat (2012). Prior to trial in the County Court of St. Lucie County, Norman filed five motions to dismiss and challenged the constitutionality of section 790.053 on various grounds. *See Norman*, 159 So.3d at

209. The county court reserved ruling on Norman's motions to dismiss until after the jury trial.

After the jury found Norman guilty of the sole count of openly carrying a firearm in violation of section 790.053, the county court denied Norman's motions to dismiss, but certified the following three questions of great public importance to the Fourth District:

> I. Is Florida's statutory scheme related to the open carry of firearms constitutional?
>
> II. Do the exceptions to the prohibition against open carry constitute affirmative defenses to a prosecution for a charge of open carry, or does the State need to prove beyond a reasonable doubt that a particular defendant is not conducting himself or herself in the manner allowed[, meaning that they are elements of the crime]?
>
> III. Does the recent "brief and open display" exception unconstitutionally infect the open carry law by its vagueness?

Id. Thereafter, the county court withheld adjudication and imposed a $300 fine, along with court costs.

In answering the certified questions, the Fourth District concluded that it need not "address whether the 'brief and open display' exception unconstitutionally infects the open carry law by its vagueness because under the facts of the case this exception did not apply to [Norman.]" *Id.* at 209–10. Norman does not challenge this conclusion before this Court. In analyzing the two other certified questions, which Norman does challenge, the Fourth District affirmed the trial court's rulings "by holding that section 790.053, which generally prohibits the open carrying of firearms, is constitutional," and that "exceptions to the prohibition against open carry constitute affirmative defenses to a prosecution for a charge of open carry." *Id.* at 209.

Addressing the constitutionality of section 790.053, the Fourth District applied "a two-step analysis" that has "been employed by the majority of the federal circuit courts to consider Second Amendment challenges since the Supreme Court's decision in [*District of Columbia v.*] *Heller*, [554 U.S. 570 (2008)]." *Norman*, 159 So.3d at 210 & n.2. This two-step analysis requires first determining "whether the challenged law burdens conduct protected by the Second Amendment based on a historical understanding of the scope of the [Second Amendment] right, or whether the challenged law falls within a well-defined and narrowly limited category of prohibitions that have been historically unprotected." *Id.* at 210 (quoting *Jackson v. City & Cty. of San Francisco*, 746 F.3d 953, 960 (9th Cir. 2014)) (alteration in original). The second step determines the appropriate level of scrutiny to apply to the challenged law if the law burdens conduct falling under the scope of the Second Amendment right. *Id.* at 210–11.

The Fourth District concluded that under the first prong of its analysis, section 790.053 burdens the right, but "does not improperly infringe on Florida's constitutional guarantee, nor does it infringe on 'the *central component*' of the Second Amendment—the right of self-defense" because a citizen may still carry a firearm under the concealed carry licensing scheme. *Id.* at 219 (quoting *Heller*, 554 U.S. at 599). The Fourth District then interpreted *Heller* to establish "that Second Amendment challenges are no longer susceptible to a rational-basis review." *Id.* at 220 (citing *Heller*, 554 U.S. at 628 n.27). After reviewing various federal circuit court decisions that have considered challenges to laws impacting the Second Amendment right, the Fourth District concluded that "intermediate scrutiny is the proper standard to apply to section 790.053." *Id.* at 222.

In applying the intermediate scrutiny test, the Fourth District concluded that the State's interest of public safety was "compelling." *Id.* As to the second prong, whether a reasonable fit existed between the challenged law and the State's asserted objectives, the Fourth District noted the difficulty of obtaining empirical proof of regulation efficacy, but nonetheless concluded that this second prong of the intermediate scrutiny test was met because "courts have traditionally been more deferential to the legislature in this area." *Id.* at 223. Therefore, the Fourth District concluded that section 790.053 passed the intermediate scrutiny test. *Id.*

The Fourth District then considered Norman's other constitutional challenges to section 790.053: that the law was unconstitutionally overbroad and that Florida's shall-issue concealed-carry licensing scheme was not an alternative channel to exercise the Second Amendment right, making the open carrying of a firearm the only available avenue for exercising the right. *Id.* at 223, 225. The Fourth District declined "the invitation to consider [Norman's] challenge to Florida's open carry restriction using an overbreadth analysis." *Id.* at 225. As to Norman's other constitutional challenge to section 790.053, the Fourth District concluded that "open carry is not the only practical avenue by which [Norman] may lawfully carry a gun in public for self-defense. Through its 'shall-issue' permitting scheme, Florida has provided a viable alternative outlet to open firearms carry which gives practical effect to its citizens' exercise of their Second Amendment rights." *Id.* at 226.

Addressing the other two certified questions, the Fourth District concluded that under *Hodge v. State*, 866 So.2d 1270 (Fla. 4th DCA 2004), since "the exceptions are not in the enacting clause of section 790.053, but are contained within a separate statute altogether," the exceptions are affirmative defenses. *Norman*, 159 So.3d at 226. Finally, in addressing the last certified question, the Fourth District concluded that Norman lacked standing to challenge the "brief and open display" exception because the county court made a finding of fact that there was no credible evidence that Norman's firearm could have been concealed before his arrest considering his manner of dress. *Id.* at 227. Norman petitioned this Court to review the Fourth District's decision, and we accepted jurisdiction.

ANALYSIS

The issue we address is whether Florida's Open Carry Law, which prohibits openly carrying a firearm subject to sixteen statutory exceptions, violates the Second Amendment to the United States Constitution or article I, section 8, of the Florida Constitution. The constitutional validity of a law is a legal issue subject to de novo review. *See Crist v. Ervin*, 56 So.3d 745, 747 (Fla. 2010)....

I. CHAPTER 790, FLORIDA STATUTES

Florida's statutory scheme for regulating the manner of carrying firearms has existed in its current state for almost three decades. In 1987, the Florida Legislature passed the Jack Hagler Self-Defense Act, ch. 87-24, Laws of Fla. (1987) ("the Act"), amending section 790.06, Florida Statutes (1985). The former section 790.06 authorized local governments to issue concealed-carry licenses to applicants based on the applicant's "good moral character" and other varying criteria. § 790.06, Fla. Stat. (1985). The Act streamlined Florida's licensing scheme for carrying concealed firearms by authorizing the State to issue concealed-carry licenses, instead of local governments. At that time, Florida became one of the first states to allow the concealed carrying of firearms by a state-run licensing scheme. Notable for our purposes here, Florida's "shall-issue" permitting scheme leaves no discretion to the State in issuing concealed-carry licenses, provided the applicant meets certain objective, statutory criteria. *See* § 790.06, Fla. Stat. (2012).

Shortly after the Act went into effect, the Legislature passed in a special session House Bill 28-B, which prohibited the open carrying of firearms. *See* ch. 87-537, Laws of Fla. (1987). House Bill 28-B was later codified in section 790.053, Florida Statutes (1987). Representative Ronald C. Johnson, a member of the Florida House of Representatives and the sponsor of the Act, spoke on the floor of the House of Representatives and implored his colleagues to vote in favor of House Bill 28-B because "a problem ha[d] arisen in the minds of the public," concerning Florida's gun laws. This problem was brought to light in a letter Florida's then attorney general wrote to Florida's then governor, and by contemporaneous news reports that claimed that, with the recent passage of the Act, Florida law now allowed the open carrying of firearms in public. Representative Johnson stated that House Bill 28-B would clarify that in Florida, "we did not then and we do not now allow for the open carry of firearms." After House Bill 28-B passed unanimously, Representative Johnson thanked his colleagues for their vote, stating that the Legislature had reaffirmed in the eyes of the public that Florida was a "safe place for individuals to live, and an excellent place for people to visit." The Senate unanimously voted the following day to approve the concurring bill. Therefore, it is apparent that in enacting a uniform, objective firearm licensing scheme that would allow greater availability of firearms to the public, the Legislature considered it necessary to prohibit the open carrying of firearms, subject to certain enumerated exceptions.

Florida's Open Carry Law provides in its entirety:

(1) Except as otherwise provided by law and in subsection (2), it is unlawful for any person to openly carry on or about his or her person any firearm or electric weapon or device. It is not a violation of this section for a person licensed to carry a concealed firearm as provided in s. 790.06(1), and who is lawfully carrying a firearm in a concealed manner, to briefly and openly display the firearm to the ordinary sight of another person, unless the firearm

is intentionally displayed in an angry or threatening manner, not in necessary self-defense.

(2) A person may openly carry, for purposes of lawful self-defense:

(a) A self-defense chemical spray.

(b) A nonlethal stun gun or dart-firing stun gun or other nonlethal electric weapon or device that is designed solely for defensive purposes.

(3) Any person violating this section commits a misdemeanor of the second degree, punishable as provided in s. 775.082 or s. 775.083.

§ 790.053, Fla. Stat. (2012).

In chapter 790, the Legislature enunciated a "Declaration of Policy" with regard to the "Lawful ownership, possession, and use of firearms and other weapons":

> The Legislature finds as a matter of public policy and fact that it is necessary to promote firearms safety and to curb and prevent the use of firearms and other weapons in crime and by incompetent persons without prohibiting the lawful use in defense of life, home, and property, and the use by United States or state military organizations, and as otherwise now authorized by law, including the right to use and own firearms for target practice and marksmanship on target practice ranges or other lawful places, and lawful hunting and other lawful purposes.

§ 790.25(1), Fla. Stat. (2012).

Further, section 790.25(4) addresses the construction to be given to chapter 790, and provides in pertinent part:

> This act shall be liberally construed to carry out the declaration of policy herein and in favor of the constitutional right to keep and bear arms for lawful purposes. This act is supplemental and additional to existing rights to bear arms now guaranteed by law and decisions of the courts of Florida, and nothing herein shall impair or diminish any of such rights.

Id. § 790.25(4).

Except for the "brief[] and open[] display" provision added to the law in 2011, Florida's Open Carry Law has remained substantively unchanged since its passage in 1987. See ch. 2011-145, § 1, Laws of Fla. (2011). Under Florida's current statutory scheme, specifically Florida's Open Carry Law, openly carrying a firearm is illegal outside of the enumerated exceptions. See § 790.053. However, Florida's Open Carry Law does not diminish an individual's ability to carry a firearm for self-defense, so long as the firearm is carried in a concealed manner and the individual has received a concealed-carry license. Id. § 790.06(2).

As explained above, Florida's "shall-issue" licensing scheme provides almost every individual the ability to carry a concealed weapon. The statute merely requires the applicant to provide a statement that he or she "[d]esires a legal means to carry a concealed weapon or firearm for lawful self-defense" and that the applicant meets certain objective requirements. *Id.* These objective requirements include that the applicant is not a convicted felon, has not been committed to a mental institution, and has demonstrated competence with handling a firearm. *Id.* Thus, under Florida's "shall-issue" licensing scheme, the State has no discretion in issuing licenses and may not withhold a license from an individual based on any subjective beliefs, provided the applicant meets the objective, statutory requirements. *See id.*

In short, chapter 790 allows anyone with a concealed-carry license, which are granted liberally, to carry a firearm in public, so long as the firearm is concealed. Having explained Florida's Open Carry Law, we next explain the history and scope of the constitutional rights, both federal and state, at issue in this case.

II. FEDERAL AND STATE CONSTITUTIONAL RIGHT TO BEAR ARMS

Norman challenges the constitutionality of Florida's Open Carry Law under both the Second Amendment to the United States Constitution and article I, section 8, of the Florida Constitution. We explain below the history and scope of these rights, both through constitutional text and case law. Put simply, Florida's right provides explicitly to Floridians what the United States Supreme Court has interpreted the federal right to guarantee—an individual right to bear arms for self-defense, subject to legislative regulation.

A. History and Scope of the Right Provided by the Second Amendment to the United States Constitution

The Second Amendment to the United States Constitution states, in full:

> A well regulated Militia, being necessary to the security of a free State, the right of the people to keep and bear Arms, shall not be infringed.

In 2008, in *District of Columbia v. Heller,* the United States Supreme Court thoroughly analyzed the history of this constitutional guarantee in reviewing the constitutionality of a District of Columbia law that entirely banned the possession of handguns in the home and required that firearms otherwise lawfully allowed to be kept in the home be rendered inoperable. 554 U.S. at 628. In a 5–4 decision, the Court invalidated the District of Columbia law, *id.* at 592, 635, and concluded that the Second Amendment provides an individual right to bear arms that is grounded in self-defense. *Id.* at 599 (noting that the "*central component*" of the Second Amendment was and remains self-defense). One basis for the Court's conclusion that the Second Amendment guarantees an individual right, not connected to service in a militia, was a review of post-Civil War legislation that concerned "how to secure constitutional rights for newly freed slaves." *Id.* at 614. As the *Heller* Court explained, "[b]lacks were routinely disarmed by Southern States after the Civil War." *Id.*

After determining that the Second Amendment guarantees an individual right, in *Heller* the majority avoided explicitly "establish[ing] a level of scrutiny for evaluating Second Amendment restrictions." 554 U.S. at 634. Instead, the Court stated that the law at issue in *Heller* would fail under "any of the standards of scrutiny [the Court has] applied to enumerated constitutional rights." *Id.* at 628. However, the Court explicitly noted that the Second Amendment's individual right is not unlimited, and, historically, the right has been subject to laws prohibiting how firearms are carried, including antebellum laws prohibiting the concealed carrying of weapons. *Id.* at 626–27. Indeed, as one scholar has explained, "[e]ven in Dodge City, that epitome of the Wild West, gun carrying was prohibited." Saul Cornell, *The Right to Carry Firearms Outside of the Home: Separating Historical Myths from Historical Realities*, 39 Fordham Urb. L.J. 1695, 1724 (2012).

Two years after *Heller*, in *McDonald v. City of Chicago*, 561 U.S. 742 (2010), the United States Supreme Court considered a broad-sweeping handgun ban in Chicago, which was "similar to the District of Columbia's" that was at issue in *Heller* because it prevented possession of "any firearm unless such person is the holder of a valid registration certificate for such firearm." *Id.* at 750 (quoting Chicago, Ill., Municipal Code § 8-20-040(a) (2009)). Relying on *Heller*, the *McDonald* Court struck down the handgun ban at issue. *Id.* at 791. In reviewing the handgun ban, the Court noted that its previous decision in *Heller* "protects the right to possess a handgun in the home for the purpose of self-defense," *id.* and the plurality opinion "recognized that the right to keep and bear arms is not 'a right to keep and carry any weapon whatsoever in any manner whatsoever and for whatever purpose.'" *Id.* at 786 (quoting *Heller*, 554 U.S. at 626). Significantly, after an exhaustive review of its selective incorporation jurisprudence, the Court applied the Second Amendment to the States via the Due Process Clause of the Fourteenth Amendment. *Id.* at 791.

Recently, the United States Supreme Court shed further light on the scope of the Second Amendment in *Caetano v. Massachusetts*, ___ U.S. ___, 136 S.Ct. 1027 (2016). In *Caetano*, the Court reviewed a judgment of the Supreme Judicial Court of Massachusetts upholding a Massachusetts law prohibiting the possession of stun guns, reasoning "stun gun[s] [were not] the type of weapon contemplated by Congress in 1789 as being protected by the Second Amendment." 136 S.Ct. at 1027 (quoting *Commonwealth v. Caetano*, 470 Mass. 774, 26 N.E.3d 688, 691 (2015)). On review, the Supreme Court vacated the judgment, finding that this explanation contradicted *Heller*'s "statement that the Second Amendment 'extends ... to ... arms ... that were not in existence at the time of the founding." *Id.* at 1028 (quoting *Heller*, 554 U.S. at 582). Thus, the *Caetano* Court confirmed that the Second Amendment is a right evolving with advances in technology. *See id.*

The Court also recently considered "whether a misdemeanor conviction for recklessly assaulting a domestic relation disqualifies an individual from possessing a gun under [a federal law prohibiting possession of firearms by persons previously convicted of a misdemeanor crime of domestic violence]." *Voisine v. United States*, ___ U.S. ___, 136 S.Ct. 2272, 2277–78 (2016). Importantly, in holding that the federal law applied to reckless assaults in addition to knowing or intentional ones, the Court chose not to address Voisine's claim that the law violated the Second Amendment and, instead, resolved the issue on statutory interpretation grounds. *See id.* at 2278–80. *But see id.* at 2290 (Thomas, J., dissenting) (noting that the majority's statutory construction of the statute at issue improperly extended the "statute into ... constitutionally problematic territory").

While the Supreme Court in *Heller* and *McDonald* struck down laws that, by design and effect, totally prohibited the use of operable firearms in the home, the Court has not further defined the scope of the Second Amendment to preclude laws regulating the *manner* of how arms are borne. Indeed, the Court acknowledged that its decision in *Heller* left "many applications of the right to keep and bear arms in doubt," 554 U.S. at 635, and clarified in *Caetano* that the right evolves with advances in technology. *See* 136 S.Ct. at 1028.

In the eight years since *Heller*, federal circuit courts have considered an array of Second Amendment challenges to laws regulating the manner and use of firearms. For instance, the Second, Third, Fourth, Ninth, and Tenth Circuits have all considered and upheld state laws either prohibiting entirely the concealed carrying of firearms or requiring a demonstration of "good cause" or a "justifiable need" before a person is licensed to carry concealed firearms. Some federal circuit courts have held that laws prohibiting the concealed carrying of firearms without first demonstrating a subjective "good cause," did not even implicate the Second Amendment. For instance, the Ninth Circuit in *Peruta v. County of San Diego*, 824 F.3d 919 (9th Cir. 2016), conducted a historical examination of the Second Amendment and, based on this historical analysis, held "that the Second Amendment right to keep and bear arms does not include, in any degree, the right of a member of the general public to carry concealed firearms in public." *Id.* at 939. The Tenth Circuit has also held "that the concealed carrying of firearms falls outside the scope of the Second Amendment's guarantee," but did not conduct a historical examination of the Second Amendment right as the Ninth Circuit conducted in *Peruta. Peterson v. Martinez*, 707 F.3d 1197, 1212 (10th Cir. 2013). In *Peterson*, the petitioner challenged a residency requirement of Colorado's "shall issue" permitting scheme for the concealed carrying of firearms as violating the Second Amendment, even though Colorado law permitted nonresidents to openly carry firearms in the state. *Id.* at 1209. Importantly, the Tenth Circuit did not premise its holding on the fact that residents and nonresidents of Colorado may openly carry. *See id.*

Similarly, the Fourth Circuit considered a Maryland law requiring that handgun permits be issued only to individuals with "good-and-substantial-reason" to wear, carry (open or concealed), or transport a handgun. *Woollard v. Gallagher*, 712 F.3d 865, 868 (4th Cir. 2013). Unlike the Ninth and Tenth Circuits, however, the Fourth Circuit "refrain[ed] from any assessment of whether Maryland's good and substantial reason requirement for obtaining a handgun permit implicate[d] Second Amendment protections," but concluded that the law nevertheless passed constitutional muster under intermediate scrutiny. *Id.* at 876.

In holding that the law passed intermediate scrutiny, the Fourth Circuit noted that "intermediate scrutiny applies to laws burdening any right to carry firearms outside the home, where 'firearm rights have always been more limited, because public safety interests often outweigh individual interests in self-defense.'" *Id.* at 882 (quoting *United States v. Masciandaro*, 638 F.3d 458, 470 (4th Cir. 2011)). The Third Circuit considered a similar, subjective "justifiable need" restriction on carrying handguns in public (without distinguishing between open and concealed carrying) in *Drake v. Filko*, 724 F.3d 426 (3d Cir. 2013), and concluded that the law did "not burden conduct within the scope of the Second Amendment's guarantee." *Id.* at 429. Regardless, the Third Circuit held that even if the "justifiable need" restriction was not presumptively lawful, it would still pass intermediate scrutiny. *Id.* at 430. The Third Circuit noted that the law "fits comfortably within the longstanding tradition of regulating the public carrying of weapons for self-defense. In fact, it does not go as far as some of the historical bans on public carrying; rather, it limits the opportunity for public carrying to those who can demonstrate a justifiable need to do so." *Id.* at 433.

In contrast, the Second Circuit concluded that New York's "proper cause" restriction to obtain a license to carry a concealed firearm implicated the Second Amendment in *Kachalsky v. County of Westchester*, 701 F.3d 81, 93 (2d Cir. 2012). However, like its sister courts that have subjected laws regulating the carrying of firearms in public to some level of scrutiny, the Second Circuit held that the "proper cause" restriction passed intermediate scrutiny. *Id.* at 96, 100. Explaining that the law passed intermediate scrutiny, the Second Circuit noted that "extensive state regulation of handguns has never been considered incompatible with the Second Amendment or, for that matter, the common-law right to self-defense. This includes significant restrictions on how handguns are carried, complete prohibitions on carrying the weapon in public, and even in some instances, prohibitions on purchasing handguns." *Id.* at 100. Therefore, federal circuit courts have found restrictions on the public carrying of firearms as not only surviving intermediate scrutiny, but, in some instances, not even implicating the Second Amendment right at all. *See Drake*, 724 F.3d at 429–30.

B. History and Scope of the Right Provided by Article I, Section 8, of the Florida Constitution

Not only is the Federal right to bear arms applicable to the states under *McDonald* by selective incorporation through the Due Process Clause of the Fourteenth Amendment, but the Florida Constitution includes a separate constitutional right to bear arms in article I, section 8. Specifically, the Florida Constitution provides:

> The right of the people to keep and bear arms in defense of themselves and of the lawful authority of the state shall not be infringed, *except that the manner of bearing arms may be regulated by law.*

Art. I, § 8(a), Fla. Const. (emphasis added). In contrast to the federal right, Florida's Constitution explicitly states that the purpose of the constitutional right is self-defense while simultaneously expressly limiting that right by providing the Legislature the authority to regulate the manner of bearing arms.

This constitutional right has endured in Florida — with only a small gap — since 1838 when Florida's Constitution was adopted by the then Territory of Florida. *Fla. Carry v. Univ. of N. Fla.*, 133 So.3d 966, 983–84 (Fla. 1st DCA 2013) (Makar, J., concurring). When Florida's current Constitution was adopted in 1968, the explicit right of the Legislature to regulate the manner in which arms are borne first announced in the 1885 Constitution remained.

Near the turn of the twentieth century, in one of this Court's earliest decisions interpreting Florida's constitutional right to keep and bear arms for self-defense, this Court recognized in *Carlton v. State*, 63 Fla. 1, 58 So. 486 (1912), that article I, section 20, the precursor to today's constitutional right, which was contained in the 1885 Constitution's Declaration of Rights, was "intended to give the people the means of protecting themselves against oppression and public outrage, and was not designed as a shield for the individual man, who is prone to load his stomach with liquor and his pockets with revolvers or dynamite, and make of himself a dangerous nuisance to society." *Id.* at 488.

A former member of this Court also echoed the *Heller* Court's statement that some early gun laws were enacted with a racial motivation in mind. As Justice Buford explained in *Watson v. Stone*, 148 Fla. 516, 4 So.2d 700 (1941), when concurring specially in a decision of this Court, which applied the rule of lenity to strictly construe the predecessor of section 790.05 in favor of the defendant:

> *The original Act of 1893 was passed when there was a great influx of negro laborers in this State drawn here for the purpose of working in turpentine and lumber camps. The same condition existed when the Act was amended in 1901 and the Act was passed for the purpose of disarming the negro laborers and to thereby reduce the unlawful homicides that were prevalent in turpentine and saw-mill camps and to give the white citizens in sparsely settled areas a better feeling of security.* The statute was never intended to be applied to the white population and in practice has never been so applied. We have no statistics available, but it is a safe guess to assume that more than 80% of the white men living in the rural sections of Florida have violated this statute. It is also a safe guess to say that not more than 5% of the men in Florida who own pistols and repeating rifles have ever applied to the Board of County Commissioners for a permit to have the same in their possession and there had never been, within my knowledge, any effort to enforce the provisions of this statute as to white people, because it has been generally conceded to be in contravention of the Constitution and non-enforceable if contested.

Id. at 703 (Buford, J., concurring specially) (emphasis added).

Consistent with the plain language of article I, section 8, and its predecessor providing that the Legislature may regulate the manner and use of firearms, as well as the *Heller* Court's interpretation of the federal right as not unlimited, the Legislature has enacted various laws regulating the manner in which arms are carried. This Court has upheld these various regulations of this constitutional right upon challenge. For instance, in *Nelson v. State*, 195 So.2d 853 (Fla. 1967), this Court concluded that the "statutory prohibition of possession of a pistol by one convicted of a felony, civil rights not restored, [was] a reasonable public safeguard." *Id.* at 855–56. Then, in *Rinzler v. Carson*, 262 So.2d 661 (Fla. 1972), this Court upheld a statute that barred the usage of an entire class of firearms, explaining that "[a]lthough the Legislature may not entirely prohibit the right of the people to keep and bear arms," pursuant to article I, section 8, "it can determine that certain arms or weapons may not be kept or borne by the citizen." *Id.* at 665. In doing so, the Court did not apply any level of scrutiny and noted that it had previously upheld other regulations enacted by the Legislature that regulated the use and manner of bearing specific weapons. *Rinzler*, 262 So.2d at 665–66.

As we recognized in *Rinzler*, inherent in the holdings of these cases is the acknowledgment that under the Florida Constitution, *"the right to keep and bear arms is not an absolute right,* but is one which is subject to the right of the people through their legislature to enact valid police regulations to promote the health, morals, safety and general welfare of the people." *Id.* at 666 (emphasis added). In light of *Heller*'s clarification that the federal right under the Second Amendment is not unlimited, the Florida right is, thus, consistent with the federal right.

III. DETERMINING THE APPROPRIATE LEVEL OF SCRUTINY

In reviewing Norman's claim that section 790.053 violates the Second Amendment to the United States Constitution, we apply the two-step analysis that has been employed by the United States Court of Appeals for the Eleventh Circuit in *Georgia Carry.Org, Inc. v. U.S. Army Corps of Eng'rs*, 788 F.3d 1318, 1322 (11th Cir. 2015), and nearly every other federal circuit court of appeal after *Heller* and *McDonald* to determine the appropriate the level of scrutiny. The Fourth District expressly applied this two-step inquiry in *Norman*, 159 So.3d at 210–11. As the Fourth District explained, under this two-step analysis:

> First, we determine "whether the challenged law burdens conduct protected by the Second Amendment based on a historical understanding of the scope of the [Second Amendment] right, or whether the challenged law falls within a well-defined and narrowly limited category of prohibitions that have been historically unprotected." *Jackson*, 746 F.3d at 960 (alteration in original) (citations omitted) (internal quotation marks omitted). To answer this question, "we ask whether the regulation is one of the presumptively lawful regulatory measures identified in *Heller*[], or whether the record includes persuasive historical evidence establishing that the regulation at issue imposes prohibitions that fall outside the historical scope of the Second Amendment." *Id.* (citations omitted) (internal quotation marks omitted). If the provision is not "within the historical scope of the Second Amendment," *id.* then it is constitutional. *See id.*; *see also Nat'l Rifle Ass'n*, 700 F.3d at 195. If it is within the scope, we must proceed to the second step of the analysis.

> At step two, we must "determine the appropriate level of scrutiny" to apply to the provision at issue. *Jackson*, 746 F.3d at 960.

Norman, 159 So.3d at 210–11.

In this case, the first prong is met. Florida's Open Carry Law, which regulates the manner of how arms are borne, imposes a burden on conduct falling within the scope of the Second Amendment. The law prohibits, in most instances, one manner of carrying arms in public, thereby implicating the "central component" of the Second Amendment—the right of self-defense. Thus, we turn to step two.

We must next determine the appropriate level of scrutiny to apply in reviewing the validity of Florida's Open Carry Law, codified in section 790.053. As the *Heller* Court explained, there are three "traditionally expressed levels" of scrutiny: rational basis, intermediate scrutiny, and strict scrutiny. *Heller*, 554 U.S. at 634. As this Court has clarified, "[e]ach level has a concomitant presumption of validity or invalidity and standard of proof." *N. Fla. Women's Health & Counseling Servs., Inc. v. State*, 866 So.2d 612, 625 (Fla. 2003). Rational basis review is the most deferential to the State, as "a relatively relaxed standard reflecting the Court's awareness that the drawing of lines that create distinctions is peculiarly a legislative task and an unavoidable one." *Mass. Bd. of Retirement v. Murgia*, 427 U.S. 307, 314 (1976). Although *Heller* provided little guidance to courts reviewing constitutional challenges to gun regulations under the Second Amendment, it foreclosed subjecting the kind of regulation at issue here to rational basis review. *See Heller*, 554 U.S. at 628 n.27 ("If all that was required to overcome the right to keep and bear arms was a rational basis, the Second Amendment would be redundant with the separate constitutional prohibitions on irrational laws, and would have no effect."). Therefore, we are left to choose between strict and intermediate scrutiny.

On the opposite end of the spectrum of constitutional analysis from rational basis review is strict scrutiny, the most rigorous level of review. *See Korematsu v. United States*, 323 U.S. 214, 216 (1944); *see also N. Fla. Women's Health*, 866 So.2d at 625. If a law impairs the exercise of a fundamental right, it must pass strict scrutiny. *See, e.g., Washington v. Glucksberg*, 521 U.S. 702, 720–21 (1997). The law is presumptively unconstitutional. *See N. Fla. Women's Health*, 866 So.2d at 625 n.16. Laws reviewed under strict scrutiny must "further[] a compelling interest" and be "narrowly tailored to achieve that interest." *Citizens United v. Fed. Election Comm'n*, 558 U.S. 310, 340 (2010) (quoting *Federal Election Comm'n v. Wis. Right to Life, Inc.*, 551 U.S. 449, 464 (2007)); *see also D.M.T. v. T.M.H.*, 129 So.3d 320, 339 (Fla. 2013) ("Strict scrutiny ... requires the State to prove that the legislation furthers a compelling governmental interest through the least intrusive means."). When a law is reviewed under strict scrutiny, the State bears the burden of proving its validity. *Fisher v. Univ. of Tex. at Austin*, ___ U.S. ___, 133 S.Ct. 2411, 2421 (2013).

Somewhere between rational basis review and strict scrutiny is intermediate scrutiny. Under this less rigorous standard, the challenged law "must be substantially related to an important governmental objective." *Clark v. Jeter*, 486 U.S. 456, 461 (1988). While the State still bears the burden under this standard, the relationship between the Legislature's ends and means need only be a "reasonable fit." *Chester*, 628 F.3d at 683 (citing *Bd. of Trustees of State Univ. of N.Y. v. Fox*, 492 U.S. 469, 480 (1989)).

As the Fourth District explained, in deciding whether strict or intermediate scrutiny is appropriate to apply to Second Amendment challenges, federal courts

> look at "(1) 'how close the law comes to the core of the Second Amendment right [of self-defense]' and (2) 'the severity of the law's burden on the right.'" [*Jackson*, 746 F.3d] at 960–61 (quoting *Chovan*, 735 F.3d at 1138). Moreover, in applying step two, we remain mindful that "[a] law that imposes such a se-

vere restriction on the core right of self-defense that it 'amounts to a destruction of the [Second Amendment] right,' is unconstitutional under any level of scrutiny." *Id.* at 961 (alteration in original) (quoting *Heller*[], 554 U.S. at 629).

Norman, 159 So.3d at 210–11. This guide is informed by *Heller*'s emphasis on "the weight of the burden imposed by the D.C. gun laws." *United States v. Decastro*, 682 F.3d 160, 166 (2d Cir. 2012). The D.C. gun laws invalidated by *Heller* made "it *impossible* for citizens to use [handguns] for the core lawful purpose of self-defense." *Heller*, 554 U.S. at 630 (emphasis added). Thus, if the law leaves open an alternative outlet to exercise the right—here, Florida's shall-issue concealed-carry licensing scheme—then the law is "less likely to place a severe burden on the Second Amendment right than those which do not." *Jackson*, 746 F.3d at 961 (citing [*United States v.*] *Marzzarella*, 614 F.3d at 97).

As to the first prong, Florida's Open Carry Law is related to the core of the constitutional right to bear arms for self-defense because it prohibits the open carrying of firearms in public where a need for self-defense exists. *See, e.g., Moore v. Madigan*, 702 F.3d 933, 937 (7th Cir. 2012) ("To confine the right to be armed to the home is to divorce the Second Amendment from the right of self-defense described in *Heller* and *McDonald*."). However, Florida's Open Carry Law is not so close to the "core" of this right as to prevent people from defending themselves. Indeed, under Florida's permissive "shall-issue" licensing scheme, most individuals are not prevented from carrying a firearm in public for self-defense.

Turning to the second prong, which is the severity of the law's burden on the right, as the Fourth District recited, "we remain mindful that '[a] law that imposes such a severe restriction on the core right of self-defense that it "amounts to a destruction of the [Second Amendment] right," (quoting *Jackson*, 746 F.3d at 961) is unconstitutional under any level of scrutiny.'" *Norman*, 159 So.3d at 211. However, if the regulation leaves open an alternative outlet to exercise the right, then the regulation is "less likely to place a severe burden on the ... right than those which do not." *Jackson*, 746 F.3d at 961 (citing *Marzzarella*, 614 F.3d at 97); *Decastro*, 682 F.3d 160, 166, 168 (2d Cir. 2012). As we have explained, Florida's permissive, shall-issue, concealed-carry licensing scheme clearly "leave[s] open alternative channels" to exercise the right. *Jackson*, 746 F.3d at 961 (citing *Marzzarella*, 614 F.3d at 97).

Significantly, unlike the laws at issue in *Heller* and *McDonald*, which completely banned the possession of handguns in one's home, Florida's Open Carry Law regulates only <u>how</u> firearms are borne in public. Because this law does not amount to an entire ban on a class of guns or completely prohibit the bearing of firearms in public and does not affect the right to keep arms in one's home, "where the need for defense of self, family, and property is most acute," *Heller*, 554 U.S. at 628, we conclude that Florida's Open Carry Law does not severely burden the right. As the Third Circuit Court of Appeals has explained, a law that "was neither designed to nor has the effect of prohibiting the possession of any class of firearms ... is more accurately characterized as a regulation of the manner in which persons may lawfully exercise their Second Amendment rights." *Marzzarella*, 614 F.3d at 97.

Thus, like every federal circuit court that has reviewed a challenged law that closely relates to the Second Amendment but does not completely ban the possession or use of firearms, we conclude that intermediate scrutiny is appropriate. The Tenth Circuit cogently set forth the reason why intermediate scrutiny, rather than strict scrutiny, is more appropriate for reviewing laws regulating the use of firearms. As the Tenth Circuit explained when it considered a Second Amendment challenge to a federal regulation prohibiting the storage and carriage of firearms on property owned by the United States Postal Service, "[i]ntermediate scrutiny makes sense in the Second Amendment context," because

> [t]he right to carry weapons in public for self-defense poses inherent risks to others. Firearms may create or exacerbate accidents or deadly encounters, as the longstanding bans on private firearms in airports and courthouses illustrate. The risk inherent in firearms and other weapons distinguishes the Second Amendment right from other fundamental rights that have been held to be evaluated under a strict scrutiny test, such as the right to marry and the right to be free from viewpoint discrimination, which can be exercised without creating a direct risk to others. Intermediate scrutiny appropriately places the burden on the government to justify its restrictions, while also giving governments considerable flexibility to regulate gun safety.

Bonidy v. U.S. Postal Serv., 790 F.3d 1121, 1126 (10th Cir. 2015) (emphasis added).

In accordance with the federal courts that have considered the issue and in accordance with the analytical framework set forth by the Fourth District in *Norman*, we review section 790.053—Florida's Open Carry Law—under intermediate scrutiny.

IV. REVIEWING SECTION 790.053 UNDER INTERMEDIATE SCRUTINY

As we have explained, under intermediate scrutiny, the challenged law "must be substantially related to an important governmental objective." *Clark*, 486 U.S. at 461; *see also T.M v. State*, 784 So.2d 442, 443 n.1 (Fla. 2001). While the terminology may at times differ, intermediate scrutiny requires "the asserted governmental end to be more than just legitimate, either 'significant,' 'substantial,' or important," and requires that "the fit between the challenged regulation and the asserted objective be reasonable, not perfect." *Marzzarella*, 614 F.3d at 98.

Regarding the first prong of the intermediate scrutiny test—whether the law has an "important governmental objective"—the governmental interests furthered by section 790.053 are undoubtedly important. *Clark*, 486 U.S. at 461. The Legislature, in its "Declaration of Policy" regarding the "Lawful ownership, possession, and use of firearms and other weapons," under chapter 790 found: "[A]s a matter of public policy[,] … it is necessary to promote firearms safety and to curb and prevent the use of firearms and other weapons in crime and by incompetent persons without prohibiting the lawful use in defense of life, home, and property…." § 790.25(1), Fla. Stat. (2012). As section 790.25(4) states, the provisions of chapter 790 "shall be liberally construed to carry out the declaration of policy." Likewise, the United States Supreme Court has stated that the "'legitimate and compelling state interest' in protecting the community from crime cannot be doubted." *Schall v. Martin*, 467 U.S. 253, 264 (1984) (quoting *De Veau v. Braisted*, 363 U.S. 144, 155 (1960)). Thus, we conclude that the State has satisfied the first prong of intermediate scrutiny, as the government's interest in ensuring public safety by reducing firearm-related crime is undoubtedly critically important.

As to the second prong of intermediate scrutiny, our task is to determine whether section 790.053 "reasonably fits" or "substantially relates" to the stated government purpose of public safety and reducing gun violence. We conclude that it does. The State, in briefing before this Court, contends that by restricting open carry, but permitting concealed carry:

> [T]he Legislature has reasonably concluded that concealed carry serves the State's interests, while open carry does not. An armed attacker engaged in the commission of a crime, for example, might be more likely to target an open carrier than a concealed carrier for the simple reason that a visibly armed citizen poses a more obvious danger to the attacker than a citizen with a hidden firearm.

… Norman contends that the State has not produced evidence that Florida's Open Carry Law reasonably fits the State's important government interest. However, under intermediate scrutiny review, the State is not required to produce evidence in a manner akin to strict scrutiny review.

Consistent with the government's "considerable flexibility to regulate gun safety," *Bonidy*, 790 F.3d at 1126, when reviewing challenged gun regulations under intermediate scrutiny, federal courts have upheld gun regulations by the government if they reasonably comport with important governmental interests, even if the government did not justify the restriction with data or statistical studies.

Indeed, in *Masciandaro*, the Fourth Circuit upheld under intermediate scrutiny a federal regulation prohibiting the carrying or possessing of a loaded handgun in a motor vehicle in a national park because the Secretary of the Interior "could have reasonably concluded" that the regulation was reasonably adapted to the substantial government interest of public safety. 638 F.3d at 473. Similarly, in *Williams*, the Seventh Circuit upheld under intermediate scrutiny a federal law dispossessing felons of firearms, concluding that the government had proven that the law was substantially related to the important governmental interest of preventing felons access to guns by merely "pointing to [the challenger's] own violent past." 616 F.3d at 693.…

Thus, our review of the post-*Heller* jurisprudence leads us to conclude that when reviewing under intermediate scrutiny Second Amendment challenges to laws regulating the manner of how firearms are borne, "courts have traditionally been more deferential to the legislature in this area." *Norman*, 159 So.3d at 223. This is especially so when considering that "[r]eliable scientific proof regarding the efficacy of prohibiting open carry is difficult to obtain." *Id.* n.14. Therefore, we agree with the Fourth District and are satisfied that the State's prohibition on openly carrying firearms in public with specified exceptions—such as authorizing the open carrying of guns to and from and during lawful recreational activities—while still permitting those guns to be carried, albeit in a concealed manner, reasonably fits the State's important government interests of public safety and reducing gun-related violence.

Accordingly, we hold that section 790.053 survives intermediate scrutiny review and is not unconstitutional under the Second Amendment. Our review of section 790.053 does not end here, though, as we must also analyze whether section 790.053 is unconstitutional under Florida's freestanding constitutional right to keep and bear arms for self-defense.

V. FLORIDA CONSTITUTIONAL CHALLENGE TO SECTION 790.053

We have already determined that Florida's Open Carry Law survives intermediate scrutiny when considering whether the law violates the Second Amendment. We next consider whether Florida's freestanding constitutional right to keep and bear arms for self-defense, subject to the explicit grant of legislative authority to regulate how those arms are kept and borne, provides more constitutional rights than provided by the Second Amendment. Norman contends that it does because article I, section 8, is part of the Florida Constitution's Declaration of Rights, "a series of rights so basic that the framers of our Constitution accorded them a place of special privilege." *Traylor v. State*, 596 So.2d 957, 963 (Fla. 1992).

Significantly unlike other rights contained in Florida's declaration of rights, however, the plain language of article I, section 8, of the Florida Constitution explicitly authorizes the Legislature to regulate the manner of exercising the right to keep and bear arms for self-defense. Because we have already determined that the Open Carry Law merely regulates one manner of carrying firearms in public, we reject Norman's argument that this law regulating how firearms are carried in public warrants strict scrutiny review under Florida's constitutional right. Accepting such an argument would render every law regulating the use and manner of firearms presumptively unconstitutional, thereby rendering meaningless the text of article I, section 8, authorizing the Legislature to regulate firearms.

Indeed, our conclusion that laws regulating the manner and use of firearms do not actually implicate Florida's freestanding constitutional right, triggering strict scrutiny review, is borne out by this Court's precedent upholding against constitutional challenges laws on the keeping and bearing of arms without subjecting the laws to any form of heightened scrutiny. *See Rinzler*, 262 So.2d at 664 (upholding constitutionality of statute making it unlawful for any person to "possess[ ] or control any short-barreled rifle, short-barreled shotgun, or machine gun which is, or may readily be made, operable") (quoting § 790.0221, Fla. Stat. (Supp. 1970)); *Nelson*, 195 So.2d at 856 (upholding constitutionality of statute making it unlawful for convicted felons to possess a pistol, sawed-off rifle, or sawed-off shotgun); *Davis* [*v. State*], 146 So.2d at 895 (holding valid law making it a criminal offense to carry in one's manual possession a pistol, Winchester rifle or other repeating rifle in county without a license from county commissioners). Therefore, we conclude that section 790.053, which regulates one manner of carrying arms in public, is not subject to strict scrutiny review. Accordingly, consistent with our conclusion that section 790.053 passes constitutional muster under intermediate scrutiny, and therefore does not violate the Second Amendment, we hold that section 790.053 does not violate article I, section 8, of the Florida Constitution under the same standard.

CONCLUSION

We hold that section 790.053 does not unconstitutionally infringe on the Second Amendment right to bear arms, as interpreted by the United States Supreme Court in *Heller* and *McDonald*, or the Florida Constitution's freestanding right to bear arms subject to the Legislature's authority to regulate the use and manner of doing so. Because section 790.053 regulates only one manner of bearing arms and does not impair the exercise of the fundamental right to bear arms, we approve the Fourth District's well-reasoned decision in *Norman* upholding the constitutionality of section 790.053 under intermediate scrutiny.

It is so ordered.

LABARGA, C.J., and QUINCE, J., concur.

LEWIS, J., concurs in result.

CANADY, J. [Justice Canady, joined by Justice Polston, dissented with an opinion relying exclusively on the Second Amendment jurisprudence of the U.S. Supreme Court. For that reason, the dissent is not included here.]

G. Article I, Section 10 — Prohibited Laws

i. *Ex Post Facto* Laws

This provision is adopted from the 1885 Constitution, but some such prohibition has been included in all earlier Florida Constitutions. Note the similar prohibitions in Article I, Section 10 of the U.S. Constitution.

Shenfield v. State

44 So. 3d 96 (Fla. 2010)

CANADY, C.J.

In this case, we consider whether a statutory amendment relating to the circumstances in which a probationary period is tolled pending consideration of an alleged probation violation may constitutionally be applied to a probationer who was placed on probation before the amendment became effective. We have for review the decision of the Fourth District Court of Appeal in *Shenfeld v. State*, 14 So.3d 1021 (Fla. 4th DCA 2009), in which the Fourth District certified that its decision is in direct conflict with the decisions of the First District Court of Appeal in *Harris v. State*, 893 So.2d 669 (Fla. 1st DCA 2005), and *Frye v. State*, 885 So.2d 419 (Fla. 1st DCA 2004). We have jurisdiction. *See* art. V, § 3(b)(4), Fla. Const. For the reasons that follow, we agree with the Fourth District that the application of the statutory amendment to a probationer who was placed on probation before the amendment became effective did not violate the constitutional prohibition of ex post facto laws.

I. BACKGROUND

In July 2002, Jason Shenfeld pleaded guilty to a robbery committed earlier that year. In September 2002, the trial court adjudicated Shenfeld guilty, sentenced him to five years' incarceration, suspended the sentence, and ordered him to serve five years of drug offender probation. In 2004, Shenfeld filed a motion to terminate his probation. The trial court declined to terminate probation, but it modified Shenfeld's probation to administrative probation. On July 23, 2007, before Shenfeld's probation expired, an affidavit of violation of probation was filed, alleging that Shenfeld had committed several violations by committing new crimes. Shenfeld had been arrested without a warrant for allegedly committing first-degree murder, sexual battery, and false imprisonment on July 21, 2007. On October 1, 2007, after Shenfeld's probation would have expired absent tolling, an amended affidavit was filed. The amended affidavit changed the dates of Shenfeld's alleged violations. *Shenfeld*, 14 So.3d at 1023.

When Shenfeld was placed on probation, section 948.06(1), Florida Statutes (2001), provided that "[u]pon the filing of an affidavit alleging a violation of probation or community control and following issuance of a warrant under s. 901.02, the probationary period is tolled until the court enters a ruling on the violation." Florida district courts of appeal held that under the 2001 version of section 948.06(1), "[b]oth the filing of an affidavit of violation and the issuance of an arrest warrant are required to toll the probationary period, and the mere filing of the affidavit is insufficient." *Jones v. State*, 964 So.2d 167, 170 (Fla. 5th DCA 2007) (citing *Sepulveda v. State*, 909 So.2d 568, 570 (Fla. 2d DCA 2005)). In 2007, the Legislature amended section 948.06(1) to allow for tolling of the probationary period "[u]pon the filing of an affidavit alleging a violation of probation or community control and following issuance of a warrant under s. 901.02, a warrantless arrest under this section, or a notice to appear under this section." § 948.06(1)(d), Fla. Stat. (2007). This amendment became effective June 20, 2007. Ch. 2007-210, § 7, at 1938, Laws of Fla. The amended statute thus was in effect when Shenfeld violated his probation.

Relying on the 2001 version of section 948.06(1), Shenfeld moved to dismiss the affidavits of violation of probation. Shenfeld contended that because he was arrested without a warrant and no arrest warrant for the violations was issued during his probationary period, his probation was never tolled and the trial court lacked jurisdiction to revoke his probation once the probationary period expired. Shenfeld further asserted that application of the 2007 version of section 948.06(1) to him was an ex post facto violation.

The trial court denied Shenfeld's motion to dismiss, explaining that its denial was on the basis that the original affidavit of violation was timely and the amended affidavit did not allege new charges. The trial court did not expressly address Shenfeld's argument that because no arrest warrant was issued, his probation was not tolled and the trial court lacked jurisdiction to revoke his probation. After an evidentiary hearing, the trial court found that Shenfeld had violated his probation and revoked that probation. The trial court sentenced Shenfeld to fifteen years in prison. *Shenfeld*, 14 So.3d at 1023.

Shenfeld appealed his sentence and the trial court's ruling on his motion to dismiss to the Fourth District Court of Appeal. Shenfeld argued that the trial court violated the prohibition on ex post facto laws by retroactively applying section 948.06(1), Florida Statutes (2007), in his case. Shenfeld continued to assert his argument that had the trial court applied the probation tolling statute that was in effect when he was originally placed on probation, the trial court would not have had jurisdiction to consider the alleged violations of probation. The Fourth District concluded that the application of section 948.06(1), Florida Statutes (2007), to Shenfeld's revocation of probation proceeding was not an ex post facto violation because it determined that the 2007 amendment to section 948.06(1) was procedural in effect. The Fourth District reasoned that the revision was procedural in nature because the purpose and effect of the amendment was to toll the probationary period in order to allow the alleged violations of probation to be heard. Accordingly, the Fourth District concluded that the trial court had jurisdiction to revoke Shenfeld's probation and sentence him. *Shenfeld*, 14 So.3d at 1023–24.

II. ANALYSIS

On appeal, Shenfeld contends that the 2007 version of section 948.06(1) could not constitutionally be applied to him and that the trial court therefore erred in denying his motion to dismiss. Specifically, Shenfeld asserts that the ex post facto clauses of the United States Constitution and the Florida Constitution prohibit retroactive application of section 948.06(1), Florida Statutes (2007), in his revocation of probation proceeding. The State contends that section 948.06(1), Florida Statutes (2007), was not applied retroactively in this case and, alternatively, that if the statute was applied retroactively, the application was constitutional.

The United States Constitution provides that "[n]o State shall ... pass any ... ex post facto Law." U.S. Const. art. I, § 10, cl. 1. The Florida Constitution similarly states that "[n]o ... ex post facto law ... shall be passed." Art. I, § 10, Fla. Const.

The constitutional prohibition of ex post facto laws forbids the enactment of "laws with certain retroactive effects." *Stogner v. California*, 539 U.S. 607, 610 (2003). The four categories "of *ex post facto* laws set forth by Justice Chase more than 200 years ago in *Calder v. Bull*[, 3 U.S. (3 Dall.) 386 (1798),]" have been "recognized as providing an authoritative account of the scope of the *Ex Post Facto* Clause." *Stogner*, 539 U.S. at 611. These are the four categories set forth by Justice Chase:

> 1st. Every law that makes an action done before the passing of the law, and which was innocent when done, criminal; and punishes such action. 2d. Every law that aggravates a crime, or makes it greater than it was, when committed. 3d. Every law that changes the punishment, and inflicts a greater

punishment, than the law annexed to the crime, when committed. 4th. Every law that alters the legal rules of evidence, and receives less, or different, testimony, than the law required at the time of the commission of the offense, in order to convict the offender.

Id. at 612 (quoting *Calder*, 3 U.S. (3 Dall.) at 390–91) (emphasis removed). All ex post facto claims must be evaluated in the light of these four categories. In determining whether an ex post facto violation has occurred, it is "a mistake to stray beyond *Calder*'s four categories." *Carmell v. Texas*, 529 U.S. 513, 539 (2000) (emphasis removed).

It is evident that the four *Calder* categories do not encompass every law effective after the commission of an offense and applied in the proceedings regarding the offense. The prohibition of ex post facto laws thus "does not give a criminal a right to be tried, in all respects, by the law in force when the crime charged was committed." *Dobbert v. Florida*, 432 U.S. 282, 293 (1977) (quoting *Gibson v. Mississippi*, 162 U.S. 565, 590 (1896)). And the mere fact that a statutory change "[alters] the situation of a party to his disadvantage" is not sufficient to bring that change within the scope of the ex post facto clause. *Collins v. Youngblood*, 497 U.S. 37, 50 (1990) (quoting from and overruling *Kring v. Missouri*, 107 U.S. 221, 235 (1883)). Detriment to the defendant is necessary but not sufficient to establish an ex post facto violation. "[E]ven if a law operates to the defendant's detriment, the *ex post facto* prohibition does not restrict 'legislative control of remedies and modes of procedure which do not affect matters of substance.'" *Miller v. Florida*, 482 U.S. 423, 433 (1987) (quoting *Dobbert*, 432 U.S. at 293); *see also Beazell v. Ohio*, 269 U.S. 167, 171 (1925). Such matters of substance are implicated only when the law falls within one of the four *Calder* categories.

The 2007 revision to section 948.06(1) at issue here is a matter of procedure that does not fall within any of those categories. The statutory provision expanding the circumstances under which a probationary term could be tolled "neither made criminal a theretofore innocent act [first category], nor aggravated a crime previously committed [second category], nor provided greater punishment [third category], nor changed the proof necessary to convict [fourth category]." *Dobbert*, 432 U.S. at 293. Instead, the statutory change simply altered the "modes of procedure" governing the adjudication of probation violations by permitting the tolling of a probationary term without the issuance of an arrest warrant.

Shenfeld's reliance on *State v. Williams*, 397 So.2d 663 (Fla.1981), is unavailing. In *Williams*, this Court held that a statute—enacted after the commission of the charged offense—which allowed the trial court to retain jurisdiction over the first third of the defendant's statutory maximum sentence could not be constitutionally applied retroactively. The trial court's retention of jurisdiction gave it the authority to bar the defendant's parole or gain-time release. This Court explained that retroactive application of the statute would attach "the legal consequences of the trial court's parole veto and no gain-time release to those who committed crimes before the provision's effective date" and that as a consequence "the prisoners' sentences are enhanced." *Id.* at 665. The statutory change at issue in *Williams* thus fell squarely within *Calder*'s third category — that is, laws inflicting "a greater punishment" than was applicable to the offense at the time it was committed. The statutory revision at issue in this case, in contrast, did nothing to increase the punishment applicable to Shenfeld.

The statutory change challenged by Shenfeld is akin to a statutory extension of a statute of limitations which becomes effective before the statute has run. Such a statutory change — unlike a statute reviving a previously time-barred prosecution — does not fall within the scope of any of the four *Calder* categories. *See Stogner*, 539 U.S. at 613, 632–33 (stating that "[a]fter (but not before) the original statute of limitations had expired, a party such as Stogner was not 'liable to any punishment'" and concluding "that a law enacted after expiration of a previously applicable limitations period violates the *Ex Post Facto* Clause when it is applied to revive a previously time-barred prosecution"); *Reino v. State*, 352 So.2d 853, 861 (Fla.1977) (recognizing that "the legislature could have amended [the statute of limitations] retroactively" with respect to crimes for which "[p]rosecution was not yet barred"). The probation statute amendment here became effective before Shenfeld's probationary term had expired. If the time for bringing criminal charges may constitutionally be extended before the prosecution has been time-barred, it follows that a provision for tolling may be applied to a probationary term that has not yet expired.

III. CONCLUSION

We approve the decision of the Fourth District. The 2007 revision to section 948.06(1), Florida Statutes (2007), was procedural in nature. Its application in Shenfeld's revocation of probation proceeding did not violate the prohibition on ex post facto laws.

It is so ordered.

PARIENTE, LEWIS, QUINCE, POLSTON, LABARGA, and PERRY, JJ., concur.

ii. Abrogation of Contracts

Pomponio v. Claridge of Pompano Condominium

378 So. 2d 774 (Fla. 1979)

ENGLAND, Chief Justice.

The present cause is before us to determine the constitutionality of section 718.401(4), Florida Statutes (1977), which provides for the deposit of rents into the registry of the court during litigation involving obligations under a condominium lease. We have jurisdiction pursuant to article V, section 3(b)(1) of the Florida Constitution. The question of whether this statute impermissibly impairs the obligation of contracts in violation of article I, section 10 of the Florida and federal constitutions ... is now squarely presented.

The Claridge of Pompano Condominium, Inc., ("the Association") and several individual unit owners who are members of the Association brought suit against the developer of the condominium and the lessors of a ninety-nine year recreational lease associated with the condominium.[26] The Association, as a representative of the unit owners, is the named lessee under the recreational lease. As required by section 718.401(4), the trial court granted the Association and unit owners' motion to permit payment of rents into the registry of the court, despite the developer and lessors' contention that the provision is unconstitutional. By this appeal, the developer and lessors seek to have the ruling reversed. We hold that the statute is unconstitutional.

The parties argue, respectively, that the rent deposit statute either permissibly modifies a contractual remedy or impermissibly impairs substantial contract rights and obligations. Yet a proper analysis of this issue cannot hinge exclusively on any supposed distinction between "remedies" and "obligations." The United States Supreme Court has discarded this distinction as "an outdated formalism,"[27] and we choose to do likewise. To formulate a more logical approach to the question of impairment, it is necessary at the outset to examine the interpretive development of the contract clause in the decisions of the United States Supreme Court.

While the intent of the framers with respect to the contract clause has generated considerable speculation, its origins remain too obscure to be of any assistance in its construction. It is nonetheless clear that in the early decisions of the United States Supreme Court the clause was interpreted literally as a strict prohibition.[28] As with other seemingly absolute constitutional provisions, however, it soon became evident that some degree of flexibility would have to be read into the clause to ameliorate the harshness of such rigid application. In order to accommodate necessary legislation without deviating from the principle that all laws impairing the obligations of contract are constitutionally prohibited, the Court developed two basic analytical devices the "obligation-remedy" distinction and the "reserved powers" doctrine both of which dominated contract clause interpretation for the next century.

The "Obligation-Remedy" Test

Home Building & Loan Association v. Blaisdell, 290 U.S. 398 (1934), is the most important case in the history of contract clause interpretation.[29] In *Blaisdell*, the

---

26. [FN3.] Although the Pompano lease was executed prior to the enactment of section 718.401(4) or its predecessor, section 711.63(4), Florida Statutes (1975), the Court specifically held in *Century Village*[, *Inc. v. Wellington, E, F, K, L, H, J, M, & G, Condominium Ass'n*, 361 So. 2d 128 (Fla. 1978),] that this provision was intended by the legislature to be applied retroactively. Unlike the lease considered in *Century Village*, the present condominium lease does not incorporate statutory amendments enacted subsequent to the contract's execution.

27. [FN4.] *United States Trust Co. v. New Jersey*, 431 U.S. 1, 19 (1977).

28. [FN6.] See, e.g., *Trustees of Dartmouth College v. Woodward*, 17 U.S. (4 Wheat.) 518 (1819). Until the late nineteenth century, the contract clause was the subject of the Court's attention more frequently than any other provision except the commerce clause, B. Wright, *The Contract Clause of the Constitution* 91–92 (1938), and as the Court itself recently observed, "it was perhaps the strongest single constitutional check on state legislation during our early years as a Nation...." *Allied Structural Steel Co. v. Spannaus*, 438 U.S. 234, 241 (1978).

29. [FN9.] The United States Supreme Court has itself stated that "(t)he *Blaisdell* opinion ... amounted to a comprehensive restatement of the principles underlying the application of the Contract Clause," *City of El Paso v. Simmons*, 379 U.S. 497, 508 (1965), and "is regarded as the leading case in

Court upheld a mortgage moratorium statute that Minnesota had enacted to provide relief for homeowners threatened with foreclosure. The statute enabled a court to extend the time for redemption beyond that provided for in the mortgage contract. Though the statute directly affected lenders' foreclosure rights, the Court ruled that it did not violate the contract clause, reasoning that "the state ... continues to possess authority to safeguard the vital interests of its people." 290 U.S. at 434.

In its decision, the *Blaisdell* majority traced the judicial history of the obligation-remedy distinction and the reserved powers doctrine in contract clause analysis. It then concluded:

> It is manifest from this review of our decisions that there has been a growing appreciation of public needs and of the necessity of finding ground for a rational compromise between individual rights and public welfare....
>
> It is no answer to say that this public need was not apprehended a century ago, or to insist that what the provision of the Constitution meant to the vision of that day it must mean to the vision of our time.... "The case before us must be considered in the light of our whole experience and not merely in that of what was said a hundred years ago."[30]

Having jettisoned the analytical framework which governed prior contract clause cases, the Court formulated a new test against which legislation would be measured:

> The question is not whether the legislative action affects contracts incidentally, or directly or indirectly, but whether the legislation is addressed to a legitimate end and the measures taken are reasonable and appropriate to that end.[31]

Thus, beginning with *Blaisdell*, the Court began to permit certain "reasonable" impairments of contractual obligations. This new and more flexible approach to contract clause analysis later was refined and developed by the Court in three major cases.

The Evolving "Reasonableness" Test

In *City of El Paso v. Simmons*, 379 U.S. 497 (1965), the Court stated that it would not even "pause to consider ... again the dividing line under federal law between 'remedy' and 'obligation'...." 379 U.S. at 506. Instead, the majority noted that "decisions dating from (*Blaisdell*) have not placed critical reliance on the distinction between

---

the modern era of Contract Clause interpretation." *United States Trust Co. v. New Jersey*, 431 U.S. 1, 15 (1977).

30. [FN13.] *Id.* at 442–43 (quoting from *Missouri v. Holland*, 252 U.S. 416 (1920)).

31. [FN14.] 290 U.S. at 438. In our opinion, however, there is considerable merit to the argument that, without regard to the particular approach which it claimed to be applying, the Court both before and after *Blaisdell* actually proceeded to work practical solutions based on the facts and circumstances of each case. See Comment, *The Role of the Contract Clause in Municipalities' Relations with Creditors*, 1976 Duke L.J. 1321, 1327. If this theory is correct, then the "new test" unveiled in *Blaisdell* was really no more than an attempt to restate what the Court had actually been doing all along, with an implicit admission that the traditional obligation-remedy distinction had been used merely for the purpose of post-analytical labelling and categorization.

obligation and remedy," and proceeded to demonstrate that its post-Depression rulings had been made "without any regard to whether the measure was substantive or remedial." *Id.* at 506–07 n.9. Recognizing that "'(t)he Constitution is "intended to preserve practical and substantial rights, not to maintain theories,"'"[32] the Court in *Simmons* clearly refuted the notion that statutes could be properly measured by any criteria other than reasonableness:

> This Court's decisions have never given a law which imposes unforeseen advantages or burdens on a contracting party constitutional immunity against change.... Laws which restrict a party to those gains reasonably to be expected from the contract are not subject to attack under the Contract Clause, notwithstanding that they technically alter an obligation of a contract.[33]

In resolving the controversy before it, the *Simmons* majority applied what Justice Black decried in dissent as a "balancing" test,[34] giving due consideration for the "buyer's undertaking," whether "the buyer was substantially induced to enter into these contracts" because of the promise, and the significance of the "State's vital interest,"[35] and concluded that the Texas statute at issue was constitutionally permissible because "(t)he measure taken ... was a mild one indeed, hardly burdensome to the purchaser..., but nonetheless an important one to the State's interest."[36]

The next major decision in the interpretive development of the contract clause was *United States Trust Co. v. New Jersey*, 431 U.S. 1(1977).[37] The Court's analysis in *United States Trust* both expanded upon the "balancing" test of *Simmons* and refined the "reasonableness" standard of *Blaisdell*:

> (a) finding that there has been a technical impairment is merely a preliminary step in resolving the more difficult question whether that impairment is permitted under the Constitution.
>
> ... (T)he Contract Clause limits otherwise legitimate exercises of state legislative authority, and the existence of an important public interest is not always sufficient to overcome that limitation.... Moreover, the scope of the

---

32. [FN19.] *Id.* at 515 (quoting from *Faitnote Iron & Steel Co. v. City of Asbury Park*, 316 U.S. 502, 514 (1942)).

33. [FN20.] 379 U.S. at 515.

34. [FN21.] *Id.* at 517, 528–33 (Black, J., dissenting).

35. [FN22.] *Id.* at 514–15.

36. [FN23.] *Id.* at 516–17.

37. [FN24.] In *United States Trust*, the Court had this to say about the obligation-remedy distinction:

> (I)t was ... recognized very clearly that the distinction between remedies and obligations was not absolute.... More recent decisions have not relied on the remedy/obligation distinction, primarily because it is now recognized that obligations as well as remedies may be modified without necessarily violating the Contract Clause.
>
> Although now largely an outdated formalism, the remedy/obligation distinction may be viewed as approximating the result of a more particularized inquiry into the legitimate expectations of the contracting parties.

431 U.S. at 19 n.17 (citations omitted and emphasis added).

State's reserved power depends on the nature of the contractual relationship with which the challenged law conflicts.

> … The Court in *Blaisdell* recognized that laws intended to regulate existing contractual relationships must serve a legitimate public purpose…. Legislation adjusting the rights and responsibilities of contracting parties must be upon reasonable conditions and of a character appropriate to the public purpose justifying its adoption.[38]

The Court concluded that the correct standard to be employed in assessing the validity of legislation affecting a state's own contracts is that:

> (a)s with laws impairing the obligations of private contracts, *an impairment may be constitutional if it is reasonable and necessary to serve an important public purpose.*[39]

In finding that the challenged statute did not satisfy this test, the Court emphasized that while "(t)he extent of impairment is certainly a relevant factor in determining its reasonableness," an enactment cannot be considered "necessary" if the legislature "without modifying the covenant at all, … could have adopted alternative means of achieving their … goals," because "a State is not free to impose a drastic impairment when an evident and more moderate course would serve its purposes equally well."[40]

In its most recent pronouncement on the subject, *Allied Structural Steel Co. v. Spannaus*, 438 U.S. 234 (1978), the Court invalidated a Minnesota law which retroactively imposed upon certain private companies with voluntary pension plans additional obligations as to employees who would not have been entitled to such benefits under the original terms of the plan. Without any mention of the obligation-remedy distinction, the majority reviewed the underpinnings of the Court's post *Blaisdell* decisions and formulated its statement of the proper approach to contract clause challenges thusly:

> In applying these principles to the present case, the first inquiry must be whether the state law has, in fact, operated as a substantial impairment of a contractual relationship. *The severity of the impairment measures the height of the hurdle the state legislation must clear. Minimal alteration of contractual obligations may end the inquiry at its first stage. Severe impairment, on the other hand, will push the inquiry to a careful examination of the nature and purpose of the state legislation.*[41]

Several factors to be considered in this balancing test were identified in *Spannaus*:

> (a) Was the law enacted to deal with a broad, generalized economic or social problem?[42]

---

38. [FN25.] *Id.* at 21–22.
39. [FN26.] 431 U.S. at 25 (emphasis added).
40. [FN27.] *Id.* at 27–31.
41. [FN28.] 438 U.S. at 244–45 (footnotes omitted and emphasis added).
42. [FN29.] *Id.* at 250 (citing *Home Bldg. & Loan Ass'n v. Blaisdell*, 290 U.S. 398, 445 (1934)).

(b) Does the law operate in an area which was already subject to state regulation at the time the parties' contractual obligations were originally undertaken, or does it invade an area never before subject to regulation by the state?[43]

(c) Does the law effect a temporary alteration of the contractual relationships of those within its coverage, or does it work a severe, permanent, and immediate change in those relationships irrevocably and retroactively?[44]

Analysis and Conclusion

We recognize that this Court, when construing a provision of the Florida Constitution, is not bound to accept as controlling the United States Supreme Court's interpretation of a parallel provision of the federal Constitution. Yet such rulings have long been considered helpful and persuasive, and are obviously entitled to great weight.[45] With this in mind, we now choose to adopt an approach to contract clause analysis similar to that of the United States Supreme Court. That Court's decisions[46] in this area of law convince us that such an approach is the one most likely to yield results consonant with the basic purpose of the constitutional prohibition.

In our view, any realistic analysis of the impairment issue in Florida must logically begin both with *Yamaha Parts Distributors Inc. v. Ehrman*, 316 So. 2d 558 (Fla. 1975), which applied the well-accepted principle that virtually no degree of contract impairment is tolerable in this state, and with the notion enunciated in *Louisiana ex rel. Ranger v. New Orleans*, 102 U.S. 203 (1880), that "he who pays too late, pays less."[47] These concepts direct our inquiry to the actual effect of the rent deposit statute on the lessor's contractual right to receive its bargained-for rent. That effect, when fully analyzed, persuades us that in the absence of contractual consent significant contract rights are unreasonably impaired by the statute's operation.

Preliminarily, it should be noted that the deposit into court of moneys which one or another contract litigant may withdraw only after incurring some legal cost or a modest delay is constitutionally permissible. Our conclusion in *Yamaha* that "virtually" no impairment is tolerable necessarily implies that some impairment is tolerable, although perhaps not so much as would be acceptable under traditional federal contract clause analysis.

To determine how much impairment is tolerable, we must weigh the degree to which a party's contract rights are statutorily impaired against both the source of authority under which the state purports to alter the contractual relationship and the evil which it seeks to remedy. Obviously, this becomes a balancing process to determine

---

43. [FN30.] *Id.* (citing *Veix v. Sixth Ward Bldg. & Loan Ass'n*, 310 U.S. 32, 38 (1940)).

44. [FN31.] *Id.* (citing *United States Trust Co. v. New Jersey*, 431 U.S. 1, 22 (1977)).

45. [FN32.] See, *e.g.*, *Dudley v. Harrison, McCready & Co.*, 127 Fla. 687, 699, 173 So. 820, 825 (1937); *State v. Hetland*, 366 So.2d 831, 836 (Fla. 2d DCA 1979); *Leveson v. State*, 138 So.2d 361, 364 (Fla. 3d DCA 1962); *Houston v. State*, 113 So.2d 582, 584–85 (Fla. 1st DCA 1959).

46. [FN33.] See notes 9-31 and accompanying text *supra*.

47. [FN36.] *Id.* at 207. As applied to this rent deposit statute, the rubric should be rephrased to read that "he who receives payment too late, receives less."

whether the nature and extent of the impairment is constitutionally tolerable in light of the importance of the state's objective, or whether it unreasonably intrudes into the parties' bargain to a degree greater than is necessary to achieve that objective.

Section 718.401(4), of course, does more than provide a procedure for the deposit of rents subject to disbursement upon compliance with some procedural showing or its equivalent.[48] This statute potentially allows the retention in court of at least some portion of the deposited rent during the entire term of litigation. Barring the current use of court-retained rent moneys is an economic deprivation for which a landlord obviously has not bargained, producing potential erosion of value (at least in our persistently inflationary economy) which goes beyond mere inconvenience. To this extent at least, the statute "impairs" the landlord's contract.[49]

The degree of impairment created by section 718.401(4) is confined to amounts deemed by the legislature not to be essential to the maintenance of the property in dispute. Withdrawals are authorized for amounts "necessary for payment of taxes, mortgage payments, maintenance and operating expenses, and other necessary expenses incident to maintaining and equipping the leased facilities."[50] This formulation precludes a uniform level of impairment in each case, inasmuch as the impairment in any particular situation will depend directly on the disparity between the contract amount of rent and the landlord's property maintenance obligations that is, the lessor's built-in profit.[51] In this formulation, of course, all other needs or desires of the lessor for its promised rents are wholly ignored.[52]

---

48. [FN40.] Contrast, for example, sections 76.18 and 76.19, Florida Statutes (1977), which authorize a bond to free property from an attachment.

49. [FN41.] In *State ex rel. Women's Benefit Ass'n v. Port of Palm Beach Dist.*, 121 Fla. 746, 759, 164 So. 851, 856 (1935), we said: To "impair" has been defined as meaning to make worse; to diminish in quantity, value, excellency or strength; to lessen in power; to weaken. Whatever legislation lessens the efficacy of the means of enforcement of the obligation is an impairment. Also if it tends to *postpone or retard* the enforcement of the contract, it is an impairment. (Emphasis in the original).

50. [FN42.] It is unclear whether funds may be withdrawn from the deposited rents in order to improve the leased premises. One incidental effect of the uncertainty could well be that lessees' prospects for promised additional (or improved) facilities, such as tennis courts, swimming pools, or meeting halls, may be thwarted by a suit instituted by some unit owners which requires significant rent deposits.

51. [FN43.] As a practical matter, the amount of "spread" will also vary from month to month depending upon such factors as seasonal maintenance needs and due dates for tax or mortgage payments. Thus, in some months the landlord may be able to withdraw virtually all, and in others none, of the rent deposits.

52. [FN44.] See note 48 *infra*. The present lessors, in fact, would seem to be effectively barred from any disbursement under the statute in its present form. Section 718.401(4) provides that the "unit owner or association shall pay (rents) into the registry of the court." The provision permits disbursement of these rents, however, only "(w)hen the unit owner has deposited the required funds." As the Court stated in *Century Village*, the terms "unit owner" and "association" are not interchangeable. 361 So.2d at 133–34. Were the present statute read as it seemingly was intended, rents deposited by the Association would be totally inaccessible to the lessor. The precise terms of the present statute need not be interrelated, however, since it impermissibly impairs the obligation of contracts even if the restricted withdrawal privilege were available.

On the other side of the ledger is the state's interest in requiring a unit owner's deposit of leasehold rents into court during the course of litigation. This provision rests on the state's exercise of its police power to promote the health, safety, and welfare of its citizens. While the specific objectives for section 718.401(4) are neither expressly articulated nor plainly evident from a reading of the statute,[53] the litigants have suggested that the legislature's concern was the protection of unit owners from the lessor's foreclosure for non-payment of rent during the pendency of the litigation. To this assertion we have two answers. There is to our knowledge neither a documented threat of massive condominium foreclosures in Florida nor any documentation of the underlying premise that unit owners would withhold rents from landlords pending litigation with them.

We believe that the balance between the state's probable objectives and its method of implementation, on the one hand, and the degree of contract impairment inflicted in furtherance of its policy, on the other, favors preservation of the contract over this exercise of the police power. Bearing on our view is the fact that the manner in which the police power has been wielded here is not the least restrictive means possible. See *City of El Paso v. Simmons*, 379 U.S. 497, 516–17 (1965). Contrast, for example, Florida's Residential Landlord and Tenant Act, which similarly requires the payment of rent into the court's registry during the pendency of a lawsuit between parties to the lease,[54] but which authorizes the court to disburse to a landlord all or any portion of the funds on deposit upon a showing of "actual danger of loss of the premises or *other personal hardship resulting from the loss of rental income from the premises.*"[55] In that statute the legislature has acknowledged that the consequences of rent detention may extend to a deprivation of sums needed for purposes other than the preservation of the controverted property. The severity of impairment wreaked by section 718.401(4) would have been mitigated by a "personal hardship" provision like that in the landlord-tenant act, but none is present.[56]

Therefore, in the face of an express constitutional prohibition against any law "impairing the obligation of contracts,"[57] the state's justification for an exercise of the police power to impair the lessor's contractual bargain does not, in our opinion, pro-

---

53. [FN45.] By contrast, the legislative intent in *Blaisdell* was spelled out in the statute, 290 U.S. at 416, and in the *Women's Benefit Ass'n* case, there were reports of the emergency conditions to document the legislative history and intended effect of the constitutional amendment at issue. 121 Fla. at 765–66, 164 So. at 858 (Buford, J., dissenting).

54. [FN46.] § 83.60(2), Fla.Stat. (1977).

55. [FN47.] § 83.61, Fla.Stat. (1977) (emphasis supplied).

56. [FN48.] As the United States Supreme Court has observed:
The severity of an impairment of contractual obligations can be measured by the factors that reflect the high value the Framers placed on the protection of private contracts. Contracts enable individuals to order their personal and business affairs according to their particular needs and interests. Once arranged, those rights and obligations are binding under the law, and the parties are entitled to rely on them.
Allied Structural Steel Co. v. Spannaus, 438 U.S. 234, 245 (1978).

57. [FN49.] U.S.Const. art. I, § 10, cl. 1; art. I, § 10, Fla.Const.

vide sufficient countervailing considerations. As applied retroactively, absent a lessor's express consent to its incorporation into the terms of the contract, the statute is invalid. Accordingly, the trial court's order authorizing payment of rents into the registry of the court is hereby vacated.

It is so ordered.

BOYD, OVERTON and SUNDBERG, JJ., concur.

OVERTON, J., concurs specially with an opinion. [omitted]

ADKINS, J., concurs in result only.

ALDERMAN, J., dissents. [omitted]

Questions

1. a. What is the principal basic tenet behind the Court's decision (i.e., in all "impairment" cases)?

    b. What are the factors "balanced" by the Court?

2. Would Justice Overton concur with the opinion if the prime rate were 2%? Why?

H. Article I, Section 21 — Access to Courts

A similar provision was found in the 1885 Constitution, and parallel provisions existed in all earlier Florida Constitutions. There is no comparable provision in the U.S. Constitution. Talbot "Sandy" D'Alemberte noted of the Access to Courts provision that it is derived from a provision in the Magna Carta which required "that courts be open and that justice be available without impediments."[58]

Kluger v. White
281 So. 2d 1 (Fla. 1973)

ADKINS, Justice.

This is an appeal from an order of dismissal entered for defendants and against plaintiff in this property damage action by the Dade County Circuit Court, specifically passing upon the constitutionality of Fla. Stat. § 627.738, F.S.A. We have jurisdiction pursuant to Fla. Const., art. V, § 3(b)(1), F.S.A.

The cause of action arose from an automobile collision between a car owned by appellant, and driven by her son, and one owned by appellee, and driven by another person. The amended complaint filed by appellant alleged that the driver of appellee's car was negligent and had been formally charged with failure to yield the right of way; that there were no personal injuries; that there were damages to appellant's car to the extent of $774.95; and that the fair market value of the car was $250.00.

---

58. *See* TALBOT D'ALEMBERTE, THE FLORIDA STATE CONSTITUTION: A REFERENCE GUIDE (1991).

Appellant was insured with appellee, Manchester Insurance and Indemnity Company, but the policy did not provide for 'basic or full' property damage coverage. Appellant alleged that the Manchester agent had not specifically explained to her the possible results of failing to include property damage coverage.

Fla. Stat. § 627.738, F.S.A., provides, in effect, that the traditional right of action in tort for property damage arising from an automobile accident is abolished, and one must look to property damage with one's own insurer, unless the plaintiff is one who

(1) has chosen not to purchase property damage insurance, and

(2) has suffered property damage in excess of $550.00.

In total, Fla. Stat. § 627.738, F.S.A., provides:

"(1) The owner of a motor vehicle as defined in § 627.732 is not required to maintain security with respect to property damage to his motor vehicle, but may elect to purchase either full or basic coverage for accidental property damage to his motor vehicle.

"(2) Every insurer providing security under §§ 627.730–627.741 shall offer the owner either full or basic coverage for accidental property damage to the insured motor vehicle, as follows:

"(a) Full coverage shall provide insurance without regard to fault for accidents occurring within the United States or its territories or possessions or Canada.

"(b) Basic coverage shall be limited to insurance against damage caused by the fault of another resulting from contact between the insured vehicle and a vehicle with respect to which security is required under §§ 627.730–627.741.

"(3) The insurer may include within the terms and conditions applicable to full or basic coverage such other provisions as it customarily applies to collision coverage for private passenger automobiles in other states, including deductibles without limitation.

"(4) Every owner, registrant, operator, or occupant of a motor vehicle with respect to which security has been provided as required by §§ 627.730–627.741, and every other person or organization legally responsible for the acts or omissions of such an owner, registrant, operator, or occupant, is hereby exempted from tort liability for damages because of accidental property damage to motor vehicles arising out of the ownership, operation, maintenance, or use of such motor vehicle in this state. However, a person shall not be exempt from such liability if he was operating the motor vehicle without the express or implied consent of its owner or an insured under the owner's policy or if his willful and wanton misconduct was the proximate cause of the accident. This exemption applies only with respect to property damage to motor vehicles subject to §§ 627.730–627.741 but shall not be applicable as to a motor vehicle damaging a parked vehicle.

"(5) Notwithstanding subsection (4), an owner who has elected not to purchase insurance with respect to property damage to his motor vehicle may maintain an action of tort therefor against the owner, registrant, operator or occupant of a motor vehicle causing such damage if such damage exceeds five hundred and fifty dollars, and the insurer of an owner who has elected to purchase full or basic collision coverage for his motor vehicle shall have right, if the damage to such motor vehicle exceeds the above amount, to recover the amount of the benefits it has paid and, on behalf of its insured, any deductible amount from the insurer of the owner, registrant, operator, or occupant of a motor vehicle causing such damage. The issues of liability in such a case and the amount of recovery shall be decided on the basis of tort law, and shall be determined by agreement between the insurers involved or, if they fail to agree, by arbitration." *"Not Yet Decided"*

The appellant in the case *sub judice* falls into that class of accident victims with no recourse against any person or insurer for loss caused by the fault of another, taking her allegations as true. She did not choose to purchase either 'full or basic coverage for accidental property damage' to her automobile, and her damages were the fair market value of her automobile since repair costs cannot be recovered where they exceed the fair market value of the automobile before the collision. Blashfield, *Automobile Law*, Vol. 15, § 480.1, and 25 C.J.S. Damages § 82.

Appellant has raised numerous constitutional challenges to Fla. Stat. § 627.738, F.S.A. As appellant points out in her brief, the issues are limited to the single statute dealing with property damage, and the remainder of the Florida Automobile Reparations Act is not under consideration in the case *sub judice.* — *"Not Yet Decided"*

It is likewise unnecessary for this Court to consider but one of the constitutional issues raised by appellant, for we find, as explained below, that Fla. Stat. § 627.738, F.S.A., fails to comply with a reasonable interpretation of Fla. Const., art. I, § 21, F.S.A., which reads as follows:

"The courts shall be open to every person for redress of any injury, and justice shall be administered without sale, denial or delay."

This Court has never before specifically spoken to the issue of whether or not the constitutional guarantee of a 'redress of any injury' (Fla. Const., art. I, § 21, F.S.A.) bars the statutory abolition of an existing remedy without providing an alternative protection to the injured party.

Corpus Juris Secundum provides:

"A constitutional provision insuring a certain remedy for all injuries or wrongs does not command continuation of a specific statutory remedy. However, in a jurisdiction wherein the constitutional guaranty applies to the legislature as well as to the judiciary, ... it has been held that the guaranty precludes the repeal of a statute allowing a remedy where the statute was in force at the time of the adoption of the Constitution. Furthermore, ... the guaranty also prevents, in some jurisdictions, the total abolition of a common-law remedy." 16A C.J.S. Constitutional Law s 710, pp. 1218–1219.

This Court has held that the Declaration of Rights of the Constitution of the State of Florida does apply to State government and to the Legislature. *Spafford v. Brevard County*, 92 Fla. 617, 110 So. 451 (1926). The right to a cause of action in tort for negligent causation of damage to an automobile in a collision was recognized by statute prior to the adoption of the 1968 Constitution of the State of Florida, as evidenced by the fact that Fla. Stat. §627.738, F.S.A., the statute under attack, specifically exempts owners and drivers of automobiles from tort liability for such damages. In addition, the cause of action for damage to property by force or violence — trespass *vi et armis* — was one of the earliest causes of action recognized at English Common Law.

It is essential, therefore, that this Court consider whether or not the Legislature is, in fact, empowered to abolish a common law and statutory right of action without providing an adequate alternative.

Upon careful consideration of the requirements of society, and the ever-evolving character of the law, we cannot adopt a complete prohibition against such legislative change. Nor can we adopt a view which would allow the Legislature to destroy a traditional and long-standing cause of action upon mere legislative whim, or when an alternative approach is available.

We hold, therefore, that where a right of access to the courts for redress for a particular injury has been provided by statutory law predating the adoption of the Declaration of Rights of the Constitution of the State of Florida, or where such right has become a part of the common law of the State pursuant to Fla. Stat. §2.01, F.S.A., the Legislature is without power to abolish such a right without providing a reasonable alternative to protect the rights of the people of the State to redress for injuries, unless the Legislature can show an overpowering public necessity for the abolishment of such right, and no alternative method of meeting such public necessity can be shown.

It is urged that this Court has previously approved action by the Legislature which violated the rule which we have laid down. We disagree.

In *McMillan v. Nelson*, 149 Fla. 334, 5 So.2d 867 (1942), this Court approved the so-called "Guest Statute" which merely changed the degree of negligence necessary for a passenger in an automobile to maintain a tort action against the driver. It did not abolish the right to sue, and does not come under the rule which we have promulgated.

Workmen's compensation abolished the right to sue one's employer in tort for a job-related injury, but provided adequate, sufficient, and even preferable safeguards for an employee who is injured on the job, thus satisfying one of the exceptions to the rule against abolition of the right to redress for an injury.

The Legislature in 1945 enacted Fla. Stat. Ch. 771, F.S.A., which abolishes the rights of action to sue for damages for alienation of affections, criminal conversation, seduction or breach of promise. This Court upheld the validity of the chapter in *Rotwein v. Gersten*, 160 Fla. 736, 36 So.2d 419 (1948). The Court opined:

"The causes of action proscribed by the act under review were a part of the common law and have long been a part of the law of the country. They have no doubt served a good purpose, but *when they become an instrument of extortion and blackmail, the legislature has the power to, and may, limit or abolish them*" (emphasis supplied) (p. 421).

Thus, in abolishing the right of action for alienation of affections, etc., the Legislature showed the public necessity required for the total abolition of a right to sue.

The Legislature has not presented such a case in relation to the abolition of the right to sue an automotive tortfeasor for property damage. Nor has alternative protection for the victim of the accident been provided, as evidenced by the facts here before the Court.

Had the Legislature chosen to require that appellant be insured against property damage loss—as is, in effect, required by Fla. Stat. § 627.733, F.S.A., with respect to other possible damages—the issues would be different. A reasonable alternative to an action in tort would have been provided and the issue would have been whether or not the requirement of insurance for all motorists was reasonable. That issue is not before us.

Retaining the right of action for damages over $550.00 (Fla. Stat. § 627.738(5), F.S.A.) does not correct the constitutional infirmity, but merely gives rise to another argument, that appellant has been deprived of the equal protection of the law solely on the basis of the value of her automobile in violation of Fla. Const., art. I, § 2, F.S.A., and U.S. Const., amend. XIV, § 1. It is unnecessary to reach the merits of this contention because the statute under consideration has already failed constitutional muster on other grounds.

Accordingly, the decision of the trial court holding Fla. Stat. § 627.738, F.S.A., to be constitutional and denying appellant a cause of action against appellee is reversed, and the cause is remanded for further proceedings not inconsistent herewith.

It is so ordered.

ROBERTS, ERVIN and McCAIN, JJ., concur.

BOYD, J., dissents with opinion.

CARLTON, C.J., and DEKLE, J., dissent and concur with BOYD, J.

BOYD, Justice (dissenting):

I dissent.

The judgment of the trial court should be affirmed for the following reasons:

The first reason is relatively simple. Plaintiff sought a judgment against defendant Manchester Insurance and Indemnity Company, from which she had acquired an automobile insurance policy, which admittedly did not protect her against the loss of her car by collision. She had signed a waiver, declining to purchase property damage insurance, after such coverage was offered to her, as provided by law. Since the offer of property insurance protection was made to plaintiff, and since she rejected that offer, the claim against the company that it was negligently liable for her losses was properly dismissed as being without merit.

The second reason we should affirm the judgment of the trial court reaches the Constitutional question involved. The question as to the constitutionality of the section of the statute denying plaintiff the opportunity to sue defendant White, on the ground that plaintiff had declined to purchase her own collision insurance, and was, therefore, her own insurer to the extent of $550.00, is one of great importance.

Plaintiff claims that the statute, by denying her the opportunity to litigate against defendant White, violates § 21 of Article I of the Constitution of the State of Florida,[59] by denying 'redress for an injury.' This Court must determine whether the statute does indeed deny access to the courts in such a manner as to conflict with the foregoing constitutional provision. Obviously, a literal and dogmatic construction of said provision would deny both the Legislature and the Court the power to impose reasonable and logical limitations on the constitutional right to use the courts of Florida. It, of course, is assumed that the citizens who adopted the 1968 Constitution intended that the language therein be given the same construction as similar language in the prior Constitution of 1885.[60]

This Court has held that the right to maintain litigation is not absolute but, rather, is subject to reasonable restraints. We have repeatedly upheld statutes of limitation, which prevented aggrieved persons from litigating for redress of injury, unless the suits were filed within a time specified by Statute.[61]

In some instances, we have followed the principles of the Common Law to bar certain actions where, admittedly, wrongs have occurred. In *Orefice v. Albert*,[62] we noted that:

> "It is an established policy, evidenced by many decisions, that suits will not be allowed in this state among members of a family for tort. Spouses may not sue each other, nor children their parents. The purpose of this policy is to protect family harmony and resources...."[63]

In other instances, the law of Florida contains many decisions which have upheld the constitutional validity of legislation modifying Common Law causes of action.

---

59. [FN2.] "The courts shall be open to every person for redress of any injury, and justice shall be administered without sale, denial or delay."

60. [FN3.] § 4 of the Declaration of Rights in the 1885 Constitution provided:
"All courts in this State shall be open, so that every person for any injury done him in his lands, goods, person or reputation shall have remedy, by due course of law, and right and justice shall be administered (sic) without sale, denial or delay."

61. [FN4.] See, *e.g.*, *In re Brown's Estate*, 117 So.2d 478 (Fla.1960); *Campbell v. Horne*, 147 Fla. 523, 3 So.2d 125 (1941). Both of these cases were decided in light of Art. III, § 33 of the 1885 Constitution.
"No statute shall be passed lessening the time within which a civil action may be commenced on any cause of action existing at the time of its passage."
The current applicable provision, Art. III, § 11(a)(7) of the 1968 Constitution, retains only one restriction upon the Legislature's power to alter the statutes of limitation—that such alteration may not be accomplished by means of a special law.

62. [FN5.] 237 So.2d 142 (Fla.1970).

63. [FN6.] *Id.* at 145.

In most of those decisions, the party presenting a constitutional challenge presented arguments similar to those of plaintiff in the present case. For example, in *Rotwein v. Gersten*,[64] legislation which completely abolished the causes of action for alienation of affections, criminal conversation, seduction, and breach of contract to marry was held to be proper and not prohibited by constitutional limitations. In *Rotwein*, this Court clearly stated that an individual does not have a vested interest or property right in a Common Law cause of action, and further noted that when a Common Law cause of action becomes an instrument of abuse, the Legislature can enact the necessary modifications.

The Florida "Guest Statute"[65] was also upheld in the face of constitutional attacks prior to its recent repeal by the Legislature. Prior to the enactment of the "Guest Statute," an individual could maintain a Common Law cause of action for the negligence of a driver of the vehicle in which he was riding. The "Guest Statute" modified such cause of action by relieving the driver from tort liability for ordinary negligence. In *McMillan v. Nelson*,[66] constitutional challenges were presented, urging, among other things, that the legislation deprived individuals of remedy under law, and violated equal protection and due process requirements. This Court rejected such arguments, and upheld the validity of the statute.

Finally, another instance of the latter type is the Workmen's Compensation Act.[67] Under that Act, an injured workman is provided a schedule of benefits from his employer without reference to the cause of injuries arising out of the course of his employment. The concept of 'fault' has been eliminated. Despite the fact that they modify Common Law causes of action, such laws have universally been held to be a legitimate and constitutional exercise of legislature power.[68]

Recently, in the landmark decision of *Pinnick v. Cleary*,[69] the Supreme Judicial Court of Massachusetts upheld that state's newly-enacted no-fault insurance law. As Florida's law provides that those Who decline to purchase property insurance coverage may sue to recover for collision damage only when such damage exceeds $550.00, the Massachusetts law, in an analogous manner, provided that those Who elected a deductible in their otherwise compulsory medical payments coverage, could sue to recover for "pain and suffering" only when total medical expenses exceeded $500.00. The Massachusetts court noted that:

> "The only limitation imposed by c. 670 on the potential plaintiff's prior right of recovery at common law is the elimination of damages for 'pain and suffering, including mental suffering associated with * * * injury' except in

64. [FN7.] 160 Fla. 736, 36 So.2d 419 (1948).

65. [FN8.] Section 320.59, Florida Statutes, 1971—repealed by § 1, ch. 72-1, Laws of Florida.

66. [FN9.] 149 Fla. 334, 5 So.2d 867 (1942).

67. [FN10.] Chapter 440, Florida Statutes, 1971, F.S.A.

68. [FN11.] See, *e.g., Mullarkey v. Florida Feed Mills, Inc.*, 268 So.2d 363 (Fla.1972); *Carter v. Sims Crane Service, Inc.*, 198 So.2d 25 (Fla.1967); *Wilson v. McCoy Mfg. Co.*, 69 So.2d 659 (Fla.1954); *South Atlantic S.S. Co. v. Tutson*, 139 Fla. 405, 190 So. 675 (1939).

69. [FN12.] 271 N.E.2d 592 (Mass.1971).

certain specified categories of cases. Section 5 of c. 670 provides generally that the reasonable and necessary medical expenses incurred by a plaintiff in the treatment of his injuries must be over $500 to permit recovery for pain and suffering. However, recognizing that certain types of injuries could entail considerable pain and suffering which would warrant monetary compensation regardless of medical expense incurred, the Legislature provided by way of exception to the general rule that damages for pain and suffering could be sought in all cases involving five designated types of injuries. These are a fracture, injury causing death, injury consisting in whole or in part of loss of a body member, permanent and serious disfigurement, and injury resulting in loss of sight or hearing as elsewhere defined in the General Laws. The victim whose injury falls outside these categories and whose medical expenses are less than $500 cannot recover at all for pain and suffering. *However, it is still possible for the person who desires to assure for himself recovery in excess of his out-of-pocket costs to do so. Just as he may elect a deductible if he has medical payments insurance to avoid duplicate recovery for medical expenses, so he may choose to keep both forms of insurance in full precisely to allow himself double recovery of these expenses.* Other forms of duplicate coverage are equally possible. It is true that the amount of excess he will receive thereby will bear no necessary relation to the value of his pain and suffering as arbitrarily set by a jury but, on the other hand, he is assured of some profit over out-of-pocket expenses in every motor vehicle accident. This certainty he was never afforded by his prior 'right' to recovery for pain and suffering in a suitable case, which in order to be realized even in such a case had to be actively pursued at considerable expense."[70]

Additionally, the *Pinnick* case is of particular interest because the arguments raised against the Massachusetts law mirror those made against the Florida law. It was argued that the Massachusetts law was defective in that it altered a vested property right, i.e., the tort action. The Massachusetts court rejected this argument:

"In arguing that the cause of action affected by c. 670 constitutes a vested property right, the plaintiff seems to ignore the distinction between a cause of action which has accrued and the expectation which every citizen has if a legal wrong should occur to find redress according to the rules of statutory and common law applicable at that time. The Legislature is admittedly restricted in the extent to which it can retroactively affect common law rights of redress which have already accrued. However, there is authority in abundance for the proposition that '(n)o person has a vested interest in any rule of law entitling him to insist that it shall remain unchanged for his benefit.' *New York Cent. R.R. v. White*, 243 U.S. 188, 198; *Munn v. Illinois*, 94 U.S. 113, 134...."[71]

---

70. [FN13.] *Id.* at 598–599. (Footnotes omitted) (Emphasis supplied.)
71. [FN14.] *Id.* at 599–600.

It was also argued that the Massachusetts law was defective in that it did not provide for a reasonable substitution for prior rights under the Common Law. The Massachusetts Court also rejected this argument:

> "We are urged to apply a test derived largely from the suggestion in *New York Cent. R.R. v. White*, 243 U.S. 188, 201..., that a State might not have the power under the due process clause 'suddenly (to) set aside all common-law rules respecting liability as between employer and employee, without providing a reasonably just substitute. * * * (I)t perhaps may be doubted whether the State could abolish all rights of action on the one hand, or all defenses, on the other, without setting up something adequate in their stead.' The proposed test may best be considered and understood, therefore, in the light of the facts before the court in that case.

> "The Workmen's Compensation Act dealt with in the *White* case substituted an administrative system of compensation for the common law rights of employees engaged in hazardous employments. The new system was compulsory on both employers and employees. The employee injured or killed in the course of his employment was entitled to a fixed compensation according to a prescribed schedule without regard to fault in almost every case. At common law the employee's rights against his employer were considerably circumscribed in fact by certain defences available to the employer. *Where he could succeed in making out a case, however, the employee stood to gain a great deal more from a jury than he would receive under workmen's compensation.* Viewing the overall operation and effect of the statute on both parties affected by it, the court indicated that the exchange of rights was adequate. With respect to the statute's effect on employees, it gave the following reasons: *'If the employee is no longer able to recover as much as before in case of being injured through the employer's negligence, he is entitled to moderate compensation in all cases of injury, and has a certain and speedy remedy without the difficulty and expense of establishing negligence or proving the amount of the damages.'* P. 201, 37 S.Ct. p. 252.

> "It is immediately apparent that c. 670 alters prior legal rights to a much less drastic extent than did the act involved in the *White* case."[72]

Finally, it was argued that the Massachusetts law was defective in that it conflicted with a Massachusetts constitutional provision, quite similar to Florida's Article I, Section 21, guaranteeing "redress for an injury.[73] This argument, too, was rejected by the Massachusetts court:

---

72. [FN15.] *Id.* at 605–606. (Footnotes omitted) (Emphasis supplied.)

73. [FN16.] Mass.Const., pt. 1 Art. XI, providing:

"Every subject of the commonwealth ought to find a certain remedy, by having recourse to the laws, for all injuries or wrongs which he may receive in his person, property, or character. He ought to obtain right and justice freely, and without being obliged to purchase it; completely, and without any denial; promptly, and without delay; conformably to the laws."

"Article 11 of the Declaration of Rights guarantees 'a certain remedy, by having recourse to the laws, for all injuries or wrongs which * * * (one) may receive * * *.' The article is clearly directed toward the preservation of procedural rights and has been so construed. See, e.g., *Cressey v. Erie R.R.*, 278 Mass. 284, 291, 180 N.E. 160; *Universal Adjustment Corp. v. Midland Bank, Ltd.*, 281 Mass. 303, 320, 184 N.E. 152; *Commonwealth v. Hanley*, 337 Mass. 384, 387, 149 N.E.2d 608. The only intimation which has been cited to us that it might have ramifications in the area of substantive rights is a dictum in *Commonwealth v. Boston Transcript Co.*, 249 Mass. 477, 482, 144 N.E. 400, that the Legislature might be precluded under art. 11 from abolishing an action for libel in certain circumstances as it had purported to do. However, changes in prior law are necessary in any ordered society, and to argue that art. 11 prohibits alterations of common law rights as such, especially in the face of the specific provision to the contrary in art. 6, flies in the face of all reason and precedent. To the extent that the dictum in the *Boston Transcript* case is to the contrary we decline to follow it."[74]

This Court is compelled to take notice of the controversy which existed for long years, relating to insurance rates and practices. A high percentage of the cases in Florida courts arose from tort claims, and these cases imposed upon the litigants the burdens of investigation of accidents, trials, appeals, and attendant legal fees. During all of this process, of course, the victims entitled to economic relief were required to 'sweat out' the outcome. A better system was not only needed, but became mandatory. After extensive investigation, hearings, and study, the Legislature enacted the present no-fault law. Prior to the enactment of our Workmen's Compensation Laws, similar legal machinations commonly caused long delays, and injured employees (in situations analagous to those injured or damaged by automobiles, and seeking redress under our insurance laws prior to the enactment of the no-fault law) were often required to accept unjust amounts in quick settlements to prevent long delays. For the greater good of society and social justice, the Legislature thus enacted both our Workmen's Compensation Law, and the no-fault insurance statute *sub judice*.

Surely the Legislature could have made it mandatory for all automobile owners to acquire collision insurance.[75] Obviously, if the state can require an owner to acquire insurance to absorb his losses, it can permit that same owner, at his discretion, either to acquire said insurance, or to be his own insurer.

I believe that the trial court was correct in dismissing the complaint and holding Section 627.738, Florida Statutes, 1971, F.S.A., constitutional. The judgment of the trial court should be affirmed.

I therefore dissent to the majority opinion.

CARLTON, C.J., and DEKLE, J., concur.

---

74. [FN17.] 271 N.E.2d at 600. (Footnote omitted.)

75. [FN18.] *Cf.*, *Williams v. Newton*, 236 So.2d 98 (Fla.1970), discussing the validity of Chapter 324, Florida Statutes, F.S.A., the Financial Responsibility Law.

Questions

1. How does the access-to-courts provision limit the state Legislature's power?

2. What is the "cut-off" date to which the Court must look when deciding cases dealing with access to courts?

3. How can the Legislature override the access-to-courts restriction?

4. According to the dissent, what are the "magic words" which determine whether the Legislature has run afoul of the access-to-courts provision?

5. What would the outcome of the case be if the Legislature amended the statute and allowed access to the courts only for persons who suffer damage to property as a result of the other driver's wanton and willful disregard?

6. What is the test for access to the courts?

Lasky v. State Farm Insurance Co.

296 So. 2d 9 (Fla. 1974)

DEKLE, Justice.

This appeal comes to us directly from the Circuit Court in and for Broward County and involves the constitutional validity of F.S. §§ 627.737 and 627.738, F.S.A., these being the portions of the 1972 Florida Automobile Reparations Reform Act (hereinafter referred to as the "no-fault" insurance act) providing for tort immunity in certain specified circumstances. Inasmuch as the trial court, in dismissing the action, expressly held the statutes in question to be constitutionally valid in the face of appellants' challenge, our jurisdiction has properly been invoked under Article V, § 3(b)(1), F.S.A., of our state constitution.

The pleadings reflect that Appellant Ann Lasky sustained personal injuries when driving her husband's car on February 18, 1972. The Lasky car was struck by a vehicle operated by Respondent May, and was subsequently determined to be a total loss. Because the Lasky car was a 1958 Ford, its replacement value did not meet the $550.00 "threshold" requirement of our no-fault insurance law as to property damage. Mrs. Lasky's injuries did not include any compound fracture or other injury which would bring her within the provisions of § 627.737(2) allowing her to recover damages for pain and suffering, etc., in the traditional tort action; if she comes within these provisions at all, it must be by virtue of the one thousand dollar medical expense "threshold" provision of F.S. § 627.737(2), F.S.A. The Laskys filed suit specifically seeking recovery for pain and suffering and property damage. Appellees moved to dismiss the complaint on the basis that the aforementioned statutes barred recovery; this motion was granted, the trial court specifically finding the statutes in question to be constitutionally valid in the face of appellant's challenge; this direct appeal ensued.

* * *

CONSTITUTIONALITY

Appellants here present a many-faceted attack upon the constitutional validity of both F.S. § 627.737, F.S.A. (limiting damages recoverable in a tort action for personal injury by denying recovery for pain and suffering and similar intangible items of damage unless certain conditions are met) and F.S. §627.738, F.S.A. (providing an exemption from tort liability for property damage). These statutes, it is asserted, violate appellants' rights of access to the courts[76] and to trial by jury,[77] deny them due process of law and equal protection of the laws,[78] and impose unconstitutional restraints on the right of non-residents to travel.[79]

Although the appellants' challenge is directed at both sections cited above, we need not tarry over the resolution of the challenge to §627.738 (property damage), inasmuch as we have recently held this section invalid on grounds that it unconstitutionally denied the right of access to the courts under Art. I, §21, Fla. Const. *Kluger v. White*, 281 So.2d 1 (Fla.1973).

We now hold, however, that, with one exception, the personal injury aspects of F.S. §627.737, F.S.A., are valid and constitutional.

The provisions for tort immunity in personal injury cases present questions differing from those present in *Kluger*. As we noted in *Kluger*:

"Had the Legislature chosen to require that appellant be insured against property damage loss—as is, in effect, required by Fla. Stat. §627.733, F.S.A., with respect to other possible damages—the issues would be different. A reasonable alternative to an action in tort would have been provided...." 281 So.2d at 5.

Sub judice, we have exactly that situation. F.S. §627.733(1), F.S.A., requires that:

"Every owner or registrant of a motor vehicle required to be registered and licensed in this state shall maintain security as required by subsection (3) of this section in effect continuously throughout the registration or licensing period."

F.S. §627.733(3), F.S.A., requires that security be provided either by insurance for the benefits contained in the no-fault law or by such other method approved by the department of insurance as providing equivalent security. Additionally, F.S. §627.733(4), F.S.A., provides that an owner of a motor vehicle as to which security is required and who does not have such security in effect at the time of an accident has no tort immunity, but is personally liable for payment of the benefits under F.S. §627.736, F.S.A., for personal injury and has all the obligations of an insurer under the no-fault insurance act. Thus, the owner of a motor vehicle is Required to maintain security (either by insurance or otherwise) for payment of the no-fault benefits, and has no tort immunity if he fails to meet this requirement. This provides a reasonable alternative to the traditional action in tort. In exchange for his previous right to damages for pain and suffering (in the limited class of cases where recovery of these ele-

---

76. [FN3.] Such right is asserted under Art. I, §21, Fla. Const.

77. [FN4.] Asserted under Art. I, §22, Fla. Const., and the Seventh Amendment to the U.S. Const.

78. [FN5.] Asserted under Art. I, §§2 and 9, Fla. Const., and the Fourteenth Amendment to the U.S. Const.

79. [FN6.] The basis for this right is not stated, but presumably rests on the Privileges and Immunities Clause of the Fourteenth Amendment, U.S. Const. In any event, the basic right is well-established.

ments of damage is barred by §627.737), with recovery limited to those situations where he can prove that the other party was at fault, the injured party is assured of recovery of his major and salient economic losses from his own insurer.

Protections are afforded the accident victim by this Act in the speedy payment by his own insurer of medical costs, lost wages, etc., while foregoing the right to recover in tort for these same benefits and (in a limited category of cases) the right to recover for intangible damages to the extent covered by the required insurance (F.S. §627.737(1), F.S.A.); furthermore, the accident victim is assured of some recovery even where he Himself is at fault. In exchange for his former right to damages for pain and suffering in the limited category of cases where such items are preempted by the act, he receives not only a prompt recovery of his major, salient out-of-pocket losses — even where he is at fault — but also an immunity from being held liable for the pain and suffering of the other parties to the accident if they should fall within this limited class where such items are not recoverable.

In *Kluger*, we held that the provisions of F.S. §627.738, F.S.A., invalidly deprived persons of their right of access to the courts where the statute deprived a person of any and all means by which he could be made whole for property damage less than five hundred and fifty dollars in amount, resulting from a vehicular accident, unless he voluntarily elected to purchase insurance for property damage to his own vehicle. Thus a person who elected not to insure his own vehicle against property damage, and who sustained damage to his car in the amount of five hundred and forty dollars as the result of the fault of another would be without recourse against anyone under s 627.738, despite a clear loss to him and even where evidence of fault of the other party was overwhelming.

The provisions of F.S. §627.737, F.S.A., present a totally different picture. As we have noted above, insurance coverage as to the personal injury benefits provided by the no-fault insurance law is compulsory. F.S. §627.733, F.S.A. In contrast to the property damage tort immunity section, all right of recovery is not denied, but only recovery for particular intangible elements of damage in a few situations; there is no immunity from tort liability for tangible damages resulting from injury except where the benefits provided in F.S. §627.736(1), F.S.A., are payable to the injured party by his insurer or would be so payable but for an authorized deduction or exclusion. F.S. §627.737(1), F.S.A. Thus the injured party will receive such benefits as payment of his medical expenses and compensation for any loss of income and loss of earning capacity under the insurance policy he is required by law to maintain, up to applicable policy limits, and may bring suit to recover such of these damages as are in excess of his applicable policy limits.

The exemption from tort liability for intangible damages (pain and suffering, mental anguish and inconvenience) is applicable only to a limited class of cases in which the benefits for medical expenses are less than one thousand dollars.[80] In computing

---

80. [FN9.] F.S. §627.737(2), F.S.A., referring to benefits payable under F.S. §627.736(1)(a), F.S.A.

the one thousand dollar figure, a person entitled to receive free medical and surgical benefits is credited with the equivalent value of the services so provided him, as a part of the $1,000. § 627.737(2). We also deem worthy of note that § 627.736(1) and (1)(a) specify as to medical expenses that these must be such as are "reasonable" and that such expenses shall be "for Necessary medical, etc." services. Strict observance of these wise legislative predicates applying to the $1,000 level, should serve to meet the arguments that the cost to the "rich man" will easily exceed such a threshold while the services "that a poor man cannot afford will always be under the threshold." In this day of ever-increasing medical and hospital costs, the $1,000 minimum seems less than illusory.

Unlike the arbitrary dollar limitation involved in *Kluger*, the provisions here involved create a reasonable classification. By providing that suit can be brought to recover for pain and suffering in situations where the "threshold" amount of Reasonable and Necessary medical expenses has been reached, the Legislature has made a reasonable classification, a point later discussed more fully. It is also provided that even where these conditions are not present as a basis for suit by the injured party against the tortfeasor, the injured party is still entitled to receive the benefits provided by § 627.736(1) (medical bills, loss of income, etc.) from his own insurer, which benefits are payable regardless of fault.

In exchange for the loss of a former right to recover—upon proving the other party to be at fault—for pain and suffering, etc., in cases where the thresholds of the statute are not met, the injured party is assured a speedy payment of his medical bills and compensation for lost income from his own insurer, even where the injured party was himself clearly at fault. Additionally, he can recover for such expenses which are in excess of his policy limits by the traditional tort action, and may recover for intangible damage (pain and suffering, etc.) by means of such suit in all but the limited class of cases above mentioned. Considering this pattern of recovery, together with the fact that coverage is made compulsory by § 627.733, there is a clear distinction from the total deprivation of any right of recovery for property loss under $550.00 disapproved in *Kluger*. The property provisions considered in *Kluger* did not allow any reasonable alternative to the traditional tort action; the provisions of F.S. § 627.737, F.S.A., do provide a reasonable alternative to the traditional action in tort, and therefore do not violate the right of access to the courts guaranteed by Art. I, § 21, Fla. Const.

* * *

RIGHT TO TRIAL BY JURY

Appellants' next contention is that the provisions of F.S. § 627.737, F.S.A., deprive them of their right to trial by jury under Fla. Const. Art. I, § 22, and the Seventh Amendment, U.S. Const., to the extent made applicable to the states by the due process clause of the Fourteenth Amendment, U.S. Const. We disagree.

We note initially that the no-fault law does not on its face purport to deal with trial by jury in any regard, and that accordingly any such deprivation must result, if at all, from the application of the act. The only manner in which the jury trial rights of appellants[81] are involved is found in the tort liability exemption provisions; that is to say, appellants are deprived of their right to a jury trial only in those cases where preexisting tort liability has been abolished by the act, removing the cause of action which would have been triable by a jury.

Does the abrogation of an existing cause of action, triable by jury, violate the right to jury trial? If such is the case, the Legislature would lose a great deal of flexibility, for it could not enact laws such as workmen's compensation acts, which abrogate a preexisting right to jury trial. As was stated by the U.S. Supreme Court in *Mountain Timber Co. v. Washington*, 243 U.S. 219 (1917), with respect to the Washington workmen's compensation law:

> "(W)e find nothing in the *Act* that excludes a trial by jury. As between employee and employer, the act abolishes all right of recovery in ordinary cases, and therefore leaves nothing to be tried by jury." 243 U.S. at 235. (Emphasis added)

Similarly here, the no-fault act abolishes *All* right of recovery of specific items of damage in specific circumstances, and, as to those areas, leaves nothing to be tried by a jury. *See also, Opinion of the Justices*, 113 N.H. 205, 304 A.2d 881 (1973), reaching a similar result as to New Hampshire's no-fault insurance act, and our own previous decisions upholding the validity of our workmen's compensation act. While the abolition of a *Cause of action* triable by jury might in some instance be unconstitutional on another ground,[82] the present statutory provisions do not violate the *Right* to trial by jury.

DISPOSITION OF PRESENT CASE

In most circumstances, the above discussion would suffice to dispose of the case before us, since we here uphold the ruling of the trial court dismissing the complaint as filed. However, the unique circumstances involved in this case persuade us that a simple affirmance of the order appealed would be contrary to the interests of justice. As noted earlier, the appellants in this action have now in fact exceeded the one thousand dollar "threshold" requirement of F.S. §627.737(2), F.S.A., and thus would be entitled, under the act, to pursue their claims for intangible damages for pain and suffering, etc., absent the trial court's order of dismissal prior to such a showing. To allow the earlier dismissal of the complaint with prejudice to stand would have the effect of depriving the appellants of their rights under the statute by virtue of dismissal of an action that had not accrued[83] as of the time of dismissal. Under such an interpretation, the dismissal in the instant cause would bar *all* recovery despite qualification

---

81. [FN17.] We do not purport to deal today with compulsory arbitration features as to insurers, such as may be found in F.S. §627.738(5), F.S.A.

82. [FN18.] *Kluger v. White*, 281 So.2d 1 (Fla.1973).

83. [FN20.] The use of the terms "accrued" and "cause of action" in this context is different from the historical definitions, due to the possible subsequent accrual of the further cause of action at such later time as the $1,000 threshold of F.S. §627.737, F.S.A., is reached.

thereafter to sue. We find such a construction untenable and hold that the plaintiff may sue for such damages once the "threshold" has been crossed, so long as it is within the statute of limitations. Where the "threshold" amount has not yet been reached, the cause of action cannot be said to accrue until such time as the "threshold" is crossed.

Accordingly, we remand the cause to the Circuit Court in and for Broward County to proceed, upon any required amendment, based upon the benefits payable to appellants under F.S. §627.736(1)(a), F.S.A., having now exceeded in amount the sum of one thousand dollars, in order to allow an opportunity to pursue a recovery in tort of damages for pain, suffering, mental anguish and inconvenience pursuant to F.S. §627.737(2), F.S.A., as the facts may appear, and for such other and further proceedings as may be necessary, not inconsistent with this opinion.

It is so ordered.

ADKINS, C. J., and ROBERTS, McCAIN and CARLTON (Retired), JJ., concur.

ERVIN, J., concurs in part and dissents in part with opinion.

BOYD, J., dissents.

ERVIN, Justice (concurring in part and dissenting in part):

F.S. Sections 627.737 and 627.738, F.S.A. of the "no-fault act" are facially unconstitutional. Insofar as the majority holds these sections in part unconstitutional. I concur, but insofar as they hold them in part constitutional I dissent.

These sections are an unwarranted deprival of the rights of motor vehicle accident tort victims without their consent to recover their actual, traditional and long-recognized bodily injury damages in actions at law from tort feasors.

These sections though represented to provide alternative remedies for tort action recoveries are in fact special interest legislation lacking due process and equal protection, and are violative of Sections 2, 9, 21 and 22 of Article I of the Florida Constitution, and the 7th and 14th amendments to the United States Constitution. Compare such cases as *Kluger v. White* (Fla.1973), 281 So.2d 1; *Fronton, Inc. v. Fla.State Racing Comm.* (Fla.1955), 82 So.2d 520, 523; *Faircloth v. Mr. Boston Distiller Corp.* (Fla.1970), 245 So.2d 240; *Cawthon v. Town of DeFuniak Springs* (1924), 88 Fla. 324, 102 So. 50; *Gates v. Foley* (Fla.1971), 247 So.2d 40; *Carter v. State Road Department* (Fla.1966), 189 So.2d 793, and *Grace v. Howlett* (1972), 51 Ill.2d 478, 283 N.E.2d 474.

These unconstitutional sections are patently unrealistic to modern medical costs and the disparities of individual wealth. They do not adequately provide for a reasonable equivalent to a tort action recovery. Moreover, they afford only insurance coverage "up to applicable policy limits." Their chief design is to eliminate tort action recovery under the threshold of $1,000 in order to facilitate the automobile liability casualty business by greatly reducing the benefits payable by casualty companies.

This Court has consistently held that a general law which fails to operate uniformly throughout the State is unconstitutional and invalid unless it contains a classification predicated upon a reasonable basis. *State v. Newell*, 85 So.2d 124 (Fla.1956); *Baker v. Gray*, 133 Fla. 23, 182 So. 620 (1938). Where an attempted classification is arbitrary and unreasonable, in that it excludes those similarly situated from the group, and there is no rational basis for classification, the statute will not be upheld. *Fronton, Inc. v. Florida State Racing Commission*, 82 So.2d 520 (Fla.1955).

In *Daniels v. O'Connor*, 243 So.2d 144 (Fla.1971), this Court stated that it is well settled that the equal protection clause is violated when a classification made by an act is arbitrary and unreasonable. However, when the differences in treatment between those included and those excluded from the class bear a real and substantial relationship to the purposes sought to be obtained by the act, the classification is valid, as against an attack under the equal protection clause.

Under Fla. Stat. § 627.737, F.S.A., entitled "Tort Exemption," there is an exemption from tort liability for damages because of bodily injuries, sickness or disease arising out of the ownership, operation, maintenance or use of a motor vehicle in this State. However, subsection (2) of this section provides that the injured party may bring an action in tort for pain and suffering in the event that the benefits payable under the act exceed $1,000, or that the injury or disease consists in whole or in part of permanent disfigurement, a fracture to a weight-bearing bone, a compound, comminuted, displaced or compressed fracture, loss of a bodily member, permanent injury within a reasonable degree of medical probability, or permanent loss of a bodily function, or death.

It further provides that any person who is entitled to receive free medical and surgical benefits shall be deemed in compliance with the requirements of this subsection upon a showing that the medical treatment received has an equivalent value of at least $1,000. Fla. Stat. s 627.736, F.S.A., in explaining what is meant by "reasonable amount," explains that no charge may be in excess of the amount the person or institution customarily charges for like products, services and accommodations in cases involving no insurance.

It is difficult to conceive why pain endured from a fall down a flight of stairs should be assigned a higher value than if incurred in a motor vehicle accident, but even assuming, *arguendo*, that the Legislature can, in the proper exercise of its police power, separate motor vehicle accident victims into a special class, and provide for them a remedy different than that available to persons sustaining similar injuries by all other means, it must nevertheless provide equally for the members falling within the same class. Stated differently, even where a valid basis for classification exists, it is impermissible for the Legislature to discriminate between members of the class.

It is a matter so well known that the Court should take judicial notice of the fact that medical expenses vary from geographical area to geographical area and even within geographical areas; but this is not even necessary here, since the complaint as amended makes these allegations which must be accepted as true.

Thus, it is clear, and the record clearly shows, that medical expenses vary from one area to another and within areas. Likewise, some people take longer to heal than others, some are more sensitive to pain than others, and some visit physicians more frequently, while others consult the medicine chest in their home. All of this, the threshold of $1,000 would ignore. Thus, upon application of the formula, if identical twins were injured in a common accident and one was taken to a hospital in Miami and the other to a hospital in Jacksonville, both having suffered identical injuries, the twin hospitalized in Miami could reach the $1,000 threshold twice as fast as the twin who was hospitalized in Jacksonville. The same absurd consequences would flow from the application of the threshold if the same twins were placed in the same hospital with the same identical injuries, but one was placed in a private room and the other in a semi-private room or a ward. The arbitrariness of the formula would further be compounded if they had different doctors who charged different amounts, and further, if one doctor happened to be a specialist and the other a general practitioner. How can the Legislature possibly contend that a statute which would breed such results can be said to rest on a rational basis? This legislation unabashedly favors the rich—who can afford to pay and are charged and do pay higher medical fees and thus reach the threshold much faster—over the less affluent.

The Legislature can do a better job than it has done. It unblushingly has decided to flatly ignore Section 21, Art. I, Dec. of Rights, Fla. Const. providing "The courts shall be open to every person for redress of *any* injury, and justice shall be administered without sale, denial or delay." (Emphasis supplied.) The Legislature has no authority to take away the rights of the public without their consent to recover for tort injuries.

The majority opinion is difficult to understand. It agrees with *Kluger v. White*, supra, as to the unconstitutionality of the $550 floor regarding property damage, but gives its unqualified approval to the $1,000 threshold in bodily injury cases.

In the $1,000 threshold "no fault" insurance gimmick much is "dredged up" by the majority to justify contravening the Constitution. According to the majority it will do all sorts of things "includ(ing) a lessening of the congestion of the court system, a reduction in concomitant delays in court calendars, a reduction of automobile insurance premiums and an assurance that persons injured ... would receive economic aid ... in order not to drive them into dire financial circumstances with the possibility of swelling the public relief rolls...." Moreover "the tort system ... tended to promote perjury ... etc." What a bonanza and blessing "no fault" immunity is! But what about the Constitution?

The majority labors the proposition concerning medical expense for bodily injury that the poor man and rich man are on equal footing. The rationalization is that all such expenses must be reasonable. But who is to judge and police the situation to bring reasonableness to bear in so variable an area. Usually the poor man goes into the hospital ward; the affluent into the hospital room. The wealthy get the finest doctors and the better medical treatment—such are the facts of medical life. Discrimination is quite apparent in this aspect of "no-fault" when viewed in terms of reality.

It appears to me that this subject should be re-reviewed by the Legislature not only to eliminate the patent violations of constitutional provisions, but to bring the provisions of the law into conformity with the traditional rights of the average citizen to vindicate his wrongs in the courts.

There have been many complaints in latter years that the courts are being replaced by bureaucratic administration; trial by jury is "old hat," and that special interests run rampant. There is little in these "no-fault" sections to lead one to believe otherwise.

There are certain fundamental rights to redress for injury or wrongs which the Constitution precludes elimination by the Legislature. Those tort remedies which are the subject of this litigation are fundamental. There may be a few borderline classes of claims, e.g., heart balm or breach of promise or some usury causes of action which for reasons of clear public policy and obvious compelling state interest may be eliminated by the Legislature, but not those of the traditional tort kind involved in the instant case where an arbitrary threshold limit of $1000 is plucked out of the air by the Legislature.

Diamond v. Squibb & Sons, Inc.

397 So. 2d 671 (Fla. 1981)

BOYD, Justice.

This cause is before the Court on petition for certiorari to review the decision in *Diamond v. E.R. Squibb & Sons, Inc.*, 366 So.2d 1221 (Fla.3d DCA 1979). Jurisdiction is predicated on conflict with *Overland Construction Co. v. Sirmons*, 369 So.2d 572 (Fla.1979). Art. V, s 3(b)(3), Fla.Const. (1972). We conclude that under the principle laid down in *Overland*, which was decided after the decision in the case under review, the district court of appeal was in error and its decision must be quashed.

On April 1, 1977, Nina Diamond and her parents brought this action against E. R. Squibb and Sons, Inc., based on negligence and product liability. They alleged that from July 27, 1955, to April 1, 1956, Nina Diamond, while yet unborn, had administered to her a drug known as diethylstilbestrol, produced by the Squibb company under the trademark "stilbetin." They alleged further that in May, 1976, they learned that teenaged girls whose mothers had been treated with stilbetin during pregnancy were developing cancerous or pre-cancerous conditions. The complaint charged that in developing, promoting, and marketing the drug, Squibb knew or should have known that it was not safe.

The defendant Squibb moved for summary judgment on the ground that section 95.031(2), Florida Statutes (1977), was applicable and barred the action. Section 95.031(2) provides:

> Actions for products liability and fraud under subsection 95.11(3) must be begun within the period prescribed in this chapter, with the period running from the time the facts giving rise to the cause of action were discovered or should have been discovered with the exercise of due diligence, instead of running from any date prescribed elsewhere in subsection 95.11(3) but in any event within 12 years after the date of delivery of the completed product to its original purchaser or the date of the commission of the alleged fraud,

regardless of the date the defect in the product or the fraud was or should have been discovered.

In response to the motion, the plaintiffs argued that section 95.031(2), if held to apply, would have abolished their right of action thereby depriving them of due process of law and denying them access to courts in violation of article I, section 21, Florida Constitution. The circuit court ruled for defendant and entered summary judgment.

Article I, section 21, Florida Constitution, provides: "The courts shall be open to every person for redress of any injury, and justice shall be administered without sale, denial or delay."

The operation of section 95.031(2) in this case has the same effect as it had in *Overland Construction Co. v. Sirmons*, 369 So.2d 572 (Fla.1979). The statute of limitations operated there to bar the cause of action before it ever accrued, so that no judicial forum was available to the aggrieved plaintiff. A majority of the members of this Court declared the limitations period unconstitutional as applied on the ground that it violated article I, section 21, Florida Constitution.

We find that binding precedent exists because petitioners' right of action was barred before it ever existed, as in *Overland*. We therefore hold that as applied in this case, section 95.031(2) violates the Florida Constitution's guaranty of access to courts.

The district court's decision is quashed and the cause is remanded to that court with directions to vacate the judgment and remand to the circuit court for further proceedings consistent with this opinion.

It is so ordered.

SUNDBERG, C.J., and ADKINS, OVERTON and ENGLAND, JJ, concur.

McDONALD, J., concurs specially with an opinion.

ALDERMAN, J., dissents.

McDONALD, Justice, specially concurring.

I have questioned whether the doctrine articulated in *Overland Construction Co. v. Sirmons*, 369 So.2d 572 (Fla.1979), is an unwarranted curb on the legislature's power and do not embrace it.[84] I do, however, concur in the results of this decision.

The sale and ingestion of the alleged defective product took place in 1955–1956. It is alleged that the effect of that ingestion did not materialize until after the plaintiff reached puberty. In this plaintiff's case the claim would have been barred, even though the wrongful act had taken place, before the injury became evident. She had an accrued cause of action but it was not recognizable, through no fault of hers, because the injury had not manifested itself. This is different from a situation where the injury is not inflicted for more than twelve years from the sale of the product. When an

---

84. [FN*] See *Battilla v. Allis Chalmers Mfg. Co.*, 392 So.2d 874 (Fla.1980).

injury has occurred but a cause of action cannot be pursued because the results of the injury could not be discovered, a statute of limitation barring the action does, in my judgment, bar access to the courts and is constitutionally impermissive.

Questions

1. What is the important distinction between the situation in *Kluger* and that in *Lasky*, which explains the different outcomes?

2. Articulate the rule enunciated in *Squibb*.

3. Does *Squibb* contradict the Court's holding that statutes of limitation do not abrogate one's right to seek redress?

Damiano v. McDaniel
689 So. 2d 1059 (Fla. 1997)

GRIMES, Justice.

We review *Damiano v. McDaniel*, 670 So.2d 1198, 1199 (Fla. 4th DCA 1996), which certified to this Court the following question:

> IS THE MEDICAL MALPRACTICE STATUTE OF REPOSE UNCONSTI-TUTIONALLY APPLIED, AS A VIOLATION OF ARTICLE I, SECTION 21 OF THE FLORIDA CONSTITUTION, IN BARRING AN ACTION FOR MEDICAL MALPRACTICE WHERE THE INJURY, RESULTING IN AIDS, DOES NOT MANIFEST ITSELF WITHIN THE STATUTORY FOUR YEAR TERM FROM THE DATE OF THE INCIDENT RESULTING IN THE SUB-SEQUENT INFECTION?

We have jurisdiction under article V, section 3(b)(4) of the Florida Constitution.

Francine Damiano received an HIV-infected blood transfusion in June of 1986. She tested positive for HIV in April of 1990. By that time, she had infected her husband. The Damianos filed suit in 1992 against Ms. Damiano's physician, Dr. Mc-Daniel, and the blood center which had supplied the blood for her transfusion. The complaint alleged that Dr. McDaniel had negligently ordered blood transfusions for Ms. Damiano when she was not in a life-threatening situation even though he knew of the risk of HIV contamination of donated blood. The trial court entered summary judgment in favor of Dr. McDaniel on the ground that the suit was barred by the statute of repose for medical malpractice. §95.11(4)(b), Fla.Stat. (1989).[85] The Fourth

---

85. [FN1.] Section 95.11(4)(b), Florida Statutes (1989), states in relevant part:
> An action for medical malpractice shall be commenced within 2 years from the time the incident giving rise to the action occurred or within 2 years from the time the incident is discovered, or should have been discovered with the exercise of due diligence; however, *in no event shall the action be commenced later than 4 years from the date of the incident or oc-currence out of which the cause of action accrued....* In those actions covered by this paragraph in which it can be shown that fraud, concealment, or intentional misrepresentation of fact prevented the discovery of the injury within the 4-year period, the period of limitations is extended forward 2 years from the time that the injury is discovered or should have been discovered with the exercise of due diligence, but in no event to exceed 7 years from the

District Court of Appeal affirmed the summary judgment but certified the foregoing question to this Court. We find that the certified question has been resolved adversely to the Damianos by this Court's prior decisions.[86]

In *Carr v. Broward County*, 541 So.2d 92 (Fla.1989), we explained that section 95.11(4)(b) "prescribes (1) a statute of limitations of two years; (2) a statute of repose of four years absent fraud or intentional misconduct; and (3) a statute of repose of seven years where there is an allegation that fraud, concealment, or intentional misrepresentation of fact prevented discovery of the negligent conduct." *Id.* at 94. We also pointed out that the running of the statute of repose begins with the incident of malpractice. We then upheld the statute of repose against a claim that the statute unconstitutionally denied access to the courts, reasoning that the legislature had properly found an overpowering public necessity for the enactment of the statute, consistent with the principles of *Kluger v. White*, 281 So.2d 1, 4 (Fla.1973). Subsequently, in *University of Miami v. Bogorff*, 583 So.2d 1000, 1004 (Fla.1991), we held that the statute of repose may be constitutionally applied to bar claims even when the cause of action does not accrue until after the period of repose has expired.

The Damianos contend that the statute of repose did not begin to run until they were put on notice that an injury had occurred. We dispelled a similar argument in *Kush v. Lloyd*, 616 So.2d 415 (Fla.1992). In *Kush*, we addressed the application of the statute of repose to a wrongful birth malpractice action alleging negligent failure to diagnose an inheritable genetic impairment. After their first son was born with deformities, the plaintiffs underwent genetic testing but were never informed that the mother had a genetic abnormality. The suit was filed following the birth of their second genetically impaired son, seven years after the alleged malpractice incident. While recognizing that the cause of action for purposes of the statute of limitations did not accrue until the birth of the second son, *id.* at 421, we held that the suit was nevertheless barred by the statute of repose. We explained the rationale for what otherwise might appear to be a harsh result:

> [T]he medical malpractice statute of repose represents a legislative determination that there must be an outer limit beyond which medical malpractice suits may not be instituted. In creating a statute of repose which was longer

---

date the incident giving rise to the injury occurred.
(Emphasis added.) The validity of the claim against the blood center is not before us. *See Silva v. Southwest Florida Blood Bank*, 601 So.2d 1184 (Fla.1992) (section 95.11(4)(b), Florida Statutes (1991), inapplicable to claim against blood bank for delivery of tainted blood).

86. [FN2.] While this Court has not had occasion to apply the statute of repose to a malpractice case involving HIV/AIDS, the district courts of appeal have done so on several occasions. In each instance, these courts have held that the receipt of the tainted blood triggers the running of the four-year statute of repose regardless of when the victim gains knowledge of the infection. *Dampf v. Furst*, 624 So.2d 368 (Fla. 3d DCA 1993), *review denied*, 634 So.2d 623 (Fla.1994); *Padgett v. Shands Teaching Hosp. & Clinics, Inc.*, 616 So.2d 467 (Fla. 1st DCA 1993); *Doe v. Shands Teaching Hosp. & Clinics, Inc.*, 614 So.2d 1170 (Fla. 1st DCA 1993); *Whigham v. Shands Teaching Hosp. & Clinics, Inc.*, 613 So.2d 110 (Fla. 1st DCA 1993).

than the two-year statute of limitation, the legislature attempted to balance the rights of injured persons against the exposure of health care providers to liability for endless periods of time. Once we determined that the statute was constitutional, our review of its merits was complete. This Court is not authorized to second-guess the legislature's judgment.

Id. at 421–22. The same result inheres in the instant case. While the Damianos' cause of action for purposes of the statute of limitations would not have accrued until they learned that Ms. Damiano was HIV-positive, their suit was nevertheless barred by operation of the statute of repose, which began to run with the alleged incident of malpractice.

We answer the certified question in the negative and approve the decision below.[87]

It is so ordered.

OVERTON, HARDING, WELLS and ANSTEAD, JJ., concur.

KOGAN, C.J., and SHAW, J., dissent.

I. Article I, Section 22 — Right to Jury Trial

Like Article I, Section 21, this provision protects the civil justice system. A similar provision protecting the right to jury trial has appeared in all previous Florida Constitutions.

In re Forfeiture of 1978 Chevrolet Van

493 So. 2d 433 (Fla. 1986)

EHRLICH, Justice.

We have for review a decision of the Fourth District Court of Appeal, *In re Forfeiture of One 1978 Chevrolet Van*, 467 So.2d 808 (Fla. 4th DCA 1985), which directly and expressly conflicts with a decision of another district court, *Smith v. Hindery*, 454 So.2d 663 (Fla. 1st DCA 1984), on the question of whether there is a right to a jury trial under article I, section 22 of the Florida Constitution, in civil forfeiture proceedings instituted under Florida's Contraband Forfeiture Act, sections 932.701–.704, Florida Statutes (1983).[88] The district court in the instant case concluded that there is such a right. We agree and approve the decision below.

---

87. [FN4.] We reject the Damianos' reliance on *Diamond v. E.R. Squibb & Sons, Inc.*, 397 So.2d 671 (Fla.1981). That case was decided years before our decisions in *Carr v. Broward County*, 541 So.2d 92 (Fla.1989), *University of Miami v. Bogorff*, 583 So.2d 1000 (Fla.1991), *Kush v. Lloyd*, 616 So.2d 415 (Fla.1992), and *Harriman v. Nemeth*, 616 So.2d 433 (Fla.1993). Moreover, *Diamond* was a products liability action involving an entirely different statute of repose.

88. [FN1.] This act provides for seizure and forfeiture to the state of personal property which is used in the commission of a felony.

In November 1983, Lloyd Green, the respondent in this action, was arrested for the sale, delivery, or possession with intent to sell a controlled substance in violation of section 893.13(1)(a)2, Florida Statutes (1983). At the time of his arrest Green's 1978 Chevy van, .45 caliber handgun, and over $4,000 in cash were seized. Shortly after Green's arrest, the Broward County Sheriff, petitioner herein, initiated forfeiture proceedings pursuant to section 932.704, Florida Statutes (1983). Green made a timely request for a jury trial which was denied by the trial court. After a trial on the merits before the trial court, a final order of forfeiture of all the personal property at issue was entered.

On appeal, the district court held that the denial of Green's request for a jury trial was error, reversed the order of forfeiture and remanded for a jury trial.

Article I, section 22 of the Florida Constitution (1968) provides in part: "The right of trial by jury shall be secure to all and remain inviolate." Our first constitution of 1838, which became effective upon Florida's admittance to the Union in 1845, and all subsequent constitutions have contained similar provisions. This provision guarantees the right to trial by jury in those cases in which the right was enjoyed at the time this state's first constitution became effective in 1845. *State v. Webb*, 335 So.2d 826 (Fla.1976); *Carter v. State Road Department*, 189 So.2d 793 (Fla.1966); *Pugh v. Bowden*, 54 Fla. 302, 45 So. 499 (1907). With this rule in mind, the district court looked to the scholarly opinion of the United States Circuit Court for the Seventh Judicial Circuit in *United States v. One 1976 Mercedes Benz 280S*, 618 F.2d 453 (7th Cir.1980), and concluded that "the existence of forfeiture proceedings at common law with the right to jury trial supports the contention that article I, section 22, of the Florida Constitution entitles one to a jury trial in forfeiture proceedings under Chapter 932, Florida Statutes." 467 So.2d at 809.

The district court recognized that its decision was in direct conflict with that of the First District Court in *Smith v. Hindery*, 454 So.2d 663 (Fla. 1st DCA 1984). When faced with this issue, the *Smith* court concluded "[t]he Florida Contraband Forfeiture Act did not exist at common law, and there is therefore no right to a jury trial in a forfeiture proceeding under that Act." 454 So.2d at 664. The query of the *Smith* Court appears to have been whether this *specific act* existed at common law. The district court below concluded "[t]he question is not whether this specific act existed at that time, but whether forfeiture proceedings were known to the common law." 467 So.2d at 809.

The State of Florida, as amicus curiae, contends that in rem forfeiture proceedings,[89] such as those instituted pursuant to chapter 932, are not a "part of the common law," as such proceedings are statutory in nature and are not the result of judicial decision. Therefore, article I, section 22 does not secure the right to a jury trial in such proceedings. The state clearly misapprehends the scope of the term "common law" as utilized in this context.

---

89. [FN2.] The Florida Contraband Forfeiture Act provides for a statutory forfeiture in rem, against the property itself, as opposed to a common law forfeiture upon conviction which is in personam against the defendant. *See* 37 C.J.S. Forfeiture § 2 (1943).

First, we note that the term "common law" does not appear in article I, section 22 or in any prior state constitutional provision on the subject, as it does in the provision's federal counterpart. The seventh amendment to the United States Constitution provides in part:

> In Suits at common law, where the value in controversy shall exceed twenty dollars, the right of trial by jury shall be preserved....

Although the seventh amendment guarantee to the right of trial by jury is only binding upon federal courts, this Court has recognized that federal decisions construing it are helpful and persuasive in construing this state's constitutional provision of like import. *Dudley v. Harrison McCready & Co.*, 127 Fla. 687, 173 So. 820 (1937). Therefore, it is apparent to us that reference to the "common law" in regard to the right to a jury trial under our state constitution is the result of reliance on federal decisions construing that right under the seventh amendment to the United States Constitution. As used in the context of the right to a jury trial under the seventh amendment, the term "common law" is used in a jurisdictional sense "in contradistinction to equity, and admiralty, and maritime jurisprudence." *Parsons v. Bedford, Breedlove & Robeson*, 28 U.S. (3 Pet.) 433, 446 (1830). It includes not only the *lex non scripta* but also the written statutes enacted by both Parliament and Congress. *See, e.g., People v. One 1941 Chevrolet Coupe*, 37 Cal.2d 283, 231 P.2d 832, 835 (1951); *One 1976 Mercedes Benz*, 618 F.2d at 456–57.

The constitutional right to a trial by jury is not to be narrowly construed. *See Hollywood, Inc. v. City of Hollywood*, 321 So.2d 65 (Fla.1975). This right is not limited strictly to those specific proceedings in which it existed before the adoption of our constitution, but should be extended to proceedings of like nature as they may arise. *Wiggins v. Williams*, 36 Fla. 637, 18 So. 859 (1896). *Accord, People v. One 1941 Chevrolet Coupe*, 37 Cal.2d 283, 231 P.2d 832 (1951); *State v. 1920 Studebaker*, 120 Or. 254, 251 P. 701 (1926); *Colon v. Lisk*, 13 A.D. 195, 43 N.Y.S. 364, *affd*, 153 N.Y. 188, 47 N.E. 302 (1897).

In *Wiggins v. Williams* this Court stated:

> "[W]hen the right of trial by jury is secured by constitutional provision in general terms like ours, and without any qualification or restriction, it must be understood as retained in all those cases that were triable by jury according to the course of the common law. The provision in the first Constitution [securing the right of jury by trial] contemplated, without doubt, a continuation of jury trials in all cases where such was the practice at the common law, and there is nothing in the subsequent Constitutions to indicate a change of meaning in this respect." [quoting *Buckman v. State*, 34 Fla. 48, 15 So. 697 (1894).] ... The authorities, with great uniformity hold that constitutional provisions like ours were designed to preserve and guarantee the right of trial by jury in proceedings according to the course of the common law as known and practiced at the time of the adoption of the Constitution.

* * *

"[T]he Constitution was intended to provide for the future as well as the past, to protect the rights of the people by every safeguard which their wisdom and experience then approved, whether those rights then existed by rules of the common law, or might from time to time arise out of subsequent legislation. All the rights, whether then or thereafter arising, which would properly fall into those classes of rights to which by the course of the common law the trial by jury was secured, were intended to be embraced within this article. Hence, it is not the time when the violated right first had its existence, or whether the statute which gives rise to it was adopted before or after the Constitution, that we are to regard as the criterion of the extent of this provision of the Constitution, but it is the nature of the controversy between the parties, and its fitness to be tried by a jury according to the rules of the common law, that must decide the question." [quoting *Plimpton v. Town of Somerset*, 33 Vt. 283 (1860).]

36 Fla. at 650–51, 653, 18 So. at 863–64.

We cannot agree with the state that the district court "misstated" the issue presented. However, we conclude that the more precise inquiry to be made in this case is: whether under English and American practice at the time Florida's first constitution became effective in 1845, there existed a right to a jury trial in civil proceedings in rem for the enforcement of statutory forfeitures.[90]

After an exhaustive historical analysis of civil in rem forfeiture proceedings, the Seventh Circuit in *One Mercedes Benz* concluded that as of 1791, the effective date of the Bill of Rights, it was the practice in both England and America to provide for a jury trial in such proceedings. 618 F.2d at 458. Under section 9 of the Judiciary Act of 1789, as of 1791 in America, if the seizure occurred on land the trial court sat as a court of common law and the trial was by jury; if the seizure occurred on navigable waters the court sat as a court of admiralty and trial was by the court. 618 F.2d at 459. It appears that prior to 1791 all seizures in England, for violation of laws of revenue, trade and navigation were tried by a jury in the court of exchequer, according to the course of the common law. *Id.* at 462–63. It also appears the Judiciary Act of 1789 was Congress's attempt to reinstate the right to a jury trial which had been taken away from the colonists by Parliament when it placed jurisdiction over forfeiture proceedings in rem in the colonies' admiralty courts. *Id.* at 463–65.

The conclusion that prior to 1791 forfeiture proceedings within the common law jurisdiction of the United States District Courts were tried before a jury is well supported. *See, e.g., United States v. The Betsey and Charlotte*, 8 U.S. (4 Cranch) 443

90. [FN3.] We note this inquiry is similar to that employed by the Seventh Circuit in *One Mercedes Benz*. The Seventh Circuit in *One Mercedes Benz* conducted a "historical investigation" to determine "whether under English and American practice [prior to December 15, 1791, the effective date of the Bill of Rights] trial by jury was utilized in civil proceedings *in rem* for enforcement of statutory forfeitures in violation of customs laws or other statutes; or whether, on the other hand, such a proceeding fell within the scope of equity or admiralty, where jury trial was traditionally unavailable." 618 F.2d at 458 (footnotes omitted).

(1808); *C.J. Hendry Co. v. Moore*, 318 U.S. 133 (1943); Warren, *New Light on the History of the Federal Judiciary Act of 1789*, 37 Harv.L.R. 49, 74–75 (1923).

We agree with the conclusions reached by the Seventh Circuit in *One Mercedes Benz;* and, therefore, conclude that as of 1845 there was a right to a jury trial in in rem forfeiture proceedings heard in the common law courts. We note that the majority of jurisdictions which have provisions similar to article I, section 22 have likewise held that there is a right to a trial by jury in proceedings to enforce civil forfeiture statutes. *See, e.g., People v. One 1941 Chevrolet Coupe,* 37 Cal.2d 283, 231 P.2d 832 (1951); *State v. 1920 Studebaker,* 120 Or. 254, 251 P. 701 (1926); *Keeter v. State ex rel. Sage,* 82 Okl. 89, 198 P. 866 (1921); *Colon v. Lisk,* 13 A.D. 195, 43 N.Y.S. 364 (1897); *See also Commonwealth v. One 1972 Chevrolet Van,* 385 Mass. 198, 431 N.E.2d 209 (1982).

Our conclusion that article I, section 22 preserves the right to trial by jury in in rem forfeiture proceedings is further supported by section 2.01, Florida Statutes (1983). Section 2.01 provides:

> The common and statute laws of England which are of a general and not a local nature, with the exception hereinafter mentioned, down to the 4th day of July, 1776, are declared to be of force in this state; provided, the said statutes and common law be not inconsistent with the Constitution and laws of the United States and the acts of the Legislature of this state.

This provision was first enacted by the territorial government of Florida as section 1 of the Act of November 6, 1829. It expressly makes English common law and statutory law as of July 4, 1776 part of the law of Florida. *Knapp v. Fredricksen,* 148 Fla. 311, 4 So.2d 251 (1941); *State ex rel. Williams v. Coleman,* 131 Fla. 892, 180 So. 357 (1938). Generally speaking, the common practice according to the common and statutory law of England prior to July 4, 1776 remains in effect in Florida unless and until it is modified or superseded by statute. *Le Roy v. Reynolds,* 141 Fla. 586, 193 So. 843 (1940); *Banfield v. Addington,* 104 Fla. 661, 140 So. 893 (1932).

It has been argued that the summary proceeding provided under section 932.704 has effectively superseded any common law custom to provide for a jury trial in proceedings such as this. Such a result is precisely what article I, section 22 protects against. Article I, section 22 preserves the right to a trial by jury in those classes of actions where such right was recognized prior to 1845. As of 1829, the English practice of jury trial of statutory forfeiture proceedings became part of the territorial law of Florida. Our constitution preserves that right; thus, the legislature cannot abrogate it by statute.

Accordingly, we approve the decision of the district court below and disapprove any language in *Smith v. Hindery* which conflicts with this decision.

It is so ordered.

ADKINS, BOYD, OVERTON, SHAW and BARKETT, JJ., concur.

McDONALD, C.J., dissents.

Questions

1. What is the test used by the Court to determine whether petitioner was entitled to a jury trial?

2. How does the Florida provision differ from the guarantee found in the Seventh Amendment?

Broward County v. LaRosa

505 So. 2d 422 (Fla. 1987)

McDONALD, Chief Justice.

We have for review *Broward County v. La Rosa*, 484 So.2d 1374 (Fla. 4th DCA 1986), which expressly construes article I, sections 18 and 22 as well as article II, section 3 of the Florida Constitution. We have jurisdiction pursuant to article V, section 3(b)(3), Florida Constitution. The issue in this case is whether a county ordinance may constitutionally empower a local administrative agency to award actual damages, including compensation for humiliation and embarrassment, to victims of race discrimination. We hold that such an award violates both article I, section 22 and article II, section 3 of the Florida Constitution and approve the opinion of the district court.

Article I, section 1.06E of the Broward County Charter requires the county to enact provisions designed to protect its citizens from discrimination based upon religion, political affiliation, race, color, age, sex, or national origin. Pursuant to this directive, Broward County enacted the Broward County Human Rights Ordinance (ordinance) on June 2, 1978.[91] The ordinance created an administrative agency known as the Broward County Human Rights Board (board). Section 16 1/2-67(b)(8) of the ordinance provides that, if the board determines that a person has engaged in a discriminatory practice, it may order that person to take any number of affirmative corrective actions, including payment to the complainant of actual damages. This damage award may include compensation for humiliation and embarrassment suffered as a direct result of a discriminatory practice.[92]

---

91. [FN1.] Broward County, Fla., Code § 16 1/2-86 (1978). On June 9, 1983, the legislature enacted a special act known as the "Broward County Human Rights Act." Ch. 83-380, Laws of Fla. On November 6, 1984, a majority of the voters participating in a countywide referendum approved this special act. This act superceded ch. 161/2, arts. I II, and III of the Broward County Code. Accordingly, these sections of the code were repealed effective March 5, 1985. Notably, the corresponding provisions of the act and the ordinance appear identical. *Compare* ch. 83-380 Art. 3, § 7, Laws of Fla., *with* Broward County, Fla., Code § 16 1/2-67 (1978). Nevertheless, because the Broward County Human Rights Act is not at issue in the instant case and, therefore, is not before this Court, we refrain from addressing the constitutionality of this special legislative enactment.

92. [FN2.] Broward County, Fla., Code § 16 1/2-67(b) (1978), provides in pertinent part:
  (b) Affirmative action ordered under this section may include but is not limited to:
    (8) Payment to the complainant of actual damages for injury including compensation for humiliation and embarrassment suffered as a direct result of a discriminatory practice, any expense incurred by the complainant as a direct result of such discriminatory practice.

Clifton G. Smith filed a complaint against La Rosa with the board, alleging that La Rosa had refused to lease Smith an apartment because Smith was black. Following an investigation, the board determined that La Rosa had engaged in a discriminatory practice in connection with his rental housing units and ordered La Rosa either to pay Smith $4,000, representing compensation for humiliation and embarrassment, or to make available the same or a similar apartment. La Rosa filed suit in Broward County Circuit Court seeking a declaration of the ordinance's unconstitutionality and an injunction against enforcement of the final order. After a hearing, the circuit court entered a summary judgment in favor of La Rosa. On appeal the Fourth District Court of Appeal affirmed, ruling that section 16 1/2-67(b)(8) violated article I, sections 18 and 22 as well as article II, section 3 of the Florida Constitution.

Both parties agree that local governments have the power to adopt appropriate legislation to further the elimination of invidious discrimination in such essential areas of human concern as housing and employment. *See* 1984 Op.Att'y Gen.Fla. No. 84–97 (Oct. 22, 1984). The parties disagree, however, concerning whether a local government can constitutionally empower a local administrative agency to award common law money damages for noneconomic injuries such as humiliation and embarrassment. Broward County argues that both the circuit court and district court erred in finding such action constitutionally infirm. We cannot agree.

Article II, section 3, of the Florida Constitution mandates a separation of power between the three branches of state government. As the district court correctly pointed out, although the legislature has the power to create administrative agencies with quasi-judicial powers, the legislature cannot authorize these agencies to exercise powers that are fundamentally judicial in nature. *Canney v. Board of Public Instruction,* 278 So.2d 260 (Fla.1973); *La Rosa,* 484 So.2d at 1377; *Biltmore Construction Co. v. Florida Department of General Services,* 363 So.2d 851 (Fla. 1st DCA 1978). An administrative agency conducts a quasi-judicial proceeding in order to investigate and ascertain the existence of facts, hold hearings, and draw conclusions from those hearings as a basis for their official actions. *Commission on Ethics v. Sullivan,* 489 So.2d 10 (Fla.1986); *South Atlantic S.S. Co. v. Tutson,* 139 Fla. 405, 190 So. 675 (1939); *State ex rel. Department of General Services v. Willis,* 344 So.2d 580 (Fla. 1st DCA 1977). Admittedly, the boundary between judicial and quasi-judicial functions is often unclear. Nevertheless, we cannot imagine a more purely judicial function than a contested adjudicatory proceeding involving disputed facts that results in an award of unliquidated common law damages for personal injuries in the form of humiliation and embarrassment.[93]

We reject Broward County's implicit assertion that the distinction between judicial and quasi-judicial proceedings has no substantive meaning. The mere characterization of the board's power to award unliquidated damages as quasi-judicial does not change

---

93. [FN5.] We see a significant distinction between administrative awards of quantifiable damages for such items as back rent or back wages and awards for such nonquantifiable damages as pain and suffering or humiliation and embarrassment.

the fact that the power amounts to an unconstitutional delegation of judicial authority. Nor has Broward County convinced us that article II, section 3 applies only to the legislature and has no restraining effect on Broward County's actions.

The legislature created Broward County pursuant to article VIII, section 1(a) of the Florida Constitution. Therefore, as the district court aptly pointed out, "[i]f the legislature lacks the constitutional authority to establish an administrative agency empowered to try common law actions for money damages arising from humiliation and embarrassment, then surely Broward County also lacks such authority." 484 So.2d 1377–78.

Moreover, article V, section 1, Florida Constitution, provides that "[c]ommissions established by law, or administrative officers or bodies may be granted quasi-judicial power in matters connected with the functions of their offices." Clearly, this provision recognizes the distinction between judicial and quasi-judicial power and authorizes administrative agencies such as the board to be empowered only with the latter. Indeed, to interpret this constitutional provision otherwise would not only ignore its plain language, but would also vest the legislative branch with the authority to create courts other than the four types that the constitution authorizes.[94] We have previously held that such legislative action is prohibited. *Simmons v. Faust*, 358 So.2d 1358 (Fla.1978).

We also find that the section 16 1/2-67(b)(8) violates article I, section 22 of the Florida Constitution, which provides in pertinent part that "[t]he right of trial by jury shall be secure to all and remain inviolate." This provision secures the right to a jury trial in all cases that traditionally afforded a jury trial at common law. *Construction Systems & Engineering, Inc. v. Jennings Construction Corp.*, 413 So.2d 1236 (Fla. 3d DCA 1982), *review denied*, 426 So.2d 26 (Fla.1983); *Smith v. Barnett Bank*, 350 So.2d 358 (Fla. 1st DCA 1977). Broward County argues that the constitutional right to a jury trial does not apply in the instant case because common law did not recognize civil rights when Florida adopted its constitution. We reject this argument as inapplicable. Common law undeniably recognized actions for unliquidated damage awards. When a tribunal with the power to make such awards for humiliation and embarrassment tries an accused, that accused has an inalienable right to a jury trial.

We join the district court in commending Broward County for its moral commitment to eliminating invidious discrimination in important areas of human concern such as housing. Nevertheless, we also must agree with the district court that, despite the ordinance's laudatory purpose, section 16 1/2-67(b)(8) is constitutionally infirm. In light of this finding, we need not address the other issues that the county raises.

Accordingly, we approve the opinion of the Fourth District Court of Appeal.

It is so ordered.

OVERTON, EHRLICH, SHAW and BARKETT, JJ., concur.

---

94. [FN6.] Art. V, § 1, Fla. Const., provides in pertinent part that "[t]he judicial power shall be vested in a supreme court, district courts of appeal, circuit courts and county courts. No other courts may be established by the state, any political subdivision or any municipality."

Questions

1. What is the limitation placed on the Legislature by Section 22?

2. Does there have to be a specific common law cause of action in existence in order to require that a petitioner have a right to a jury trial?

J. Article I, Section 3 — Religious Freedom

All previous Florida Constitutions have contained some guarantee of religious liberty and prohibited a formal establishment of religion. However, the clause prohibiting even indirect government aid to religion comes from the 1885 Constitution.[95] In 2008, the Taxation and Budget Reform Commission proposed to eliminate this restriction, but the Florida Supreme Court invalidated the proposal as beyond the tax and budgetary remit of that commission. *See Ford v. Browning*, 992 So. 2d 132, 140–41 (Fla. 2008). In 2012, the Florida Legislature proposed an amendment to this provision which would have removed the restrictions on indirect assistance to religious organizations, but the amendment was rejected by Florida voters. The 2018 Constitution Revision Commission also considered removing the restriction, a move that prompted many citizens and government-watchdog groups to argue against such a proposal. Though it passed all committees, the full Commission failed to place this proposal on the ballot.[96]

In the following case, involving the program under which Florida students could obtain vouchers to study at private schools, including religious schools, both the trial court and the First District Court of Appeal focused on whether the voucher program fell afoul of Article I, Section 3's "no aid" provision. On appeal, the Florida Supreme Court resolved the case under Article IX, Section 1, and that Court's opinion will be dealt with later when we look at Article IX.

Bush v. Holmes
886 So. 2d 340 (1st DCA 2004) (en banc), *aff'd in part*,
919 So. 2d 392 (Fla 2006)

ON MOTION FOR REHEARING EN BANC

VAN NORTWICK, J.

Having considered en banc the arguments raised in this appeal, we withdraw our previous majority opinion and issue the following en banc opinion.

---

95. *See* FLA. CONST. OF 1885, Decl. of Rights, § 6.

96. *See* Constitution Revision Commission 2017–18, P4, Declaration of Rights, Religious freedom; sectarian aid, https://crc.law.fsu.edu/Proposals/Commissioner/2017/0004.html.

Governor John Ellis ("Jeb") Bush, Attorney General Charlie Crist, Chief Financial Officer Tom Gallagher and Commissioner of Agriculture Charles H. Bronson, as and constituting the Florida Cabinet; the Florida Department of Education; and the Florida Board of Education appeal a final summary judgment in which the trial court ruled that the Florida Opportunity Scholarship Program (OSP), section 229.0537, Florida Statutes (1999), facially violated article I, section 3 of the Florida Constitution. The central issue before us in this appeal is whether the OSP violates the last sentence of article I, section 3 of the Florida Constitution, the so-called "no-aid" provision, which mandates that "[n]o revenue of the state ... shall ever be taken from the public treasury directly or indirectly in aid ... of any sectarian institution." The appellants argue that article I, section 3, in its entirety, including the no-aid provision, imposes no greater restrictions on state aid to religious schools than does the Establishment Clause in the United States Constitution and that, as a result, the summary judgment must be reversed on the authority of the recent decision of the United States Supreme Court in *Zelman v. Simmons-Harris*, 536 U.S. 639 (2002), in which the court held an Ohio parental choice voucher program constitutional under the Establishment Clause. Further, the appellants argue that, if the no-aid provision is interpreted to prohibit the use of state funds to provide OSP vouchers for students attending sectarian schools, the provision would violate the Free Exercise Clause of the First Amendment. Because we cannot read the entirety of article I, section 3 of the Florida Constitution to be substantively synonymous with the federal Establishment Clause, we find the appellants' arguments without merit.

The first sentence of article I, section 3 of the Florida Constitution is synonymous with the federal Establishment Clause in generally prohibiting laws respecting the establishment of religion. In addition to the Establishment Clause language, article I, section 3 also includes the language of the no-aid provision, which expands the restrictions in state aid and to religion by specifically prohibiting the expenditure of public funds "directly or indirectly" to aid sectarian institutions. For a court to interpret the no-aid provision of article I, section 3 as imposing no further restrictions on the state's involvement with religious institutions than the Establishment Clause, it would have to ignore both the clear meaning and intent of the text and the unambiguous history of the no-aid provision. There is no dispute in this case that state funds are paid to sectarian schools through the OSP vouchers. Thus, we hold the OSP unconstitutional under the no-aid provision to the extent that the OSP authorizes state funds to be paid to sectarian schools. Finally, based upon the recent United States Supreme Court decision in *Locke v. Davey*, 540 U.S. 712 (2004), we hold that the no-aid provision does not violate the Free Exercise clause of the United States Constitution. Accordingly, we affirm the decision of the trial court and certify a question of great public importance to the Florida Supreme Court.

* * *

The trial court found that the "funds disbursed under the OSP emanate directly from the revenue of Florida and its political subdivisions" and that such disbursements result "in a dollar for dollar reduction in the funds of the public school or school district" where the student of the recipient parent was enrolled. Thus, the "funds are without question revenue 'taken from the public treasury' of a political subdivision" and are hence distinguishable from the type of state aid found constitutional in *Nohrr v. Brevard County Educational Facilities Authority*, 247 So.2d 304 (Fla.1971), and *Johnson v. Presbyterian Homes of Synod of Florida, Inc.*, 239 So.2d 256 (Fla.1970). The trial court expressly rejected the argument that, because state funds are disbursed to the parent or guardian of a student who then restrictively endorses the state warrant to the private school of choice, OSP does not directly or indirectly benefit any particular church, religious denomination or sectarian institution. The trial court declared section 229.0537 facially unconstitutional and enjoined appellants from taking any action to implement the OSP.

II. *The Florida Opportunity Scholarship Program*

In section 229.0537(1), Florida Statutes (1999), the Florida Legislature ... created the OSP to allow a student attending a "failing" public school to attend a private school, sectarian or non-sectarian, with the financial assistance of the state. Under the OSP, the state

> make[s] available opportunity scholarships in order to give parents and guardians the opportunity for their children to attend a public school that is performing satisfactorily or to attend an eligible private school when the parent or guardian chooses to apply the equivalent of the public education funds generated by his or her child to the cost of tuition in the eligible private school....

§ 229.0537(1), Fla. Stat. (1999). Thus, when a school is found by the state to be a "failing" school during two years of a four-year period, the school is required to notify parents and guardians of students attending such a failing school of the opportunity to enroll in a public school within the district which is not failing, or of the opportunity to receive a "scholarship," that is, a tuition voucher, by which a student may attend a private school. § 229.0537(2)–(4), Fla. Stat. (1999).

For the student attending a private school with assistance under the OSP, a state warrant is made payable to a student's parent or guardian and is mailed by the Department of Education directly to the private school chosen by the parent or guardian; the parent or guardian then is to restrictively endorse the warrant to the private school. § 229.0537(6)(b), Fla. Stat. (1999). The private schools participating in the OSP have specified requirements, including an agreement "not to compel any student attending the private school on an opportunity scholarship to profess a specific ideological belief, to pray, or to worship." § 229.0537(4), Fla. Stat. (1999).

III. *Article I, Section 3*

Article I, section 3 of the Florida Constitution provides:

> **Religious Freedom.** — There shall be no law respecting the establishment of religion or prohibiting or penalizing the free exercise thereof. Religious freedom shall not justify practices inconsistent with public morals, peace or safety. No revenue of the state or any political subdivision or agency thereof shall ever be taken from the public treasury directly or indirectly in

aid of any church, sect, or religious denomination or in aid of any sectarian institution.

As explained in the Commentary to this section, the first sentence of section 3 is "akin to the first clause in the First Amendment of the U.S. Constitution." Talbot "Sandy" D'Alemberte, *Commentary*, art. I, § 3, 25A Fla. Stat. Annot. 79 (1991). The second sentence is a continuation of the limitation on the exercise of religion which first appeared in the 1868 Florida Constitution, the so-called "Reconstructionist Constitution." *See id.* As for the third and last sentence, it is "much the same as under section 6 of the 1885 Constitution," *id.*, and there is no analogue to this provision in the federal constitution. Only the third and last sentence of article I, section 3, the no-aid provision, is pertinent in the case at bar because it is that provision which was the basis for the trial court's ruling before us.

A. *Historical Context for the No-Aid Provision.*

There exists no record from the constitutional convention that incorporated the no-aid provision into the 1885 Florida Constitution. Nevertheless, history tells us a great deal about the origins and intent of the no-aid provision which can assist us in its interpretation. *See State v. Butler*, 70 Fla. 102, 69 So. 771, 777 (Fla.1915) ("In construing and applying provisions of a Constitution the leading purpose should be to ascertain and effectuate the intent and object designed to be accomplished.... Every word of a state Constitution should be given its intended meaning and effect....").

Florida's no-aid provision was adopted into the 1868 Florida Constitution during the historical period in which so-called "Blaine Amendments" were commonly enacted into state constitutions. The primary purpose of these amendments to the various state constitutions was to bar the use of public funds to support religious schools. Justice Brennan discussed this history, observing that the "subsidy of sectarian educational institutions became embroiled in bitter controversies very soon after the Nation was formed." *Lemon v. Kurtzman*, 403 U.S. 602, 645 (1971) (Brennan, J., concurring). Into the 19th century, state governments looked to the church to provide education, often with government aid, and political disputes frequently arose over which churches or sectarian organizations should receive public assistance. *Id.* at 645–46....

Given this historical context and the highly restrictive language in Florida's no-aid provision, the drafters of the no-aid provision clearly intended at least to prohibit the direct or indirect use of public monies to fund education at religious schools.

In addition, the legislative history of the most recent general revision of the Florida Constitution in 1966–68, included in pertinent part in the record on appeal, confirms that the no-aid language was intended to impose restrictions beyond what is restricted by the federal Establishment Clause. The proposed revised Constitution forwarded to the Florida Legislature by the Constitution Revision Commission ("CRC") omitted what is now the final sentence of article I, section 3. *See Fla. H.R. Jour.* 1–3 (Extra.Sess.1967). This omission would have had the effect of equating the language of article I, section 3 with the language of the federal Establishment Clause. The legislature revised the CRC's draft, however, to retain the no-aid prohibition in addition to the Establishment Clause language. *See* H. Amend. 3 to Fla. H.R. 3-XXX (1967). By retaining the specific prohibition on using public funds to support sectarian institutions contained in the 1885 Constitution in addition to the Establishment Clause language, the legislature—and subsequently the electorate, which ratified the Constitution of 1968—made clear that article I, section 3 necessarily imposes restrictions beyond the Establishment Clause.

B. *The Language of the No-Aid Provision.*

Our interpretation of the no-aid provision must start with its text. *See Florida Soc'y of Ophthalmology v. Florida Optometric Ass'n*, 489 So.2d 1118, 1119 (Fla.1986) ("Any inquiry into the proper interpretation of a constitutional provision must begin with an examination of that provision's explicit language.").... The constitutional prohibition in the no-aid provision involves three elements: (1) the prohibited state action must involve the use of state tax revenues; (2) the prohibited use of state revenues is broadly defined, in that state revenues cannot be used "directly or indirectly in aid of" the prohibited beneficiaries; and (3) the prohibited beneficiaries of the use of state revenues are "any church, sect or religious denomination" or "any sectarian institution." We will examine each element separately.

Use of State Revenues. First, the no-aid provision focuses on the use of state funds to aid sectarian institutions, not on other types of support. As the trial court found, it is undisputed that the OSP uses state revenues to fund vouchers that are paid to private schools chosen by the parents or guardians of students. It is this use of state revenues which distinguishes the OSP from the facts in other cases in which the state has provided assistance to a religious or secular institution. *See* section IV below.

Directly or Indirectly. Second, the express prohibition of direct and indirect aid to churches, religions, sects or sectarian institutions in the no-aid provision evidences a clear intent by the drafters to bar a broad range of uses of state revenues to benefit sectarian organizations. The common meaning of "indirect" is "[n]ot directly planned for; secondary: *indirect benefits.*" *American Heritage Dictionary of the English Language*, 670 (1979) (emphasis added). Thus, the legislature need not use state revenues to provide direct financial aid to sectarian institutions for the OSP to violate the no-aid provision. An indirect or secondary benefit to sectarian institutions from the use of state funds would be sufficient to violate the provision.

Appellants argue that the OSP does not constitute direct or indirect aid to any sectarian institution because the vouchers are made payable to parents, who make the choice of the school in which to enroll their children. Even though the OSP gives parents and guardians a choice as to which school to apply a tuition voucher, under the OSP statute the parents must restrictively endorse the voucher to the school, and the voucher funds are then paid by the state to the school. Because of the broad language of the no-aid provision, prohibiting the use of state revenues "directly and indirectly" in aid of secular institutions, such an indirect path for the aid does not remove the OSP from the restrictions of the no-aid provision.

Appellants further argue that the funds from the OSP vouchers do not even incidentally benefit sectarian schools receiving the voucher payments. Appellants reason that, because the record in this case shows that voucher payments to schools do not cover the full cost of educating the student and the "shortfall" in the cost is subsidized by the schools or another source, the voucher payments cannot constitute "aid" as a matter of law. We cannot agree, and adopt the reasoning of the trial court set forth in the order on appeal:

> ... It cannot be logically, legally, or persuasively argued that the receipt of these funds does not aid or assist the institution in a meaningful way. The entire educational mission of these schools, including the religious education component, is advanced and enhanced by the additional, financial support received through operation of the Opportunity Scholarship Program.

Any Sectarian Institution. Third, the no-aid provision prohibits not only aid to "any church, sect or religious denomination," but also aid to "any sectarian institution." Thus, the no-aid provision does not create a constitutional bar to the payment of an OSP voucher to a non-sectarian school, if the state funds do not aid indirectly a religion, church or sect which owns or operates the school. On the other hand, because an OSP voucher is used to pay the cost of tuition, any disbursement made under the OSP and paid to a sectarian or religious school is made in aid of a "sectarian institution," the school itself, even if it can be shown that no voucher funds benefit or support a church or religious denomination. *See State ex rel. Gallwey v. Grimm*, 146 Wash.2d 445, 48 P.3d 274, 279 (2002) ("Neither party seriously disputes that the EOG Program [which provides tuition grants for upper division course work for use at public or private institutions to students who have completed an associate of arts degree or its equivalent and are considered financially needy] supports the subject colleges and universities with public funds.")....

The appellants do not dispute that sectarian schools receive state funds from OSP vouchers. The record reflects that the vast majority of the schools receiving state funds from OSP vouchers at the time of the hearing below are operated by religious or church groups with an intent to teach to their attending students the religious and sectarian values of the group operating the school. Evidence of record demonstrates, for example, that during the OSP's first three years, ninety percent of the students in Escambia County who utilized an OSP voucher were enrolled in a school operated by the Diocese of Pensacola-Tallahassee, a unit of the Catholic Church. The record further reflects that the mission of the Pensacola-Tallahassee Diocesan school system, according to its written Mission Statement, is

> to collaborate with parents in the Christian formation of students passing on to them the message of Christ taught by the Catholic Church. This is done in the context of Christian community which worships together, fosters service and strives to achieve academic excellence.

The Diocese's "Philosophy of Education" is stated, in part, as follows:

> The Diocese of Pensacola-Tallahassee sponsors pre-schools, elementary and secondary schools in Northwest Florida, dedicated to forming youth in the Catholic faith, developing Gospel values and fostering academic excellence.

V. *Article I, Section 3 of the Florida Constitution is More Restrictive than First Amendment of United States Constitution*

Appellants argue that article I, section 3 of the Florida Constitution should be interpreted in a manner substantively synonymous with the Establishment Clause of the First Amendment. We cannot agree. For a court to interpret the no-aid provision as adding nothing substantive to article I, section 3 of the Florida Constitution would require that court to ignore the clear meaning of the text of the provision and its formative history....

In *Silver Rose Entertainment, Inc. v. Clay County*, 646 So.2d 246, 250-1 (Fla. 1st DCA 1994), *rev. denied*, 658 So.2d 992 (Fla.1995), we explained that article I, section 3 utilizes the test established in *Lemon v. Kurtzman*, 403 U.S. at 612–13, so that a statute which "passes muster under article I, section 3 of the Florida Constitution necessarily meets the federal Establishment Clause tests." However, we noted that, in addition to the three-stage *Lemon* test,[97] article I, section 3 "adds a fourth: The statute must not authorize the use of public moneys, directly or indirectly, in aid of any sectarian institution." *Silver Rose*, 646 So.2d at 251; *see also Rice v. State*, 754 So.2d 881, 883 (Fla. 5th DCA), *rev. denied*, 779 So.2d 272 (Fla.2000).

... If article I, section 3 of the Florida Constitution was coterminous with the First Amendment to the United States Constitution, our inquiry in this case would be decidedly different, and a reversal would be mandated under *Zelman*. If we were resolving this case purely on Establishment Clause principles, the fact that the OSP program on its face has a religiously neutral purpose — to aid children in failing public schools — and the fact that the OSP gives parents or guardians the freedom of choice in selecting an alternative to a failing public school, would be dispositive factors, without regard to whether a disbursement was made directly to a parent or guardian rather than the school....

However, article I, section 3 of Florida's Constitution is plainly not identical to the First Amendment. As explained in *Silver Rose* and in section III above, unlike the First Amendment and the first sentence of article I, section 3, the no-aid provision contains a broad prohibition against the expenditure of state revenues. It prohibits the use of state funds either "directly or indirectly in aid of" not only churches, religions, and sects, but any sectarian institution....

---

97. [FN12.] The three Establishment Clause tests set forth in *Lemon* are: "First, the statute must have a secular legislative purpose; second, its principal or primary effect must be one that neither advances nor inhibits religion, *Board of Education v. Allen*, 392 U.S. 236, 243 (1968); finally, the statute must not foster 'an excessive government entanglement with religion.' *Walz* [*v. Tax Com. of New York*, 397 U.S.] at 674." *Lemon*, 403 U.S. at 612–13.

VIII. Conclusion and Certified Question.

In summary, we affirm the final summary judgment on appeal and hold that section 229.0537, Florida Statutes (1999), violates the no-aid provision found in the last sentence of article I, section 3 of the Florida Constitution because the OSP uses state revenues to aid sectarian schools. We also hold that the no-aid provision does not violate the federal Free Exercise Clause.

As did the trial court, we recognize the salutary public policy supporting the OSP legislation to enhance the educational opportunity of children trapped in substandard schools. Nevertheless, courts do not have the authority to ignore the clear language of the Constitution, even for a popular program with a worthy purpose. If Floridians wish to remove or lessen the restrictions of the no-aid provision, they can do so by constitutional amendment. *See* art. XI, Fla. Const.

* * *

ERVIN, ALLEN, WEBSTER, DAVIS, BENTON, PADOVANO, and BROWNING, JJ., concur.

BENTON, J., concurs with an opinion in which ALLEN, DAVIS, PADOVANO, and BROWNING, JJ., concur.

WOLF, C.J., concurs in part and dissents in part with an opinion. [omitted]

POLSTON, J., dissents with an opinion in which BARFIELD, KAHN, LEWIS, and HAWKES, JJ., concur.

* * *

POLSTON, J., dissenting.

Appellants argue that the trial court erroneously ruled in its final summary judgment that the Florida Opportunity Scholarship Program, section 229.0537, Florida Statutes (1999), violates Article I, § 3 of the Florida Constitution and is therefore unconstitutional. I agree with appellants that the Opportunity Scholarship Program is constitutional and would reverse....

The majority opinion is seriously flawed because it (i) fails to distinguish controlling Florida Supreme Court precedent, (ii) erroneously rules that the choice by the parents and guardians of the children benefitting from the program has no effect on the analysis of Article I, § 3, (iii) ignores the federal constitutional Establishment Clause analysis addressing indirect aid, thereby incorrectly ruling that the analysis of Article I § 3 is different from the federal constitution, and (iv) discriminates against religion in violation of the United States and Florida Free Exercise Clauses.

I disagree with the majority because I am of the view that the Establishment Clause of the Florida Constitution, which includes the no-aid language in Article I, § 3, as interpreted by the Florida Supreme Court, means the same as the Establishment Clause in the United States Constitution, as interpreted by the United States Supreme Court.

Therefore, I respectfully dissent.

I. SCHOOLS ARE NOT DIFFERENT UNDER ART. I, § 3

Appellant Attorney General Robert A. Butterworth argued that a general application of the trial court's construction of Article I, § 3, "would prohibit any religious institution from acting as a government service provider or participating in secular general welfare programs where there is only an incidental benefit to religion." There is no distinction between this Opportunity Scholarship Program and the state Medicaid program that funds religiously affiliated or operated health care institutions providing free or subsidized medical care (e.g., St. Mary's Hospital in West Palm Beach and Baptist Medical Center in Jacksonville). Other examples are legislative programs providing public funds to any public or private person or organization for preservation of historic structures, rent paid to churches for use of their facilities as polling places, and government subsidized pre-K or childcare programs operated by churches or faith-based organizations.

The Attorney General identified various legislative programs, in addition to Opportunity Scholarships, that eligible persons may utilize at private educational institutions across Florida, including those that are religiously affiliated or operated: Florida Bright Futures Scholarship Program, John M. McKay Scholarships for Students with Disabilities Program, Florida Private Student Assistance Grant Program, William L. Boyd, IV, Florida Resident Access Grants, Florida Partnership for School Readiness, Florida Postsecondary Student Assistance Grant Program, Jose Marti Scholarship Challenge Grant Program, Mary McLeod Bethune Scholarship Program, Critical Teacher Shortage Student Loan Forgiveness Program, and the Minority Teacher Education Scholars Program. No fewer than 23 religiously affiliated or operated private four-year universities in Florida are eligible to receive Bright Futures scholarship funds.

According to the Attorney General, the legislature has programs that provide funds directly to religiously affiliated educational institutions, stating that "in 2002, the Historically Black College and University Library Improvement Program provide[d] $8,974,038 in direct aid for library development to three religiously affiliated or operated private colleges: Bethune-Cookman College, Edward Waters College, and Florida Memorial College."

The majority states that its holding is premised on the history and intent of Florida's no-aid provision, as originally enacted, to prohibit the state from using its revenue to benefit religious schools, and then cautions that the holding "should not in any way be read as a comment on the constitutionality of any other government program or activity which involves a religious or sectarian institution." In other words, the majority says that schools are different under Article I, § 3. However, there is nothing in the language of Article I, § 3 indicating that it applies only to schools.

Moreover, there is no constitutional history indicating that it was the original intent of the drafters that Article I, § 3 apply only to schools. There is no record of the Florida 1885 Constitution Convention that adopted the relevant language. Because the constitutional history is completely silent on intent, the majority is correct in its characterization of the history of the no-aid provision as "unambiguous." It unambiguously provides no help in construing the language of Article I, § 3. We should not assume intent without more than we have before us....

Schools are not different. The constitutionality of this Opportunity Scholarship Program should be treated the same as other programs under Article I, § 3....

VII. THE MAJORITY'S RULING DISCRIMINATES AGAINST RELIGION IN VIOLATION OF FLORIDA'S FREE EXERCISE CLAUSE

The trial court, and the majority, simply rule that Florida's Establishment Clause, including the no-aid language, must be afforded great weight, without making any attempt to reconcile it with Florida's Free Exercise Clause. *See Local Union No. 519 v. Robertson*, 44 So.2d 899, 903 (Fla.1950) (ruling that when constitutional interests are competing, they should be harmonized to give effect to each). The trial court's interpretation of the no-aid language in the last sentence of Article I, § 3 erroneously conflicts with the Free Exercise Clause of the Florida Constitution. *See Chiles [v. Phelps]*, 714 So.2d at 459 (Fla.1998) (ruling that the Florida Constitution should not be read in a conflicting manner); *Capital City Country Club [v. Tucker]*, 613 So.2d at 452 [(Fla. 1993)].

Ignoring the Free Exercise Clause of Florida's Constitution in the first sentence of Article I, § 3, the trial court stated that the only portion of Article I, § 3 that had any relevance to the proceeding was the last sentence. The first sentence states: "There shall be no law respecting the establishment of religion or prohibiting or penalizing the free exercise thereof." The phrase "or penalizing" is not explicitly stated in the United States Constitution's Free Exercise Clause. To the extent that appellees argue that the additional no-aid language in Florida's Establishment Clause should be read as more restrictive, this additional language in the Free Exercise Clause should also be read as more restrictive. Instead of applying the same legal reasoning to both the Establishment Clause and Free Exercise Clause, the majority ignores this different language and states, without any analysis, that Florida's Free Exercise Clause means the same as the United States Constitution....

The Florida Constitution should not be construed in a manner that tips the scales of neutrality in favor of more restrictions and less free exercise of religion. I decline to do so.

Conclusion

I conclude that the trial court erred by granting final summary judgment in favor of appellees because the Opportunity Scholarship Program, section 229.0537, Florida Statutes (1999), does not violate Article I, § 3 of the Florida Constitution. Therefore, I respectfully dissent.

BARFIELD, KAHN, LEWIS, and HAWKES, JJ., concur.

Council for Secular Humanism, Inc. v. McNeil

44 So. 3d 112 (1st DCA), *rev. denied*, 41 So. 3d 215 (Fla. 2010)
Revised Opinion on Appellees' Motions for Rehearing
En Banc and to Certify Question

VAN NORTWICK, J.

Walter A. McNeil, Prisoners of Christ, Inc., and Lamb of God Ministries, Inc., appellees, have moved for rehearing en banc of our previous opinion in this proceeding, *Council for Secular Humanism, Inc. v. McNeil*, 34 Fla. L. Weekly D2557, 2009 WL 4782384 (Fla. 1st DCA December 15, 2009), and to certify a question of great public importance. By separate order, the court denies the motion for rehearing en banc. We withdraw our prior opinion, substitute the following opinion, and certify a question.

The Council for Secular Humanism, Inc., (CSH), Richard Hull and Elaine Hull appeal a final judgment on the pleadings on their amended petition seeking to have the trial court prohibit, on state constitutional grounds, appellee Walter A. McNeil, as Secretary of the Department of Corrections, from using State funds pursuant to sections 944.473 and 944.4731, Florida Statutes (2007), to support the faith-based substance abuse transitional housing programs of appellees Prisoners of Christ, Inc. (Prisoners) and Lamb of God Ministries, Inc. (Lamb of God). Count I of the amended petition alleged that payments to these organizations constituted payments to churches, sects, religious sects, religious denominations or sectarian institutions contrary to the so-called "no-aid" provision in Article I, section 3 of the Florida Constitution. Count II challenged the contracts which were entered into with these faith-based institutions under the same constitutional provision. Count III sought to bar the secretary from delegating government authority and powers to chaplains pursuant to section 944.4731(6)(a), which requires that, prior to placement of an offender in a faith-based substance abuse transitional housing program, a transition assistant specialist must consult with a chaplain if an inmate requests and is approved for placement. The trial court entered a final judgment on the pleadings in favor of appellees on all counts.

As to Count I, we reverse the order under review because the trial court erred in ruling that the no-aid provision was limited to the school context and, thus, did not apply to sections 944.473 and 944.4731. As to Count II, we affirm the trial court's determination that appellants lack taxpayer standing to pursue the Count II claims because those claims did not constitute a challenge to the government's taxing and spending powers. Finally, with respect to Count III, we hold that the amended petition does not state a cause of action under Article I, section 3, based on the alleged unlawful delegation of authority to prison chaplains. Accordingly, we affirm in part, reverse in part, and remand for further proceedings.

Count I

In passing on a motion for judgment on the pleadings, "all well pleaded material allegations of the complaint and all fair inferences to be drawn therefrom must be taken as true and the inquiry is whether the plaintiff has stated a cause of action by his complaint." *Martinez v. Florida Power & Light Co.*, 863 So.2d 1204, 1205 (Fla.2003) (quoting *Reinhard v. Bliss*, 85 So.2d 131, 133 (Fla.1956)). "The allegations of the defendant's answer are of no avail to him at a hearing on a defendant's motion for decree on the pleadings." *Id.*

As alleged in the amended petition, CSH is a nonprofit New York corporation registered to do business in Florida and is a Florida taxpayer. CSH alleges that it was formed to foster religious liberty by promoting the enforcement of the principle of separation of church and state. The Hulls are Florida taxpayers residing in Leon County and members of CSH. Prisoners and Lamb of God are both Florida nonprofit corporations which describe themselves as "ministries."

McNeil, as Secretary of the Department of Corrections, entered into contracts with Prisoners and Lamb of God under which these entities were obligated to provide faith-based substance abuse post-release transitional housing program services in return for which the ministries would be paid $20 per day per prisoner assigned to the programs. In their amended petition, appellants allege that these appellees are sectarian religious institutions which use Christian doctrine to carry out their work with participants in the substance abuse transitional programs; "that the faith-based component of the state-funded programs they provide includes teaching of Christian doctrine and attempts to encourage program participants to change their character by faith in Jesus Christ and other Christian doctrines;" that Prisoners is a member of the Coalition of Prison Evangelists; and that Lamb of God works in partnership with the Church in the Woods at Freedom Ranch, a Christian church operated by John Glenn, founder of Alpha Ministries, which appellants allege is an explicitly Christian organization. Finally, appellants allege that sections 944.473 and 944.4731 authorize the "payment of funds from the public coffers" to these "sectarian institutions" in violation of Article I, section 3.

Section 944.473(2)(a) requires inmates who meet certain criteria to "participate in substance abuse program services when such services are available." Section 944.473(2)(c) provides that "[w]hen selecting contract providers to administer substance abuse treatment programs, the department shall make every effort to consider qualified faith-based service groups on an equal basis with other private organizations." Section 944.4731(3)(a) adds that "contingent upon funding, the department shall enter into contracts with multiple providers who are private organizations, including faith-based service groups, to operate substance abuse transition housing programs ..." Section 944.4731(3)(b) requires that the department "ensure that an offender's faith orientation, or lack thereof, will not be considered in determining admission to a faith-based program and that the program does not attempt to convert an offender toward a particular faith or religious preference."

In our en banc decision in *Bush v. Holmes*, 886 So.2d 340 (Fla. 1st DCA 2004), this court addressed the constitutionality of the Florida Opportunity Scholarship Program (OSP) and held that the no-aid provision of Article I, section 3, which mandates that "[n]o revenue of the state ... shall ever be taken from the public treasury directly or indirectly in aid ... of any sectarian institution," prohibited those sectarian schools from receiving funds from the State through the OSP voucher program provided for in section 229.0537, Florida Statutes (1999). In *Holmes*, we explained:

The constitutional prohibition in the no-aid provision involves three elements: (1) the prohibited state action must involve the use of state tax revenues; (2) the prohibited use of state revenues is broadly defined, in that state revenues cannot be used "directly or indirectly in aid of" the prohibited beneficiaries; and (3) the prohibited beneficiaries of the use of state revenues are "any church, sect, or religious denomination" or "any sectarian institution."

886 So.2d at 352.

Upon review in *Bush v. Holmes*, 919 So.2d 392 (Fla.2006), the Florida Supreme Court did not reach the issue addressed by this court in *Holmes*. Rather, the court held that the OSP was facially unconstitutional under the provisions of Article 9, section 1(a) of the Florida Constitution. The Court neither approved nor disapproved of this court's decision in *Holmes*, 919 So.2d at 413. Thus, this court's majority opinion in *Holmes*, construing Article I, section 3, remains controlling law.

In the case under review, appellees argued below and argue on appeal that the no-aid provision and this court's decision in *Holmes* was limited explicitly to the school context and, thus, did not apply to the instant case. In its final judgment on the pleadings, the trial court accepted appellees' argument and ruled [that *Holmes* applied only in the context of schools].

This restrictive reading of the no-aid provision and *Holmes* was error. *Holmes* governs the case under review. Thus, we reverse the final judgment on the pleadings as to Count I.

Our *Holmes* decision did not limit its analysis to a "schools only" context. Further, nothing in the text of Florida's no-aid provision limits its application to the school context. As we discussed in *Holmes, id.* at 349–50, many state constitutions contain restrictions on state funding to religions or religious institutions, although the Florida no-aid provision is among the most restrictive. Some states limit the restriction to public funding of sectarian schools. The Alabama Constitution, for example, provides that "[n]o money raised for the support of the public schools shall be appropriated to or used for the support of any sectarian or denominational school." Ala. Const. Art. XIV, § 263; *see generally* Mark Edward DeForrest, *An Overview and Evaluation of State Blaine Amendments: Origins, Scope, and First Amendment Concerns*, 26 Harv. J.L. & Pub. Pol'y 551, 576–88 (2003). In contrast, the Florida no-aid provision broadly prohibits the use of public funds "in aid of any church, sect, or religious denomination or in aid of any sectarian institution." Fla. Const., Art. I, § 3.

In granting the judgment on the pleadings below, because the trial court ruled that the no-aid provision did not apply outside of the school context, it utilized an Establishment Clause analysis to conclude that the subject program in this case and the contracts entered into pursuant to that program are not unconstitutional. The trial court found that, the language in section 944.473(2)(c), which directs DOC to consider faith-based service groups on an equal basis with other private organizations, was merely an expression of a nondiscrimination policy that would prevent the state from excluding groups based on religion.

The appellants' claims in Count I are based solely on the no-aid provision in Florida's constitution, not the state or federal Establishment Clauses. Thus, we do not address the trial court's Establishment Clause analysis. As this court explained in *Holmes*, Article I, section 3 of the Florida Constitution is not "substantively synonymous with the federal Establishment Clause." 886 So.2d at 344. While the first sentence of Article I, section 3 is consistent with the federal Establishment Clause by "generally prohibiting laws respecting the establishment of religion," the no-aid provision of Article I, section 3 imposes "further restrictions on the state's involvement with religious institutions than [imposed by] the Establishment Clause." *Id.* Specifically, the state may not use tax revenues to "directly or indirectly" aid "any church, sect, or religious denomination or any sectarian institution." As we noted in *Holmes*, 886 So.2d at 359–360, the United States Supreme Court has recognized that state constitutional provisions such as Florida's no-aid provision are "far stricter" than the Establishment Clause, *Witters v. Washington Department of Services for the Blind*, 474 U.S. 481, 489 (1986), and "draw[] a more stringent line than that drawn by the United States Constitution." *Locke v. Davey*, 540 U.S. 712, 722 (2004).

Appellees assert that, even if Prisoners and Lamb of God are considered sectarian institutions, paying them to provide social services to inmates under the programs does not violate the no-aid provision. We agree that Florida's no-aid provision does not create a per se bar to the state providing funds to religious or faith-based institutions to furnish necessary social services. As we explained in dicta in *Holmes*, 886 So.2d at 362, "nothing in the Florida no-aid provision would create a constitutional bar to state aid to a non-profit institution that was not itself sectarian, even if the institution is affiliated with a religious order or religious organization." Thus, allegations that government funds are paid to a religious entity to provide social services are not sufficient, standing alone, to state a cause of action under the no-aid provision. A government program that merely purchases at market prices secular services or products from a church, synagogue, or mosque would not, by itself, violate the no-aid provision. On the other hand, simply because a sectarian organization is paid to provide social services for the state, does not remove such social services program from examination under the no-aid provision. Given the text of the no-aid provision, *id.* at 353–54, we conclude that the overriding purpose of the provision is to prohibit the use of state funds to promote religious or sectarian activities. Thus, to violate the no-aid provision, in addition to providing social services, the government-funded program must also advance religion. In determining whether such programs violate the no-aid provision, the inquiry necessarily will be case-by-case and will consider such matters as whether the government-funded program is used to promote the religion of the provider, is significantly sectarian in nature, involves religious indoctrination, requires participation in religious ritual, or encourages the preference of one religion over another.[98]

---

98. [FN. 4.] We note that, "[t]he teaching of moral values, and creating a comprehensive rehabilitation program intentionally focused on moral values and character development, need not imply indoctrination into a religious faith." *Ams. United for Separation of Church and State v. Prison Fellowship*

In the amended petition, the appellants allege that not only are Prisoners and Lamb of God sectarian institutions, but the programs themselves are fundamentally carried out in a sectarian manner in violation of Article I, section 3. Appellants assert that these allegations are sufficient to state a cause of action under the no-aid provision. Below, appellees did not raise the sufficiency of the allegations of the amended petition under the no-aid provision and, understandably, the issue was not addressed by the trial court. Accordingly, we decline to do so now.

Appellees also argue that, if the no-aid provision bars religious entities from participating in state contracting, it would violate the Federal Establishment and Free Exercise Clauses. We do not agree. First, as we conclude above, the no-aid provision does not constitute a per se bar to state or local government contracting with religious entities for the provision of goods and services. Second, if, based upon the facts of a particular case, a court found the program in violation of the no-aid provision, such a decision would not violate the Federal Establishment and Free Exercise Clauses. As we explained in detail in *Holmes*, 886 So.2d at 362–66, the United States Supreme Court has recognized that a state constitutional provision, like Florida's no-aid provision, can bar state financial aid to religious institutions without violating either the Establishment Clause or Free Exercise Clause. *Locke*, 540 U.S. at 725. As the Court explained, "there are some state actions permitted by the Establishment Clause but not required by the Free Exercise Clause," *id.* at 719, and states are free to "draw[] a more stringent line than drawn by the United States Constitution...." *Id.* at 722.

Because our decision in this case is the first instance in which the Florida no-aid provision has been applied outside of the school context and because our decision could affect the manner in which the state contracts for social services, we certify the following question of great public importance under rule 9.330, Florida Rules of Appellate Procedure:

> WHETHER THE NO-AID PROVISION IN ARTICLE I, SECTION 3 OF THE FLORIDA CONSTITUTION PROHIBITS THE STATE FROM CON-TRACTING FOR THE PROVISION OF NECESSARY SOCIAL SERVICES BY RELIGIOUS OR SECTARIAN ENTITIES?

Count III

In Count III, CSH and the Hulls have alleged that section 944.4731(6)(a)[99] provides a "chaplain" with important government powers with respect to the placement of offenders in substance abuse transitional programs. They allege:

Ministries, 432 F.Supp.2d 862, 875, n. 12 (S.D.Iowa 2006), *affirmed in part, rev'd in part*, 509 F.3d 406 (8th Cir.2007). Further, as asserted by appellees, the services received by the state under the programs certainly may serve legitimate penological goals. The question raised in the instant case is not whether the programs at issue serve a public purpose, but whether they violate the no-aid provision. As we observed in Holmes, "courts do not have the authority to ignore the clear language of the Constitution, even for a popular program with a worthy purpose." *Holmes*, 886 So.2d at 366–67.

99. [FN 6.] Section 944.4731(6)(a) provides:

(a) The transition assistance specialist and the chaplain shall provide a list of contracted private providers, including faith-based providers, to the offender and facilitate the appli-

This delegation of government authority to a religious official violates Article I, Section 3 of the Florida Constitution, as it unconstitutionally substitutes the judgment of a religious authority for the decision-making of secular public officials. Moreover, any use of public funds to pay the chaplain designated in Florida Statutes § 944.4731(6) similarly violates Article I, section 3 of the Florida Constitution.

They sought "a temporary and permanent injunction preventing [McNeil] from delegating government authority and powers to the chaplain, including, but not limited to, the authority to be consulted prior to the placement of any offender in faith-based substance abuse transitional housing programs."

These allegations do not state a cause of action under either the Federal Establishment Clause or Article I, section 3 of the Florida Constitution. Appellants have not alleged that the acts of these chaplains establish a religion. In addition, the state's employment of a chaplain does not violate the Establishment Clause. *Marsh v. Chambers*, 463 U.S. 783 (1983). Moreover, the mere fact that public funds are used to pay a chaplain does not establish a cause of action under Florida's no-aid provision. The individual chaplains are not a church, sect, religious denomination or sectarian institution. Further, appellants do not allege that that employment of a chaplain is "in aid of any church, sect, or religious denomination or in aid of any sectarian institution."

AFFIRMED in part, REVERSED in part, and REMANDED for further proceedings consistent with this opinion; question certified. No further motions for rehearing will be entertained.

PADOVANO, J., and BROWNING, JR., EDWIN J., Senior Judge, concur.

On Motion for Rehearing En Banc

The motion for rehearing en banc filed by appellees on December 29, 2009, the response of the appellants thereto, and the request for a vote by a judge in regular active service on this court have been considered by all judges of the court who are in regular active service and who are not disqualified. *See* rule 9.331(d)(a), Fla. R.App. P. Less than a majority of those judges have voted in favor of rehearing en banc. Accordingly, the motion for rehearing en banc is denied.

WOLF, KAHN, WEBSTER, BENTON, VAN NORTWICK, PADOVANO and CLARK, JJ., concur. LEWIS and WETHERELL, JJ., dissent. THOMAS, J., dissents with opinion with which HAWKES, C.J., and ROBERTS, ROWE and MARSTILLER, JJ., concur. [Omitted.]

---

cation process. The transition assistance specialist shall inform the offender of program availability and assess the offender's need and suitability for substance abuse transition housing assistance. If an offender is approved for placement, the specialist shall assist the offender and coordinate the release of the offender with the selected program. If an offender requests and is approved for placement in a contracted faith-based substance abuse transition housing program, the specialist must consult with the chaplain prior to such placement. A right to substance abuse program services is not stated, intended, or otherwise implied by this section.

THOMAS, J., dissenting.

I respectfully dissent from this court's decision to deny rehearing en banc, pursuant to Florida Rule of Appellate Procedure 9.331. This is undeniably a case of exceptional importance, and we should rehear this case *en banc,* and recede from our prior incorrect decision in *Bush v. Holmes,* 886 So.2d 340 (Fla. 1st DCA 2004) (en banc), *aff'd on other grounds,* 919 So.2d 392 (Fla.2006). That decision is controlling in this case, absent *en banc* review. The panel's opinion here will apply *Holmes* for the first time beyond the context of school vouchers, thus potentially jeopardizing a wide range of governmental social welfare programs, including faith-based placement programs for foster children, faith-based prison programs, and other State contracts with faith-based providers, as Judge Polston predicted in his dissenting opinion in *Holmes. Id.* at 376. This impact will occur despite statutory protections that prohibit a program provider from attempting to convert the program's beneficiaries. *See* § 944.4731, Fla. Stat.

We should grant Appellee's Motion for Rehearing En Banc, recede from *Holmes,* adopt Judge Wolf's concurring and dissenting opinion in *Holmes,* and hold that a No-Aid violation occurs only where a governmental contract fails to include a legitimate *quid pro quo.*

Commentary

The U.S. Supreme Court in *Trinity Lutheran Church of Columbia v. Comer,* 137 S. Ct. 2012 (2017), struck down a Missouri state grant program that resurfaced children's playgrounds with recycled rubber because the program forbade any assistance to church-run preschools. The Missouri constitutional provision is similar to Florida's in prohibiting indirect assistance to religion. In 2019, the U.S. Supreme Court granted certiorari in a case where the Montana Supreme Court used that state's no-aid provision to invalidate a state scholarship tax credit program which allowed funds to go to students attending religious schools. *See Espinoza v. Montana Dept. of Revenue,* 435 P.2d 603 (Mont. 2018), *cert. granted,* 139 S. Ct. 2777 (2019). In *Espinoza v. Montana Department of Revenue,* 140 S. Ct. 2246 (2020), the U.S. Supreme Court, by a 5–4 vote, held that the application of Montana's no-aid provision to prevent tax credit funds being used for students attending religious schools violated the Free Exercise Clause of the First Amendment. Read the following excerpt from the U.S. Supreme Court's opinion in *Espinoza.*[100] To what degree is the Florida no-aid provision still viable?

Espinoza v. Montana Department of Revenue
140 S. Ct. 2246 (2020)

* * *

---

100. *But see Carson v. Makin,* Case No. 19-1746, 2020 WL 6335999, *9–10 (1st Cir., Oct. 29, 2020) (upholding the no-aid provision in the Maine Constitution as a valid restriction on public funds being used to support advancement of religion).

II

A

The Religion Clauses of the First Amendment provide that "Congress shall make no law respecting an establishment of religion, or prohibiting the free exercise thereof." We have recognized a " 'play in the joints' between what the Establishment Clause permits and the Free Exercise Clause compels." *Trinity Lutheran Church of Columbia, Inc. v. Comer*, 137 S.Ct. 2012, 2019 (2017) (quoting *Locke v. Davey*, 540 U.S. 712, 718 (2004)). Here, the parties do not dispute that the scholarship program is permissible under the Establishment Clause. Nor could they. We have repeatedly held that the Establishment Clause is not offended when religious observers and organizations benefit from neutral government programs. See, *e.g.*, *Locke*, 540 U.S. at 719; *Rosenberger v. Rector and Visitors of Univ. of Va.*, 515 U.S. 819, 839 (1995). See also *Trinity Lutheran*, 137 S.Ct., at 2019–2020 (noting the parties' agreement that the Establishment Clause was not violated by including churches in a playground resurfacing program). Any Establishment Clause objection to the scholarship program here is particularly unavailing because the government support makes its way to religious schools only as a result of Montanans independently choosing to spend their scholarships at such schools. See *Locke*, 540 U.S. at 719; *Zelman v. Simmons-Harris*, 536 U.S. 639, 649–653 (2002). The Montana Supreme Court, however, held as a matter of state law that even such indirect government support qualified as "aid" prohibited under the Montana Constitution.

The question for this Court is whether the Free Exercise Clause precluded the Montana Supreme Court from applying Montana's no-aid provision to bar religious schools from the scholarship program. For purposes of answering that question, we accept the Montana Supreme Court's interpretation of state law—including its determination that the scholarship program provided impermissible "aid" within the meaning of the Montana Constitution—and we assess whether excluding religious schools and affected families from that program was consistent with the Federal Constitution.

The Free Exercise Clause, which applies to the States under the Fourteenth Amendment, "protects religious observers against unequal treatment" and against "laws that impose special disabilities on the basis of religious status." *Trinity Lutheran*, 137 S.Ct., at 2021 (internal quotation marks and alterations omitted)....

Most recently, *Trinity Lutheran* distilled these and other decisions to the same effect into the "unremarkable" conclusion that disqualifying otherwise eligible recipients from a public benefit "solely because of their religious character" imposes "a penalty on the free exercise of religion that triggers the most exacting scrutiny." 137 S.Ct., at 2021. In *Trinity Lutheran*, Missouri provided grants to help nonprofit organizations pay for playground resurfacing, but a state policy disqualified any organization "owned or controlled by a church, sect, or other religious entity." *Id.*, 137 S.Ct., at 2017. Because of that policy, an otherwise eligible church-owned preschool was denied a grant to resurface its playground. Missouri's policy discriminated against the Church "simply because of what it is—a church," and so the policy was subject to the "strictest scrutiny," which it failed. *Id.*, 137 S.Ct., at 2022–2025. We acknowledged that the State had not "criminalized" the way in which the Church worshipped or "told the Church that it cannot subscribe to a certain view of the Gospel." *Id.*, 137 S.Ct., at 2022. But the State's discriminatory policy was "odious to our Constitution all the same." *Id.*, 137 S.Ct., at 2025.

Here too Montana's no-aid provision bars religious schools from public benefits solely because of the religious character of the schools. The provision also bars parents who wish to send their children to a religious school from those same benefits, again solely because of the religious character of the school. This is apparent from the plain text. The provision bars aid to any school "controlled in whole or in part by any church, sect, or denomination." Mont. Const., Art. X, §6(1). The provision's title—"Aid prohibited to sectarian schools"—confirms that the provision singles out schools based on their religious character. *Ibid.* And the Montana Supreme Court explained that the provision forbids aid to any school that is "sectarian," "religiously affiliated," or "controlled in whole or in part by churches." 393 Mont. at 464–467, 435 P.3d at 612–613. The provision plainly excludes schools from government aid solely because of religious status. See *Trinity Lutheran*, 137 S.Ct., at 2019–2021.

* * *

B

Seeking to avoid *Trinity Lutheran*, the Department contends that this case is instead governed by *Locke v. Davey*, 540 U.S. 712 (2004). *Locke* also involved a scholarship program. The State of Washington provided scholarships paid out of the State's general fund to help students pursuing postsecondary education. The scholarships could be used at accredited religious and nonreligious schools alike, but Washington prohibited students from using the scholarships to pursue devotional theology degrees, which prepared students for a calling as clergy. This prohibition prevented Davey from using his scholarship to obtain a degree that would have enabled him to become a pastor. We held that Washington had not violated the Free Exercise Clause.

Locke differs from this case in two critical ways. First, *Locke* explained that Washington had "merely chosen not to fund a distinct category of instruction": the "essentially religious endeavor" of training a minister "to lead a congregation." *Id.*, at 721. Thus, Davey "was denied a scholarship because of what he proposed to do—use the funds to prepare for the ministry." *Trinity Lutheran*, 137 S.Ct., at 2023–2024. Apart from that narrow restriction, Washington's program allowed scholarships to be used at "pervasively religious schools" that incorporated religious instruction throughout their classes. *Locke*, 540 U.S. at 724–725. By contrast, Montana's Constitution does not zero in on any particular "essentially religious" course of instruction at a religious school. Rather, as we have explained, the no-aid provision bars all aid to a religious school "simply because of what it is," putting the school to a choice between being religious or receiving government benefits. *Trinity Lutheran*, 137 S.Ct., at 2023. At the same time, the provision puts families to a choice between sending their children to a religious school or receiving such benefits.

Second, *Locke* invoked a "historic and substantial" state interest in not funding the training of clergy, 540 U.S. at 725, explaining that "opposition to … funding 'to support church leaders' lay at the historic core of the Religion Clauses," *Trinity Lutheran*, 137 S.Ct., at 2023 (quoting *Locke*, 540 U.S. at 722). As evidence of that tradition, the Court in *Locke* emphasized that the propriety of state-supported clergy was a central subject of founding-era debates, and that most state constitutions from that era prohibited the expenditure of tax dollars to support the clergy. See *id.*, at 722–723.

But no comparable "historic and substantial" tradition supports Montana's decision to disqualify religious schools from government aid. In the founding era and the early 19th century, governments provided financial support to private schools, including denominational ones. "Far from prohibiting such support, the early state constitutions and statutes actively encouraged this policy." L. Jorgenson, *The State and the Non-Public School*, 1825–1925, p. 4 (1987)….

… In addition, many of the no-aid provisions belong to a more checkered tradition shared with the Blaine Amendment of the 1870s. That proposal—which Congress nearly passed—would have added to the Federal Constitution a provision similar to the state no-aid provisions, prohibiting States from aiding "sectarian" schools. See *Mitchell v. Helms*, 530 U.S. 793, 828 (2000) (plurality opinion). "[I]t was an open secret that 'sectarian' was code for 'Catholic.'" *Ibid.*; see Jorgenson, *supra*, at 70. The Blaine Amendment was "born of bigotry" and "arose at a time of pervasive hostility to the Catholic Church and to Catholics in general"; many of its state counterparts have a similarly "shameful pedigree." *Mitchell*, 530 U.S. at 828–829 (plurality opinion); see Jorgenson, *supra*, at 69–70, 216; Jeffries & Ryan, *A Political History of the Establishment Clause*, 100 Mich. L. Rev. 279, 301–305 (2001). The no-aid provisions of the 19th century hardly evince a tradition that should inform our understanding of the Free Exercise Clause….

K. Article I, Section 9 — Due Process

A comparable clause has appeared in all previous Florida Constitutions. As with the federal Constitution, this guarantee includes both substantive and procedural due process protections for Florida citizens. In the following case, consider whether the Florida Constitution provides greater rights than those provided by the U.S. Constitution, and consider as well what test applies.

State v. Smith

547 So. 2d 13 (Fla. 1989)

BARKETT, Justice.

We have for review *Smith v. State*, 501 So.2d 657 (Fla. 4th DCA 1987), which certified the following question of great public importance:

WHETHER, PRIOR TO THE INITIATION OF FORMAL ADVERSARY JUDICIAL PROCEEDINGS IN THE FORM OF AN INDICTMENT OR IN-

FORMATION, AN ACCUSED HAS A CONSTITUTIONAL RIGHT TO COUNSEL AT A COMPELLED LINEUP?

Id. at 658. Because of the particular facts of this case, we rephrase the question as follows:

MUST EVIDENCE BE SUPPRESSED THAT WAS OBTAINED THROUGH AN EX PARTE ORDER COMPELLING AN ACCUSED ALREADY IN PO-LICE CUSTODY TO PARTICIPATE IN A POLICE LINEUP?

We have jurisdiction. Art. V, §3(b)(4), Fla. Const. We find that the due process clause of the Florida Constitution forbids a lineup conducted under these circumstances. Accordingly, we answer the rephrased certified question in the affirmative, and approve the result reached below. *See* art. I, §9, Fla. Const.

I.

Around 1:00 on the morning of February 28, 1983, two men held up a convenience store at gunpoint, absconding with cash, money orders, and various other items. One man entered the store, bought a few items, and left. As he left, the second man entered and proceeded to rob the store clerk, Seepersaud Schive Charan. Charan immediately reported the robbery and gave a description of both men and their car to the police. The man who did the taking was described as "between 140, 180 pounds, 5 feet 6 inches to 6 feet, black male, 23–25 [years old]." A few minutes after the police alert, an officer spotted two men at a nearby apartment building walking away from a car that fit the description of the car used in the robbery. The officer followed one of the men up some stairs and returned him to the parking lot where Charan identified him as the man who had first entered the store. The man Charan identified was not Respondent, Sylester Earl Smith ("Respondent"), but rather Sylvester Smith ("SylVester"), Respondent's brother.[101]

The next day, Terry Lamar Green was arrested in connection with the robbery after he tried to cash one of the stolen money orders. Two days later, Charan identified Green from a photo display as the second robber, the man who actually did the taking. Charan now described the second robber as 5 feet 6 inches tall and 145 pounds, a description that fit Green.[102] Based upon the photo identification and description, Sergeant Carroll, the detective in charge of the robbery, initiated the filing of a robbery charge against Green. In the meantime, however, SylVester had been questioned by the state attorney and had placed the blame for the robbery on his brother, Respondent. Green was then released and Respondent arrested.

On March 15, Respondent appeared before the county court for a first appearance hearing. The record indicates that counsel was not appointed at that proceeding and contains a notation that Respondent would retain his own attorney. After this hearing,

---

101. [FN2.] The names are confusing. Respondent's name, Sylester, does not have the "v" which his brother's name has.

102. [FN3.] The photograph showed Green only from the neck up.

Tens of 4th + 6th holdings

Respondent was asked to stand in a lineup but he refused. On March 24, without notice to Respondent, the state's attorney obtained an ex parte court order compelling Respondent's appearance at a lineup on that same day. Respondent was not represented by counsel at the hearing on the state's motion to compel.

After obtaining the order to compel, the state's attorney advised the public defender's office that a lineup was going to be held but was told that Respondent had his own attorney. Respondent stated prior to the lineup that he did not know who his attorney was. The lineup was conducted without counsel and Charan picked Respondent. After the lineup, Charan was deposed. He now described the robber as about 5 feet 7 inches tall and weighing 185 pounds, a description which fit Respondent. On March 28, an information was filed formally charging Respondent with the robbery.

Prior to trial, Respondent filed a motion to suppress the lineup identification. At the suppression hearing, Sergeant Carroll testified that prior to the lineup, he told Charan there was a new suspect and the person Charan had picked out from the photographs would not be in the lineup.[103] Charan, however, denied he was told there was a different suspect for the live lineup. Sergeant Carroll also testified that immediately after the lineup, Charan said he had recognized Respondent by the wide scar on his right arm. The trial court denied the motion, finding that no constitutional rights had been violated.

At trial, the state's evidence against Respondent consisted of the testimony of Charan and Sergeant Carroll relative to the lineup identification, Charan's in-court identification, and SylVester's testimony. Sergeant Carroll repeated his pretrial testimony except this time he equivocated as to whether he had told Charan that the police had a new suspect for the live lineup. Charan again stated that he had not been told that the lineup would not include the person he had identified in the photo display. When Charan identified Respondent in court, he pointed out the scar on Respondent's arm, stating that he saw the scar at the robbery. He denied seeing the scar at the lineup.

According to SylVester, who testified in exchange for a recommendation of probation on the same charge, he and Respondent went to the store to get beer. Although he knew Respondent intended to rob, SylVester said he did not. He went into the store twice, to buy something and then to get some change. After he got the change, Respondent told him to leave and he drove to their apartment a few blocks away. He returned a few minutes later and found Respondent hiding in some bushes between their apartment and the store.

In its case, the defense introduced the photo display from which the store clerk had selected the picture of Terry Lamar Green as the second robber.

---

103. [FN4.] Because it is not essential to the disposition of this case, we do not reach the question of whether the lineup procedures used in this instance was unduly suggestive and therefore inadmissible.

< very well could have been

The jury found Respondent guilty as charged. After the verdict but prior to sentencing, Respondent submitted to the trial court the results of a polygraph examination he had taken on October 16, 1983, showing that he did not commit the robbery in question. He also requested a new trial based upon the fact that yet another brother, Billie Joe Smith, who also fit the description of the robber given by Charan at trial, had been arrested and charged with robbing another convenience store later the same day, in the same vicinity, and with a similar method of operation. That motion was denied.

On appeal, the Fourth District reversed the trial court but certified the case as involving a question of great public importance. *Smith,* 501 So.2d at 658.

II.

One of the most fundamental principles of Anglo-American jurisprudence is the guarantee of due process. The concept was first articulated in a written legal document in article 39 of Magna Charta[104] when promulgated by King John of England on June 15, 1215. Since that time, the concept of due process has been embodied in every great charter produced by modern Western democracies. Both the fifth and fourteenth amendments of the federal Constitution, as well as article I, section 9 of the Florida Constitution, embody the concept and make it binding upon the courts of Florida. It is one of the central tenets of the organic law of this state, and one that restricts the power of all three branches of government. As a concept rooted in the Anglo-American tradition of ordered liberty, due process is a transcendent principle of both natural and positive law, against which even the enactments of the legislature or the pronouncements of the courts will be measured.

Due process rests primarily on the concept of fundamental fairness. On several occasions we have cited with approval the statements made by Daniel Webster in *Trustees of Dartmouth College v. Woodward,* 17 U.S. (4 Wheat.) 518, 580–582 (1819) (cited with approval in *State ex rel. Munch v. Davis,* 143 Fla. 236, 196 So. 491 (1940), and *Fiehe v. R.E. Householder Co.,* 98 Fla. 627, 125 So. 2 (1929)), where he said that due process

> hears before it condemns; … proceeds upon inquiry, and renders judgment only after trial. The meaning is that every citizen shall hold his life, liberty, property, and immunities, under the protection of the general rules which govern society.

Elsewhere, we have stated that

> "[t]he essential elements of due process of law are notice, and an opportunity to be heard and to defend in an orderly proceeding adapted to the nature of the case.... [I]t is a rule as old as the law that no one shall be personally

---

104. [FN5.] Article 39 required that no person could be subjected to a loss of rights except according to the law of the land. C. Holt, *Magna Charta* 326–27 (1965).

bound until he has had his day in court, by which is meant, until he has been duly cited to appear, and has been afforded an opportunity to be heard. Judgment without such citation and opportunity wants all the attributes of a judicial determination; it is judicial usurpation and oppression and can never be upheld where justice is fairly administered."

Fiehe, 98 Fla. at 636, 125 So. at 7 (quoting 6 R.C.L. 446 (1915)). Due process, then, embodies at least two general concepts: the right to adequate advance notice and a meaningful right to be heard *before* a tribunal takes action.

The proceedings that resulted in Respondent's compelled participation in this police lineup offend both of these concepts. At Respondent's first hearing, he indicated that he would retain his own attorney. Consequently, no attorney was appointed by the court. After this initial hearing, Respondent refused to participate in a police lineup. Over a week later, the trial court at the instance of the state entered an ex parte order compelling Respondent to participate in a lineup. Respondent received no notice of the hearing or of the state's motion to compel. Since he had not yet retained counsel, he was unrepresented before the court. Thus, he was precluded from expressing his objections to the lineup procedure in any meaningful manner. Indeed, this ex parte procedure did not even afford Respondent an opportunity to explain whether he was having difficulty obtaining private counsel.

We cannot countenance an ex parte court hearing requesting a lineup against a criminal defendant already in custody. Such a procedure offends the most basic concepts of due process and ordered liberty embodied in article I, section 9 of the Florida Constitution. Thus, the compelled lineup conducted in this instance was unconstitutional. Art. I, §9, Fla. Const. Any consequences flowing from the unlawful lineup were fruit of the poisonous tree and should have been suppressed at trial. *See Caplan v. State*, 531 So.2d 88 (Fla.1988), *cert. denied*, 489 U.S. 1099 (1989).

III.

We now address the legal consequences of the unconstitutional lineup. For this limited purpose, we adopt the principles enunciated in *United States v. Wade*, 388 U.S. 218 (1967), and *Gilbert v. California*, 388 U.S. 263 (1967), which we find to be applicable to the violation of Florida due process law that occurs in ex parte proceedings of this type. We address separately the lineup identification and the in-court identification.

Under *Gilbert*, evidence of an unconstitutional pretrial lineup identification is *per se* inadmissible. If admitted, the accused is entitled to a new trial unless the state carries its burden of showing on appeal that the error was harmless beyond a reasonable doubt. 388 U.S. at 274. We believe the harmless error standard employed by Florida under *State v. DiGuilio*, 491 So.2d 1129 (Fla.1986), should be the proper method of gauging this question. *DiGuilio* requires the state, as the beneficiary of the error, to prove beyond a reasonable doubt that the error did not contribute to the verdict, or alternatively, that there is no reasonable possibility the error contributed to conviction. *Id.* at 1135.

We cannot find the error harmless in this case. Other than the identification testimony, the only evidence against Respondent was the codefendant SylVester's testimony. There was no physical evidence to corroborate Respondent's participation in the robbery. In fact, the stolen money orders were found on Terry Green, the first man identified. The fact that SylVester agreed to testify in exchange for a plea agreement and also apparently in order to get out of jail casts considerable doubt upon his credibility.

The lineup evidence unquestionably bolstered Charan's in-court identification. Given Charan's prior identification of someone else and the suspect nature of the codefendant's testimony, we believe there is a reasonable probability that the improper lineup evidence "contributed to the conviction." *DiGuilio*, 491 So.2d at 1135. Respondent thus is entitled to a new trial.

At Respondent's new trial, the burden will be on the state to establish by clear and convincing evidence that Charan's in-court identification rested upon his observations during the robbery, independent from and untainted by the unconstitutional lineup.[105] *Wade*, 388 U.S. at 240. If the state fails to meet its burden, Charan will not be permitted to identify Respondent.

For the foregoing reasons, the result reached below is approved.

It is so ordered.

OVERTON, SHAW, GRIMES and KOGAN, JJ., concur.

EHRLICH, C.J., concurs in result only.

McDONALD, J., dissents.

Questions

1. What are the two due process concerns raised in this case?

2. Is the federal Constitution's due process standard different from Florida's standard?

3. At the new trial, what will the state have to establish before the court will allow Charan's in-court identification, and by what standard?

---

105. [FN6.] In *United States v. Wade*, 388 U.S. 218, 241 (1967), the Supreme Court outlined a number of factors to be considered in making this determination: the prior opportunity the witness had to observe the alleged criminal act; the existence of any discrepancy between any pre-lineup description and the defendant's actual description; any identification prior to the lineup of another person; any identification by picture of the defendant prior to the lineup; failure to identify the defendant on a prior occasion; any time lapse between the alleged act and the lineup identification; and any other factors raised by the totality of the circumstances that bear upon the likelihood that the witness' in-court identification is not tainted by the illegal lineup and does, in fact, have an independent source. We adopt this nonexclusive list of factors as a matter of Florida law in gauging errors of the type involved in this case. Art. I, § 9, Fla. Const.

L. Article I, Section 17 — Excessive Punishments

A similar provision appeared in all previous Florida Constitutions. The current provision was amended in 2002 after a previous 2000 amendment was struck from the Florida Constitution, because the Supreme Court found that the ballot title and summary did not clearly inform voters about the substance of the amendment.[106] The 2002 amendment is another linkage amendment which ties the meaning of "cruel and unusual" as used in the Florida Constitution to the jurisprudence of the U.S. Supreme Court's interpretation of the Eighth Amendment to the U.S. Constitution.

The first case came before the legislative amendment and the Court's decision in this case prompted the Legislature to propose the linkage amendment to Article I, Section 17.

Jones v. State

701 So. 2d 76 (Fla. 1997), *cert. denied*, 523 U.S. 1014 (1998)

PER CURIAM.

Leo Alexander Jones, at a time when he was under warrant of death, filed a petition to invoke this Court's all writs jurisdiction, seeking a determination of whether electrocution in Florida is cruel and unusual punishment under the Eighth and Fourteenth Amendments of the United States Constitution and cruel or unusual punishment under article I, section 17 of the Florida Constitution.

In addition to arguing that execution per se is cruel and unusual punishment, he pointed to the circumstances surrounding the recent execution of Pedro Medina [where flames were seen near the headpiece of the electric chair and smoke came from the headpiece] to support his contention that execution in Florida's electric chair in its present condition is cruel and unusual punishment. This Court rejected Jones's claim that execution was per se cruel or unusual punishment. However, the Court relinquished jurisdiction to the trial court to conduct an evidentiary hearing on Jones's claim that electrocution in Florida's electric chair in its present condition is cruel or unusual punishment. In order to provide the time necessary for the hearing, we stayed Jones's pending execution.

After a four-day hearing, the trial court entered an order denying the petitioner's claim. On appeal from that order, Jones argued that the trial judge had erroneously denied his motion for continuance. Jones asserted that none of his expert witnesses could be available to testify at the scheduled hearing. He also complained that during the course of the hearing, new written protocols for carrying out executions were then

---

106. *See Armstrong v. Harris*, 773 So. 2d 7 (Fla. 2000). We will look at this case when we consider legislative amendments to the Constitution in our discussion of Article XI.

being developed based on recommendations of engineers who had examined the electric chair and that Jones's attorneys did not receive the new protocols until the second day of the hearing. As a consequence, he claimed that he was unable to effectively cross-examine the state's experts concerning these protocols. In addition, it was not until after the hearing that the State also provided Jones's attorneys with requested chart recordings pertaining to the performance of the electric chair during Medina's execution. In view of these circumstances, we once again relinquished jurisdiction to the trial court to hold an additional hearing in which the parties could present additional testimony and evidence, including the testimony of any witnesses who had testified at the previous hearing and that Jones could require two engineers who had testified for the State at the previous hearing to be present and undergo cross-examination. At the conclusion of the hearing, the trial judge was directed to consider the testimony and evidence presented at both hearings and enter a new order on the claim that electrocution in Florida's electric chair in its present condition is cruel or unusual punishment.

By subsequent order, we permitted Jones's experts to examine Florida's electrocution equipment and to witness the testing thereof by appropriate Florida officials. We also permitted Jones's attorneys to have access to certain requested evidentiary items concerning Medina's execution.

A second four-day evidentiary hearing was held. During the course of the two hearings, many witnesses testified and each side presented expert testimony from doctors and engineers. Thereafter, the trial judge entered a twenty-six page final order denying Jones's claim that Florida's electric chair in its present condition was unconstitutional. In the order of denial, the judge made several significant findings of fact which may be summarized as follows:

1. The procedures used in the last seventeen Florida executions have been consistently followed, and no malfunctions occurred until the execution of Pedro Medina.

2. The flame and smoke observed during Medina's execution were caused by insufficient saline solution on the sponge in the headpiece of the electric chair.

3. Medina's brain was instantly and massively depolarized within milliseconds of the initial surge of electricity. He suffered no conscious pain.

4. Consistent with recommendations of experts appointed by the Governor following Medina's execution, the Department of Corrections has now adopted as a matter of policy written "Testing Procedures for Electric Chair" and "Electrocution Day Procedures."

5. Florida's electric chair—its apparatus, equipment, and electric circuitry— is in excellent condition.

6. Florida's death chamber staff is qualified and competent to carry out executions.

7. All inmates who will hereafter be executed in Florida's electric chair will suffer no conscious pain.

The trial judge made the following conclusions of law:

1. Cruel or unusual punishment is defined by the Courts as the wanton infliction of unnecessary pain. *Gregg v. Georgia*, 428 U.S. 153 (1976); *Louisiana ex rel. Francis v. Resweber*, 329 U.S. 459 (1947).

2. Florida's electric chair, in past executions, did not wantonly inflict unnecessary pain, and therefore, did not constitute cruel or unusual punishment.

3. Florida's electric chair, as it is to be employed in future executions pursuant to the Department of Corrections' written testing procedures and execution day procedures, will result in death without inflicting wanton and unnecessary pain, and therefore, will not constitute cruel or unusual punishment.

4. Florida's electric chair in its present condition does not constitute cruel or unusual punishment.

5. During the hearing it has been strongly suggested and inferred by Jones that Florida's electric chair as the method of judicial execution should be abandoned in favor of judicial execution by lethal injection. Such a move to adopt lethal injection is not within the constitutional prerogative of the Courts of this State, but rather lies solely within the prerogative of the Legislature of the State of Florida.

Jones's first point on appeal pertains to the testimony of State witness Dr. Michael Morse, who qualified as an expert in the field of electrical engineering with particular reference to the application of engineering science to the human body. In the first hearing, Morse testified that Medina had been rendered instantly unconscious and unable to feel pain. On cross-examination, he stated that he could not say with one hundred percent certainty how the electric current distributed itself during an execution. Pursuant to our order, the State arranged for Dr. Morse to be present at the second hearing so that Jones's counsel could further cross-examine him. During the second hearing, Jones's counsel announced that he did not need Dr. Morse present for further cross-examination. However, the State later called Morse to the stand and asked if he had done further research in trying to determine where the current goes when it leaves the headpiece. He said he had utilized a document prepared by Dr. John Wikswo and carried it forward to conclude that in his opinion somewhere between one-third and two-thirds of the current would flow to the brain during an execution in the electric chair. This testimony was apparently presented to rebut testimony from one of Jones's witnesses that a much smaller amount of current would pass directly to the brain during an execution. There was no objection to this testimony, and Morse was cross-examined on this and other matters. At the request of Jones's counsel the court asked Morse to retrieve the Wikswo article for Jones's counsel.

Morse furnished a copy of the article to Jones's counsel at the beginning of the hearing on the following morning, and the court released Morse from attendance so that he could remain in the courtroom if he wished. Later that morning, Jones's

Bd did
FL have
Daubert den?

counsel filed a motion to strike Morse's testimony concerning current flow to the brain because the research on which it was based as well as the research contained in Wikswo's article was novel scientific evidence which had not been shown to have been accepted in the scientific community under the rationale of *Frye v. United States*, 293 F. 1013 (D.C.Cir.1923). The trial judge denied the motion as being untimely since Dr. Morse had completed his testimony and been released as a witness before any objection was raised.

Jones argues that because Morse was still in attendance in the courtroom, the judge's ruling was in error. However, as in the case of other objections to expert testimony, a *Frye* objection is waived unless it is made at the time the testimony is offered. *Jordan v. State*, 694 So.2d 708 (Fla.1997); *Hadden v. State*, 690 So.2d 573 (Fla.1997). In any event, there is nothing in the findings of the judge's order which suggests that he relied on the disputed testimony. Moreover, that portion of Morse's testimony to which Jones objected was not probative of the issue this Court had directed the trial judge to decide, i.e., whether Florida's electric chair in its present condition constituted cruel or unusual punishment. We also reject Jones's second and corollary argument that the trial judge erred in refusing to grant a continuance so he would be able to present the testimony of Wikswo to demonstrate that Morse had misconstrued what he had said in his article.

Jones states his third argument as follows: "Although the proper constitutional analysis holds that a deliberate indifference to a risk of pain renders a method of punishment cruel, Judge Soud erroneously required Mr. Jones to show that Medina and other judicial [sic] electrocuted persons experienced conscious pain." He cites *Farmer v. Brennan*, 511 U.S. 825 (1994), for the proposition that a state official's failure to prevent harm to prisoners constitutes cruel and unusual punishment if the official shows deliberate indifference to the prisoner's well-being. He then jumps to the conclusion that the State of Florida has shown deliberate indifference through its executions. This contention is totally without merit. In order for a punishment to constitute cruel or unusual punishment, it must involve "torture or a lingering death" or the infliction of "unnecessary and wanton pain." *Gregg v. Georgia*, 428 U.S. 153 (1976); *Louisiana ex rel. Francis v. Resweber*, 329 U.S. 459 (1947). As the Court observed in *Resweber*: "The cruelty against which the Constitution protects a convicted man is cruelty inherent in the method of punishment, not the necessary suffering involved in any method employed to extinguish life humanely." *Id.* at 464, 67 S.Ct. at 376. There was substantial evidence presented in this case that executions in Florida are conducted without any pain whatsoever, and this record is entirely devoid of evidence suggesting deliberate indifference to a prisoner's well-being on the part of state officials.

Jones also argues that the trial judge erred in refusing to admit and consider evidence that execution in Florida is unusual because there is a trend away from execution through the use of the electric chair as a means of capital punishment and because only six states currently employ the electric chair as a means of execution. The trial judge properly excluded this evidence as being beyond the scope of the issue which he had been assigned to decide. Our previous ruling that execution by the use of the electric chair is not per se unconstitutional subsumed the argument that Jones now makes. *See Campbell v. Wood*, 18 F.3d 662, 682 (9th Cir.1994) ("We cannot conclude that judicial hanging is incompatible with evolving standards of decency simply because few states continue the practice."); *Hunt v. Nuth*, 57 F.3d 1327, 1338 (4th Cir.1995) ("[T]he existence and adoption of more humane methods [of execution] does not automatically render a contested method cruel and unusual.").

In his fifth argument, Jones contends that Dr. Sperry was called as a witness by the State in violation of the attorney-client privilege. As a consequence of the flame and smoke which accompanied Medina's execution, the State asked two doctors to conduct an autopsy. At the request of Jones, two doctors selected by his attorney were also permitted to participate in the autopsy. Dr. Sperry was one of the doctors selected by Jones's attorneys for this purpose. Following the autopsy, all four doctors jointly signed the autopsy report. At the second hearing, the State proposed to call Dr. Sperry as a witness. Jones objected on the grounds of attorney-client privilege. At the hearing on this motion, the judge heard testimony as to the nature of Dr. Sperry's employment by Jones's attorneys. The trial judge found no attorney-client relationship that would preclude the testimony of Dr. Sperry. The judge found that Dr. Sperry had received no instructions not to discuss his findings with other pathologists or the state attorneys. The judge also ruled that he would find that any privilege that might have existed had been waived under the circumstances because Jones's attorneys did not object when Dr. Sperry answered questions and spoke at the meetings which took place before and after the autopsy at which Jones's lawyers attended.

In view of the judge's findings, which were supported by the record, we hold that no error occurred. Section 90.502, Florida Statutes (1995), pertaining to the lawyer-client privilege, protects confidential communications. The testimony by Dr. Sperry at the hearing did not pertain to communications with Jones's lawyers. We reject Jones's reliance on those cases which hold that a confidential mental health expert who is retained by defense counsel and who secures confidential information from the defendant cannot be called to testify by the State. *E.g., Lovette v. State*, 636 So.2d 1304 (Fla.1994). Dr. Sperry's testimony was limited to participation in the autopsy and his opinions concerning the effect of execution upon those being executed. *See Rose v. State*, 591 So.2d 195, 197–98 (Fla. 4th DCA 1991) (no error in permitting the medical examiner originally hired by the defense but not called as a witness to testify on behalf of the State where no confidential communications were passed between doctor and defendant's attorney).

In his sixth point on appeal, Jones attacks a number of evidentiary rulings made by the trial judge during the course of the hearing. None of these rulings individually or collectively were of such moment as to affect the outcome of this case and need not be discussed.

Finally, we reject Jones's contention that the trial judge's bias rendered him incapable of conducting a full and fair hearing.

There is competent substantial evidence in the record to support the order of the trial judge. We hold that electrocution in Florida's electric chair in its present condition is not cruel or unusual punishment. We hereby vacate Jones's stay of execution.

OVERTON, GRIMES, HARDING and WELLS, JJ., concur.

HARDING, J., specially concurring with an opinion in which OVERTON, J., concurs.

KOGAN, C.J., dissents with an opinion in which SHAW and ANSTEAD, JJ., concur.

SHAW, J., dissents with an opinion in which KOGAN, C.J., and ANSTEAD, J., concur.

ANSTEAD, J., dissents with an opinion in which KOGAN, C.J., and SHAW, J., concur. [omitted]

HARDING, Justice, specially concurring.

I concur with the majority that Florida's electric chair, in its current condition, does not violate either the United States Constitution's ban on cruel and unusual punishment or the Florida Constitution's ban on cruel or unusual punishment. I write separately to encourage the legislature to amend section 922.10, Florida Statutes (Supp.1996), to provide that a death sentence may be executed *either* by electrocution or by lethal injection. I believe that such an amendment would avert a possible constitutional "train wreck" if this or any other court should ever determine that electrocution is unconstitutional.

OVERTON, J., concurs.

SHAW, Justice, dissenting.

Florida's electric chair was commissioned by the legislature in 1923 as a humane alternative to hanging, and legend has it that the chair, which was built the next year and nicknamed "Old Sparky," was a home-made affair, fashioned by inmates on-site from a single oak tree. Because of the spate of malfunctions in this jerry-built and now-dated chair, I find that execution by electrocution as currently practiced in this state no longer serves a humane purpose and in fact violates the prohibition against "cruel or unusual" punishment contained in the Florida Constitution.

I. CRUEL OR UNUSUAL PUNISHMENT

The people of Florida, through the legislature, have designated the death penalty as an appropriate punishment for certain crimes, *see* § 775.082, Fla. Stat. (1995), and with this I have no quarrel—the people of Florida have spoken, and I have sworn to uphold the law. To survive constitutional review, however, a method of execution must conform with both the state and federal constitutions, and I am similarly oath-bound to uphold the principles of these charters.

The United States Supreme Court has not reviewed a method of execution under the federal constitution in over a hundred years and the lower federal courts are in disaccord in this area, offering scant guidance to the states. When determining matters of basic rights, Florida courts are bound under federalist principles to look first to our state constitution:

When called upon to decide matters of fundamental rights, Florida's state courts are bound under federalist principles to give primacy to our state Constitution and to give independent legal import to every phrase and clause contained therein.

Traylor v. State, 596 So.2d 957, 962 (Fla.1992). If a government practice fails under the Florida Constitution, no further analysis is necessary under the federal charter.

Article I, section 17, Florida Constitution, proscribes punishments that are "cruel or unusual":

SECTION 17. Excessive punishments.—Excessive fines, cruel or unusual punishment, attainder, forfeiture of estate, indefinite imprisonment, and unreasonable detention of witnesses are forbidden.

Art. I, § 17, Fla. Const. While some degree of suffering is inherent in any method of execution, the "cruel or unusual" prohibition bars those methods that fall below the constitutional floor.

Significantly, the framers of article I, section 17 of the Florida Constitution articulated the "cruel or unusual" prohibition in the alternative, and this Court has given the provision a literal interpretation: The State is forbidden from imposing punishments that are either cruel or unusual. Further, the prohibition contains no limiting language and, by its plain words, bars punishments that are cruel or unusual in any manner. Thus, if the Florida prohibition is to have meaning, it must at a minimum bar any punishment that is impermissibly cruel either on its face or in its effect, as well as any punishment that is unusual. To comport with the Florida Constitution, a method of execution must meet these minimum criteria as explained below.

To meet the requirement that a punishment not be cruel on its face, a method of execution should entail no unnecessary violence or mutilation[.] *Glass [v. Louisiana]*, 471 U.S. at 1085 (Brennan, J., dissenting). The guillotine is an example of a method that would fail under this prong, for while beheading results in a quick, relatively painless death, it involves frank violence (i.e., gross laceration and blood-letting) and mutilation (i.e., decapitation) and thus is facially cruel.

Next, to meet the requirement that a punishment not be cruel in its effect, a method of execution should inflict no unnecessary pain. As the United States Supreme Court stated: "The traditional humanity of modern Anglo-American law forbids the infliction of unnecessary pain in the execution of the death sentence." *Resweber*, 329 U.S. at 463.

The all-important consideration is that the execution shall be so instantaneous and substantially painless that the punishment shall be reduced, as nearly as possible, to no more than that of death itself.

Id. at 474 (Burton, J., dissenting). California's gas chamber would fail here, for while lethal gas as applied in California involves minimal violence and mutilation, it inflicts substantial pain (i.e., intense visceral pain from oxygen deprivation) and results in a slow, lingering death akin to artificial drowning (i.e., the inmate may remain conscious for several minutes) and thus is cruel in its effect. Execution by gas is to be distinguished from lethal injection, which is generally considered painless.

Section 17 of the Florida Constitution also prohibits "unusual" punishments, and giving the word "unusual" its plain meaning, I know of no better yardstick for measuring this criterion than to compare the method of punishment under review against those methods currently available in other states or Western nations. While I would find lack of approval in a majority of jurisdictions a strong indicator that a method is impermissibly unusual, I recognize that this is not dispositive but rather is simply one factor—albeit a significant one—to be considered.

II. FLORIDA'S ELECTRIC CHAIR

While the people of Florida have designated capital punishment as an appropriate sanction for certain crimes, the legislature has implemented electrocution as the sole method of execution in this State. *See* § 922.10, Fla. Stat. (Supp.1996). In light of recent malfunctions in Florida's electric chair, this method of execution, in my opinion, entails unnecessary violence and mutilation and thus is unconstitutionally cruel on its face—not unlike the guillotine which was abandoned years ago in its country of origin, France, notwithstanding its efficiency in getting the grisly job done with dispatch and minimal pain.

III. CONCLUSION

The execution of a condemned man or woman is an extraordinarily solemn undertaking reluctantly assumed by the State at the behest of the people—no task is more somber or weighty for the State than the purposeful killing of one of its own. It is no circus. The constitutional tolerance for error in an execution is not boundless, for the Florida Constitution embodies all that is good and decent in the law and has no truck with the wanton infliction of violence or mutilation or pain that characterized executions in ages past—whether inherent in the method of execution or arising from "human error" or from simple indifference.

Execution by electrocution is a spectacle whose time has passed—like the guillotine or public stoning or burning at the stake. Deborah Denno and other experts have submitted sworn affidavits attesting to the following statistics concerning electrocution: Electrocution was first adopted by a state as a method of execution in 1888 and last adopted in 1949, at which time twenty-six states used it; since 1949 (i.e., almost half a century ago), no state has adopted electrocution and twenty states have dropped it; of thirty-eight states that currently authorize execution, only six (Alabama, Florida, Georgia, Kentucky, Nebraska, and Tennessee) require electrocution; of these six, two (Kentucky and Tennessee) have not executed any prisoners since the United States Supreme Court lifted its ban on capital punishment in 1976; four additional states (Arkansas, Ohio, South Carolina, and Virginia) offer electrocution as an option; of these four, one (Ohio) has not executed any prisoners since 1976; of approximately 140 countries outside the United States that impose capital punishment, none impose electrocution; in short, *only four governments in the entire world (Alabama, Florida, Georgia, and Nebraska) impose electrocution exclusively;* as a postscript—both the

Humane Society of the United States and the American Veterinarian Medical Association condemn electrocution as a method of euthanasia for animals.

Florida's electric chair, by its own track record, has proven itself to be a dinosaur more befitting the laboratory of Baron Frankenstein than the death chamber of Florida State Prison. Because electrocution is the sole means of execution approved for use in Florida, the legislature has, so to speak, placed all its constitutional eggs in this one basket. As a result, any infirmity in this method cannot be mitigated at this time by the presence of an acceptable alternative. Such an all-or-nothing approach has proved fatal to the capital sentencing scheme in other states.

In sum, while the people of Florida have determined that capital punishment is a proper sanction for certain crimes, the legislature has authorized a single method of execution and this method has resulted in botched executions in eleven percent of cases in recent years—producing impermissible violence and mutilation. This, in my opinion, puts the burden back on the legislature to implement an alternative method—one that comports with the Florida Constitution. While the Florida Constitution does not—by any means—guarantee that no inmate executed in Florida will suffer, it *does* guarantee that none will be needlessly brutalized or mutilated.

KOGAN, C.J., and ANSTEAD, J., concur.

Valle v. State

70 So. 3d 530 (Fla.), *cert. denied*, 564 U.S. 1067 (2011)

PER CURIAM.

Manuel Valle, a prisoner under sentence of death, appeals the denial of his amended successive motion for postconviction relief filed pursuant to Florida Rule of Criminal Procedure 3.851. We have jurisdiction. *See* art. V, § 3(b)(1), Fla. Const. On June 30, 2011, the Governor signed a death warrant for Valle, and he was scheduled to be executed on August 2, 2011. Valle subsequently sought postconviction relief in the circuit court, raising numerous claims, including an Eighth Amendment challenge to the Florida Department of Correction's (DOC) June 8, 2011, lethal injection protocol, which replaced the first drug in its three-drug sequence, sodium thiopental, with another drug, pentobarbital sodium (pentobarbital). Under this claim, Valle primarily argued that due to "serious concerns" regarding the efficacy of pentobarbital to render an inmate unconscious, the DOC's use of that drug in the protocol constitutes cruel and unusual punishment. After the circuit court summarily denied relief on his claims, this Court granted Valle's motion for a stay of execution, in part, until September 1, 2011, and temporarily relinquished jurisdiction for the narrow purpose of holding an evidentiary hearing on Valle's claim regarding the efficacy of pentobarbital as an anesthetic in the amount prescribed by Florida's protocol. Following an evidentiary hearing, the circuit court again denied relief. For the reasons set forth below, we now affirm the circuit court's orders and vacate the temporary stay of execution.

ANALYSIS

Constitutionality of Florida's Lethal Injection Procedures

In this claim, Valle raises various challenges to the constitutionality of Florida's lethal injection procedures, but the bulk of his argument focuses on the DOC's June 8, 2011, substitution of five grams of pentobarbital for five grams of sodium thiopental as the first of three drugs used in the lethal injection protocol. In Florida, the first drug is used to anesthetize the condemned inmate prior to the administration of the final two drugs in the three-drug sequence, pancuronium bromide (a paralytic agent that can stop respiration) and potassium chloride (a substance that will cause the heart to stop). Valle acknowledges that aside from substituting pentobarbital for sodium thiopental, both of which are barbiturates, Florida's lethal injection protocol has remained unaltered since this Court's decision in *Lightbourne* [*v. McCollum*, 969 So. 2d 326 (Fla. 2007)], which upheld the August 2007 lethal injection protocol against a similar constitutional challenge. He therefore argues that the DOC's plan to use pentobarbital constitutes cruel and unusual punishment because as a result of the substitution, he may remain conscious after being injected with pentobarbital, thereby subjecting him to significant pain during the administration of the final two drugs. As presented, the DOC's recent replacement of sodium thiopental with pentobarbital in Florida's three-drug lethal injection sequence is the primary claim underlying Valle's Eighth Amendment challenge.

Pursuant to this Court's order of relinquishment, the circuit court conducted a two-day evidentiary hearing, which included the admission of expert testimony from both parties, letters authored by Lundbeck, and eyewitness testimony from individuals who were present during the executions of Alabama inmate Eddie Powell and Georgia inmate Roy Blankenship. After receiving this evidence, the circuit court denied relief, concluding that the substitution of pentobarbital as an anesthetic did not violate the Eighth Amendment because the evidence failed to establish that the intravenous administration of pentobarbital creates a substantial risk of serious harm. After a thorough review of the record, we affirm the circuit court's denial.

This Court has previously recognized its duty "to ensure that the method used to execute a person in Florida does not constitute cruel and unusual punishment." *Lightbourne*, 969 So.2d at 349. To fulfill its obligation, this Court is guided by article I, section 17 of the Florida Constitution, which provides that "[a]ny method of execution shall be allowed, unless prohibited by the United States Constitution." Specifically, Florida's provision on the prohibition against cruel and unusual punishment "shall be construed in conformity with decisions of the United States Supreme Court which interpret the prohibition against cruel and unusual punishment provided in the Eighth Amendment to the United States Constitution." Art. I, § 17, Fla. Const. Therefore, in accordance with our state constitution, this Court is bound by the precedent of the Supreme Court regarding challenges to this state's chosen method of execution. *See Lightbourne*, 969 So.2d at 335 ("[W]e must evaluate whether lethal injection is unconstitutional 'in conformity with decisions of the United States Supreme Court.'") (quoting art. 1, § 17, Fla. Const.)).

The parties agree that Valle's various challenges to the DOC's lethal injection procedures are governed by the Supreme Court's plurality decision in *Baze v. Rees*, 553 U.S. 35 (2008), which defined the contours of a condemned inmate's burden of proof for mounting a successful Eighth Amendment challenge to a state's lethal injection protocol. Although acknowledging that "subjecting individuals to a risk of future harm—not simply actually inflicting pain—can qualify as cruel and unusual punishment," the Supreme Court in *Baze* explained that to prevail on such a claim, condemned inmates must demonstrate that "the conditions presenting the risk must be 'sure or very likely to cause serious illness and needless suffering,' and give rise to 'sufficiently imminent dangers.'" 553 U.S. at 49–50 (quoting *Helling v. McKinney*, 509 U.S. 25, 33, 34–35 (1993)) (plurality opinion); *see also Brewer v. Landrigan*, ___ U.S. ___, 131 S.Ct. 445, 445 (2010) ("[S]peculation cannot substitute for evidence that the use of the drug is 'sure or very likely to cause serious illness and needless suffering.'" (quoting *Baze*, 553 U.S. at 50)). That is, "there must be a 'substantial risk of serious harm,' an 'objectively intolerable risk of harm' that prevents prison officials from pleading that they were 'subjectively blameless for purposes of the Eighth Amendment.'" *Baze*, 553 U.S. at 50 (quoting *Farmer v. Brennan*, 511 U.S. 825, 842, 846 & n. 9 (1994)). This standard imposes a "heavy burden" upon the inmate to show that lethal injection procedures violate the Eighth Amendment. *Id.* at 53 (quoting *Gregg v. Georgia*, 428 U.S. 153, 175 (1976)).

Cognizant of this standard, we now turn to Valle's challenge to the DOC's substitution of pentobarbital for sodium thiopental. In the lethal injection context, "the condemned inmate's lack of consciousness is the focus of the constitutional inquiry." *Ventura* [*v. State*], 2 So.3d at 200; *see also Schwab* [*v. State*], 995 So.2d at 924, 927 (adopting the trial court's order, which stated that "the critical Eighth Amendment concern is whether the prisoner has, in fact, been rendered unconscious by the first drug"). As we explained in *Lightbourne*, "[i]f the inmate is not fully unconscious when either pancuronium bromide or potassium chloride [the second and third drugs in the protocol] is injected, or when either of the chemicals begins to take effect, the prisoner will suffer pain." 969 So.2d at 351; *see also Baze*, 553 U.S. at 53 ("[F]ailing a proper dose of sodium thiopental that would render the prisoner unconscious, there is a substantial, constitutionally unacceptable risk of suffocation from the administration of pancuronium bromide and pain from the injection of potassium chloride.").

In order to show the risks of using pentobarbital as a substitute, Valle relies extensively on the testimony of Dr. Waisel, who testified that pentobarbital and sodium thiopental are not interchangeable barbiturates, that five grams of sodium thiopental are not proportionally equivalent to five grams of pentobarbital, and that due to a lack of research, he would be unable to determine a dose of pentobarbital that would properly anesthetize an individual. Instead, he could only testify as to the amount needed to sedate someone. According to Dr. Waisel, a sedated patient may still be responsive while an anesthetized patient may be unconscious enough to undergo an open-chest surgery. In his opinion, the allowable upper dose needed to sedate a person would fall between 200 and 500 milligrams of pentobarbital, but he acknowledged that the amount used by the DOC for anesthetizing an inmate is 5000 milligrams. Although Dr. Waisel identified the use of pentobarbital to induce anesthesia as "off label," since the drug's package insert does not mention induction of anesthesia as an indication, he testified that there are legitimate "off-label" uses for drugs. In fact, Dr. Waisel agreed that pentobarbital is used as part of physician-assisted suicide and animal euthanasia procedures. In sum, Dr. Waisel opined that because there is insufficient data regarding the use of pentobarbital as an anesthetic, there would be no way to know, in any given case, how an overdose of the drug will affect healthy inmates.

In opposition, the State presented the testimony of Dr. Dershwitz, who testified that 5000 milligrams of pentobarbital, as provided for in the DOC's lethal injection protocol, is "far in excess of the dose that would be used in a human for any reason." According to Dr. Dershwitz, that dosage of pentobarbital is lethal standing alone, and when administered, the drug will induce a total flat line on the electroencephalogram (EEG) in brain activity, meaning that the person into whom the drug is injected will have no perception or sensation. Although Dr. Dershwitz acknowledged that the FDA had not approved pentobarbital for use in lethal injections, like Dr. Waisel, he explained that its use for such purposes was considered "off label" and that using a drug in an "off-label" manner is "common in medicine."

In reviewing this portion of Valle's claim, the circuit court credited the testimony of Dr. Dershwitz over that of Dr. Waisel, specifically finding Dr. Dershwitz's testimony to be "credible and persuasive" and Dr. Waisel's testimony to be "based on speculation" and "therefore, inherently unreliable." As we have previously explained, where "the trial court's findings are supported by competent substantial evidence, this Court will not substitute its judgment for that of the trial court on questions of fact, likewise of the credibility of the witnesses as well as the weight to be given to the evidence by the trial court." *Provenzano v. State*, 761 So.2d 1097, 1099 (Fla.2000) (quoting *Blanco v. State*, 702 So.2d 1250, 1252 (Fla.1997)); *see id.* at 1098–99 (applying competent, substantial evidence standard to review Provenzano's Eighth Amendment challenge to Florida's lethal injection procedure following an evidentiary hearing on the issue). In applying this standard, "[w]e recognize and honor the trial court's superior vantage point in assessing the credibility of witnesses and in making findings of fact." *Porter v. State*, 788 So.2d 917, 923 (Fla.2001). This stems from our recognition that "the trial court is in the best position to evaluate the credibility of witnesses, and appellate courts are obligated to give great deference to the findings of the trial court." *Durousseau v. State*, 55 So.3d 543, 562 (Fla.2010), *petition for cert. filed*, No. 10-10518 (U.S. May 10, 2011).

Based upon the testimony presented, the circuit court concluded that Dr. Dershwitz "refuted any suggestion that the dose of pentobarbital in the Florida lethal injection protocol would leave an inmate conscious and able to experience pain and suffering during the lethal injection process." The circuit court's findings are borne out by the testimony and are well-supported by the record. While Dr. Waisel opined that he would be unable to determine whether pentobarbital would produce its intended effect (i.e., to anesthetize the inmate before the administration of the last two drugs in the three-drug sequence), in the end, he did not testify that the drug would fail to do so. By asserting that no evidence exists concerning whether pentobarbital will render an inmate unconscious, Valle has failed to meet his burden of proof.[107] As the circuit court correctly recognized, Dr. Waisel's asserted lack of knowledge about pentobarbital's effects falls short of the heavy burden of affirmatively showing that the drug is sure or very likely to cause serious illness and needless suffering or that its use will result in a substantial risk of serious harm. *See DeYoung v. Owens*, 646 F.3d 1319, 1326 n. 4 (11th Cir.2011) ("DeYoung also alleges that pentobarbital has not been sufficiently tested for its ability to cause an anesthetic coma in fully conscious persons. However, DeYoung's expert candidly admits he does not know how the State's dosage of pentobarbital will affect inmates because he claims there is no way to know. This asserted *lack* of knowledge obviously cannot satisfy DeYoung's burden of affirmatively showing that a substantial risk of serious harm exists.").

Despite Dr. Dershwitz's testimony, Valle also relies on a collection of letters sent from Lundbeck, the manufacturer of pentobarbital, to the DOC and the Governor stating that the use of pentobarbital outside of the approved label has not been established, and that consequently, Lundbeck could not assure the associated safety and efficacy profiles in such instances. These letters further requested that this state stop using pentobarbital to execute prisoners.

The circuit court concluded that these letters carried no weight and exhibited no legal value because "[t]here was no mention of medical evidence or anything relevant to the court's inquiry." We agree. The experts for both Valle and the State recognized that a variety of drugs have acceptable "off-label" uses. Lundbeck's opposition to the use of pentobarbital and asserted lack of information as to the drug's efficacy and safety for use in lethal injections do nothing to establish a substantial risk of serious harm. *See, e.g., West v. Brewer*, No. CV-11-1409-PHX-NVW, 2011 WL 2836754, at *8 (D.Ariz. July 18, 2011) (finding the manufacturer's "warning" against the use of pentobarbital in executions unpersuasive since it did not establish a substantial risk of harm), *aff'd*, 652 F.3d 1060 (9th Cir. 2011); *Powell v. Thomas*, 784 F.Supp.2d 1270, 1281 n. 7 (M.D.Ala. 2011) ("Williams emphasizes that the manufacturer of pentobarbital has pronounced that it is opposed to its drug being used for executions, but fails to demonstrate how that fact is in any way relevant to the issues and his burden."), *aff'd*, 641 F.3d 1255 (11th Cir.), *cert. denied*, ___ U.S. ___, 131 S.Ct. 2487 (2011).

To further buttress his assertion that the drug's substitution amounts to an Eighth Amendment violation, Valle points to the recent executions of Alabama inmate Eddie Powell and Georgia inmate Roy Blankenship. Valle contends that Alabama's and Georgia's use of pentobarbital to execute inmates resulted in botched executions or executions that did not go according to plan. With respect to the Powell execution, Valle presented the testimony of Powell's attorney, Matt Schulz, who was able to observe

---

107. [FN 1.] Valle also overlooks the fact that the portion of Florida's lethal injection protocol ensuring that an inmate is unconscious prior to the administration of the second and third drugs has not been altered since we approved the August 2007 protocol in Lightbourne. Under the current protocol, if the administration of pentobarbital does not render Valle unconscious, he will not be injected with the final two drugs, and the execution will be suspended until Valle is unconscious.

Powell's left side, face, and right arm during the execution. As Schulz explained, after the warden permitted Powell to recite his last words, the warden walked behind Powell and made an announcement that the execution was to be carried out; the intravenous (IV) lines ran into a wall, which led to a room outside the execution chamber. Schulz testified that he could not see the drugs being administered and did not know when the injections began. After the warden left the execution chamber, Schulz explained, a chaplain took Powell's left hand and spoke to Powell for around thirty seconds to a minute, during which Powell turned to Schulz, "nodded a little bit and then took a deep breath and laid his head back."

By Schulz's account, approximately one minute later, Powell suddenly jerked his head up, it appeared as though his upper body was pressing against the restraints, and he looked around with confusion. Schulz asserted that Powell clenched his jaw, flexed his muscles, and his arteries bulged. This episode lasted approximately one minute, and then Powell's eyes glazed over, rolled back into his head, and then his head rested. As Schulz described it, after a few minutes, a guard approached Powell, yelled his name three times, and then ran his finger over Powell's left eyelash; Powell did not respond to the guard's actions. After a couple of minutes, Schulz noticed that Powell's eyes were slightly opened, although Schulz did not actually see at what point they opened. Schulz also did not see Powell's eyes close, but remembered that by the end of the procedure, which lasted around twenty to twenty-five minutes, Powell's eyes were fully closed.

The circuit court rejected Schulz's testimony as speculative and concluded that "[e]ven if the entire situation lasted one minute, it certainly does not establish that [Powell] suffered to establish an Eighth Amendment claim."

We accept the circuit court's findings as supported by competent, substantial evidence.

As to the Blankenship execution, Valle again relies on the testimony of Dr. Waisel, who was not present at the execution but testified that Blankenship "suffered extremely." After reviewing various materials, Dr. Waisel opined that based on reports, Blankenship looked at his arms with discomfort and pain, grimaced, jerked his head up, and continued breathing and mouthing words for up to what was reported to be three minutes. Dr. Waisel explained that Blankenship's movement should have stopped fifteen seconds after the pentobarbital reached his body, and given that Blankenship's body movements lasted for three minutes, the drug did not work as it was intended. Dr. Waisel never opined as to what time the pentobarbital was actually administered.

To rebut Dr. Waisel's testimony, the State presented the eyewitness testimony of John Harper and Dr. Jacqueline Martin. According to Harper, who works for the Georgia Department of Corrections, Blankenship had an IV line running into each of his arms. Harper observed Blankenship look at his left arm about five seconds after the start of the first syringe, which was injected into Blankenship's right arm. Harper testified that within ten seconds of the first drug's administration, Blankenship appeared to be unconscious, and other than Blankenship looking at his left arm and making what he described as a "grunt" sound, he did not observe anything else. Similarly, Dr. Martin stated that two or three minutes after the warden left the execution chamber, Blankenship looked at his left arm, moved his mouth, looked at his right arm, put his head down on a pillow, and then did not move. She observed no obvious signs of distress or facial features indicating pain, and in her medical opinion, Blankenship was not in pain during the execution.

In reviewing the above testimony, the circuit court determined that the State presented two "very credible witnesses" who testified consistently with one another and found that that there was no indication that Blankenship experienced pain or suffering.

The circuit court's resolution of this issue is supported by competent, substantial evidence.

Valle attempts to use the Powell and Blankenship executions to show that the administration of pentobarbital does not adequately render an inmate unconscious. However, the record before this Court supports the circuit court's findings to the contrary. Nevertheless, even if we were to assume that problems arose during the course of the Blankenship and Powell executions, the United States Supreme Court has advised that "an isolated mishap alone does not give rise to an Eighth Amendment violation, precisely because such an event, while regrettable, does not suggest cruelty, or that the procedure at issue gives rise to a 'substantial risk of serious harm.'" *Baze*, 553 U.S. at 50 (quoting *Farmer*, 511 U.S. at 842. Thus, Valle has failed to satisfy the *Baze* standard, which requires proof that the replacement of the drug is "*sure or very likely* to cause serious illness and needless suffering." *Id.* (quoting *Helling*, 509 U.S. at 34).

Valle does not, however, premise his Eighth Amendment claim solely on the DOC's recent substitution of pentobarbital for sodium thiopental. Rather, Valle contends that the substitution of the drug, *coupled* with inadequate procedural safeguards and a cavalier attitude toward lethal injection, puts him at risk of serious harm. Specifically, Valle notes the existence of various inadequacies in Florida's lethal injection procedures, including how the drugs are administered and the manner in which consciousness is assessed and monitored. Referring to what he describes as Florida's unique history of deviating from written execution protocols and citing to the Angel Diaz execution in 2006 as one example, Valle also asserts inadequate qualifications, certification, training, and experience of execution team members, inadequate monitoring of the IV lines, and the DOC's failure to conduct a meaningful review and certification of its process.

Because Valle agrees that other than replacing sodium thiopental with pentobarbital, the DOC's June 2011 protocol is identical to the August 2007 lethal injection protocol that this Court upheld in *Lightbourne*, the circuit court did not err in summarily denying this portion of Valle's claim. The factual circumstances surrounding the execution of Diaz were thoroughly litigated in *Lightbourne*, and since that time, there have been five executions without subsequent allegations of newly discovered problems with Florida's lethal injection process. *See Tompkins v. State*, 994 So.2d 1072, 1081–82 (Fla.2008) (affirming summary denial of challenge to lethal injection procedures and noting that after the *Lightbourne* decision, two executions had been conducted in Florida with no subsequent allegations of problems giving rise to the investigations following the Diaz execution). The remaining aspects of the protocol to which Valle currently takes issue were rejected on the merits in *Lightbourne*, 969 So.2d at 350–53, and in subsequent cases. *See, e.g., Baze*, 553 U.S. at 53–61 (rejecting claims regarding the inadequate administration of the lethal injection protocol, the risk that the procedures will not be properly followed, the absence of additional monitoring by trained personnel, inadequate training, issues with the placement and monitoring of IV lines, the lack of professional medical experience, and the need for a significant consciousness test); *Troy v. State*, 57 So.3d 828, 839–40 (Fla.2011) (rejecting Troy's claims regarding deficiencies in Florida's lethal injection protocol including that the protocol fails to require that the execution team and the medical personnel who perform lethal injection have appropriate training, credentials, and supervision, fail to require adequate record-keeping and an adequate review and certification process, and fail to require adequate standards to manage complications inherent in the procedure).

As recognized above, the *Baze* standard requires proof that Florida's lethal injection procedures are sure or very likely to cause serious illness and needless suffering or will result in a substantial risk of serious harm. *See* 553 U.S. at 50. After reviewing the evidence and testimony presented below, we conclude that Valle has failed to satisfy the "heavy burden" that Florida's current lethal injection procedures, as implemented by the DOC, are constitutionally defective in violation of the Eighth Amendment of the United States Constitution. We thus affirm the circuit court's orders.

* * *

The Governor's Discretion to Sign Death Warrants

Next, Valle asserts that Florida's death penalty structure violates the Eighth and Fourteenth Amendments because by being able to sign a death warrant, the Governor has the absolute discretion to decide who lives and who dies. This, Valle contends, is contrary to the Eighth Amendment requirement that there be a principled way to distinguish between who is executed and who is not. In *Marek v. State*, 8 So.3d 1123, 1129–30 (Fla.2009), we rejected a similar constitutional challenge to Florida's clemency process and declined to "second-guess" the application of the exclusive executive function of clemency. While our decision in *Marek* was pending, Marek filed another successive postconviction motion, specifically contending that the manner in which the Governor determined that a death warrant should be signed was arbitrary and capricious. This Court affirmed the denial of relief, explaining in more detail:

> Marek argues that Florida's clemency process, *particularly the Governor's authority to sign warrants,* is unconstitutional because it does not provide sufficient due process to the condemned inmate. He asserts that public records documenting that the Governor reviewed Marek's case in September 2008 without input from Marek demonstrate that he was denied due process. Marek contends that because he did not obtain the public records until April 27, 2009, he could not have raised this claim in a prior proceeding. However, Marek did raise this claim in his second successive postconviction proceeding. *In that proceeding, Marek analogized the Governor's decision to sign his death*

warrant to a lottery and contended that Florida's clemency process was one-sided, arbitrary, and standardless. This Court rejected Marek's challenges as meritless. The current claim raises the same legal challenge this Court previously considered.

Marek v. State, 14 So.3d 985, 998 (Fla.) (emphasis added) (citation omitted) (citing *Marek*, 8 So.3d at 1129–30), *cert. denied*, ___ U.S. ___, 130 S.Ct. 40 (2009).

In essence, Valle raises a claim similar to Marek's and is asking this Court to second-guess the Governor's decision in determining *when* to sign Valle's death warrant because other inmates were also eligible for a death warrant. However, this Court has always proceeded very carefully in addressing such a claim since it triggers separation of powers concerns. *See, e.g., Johnston [v. State]*, 27 So.3d at 26 ("[W]e decline to depart from the Court's precedent, based on the doctrine of separation of powers, in which we have held that it is not our prerogative to second-guess the executive on matters of clemency in capital cases."); *In re Advisory Opinion of the Governor*, 334 So.2d 561, 562–63 (Fla.1976) ("This Court has always viewed the pardon powers expressed in the Constitution as being peculiarly within the domain of the executive branch of government."). Here, Valle has not provided any reason for this Court to depart from its precedents, and we therefore affirm the circuit court's denial of relief.

Length of Time on Death Row

Valle next contends that the circuit court erred in summarily denying his claim that the thirty-three years he has spent on death row constitutes cruel and unusual punishment. Under this Court's clear precedent, Valle's claim is facially invalid, and the circuit court did not err in summarily denying relief. In *Tompkins*, this Court observed that "no federal or state court has accepted the argument that a prolonged stay on death row constitutes cruel and unusual punishment, especially where both parties bear responsibility for the long delay." 994 So.2d at 1085 (quoting *Booker v. State*, 969 So.2d 186, 200 (Fla.2007)). In line with *Tompkins*, this Court has repeatedly held this claim to be meritless. *See, e.g., id.* (rejecting claim that twenty-three years on death row constituted cruel and unusual punishment); *Booker*, 969 So.2d at 200 (rejecting claim that almost thirty years on death row constituted cruel and unusual punishment); *Gore v. State*, 964 So.2d 1257, 1276 (Fla.2007) (rejecting claim that twenty-three years on death row constituted cruel and unusual punishment); *Rose v. State*, 787 So.2d 786, 805 (Fla.2001) (holding as without merit cruel and unusual punishment claim of death row inmate under death sentence since 1977).

Furthermore, while Valle asserts that the State repeatedly botched his trials and resentencings during his first ten years on death row, thereby extending the length of his incarceration, he has contributed to the remaining twenty-three years of delay in his execution. Since his death sentence became final in 1991, Valle has continued to exercise his constitutional rights in challenging his convictions and sentence. He filed a postconviction motion in state court, multiple habeas petitions in this Court, and a habeas petition in federal court, the denial of which was affirmed on appeal in 2006. Valle "cannot now contend that his punishment has been illegally prolonged because the delay in carrying out his sentence is in large part due to his own actions in challenging his conviction[s] and sentence." *Tompkins*, 994 So.2d at 1085. Therefore, the circuit court did not err in summarily denying Valle's claim.

* * *

CONCLUSION

In accordance with our analysis above, we affirm the circuit court's denial of post-conviction relief. No motion for rehearing will be entertained by this Court. The mandate shall issue immediately. We hereby lift the temporary stay imposed by this Court on July 25, 2011.

It is so ordered.

CANADY, C.J., and PARIENTE, LEWIS, QUINCE, POLSTON, LABARGA, and PERRY, JJ., concur.

M. Article I, Section 24 — Access to Public Records and Meetings

Florida's original Sunshine Law, codified in Chapter 119, Florida Statutes, dates back to 1967. The 1977–78 Constitution Revision Commission proposed a constitutional right of access to public records as two separate provisions, but these proposals were rejected by voters. In 1992, the Florida Supreme Court, ruling on separation of powers grounds, found that the Sunshine Law did not apply to the Legislature or to constitutional officers of other branches of state government. *See Locke v. Hawkes*, 595 So. 2d 32 (Fla. 1992). The decision prompted the Legislature to submit this amendment, which was adopted by Florida voters in November 1992.

Campus Communications v. Earnhardt
821 So. 2d 388 (5th DCA), *rev. denied*, 848 So. 2d 1153 (Fla. 2002), *cert. denied*, 540 U.S. 1049 (2003)

SAWAYA, J.

Campus Communications, Inc. (Campus) appeals the final judgment finding Chapter 2001-1, codified at section 406.135, Florida Statutes (2001), constitutional and retroactively applicable to the request made by Campus to view and copy the autopsy photographs of R. Dale Earnhardt. We affirm.

Factual Background and Issues

Mr. Earnhardt was a famous and very successful race car driver who became involved in a fatal crash during the Daytona 500 race on February 18, 2001. He was taken to Halifax Medical Center where, sadly, life-saving efforts were unsuccessful. Mr. Earnhardt was pronounced dead on that same date.

An autopsy was performed on February 19, 2001, by an assistant to the Volusia County Medical Examiner in accordance with Florida law governing accidental deaths.[108] In performing the autopsy, thirty-three photographs were taken which, according to the uncontradicted testimony of the medical examiner, were not of "diagnostic quality" and were taken solely as a back-up to the dictation system utilized by the medical examiner to record his findings for inclusion in a written autopsy report.

The written autopsy report, post-crash photographs of Mr. Earnhardt's car, a toxicology report and a sketch showing the markings on Mr. Earnhardt's body were promptly made available to the public. The autopsy photographs, however, were not released because on February 22, 2001, Mrs. Earnhardt sought and obtained an ex parte injunction precluding the medical examiner from releasing them. This injunction was obtained before any request for access to the photographs was made.

On February 23, 2001, the Orlando Sentinel newspaper requested the autopsy photographs. Michael Uribe, who operates a for-profit website on which he publishes celebrity autopsy photographs, also made a request for the photographs. Mr. Uribe had previously published the autopsy photographs of Neil Bonnett and Rodney Orr, both of whom were race car drivers killed in crashes at the Daytona International Speedway. Both requests were denied pursuant to the injunction.

The medical examiner, the Earnhardts and the newspaper interests represented by the Orlando Sentinel subsequently entered into a mediation agreement whereby they agreed that the photographs would be examined by an expert in biomechanics who would issue a report and, thereafter, the photographs would be permanently sealed. Neither Campus nor Mr. Uribe participated in the mediated settlement and on the same day the agreement was reached, Campus made its request for the photographs.

On March 29, 2001, the Florida Legislature enacted section 406.135, which was signed by Governor Bush and became effective on that same date. Upon passage of the statute, the Earnhardts amended their request to include permanent injunctive relief under the statute. Campus filed a cross-claim against the medical examiner seeking an order under the Public Records Act requiring the medical examiner to allow inspection and copying of the photographs. Trial subsequently commenced, evidence and testimony were presented, and the trial court rendered its decision finding the statute constitutional and retroactively applicable to the requests made by Campus and Mr. Uribe.

The issues we are confronted with in the instant proceedings are 1) whether section 406.135 is overly broad and therefore unconstitutional; 2) whether the statute should be applied retroactively; and 3) whether the trial court erred in finding that Campus

---

108. [FN2.] Section 406.11(1)(a)2., Florida Statutes (2001), provides that if a human being dies by accident in the State of Florida, the medical examiner of the district in which the death occurred or where the body is found "shall determine the cause of death and shall, for that purpose, make or have performed such examinations, investigations, and autopsies as he or she shall deem necessary or as shall be requested by the state attorney...."

failed to establish good cause under the statute to allow inspection and copying of the photographs. We will proceed to address each issue in the order presented.

Constitutionality of the Statute

General Principles and Legislative Findings

We begin our analysis with the generally accepted principle that "all laws are presumed constitutional" and "[t]he burden rests on the party challenging the law to show that it is invalid." *Chicago Title Ins. Co. v. Butler*, 770 So.2d 1210, 1214 (Fla.2000) (citations omitted). If any doubt exists as to the validity of a law, it must be resolved in favor of constitutionality where reasonably possible. *L.B. v. State*, 700 So.2d 370 (Fla.1997); *Department of Law Enforcement v. Real Prop.*, 588 So.2d 957, 961 (Fla.1991).

Both the Florida Constitution and the Public Records Act allow for the creation of exemptions to the Act by the Legislature, provided the newly enacted exemption 1) serves an identifiable public purpose and 2) is no broader than necessary to meet that public purpose. Art. I, § 24(c), Fla. Const.; § 119.15(4)(b), Fla. Stat. (2001). As to the first requirement, the Legislature must specifically state the public necessity which justifies the exemption. Art. 1, § 24(c), Fla. Const. In order to fulfill these constitutional and statutory requirements, the Legislature made the following findings:

> The Legislature finds that it is a public necessity that photographs and video and audio recordings of an autopsy be made confidential and exempt from the requirements of section 119.07(1), Florida Statutes, and Section 24(a) of Article I of the State Constitution. The Legislature finds that photographs or video or audio recordings of an autopsy depict or describe the deceased in graphic and often disturbing fashion. Such photographs or video or audio recordings may depict or describe the deceased nude, bruised, bloodied, broken, with bullet or other wounds, cut open, dismembered, or decapitated. As such, photographs or video or audio recordings of an autopsy are highly sensitive depictions or descriptions of the deceased which, if heard, viewed, copied or publicized, could result in trauma, sorrow, humiliation, or emotional injury to the immediate family of the deceased, as well as injury to the memory of the deceased. The Legislature notes that the existence of the World Wide Web and the proliferation of personal computers throughout the world encourages and promotes the wide dissemination of photographs and video and audio recordings 24 hours a day and that widespread unauthorized dissemination of autopsy photographs and video and audio recordings would subject the immediate family of the deceased to continuous injury. The Legislature further notes that there continue to be other types of available information, such as the autopsy report, which are less intrusive and injurious to the immediate family members of the deceased and which continue to provide for public oversight. The Legislature further finds that the exemption provided in this act should be given retroactive application because it is remedial in nature.

Ch. 2001-1, § 2, at 2, Laws of Fla.

We will address the specificity requirement first.

The Specificity Requirement

As to the requirement that the exemption serve an identifiable public purpose, the Legislature must "state with specificity the public necessity justifying the exemption." Art. I, §24(c), Fla. Const. We find that chapter 2001-1, Laws of Florida, clearly satisfies this requirement. The legislative findings detail the graphic and often gruesome nature of such autopsy photographs and the trauma and emotional injury the immediate family of the deceased would likely suffer if these records were disclosed and disseminated to the public. The Legislature also recognizes the potential for exacerbation of such injury in light of the ever increasing use of the Internet and the proliferation of personal computers. These findings are supported by the evidence and testimony introduced in the proceedings before the trial court.

We need not address the specificity requirement any further because Campus does not forcefully challenge the Legislature's statement of public necessity. Rather, Campus focuses on the argument that the exemption is overly broad.

The Exemption Must Not Be Overly Broad

Campus contends that section 406.135 is unconstitutional because it is broader than necessary to meet the statute's public purpose. Specifically, Campus argues that the finding made by the Legislature that some photographs "may" show gruesome scenes and that trauma "could" result from publication of the autopsy photographs is explicit recognition that photographs are not always gruesome and that trauma does not always result from their viewing. Therefore, Campus asserts, the Legislature exempted more records than were necessary to serve the purpose of the statute. We disagree that the statute is overly broad.

We find the scope of section 406.135 to be specific and narrow: it applies only to autopsy photographs and audio and video recordings of the autopsy. It does not apply to other records of the autopsy such as the written autopsy report and, therefore, those materials remain unrestricted public records. Moreover, in the instant case, the trial court found that there was no information that could be obtained from the autopsy photographs of Mr. Earnhardt that was not contained in the autopsy report which was published to the parties and the public.

Equally important, despite the fact that autopsy photographs and audio and video recordings are no longer considered unrestricted public records, is the inclusion of the good cause provisions which do allow the publication of these restricted records if the statutory criteria are established. *See* §406.135(2)(a), Fla. Stat. (2001). Thus the fact that the Legislature used "may," "could" and "often" is not evidence that the exemption is overly broad, but rather a recognition that circumstances may exist which would justify disclosure of autopsy photographs and audio and video recordings upon a showing of good cause. Moreover, use of the absolute terminology advocated by Campus such as "would," "always" and "must" would foreclose the possibility that disclosure could be made even upon a showing of good cause.

We find *Bryan v. State*, 753 So.2d 1244 (Fla.), *cert. denied*, 528 U.S. 1185 (2000), analogous to the instant case. In *Bryan*, the court analyzed a public records exemption provided in section 945.10(1)(e), Florida Statutes (1999), which exempted from disclosure records and information of the Department of Corrections "which if released would jeopardize a person's safety." The Legislature had justified the adoption of this exemption by stating that "it is a public necessity that the department records ... remain confidential and exempt from public disclosure ... because to provide otherwise would *in some cases* conflict with other existing law or would reveal information that would jeopardize the safety of the guards, inmates, and others." *Id.* at 1250 (emphasis supplied). The legislative findings in *Bryan* that disclosure of the information "in some cases" would jeopardize an individual's safety could be considered constitutionally infirm on the same grounds advanced by Campus in the instant case, but the supreme court approved the exemption as being "supported by a thoroughly articulated public policy." *Id.* at 1251 (footnote omitted). Like the court in *Bryan*, we find the exemption provided in section 406.135 to be supported by a thoroughly articulated public policy and reject the argument that it is overly broad.

Campus next assails the "good cause" provision of the statute, protesting that the Legislature did not define this term. We find that this argument lacks merit because the statute requires consideration of specific criteria to determine whether good cause has been shown. *See* § 406.135(2)(a), Fla. Stat. (2001). Moreover, good cause is not a novel concept to our jurisprudence. Florida courts have applied good cause provisions in a variety of contexts, including the Public Records Act. *See, e.g.,* § 119.07(7)(a), Fla. Stat. (2001); *Department of Health & Rehabilitative Servs. v. Gainesville Sun Publ'g Co.,* 582 So.2d 725 (Fla. 1st DCA 1991). Therefore, the statute is not invalid because it fails to specifically define a term for which the courts already know the meaning.

We find that section 406.135 serves an identifiable public purpose, is no broader than necessary to meet that public purpose and was enacted in accordance with the constitutional and legislative requirements we have previously discussed. The presumption of constitutionality has not been overcome by Campus. Therefore, we conclude that section 406.135 is constitutional. [The Court found that the legislation was remedial and that retroactive application did not abrogate any vested rights.]

The last issue we must address is whether the trial court erred in finding that Campus failed to establish good cause under section 406.135.

Good Cause

Campus argues that even if section 406.135 is constitutional, the trial court erred in finding that Campus failed to establish good cause for release of the photographs. The statute requires consideration of the following factors in determining good cause: 1) whether disclosure is necessary so that the public can evaluate the government's performance; 2) the seriousness of the intrusion into the family's right to privacy; 3) whether disclosure is the least intrusive method available; and 4) the availability of similar information in other public records, regardless of form. § 406.135(2)(a), Fla. Stat. (2001).

As to the first factor, while the public obviously has a great interest in making certain its government, the medical examiner in the instant case, carries out its duties in a responsible fashion, that interest cannot be served by viewing the autopsy photographs of Mr. Earnhardt because the uncontradicted testimony establishes that the photographs are not of diagnostic quality. Moreover, the testimony further establishes that there is nothing that can be discerned from the photographs that is not contained in the autopsy report and other materials that have been released to Campus and the public. If it cannot be determined from the photographs that the cause of death was anything other than what the medical examiner concluded, the photographs will not aid in assuring that the government is performing up to the required standard. Regarding the argument advanced by Campus that the photographs are needed to evaluate NASCAR safety requirements, the trial court found, and we agree, that the safety requirements of NASCAR, a private entity, do not implicate the public's interest in evaluating governmental performance sufficient to release the photographs.

The second factor weighs very heavily in favor of nondisclosure. The medical examiner testified that the photographs were "gruesome, grisly and highly disturbing," and the physician attending Mr. Earnhardt after the accident confirmed this. The trial court found that such publication would "be an indecent, outrageous, and intolerable invasion, and would cause deep and serious emotional pain, embarrassment, humiliation and sadness to Dale Earnhardt's surviving family members." It is evident from our review of the record that the publication of the nude and dissected body of Mr. Earnhardt would cause his wife and children pain and sorrow beyond the poor power of our ability to express in words.

Regarding the third factor, the trial court found that there were no less intrusive means available for preventing trauma to the Earnhardt family. Campus argues that inspection alone would not cause a serious intrusion into the privacy rights of the Earnhardt family. However, the trial court rejected this argument, finding that the mere knowledge that the photographs would be accessible for inspection was the cause of overwhelming distress to the Earnhardt family.

The fourth factor also weighs in favor of nondisclosure. As we previously stated, the autopsy report and other information was made available to the public and, given the poor quality of the photographs and the fact that they were only made as a back-up to the medical examiner's dictation system, disclosure of the photographs would reveal nothing that is not contained in the autopsy records that were released.

The standard of review regarding issues of good cause requires us to determine whether the trial court abused its discretion in making its decision. *See Palokonis v. EGR Enters. Inc.*, 652 So.2d 482 (Fla. 5th DCA 1995); *Williams v. Estate of Williams*, 493 So.2d 44 (Fla. 5th DCA 1986). Based on our thorough review of the record in the instant case and our analysis of this issue, we conclude that the trial court did not abuse its discretion in finding that Campus failed to establish good cause under section 406.135.

Conclusion

The Florida Constitution gives every citizen the right to inspect and copy public records so that all may have the opportunity to see and know how the government functions. It is also a declared constitutional principle that every individual has a right of privacy, and while our constitution does not catalogue every matter that one can hold as private, autopsy photographs which display the remains of a deceased human being is certainly one of them. But we need not say so because the Legislature has said so and that is its prerogative, not ours. Thus our function here has not been to weigh these two constitutional rights with respect to autopsy photographs and determine whether the right that helps ensure an open government freely accessible by every citizen is more significant or profound than the right that preserves individual liberty and privacy. Rather, our function has been to determine whether the Legislature has declared that the latter prevails over the former in a manner that is consistent with the constitutional provisions that bestow upon it the power to do so. We have fulfilled our judicial responsibility in this matter by determining whether section 406.135 was constitutionally enacted and whether it was properly applied under the facts and circumstances of the instant case. Having concluded that it was, we affirm the judgment under review.

We conclude our judicial responsibility by certifying to the Florida Supreme Court the following questions to be of great public importance:

1. IS SECTION 406.135 CONSTITUTIONAL?
2. IF SECTION 406.135 IS CONSTITUTIONAL, SHOULD IT BE APPLIED RETROACTIVELY?

AFFIRMED; QUESTIONS CERTIFIED.

PETERSON and GRIFFIN, JJ., concur.

Sarasota Herald-Tribune v. State

924 So. 2d 8 (2d DCA), *rev. denied*, 918 So. 2d 293 (Fla. 2005),
cert. denied, 546 U.S. 1135 (2006)

ALTENBERND, Judge.

The Sarasota Herald-Tribune, Tampa Tribune, WFLA-TV News Channel 8, and The Herald (the Media) petition this court to review an order entered by the trial court that excludes the press from viewing and inspecting crime scene photographs, crime scene videotapes, and autopsy photographs that were admitted into evidence in open court during the criminal trial of Joseph P. Smith for the murder of Carlie Brucia. The order actually prevents all members of the public from viewing these exhibits. We conclude that the statutes relied upon by the trial court to bar examination of this evidence by the Media do not apply to these exhibits that have been formally introduced into evidence in a pending criminal trial. Instead, the trial court was required to apply the analysis set forth in Florida Rule of Judicial Administration 2.051(c), which essentially codifies the holdings in *Barron v. Florida Freedom Newspapers, Inc.*, 531 So.2d 113 (Fla.1988), and *Miami Herald Publishing Co. v. Lewis*, 426 So.2d 1 (Fla.1982). Under that analysis, we conclude that the four members of the

Media who have asked to view the evidence have been improperly excluded from viewing it.

We emphasize that we are not holding that the Media is entitled to copies of this evidence or to publish it. The Media has not sought that relief and does not suggest that it has any interest in seeking that relief. We also emphasize that we are not holding that the trial court must make this evidence generally available for easy viewing by large numbers of people. Finally, our holding is limited to exhibits actually introduced into evidence. We have not been asked to determine any issue concerning exhibits that may have been identified but not admitted for use and examination by the jury, or concerning documents that were disclosed earlier in these proceedings and not used for any purpose during the trial.

I. PROCEEDING IN TRIAL COURT LEADING UP TO THIS APPELLATE PROCEEDING

The State indicted Joseph P. Smith, alleging that he kidnapped, sexually assaulted, and murdered a young girl, Carlie Brucia, on February 1, 2004. It is undisputed that many of the crime scene photographs and autopsy photographs related to these crimes are disturbing. Prior to the jury trial, the trial court entered orders restricting access to some of the documents that might otherwise have been accessible as court records. The Media did not challenge those orders.

At trial, however, the Media sought access to crime scene photographs, crime scene videotapes, and autopsy photographs that were actually introduced into evidence. The State did not wish to have the exhibits made public. The Media argued that the trial court should enter an order containing restrictions similar to those imposed by Judge Stan Morris in the trial of Danny Rolling, which would have permitted the Media to view and inspect the exhibits. *See State v. Rolling*, 22 Media L. Rep. (BNA) 2264, 1994 WL 722891 (Fla. 8th Cir.Ct.1994). Ultimately, the trial court was persuaded that the enactment of section 406.135, Florida Statutes (2005), and certain provisions in chapter 119, Florida Statutes (2005), required it to enter an order more restrictive than the order entered in the *Rolling* case. On November 10, the trial court orally ruled that it would bar all press and public access to certain exhibits that had been introduced into evidence. The evidence at issue includes five crime scene photographs that were admitted into evidence as State's exhibits 30, 32, 34, 35a, and 36. It also includes thirteen autopsy photographs that were admitted into evidence as State's exhibits 39–46, 48, 50, 51, 53, and 56. Finally, there is a videotape that was marked for identification as State's exhibit 31, but was redacted prior to admission into evidence. This court is uncertain whether the redacted videotape was introduced into evidence under a different exhibit number.

The Media challenged the trial court's oral ruling by filing a petition in this court pursuant to Florida Rule of Appellate Procedure 9.100(d), which permits expedited review of orders excluding the press. We instructed the trial court to render a written order, which was entered on November 17, 2005. Thus, the order that we are reviewing in this case pursuant to rule 9.100(d) is the order of November 17, 2005.

Both the State and Mr. Smith have responded to the Media's petition, supporting the trial court's order. The State argues that the Media cannot bring this challenge because the Media did not challenge the earlier orders restricting access to documents pretrial. We conclude that the orders addressing pretrial issues are not dispositive of the Media's right to view exhibits introduced into evidence during a public, criminal trial.

II. THE CONSTITUTIONAL DIMENSIONS OF THIS CASE

The broadest issue in this case is whether the State can rely upon secret evidence to obtain a conviction for a capital offense. Although Mr. Smith's trial has been broadcast on television and conducted in an open, public courtroom, these specific items of evidence have been concealed from all members of the public and the press. The disputed photographs are not in this court's record, and we have not chosen to view them. Nevertheless, we can fully understand that they must be extraordinarily distressing to family and friends of the young victim. However, these photographs are evidence in a trial where the State, on behalf of the people, is using its power to pursue the most extreme penalties. Secret evidence is the hallmark of an oppressive regime; it is not a policy generally acceptable in a free society with courts that must be open to the people to assure the legitimacy of those courts and the fairness of the proceedings that occur therein.

As a result of these concerns, the Media has challenged the trial court's ruling at a constitutional level. There is strong support for this argument. As the United States Supreme Court stated in *Craig v. Harney*, 331 U.S. 367, 374 (1947): "A trial is a public event. What transpires in the court room is public property.... There is no special perquisite of the judiciary which enables it, as distinguished from other institutions of democratic government, to suppress, edit, or censor events which transpire in proceedings before it."

Allowing the public access to all aspects of a criminal trial "enhances the quality and safeguards the integrity of the factfinding process, with benefits to both the defendant and to society as a whole." *Globe Newspaper Co. v. Superior Court*, 457 U.S. 596, 606 (1982) (citing *Richmond Newspapers, Inc. v. Virginia*, 448 U.S. 555, 569 (1980)). When the media attends a trial and reports on the proceedings, a larger segment of the public is afforded this important access.

> The open trial thus plays as important a role in the administration of justice today as it did for centuries before our separation from England. The value of openness lies in the fact that people not actually attending trials can have confidence that standards of fairness are being observed; the sure knowledge that *anyone* is free to attend gives assurance that established procedures are being followed and that deviations will become known. Openness thus enhances both the basic fairness of the criminal trial and the appearance of fairness so essential to public confidence in the system. *Richmond Newspapers, Inc. v. Virginia*, 448 U.S. at 569–571.

Press-Enter. Co. v. Superior Court, 464 U.S. 501, 508 (1984).

Although the openness of criminal trial proceedings helps to ensure fairness to the accused and provides the public with an assurance of that fairness, certain limited circumstances can exist in which a court would be justified in closing aspects of a proceeding to public scrutiny. *Press-Enter. Co. v. Superior Court*, 478 U.S. 1, 9 (1986). "In such cases, the trial court must determine whether the situation is such that the rights of the accused override the qualified First Amendment right of access." *Id.*

> The presumption of openness may be overcome only by an overriding interest based on findings that closure is essential to preserve higher values and is narrowly tailored to serve that interest. The interest is to be articulated along with findings specific enough that a reviewing court can determine whether the closure order was properly entered.

Press-Enter., 464 U.S. at 510. "But the circumstances under which the press and public can be barred from a criminal trial are limited; the State's justification in denying access must be a weighty one." *Globe*, 457 U.S. at 606. "Where ... the State attempts to deny the right of access in order to inhibit the disclosure of sensitive information, it must be shown that the denial is necessitated by a compelling governmental interest, and is narrowly tailored to serve that interest." *Id.* at 606–07.

This case is somewhat unusual because the "compelling governmental interest" that may justify a restriction on disclosure does not primarily involve the defendant's privacy or his right to a fair trial. *See, e.g., United States v. Posner*, 594 F.Supp. 930 (S.D.Fla.1984). Instead, the interest to be protected is the privacy of the victim's family and friends. The supreme court has recognized that article I, section 23 of the Florida Constitution can form a constitutional basis for closure of court records or proceedings. *See Barron*, 531 So.2d at 118. Nevertheless, the privacy interests of persons who are family or friends of the victims of well-publicized crimes would seem to be a difficult interest to balance against the interests favoring public trial.

Although the facts of the petition and the order on review raise these important constitutional questions, we are required, whenever possible, to resolve a dispute without reaching the constitutional issues and without declaring statutes unconstitutional. *See Singletary v. State*, 322 So.2d 551 (Fla.1975). In its November 17, 2005, order, the trial court concluded that the specific exhibits were exempt and confidential, relying on the content of section 406.135 and chapter 119, Florida Statutes (2005). Without regard to their constitutionality, these statutes on their face do not render these exhibits confidential. Accordingly, resolution of this petition does not require that we review the constitutional sufficiency of any statute.

III. SECTION 406.135, FLORIDA STATUTES (2005)

Section 406.135 was enacted in response to efforts by some to obtain copies of autopsy photographs concerning the death of Dale Earnhardt. *See Campus Commc'ns, Inc. v. Earnhardt*, 821 So.2d 388 (Fla. 5th DCA 2002). Subsection 1 of that statute unambiguously states: "A photograph or video or audio recording of an autopsy *in the custody of a medical examiner* is confidential and exempt from the requirements of s. 119.07(1) and s. 24(a), Art. I of the State Constitution." (Emphasis supplied.)

The exhibits in evidence in the trial court are not in the custody of a medical examiner as the records of the county medical examiner; they are in the custody of the clerk of court as circuit court records.

Moreover, section 406.135(3)(c) states that

a criminal ... proceeding is exempt from this section, but unless otherwise exempted, is subject to all other provisions of chapter 119, provided however that this section does not prohibit a court in a criminal ... proceeding upon good cause shown from restricting or otherwise controlling the disclosure of an autopsy, crime scene, or similar photograph or video or audio recordings in the manner prescribed herein.

Thus, the statute expressly exempts criminal court proceedings from its application. The legislature directs the reader to chapter 119 to determine whether it may provide some other applicable exemption. Although section 406.135 may not "prohibit" a court in a criminal proceeding upon good cause shown from restricting or otherwise controlling the disclosure of an autopsy, crime scene, or similar photograph or video or audio recordings in the manner prescribed in that statute, as we will soon discover the regulation of the trial court in this function is controlled by rule 2.051, which establishes different tests to comply with constitutional requirements. Thus section 406.135 does not render these court exhibits confidential. If any statute accomplishes that act, it must be a provision in chapter 119.

IV. CHAPTER 119, FLORIDA STATUTES (2005)

The State argues that section 119.071(2)(h) provides the necessary exemption. That statute states:

(h) 1. Any criminal intelligence information or criminal investigative information including the photograph, name, address, or other fact or information which reveals the identity of the victim of the crime of sexual battery as defined in chapter 794; the identity of the victim of a lewd or lascivious offense committed upon or in the presence of a person less than 16 years of age, as defined in chapter 800; or the identity of the victim of the crime of child abuse as defined by chapter 827 and any criminal intelligence information or criminal investigative information or other criminal record, including those portions of court records and court proceedings, which may reveal the identity of a person who is a victim of any sexual offense, including a sexual offense proscribed in chapter 794, chapter 800, or chapter 827, is exempt from s. 119.07(1) and s. 24(a), Art. I of the State Constitution.

2. In addition to subparagraph 1., any criminal intelligence information or criminal investigative information that is a photograph, videotape, or image of any part of the body of the victim of a sexual offense prohibited under chapter 794, chapter 800, or chapter 827, regardless of whether the photograph, videotape, or image identifies the victim, is confidential and exempt from s. 119.07(1) and s. 24(a), Art. I of the State Constitution. This exemp-

tion applies to photographs, videotapes, or images held as criminal intelligence information or criminal investigative information before, on, or after the effective date of the exemption.

Both subparagraphs of this statute apply to "criminal intelligence information or criminal investigative information." Those terms are defined in section 119.011(3), Florida Statutes (2005). That statute states:

(3)(a) "Criminal intelligence information" means information with respect to an identifiable person or group of persons collected by a criminal justice agency in an effort to anticipate, prevent, or monitor possible criminal activity.

(b) "Criminal investigative information" means information with respect to an identifiable person or group of persons compiled by a criminal justice agency in the course of conducting a criminal investigation of a specific act or omission, including, but not limited to, information derived from laboratory tests, reports of investigators or informants, or any type of surveillance.

The photographs at issue do not seem to fall within the definition of "criminal intelligence information." They do arguably fall within the definition of "criminal investigative information." The definition does not expressly discuss exhibits in public trials, but section 119.011(4)(a) defines a "criminal justice agency" to include a "court."[109] Assuming without deciding that the exhibits introduced into evidence in this case may fall within this definition, section 119.07(6) provides:

Nothing in this chapter shall be construed to exempt from subsection (1) a public record that was made a part of a court file and that is not specifically closed by order of court, except ... information or records that may reveal *the identity of a person who is a victim* of a sexual offense as provided in s. 119.071(2)(h).

(Emphasis supplied.) Subsection (1) contains the provisions permitting inspection of public records. Thus, because the photographs at issue in this case are part of a court file, they are not exempt unless they fall within the exception described in section 119.07(6) concerning records that reveal the identity of a victim.

The records at issue in the trial court may come within the description in section 119.071(2)(h)(2), but they do not come within the description in section 119.071(2)(h)(1). That is to say, practically everyone in this country already knows the name of this unfortunate child and the fact that she was a victim of a sexual offense. At this point no public record can be held secret because it might reveal the well-known fact that Carlie Brucia was the victim of a sexual offense. *See Staton v. McMillan*, 597 So.2d 940 (Fla. 1st DCA 1992) (statutory exemptions from disclosure under Public Records Act do not apply if information has already been made public).

---

109. [FN2.] This court and the supreme court have held that clerks of circuit court are not subject to the chapter 119, the Public Records Act. *See Times Publ'g Co. v. Ake*, 645 So.2d 1003 (Fla. 2d DCA 1994), *approved*, 660 So.2d 255 (Fla.1995). For purposes of this expedited opinion, we merely assume without deciding that these statutes could apply in this specific context.

Thus, the exception contained in section 119.07(6) does not apply. Nothing in chapter 119 exempts from disclosure these exhibits that have been made a part of a court file.

V. FLORIDA RULE OF JUDICIAL ADMINISTRATION 2.051

Thus, if any lawful basis exists to maintain the secrecy of these photographs, it must be derived from another source. The only remaining possibility, not expressly addressed by the trial court, is rule 2.051. Rule 2.051(c)(9)(A)(v) does contain a ground that would permit some protection to these photographs. It states:

> (c) **Exemptions.** The following records of the judicial branch shall be confidential....
>
> ....
>
> (9) Any court record determined to be confidential in case decision or court rule on the grounds that
>
> (A) confidentiality is required to
>
> ....
>
> (v) avoid substantial injury to innocent third parties;....

The exemption, however, must be implemented with significant procedural safeguards to protect the constitutional rights discussed in section I of this opinion. Thus, the rule continues:

> (B) the degree, duration, and manner of confidentiality ordered by the court shall be no broader than necessary to protect the interests set forth in subdivision (A);
>
> (C) no less restrictive measures are available to protect the interests set forth in subdivision (A); and
>
> (D) except as provided by law or rule of court, reasonable notice shall be given to the public of any order closing any court record.

The trial court's order considered the "good cause" requirements in section 406.135, but did not consider the requirements of this rule. The trial court imposed a total ban on public viewing of this evidence, reasoning that the public should simply trust the testimony of the medical examiner who relied upon the undisclosed photographs because any further disclosure of the photographs would upset the victim's family. It further concluded that no less intrusive means existed to prevent harm to the family, and that other public records were available that provided detailed written descriptions of the photographs so that they did not need to be viewed.

With all due respect both to the trial court and the victim's family, these photographs have already been viewed by various people in law enforcement, by court personnel and lawyers, by this jury, and presumably by the grand jury. We can well understand that the family does not wish to have these photographs published in the press or on the internet; no one intends to let that happen. At this point, four representatives of the press are requesting the right to have four professional journalists view these photographs merely to confirm the accuracy of the verbal descriptions provided by witnesses under oath in the courtroom. We respect the privacy interests of the victim's family, but less restrictive measures exist to protect those interests while also protecting the competing interests engendered by a public trial.[110]

V. CONCLUSION

We do not mandate that the trial court enter any specific order pursuant to rule 2.051, except that the order must make provision for each of the petitioners in this proceeding to be allowed to have one professional journalist view these exhibits. We previously entered an unpublished order quashing the trial court's order. We stayed that order pending the issuance of this opinion. To permit an orderly resolution of this matter, in light of the Thanksgiving holidays and the resumption of the penalty phase in this case, this court stays the effect of this opinion until 1:30 p.m. on Monday, November 28, 2005, to permit the respondents to seek a further stay from the supreme court. Unless a stay is entered by the supreme court, the trial court must allow the Media to view these exhibits on November 28 even if motions for rehearing are filed in this court or our mandate has not issued.

The petition for review of order excluding press is granted.

VILLANTI, J., Concurs.

CASANUEVA, J., Concurs with opinion. [omitted]

Article I, Section 24 also mandates that meetings where public business is being transacted must be open to the public. The following case involved the issuance of revenue bonds by the City of Sarasota and Sarasota County to provide spring training facilities for the Baltimore Orioles. The bonding issue will be dealt with later when we look at Article VII. However, the case also involved a claim that the City and County failed to comply with the open meetings requirement of the Sunshine Law in the course of negotiations with the baseball team. The Supreme Court provides a good summary of what the Sunshine Law requires.

Sarasota Citizens v. City of Sarasota

48 So. 3d 755 (Fla. 2010)

PER CURIAM.

Sarasota Citizens for Responsible Government, et al., (collectively referred to as "Citizens") appeal a trial court's judgment validating bonds proposed for issuance by the City of Sarasota and the County of Sarasota in furtherance of an agreement bringing the Baltimore Orioles to Sarasota for spring training. On appeal in this

---

110. [FN3.] It is worth noting that the introduction of "gruesome" photographs is often an issue raised on appeal, especially in criminal cases. *See, e.g., Rodriguez v. State*, 919 So.2d 1252, (Fla. 2d DCA 2005); *Rose v. State*, 787 So.2d 786 (Fla.2001). Although the issue is rarely successful, it would be disturbing if this court or the supreme court were to reverse a criminal conviction based on the gruesomeness of photographs that no member of the public had ever seen.

Court, Citizens only allege Sunshine Law violations by the County. They do not challenge any other aspect of the bond validation proceedings, and they do not appeal the trial court's determination that the City did not violate the Sunshine Law. For the reasons explained below, we affirm the trial court.

I. BACKGROUND

As the trial court summarized,

> [t]he Sarasota County Board of County Commissioners [Board] entered into a Memorandum of Understanding (MOU) with the Baltimore Orioles (Orioles) in July, 2009. The MOU obligated the Orioles, among other things, to relocate to Sarasota for spring training. Sarasota County is obligated to fund construction of facilities/facility improvements at the Ed Smith complex, the location within the City of Sarasota where the Orioles are obligated to conduct spring training activities, and other facilities located elsewhere in the County.
>
> * * *
>
> In November, 2008, the [Board] instructed the County Administrator, James Ley, to initiate negotiations with the Orioles. Mr. Ley delegated this task to Deputy County Administrator David Bullock (Bullock). Negotiations between the County and Orioles began immediately and continued until the terms of the MOU were finalized in July, 2009. The MOU was approved by the [Board] at a public meeting on July 22, 2009. At that public hearing, the [Board] adopted an amended or modified Tourist Development Tax Ordinance, in part to provide part of the County's funding obligation under the MOU; approved an Interlocal Agreement with the City which included an obligation of the City to convey the Ed Smith complex to the County, to transfer funds to the County to offset part of the cost of construction and to undertake responsibility for environmental remediation, if required, at the complex; and adopted a resolution authorizing issuance of bonds for the purpose of financing costs associated with the improvements required by the MOU. Simultaneously, the City also authorized issuance of bonds to fulfill its obligations pursuant to the [I]nterlocal [A]greement.
>
> * * *

The terms of the MOU and Interlocal Agreement were the result of extensive negotiations. In furtherance of the Board's directive to begin negotiations with the Orioles, Bullock retained two consultants for their baseball expertise and also consulted with County staff, including the County's chief financial officer, the County's attorney, the County's parks and recreation director, and a County planning coordinator. Bullock's communications and discussions with these individuals were not advertised or otherwise treated as public meetings.

The negotiations with the Orioles took place intermittently over a series of months through meetings, phone calls, and e-mailed documents involving different individuals, all coordinated by Bullock. *** The negotiations with the Orioles took place alongside a series of discussions by the Board at its public meetings. *** At various points after the start of negotiations with the Orioles in November 2008, e-mails from constituents or others to members of the Board regarding the Orioles were copied to other Board members and sometimes included the reactions from other Board members. In at least one e-mail correspondence, a comment was directly addressed from one Board member to another. The last e-mail among Board members produced at trial was sent on April 12, 2009.

* * *

Ultimately, these negotiations and meetings resulted in Board action on July 22, 2009. On that date, the Board held a public hearing that lasted over four hours. The Board heard from approximately forty citizens, including several representatives of Citizens. Bullock and staff gave a presentation on the provisions of the proposed documents and answered questions posed by the Board.

Then, on February 19, 2010, after Citizens filed a suit alleging Sunshine Law violations against the City and the County, the Board held another public hearing for the reconsideration and ratification of the Interlocal Agreement, the MOU, and related actions. The Board also adopted a new resolution authorizing the sale of bonds to finance the County's portion of the facility renovations.

* * *

After a four-day bench trial, the trial court validated the County's and the City's proposed bonds and denied Citizens' complaint. On appeal in this Court, Citizens allege that the trial court erred in ruling that (a) Bullock's consultations were not required to be in the sunshine, (b) the one-on-one staff briefings of County Board members prior to the July 22, 2009 public meeting were not a violation of the Sunshine Law, and (c) any e-mail violations were cured by the Board's public meetings.

II. THE NEGOTIATIONS TEAM

Citizens contend that the trial court erred when ruling that Bullock and the individuals he consulted in negotiating with the Orioles (the so-called negotiations team) were not a board or commission subject to the Sunshine Law. However, we agree with the City and County and affirm the trial court.

* * *

This appeal regarding alleged Sunshine Law violations only concerns ... whether the authorization complies with the requirements of law.

Article I, section 24(b) of the Florida Constitution provides:

All meetings of any collegial public body of the executive branch of state government or of any collegial public body of a county, municipality, school district, or special district, at which official acts are to be taken or at which public business of such body is to be transacted or discussed, shall be open and noticed to the public and meetings of the legislature shall be open and noticed as provided in Article III, Section 4(e), except with respect to meetings exempted pursuant to this section or specifically closed by this Constitution.

And section 286.011, Florida Statutes (2009), commonly known as the Government in the Sunshine Law, provides in part:

> All meetings of any board or commission of any state agency or authority or of any agency or authority of any county, municipal corporation, or political subdivision, except as otherwise provided in the Constitution, at which official acts are to be taken are declared to be public meetings open to the public at all times, and no resolution, rule, or formal action shall be considered binding except as taken or made at such meeting. The board or commission must provide reasonable notice of all such meetings.

Because section 286.011 "was enacted in the public interest to protect the public from 'closed door' politics ... the law must be broadly construed to effect its remedial and protective purpose." *Wood v. Marston*, 442 So.2d 934, 938 (Fla.1983). As this Court has explained,

> [t]he statute should be construed so as to frustrate all evasive devices. This can be accomplished only by embracing the collective inquiry and discussion stages within the terms of the statute, as long as such inquiry and discussion is conducted by any committee or other authority appointed and established by a governmental agency, and relates to any matter on which foreseeable action will be taken.

Town of Palm Beach v. Gradison, 296 So.2d 473, 477 (Fla.1974). "Mere showing that the government in the sunshine law has been violated constitutes an irreparable public injury...." *Id.* Therefore, where officials have violated section 286.011, the official action is void ab initio. *Id.*

All governmental authorities in Florida are subject to the requirements of the Sunshine Law unless specifically exempted. *See* art. I, § 24(c), Fla. Const. The requirements may also apply to committees subordinate to or selected by traditional governmental authorities. This Court in *Wood* explained that the dispositive question is whether "decision-making authority" has been delegated to the committee. 442 So.2d at 939. Where the committee has been delegated decision-making authority, the committee's meetings must be open to public scrutiny, regardless of the review procedures eventually used by the traditional governmental body. *See id.* at 939–40 ("Where a body merely reviews decisions delegated to another entity, the potential for rubber-stamping always exists. To allow a review procedure to insulate the decision itself from public scrutiny invites circumvention of the Sunshine Law."). In contrast, a committee is not subject to the Sunshine Law if the committee has only been delegated information-gathering or fact-finding authority and only conducts such activities. *See id.* at 940–41.... Whether, in fact, the delegation is a delegation of decision-making authority or fact-finding authority is evaluated according to the "nature of the act performed, not on the make-up of the committee or the proximity of the act to the final decision." *Wood*, 442 So.2d at 939 (emphasis omitted).

In this case, the trial court's order included factual findings regarding the roles of the individuals Bullock consulted when negotiating with the Orioles. Specifically, the trial court found that "the people and entities Bullock met with … operated in the roles of advisor, consultant and facilitator to assist him in the performance of his duty to negotiate with the Orioles." The trial court found that these individuals "did not deliberate with, or without, him." "Bullock retained and exercised the ultimate authority to negotiate the terms of the MOU that would be submitted to the [Board] for consideration."

These factual findings are supported by competent substantial evidence in the record. See Lyon [v. Lake County], 765 So.2d at 790 [(Fla. 5th DCA 2000)] (reviewing trial court's factual finding that a meeting was informational for competent substantial evidence in the record). For example, Bullock testified that there was never a committee formed to negotiate any aspects of the MOU. Bullock also testified that he only consulted with the County's chief financial planning officer for information regarding potential funding and financing mechanisms and that the County's parks and recreation director "would provide information because this is essentially a recreational facility." Additionally, the County's project coordinator testified that she provided staff support by making copies, typing letters, and scheduling meeting rooms. There was also testimony from the County Administrator that the baseball experts' responsibilities were "to advise staff as to the makeup of what should be [in] an MOU, the issues to be aware of[, and] to provide some comparative analysis of other such deals around the country." And individual members of the so-called negotiating team testified that they were not delegated any authority to negotiate with the Orioles and that everything was under the direction of Bullock. Therefore, there is competent substantial evidence in the record to support the trial court's findings that the individuals consulted by Bullock performed an informational and fact-finding role in assisting Bullock.

Because the individuals consulted by Bullock served an informational role, the so-called negotiations team did not constitute an advisory committee subject to the requirements of the Sunshine Law. As explained above, only advisory committees acting pursuant to a delegation of decision-making authority by the governmental entity are subject to the open meetings requirement of section 286.011. Advisory committees functioning as fact-finders or information gatherers are not subject to section 286.011. See Lyon, 765 So.2d at 789; Cape Publ'ns, Inc. v. City of Palm Bay, 473 So.2d 222 (Fla. 5th DCA 1985); Bennett v. Warden, 333 So.2d 97 (Fla. 2d DCA 1976). This is not a situation where Bullock and the individuals he consulted made joint decisions. Cf. Dascott v. Palm Beach County, 877 So.2d 8 (Fla. 4th DCA 2004). Instead, these individuals were simply providing advice and information, which does not make the negotiations team a board or commission subject to the Sunshine Law. See, e.g., McDougall v. Culver, 3 So.3d 391, 393 (Fla.2d DCA 2009) ("[T]he senior officials provided only a recommendation to the Sheriff but they did not deliberate with him nor did they have decision-making authority. Therefore, we conclude that the use of the memoranda did not violate the Sunshine Law."); Jordan v. Jenne, 938 So.2d 526, 530 (Fla. 4th DCA 2006) ("Because the [group] provided only a mere recommendation to the inspector general and did not deliberate with the inspector general, the ultimate authority on termination, we conclude that the [group] does not exercise decision-making authority so as to constitute a 'board' or 'commission' within the meaning of section 286.011, and as a result, its meetings are not subject to the Sunshine Act.").

* * *

Accordingly, this Court affirms the trial court's ruling regarding Bullock and the individuals he consulted while negotiating with the Orioles.

III. ONE-ON-ONE BRIEFINGS

Citizens next argue that the trial court erred in determining that the private staff briefings of individual board members in preparation for the July 22, 2009 public hearing did not violate the Sunshine Law. We agree with the contrary arguments of the City and County and affirm the trial court.

This Court has explained that meetings within the meaning of the Sunshine Law include any gathering, formal or informal, of two or more members of the same board or commission "where the members deal with some matter on which foreseeable action will be taken by the Board." *Tolar v. School Bd. of Liberty County*, 398 So.2d 427, 428 (Fla.1981); *see also Bd. of Pub. Instruction v. Doran*, 224 So.2d 693, 698 (Fla.1969). However, public officials may call upon staff members for factual information and advice without being subject to the Sunshine Law's requirements. *See Occidental Chem. Co. v. Mayo*, 351 So.2d 336, 342 (Fla.1977); *Wood*, 442 So.2d at 940 ("The Second District found no violation, holding, *inter alia,* that the meetings were not decision-making in nature, but were 'for the purpose of "fact-finding" to assist him in the execution of [his] duties,' [*Bennett*,] 333 So.2d at 99, and we approve the holding that such fact-finding staff consultations are not subject to the Sunshine Law.").

Here, Bullock, individually and assisted by other County staff, held one-on-one meetings in the two- or three-day period immediately preceding the Board's public meeting on July 22, 2009. These meetings were informational briefings regarding the contents of the MOU, where Bullock would also ask if the individual members had any questions about the MOU. There is no evidence that Bullock or other County staff communicated what any commissioner said to any other commissioner.

These informational briefings for individual members of the Board were not violations of the Sunshine Law. As this Court has explained,

> members of a collegial administrative body are not obliged to avoid their staff during the evaluation and consideration stages of their deliberations. Were this so, the value of staff expertise would be lost and the intelligent use of employees would be crippled.

Occidental, 351 So.2d at 342 n. 10. Therefore, we affirm the trial court's ruling regarding these one-on-one meetings.

IV. E-MAILS

Lastly, Citizens contend that the trial court erred by ruling that any violations committed in e-mail discussions between board members were cured by the Board's public meetings that were held up to and including July 22, 2009. Agreeing with the contrary arguments of the City and County, we affirm the trial court.

In *Tolar*, 398 So.2d at 429, this Court held that Sunshine Law violations can be cured by "independent, final action in the sunshine," which this Court distinguished from mere ceremonial acceptance or perfunctory ratification of secret actions and decisions. *See also Zorc v. City of Vero Beach*, 722 So.2d 891, 903 (Fla. 4th DCA 1998) ("[O]nly a *full*, open hearing will cure a defect arising from a Sunshine Law violation. Such violation will not be cured by a perfunctory ratification of the action taken outside of the sunshine."); *Monroe County v. Pigeon Key Historical Park, Inc.*, 647 So.2d 857, 861 (Fla. 3d DCA 1994) ("Governmental actions will not be voided whenever governmental bodies have met in secret where sufficiently corrective final action has been taken.").

In *Tolar*, a school superintendent-elect met privately with school board members and discussed, among other things, the removal of Tolar as director of administration and abolition of his position. 398 So.2d at 427. At a subsequent public meeting in which Tolar was present and "given full opportunity to express his views," the school board members voted to transfer Tolar to another position and abolish his position. *Id.* Tolar sued for injunctive relief, alleging a violation of section 286.011. *Id.* As this Court noted, "By the express terms of section 286.011, any resolution, rule, regulation, or formal action taken at these secret meetings would not be binding." *Id.* at 428. Yet this Court declined to invalidate the action taken by the school board. *Id.* Instead, this Court distinguished *Tolar* from its previous holding in *Gradison*, 296 So.2d 473, where this Court held void formal action that "was merely the crystallization of secret decisions." *Tolar*, 398 So.2d at 428.

As explained in *Tolar*, the *Gradison* holding invalidating what was merely a summary approval of secret decisions

> does not mean, however, that public final action of the Board will always be void and incurable merely because the topic of the final public action was previously discussed at a private meeting....

>   * * *

> ... [H]ere[,] the Board took independent, final action in the sunshine in voting to abolish the position. The Board's action was not merely a ceremonial acceptance of secret actions and was not merely a perfunctory ratification of secret decisions at a later meeting open to the public.

398 So.2d at 428–429.

In this case, e-mails from constituents to members of the Board were copied to other members and sometimes led to comments between Board members regarding the topic of bringing the Orioles to Sarasota for spring training. The last such e-mail exchange, which possibly violated the Sunshine Law, occurred on April 12, 2009. However, the Board conducted multiple public meetings subsequent to that April 12 exchange where the topic of Orioles spring training was discussed and considered. For example, on April 14, 2009, the Board publicly rejected a commissioner's detailed proposal for an agreement with the Orioles as well as another commissioner's alternative proposal. Then, on May 13, 2009, the Board publicly discussed stadium costs and financing and directed the County Administrator to proceed with negotiations providing funding in the amount of $28.2 million contingent upon specific terms relating to operations and maintenance, advertising, construction management, stadium uses, property taxes, terms of occupancy, and the Cal Ripken youth facility. Then, on May 26, 2009, the Board considered the Orioles' response as well as funding sources for the renovation of the stadium. One commissioner noted that she "could handle" another $3 million in addition to the prior $28.2 million offer. Ultimately, on July 22, 2009, the Board held a properly noticed public hearing and approved the MOU and the Interlocal Agreement after a multi-hour discussion. In fact, representatives of Citizens spoke at that July 22 hearing as well as the prior meeting on May 26.

Based upon the fact that, subsequent to the last possibly violative e-mail, multiple proposals were discussed and rejected before one was finally approved, it is clear the Board took independent, final action in the sunshine regarding Orioles spring training in Sarasota. This simply is not the case of a "ceremonial acceptance of secret actions [or] merely a perfunctory ratification of secret decisions at a later meeting open to the public." *Tolar*, 398 So.2d at 429. Therefore, any possible e-mail violations were cured.

CONCLUSION

We affirm the trial court's judgment validating bonds proposed for issuance by the City of Sarasota and the County of Sarasota in furtherance of the agreement bringing the Baltimore Orioles to Sarasota for spring training. Because Bullock's so-called negotiations team only served an informational role, it was not subject to the requirements of the Sunshine Law. The County also did not violate the Sunshine Law when Bullock, assisted by other County staff, briefed individual Board members prior to the July 22, 2009 public meeting. Finally, any possible violations that occurred when Board members circulated e-mails among each other were cured by subsequent public meetings regarding the negotiations and agreement with Orioles.

It is so ordered.

CANADY, C.J., and PARIENTE, LEWIS, QUINCE, POLSTON, LABARGA, and PERRY, JJ., concur.

Article II

Section 3 — Separation of Powers

A. Delegation of Legislative Power
  1. *Askew v. Game & Fresh Water Fish Comm'n*, 336 So. 2d 556 (Fla. 1976).
  2. *Askew v. Cross Key Waterways*, 372 So. 2d 913 (Fla. 1978).
  3. *Chiles v. Children A, B, C, D, E & F*, 589 So. 2d 260 (Fla. 1991).
B. Improper Delegation of Judicial Power
  4. *E.Y. v. State*, 390 So. 2d 776 (Fla. 3d DCA 1980).
  5. *Carnegie v. State*, 473 So. 2d 782 (Fla. 1985).
C. Encroachment by One Branch on the Authority of Another Branch
  i. By Executive on Legislature
    6. *Florida House of Representatives v. Crist*, 999 So. 2d 601 (Fla. 2008).
  ii. By Legislature on Executive
    7. *Jones v. Chiles*, 638 So. 2d 48 (Fla. 1994).
  iii. By Legislature and Executive on Judiciary
    8. *Bush v. Schiavo*, 885 So. 2d 321 (Fla. 2004).

Article II of the Florida Constitution includes general provisions relating to the state's boundaries and capital, as well as other miscellaneous provisions that will be considered together with the miscellaneous provisions of Article X. This chapter will examine Article II, Section 3, which addresses the fundamental principle of separation of powers. Article II, Section 3 provides, "The powers of the state government shall be divided into legislative, executive and judicial branches. No person belonging to one branch shall exercise any powers appertaining to either of the other branches unless expressly provided herein." A similar provision has been found in all previous Florida Constitutions.[1]

As the cases show, there are important differences between the separation of powers as it applies to the federal government under the U.S. Constitution and that applied

---

1. *See, e.g.*, FLA. CONST. OF 1838, art. II; FLA. CONST. OF 1861, art. II, §§ 1, 2; FLA. CONST. OF 1865, art. II, §§ 1, 2; FLA. CONST. OF 1868, art. III; FLA. CONST. OF 1885, art. II. The wording of the 1885 Constitution is typical and illustrates the similarity with the current provision:
   Article II. Distribution of Power.
   The powers of the government of the State of Florida shall be divided into three departments: Legislative, Executive and Judicial; and no person properly belonging to one of the departments shall exercise any powers appertaining to either of the others, except in cases expressly provided for by this Constitution.
FLA. CONST. OF 1885, art. II.

by the Florida courts under the explicit provision of the Florida Constitution.[2] Separation of powers recognizes that each branch of government has distinct responsibilities and powers that are constitutionally entrusted to that branch. A major goal for this separation is to avoid excessively centralized power and maintain the balance of authority between the branches of government. This balance between the branches prevents any one branch from acting without checks.

Article II, Section 3 consists of two main prohibitions. The concept of "delegation of power" restricts one branch's ability to assign to any other branch some of its essential functions and, thereby, frustrate the balance of power. In other words, one branch may not give away its core functions to another branch of state government. Also, one branch may not "encroach" on the constitutional authority of another branch. In other words, one branch may not take the authority granted by the Florida Constitution to another branch.

Although "separation" and "delegation" are the mainstays of Article II, you will see their pivotal role in other constitutional provisions, in particular within Articles III, IV and V, which directly describe the powers of the Legislative, Executive and Judicial branches.

A. Delegation of Legislative Power

Askew v. Game & Fresh Water Fish Comm'n

336 So. 2d 556 (Fla. 1976)

BOYD, Justice.

In this proceeding we are reviewing by direct appeal an order from the Circuit Court of Leon County, Second Judicial Circuit of Florida, which initially and directly passed on the validity of several state statutes and construed a provision of the state Constitution. We have jurisdiction.

The cause arose when The Bream Fisherman's Association sought to enjoin the Department of Natural Resources, State of Florida, from introducing a species of fish, the White Amur, into the waters of Deer Point Lake in Bay County. The Department acted under Sections 372.26, 372.925, Florida Statutes (1973), and Section 372.931, as amended by Chapter 74-65, Laws of Florida, which collectively permit the Department to control aquatic weeds in Florida by means of introducing fish into Florida waters without obtaining a permit from the Game and Fresh Water Fish Commission. The Commission, too, brought suit for a permanent injunction against the Department and the case was consolidated with the Association's case.

---

2. Professor Alan Tarr has theorized that one reason for the looser understanding of separation of powers at the federal level lies in the understanding of "enumerated powers" as a limitation under the U.S. Constitution. *See* G. Alan Tarr, *Interpreting the Separation of Powers in State Constitutions*, 59 N.Y.U. ANN. SURVEY OF AMERICAN L. 329, 329–30 (2003). The states, however, exercise plenary power except where limited by the federal or state constitutions. *See id.*

As it existed on November 26, 1974, Article IV, Section 9 of the Florida Constitution stated:

> "§ 9. *Game and fresh water fish commission.* There shall be a game and fresh water fish commission, composed of five members appointed by the governor for staggered terms of five years. The commission shall exercise the nonjudicial powers of the state with respect to wild animal life and fresh water aquatic life, except that all license fees for taking wild animal life and fresh water aquatic life and penalties for violating regulations of the commission shall be prescribed by specific statute."

The order of the Circuit Court construed the above constitutional provision to find the following unconstitutional: the exemption sentence of Section 372.26; Section 372.925 as it applies to fresh water aquatic life; and Section 372.931 as amended by Chapter 74-65, Laws of Florida, on its face.

We agree with the Circuit Court that, standing alone, the former Article IV, Section 9 of the Florida Constitution would require that the challenged statutes be held unconstitutional. However, there is another provision of the Constitution, not mentioned in the order of the Circuit Court, which must be considered. Article II, Section 7, Florida Constitution, states:

> "§ 7. *Natural resources and scenic beauty.* It shall be the policy of the state to conserve and protect its natural resources and scenic beauty. Adequate provision shall be made by law for the abatement of air and water pollution and of excessive and unnecessary noise."

In construing the Constitution every section should be considered so that the Constitution will be given effect as a harmonious whole. A construction which would leave without effect any part of the Constitution should be rejected. *State v. Bryan*, 50 Fla. 293, 39 So. 929 (Fla.1905). Were we to hold the challenged statutes unconstitutional the Legislature would be stripped of its power in many instances to carry out the policy of abatement of water pollution, as embodied in Article II, Section 7. Consequently we construe former Article IV, Section 9 and Article II, Section 7 together to hold the challenged statutes to be constitutional.

The order of the Circuit Court is reversed and the cause remanded for proceedings consistent with this opinion.

It is so ordered.

OVERTON, C.J., and ADKINS, SUNDBERG and HATCHETT, JJ., concur.

ENGLAND, J., concurs in result only.

Questions

1. How does this case implicate Article II, Section 3?

2. Do you think the drafters of Article IV, Section 9 intended this decision? (And why?)

3. Consider the advantages and disadvantages of Article II, Section 7. (Think as an environmentalist and as an administrator!)

Askew v. Cross Key Waterways

372 So. 2d 913 (Fla. 1978)

SUNDBERG, Justice.

We deal today with the constitutionality of the provisions of Section 380.05(1), Florida Statutes (1975), for designation of areas of critical state concern by use of the criteria stated in Section 380.05(2)(a) and (b), Florida Statutes (1975). The issue reaches us by appeal from two separate decisions of the District Court of Appeal, First District,[3] which have been consolidated for review by this Court. Because each case was ultimately disposed of upon the constitutional invalidity of the aforementioned statutory provisions jurisdiction reposes in this Court pursuant to Article V, Section 3(b)(1), Florida Constitution.

Responding to the policy and mandate contained in Article II, Section 7, Florida Constitution, in 1972 the legislature enacted the "Florida Environmental Land and Water Management Act," Chapter 72-317, Laws of Florida, Chapter 380, Florida Statutes, Section 380.05(1)(a) of the enactment empowers the Division of State Planning to recommend areas of critical state concern to the Governor and cabinet acting as the Administration Commission.[4] In its recommendation the Division of State Planning must designate the boundaries of the proposed area of critical state concern, explain the reasons for its conclusion that the area is of critical concern to the state or region, the dangers which would result from uncontrolled or inadequate development of the area, and the advantages to be gained from the development of the area in a coordinated manner. In addition, the Division of State Planning recommends specific principles for guiding the development of the proposed area.

Section 380.05(2), Florida Statutes (1975), enunciates the criteria which the Division of State Planning shall utilize in determining whether to recommend designation of a particular area as one of critical state concern:

(2) An area of critical state concern may be designated only for:

(a) An area containing, or having a significant impact upon, environmental, historical, natural, or archaeological resources of regional or statewide importance.

---

3. [FN1.] *Cross Key Waterways v. Askew*, 351 So.2d 1062 (Fla. 1st DCA 1977); *Postal Colony Co., Inc. v. Askew*, 348 So.2d 338 (Fla. 1st DCA 1977).

4. [FN4.] Art. IV, §4, Fla.Const.; §§ 20.03(1), 20.31(2), Fla.Stat. (1975).

(b) An area significantly affected by, or having a significant effect upon, an existing or proposed major public facility or other area of major public investment.

(c) A proposed area of major development potential, which may include a proposed site of a new community, designated in a state land development plan.

Prior to submitting a recommendation with respect to an area of critical state concern to the Administration Commission, the Division of State Planning must give notice to all local governments and regional planning agencies included within the proposed boundaries, including any notice required by Chapter 120, Florida Statutes (1975), the Administrative Procedure Act, the provisions of which govern the actions taken by the Division of State Planning and the Administration Commission under Chapter 380. Section 380.05(4) and (8), Florida Statutes (1975); Section 120.72, Florida Statutes (1975).

Within 45 days after receiving the recommendations of the Division of State Planning, the Administration Commission must either reject the recommendations or adopt them with or without modification. Thereafter, by rule, the Administration Commission designates the area of critical state concern and approves the principles for guiding development of the designated area. Section 380.05(1)(b), Florida Statutes (1975). The Administration Commission is statutorily prohibited from designating more than five percent, in the aggregate, of the land within the state (approximately 1.8 million acres) as an area of critical state concern. Section 380.05(17), Florida Statutes (1975).

Section 380.05(5) provides that:

After the adoption of a rule designating an area of critical state concern the local government having jurisdiction may submit to the state land planning agency its existing land development regulations for the area, if any, or shall prepare, adopt and submit new or modified regulations, taking into consideration the principles (for guiding development) set forth in the rule designating the area as well as the factors that it would normally consider.

Subsection (7) of Section 380.05 directs the Division of State Planning to provide technical assistance to the local government in the preparation of the proposed land development regulations. If the Division of State Planning determines that the land development regulations submitted by the local government comport with the principles for guiding development, it shall by rule approve the locally-promulgated land development regulations. Section 380.05(6). The regulations are not effective until the Division of State Planning's rule approving them becomes effective which, under Section 120.54(11), Florida Statutes (1975), is 20 days after it is filed with the Secretary of State.

If the relevant local government fails to propose land development regulations within six months of adoption of the rule designating the area of critical state concern or, if such regulations have been proposed but the Division of State Planning concludes that they do not comply with the principles for guiding development for the area, within 120 days thereafter the Division of State Planning must recommend land development regulations to the Administration Commission. Section 380.05(8). The Administration Commission is allowed forty-five days after the receipt of recommended regulations, if any, from the Division of State Planning within which to reject the same or adopt them with or without modification. The Administration Commission must establish the land development regulations, by rule, within the forty-five day period as well. This rule must specify to what extent the regulations will supersede or supplement local land development regulations. Section 380.05(8). Although the regulations are administered by the local government, the Division of State Planning may initiate judicial proceedings to compel their enforcement if it concludes that local administration is inadequate. Section 380.05(8) and (9). Chapter 380 possesses the flexibility to conform to changed needs and conditions of a designated area of critical state concern by permitting the local government to propose new land development regulations after the initial regulations have been approved by the Division of State Planning or the Administration Commission. Section 380.05(10). It is essential under the statutory scheme that land development regulations become effective within twelve months after the adoption of the rule designating the area of critical state concern. If this condition is not fulfilled, the designation terminates and the area may not be redesignated for a period of one year after the termination. Section 380.05(12).

The Act affects regulation of virtually all development in an area of critical state concern: all building, mining, and changes in the use or appearance of land, water and air and appurtenant structures; material increases in the density of its use; alteration of shores and banks; drilling; structural demolition; clearing adjunct to construction; and deposit of waste or fill. Excepted are work by road agencies and other utilities; structural maintenance affecting only the interior or the color or exterior decoration of a structure; the use of structures for customary dwelling purposes; changes of usage within the same regulated class of use; changes in ownership; and changes in rights of access, riparian rights, easements and covenants affecting rights and land. Section 380.04.

The controversy before us results from actions taken by the Administration Commission of the Department of Administration in designating the Green Swamp area of critical state concern and the Florida Keys area of critical state concern and, in the case of the former, adopting land development regulations.

Green Swamp Area of Critical State Concern.

The Administration Commission adopted Chapter 22F-5, Florida Administrative Code, on July 16, 1974, which rule designated the Green Swamp area of critical state concern[5] and adopted principles for guiding development related thereto. After hearings on proposed land development regulations for the area, the Administration Commission on June 17, 1975, adopted amended land development regulations.

---

5. [FN8.] Composed of 322,690 acres in Polk and Lake Counties.

Subsequent to that date a challenge to the land development regulations was filed but was denied by a hearing officer on June 27, 1975. On June 30, 1975, the land development regulations were filed with the Secretary of State as Chapters 22F-6 and 22F-7, Florida Administrative Code. However, it was brought to the attention of the Administration Commission that Section 120.54(11), Florida Statutes (1975), which provides that regulations are "effective" twenty days after they are filed, might preclude the land development regulations from becoming effective within twelve months of adoption of the rule designating the area of critical state concern as mandated by Section 380.05(12), Florida Statutes (1975). Apprehensive concerning the effect of Section 120.54(11) upon the efficacy of the regulations, the Administration Commission met on July 15, 1975, declared an emergency pursuant to Section 120.54(8)(a), Florida Statutes (1975), and approved land development regulations identical to Chapters 22F-6 and 22F-7. These regulations were filed as emergency rule Chapters 22 FER-75-1 through 30, Florida Administrative Code. Individual and corporate parties to the rulemaking proceedings petitioned the district court for review of the described final agency rulemaking action. Although the petitioners attacked the land development regulations on constitutional and several statutory grounds, the district court disposed of the case on a single statutory issue and expressly reached none other. The court held that the emergency rules adopting the land development regulations were not effective because there was no demonstrated "immediate danger to the public health, safety, or welfare" as required by Section 120.54(8)(a). It concluded further that the land development regulations adopted as Chapters 22F-6 and 22F-7 did not become effective within the time imposed by Section 380.05(12) and, therefore, the designation made by Chapter 22F-5 terminated.

On petition for rehearing the Administration Commission raised for the first time the issue of the intervening rule challenge under Section 120.54(3). However, the court declined to consider the issue because of Florida Appellate Rule 3.14(b) and because of its decision in *Cross Key Waterways, Inc. v. Askew*, [351 So.2d 1062 (Fla. 1st DCA 1977)], holding unconstitutional the provision by Section 380.05(1) for designation of areas of critical state concern through use of the criteria stated in Section 380.05(2)(a) and (b). Thus, the fundamental constitutional ground avoided in the principal opinion was the basis for disposition of the case on rehearing.

Florida Keys Area of Critical State Concern.

On March 3, 1975, the Division of State Planning issued its report to the Administration Commission recommending that a substantial portion of the Florida Keys be declared an area of critical state concern. The Administration Commission held a public meeting in Key West on March 28, 1975, to receive comment on the recommendation of the Division of State Planning. The meeting was conducted in accordance with Section 120.54, Florida Statutes (1975), related to rulemaking procedures, and revisions in the recommendation of the Division of State Planning were proposed. Subsequently, "issue papers" were prepared and submitted by the Division of State Planning in response to questions raised at the March 28, 1975, meeting. After an oral request that the proceedings held on March 28, 1975, be conducted in accordance with the provisions of Section 120.57, Florida Statutes (1975), on April 14, 1975, appellees filed a written petition requesting that further proceedings scheduled for the following day be conducted in the formal manner prescribed by Section 120.57. Appellees asserted that their substantial interests would be affected and that a rulemaking proceeding pursuant to Section 120.54 did not provide adequate opportunity to protect those interests. At the proceedings conducted on April 15, 1975, the petition for a Section 120.57 hearing was denied due to the purported failure of appellees to establish that proceedings pursuant to Section 120.54 were inadequate to protect their interests. At the close of this meeting, the Administration Commission approved the proposed rule designating virtually all of the Keys[6] as an area of critical state concern. On April 25, 1975, the rule designating the area of critical state concern together with accompanying principles for guiding development were filed with the Secretary of State and ultimately published as Chapter 22F-8, Florida Administrative Code.

Timely petitions for review of this agency action were lodged with the District Court of Appeal, First District, by appellees. In ruling upon a motion to dismiss, the district court confirmed the standing of appellees to seek review of the agency action.

As mentioned above the district court held that the Section 380.05(2)(a) and (b) standards for exercise of the Section 380.05(1) power to designate areas of critical state concern are inadequate and that the delegation consequently offends Article II, Section 3, Florida Constitution. Accordingly, the court quashed Rule 22F-8. However, the district court expressly resolved all other issues raised, including the form of the proceedings, adversely to appellees.

The Consolidated Cases

While numerous issues are raised in these consolidated appeals we, like the District Court of Appeal, First District, find the issue of the constitutionality of the delegation of power to the Administration Commission to be dispositive. Therefore, except as otherwise herein expressly mentioned, we refrain from passing upon any other issues raised.

At contest here are the competing philosophies which underlie two provisions of our fundamental document of government and the attempt by the legislature to accommodate those philosophies through the enactment of Section 380.05(2)(a) and (b), Florida Statutes (1975). Article II, Section 7, Florida Constitution, enunciates the policy of the State to conserve and protect its natural resources and scenic beauty. Nonetheless, in implementing this policy due regard must be had for the admonition of Article II, Section 3, Florida Constitution:

> Branches of government. The powers of the state government shall be divided into legislative, executive and judicial branches. No person belonging to one

---

6. [FN10.] "All lands in Monroe County, except: (1) that portion … included within … the Everglades National Park and areas north of said Park; (and) (2) all lands seaward of mean high water that are owned by local, state, or federal governments." Ch. 22F-8, Fla. Admin.Code.

branch shall exercise any powers appertaining to either of the other branches unless expressly provided herein.

Appellants urge two propositions upon us. First, that the provisions of Section 380.05(2)(a) and (b) set forth adequate criteria for exercise of the power delegated by Section 380.05(1) when measured against the case law which construes the operation of Article II, Section 3. This argument is bolstered by the decisions from this Court which recognize that the specificity of standards and guidelines may depend upon the subject matter dealt with and the degree of difficulty involved in articulating finite standards. See, e.g. *Straughn v. K & K Land Management, Inc.*, 326 So.2d 421 (Fla.1976); *State Dept. of Citrus v. Griffin*, 239 So.2d 577 (Fla.1970). Second, it is asserted that the modern trend in administrative law is to relax the doctrine of unlawful delegation of legislative power in favor of an analysis which focuses upon the existence of procedural safeguards in the administrative process as opposed to standards enunciated by the legislature. See *Butler v. United Cerebral Palsy of Northern Ky., Inc.*, 352 S.W.2d 203 (Ky.1961); *Warren v. Marion County*, 353 P.2d 257 (Or.1960); *Barry and Barry, Inc. v. State of Washington Dept. of Motor Vehicles*, 81 Wash.2d 155, 500 P.2d 540 (1972); *Schmidt v. Dept. of Resource Development*, 39 Wis.2d 46, 158 N.W.2d 306 (1968); K. Davis, *Administrative Law of the Seventies*, § 2.04, at 30 (1976). Appellants maintain that the broad statement of policy contained in Sections 380.05(1) and 380.05(2)(a) and (b) coupled with the administrative safeguards imposed by Chapter 120, Florida Statutes (1975), alleviates any objection that the Administration Commission will act arbitrarily or capriciously in performing the function assigned by the legislature.

Dealing with these propositions in the order presented, we first conclude that we must concur with the able opinion of the District Court of Appeal, First District, in *Cross Key Waterways v. Askew* insofar as it finds the standards and guidelines of Section 380.05(2)(a) and (b) to be deficient when assessed in light of prior case law. See *D'Alemberte v. Anderson*, 349 So.2d 164 (Fla.1977); *Lewis v. Bank of Pasco County*, 346 So.2d 53 (Fla.1977); *Sarasota County v. Barg*, 302 So.2d 737 (Fla.1974); *Conner v. Joe Hatton, Inc.*, 216 So.2d 209 (Fla.1968); *State v. Atlantic Coast Line Ry.*, 56 Fla. 617, 47 So. 969 (1908). A corollary of the doctrine of unlawful delegation is the availability of judicial review. In the final analysis it is the courts, upon a challenge to the exercise or nonexercise of administrative action, which must determine whether the administrative agency has performed consistently with the mandate of the legislature. When legislation is so lacking in guidelines that neither the agency nor the courts can determine whether the agency is carrying out the intent of the legislature in its conduct, then, in fact, the agency becomes the lawgiver rather than the administrator of the law.

The criteria for designation of an area of critical state concern set forth in Section 380.05(2)(a) and (b) are constitutionally defective because they reposit in the Administration Commission the fundamental legislative task of determining which geographic areas and resources are in greatest need of protection. As pointed out by Judge Smith below, the procedure envisioned by Sections 380.05(1) and (2) makes it impossible for a reviewing court to ascertain whether the priorities recognized by the Administration Commission comport with the intent of the legislature:

> The greater deficiency of Section 380.05(2), subsection (a), is that it does not establish or provide for establishing priorities or other means for identifying and choosing among the resources the Act is intended to preserve. That subsection lacks the specificity of the Big Cypress designation, the predictability of a legislatively approved comprehensive plan which confines subsection (c) criteria, the rule standards required for Section 380.10 identification of developments of regional impact, and any other standards for the necessary choice. The Act treats alike, as fungible goods, disparate categories of environmental, historical, natural and archaeological resources of regional or statewide importance and all of Florida's manifold resources within those vast categories. Up to the acreage limit, the Commission is empowered to supersede as it chooses the local governments regulating development in historic Pensacola or St. Augustine, or at the shores of the Atlantic and Gulf of Mexico to a depth of a thousand feet, or in all acreage on the Suwannee and St. Johns and their tributaries or, indeed, in all the Florida Keys. If Cedar Key, Ybor City, Palm Beach and the path of the King's Road are found to be historic resources of satisfactory importance, they too may be designated. Subsection (a) reaches beyond those areas to include, as similarly eligible for designation, areas which for unstated reasons "impact" valued resources elsewhere. Subsection (b) expands the choice to include areas which in unstated ways affect or are affected by any "major public facility" which is defined in Section 380.031(10), or any "major public investment," which is not.

351 So.2d at 1069 (footnotes omitted).

We emphasize that it is not the legislature's use of the phrases "containing, or having a significant impact upon, environmental, historical, natural, or archaeological resources of regional impact" nor "significantly affected by, or having a significant effect upon, an existing or proposed major public facility or other area of major public investment" which faults the legislation.... As suggested by the district court of appeal such "approximations of the threshold of legislative concern" are not only a practical necessity in legislation, but they are now amenable to articulation and refinement by policy statements adopted as rules under the 1974 Administrative Procedure Act, Chapter 120, Florida Statutes. The benefits of the current version of Chapter 120 were not available at the time of the *Barg* decision. The deficiency in the legislation here considered is the absence of legislative delineation of priorities among competing areas and resources which require protection in the State interest.

We are told by appellants that the standards in Section 380.05(2)(a) and (b) are no less definite than the guidelines of Sections 501.204 and 501.205, Florida Statutes (1975), which were upheld against a similar constitutional attack in *Dept. of Legal Affairs v. Rogers*, 329 So.2d 257 (Fla.1976). The sections in question made unlawful "unfair ... acts or practices in the conduct of any trade or commerce" and provided for the adoption by the cabinet of "rules ... which prohibit with specificity acts or practices that violate this part ..." However, the legislation in question contained the admonition that in construing the Act great weight and consideration should be given to the interpretation of similar terms in the Federal Trade Commission Act (15 U.S.C. 45(a)(1)) by the Federal Trade Commission and the federal courts. Furthermore, the rules promulgated by the cabinet are required to be consistent with the rules, regulations, and decisions of the Federal Trade Commission and the federal courts in interpreting the provisions of the federal act. Appellants stress the language of Mr. Justice England's concurring opinion, in which this author joined, that:

> (F)lorida's declaration of commercial policy need not be made rigid to the point of ineffectiveness, but may be "fleshed out" by administrative action to meet changing circumstances within our borders.

329 So.2d at 269.

However, for an administrative agency to "flesh out" an articulated legislative policy is far different from that agency making the initial determination of what policy should be. In the cases under review the Administration Commission has in fact exercised the policy role in the first instance of determining which areas of this State and the resources therein are of critical state concern. It has then proceeded, pursuant to the other provisions of Section 380.05, to promulgate principles for guiding development and to adopt or approve land development regulations. Under the provisions of Section 380.05, the Administration Commission "fleshes out" what it has in the first instance conceived. In the words of Justice Whitfield in *State v. Atlantic Coast Line Ry., supra*, the function of the Administration Commission under Section 380.05(1) and (2)(a) and (b) involves the exercise of primary and independent discretion rather than the determination "within defined limits, and subject to review, (of) some fact upon which the law by its own terms operates...." 47 So. at 972. In contrast, by The Big Cypress Conservation Act of 1973, Section 380.055, Florida Statutes (1975), the legislature conceived the areas of critical state concern and left to the Division of State Planning and the Administration Commission the task of "fleshing out" through adoption of land development regulations.

Our research in other jurisdictions fails to disclose one instance in which the legislative branch has unconditionally delegated to an agency of the executive branch the policy function of designating the geographic area of concern which will be subject to land development regulation by the agency. For example, in *CEEED v. California Coastal Zone Conservation Commission*, 43 Cal.App.3d 306, 118 Cal.Rptr. 315 (Dist.Ct.App.1974), the California court sustained against an unlawful delegation attack broad powers of regional commissions to issue development permits within the California coastal zone designated by the Coastal Conservation Act of 1972. Any development in the designated coastal area was subject to permitting by an appropriate regional commission pending formulation and submission for adoption by the legislature of a comprehensive California Coastal Zone Conservation Plan. The court approved the standard in the Act, which required a finding before permitting, that " ... the development will not have any substantial adverse environmental or ecological effect" and that " ... the development is consistent with, the findings and declarations set forth in Section 27001 and with the objectives set forth in Section 27302." It dealt with the delegation issue in the following language:

> The constitutional doctrine prohibiting delegation of legislative power rests on the premise that the Legislature may not abdicate its responsibility to resolve the "truly fundamental issues" by delegating that function to others or by failing to provide adequate directions for the implementation of its declared policies. (Citations omitted) Consequently, where the Legislature makes the fundamental policy decision and delegates to some other body the task of implementing that policy under adequate safeguards, there is no violation of the doctrine. (Citations omitted.)

* * *

> The "substantial adverse environmental or ecological effect" standard is more specific than the broad "health, safety, or general welfare" guideline upheld in Candlestick and the cases cited above. (*Candlestick Properties, Inc. v. San Francisco Bay CND Commission*, 11 Cal.App.3d 557, 89 Cal.Rptr. 897 (Dist.Ct.App.1970)). Although application of the standard calls for the exercise of judgment and discretion, by the very nature of the legislative goals, considerable discretion must of necessity be vested in the Commission. As the court in *Friends of Mammoth v. Board of Supervisors*, 8 Cal.3d 247, 271, 104 Cal.Rptr. 761, 777, 502 P.2d 1049, 1065, said of the "significant effect on the environment" phrase in the California Environmental Quality Act: "To some extent this is inevitable in a statute which deals, as the EQA must, with questions of degree." The statutory criteria to be observed by the Commission and the regional commissions in carrying out the tasks delegated to them clearly satisfy constitutional requirements. The fact that the Commission is required to weigh complex factors in determining whether a development will have a substantial adverse environmental or ecological effect does not, as plaintiffs charge, mean that unbridled discretion has been conferred on it. A statute empowering an administrative agency to exercise a judgment of a high order in implementing legislative policy does not confer unrestricted powers. (Citations omitted.)

118 Cal.Rptr. at 329–330.

The language of the California court is not dissimuar to that used by Justice Whitfield in *State v. Atlantic Coast Line Ry.*, *supra*. However, the striking difference between the California Act and the statutory scheme here under consideration lies in the fact that the California Act geographically circumscribed by its own terms both the coastal zone and the area within the coastal zone within which the regional commissions were authorized to require development permitting. Furthermore, the permitting function was an interim measure pending adoption by the legislature of a comprehensive Coastal Zone Conservation Plan.

In *J.M. Mills, Inc. v. Murphy*, 116 R.I. 54, 352 A.2d 661 (1976), the Rhode Island Supreme Court dealt with the validity of the Fresh Water Wetlands Act. The Act provides for regulation of all fresh water wetlands. The Act defines its geographical jurisdiction, declares the state policy with regard to wetlands, and requires the approval of both the Director of the Department of Natural Resources and the municipality in which the land is located before wetlands may be altered. Plaintiff landowner sought a declaratory judgment challenging the functions vested in the Director and the municipalities as being an unlawful delegation of legislative power. On appeal by the plaintiff from an adverse decision in the trial court, the supreme court affirmed. After noting that the nondelegation doctrine has been relaxed of late, the court reasoned that the adequacy of legislative standards could best be measured against the intended purpose of the legislation. Having enunciated these general principles the court stated:

> With these general principles in mind, we proceed to consider the validity of a delegation of authority to the director of the Department of Natural Resources to disapprove applications to alter fresh water wetlands. Section 2-1-21 requires anyone who would alter the character of a wetland to obtain the approval of the director and fixes the governing standard as the "best public interest." The plaintiffs argue that this is not a meaningful standard. In response to this contention, we first note that the director is given jurisdiction over only a very limited area, wetlands. The term "wetlands" is precisely defined in 2-1-20. In a previous case where this court found a valid delegation of authority to the Blackstone Valley Sewer District Commission, *City of Central Falls v. Halloran*, 94 R.I. 189, 179 A.2d 570 (1962), we *placed great weight on the fact that the administrative agency was given discretion to act only in a well-defined geographical area.* Here, also, the scope of administrative authority is clearly confined.

352 A.2d at 666 (emphasis supplied).

It is apparent that the Rhode Island court was materially influenced by the fact that the administrative agency was granted discretion to act only in a geographical area well-defined by the legislature.

To the same effect is the case of *Toms River Affiliates v. Dept. of Environmental Protection*, 140 N.J.Super. 135, 355 A.2d 679 (1976), upholding against constitutional attack the New Jersey Coastal Area Facility Review Act. The Act establishes boundaries for the "coastal area" of the state and declares that this area constitutes "an exceptional, unique, irreplaceable and delicately balanced physical, chemical and biologically acting and interacting natural environmental resource...." The State Department of Environmental Protection is designated as the agency to administer the Act and is granted authority to adopt rules and regulations to effectuate its purposes. After declaring the purposes of the legislation, the Act proceeds to list the facilities subject to its provisions. In denying the challenge that the Act does not provide adequate standards for its administration, the New Jersey court approved some rather nonspecific standards when coupled with procedural safeguards designed to insure against unreasonable and unwarranted administrative action. Nonetheless, the geographic area to be regulated by the administrative agency was discreetly defined by the Act.

In 1974, Massachusetts enacted St.1974, c. 637, "An act protecting land and water on Martha's Vineyard" which is patterned after The American Law Institute, Model Land Development Code. ALI, *A Model Land Development Code*, Art. 7 (1976). Section 380.05, Florida Statutes (1975), was likewise modeled after an earlier draft of Article 7 of the American Law Institute Model Code. The Martha's Vineyard Act was the subject of litigation in *Island Properties, Inc. v. Martha's Vineyard Commission*, 361 N.E.2d 385 (Mass.1977). The test in this case did not touch upon the subject of unlawful delegation and, therefore, the decision is not persuasive in the instant cases. It is instructive to note, however, that in implementing the ALI model code the Massachusetts legislature expressly delineated the geographical area of Martha's Vineyard within which the Martha's Vineyard Commission is authorized to designate districts of critical planning concern. Under the terms of the Massachusetts act the commission was charged with developing standards and criteria for identification of areas of critical planning concern within the boundaries of the island, which standards and criteria were subject to and received the approval of the Secretary of Communities and Development. The Massachusetts scheme, then, is similar to that adopted by the Florida Legislature for the "Big Cypress Area" (Section 380.055) insofar as establishment of the geographic perimeters in which the agency may exercise its discretion is concerned.

The second prong of appellants' argument is based upon a thesis for delegation of legislative power developed and espoused by Professor Kenneth Culp Davis of the University of Chicago College of Law. See Davis, *Administrative Law of the Seventies, supra*. Professor Davis maintains that there should be a shift in emphasis from legislatively imposed standards for administrative action to procedural safeguards in the administrative process. He supports his rationale by citation to federal decisions as well as decisions from a minority of state court jurisdictions. His premises are that (1) strict adherence to the nondelegation doctrine would stultify the administrative process; (2) the doctrine, in fact, has been used as a label to invalidate legislation of which courts disapprove without any rational distinction between standards approved and those disapproved; and (3) the danger of arbitrary or capricious administrative action is best met through procedural due process safeguards in the administrative process.

The Davis view is probably best demonstrated in the case of *Barry & Barry, Inc. v. State of Washington, Dept. of Motor Vehicles, supra*, wherein the Washington court stated:

We are convinced and have no hesitancy in saying that the strict requirement of exact legislative standards for the exercise of administrative authority has ceased to serve any valid purpose. In addition to lacking purpose, the doctrine in several respects impedes efficient government and conflicts with the public interest in administrative efficiency in a complex modern society.

* * *

Second, requiring the legislature to lay down exact and precise standards for the exercise of administrative authority destroys needed flexibility....

Finally, a strictly construed standards doctrine is logically unsound and legally meaningless. The needs and demands of modern government require the delegation of legislative power without *specific* guiding standards.... We think that it is time to abandon the notion that the presence or absence of vague verbalisms like "public interest" or "just and reasonable" make all the difference between valid legislation and unlawful delegation.

500 P.2d 540, at 543 (emphasis in original).

The court went on to say that the focus should be on administrative safeguards and administrative standards. Relying upon United States Supreme Court decisions in reaching its result, the court concluded that the Washington constitution requires no different result than that reached under the United States Constitution:

It may be argued that whatever the freedom of the federal courts to ignore the requirement of precise legislative standards for delegated authority, its continued existence is mandated in the state of Washington by Const. art. 2, § 1 (amendment 7), which provides that "(t)he legislative authority of the state of Washington shall be vested in the legislature...." However, there is a similar provision in U.S. Const. art. 1, § 1: "(a)ll legislative Powers herein granted shall be vested in a Congress of the United States...." The Supreme Court of the United States has not regarded this provision as prohibitory in upholding the delegations of legislative authority without meaningful standards in the above-mentioned decisions in *American Trucking Associations* (*American Trucking Associations, Inc. v. Atchison, Topeka & Santa Fe Railway*, 387 U.S. 397 (1967)), and *Southwestern Cable Co.* (*U. S. v. Southwestern Cable Co.*, 392 U.S. 157 (1968)).

In our judgment, these provisions of the Washington State and United States constitutions mean only that legislative power is delegated *initially and fundamentally* to the legislative bodies. We believe that one of the legislative powers granted by these provisions is the power to determine the amount of discretion an administrative agency should exercise in carrying out the duties granted to it by the legislature. To construe these provisions as confining the exercise of legislative power to the legislative bodies, would be to read them as limitations of power rather than as grants of power. We may assume that if the framers had intended to so limit the power of the legislative bodies, they would have done so expressly, rather than by implication.

500 P.2d at 544 (emphasis in original).

It should be noted that Article II, Section 3, Florida Constitution, contrary to the Constitutions of the United States and the State of Washington, does by its second sentence contain an express limitation upon the exercise by a member of one branch of any powers appertaining to either of the other branches of government. While other jurisdictions which subscribe to the Davis thesis have constitutional provisions similar to Article II, Section 3, Florida Constitution, the precise issue of the meaning of the limiting language is not discussed.

Although the Davis view is an entirely reasonable one as demonstrated by its adoption in the federal courts and a minority of state jurisdictions, nonetheless, it clearly has not been the view in Florida. See Davis, *Administrative Law of the Seventies, supra,* at 32. Should this Court, then, accept the invitation of appellants to abandon the doctrine of nondelegation of legislative power which is not only firmly embedded in our law, but which has been so continuously and recently applied? See, e.g., *D'Alemberte v. Anderson; Lewis v. Bank of Pasco County, supra.* We believe *stare decisis* and reason dictate that we not.

Regardless of the criticism of the courts' application of the doctrine, we nevertheless conclude that it represents a recognition of the express limitation contained in the second sentence of Article II, Section 3 of our Constitution. Under the fundamental document adopted and several times ratified by the citizens of this State, the legislature is not free to redelegate to an administrative body so much of its lawmaking power as it may deem expedient. And that is at the crux of the issue before us. Appellants argue that Section 380.05 requires that all land development regulations be consistent with the principles for guiding development which are adopted contemporaneously with the designation of an area of critical state concern and, therefore, there can be no abuse in the process. We concur that the provisions of Section 380.05 coupled with Chapter 120, Florida Statutes, are calculated to assure procedural due process. Nonetheless, the standard by which land development regulations are to be measured is not a standard articulated by the legislature but one determined by the Administration Commission through formulation of principles for guiding development. In short the primary policy decision of the area of critical state concern to be designated as well as the principles for guiding development in that area are the sole province of an administrative body. From that determination all else follows. This does not comport with the dictates of *State v. Atlantic Coast Line Ry. Co., supra,* and its progeny. Flexibility by an administrative agency to administer a legislatively articulated policy is essential to meet the complexities of our modern society, but flexibility in administration of a legislative program is essentially different from reposing in an administrative body the power to establish fundamental policy.

In our consideration of this issue, we have not overlooked the decision of the United States Supreme Court in *Penn Central Transportation Co. v. City of New York,* 438 U.S. 104 (1978), cited by appellants as supplemental authority. This decision deals with the designation of Grand Central Terminal as a "landmark" by the Landmarks Preservation Commission under New York City's Landmarks Preservation Law. Neither in the state courts nor in the United States Supreme Court was the issue of unlawful delegation raised or considered. The issues decided were whether the application of the Landmarks Preservation Law had taken the owners' property without just compensation in violation of the Fifth and Fourteenth Amendments and arbitrarily deprived them of their property without Due Process of Law in violation of the Fourteenth Amendment. Hence, the *Penn Central* case is inapposite.

It is submitted by appellants that the provisions of Section 11.60(2)(i), Florida Statutes (1977), will cure any lack of adequate standards or guidelines in the subject legislation. By Section 11.60(2)(i), the joint Administrative Procedures Committee of the legislature is given standing to seek review in the courts of this State of the validity or invalidity of any administrative rule. However, this offers no panacea because the ability of the committee to maintain proceedings for review of a rule does not make binding upon the courts the view asserted by the committee. It is still necessary for the court to measure the validity or invalidity of the administrative action against the standards and guidelines articulated in the legislation under which the agency acts.

Accordingly, until the provisions of Article II, Section 3 of the Florida Constitution are altered by the people we deem the doctrine of nondelegation of legislative power to be viable in this State. Under this doctrine fundamental and primary policy decisions shall be made by members of the legislature who are elected to perform those tasks, and administration of legislative programs must be pursuant to some minimal standards and guidelines ascertainable by reference to the enactment establishing the program. The criteria contained in Section 380.05(2)(a) and (b), Florida Statutes (1975), do not comply with this constitutional imperative.

Our decision today need not impair the ability of our state government to protect the resources and facilities described in Section 380.05(2)(a) and (b), however. In complying with the policy and mandate of Article II, Section 7, Florida Constitution, the legislature need only exercise its constitutional prerogative and duty to identify and designate those resources and facilities. It may be done in advance as with the Big Cypress area of critical state concern, Section 380.055, Florida Statutes (1975), or through ratification of administratively developed recommendations as in the case of the California Coastal Zone Conservation Plan, *CEEED v. California Coastal Zone Conservation Commission, supra*. In either case the ultimate selection of priorities for areas of critical state or regional concern will rest with representatives of our government charged with such responsibilities under our Constitution.

The decisions of the District Court of Appeal, First District, are affirmed.

It is so ordered.

ADKINS, BOYD, HATCHETT and ALDERMAN, JJ., concur.

ENGLAND, C.J., concurs with an opinion, with which ADKINS, J., concurs.

OVERTON, J., concurs in result only.

ENGLAND, Chief Justice, concurring.

I sincerely hope that the significance of our decision today is not lost in a debate concerning its effect on the Environmental Land and Water Management Act. Justice Sundberg has revitalized a vastly more important doctrine one that guarantees that Florida's government will continue to operate only by consent of the governed. He is saying, quite simply, that whatever may be the governmental predilections elsewhere, in Florida no person in one branch of our government may by accident or by assignment act in a role assigned by the Constitution to persons in another branch.

Law giving, the power involved here, is a responsibility assigned to the legislature, and that body is prohibited from relegating its responsibility wholesale to persons, whether elected or appointed, whose duties are simply to see that the laws are observed. The people of Florida placed that restraint on the legislature, as they had every right to do. People in other states may not restrict their public officials to this extent, but their authority to do so, and the effect of their doing so, are readily acknowledged even in states without a similar constitutional limitation....

In my opinion, Florida's unique constitutional directive that governmental powers should not be aggregated in one branch, by usurpation, inadvertence or knowing delegation, experiences a refreshing resurgence from Justice Sundberg's opinion.

ADKINS, J., concurs.

Questions

1. Identify the "players" in this case and the branch of government to which each belongs.

2. According to the Court, why is Florida Statutes § 380.05(2)(a) & (b) deficient?

3. According to the Court, what is the outermost limit that the executive agency can engage in, with regard to policy?

4. Under Florida's "Nondelegation Doctrine," if the Legislature wishes to delegate authority to an administrative agency, what should the Legislature include in the grant of delegation?

5. What is the premise underlying Florida's "Nondelegation Doctrine"?

Chiles v. Children A, B, C, D, E & F

589 So. 2d 260 (Fla. 1991)

BARKETT, Justice.

We have for review the order of the Eleventh Judicial Circuit, in and for Dade County, Florida, in which the court declared unconstitutional sections 216.011(1)(*ll*) and 216.221, Florida Statutes (1989). The order was appealed to the Third District Court of Appeal which, without deciding the merits, certified the issue to this Court as a matter of great public importance requiring immediate resolution. *Chiles v. Children A, B, C, D, E, and F*, No. 91-2530 (Fla. 3d DCA Oct. 21, 1991).

Appellees, six of Florida's foster children (hereinafter "children"), sought declaratory and injunctive relief against the State's Governor, Secretary of State, Attorney General, Comptroller, Treasurer, Commissioner of Agriculture, Commissioner of Education, and all as members of the Administration Commission (hereinafter "Commission").[7] The trial court granted the children's request and held sections 216.011(1)(*ll*) and 216.221, Florida Statutes (1989), unconstitutional and enjoined the Commission from attempting to restructure the 1991 Appropriations Act pursuant to the budget reduction procedure established in chapter 216.

The state action that precipitated this case was the Governor's determination of an estimated $621.7 million general revenue shortfall in the fiscal 1991–92 state budget. In September 1991, the Governor directed all "state agencies," which by leg-

7. [FN2.] The Administration Commission is created pursuant to section 14.202, Florida Statutes (1989), as part of the Executive Office of the Governor and is composed of the Governor and Cabinet.

islative definition in section 216.011(1)(*ll*), Florida Statutes (1989), includes the judicial branch, to prepare revised financial plans that would reduce their current operating budgets. On October 22, 1991, the Administration Commission[8] adopted the Governor's recommendations reducing the budgets established by the 1991 Appropriations Act, chapter 91-193, section 1, Laws of Florida.

Initially, the Commission challenges the appropriateness of the trial court order granting the children's request for declaratory relief.[9] The purpose of declaratory relief is "to afford relief from insecurity and uncertainty with respect to rights, status, and other equitable or legal relations" and thus the declaratory judgment statute is to be construed liberally. § 86.101, Fla.Stat. (1989). This Court has held that to "entertain a declaratory action regarding a statute's validity, there must be a bona fide need for such a declaration based on present, ascertainable facts or the court lacks jurisdiction to render declaratory relief." *Martinez v. Scanlan*, 582 So.2d 1167, 1170 (Fla.1991). Additionally, this Court has upheld a grant of declaratory relief when the cause involved the public interest in the settlement of controversies in the operation of essential governmental functions and in the disbursement of public funds. *See Overman v. State Bd. of Control*, 62 So.2d 696 (Fla.1952). We find the children have demonstrated the existence of present ascertainable facts which were sufficient to permit the trial court to afford declaratory relief.

The central issue in this case is whether the legislature, in passing section 216.221, violated the doctrine of separation of powers by assigning to the executive branch the broad discretionary authority to reapportion the state budget. Section 216.221(2), Florida Statutes (1989), provides in relevant part:

> If, in the opinion of the Governor, after consultation with the revenue estimating conference, a deficit will occur in the General Revenue Fund, he shall so certify to the commission. *The commission may, by affirmative action, reduce all approved state agency budgets and releases by a sufficient amount to prevent a deficit in any fund.*

(Emphasis added.)

The principles underlying the governmental separation of powers antedate our Florida Constitution and were collectively adopted by the union of states in our federal constitution. *See Mistretta v. United States*, 488 U.S. 361, 380 (1989). The fundamental concern of keeping the individual branches separate is that the fusion

---

8. [FN3.] The vote was by a majority that did not include the Secretary of State or the Commissioner of Education.

9. [FN5.] The Commission does not contend that the children lack standing to challenge the statute in their capacity as taxpayers. This Court has long held that a citizen and taxpayer can challenge the constitutional validity of an exercise of the legislature's taxing and spending power without having to demonstrate a special injury. *Brown v. Firestone*, 382 So.2d 654 (Fla.1980); *Department of Admin. v. Horne*, 269 So.2d 659 (Fla.1972); *see Rosenhouse v. 1950 Spring Term Grand Jury*, 56 So.2d 445 (Fla.1952); *Yon v. Orange County*, 43 So.2d 177 (Fla.1949); *State ex rel. Hill v. Cone*, 140 Fla. 1, 191 So. 50 (1939). The budget reductions ordered pursuant to section 216.221, Florida Statutes (1989), go to the very heart of the legislature's taxing and spending power, and thus the children have standing to invoke this constitutional challenge.

of the powers of any two branches into the same department would ultimately result in the destruction of liberty. *E.g., Ponder v. Graham,* 4 Fla. 23, 42–43 (1851); *see The Federalist No.* 47 (James Madison), *No.* 51 (Alexander Hamilton or James Madison).

The separation of powers doctrine is expressly codified in the Florida Constitution in article II, section 3:

> The powers of the state government shall be divided into legislative, executive and judicial branches. *No person belonging to one branch shall exercise any powers appertaining to either of the other branches unless expressly provided herein.*

(Emphasis added.) The doctrine encompasses two fundamental prohibitions. The first is that no branch may encroach upon the powers of another. *See, e.g., Pepper v. Pepper,* 66 So.2d 280, 284 (Fla.1953). The second is that no branch may delegate to another branch its constitutionally assigned power. *See, e.g., Smith v. State,* 537 So.2d 982, 987 (Fla.1989). This case presents a separation of powers problem of the second type: a delegation of the legislative function.

Almost 300 years ago, in his *Second Treatise of Government,* John Locke explained the reasons for prohibiting such delegations of legislative authority:

> The legislative cannot transfer the power of making laws to any other hands; for it being but a delegated power from the people, they who have it cannot pass it over to others. The people alone can appoint the form of the commonwealth, which is by constituting the legislative and appointing in whose hands that shall be. And when the people have said, we will submit to rules and be governed by laws made by such men, and in such forms, nobody else can say other men shall make laws for them; nor can the people be bound by any laws but such as are enacted by those whom they have chosen and authorized to make laws for them. The power of the legislative, being derived from the people by a positive voluntary grant and institution, can be no other than what that positive grant conveyed, which being only to make *laws,* and not to make *legislators, the legislative can have no power to transfer their authority of making laws and place it in other hands.*

John Locke, *Two Treatises of Government* 193 (Thomas I. Cook ed., Hafner Publishing Co. 1947) (emphasis added).

This Court has repeatedly held that, under the doctrine of separation of powers, the legislature may not delegate the power to enact laws or to declare what the law shall be to any other branch. Any attempt by the legislature to abdicate its particular constitutional duty is void. *Pursley v. City of Fort Myers,* 87 Fla. 428, 432, 100 So. 366, 367 (1924); *Bailey v. Van Pelt,* 78 Fla. 337, 350, 82 So. 789, 793 (1919). As recently as 1978, in *Askew v. Cross Key Waterways,* 372 So.2d 913, 920–21 (Fla.1978), we reaffirmed that the legislature, under article II, section 3 of our constitution, may not delegate its lawmaking function to another branch notwithstanding policy considerations or the fiscal operations of other states which do not have Florida's constitutional prohibitions against the delegation of powers. Thus we must ascertain whether section 216.221(2) delegates the legislative responsibility to establish law.

Article III, sections 1 and 7 assign to the legislature the responsibility for passage of all bills into law, regardless of their subject matter. Article III, section 8 sets forth the procedure for the executive power to approve or veto legislation of both nonappropriations and appropriations bills. Article IV, section 1(e) imposes a duty on the Governor to inform the legislature at least once in each regular session of the condition of the state. The Governor may also propose "reorganization of the executive department as will promote efficiency and economy, and recommend measures in the public interest." *Id.* These provisions, read in *pari materia*, constitute the full constitutional allocation of the executive and legislative responsibilities concerning legislation generally and appropriations bills specifically.

More specifically, the constitution provides that "[n]o money shall be drawn from the treasury except in pursuance of appropriation made *by law*," art. VII, § 1(c), Fla. Const. (emphasis added), and that "[p]rovision shall be made *by law* for raising sufficient revenue to defray the expenses of the state for each fiscal period." Art. VII, § 1(d), Fla. Const. (emphasis added).

Based on all these constitutional provisions, this Court has long held that the power to appropriate state funds is *legislative* and is to be exercised *only* through duly enacted *statutes*. *State ex rel. Davis v. Green*, 95 Fla. 117, 127, 116 So. 66, 69 (1928). As we stated in *State ex rel. Kurz v. Lee*:

> The object of a constitutional provision requiring an appropriation made by law as the authority to withdraw money from the state treasury is to prevent the expenditure of the public funds already in the treasury, or potentially therein from tax sources provided to raise it, without the consent of the public given by their representatives in formal legislative acts. *Such a provision secures to the Legislative (except where the Constitution controls to the contrary) the exclusive power of deciding how, when, and for what purpose the public funds shall be applied in carrying on the government.*

121 Fla. 360, 384, 163 So. 859, 868 (1935) (emphasis added). Furthermore, the power to *reduce* appropriations, like any other lawmaking, is a *legislative function*. *See Florida House of Representatives v. Martinez*, 555 So.2d 839, 845 (Fla.1990).

The Commission concedes that the power to legislate and to appropriate funds is initially vested in the legislature, but argues that the Governor has been made a part of the lawmaking process by the express provisions of article III, section 8 of the constitution. The article to which the Commission refers, however, is the provision which simply authorizes the Governor to *veto* legislation. We have previously made clear:

> "[T]he veto power is intended to be a negative power, the power to nullify, or at least suspend, legislative intent. It is not designed to alter or amend legislative intent."

Martinez, 555 So.2d at 843 (quoting *Brown v. Firestone*, 382 So.2d 654, 664 (Fla.1980)) (emphasis altered from original). Thus, it is well settled that the executive branch does not have the power to use the veto to restructure an appropriation. It follows that the legislature cannot provide by statute for the Governor and Cabinet to do at a later date what is forbidden by constitution during the initial appropriations process. Thus, although the constitution provides for executive branch participation in the lawmaking process through the exercise of the Governor's veto power, article III, section 8 does not authorize the legislature to delegate to the executive branch its authority to make decisions regarding the purposes for which public funds may or may not be applied. *Lee; Green.*

The Commission nevertheless argues that the ability to balance the budget through the reduction process of chapter 216 does not encompass a delegation of legislative power. Rather, it contends that reducing the budget is not the same as "appropriating."

We construe the power granted in section 216.221(2) as precisely the power to appropriate. The legislative responsibility to set fiscal priorities through appropriations is totally abandoned when the power to reduce, nullify, or change those priorities is given over to the total discretion of another branch of government.[10] Moreover, the constitutional efforts to set forth a deliberate veto and enforcement mechanism for the executive branch would seem an elaborate exercise in futility if the Governor and Cabinet, by stroke of the executive pen, could excise whole portions of the appropriations act and totally restructure legislative priorities. To permit the Commission to reduce specific appropriations in general appropriations bills would allow the legislature to abdicate its lawmaking function and would enable another branch to amend the law without resort to the constitutionally prescribed lawmaking process. This delegation strikes at the very core of the separation of powers doctrine, and for this reason section 216.221 must fail as unconstitutional.

The facts of the present case are analogous to the facts of a number of previous decisions invalidating legislative delegations under the doctrine of separation of powers. In *Askew v. Cross Key Waterways* this Court addressed the constitutionality of sections 380.051(1) and 380.05(2)(a) and (b), Florida Statutes (1975), empowering the Administration Commission, acting on recommendation of the Division of State Planning, to designate certain geographical areas as being of critical state concern and to promulgate regulations for coordinated development of those lands. We declared those sections unconstitutional under article II, section 3 "because they reposit in the Administration Commission the fundamental legislative task of determining which geographic areas and resources are in greatest need of protection." 372 So.2d at 919. We held that

> until the provisions of Article II, Section 3 of the Florida Constitution are altered by the people we deem the doctrine of nondelegation of legislative power to be viable in this State. Under this doctrine *fundamental and primary policy decisions shall be made by members of the legislature who are elected to perform those tasks,* and administration of legislative programs must be pur-

---

10. [FN7.] As noted in several amicus briefs, some of the Commission's reductions totally eliminate legislatively established programs. For example, the Emergency Financial Assistance for Housing Programs mandated by the legislature to address this state's housing needs would be *completely* abolished.

suant to some minimal standards and guidelines ascertainable by reference to the enactment establishing the program.

Id. at 925 (emphasis added).

In *Orr v. Trask,* 464 So.2d 131, (Fla.1985), this Court invalidated the Governor's attempt to extinguish the term of office of the deputy commissioner of workers' compensation. The Governor purported to be acting pursuant to the 1983 General Appropriations Act which reduced the number of deputy commissioner positions from five to four. The issue was whether the proviso in the appropriations act furnished legal authority for the Governor to truncate Trask's term of office. The Court concluded that it did not, holding that although "it was not necessary for the legislature to make the actual selection of the deputy positions to be abolished; it was ... necessary that the legislature furnish ascertainable minimal criteria and guidelines on how the selection was to be made." *Id.* at 134–35. Thus, because the appropriations act did not furnish guidelines to the Governor as to the criteria to be used in reducing the number of deputy positions, the authorization for such reduction in the appropriations act violated the separation of powers doctrine in article II, section 3. *Id.*

In *Lewis v. Bank of Pasco County,* 346 So.2d 53, 54 (Fla.1976), the Court adopted in full the opinion of the Second Judicial Circuit declaring section 658.10(1), Florida Statutes (1975), unconstitutional. At issue in *Lewis* was a statute granting to the Comptroller the authority to release to the public and the news media otherwise confidential bank or trust company records. The trial court invalidated the statute under the doctrine of separation of powers as " 'attempting to grant to the ... [Comptroller] the power to say *what the law shall be.*' " 346 So.2d at 56 (quoting *Sarasota County v. Barg,* 302 So.2d 737 (Fla.1974)). To quote the trial court:

> As the statute is written, it makes a vast volume of private records, necessarily subject to governmental inspection confidential, but then gives the Comptroller unrestricted and unlimited power to exempt particular records and items of information from the operation of that provision of the statute making them confidential.
>
> In other words, the Department [of Banking] is given power from day to day to say what is the law as to the confidential nature of any records of banks which the Department has the right to inspect or include in the reports of bank examinations.
>
> The Constitution does not permit this delegation of legislative power.

Id. 346 So.2d at 55.

Each of the cases cited above, *Askew, Orr,* and *Lewis,* describes a situation in which there is inadequate legislative direction to the executive branch to carry out the ultimate policy decision of the legislature. They left total discretion to executive branch officials. That is, the statutes did not indicate *which* land to designate as areas of critical state concern in *Askew,* or *which* position to cut in *Orr,* or *which* confidential information could be released in *Lewis.* Likewise, in this case, section 216.221 does not indicate *which* budgeting priorities to maintain or to cut from the original appropriation.

The Commission argues that *State ex rel. Caldwell v. Lee*, 157 Fla. 773, 27 So.2d 84 (1946), supports the constitutionality of the delegation in the present case. We find *Caldwell* inapposite because that case dealt with the delegation of authority over "unneeded balances or surpluses" to be applied in accordance with specified legislative intent. In *Caldwell*, a prerequisite to the board's use of the funds was that all legislative priorities and mandates established in the appropriations act had to be met before the board could act. In this case, no surpluses have been claimed to exist, and the facts indicate that entities of state government will not even be able to fulfill their legal responsibilities. Moreover, there is no express legislative policy that is being carried out. It is, in fact, the Commission which is setting policy.

We note again that it is the legislature's constitutional duty to determine and raise the appropriate revenue to defray the expenses of the state. Art. VII, § 1(d), Fla. Const. ("Provision shall be made *by law* for raising sufficient revenue to defray the expenses of the state for each fiscal period.") (emphasis added). This provision directs the legislature—the only branch with the power to make *law*—and not the executive, to make appropriations for revenue. By its plain wording, article VII, section 1(d) does *not* authorize the Governor to reduce expenses or to reduce appropriations in order to balance the budget. Rather, quite clearly, it requires the legislature either to reduce the appropriations or to raise "sufficient revenue" to satisfy the appropriations it deems necessary to run the government.

Under any working system of government, one of the branches must be able to exercise the power of the purse, and in our system it is the legislature, as representative of the people and maker of laws, including laws pertaining to appropriations, to whom that power is constitutionally assigned. We do not today state that the Governor and Cabinet have no role to play in the budgetary process. For example, section 216.292, Florida Statutes (1989), provides for limited transfers within budget entities under specific circumstances.

Furthermore, the Governor is not without recourse if he or she determines that an appropriation has been erroneously or irresponsibly made such that sufficient revenue to defray the expenses of the state for the fiscal period in question will not be available. As we have observed, the Governor may, pursuant to article III, section 8, veto a bill at the time of its passage or, in fulfillment of the duty to take care that the laws are faithfully executed under article IV, section 1(a), and in exercise of the authority granted under article III, section 3(c)(1), call the legislature into special session to balance the budget for the remainder of the fiscal period. The Governor and Cabinet, sitting as the Administration Commission, however, may not be assigned the task of redrafting the appropriations bill once it has passed the legislature and has been approved by the Governor, an avenue that section 216.221 attempts to open for the Commission.

The constitution specifically provides for the legislature alone to have the power to appropriate state funds. More importantly, only the legislature, as the voice of the people, may determine and weigh the multitude of needs and fiscal priorities of the State of Florida. The legislature must carry out its constitutional duty to establish fiscal priorities in light of the financial resources it has provided.

Consequently, we find that section 216.221 is an impermissible attempt by the legislature to abdicate a portion of its lawmaking responsibility and to vest it in an executive entity. In the words of John Locke, the legislature has attempted to make *legislators,* not *laws.* As a result, the powers of both the legislative and executive branches are lodged in one body, the Administration Commission. This concentration of power is prohibited by any tripartite system of constitutional democracy and cannot stand.

This is not to say that the legislature cannot permit another branch or agency to respond to a budget crisis caused by unexpected events between legislative sessions. The legislature can delegate functions so long as there are sufficient guidelines to assure that the legislative intent is clearly established and can be directly followed in the event of a budget shortfall.[11] Carefully crafted legislation establishing, among other things, the extent to which appropriations may be reduced, coupled with a recitation of reduction priorities and provisions for legislative oversight, might pass facial constitutional muster. What the legislature *cannot* do is delegate its policy-making responsibility.

We likewise affirm the trial court's judgment finding that section 216.011(1)(*ll*), Florida Statutes (1989), which defines the term "state agency" as used throughout chapter 216, is also unconstitutional. Section 216.011(1)(*ll*) provides:

> "State agency" or "agency" means any official, officer, commission, board authority, council, committee, or department of the executive branch, or the judicial branch, as herein defined, of state government.[12]

This section, on its face, flagrantly violates the doctrine of separation of powers. The inclusion of the judicial branch within the definition of "state agency," and hence the placing of the judiciary's fiscal affairs under the management of the executive branch, disregards the constitutional mandate of coordinate power-sharing. Under the constitution, the judiciary is a coequal branch of the Florida government vested with the sole authority to exercise the judicial power. Art. V, § 1, Fla. Const. In accordance with the constitution, it is the chief justice of the supreme court who is the chief administrative officer of the judicial system. Art. V, § 2(b), Fla. Const. Because section 216.011(1)(*ll*) encompasses the judicial branch within its definition of "state agency," it violates the constitutional doctrine of separation of powers. Thus, all other sections of chapter 216 which, by operation of section 216.011(1)(*ll*), subject the judicial branch to executive oversight, are also unconstitutional.

The legislature was obviously cognizant of separation of powers principles in drafting section 216.011(1)(*ll*), as evidenced by the fact that the legislature itself is conspicuously absent from the definition of "state agency." Indeed, while section 216.011(1)(*ll*) treats the judicial branch as a subordinate agency subject to executive authority, the legislative

---

11. [FN9.] We reject the Commission's assertion that section 216.221 contains sufficient guidelines.

12. [FN10.] Section 216.011(1)(s), Florida Statutes (1989), defines "judicial branch" to include "the various officers, courts, commissions, or other units of the judicial branch of state government supported in whole or in part by appropriations made by the Legislature."

branch, throughout chapter 216, is expressly exempted from similar executive control. For example, section 216.081(2), Florida Statutes (1989), provides:

> All of the data relative to the legislative branch shall be for information and guidance in estimating the total financial needs of the state for the ensuing biennium; *none of these estimates shall be subject to revision or review by the Governor,* and they *must* be included in his recommended budget.

(Emphasis added.) Apparently, the legislature recognized the threat to its own constitutional sovereignty and, in passing chapter 216, excluded itself from executive review. In doing so, the legislature has only succeeded in emphasizing the constitutional infirmity of attempting to relocate, by legislative fiat, the coequal powers of the judiciary within the executive branch. But the legislature cannot, short of constitutional amendment, reallocate the balance of power expressly delineated in the constitution among the three coequal branches. The judicial branch cannot be subject in any manner to oversight by the executive branch. The submission of the judicial budget, like the legislature's, may be provided to the Governor for information and guidance, but cannot be subject to revision, reduction, or review by the Governor. Moreover, to maintain the independence of the judiciary, any reduction in the judicial budget mandated by the legislature must be made by the chief justice and cannot be delegated to the executive branch.

Finally, we note that even absent the constitutional infirmities of chapter 216, any substantial reductions of the judicial budget can raise constitutional concerns of the highest order. This Court has an independent duty and authority as a constitutionally coequal and coordinate branch of the government of the State of Florida to guarantee the rights of the people to have access to a functioning and efficient judicial system.[13] Article I, section 21 of the Florida Declaration of Rights provides that "[t]he courts *shall* be open to every person for redress of any injury, and justice *shall* be administered without sale, denial or delay." (Emphasis added.)

We are not unmindful of the difficult conditions which precipitated the Commission's actions and we recognize that the Commission has acted in good faith in attempting to address the fiscal crisis which besets this state. We are, however, called upon to rule based on legal principles which are enduring and cannot be bent to accomplish transient needs. Otherwise, we in the judiciary would be arrogating to ourselves, not merely the power of the legislature to make laws, but the power of the people to change the constitution. It would indeed be easier and more practical to permit the Commission to rewrite the appropriations bill. We are prohibited by our constitution from doing so.

Accordingly, we affirm the trial court's order holding sections 216.011(1)(*ll*) and 216.221, Florida Statutes (1989), unconstitutional as a violation of the doctrine of separation of powers.

---

13. [FN11.] We recognize that there may be items placed in the judicial budget that, although they serve important governmental functions, are not absolutely essential to the constitutional duties of the judiciary.

Any budgetary actions taken pursuant to these statutes subsequent to the injunctive relief granted by the trial judge cannot be implemented.

It is so ordered.

SHAW, C.J., and GRIMES, KOGAN and HARDING, JJ., concur.

OVERTON, J., concurs with an opinion.

McDONALD, J., dissents with an opinion.

NO MOTION FOR REHEARING WILL BE ALLOWED.

OVERTON, Justice, concurring.

I fully concur in the majority opinion. I write only to emphasize that the reason section 216.221(2), Florida Statutes (1989), is unconstitutional is because it grants the Governor and Cabinet unlimited legislative policy-making discretion. Other states apparently have addressed the issue of budget adjustments in a constitutional manner without requiring a special legislative session. The extent of the Governor's and Cabinet's legislative policy-making authority granted by section 216.221(2) is illustrated by the total elimination of funds appropriated by the legislature for emergency housing for homeless families with children, as well as the elimination of a special appropriation for additional aid to dependent children. Each of these decisions is not a minor adjustment in the budget; they substantially affect legislative intent and effectively repeal legislative action.

As noted by Justice McDonald in his dissent, there clearly is a need to maintain a balanced budget, but this statute, and the broad authority it gives to the Governor and the Cabinet, is not the only manner in which budget adjustments can be made. Former Speaker of the House Jon Mills, as an amicus curiae, citing a National Conference of State Legislatures study relating to legislative budget procedures in the fifty states, noted that other states have addressed this problem in more restrictive ways without having to call the legislative body into session. While section 216.221(2) is unconstitutional, it does not mean that the legislature must reconvene every time there is a need for budget adjustments. I believe the legislature can establish a process with specific guidelines for making budget adjustments that is constitutional.

McDONALD, Justice, dissenting.

Section 216.221, Florida Statutes (1989), involves a statutory scheme which permits the reasonable exercise of appropriately shared authority between the executive and legislative branches. The need to maintain a balanced budget is one which is strongly ensconced in Florida's history; it is a protection for the public, and particularly for future generations, which must be guaranteed to the greatest extent possible. Section 216.221 provides the framework for such protection and I believe it is constitutional. This section does not constitute an unconstitutional delegation of legislative power to the Commission, even as applied to reduce the amount of money released to the judicial branch of government.

The balanced budget measure of the Florida Constitution, article VII, section 1(d) is found in neither the legislative nor executive article of the Constitution. Hence, the Constitution imposes the obligation to operate within a balanced budget upon all entities and agencies of state government. One plain mandate of article VII, section 1(d) is to impose upon the legislature the initial requirement to adopt a balanced budget and provide sufficient funds to finance it. Nevertheless, the Constitution anticipates that a post-adoption budget deficit may occur and imposes correlative powers and responsibilities in the Governor to deal with a deficit in the absence of legislative action. More specifically, the Governor is vested with the "supreme executive power" of the state and is charged by the Constitution with the responsibility to "take care that the laws be faithfully executed." Art. IV, § 1(a), Fla. Const.

It cannot be denied that the balanced budget provision of the Florida Constitution is a state law of great weight and importance. It necessarily follows that the Governor, acting with the Commission, is both obligated and empowered by the Constitution itself to assure that the balanced budget mandate of the Constitution is faithfully executed. If the legislature were to refuse to adopt measures necessary to balance an unbalanced budget, the Governor would not be relieved of the constitutional obligation to employ the supreme executive power of the state to assure the budget was balanced. The mandates of the Constitution prevail over both the legislative and executive branches of government. In that regard section 216.221(1) is declarative of the constitutional power and responsibility reposed in the Governor.

The present controversy is not one involving the unwelcome intrusion of one branch on another. In *State v. Lee*, 157 Fla. 773, 27 So.2d 84 (1946), we held that a law allowing for the transfer of funds among budget entities was not an unlawful exercise of legislative power by the executive. A transfer from fund to fund or program to program is certainly more a matter of quasi-legislative action than is the reduction of an appropriation which by law is a maximum appropriation. There must be a guard standing at the door to prevent the expenditure of funds which are not on hand and are not forthcoming. The legislation under attack recognizes this.

My colleagues declare section 216.221 unconstitutional because they perceive the Commission as performing a legislative function or doing so with inadequate guidance. Although neither the Governor nor the Attorney General complains, I have some residual doubts that the Commission should be involved, but have no doubt that the Governor has a constitutional obligation to preclude the expenditure of funds in excess of revenue. Should the statute fall, he still has this constitutional mandate to assure that no more money is spent than is taken in. Thus, I see little to gain by striking down section 216.221.

For budgetary purposes alone, I believe it permissible to define the judicial branch as a state agency and subject to all of the laws relative to the budget process.

I would reverse the decision under review and find the statutes under review constitutional.

Commentary and Questions

"Over-delegation" by the legislature means giving away legislative functions, which is unconstitutional because it violates separation of powers.

1. What was the Administration Commission's two-step argument?

2. According to the majority opinion, how did the legislature "go astray" in the contested statutes?

3. According to the majority, what is the Governor's role in the appropriations process?

4. Under both *Cross Keys* and this case, what does the Court look for when reviewing a "delegation case"?

5. Why does the majority rule § 216.041(1)(*ll*), Florida Statutes, unconstitutional?

6. How does Justice Overton suggest dealing with a budget shortfall without reconvening the Legislature?

7. Trace the "steps" in dissenting Justice McDonald's argument upholding § 216.221's constitutionality?

B. Improper Delegation of Judicial Power

Even though it rarely occurs, courts are forbidden from delegating their inherent judicial authority to agencies of the executive branch.

E.Y. v. State

390 So. 2d 776 (Fla. 3d DCA 1980)

NESBITT, Judge.

The appellant, pursuant to Section 812.13, Florida Statutes (1977), challenges his adjudication of delinquency arising out of robbery charges filed against him. Appellant contends the evidence is insufficient to show that the robbery was accompanied by any force or violence. *McCloud v. State*, 335 So. 2d 257 (Fla. 1976); *Mims v. State*, 342 So. 2d 116 (Fla. 3d DCA 1977); Fla. Std. Jury Instr. (Crim.) (Robbery) 2.06 and 2.07.

The pertinent testimony showed that the appellant snatched a purse from the hand of the victim, an elderly woman who was walking on a sidewalk on Miami Beach. She was confronted by the defendant and his companion on the sidewalk. The victim described the scene as "a very small sidewalk, and on one side are the gates and on the right side are the cars, and I couldn't go anywhere." She testified that the defendant approached on the left "(a)nd this boy took my purse out of my hand (referring to the defendant). I was scared and I couldn't see anything, and I was in a state of shock for a moment."

It is obvious that upon having her path blocked by the defendant and his companion, this elderly lady was intimidated at the moment of, or slightly prior to, this event.

On cross-examination, the victim indicated that her state of mind described above occurred contemporaneously with the act. Under these circumstances, we find the testimony was sufficient to show that the violence or intimidation preceded or was contemporaneous with the taking. *Montsdoca v. State*, 84 Fla. 82, 93 So. 157 (1922).

… Consequently, this court will not substitute its judgment for that of the trier of fact nor pit its judgment against those determinations of fact properly rendered by the trier of fact. *State v. Smith*, 249 So.2d 16 (Fla.1971). All conflicts and reasonable inferences therefrom are resolved to support the judgment of conviction. *Wooten v. State*, 361 So.2d 167 (Fla. 3d DCA 1978); *Dawson v. State*, 338 So.2d 242 (Fla. 3d DCA 1976); *Starling v. State*, 263 So.2d 645 (Fla. 3d DCA), *cert. denied*, 268 So.2d 905 (Fla.1972).

Next, the appellant asserts the trial court erred in delegating authority to his counselor to fix restitution. The dispositional order of this court provided: "Further, said child is to pay a proportionate restitution to the victim in the amount deemed appropriate by his counselor."

In *Fresneda v. State*, 347 So.2d 1021 (Fla.1977), our Supreme Court held that, prior to restitution being ordered, a defendant must be given notice of the proposed restitution order as well as an opportunity to be heard as to the amount. Additionally, the authority to determine the amount cannot be delegated to the probationer's supervisor. *McClure v. State*, 371 So.2d 196 (Fla. 2d DCA 1979); *Kroenke v. State*, 366 So.2d 46 (Fla. 2d DCA 1978), *cert. denied*, 374 So.2d 99 (Fla.1979).

For the foregoing reasons, the appellant's adjudication of delinquency is affirmed; the order delegating judicial authority to the juvenile's counselor to determine the amount of restitution is reversed with directions to afford the juvenile an evidentiary hearing as to the amount of restitution prior to any adjudication by the court.

Affirmed in part and reversed in part.

Carnegie v. State

473 So. 2d 782 (Fla. 2d DCA 1985)

PER CURIAM.

The appellant, Michael Carnegie, appeals from the judgments and sentences entered against him on charges of battery and burglary of a dwelling. We affirm in part and reverse in part.

Appellant has raised several points on appeal, but we find merit only in his contention that the trial court erred in departing from the sentencing guidelines on the charge of burglary of a dwelling.

When sentencing appellant on the burglary charge, the court departed from the guideline recommended range of twelve to thirty months imprisonment and sentenced appellant to serve fifteen years in prison. The court did not give any reasons for its departure, but directed the state to prepare and submit written reasons for departure. The court stated that these reasons, when submitted, would be incorporated into the final judgment and sentence. The scoresheet used by the court in sentencing does not set forth any reasons for departure, but a sheet attached to the scoresheet is entitled "Submitted Reasons For Guideline Departure." Apparently, this document was submitted by the state in compliance with the court's order. It is the only statement of reasons for departure in the record.

We find that the trial court improperly delegated to the state attorney's office a responsibility which belongs exclusively to the court. See *McClure v. State*, 371 So.2d 196 (Fla.2d DCA 1979). Although oral reasons for departure, subsequently transcribed and made part of the record, are sufficient to meet the requirements of Florida Rule of Criminal Procedure 3.701(d)(11), see *Smith v. State*, 454 So.2d 90 (Fla. 2d DCA 1984), the court in this case did not articulate any reasons for departure. A mere statement by the trial court that it intends to incorporate into the judgment and sentence written reasons for departure to be submitted by the state at a later date, falls far short of meeting the requirements set forth in section 921.001(6), Florida Statutes (1983), and Florida Rule of Criminal Procedure 3.701(d)(11).

We, accordingly, reverse and remand for resentencing on the charge of burglary of a dwelling. We affirm the judgments in connection with both of the charges together with the sentence imposed on the battery charge.

Reversed and remanded for resentencing.

RYDER, C.J., and SCHOONOVER and LEHAN, JJ., concur.

C. Encroachment by Executive on Legislative Power

i. By Executive on Legislature

Florida House of Representatives v. Crist

999 So. 2d 601 (Fla. 2008)

CANTERO, J.

After almost sixteen years of sporadic negotiations with four governors, in November 2007 the Seminole Indian Tribe of Florida signed a gambling "compact" (a contract between two sovereigns) with Florida Governor Charles Crist. The compact significantly expands casino gambling, also known as "gaming," on tribal lands. For example, it permits card games such as blackjack and baccarat that are otherwise prohibited by law. In return, the compact promises substantial remuneration to the State.

The Florida Legislature did not authorize the Governor to negotiate the compact before it was signed and has not ratified it since. To the contrary, shortly after the compact was signed, the Florida House of Representatives and its Speaker, Marco Rubio, filed in this Court a petition for a writ of quo warranto disputing the Governor's authority to bind the State to the compact. We have exercised our discretion to consider such petitions, *see* art. V, §3(b)(8), Fla. Const., and now grant it on narrow grounds. We hold that the Governor does not have the constitutional authority to bind the State to a gaming compact that clearly departs from the State's public policy by legalizing types of gaming that are illegal everywhere else in the state.

In the remainder of this opinion, we describe the history of Indian gaming compacts in general and the negotiations leading up to the compact at issue. We then explain our jurisdiction to consider the petition. Finally, we discuss the applicable constitutional provisions, statutes, and cases governing our decision.

I. THE FACTUAL AND LEGAL BACKGROUND

We analyze the compact in the context of the federal regulations authorizing it as well as the background of the negotiations in this case. We first review the statutory foundation for the compact: the Indian Gaming Regulatory Act, 25 U.S.C. §§ 2701–2721 (2000) (IGRA). Next, we detail the history of the Tribe's attempts to negotiate a compact with the State. Finally, we explain the compact's relevant terms.

A. IGRA

Indian tribes are independent sovereigns. The Indian Commerce Clause of the United States Constitution grants only Congress the power to override their sovereignty on Indian lands. U.S. Const., art. I, § 8, cl. 3 ("The Congress shall have Power ... [t]o regulate Commerce with ... the Indian Tribes."); *see also California v. Cabazon Band of Mission Indians*, 480 U.S. 202, 207 (1987) (noting that tribal sovereignty is subordinate only to the federal government). Before IGRA, states had no role in regulating Indian gaming. *See Cabazon*, 480 U.S. at 202.

Congress enacted IGRA in 1988. Among other things, the statute provides "a statutory basis for the operation of gaming by Indian tribes as a means of promoting tribal economic development, self-sufficiency, and strong tribal governments." 25 U.S.C. § 2702(1). IGRA divides gaming into three classes: Class I includes "social games solely for prizes of minimal value." *Id.* § 2703(6). Class II includes "the game of chance commonly known as bingo" and "non-banked" card games—that is, games in which participants play against only each other; the host facility (the "house") has no stake in the outcome. *Id.* § 2703(7). Class III—the only type relevant here—comprises all other types of gaming, including slot machines, pari-mutuel wagering (such as horse and greyhound racing), lotteries, and "banked" card games—such as baccarat, blackjack (twenty-one), and *chemin de fer*—in which participants play against the house. *Id.* § 2703(6)–(8).

IGRA permits Class III gaming on tribal lands, but only in limited circumstances. It is lawful only if it is (1) authorized by tribal ordinance, (2) "located in a State that permits such gaming for any purpose by any person, organization, or entity," and (3) "conducted in accordance with a Tribal-State compact entered into by the Indian tribe and the State ... that is in effect." *Id.* § 2710(d)(1) (emphasis added).

IGRA provides for tribes to negotiate compacts with their host states. Upon a tribe's request, a state "shall negotiate with the Indian tribe in good faith to enter into such a compact." *Id.* § 2710(d)(3)(A) (emphasis added). If the parties successfully negotiate a compact and the Secretary of the Department of the Interior (Department) approves it, the compact takes effect "when notice of approval by the Secretary" is published in the Federal Register. *Id.* § 2710(d)(3)(B), (8).

If negotiations fail, IGRA allows a tribe to sue the state in federal court. If the state continues to refuse consent, the Secretary may "prescribe ... procedures" permitting Class III gaming. *See id.* § 2710(d)(7)(B)(vii). The United States Supreme Court has held, however—in a case involving the Seminole Tribe's attempts to offer Class III gaming in Florida—that IGRA did not abrogate the states' Eleventh Amendment immunity. *See Seminole Tribe of Fla. V. Florida,* 517 U.S. 44, 47 (1996). Therefore, states need not consent to such lawsuits. The Department later created an alternative procedure under which, when a tribe cannot negotiate a compact and a state asserts immunity, the Secretary may prescribe Class III gaming. *See* Class III Gaming Procedures, 64 Fed.Reg. 17535-02 (Apr. 12, 1999) (codified at 25 C.F.R. pt. 291 (2007)). At least one federal court, however, has held that the Secretary lacked authority to promulgate such regulations. *See Texas v. United States,* 497 F.3d 491, 493 (5th Cir.2007), *petition for cert. filed sub nom. Kickapoo Traditional Tribe of Texas v. Texas,* 76 U.S.L.W. 3471 (U.S. Feb. 25, 2008) (No. 07-1109). Therefore, their validity remains questionable.

B. The Negotiations Between the Tribe and the State

With this statutory framework in mind, we briefly describe the protracted history of the Seminole Tribe's efforts to negotiate a compact for conducting Class III gaming in Florida. These negotiations spanned sixteen years and four different governors.

The Seminole Indian Tribe is a federally recognized Indian tribe whose reservations and trust lands are located in the State. The Tribe currently operates Class II gaming facilities, offering low stakes poker games and electronically aided bingo games. The Tribe first sought a compact allowing it to offer Class III gaming in 1991. That January, the Tribe and Governor Lawton Chiles began negotiations, but they ultimately proved fruitless. That same year, the Tribe filed suit in federal court alleging that the State had failed to negotiate in good faith. As noted earlier, the Supreme Court ultimately ruled that the State could assert immunity, and it did. *See Seminole Tribe,* 517 U.S. at 47, *aff'g Seminole Tribe of Fla. v. Fla.,* 11 F.3d 1016 (11th Cir.1994).

Over the next several years, the Tribe repeatedly petitioned the Department to establish Class III gaming procedures. In 1999, the Department did so. It found the Tribe eligible for the procedures and called an informal conference, which was held in Tallahassee that December. At the State's suggestion, however, the Tribe agreed to suspend the conference, though only temporarily. In January 2001, the Secretary issued a twenty-page decision allowing the Tribe to offer a wide range of Class III games. When the State requested clarification, however, the Secretary withdrew the decision. The delay continued. Finally, five years later—in May 2006—the Department reconvened the conference in Hollywood, Florida, and in September of that year warned that if the Tribe and the State did not execute a compact within 60 days, the Department would issue Class III gaming procedures. Despite the parties' failure to negotiate a compact, however, the Department never issued procedures.

Apparently exasperated with the slow progress of the procedures, in March 2007 the Tribe sued the Department in federal court. *See Seminole Tribe of Fla. v. United States,* No. 07-60317-CIV, 2007 WL 5077484 (S.D. Fla. filed Mar. 6, 2007). The Department then urged Governor Crist to negotiate a compact, warning that if a compact was not signed by November 15, 2007, the Department would finally issue procedures. Under the proposed procedures, the State would not receive any revenue and would have no control over the Tribe's gaming operations. The Tribe would be authorized to operate slot machines and "card games," defined as "a game or series of games of poker (other than Class II games) which are played in a nonbanking manner." (Emphasis added.) Notably, the alternative procedures would not have permitted the Tribe to operate banked card games such as blackjack.[14]

On November 14—the day before the deadline—the Governor agreed to a compact with the Tribe (Compact). Five days later, the House and its Speaker, Marco Rubio, filed this petition disputing the Governor's authority to bind the State to the Compact without legislative authorization or ratification. We allowed the Tribe to join the action as a respondent.[15]

On January 7, 2008, upon publication of the Secretary's approval, the Compact went into effect. *See* Notice of Deemed Approved Tribal-State Class III Gaming Compact, 73 Fed.Reg. 1229 (Jan. 7, 2008). The parties agree, however, that the Secretary's approval does not render the petition moot.[16]

C. The Compact

The Compact recites that the Governor "has the authority to act for the State with respect to the negotiation and execution of this Compact." It covers a period of twenty-five years and allows the Tribe to offer specified Class III gaming at seven casinos in the State. It establishes the terms, rights, and responsibilities of the parties regarding such gaming. We discuss only its more relevant provisions.

The Compact authorizes the Tribe to conduct "covered gaming," which includes several types of Class III gaming: slot machines; any banking or banked card game, including baccarat, blackjack (twenty-one), and *chemin de fer;* high stakes poker games; games and devices authorized for the state lottery; and any new game authorized by Florida law. The Compact expressly does not authorize roulette- or craps-style games. The gaming is limited to seven casinos on tribal lands in six areas of the state: Okeechobee, Coconut Creek, Hollywood (two), Clewiston, Immokalee, and Tampa. Compact pt. IV.B., at 7–8.

The Compact grants the Tribe the exclusive right to conduct certain types of gaming. That is, the Tribe may conduct some Class III gaming, such as banked card games, that is prohibited under state law. Based on that "partial but substantial ex-

---

14. [FN1.] During this period, two separate but identical bills designating the Governor to negotiate and execute a compact and submit it for ratification by the legislature were not voted on by the House of Representatives. *See* Fla. SB 160 (2007); Fla. HB 209 (2007).

15. [FN2.] We also allowed other organizations to file briefs as amici curiae in support of the House: the Florida Senate, the Gulfstream Park Racing Association, and the City of Hallandale Beach.

16. [FN3.] The federal district court, however, concluded that such approval did render the Tribe's suit moot. *Seminole Tribe of Fla. v. United States*, No. 07-60317-CIV (S.D. Fla. order filed June 20, 2008). The court dismissed the Tribe's case and noted that the Tribe already had begun operating under the Compact's terms.

clusivity," the Tribe must pay the State a share of the gaming revenue. That share is based in part on amounts that increase at specified thresholds: when the Compact becomes effective, the State receives $50 million. Over the first twenty-four months of operation, it will receive another $175 million. Thereafter, for the third twelve months of operation the State will receive $150 million, and for each twelve-month cycle after that, a minimum of $100 million. If the State breaches the exclusivity provision, however—by legalizing any Class III gaming currently prohibited under state law—the Tribe may cease its payments. The Compact (attached as an appendix to this opinion) is thirty-seven pages long and contains several other provisions we need not detail here.

II. JURISDICTION

Before discussing the issue presented, we first address our jurisdiction. The House and Speaker Rubio have filed in this Court a petition for writ of quo warranto. The Governor contends that this Court lacks jurisdiction because the House does not seek either to remove him from office or to enjoin the future exercise of his authority. We conclude, however, that these are not the only grounds for issuing such a writ.

The Florida Constitution authorizes this Court to issue writs of quo warranto to "state officers and state agencies." Art. V, § 3(b)(8), Fla. Const. The term "quo warranto" means "by what authority." This writ historically has been used to determine whether a state officer or agency has improperly exercised a power or right derived from the State. *See Martinez v. Martinez*, 545 So.2d 1338, 1339 (Fla.1989); *see also* art. V, § 3(b)(8), Fla. Const. Here, the Governor is a state officer. The House challenges the Governor's authority to unilaterally execute the Compact on the State's behalf.

The Governor argues that because he already has signed the Compact, quo warranto relief is inappropriate. But the writ is not so limited. In fact, petitions for the writ historically have been filed after a public official has acted. *See, e.g., Chiles v. Phelps,* 714 So.2d 453, 455 (Fla.1998) (holding that the Legislature and its officers exceeded their authority in overriding the Governor's veto); *State ex rel. Butterworth v. Kenny,* 714 So.2d 404, 406 (Fla.1998) (issuing the writ after the Capital Collateral Regional Counsel had filed a federal civil rights suit, concluding that it had no authority to file it). The Governor's execution of the Compact does not defeat our jurisdiction....

In this case, the Secretary has approved the Compact and, absent an immediate judicial resolution, it will be given effect. In fact, according to news reports, the Tribe already has begun offering blackjack and other games at the Seminole Hard Rock Hotel and Casino. *See* Amy Driscoll, "Casino Gambling: Amid glitz, blackjack's in the cards," The Miami Herald, June 23, 2008, at B1. Thus, if indeed the Governor has exceeded his constitutional authority, a compact that violates Florida law will, nevertheless, become effective in seven casinos located on tribal lands located in the state. As in *Phelps*, therefore, the importance and immediacy of the issue justifies our deciding this matter now rather than transferring it for resolution in a declaratory judgment action.

III. DISCUSSION OF LAW

We now discuss the law that applies to this inter-branch dispute. In deciding whether the Governor or the Legislature has the authority to execute a compact, we first define a "compact" and its historical use in Florida. We then discuss how other jurisdictions have resolved this issue. Next, we review the relevant provisions of our own constitution. Finally, we explain our conclusion that the Governor lacked authority under our state's constitution to execute the Compact because it changes the state's public policy as expressed in the criminal law and therefore infringes on the Legislature's powers.

A. Compacts and their Use in Florida

A compact is essentially a contract between two sovereigns. *Texas v. New Mexico*, 482 U.S. 124, 128 (1987); *see Black's Law Dictionary* 298 (8th ed.1999) (defining a compact as "[a]n agreement or covenant between two or more parties, esp[ecially] between governments or states"). The United States Supreme Court has described compacts as "a supple device for dealing with interests confined within a region." *State ex rel. Dyer v. Sims*, 341 U.S. 22, 27 (1951). The United States Constitution provides that "[n]o State shall, without the Consent of Congress … enter into any Agreement or Compact with another State, or with a foreign Power." U.S. Const, art. I, § 10. IGRA establishes the consent of Congress to execute gaming compacts, but requires federal approval before they become effective. *See* 25 U.S.C. § 2710(d)(8).

Like many states, Florida has executed compacts on a range of subjects, including environmental control, water rights, energy, and education—more than thirty in all. The vast majority were executed with other states. In most cases, the Legislature enacted a law. *See, e.g.*, § 372.831, Fla. Stat. (2007) ("The Wildlife Violator Compact is created and entered into with all other jurisdictions legally joining therein in the form substantially as follows[.]"); § 257.28 (Interstate Library Compact); § 252.921 (Emergency Management Assistance Compact); § 322.44 (Driver License Compact). In others, the Legislature authorized the Governor to execute a compact in the form provided in a statute. *See, e.g.*, § 370.19, Fla. Stat. (2007) ("The Governor of this state is hereby authorized and directed to execute a compact on behalf of the State of Florida with any one or more of [the following states] … legally joining therein in the form substantially as follows[.]"); § 370.20 (containing the same authorization and establishing the terms for the Gulf States Marine Fisheries Compact); § 403.60 (using the same authorization language for the Interstate Environmental Control Compact, establishing its terms, and "signif[ying] in advance" the Legislature's "approval and ratification of such compact"). In a few—including a compact among the State, the Tribe, and the South Florida Water Management District regulating water use on Tribal lands—the Legislature by statute approved and ratified the compact. § 285.165, Fla. Stat. (2007). Thus, by tradition at least, it is the Legislature that has consistently either exercised itself or expressly authorized the exercise of the power to bind the State to compacts. We have found no instance in which the governor has signed a compact without legislative involvement.

Although tradition bears some relevance, it does not resolve the question of which branch actually has the constitutional authority to execute compacts in general and gaming compacts in particular. As explained above, the Compact here governs Class III gaming on certain tribal lands in Florida. The issue is whether, regardless of whether the Governor bucked tradition, he had constitutional authority to execute the Compact without the Legislature's prior authorization or, at least, subsequent ratification.

D. The Compact Violates the Separation of Powers

The House claims that the Compact violates the separation of powers on a number of grounds.[17] We find one of them dispositive. The Compact permits the Tribe to conduct certain Class III gaming that is prohibited under Florida law. Therefore, the Compact violates the state's public policy about the types of gambling that should be allowed. We hold that, whatever the Governor's authority to execute compacts, it does not extend so far. The Governor does not have authority to agree to legalize in some parts of the state, or for some persons, conduct that is otherwise illegal throughout the state.

We first discuss whether state laws in general, and gaming laws in particular, apply to Indian tribes. We next discuss Florida law on gaming. We then address the House's argument that IGRA prohibits compacts from expanding the gaming allowed under state law. Finally, we explain why the Governor lacked authority to bind the State to a compact, such as this one, that contradicts state law.

1. State Gaming Laws Apply to the Tribe

Generally, state laws do not apply to tribal Indians on Indian reservations unless Congress so provides. *McClanahan v. State Tax Comm'n of Ariz.*, 411 U.S. 164, 170 (1973). Therefore, the extent to which a state may enforce its criminal laws on tribal land depends on federal authorization. *See Seminole Tribe of Fla. v. Butterworth*, 658 F.2d 310, 312 (5th Cir.1981). Congress has, however, conferred on the states the authority to assume jurisdiction over crimes committed on tribal land, *see* Act of Aug. 15, 1953, Pub.L. No. 280 § 6, 67 Stat. 588, 590 (1953), and Florida has assumed such jurisdiction. *See* ch. 61-252, §§ 1–2, at 452–53, Laws of Fla. (codified at § 285.16, Fla. Stat. (2007)); *see also* § 285.16(2), Fla. Stat. (2007) ("The civil and criminal laws of Florida shall obtain on all Indian reservations in this state and shall be enforced in the same manner as elsewhere throughout the state."); Op. Att'y

---

17. [FN8.] The House argues that the Compact significantly changes Florida law and policy in a number of ways: it authorizes Class III slot machines outside of Broward County; it allows blackjack and other banked card games that are currently illegal throughout Florida; it provides for collection of funds from tribal casinos for State purposes under a revenue-sharing agreement and penalizes the State for any expansion of non-tribal gaming; it allows an exception to Florida's substantive right of access to public records for information dealing with Indian gaming; it changes the venue of litigation dealing with individual disputes with the tribal casinos; it sets procedures for tort remedies occurring in certain circumstances; it waives sovereign immunity to the extent that it creates enforceable contract rights between the State and the Tribe; and it establishes a regulatory mechanism to be undertaken by the Governor or his designee. Because of our resolution of this case, we need not consider whether these other provisions encroach on the legislature's policy-making authority.

Gen. Fla. 94-45 (1994) (discussing the state's jurisdiction over Indian reservations). The state's law is therefore enforceable on tribal lands to the extent it does not conflict with federal law. *See* Op. Att'y Gen. Fla. 94-45 (1994); *see also Hall v. State*, 762 So.2d 936, 936–38 (Fla. 2d DCA 2000) (holding that the circuit court had jurisdiction over a vehicular homicide on an Indian reservation); *State v. Billie*, 497 So.2d 889, 892–95 (Fla. 2d DCA 1986) (holding that a Seminole Indian was properly charged under state criminal law with killing a Florida panther on tribal land). In regard to gambling in particular, federal law provides that, except as provided in a tribal-state compact, state gambling laws apply on tribal lands. *See* 18 U.S.C. § 1166(a) (2000).

Based on these state and federal provisions, what is legal in Florida is legal on tribal lands, and what is illegal in Florida is illegal there. Absent a compact, any gambling prohibited in the state is prohibited on tribal land.

2. Florida's Gaming Laws

It is undisputed that Florida permits limited forms of Class III gaming. The state's constitution authorizes the state lottery, which offers various Class III games, and now permits slot machines in Miami-Dade and Broward Counties. *See* art. X, §§ 7, 15, Fla. Const. For a long time, the State also has regulated pari-mutuel wagering— for example, on dog and horse racing. *See* ch. 550, Fla. Stat. (2007) (governing pari-mutuel wagering).

It is also undisputed, however, that the State prohibits all other types of Class III gaming, including lotteries not sponsored by the State and slot machines outside Miami-Dade and Broward Counties. Florida law distinguishes between nonbanked (Class II) card games and banked (Class III) card games. A "banking game" is one "in which the house is a participant in the game, taking on players, paying winners, and collecting from losers or in which the cardroom establishes a bank against which participants play." § 849.086(2)(b); *see* § 849.086(1), Fla. Stat. (deeming banked games to be "casino gaming"). Florida law authorizes cardrooms at pari-mutuel facilities for games of "poker or dominoes," but only if they are played "in a nonbanking manner." § 849.086(2), Fla. Stat.; *see* § 849.086(1)–(3). Florida law prohibits banked card games, however. *See* § 849.086(12)(a), (15)(a). Blackjack, baccarat, and *chemin de fer* are banked card games. They are therefore illegal in Florida.

3. Does IGRA Permit Compacts to Expand Gaming?

Contrary to Florida law, the Compact allows banked card games such as blackjack, baccarat, and *chemin de fer*. The House argues that the Compact therefore violates IGRA itself, which permits Class III gaming only if the state "permits such gaming for any purpose by any person, organization, or entity." 25 U.S.C. § 2710(d)(1). The Governor, on the other hand, contends that, once state law permits *any* Class III gaming, a compact may allow *all* Class III gaming.

The meaning of the phrase "permits such gaming" has been heavily litigated. The question is whether, when state law permits some Class III games to be played, a tribe must be permitted to conduct only those particular games or all Class III games ...

Whether the Compact violates IGRA, however, is a question we need not and do not resolve. Given our narrow scope of review on a writ of quo warranto, the issue here is only whether the Florida Constitution grants the Governor the authority to unilaterally bind the State to a compact that violates public policy. We conclude that *even if* the Governor is correct that IGRA permits the expansion of gaming on tribal lands beyond what state law permits, such an agreement represents a significant change in Florida's public policy. It is therefore precisely the type of action particularly within the Legislature's power. We now discuss that issue.

4. The Compact Violates Florida's Public Policy on Gaming

Article II, section 3 of the Florida Constitution prohibits the executive branch from usurping the powers of another branch. Enacting laws—and especially criminal laws—is quintessentially a legislative function. *See State v. Barquet*, 262 So.2d 431, 433 (Fla.1972) ("The lawmaking function is the chief legislative power."). By authorizing the Tribe to conduct "banked card games" that are illegal throughout Florida—and thus illegal for the Tribe—the Compact violates Florida law. *See Chiles v. Children A, B, C, D, E, & F*, 589 So.2d 260, 264 (Fla.1991) ("This Court has repeatedly held that, under the doctrine of separation of powers, the legislature may not delegate the power to enact laws or to declare what the law shall be to any other branch."). The Governor's action therefore encroaches on the legislative function and was beyond his authority. Nor does it matter that the Compact is a contract between the State and the Tribe. Neither the Governor nor anyone else in the executive branch has the authority to execute a contract that violates state criminal law. *Cf. Local No. 234, United Assoc. of Journeymen & Apprentices of Plumbing & Pipefitting Industry v. Henley & Beckwith, Inc.*, 66 So.2d 818, 821 (Fla.1953) ("[A]n agreement that is violative of a provision of a constitution or a valid statute, or an agreement which cannot be performed without violating such a constitutional or statutory provision, is illegal and void."); *City of Miami v. Benson*, 63 So.2d 916, 923 (Fla.1953) ("The contract in question, that is, the acceptance by the City of the proposal made by its agent, employee or advisor, to purchase the bonds, is contrary to public policy and is, therefore, void.").

IV. CONCLUSION

We conclude that the Governor's execution of a compact authorizing types of gaming that are prohibited under Florida law violates the separation of powers. The Governor has no authority to change or amend state law. Such power falls exclusively to the Legislature. Therefore, we hold that the Governor lacked authority to bind the State to a compact that violates Florida law as this compact does. We need not resolve the broader issue of whether the Governor ever has the authority to execute compacts without either the Legislature's prior authorization or, at least, its subsequent ratification. Because we believe the parties will fully comply with the dictates of this opinion, we grant the petition but withhold issuance of the writ.

It is so ordered.

WELLS, ANSTEAD, PARIENTE, and BELL, JJ., concur.

QUINCE, C.J., concurs in result only.

LEWIS, J., concurs in result only with an opinion.

LEWIS, J., concurring in result only.

I concur in result only based upon two aspects of the majority opinion which cause concern. First, I would conclude that the majority's analysis and discussion with regard to the Governor's power to enter into a compact is overly restrictive.

THE CONSTITUTIONAL AUTHORITY OF THE GOVERNOR

I cannot agree with the analysis of the majority, which is unduly restrictive with regard to the constitutional powers of the Governor as the chief executive officer of the State of Florida. The general thrust of the majority opinion indicates that the "necessary business" clause of article IV, section 1(a) of the Florida Constitution does not authorize the Governor to bind the State to an IGRA compact, and the opinion relies upon foreign cases which suggest similar limitations upon the actions of governors in other jurisdictions. I disagree and instead conclude that, if the Compact had not granted and authorized certain types of Class III gaming that are specifically prohibited by state law, the Governor would have been authorized—pursuant to the necessary-business clause—to enter into a compact on behalf of the State without either legislative authorization or ratification under the circumstances presented by the instant case. *See Dewberry v. Kulongoski*, 406 F.Supp.2d 1136, 1154 (D.Or.2005) (determining that the execution of a gaming compact was "necessary business" that the governor was authorized to transact under an identical constitutional provision). To the extent the majority suggests otherwise, I disagree.

While I agree that the Governor may not bind the State to a compact that *specifically conflicts with existing state law,* in my view the constitutional provision does afford the Governor a field of operation to enter into a binding compact under circumstances in which the other branches of government have ignored a problem or neglected to act and have thereby created a void by governmental inaction or a total vacuum in an area that will likely create or produce a negative impact for Florida and the citizens of this State. This power is particularly applicable when that void or vacuum has existed with regard to a known problem or issue for an extensive period of time and adverse consequences are reasonably imminent. Here, despite the fact that this gaming issue existed and the Tribe actively sought to negotiate resolution in a compact for almost sixteen years, the Legislature—having full access to the information and issues—did not act. In an effort to protect Florida and the citizens of this State from the results of the federal Department's clear statement that it would issue Class III gaming procedures (under which the State would receive no revenue and possess no control over the Tribe's gaming operations) and the pending legal action, the Governor negotiated a compact. Under these imminent circumstances, the Governor's action constituted "necessary business," which that office was required to address in an attempt to protect the public interest. To hold otherwise would strip the necessary-business clause of any meaningful field of operation. *See Broward County v. City of*

Ft. Lauderdale, 480 So.2d 631, 633 (Fla.1985) ("[A] construction of the constitution which renders superfluous, meaningless or inoperative any of its provisions should not be adopted by the courts.").

In my view, the Governor generally possesses the authority to act under a broad range of circumstances where the failure of the other branches of government to act for an extended period of time imminently threatens harm. This may conceivably address matters such as the quality of life, health, or welfare of the citizens of Florida. For example, an emergency that threatens imminent harm to the quality of air or water in Florida may constitute "necessary business" for the Governor depending on the circumstances presented. Further, the Governor is bound by our state Constitution to "take care that the laws be faithfully executed." Art. IV, § 1(a), Fla. Const. In my view, this duty includes the negotiation of inter-sovereign compacts that (1) are consistent with preexisting state law and (2) further the interests of the State of Florida. These constitutional provisions should be interpreted to afford the Governor the power and authority to negotiate with another sovereign concerning those issues that significantly impact this State and the general well-being of the State even without legislative authorization or ratification under certain circumstances.

CONCLUSION

The jurisdictionally based question framed by the House and Speaker Rubio should be answered. The Governor possesses the authority under the Florida Constitution to enter into Indian-gaming compacts. Here, however, he *erroneously exercised* that authority because the Compact impermissibly included authorization of Class III gaming specifically prohibited under state law. It is undisputed that the Legislature has acted in this area, and for this reason, I concur in the result of the majority. However, I disagree with the overly restrictive suggestion of the majority and generally conclude that where inaction by the other branches of government for an extended period of time has produced a vacuum under circumstances such as these, the Governor is constitutionally authorized to act under the necessary-business clause to protect the well-being of the State of Florida.

ii. By Legislature on Executive Branch

Jones v. Chiles

638 So. 2d 48 (Fla. 1994)

OVERTON, J.

John Paul Jones, Jr., a compensation claims judge, petitions for a writ of mandamus, asking this Court to require Lawton M. Chiles, Governor of the State of Florida, to reappoint him to office as required by the reappointment procedure set forth in section 440.45, Florida Statutes (1991). We have jurisdiction under article V, section 3(b)(8), of the Florida Constitution. We find that the portion of section 440.45(2) that eliminates the Governor's choice in the reappointment of a compensation claims judge is invalid, because it unconstitutionally encroaches on the power of the Governor to appoint executive branch officers. For the reasons expressed, we deny the petition.

The undisputed facts of this case are as follows. In 1972, Jones was appointed to a four-year term as a compensation claims judge to hear workers' compensation cases. Shortly thereafter, the legislature created a process for the merit selection and retention of compensation claims judges. *See* § 440.45, Fla. Stat. (1975). Under that process, each appellate district had a judicial nominating commission. For initial appointments, the commission submitted to the Governor a list containing the names of three lawyers, and the Governor appointed one of those lawyers to serve a four-year term as a compensation claims judge. Before the expiration of a judge's four-year term, the commission voted whether to retain the judge for another term. If the commission voted not to retain the judge, then the Governor could not reappoint the judge. If the commission voted to retain the judge, then the Governor was required to reappoint the judge to another four-year term. Under this process, Jones has been reappointed to five four-year terms since his initial appointment and was last reappointed by Governor Martinez in 1988.

In 1990, the legislature created a statewide nominating commission to replace the existing district judicial nominating commissions for workers' compensation judges. The retention process remained the same. *See* § 440.45, Fla. Stat. (1991). In 1992, the new statewide nominating commission voted 8–6 to retain Jones. Governor Chiles, however, has not reappointed Jones to office and has advised that he will not do so. At this time, Jones remains in office, is still performing his duties, and is being paid his state salary. He now files this petition for a writ of mandamus, asking this Court to require the Governor to reappoint him to office as mandated by section 440.45.

Section 440.45 provides in pertinent part as follows:

(1) The Governor shall appoint as many full-time judges of compensation claims to the workers' compensation trial courts as may be necessary to effectually perform the duties prescribed for them under this chapter. The Governor shall initially appoint a judge of compensation claims from a list of at least three persons nominated by a statewide nominating commission. The statewide nominating commission shall be composed of the following: five members, one of each who resides in each of the territorial jurisdictions of the district courts of appeal, appointed by the Board of Governors of The Florida Bar from among The Florida Bar members who are actively engaged in the practice of law; five electors, of each who resides in each of the territorial jurisdictions of the district courts of appeal, appointed by the Governor; and five electors, one of each who resides in each of the territorial jurisdictions of the district courts of appeal, and who are not members of The Florida Bar, selected and appointed by a majority vote of the other ten members of the commission. The meetings and determinations of the nominating commission as to the judges of compensation claims shall be open to the general

public. No person shall be nominated or appointed as a full-time judge of compensation claims who has not had 5 years' experience in the practice of law in this state; and no judge of compensation claims shall engage in the private practice of law during a term of office. The Governor may appoint any former judge of compensation claims to serve as a judge of compensation claims pro hac vice to complete the proceedings on any claim with respect to which the judge of compensation claims had heard testimony and which remained pending at the time of the expiration of the judge of compensation claims' term of office. However, no former judge of compensation claims shall be appointed to serve as a judge of compensation claims pro hac vice for a period to exceed 60 successive days.

(2) Each full-time judge of compensation claims shall be appointed for a term of 4 years, but during the term of office may be removed by the Governor for cause. *Prior to the expiration of the term of office of the judge of compensation claims, the conduct of such judge of compensation claims shall be reviewed by the statewide nominating commission, which commission shall determine whether such judge of compensation claims shall be retained in office.* Evaluation forms to be considered by the commission shall be prepared by the Chief Judge, shall be completed anonymously by each attorney within 45 days from the date of any hearing in which he has participated, and shall be forwarded to the statewide nominating commission. Included in the evaluation shall be questions relating to timeliness of decisions; diligence, availability, and punctuality; neutrality and objectivity regarding legal issues; knowledge and application of law; courtesy toward litigants, witnesses, and lawyers; judicial demeanor; and willingness to ignore irrelevant considerations such as race, sex, religion, politics, identity of lawyers, or parties. A report of the decision shall be furnished to the Governor no later than 6 months prior to the expiration of the term of the judge of compensation claims. *If the statewide nominating commission votes not to retain the judge of compensation claims, the judge of compensation claims shall not be reappointed but shall remain in office until a successor is appointed and qualified. If the statewide nominating commission votes to retain the judge of compensation claims in office, then the Governor shall reappoint the judge of compensation claims for a term of 4 years.* Judges of compensation claims shall be subject to the jurisdiction of the Judicial Qualifications Commission.

(3) The judges of compensation claims shall be within the Department of Labor and Employment Security under the secretary of that department.

(Emphasis added.)

As the underlined portion of section 440.45 indicates, "if the statewide nominating commission votes to retain the judge of compensation claims in office, then the governor *shall* reappoint the judge of compensation claims for a term of four years." (Emphasis added.) Because of this language in the statute, Jones maintains that the Governor must perform the ministerial act of reappointing him given that the nominating commission has voted to retain him in office. The Governor, on the other hand, argues that he need not reappoint Jones to office as required by section 440.45 because the statute violates the separation of powers doctrine by unconstitutionally depriving him of his gubernatorial prerogative to appoint executive branch officers.

As noted, under the statute the Governor has no choice in whether to reappoint a judge of compensation claims; the Governor is required to reappoint a judge of compensation claims once the nominating commission has voted to retain that judge in office. The question, then, is whether the statute is unconstitutional as asserted by the Governor. A number of provisions of the Florida Constitution are applicable in answering this question.

By law, compensation claims judges fall under the Workers' Compensation Division of the Department of Labor and Employment Security. *See* §§ 20.171(d), 440.45, Fla. Stat. (1991). The Department of Labor and Employment Security is one of the twenty-five *executive departments* provided for in article VI, section 6, of the Florida Constitution. As the chief executive officer in whom the supreme executive power is vested, the Governor has direct supervision over all executive departments unless the legislature places that supervision in the hands of one of the following other executive officers: the lieutenant governor, the governor and cabinet, a cabinet member, or an officer or board appointed by and serving at the pleasure of the governor. *See* art. IV, §§ 1(a), 6, Fla. Const. Inherent in that direct supervisory authority is the power to appoint executive officers to public office.

Under section 20.171, the Department of Labor and Employment Security comes under the direct supervision of the Secretary of Labor and Employment Security, an officer who is appointed by and serves at the pleasure of the Governor. As such, only the Governor or the Secretary of Labor and Employment Security, subject to the Governor's approval, would have the power to appoint judges of compensation claims. The legislature, under section 440.45, directs the Governor to "appoint as many full-time judges of compensation claims to the workers' compensation trial courts as may be necessary to effectually perform the duties prescribed for them." Consequently, the Governor alone is the executive officer in whom the power of appointment of compensation claims judges is vested. The only restriction that may be placed on that appointment power is that confirmation by the senate or the approval of three members of the cabinet may be required by law. Art. IV, § 6(a), Fla. Const. Additionally, because article III, section 13, of the Florida Constitution, expressly limits the terms of public officers to four years unless otherwise specified in the constitution, and because the Governor is the chief executive officer in whom the power to appoint compensation claims judges is vested, a new appointment by the Governor is required for compensation claims judges every four years. Under the reappointment provisions of section 440.45(2), however, the legislature has provided that reappointment of compensation claims judges is to be by majority vote of the statewide nominating commission. Because under section 440.45 the Governor must reappoint a judge of compensation claims if the statewide nominating commission votes to retain such judge, the Governor's act in reappointing a judge of compensation claims is purely ministerial. This procedure effectively eliminates the power of the Governor to reappoint compensation claims judges as officers of the executive branch.

Jones, nevertheless, maintains that the Governor has no constitutional right to appoint compensation claims judges because, although compensation claims judges are technically executive branch officers, they are, in reality, judicial officers inasmuch as they exercise quasi-judicial powers; they function exclusively as judicial officers; and they are governed by Supreme Court rules. Consequently, Jones asserts, the Governor has no constitutional appointment power in the reappointment of compensation claims judges.

As noted above, in Florida, the legislature has chosen to place compensation claims judges within the executive branch as part of the Department of Labor. Although, in the past, this Court has acknowledged that judges of compensation claims perform a quasi-judicial function, we have repeatedly acknowledged that those judges are still members of the executive branch.... Although we did acknowledge in *Orr v. Trask*, 464 So. 2d 131 (Fla. 1985), that, under section 440.45, the decision to reappoint an incumbent rests entirely with the nominating commission, we were simply reiterating the requirements of the statute in ruling on the removal power of the Governor; we were not ruling, as we do today, on the constitutionality of the exclusive reappointment power given to the nominating commission. We find that compensation claims judges are executive branch officials, not judicial branch officials. Having determined that judges of compensation claims fall within the authority of the executive branch, we conclude that section 440.45(2) violates the separation of powers doctrine to the extent that it deprives the Governor of his power to appoint and reappoint.

Jones contends that this holding will compromise the position of compensation claims judges because it will make those judges beholden to the Governor. We note, however, that, in 1993, the legislature itself amended section 440.45, effective January 1, 1994, to eliminate the power of the statewide nominating commission to reappoint judges of compensation claims and to provide the Governor with that power instead. *See* ch. 93-415, § 40, Laws of Fla. Additionally, it is the legislature that has chosen to place compensation claims judges and the adjudication of workers' compensation claims within the executive branch. If it so desired, the legislature could completely eliminate compensation claims judges as executive branch officials and place the adjudication of workers' compensation cases within the judicial branch by providing that jurisdiction of those cases is to be in placed in either the county or circuit courts.... Consequently, no provision exists to prohibit the legislature from placing the jurisdiction of workers' compensation claims within either the county or circuit courts.

In conclusion, we find the portion of section 440.45(2) that eliminates the Governor's choice in the reappointment of a compensation claims judge to be invalid because it unconstitutionally encroaches on the power of the Governor to appoint executive branch officers. Having made this determination, we find that the Governor is free to proceed under the new appointment procedure set forth in chapter 93-415, section 40, Laws of Florida, in filling Jones' position. The Governor has made no objection to the new appointment process set forth in that provision and, under that process, he is allowed to make the final choice in filling Jones' position by choosing from the qualified individuals submitted to him by the nominating commission. Further, under the unique circumstances of this case, we find that Jones and like-situated compensation claims judges should continue to serve as compensation claims judges in a de facto capacity until the Governor fills their positions under the provisions of chapter 93-415.

Accordingly, for the reasons expressed, the petition for a writ of mandamus is denied.

It is so ordered.

GRIMES, C.J., and SHAW, KOGAN and HARDING, JJ., and McDONALD, Senior Justice, concur.

iii. By Legislature on Judiciary

Bush v. Schiavo

885 So. 2d 321 (Fla. 2004)

PARIENTE, C.J.

The narrow issue in this case requires this Court to decide the constitutionality of a law passed by the Legislature that directly affected Theresa Schiavo, who has been in a persistent vegetative state since 1990. This Court, after careful consideration of the arguments of the parties and amici, the constitutional issues raised, the precise wording of the challenged law, and the underlying procedural history of this case, concludes that the law violates the fundamental constitutional tenet of separation of powers and is therefore unconstitutional both on its face and as applied to Theresa Schiavo. Accordingly, we affirm the trial court's order declaring the law unconstitutional.

FACTS AND PROCEDURAL HISTORY

The resolution of the discrete separation of powers issue presented in this case does not turn on the facts of the underlying guardianship proceedings that resulted in the removal of Theresa's nutrition and hydration tube. The underlying litigation, which has pitted Theresa's husband, Michael Schiavo, against Theresa's parents, turned on whether the procedures sustaining Theresa's life should be discontinued. However, the procedural history is important because it provides the backdrop to the Legislature's enactment of the challenged law. We also detail the facts and procedural history in light of the Governor's assertion that chapter 2003-418, Laws of Florida (hereinafter sometimes referred to as "the Act"), was passed in order to protect the due process rights of Theresa and other individuals in her position. [The facts of this case, including Theresa Schiavo's injury and the litigation between her husband and her parents over the husband's decision to remove her feeding tube, are presented fully in the case *In re Guadianship of Schiavo*, 916 So. 2d 814 (Fla. 2d DCA 2005), which was included in Article I of this casebook.]

... We denied review [of the decision by her husband to remove her feeding tube], *see In re Guardianship of Schiavo*, 855 So. 2d 621 (Fla. 2003), and Theresa's nutrition and hydration tube was removed on October 15, 2003.

On October 21, 2003, the Legislature enacted chapter 2003-418, the Governor signed the Act into law, and the Governor issued executive order No. 03-201 to stay the continued withholding of nutrition and hydration from Theresa. The nutrition and hydration tube was reinserted pursuant to the Governor's executive order.

On the same day, Michael Schiavo brought the action for declaratory judgment in the circuit court. Relying on undisputed facts and legal argument, the circuit court entered a final summary judgment on May 6, 2004, in favor of Michael Schiavo, finding the Act unconstitutional both on its face and as applied to Theresa. Specifically, the circuit court found that chapter 2003-418 was unconstitutional on its face as an unlawful delegation of legislative authority and as a violation of the right to privacy, and unconstitutional as applied because it allowed the Governor to encroach upon the judicial power and to retroactively abolish Theresa's vested right to privacy.[18]

ANALYSIS

We begin our discussion by emphasizing that our task in this case is to review the constitutionality of chapter 2003-418, not to reexamine the guardianship court's orders directing the removal of Theresa's nutrition and hydration tube, or to review the Second District's numerous decisions in the guardianship case. Although we recognize that the parties continue to dispute the findings made in the prior proceedings, these proceedings are relevant to our decision only to the extent that they occurred and resulted in a final judgment directing the withdrawal of life-prolonging procedures.

The language of chapter 2003-418 is clear. It states in full:

Section 1. (1) The Governor shall have the authority to issue a one-time stay to prevent the withholding of nutrition and hydration from a patient if, as of October 15, 2003:

(a) That patient has no written advance directive;

(b) The court has found that patient to be in a persistent vegetative state;

(c) That patient has had nutrition and hydration withheld; and

(d) A member of that patient's family has challenged the withholding of nutrition and hydration.

(2) The Governor's authority to issue the stay expires 15 days after the effective date of this act, and the expiration of the authority does not impact the validity or the effect of any stay issued pursuant to this act. The Governor may

---

18. [FN 2] Because we find the separation of powers issue to be dispositive in this case, we do not reach the other constitutional issues addressed by the circuit court.

lift the stay authorized under this act at any time. A person may not be held civilly liable and is not subject to regulatory or disciplinary sanctions for taking any action to comply with a stay issued by the Governor pursuant to this act.

(3) Upon issuance of a stay, the chief judge of the circuit court shall appoint a guardian ad litem for the patient to make recommendations to the Governor and the court.

Section 2. This act shall take effect upon becoming a law.

Ch. 2003-418, Laws of Fla. Thus, chapter 2003-418 allowed the Governor to issue a stay to prevent the withholding of nutrition and hydration from a patient under the circumstances provided for in subsections (1)(a)–(d). Under the fifteen-day sunset provision, the Governor's authority to issue the stay expired on November 5, 2003. *See id.* The Governor's authority to lift the stay continues indefinitely.

SEPARATION OF POWERS

The cornerstone of American democracy known as separation of powers recognizes three separate branches of government—the executive, the legislative, and the judicial—each with its own powers and responsibilities. In Florida, the constitutional doctrine has been expressly codified in article II, section 3 of the Florida Constitution, which not only divides state government into three branches but also expressly prohibits one branch from exercising the powers of the other two branches.

"This Court ... has traditionally applied a strict separation of powers doctrine," *State v. Cotton*, 769 So. 2d 345, 353 (Fla. 2000), and has explained that this doctrine "encompasses two fundamental prohibitions. The first is that no branch may encroach upon the powers of another. The second is that no branch may delegate to another branch its constitutionally assigned power." *Chiles v. Children A, B, C, D, E, & F*, 589 So. 2d 260, 264 (Fla. 1991) (citation omitted).

The circuit court found that chapter 2003-418 violates both of these prohibitions, and we address each separately below. Our standard of review is de novo. *See Major League Baseball v. Morsani*, 790 So. 2d 1071, 1074 (Fla. 2001) (stating that a trial court's ruling on a motion for summary judgment posing a pure question of law is subject to de novo review).

Encroachment on the Judicial Branch

We begin by addressing the argument that, as applied to Theresa Schiavo, the Act encroaches on the power and authority of the judicial branch. More than 140 years ago this Court explained the foundation of Florida's express separation of powers provision:

> The framers of the Constitution of Florida, doubtless, had in mind the omnipotent power often exercised by the British Parliament, the exercise of judicial power by the Legislature in those States where there are no written Constitutions restraining them, when they wisely prohibited the exercise of such powers in our State.

That Convention was composed of men of the best legal minds in the country—men of experience and skilled in the law—who had witnessed the breaking down by unrestrained legislation all the security of property derived from contract, the divesting of vested rights by doing away the force of the law as decided, the overturning of solemn decisions of the Courts of the last resort, by, under the pretence of remedial acts, enacting for one or the other party litigants such provisions as would dictate to the judiciary their decision, and leaving everything which should be expounded by the judiciary to the variable and ever-changing mind of the popular branch of the Government.

Trustees Internal Improvement Fund v. Bailey, 10 Fla. 238, 250 (1863). Similarly, the framers of the United States Constitution recognized the need to establish a judiciary independent of the legislative branch. Indeed, the desire to prevent Congress from using its power to interfere with the judgments of the courts was one of the primary motivations for the separation of powers established at this nation's founding. *Plaut v. Spendthrift Farm, Inc.*, 514 U.S. 211, 221–22 (1995).

Under the express separation of powers provision in our state constitution, "the judiciary is a coequal branch of the Florida government vested with the sole authority to exercise the judicial power," and "the legislature cannot, short of constitutional amendment, reallocate the balance of power expressly delineated in the constitution among the three coequal branches." *Children A, B, C, D, E, & F*, 589 So. 2d at 268–69; *see also Office of State Attorney v. Parrotino*, 628 So. 2d 1097, 1099 (Fla. 1993) ("[T]he legislature cannot take actions that would undermine the independence of Florida's judicial ... offices.").

As the United States Supreme Court has explained, the power of the judiciary is "not merely to rule on cases, but to decide them, subject to review only by superior courts" and "having achieved finality ... a judicial decision becomes the last word of the judicial department with regard to a particular case or controversy." *Plaut*, 514 U.S. at 218–19, 227. Moreover, "purely judicial acts ... are not subject to review as to their accuracy by the Governor." *In re Advisory Opinion to the Governor*, 213 So. 2d 716, 720 (Fla. 1968); *see also Children A, B, C, D, E, & F*, 589 So. 2d at 269 ("The judicial branch cannot be subject in any manner to oversight by the executive branch.").

In *Advisory Opinion*, the Governor asked the Court whether he had the "constitutional authority to review the judicial accuracy and propriety of [a judge] and to suspend him from office if it does not appear ... that the Judge has exercised proper judicial discretion and wisdom." 213 So. 2d at 718. The Court agreed that the Governor had the authority to suspend a judge on the grounds of incompetency "if the physical or mental incompetency is established and determined within the Judicial Branch by a court of competent jurisdiction." *Id.* at 720. However, the Court held that the Governor did not have the power to "review the judicial discretion and wisdom of a ... Judge while he is engaged in the judicial process." *Id.* The Court explained that article V of the Florida Constitution provides for appellate review for the benefit of litigants aggrieved by the decisions of the lower court, and that "appeal is the exclusive remedy." *Id.*

In this case, the undisputed facts show that the guardianship court authorized Michael to proceed with the discontinuance of Theresa's life support after the issue was fully litigated in a proceeding in which the Schindlers were afforded the opportunity to present evidence on all issues. This order as well as the order denying the Schindlers' motion for relief from judgment were affirmed on direct appeal. *See Schiavo I*, 780 So. 2d at 177; *Schiavo IV*, 851 So. 2d at 183. The Schindlers sought review in this Court, which was denied. Thereafter, the tube was removed. Subsequently, pursuant to the Governor's executive order, the nutrition and hydration tube was reinserted. Thus, the Act, as applied in this case, resulted in an executive order that effectively reversed a properly rendered final judgment and thereby constituted an unconstitutional encroachment on the power that has been reserved for the independent judiciary. *Cf. Bailey*, 10 Fla. at 249–50 (noting that had the statute under review "directed a rehearing, the hearing of the case would necessarily carry with it the right to set aside the judgment of the Court, and there would be unquestionably an exercise of judicial power").

The Governor and amici assert that the Act does not reverse a final court order because an order to discontinue life-prolonging procedures may be challenged at any time prior to the death of the ward. In advancing this argument, the Governor and amici rely on the Second District's conclusion that as long as the ward is alive, an order discontinuing life-prolonging procedures "is subject to recall and is executory in nature." *Schiavo II*, 792 So. 2d at 559. However, the Second District did not hold that the guardianship court's order was not a final judgment but, rather, that the Schindlers, as interested parties, could file a motion for relief from judgment under Florida Rule of Civil Procedure 1.540(b)(5) if they sufficiently alleged that it is no longer equitable that the judgment have prospective application. *See id.* at 561. Rule 1.540(b) expressly states that a motion filed pursuant to its terms "does not affect the finality of a judgment." Further, the fact that a final judgment may be subject to recall under a rule of procedure, if certain circumstances can be proved, does not negate its finality. Unless and until the judgment is vacated by judicial order, it is "the last word of the judicial department with regard to a particular case or controversy." *Plaut*, 514 U.S. at 227.

Under procedures enacted by the Legislature, effective both before the passage of the Act and after its fifteen-day effective period expired, circuit courts are charged with adjudicating issues regarding incompetent individuals. The trial courts of this State are called upon to make many of the most difficult decisions facing society. In proceedings under chapter 765, Florida Statutes (2003), these decisions literally affect the lives or deaths of patients. The trial courts also handle other weighty decisions affecting the welfare of children such as termination of parental rights and child custody. *See* § 61.13(2)(b)(1), Fla. Stat. (2003) ("The court shall determine all matters relating to custody of each minor child of the parties in accordance with the best interests of the child and in accordance with the Uniform Child Custody Jurisdiction and Enforcement Act."); § 39.801(2), Fla. Stat. (2003) ("The circuit court shall have exclusive original jurisdiction of a proceeding involving termination of parental rights."). When the prescribed procedures are followed according to our rules of court and the governing statutes, a final judgment is issued, and all post-judgment procedures are followed, it is without question an invasion of the authority of the judicial branch for the Legislature to pass a law that allows the executive branch to interfere with the final judicial determination in a case. That is precisely what occurred here and for that reason the Act is unconstitutional as applied to Theresa Schiavo.

Delegation of Legislative Authority

In addition to concluding that the Act is unconstitutional as applied in this case because it encroaches on the power of the judicial branch, we further conclude that the Act is unconstitutional on its face because it delegates legislative power to the Governor. The Legislature is permitted to transfer subordinate functions "to permit administration of legislative policy by an agency with the expertise and flexibility to deal with complex and fluid conditions." *Microtel, Inc. v. Fla. Public Serv. Comm'n*, 464 So. 2d 1189, 1191 (Fla. 1985). However, under article II, section 3 of the constitution the Legislature "may not delegate the power to enact a law or the right to exercise unrestricted discretion in applying the law." *Sims v. State*, 754 So. 2d 657, 668 (Fla. 2000). This prohibition, known as the nondelegation doctrine, requires that "fundamental and primary policy decisions ... be made by members of the legislature who are elected to perform those tasks, and [that the] administration of legislative programs must be pursuant to some minimal standards and guidelines ascertainable by reference to the enactment establishing the program." *Askew v. Cross Key Waterways*, 372 So. 2d 913, 925 (Fla. 1978); *see also Avatar Dev. Corp. v. State*, 723 So. 2d 199, 202 (Fla. 1998) (citing *Askew* with approval). In other words, statutes granting power to the executive branch "must clearly announce adequate standards to guide ... in the execution of the powers delegated. The statute must so clearly define the power delegated that the [executive] is precluded from acting through whim, showing favoritism, or exercising unbridled discretion." *Lewis v. Bank of Pasco County*, 346 So. 2d 53, 55–56 (Fla. 1976). The requirement that the Legislature provide sufficient guidelines also ensures the availability of meaningful judicial review:

> In the final analysis it is the courts, upon a challenge to the exercise or nonexercise of administrative action, which must determine whether the administrative agency has performed consistently with the mandate of the legislature. When legislation is so lacking in guidelines that neither the agency nor the courts can determine whether the agency is carrying out the intent of the legislature in its conduct, then, in fact, the agency becomes the lawgiver rather than the administrator of the law.

Askew, 372 So. 2d at 918–19.

We have recognized that the "specificity of the guidelines [set forth in the legislation] will depend on the complexity of the subject and the 'degree of difficulty involved in articulating finite standards.'" *Brown v. Apalachee Regional Planning Council*, 560 So. 2d 782, 784 (Fla. 1990) (quoting *Askew*, 372 So. 2d at 918). However, we have also made clear that "even where a general approach would be more practical than a detailed scheme of legislation, enactments may not be drafted in terms so general and unrestrictive that administrators are left without standards for the guidance of their official acts." *State Dep't of Citrus v. Griffin*, 239 So. 2d 577, 581 (Fla. 1970).

In both *Askew* and *Lewis*, this Court held that the respective statutes under review violated the nondelegation doctrine because they failed to provide the executive branch with adequate guidelines and criteria....

In this case, the circuit court found that chapter 2003-418 contains no guidelines or standards that "would serve to limit the Governor from exercising completely unrestricted discretion in applying the law to" those who fall within its terms. The circuit court explained:

> The terms of the Act affirmatively confirm the discretionary power conferred upon the Governor. He is given the "authority to issue a one-time stay to prevent the withholding of nutrition and hydration from a patient" under certain circumstances but, he is not required to do so. Likewise, the act provides that the Governor "*may* lift the stay authorized under this act at any time. The Governor *may* revoke the stay upon a finding that a change in the condition of the patient warrants revocation." (Emphasis added). In both instances there is nothing to provide the Governor with any direction or guidelines for the exercise of this delegated authority. The Act does not suggest what constitutes "a change in condition of the patient" that could "warrant revocation." Even when such an undefined "change" occurs, the Governor is not compelled to act. The Act confers upon the Governor the unfettered discretion to determine what the terms of the Act mean and when, or if, he may act under it.

We agree with this analysis. In enacting chapter 2003-418, the Legislature failed to provide any standards by which the Governor should determine whether, in any given case, a stay should be issued and how long a stay should remain in effect. Further, the Legislature has failed to provide any criteria for lifting the stay. This absolute, unfettered discretion to decide whether to issue and then when to lift a stay makes the Governor's decision virtually unreviewable.

The Governor asserts that by enacting chapter 2003-418 the Legislature determined that he should be permitted to act as proxy for an incompetent patient in very narrow circumstances and, therefore, that his discretion is limited by the provisions of chapter 765. However, the Act does not refer to the provisions of chapter 765. Specifically, the Act does not amend section 765.401(1), Florida Statutes (2003), which sets forth an order of priority for determining who should act as proxy for an incapacitated patient who has no advance directive. Nor does the Act require that the Governor's decision be made in conformity with the requirement of section 765.401 that the proxy's decision be based on "the decision the proxy reasonably believes that patient would have made under the circumstances" or, if there is no indication of what the patient would have chosen, in the patient's best interests. § 765.401(2)–(3), Fla. Stat. (2003). Finally, the Act does not provide for review of the Governor's decision as proxy as required by section 765.105, Florida Statutes (2003). In short, there is no indication in the language of chapter 2003-418 that the Legislature intended the Governor's discretion to be limited in any way. Even if we were to read chapter 2003-418 in pari materia with chapter 765, as the Governor suggests, there is nothing in chapter 765 to guide the Governor's discretion in issuing a stay because chapter 765 does not contemplate that a proxy will have the type of open-ended power delegated to the Governor under the Act.

We also reject the Governor's argument that this legislation provides an additional layer of due process protection to those who are unable to communicate their wishes regarding end-of-life decisions. Parts I, II, III, and IV of chapter 765, enacted by the Legislature in 1992 and amended several times, provide detailed protections for those who are adjudicated incompetent, including that the proxy's decision be based on what the patient would have chosen under the circumstances or is in the patient's best interest, and be supported by competent, substantial evidence. *See* §765.401(2)–(3). Chapter 765 also provides for judicial review if "the patient's family, the health care facility, or the attending physician, or any other interested person who may reasonably be expected to be directly affected by the surrogate or proxy's decision ... believes [that] the surrogate or proxy's decision is not in accord with the patient's known desires or the provisions of this chapter." §765.105(1), Fla. Stat. (2003).

In contrast to the protections set forth in chapter 765, chapter 2003-418's standardless, open-ended delegation of authority by the Legislature to the Governor provides no guarantee that the incompetent patient's right to withdraw life-prolonging procedures will in fact be honored. *See In re Guardianship of Browning*, 568 So. 2d 4, 12 (Fla. 1990) (reaffirming that an incompetent person has the same right to refuse medical treatment as a competent person). As noted above, the Act does not even require that the Governor consider the patient's wishes in deciding whether to issue a stay, and instead allows a unilateral decision by the Governor to stay the withholding of life-prolonging procedures without affording any procedural process to the patient.

Finally, we reject the Governor's argument that the Legislature's grant of authority to issue the stay under chapter 2003-418 is a valid exercise of the state's *parens patriae* power. Although unquestionably the Legislature may enact laws to protect those citizens who are incapable of protecting their own interests, *see, e.g., In re Byrne*, 402 So. 2d 383 (Fla. 1981), such laws must comply with the constitution. Chapter 2003-418 fails to do so.

Moreover, the argument that the Act broadly protects those who cannot protect themselves is belied by the case-specific criteria under which the Governor can exercise his discretion. The Act applies only if a court has found the individual to be in a persistent vegetative state and food and hydration have been ordered withdrawn. It does not authorize the Governor to intervene if a person in a persistent vegetative state is dependent upon another form of life support. Nor does the Act apply to a person who is not in a persistent vegetative state but a court finds, contrary to the wishes of another family member, that life support should be withdrawn. In theory, the Act could have applied during its fifteen-day window to more than one person, but it is undeniable that in fact the criteria fit only Theresa Schiavo.

In sum, although chapter 2003-418 applies to a limited class of people, it provides no criteria to guide the Governor's decision about whether to act. In addition, once the Governor has issued a stay as provided for in the Act, there are no criteria for the Governor to evaluate in deciding whether to lift the stay. Thus, chapter 2003-418 allows the Governor to act "through whim, show[] favoritism, or exercise unbridled discretion," *Lewis*, 346 So. 2d at 56, and is therefore an unconstitutional delegation of legislative authority.

CONCLUSION

We recognize that the tragic circumstances underlying this case make it difficult to put emotions aside and focus solely on the legal issue presented. We are not insensitive to the struggle that all members of Theresa's family have endured since she fell unconscious in 1990. However, we are a nation of laws and we must govern our decisions by the rule of law and not by our own emotions. Our hearts can fully comprehend the grief so fully demonstrated by Theresa's family members on this record. But our hearts are not the law. What is in the Constitution always must prevail over emotion. Our oaths as judges require that this principle is our polestar, and it alone....

The continuing vitality of our system of separation of powers precludes the other two branches from nullifying the judicial branch's final orders. If the Legislature with the assent of the Governor can do what was attempted here, the judicial branch would be subordinated to the final directive of the other branches. Also subordinated would be the rights of individuals, including the well established privacy right to self determination. *See Browning*, 568 So. 2d at 11–13. No court judgment could ever be considered truly final and no constitutional right truly secure, because the precedent of this case would hold to the contrary. Vested rights could be stripped away based on popular clamor. The essential core of what the Founding Fathers sought to change from their experience with English rule would be lost, especially their belief that our courts exist precisely to preserve the rights of individuals, even when doing so is contrary to popular will.

The trial court's decision regarding Theresa Schiavo was made in accordance with the procedures and protections set forth by the judicial branch and in accordance with the statutes passed by the Legislature in effect at that time. That decision is final and the Legislature's attempt to alter that final adjudication is unconstitutional as applied to Theresa Schiavo. Further, even if there had been no final judgment in this case, the Legislature provided the Governor constitutionally inadequate standards for the application of the legislative authority delegated in chapter 2003-418. Because chapter 2003-418 runs afoul of article II, section 3 of the Florida Constitution in both respects, we affirm the circuit court's final summary judgment.

It is so ordered.

WELLS, ANSTEAD, LEWIS, QUINCE, CANTERO and BELL, JJ., concur.

Article III

Legislature

Introduction

The legislative article recognizes the enormous authority of the Florida Legislature. Historically, the executive in Florida was limited because of post-Reconstruction fears of centralized power and the preferences of Floridians. Additionally, the Legislature had substantial authority over local governments through a local bill process that essentially reduced counties to local fiefdoms of their legislators. That changed with the 1968 Constitution, which granted home rule to local governments, discussed in Article VIII. At the same time, however, the 1968 Constitution changed the Legislature's sessions from biannual to annual. And, though from time to time amendments have been proposed to make the Legislature unicameral, it has remained bicameral since its inception.

The story of Article III is one of institutional struggle. The Legislature is given substantial power, and those in power have rarely surrendered or reduced that power. The result has been struggles between the executive and the Legislature even when both entities are controlled by the same political party. There are similar struggles between local governments and the Legislature—some of which are resolved by Article III.

Citizens turn to the courts to challenge legislative actions. As a result, there is a continuing tension between the courts and the Legislature. The courts have the authority and responsibility to determine if legislative actions are unconstitutional. The legislative branch is of course limited by the Constitution, and the courts are the referees of those violations.

Finally, Florida has a constitutional initiative process that allows citizens to change policies through the Constitution. As this process has played out between 1990 and 2020, those initiatives have often reflected a belief by citizens that the Legislature did not respond to the people's wishes. Once a policy is in the Constitution, however it got there, the Legislature cannot violate constitutional policy. Therefore, as is discussed later in this chapter, the Legislature did not generally favor constitutional restrictions on its authority to draft redistricting plans. However, a citizen's initiative placed new restrictions on the apportionment process, the Legislature had to follow those new constitutional policies, and those policies were enforced by the courts. The Constitution is the supreme law of the state; the courts interpret the Constitution, and the Legislature is subject to that interpretation.

The cases in this Article are divided into four sections: Legislative Process, Executive Review, Relationship with Local Government, and Apportionment.

Legislative Process addresses the procedural requirements and limitations on the Legislature. For example, under the single subject rule, legislation cannot deal with more than one subject. Executive Review addresses the issue of veto. The Florida Governor's veto authority under the Florida Constitution differs from that granted to the President by the U.S. Constitution in that the Governor has line item veto authority over appropriations, and the President of the United States does not.

Partial veto; cancelling specific provisions of a bill veto veto-ing the whole bill

The Constitution defines and limits legislative authority over local governments—another historically thorny area. The Legislature formerly passed local bills that superseded local authority on many purely local matters or passed local laws that changed the laws—for example hunting laws—only in one geographic part of the state.

Reapportionment is a central aspect of defining governmental authority. The Legislature has a constitutional duty to reapportion itself after each decennial census. Concerns about this process, including attempts to weaken minority voting rights or to favor incumbents, have produced some guardrails and limitations over how these legislative lines are drawn.

A. Legislative Process

i. Article III, Section 6—Laws (Single Subject Rule for General Legislation)

No Legislation can only be about one subject matter

The single subject rule is really a rule of procedure that has been constitutionalized. The logic is clear. Compelling a vote or decision on two unrelated subjects combined is unfair and produces illogical results. For example, combining a vote to increase criminal penalties for robbery with a change in policy on septic tanks is not a good process.

It is interesting that there is essentially a statute of limitations on challenges for failure to comply with the legislative single subject rule. If the session law is not challenged and the act is codified into the Florida Statutes a year later, it is too late to bring a single subject challenge.

Santos v. State

380 So. 2d 1284 (Fla. 1980)

BOYD, Justice.

This cause is before the Court on appeal from a judgment of the County Court of Orange County. The trial court passed upon the constitutionality of a state statute. We have jurisdiction. Art. V, s 3(b)(1), Fla. Const.

The appellant was charged with the crimes of driving while intoxicated and driving with unlawful blood alcohol level in violation of section 316.193, subsections (1) and (3) respectively, Florida Statutes (1977). The judgment from which this appeal is brought was rendered upon a plea of nolo contendere. Prior to his change of plea from not guilty to nolo contendere, the appellant moved: (1) to dismiss the information on the ground that section 316.193 is unconstitutional and on the ground that one of the offenses charged is a lesser included offense of the other; (2) to suppress evidence; and (3) for discharge under the speedy trial rule.

The trial court denied the motion to dismiss, upholding the statute's constitutionality and ruling that the appellant could be charged with both offenses. The court subsequently dismissed the charge of driving while intoxicated. Thus the appellant's contention that he could not properly be charged with both offenses became moot. The court also denied the motion to suppress and for discharge. The appellant pled nolo contendere to the unlawful blood alcohol level charge, was adjudicated guilty and sentenced.

The appellant presents three issues. He contends that section 316.193, Florida Statutes (1977), violates article III, section 6 of the Florida Constitution. He contends that the court erred in denying his motion to suppress evidence. He contends, finally, that the court erred in denying his motion for discharge pursuant to the speedy trial rule.

At the time the appellant changed his plea to nolo contendere, he specifically reserved for appeal only the court's ruling on his motion to dismiss. A plea of nolo contendere forecloses the appeal of any issue, other than the facial sufficiency of the charging document, that is not specifically reserved for appellate review. *Hand v. State*, 334 So.2d 601 (Fla. 1976); *State v. Ashby*, 245 So.2d 225 (Fla. 1971). Therefore, we will only consider the issue of the statute's constitutionality under article III, section 6.

Article III, section 6 provides in pertinent part: "Every law shall embrace but one subject and matter properly connected therewith, and the subject shall be briefly expressed in the title." The appellant contends that section 316.193 embraces more than one subject and therefore violates the single-subject requirement for laws. In support of this contention, he asserts that it is improper for section 316.193(1) and (3) to create two separate and distinct offenses. This argument is without merit.

The quoted portion of article III, section 6 contains two essential requirements. The requirement that the subject of a law be briefly expressed in the title serves the purpose of providing notice to interested persons of the contents of an enactment. *State v. McDonald*, 357 So.2d 405 (Fla. 1978); *Knight & Wall Co. v. Bryant*, 178 So.2d 5 (Fla. 1965). The purpose of the requirement that each law embrace only one subject and matter properly connected with it is to prevent subterfuge, surprise, "hodge-podge" and log rolling in legislation. *State v. Lee*, 356 So.2d 276 (Fla. 1978); *Lee v. Bigby Electric Co.*, 136 Fla. 305, 186 So. 505 (1939). The purposes sought to be achieved by these constitutional restrictions are satisfied if each enactment of the legislature embraces "but one subject and matter properly connected therewith" and the subject is "briefly expressed in the title." Art. III, s 6, Fla. Const. When laws passed by the legislature are being codified for publication in the Florida Statutes, these restrictions do not apply. The legislature is free to use whatever classification system it chooses. Article III, section 6 does not require sections of the Florida Statutes to conform to the single-subject requirement. The requirement applies to "laws" in the sense of acts of the legislature.

The offense proscribed by section 316.193(1), Florida Statutes (1977), was established by chapter 71-135, Laws of Florida. This act of the legislature is called the Florida Uniform Traffic Control Law. It regulates the use of the public roads of the state. It embraces only that subject and matters properly connected therewith. The offense proscribed by section 316.193(3) was created by chapter 74-384, Laws of Florida. That law embraces the subject of driving while under the influence of alcohol and matters properly connected therewith.

We hold that neither of the laws at issue here violates article III, section 6. The judgment of the county court is affirmed.

It is so ordered.

ENGLAND, C.J., and ADKINS, OVERTON, SUNDBERG, ALDERMAN and Mc-DONALD, JJ., concur.

Questions

1. What was Appellant's argument?

2. According to the Court, how had Appellant misconstrued Section 6?

Loxahatchee River Environmental Control District v. School Board of Palm Beach County

515 So. 2d 217 (Fla. 1987)

GRIMES, Justice.

This is a petition for review of the decision in *Loxahatchee Environmental Control District v. School Board*, 496 So.2d 930 (Fla. 4th DCA 1986), upholding the constitutionality of section 235.26(1), Florida Statutes (1981). We have jurisdiction under article V, section 3(b)(3), of the Florida Constitution.

The Loxahatchee River Environmental Control District (District) operates a regional sewage and sanitation treatment facility which serves property owners in portions of Palm Beach and Martin counties. This case resulted from a dispute over whether the Palm Beach County School Board (Board) was required to pay certain fees to the District as a prerequisite for the right to connect a school to the District's wastewater system when it reaches the environs of the school. A more detailed explanation of the facts may be found in the opinion of the district court of appeal. The resolution of the dispute turned on whether section 235.26(1) exempted the Board from paying the fees. Both the trial court and the district court of appeal upheld the constitutionality of the statute and ruled that the statute relieved the Board of the requirement to pay the fees.

... We address only the Board's contention with respect to article III, section 6 of the Florida Constitution....

Section 235.26(1), which is part of the statute directing the State Board of Education to adopt a uniform state building code for planning and construction of public educational facilities, reads as follows:

(1) UNIFORM BUILDING CODE. — All public educational and ancillary plants constructed by a board, except the Board of Regents, shall conform to the State Uniform Building Code for Public Educational Facilities Construction, and such plants are exempt from all other state, county, district, municipal, or local building codes, interpretations, building permits, and assessments of fees for building permits, ordinances, *and impact fees or service availability fees.* Any inspection by local or state government shall be based on the Uniform Building Code as prescribed by rule. Each board shall provide for periodic inspection of the proposed educational plant during each phase of construction to determine compliance with the Uniform Building Code.

(Emphasis added.) The italicized language was added by chapter 81-223, Laws of Florida. The District contends that the title of chapter 81-223 failed to give the notice required by article III, section 6 of the Florida Constitution with respect to the added language.

The pertinent portion of article III, section 6, reads as follows:

Every law shall embrace but one subject and matter properly connected therewith, and the subject shall be briefly expressed in the title.

While inclining toward the position that the title was adequate, the district court declined to specifically reach that conclusion. Rather, the court held that once the challenged law had been reenacted as a portion of the Florida Statutes, it was not subject to challenge under article III, section 6.

At every odd-year regular session, the legislature, as part of its program of continuing revision, adopts the laws passed in the preceding odd year as official statute laws and directs that they take effect immediately under the title of "Florida Statutes" dated the current year.[1] In *Santos v. State,* 380 So.2d 1284 (Fla.1980), this Court held that when laws passed by the legislature are adopted and codified in this manner, the restrictions of article III, section 6, pertaining to one subject matter and notice in the title no longer apply. *Accord State v. Combs,* 388 So.2d 1029 (Fla.1980). While both of those cases were considering alleged violations of the single subject rule, the principle clearly applies to the requirement for the subject of the legislation to be "briefly expressed in the title."

Notwithstanding, the District argues that this cannot be the law because otherwise cases such as *Bunnell v. State,* 453 So.2d 808 (Fla.1984), would not have been rendered. In *Bunnell,* the defendant had been charged with violating a recently enacted 1981 statute pertaining to obstruction of justice by giving false information. The Court held that the law had been enacted in violation of the one subject provision of article III, section 6. The decision was rendered on July 19, 1984, at a time after the law had been reenacted as a portion of the Florida Statutes, but the opinion did not mention this fact.

We believe that the two principles can be reconciled. A law passed in violation of the requirements of article III, section 6, is invalid until such time as it is reenacted for codification into the Florida Statutes. *See Thompson v. Intercounty Tel. & Tel. Co.,* 62 So.2d 16 (Fla.1952). Thus, the statute cannot be considered with reference to what has occurred prior to that time. In Bunnell's case, the conduct for which he was being charged occurred before the statute was adopted and codified. Hence, principles of ex post facto prevented the law from applying to him.

In the instant case, the dispute arose in the fall of 1981, before Chapter 81-223 had been reenacted. If the law were held to violate article III, section 6, the Board

---

1. [FN *] A more complete explanation of this procedure may be found in the Preface to the official Florida Statutes.

would not have been exempt from the payment of the fees at that time. Therefore, even though the Board would be under no obligation to pay such fees once the statute was reenacted, we think it advisable to address the sufficiency of the title of chapter 81-223 with respect to the notice required by article III, section 6.

The language in the lengthy title to chapter 81-223 pertinent to the challenged amendment reads:

> An act relating to educational facilities construction and funding; amending, creating and repealing various sections in chapter 235, Florida Statutes ... modifying certain standards relating to safety, sanitation, sites, coordination of local construction planning, facilities design, construction techniques, new construction, day labor projects, and the State Uniform Building Code ... reviving and readopting certain sections of chapter 235, Florida Statutes.

In addressing the contention that a statute violated article III, section 6, this Court has said:

> The title of a statute need not index all of the statute's contents. The proper test is whether the title is so worded as not to mislead a person of average intelligence as to the scope of the enactment and is sufficient to put that person on notice and cause him to inquire into the body of the statute itself.

Williams v. State, 370 So.2d 1143, 1144 (Fla.1979). Measured by this criterion, we believe that the reference to modifying certain standards relating to the State Building Code constituted sufficient notice for purposes of article III, section 6. In fact, the District does not argue that the title gave insufficient notice of adding impact fees or service availability fees, as such, to the list of fee exemptions already in the statute. Rather, the District contends that if the language added to section 235.26(1) is construed to include utility charges as well as building related fees, the title gave inadequate notice because there was no reference to utilities. We are not persuaded by the District's argument.

In *Contractors & Builders Association v. City of Dunedin,* 329 So.2d 314 (Fla.1976), this Court upheld the collection of "impact fees." There, the fees were imposed upon the issuance of building permits and earmarked for capital improvements to the water and sewage systems which were operated by the City of Dunedin. We believe that the impact fees and service availability fees charged by utility companies, such as the District, are not so different from those charged by municipalities to pay for capital improvements to water and sewer services as to require a specific reference to the word "utility" in the title of the act.

* * *

We approve the decision of the district court of appeal.

It is so ordered.

McDONALD, C.J., and OVERTON, EHRLICH, SHAW, BARKETT and KOGAN, JJ., concur.

ii. Article III, Section 12 — Appropriation Bills (Single Subject)

This provision has the same basic logic as the single subject rule for general legislation. However, it guards against an additional legislative trick. The trick is to try to divert money in the appropriations process from a statutory source that will not be easily identified in the review of a 2,000-page appropriations bill.

The logic behind the single subject rule for appropriations bills is that appropriations bills are measures to direct expenditures for a period of time, i.e., one year. The provision mandates that short term fiscal measures cannot be used to change policy "on any other subject." The *Florida Defenders of the Environment* case below is a perfect example of why this rule exists. The diversion of funds essentially amends a statute without going through the amendatory process.

City of North Miami v. Florida Defenders of the Environment

481 So. 2d 1196 (Fla. 1985)

ADKINS, Justice.

We have for review *Florida Defenders of the Environment, Inc. v. Graham*, 462 So.2d 59 (Fla. 1st DCA 1984), in which the district court declared appropriation Item 1312A of chapter 83-300, Laws of Florida, invalid. We have jurisdiction. Art. V, § 3(b)(1), Fla. Const.

Item 1312A of the 1983 General Appropriations Act provided for the appropriation of $8,500,000 from the Conservation and Recreation Lands Trust Fund (CARL Fund), to the Special Acquisition Trust Fund. Such funds were to be used in the state's purchase of the "Interama Lands" from the City of North Miami. The purposes for which CARL Fund monies may be spent are specifically limited in section 253.023(3), Florida Statutes (1981). The procedures for selecting those lands to be purchased with CARL Fund monies are prescribed by section 259.035, Florida Statutes (1981).

Article III, section 6, Florida Constitution, provides:

> Every law shall embrace but one subject and matter properly connected therewith, and the subject shall be briefly expressed in the title.... Laws to revise or amend shall set out in full the revised or amended act, section, subsection or paragraph of a subsection....

Article III, section 12, Florida Constitution, provides "laws making appropriation ... shall contain provisions on no other subject."

We hold that Item 1312A violates article III, sections 6 and 12 of the Florida Constitution because it is an appropriations bill that changes and amends existing law on subjects other than appropriations, *see Brown v. Firestone*, 382 So.2d 654 (Fla.1980), and unlawfully alters a statutory distribution formula. *See Gindl v. Department of Education*, 396 So.2d 1105, 1106 (Fla.1979).

Accordingly, we affirm the decision of the district court directing the comptroller to disregard appropriation 1312A and the secretary of state to strike it from chapter 83-300.

It is so ordered.

BOYD, C.J., and OVERTON, McDONALD, EHRLICH and SHAW, JJ., concur.

Question

1. According to the Court, what was the "conflict" that violated Section 12 in this case?

iii. Article III, Section 4 — Quorum and Procedure

The Legislature makes its own rules. The issue in this case, and in the ones that follow dealing with Article III, Section 5, involve separation of powers.

Moffitt v. Willis
459 So. 2d 1018 (Fla. 1984)

ADKINS, Justice.

We have before us an original proceeding on suggestion for a writ of prohibition which would quash an order of the circuit court judge wherein he determined the circuit court had the jurisdiction to rule on a complaint against the legislature. We have jurisdiction. Art. V, §3(b)(7), Fla.Const.

In January 1982, the Miami Herald Publishing Company and twelve other newspaper publishing companies sued the petitioners, H. Lee Moffitt, as Speaker of the House of Representatives and Curtis Peterson, as President of the Senate, for declaratory judgment. The complaint filed in that action alleges that during May and June of 1981, secret meetings of committees of the legislature occurred in violation of legislative rules and the first and fourteenth amendments to the United States Constitution; article II, section 8, Florida Constitution; article III, Florida Constitution; section 11.142, Florida Statutes (1981); and section 286.011 and 286.012, Florida Statutes (1981).

Petitioners filed a motion to dismiss the complaint on the ground that the circuit court lacked jurisdiction over the subject matter under the constitutional doctrine of separation of powers because the complaint relates to the Florida Senate and the Florida House of Representatives. A hearing on the motion was held before the respondent, the Honorable Ben C. Willis. Judge Willis ordered that the newspaper publishing companies were entitled to a ruling under chapter 86, Florida Statutes (1981), as to the allegations in the complaint relating to the first amendment to the United States Constitution and the corresponding provision of the Florida Constitution, article I, section 4, Florida Constitution, and also as to section 11.142, Florida Statutes (1981).

The petitioners are now seeking a writ of prohibition to have Judge Willis' order quashed and to have the complaint dismissed. We have permitted the newspaper publishing companies to intervene in this cause.

We agree with the petitioners, grant their petition and direct the dismissal of the civil action pending in the second judicial circuit which is the subject matter of this petition.

One of the issues we are faced with in this case is the jurisdiction of this Court to prohibit proceedings in the circuit court. The intervenors argue that should we determine that our jurisdiction to issue writs of prohibition is now coextensive with that of the district courts of appeal, in respect to circuit court proceedings, forum shopping in the appellate structure and even successive applications to this and other courts may be the result. We disagree.

* * *

In *State ex rel. Sarasota County v. Boyer*, 360 So.2d 388 (Fla.1978), we fully discussed our jurisdiction to issue writs of prohibition. We stated that, inasmuch as we cannot know with certainty whether we have appellate jurisdiction over the decision until it has been decided and that at that point we could not issue a preventive to undo what has been done, the answer is that it is only necessary to show that on the face of the matter it appears that a lower court is about to act in excess of its jurisdiction in a case which is likely to come within our jurisdiction to review. *Id.* at 392. Although that case involved the district court, the same rationale applies to our jurisdiction to issue the writ to a circuit court. In *Tsavaris v. Scruggs*, 360 So.2d 745 (Fla.1977), we found that this Court had jurisdiction to issue a writ of prohibition to a trial court in a case where the defendant had been indicted for first-degree murder. We could not know whether conviction would result in a sentence of death, but we knew the possibility of a death sentence was real since the crime charged was a capital offense. We have also on many occasions considered an original petition for writ of prohibition asking us to restrain a criminal court of record from proceeding to try a cause. In those instances, the issue presented was the defendant's constitutional right to a speedy trial. *See, e.g., Lowe v. Price*, 437 So.2d 142 (Fla.1983); *Pena v. Schultz*, 245 So.2d 49 (Fla.1971); *Loy v. Grayson*, 99 So.2d 555 (Fla.1957).

We are now presented with a case in which the trial judge has issued an order, in response to a motion to dismiss, which states that the plaintiffs are entitled to a ruling as to the allegations relating to the first amendment of the United States Constitution and article I, section 4 of the Florida Constitution. The defendants, the petitioners here, argue that the trial court lacks jurisdiction because article II, section 3 of the Florida Constitution mandates separation of powers. It is clear to us that if this case were to proceed to trial and then to appeal at the district court, it is most likely that some provision of the state or federal constitution would be construed. The case would then come within our jurisdiction to review. In keeping with our holding in *Sarasota County v. Boyer*, we have jurisdiction to issue a writ of prohibition in this instance.

The fundamental argument raised by the petitioners is that the circuit court does not have jurisdiction to determine and declare the meaning and application of the rules and procedures of the Florida Senate and the Florida House of Representatives. Petitioners maintain that the authority of each house of the legislature, vis-a-vis article III, section 4(a) and article II, section 3 of the Florida Constitution, to determine its own internal procedure is at issue and that neither the constitutionality of any enacted statute, nor any policy commitment of the state of Florida, nor the balancing of compelling interests of the state are at issue. We agree with the petitioners' contentions.

At the outset, we reassert that our duty in this cause is to determine whether the circuit court has the *jurisdiction*. We do not propose to address the merits of the case in the process.

In order to determine jurisdiction we must first identify the precise activity complained of in the suit below. The publishing companies allege that certain groups of individuals, which they identify as house and senate committees, held secret closed meetings during the 1981 legislative session. They do not complain of or challenge any specific act or law promulgated by the legislature. Rather, the complaint is that the house and senate violated their own rules of procedure. Rule 2.13 of the Rules of the Florida Senate provides in part that "all committee meetings shall be open to the public." Rule 6.25 of the Rules of the Florida House of Representatives provides in part that "all meetings of all committees shall be open to the public at all times." The publishing companies further assert that the legislature is required to conduct its business according to its rules pursuant to section 11.142, Florida Statutes (1981), which provides:

> Each standing and select committee shall meet at such times as it shall determine and shall abide by the general rules and regulations adopted by its respective house to govern the conduct of meetings by such committee.

Several federal and state constitutional provisions are also assertedly being violated by the activity.

The petitioners have never conceded that the meetings complained of were secret legislative committee meetings. In our view, a judicial determination of this matter hinges on the meaning of legislative committee meeting and what activity constitutes such a meeting. At this point, the judiciary comes into head-to-head conflict with the legislative rulemaking prerogative.

Article III, section 4(a) of the Florida Constitution gives each house the power to determine its own rules of procedure. As historically interpreted by this Court, this provision gives each house the power and prerogative not only to adopt, but also to interpret, enforce, waive or suspend whatever procedures it deems necessary or desirable so long as constitutional requirements for the enacting of laws are not violated. *See, e.g., State ex rel. X-Cel Stores, Inc. v. Lee,* 122 Fla. 685, 166 So. 568 (1936); *State ex rel. Landis v. Thompson,* 120 Fla. 860, 163 So. 270 (1935) (wherein we stated that under the constitution the legislature determines and enforces the rules of its own proceedings). In *Crawford v. Gilchrist,* 64 Fla. 41, 54–55, 59 So. 963, 968 (1912), we said that:

The provision that each house *"shall* determine the rules of its proceedings," does not restrict the power given to the mere formulation of standing rules, or to the proceedings of the body in ordinary legislative matters; but, *in the absence of constitutional restraints,* and when exercised by a majority of a constitutional quorum, such authority extends to the determination of the propriety and effect of any action as it is taken by the body as it proceeds in the exercise of any power, in the transaction of any business, or in the performance of any duty conferred upon it by the constitution.

It is the final product of the legislature that is subject to review by the courts, not the internal procedures. As we stated in *General Motors Acceptance Corp. v. State,* 152 Fla. 297, 303, 11 So.2d 482, 485 (1943), the legislature has the power to enact measures, while the judiciary is restricted to the construction or interpretation thereof.

Section 11.142 of the Florida Statutes provides that the committees shall abide by the house and senate rules. While the judiciary certainly has the power to determine what effect a statute has and to whom it applies as well as its constitutionality, that is not the issue before us today. We are not confronted with whether a statute applies, rather we are asked to allow the courts to determine when and how legislative rules apply to members of the legislature. The constitutionality of the rules themselves is not challenged here. The only issue argued is that of the propriety and constitutionality of certain internal activities of members of the legislature. It is a legislative prerogative to make, interpret and enforce its own procedural rules and the judiciary cannot compel the legislature to exercise a purely legislative prerogative. *See Dade County Classroom Teachers Association v. Legislature,* 269 So.2d 684, 686 (Fla.1972).

The intervenors rely on several cases to support the circuit court's jurisdiction. We find their reliance to be misplaced inasmuch as each of the cases cited involves an activity by the legislative branch which reaches out to effect some action or result outside of the legislature itself and therefore beyond their internal procedures. *Forbes v. Earle,* 298 So.2d 1 (Fla.1974) (the court did not lack the subject matter jurisdiction to determine the extent of a committee's power to issue a subpoena binding on the Judicial Qualifications Commission); *Johnson v. McDonald,* 269 So.2d 682 (Fla.1972) (court had jurisdiction to declare the power of a sub-committee to issue a subpoena duces tecum); *Hagaman v. Andrews,* 232 So.2d 1 (Fla.1970) (court determined the power of a committee chairman to subpoena bank records); *Johnston v. Gallen,* 217 So.2d 319 (Fla.1969) (court had jurisdiction to determine the power of the speaker of the house to create a select committee, having investigatory powers, between sessions).

Just as the legislature may not invade our province of procedural rulemaking for the court system, we may not invade the legislature's province of internal procedural rulemaking. *See, e.g., State v. Garcia,* 229 So.2d 236 (Fla.1969); *State v. Robinson,* 132 So.2d 156 (Fla.1961); *Hay v. Isetts,* 98 Fla. 1026, 125 So. 237 (1929). A member of the legislature can raise a point of order regarding a violation of any of the rules of the house or senate. That is the proper forum for determining the propriety of the activities complained of in the suit below.

Therefore, we find that the circuit court lacks jurisdiction to proceed in this matter. We withhold issuance of a writ of prohibition with the confidence that the respondent will comply with the dictates of this opinion.

It is so ordered.

ALDERMAN, EHRLICH and SHAW, JJ., concur.

BOYD, Chief Justice, concurring in part and dissenting in part [omitted].

Questions

1. According to the Court, what is the issue in this case?

2. When does the Court have jurisdiction to "interfere" in the Legislature's internal process?

iv. Article III, Section 5 —
Investigations and Witnesses

Florida House of Representatives v. Expedia, Inc.
85 So. 3d 517 (Fla. 1st DCA 2012)

PADOVANO, J.

The issue before the court is whether a member of the Florida House of Representatives and his aide are entitled to claim legislative privilege as a ground for refusing to testify in a civil case. A legislative privilege existed under the common law, and we conclude that it continues to apply in Florida by general legislation adopting the common law. We also conclude that a legislative privilege is implicit in the separation of powers provision of the Florida Constitution. Because the testimony to be given in this case is within the scope of the privilege, we hold that the subpoenas at issue must be quashed.

The controversy over the existence of a legislative privilege arose from two tax cases, both of which are pending in the circuit court for Leon County. In these cases, Expedia and other online travel companies filed complaints against Broward County and Osceola County to challenge the assessment of tourist development taxes. The counties filed counterclaims alleging, among other things, that the travel companies had evaded their obligations to pay the taxes.

In the course of related tax litigation in Georgia, Expedia was ordered to produce certain internal documents, including written communications prepared by its law firm and its accountants. These documents were confidential but they were disclosed to opposing counsel in the Georgia litigation under a protective order. Subsequently, the lawyer for Broward County came into possession of the documents and sought to use them as evidence in the Florida cases. The trial court ruled that the documents were privileged and that they would not be admissible in evidence, in the absence of a showing that Expedia had waived the privilege.

Meanwhile, the Florida Legislature was considering a bill that would have afforded favorable tax treatment to hotel bookings made by Expedia and other online travel companies. Rick Kriseman, a member of the Florida House of Representatives, opposed the bill. The lawyer for Broward County provided Representative Kriseman with the Expedia documents that were to remain confidential under the terms of the Georgia protective order. Representative Kriseman then forwarded the documents to all of the members of the Florida House of Representatives and made them available, as well, to certain members of the press.

Following the dissemination of the documents, the lawyers for Expedia obtained subpoenas directing Representative Kriseman and his aide, David Flintom, to appear for depositions. They wanted to ask these two men how they obtained the documents. The Florida House of Representatives moved to quash the subpoenas on the ground that Representative Kriseman and his aide were protected by legislative immunity. Expedia argued that the testimony to be elicited was necessary to prove that it had not provided the documents independently of the lawyer for Broward County, and thereby to establish that it had not waived the privilege protecting the documents.

The trial court denied the motion to quash in part and held that the depositions could go forward on a limited basis. The court ruled that the lawyers for Expedia could ask Representative Kriseman and Mr. Flintom whether Expedia or any of its agents had independently provided the documents at issue. In that event, the lawyers could ask Representative Kriseman and Mr. Flintom what they had done with the documents once they received them. The court emphasized the narrow scope of the permissible inquiry and stated that no questions could be asked pertaining to the thoughts, opinions, or legislative activities of the witnesses.

The House of Representatives filed a petition for writ of prohibition in this court on behalf of Representative Kriseman and his aide, to prevent the trial court from going forward with the depositions. We treat the petition for writ of prohibition as an appeal from a final order. *See* Fla. R.App. P. 9.040(c) (stating that "[i]f a party seeks an improper remedy, the cause shall be treated as if the proper remedy had been sought").

* * *

We begin our analysis on the merits of the appeal by observing that the Florida courts have not yet directly held that a member of the state legislature is entitled to claim a testimonial privilege. The subject was discussed in *Girardeau v. State*, 403 So.2d 513 (Fla. 1st DCA 1981) and *City of Pompano Beach v. Swerdlow Lightspeed Management Co., LLC*, 942 So.2d 455 (Fla. 4th DCA 2006), but in each of those cases the court stopped short of holding that a legislative privilege exists. In *Girardeau*, the court concluded that it was not necessary to recognize the existence of such a privilege, because it could not be asserted in any event to withhold information from a grand jury investigating a crime. And the court declined to reach the issue on the merits in *Swerdlow*, concluding that it had been presented prematurely.

Although the issue has not been squarely addressed in Florida, there is ample authority in American law for the proposition that a member of the legislative branch has a right to assert a legislative privilege. The testimonial privilege that protects a legislator from the command of a subpoena issued in a civil case is closely related to the immunity that protects a legislator from civil liability. These protections are based on the same policy considerations. As we shall explain, the privileges and immunities afforded to all government officials, including those who serve in the legislative branch, arise from the common law.

The principle of legislative immunity was so well established in English and American law that it was incorporated into the United States Constitution. In the leading case of *Tenney v. Brandhove*, 341 U.S. 367, (1951), the Court held that Article I, section 6 of the United States Constitution creates a form of legislative immunity. The applicable portion of this article, popularly known as the "Speech or Debate Clause," provides in pertinent part that "in all Cases, except Treason, Felony and Breach of the Peace, [senators and representatives shall] be privileged from Arrest during their Attendance at the Session of their respective Houses, and in going to and returning from the same; and for any Speech or Debate in either House, they shall not be questioned in any other Place."

The *Tenney* case dealt with immunity from suit, but the Supreme Court subsequently held in *Gravel v. United States*, 408 U.S. 606 (1972), that the Speech or Debate Clause also creates a testimonial privilege. In that case, a United States Senator was subpoenaed before a grand jury to give information relating to classified documents known as the Pentagon Papers. One of the matters under consideration by the grand jury was whether the senator had leaked the documents to a newspaper. The Court acknowledged the existence of the testimonial privilege but concluded that the senator was not entitled to rely on it under the facts of the case, because the subject matter of the inquiry—whether he had leaked the documents to the press—was not within the legitimate sphere of congressional activities and because the privilege cannot be used, in any event, as a shield against the commission of a crime.

The Florida Constitution does not include a version of the Speech or Debate Clause, but the decisions in *Tenney* and *Gravel* are significant to our analysis, nonetheless. These decisions illustrate that the Speech or Debate Clause is based on legislative privileges and immunities that are firmly rooted in the common law. As the Supreme Court explained in *Tenney*, "The privilege of legislators to be free from arrest or civil process for what they say or do in legislative proceedings has taproots in the Parliamentary struggles of the Sixteenth and Seventeenth Centuries." *Tenney*, 341 U.S. at 372.

The Speech or Debate clause is limited by its terms to members of Congress, yet the court in *Tenney* applied the underlying common law principles to conclude that members of the California Legislature were immune from liability in a civil suit. Subsequently, the Court extended legislative immunity to local legislative officials, *see Bogan v. Scott-Harris*, 523 U.S. 44 (1998), and to non-legislators legitimately engaged in a legislative function. *See Supreme Court of Virginia v. Consumers Union of the United States*, 446 U.S. 719 (1980).

The principles that give rise to the need to immunize legislators are the same as those that justify immunity for members of other branches of government. Judges are immune from suit, *see Pierson v. Ray,* 386 U.S. 547 (1967); *Mireles v. Waco,* 502 U.S. 9 (1991), and judicial immunity, like legislative immunity, is based on principles developed in the common law. *See Forrester v. White,* 484 U.S. 219 (1988). Our supreme court noted in *Office of State Attorney, Fourth Judicial Circuit of Florida v. Parrotino,* 628 So.2d 1097, 1099 (Fla.1993), that the English courts had held that "absolute immunity was conferred upon judges acting within their lawful powers, even where the actions allegedly involved serious misconduct," and that this principle "was directly imported into the law of the United States as the common-law basis for judicial immunity."

This common law principle is most often used to immunize a judge from liability in civil litigation, but it has also been used to support the proposition that a judge cannot be compelled to testify about his or her thought process in making a decision in a case. *See State v. Lewis,* 656 So.2d 1248 (Fla.1994) (stating that a judge may not be examined as to his or her thought process in making a decision); *Department of Highway Safety and Motor Vehicles v. Marks,* 898 So.2d 1063 (Fla. 5th DCA 2005) (holding that a hearing officer acting in a judicial capacity was entitled to claim judicial immunity and could not be compelled to give testimony about his mental process in deciding a case).

We can draw the same analogy to the protections afforded to public officials in the executive branch of the government, as these protections are also based on the common law. In *Spalding v. Vilas,* 161 U.S. 483 (1896), the court held that the postmaster general was immune from civil suit. Drawing on principles of immunity developed in English cases at common law, the Court concluded that it is necessary to protect executive branch officials in order to ensure the proper functioning of the government. These common law principles evolved into the modern rules of law pertaining to absolute immunity, *see Nixon v. Fitzgerald,* 457 U.S. 731 (1982), and good faith immunity. *See Mitchell v. Forsyth,* 472 U.S. 511 (1985).

Additionally, as with their counterparts in the judiciary and the legislature, public officials in the executive branch are entitled to a testimonial privilege. *See United States v. Nixon,* 418 U.S. 683 (1974) (recognizing the existence of executive privilege but holding that it is not absolute, in that it cannot be asserted to shield evidence of a crime); *Cheney v. United States Dist. Ct. for the Dist. of Columbia,* 542 U.S. 367 (2004); *Dep't of Health & Rehab. Servs. v. Brooke,* 573 So.2d 363 (Fla. 1st DCA 1991) (holding that the head of a state administrative agency was protected by executive privilege and could not be forced to appear in court and answer questions about funding of the agency).

It is clear from these authorities that the privileges and immunities protecting all public officials, including members of the legislature, arise from the common law. The significance of this point is simply this: if legislative privileges and immunities existed under the common law, they continue to exist, apart from specific constitutional provisions like the Speech or Debate Clause, to the extent that a state continues to recognize the common law.

Section 2.01, Florida Statutes, provides in material part that "[t]he common law and statute laws of England which are of a general and not a local nature ... are declared to be of force in this state; provided, the said statutes and common law [are] not inconsistent with the Constitution and laws of the United States and the acts of the Legislature of this state." It follows from this language that if legislative immunity existed under the common law of England, it continues to exist in Florida. Because we know of no law abrogating the common law on this point, we conclude that Florida legislators continue to enjoy legislative immunity under state law.

As an independent ground for our decision, we conclude that legislative privilege exists by virtue of the separation of powers provision of the Florida Constitution. This constitutional issue is closely related to the common law issues we have discussed. One purpose of common law legislative immunity was to protect the independence of the legislature. Another purpose was to "reinforce the separation of powers" between the branches of government. *Fowler-Nash v. Democratic Caucus of Pa. House of Representatives*, 469 F.3d 328, 331 (3d Cir.2006).

Article II, section 3 of the Florida Constitution states, "The powers of the state government shall be divided into legislative, executive and judicial branches. No person belonging to one branch shall exercise any powers appertaining to either of the other branches unless expressly provided herein." The importance of this provision cannot be overstated. Our supreme court described the separation of powers as "the cornerstone of American democracy." *Bush v. Schiavo*, 885 So.2d 321, 329 (Fla.2004). In the *Schiavo* case, the court also stated that Florida has traditionally applied a "strict separation of powers doctrine." *Id.* at 329. Strict enforcement of the provision is necessary in part to ensure that one branch of the government does not encroach on powers vested exclusively in another.

We suggested in *Girardeau* that the separation of powers provision in Article II, section 3 would support a claim of legislative privilege. *Girardeau*, 403 So.2d at 516. This reasoning is legally sound, and we now adopt it as part of the basis for this decision. The power vested in the legislature under the Florida Constitution would be severely compromised if legislators were required to appear in court to explain why they voted a particular way or to describe their process of gathering information on a bill. Our state government could not maintain the proper "separation" required by Article II, section 3 if the judicial branch could compel an inquiry into these aspects of the legislative process.

Because the right to assert a legislative privilege arises from the state constitution as well as the common law, it is among those privileges that exist independently of the Florida Evidence Code. Section 90.501, Florida Statutes limits the testimonial privileges that are available to those that are listed in the Evidence Code. Legislative privilege is not listed in the Code but it falls within the exception for those privileges that "arise from the Constitution of the United States or of the State of Florida." *See* § 90.501, Fla. Stat. Because it arises from the separation of powers provision in Article II, section 3, as we have explained, it continues to exist notwithstanding the fact that it is not among the testimonial privileges identified in the Code.

Although there is no judicial precedent in Florida for legislative immunity, there is no reason why we should not now recognize that it exists. Nor do we see any reason why this form of immunity, like the others, should not also include a privilege that can be asserted against the obligation that would otherwise exist to give compelled testimony in a civil case. In *Gravel*, the United States Supreme Court treated legislative testimonial privilege as a necessary incident of the legislative immunity it had previously recognized in *Tenney*, and we believe the same logic applies here. If legislators are immune from civil liability for actions taken in the course of their legislative duties, they are also entitled to refuse to testify about the performance duties.

This leads us to the question of whether the testimony to be elicited in the present case falls within the scope of the privilege. We conclude that it does. The documents that are the subject of the inquiry were acquired and distributed in the course of a debate within the House of Representatives on the merits of a pending bill. Gathering information pertaining to potential legislation and sharing it with colleagues is an essential part of the legislative process. Thus, it is clear that Representative Kriseman and his aide were performing a legitimate legislative function. *See Kamplain v. Curry County Bd. of Comm'rs*, 159 F.3d 1248, 1251 (10th Cir.1998) (stating that the courts apply a functional test in determining whether the privilege applies). Hence, the testimony Expedia wishes to elicit is protected.

Furthermore, we have little doubt that the privilege may be asserted by legislative staff members as well as the legislators themselves. The reason for affording a legislative privilege could be subverted entirely if an aide could be forced to disclose that which the senator or representative would be entitled to keep private. *See Gravel*, 408 U.S. at 628 (holding that the privilege applied to both the senator and his aide). It follows that Mr. Flintom is entitled to assert the privilege just as it may be asserted by Representative Kriseman.

The legislative privilege we have recognized in this case is not absolute. On this point, we adhere to our decision in *Girardeau* that the privilege could not be used to withhold evidence of a crime. An absolute testimonial privilege is not available even to the President of the United States. *See United States v. Nixon, supra.* The court will always have to make a preliminary inquiry to determine whether the information is within the scope of the privilege and whether the need for privacy is outweighed by a more important governmental interest.

No such interest has been demonstrated in the present case. Expedia claims that it needs to ask whether the documents were provided to Representative Kriseman by any of its own agents. This is a curious question, given the fact that the parties acknowledge that the documents were in fact provided by the lawyer for Broward County. Nevertheless, Expedia claims that it is necessary to prove that it did not provide the documents independently, so that it can refute a claim that it had waived the attorney-client privilege with respect to the documents. The problem with this claim is that the burden of proving a waiver is on the counties. Expedia is attempting to refute a fact that has not yet been proven and, as it appears from this record, may never be proven.

In summary, we hold that Representative Kriseman and Mr. Flintom are entitled to assert a legislative privilege. Because the questions to be asked of them regarding the documents they received and the actions they took in connection with a bill pending in the legislature are within the scope of the privilege, they cannot be compelled to testify. For these reasons, we reverse with instructions to quash the subpoenas.

Reversed.

WOLF and MARSTILLER, JJ., concur.

League of Women Voters of Florida v. Florida House of Representatives

132 So. 3d 135 (Fla. 2013)

PARIENTE, J.

Does enforcement of the explicit prohibition in the Florida Constitution against partisan political gerrymandering and improper discriminatory intent in redistricting outweigh a claim of an absolute legislative privilege? Specifically, the issue presented to the Court is whether Florida state legislators and legislative staff members have an absolute privilege against testifying as to issues *directly* relevant to whether the Legislature drew the 2012 congressional apportionment plan with unconstitutional partisan or discriminatory "intent." *See* art. III, § 20(a), Fla. Const.

This Court is charged with the solemn obligation to ensure that the constitutional rights of its citizens are not violated and that the explicit constitutional mandate to outlaw partisan political gerrymandering and improper discriminatory intent in redistricting is effectively enforced. While the Legislature asserts that the challengers should be precluded from accessing relevant discovery information because it is absolutely privileged, we conclude that there is no unbending right for legislators and legislative staff members to hide behind a broad assertion of legislative privilege to prevent the discovery of relevant evidence necessary to vindicate the explicit state constitutional prohibition against unconstitutional partisan political gerrymandering and improper discriminatory intent.

This Court has held, in interpreting the constitutional redistricting "intent" standard, that "the focus of the analysis must be on both direct and circumstantial evidence of intent." *In re Senate Joint Resolution of Legislative Apportionment 1176 (Apportionment I)*, 83 So.3d 597, 617 (Fla.2012). Further, this Court has stated that "there is no acceptable level of improper intent." *Id.* As Chief Judge Benton aptly observed in his dissenting opinion to the First District Court of Appeal's decision below, "[t]he enactment of article III, section 20 of the Florida Constitution makes plain that how and why the Legislature redistricts is a matter of paramount public concern." *Fla. House of Reps. v. Romo*, 113 So.3d 117, 131 (Fla. 1st DCA 2013) (Benton, C.J., dissenting).

In this opinion, we decide for the first time that Florida should recognize a legislative privilege founded on the constitutional principle of separation of powers, thus rejecting the challengers' assertion that there is no legislative privilege in Florida. We also hold, however, that this privilege is not absolute where, as in this case, the purposes underlying the privilege are outweighed by the compelling, competing interest of effectuating the *explicit* constitutional mandate that prohibits partisan political gerrymandering and improper discriminatory intent in redistricting. We therefore reject the Legislature's argument that requiring the testimony of individual legislators and legislative staff members will have a "chilling effect" among legislators in discussion and participation in the reapportionment process, as this type of "chilling effect" was the precise purpose of the constitutional amendment outlawing partisan political gerrymandering and improper discriminatory intent.

We also unequivocally reject the dissent's hyperbolic assertion that our decision "grievously violates the constitutional separation of powers," dissenting op. at 156, by recognizing a legislative privilege but concluding that it is not absolute as to enforcing this explicit constitutional mandate. To the contrary, we strike the appropriate balance between respecting the separation of powers and fulfilling this Court's obligation to uphold the citizens' explicit constitutional protection against partisan political gerrymandering and improper discriminatory intent in redistricting.

Accordingly, we quash the First District's decision in *Florida House of Representatives v. Romo,* 113 So.3d 117 (Fla. 1st DCA 2013), which erroneously afforded legislators and legislative staff members the absolute protection of a legislative privilege. We approve the circuit court's order permitting the discovery of information and communications, including the testimony of legislators and the discovery of draft apportionment plans and supporting documents, pertaining to the constitutional validity of the challenged apportionment plan. Further, we emphasize that the circuit court is not constrained by this opinion from considering, as discovery proceeds, how a specific piece of information protected by the privilege fits into the balancing approach set forth in this opinion.

FACTS AND BACKGROUND

In February 2012, the Florida Legislature approved the decennial plan apportioning Florida's twenty-seven congressional districts, based on population data derived from the 2010 United States Census. Soon after its adoption, two separate groups of plaintiffs filed civil complaints in circuit court, which were later consolidated, challenging the constitutionality of the plan under new state constitutional redistricting standards approved by the Florida voters in 2010 and now enumerated in article III, section 20, of the Florida Constitution. Those standards, governing the congressional reapportionment process, appeared on the 2010 general election ballot as "Amendment 6" and, together with their identical counterparts that apply to legislative reapportionment ("Amendment 5"), were generally referred to as the "Fair Districts" amendments.[2] All together, these "express new standards imposed by the voters clearly act as a restraint on legislative discretion in drawing apportionment plans." *Apportionment I,* 83 So.3d at 599.

---

2. [FN 1.] Amendment 5 is now codified in article III, section 21, of the Florida Constitution. The standards in article III, section 20—governing congressional reapportionment—and those in article III, section 21—governing legislative reapportionment—are identical.

The Florida Constitution's Redistricting Standards

Article III, section 20, of the Florida Constitution prohibits the Legislature from drawing an apportionment plan or individual district "with the intent to favor or disfavor a political party or an incumbent" and "with the intent or result of denying or abridging the equal opportunity of racial or language minorities to participate in the political process or to diminish their ability to elect representatives of their choice." Art. III, § 20(a), Fla. Const. Specifically, this constitutional provision provides in its entirety as follows:

In establishing congressional district boundaries:

(a) No apportionment plan or individual district shall be drawn with the intent to favor or disfavor a political party or an incumbent; and districts shall not be drawn with the intent or result of denying or abridging the equal opportunity of racial or language minorities to participate in the political process or to diminish their ability to elect representatives of their choice; and districts shall consist of contiguous territory.

(b) Unless compliance with the standards in this subsection conflicts with the standards in subsection (a) or with federal law, districts shall be as nearly equal in population as is practicable; districts shall be compact; and districts shall, where feasible, utilize existing political and geographical boundaries.

(c) The order in which the standards within subsections (a) and (b) of this section are set forth shall not be read to establish any priority of one standard over the other within that subsection.

Art. III, § 20, Fla. Const.

* * *

The Current Dispute

In the consolidated circuit court lawsuit challenging the validity of the 2012 congressional apportionment plan under the Florida Constitution's redistricting standards, the challengers allege that the congressional apportionment plan and numerous individual districts violate the article III, section 20, standards by impermissibly favoring Republicans and incumbents, by intentionally diminishing the ability of racial and language minorities to elect representatives of their choice, and by failing to adhere to the requirement that districts be compact and follow existing political and geographical boundaries where feasible. The challengers seek both a declaratory judgment invalidating the entire plan, or at least the specific districts challenged, as well as a permanent injunction against conducting any future elections using the congressional district boundaries established by the 2012 apportionment plan.

As part of ongoing pretrial civil discovery—and specifically in an effort to uncover and demonstrate alleged unconstitutional partisan or discriminatory intent in the congressional apportionment plan—the challengers sought information from the Legislature and from third parties regarding the 2012 reapportionment process. From third-party discovery, the challengers uncovered communications between the Legislature and partisan political organizations and political consultants, which they allege reveal a secret effort by state legislators involved in the reapportionment process to favor Republicans and incumbents in direct violation of article III, section 20(a). The challengers have also taken deposition testimony from numerous third-party witnesses as to their involvement in the redistricting process and their communications with state legislators and legislative staff members, and have been provided with e-mail communications between legislators and legislative staff, as well as other public records from the Legislature.

In order to further develop and discover evidence concerning their claim of unconstitutional legislative intent in violation of article III, section 20(a), the challengers served a notice of taking depositions of the then-state Senate Majority Leader, an administrative assistant to the Senate Reapportionment Committee, and the staff director of the House Redistricting Committee. Thereafter, the Legislature filed a "Motion for Protective Order Based on Legislative Privilege," in which it requested the circuit court to enter an order "declaring that (i) no legislators or legislative staff may be deposed, and (ii) unfiled legislative draft maps and supporting documents are not discoverable." The Legislature's motion for a protective order was filed in direct response to the challengers' notice of taking depositions; however, the Legislature sought to more generally prevent the depositions of *any* legislators and legislative staff, as well as the "discovery of legislatively drawn draft redistricting plans that were never filed as bills."

The circuit court granted in part and denied in part the Legislature's motion for a protective order. The circuit court determined that, although a legislative privilege exists in Florida, the privilege is not absolute and "must be balanced against other compelling government interests." Finding it "*difficult to imagine a more compelling, competing government interest* than that represented by the [challengers'] claim," the circuit court drew a distinction between "subjective" thoughts or impressions of legislators and the thoughts or impressions shared with legislators by staff or other legislators, and "objective" information or communication that "does not encroach" into those thoughts or impressions. (Emphasis added.) In drawing this distinction, the circuit court observed that "there are some categories of information and communications that are most in need of the protection offered by the privilege and some that are less in need of such protection."

Accordingly, because "the motive or intent of legislators in drafting the reapportionment plan is one of the specific criteria to be considered when determining the constitutional validity of the plan," and because the information sought by the challengers "is certainly relevant and probative of intent," the circuit court held that all objective" information or communications "should not be protected by the privilege." However, the circuit court cautioned that any individual legislators or legislative staff members who assert a claim of legislative privilege "shall not be deposed regarding their 'subjective' thoughts or impressions or regarding the thoughts or impressions shared with them by staff or other legislators." The circuit court also determined that the same dichotomy applied to the production of documents. It therefore ordered the Legislature to produce all requested documents that do not contain "subjective" information and to schedule an in camera review as to any disputed documents.

On a petition for a writ of certiorari to review the circuit court's non-final order, the First District, relying on its prior decision in *Florida House of Representatives v. Expedia, Inc.*, 85 So.3d 517 (Fla. 1st DCA 2012), which was the first published Florida case to explicitly recognize the existence of a legislative privilege in Florida, concluded that the circuit court's order departed from the essential requirements of law when it allowed the challengers to depose legislators and legislative staff members "on any matter pertaining to their activities in the reapportionment process." *Romo*, 113 So.3d at 123. The First District reasoned that the legislative privilege "equally protects 'subjective' information, such as the legislator's rationale or motivation for proposing or voting on a piece of legislation, and 'objective' information, such as the data or materials relied on by legislators and their staff in the legislative process." *Id.* Thus, the First District quashed the circuit court's order "insofar as it permits [the challengers] to depose legislators and legislative staff members concerning the reapportionment process and insofar as it requires production of draft maps and supporting documents for an in camera review under the erroneous, unworkable objective/subjective dichotomy." *Id.* at 128.

Chief Judge Benton dissented, observing in part that "[p]artisan political shenanigans are not 'state secrets,'" and that, at this stage of the litigation, "it is impossible to say that any question [the challengers] would actually have asked would be objectionable." *Id.* at 130–31 (Benton, C.J., dissenting). Subsequently, after both groups of challengers in the consolidated litigation below sought review, we exercised our discretion to accept jurisdiction to review the First District's decision because that decision expressly affects a class of constitutional officers—namely, legislators—and because this Court has never considered whether a legislative privilege exists, which is clearly an important issue to resolve. *See* art. V, §3(b)(3), Fla. Const.

ANALYSIS

The questions we confront require this Court to interpret the Florida Constitution to determine whether a legislative privilege exists and to define the parameters of that privilege as applied in this case. These are pure questions of law that are subject to de novo review.

We hold, first, that a legislative privilege exists in Florida, based on the principle of separation of powers codified in article II, section 3, of the Florida Constitution. However, we conclude that this privilege is not absolute and may yield to a compelling, competing interest. We then proceed to review whether a compelling, competing interest exists in this case. Finally, we explain why we embrace the circuit court's balancing approach at this stage of the litigation, which determined that the compelling, competing constitutional interest present here outweighs the purposes underlying the privilege, therefore allowing discovery but retaining the right of an individual legislator or legislative staff member to assert the privilege as to his or her thoughts or impressions or the thoughts or impressions shared with legislators by staff or other legislators.

I. Florida's Legislative Privilege

The challengers contend that this Court should not recognize a legislative privilege because the Florida Constitution lacks a Speech or Debate Clause, which is the constitutional provision upon which the legislative privilege is traditionally premised. This clause, which generally states that legislators shall in all cases except treason, felony, or breach of the peace, not be questioned in any other place for any speech or debate in either legislative chamber, is the general justification that the federal courts and other states with a state-specific clause have utilized in recognizing the legislative privilege. *See City of Pompano Beach v. Swerdlow Lightspeed Mgmt. Co.*, 942 So.2d 455, 457 (Fla. 4th DCA 2006) ("The federal courts which have acknowledged and applied the privilege have done so based largely on the Speech and Debate Clause in Article I, section 6, of the United States Constitution, which protects federal legislators from suits."); *Kerttula v. Abood*, 686 P.2d 1197, 1205 (Alaska 1984) (applying Alaska's state constitutional version of the Speech or Debate Clause to preclude the deposition of a state legislator).

In contrast to the vast majority of states, the Florida Constitution does not include a Speech or Debate Clause and has not included one since the clause was omitted during the 1868 constitutional revision. In fact, Florida is one of only two states in the country that lacks either a state constitutional Speech or Debate Clause or a provision protecting legislators from arrest during legislative session.

Coupled with the absence of a Speech or Debate Clause in the Florida Constitution is the presence of Florida's broad constitutional right of access to public records, set forth in article I, section 24, and right to transparency in the legislative process, codified in article III, section 4. Specifically regarding the Legislature, the Florida Constitution mandates as follows:

> [A]ll prearranged gatherings, between more than two members of the legislature, or between the governor, the president of the senate, or the speaker of the house of representatives, the purpose of which is to agree upon formal legislative action that will be taken at a subsequent time, or at which formal legislative action is taken, regarding pending legislation or amendments, shall be reasonably open to the public.

Art. III, §4(e), Fla. Const. Further, article I, section 24(a), which "specifically includes the legislative" branch, provides that "[e]very person has the right to inspect or copy any public record made or received in connection with the official business of any public body" of the state. Art. I, §24(a), Fla. Const.

Thus, the absence of a Speech or Debate Clause and the strong public policy, as codified in our state constitution, favoring transparency and public access to the legislative process, are factors weighing against recognizing a legislative privilege in Florida. Florida statutes also do not provide for a legislative privilege. Further, any common law legislative privilege has been abolished by a provision in the Florida Evidence Code providing that Florida law recognizes only privileges set forth by statute or in the state or federal constitutions.[3]

These factors, however, are not conclusive because there is another important factor that weighs in favor of recognizing the privilege—the doctrine of separation of powers. It is through this separate and important constitutional principle, which is codified in article II, section 3, of the Florida Constitution, that we recognize a legislative privilege under Florida law.

Forty states, including Florida, have a specific state constitutional provision recognizing the separation of powers between the three branches of government. Article II, section 3, of the Florida Constitution, which is Florida's separation of powers provision, provides as follows:

> The powers of the state government shall be divided into legislative, executive and judicial branches. No person belonging to one branch shall exercise any powers appertaining to either of the other branches unless expressly provided herein.

Art. II, §3, Fla. Const.

In *Expedia,* which was the first published case to analyze and recognize the existence of a legislative privilege in Florida, the First District concluded that the state constitutional separation of powers provision provides an independent basis to recognize a legislative privilege under Florida law. 85 So.3d at 524. The issue in *Expedia* was whether a legislator and a member of the legislator's staff could be deposed in tax-related litigation so that a party in the lawsuit could "refute a claim that it had waived the attorney-client privilege" as to several documents the legislator had obtained. *Id.* at 525. The First District held that the legislator and his aide were entitled to assert a legislative privilege against the compelled testimony and that there was no compelling interest in seeking the depositions because the party seeking them was "attempting to refute a fact that has not yet been proven, and, as it appears from this record, may never be proven." *Id.*

Although *Expedia* was the first published Florida case to explicitly conclude that state legislators may assert a legislative privilege, various Florida circuit courts have, in unpublished orders over the years, quashed subpoenas requesting the testimony of state legislators or legislative staff members for various reasons. For example, in 2003, a circuit court quashed a subpoena seeking to elicit the intent, purpose, or motive behind a particular state senator's introduction of certain amendments to a 2002 piece of legislation. *See* Order Granting Motion to Quash, *Billie v. State,* No. 02-499-CA (Fla. 17th Cir.Ct. Feb. 7, 2003). None of these orders specifically analyzed the legislative privilege, however, and most have been premised on the tenet that an individual legislator's testimony as to individual intent is usually irrelevant in a typical

---

3. [FN 8.] *See Marshall v. Anderson,* 459 So.2d 384, 387 (Fla. 3d DCA 1984) (stating that the adoption of section 90.501, Florida Statutes (1981), "abolishe[d] all common-law privileges existing in Florida," making "the creation of privileges dependent upon legislative action or pursuant to the Supreme Court's rule-making power" (quoting Law Revision Council Note)).

lawsuit challenging a statute. These orders nevertheless support the premise that the judicial branch has respected the separation of powers between the three branches of government, particularly where no compelling interest in seeking the testimony has been demonstrated.

Such respect between the three branches is inherent in our democratic system of government. This Court has previously described the constitutional tenet of separation of powers as "[t]he cornerstone of American democracy," *Bush v. Schiavo,* 885 So.2d 321, 329 (Fla.2004), and has explained that article II, section 3, which is the state constitutional separation of powers provision, "encompasses two fundamental prohibitions. The first is that no branch may encroach upon the powers of another. The second is that no branch may delegate to another branch its constitutionally assigned power." *Chiles v. Children A, B, C, D, E, & F,* 589 So.2d 260, 264 (Fla.1991). Indeed, as pointed out by several former presiding officers of the Legislature in their amicus curiae brief filed in this case, "the legislative privilege is critical to a proper separation of powers, upon which our system of government is built."

Accordingly, because of the role that the principle of separation of powers plays in the structure of Florida's state government, as embodied in article II, section 3, of our state constitution, we reject the challengers' contention that there is no legislative privilege in Florida and hold that state legislators and legislative staff members do possess a legislative privilege under Florida law. This privilege is based on the principle that "no branch may encroach upon the powers of another," *Chiles,* 589 So.2d at 264, and on inherent principles of comity that exist between the coequal branches of government. In other words, "the privilege can be said to derive from the supremacy of each branch within its own assigned area of constitutional duties." *United States v. Nixon,* 418 U.S. 683, 705 (1974).

Several reasons support recognition of a legislative privilege. The most obvious is the practical concern of protecting the integrity of the legislative process by not unnecessarily interfering with the Legislature's business. As the circuit court cogently articulated, "[l]egislators could not properly do their job if they had to sit for depositions every time someone thought they had information that was relevant to a particular court case or administrative proceeding." In addition, other reasons for recognizing a privilege include the "historical policy ... of protecting disfavored legislators from intimidation by a hostile executive" and protecting legislators "from the burdens of forced participation in private litigation." *Kerttula,* 686 P.2d at 1202. These other policies undergirding the legislative privilege aim to ensure that the separation of powers is maintained so that the Legislature can accomplish its role of enacting legislation in the public interest without undue interference.

Although separation of powers principles require deference to the Legislature in refusing to provide compelled testimony in a judicial action, we emphasize that the legislative privilege is not absolute. As the United States Supreme Court has noted in determining that the President of the United States does not enjoy an absolute privilege of immunity from judicial process in all circumstances, "when the privilege depends solely on the broad, undifferentiated claim of public interest ... a confrontation with other values arises." *Nixon*, 418 U.S. at 706. This public interest component is especially true in Florida, where one of our state constitutional values is a strong and well-established public policy of transparency and public access to the legislative process, which is enshrined in the Florida Constitution.

Indeed, the proposition that a legislative privilege is not absolute, particularly where another compelling, competing interest is at stake, is not a novel one. For example, in *United States v. Gillock*, 445 U.S. 360, 369, 372 (1980), the Supreme Court acknowledged the need to avoid unnecessary intrusion by the executive or judicial branches into the "affairs of a coequal branch," as well as the Court's "sensitivity to interference with the functioning of state legislators." However, the Court concluded nevertheless that "although principles of comity command careful consideration, ... where important federal interests are at stake, as in the enforcement of federal criminal statutes, comity yields." *Id.* at 373. The Court stated as follows:

> We recognize that denial of a privilege to a state legislator may have some minimal impact on the exercise of his legislative function; however, similar arguments made to support a claim of Executive privilege were found wanting in *United States v. Nixon*, 418 U.S. 683 (1974), when balanced against the need of enforcing federal criminal statutes. There, the genuine risk of inhibiting candor in the internal exchanges at the highest levels of the Executive Branch was held insufficient to justify denying judicial power to secure all relevant evidence in a criminal proceeding. *See also United States v. Burr*, 25 F.Cas. 187 (No. 14,694) (C.C.Va.1807). Here, we believe that recognition of an evidentiary privilege for state legislators for their legislative acts would impair the legitimate interest of the Federal Government in enforcing its criminal statutes with only speculative benefit to the state legislative process.

Id. While the interest implicated in this case is not the enforcement of the criminal laws, this case involves the vindication of an explicit constitutional prohibition against partisan political gerrymandering and a constitutional restraint on the Legislature's actions—a public interest that is also compelling.

As the First District itself has recognized, there may be a compelling, competing interest in a particular case that outweighs the purposes underlying the privilege. *See Expedia*, 85 So.3d at 525. When the legislative privilege is asserted, therefore, courts must engage in an inquiry to determine both if the privilege applies to protect the particular information being sought and the reason the information is being sought.[4] This inquiry is a two-step process.

---

4. [FN 11.] This case does not involve legislative immunity, nor does it involve the liability of any individual legislator. We note that the legislative privilege (that is, an evidentiary privilege against compelled judicial process) is different than legislative immunity from suit, even though federal courts have held that the legislative privilege is derived from the principles underlying legislative immunity. *See Gravel v. United States*, 408 U.S. 606, 615 (1972). These principles are based on the United States Constitution's Speech or Debate Clause, see U.S. Const. art. I, §6, cl. 1, and arise out of "the Parliamentary struggles of the Sixteenth and Seventeenth Centuries." *Tenney v. Brandhove*, 341 U.S. 367, 372 (1951).

The first step is to determine whether the information sought falls within the scope of the privilege. This is an important determination because, for example, information concerning evidence of a crime would not be covered by the legislative privilege. For purposes of our analysis in this case, however, we assume that all of the information being sought by the challengers, which relates to functions undertaken by legislators and legislative staff during the course of their legitimate legislative duties, would fall within the scope of the privilege. We therefore proceed to the next step.

Once a court determines that the information being sought is within the scope of the legislative privilege, the court then must determine whether the purposes underlying the privilege—namely, the deference owed by each coequal branch of government to the others and the practical concerns of legislators' abilities to perform their legislative functions free from the burdens of forced participation in private litigation—are outweighed by a compelling, competing interest. With this in mind, we next address the compelling, competing interest asserted in this case. Then, we analyze whether this compelling, competing interest outweighs the purposes underlying the privilege.

II. The Compelling, Competing Interest

The compelling, competing interest in this case is ensuring compliance with article III, section 20(a), which specifically outlaws improper legislative "intent" in the congressional reapportionment process. The language of article III, section 20(a), explicitly places legislative "intent" at the center of the litigation. Indeed, as the circuit court succinctly stated, it is "difficult to imagine a more compelling, competing government interest" than the interest represented by the challengers' article III, section 20(a), claims. The circuit court explained this finding as follows:

> [The challengers' claim] is based upon a specific constitutional direction to the Legislature, as to what it can and cannot do with respect to drafting legislative reapportionment plans. It seeks to protect the essential right of our citizens to have a fair opportunity to select those who will represent them. In this particular case, the motive or intent of legislators in drafting the reapportionment plan is one of the specific criteria to be considered when determining the constitutional validity of the plan. The information sought is certainly relevant and probative of intent. Frankly, if the compelling government interest in this case does not justify some relaxing of the legislative privilege, then there's probably no other civil case which would.

The first-tier requirements in article III, section 20, provide that "[n]o apportionment plan or individual district shall be drawn with the intent to favor or disfavor a political party or an incumbent." Art. III, § 20(a), Fla. Const. We recently explained that, in enacting these constraints on the Legislature's reapportionment of congressional and state legislative districts, "the framers and voters clearly desired more judicial scrutiny" of the apportionment plans, "not less." *Apportionment III,* 118 So.3d at 205 [*Florida House of Representatives v. League of Women Voters of Florida*]. Indeed, as this Court has previously noted, "[t]he new requirements dramatically alter the landscape with respect to redistricting by prohibiting practices that have been acceptable in the past.... By virtue of these additional constitutional requirements, the parameters of the Legislature's responsibilities under the Florida Constitution" and therefore the scope of judicial review of the validity of an apportionment plan "have plainly increased, requiring a commensurately more expanded judicial analysis of legislative compliance." *Apportionment I*, 83 So.3d at 607 [*In re Senate Joint Resolution of Legislative Apportionment 1176*].

Although the dissent relies heavily on the historical roots of the legislative privilege and the United States Supreme Court's decision in *Tenney*, 341 U.S. 367, *Tenney* was "a civil action brought by a private plaintiff to vindicate private rights." *Gillock*, 445 U.S. at 372. Specifically, the issue in *Tenney* was whether an individual plaintiff could maintain a cause of action for monetary damages against members of the California state legislature's "Fact-Finding Committee on Un-American Activities" after the committee held a hearing that the plaintiff alleged was designed "to intimidate and silence [him] and deter and prevent him from effectively exercising his constitutional rights of free speech and to petition the Legislature." *Tenney*, 341 U.S. at 369, 371.

The compelling, competing interest in this case is a far cry from the interests implicated in *Tenney*. Unlike the plaintiff in *Tenney*, the challengers seek not to vindicate private rights, but to determine whether the Florida Legislature violated an explicit constitutional provision outlawing improper partisan and discriminatory intent in the redistricting process. The challengers do not seek monetary damages, but instead challenge whether the congressional districts in which citizens exercise their fundamental democratic right to elect representatives of their choice were drawn in compliance with the Florida Constitution.

In order to fully effectuate the public interest in ensuring that the Legislature does not engage in unconstitutional partisan political gerrymandering, it is essential for the challengers to be given the opportunity to discover information that may prove any potentially unconstitutional intent. The challengers assert that documents they have so far uncovered, primarily through third-party discovery, reveal direct, secret communications between legislators, legislative staff members, partisan organizations, and political consultants. In addition, because of Florida's broad public records laws, the challengers have received 16,000 e-mails, including e-mails between legislators and legislative staff, as part of the discovery process. Contrary to the Legislature's argument, the fact that the challengers have already discovered communications between legislators and legislative staff, as well as between legislators, legislative staff members, and outside political consultants, related to the congressional apportionment plan, at least in part because Florida's strong public records constitutional provision requires it, does not make the depositions sought any less important to the critical issue of intent that is the focus of the challengers' article III, section 20(a), claims.

If the Legislature alone is responsible for determining what aspects of the reapportionment process are shielded from discovery, the purpose behind the voters' enactment of the article III, section 20(a), standards will be undermined....

Legislature held public hearings; but still could be violating FL Const.

In *Apportionment I*, we acknowledged the Legislature for engaging in extensive public hearings as indicative of an unprecedented transparent reapportionment process. *See Apportionment I*, 83 So.3d at 664 ("We commend the Legislature for holding multiple public hearings and obtaining public input."); *see also id.* at 637 n. 35 (noting that the Legislature held twenty-six hearings at different locations around the state, during which the public had the opportunity to provide recommendations for the legislative and congressional apportionment plans). However, if evidence exists to demonstrate that there was an entirely different, separate process that was undertaken contrary to the transparent effort in an attempt to favor a political party or an incumbent in violation of the Florida Constitution, clearly that would be important evidence in support of the claim that the Legislature thwarted the constitutional mandate.

We reject the approach of the dissenting opinion, which contends that a broad claim of an absolute legislative privilege should prevent this discovery, and emphasize that this Court's first obligation is to give meaning to the explicit prohibition in the Florida Constitution against improper partisan or discriminatory intent in redistricting. The existence of a separate process to draw the maps with the intent to favor or disfavor a political party or an incumbent is precisely what the Florida Constitution now prohibits. This constitutional mandate prohibiting improper partisan or discriminatory intent in redistricting therefore requires that discovery be permitted to determine whether the Legislature engaged in actions designed to circumvent the constitutional mandate.

* * *

This Court has explained that the "intent" standard "applies to both the apportionment plan as a whole and to each district individually," and that "there is no acceptable level of improper intent." *Apportionment I*, 83 So.3d at 617. Thus, the communications of individual legislators or legislative staff members, if part of a broader process to develop portions of the map, could directly relate to whether the plan as a whole or any specific districts were drawn with unconstitutional intent.

Not a typical case

As another court has explained in evaluating a similar claim, "[t]his is not … 'the usual "deliberative process" case in which a private party challenges governmental action … and the government tries to prevent its decision-making process from being swept up unnecessarily into [the] public [domain].'" *Comm. for a Fair & Balanced Map v. Ill. State Bd. of Elections*, No. 11-C-5065, 2011 WL 4837508, at *8 (N.D.Ill.2011) (quoting *United States v. Bd. of Ed. of City of Chicago*, 610 F.Supp. 695, 700 (N.D.Ill.1985)). Instead, "the decisionmaking process … [itself] *is* the case." *Id.* The same court also noted that cases concerning voting rights, "although brought by private parties, seek to vindicate public rights" and are, in this respect, "akin to criminal prosecutions." *Id.* at *6.

* * *

Having concluded that this case presents a compelling, competing interest against application of an absolute legislative privilege, we now address the critical issue of whether this interest outweighs the purposes underlying the privilege.

III. The Balancing Approach

In this case, the circuit court determined that the legislative privilege does not shield most information or communications regarding the congressional apportionment process, but does protect the thoughts or impressions of individual legislators and legislative staff members at this stage of the litigation. We embrace the circuit court's balancing approach. We conclude that the compelling, competing constitutional interest in prohibiting the Legislature from engaging in unconstitutional partisan political gerrymandering outweighs the purposes underlying the legislative privilege as to all discovery, except to the extent that the circuit court protected the thoughts or impressions of individual legislators or legislative staff at this stage of the litigation. This is not a bright line, however, and involves a balancing of interests as specific questions are posed and additional discovery information is received in this case. The circuit court therefore is not constrained by this opinion from considering, as discovery proceeds, how a specific piece of information protected by the privilege fits into this balancing approach.

* * *

We also reject the Legislature's argument that this Court should apply an absolute privilege and preclude the discovery sought because all courts that have considered this issue have precluded similar discovery. First, we note that this Court has never had the occasion to specifically consider whether a legislative privilege exists in Florida and to delineate its boundaries, and, as we have explained, Florida stands apart from many other states in lacking a constitutional Speech or Debate Clause.

Second, although the Legislature has made a point of arguing that no court anywhere has ever allowed a legislator to be deposed regarding the legislative process outside of the criminal context, the Legislature also has candidly admitted that no court in a state with a constitutional provision similar to Florida's, which explicitly prohibits improper intent or purpose in redistricting, has ever addressed this particular issue. Thus, despite the Legislature's claim that no court in any of these states has ever permitted the compelled testimony of a state legislator, no court in any of these states has ever expressly prohibited it either. In other words, there is no precedent on this issue in the narrow context of a constitutional provision that explicitly prohibits improper legislative intent in redistricting.

To say, as the dissent does, that our decision stands alone "in the recorded history of our Republic" in compelling legislators to be interrogated "in a civil case concerning their legislative activities," dissenting op. at 156, fails to take into account that this case is unlike any other "civil" case involving the legislative privilege. In contrast to traditional civil cases, this case concerns an issue of first impression involving an explicit state constitutional prohibition against partisan political gerrymandering and improper discriminatory intent.

We likewise reject the dissent's reliance on a single case decided by a federal district court judge, who determined the scope of the federal legislative privilege in the context of preclearance review under the Federal Voting Rights Act. *See Florida v. United States,* 886 F.Supp.2d 1301, 1302 (N.D.Fla.2012). Although legislative purpose may be a relevant factor in a discriminatory intent challenge brought pursuant to the Federal Voting Rights Act, challenges under the federal statute primarily involve "effect" rather than "intent," which is an easier standard to establish since it does not involve probing the motives behind the plan. *See, e.g., Thornburg v. Gingles,* 478 U.S. 30 (1986). In addition, federal courts have long recognized the existence of a federal legislative privilege based on the explicit text of the Speech or Debate Clause of the United States Constitution and through federal common law—neither of which applies to an action in state court based on a specific prohibition in the state constitution.

* * *

As to the procedure to determine whether the draft apportionment plans and supporting documents should be produced, we reject the First District's reasoning and approve the circuit court's approach. As the circuit court stated:

Florida has a long and rich tradition of open government and the case law in this area suggests that questions about the interpretation of the Public Records Act should be resolved in favor of access by the public. Any specific exemptions are therefore to be strictly construed. Noting the legislative history of the exemption under which the [Legislature] seek[s] protection, I conclude that their very broad interpretation of the exemption is not supported by the language of the statute nor the case law in this area. The [challengers'] interpretation might be a little too narrow, as they suggest that once any plan has been passed, any documents that might have been exempted from the act, are no longer so.

It is difficult for me to know where to draw the line between the plan that was actually proposed and adopted by the legislature and any other draft of a plan. The [challengers'] argument is that the entire process is designed to create a plan, not several plans. Without having precise knowledge of how plans are proposed, discussed, and developed, it is difficult for me to evaluate that assertion. The only way I know how to do so is to have any disputed documents presented to me in camera, with explanatory testimony as to their nature and how they compare or contrast with the plan ultimately adopted.

We agree that the first issue to be decided is whether the draft plans fall within the scope of the public records exemption in section 11.0431(2)(e), Florida Statutes (2012), and that this exemption should be strictly construed in favor of disclosure. *See Rameses, Inc. v. Demings,* 29 So.3d 418, 421 (Fla. 5th DCA 2010) ("In light of the policy favoring disclosure, the Public Records Act is construed liberally in favor of openness, and exemptions from disclosure are construed narrowly and limited to their designated purpose."). However, even if the circuit court concludes, after undertaking an in camera review of any disputed documents, that the draft plans are exempt from public records disclosure, the circuit court should still require the Legislature to produce the draft apportionment maps and supporting documents under appropriate litigation discovery rules, to the extent these documents do not contain information regarding individual legislators' or legislative staff members' thoughts or impressions. *See Dep't of High. Saf. & Motor Veh. v. Krejci Co.,* 570 So.2d 1322, 1325 (Fla. 2d DCA 1990) (determining that a statutory exemption from public records disclosure is not a per se bar to insulate records from discovery in a civil action); *see also* Fla. R. Civ. P. 1.280(b)(1) ("Parties may obtain discovery regarding *any matter, not privileged,* that is relevant to the subject matter of the pending action. . . ." (emphasis added)).

We emphasize that this case presents novel issues of law and the first circuit court litigation under the new article III, section 20(a), redistricting standards. Indeed, the specific claims raised by the challengers in this case are first of their kind claims under the Florida Constitution that require considerable factual development. *See Apportionment III,* 118 So.3d at 210. Given that the record at this time does not indicate that the challengers "have so much as framed the questions to be asked on deposition," *Romo,* 113 So.3d at 130 (Benton, C.J., dissenting), the challengers should not be prevented from developing evidence to support their constitutional claims.

Although the dissent criticizes our approval of the dichotomy between discoverable and non-discoverable information as having no principled basis, we approve the distinction drawn in the well-reasoned order of the circuit court, recognizing that this order was entered in anticipation of the depositions being set and the types of questions that could be posed. As Chief Judge Benton pointed out, "[a]ctually knowing what questions the litigants intended to ask could well shed an invaluable light on these important issues." *Id.* at 133. Without the depositions having taken place and specific objections raised, this Court can rule only on issues that are before us.

While the Florida Constitution authorizes the Legislature to adopt redistricting plans, it places significant limitations on how the redistricting plans are drawn and therefore the power is vested in the courts to determine the constitutionality of those plans. Accordingly, for all these reasons, we conclude that the circuit court recognized the proper balance in determining what information is protected by the legislative privilege at this stage of the litigation and what information the challengers should be permitted to discover. Because we conclude that the circuit court committed no error of law in its order, we also necessarily conclude that the First District erred in granting certiorari review of that non-final order because the circuit court's order did not depart from the essential requirements of law, a necessary prerequisite for granting certiorari relief. *See Citizens Prop. Ins. Corp. v. San Perdido Ass'n,* 104 So.3d 344, 351 (Fla.2012).

In sum, we hold that individual legislators may waive their privilege, or legislators and legislative staff members may assert a claim of legislative privilege at this stage of the litigation only as to any questions or documents revealing their thoughts or impressions or the thoughts or impressions shared with legislators by staff or other legislators, but may not refuse to testify or produce documents concerning any other information or communications pertaining to the 2012 reapportionment process. Further, we emphasize that the circuit court is not constrained by this opinion from considering, as discovery proceeds, how a specific piece of information protected by the privilege fits into the balancing approach embraced herein.

* * *

It is so ordered.

CANADY, J., dissenting.

In this case, for the first time in the recorded history of our Republic, a court has ruled that state legislators are required to submit to interrogation in a civil case concerning their legislative activities. I dissent from this unprecedented decision—a decision which effectively abrogates the well-established common law legislative privilege and grievously violates the constitutional separation of powers. I would approve the First District Court of Appeal's cogent decision.

I.

The legislative privilege—which the majority reduces to a matter of judicial discretion—is firmly rooted in the English common law and inherent in the constitutional separation of powers. In *Tenney v. Brandhove*, 341 U.S. 367 (1951), the United States Supreme Court explained the historical origins of the privilege.

> The privilege of legislators to be free from ... civil process for what they do or say in legislative proceedings has taproots in the Parliamentary struggles of the Sixteenth and Seventeenth Centuries.... In 1689, the Bill of Rights declared in unequivocal language: "That the Freedom of Speech, and Debates or Proceedings in Parliament, ought not to be impeached or questioned in any Court or Place out of Parliament."

Id. at 372 (quoting 1 Wm. & Mary, Sess. 2, c.II). Central elements of the Bill of Rights of 1689 were a provision abolishing the royal suspending power—that is, the monarch's asserted power to suspend the operation of laws without the consent of Parliament—and the provision recognizing the legislative privilege. "Together, the two provisions preserved the freedom of legislative debate and the force of legislative enactment, thus assuring the functional independence of Parliament in a system of separate powers." Robert J. Reinstein & Harvey A. Silverglate, *Legislative Privilege and the Separation of Powers,* 86 Harv. L.Rev. 1113, 1135 (1973). Along with the other provisions of the English Bill of Rights, Magna Charta, and the writ of habeas corpus, the legislative privilege stands as a component in "a towering common law lighthouse of liberty." *Boumediene v. Bush,* 553 U.S. 723, 845 (2008) (Scalia, J., dissenting) (quoting Akhil Reed Amar, *Sixth Amendment First Principles,* 84 Geo. L.J. 641, 663 (1996)). The legislative privilege undeniably is one of "the presuppositions of our political history." *Tenney,* 341 U.S. at 372.

As *Tenney* recognizes, "[t]he claim of an unworthy purpose does not destroy the privilege." 341 U.S. at 377. The privilege exists so that legislators will be "immune from deterrents to the uninhibited discharge of their legislative duty, not for their private indulgence but for the public good." *Id.* "The privilege would be of little value if [legislators] could be subjected to the cost and inconvenience and distractions of a trial upon a conclusion of the pleader, or to the hazard of a judgment against them based upon a jury's [or judge's] speculation as to motives." *Id.* Any impairment of the legislative privilege threatens both to undermine the ability of legislators to carry out their constitutional duties and to weaken the constitutional separation of powers.

The autonomy of the core internal operations of the legislative branch is a bulwark of the separation of powers. That autonomy is violated by the intrusion of the judicial branch into the internal operations of the legislative process. When the constitutional autonomy of one branch is breached by another branch, the separation of powers is violated. Florida law has recognized that the judicial branch should not intrude into the internal operations of the legislative branch. "Florida courts have full authority to review the final product of the legislative process, but they are without authority to review the internal workings of [the Legislature]." *Fla. Senate v. Fla. Pub. Emps. Council 79*, 784 So.2d 404, 409 (Fla.2001); *see also Moffitt v. Willis*, 459 So.2d 1018, 1022 (Fla.1984) (rejecting judicial inquiry into "the propriety and constitutionality of certain internal activities of members of the legislature").

Due respect for the separation of powers precludes the judicial branch from requiring that legislators and legislative employees submit to an inquisition conducted to ferret out evidence of an improper purpose in the legislative process. As the Supreme Court stated in *Tenney*, the view that it is "not consonant with our scheme of government for a court to inquire into the motives of legislators, has remained unquestioned." 341 U.S. at 377 (citing *Fletcher v. Peck*, 10 U.S. (6 Cranch) 87, 130 (1810)). Courts are highly sensitive to the fact that "judicial inquiries into legislative … motivation represent a substantial intrusion into the workings of [an]other branch[] of government." *Vill. of Arlington Heights v. Metro. Hous. Dev. Corp.*, 429 U.S. 252, 268 n. 18 (1977). That is why the majority has been unable to cite any decision in which a legislator has been required to provide testimony in a civil case regarding the legislative process. The best that the petitioners offer is an unreported federal trial court order compelling a legislative staff member to submit to a deposition. *See Baldus v. Members of Wis. Gov't Accountability Bd.*, 2011 WL 6122542 (E.D.Wis.2011).

Contrary to the majority's suggestion, *Tenney*'s recognition of the important purpose of the legislative privilege is by no means undermined by *United States v. Gillock*, 445 U.S. 360 (1980), where the Supreme Court held that the legislative privilege was not applicable in a federal criminal prosecution of a state legislator. In *Gillock*, the Supreme Court reasoned that "the separation of powers doctrine [] gives no support to the grant of a privilege to state legislators in federal criminal prosecutions" because "federal interference in the state legislative process is not on the same constitutional footing with the interference of one branch of the Federal Government in the affairs of a coequal branch." 445 U.S. at 370.

Given "the absence of a constitutional limitation on the power of Congress to make state officials, like all other persons, subject to federal criminal sanctions," the Supreme Court concluded that no basis existed "for a *judicially created limitation* that handicaps proof of the relevant facts." *Id.* at 374 (emphasis added). *Gillock* thus does not address the role that the legislative privilege plays in the separation of powers between the legislative and judicial branches. Instead, *Gillock* is a case about the scope of federal legislative power vis-à-vis state legislators. In *Gillock*, the recognition of the legislative privilege would have required "a judicially created limitation" impinging on the prosecution of federal offenses created by Congress. Here, however, it is the majority's failure to honor the legislative privilege that has required "a judicially created limitation" on the legislative privilege—a privilege that is rooted in the English common law and inherent in the constitutional separation of powers.

The absence of persuasive authority justifying the compelled deposition of state legislators was recently recognized by Judge Robert L. Hinkle in *Florida v. United States,* 886 F.Supp.2d 1301 (N.D.Fla.2012), a case arising under section 5 of the Voting Rights Act of 1965, 42 U.S.C. §§ 1973(a)–1973(q) (2006). Although Judge Hinkle recognized that in Voting Rights Act cases, as in equal protection cases, "the critical question often is whether the legislature acted with a discriminatory purpose," he held that legislators and legislative staff could not be compelled to testify. He observed:

> The considerations that support the result include the burden that being compelled to testify would impose on state legislators, the chilling effect the prospect of having to testify might impose on legislators when considering proposed legislation and discussing it with staff members, and perhaps most importantly, the respect due a coordinate branch of government. Legislators ought not call unwilling judges to testify at legislative hearings about the reasons for specific judicial decisions, and courts ought not compel unwilling legislators to testify about the reasons for specific legislative votes. Nothing in the Voting Rights Act suggests that Congress intended to override this long-recognized legislative privilege.

Florida, 886 F.Supp.2d at 1303.

II.

The majority recognizes "that a legislative privilege exists in Florida, based on the principle of separation of powers codified in article II, section 3, of the Florida Constitution" but concludes "that this privilege is not absolute and may yield to a compelling, competing interest." Majority op. at 143. The majority holds that a compelling, competing interest is operative here because with the passage of article III, section 20, Florida Constitution, "'the framers and the voters clearly desired more judicial scrutiny' of the [redistricting] plans, 'not less.'" Majority op. at 148 (quoting *Fla. House of Representatives v. League of Women Voters of Fla.,* 118 So.3d 198, 205 (Fla.2013)). The majority adopts a "balancing approach"—applicable to both depositions and document production—under which "most information or communications regarding the congressional [redistricting] process" are discoverable, but the "thoughts or impressions of individual legislators and legislative staff members" are not subject to discovery "at this stage of the litigation." Majority op. at 151. The majority also holds that "any common law legislative privilege has been abolished by" the Florida Evidence Code. Majority op. at 144.

The majority's conclusion that the common law legislative privilege has been abolished is unwarranted. Section 90.501, Florida Statutes (2013), which the majority relies on to support this conclusion, simply provides that no evidentiary privilege exists other than those "provided by [chapter 90], any other statute, or the Constitution of the United States or of the State of Florida." The English common law legislative privilege, however, is given the force of law in Florida by the terms of another statute. Section 2.01, Florida Statutes (2013), provides that the general "common and statute laws of England ... down to the 4th day of July, 1776, are declared to be in force in this state" to the extent they are "not inconsistent with the Constitution and laws of the United States and the acts of the Legislature of this state." Section 90.501 does nothing to abolish any privilege established in Florida law by section 2.01. By the plain terms of section 2.01, the legislative privilege contained in the Bill of Rights of 1689 is in force under Florida law.

The majority is correct in acknowledging that the legislative privilege is inherent in the separation of powers under Florida's Constitution. But the majority errs in reducing the constitutional legislative privilege to a matter of unfettered judicial discretion. Like the presumption of constitutionality historically applied to redistricting plans passed by the Florida Legislature but effectively abrogated by this Court last year, what now remains of the legislative privilege in this context promises to be swiftly vanishing. There is an unmistakable signal in the majority's statements that the "thoughts or impressions of individual legislators and legislative staff members" are not discoverable *"at this stage of the litigation"* and that the circuit court "is *not constrained* by [the majority's] opinion from considering, as discovery proceeds, how a specific piece of information protected by the privilege fits into this balancing approach" adopted by the majority. Majority op. at 151 (emphasis added). To the extent that the improper motivations of individual legislators are a legal basis for determining that a constitutional violation by the Legislature has occurred—a point the majority assumes but does not establish—it is unclear what rationale exists for holding that the "thoughts and impressions" of individual legislators are protected from discovery. It would seem to be axiomatic that an individual's improper motivation will be reflected in that individual's "thoughts and impressions." Although the majority adopts the thoughts-and-impressions limitation "at this stage of the litigation," the majority certainly has not articulated a specific rationale for the limitation. Majority op. at 151. The tenuousness of the limitation is manifest; there is no reason to believe that the limitation will long survive.

The majority's balancing approach boils down to the exercise of unfettered judicial discretion: the legislative privilege inherent in the separation of powers will give way to the extent that an entirely subjective judicial determination requires that the privilege must give way. This is not the way that one branch of government should approach the acknowledged constitutional privilege of an equal and coordinate branch of government. When the judicial branch is called on to consider the scope of a privilege granted by the Constitution to another branch of government, it is incumbent upon the judicial branch to articulate clearly grounded, objective rules that can be applied without the suggestion that the coordinate branch's privilege is subject to diminishment or abrogation through the unfettered discretion of judges. At no time would it be more appropriate to pay heed to the maxim that "he is the best judge who leaves the least to his own discretion." In a context such as this—where the internal functioning of a coordinate branch of government is at issue — due respect for the separation of powers requires that judicial restraint be at its zenith. Unfortunately, the balancing approach adopted by the majority represents the nadir of judicial restraint.

Nothing in article III, section 20, justifies this evisceration of the constitutional legislative privilege. The majority's assertion that the constitutional legislative privilege is restricted by the desire of the voters for "more judicial scrutiny" is based purely on supposition. Majority op. at 148. The text of article III, section 20, provides directives to the Legislature regarding the redistricting process but says nothing about judicial scrutiny or the legislative privilege. Therefore, any impact of the adoption of this constitutional provision on the constitutional legislative privilege could arise only by implication. But the annulment or the fundamental alteration of an essential component of the constitutional separation of powers does not properly arise by implication....

The view adopted by the majority works a radical change in the relationship between the judicial branch and the legislative branch by thrusting judicial officers into the internal workings of the legislative process. Such a radical alteration in the operation of the separation of powers should not be accomplished absent the clear assent of the people of Florida. No such assent was manifested by the adoption of article III, section 20. Nothing in the text of the proposed amendment — much less the ballot summary — informed the voters that this alteration would be a consequence of the adoption of the amendment by the people. When the validity of the ballot summary was under consideration in this Court, the sponsor of the proposed amendment argued that the proposal "*changes no judicial functions whatsoever*" and has "*no effects on judicial functions.*" Amended Answer Brief of Sponsor at 7, 15 n. 2, *Advisory Op. to Atty. Gen. re Standards for Establishing Legislative District Boundaries (Legislative District Boundaries),* 2 So.3d 175 (Fla.2009) (emphasis added). The Court's plurality opinion approving the ballot summary concluded that the proposed amendment "*do[es] not alter the functions of the judiciary.*" *Legislative District Boundaries,* 2 So.3d at 183 (emphasis added). But now the Court has effectively accepted the petitioners' argument in this case that "[a]rticle III, section 20, *revised the balance of powers* in the redistricting context" and created a "*new arrangement*" requiring an aggressive judicial role. Petitioners' Initial Brief on the Merits at 19, *League of Women Voters of Fla. v. Fla. House of Representatives,* No. SC13-949, *review granted,* 122 So.3d 868 (Fla.2013) (table) (emphasis added). A revision of the "balance of powers" between the judicial and legislative branches should not be brought about by stealth.

* * *

POLSTON, C.J., concurs.

B. Executive Review

i. Article III, Section 8 —
Executive Approval and Veto

The line item veto provides authority to a Florida Governor that the President of the United States does not have. The veto process naturally produces tension between the branches, and the judiciary is asked to referee the conflicts. The rules of this game try to find a balance that does not grant too much power to the Governor while at the same time avoids legislative tricks that would hide certain appropriations from the Governor's veto pen.

Martinez v. Florida Legislature
542 So. 2d 358 (Fla. 1989)

McDONALD, Justice.

The First District Court of Appeal has certified the trial court's final judgment in this cause as involving issues of great public importance which require immediate resolution. We have jurisdiction pursuant to article V, section 3(b)(5) of the state constitution. At issue are Governor Martinez' vetoes of portions of specific appropriations. We find an improper exercise of the gubernatorial veto and affirm the trial court's rulings.

On June 8, 1988 the legislature adopted chapter 88-555, Laws of Florida, the general appropriations act of 1988. On June 29 Governor Martinez vetoed more than 150 specific line item appropriations contained in that act. He also vetoed five portions of specific appropriations. In September the legislature and five of its members,[5] in their official capacity and as citizens and taxpayers, petitioned this Court for a writ of mandamus to expunge the five partial vetoes. This Court granted Martinez' motion to dismiss in favor of a declaratory judgment action in circuit court.

The legislature then brought suit in circuit court to have the partial vetoes declared unconstitutional. As affirmative defenses, Martinez claimed: 1) the legislative intent documents (the statement of intent and legislative working papers), containing the five disputed items, constituted specific appropriations and had been incorporated by reference into the general appropriations bill by a letter from the chairs of the legislative appropriations committees;[6] 2) the suit failed to state a cause of action; and 3) the in-

---

5. [FN 1.] Jon L. Mills, Tom Gustafson, Samuel P. Bell, III, John W. Vogt, and Robert (Bob) Crawford.

6. [FN 2.] The text of the transmittal letter, signed by Samuel P. Bell, III, and James A. Scott, the respective appropriations committees' chairmen, reads as follows:

> Pursuant to the provisions of Section 216.181(1), Florida Statutes, we are jointly transmitting herewith the General Appropriations Act, Summary Statement of Intent, and detailed legislative intent in the form of computerized workpapers (D-3A's) for each department. These workpapers are provided through computer releases and reflect the Agency's Request, Governor's Recommendation and Legislative Appropriations. The summary document compares the Governor's Amended Budget Recommendations to the funds appro-

dividual legislators lacked standing to sue. Martinez also counterclaimed against the individual legislators for a declaration of the legal effect and significance of the legislative intent documents. Finally, Martinez cross-claimed against the secretary of state (Smith) and comptroller (Lewis) as to the significance of the intent documents and the constitutionality of the implementing and conforming acts (chapters 88-556 and 88-557, Laws of Florida) pertaining to the general appropriations act.

The legislature moved for final summary judgment, the individual legislators moved to dismiss the counterclaim, and Smith and Lewis moved to abate consideration of the cross-claim pending disposition of the main action. The court heard the legislature's motions for summary judgment and dismissal on December 22. A week later the court ruled in the legislature's favor and ordered Smith to expunge the five partial vetoes from the state records. The court also dismissed the counterclaim with prejudice and declared the cross-claim moot. Martinez appealed to the first district, which, upon the legislature's petition, certified the case to this Court.

Section 8(a) of article III, Florida Constitution, provides that "[t]he governor may veto any specific appropriation in a general appropriation bill, but may not veto any qualification or restriction without also vetoing the appropriation to which it relates." The basic requirements for a veto, therefore, are 1) a specific appropriation which is part of 2) an appropriations bill. We agree with the trial court and the legislature that the vetoes at issue do not meet those requirements.

The instant vetoes dealt with one appropriation to the Department of Agriculture and Consumer Services (number 118) and four appropriations to the Department of Education (numbers 528, 529, and 530). Each veto message begins the same: "The portion of Specific Appropriation," and each removes only part, not all, of an appropriation line in chapter 88-555. The first message vetoes $500,000 from the $7,400,000 appropriated in item 118....

---

priated for the 1988–89 Fiscal Year. Pursuant to Chapter 216, Florida Statutes, the Appropriations Act and the intent documents are to be considered the original approved budget for operational and fixed capital outlay expenditures for each state agency. Copies of the computerized workpapers have been provided to the Office of the Auditor General.

In addition to the General Appropriations Act and Summary Statement of Intent, [chapter 88–556, Laws of Florida], implementing and administering the General Appropriations Act, and [chapter 88-557, Laws of Florida], conforming statutes, should be used to interpret legislative intent.

Ch. 216, Fla.Stat. (Supp.1988), sets out the general state budget process. Under it state agencies submit budget requests to the legislature and to the Executive Office of the Governor by November 1 of each even-numbered year. §216.023. The executive office makes a detailed study of each agency and prepares an analysis of the legislative budget requests for the governor, §216.151, who, 45 days before the session begins in odd-numbered years, sends a recommended budget to the legislature. §216.162. After the legislature enacts the general appropriations bill, that bill, along with the statement of intent and working papers, is transmitted back to the governor and state agencies for implementation. §216.181(1). The general appropriations act and supporting documents are the agencies' original approved operating budgets. §216.181(3). Changes in appropriations may be approved by the executive office or by the administration commission. E.g., §§216.181(2), (8), (9), 216.292.

The vetoed items are not listed in chapter 88-555. Instead, they appear in the summary statement of intent and computerized working papers, the so-called intent documents. Martinez argues that the statement of intent is an element of the general appropriations bill and that the letter transmitting the intent documents expressly incorporated the working papers into that bill. Therefore, according to the governor, any item in the working papers or statement of intent is subject to being vetoed as if it were a specific line item in chapter 88-555. The legislature, on the other hand, argues that, because they appear in working documents not adopted by the legislature, the vetoed items are not specific, identifiable appropriations adopted by the legislature in the general appropriations bill and that these vetoes do not meet the constitutional requirements.

Both sides rely on *Brown v. Firestone*, 382 So.2d 654 (Fla.1980), in which this Court considered another challenge to the gubernatorial veto. Specifically, we had to decide if the veto could be exercised on provisos, contained within the appropriations bill and relating to specific appropriation lines, directing how portions of specific appropriations were to be spent. In *Brown* we defined a specific appropriation as "an identifiable, integrated fund which the legislature has allocated for a specific purpose." *Id.* at 668. If a qualification or restriction in an appropriations bill sets apart an identifiable sum of money, that fund will be considered to be a specific appropriation because "it will most likely be the smallest identifiable fund to which the qualification logically relates." *Id.* We held that "[i]f the legislature deems it wise to appropriate a specific fund in a qualification or restriction, then the governor will be able to veto that qualification as a specific appropriation, just as he could have done had the legislature listed the fund as a separate line item." *Id.*

Martinez argues that *Brown* allows him to trace back from the broad line item appropriations through the summary statement of intent to the smallest identifiable funds in the legislative working papers. The legislature points out, however, that *Brown* explores the limits of the legislature's power to enact general appropriation law and the gubernatorial veto power and recognizes that single appropriation items can "be either general or quite specific depending upon the degree of particularization employed by the legislature." *Id.* at 666. The vetoed items are unspecified parts of specific appropriations in chapter 88-555, and, therefore, the legislature contends that Martinez could veto the entire line items or nothing at all.

"[M]oney can be appropriated by the legislature only by means of a bill by it *enacted into law* with the formalities prescribed by the constitution for enacting bills into *laws*." *In re Advisory Opinion*, 43 Fla. 305, 309, 31 So. 348, 349 (1901) (emphasis in original). The heart of this matter is whether the statement of intent and the legislative working papers are part of the general appropriations bill enacted by the legislature. If they were not part of the general appropriations bill, the veto cannot reach them because the constitution permits the governor to veto only specific appropriations in a general appropriations bill.

The statement of intent comes from section 216.181(1), Florida Statutes (Supp.1988), which provides in part:

> The statement of intent may not allocate or appropriate any funds, or amend or correct any provision, in the General Appropriations Act, but may provide additional direction and explanation to the Executive Office of the Governor, the Administration Commission, and each affected state agency relative to the purpose, objectives, spending philosophy, and restrictions associated with any specific appropriation category. The statement of intent shall compare the request of the agency or the recommendation of the Governor to the funds appropriated for the purpose of establishing intent in the development of the approved operating budget.

Martinez argues that, regardless of what section 216.181(1) says, the statement of intent and working papers are, in reality, integral parts of the general appropriations act. The legislature, however, claims that the statute is unambiguous and, on its face, demonstrates the intent that the statement of intent and the working papers are not part of the appropriations bill.

We agree with the legislature. The statement of intent "may not allocate or appropriate any funds, or amend or correct any provision, in the General Appropriations Act." § 216.181(1). This language is unequivocal and unambiguous. The intent documents have not been enacted into law, they are not part of the general appropriations bill, and the gubernatorial veto cannot reach them.

This holding raises the question of what are the statement of intent and the working papers if they are not part of the appropriations act. Martinez claims that, if they are not part of that act, their provisions are directory, not mandatory, and cannot be binding. The legislature, on the other hand, argues that the effect and significance of the statement of intent and working papers can only be determined in a declaratory judgment action, brought by the governor, to resolve that issue.

Be that as it may, this issue needs to be resolved, and we have decided to consider it. We find the statement of intent and working papers to be what they appear to be, a manifestation of how the legislature thinks, in its considered opinion as a representative of the people, appropriations should be spent. Those documents have not been enacted into law, however, and, thus, cannot have the force of law. Unless a specific appropriation is in a general appropriations bill or a specific legislative act, it is unenforceable. "The governor's veto power is balanced against the legislature's power." *Thompson v. Graham,* 481 So.2d 1212, 1215 (Fla.1985). The legislature cannot give the force of law to something which it refuses to enact into law. Although the legislature's intent is evidenced by the statement of intent and the working papers, the provisions in those documents cannot be binding. They are not equivalent to proviso language contained in a general appropriations bill enacted by the legislature.

Because the statement of intent and the working papers are not part of the appropriations bill, items in them cannot be vetoed. We therefore affirm the trial court's ruling that the partial vetoes of line items 118, 528, 529, and 530 be expunged from the state records. We also hold that, although persuasive, the statement of intent and working papers are directory, not mandatory.

It is so ordered.

EHRLICH, C.J., and OVERTON, SHAW, BARKETT, GRIMES and KOGAN, JJ., concur.

Florida House of Representatives v. Martinez

555 So. 2d 839 (Fla. 1990)

KOGAN, Justice.

The Florida House of Representatives petitions for a writ of mandamus ordering the Florida Secretary of State to expunge from his official records gubernatorial vetoes directed at portions of the 1989 appropriations act, chapter 89-253, Laws of Florida (the "Act"). Petitioners also request that, in the same writ, we order the Florida Comptroller to make other adjustments to state financial records to reflect these expunctions. We have jurisdiction. Art. V, § 3(b)(8), Fla. Const.

I.

The sources of the present controversy are vetoes issued by Governor Bob Martinez that purport to nullify seven portions of the Act. Members of the House of Representatives challenge these vetoes as a violation of the Florida Constitution.

Veto number one was directed at the following language in the Act:

Specific Appropriation 5

5 Lump Sum

Salary Increases

From General Revenue Fund 76,411,208

From Educational Enhancement Fund 6,433,236

From Trust Funds. 21,632,810

. . . .

Funds are provided in Specific Appropriation 5 for adjustments to selected legal positions in the Florida Department of Legal Affairs, to be distributed at the discretion of the Attorney General. The effective date of any salary adjustments given in accordance with this provision shall be January 1, 1990. The Attorney General is authorized to exceed the maximum of the pay grade for up to eight Assistant Attorney General positions.

The Governor gave the following reason for his veto in his Veto Message:

Proviso language in Section 1.1.2.D.2), [sic] paragraph 3, on pages 293 and 294, providing for salary adjustments to selected positions in the Department of Legal Affairs, is hereby vetoed. The funds appropriated for this purpose in Appropriation 5 are $300,000 from the General Revenue Fund and $61,070 from Trust Funds. These increases are in addition to the 4% pay increases provided for all Selected Exempt Service employees. It is inappropriate and inequitable to provide certain employees with extra benefits.

Veto number two was directed at the following language in the Act:

Specific Appropriation 500

500 Specific Categories

Grants and aids—Dropout Prevention

From Educational Enhancement Trust................11,494,153

From the funds provided in Specific Appropriation 500:

....

19. $4,000,000 is for Florida First Start as described in CS/HB 1160 or similar legislation and $100,000 shall be allocated for the Toddler Intervention program (TIP) in Dade County.

The Governor's Veto Message contained the following relevant statement:

Proviso language following Appropriation 500 on page 84 appropriating $3,900,000 from the Educational Enhancement Trust Fund for Florida First Start is hereby vetoed. This appropriation creates the Florida First Start Program for handicapped and at-risk children from birth to age three. The specific program objectives and services to be provided are not educational, but are social services more properly delivered by the Department of Health and Rehabilitative Services. The projected cost to fully implement this program is in excess of $80 million. Before a new program of this magnitude is begun, an in-depth analysis of current programs at the local, state and federal levels should be conducted. Currently, the Department of Education is developing a comprehensive, coordinated system of early intervention services for handicapped and at-risk children aged 0 to 3 funded by a federal grant under PL99-457, Part H—Infants and Toddlers Program. First Start may duplicate and conflict with this effort.

Veto number three....

Veto number four....

Veto number five was directed at the following proviso language in the Act:

Upon termination of employees in the Senior Management Service, Selected Exempt Service, or positions with comparable benefits, payments for unused annual leave credits accrued on the member's last anniversary date shall be prorated at the rate of one-twelfth (1/12) of the last annual amount credited for each month, or portion thereof, worked subsequent to the member's last anniversary date.

The Governor's Veto Message contained the following relevant statement:

Proviso language in Section 1.1.5., paragraph 4, on page 296, authorizing funds to be used for purposes other than for the payment for unused annual leave credits for employees in the Senior Management Service and Selected Exempt Service, is hereby vetoed, and no funds provided in any agency budget, to the extent they are identified by this language, shall be utilized for such purposes. Limiting this benefit would not only impair the contract the State has with its present senior-level managers, but also would seriously undermine State government's ability to attract other high level senior managers.

Veto number six was directed at the following language in the Act:

Specific Appropriation 1539

1539 Lump Sum

    Senate

    From General Revenue Fund........................22,838,383

    ....

The Legislature may pay, from funds appropriated to the legislative branch, the reasonable costs that are incurred by members or employees of the legislature in excess of the level of benefits available under the state health plan for alcohol dependency treatment and rehabilitation programs.

The Governor's veto message contained the following relevant language:

Proviso language in the third paragraph following Appropriation 1539 on page 248 and $1 from the General Revenue Fund to allow members or employees of the legislative branch additional benefits for the treatment of alcohol dependency is hereby vetoed. This proviso language would permit unequal treatment of State employees and officials in regard to their health insurance since only members or employees of the legislative branch would be eligible for the additional benefits.

Veto number seven was directed at the following portion of the Act:

Specific Appropriation 1578

Other Personal Services

    From General Revenue Fund 3,113,503

    From Forfeited Property Trust Fund 333,444

    From Internal Improvement Trust Fund 970,752

Funds in Specific Appropriation 1578, include $455,000 from the General Revenue Fund for a feasibility and needs assessment study to be conducted by the Florida Resources and Environmental Analysis Center of Florida State University concerning the implementation of a statewide Geographic Information System. The study shall be completed and its results reported to the Speaker of the House of Representatives and to the President of the Senate no later than December 31, 1990. In addition, an interim report shall be provided to the Speaker and the President no later than March 15, 1990. The study shall include but not be limited to an assessment of short and long term implementation costs and objectives, impact and effects on local governments and appropriate state agencies, staffing and training requirements, technical specifications, and a timetable for implementation.

The Governor's Veto Message contained the following relevant statement:

> Appropriation 1578 and associated proviso language on pages 253 and 254 appropriating $3,113,503 from the General Revenue Fund for modernization of State land records and a feasibility and needs assessment study by Florida State University concerning the implementation of a statewide Geographic Information System is hereby vetoed. The Department of Natural Resources' Legislative Budget Request stated that the modernization project would be done in three phases at a total cost of $8.1 million. With the $959,600 appropriated for this project in Fiscal Year 1988–89, the Department contracted with Florida State University to conduct a needs assessment to determine the scope of the project, design the project, and complete a pilot demonstration project. The needs assessment, dated May 5, 1989, reveals that the total project is estimated to cost $32,315,000, and will take eleven years to complete. Before any further State funds are appropriated for this purpose, the Trustees of the Internal Improvement Trust Fund and the Legislature should thoroughly review the proposed scope and timing of the project to determine if it is in the best interest of the State. If it is determined that such a project is warranted, it should be funded from trust funds set aside for land management purposes, and competitively bid to allow participation from the private and public sector. The proviso language appropriates $455,000 for a feasibility and needs assessment study which is duplicative of the purpose of the Growth Management Date [sic] Network Coordinating Council created in section 282.043, Florida Statutes. The Council, composed of nine State agencies, is charged by statute with developing criteria, policies and procedures for the prescribed and preplanned transmission of growth management data among State and local agencies. In an October 1988 report adopted by the Governor and Cabinet, the Council specified procedures which are being implemented to develop a Statewide Geographic Information System.

II.

Initially, the Governor challenges the standing of petitioners to bring this action in their capacities as officers of the Florida House of Representatives. However, the Governor does not contend that petitioners lack standing to raise this question individually, in their capacities as taxpayers of the state. Unquestionably they do. *Brown v. Firestone,* 382 So.2d 654, 662 (Fla.1980). Accordingly, the present petition is properly before this Court.

III.

The substantive issues raised by the parties involve the interpretation of article III, section 8(a) of the Florida Constitution, which provides in pertinent part:

> The governor may veto any specific appropriation in a general appropriation bill, but may not veto any qualification or restriction without also vetoing the appropriation to which it relates.

In the past, we have attempted to delineate the scope of this constitutional restriction on the Governor's veto power. In *Brown*, for instance, we began with the following proposition:

> [T]he veto power is intended to be a negative power, the power to nullify, or at least suspend, legislative intent. *It is not designed to alter or amend legislative intent.*

382 So.2d at 664 (emphasis added). Elaborating on this point, we stated:

> If the legislature makes a specific appropriation, even if it be substantial, and if the legislature attaches a rationally and directly related qualification or restriction to that appropriation, then [the Constitution] requires the governor to make the hard choice whether to give up the appropriation entirely or to follow the legislative direction for its use.

Id. at 667. Thus, under the Florida Constitution, the veto power does not embrace authority to nullify a qualification or restriction *unless* the Governor simultaneously nullifies the related fund of money. Art. III, § 8(a), Fla. Const.

Perhaps the most difficult issue raised by the constitutional restriction, however, is the exact meaning of the term "specific appropriation." In attempting to resolve this question, we adopted the following rule in *Brown*:

> A specific appropriation is an identifiable, integrated fund which the legislature has allocated for a specified purpose.

Brown, 382 So.2d at 668. This rule, while simple in theory, has been somewhat more difficult to apply in actual practice. The present controversy shows that it now needs refinement.

As is obvious from a review of recent appropriations laws, the legislature frequently appropriates large sums of money under a vague or broad line-item category and then specifies in proviso language the precise way this money may be spent. The problem is to determine when this proviso language has identified a sum of money and its purpose with sufficient definiteness that the language has become a "specific appropriation" within the meaning of the constitution.

There is no problem when proviso language expressly breaks the line item into a definite unit intended for a stated purpose. Such a proviso for all practical purposes constitutes a specific appropriation, as we stated in *Brown*. This is a necessary conclusion. If we were to adopt a rule that forbade the Governor to veto such proviso language, then the legislature easily could construct a "veto-proof" appropriations act merely by hiding the actual appropriations inside a mass of proviso language appearing under a few vague line items. Such a result would violate the intent of the framers in adopting article III, § 8(a), and would seriously diminish the executive's powers.

At the other extreme, however, is proviso language that does not identify a sum of money at all, but merely specifies that some *unidentified* portion of the line item shall or may be used for particular purposes. Such proviso language lies at the very heart of the legislative power to appropriate funds, as representatives of the people, and to attach qualifications to the use of those funds. Permitting the Governor to veto language of this type would rob the legislature of its authority.

Both of these extremes must be avoided.

IV.

We have no doubt that vetoes one, five and six quoted earlier in this opinion are unconstitutional under the analysis we have just surveyed. The Governor conceded as much in oral argument.

Veto number one was directed at proviso language authorizing the Attorney General to exceed the maximum pay grade for eight specific employee positions. No sum of money is identified anywhere in the proviso itself or elsewhere in the Act. Nevertheless, the Governor unilaterally has assigned a value of $361,070 to this proviso and argues in his response that he thus has "sought to identify the funds attributable to that proviso as directed by this Court's decision in *Brown v. Firestone.*"

However, nothing in *Brown* authorizes the Governor to assign value to a proviso if the legislature itself has not done so. Investing the Governor with this power would permit him to fabricate an "integrated fund" out of virtually any proviso or portion of a proviso merely by supplying his own "estimate" of its monetary cost. This would intrude too greatly upon the legislative prerogative, no matter how accurate the Governor's monetary estimate might be. We thus conclude that, before the Governor may veto specific proviso language, that language *on its face* must create an identifiable integrated fund—an exact sum of money—that is allocated for a specific purpose. The proviso in veto number one does not meet this test, and the veto thus fails.

Similarly, veto number five was directed at a proviso establishing conditions under which certain workers will be paid for unused annual leave credits on termination. This proviso does not identify an exact sum of money, nor does the Governor attempt to disclose such a sum in his Veto Message. Accordingly, this veto fails under the analysis in *Brown.*

Veto number six was directed at a proviso creating special benefits for the treatment of alcohol dependency for members and employees of the legislature. The Governor's Veto Message vetoes the proviso "and $1 from the General Revenue Fund." Again, this appears to be an impermissible attempt, however unrealistic, to estimate the value of the proviso language. The Governor now concedes in his response that "he failed to veto the funds to which the proviso language relates." Indeed, he could not have done so, since the proviso itself specifies no such sum. Accordingly, this veto also fails.

V.

Veto number two involves proviso language creating an appropriation totaling $4,000,000, which was further divided into two separate units. The first of these units consisted of $100,000 expressly earmarked for the Toddler Intervention Program in

Dade County. The second consisted of the remainder of the appropriation—or $3,900,000—expressly earmarked for the Florida First Start Program. The Governor's Veto Message by its plain language sought to eliminate the latter but not the former.

We believe this is an acceptable exercise of the veto power. Although the figure $3,900,000 does not expressly appear in the Act, that sum nevertheless is unquestionably the amount appropriated for the Florida First Start program. The elements required by *Brown*—an integrated identifiable fund allocated for a specified purpose—clearly exist on the face of the Act. Accordingly, the Governor's veto of this $3,900,000 appropriation will be sustained.

VI.

The next group of vetoes—numbers three, four and seven—share a common characteristic. In each of these, the Governor did not veto the entire sum of money appropriated for a single stated purpose in the line item. Rather, he vetoed only those portions that had been appropriated from specific funding sources. In each instance, the Act provided an exact sum of money that would be taken from each of these funding sources. And in each instance, money derived from other funding sources was not vetoed, thus leaving the line item partially funded.

* * *

Similarly, veto number seven was directed in part at $3,113,503 taken from the General Revenue Fund to pay for Other Personnel Services for the Department of Natural Resources. However, two other funding sources for this line item remained intact. Although the Act itself does not provide any more precise purpose, the Governor's Veto Message stated that at least some of this money would be used to modernize state land records—a purpose to which he objected.

The Governor now argues that these vetoes must be sustained because they were directed at identifiable sums of money allocated for a specific purpose. Petitioners argue that this is not a proper interpretation of *Brown*.

We agree with petitioners. The Governor's veto powers must be interpreted in light of the policies underlying Florida's doctrine of separation of powers. *See* Art. II, § 3, Fla. Const. The constitution commands not merely that there must be three branches of government, but that "[n]o person belonging to one branch shall exercise any powers appertaining to either of the other branches unless expressly provided herein." *Id.* In light of this strong policy, we believe the veto power must be construed in such a way as to maintain the vigor of the legislative branch, and that the legislative power must be construed so as to preserve the viability of the executive. We must strike a balance.

It now is well settled that the veto power may be used only to nullify or suspend, not to reduce or modify an appropriation. *Brown.* What the Governor requests is little different than the power *to reduce.* In each of the line items at issue here, the legislature has identified only one purpose, which will be achieved with sums taken from several separate funding sources. The Governor argues essentially that we must consider each of these sources to be a "fund" subject to veto. We, however, believe that the existence of such a fund cannot be determined solely by reference to the fact that a specific sum is stated in the Act itself. There also must be consideration of the legislature's *purpose*.

While the definition of "specific appropriation" contained in *Brown* did not directly address the issue presented by vetoes three, four, and seven, the requirement of an "integrated fund" mandates the result we reach today. *See Brown.* In a practical sense, a fund is not "integrated" — it is not a "specific appropriation" — unless it consists of all those elements necessary to achieve the stated purpose. This is true even if those individual elements are precise sums of money taken from different funding sources. If the legislature's purpose is to expend a specific amount of money for a single stated purpose, then the Governor has no authority to reduce that amount by vetoing one of several funding sources. The Governor must veto all or none.

Any requirement less than this would seriously erode the legislature's power to decide the level of appropriations. Permitting the vetoing of individual funding sources comes too close to authorizing the Governor to reduce appropriations. We thus conclude that vetoes number three and four fail, and that veto number seven fails to the extent it attempts to eradicate the $3,113,503 funding source. Art. II, §3, Fla. Const.; Art. III, §8, Fla. Const.

VII.

Finally, veto number seven also was directed at a proviso specifying that $455,000 be used to study the need for a statewide Geographic Information System. Petitioners in their brief have conceded that the proviso setting aside $455,000 was subject to the line-item veto. However, they apparently argue that the entire veto must fail because of the impropriety in vetoing the $3,113,503 funding source, which we have analyzed above. The Governor on the other hand argues that the only issue before this Court is the propriety of vetoing the funding source itself.

We agree with the Governor. Read in its totality, the Veto Message indicates that veto number seven was directed at two distinct elements of the Act: the eradication of the $3,113,503 funding source and the $455,000 appropriated for a study of a Geographic Information System. The two are not so closely related as to be inseparable. We thus are inclined to treat veto number seven as two separate vetoes inartfully combined into one. On that basis and in light of petitioners' concession, we conclude that veto number seven is valid solely to the extent that it disapproved the $455,000 study.

VIII.

For the foregoing reasons, we grant in part and deny in part petitioners' request for a writ of mandamus. On the date this opinion becomes final, the Secretary of State shall expunge from the official records of the state those vetoes found to be improper in this opinion, and the Governor and Comptroller shall take all actions necessary to ensure that these expunctions are reflected in the financial operations of the state. Trusting that respondents will fully comply with the views expressed in this opinion, we withhold issuance of the writ.

It is so ordered.

EHRLICH, C.J., and OVERTON, SHAW and BARKETT, JJ., concur.

McDONALD, Justice, concurring in part and dissenting in part.

In this action members of the House of Representatives seek a writ of mandamus to compel the Secretary of State to expunge vetoes of the Governor from the official records of the state and to direct the Comptroller to take appropriate actions with such order. The petitioners contend that seven gubernatorial vetoes pertaining to the General Appropriations Act of 1984, Senate Bill 1500, are invalid. The Secretary of State and the Comptroller take no position of the claims; the Governor argues that the vetoes should be sustained, or, in the alternative, certain proviso language in the appropriation act should be stricken as unconstitutional.

Vetoes number one, five, and six can and should be reviewed together. These three vetoes clearly do not challenge "specific appropriations" as that term is used in article III, section 8 of the Florida Constitution. Article III, section 8 provides in pertinent part: "The governor may veto any specific appropriation in a general appropriation bill, but may not veto any qualification or restructuring without also vetoing the appropriation to which it relates." In *Brown v. Firestone*, 382 So.2d 654 (Fla.1980), we defined "specific appropriation" which is subject to veto as follows:

> In the context of a qualification or restriction, *a specific appropriation is the smallest identifiable fund* to which a qualification or restriction is or can be directly and logically related. In practical effect this means that in most cases *where a qualification or restriction includes the setting apart of an identifiable sum of money, that fund will be considered a specific appropriation*, since it will most likely be the smallest identifiable fund to which the qualification logically relates.

Id. at 668 (emphasis supplied). In *Martinez v. The Florida Legislature*, 542 So.2d 358 (Fla.1989), we again recited this definition and further stated:

> If a qualification or restriction in an appropriations bill sets apart an identifiable sum of money, that fund will be considered to be a specific appropriation because "it will most likely be the smallest identifiable fund to which the qualification logically relates." We held that "[i]f the legislature deems it wise to appropriate a specific fund in a qualification or restriction, then the governor will be able to veto that qualification as a specific appropriation, just as he could have done had the legislature listed the fund as a separate line item."

Id. at 360 (quoting *Brown*, 382 So.2d at 668).

The legislature's provisos referred to in the Governor's vetoes one, five, and six do not comport with this definition. They do not refer to an identifiable sum. The Governor's concerns over the constitutionality or wisdom of such provisions cannot be reached by the use of veto. *Brown.* The Governor's remedies are limited to vetoing the entire item to which such refers or seeking a declaration in the courts in reference thereto.

The appropriation which was the subject of veto number three designated $74,600 for expenses to be derived from infrastructure funds. In *Brown* we considered proviso language, while here we consider the effect of a directive that a specified amount of money come from a particular funding source to be spent for a specified purpose. An appropriation designating that X amount of dollars are appropriated for a designated purpose, but that Y dollars shall be derived from source Z, has the constitutional equivalency of saying that X number of dollars are appropriated, but, of that amount, Y number of dollars shall be spent in a designated manner. Each is a clearly defined fund and specifically referenced. Under *Brown* the sum of $74,600 was a specific line item separated from the other funds. Because it was a specific appropriation, the Governor could veto it.

Veto number four is similar. A segregated line item appropriation of $80,000, to be derived from a particular revenue source, was vetoed. This appropriation was clearly identified and subject to veto.

Veto number seven was more substantial in terms of dollars. The sum of $3,113,503 for Other Personnel Services was specifically appropriated. The Governor vetoed it and stated his reason. The fact that he did not veto the line items of $332,444 and $970,752 should not affect his veto of the line item of $3,113,503.

Veto number two is in a little different posture. The Governor's veto message on this item is somewhat confusing in that it is not clear whether the $4,000,000 appropriation was to be vetoed, or whether $3,900,000 of that amount was the subject of veto. Because the $4,000,000 contained a proviso that $100,000 would be used for a specific purpose, the petitioners contend that the Governor could veto the $4,000,000 or the $100,000, but not $3,900,000. Reading the veto message in its totality, I believe the clear intent of the Governor was to veto the entire $4,000,000. I also believe, however, that because the $100,000 proviso created a lesser identifiable sum, it would not be improper to veto the $3,900,000 of the $4,000,000 fund. My colleagues would give the benefit of doubt on whether the veto was for $4,000,000 or for $3,900,000 to the legislature and uphold the $3,900,000 veto only. I am content with this.

In summary, I would rule invalid the vetoes of items one, five, and six, but uphold the vetoes on items three, four, and seven. On veto number two, I would sustain the $4,000,000 veto except for $100,000 for the Toddler Intervention Program (TIP) in Dade County.

GRIMES, Justice, concurring in part, dissenting in part.

I agree that the governor could not legally exercise vetoes numbered one, five, and six for the reasons expressed in the majority opinion. If the governor believes that the appropriations to which these vetoes were directed are unconstitutional, his recourse lies in the filing of a suit for declaratory decree in circuit court. *Brown v. Firestone*, 382 So.2d 654 (Fla.1980). I also agree that the governor could legally exercise veto number two directed to $3,900,000 appropriated for the Florida First Start program.

The legality of vetoes number three, four, and seven essentially depends upon the definition of appropriation. In *Brown*, we said:

A specific appropriation is an identifiable, integrated fund which the legislature has allocated for a specified purpose.

382 So.2d at 668. The appropriations which were the subject of vetoes three, four, and seven meet this definition. The majority has mistakenly read into the definition a proviso that no other funds may be appropriated for the same purpose.

For example, no one could dispute the validity of veto number three if the appropriation from the State Infrastructure Fund of $74,000 stood alone as the appropriation for expenses of the Division of Motor Pool. The fact that monies are appropriated from other funds also to pay expenses of the Division of Motor Pool does not have the effect of causing the separate line item of $74,600 to be lumped into the other appropriations. The fallacy of the legislature's position on this point becomes particularly clear when it is noted that the total expenses of $2,673,934 appropriated for the Division of Motor Pool does not even appear in appropriation 749. Rather, the four funding sources from which the monies are appropriated are listed as separate line items.

The same rationale applies to vetoes four and seven. Accordingly, I would also uphold vetoes three, four, and seven.

Questions

1. Why did the Court find that the Governor's vetoes number 1 and 6 were unconstitutional?

2. Why was the Governor's veto number 5 held unconstitutional?

3. Why did the Court hold that veto number 2 was constitutional?

4. Why did veto numbers 3, 4 and 7 fail?

5. How did the Court rescue the Governor's veto of $455,000 for the study of a Geographic Information System, as part of veto number 7?

Thompson v. Graham

481 So. 2d 1212 (Fla. 1985)

McDONALD, Justice.

We have before us a petition for a writ of mandamus asking that we direct the secretary of state to expunge certain of the governor's vetoes from the state's official records. We have jurisdiction pursuant to article V, section 3(b)(8), Florida Constitution, and we decline to issue the writ.

The 1985 legislature enacted committee substitute for senate bill 848, a bill which amended chapters 235 and 203, Florida Statutes, and which authorized and provided funds for specific public education capital outlay (PECO) projects. In June 1985 the governor vetoed several of the specific appropriations in section 35 of CS/SB 848. Claiming that CS/SB 848 is not a general appropriations bill and, therefore, is not subject to the governor's line item veto provided for in article III, section 8(a) of the state constitution, the Florida House of Representatives filed this petition for writ of mandamus. The governor responded to the petition and also filed a motion to dismiss claiming that the house lacks both capacity to sue and standing to seek the requested relief. Thompson, speaker of the house, then joined the suit, petitioning as a citizen and taxpayer of the state.[7] We disagree with Thompson and hold that the appropriations contained in CS/SB 848 are subject to the line item veto.

1968 Constitution, in dealing with vetoes, provides:

> In all cases except general appropriations bills, the veto shall extend to the entire bill. The governor may veto any specific appropriation in a general appropriation bill, but may not veto any qualification or restriction without also vetoing the appropriation to which it relates.

Art. III, §8(a), Fla. Const. Article IV, section 18 of the predecessor 1885 Florida Constitution provided in part: "The Governor shall have power to disapprove of any item or items of any bills making appropriations of money embracing distinct items."

In *Brown v. Firestone*, 382 So.2d 654 (Fla.1980), we noted the concerns of the Constitutional Revision Commission about this Court's decision in *Green v. Rawls*, 122 So.2d 10 (Fla.1960), which seemingly construed article IV, section 18 to authorize the governor to veto an appended qualification in the use of an appropriated item without vetoing the appropriation itself. We concluded that "the principal motivation behind revision of article IV, section 18, was to prevent the governor from altering legislative intent by requiring him to veto both a qualification or restriction and the appropriation to which it relates. 382 So.2d at 668. It was "to prevent the creative exercise of the gubernatorial veto." *Id.* at 667. In *Brown* we made it clear that under the current veto provision the governor cannot do this. He must accept the appropriation with the qualification or must reject it all. We do not believe the 1968 change otherwise modified the governor's veto powers as it related to appropriations.

Chapter 216, Florida Statutes (1983), sets out the general state budget process. That chapter defines an appropriations act as

> the authorization of the Legislature, based upon legislative budgets..., for the expenditure of amounts of money by an agency and the legislative branch for stated purposes in the performance of the functions it is authorized by law to perform.

§216.011(1)(c), Fla.Stat. (1983). By statute the commissioner of education is directed to submit a budget covering PECO projects to the legislature, which budget request will include the amounts of needed appropriations. §235.41, Fla.Stat. (1983). Moreover, chapter 235 defines a capital project, for PECO purposes, as

---

7. [FN 2.] Because Thompson as a citizen and taxpayer of the state clearly has standing to bring this suit, *Brown v. Firestone*, 382 So.2d 654 (Fla.1980); *Department of Administration v. Horne*, 269 So.2d 659 (Fla.1972), we need not decide in this opinion the question of whether the house, or Thompson as speaker of the house, has capacity or standing to bring this action. Thus, we decide this case as though Thompson were the sole petitioner. We reserve the right, at our option, to deal with this issue by separate order.

"sums of money appropriated from the Public Education Capital Outlay and Debt Service Trust Fund to the state system of public education and other educational agencies as authorized by the legislature." § 235.011(2), Fla.Stat. (1983). Finally, an appropriation is defined as "a legal authorization to make expenditures for specific purposes within the amounts authorized in the appropriations act." § 216.011(1)(b), Fla.Stat. (1983).

In its title CS/SB 848 states that it is an act "authorizing and providing funding for specified public educational capital outlay projects." The definitions set out lead to the conclusion that, in the context of this PECO bill, "authorizing and providing funding" is simply another way of saying "appropriating" and in our opinion comes within the definition of a general appropriations bill as it relates to the governor's veto power.

Thompson, to support his contention that CS/SB 848 is not a general appropriations bill, cites *Bengzon v. Secretary of Justice*, 299 U.S. 410 (1937). In *Bengzon* the Governor-General of the Philippines used his line item veto to strike a single section, dealing with gratuities for justices of the peace, from a twelve-section act. The Court found the act not to be an appropriations bill on which the line item veto could be used. In so holding the Court defined both what an appropriations bill is and is not:

> The term "appropriation act" obviously would not include an act of general legislation; and a bill proposing such an act is not converted into an appropriation bill simply because it has engrafted upon it a section making an appropriation. An appropriation bill is one the primary and specific aim of which is to make appropriations of money from the public treasury.

Id. at 413. The Court then went on and stated: "To say otherwise would be to confuse an appropriation bill proposing sundry appropriations of money with a bill proposing sundry provisions of general law and carrying an appropriation as an incident." *Id.*

Seizing on the fact that only one of CS/SB 848's sections, covering twelve of the act's eighty pages, authorizes expenditure of funds, Thompson argues that any appropriations in the PECO bill are mere incidents to substantive legislation. Section 35 of CS/SB 848, however, contains eighty-six specific items and authorizes the expenditure of over a half billion dollars. We simply do not see how these appropriations are merely "incidental" and necessary solely to implement a substantive law as was the case in *Bengzon*. Each appropriated item is a distinct project and not dependent on any other; collectively, the allocated funds amount to a general appropriation for educational capital outlay. Except for the fact that each is an educational project item, there is no direct relationship between those items vetoed by the governor and those allowed to become law.

Article III, section 8(a) gives the governor the power to "veto any specific appropriation in a general appropriation bill." "An item of an appropriation bill obviously means an item which in itself is a specific appropriation of money, not some general provision of law which happens to be put into an appropriation bill." *Bengzon,* 299 U.S. at 414–15.

Thompson argues that holding CS/SB 848 subject to the line item veto will infringe upon the legislature's prerogative to write the laws and to establish funding priorities. We do not agree. The veto power, while it can be used to nullify or suspend legislative intent, cannot be used to alter or amend legislative intent. *Brown v. Firestone.* The governor may not reassign vetoed moneys to other uses; he can neither create projects nor require the legislature to do so. The funds vetoed in this appropriation remain unexpended rather than being used for a different purpose.

The governor's veto power is balanced against the legislature's power. To do as this petition requests would have a chilling effect on this balance of power. We hold that the governor had the power to exercise the line item veto as to CS/SB 848, and we decline to issue the requested writ.

It is so ordered.

BOYD, Chief Justice, concurring.

The issue before the Court is whether the gubernatorial item veto provided for by article III, section 8(a) of the Florida Constitution with regard to "general appropriation bills" is applicable to chapter 85-116, Laws of Florida. Article III, section 8(a) gives the Governor the authority to veto "any specific appropriation in a general appropriation bill." The Governor's position is that the several specific authorizations of capital projects set forth in section 35 of chapter 85-116 are specific appropriations in a general appropriation bill and are thus subject to the item veto. At the very least it cannot be said that it is clear the Governor has exceeded his authority in vetoing various specific provisions of chapter 85-116. I therefore concur in the Court's denial of the petition for a writ of mandamus.

Chapter 85-116 amends various parts of chapters 203, 235, and 236, Florida Statutes (1983), including those portions of chapter 235 comprising the Educational Facilities Act of 1981. Chapter 85-116 also contains legislative authorizations for the funding of certain capital projects by the Public Education Capital Outlay and Debt Service Trust Fund. It might be suggested that chapter 85-116 violates the constitutional restriction in article III, section 6, Florida Constitution, requiring that "[e]very law shall embrace but one subject and matter properly connected therewith." *See, e.g., Department of Education v. Lewis,* 416 So.2d 455 (Fla.1982); *Brown v. Firestone,* 382 So.2d 654 (Fla.1980). On the other hand, it can very reasonably be argued that everything in chapter 85-116 embraces the single subject of public educational facilities to be constructed in the State of Florida or matters "properly connected therewith." In any event, we need not decide the question of the law's compliance with article III, section 6 because that question is not before us.

The position of the House of Representatives and its Speaker is that the several specific authorizations of capital projects in the act are not appropriations in the constitutional sense, and that the fact that there are numerous such authorizations does not transform chapter 85-116 into a "general appropriation bill." In the House's view, the references to funding of specific projects in chapter 85-116 are "authorizations" within the meaning of article XII, section 9(a)(2), Florida Constitution, rather than appropriations. Pursuant to these authorizations, the House points out, the State Board of Education can disburse no more than the authorized amount on each of the authorized projects. The funding for the authorized projects is not derived from legislative appropriations for current expenses of the state but rather from bonds issued by the State Board of Education. The bonds are in turn retired by means of periodic payments from the Public Education Capital Outlay and Debt Service Trust Fund.

Article XII, section 9(a) establishes the capital outlay trust fund and designates a certain regular periodic revenue source, the gross receipts tax, for deposit into the fund. Article XII, section 9(a)(2) provides in part that "no bonds, except refunding bonds, shall be issued, and no proceeds shall be expended for the cost of any capital project, unless such project has been authorized by the legislature." It is in pursuance of this provision that the legislature must provide authorization for capital projects to be financed by the capital outlay trust fund and that is what the legislature did in chapter 85-116. After the legislature has given its approval to such projects, the State Board of Education and the Commissioner of Education proceed to arrange for their funding as provided by the substantive provisions of the Florida School Code. *See* §§ 235.41, 235.42, 235.4235, 235.435, Fla.Stat. (1983). Thus the House concludes that the items the Governor vetoed were authorizations of projects to be financed through constitutionally sanctioned bonded indebtedness and not direct appropriations for expenditures on current government expenses.

Regardless of whether the money for the capital projects is to come from the expenditure of current revenues or from bond proceeds to be repaid by future revenues, it seems clear that the "authorizations" in section 35 of chapter 85-116 are appropriations of state taxpayers' money to the state budget for the purpose of meeting the current expenses of the state. The gross receipts tax provided by chapter 203, Florida Statutes (1983), and placed in the capital outlay trust fund pursuant to article XII, section 9(a) of the constitution, is imposed upon suppliers of certain kinds of utility services but is passed on to the general consuming public. Expenditures financed by bonds to be repaid by the trust fund are no less the resources of Florida's taxpayers than current revenues raised by the general sales tax. I can see no reason to distinguish these two kinds of expenditures for purposes of the veto power. Thus I conclude that such authorizations are "specific appropriations" within the meaning of article III, section 8. As for the question of whether they are "specific appropriations in a general appropriation bill," it is important to note that nothing in the Constitution or laws of Florida requires the legislature to adopt "appropriations for salaries of public officers and other current expenses of the state," art. III, § 12, Fla.Const., in a single general appropriations bill. The fact that chapter 85-116 authorizes expenditure of state funds on over eighty separate projects for a total of approximately $500,000,000 in the current fiscal year is enough to make it a general appropriations bill for purposes of article III, section 8.

For the foregoing reasons I concur in the Court's judgment upholding the Governor's vetoes and denying the petition for writ of mandamus.

SHAW, Justice, concurring specially.

The legislative act at issue, a committee substitute for Senate Bill 848 enacted by both houses, can be summarized as follows: Sections 1–27 contain substantial substantive amendments to chapter 235, Florida Statutes, entitled Educational Facilities Act; sections 28–32 amend various provisions of chapter 203, Florida Statutes, entitled Gross Receipts Tax; section 33 contains a severability clause; section 34 amends section 236.25, Florida Statutes (Supp.1984), entitled District School Tax; section 35 appropriates over a half billion dollars for certain educational purposes during fiscal year 1985–86 and specifies various sums of money from this appropriation to be spent for selected purposes; section 36 makes section 216.301(3)(a), Florida Statutes, applicable to chapter 84-542, Laws of Florida; section 37 appropriates $77,604,498 pursuant to section 216.301(2)(a), Florida Statutes; sections 38–41 pertain to special authorizations for selected educational institutions; and section 42 provides for an effective date of not later than 1 July 1985.

As in *Brown v. Firestone*, 382 So.2d 654 (Fla.1980), we are called on to "define and delineate the relationship between the gubernatorial veto power and the legislature's authority to enact general appropriations law." *Id.* at 663. The Governor has exercised a line item veto of certain specific appropriations in section 34 of the act, purportedly under the authority of article III, section 8(a) of the Florida Constitution. Petitioner challenges these vetoes on the ground that this act is not a general appropriations act and, thus, the Governor does not have the power to veto specific appropriations. It is the position of petitioner that the Governor may only veto or approve the act in its entirety. I write separately because, in my view, neither the majority nor the dissenters have fully analyzed the various constitutional provisions bearing on this controversy. For the reasons below, regardless of whether the act is treated as a general act or an appropriations act, I conclude that it contains more than one subject and thus violates either section 6 or section 12 of article III of the Florida Constitution.

In *Brown v. Firestone*, the Governor vetoed, inter alia, two provisos relating to specific appropriations in the General Appropriations Act of 1979, but not the specific appropriations themselves. It was the Governor's position that these provisions unconstitutionally violated article III, section 12 by attempting either to enact law on other subjects in an appropriations bill or to repeal or suspend existing law in an appropriations bill. It was the position of the petitioners in *Brown* that the Governor violated the provisions of article III, section 8(a), by vetoing the provisos without vetoing the specific appropriations to which they related. Because of the peculiar posture of the controversy in *Brown*, we recognized that we were in a quandary: if we looked first to the legislative provisos and found them unconstitutional, the propriety of the Governor's vetoes would be immaterial; if we looked first at the propriety of the Governor's vetoes and held them to be constitutional, the validity of the provisos would be immaterial. Our resolution of this quandary was "to consider the validity of both the vetoes and the legislative provisos to which they relate" in the hope "that our efforts will serve to illuminate and clarify the intrinsic elements of this complex problem." *Brown v. Firestone* at 663. In my view, we are faced with a similar dilemma here: if the act unconstitutionally contains more than one subject, the propriety of the Governor's vetoes are immaterial; if we restrict ourselves to the constitutionality of the vetoes, the validity of the act is not at issue. It is my view, however, that as in *Brown v. Firestone,* we should address both of these issues.

[Discussion of Section 6 omitted.]

On the issue of the Governor's line item veto power, I find that "general appropriation bills" as used in section 8(a) is indistinguishable from "[l]aws making appropriations for salaries of public officers and other current expenses of the state" as used in section 12. I agree with respondent that the Governor's line item veto power is not affected by the number of general appropriations bills which the legislature, in its discretion, may choose to pass and send to the Governor for review. Whether there be one or many general appropriations bills, the Governor may veto specific appropriations subject to the constraints of *Brown v. Firestone.*

In summary, as discussed above, I would affirm the Governor's veto power....

ADKINS, Justice, dissenting.

I dissent. Article IV, section 18, Florida Constitution (1885) provided:

> The Governor shall have power to disapprove of *any item or items of any bills making appropriations* of money embracing distinct items, and the part or parts of the bill approved shall be the law, and the item or items of appropriation disapproved shall be void, unless repassed according to the rules and limitations prescribed for the passage of other bills over the Executive veto. (Emphasis supplied.)

The Constitution was revised in 1968. Article III, section 8, Florida Constitution (1968) authorizing executive veto, contains the following:

> In all cases except general appropriation bills, the veto shall extend to the entire bill. The governor may veto any specific appropriation in a *general* appropriation bill, but may not veto any qualification or restriction without also vetoing the appropriation to which it relates. (Emphasis supplied.)

The majority sees no change in these provisions. Common sense dictates a different construction. As stated by Talbot "Sandy" D'Alemberte in his Commentary about Article III, section 8, 25A Florida Statutes Annotated 674:

> The scope of the executive veto power over appropriations was apparently broader under Section 18, Article IV of the 1885 Constitution. There, he was given "power to disapprove of any item or items of any bills making appropriations of money embracing distinct items ..." "Any bills" is certainly broader than the phrase "general appropriation bills."

The majority opinion refuses to recognize the common acceptance and definition of "General Appropriation." This gives an unfortunate result.

We have said:

> Provisions in a General Appropriations Bill on any subject other than "appropriations for salaries of public officers and other current expenses of the State" and matters reasonably related thereto are invalid and are not law.

In re Opinion to the Governor, 239 So.2d 1 (Fla.1970).

CS/SB 848 deals with subjects other than appropriations. The majority opinion construes this law as a "general appropriations law," but fails to explain the effect of Article III, section 12, Florida Constitution, which reads:

> Laws making appropriations for salaries of public officers and other current expenses of the state shall contain provisions on no other subject.

It is fundamental that the legislature can exercise any power not prohibited by the Constitution, while the governor can exercise only those powers granted by the Constitution. The majority opinion qualifies this rule, so that the governor may now exercise such powers as may be granted by the Constitution or the Supreme Court.

EHRLICH, Justice, dissenting.

With all deference to my brethren of the majority, I do not believe they have made a proper analysis of the provisions of our state constitution which control the outcome of this case. Nowhere in the majority opinion is there a discussion of what is a "general appropriation bill." Seemingly, the Court is saying that an appropriation bill is an appropriation bill and that all appropriation bills are the same and that hence the governor's line item veto is applicable to any appropriation bill. I do not believe this is the case.

Article III, section 8(b) gives the governor the authority to "veto any specific appropriation in a general appropriation bill." In all other cases, the governor's veto extends to the entire bill. The issue before us is whether CS/SB 848 is "a general appropriation bill" within the meaning of article III, section 8(a). Unfortunately, the Constitution does not supply us with a clear definition of that term.

Article III, section 12 provides "Laws making appropriations for salaries of public officers and other current expenses of the state shall contain provisions on no other subject." This Court had occasion to construe that identical language which was contained in article III, section 30, of the 1885 constitution in the case of *Amos v. Moseley,* 74 Fla. 555, 77 So. 619 (1917):

> This provision of the Constitution must be considered in its entirety, and, when so construed, it becomes apparent that *it refers to what is known as the general appropriation bill.* No more apt words than "salaries of public officers and other current expenses of the state" could be used to describe the law in which such appropriations are made at each legislative session.

Id. at 570, 77 So. at 623 (emphasis supplied).

I accept this Court's early definition that the general appropriation bill is one that makes appropriations for salaries of public officers and other current expenses of the state. CS/SB 848 is clearly not a general appropriation bill. It is indeed an appropriation bill because it does appropriate money for Florida's educational system, but does not provide for salaries of public officers and other current expenses.

Narrowly construing what constitutes a "general appropriation bill" for purposes of article III, sections 8(b) and 12, correctly balances the competing public policies at issue here. The sections are designed to prevent the legislature from logrolling when its power to do so is strongest, i.e. when appropriations for salaries and current expenses are made. Without the limitation on legislative drafting in section 12, the legislature would be able to impose all but the most objectionable measures upon the people of this state, effectively denying them the protection of the gubernatorial veto. Without gubernatorial power to line-item veto general appropriation bills pursuant to section 8(b), the legislature would likewise be able to authorize all but the most objectionable expenditures. In both cases, the governor would have the draconian choice of paralyzing the day-to-day operations of the entire state government by vetoing the entire bill, or abrogating his constitutional duty to serve as a check to unfettered legislative power.

When an appropriations bill is not a general appropriation bill, i.e. when it is not one appropriating salaries and current expenses, the threat of unfettered legislative power is lessened. Such appropriations bills concern matters other than day-to-day operations of all or a substantial part of state government. The choice imposed on the governor and the necessity for deviating from the normal system of checks and balances are less compelling. The single-subject provision of article III, section 6, guarantees that appropriation bills other than general appropriation bills, regardless of whether they contain matter other than appropriations, will be of limited scope, and thus a veto will have only limited impact.

If one were to construe the term "general appropriation bill" as broadly as the majority does here, then there is little to distinguish, on policy grounds, between allowing the governor to line-item veto any appropriation, and denying him the power to veto only sections of non-appropriation bills. Partial veto of bills is denied because allowing the governor to do so would give him the power in effect to rewrite legislation to his own liking. This would disrupt the balance of power in favor of the executive. I conclude the power to line-item veto appropriations in this case is such a disruption clearly not intended by the framers. This is especially clear in light of the narrow interpretation of "general appropriation bill" found in *Amos* and the cases cited therein, an interpretation the framers of the 1968 constitution presumably understood and were free to alter, had they so desired.

It is my opinion, therefore, that the veto proscription contained in article III, section 8(b) is applicable to the vetoes in question.

I therefore dissent.

ADKINS, J., concurs.

Questions

1. When is an act of legislation an appropriations bill?

2. What guideline does the Court try to articulate in helping the Legislature and executive determine when a bill is an appropriation bill?

3. What did the petitioner argue?

4. What facts caused the Court to reject petitioner's argument?

5. What issue does Justice Shaw address in his concurrence?

6. According to Justice Ehrlich:

a. What is a general appropriation bill?

b. Why should "appropriation bills" be narrowly defined?

c. What is the flaw in the majority's definition of a general appropriation bill?

d. What should be the outcome of this case?

Florida Society of Ophthalmology v. Florida Optometric Association

489 So. 2d 1118 (Fla. 1986)

BARKETT, Justice.

This cause is before us pursuant to jurisdiction granted in article V, section 3(b)(4), Florida Constitution. The First District Court of Appeal certified this case as presenting a question of great public importance. *Florida Optometric Association v. Firestone,* 465 So.2d 1319 (Fla. 1st DCA 1985). The principal question presented is whether the Florida Constitution affords the governor seven or fifteen days to veto a bill presented to him after the legislature has adjourned sine die. *[indefinitely]*

In May of 1983, the Florida House and Senate passed SB 168 which provides, *inter alia,* that certain optometrists may administer, use, and prescribe medicinal drugs. The House and Senate adjourned sine die the 1983 regular session on June 13, 1983. On June 14, 1983, the Legislature presented SB 168 to the governor. Fifteen days later, on June 29, 1983, the governor vetoed the bill. The Senate took no action on the bill subsequent to the gubernatorial veto.

The Florida Optometric Association, respondents herein, petitioned the trial court for a writ of mandamus ordering the Florida Secretary of State to publish SB 168 as a law of the state. The association claimed that the governor's veto of the bill was untimely and therefore ineffectual. The circuit court dismissed the association's petition with prejudice. On appeal, the First District Court reversed the order of dismissal, remanded the cause to the circuit court with directions that the writ be issued, and certified to this Court the following question as being of great public importance:

Whether Article III, section 8(a), Florida Constitution, allows the governor seven or fifteen consecutive days to act on a bill presented to him after the legislature adjourns sine die, and, if he is allowed only seven days thereafter, should the effect of an opinion so holding have only prospective application?

Article III, section 8(a) provides, in part:

Every bill passed by the legislature shall be presented to the governor for his approval and shall become a law if he approves and signs it, or fails to veto it within seven consecutive days after presentation. If during that period or on the seventh day the legislature adjourns sine die or takes a recess of more than thirty days, he shall have fifteen consecutive days from the date of presentation to act on the bill.

Any inquiry into the proper interpretation of a constitutional provision must begin with an examination of that provision's explicit language. If that language is clear, unambiguous, and addresses the matter in issue, then it must be enforced as written. *See, e.g. Plante v. Florida Commission on Ethics,* 354 So.2d 87, 89 (Fla. 1st DCA 1977).

The provision in question, however, does not explicitly address the situation before us in which a bill is presented to the governor after the legislature has adjourned sine die. We recognize the rule that constitutional language must be allowed to "speak for itself." Application of that rule, however, must be tempered by judicial deference to offsetting and equally constraining rules. We refer to two fundamental principles of constitutional adjudication. First, constitutions "receive a broader and more liberal construction than statutes." *State Highway Commission v. Spainhower,* 504 S.W.2d 121, 125 (Mo.1973). Second, constitutional provisions should not be construed so as to defeat their underlying objectives. *Plante v. Smathers,* 372 So.2d 933, 936 (Fla.1979); *State ex rel. Dade County v. Dickinson,* 230 So.2d 130, 135 (Fla.1969).

Constitutions are "living documents," not easily amended, which demand greater flexibility in interpretation than that required by legislatively enacted statutes. Consequently, courts are far less circumscribed in construing language in the area of constitutional interpretation than in the realm of statutory construction. *See Malnak v. Yogi,* 592 F.2d 197, 204 (3d Cir.1979). When adjudicating constitutional issues, the principles, rather than the direct operation or literal meaning of the words used, measure the purpose and scope of a provision. . .

An essential purpose of veto provisions such as that found in article III, section 8(a) is to safeguard the executive's opportunity to consider all bills presented to him. *See Edwards v. United States,* 286 U.S. 482, 486 (1932). Typically, a plethora of bills is passed and then presented to the executive at the end of a legislative session. The article III, section 8(a) grant of additional time to veto such bills is designed to afford the governor ample opportunity to review this last-minute legislative onslaught.

It is evident from the record that in a typical session of the Florida legislature some 60 percent of all bills passed during the session are presented to the governor just before or immediately after adjournment, with the bulk submitted after adjournment. The record further discloses that, in every year from 1979 to 1983, the omnibus general appropriations bill was presented to the executive post-adjournment. The governor's need for additional time to review legislation is, therefore, the most pronounced in regard to those bills presented after adjournment.

In order to give full effect to the constitutional objective that the governor be afforded additional opportunity to review legislation when his time constraints are the most severe, article III, section 8(a) must be read as allotting the governor fifteen days to veto those bills presented to him after adjournment sine die. The provision's design would be thwarted were the governor allowed only seven days to review what is generally the majority of the bills presented, and allowed fifteen days to review what is, in most years, a smaller number of bills presented during the last week of the session.

The Supreme Court, in *Wright v. United States,* 302 U.S. 583 (1938), was called upon to construe the executive's veto power narrowly. The Court refused and stated that it would not adopt any construction which would frustrate the veto provision's cardinal objective that the executive be afforded suitable opportunity to review those bills presented to him. *Id.* at 596. We find ourselves facing a similar request, and we respond with a like answer. We will not construe article III, section 8(a) in a manner that defeats its underlying constitutional objective. Rather, we interpret the provision as affording the governor fifteen days (from presentment) to veto those bills submitted after the legislature has adjourned sine die.

Our holding is supported not only by the maxims of constitutional construction discussed above, but by others as well. If a constitutional provision is silent on a given issue, or if its literal language clashes irreconcilably with its obvious purpose, then courts may resort to consideration of historical evidence concerning the intent of those who drafted and adopted that provision. The various historical materials in the record relevant to the drafting of article III, section 8(a) leave no doubt but that the drafters never intended that the governor be limited to seven days to review bills presented after adjournment sine die.

Additionally, our holding is supported by that rule of constitutional interpretation which provides that the construction traditionally given to a provision by those officers affected thereby is presumably correct. In *Amos v. Moseley,* 74 Fla. 555, 77 So. 619, 625 (1917), we noted that

> where there has been a practical construction, which has been acquiesced in for a considerable period, considerations in favor of adhering to this construction sometimes present themselves to the courts with a plausibility and force which it is not easy to resist. Indeed, where a particular construction has been generally accepted as correct, and especially when this has occurred contemporaneously with the adoption of the Constitution ... it is not to be denied that a strong presumption exists that the construction rightly interprets the intention. And where this has been given by officers in the discharge of their official duty ... the argument ab inconvenienti is sometimes allowed to have very great weight.

We recently restated this principle more emphatically when we held that such established constructions of constitutional provisions are "presumptively correct unless manifestly erroneous." *State v. Kaufman,* 430 So.2d 904, 907 (Fla.1983). *See also Vinales v. State,* 394 So.2d 993, 994 (Fla.1981); *Brown v. Firestone,* 382 So.2d 654, 671 (Fla.1980). The record discloses unequivocally that both the governor and the legislature have consistently construed article III, section 8(a) as affording the executive fifteen days to veto bills presented to him after adjournment sine die. Indeed, this Court, in an advisory opinion, computed the days available for veto of a bill presented after adjournment as fifteen and not seven. *In re Advisory Opinion to the Governor,* 374 So.2d 959 (Fla.1979).

Accordingly, we hold that the governor's June 29, 1983 veto of SB 168 was a timely, effective exercise of the gubernatorial veto power under article III, section 8(a) of the Florida Constitution, and quash the decision of the district court below.

It is so ordered.

EHRLICH, Justice, specially concurring.

I concur with the decision of the Court, and while I do not fault the reasoning of the opinion, my analysis differs but reaches the same result.

I quite agree with the majority that "the various historical materials in the record relevant to the drafting of article III, section 8(a) leave no doubt that the drafters never intended that the governor be limited to seven days to review bills presented after adjournment sine die." I also agree that the record discloses unequivocally that both the governors and the legislatures since the adoption of the 1968 Constitution "have consistently construed article III, section 8(a) as affording the executive fifteen days to veto bills presented to him after adjournment sine die." It is also quite clear that the only changes from the 1885 provision that the drafters sought to make related to the time the governor had within which to veto and when that time began to run.

Article III, section 8(a) of the 1968 Constitution was assimilated from article III, section 28 and article IV, section 18 of the 1885 Constitution. Article III, section 28 provided that the governor had five days, exclusive of Sunday, after presentment within which to veto a bill passed by the legislature, and that if the legislature, by its final adjournment, prevented such action, the governor had twenty days after adjournment within which to veto the bill. Article III, section 28 was silent as to the number of days the governor had to act on a bill presented to him after adjournment.

We can take judicial notice that under the 1885 Constitution, bills were presented to the governor after adjournment and vetoed at a point in time in excess of five days after adjournment. I can find no reported case where any such veto was challenged in the appellate courts of Florida on the ground that the governor only had five days after adjournment within which to exercise his veto power. It was obviously accepted by both the legislatures and the governors who served under the 1885 Constitution that the five day veto provision of article III, section 28 was not applicable to bills presented to the governor after adjournment, and that the governor had twenty days after adjournment to exercise his veto power as to such bills.

The Florida Constitutional Revision Commission, which included within its membership two justices and one retired justice of this Court, recommended no substantive change in article III, section 28 of the 1885 Constitution. I can find no draft which contains a proposal that expressly provides a post-adjournment period for gubernatorial veto of a bill. All drafts have the format of article III, section 28 of the 1885 Constitution which is carried over into article III, section 8 of the 1968 Constitution, namely, a stated period of time within which the governor must act, but that if within such period the legislature adjourns, or recesses, then the governor has a longer period of time within which to veto.

The revised Constitution as proposed by the Constitutional Revision Commission was put in its final form by the drafting and style committee of the Commission composed of circuit court judge Hugh Taylor, Chairman, district court of appeal judge, Thomas H. Barkdull, Jr., and Senator John E. Mathews, Jr. Article III, section 8(a) as proposed to the legislature by the Constitutional Revision Commission provided in pertinent part:

> Every bill passed by the legislature shall be presented to the governor for his approval and shall become a law if he approves and signs it, or fails to veto it within seven days after presentation. If during that period the legislature adjourns sine die or takes a recess of more than thirty days, he shall have twenty days from the date of adjournment or recess to act on the bill.

This proposal was amended by the legislature to its present form, with the following time changes: It increased the period for the governor's consideration from five to seven consecutive days, and provided that if during such period, or on the seventh day, the legislature adjourns sine die or takes a recess of more than thirty days, the time within which the governor is required to act is reduced from twenty days to fifteen consecutive days. Such time was to run from the date of presentation rather than from the date of adjournment or recess.

At the time the 1968 Constitution was presented to the electors of Florida for their consideration, it was explained in an official publication of the Florida Legislature that the new article III, section 8(a) was a redraft of and a combination of article III, section 28 and article IV, section 18 of the 1885 Constitution. The explanation and analysis in relevant part was:

EXECUTIVE APPROVAL AND VETO.

> Section 8. Redrafts and combines the provisions of Section 28, Article III and Section 18, Article IV of the present Constitution. *Permits veto during session within seven consecutive days after presentation,* instead of the present "five days (Sunday excepted)." *Fifteen day period, from date of presentation, for Governor to act on bills is authorized when the Legislature recesses for more than thirty (30) days, or upon sine die adjournment. Present provisions allow the Governor twenty days (20) after adjournment.* (emphasis supplied)

Article III, section 8(a) makes no specific mention of the number of days the governor has to act on a bill if presented to him after the legislature has adjourned. There are really three periods of time encompassed within section 8(a), the first 53 days, the last 7 days of the session where the Legislature either adjourns sine die or takes a recess of more than 30 days, and post-adjournment. We know from the record that post-adjournment presentation of bills is a very critical period with respect to executive approval and vet

The first sentence of article III, section 8(a) provides that the governor has seven days after presentation within which to veto a bill. That sentence is silent on whether the legislature has to be in session or can be in adjournment to be applicable. However, the second sentence of section 8(a) gives meaning to the first sentence, and provides that if within the seven day period after presentation to the governor, the legislature adjourns sine die or takes a recess for more than 30 days, the governor has fifteen consecutive days from the date of presentation to act on the bill. Since the second sentence addresses the last seven days of the session and treats the veto period differently than it is treated in the first sentence, the latter has to refer to the period when the legislature is in session, exclusive of the last seven days. The second sentence relates to all other periods, the last seven days expressly, and by implication post-adjournment. This analysis is consistent with and supported by the analysis made by the Legislative Reference Bureau cited above.

Article III, section 28 of the 1885 Constitution was likewise silent as to the number of days the governor had to act on a bill presented to him after the legislature has adjourned. The second sentence of that section provided that the governor had five days, Sunday excepted, within which to veto a bill. That sentence is also silent on whether the legislature had to be in session to be applicable. Here again, the third sentence gives meaning to the second sentence and provided that if the legislature, by its final adjournment, prevented such action, the governor had twenty days after adjournment within which to veto. Since the third sentence, in effect addresses the last five days of the session and treats the veto period differently than it is treated in the second sentence, the latter also has to refer to the period when the legislature is in session, exclusive of the last five days. . . . The third sentence relates to all other periods, the last five days expressly, and likewise by implication post-adjournment.

The district court of appeal's analysis of article III, section 8(a) admittedly has superficial credibility and charm. According to the district court of appeal, under article III, section 8(a) the governor has seven days to veto, but there are two exceptions which, if they occur during the seven day period after presentation, operate to extend such period: 1) the legislature's adjourning sine die, and 2) the legislature's recessing more than 30 days. According to that analysis if either of these events occurs, the governor has an additional eight days or a total of fifteen consecutive days from the date of presentment, to exercise his veto. In the case at bar neither of the two exceptions took place and therefore, since the bill was presented to the governor after adjournment, he had only seven days to veto.

If we apply the district court of appeal's analysis to article III, section 28 of the 1885 Constitution, we come up with the same result. The governor would have had five days to veto instead of twenty days.

Applying the district court of appeal's analysis to the current constitutional provision leads to absolutely absurd results. For example, if the bill is presented to the governor on the 59th day of the session, he has fifteen days after presentment to veto it, but if presented to him one day after adjournment, he has only seven days to veto it. In the hypothetical, a difference of two days in presentment, means a reduction of eight days within which the governor can exercise his veto power. I cannot believe that the distinguished constitutional lawyers and jurists who recommended the change, and the legislature which approved the change for submission to the people of Florida in a general election, intended such counterproductive results. The record clearly indicates otherwise.

On the basis of the foregoing, I am of the opinion that the governor's veto in question was timely.

BOYD, Chief Justice, dissenting.

The result that the majority reaches is reasonable and logical. It could well be suggested that the majority's reasoning and conclusion should have been provided for in the Constitution. It can well be argued that such reasoning and result should be incorporated into the Florida Constitution by amendment. The only problem with the Court's conclusion is that as presently written, the plain and unambiguous language of the constitution dictates a different result. Thus there is no room for constitutional interpretation or construction, nor for policy arguments of any kind.

The constitutional language set forth [in article III section 8(a)] clearly provides that the bill "shall become a law" if the governor "fails to veto it within seven consecutive days after presentation." There are two, and only two, exceptions to the seven-day time limit. These are: (1) when, during the seven consecutive days following presentation, the legislature adjourns *sine die;* and (2) when, during the seven consecutive days following presentation, the legislature takes a recess of more than thirty days. If neither of the two exceptions occurs with regard to a given bill, then the bill in question "shall become a law if" the governor "fails to veto it within seven consecutive days after presentation."

Did either of the two exceptional situations occur here to activate the increased time allowed after presentation for exercise of the gubernatorial veto power? The answer, as clearly shown by the record, is no. Therefore the period in which the governor had the power to veto the bill expired at the end of the seventh consecutive day following the presentation of the bill to the governor.

The power of the judiciary to interpret or construe the constitution depends on the existence of some uncertainty or ambiguity in the constitutional language. *City of St. Petersburg v. Briley, Wild & Associates, Inc.,* 239 So.2d 817 (Fla.1970). In the absence of any such ambiguity, courts have only the authority to apply the plain language and to enter judgments as thus mandated.[8] If the governor should have fifteen days to consider a bill presented him after the legislature has adjourned, a proposal for amendment of the constitution to so provide should be presented to the people for electoral adoption.

---

8. [FN *] Petitioners seek to create an ambiguity by arguing that the framers did not contemplate the situation where bills are presented after adjournment. However, respondents more convincingly point out that the framers did contemplate presentation after adjournment, as is evident in article III, section 7, which provides for signature of bills by legislative presiding officers "during the session or as soon as practicable after … adjournment sine die."

For the foregoing reasons I respectfully dissent and would approve the decision of the district court of appeal, with one qualification. While I would hold that the respondents, who timely challenged the veto that affected them, are entitled to have the veto of 1983 Senate Bill 168 declared void and the bill declared to be a law, I would otherwise give the holding prospective effect only. Governors serving since 1968 have acted under the erroneous belief that they had fifteen days to veto bills presented after adjournment. The possibility of application of a contrary holding to long-past vetoes would create uncertainty and confusion in the law.

ADKINS, J., concurs.

C. Relationship with Local Governments

State constitutions must define local government authority and the relationship of local governments to the state. Local governments are a pillar of democratic governance and, indeed, performing the day-to-day tasks of government that most citizens can see and provide access to local officials that is more difficult and less personal on the state and national level. There is a tension between the Legislature and local governments.

Special laws are a means for the Legislature to enact policies that affect localities in distinct and different ways. There are valid reasons for many of these special or local laws. For example, following the local law process, a local bill may establish an airport authority to manage and run an airport. However, certain local bills are prohibited for logical reasons. Different criminal laws in different counties would be a disaster. The list of prohibited special laws in Article III, Section 11 exists for a reason. The Legislature abused the process and engaged in all sorts of intervention in local policies that would be inappropriate in a modern society. For example, a local bill would be passed to preserve the clarity of a stream in a particular district while general laws that would provide similar protection statewide were defeated.[9]

i. Article III, Section 10 — Special Laws

St. Johns River Water Management District v. Deseret Ranches of Florida, Inc.

421 So. 2d 1067 (Fla. 1982)

[A separate aspect of this case is treated in the chapter on Article VII.]

ALDERMAN, Chief Justice.

St. Johns appeals the decision of the District Court of Appeal, Fifth District, holding chapter 77-382, Laws of Florida, which created the Greater St. Johns River

---

9. Mary E. Adkins, Making Modern Florida: How the Spirit of Reform Shaped a New State Constitution (Gainesville: University Press of Florida 2016), 17.

Basin, unconstitutional as a local law enacted without the notice required by article III, section 10, Florida Constitution.... We hold that chapter 77-382 is a constitutional, properly enacted general law and reverse that portion of the Fifth District's opinion holding to the contrary....

In 1979, Deseret Ranches of Florida, a landowner in Orange, Osceola, and Brevard Counties, filed suit for declaratory relief on behalf of all persons against whom ad valorem taxes and permit application fees were assessed in those counties by the St. Johns River Water Management District. Deseret contended that the Greater St. Johns River Basin, created by chapter 77-382, Laws of Florida,[10] was unconstitutionally established ...

The district court granted certiorari and held that because chapter 77-382 does not operate uniformly throughout the state but rather applies only to those inhabitants and property owners in the District who are not within the Oklawaha Basin, it is a local law enacted in violation of article III, section 10, Florida Constitution, which requires that notice of intention to seek enactment of a special law be published in the manner provided by general law....

Upon consideration of petitions for rehearing and clarification, the Fifth District decided that its holding as to the unconstitutionality of chapter 77-382 should operate prospectively, thereby entitling the Basin to receive ad valorem taxes accruing on January 1, 1981. 406 So.2d at 1142–43.

We initially address the issue of whether chapter 77-382 is unconstitutional on the basis that it was enacted without the notice required by article III, section 10, which provides:

> Special laws.—No special law shall be passed unless notice of intention to seek enactment thereof has been published in the manner provided by general law. Such notice shall not be necessary when the law, except the provision for referendum, is conditioned to become effective only upon approval by vote of the electors of the area affected.

In order to determine whether this notice was necessary, we must decide whether chapter 77-382 is a special law within the contemplation of article III, section 10. In

---

10. [FN 1.] Chapter 77-382, Laws of Florida, provides in pertinent part:
Section 1. Subsection (8) of section 373.0693, Florida Statutes, 1976 Supplement, is amended to read:
373.0693 Basins; basin boards.—
....

    (a) On July 1, 1977, the entire area of the St. Johns River Water Management District, less those areas in the Oklawaha Basin, shall be formed into a subdistrict or basin of the St. Johns River Water Management District. Such area shall be designated as the Greater St. Johns River Basin.

    (b) The governing board of the St. Johns River Water Management District shall also serve as the governing board of the Greater St. Johns River Basin.

view of the nature and history of this enactment, we hold that it is a general law rather than a special law. Chapter 77-382 was enacted as an amendment to chapter 373, Florida Statutes, and we must construe it in conjunction with that chapter. Recognizing that the waters in the state are among Florida's basic resources, the Florida Legislature, through chapter 373, "The Florida Water Resources Act," provided a comprehensive statewide plan for the conservation, protection, management, and control of state waters. § 373.016. This statutory plan, created by general law (chapter 72-299, Laws of Florida), provides that the state be divided into five water management districts and that lands within each district be further divided into subdistricts or basins. §§ 373.069 and 373.0693. The present districts and basins, with the exception of the Greater St. Johns River Basin, were created pursuant to chapter 76-243, Laws of Florida, which is a general law. Although the Greater St. Johns River Basin was the only basin created in 1977, there is no reasonable basis for characterizing its enacting legislation any differently than the legislation creating the other basins. Although enacted in different years and applicable to different geographical areas of the state, both laws became integral parts of Florida's comprehensive water management plan affecting people statewide.

Although there is no definition of general or local law in the constitution, in our early case of *State ex rel. Gray v. Stoutamire*, 131 Fla. 698, 179 So. 730, 733 (1938), we defined the terms "special or local laws" as used in the constitution and said that they "refer ordinarily to law relating to entities, interests, rights, and functions other than those of the State, since the organic law does not contemplate or require previous publication of notice of proposed laws for the exercise of State powers and functions though they may be more or less local or special in their operation or objects." (Emphasis supplied.) In the present case, the statewide water management plan created and implemented by chapter 373 is primarily a state function serving the state's interest in protecting and managing a vital natural resource. In fact, the Fifth District in the present case took notice of the interrelationships of various areas of the state and found that water management districts further the state functions of water resource conservation, control, planning, and development. 406 So.2d at 1140.

We have repeatedly held that a law does not have to be universal in application to be a general law if it materially affects the people of the state. *Cantwell v. St. Petersburg Port Authority*, 155 Fla. 651, 21 So.2d 139, 140 (1945). *See also Cesary v. Second National Bank of North Miami*, 369 So.2d 917 (Fla.1979). For example, in *State v. Florida State Turnpike Authority*, 80 So.2d 337 (Fla.1955), the State, in contesting a bond validation, contended that the law authorizing the turnpike and establishing the Authority was a local or special law because the legislature directed that the "partpike" be presently built through only a small part of the state and the improvements would affect only the counties located between Broward and St. Lucie. In rejecting this contention, we stated:

> The Turnpike Authority is a State agency charged with creating a highway that is bound, it seems to us, to affect traffic statewide. As a main artery to

facilitate the flow of travel northward and southward not only by residents but by those who make up one of the principal industries of the State, the tourist industry, not to mention the many businesses incident to the use of the motor vehicle, whether by resident or visitor, the entire State, will be affected. It is our opinion that such a turnpike may no more logically be said to be local than the aorta may be said to perform a local function independent of other blood vessels of the human body.

We think our opinion in *Cantwell v. St. Petersburg Port Authority,* 155 Fla. 651, 21 So.2d 139, is much more relevant. The Railroad Commission had been authorized to grant franchises for the construction of bridges, ferries, and so on, over bays and inlets connected with the Gulf of Mexico.

The Act was attacked on the ground that it was a local law attempted to be enacted without regard for the constitutional requirements. The court observed that although many counties in the State were not adjacent to the Gulf, many of them were, and that the Gulf affected the people of the counties it did not touch. The court remarked: "It may therefore be said to affect directly or indirectly every citizen of the state."

80 So.2d at 343–44. Because of the statewide impact of the Water Resources Act and because of the contribution made by each and every water management district and basin to the overall water management plan, we hold that chapter 77-382 is a general law properly enacted by the Florida Legislature.

* * *

It is so ordered.

ADKINS, BOYD, OVERTON and McDONALD, JJ., concur.

ii. Article III, Section 11 — Prohibited Special Laws

Cesary v. Second National Bank of North Miami

369 So. 2d 917 (Fla. 1979)

ALDERMAN, Justice.

This cause is before us for consideration of the following questions certified to us by the United States Court of Appeals for the Fifth Circuit pursuant to rule 4.61, Florida Appellate Rules:

1. Does Section 656.17(1), which sets the allowable interest rate for Morris Plan banks and industrial savings banks, violate Article III, Section 11(a)(9), Florida Constitution?

2. Do the special provisions of existing statutory law referred to in Section 687.031, which creates statutory exceptions to the general law of Florida governing interest and usury, violate Article III, Section 11(a)(9), as being special laws fixing interest rates on private contracts?

We answer both questions negatively and hold that neither section 656.17(1)[11] nor section 687.031,[12] Florida Statutes (1975), violates article III, Section 11(a)(9), Florida Constitution.

Ann Cesary brought a suit against The Second National Bank of North Miami in her own behalf and on behalf of those individuals who have borrowed less than $500,000 from the Bank who have paid interest thereon within a period of two years last past the date of filing this action where interest has been charged in excess of ten percent per annum. Cesary borrowed $8,800.44 from the Bank, evidenced by a promissory note dated March 29, 1972, which on its face provides for an interest rate of eleven percent per annum. Under the provisions of 12 U.S.C. s 85 (1945), the Bank was entitled to receive interest at the maximum rate allowed by Florida law. Cesary contended that under the Florida usury statute, the note was usurious on its face. The Bank defended the action on the basis of section 687.031, Florida Statutes, which allows the charging of interest in excess of ten percent for loans arising under one or more statutory exceptions outlined elsewhere in the Florida Statutes. The Bank argued that its loan fits into the exception provided in section 656.17(1) for industrial savings banks and Morris Plan banks, and that since the exception permits a 14.3 annual percentage rate, the eleven percent rate charged Cesary was not usurious. Cesary did not contest that the loans fall into the exception created by sections 656.17(1) and 687.031. Rather, she contended that these two statutory provisions are special laws prohibited by article III, section 11(a)(9), Florida Constitution, which provides:

---

11. [FN 1.] Section 656.17(1) provides:
LOANS; SECURITY REQUIRED, INTEREST AND CHARGES. The right to lend money upon the security of comakers, personal chattels, or other property and to take, receive, reserve, and charge for such loans or discounts made or upon any notes, bills of exchange, or other evidences of debt, a discount not to exceed 8 percent per annum upon the total amount of the loan from the date thereof until the maturity of the final installment, notwithstanding that the principal amount of such loan is required to be repaid in installments, plus an additional charge not to exceed 2 percent of the principal amount of any loan, which additional charge shall be for investigating the character of the individual applying for the loan, the security submitted and all other costs in connection with the making of such loans, all which charges and discounts may be collected at the time the loan is made. No other charge of any kind or nature whatsoever, by whatsoever purpose or name designated, shall be made; provided, however, that when a loan is of such character as to necessitate the filing or recording of a legal instrument, an additional charge may be made for such filing or recording, providing such charge is actually paid to the proper public officials; also borrower may be required to pay abstract costs, reasonable attorney's fees, documentary stamp taxes, other taxes, premiums on insurance, and other similar charges, if the bank deems the same necessary for the protection and security of said loan.
12. [FN 2] Section 687.031 provides:
Construction, ss. 687.02 and 687.03. Sections 687.02 and 687.03 shall not be construed to repeal, modify or limit any or either of the special provisions of existing statutory law creating exceptions to the general law governing interest and usury and specifying the interest rates and charges which may be made pursuant to such exceptions, including but not limited to those exceptions which relate to banks, Morris Plan banks, discount consumer financing, small loan companies and domestic building and loan associations.

(a) There shall be no special law or general law of local application pertaining to:

(9) creation, enforcement, extension or impairment of liens based on private contracts, or fixing of interest rates on private contracts....

Holding these two statutes constitutional, the United States District Court for the Southern District of Florida entered summary judgment for the Bank. That court said:

The statutory exceptions to the Florida interest and usury law noted in Florida Statute s 687.031 are not special laws in the prohibited constitutional sense in that they have uniform operation throughout the State of Florida. A special law is one designed to operate on particular persons or things or one that operates upon classified persons or things, when classification is not permissible or the classification adopted is illegal. A general law is one relating to subjects or persons based upon proper distinctions and differences that adhere in or are peculiar or appropriate to such subject or persons. Laws based upon proper classifications may be general laws even though limited to a part of the people. Wide discretion is granted to the legislature in resorting to classification. The burden of showing that the classification provided for does not rest upon any reasonable basis, but is essentially arbitrary, is the burden of the party attacking the classification in the statute. *Anderson v. Board of Public Instruction*, (102 Fla. 695,) 136 So. 334, *State ex rel. Landis v. Harris*, (120 Fla. 555,) 163 So. 237. Uniformity of operation of a statute as required by the Florida Constitution does not require universality of operation, *Lykes Bros. v. Bigby*, 155 Fla. 580, (21 So.2d 37,) but rather reasonable classification as to subject matter. *Cates v. Heffernan*, (154 Fla. 422,) 18 So.2d 11.

This Court is not able on the basis of its judicial knowledge to determine that the grounds justifying the particular classifications and distinctions created by the Florida legislature for the exceptions to the general law governing interest and usury are unreasonable, and there is no substantial basis for holding Florida Statute 687.031 and the exceptions noted therein unconstitutional.

No. 75-654 (S.D.Fla. Order Determining Constitutionality, Oct. 22, 1975).

Cesary appealed to the United States Circuit Court, Fifth Circuit, which in turn has certified to us the questions regarding the constitutionality of these statutes.

Cesary argues that the exceptions to the Florida usury statute are special laws in violation of article III, section 11(a)(9), because they benefit special groups, the lenders who operate under the exception, and that, therefore, the loan obtained by her from the Bank was usurious. She states that the purpose of the usury law is to protect the borrower from unconscionable lenders and the validity of the classification created by the challenged statutes should be tested in light of this purpose. Analyzing the amount of interest which may be charged by various lenders including small loan companies, credit unions, industrial savings, and savings associations under the general statutory scheme, she submits that the amount of interest permitted to be charged for the same amount of loan depends upon who the lender is and not upon the character of the borrower, the amount of loan, or security pledged. She contends that this statutory scheme has as its purpose the benefit of certain lenders and not the protection of the borrower and that these exceptions are simply special laws. She asserts that the legislature can classify by the type of borrower, type of loan, or amount of loan but cannot constitutionally classify according to the type of lender.

In response, The Second National Bank argues that these statutory exceptions are not special laws in the prohibited constitutional sense since they operate uniformly throughout the State of Florida. It contends that this state has for years permitted banks and other regulated lenders to charge interest on smaller loans at rates greater than ten percent per annum. Relying on the following definition of special law: "A statute which relates to persons or things as a class is a general law, while a statute which relates to particular persons or things of a class is special," it contends that the laws in question are general laws. Reciting that this Court has long recognized the authority of the legislature to create different classifications of lenders, rates, and limits in regulating usury, it states that the legislature has reasonably classified regulated lenders and that Cesary has failed to carry her burden of proof to show otherwise. It maintains that different types of credit transactions involve different types of risks and different costs, that small loans involve greater risk and cost than commercial loans to an established business, that revolving charge accounts of credit card plans involve more risk than a loan of $20,000 to a bank's regular customer. It submits that the subject legislation is a valid and constitutional balancing of the need for reasonable, convenient credit, the need to protect the borrower, costs of credit arrangements, the risk of nonpayment, the nature of the lender's business, and the extent of existing government regulation.

We concur with the rationale of the trial court and agree with Second National Bank that the classifications created by the legislature through enactment of sections 687.031 and 656.17(1) are reasonable and that these laws are general laws which operate uniformly throughout the state upon these classifications.

Although there is no definition of general or special law in the constitution,[13] this Court in *Bloxham v. Florida Central & Peninsular Railroad*, 35 Fla. 625, 732-33, 17 So. 902, 924–25 (1895), explained what is meant by special law as used in the context of article III, section 11, as follows:

> A statute which relates to persons or things as a class is a general law, while a statute which relates to particular persons or things of a class is special, and comes within the constitutional prohibition." It might be that the railroad of the complainant is the only property affected by the act. Such a state of affairs would not make it a special law. Speaking upon a similar contention, this court has also quoted with approval, in the case of *Ex parte Wells, supra,*

---

13. [FN 3.] Article X, section 12(g), Florida Constitution, merely provides: " 'Special law' means a special or local law."

from the supreme court of New Jersey, the following language: "A law so framed (i.e. general in its terms) is not a special or local law, but a general law, without regard to the consideration that within the state there happens to be but one individual of the class, or one place where it produces effects." It has also been said, as applied to statutes, that the word "general," as distinguished from "special," means all of a class, instead of part of a class. 23 Am. & Eng.Enc.Law, p. 148, and authorities cited. In the case of *McAunich v. Railroad Co.*, 20 Iowa 338, it is said, speaking of statutes of this character: "These laws are general and uniform, not because they operate upon every person in the state, for they do not, but because every person who is brought within the relations and circumstances provided for is affected by the law. They are general and uniform in their operation upon all persons in the like situation, and the fact of their being general and uniform is not affected by the number of persons within the scope of their operation.

The uniformity of operation throughout the state required by this constitutional provision does not mean universality of operation over the state. Reasonable classification as to subject matter is permitted. *Cates v. Heffernan*, 154 Fla. 422, 18 So.2d 11 (1944). Justice Terrell in *Cantwell v. St. Petersburg Port Authority*, 155 Fla. 651, 653, 21 So.2d 139, 140 (1945), explained:

A law does not have to be universal in application to be a general law. Laws relating to the location of the capital of the state, the state university, the state prison farm, the hospital for the insane and other state institutions are local in character but general in application and are regarded as general laws. The act under consideration is easily within this class.

"Classification" is the grouping of things because they agree with one another in certain particulars and differ from other things in those same particulars. *Anderson v. Board of Public Instruction*, 102 Fla. 695, 136 So. 334 (1931). This Court has ofttimes recognized the wide discretion of the legislature in formulating classifications when establishing regulations for the public welfare but has also acknowledged that statutory classifications must be reasonable and must be based upon some difference bearing a reasonable and just relationship to the subject matter regulated. *Carter v. Norman*, 38 So.2d 30 (Fla.1948); *State ex rel. White v. Foley*, 132 Fla. 595, 182 So. 195 (1938). A statute which relates to subjects, persons, or things as a class, based upon proper differences which are inherent in or peculiar to the class is, a general law. *State ex rel. Gray v. Stoutamire*, 131 Fla. 698, 179 So. 730 (1938).

The determination of the maximum amount of interest which may be charged for the use of money loaned is within the police power of the state, and the details of the legislation and exceptions to be made rest within discretion of the state legislature. *Griffith v. Connecticut*, 218 U.S. 563 (1910). When dealing with usury questions and classifications established by the legislature relating thereto, the legislature has a great deal of discretion, and its classifications will not be disturbed unless clearly unconstitutional. *Edwards v. State*, 62 Fla. 40, 56 So. 401 (1911). The legislature enacted the usury laws to remedy an existing evil, and it has the authority to classify regulatory enactments with reference to degrees of evil. *Beasley v. Cahoon*, 109 Fla. 106, 147 So. 288 (1933).

A party who challenges the classification of a statute has the burden of proving that the classification therein does not rest upon any reasonable basis and is therefore arbitrary. *Anderson v. Board of Public Instruction, supra.* Cesary failed to show that the grounds justifying the particular classifications created by the legislature for exceptions to the general law governing interest and usury are unreasonable.

The classifications of lenders created by sections 687.031 and 656.17(1) have a basis in real differences of conditions affecting the subject matter regulated. In establishing these classifications, the legislature considered the need for convenient, reasonable credit for as broad a group of borrowers as possible; the need to protect necessitous borrowers from overreaching "loanshark" type lenders; the costs of different credit arrangements, including substantial bookkeeping and computer costs involved in smaller loans; the risk of nonpayment; the nature of the lender's business and the degree of existing government regulation of that business; and the nature and needs of the borrower. For each classification of lender, the legislature has established a particularized regulatory procedure relating not only to the allowable interest rates but also to the type of security which may be taken, the length of terms over which repayment can be made, the charges and costs which may be assessed, and the penalties to be imposed if any of the regulatory provisions are violated.

Accordingly, we answer the certified questions in the negative. Neither section 656.17(1) nor section 687.031 violates article III, section 11(a)(9), Florida Constitution.

ENGLAND, C.J., and ADKINS, BOYD, OVERTON, SUNDBERG and HATCHETT, JJ., concur.

Questions

1. a. What is a special law?

    b. What is a special law under Section 11?

2. Does Section 11 only prohibit "special laws"?

3. According to Appellant, how did §656.13 & §687.031 violate Section 11?

4. What is the two-prong test used by the Court to assess the statutes' constitutionality?

5. What is the procedural posture of this case?

D. Apportionment

i. Article III, Section 16 — Apportionment

Apportionment is a mandatory task in every state. Redistricting of congressional seats and reapportionment of state legislatures are among the most contentious debates in legislatures. In fact, in some states, apportionment is now done by independent commissions or other entities in order to avoid the partisan and personal fights that apportionment brings.

As we have seen in the introduction to this book, Florida has its own history of being one of the most malapportioned states up through the 1960s. Only upon the direction of the U.S. Supreme Court in the aftermath of cases like *Baker v. Carr*, 369 U.S. 186 (1962), *Reynolds v. Sims*, 377 U.S. 533 (1965), and Florida's own *Swann v. Adams*, 385 U.S. 440 (1967), was Florida compelled to conform to the constitutional principle of one person, one vote.

Under the 1968 Constitution, Florida included certain specific criteria which the Legislature needed to follow when reapportioning legislative seats. However, in 2010, a citizens' initiative called "Fair Districts" added additional criteria, including one mandating that new districts neither favor nor disfavor incumbents. As the following cases show, courts and the Legislature have since wrestled with how to implement these criteria.

In re Senate Joint Resolution of Legislative Apportionment 1176

83 So. 3d 597 (Fla. 2012)

PARIENTE, J.

With the goal of reforming this state's legislative apportionment process, in 2010, the Florida voters approved an amendment to the Florida Constitution establishing stringent new standards for the once-in-a-decade apportionment of legislative districts. These express new standards imposed by the voters clearly act as a restraint on the Legislature in drawing apportionment plans. After the Legislature draws the apportionment plans, this Court is required by the Florida Constitution to review those plans to ensure their compliance with the constitution. In this review, we are obligated to interpret and apply these standards in a manner that gives full effect to the will of the voters. In order to do so, our review necessarily becomes more extensive than in decades past.

For the reasons set forth in this opinion, we declare the plan apportioning districts for the Florida House of Representatives to be constitutionally valid under the Florida Constitution. We declare the plan apportioning the districts for the Florida Senate to be constitutionally invalid under the Florida Constitution. The Legislature is now tasked by the Florida Constitution with adopting a new joint resolution of apportionment "conforming to the judgment of the supreme court" as set forth in article III, section 16(d).

I. INTRODUCTION

The once-in-a-decade process of redistricting follows the United States Census Bureau's release of new census data. Article III, section 16, of the Florida Constitution expressly entrusts the Legislature with the obligation to redraw this state's legislative districts and expressly entrusts this Court with the mandatory obligation to review the Legislature's decennial apportionment plans. The Florida House of Representatives and the Florida Senate must adopt a joint resolution apportioning the legislative districts in accordance with federal and state constitutional requirements. *Id.* After the Legislature adopts a joint resolution of apportionment, the Florida Constitution requires the Attorney General to petition this Court for a declaratory judgment to determine the validity of the Legislature's apportionment plans as enacted. Art. III, § 16(c), Fla. Const. Within thirty days of receiving the Attorney General's petition, and after permitting adversary interests to present their views, the Court has a mandatory obligation under the Florida Constitution to render a declaratory judgment determining the validity of the Legislature's apportionment plans. *Id.*

Before 2010, this Court held that Florida's constitutional requirements guiding the Legislature during the apportionment process were "not more stringent than the requirements under the United States Constitution." *In re Constitutionality of House Joint Resolution 1987 (In re Apportionment Law—2002)*, 817 So.2d 819, 824 (Fla.2002). Under this construction of the Florida Constitution, we reviewed legislative apportionment plans to determine whether those plans complied with (1) the general provisions of the United States Constitution, which set forth the one-person, one-vote standard under the Equal Protection Clause, and (2) the specific provisions of the state constitution, article III, section 16(a), requiring districts to be "consecutively numbered" and to consist of "contiguous, overlapping or identical territory."

On November 2, 2010, the voters approved Amendment 5 (Fair Districts Amendment) for inclusion in the Florida Constitution, greatly expanding the standards that govern legislative apportionment. When approving the Fair Districts Amendment for placement on the 2010 ballot, this Court explained that the "overall goal" of the Amendment was twofold: "[T]o require the Legislature to redistrict in a manner that prohibits favoritism or discrimination, while respecting geographic considerations" and "to require legislative districts to follow existing community lines so that districts are logically drawn, and bizarrely shaped districts ... are avoided." *Advisory Op. to Atty. Gen. re Standards for Establishing Legislative Dist. Boundaries,* 2 So.3d 175, 181, 187–88 (Fla.2009) (plurality opinion). After its passage, the Fair Districts Amendment was codified as article III, section 21, of the Florida Constitution.

With the advent of the Fair Districts Amendment, the Florida Constitution now imposes more stringent requirements as to apportionment than the United States Constitution and prior versions of the state constitution. The new standards enumerated in article III, section 21, are set forth in two tiers, each of which contains three requirements. The first tier, contained in section 21(a), lists the following requirements: (1) no apportionment plan or district shall be drawn with the intent to favor or disfavor a political party or an incumbent; (2) districts shall not be drawn with the intent or result of denying or abridging the equal opportunity of racial or language minorities to participate in the political process or to diminish their ability to elect representatives of their choice; and (3) districts shall consist of contiguous territory. The second tier, located in section 21(b), lists three additional requirements, the compliance with which is subordinate to those listed in the first tier of section 21 and to federal law in the event of a conflict: (1) districts shall be as nearly equal in population as is practicable; (2) districts shall be compact; and (3) where feasible, districts shall utilize existing political and geographical boundaries. *See* art. III, §21(b), Fla. Const. The order in which the constitution lists the standards in tiers one and two is "not [to] be read to establish any priority of one standard over the other within that [tier]." Art. III, §21(c), Fla. Const.

These express new standards imposed by the voters clearly act as a restraint on legislative discretion in drawing apportionment plans. In this original declaratory judgment proceeding, we must define these new standards for the first time since the passage of the Fair Districts Amendment. Although this Court's role is unquestionably circumscribed by the extremely short time frame set forth in article III, section 16(c), of the Florida Constitution, such a limitation cannot deter the Court from its extremely weighty responsibility entrusted to us by the citizens of this state through the Florida Constitution to interpret the constitutional standards and to apply those standards to the legislative apportionment plans.

When interpreting constitutional provisions, this Court endeavors to ascertain the will of the people in passing the amendment. We follow the approach that has been consistently undertaken when interpreting constitutional provisions:

> The fundamental object to be sought in construing a constitutional provision is to ascertain the intent of the framers and the provision must be construed or interpreted in such manner as to fulfill the intent of the people, never to defeat it. Such a provision must never be construed in such manner as to make it possible for the will of the people to be frustrated or denied.

Pleus v. Crist, 14 So.3d 941, 944–45 (Fla.2009); *Zingale v. Powell,* 885 So.2d 277, 282 (Fla.2004) (quoting *Gray v. Bryant,* 125 So.2d 846, 852 (Fla.1960)); *Caribbean Conservation Corp. v. Fla. Fish & Wildlife Conservation Comm'n,* 838 So.2d 492, 501 (Fla.2003).

This Court's duty to measure the Legislature's apportionment plans with the yardstick of express constitutional provisions arises from the "well settled" principle that "the state Constitution is not a grant of power but a limitation upon power." *In re Apportionment Law Senate Joint Resolution No. 1305, 1972 Regular Session (In Re Apportionment Law — 1972),* 263 So.2d 797, 805 (Fla.1972). With the recent addition of section 21 to article III of the Florida Constitution, the Legislature is governed by a different and more comprehensive constitutional measurement than before — the limitations on legislative authority in apportionment decisions have increased and the constitutional yardstick has more measurements.

In addition to measuring the Legislature's compliance with these standards, we recognize the crucial role legislative apportionment plays with respect to the right of citizens to elect representatives. Indeed, the right to elect representatives — and the process by which we do so — is the very bedrock of our democracy. To ensure the protection of this right, the citizens of the state of Florida, through the Florida Constitution, employed the essential concept of checks and balances, granting to the Legislature the ability to apportion the state in a manner prescribed by the citizens and entrusting this Court with the responsibility to review the apportionment plans to ensure they are constitutionally valid. The obligations set forth in the Florida Constitution are directed not to the Legislature's right to draw districts, but to the people's right to elect representatives in a fair manner so that each person's vote counts equally and so that all citizens receive "fair and effective representation." Once validated by the Court, the apportionment plans, which redraw each of the 40 Senate districts and each of the 120 House districts, will have a significant impact on the election of this state's elected representatives for the next decade.

On February 9, 2012, the Legislature passed Senate Joint Resolution 1176 (Joint Resolution), apportioning this state into 120 House districts and 40 Senate districts. The next day, the Attorney General fulfilled her constitutional obligation by filing a petition in this Court for a declaratory judgment to determine the validity of the legislative apportionment plans contained within the Joint Resolution. Following the Attorney General's filing, this Court "permit[ted] adversary interests to present their views" as required by article III, section 16(c). Under this Court's plenary authority to review legislative apportionment plans, we now have "jurisdiction to resolve all issues by declaratory judgment arising under article III, section 16(c), Florida Constitution." *In re Apportionment Law Appearing as Senate Joint Resolution 1 E, 1982 Special Apportionment Session (In re Apportionment Law—1982)*, 414 So.2d 1040, 1045 (Fla.1982).

We have carefully considered the submissions of both those supporting and opposing the plans. We have held oral argument. For the reasons more fully explained below, we conclude that the Senate plan is facially invalid under article III, section 21, and further conclude that the House plan is facially valid. We agree with the position of the House that the House plan can be severed from the Senate plan. In accordance with article III, section 16(c), of the Florida Constitution, the Court enters a declaratory judgment determining that the apportionment plan for the House of Representatives as contained in Senate Joint Resolution 1176 is constitutionally valid and determining that the apportionment plan for the Senate as contained in Senate Joint Resolution 1176 is constitutionally invalid.

* * *

III. ANALYSIS

A. STANDARD AND SCOPE OF REVIEW

The overarching question to be considered by the Court in this declaratory judgment proceeding is the constitutional validity of the plans contained within the Legislature's joint resolution of apportionment. *See In re Apportionment Law—2002*, 817 So.2d at 824; *In re Apportionment Law—1982*, 414 So.2d at 1052. The validity of the joint resolution is determined by examining whether the Legislature has operated within the constitutional limitations placed upon it when apportioning the state's legislative districts. The newly added constitutional standards are directly related to ensuring that the process by which citizens choose their elected officials is fair.

* * *

The recognition of the critical importance of redistricting in ensuring the basic rights of citizens to vote for the representatives of their choice is highlighted by a series of voting cases from the United States Supreme Court, most notably in *Reynolds v. Sims*, 377 U.S. 533 (1964):

> [T]he right of suffrage is a fundamental matter in a free and democratic society. Especially since the right to exercise the franchise in a free and unimpaired manner is preservative of other basic civil and political rights, any alleged infringement of the right of citizens to vote must be carefully and meticulously scrutinized....
>
> ....
>
> ... To the extent that a citizen's right to vote is debased, he is that much less a citizen.

Id. at 561–62, 567.

* * *

Throughout these proceedings, the Attorney General, the Senate, and the House have asserted that the Legislature should have full discretion in balancing the constitutional criteria that apply to apportioning legislative districts. However, when addressing similar arguments that state legislatures should have full discretion in considering such matters, the United States Supreme Court in *Reynolds* eloquently stated: "We are cautioned about the dangers of entering into political thickets and mathematical quagmires. Our answer is this: a denial of constitutionally protected rights demands judicial protection; our oath and our office require no less of us." 377 U.S. at 566.

* * *

Even though we continue to recognize the presumption of validity that governs ordinary legislative acts, the operation of this Court's process in apportionment cases is far different than the Court's review of ordinary legislative acts, and it includes a commensurate difference in our obligations....

This Court in *In re Apportionment Law—1972*, 263 So.2d at 806, while cognizant that "[t]he propriety and wisdom of legislation are exclusively matters for legislative determination," also recognized that the Legislature's authority was not unbridled. The Court observed that, although "in accordance with the doctrine of separation of powers, [it would] not seek to substitute its judgment for that of another coordinate branch of the government," pursuant to that same constitutional doctrine, the Court was also responsible for measuring legislative acts "with the yardstick of the Constitution." *Id.*

* * *

Because "legislative reapportionment is primarily a matter for legislative consideration and determination," *In re Apportionment Law—1972*, 263 So.2d at 799–800, this Court will defer to the Legislature's decision to draw a district in a certain way, so long as that decision does not violate the constitutional requirements. With an understanding that the Court's responsibility is limited to ensuring compliance with constitutional requirements, and endeavoring to be respectful to the critically important role of the Legislature, the Court has previously acknowledged that its duty "is not to select the best plan, but rather to decide whether the one adopted by the legislature is valid." *In re Apportionment Law—1992*, 597 So.2d at 285.

This principle is in keeping with the United States Supreme Court's decision in *Perry v. Perez,* ____ U.S. ____, 132 S.Ct. 934, 941 (2012), which stated that "redistricting ordinarily involves criteria and standards that have been weighed and evaluated by the elected branches in the exercise of their political judgment." In *Perez,* when it became clear that a state's redistricting plan would not obtain preclearance under Section 5 of the Voting Rights Act, a federal district court drew an interim redistricting plan without giving deference to the state's policy choices. In reversing the federal court's drawing of the plan, the Supreme Court explained that a federal district court may not wholly disregard policy choices made by a state's legislature, where those policy choices are not inconsistent with the United States Constitution or the Voting Rights Act. *Id.* at 943. The Supreme Court held that a "state plan serves as a starting point" for a federal district court because "[i]t provides important guidance that helps ensure that the district court appropriately confines itself to drawing interim maps ... without displacing legitimate state policy judgments with the court's own preferences." *Id.* at 941.

Perez is in conformity with the federal judiciary's strong preference to yield to states in making initial redistricting decisions as long as there is no violation of either the United States Constitution or the Voting Rights Act. As was emphasized in *Scott v. Germano* over 45 years ago, the "power of the judiciary of a State to require valid reapportionment or to formulate a valid redistricting plan has not only been recognized by [the United States Supreme] Court but appropriate action by the States in such cases has been specifically encouraged." *Germano,* 381 U.S. at 409.

Any attempt to use *Perez* in support of an argument that the state judiciary is constrained in performing its constitutionally mandated review takes the holding of *Perez* out of context. In contrast to *Perez,* this Court's initial review of the Legislature's joint resolution of apportionment does not require any balancing of concerns for federal versus state sovereignty. Nor is this Court engaged at this point in redrawing the plans. Rather, this Court is *required* by the state constitution to evaluate whether the Legislature's apportionment plans conflict with Florida's express constitutional standards. *See* art. III, § 16(c), Fla. Const. The Supreme Court's concerns in *Perez* regarding judicial overreach by the federal court in redrawing the state's apportionment plan do not apply to this original state proceeding, during which this Court is mandated to assess the Legislature's compliance with constitutional standards. At this juncture, the Court plays no role in drawing the Legislature's apportionment plans, and the deference owed by the federal courts to the state in the drawing of the plan is not implicated.

In our initial review of the Legislature's plan, we recognize the limitations of this Court's responsibilities. At the same time, we acknowledge and accept our paramount responsibility in apportionment, as set forth by the Florida Constitution, to ensure that the adopted plans comply with the constitutionally required mandates. "In other words, it is this Court's duty to enforce adherence to the constitutional requirements and to declare a redistricting plan that does not comply with those standards unconstitutional." *In re Legislative Districting of State*, 370 Md. 312, 805 A.2d 292, 316 (2002).

Where the legislative decision runs afoul of constitutional mandates, this Court has a constitutional obligation to invalidate the apportionment plan. To accept the Legislature's assurances that it followed the law without any type of inquiry or any type of meaningful review by this Court would render the Court's review of the new constitutional standards, and whether the Legislature complied with the new standards, essentially meaningless. To accept the Legislature's and Attorney General's position that this Court should not undertake a meaningful review of compliance with the new constitutional standards in this proceeding, but instead await challenges brought in trial courts over a period of time, would be an abdication of this Court's responsibility under the Florida Constitution. This approach would also create uncertainty for the voters of this state, the elected representatives, and the candidates who are required to qualify for their seats.

The question then becomes how this Court will accomplish its review in a meaningful way given the nature of this constitutionally required proceeding. Undoubtedly, this Court is limited by time to be able to relinquish for extensive fact-finding as we have undertaken in other original proceedings, or to appoint a commissioner to receive testimony and refer the case back to the appellate court together with findings that are advisory in nature only. A review of prior reapportionment decisions from 1972, 1982, and 1992 reveals that in the past, the Court has retained exclusive state jurisdiction to allow challenges to be later brought, and then, on one occasion, the Court appointed a commissioner to conduct fact-finding on a specific challenge pursuant to our apportionment original jurisdiction.

In light of two distinct developments, our past approach is not determinative of our review in this post-2010 case. The first development, as mentioned above, is that in 2010, the voters imposed upon the Legislature explicit, additional state constitutional standards. In contrast to 2002, where the challenges exceeded our limited scope of review because they were based on violations of federal law, the challenges in 2012 are based specifically on allegations that the plans facially violate the requirements of the new provisions of our state constitution.

The second development is that technology has continued to advance in the last decade, allowing this Court to objectively evaluate many of Florida's constitutionally mandated criteria without the necessity of traditional fact-finding, such as making credibility determinations of witnesses. In furtherance of the goal to conduct an objective evaluation of the plans, the Court required all plans, including alternative plans, to be submitted electronically in .doj format, allowing for every party and the Court to evaluate the plans using the same statistical analysis and data reports. To ensure that the Court would have the means to objectively evaluate the plans, the

Court specified in its order the manner in which the House and Senate plans should be submitted to the Court in .doj format:

> For each plan file submitted for the newly created apportionment plans, the Attorney General is directed to specify the software used to create the plan, the data and criteria used in drafting the plan, the source of the data used in drafting the plan, and any other relevant information. The Attorney General is also directed to file along with the plan statistical reports for both the new plans and the last legally enforceable plans in searchable Portable Document Format (PDF), which include at a minimum the following from the 2010 Census: the population numbers in each district, the total voting age population (VAP) in each district, and the VAP of each racial and ethnic group in each district. Reports with additional information and statistics (e.g., compactness measurements), and reports for prior apportionment plans, may also be submitted in searchable PDF format.

> The Attorney General is also directed to provide the Court with maps of the House and Senate apportionment plans depicting the new districts, which shall include maps depicting the entire state as well as regional maps. In addition to the maps depicting the districts, the Attorney General may also file maps depicting the apportionment plans with data overlays. For each such map, the Attorney General is directed to specify the data depicted in the data overlay and the source of that data. The Attorney General may also file maps other than maps depicting the new apportionment plans, including maps of prior apportionment plans with or without any data overlays.

In re Joint Resolution of Legislative Apportionment, No. SC12-1 (Fla. Sup.Ct. order filed Jan. 25, 2012). As for parties, the Court permitted the filing of alternative plans and ordered the parties to comply with the following requirements:

> Parties submitting alternative plans must submit the alternative plans electronically in .doj format....

> For each plan file submitted, the submitting party must specify the software used to create the plan, the data and criteria used in drafting each plan, the source of the data used in drafting the plan, and any other relevant information. The submitting party shall also specify whether the alternative plan is a partial or complete plan, and the population deviation for each district in the plan; if a partial plan is submitted, the submitting party must specify what county or counties are included in the partial plan. Parties may also submit statistical reports related to each submitted plan in searchable PDF format.

> For each submitted alternative plan, the submitting party must file map(s) depicting the alternative plan districts with this Court. At least one map shall be filed that reflects the entire alternative plan. The submitting party may file additional maps showing regions or areas of interest. In addition to maps depicting the districts of the alternative plan, the submitting party may also

file maps depicting the apportionment plans with data overlays, including maps of the prior plans. Each such map shall specify the data depicted in the data overlay and the source of that data. For each map filed with the Court, the submitting party shall file the map in electronic PDF format and provide the Court with fifteen (15) color paper copies.

Id. The only opponent in this case to submit an alternative plan was the Coalition, which submitted two alternative plans to this Court: an alternative Senate plan and an alternative House plan.[14]

The Court permitted alternative plans because alternative plans may be offered as relevant proof that the Legislature's apportionment plans consist of district configurations that are not explained other than by the Legislature considering impermissible factors, such as intentionally favoring a political party or an incumbent.[15] The Legislature is not obligated to accept alternative plans; this Court, however, may review them to evaluate whether the Legislature's adopted plans are contrary to law. *See, e.g., Holt,* 38 A.3d at 755, 2012 WL 360584, at *36 (explaining that alternative plans may be used as proof that the final plan "contained subdivision splits that were not absolutely necessary").

In furtherance of our goal to ensure that the Court had complete information, at the Court's direction, the Attorney General filed an appendix to the petition for declaratory judgment and filed the apportionment plans electronically in .doj format, which would allow this Court and the challengers to perform an objective statistical analysis of the plans submitted by using standard redistricting software. The House and Senate each developed and utilized its own web-based redistricting software, MyDistrictBuilder and District Builder, respectively. This Court had access to both MyDistrictBuilder and District Builder as well as the data in the House program, which included census data, American Community Survey data, and voter registration and elections data. We have also received the incumbent addresses upon which the challengers based their claims that districts were drawn to favor incumbents.[16]

---

14. [FN 10.] After the deadline for the submission of briefs and alternative plans had passed, the Coalition sought to file a supplemental appendix, including a revised alternative House plan. The Court denied that request, and the supplemental appendix was stricken. *See In re Joint Resolution of Legislative Apportionment,* No. SC12-1 (Fla. Sup.Ct. order filed Feb. 22, 2012).

15. [FN 11.] In 1982, this Court concluded that because the proceeding was limited to reviewing the facial constitutional validity of the joint resolution, "the suggestion that we should adopt an alternative plan [was] not permissible in these proceedings." *In re Apportionment Law—1982,* 414 So.2d at 1052. We did not conclude that alternative plans were impermissible for the purposes of constitutional comparison. With the advent of the new amendment codified in article III, section 21, of the Florida Constitution, portions of which bear a striking resemblance to the Federal Voting Rights Act, we deem it necessary, as we did in 1992, to review alternative apportionment plans to assess effect and intent. *See In re Apportionment Law—1992,* 597 So.2d at 282 n. 7 (permitting all interested parties to file alternative apportionment plans in support of their arguments with respect to whether or not the Joint Resolution impermissibly discriminated against a minority group).

16. [FN 12.] We ordered the production of the incumbents' addresses upon which the opponents rely in their arguments. *See In re Joint Resolution of Legislative Apportionment,* No. SC12-1, Order on Incumbents' Addresses (Fla. Sup.Ct. order filed Feb. 21, 2012). The Attorney General, Florida Senate,

The type of information available for this original review is objective data. In performing its objective analysis of the data, the Court did not rely on the figures or statistical analysis contained in the appendices filed by the FDP or the Coalition. Instead, the Court utilized the MyDistrictBuilder and District Builder software applications to evaluate the Legislature's apportionment plans and the Coalition's alternative plans. The Court utilized both software applications to evaluate voting-age population[17] and to conduct a visual inspection of the districts. All of the maps depicting districts contained in this opinion were obtained using District Builder, except for a map depicting the City of Lakeland. This Court utilized MyDistrictBuilder when analyzing undisputed voter registration and election data because MyDistrictBuilder contained that data, but District Builder did not.[18] Specifically, this Court utilized the registration and election data to conduct an analysis of minority voting behavior in evaluating challenges to individual districts. Further, this Court utilized this data to examine the overall political composition of the House and Senate plans, as well as the political composition of each challenged district.

The Court additionally acquired Maptitude for Redistricting and inputted into Maptitude the voter registration, political, and elections data utilized by MyDistrict-Builder. The Court also inputted the incumbent addresses into Maptitude. The Court utilized Maptitude to conduct additional evaluation of the plans, such as the location of incumbents' addresses and calculations of the percentage of prior population retained by a district. This Court also examined graphical data overlays of voting-age population using Maptitude in evaluating certain challenged districts. Finally, the Court used ESRI Redistricting, also acquired by the Court, to generate compactness scores using compactness measurements of Reock and Area/Convex Hull, compactness measures that were used by the House in its plan data reports.

---

and Florida House of Representatives were given the opportunity to advise the Court regarding whether any of the addresses were inaccurate and, if so, to provide the correct address.

17. [FN 14.] The voting-age population numbers contained in MyDistrictBuilder were consistent with those contained in District Builder. With respect to the Legislature's apportionment plans, these voting-age population numbers were also consistent with the Attorney General's appendix.

18. [FN 15.] The House recognized that this data was required in order to evaluate compliance with Florida's minority voting protection provision as well as the Federal Voting Rights Act, and it included the data in MyDistrictBuilder. *See* Open Data and Code for MyDistrictBuilder, http://my districtbuilder.wordpress.com/opendata (last visited Mar. 6, 2012) ("Elections data is required to comply with: Sections 2 and 5 of the federal Voting Rights Act; and Florida's Constitution, Article III, Sections 20(a) and 21(a), which both read, 'districts shall not be drawn with the intent or result of denying or abridging the equal opportunity of racial or language minorities to participate in the political process or to diminish their ability to elect representatives of their choice'"). The Senate chose to omit this data from District Builder. The District Builder Help Manual states: "Recent changes to the Florida Constitution require that districts not be 'drawn with the intent to favor or disfavor a political party or an incumbent.'... With this new language, the mere presence of political metrics in the interface for building districts could create a perception, unsubstantiated and inaccurate though it may be, that partisan factors influenced how districts were drawn. The Senate, in an abundance of caution, therefore departed from traditional practice and chose to omit voter registration counts and election results from District Builder's dashboard." District Builder Help Manual, https://db10.flsen-ate. gov/db1/help (last visited Mar. 6, 2012).

The controversy between the parties, set forth primarily by the House and Senate, is that no conclusion as to intent to favor a political party or incumbent can be made. The challengers contend that this Court is able to perform its review based on an assessment of statistical analysis, a visual examination of the plans, and an evaluation of legislative history. The challengers contend that this evidence will enable the Court to discern intent to favor or disfavor a political party or an incumbent because intent can be inferred from effect. We will discuss these arguments in more detail when we analyze the specific standards and apply them to the House and Senate plans.

Finally, we have the guidance of the many state courts that have similar provisions providing their respective state supreme courts with original jurisdiction. Those courts have, over the years, both validated and invalidated plans based on many of the same criteria now contained in Florida's constitution. As in those states, the Florida Constitution "expressly entrusts to this Court the responsibility, upon proper petition, to review the constitutionality of districting plans prepared and enacted by the political branches of government and the duty to provide appropriate relief when the plans are determined to violate the United States and [Florida] Constitutions." *In re Legislative Districting of State*, 370 Md. 312, 805 A.2d 292, 316 (2002).

With our important responsibility to ensure that the joint resolution of apportionment comports with both the United States and Florida Constitutions, and with full awareness of the inherent limitations in the process set out in the state constitution, we undertake our constitutionally mandated review of the facial validity of the Senate and House plans contained within Senate Joint Resolution 1176.

B. THE STANDARDS GOVERNING OUR ANALYSIS

Although this is the fifth time the Court has had the responsibility to undertake its constitutionally mandated review of legislative apportionment, it is the first time that the Court has been charged with defining and applying the criteria of article III, section 21. This Court's interpretation of the language contained in sections 16(a) and 21 of article III begins with the basic principles spelled out by this Court in its 1972 apportionment decision:

> Every word of the Florida Constitution should be given its intended meaning and effect. In construing constitutions, that construction is favored which gives effect to every clause and every part of it. A construction which would leave without effect any part of the language used should be rejected if an interpretation can be found which gives it effect.

In re Apportionment Law—1972, 263 So.2d at 807.

In accord with those tenets of constitutional construction, this Court "endeavors to construe a constitutional provision consistent with the intent of the framers and the voters." *Zingale*, 885 So.2d at 282 (quoting *Caribbean Conservation Corp.*, 838 So.2d at 501). In ascertaining the intent of the voters, the Court may examine "the purpose of the provision, the evil sought to be remedied, and the circumstances leading to its inclusion in our constitutional document," *In re Apportionment Law—1982*,

414 So.2d at 1048, with the view that a constitutional amendment must be assessed "in light of the historical development of the decisional law extant at the time of its adoption." *Jenkins v. State*, 385 So.2d 1356, 1357 (Fla.1980).

Guided by both this Court's precedent and a proper construction of the pertinent provisions contained within article III, we must determine whether the Legislature's joint resolution is facially consistent with the specific constitutionally mandated criteria under the federal and state constitutions. The Federal Equal Protection Clause requires that districts conform to the one-person, one-vote standard. Article III, section 16(a), requires the Legislature to apportion both the Senate and the House in "consecutively numbered ... districts of either contiguous, overlapping or identical territory."

The new standards enumerated in article III, section 21, are set forth in two tiers, each of which contains three requirements. The first tier, contained in section 21(a), lists the following requirements: (1) no apportionment plan or district shall be drawn with the intent to favor or disfavor a political party or an incumbent; (2) districts shall not be drawn with the intent or result of denying or abridging the equal opportunity of racial or language minorities to participate in the political process or to diminish their ability to elect representatives of their choice; and (3) districts shall consist of contiguous territory. *See* art. III, §21(a), Fla. Const. The second tier, located in section 21(b), enumerates three additional requirements in drawing district lines, the compliance with which is subordinate to those listed in the first tier of section 21 and to federal law in the event of conflict: (1) districts shall be as nearly equal in population as is practicable; (2) districts shall be compact; and (3) where feasible, districts shall utilize existing political and geographical boundaries. *See* art. III, §21(b), Fla. Const. The order in which the constitution lists the standards in tiers one and two is "not [to] be read to establish any priority of one standard over the other within that [tier]." Art. III, §21(c), Fla. Const.

We interpret the specific constitutional directive that tier two is subordinate to tier one in the event of conflict to mean that the Legislature's obligation is to draw legislative districts that comport with all of the requirements enumerated in Florida's constitution. However, should a conflict in application arise, the Legislature is obligated to adhere to the requirements of section 21(a) (tier one) and then comply with the considerations in section 21(b) (tier two) to the extent "practicable" or "feasible," depending on the wording of the specific constitutional standard. With this basic framework in mind, we interpret the standards, beginning with the newly enacted tier-one standards and then moving to the newly enacted tier-two standards. After we explain and interpret the standards, we set forth how the standards interact for purposes of evaluating the apportionment plans.

1. Tier-One Standards

a. Intent to Favor or Disfavor a Political Party or an Incumbent

The first of the new and significantly different requirements in our state constitution is the provision in article III, section 21(a), providing that "[n]o apportionment plan or district shall be drawn with the intent to favor or disfavor a political party or an incumbent." . . .

This new requirement in Florida prohibits what has previously been an acceptable practice, such as favoring incumbents and the political party in power. *See, e.g., In re Apportionment Law—1992*, 597 So.2d at 285. The desire of a political party to provide its representatives with an advantage in reapportionment is not a Republican or Democratic tenet, but applies equally to both parties. Thus, in 1992, when the Democrats were in control of the Legislature and, by default, the redistricting process, we rejected a claim of impermissible political gerrymandering, stating in full:

> Finally, several of the opponents observe that the Joint Resolution is nothing more than a gerrymandering effort by the Democratic majority of the legislature to protect Democratic incumbents. We have little doubt that politics played a large part in the adoption of this plan. However, the protection of incumbents, standing alone, is not illegal, and none of the opponents seriously contend that the Joint Resolution is invalid because of political gerrymandering.

Id.

A decade later, when faced with a claim that the Republican majority of the Legislature had improperly limited input from Democratic members, the United States District Court for the Southern District of Florida similarly observed that the "raw exercise of majority legislative power does not seem to be the best way of conducting a critical task like redistricting, but it does seem to be an unfortunate fact of political life around the country." *Martinez v. Bush*, 234 F.Supp.2d 1275, 1297 (S.D.Fla.2002).

"The term 'political gerrymander' has been defined as '[t]he practice of dividing a geographical area into electoral districts, often of highly irregular shape, to give one political party an unfair advantage by diluting the opposition's voting strength.'" *Vieth v. Jubelirer*, 541 U.S. 267, 271 n. 1 (2004) (plurality opinion) (quoting *Black's Law Dictionary* 696 (7th ed. 1999)). While some states have sought to minimize the political nature of the apportionment process by establishing independent redistricting commissions to redraw legislative districts, Florida voters have instead chosen to place restrictions on the Legislature by constitutional mandate in a manner similar to the constitutions of other states.

The Florida Constitution now expressly prohibits what the United States Supreme Court has in the past termed a proper, and inevitable, consideration in the apportionment process. *See, e.g., Vieth*, 541 U.S. at 286 (plurality opinion) ("[P]artisan districting is a lawful and common practice. . . ."); *Miller v. Johnson*, 515 U.S. 900, 914 (1995) ("[R]edistricting in most cases will implicate a political calculus in which various interests compete for recognition. . . .").

Florida's express constitutional standard, however, differs from equal protection political gerrymandering claims under either the United States or Florida Constitutions. Political gerrymandering claims under the Equal Protection Clause of the United States Constitution focus on determining when partisan districting as a permissible exercise "has gone too far," *Vieth*, 541 U.S. at 296 (plurality opinion), so as to "degrade a voter's or a group of voters' influence on the political process as a whole." ...

In contrast to the federal equal protection standard applied to political gerrymandering, the Florida Constitution prohibits drawing a plan or district with the intent to favor or disfavor a political party or incumbent; there is no acceptable level of improper intent. It does not reference the word "invidious" as the term has been used by the United States Supreme Court in equal protection discrimination cases, *see, e.g., Brown v. Thomson*, 462 U.S. 835, 842 (1983), and Florida's provision should not be read to require a showing of malevolent or evil purpose. Moreover, by its express terms, Florida's constitutional provision prohibits intent, not effect, and applies to both the apportionment plan as a whole and to each district individually.

We recognize that any redrawing of lines, regardless of intent, will inevitably have an *effect* on the political composition of a district and likely whether a political party or incumbent is advantaged or disadvantaged. In fact, a plurality of the Supreme Court has quoted "one of the foremost scholars of reapportionment" as observing that "*every line drawn aligns partisans and interest blocs in a particular way different from the alignment that would result from putting the line in some other place.*" [*Davis v.*] *Bandemer*, 478 U.S. at 129 n. 10 (quoting Robert G. Dixon, Jr., *Fair Criteria and Procedures for Establishing Legislative Districts 7–8, in Representation and Redistricting Issues* (Bernard Grofman, et al. eds. 1982)). In short, redistricting will inherently have political consequences, regardless of the intent used in drawing the lines. Thus, the focus of the analysis must be on both direct and circumstantial evidence of intent. *See, e.g., Vill. of Arlington Heights v. Metro. Housing Dev. Corp.*, 429 U.S. 252, 266 (1977).

* * *

This Court has before it objective evidence that can be reviewed in order to perform a facial review of whether the apportionment plans as drawn had the impermissible intent of favoring an incumbent or a political party. While we agree that the standard does not prohibit political effect, the effects of the plan, the shape of district lines, and the demographics of an area are all factors that serve as objective indicators of intent.... One piece of evidence in isolation may not indicate intent, but a review of all of the evidence together may lead this Court to the conclusion that the plan was drawn for a prohibited purpose.

With respect to intent to favor or disfavor an incumbent, the inquiry focuses on whether the plan or district was drawn with this purpose in mind. As explained by the Eleventh Circuit Court of Appeals in upholding this specific constitutional provision as applied to Florida's congressional redistricting, "the incumbency provision is neutral on its face, explicitly requiring that lines not be designed to help or handicap particular candidates based on incumbency or membership in a particular party. Far from 'dictat[ing] electoral outcomes,' the provision seeks to maximize electoral possibilities by leveling the playing field." *Brown*, 668 F.3d at 1285.

At the outset, objective indicators of intent to favor or disfavor a political party can be discerned from the Legislature's level of compliance with our own constitution's tier-two requirements, which set forth traditional redistricting principles. A disregard for these principles can serve as indicia of improper intent....

The tier-two requirements of article III, section 21(b), are meant to restrict the Legislature's discretion in drawing irregularly shaped districts; strict compliance with their express terms may serve to undercut or defeat any assertion of improper intent. *Cf. Miller*, 515 U.S. at 916 (stating that in racial gerrymandering context where race-neutral considerations are the basis for redistricting, and are not subordinated to race, a State can "defeat a claim that a district has been gerrymandered on racial lines"); *Vieth*, 541 U.S. at 335 (Stevens, J., dissenting) (stating in proposing a standard for political gerrymandering claims that "[j]ust as irrational shape can serve as an objective indicator of an impermissible legislative purpose, other objective features of a districting map can save the plan from invalidation"). However, where the shape of a district in relation to the demographics is so highly irregular and without justification that it cannot be rationally understood as anything other than an effort to favor or disfavor a political party, improper intent may be inferred.

In making this assessment, we evaluate the shapes of districts together with undisputed objective data, such as the relevant voter registration and elections data, incumbents' addresses, and demographics, as well as any proffered undisputed direct evidence of intent. We note that the Court has access to the same voter registration and election data used by the House in its redistricting software.

Similar to the partisan inquiry, the inquiry for intent to favor or disfavor an incumbent focuses on the shape of the district in relation to the incumbent's legal residence, as well as other objective evidence of intent. Objective indicators of intent may include such factors as the maneuvering of district lines in order to avoid pitting incumbents against one another in new districts or the drawing of a new district so as to retain a large percentage of the incumbent's former district. When analyzing whether the challengers have established an unconstitutional intent to favor an incumbent, we must ensure that this Court does not disregard obvious conclusions from the undisputed facts.

The Court emphasizes that mere access to political data cannot presumptively demonstrate prohibited intent because such data is a necessary component of evaluating whether a minority group has the ability to elect representatives of choice— a required inquiry when determining whether the plan diminishes a protected group's ability to elect a candidate of choice. *See* Guidance Concerning Redistricting Under Section 5 of the Voting Rights Act, 76 Fed. Reg. 7470, 7471 (Feb. 9, 2011) (DOJ Guidance Notice) (United States Department of Justice guidance notice requiring a functional analysis of voting behavior to determine whether retrogression has occurred). Likewise, the fact that the Senate or House, or their staff, may or may not have had the incumbents' addresses is not determinative of intent or lack of intent. And, as discussed in the challenges section below, the fact that there were more registered Democrats than registered Republicans in this state, but that there are more Republican-performing districts than Democratic-performing districts in both the newly drawn Senate and House plans, does not permit a conclusion of unlawful intent in this case. Rather, when the Court analyzes the tier-two standards and determines that specific districts violate those standards without any other permissible justification, impermissible intent may be inferred.

b. Minority Voting Protection

The next newly added provision in article III, section 21(a), provides that "districts shall not be drawn with the intent or result of denying or abridging the equal opportunity of racial or language minorities to participate in the political process *or* to diminish their ability to elect representatives of their choice." (Emphasis added.) The emphasized "or" separates two clauses in the preceding sentence, and each clause shares the same negative verb, "shall not be drawn." As a plurality of this Court explained in *Standards for Establishing Legislative District Boundaries,* 2 So.3d at 189 (plurality opinion), "[t]his verb modifies both clauses, thereby indicating that both clauses impose a restrictive imperative, *each of which must be satisfied.*" Accordingly, this portion of section 21(a) imposes two requirements that plainly serve to protect racial and language minority voters in Florida: prevention of impermissible vote dilution and prevention of impermissible diminishment of a minority group's ability to elect a candidate of its choice.

The dual constitutional imperatives "follow[] almost verbatim the requirements embodied in the [Federal] Voting Rights Act." *Brown,* 668 F.3d at 1280. The first imperative, that "districts shall not be drawn with the intent or result of denying or abridging the equal opportunity of racial or language minorities to participate in the political process," art. III, § 21(a), Fla. Const., is essentially a restatement of Section 2 of the Voting Rights Act (VRA), which prohibits redistricting plans that afford minorities "less opportunity than other members of the electorate to participate in the political process." 42 U.S.C. § 1973(b) (2006). Section 2 relates to claims of impermissible vote dilution.

Florida's second imperative, that "districts shall not be drawn ... to diminish [racial or language minorities'] ability to elect representatives of their choice," art. III, § 21(a), Fla. Const., reflects the statement codified in Section 5 of the VRA prohibiting apportionment plans that have "the purpose of or will have the effect of diminishing the ability of any citizens ... on account of race or color ... to elect their preferred candidates of choice." 42 U.S.C. § 1973c(b) (2006). Section 5 attempts to eradicate impermissible retrogression in a minority group's ability to elect a candidate of choice. Although Section 5 applies only to "covered jurisdictions," Florida's constitutional prohibition applies to the entire state.

Consistent with the goals of Sections 2 and 5 of the VRA, Florida's corresponding state provision aims at safeguarding the voting strength of minority groups against both impermissible dilution and retrogression. Interpreting Florida's minority voting protection provision in this manner gives due allegiance to the principles of constitutional construction, under which the Court considers "the purpose of the provision, the evil sought to be remedied, and the circumstances leading to its inclusion in our constitutional document." *In re Apportionment Law—1982,* 414 So.2d at 1048....

Moreover, all parties to this proceeding agree that Florida's constitutional provision now embraces the principles enumerated in Sections 2 and 5 of the VRA. Because

Sections 2 and 5 raise federal issues, our interpretation of Florida's corresponding provision is guided by prevailing United States Supreme Court precedent. This approach not only corresponds to the manner in which this Court addressed Federal VRA claims in 1992, *see In re Apportionment Law — 1992*, 597 So.2d at 280–82, but it squares with how other jurisdictions have interpreted comparable state provisions.

Florida's provision is unique among the states in that it incorporates language from the VRA but does not explicitly reference the VRA. We therefore review the language of Sections 2 and 5, and how each has been judicially interpreted, to give meaning to our state counterpart. The Court nonetheless recognizes our independent constitutional obligation to interpret our own state constitutional provisions.

In our review, we conclude that in applying the federal provisions to the challenges and legislative justifications, the Court must necessarily approach the application of each federal provision differently due to the manner in which the Court reviews Florida's constitutional provisions in a facial review of the apportionment plans. For example, in this case, the House and Senate use Florida's minority voting protection provision as a justification for the manner in which they drew specific districts. The challengers, on the other hand, urge the Court to conclude that many of the districts were drawn to impermissibly dilute the voting strength of minorities and, in turn, the voting strength of the Democratic Party.

In contrast to the posture of the case in which this Court reviews Florida's minority voting protection provision, Section 2 claims under the VRA are brought by plaintiffs who challenge the apportionment plan on the grounds of impermissible vote dilution. Section 5 of the VRA applies only to covered jurisdictions that must obtain preclearance by the Department of Justice before an apportionment plan goes into effect; in Florida, only five counties are covered, not the entire state.

As explained by the United States Supreme Court, the VRA "was designed by Congress to banish the blight of racial discrimination in voting," *South Carolina v. Katzenbach*, 383 U.S. 301, 308 (1966), and to help effectuate the Fifteenth Amendment's guarantee that no citizen's right to vote shall "be denied or abridged ... on account of race, color, or previous condition of servitude." *Voinovich v. Quilter*, 507 U.S. 146, 152 (1993) (quoting U.S. Const. amend. XV). Sections 2 and 5 of the VRA "combat different evils," *Reno v. Bossier Parish Sch. Bd.*, 520 U.S. 471, 477 (1997), and "differ in structure, purpose, and application." *Georgia v. Ashcroft*, 539 U.S. 461, 478 (2003) (quoting *Holder v. Hall*, 512 U.S. 874, 883 (1994) (plurality opinion)). Section 2, specifically, applies nationwide and provides that "[n]o voting qualification or prerequisite to voting or standard, practice, or procedure shall be imposed or applied by any State or political subdivision in a manner which results in a denial or abridgement of the right of any citizen of the United States to vote on account of race or color." 42 U.S.C. § 1973(a) (2006).

A denial or abridgement of the right to vote in violation of Section 2 occurs when

based on the totality of circumstances, it is shown that the political processes leading to nomination or election in the State or political subdivision are not equally open to participation by members of a class of citizens protected by subsection (a) of this section in that its members have less opportunity than other members of the electorate to participate in the political process and to elect representatives of their choice.

Id. § 1973(b). Section 2 thus prohibits any practice or procedure that, when "'interact[ing] with social and historical conditions,' impairs the ability of a protected class to elect its candidate of choice on an equal basis with other voters." *Voinovich,* 507 U.S. at 153 (quoting *Thornburg v. Gingles,* 478 U.S. 30, 47 (1986)). Importantly, Section 2 employs a "results" test, under which proof of discriminatory intent is not necessary to establish a violation of the section. *Chisom v. Roemer,* 501 U.S. 380, 395 (1991); *see also Bossier Parish Sch. Bd.,* 520 U.S. at 482 ("[P]roof of discriminatory intent is not required to establish a violation of Section 2.").

The United States Supreme Court has commonly referred to one such prohibited practice or procedure under Section 2 as "vote dilution," which is the practice of reducing the potential effectiveness of a group's voting strength by limiting the group's chances to translate the strength into voting power. *Shaw* [*v. Reno*], 509 U.S. at 641. "[T]he usual device for diluting the minority voting power is the manipulation of district lines" by either fragmenting the minority voters among several districts where a bloc-voting majority can routinely outvote them or "packing" them into one or a small number of districts to minimize their influence in adjacent districts. *Voinovich,* 507 U.S. at 153–54. For instance, under the interpretation of federal law, impermissible "packing" might occur when a minority group has "sufficient numbers to constitute a majority in three districts" but is "packed into two districts in which it constitutes a super-majority." *Id.* at 153.

The Supreme Court's leading case interpreting Section 2, *Gingles,* 478 U.S. at 50, set out three "necessary preconditions" that a plaintiff is required to demonstrate before he or she can establish that a legislative district must be redrawn to comply with Section 2. These preconditions require an individual challenging the plan to show that: (1) a minority population is "sufficiently large and geographically compact to constitute a majority in a single-member district"; (2) the minority population is "politically cohesive"; and (3) the majority population "votes sufficiently as a bloc to enable it ... usually to defeat the minority's preferred candidate." *Id.* at 50–51. When the three *Gingles* preconditions are met, courts must then assess the totality of the circumstances to determine if the Section 2 "effects" test is met—that is, if minority voters' political power is truly diluted. *Johnson v. De Grandy,* 512 U.S. 997, 1013 (1994).

A successful vote dilution claim under Section 2 requires a showing that a minority group was denied a majority-minority district that, but for the purported dilution, could have potentially existed. *See id.* at 1008 ("[T]he first *Gingles* condition requires the possibility of creating more than the existing number of reasonably compact districts with a sufficiently large minority population to elect candidates of its choice."). Majority-minority districts are ones "in which a majority of the population is a member of a specific minority group." *Voinovich,* 507 U.S. at 149; *see also Bartlett v. Strickland,*

556 U.S. 1, 13 (2009) (plurality opinion) ("In majority-minority districts, a minority group composes a numerical, working majority of the voting-age population.").

By contrast, a crossover or coalition district "is one in which minority voters make up less than a majority of the voting-age population" but are, at least potentially, "large enough to elect the candidate of [their] choice with help from voters who are members of the majority and who cross over to support the minority's preferred candidate." *Bartlett*, 556 U.S. at 13. Influence districts are districts in which a minority group can influence the outcome of an election even if its preferred candidate cannot be elected. *Id.*

The showing of either an additional minority influence district or a crossover district, as opposed to an actual majority-minority district, is insufficient for Section 2 purposes; what is required is that "the minority population in the potential election district [be] greater than 50 percent." *Id.* at 19–20. Moreover, while "there is no § 2 right to a [minority] district that is not reasonably compact, the creation of a non-compact district does not compensate for the dismantling of a compact [minority] opportunity district." *League of United Latin Am. Citizens v. Perry*, 548 U.S. 399, 430–31 (2006). As the United States Supreme Court has explained, "[t]he practical consequence of drawing a district to cover two distant, disparate communities is that one or both groups will be unable to achieve their political goals." *Id.* at 434. Therefore, with respect to the compactness inquiry for Section 2 purposes specifically, there would be "no basis to believe a district that combines two farflung segments of a racial group with disparate interests provides the opportunity that § 2 requires or that the first *Gingles* condition contemplates." *Id.* at 433.

Most recently, in *Perez*, 132 S.Ct. at 944, an eight-justice majority of the Supreme Court cited to the plurality decision in *Bartlett*, 556 U.S. at 13–15 (declining to recognize a Section 2 claim where the district was composed of only 39% black voting-age population), to hold that a federal district court would have no basis for drawing a districting plan to create a "minority coalition opportunity district." The *Perez* decision is of course binding precedent only as to the interpretation of Section 2 jurisprudence under the VRA and was specifically concerned with limiting the circumstances under which a federal district court could draw an interim apportionment plan.

Unlike the posture of a Section 2 VRA claim before a federal court, the Florida Supreme Court is charged with analyzing the apportionment plan to determine compliance with all constitutional provisions. Florida's provision now codifies these Section 2 principles, but the question is whether those principles set a floor, as well as a ceiling, for our interpretation of Florida's constitution—whether there would be a violation of Florida's minority protection provision with respect to vote dilution if the plan could be drawn to create crossover districts or even influence districts. The challengers assert that by overly packing minorities into single districts, the Legislature has acted to minimize the influence of not only minorities, but also Democrats in the surrounding districts. Where that claim has been made, we will consider that specific argument when reviewing the district challenges below.

In contrast to vote dilution claims under Section 2, Section 5 of the VRA is limited to particular "covered jurisdictions" and relates to claims of retrogression in the position of racial minorities with respect to their effective exercise of the electoral franchise. *Ashcroft*, 539 U.S. at 478. Section 5 "suspend[s] all changes in state election procedure," including redistricting plans, in jurisdictions covered by the VRA "until they are submitted to and approved by a three-judge Federal District Court in Washington, D.C., or the Attorney General" of the United States. *Nw. Austin Mun. Util. Dist. No. One v. Holder*, 557 U.S. 193 (2009); *see also Beer v. United States*, 425 U.S. 130, 133 (1976). Florida is not a covered jurisdiction for the purposes of Section 5, but the state does include five covered counties: Collier, Hardee, Hendry, Hillsborough, and Monroe. Florida's new constitutional provision, however, codified the non-retrogression principle of Section 5 and has now extended it statewide. In other words, Florida now has a statewide non-retrogression requirement independent of Section 5.

Preclearance under Section 5 is granted only if the change "neither has the purpose nor will have the effect of denying or abridging the right to vote on account of race or color." *Nw. Austin*, 129 S.Ct. at 2509 (quoting 42 U.S.C. § 1973c(a) (2006)). A violation can be shown where the drawing of the district lines has "the purpose of or will have the effect of diminishing the ability of any citizens ... on account of race or color, or [membership in a language minority group], to elect their preferred candidates of choice." 42 U.S.C. § 1973c(b).[19] The primary objective of Section 5 is to avoid retrogression. "[A] plan has an impermissible [retrogressive] 'effect' under § 5 only if it 'would lead to a retrogression in the position of racial minorities with respect to their effective exercise of the electoral franchise.'" *Bossier*, 520 U.S. at 478 (quoting *Beer*, 425 U.S. at 141). The existing plan of a covered jurisdiction serves as the "benchmark" against which the " 'effect' of voting changes is measured." *Id.*

In its 2006 reauthorization, Congress amended Section 5 to add the express prohibition against "diminishing the ability" of minorities "to elect their preferred candidate" as a response to the United States Supreme Court's 2003 decision in *Ashcroft*. This amended language mirrors the language of Florida's provision. Before the amendment to Section 5, the *Ashcroft* Court concluded that Section 5 granted to covered jurisdictions the discretion to trade off "safe" districts with "influence or coalition districts," particularly if the new plan did not "change[] the minority group's opportunity to participate in the political process." 539 U.S. at 482.

Disagreeing with the United States Supreme Court's interpretation, Congress overruled *Ashcroft*, concluding that "trade-offs" that "would allow the minority community's own choice of preferred candidates to be trumped by political deals struck by State legislators purporting to give 'influence' to the minority community while removing that community's ability to elect candidates" were "inconsistent with the orig-

---

19. [FN 26.] While Florida's provision borrows language from Section 5, it does not incorporate the portion of Section 5 placing the burden of proof on the covered jurisdiction to establish the requirements necessary to obtain preclearance.

inal and current purpose of Section 5." H.R.Rep. No. 109-478, at 44 (2006). As Congress explained, the new "Section 5 [was] intended to be specifically focused on whether the electoral power of the minority community [was] more, less, or just as able to elect a preferred candidate of choice after a voting change as before." *Id.* at 46. That is, "[v]oting changes that leave a minority group less able to elect a preferred candidate of choice, either directly or when coalesced with other voters, cannot be precleared under Section 5." *Id.* The United States Supreme Court has yet to interpret this aspect of Congress's 2006 amendment.

Just as Section 2 jurisprudence guides the Court in analyzing the state vote dilution claims, when we interpret our state provision prohibiting the diminishment of racial or language minorities' ability to elect representatives of choice, we are guided by any jurisprudence interpreting Section 5. However, the Court must remain mindful that we are interpreting an independent provision of the state constitution.

Certainly, by including the "diminish" language of recently amended Section 5, Florida has now adopted the retrogression principle as intended by Congress in the 2006 amendment. Accordingly, the Legislature cannot eliminate majority-minority districts or weaken other historically performing minority districts where doing so would actually diminish a minority group's ability to elect its preferred candidates. In other words, in addition to majority-minority districts, coalition or crossover districts that previously provided minority groups with the ability to elect a preferred candidate under the benchmark plan must also be recognized. *See Texas v. United States,* No. 11-1303 (TBG-RMC-BAH), 2011 WL 6440006, at *18–19, 831 F.Supp.2d 244, 265–68 (D.D.C. Dec. 22, 2011) (concluding that minority coalition districts are also included in the calculation of whether a new districting plan diminishes the ability of a minority group to elect a candidate of choice). We nonetheless conclude that under Florida's provision, a slight change in percentage of the minority group's population in a given district does not necessarily have a cognizable effect on a minority group's ability to elect its preferred candidate of choice. This is because a minority group's ability to elect a candidate of choice depends upon more than just population figures.

To undertake a retrogression evaluation requires an inquiry into whether a district is likely to perform for minority candidates of choice. This has been termed a "functional analysis," requiring consideration not only of the minority population in the districts, or even the minority voting-age population in those districts, but of political data and how a minority population group has voted in the past. The United States Department of Justice (DOJ) has defined what a functional analysis of electoral behavior entails:

In determining whether the ability to elect exists in the benchmark plan and whether it continues in the proposed plan, the Attorney General does not rely on any predetermined or fixed demographic percentages at any point in the assessment. Rather, in the Department's view, this determination requires a functional analysis of the electoral behavior within the particular jurisdiction or election district.... [C]ensus data alone may not provide sufficient indicia of electoral behavior to make the requisite determination. Circumstances, such as differing rates of electoral participation within discrete portions of a population, may impact on the ability of voters to elect candidates of choice, even if the overall demographic data show no significant change.

> Although comparison of the census population of districts in the benchmark and proposed plans is the important starting point of any Section 5 analysis, additional demographic and election data in the submission is often helpful in making the requisite Section 5 determination.... Therefore, election history and voting patterns within the jurisdiction, voter registration and turnout information, and other similar information are very important to an assessment of the actual effect of a redistricting plan.

DOJ Guidance Notice, 76 Fed. Reg. at 7471; *see also Texas,* 831 F.Supp.2d at 262–66, 2011 WL 6440006, at *15–18 (proposing a functional test similar to that of the DOJ).

We recognize that in certain situations, compactness and other redistricting criteria, such as those codified in tier two of article III, section 21, of the Florida Constitution, will be compromised in order to avoid retrogression. Indeed, the DOJ has even noted that "compliance with Section 5 of the Voting Rights Act may require the jurisdiction to depart from strict adherence to certain of its redistricting criteria. For example, criteria that require the jurisdiction to ... follow county, city, or precinct boundaries ... or, in some cases, require a certain level of compactness of district boundaries may need to give way to some degree to avoid retrogression." DOJ Guidance Notice, 76 Fed. Reg. at 7472. Tier two of article III, section 21, specifically contemplates this need, but only to the extent necessary. Therefore, as does the DOJ, in making our own assessment, we will rely upon "alternative or illustrative plans ... *that make the least departure from [Florida's] stated redistricting criteria needed to prevent retrogression." Id.* (emphasis added).

* * *

If the Legislature is utilizing its interest in protecting minority voting strength as a shield, this Court must be able to undertake a review of the validity of that reason. Therefore, by the very nature of the challenges and the reasons advanced for the shape of the districts, it is necessary to perform a facial review and analyze the objective data that we have available. Because a minority group's ability to elect a candidate of choice depends upon more than just population figures, we reject any argument that the minority population percentage in each district as of 2002 is somehow fixed to an absolute number under Florida's minority protection provision.

To hold otherwise would run the risk of permitting the Legislature to engage in racial gerrymandering to avoid diminishment. However, the United States Supreme Court has cautioned: "[W]e do not read ... any of our other § 5 cases to give covered jurisdictions *carte blanche* to engage in racial gerrymandering in the name of non-retrogression. A reapportionment plan would not be narrowly tailored to the goal of avoiding retrogression if the State went beyond what was reasonably necessary to avoid retrogression." *Shaw,* 509 U.S. at 655. This is especially true in light of the United States Supreme Court's admonition:

> Racial classifications of any sort pose the risk of lasting harm to our society. They reinforce the belief, held by too many for too much of our history, that individuals should be judged by the color of their skin. Racial classifications with respect to voting carry particular dangers. Racial gerrymandering, even for remedial purposes, may balkanize us into competing racial factions; it threatens to carry us further from the goal of a political system in which race no longer matters—a goal that the Fourteenth and Fifteenth Amendments embody, and to which the Nation continues to aspire. It is for these reasons that race-based districting by our state legislatures demands close judicial scrutiny.

Id. at 657.

In a manner consistent with what is required to determine whether a district is likely to perform for minority candidates of choice, the Court's analysis of this claim and any defense for the manner in which the district was drawn will involve the review of the following statistical data: (1) voting-age populations; (2) voting-registration data; (3) voting registration of actual voters; and (4) election results history. This approach is analogous to the review we undertook in 1992 of objective statistical data in order to facially decide Section 2 claims. There, when analyzing whether the joint resolution complied with Section 2 of the VRA, this Court held that its "analysis [would] include a consideration of all statistical data filed herein, including a breakdown of white, black, and Hispanic voting-age populations and voting registrations in the legislative districts contained in the Joint Resolution and in other proposed plans, none of which [were] disputed." *In re Apportionment Law—1992,* 597 So.2d at 282 (footnotes omitted).

Based on the foregoing, we analyze Florida's minority voting protection provision as safeguarding the voting strength of minority groups against impermissible dilution and retrogression.

c. Contiguity

The third of the tier-one standards is contiguity. The requirement that districts shall consist of contiguous territory exists in both sections 16(a) and 21(a) of article III. By including this standard in the first subsection of the new amendment, the voters made clear their intention to establish that the section 21(b) standards of compactness, nearly equal population, and utilizing political and geographical boundaries are subservient to the contiguity requirement.

This Court has defined contiguous as "being in actual contact: touching along a boundary or at a point." *In re Apportionment Law—2002,* 817 So.2d at 827 (quoting *In re Apportionment Law—1992,* 597 So.2d at 279). "A district lacks contiguity 'when a part is isolated from the rest by the territory of another district' or when the lands 'mutually touch only at a common corner or right angle.'" *Id.* (quoting *In re Apportionment Law—1992,* 597 So.2d at 279). No party has advocated that the interpretation of this constitutional provision has changed, and we interpret the clause in section 21(a) consistent with our previous interpretation of whether a district is contiguous under section 16(a).

2. Tier-Two Standards

We now turn to a discussion of the tier-two standards, which require that "districts shall be as nearly equal in population as is practicable," that "districts shall be compact," and that "districts shall, where feasible, utilize existing political and geographical boundaries." Art. III, §21(b), Fla. Const. Strict adherence to these standards must yield if there is a conflict between compliance with them and the tier-one standards.

a. As Nearly Equal in Population as Practicable

Although the express requirement of equal population is new to the Florida Constitution, this Court's precedent establishes the importance of the federal one-person, one-vote requirement as both an apportionment principle and a proper starting point in judicial analysis. We evaluate this federal principle in conjunction with the newly enacted state constitutional requirement set forth in article III, section 21(b), requiring districts to be "as nearly equal in population as is practicable."

* * *

Although requiring mathematical exactness for congressional districts, the United States Supreme Court has also explained that mathematical precision under the one-person, one-vote requirement is not paramount for state legislative districts when it must yield to other legitimate redistricting objectives, such as compactness and maintaining the integrity of political subdivisions:

> [S]ome deviations from population equality may be necessary to permit States to pursue other legitimate objectives such as "maintain[ing] the integrity of various political subdivisions" and "provid[ing] for compact districts of contiguous territory." *Reynolds, supra* at 578. As the Court stated in *Gaffney,* "a[n] unrealistic overemphasis on raw population figures, a mere nose count in the districts, may submerge these other considerations and itself furnish a ready tool for ignoring factors that in day-to-day operation are important to an acceptable representation and apportionment arrangement." 412 U.S. at 749.

Brown v. Thomson, 462 U.S. 835, 842 (1983) (alterations in original).

Applying that body of law during the 2002 apportionment cycle before the most recent constitutional amendment, this Court rejected the argument that the one-person, one-vote standard would require the Legislature to utilize advanced computer technology to design districts "in exactly the same numerical size." *In re Apportionment Law—2002,* 817 So.2d at 826. We concluded that "[e]ven if the advent of computer-based redistricting software [had] lowered the maximum permissible deviation, ... the relatively minor deviation before us in [that] case [did] not lead to the conclusion that either the House or Senate plans [were] facially in violation of the one-person, one-vote requirement." *Id.* at 827. There, the House plan had a maximum percentage deviation between the largest and smallest number of people per representative (statistical overall range) of 2.79%, and the Senate plan had a maximum percentage deviation between the largest and smallest number of people per representative (statistical overall range) of 0.03%. *Id.* at 826.

Now, the Florida voters have expressly spoken on the issue of population equality in Florida's redistricting process. Article III, section 21(b), requires districts to be "as nearly equal in population as is practicable." To interpret this provision, we apply the principles governing constitutional construction. The Court "endeavors to construe a constitutional provision consistent with the intent of the framers and voters," *Zingale,* 885 So.2d at 282, and in construing the language of the Florida Constitution, "[e]very word of the Florida Constitution should be given its intended meaning and effect." *In re Apportionment Law — 1972,* 263 So.2d at 807.

Florida's standard unmistakably uses the same language that the Supreme Court has used when interpreting the federal equal protection one-person, one-vote standard. *See In re Apportionment Law — 2002,* 817 So.2d at 826 (describing the federal one-person, one-vote criteria as requiring the Legislature to construct districts "as nearly of equal population as is practicable" (quoting *In re Apportionment Law — 1992,* 597 So.2d at 279)). Further, this Court has relied on Supreme Court precedent to interpret the one-person, one-vote standard in a like manner.

The FDP and the Coalition assert that Florida's equal population requirement imposes a stricter standard than this Court has previously employed. The challengers' assertion therefore raises the question of whether compliance with the standard under the Florida Constitution is measured differently than how it has been measured under the United States Constitution; in other words, whether the Legislature has less room for flexibility in population deviation among the legislative districts because the requirement is now enshrined in the Florida Constitution.

We resolve this question by concluding that the voters' inclusion of this standard in the second tier of article III, section 21, recognizes that, as under the federal constitution, strict and unbending adherence to the equal population requirement will yield to other redistricting considerations, but that those considerations must be based on the express constitutional standards. The Florida Constitution embraces this construction, expressly mandating that the equal population requirement give way to contiguity, the prohibition against the intent to favor an incumbent or political party, and the need to comply with the minority-protection provision. In addition, article III, section 21, instructs that Florida's equal population requirement be balanced with both compactness and the use of political and geographical boundaries.

The United States Supreme Court has long recognized that although the Equal Protection Clause requires state legislatures to make an "honest and good faith effort" to construct districts "as nearly of equal population as is practicable," there are legitimate reasons for states to deviate from creating districts with perfectly equal populations, including maintaining the integrity of political subdivisions and providing compact and contiguous districts. *Sims,* 377 U.S. at 577; *see also Brown,* 462 U.S. at 842.

We imbue Florida's provision with the same meaning, subject to this important caveat. Because obtaining equal population "if practicable" is an explicit and important constitutional mandate under the Florida Constitution, any deviation from that goal of mathematical precision must be based upon compliance with other constitutional standards. Accordingly, compliance with Florida's equal population standard must be assessed in tandem with the other constitutional considerations.

b. Compactness

Compactness is the second of the tier-two standards. Because the requirement that districts "shall be compact" is a new constitutional requirement, the Court begins by defining it. Before 2010, "neither the United States nor the Florida Constitution require[d] that the Florida Legislature apportion legislative districts in a compact manner." *In re Apportionment Law—2002*, 817 So.2d at 831. Now, however, the Florida Constitution expressly requires that "districts shall be compact." Art. III, § 21(b), Fla. Const. Although compactness is a new constitutional requirement in Florida, compactness is a well-recognized and long-standing constitutional standard in at least twenty state constitutions and at least six state statutes.

In defining this standard, as with the other standards, we start with the proposition that in interpreting constitutional provisions,

> [f]irst and foremost, this Court must examine the actual language used in the constitution. "If that language is clear, unambiguous, and addresses the matter in issue, then it must be enforced as written." The words of the constitution "are to be interpreted in their most usual and obvious meaning, unless the text suggests that they have been used in a technical sense." Additionally, this Court "endeavors to construe a constitutional provision consistent with the intent of the framers and the voters." Constitutional provisions "must never be construed in such manner as to make it possible for the will of the people to be frustrated or denied."

Lewis v. Leon Cnty., 73 So.3d 151, 153–54 (Fla.2011). Thus, a fundamental tenet of constitutional construction applicable in our analysis is that the Court will construe a constitutional provision in a manner consistent with the intent of the framers and the voters and will interpret its terms in their most usual and obvious meaning.

The Senate contends that this Court should not undertake to define compactness and instead leave that task to the Legislature. The Senate asserts that "compactness is ... the paradigmatic example of an elusive concept with no precise meaning." However, as is universally recognized, it is the exclusive province of the judiciary to interpret terms in a constitution and to define those terms. *See Lawnwood Medical Ctr., Inc. v. Seeger*, 990 So.2d 503, 510 (Fla.2008) ("[I]t is the duty of this Court to determine the meaning of this constitutional provision."); *Stephenson v. Bartlett*, 355 N.C. 354, 562 S.E.2d 377, 384 (2002) (noting during the review of a legislative apportionment plan that "it is emphatically the province and duty of the judicial department to say what the law is" (quoting *Marbury v. Madison*, 5 U.S. (1 Cranch) 137, 177 (1803))).

This is particularly the case with the new constitutional standards on apportionment because the standards serve as a limit on the exercise of the Legislature's authority. Further, it is incumbent upon this Court to define the term in accordance with the intent of the voters, which, in this case, was to require the Legislature to redistrict in a manner that prohibits favoritism or discrimination. *See Ervin v. Collins*, 85 So.2d 852, 855 (Fla.1956) ("We are called on to construe the terms of the Constitution, an instrument from the people, and we are to effectuate their purpose from the words employed in the document.").

A compactness requirement serves to limit partisan redistricting and racial gerrymanders. In fact, as the Illinois Supreme Court recognized, "compactness is 'almost universally recognized' as an appropriate anti-gerrymandering standard." *Schrage v. State Bd. of Elections*, 88 Ill.2d 87, 58 Ill.Dec. 451, 430 N.E.2d 483, 486 (1981) (quoting James M. Edwards, *The Gerrymander and "One Man, One Vote"*, 46 N.Y.U. L.Rev. 879, 893 (1971)); *Pearson [v. Koster]*, 359 S.W.3d at 38, 2012 WL 131425, at *2 [(Mo.)] (holding that the purpose of the constitutional requirements that districts be contiguous, compact, and nearly equal in population is "to guard, as far as practicable, under the system of representation adopted, against a legislative evil, commonly known as 'gerrymander'" (quoting [*State ex rel. Barrett v.*] *Hitchcock*, 146 S.W. at 61 [(Mo. 1916)])).

* * *

We conclude that the language of the Florida Constitution does not give the term "compact" such an expansive meaning. If we were to include "communities of interest" within the term "compactness," the Court would be adding words to the constitution that were not put there by the voters of this state. In construing the words used in the constitution, the Court is not at liberty to add words and terms that are not included in the text of the constitution. *See Pleus*, 14 So.3d at 945 ("We remain mindful that in construing a constitutional provision, we are not at liberty to add words that were not placed there originally or to ignore words that were expressly placed there at the time of adoption of the provision.").

Expanding the definition of compactness to include factors such as the ability to access and communicate with elected officials and their ability to relate and interact with one another would be contrary to the average voter's understanding of compactness and would be contrary to the usual and ordinary meaning of the word. In fact, using such a broad definition of this term would almost read out the requirement of compactness—enlarging this term to such a degree that it would frustrate the will of the people in passing this constitutional amendment. Accordingly, we hold that when reviewing compactness, the term should be construed to mean geographical compactness.

Our consideration of the term "compact" as a geographical concept raises the issues of how it is to be measured and how other constitutional considerations will impact that measurement. The Senate and the Attorney General again urge the Court not to undertake a compactness assessment because determining whether an apportionment plan complies with this principle exceeds the scope of this Court's limited review. The Senate specifically contends that compactness has no precise definition and, further, that this Court is incapable of determining whether the shape of the district is irregular due to other considerations that must go into the apportionment process, like equal population, protecting minority voting rights, and utilizing geographical and political boundaries. Since all of these policies must be balanced, the Senate maintains, Florida courts should simply defer to the Legislature's judgment.

Contrary to the Senate's and the Attorney General's assertions, compactness does not require such a unique and factual determination that appellate courts are completely unable to review the matter absent a trial record. A significant number of states mandate that during the apportionment process districts be drawn compactly, and at least fourteen of those states vest original jurisdiction to review legislative apportionment in the state supreme court. Given that other state supreme courts have accomplished a similar task without much difficulty, we reject any suggestion that this Court lacks a similar ability to evaluate whether the Legislature complied with the compactness requirement in Florida. Having made that determination, we decide how this Court will go about measuring compactness.

As a geographical inquiry, a review of compactness begins by looking at the "shape of a district"; the object of the compactness criterion is that a district should not yield "bizarre designs." *Hickel* [*v. Southeast Conference*], 846 P.2d at 45 [(Alaska 1992)]; *see also Kilbury* [*v. Franklin County*], 90 P.3d at 1077 [(Wash. 2004)] ("[T]he phrase 'as compact as possible' does not mean 'as small in size as possible,' but rather 'as regular in shape as possible.'"). Compact districts should not have an unusual shape, a bizarre design, or an unnecessary appendage unless it is necessary to comply with some other requirement. *Hickel,* 846 P.2d at 45 ("Compact districting should not yield 'bizarre designs.'"); *Schrage,* 58 Ill.Dec. 451, 430 N.E.2d at 487 ("A visual examination of Representative District 89 reveals a tortured, extremely elongated form which is not compact in any sense."); *In re Livingston,* 96 Misc. 341, 160 N.Y.S. 462, 469–70 (N.Y.Sup.Ct.1916) (noting that the challenged district was "most irregular in shape [and] really grotesque," and holding that "[i]f the constitutional provision relating to compactness means anything, this district, as laid out, manifestly does not conform to it"); *see also Shaw,* 509 U.S. at 635–36, 113 S.Ct. 2816 (describing a snake-like district that was drawn so bizarrely that it "inspired poetry: 'Ask not for whom the line is drawn; it is drawn to avoid thee'" (quoting Bernard Grofman, *Would Vince Lombardi Have Been Right If He Had Said: 'When It Comes to Redistricting, Race Isn't Everything, It's the Only Thing'?,* 14 Cardozo L.Rev. 1237, 1261 n. 96 (1993))).

In addition to a visual examination of a district's geometric shape, quantitative geometric measures of compactness have been used to assist courts in assessing compactness.[20] In fact, there is commonly used redistricting software that includes tools designed to measure compactness. The House actually used two such measurements.

20. [FN 34.] *See, e.g., League of United Latin Am. Citizens v. Perry,* 548 U.S. 399, 455 n. 2 (2006) (Stevens, J., concurring in part and dissenting in part) ("[T]wo standard measures of compactness are the perimeter-to-area score, which compares the relative length of the perimeter of a district to its area, and the smallest circle score, which compares the ratio of space in the district to the space in the smallest circle that could encompass the district."); *Vieth,* 541 U.S. at 348 (Souter, J., dissenting) ("[C]ompactness ... can be measured quantitatively in terms of dispersion, perimeter, and population ratios, and the development of standards would thus be possible.").

First, the House utilized the Reock method (circle-dispersion measurement), which measures the ratio between the area of the district and the area of the smallest circle that can fit around the district. This measure ranges from 0 to 1, with a score of 1 representing the highest level of compactness as to its scale.

Second, the House used the Area/Convex Hull method in its analysis, which measures the ratio between the area of the district and the area of the minimum convex bounding polygon that can enclose the district. The measure ranges from 0 to 1, with a score of 1 representing the highest level of compactness. A circle, square, or any other shape with only convex angles has a score of 1. Both measures used by the House have gained relatively broad acceptance in redistricting.

Despite this Court's use of visual and numerical measurements of geographic compactness, our review of that mandate cannot be considered in isolation. Other factors influence a district's compactness, including geography and abiding by other constitutional requirements such as ensuring that the apportionment plan does not deny the equal opportunity of racial or language minorities to participate in the political process or diminish their ability to elect representatives of their choice.

The Florida Constitution does not mandate, and no party urges, that districts within a redistricting plan achieve the highest mathematical compactness scores. Given Florida's unique shape, some of Florida's districts have geographical constraints, such as those located in the Florida Keys, that affect the compactness calculations. Other times, lower compactness measurements may result from the Legislature's desire to follow political or geographical boundaries or to keep municipalities wholly intact. *See, e.g., Commonwealth ex rel. Specter v. Levin*, 448 Pa. 1, 293 A.2d 15, 19 (1972) ("[A]ttempts to maintain the integrity of the boundaries of political subdivisions ... will in reality make it impossible to achieve districts of precise mathematical compactness. A great many if not most of the counties, cities, towns, boroughs, townships and wards in this Commonwealth have a geographical shape which falls far short of ideal mathematical compactness.").

Thus, if an oddly shaped district is a result of this state's "irregular geometry" and the need to keep counties and municipalities whole, these explanations may serve to justify the shape of the district in a logical and constitutionally permissible way. Nevertheless, non-compact and "bizarrely shaped districts" require close examination. As explained by the Supreme Court of Alaska in *Hickel*, if

> "corridors" of land that extend to include a populated area, but not the less-populated land around it, [the district] may run afoul of the compactness requirement. Likewise, appendages attached to otherwise compact areas may violate the requirement of compact districting.

Hickel, 846 P.2d at 45–46.

Since compactness is set forth in section 21(b), the criteria of section 21(a) must predominate to the extent that they conflict with drawing a district that is compact. However, if a district can be drawn more compactly while utilizing political and geographical boundaries and without intentionally favoring a political party or incumbent, compactness must be a yardstick by which to evaluate those other factors. Among the section 21(b) criteria, the standard for compactness is that the district "shall be compact" without qualification.

In sum, we hold that compactness is a standard that refers to the shape of the district. The goal is to ensure that districts are logically drawn and that bizarrely shaped districts are avoided. Compactness can be evaluated both visually and by employing standard mathematical measurements.

c. Utilizing Existing Political and Geographical Boundaries

In tandem with compactness, article III, section 21(b), requires that "districts shall, where feasible, utilize existing political and geographical boundaries." Unlike the mandate of compactness, this requirement is modified by the phrase "where feasible," suggesting that in balancing this criterion with compactness, more flexibility is permitted. We begin by interpreting the terms "political and geographical boundaries," remaining mindful that, as with all of the constitutional provisions, our goal is to construe the provision in "such manner as to fulfill the intent of the people, never to defeat it." *Zingale*, 885 So.2d at 282. Further, we construe the provision by looking to the "purpose of the provision, the evil sought to be remedied, and the circumstances leading to its inclusion in our constitutional document." *In re Apportionment Law—1982*, 414 So.2d at 1048.

The interpretation given by a plurality of the Court explains the purpose of this provision and the proper interpretation:

> *The purpose of the standards in section (2) of the proposals is to require legislative and congressional districts to follow existing community lines so that districts are logically drawn, and bizarrely shaped districts*—such as one senate district that was challenged in *Resolution 1987*, 817 So.2d at 824–25—are avoided. Since *the "city" and "county" terminology honors this community-based standard for drawing legislative and congressional boundaries*, and further describes the standards in terms that are readily understandable to the average voter, we conclude that the use of different terminology does not render the summaries misleading.

Standards for Establishing Legislative Dist. Boundaries, 2 So.3d at 187–88 (emphasis added). In that case, we accepted the argument that the term "political boundaries" primarily encompasses municipal or county boundaries. The FDP likewise in its brief argues that the "basic purpose of this provision is to keep communities together and sensibly adhere to natural boundaries across the state." Certainly, cities and counties would be existing political boundaries.

Consistent with this approach, the House in its brief emphasizes that the House plan was drawn with respect for county integrity, stating as follows:

> [C]ounty lines were usually preferable to other boundaries, because county lines are the most readily understood, consistently compact, functional, and stable. County boundaries are substantially less likely to change than municipal boundaries, and—unlike municipalities—all counties are con-

tiguous. Moreover, although all Floridians have a home county, millions
live outside any incorporated area. Additionally, by using a strategy of keeping counties whole, the House Map necessarily keeps many municipalities
whole within districts. And importantly, numerous Floridians advocated
an emphasis on county boundaries at the twenty-six public meetings during
the summer of 2011.

House Brief at 12–13 (footnotes omitted). The House additionally asserts that there
is an advantage in using county lines in order to further other constitutional goals
such as compactness:

[T]he House's consistent respect for county boundaries provided the additional benefit of creating compact districts. And many testified to the Legislature that their idea of compactness supported preserving county integrity
where practicable. Where county lines could not serve as the district line,
the House relied on municipal boundaries and geographic boundaries such
as railways, interstates, state roads, and rivers. Consistent with other public
testimony, the House resolved to draw accessible districts with understandable
shapes — without fingers, bizarre shapes, or "rat tails."

Id. at 13–14 (citations omitted).

On the other hand, the Senate takes the position that the "political and geographical
boundaries requirement directly presents the kind of 'fact-intensive' issues that cannot
be meaningfully reviewed in this truncated proceeding." Ironically, in contradiction
to the position of the House, the Senate asserts that "it is a 'plain fact' that boundary
requirements tend[] to conflict with compactness norms." The Senate argues that the
requirement of utilizing political boundaries is "internally inconsistent," necessitating
choices between political boundaries and geographical boundaries. Although the
House in its brief points to the "numerous Floridians" who advocated an emphasis
on county boundaries at the twenty-six public meetings, the Senate does not acknowledge that public viewpoint.

The Senate argues that since Florida's Constitution provides the Legislature with
the choice of political or geographical boundaries, the choice of boundaries was a
matter that should be left entirely to the discretion of the Legislature. During oral
argument, counsel for the Senate further alleged that Florida was "unique among the
fifty states to count geographical boundaries." In actuality, many other states have
constitutional requirements that require the consideration of geographical boundaries.
Again, consistent with the holding of other states, this Court is likewise able to evaluate
whether the Legislature complied with that requirement in Florida. Accordingly, we
turn to our construction of the meaning of "political and geographical boundaries"
as contained within our state constitution.

The Senate argues for a pick-and-choose legislative discretion regarding which
boundaries to choose from, including a very broad list that encompasses not only
easily ascertainable political boundaries, such as counties and municipalities, but extending even to "man-made demarcations," such as "well-traveled roadways." While

discretion must be afforded to accommodate for well-recognized geographical boundaries, the decision to simply use any boundary, such as a creek or minor road, would eviscerate the constitutional requirement—as well as the purpose for the requirement, which is aimed at preventing improper intent.

The Senate's approach that almost anything can be a "geographical boundary" may be why the opponents of the Senate's plan criticize the Senate's plan for not only lack of compactness but also for containing the same "finger-like extensions," "narrow and bizarrely shaped tentacles," and "hook-like shape[s]," which are constitutionally suspect and often indicative of racial and partisan gerrymandering.

We reject the Senate's view because it would render the new constitutional provision virtually meaningless and standardless. We accept the House's view of geographical boundaries that are easily ascertainable and commonly understood, such as "rivers, railways, interstates, and state roads." Together with an analysis of compactness, an adherence to county and city boundaries as political boundaries, and rivers, railways, interstates and state roads as geographical boundaries will provide a basis for an objective analysis of the plans and the specific districts drawn. In addition, we also reject the contention that following a municipal boundary will necessarily violate the compactness requirement. In a compactness analysis, we are reviewing the general shape of a district; if a district has a small area where minor adjustments are made to follow either a municipal boundary or a river, this would not violate compactness.

There will be times when districts cannot be drawn to follow county lines or to include the entire municipalities within a district. The City of Lakeland in its challenge to the Senate plan asserts a violation of this provision because the Senate plan splits the City of Lakeland into two state Senate districts. We will analyze this argument further, but certainly not every split of a municipality will violate this prohibition; the constitutional directive is only that "existing political and geographical boundaries" should be used "where feasible."

3. How These Standards Interact

Having set forth the constitutional standards, we must now decide the appropriate framework in which to evaluate how these standards interact. This includes a determination of how best to approach challenges to the joint resolution of apportionment.

An examination of the explicit language used in the Florida Constitution is the necessary starting point for any analysis of constitutional provisions. *See Zingale,* 885 So.2d at 282. The text of the constitution provides unambiguous direction for the analysis of how these constitutional standards interact. It provides that the tier-two standards are subordinate and shall give way where compliance "conflicts with the [tier-one] standards or with federal law." Art. III, § 21(b), Fla. Const. Although the tier-two standards are subordinate to the tier-one requirements, the constitution further instructs that no standard has priority over the other within each tier. *See* art. III, § 21(c), Fla. Const. Consequently, the Legislature is tasked with balancing the tier-two standards together in order to strike a constitutional result, but this Court remains "sensitive to the complex interplay of forces that enter a legislature's redistricting calculus." *Miller*, 515 U.S. at 915–16.

Florida's tier-two standards—that districts shall be as nearly equal in population as is practicable, shall be compact, and shall utilize existing political and geographical boundaries where feasible—circumscribe the Legislature's discretion in drawing district lines, requiring it to conform to traditional redistricting principles. *See id.* at 916 (defining "traditional" redistricting principles to include "compactness, contiguity, and respect for political subdivisions"); *Bush v. Vera*, 517 U.S. 952, 959–60 (1996) (plurality opinion) (noting federal district court's conclusion that "traditional redistricting principles" include "natural geographical boundaries, contiguity, compactness, and conformity to political subdivisions"). Indeed, the extent to which the Legislature complies with the sum of Florida's traditional redistricting principles serves as an objective indicator of the impermissible legislative purpose proscribed under tier one (i.e., intent to favor or disfavor a political party or an incumbent).

In other words, the goal of the tier-two requirements is "to guard, as far as practicable, under the system of representation adopted, against a legislative evil, commonly known as 'gerrymander.'" *Pearson*, 359 S.W.3d at 38, 2012 WL 131425, at *2 (quoting *Hitchcock*, 146 S.W. at 61). There is no question that the goal of minimizing opportunities for political favoritism was the driving force behind the passage of the Fair Districts Amendment. *See Standards for Establishing Legislative Dist. Boundaries*, 2 So.3d at 181 (plurality) ("The overall goal of the proposed amendments is to require the Legislature to redistrict in a manner that prohibits favoritism or discrimination, while respecting geographic considerations.").

* * *

… [T]his Court held the new standards to have "a natural relation and connection," all directed at the "overall goal of … requir[ing] the Legislature to redistrict in a manner that prohibits favoritism or discrimination, while respecting geographic considerations." *Standards for Establishing Legislative Dist. Boundaries*, 2 So.3d at 181. We agree that in the context of Florida's constitutional provision, a disregard for the constitutional requirements set forth in tier two is indicative of improper intent, which Florida prohibits by absolute terms. *See Vieth*, 541 U.S. at 335 (Stevens, J., dissenting) ("[I]rrational shape can serve as an objective indicator of an impermissible legislative purpose….."); *Schrage*, 58 Ill.Dec. 451, 430 N.E.2d at 486 ("[C]ompactness is 'almost universally recognized' as an appropriate anti-gerrymandering standard." (quoting James M. Edwards, *The Gerrymander and "One Man, One Vote,"* 46 N.Y.U. L.Rev. 879, 893 (1971))).

As was stated in *Reynolds*, 377 U.S. at 578, a "desire to maintain integrity of various political subdivisions, insofar as possible, and provide for compact districts of contiguous territory" undermines opportunities for political favoritism. Of course, the correlation between a lack of compliance with traditional redistricting principles and impermissible intent cannot be considered in isolation. In addition to prohibiting improper intent, tier one forbids the Legislature to draw districts that diminish minorities' ability to elect representatives of choice or deny minorities an equal opportunity to participate in the political process. *See* art. III, § 21(a), Fla. Const. Given this requirement, efforts to preserve or create minority districts could be misinterpreted as an action intended to favor (or disfavor) a political party or an incumbent.

* * *

In examining the reasoning behind drawing a district in a particular way, we remain cognizant that both federal and state minority voting-rights protections may require the preservation or creation of non-compact districts or may help to explain the shape of a challenged district. Therefore, the reason for drawing lines a certain way may be the result of legitimate efforts by the Legislature to comply with federal law or Florida's tier-one imperative. *Cf.* DOJ Guidance Notice, 76 Fed. Reg. 470 at 7472 ("[C]ompliance with Section 5 of the Voting Rights Act may require the jurisdiction to depart from strict adherence to certain of its redistricting criteria.").

The fact that the tier-two principles expressly yield to this requirement in tier one demonstrates that the Florida Constitution specifically contemplates this need, but only to the extent necessary. Where it can be shown that it was possible for the Legislature to comply with the tier-two constitutional criteria while, at the same time, not diminishing minorities' ability to elect representatives of choice or denying minorities an equal opportunity to participate in the political process, the Legislature's plan becomes subject to a concern that improper intent was the motivating factor for the design of the district. It is critical that the requirement to protect minority voting rights when drawing district lines should not be used as a shield against complying with Florida's other important constitutional imperatives; the Court's obligation is to ensure that "every clause and every part" of the language of the constitution is given effect where "an interpretation can be found which gives it effect." *In re Apportionment Law — 1972*, 263 So.2d at 807.

Because compliance with the tier-two principles is objectively ascertainable, it provides a good starting point for analyzing challenges to the Legislature's joint resolution. Where adherence to a tier-one requirement explains the irregular shape of a given district, a claim that the district has been drawn to favor or disfavor a political party can be defeated. Where it does not, however, further inquiry into the Legislature's intent becomes necessary.

In determining whether the plans are constitutionally valid, we have considered the role of the alternative plans submitted by the Coalition. If an alternative plan can achieve the same constitutional objectives that prevent vote dilution and retrogression of protected minority and language groups and also apportions the districts in accordance with tier-two principles so as not to disfavor a political party or an incumbent, this will provide circumstantial evidence of improper intent. That is to say, an alternative plan that achieves all of Florida's constitutional criteria without subordinating one standard to another demonstrates that it was not necessary for the Legislature to subordinate a standard in its plan.

It is with this global approach to determining the validity of the Legislature's House and Senate apportionment plans in mind that we turn to the challenges raised to the apportionment plans before this Court.

C. CHALLENGES TO THE APPORTIONMENT PLANS

1. General Challenges

We next proceed to examine the Coalition's and the FDP's arguments that they claim demonstrate improper intent on the part of the Legislature in drawing the apportionment plans.

a. Partisan Imbalance as Demonstrative of Intent

At the time the apportionment plans were drawn in 2012, of the 120 seats in the House, 39 were held by Democrats and 81 by Republicans, and of the 40 seats in the Senate, 12 were held by Democrats and 28 by Republicans. The position of Governor was held by a Republican. The Coalition and the FDP essentially allege that with the Republicans in charge of drawing the apportionment plans, the plans were drawn with the intent to favor the Republican Party.

One of the primary challenges brought by the Coalition and the FDP is that a statistical analysis of the plans reveals a severe partisan imbalance that violates the constitutional prohibition against favoring an incumbent or a political party. The FDP asserts that statistics show an overwhelming partisan bias based on voter registration and election results. Under the circumstances presented to this Court, we are unable to reach the conclusion that improper intent has been shown based on voter registration and election results.

* * *

We first address voter registration and acknowledge the reality that based on the 2010 general election data, of the voters in the state who registered with an affiliation with one of the two major parties, 53% were registered as Democrats and 47% were registered as Republicans. The challengers point out that in contrast to the statewide statistics showing that registered Democrats outnumber Republicans, the Senate and House plans contain more districts in which registered Republicans outnumber registered Democrats than vice versa. As of 2010, in the Senate plan there were 18 of 40 Senate districts (45.0%) in which registered Democrats outnumbered registered Republicans, and 22 Senate districts (55.0%) in which registered Republicans outnumbered registered Democrats. In the House plan, there were 59 of 120 House districts in which the registered Democrats outnumber registered Republicans (49.2%), and 61 districts in which registered Republicans outnumber registered Democrats (50.8%).

While Democrats outnumber Republicans statewide in voter registration, this fact does not lead to the conclusions asserted by the challengers that these statistics demonstrate that the plans were drawn with intent to favor Republicans. Although there are more registered Democrats than Republicans, as of 2010, there were over 2.5 million voters who are not registered as Democrats or Republicans. Further, voter registration is not necessarily determinative of actual election results. The actual election results show that the existence of more registered Democrats than registered Republicans statewide has not necessarily translated into Democratic Party victories in statewide elections. To illustrate, Florida last elected a Democratic governor, Lawton Chiles, in 1994.

* * *

We do not agree that the partisan imbalance in the Senate and House plans demonstrates an overall intent to favor Republicans in this case. Explanations other than intent to favor or disfavor a political party could account for this imbalance. First, it has been observed that Democrats tend to cluster in cities, which may result in a natural "packing" effect, regardless of where the lines are drawn. A plurality of the United States Supreme Court has explained:

> Whether by reason of partisan districting or not, party constituents may always wind up "packed" in some districts and "cracked" throughout others. *See* R. Dixon, Democratic Representation 462 (1968) ("All Districting Is 'Gerrymandering'"); Schuck, 87 Colum. L.Rev. at 1359. Consider, for example, a legislature that draws district lines with no objectives in mind except compactness and respect for the lines of political subdivisions. Under that system, political groups that tend to cluster (as is the case with Democratic voters in cities) would be systematically affected by what might be called a "natural" packing effect. *See Bandemer,* 478 U.S. at 159 (O'Connor, J., concurring in judgment).

Vieth, 541 U.S. at 289–90 (plurality). Second, the imbalance could be a result of a legitimate effort to comply with VRA principles or other constitutional requirements. Although the FDP summarily argues that the partisan imbalance cannot be a result of such attempts, it fails to explain why.

We reject any suggestion that the Legislature is required to compensate for a natural packing effect of urban Democrats in order to create a "fair" plan. We also reject the suggestion that once the political results of the plan are known, the Legislature must alter the plan to bring it more in balance with the composition of voters statewide. The Florida Constitution does not require the affirmative creation of a fair plan, but rather a neutral one in which no improper intent was involved.

Although we have rejected the challenge that statewide voter registration and election results demonstrate an overall intent to favor the Republican party, we evaluate these statistics when examining individual districts.

b. History of Resistance to the Amendments

The Coalition next takes issue with the fact that the Legislature "attempted every possible legal maneuver to keep the FairDistricts Amendments from becoming law" and then attempted to invalidate the congressional amendment in federal court. However, evidence that the Legislature resisted efforts to make the new constitutional standards enforceable law does not equate to evidence that the Legislature would then intentionally disregard that law once it was in effect.

c. "Gentlemen's Agreement" as Indicative of Intent

The Coalition next points to a "gentlemen's agreement" between the House and Senate, by which each chamber would "rubber stamp" the other chamber's plan, allowing each to protect its own incumbents without interference from the other. Although the Joint Resolution was passed with both chambers voting to approve the other chamber's plan, it is uncontroverted that each chamber agreed to draft its own plan without input from, debate from, or interference by the other. The challengers assert that this "gentlemen's agreement" is indicative of improper intent. The fact that the House did not debate or amend the Senate's plan or that the Senate did not debate or amend the House plan is legally irrelevant. From the beginning of the process, it was clear that each chamber would embark on its separate approach to redistricting, using different software and inputting different data. The fact that the process occurred on two different tracks without formal communication or coordination between the two chambers or that there was a "gentlemen's agreement" does not provide circumstantial evidence of improper intent.

d. Failure to Adopt the Coalition's Alternative Plans

The Coalition takes issue with the Legislature's treatment of its proposed alternative plans, which the Coalition also submitted to this Court. Specifically, the Coalition states that the Senate and House did not properly consider the Coalition's plans, which the Coalition argued contained less population deviation, were more compact, and better utilized political and geographical boundaries. We do not consider the failure of the Legislature to adopt the Coalition's alternative plans to be indicative of an improper intent.

e. Legislature's Failure to Introduce Proposed Plans at Public Hearings

In this claim, the Coalition appears to ascribe improper motive to the failure of the Legislature to introduce proposed apportionment plans during the public hearings to ensure that the plans were fully aired in public. Although a review of the public hearing testimony reveals that many individuals were upset that the Legislature was soliciting their comments in the absence of a plan, some individuals recognized that there may be legitimate reasons for the Legislature's approach. *Compare* Public Hrg. Tr. 1140 ("[W]hy couldn't the Legislature have come up with a map that we could then look at and see how it affects Wakulla County and Lafayette County and then have them testify and see what is going on[?]"); Public Hrg. Tr. 1153–54 ("This process and these hearings are very troubling. The Legislature has invited the public to comment, but you don't give us anything to comment on. Where are the maps? This isn't a conversation."); *with* Public Hrg. Tr. 1154–55 ("[I]f you would come in with maps drawn then we would be hearing from all of the naysayers that ... you met in a back room, smoke filled room and drew the maps yourself and now you are just wanting us to rubber stamp them."); Public Hrg. Tr. 2798 ("You have correctly taken a common sense approach by seeking public input before the maps are drawn and not afterwards."). More importantly, the Florida Constitution imposes no such requirement on the Legislature, and we conclude that this aspect of the process is not indicative of intent to produce partisan plans.

Having determined that none of the above general challenges should be used in this facial review of the validity of the House and Senate plans, we proceed to analyze the compliance of the House plan as a whole with the constitutional standards and then examine the challenges to the individual House districts. We then analyze the Senate plan and districts in the same manner.

2. The House Plan

a. Overall Challenges

Tier-One Requirements

Intent to favor or disfavor a political party or an incumbent. The first requirement that we address in looking at the overall plan is this important constitutional requirement, the purpose of which is to prevent the drawing of districts designed to protect a political party or an incumbent. We see no overall objective indicia of improper intent with respect to the House plan. It is undisputed that the House plan pits both Democratic and Republican incumbents against each other. While we recognize that the new districts on average retain 59.7% of the population of their predecessor districts, this fact standing alone does not demonstrate intent to favor incumbents.

Finally, as discussed below, the House plan has complied with the tier-two standards, making improper intent less likely. Indeed, the purpose of the tier-two standards—equal population, compactness, and utilizing political and geographical boundaries—is to prohibit political favoritism by constraining legislative discretion.

Florida minority voting protection provision. The FDP generally alleges that the House plan improperly over-packs black voters into minority districts to dilute their vote elsewhere. To the extent this argument is made, it is without merit. Under the House plan, there are twelve black majority-minority districts and sixteen Hispanic majority-minority districts. None of the black majority-minority districts is a super-majority district requiring the Legislature to "unpack" it on this record. As to the sixteen Hispanic majority-minority House districts, eleven do have large percentages.... These high percentages could be explained by the fact that the Hispanic population in Miami-Dade County, where these districts are located, is densely populated. The challengers have failed to establish that another majority-minority district for either black or Hispanic voters potentially could have been created. We conclude that on this record, any facial claim regarding vote dilution under Florida's constitution fails. While the Court does not rule out the potential that a violation of the Florida minority voting protection provision could be established by a pattern of overpacking minorities into districts where other coalition or influence districts could be created, this Court is unable to make such a determination on this record.

To the extent that the opponents contend that the overall House plan amounts to retrogression under the Florida Constitution, we conclude that this argument is also without merit. The record reveals that the House undertook a functional analysis when drawing its plan in order to guard against retrogression. As to black majority and crossover House districts, the fact that there is one fewer black crossover district as compared to the benchmark plan does not alter this conclusion because one additional black majority-minority district has emerged from a previously existing crossover district. Apportionment plans that increase minority voting strength are entitled to preclearance under Section 5, *see Ashcroft*, 539 U.S. at 477, 123 S.Ct. 2498, and we conclude that the same principle applies under Florida law.

With respect to House districts with sizeable Hispanic populations, we likewise conclude that there has been no unconstitutional retrogression under the Florida Constitution. Because three new Hispanic majority-minority districts have emerged from previously existing influence or crossover districts, the Hispanic influence in the remaining number of districts has shifted. No challenger has established or alleged that this change has affected the Hispanic voters' ability to elect a person of their choice in the respective districts.

Contiguity. No party challenges contiguity as to the House plan. Upon a review of the plan, we conclude that this plan does not violate the contiguity requirement under article III, sections 16(a) and 21(a), of the Florida Constitution.

Tier-Two Requirements

Equal population. In looking at this constitutional requirement, the 2010 census data shows that Florida has a total population of 18,801,310, and the ideal population for each House district is 156,678 individuals. The most populated district in the House plan is District 75, which has a population of 159,978 (an additional 3,300 individuals than the ideal, or a deviation of 2.11%), and the least populated district is District 76, which has a population of 153,745 (2,933 fewer individuals than the ideal, or a deviation of −1.87%). Thus, the total deviation is 3.97%. This is 1.18% higher than the 2.79% population deviation the Court approved in 2002.

The House aptly acknowledges that "[c]onsiderations of compactness and emphasis on county integrity, of course, had to be weighed against other considerations, including population equality." For example, the House explains that it set a population deviation upper limit that would allow Charlotte County, whose population deviated only slightly from the ideal, to remain whole.

Compactness. A visual inspection of the plan reveals that it as a whole appears to be compact and that only a few districts are highly irregular. A visual inspection of the plan reveals that there are districts that are clearly less compact than other districts, with visually unusual shapes. These include Districts 70, 88, and 117. Under the House plan, only three districts have significantly low compactness scores using both Reock and Area/Convex Hull: House Districts 88, 117, and 120. We note that Districts 70, 88, and 117 are majority-minority or minority-opportunity districts, and they are discussed more thoroughly below in conjunction with challenges to individual districts. We also note that District 120 includes the unusual geography of the Florida Keys and will therefore necessarily score low on the compactness scales.

Political and geographical boundaries. The House explains that in considering the appropriate balance of equal population, compactness, and adherence to existing boundaries, it emphasized county integrity while adhering to other tier-two standards. As explained in the House's brief: "Where practicable, it sought to keep counties whole within districts, or to wholly locate districts within counties, depending on county populations. Where not feasible, the House sought to 'anchor' districts within a county—tying the geography representing a majority or plurality of the district's residents to one county." The House also considered municipal boundaries and geographical features, but decided that "county lines were usually preferable to other boundaries." The underlying reason for this approach as expressed in the House's brief was that

> [c]ounty boundaries are substantially less likely to change than municipal boundaries, and—unlike municipalities—all counties are contiguous. Moreover, although all Floridians have a home county, millions live outside any incorporated area. Additionally, by using a strategy of keeping counties whole, the House Map necessarily keeps many municipalities whole within districts. And importantly, numerous Floridians advocated an emphasis on county boundaries at the twenty-six public meetings during the summer of 2011.

(Footnote omitted.) A review of the House plan reveals that it consistently used county boundaries where feasible, leaving thirty-seven of sixty-seven counties whole.

The House further explained that "[w]here county lines could not serve as the district line, the House relied on municipal boundaries and geographic boundaries such as railways, interstates, state roads, and rivers." As previously discussed, we have adopted the House's view of geographical boundaries as those that are easily ascertainable and commonly understood (e.g., rivers, railways, interstates, and state roads).

Conclusion as to Overall Challenges to the House Plan

A review of the House plan and the record reveals that the House engaged in a consistent and reasoned approach, balancing the tier-two standards by endeavoring to make districts compact and as nearly equal in population as possible, and utilizing political and geographical boundaries where feasible by endeavoring to keep counties and cities together where possible. Although the House plan has a higher population deviation than in the past, the House has explained that this deviation was necessary to achieve other required objectives, such as consistent use of county boundaries. The House further asserts that its "consistent respect for county boundaries provided the additional benefit of creating compact districts."

In addition, the House approached the minority voting protection provision by properly undertaking a functional analysis of voting strength in minority districts. A facial review of the House plan reveals no dilution or retrogression under the Florida Constitution. Further, we find no objective plan-wide indicia of improper attempt to favor or disfavor a political party or incumbent.

b. Challenges to Individual House Districts

We discuss the challenges to the individual House districts in turn. We conclude that the challengers have not demonstrated that any of these districts violate the Florida Constitution. [Review of most districts has been deleted for space considerations.]

House District 38

The FDP summarily alleges that District 38 retains a high percentage of the population from its predecessor district in order to benefit the incumbent in that district. However, the FDP does not point to any additional indicators of improper intent, and we deny this claim.

House District 70

The FDP contends that District 70 is non-compact and fails to utilize boundaries because it cuts across four counties (Pinellas, Hillsborough, Manatee, and Sarasota) as well as three major metropolitan areas (St. Petersburg, Bradenton, and Sarasota) and splits the town of Palmetto. The FDP also contends that District 70 is overly packed with minorities and that the House should have drawn the district with more natural boundary lines in order to allow those minorities to have a greater influence in neighboring District 71. The Coalition, on the other hand, raises no objection to this district.

District 70 is a black-opportunity district (black VAP of 45.1%; Hispanic VAP of 15.3%). It extends into four counties, taking in the areas with the highest concentration of minorities from St. Petersburg, Bradenton, and Sarasota. Significantly, part of District 70 extends into Hillsborough County, which is a covered jurisdiction under Section 5 of the VRA, and must obtain preclearance from the DOJ. District 70 is depicted below.

District 70 is strikingly similar to its predecessor district, old District 55, which has a black VAP of 49.4% and a Hispanic VAP of 13.6% and which also reached into St. Petersburg, Bradenton, and Sarasota. In adopting District 70, the Legislature stated that its intent was to comply with Section 5 of the VRA:

> [I]t is the intent of the Legislature to establish State House District 70, which is consistent with Section 5 of the federal Voting Rights Act; does not deny or abridge the equal opportunity of racial or language minorities to participate in the political process or diminish their ability to elect representatives of their choice....

Fla. S.J. Res. 1176, at 22 (Reg. Sess. 2012) (SJR 1176).

Tier-two requirements must yield when necessary to comply with federal law (here, Section 5 of the VRA) and Florida's minority voting protection provision. Although the FDP summarily asserts that District 70 is overly packed with minorities and that it could have been drawn differently to be more compact and to better utilize boundaries, the FDP has not demonstrated that this can be done without causing retrogression.

* * *

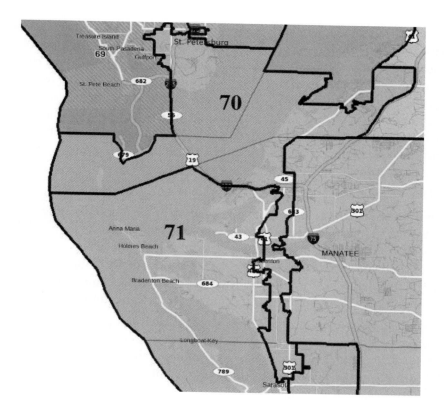

c. Conclusion as to the House Plan

We conclude that the Coalition and the FDP have not successfully demonstrated that the House plan violates one or more of the constitutional standards. In making this determination, we have reviewed the challenges to the House plan as a whole and the challenges to individual districts. Based on the nature of the review that this Court is able to perform in a facial challenge, we find that there has been no demonstrated violation of the constitutional standards in article III, section 21, and we conclude that the House plan is facially valid.

3. The Senate Plan

a. Overall Challenges

In reviewing the Senate plan, we begin by evaluating overall adherence to the constitutional requirements. Then we evaluate a claim that the Senate plan was renumbered for the purpose of favoring incumbents by allowing them to be eligible to serve for longer than they would have otherwise. Finally, we consider the challenges to individual districts brought by the Coalition, the FDP, and the City of Lakeland. We emphasize that our analysis takes into consideration both the overall challenges and the results of our analysis of challenges to individual districts. In addition, in looking at the approach used in developing the Senate plan, where appropriate, we compare it to the approach used in developing the House plan, which we have upheld. We make that comparison not because the process used by the House and its approach on compliance with the standards is the only way to approach apportionment, but because overall the House's approach to ensuring compactness and utilizing consistent political and geographical boundaries led to a plan that has withstood the challenges to its validity. Further, the House's use of political and elections data to engage in protecting minority districts allowed the House to engage in the appropriate functional analysis of the districts. Finally, we note that the process employed by the House included openly considering different plans that the Redistricting Subcommittee analyzed for factors such as compactness and note the fact that the House plan pits incumbents against one another.

Tier-One Requirements

Intent to favor or disfavor a political party or an incumbent. In evaluating the Senate plan, we first address this important constitutional requirement, the purpose of which is to prevent the drawing of a plan or districts designed to protect a political party or an incumbent. We conclude that the Senate plan is rife with objective indicators of improper intent which, when considered in isolation do not amount to improper intent, but when viewed cumulatively demonstrate a clear pattern.

First, the Coalition alleges that the Senate plan does not pit incumbents against each other, and the Senate has not contested this. This Court was provided with the addresses of 21 incumbents and has confirmed that of the addresses provided, none of the incumbents would run against another incumbent.

Second, the new districts on average are composed of 64.2% of their predecessor districts. While this percentage is just an average, our below analysis of the individual district challenges reveals that at least some incumbents appear to have been given large percentages of their prior constituencies. These percentages are of even greater concern given that the 2002 Senate plan was drawn at a time when intent to favor a political party or an incumbent was permissible and there were no requirements of compactness or utilizing existing boundaries.

Third, as discussed further below, the Senate admittedly renumbered the Senate plan in order to allow incumbents to be eligible to serve longer than they would have otherwise. Not only do we conclude that this renumbering was improper as it was intended to favor incumbents, but we note that the renumbering process indicates that the Senate specifically considered incumbent information when renumbering the districts.

Fourth, although we do not consider the partisan balance of the plan as evidence of intent, the FDP alleges that the 2012 Senate plan has two *fewer* Democratic districts than the 2002 plan based on voter registration. However, because voter registration alone is not an accurate measure of how districts perform, we do not consider this as conclusive evidence of improper intent.

Fifth, the majority (70.0%) of under-populated districts are Republican-performing districts when the 2010 gubernatorial and 2008 presidential elections are considered. Population deviations are at the heart of the requirement of one-person, one-vote, which generally requires that district populations be nearly equal to ensure that every individual's vote counts as much as any other's. Under-populated districts are comparatively over-represented. Thus, it appears that under the Senate plan, individuals residing in Republican-performing districts are over-represented as compared to individuals living in Democratic-performing districts.

Florida's minority voting protection provision. The FDP and the Coalition contend that the Senate's overall plan amounts to vote dilution and retrogression under the Florida Constitution. The Coalition further asserts that when engaging in its retrogression analysis, the Senate interpreted Florida's provision too strictly by limiting the data upon which it relied and failing to conduct the required functional analysis. While this failure is relevant to other defects in the plan, we conclude on this record that the Senate plan does not facially dilute a minority group's voting strength or cause retrogression under Florida law.

No opponent has demonstrated that the Senate plan facially dilutes minority voting strength as a whole under the Florida Constitution. The FDP has not submitted any alternative plans, and the Coalition's alternative Senate plan does not demonstrate that an additional majority-minority district can be created. While the Court does not rule out the potential that a violation of the Florida minority voting protection provision could be established by a pattern of overpacking minorities into districts where other coalition or influence districts could be created, this Court is unable to make such a determination on this record.

Nor has any challenger demonstrated that the Senate plan retrogresses as a whole under Florida law. There are as many Senate minority districts as there were under the 2002 Senate benchmark plan with what appears to be commensurate voting ability. Although there is one fewer Hispanic influence district, there are now two additional Hispanic majority-minority districts when compared to the 2002 benchmark. Districts that increase minority voting strength when compared to the benchmark are entitled to preclearance under Section 5, *see Ashcroft,* 539 U.S. at 477, and we conclude that the same principle applies under Florida law.

Contiguity. The FDP contends that the Senate plan "stretches [contiguity] to its limits," but notably does not argue that any of districts under the Senate plan are not contiguous. In looking at the Senate plan, it is clear that this plan does not violate the contiguity requirement under article III, sections 16(a) and 21(a), of the Florida Constitution.

Tier-Two Requirements

Equal population. In looking at this constitutional requirement, the 2010 census data shows that Florida has a total population of 18,801,310, and the ideal population for each Senate district is 470,033 individuals. The most populated district in the Senate plan is District 3, which has a population of 474,685 (an additional 4,652 individuals, or a deviation of 0.99%), and the least populated district is District 23, which has a population of 465,343 (4,690 fewer individuals or a deviation of −1.00%). Thus, the total deviation is 1.99%. As to Florida's standard, we must view the population deviation in conjunction with the other tier-two standards.

Compactness. The Senate contends that the Court should find that the Senate plan is facially compact because the plan is now more compact than the 2002 plan. We reject this comparison as evidence of compliance because the 2002 Senate plan had no requirement for compactness and thus cannot serve as an adequate benchmark in establishing adherence to the newly added compactness requirement.

A visual inspection of the plan reveals a number of districts that are clearly less compact than other districts, with visually bizarre and unusual shapes.... As explained above in our discussion of the standards, we reject the Senate's definition of compactness as including communities of interest.

Political and geographical boundaries. Unlike the House, the Senate did not use any consistent definition of political and geographical boundaries. Some districts adhere to county boundaries (e.g., District 5), while others freely split counties and follow a variety of roads and waterways, including minor residential roads and creeks (e.g., District 1). In some districts, the Senate constantly switched between different types of boundaries within the span of a few miles.

Conclusion as to Overall Challenges to the Senate Plan

We recognize that the Senate did not have the benefit of our opinion when drawing its plan. However, it is clear from a facial review of the Senate plan that the "pick and choose" method for existing boundaries was not balanced with the remaining tier-two requirements, and certainly not in a consistent manner. We again note that while the existing boundaries requirement is stated as "where feasible" and the equal population requirement is stated in terms of "as is practicable," the compactness requirement does not contain those modifiers; rather, the constitutional expression is that "districts *shall* be compact." The concept of "communities of interest" is not part of the constitutional term "compactness."

Although we hold that the Senate plan does not facially dilute or retrogress under Florida law as a whole, we further conclude that the Senate failed to conduct a functional analysis as to retrogression in order to properly determine when, and to what extent, the tier-two requirements must yield in order to avoid conflict with Florida's minority voting protection provision. Although the Senate touts its adherence to the recommendations of the Florida NAACP and LatinoJustice PRLDEF regarding minority districts, this does not absolve the Senate of its independent responsibility to draw an apportionment plan that adheres to *all* of the constitutional requirements.

The record is clear that in drawing districts for the 2012 apportionment cycle, the Senate employed an incorrect and incomplete retrogression analysis. Based on the record, the Senate formulated its apportionment plan without reference to election results or voter-registration and political party data; instead, it relied on voting-age population data and attempted to maintain the core of a new Senate district's predecessor district (which the Senate apparently knew had performed for a certain minority group in the past). Although it was acknowledged during the February 9, 2012, Senate floor debate that the use of voter and election performance data to safeguard minority voting opportunities is consistent with accepted practice in other states and is a data set that the DOJ uses when evaluating whether to preclear a covered jurisdiction under Section 5 of the VRA, it was also stated that the Senate need not rely on such data when undertaking its retrogression analysis. Not only does this position ignore the DOJ's guidance on this issue requiring a functional approach, *see* DOJ Guidance Letter, at 7471 ("[C]ensus data alone may not provide sufficient indicia of electoral behavior to make the requisite determination."), but it has been squarely rejected by at least one federal court. *See Texas,* 831 F.Supp.2d at 260, 2011 WL 6440006, at *12 ("[S]imple voting-age population analysis cannot accurately measure minorities' ability to elect and, therefore, Texas misjudged which districts offer its minority citizens the ability to elect their preferred candidates in both its benchmark and proposed Plans."). As a result, the Senate did not properly consider when tier-two requirements must yield in order to avoid conflict with Florida's minority voting protection provision.

Finally, applying expansive definitions to the tier-two standards and failing to follow a consistent approach in applying the standards undermine the purpose of article III, section 21, which was intended to restrict legislative discretion in an effort to level the playing field and to prevent gerrymandering....

A review of the individual districts, discussed below, reveals constitutional violations. These districts illustrate the Senate's inconsistent approach as to the tier-two standards and the ramifications of the failure to conduct a functional analysis as to retrogression.

b. Numbering Scheme

We first address the numbering of the Senate plan. With respect to numbering, the Florida Constitution states only that Senate districts shall be "consecutively numbered." Art. III, § 16(a), Fla. Const. However, because the Constitution requires that Senate terms must be staggered, the number of a Senate district determines the years in which elections must be held for that district. *See* art. III, § 15(a), Fla. Const. Here, the issue we must address is whether the Senate districts were renumbered with the intent to favor incumbents, in violation of article III, section 21(a). Specifically, the Coalition contends that by renumbering the apportionment plan so that incumbents eligible for reelection in 2012 would receive a chance to serve for a maximum of ten years, rather than eight, the Senate plan violates the prohibition on favoring incumbents.

Unquestionably, the numbering of a Senate district, whether given an odd or even number, directly affects the length of time a senator may serve. *See* art. III, § 15(a), Fla. Const. Article III, section 15(a), provides for staggered Senate terms. In accordance with that requirement, the constitution requires Senate elections to occur in particular districts in alternating general election years, with the year of the election to be determined by whether the district is designated by an odd or even number. *Id.*... The constitution further provides that at the election next following a reapportionment, some senators shall be elected for terms of two years when necessary to maintain staggered terms. *Id.*

Moreover, any senator who represents a district where a change in the district lines has resulted in a change in constituency must stand for reelection in the next general election after reapportionment. In our decision on the validity of the apportionment plan in 1982, we addressed the effect of reapportionment on "holdover Senate terms" as part of our "jurisdiction to resolve all issues ... arising under Article III, section 16(c)." *In re Apportionment Law—1982,* 414 So.2d at 1045.... [T]he Court "conclude[d] that the theoretical possibility that some current senators may be able to serve ten years in the Florida Senate is not a sufficiently important dependent matter arising under article III, section 16, Florida Constitution, that we should address it at this time." *Id.*

The question we must first answer is whether, as a result of the new requirements in article III, section 21(a), prohibiting apportionment plans that have the intent of favoring incumbents, the numbering of Senate districts is now a matter for this Court's review under article III, section 16. In light of the addition of the article III, section 21(a), provision that no "apportionment plan ... shall be drawn with the intent to favor or disfavor ... an incumbent," the challengers assert that the Senate's apportionment plan was renumbered for the benefit of incumbents, in violation of the Florida Constitution. The Senate has asserted that the provisions of article III, section 21, apply only to the drawing of district lines and not the numbering scheme.

We reject the Senate's assertion that numbering is excluded from the evaluation under the standards set forth in article III, section 21. This Court "endeavors to construe a constitutional provision consistent with the intent of the framers and the voters." *Zingale,* 885 So.2d at 282; *see also Gray,* 125 So.2d at 852. "Moreover, in construing multiple constitutional provisions addressing a similar subject, the provisions 'must be read in pari materia to ensure a consistent and logical meaning that gives effect to each provision.'" *Caribbean Conservation Corp.,* 838 So.2d at 501 (quoting *Advisory Op. to the Governor—1996 Amendment 5 (Everglades),* 706 So.2d 278, 281 (Fla.1997)).

While the introductory clause of article III, section 21, states that the provision applies "[i]n establishing legislative district boundaries," subsection (a) then states that "no apportionment *plan* or district shall be drawn with the intent to favor or disfavor ... an incumbent." (Emphasis added.) The numbers of the Senate districts are unquestionably part of the "apportionment plan" for purposes of reviewing whether the plan is designed with the intent to favor or disfavor an incumbent. The Joint Resolution necessarily defines the boundaries of each district by its number. *See, e.g.,* SJR 1176 at 52 ("District 1 is composed of: (a) That part of Escambia County consisting of: 1. All of voting tabulation districts 15, 18, 19, 20, 21...."). Further, the numbering of the districts determines the length of the terms senators will serve following apportionment, *see* art. III, § 15(a), Fla. Const., as well as the maximum length of time each senator will be eligible to serve, *see* art. VI, § 4(b)(1)–(2), Fla. Const. Thus, not only is it a matter for our review in determining the validity of the apportionment plan in light of the addition of article III, section 21, but the Legislature is prohibited from numbering the districts with the intent to favor or disfavor an incumbent. *See* art. III, 21(a), Fla. Const.

In this case, the clear intent of the constitutional provisions is to prevent the Legislature from passing an apportionment plan that has a built-in bias favoring an incumbent. Adopting a renumbering system that significantly advantages incumbents by increasing the length of time that they may serve by two years most assuredly favors incumbents....

We now turn to the Coalitions allegation that the Senate plan was in fact renumbered to benefit incumbents. Clearly, the numbering of a district determines not only the length of each senators individual term, but also determines the length of the maximum consecutive period of time a senator will be eligible to serve in the Senate. Under article VI, section 4(b), of the Florida Constitution, "No person may appear on the ballot for re-election" to the office of Florida senator "if, by the end of the current term of office, the person will have served (or, but for resignation, would have served) in that office for eight consecutive years." It should first be emphasized that the Florida Constitution does not limit senators to a maximum of eight consecutive years. Rather, the constitution prohibits anyone who has already served for eight years from standing for reelection. Conversely, any senator who has served for less than eight years is not prohibited from seeking reelection.

* * *

In this case, there is no question that district numbers were assigned with the intent to favor incumbents. The Senate Committee on Reapportionment published its first proposed plan on November 28, 2011. The plan was formally introduced at the committee's next meeting on December 6, 2011, as Senate Joint Resolution 1176. In this version of the Senate plan, the distribution of district numbers across the state was essentially unchanged from the 2002 Senate plan. Under that original numbering, at least 16 out of the 29 non-term-limited incumbents would have been eligible to serve a maximum of eight years and three incumbents would have been eligible to serve a maximum of nine years.

* * *

Article III, section 21(a), prohibits any apportionment plan from being drawn with the intent to favor an incumbent. The Senate has argued that the renumbering of its plan does not in fact "favor" incumbents; rather, the Senate maintains that the result of the numbering was merely to compensate certain incumbents who served truncated, two-year terms prior to redistricting by allowing them to serve longer terms if they are reelected. As the Senate conceded in a prior reapportionment case, however, "elected officials have no property rights to the office to which they have been elected." *In re Apportionment Law—1982*, 414 So.2d at 1046. To the contrary, it is the voters who have the rights in the process by which their representatives are elected.

The Senate's plan plainly favors certain incumbents by renumbering districts to allow them to serve longer than they would otherwise be eligible to serve. Because we conclude that the plan was drawn with the intent to favor incumbents, in violation of article III, section 21(a), we declare the renumbering in the apportionment plan to be invalid.

c. Challenges to the Senate Districts

We now turn to an examination of the challenges raised as to specific Senate districts. We first discuss the districts that we find to be in violation of the Florida Constitution. Then we discuss the district challenges that the Court rejects. Finally, we discuss the challenge brought by the City of Lakeland.

Northwest Florida: Senate Districts 1 and 3

The FDP and the Coalition contend that Districts 1 and 3 in the Panhandle violate the constitutional standards of compactness, utilizing political and geographical boundaries where feasible, and no intent to favor incumbents. Our facial review of both of these districts confirms that at least two constitutional standards were violated: compactness and utilizing existing political and geographical lines where feasible. The Senate's failure to adhere to these constitutional standards appears to be based on the erroneous belief that, in the drawing of the districts, the factor of "communities of interest" could be elevated above the constitutional mandates.

Although the Senate's stated motivation was a desire to keep coastal communities together and separate from rural communities, it is also significant that District 1 keeps 86.1% of its predecessor district (old District 4), and District 3 keeps 82.6% of its predecessor district (old District 2). Both of these percentages are far greater than the average for the Senate plan (64.2%). Because there is no constitutionally valid justification for the deviation from the constitutional standards, we are obligated to declare these districts invalid.

As the below map shows, Districts 1 and 3 are horizontal districts in northwest Florida. District 1 stretches east to west through the coastal areas of five counties, and District 3 takes in the non-coastal areas to the north of District 1.

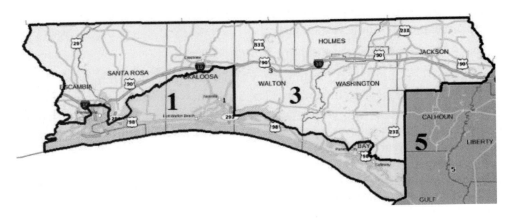

Both districts contain a majority-white voting-age population. Thus, no considerations with respect to Florida's minority voting protection provision come into play.

Both districts are visually non-compact as they stretch through the Panhandle, and the compactness measures confirm this. District 1 received a Reock score of 0.12

(closer to 1 is better), and an Area/Convex Hull score of 0.46 (closer to 1 is better). District 3 received a 0.24 Reock score and a 0.74 Area/Convex Hull score.

The districts are bounded to the east by Gulf, Calhoun, and Gadsden Counties. The more critical and constitutionally suspect boundary is the boundary between Districts 1 and 3, which follows no consistent political or geographical boundary. Instead, the district dividing line follows a variety of boundaries, switching between major roads (Interstate 10), minor roads, county lines, city boundaries, major waterways, rivers, and even creeks. It is evident that although the Senate followed numerous different boundaries when drawing Districts 1 and 3, often switching between different types of boundaries within the span of a few miles, it sacrificed compactness not to comply with the requirements of equal population or utilizing political or geographical boundaries, but rather to create a coastal district and an inland rural district.

In passing the Joint Resolution, the Legislature stated its intent was to "establish Senate District 1, which ties coastal communities of the Florida Panhandle in Escambia, Santa Rosa, Okaloosa, Walton, and Bay Counties," and to "establish Senate District 3, which ties rural Panhandle communities in Escambia, Santa Rosa, Okaloosa, Walton, Bay, Washington, Holmes, and Jackson Counties." SJR 1176 at 38. The Senate staff analysis indicates that the coastal and rural districts were created based on public testimony received by the Legislature.[21]

Although the Senate staff analysis points to selected testimony in favor of the horizontal orientation, a review of the public hearings demonstrates that the public testimony in support of horizontal coastal and rural districts was by no means unanimous. While members of the public testified that they wanted coastal areas together and separate from rural areas because of common interests, other members of the public testified in support of vertical districts that would unite counties.

We commend the Legislature for holding multiple public hearings and obtaining public input. However, the Legislature is required to follow the requirements in the constitution, including the requirements that districts be drawn "as nearly equal in population as is practicable," to be "compact," and to "where feasible, utilize existing political and geographical boundaries." Art. III, §21(b), Fla. Const. While the equal population and political and geographical boundaries requirements are stated in

---

21. [FN 46.] *See* New Senate Districts, District Descriptions (S000S9008) (Senate Staff Document), in Petition for Declaratory Judgment, Appendix at 1006, In re Senate Joint Resolution of Legislative Apportionment 1176, No. SC12-1 (Fla. Feb. 10, 2012) (Senate District Descriptions) ("The committee heard testimony at the ... public hearings and at the October 5, 2011, Senate Reapportionment Committee meeting that rural and agricultural interests in the northern part of the Panhandle have different traditions and representational needs than the urban and tourism interest in the southern part of the Panhandle. Additionally, the committee heard testimony pointing out that commerce and communication flow east and west along the main transportation corridors of the region, Interstate 10 and U.S. Highway 98, not north and south...."); *id.* ("District 1 is supported by the same testimony as District 3. Its horizontal configuration recognizes the differences between the rural North and the urban South. District 1 honors the request of members of the public who called for representation that reflects their distinct communities.").

terms of "as nearly as is practicable" or "where feasible," the compactness requirement is not modified by such qualifiers but framed in terms of "shall." As explained above, maintaining communities of interest is not a constitutional requirement, and comporting with such a principle should not come at the expense of complying with constitutional imperatives, such as compactness.

A review of the Coalition's alternative plan reveals that it was possible to draw districts in the Panhandle that are more visually compact and keep more counties together; only one county, Okaloosa County, is split in the Coalition's plan. Further, when drawing the districts to be compact and utilize consistent political boundaries, the Coalition districts also retain less of the core population of predecessor districts — 66.2% and 58.4% — closer to the average (64.2%) of the Senate plan.

The orientation of Districts 1 and 3 is in fact very similar to the composition of Districts 2 and 4 in 2002, depicted below. Although part of Okaloosa County is now included in District 1, that area consists in large part of the Eglin Air Force Base. The incumbents in Districts 1 and 3 both live in Okaloosa County and would represent largely the same constituencies as they did under the 2002 plan.

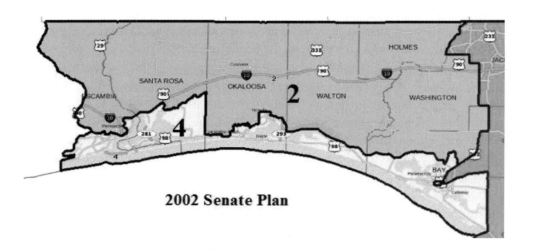

2002 Senate Plan

The drawing of the districts sacrificed compactness — a constitutional imperative — in order to keep coastal communities together. Further, although the Senate followed numerous different boundaries when drawing Districts 1 and 3, often switching between different types of boundaries within the space of a few miles, it sacrificed compactness, not in a reasoned balancing effort to comply with the requirements of equal population or to utilize political or geographical boundaries such as municipal or county boundaries, but rather to create a coastal district and an inland rural district.

We also consider it significant that in doing so, a high percentage of population from predecessor districts was retained to the benefit of the incumbents. While it is not only the fact that the districts maintained overwhelming percentages of the former core constituencies in isolation, in the context of our overall analysis of this district, it is significant. There is no valid constitutional justification for the decision to draw Districts 1 and 3 in this configuration, and we conclude that Districts 1 and 3 are constitutionally invalid.

[Further discussions of individual districts are omitted for space considerations.]

* * *

e. Conclusion as to the Senate Plan

We hold that the Senate plan is invalid. In doing so, we consider the fact that the Senate failed to conduct a functional analysis as to regression in order to properly determine when, and to what extent, the tier-two requirements must yield to avoid conflict with Florida's minority voting protection provision. Moreover, as to the requirements of compactness and utilization of existing boundaries, the Senate's expansive interpretations—interpretations we reject—and inconsistent use of these standards undermined the purpose of these requirements. Additionally, we conclude that the Senate plan is rife with objective indicators of improper intent.

We have examined and declared Senate Districts 1, 3, 6, 9, 10, 29, 30, and 34 to be in violation of constitutional requirements. We have also expressed our concerns with respect to the City of Lakeland. Finally, we declare the numbering scheme to be invalid because it was intended to benefit incumbents by making them eligible to serve for longer periods of time than they would have otherwise been eligible to serve. Accordingly, the Senate plan does not pass constitutional muster, and it is our duty under the Florida Constitution to declare it invalid.

IV. CONCLUSION

The Fair Districts Amendment changed the constitutional framework for apportionment, introducing significant reforms in the drawing of legislative districts. Before the passage of the Fair Districts Amendment in 2010, there is no question that the House and Senate plans would have passed constitutional muster and both would have been validated by this Court.

* * *

We conclude that the challengers have demonstrated that the Senate plan, but not the House plan, violates the constitutional requirements. We therefore declare the Senate plan constitutionally invalid and the House plan constitutionally valid. The language of Senate Joint Resolution 1176 establishes that the Legislature intended the Senate and House plans to be severable from each other in the event either plan was held invalid. *See* SJR 1176, § 7, at 669.

The Court recognizes that this opinion represents the first time since the passage of the Fair Districts Amendment that this Court has judicially interpreted the newly added constitutional provisions of article III, section 21. While we commend the Legislature for its efforts to interpret these standards, we also acknowledge that the Legislature lacked the benefit of our guiding construction. This Court understands that its obligations are not just to rule on the facial validity of the standards in this case, but to ensure that this decision charts a reliable course for the Legislature and the judiciary to follow in the future.

Because we have now defined Florida's new constitutional standards through this opinion, this Court has provided the Legislature with parameters for the application of the standards to the apportionment plan....

In accordance with article III, section 16(d), the Governor and the Legislature must now follow the procedures enumerated therein, which govern the process that ensues when the Supreme Court of Florida declares an apportionment plan to be constitutionally invalid.

* * *

In accordance with article III, section 16(c), of the Florida Constitution, the Court enters this declaratory judgment declaring the apportionment plan of the House of Representatives as contained in Senate Joint Resolution 1176 to be constitutionally valid under the Florida Constitution and declaring the apportionment plan of the Senate as contained in Senate Joint Resolution 1176 to be constitutionally invalid under the Florida Constitution. As contemplated by the Florida Constitution, in accordance with article III, section 16(d), the Legislature now has the task to "adopt a joint resolution conforming to the judgment of the supreme court." Art. III, § 16(d), Fla. Const.

No motion for rehearing shall be entertained. This case is final.

It is so ordered.

LEWIS, QUINCE, LABARGA, and PERRY, JJ., concur.

CANADY, C.J., concurring in part and dissenting in part.

I concur in the majority's ruling that the redistricting plan for the House of Representatives is valid, but I dissent from the ruling that the plan for the Senate is invalid. With respect to the Senate plan, I conclude that the opponents have failed to overcome the presumption that a redistricting plan adopted by the Legislature is constitutional. Because it has not been shown that the Legislature's choices in establishing the district lines in the Senate plan are without a rational basis under the applicable constitutional requirements, I would validate that plan.

I.

This Court has recognized that legislative enactments are ordinarily "clothed with a presumption of constitutionality." *Crist v. Fla. Ass'n of Criminal Def. Lawyers, Inc.,* 978 So.2d 134, 139 (Fla.2008). When the constitutional validity of a legislative enactment is challenged, "[t]o overcome the presumption [of constitutional validity], the invalidity must appear beyond reasonable doubt." *Id.* (quoting *Franklin v. State,* 887 So.2d 1063, 1073 (Fla.2004))....

In our 2002 decision we also stated that under article III, section 16, our review "is extremely limited." *In re Apportionment—2002,* 817 So.2d at 824. Recognizing the inherent limitations of a review process conducted by an appellate court during a thirty-day period, we acknowledged that we can "only pass upon the facial validity of the plan." *Id.* We specifically held that the article III, section 16, "proceeding before this Court is not the proper forum to address such a fact-intensive claim" as that presented by a claim under the Voting Rights Act of 1965, 42 U.S.C. §§ 1973–1973q (2006), or by a claim of political gerrymandering. *In re Apportionment—2002,* 817 So.2d at 831. The majority of the panel took the view that under article III, section 16, the Court had "not been afforded a structure to competently address claims that cannot be determined from the [redistricting] plan itself." *In re Apportionment—2002,* 817 So.2d at 836 (Lewis, J., concurring).

With today's decision, the majority of this Court effectively abrogates these precedents that recognized the circumscribed nature of the thirty-day review process under article III, section 16, and the presumption of constitutionality with which a legislative redistricting plan is clothed. The Court has now transformed the nature of the constitutional review process and cast aside the presumption of constitutionality. And it has done so in the absence of any argument from the opponents of the redistricting plan that we should recede from our precedent applying the presumption of constitutionality to redistricting plans.

The majority's departure from our precedents is not justified by the adoption in 2010 of article III, section 21, Florida Constitution, which created certain additional "[s]tandards for establishing legislative district boundaries." Art. III, § 21, Fla. Const. Although section 21 unquestionably altered the scope of the issues to be considered in our review of a legislative redistricting plan, nothing in section 21 changed the structure or nature of the thirty-day review process previously existing under section 16. The text of section 21 does not explicitly address the judicial review process. And it is unwarranted to conclude that section 21 implicitly altered the structure or nature of the existing constitutional review process.

It may well be that some of those who supported the adoption of section 21 desired to transform the redistricting process from what this Court has previously acknowledged it to be—"primarily a matter for legislative consideration and determination"—into a matter controlled by the largely discretionary rulings of the majority of this Court. *In re Apportionment—1972,* 263 So.2d at 799–800. A different constitutional amendment to effect such a transformation in the redistricting process might have been proposed for the consideration of Florida's voters. But the voters who adopted section 21 could not have known—from the text of the proposed amendment, much less the ballot summary—that such a transformation would be brought about by the adoption of section 21.

Weighty reasons support adhering to our precedent establishing that redistricting plans adopted by the Legislature are presumed to be constitutionally valid and that this Court should "act with judicial restraint" in our review of such plans. *In re Apportionment—1972,* 263 So.2d at 800. In *Perry v. Perez,* ___ U.S. ___, 132 S.Ct. 934, 941 (2012)—a case that was decided in January of this year presenting claims under the Voting Rights Act and the United States Constitution—the Supreme Court of the United States observed that "experience has shown the difficulty of defining neutral legal principles in this area, for redistricting ordinarily involves criteria and standards that have been weighed and evaluated by the elected branches." The Supreme Court recognized the importance of ensuring that the lower court act to vindicate federal rights "without displacing legitimate state policy judgments with the court's own preferences." *Id.* Although these observations in *Perry* are no doubt based in part on federalism concerns, it is clear that *Perry*'s concern about the "difficulty of defining neutral legal principles" to ensure that the "policy judgments" of the "the elected branches" are not displaced by judicial "preferences" is applicable to not only federal but also state judicial intervention. *Id.*

The concerns voiced by the Supreme Court in *Perry* echo concerns articulated in prior decisions where the Supreme Court considered the definition of "discernible and manageable standards by which political gerrymander cases are to be decided." *Davis v. Bandemer*, 478 U.S. 109, 123 (1986). Although a narrow majority of the Supreme Court has recognized the possibility of articulating such standards, a majority of the Supreme Court has never been able to agree on a particular test or set of tests.

In *Vieth v. Jubelirer*, 541 U.S. 267, 306–07 (2004) (Kennedy, J., concurring in the judgment), Justice Kennedy recognized the "obstacle[]" presented by the continuing "absence of rules to limit and confine judicial intervention" in the adjudication of political gerrymandering claims: "With uncertain limits, intervening courts — even when proceeding with best intentions — would risk assuming political, not legal, responsibility for a process that often produces ill will and distrust." In his opinion for the plurality in *Vieth*, Justice Scalia emphasized the importance of a solid and demonstrable criterion "to enable the state legislatures to discern the limits of their districting discretion, to meaningfully constrain the discretion of the courts, and to win public acceptance for the courts' intrusion into a process that is the very foundation of democratic decisionmaking." 541 U.S. at 291 (plurality).

* * *

The circumscribed nature of the thirty-day constitutional review process provides an additional compelling reason for not abandoning the rational-basis review required by our precedent and the acknowledgement that our review "is extremely limited." *In re Apportionment — 2002*, 817 So.2d at 824. We conduct the constitutional review process as an appellate court without the benefit of any fact-finding proceedings. We can only rely on facts that are undisputed. It is impossible for us to thoroughly evaluate disputed fact-intensive issues. We have previously recognized that the adjudication of claims arising from the provisions of the Voting Rights Act — which are analogous to the provisions of section 21(a) protecting the rights of "racial or language minorities" — often involve a "fact-intensive" inquiry which cannot be undertaken within the limits of our review pursuant to section 16. *In re Apportionment — 2002*, 817 So.2d at 829. We are similarly constrained in the evaluation of factual issues relevant to a determination of improper intent. Given the structural limitations imposed on our review, adherence to the presumption of constitutionality helps ensure that we avoid reliance on suspicion and surmise—rather than adjudicated facts—as a basis for declaring a redistricting plan constitutionally invalid.

* * *

II.

Reasonable questions and concerns can certainly be raised about certain choices the Legislature made in drawing district lines. But the proper analysis of constitutionality cannot be driven by questions and concerns. Instead, under our precedents, the analysis of constitutionality must focus on whether there is a rational relationship between the choices made by the Legislature and the constitutional standards. The majority, however, takes a very different approach than the approach required by our precedents.

The foundation of the majority's decision is constructed from three interrelated elements: (1) the effective repudiation of the presumption of constitutionality and the rational-basis scrutiny it entails; (2) the imposition of judicially created extra-constitutional constraints on the Legislature's utilization of political and geographical boundaries in the drawing of district lines; and (3) conclusions of fact based solely on suspicion and surmise.

The majority acknowledges the presumption of constitutionality but carries out its review of the Senate district plan in a manner that is heedless of the limits imposed by that presumption. The majority thus applies a strict-scrutiny analysis rather than the rational-basis review required by our precedents.

* * *

Senate District Numbering

I would reject the challenge to the numbering of districts in the Senate plan. Section 21 is a limitation on the power of the Legislature only with respect to "establishing legislative district boundaries." Art. III, § 21, Fla. Const. The prohibition on action to "favor or disfavor ... an incumbent" applies only to the manner in which district lines are "drawn." Art. III, § 21(a), Fla. Const. The numbering of the Senate districts is totally unrelated to any advantage incumbent senators will obtain vis-à-vis challenger candidates. The majority stretches the text of section 21 to reach legislative decisions that are not within the scope of section 21.

Senate Districts 1 and 3

The majority contends that Senate Districts 1 and 3 were drawn without respecting any consistent political or geographical boundary lines and that the districts are not compact. The majority rejects as illegitimate the Legislature's asserted interest in maintaining a coastal community of interest in one district and a rural community of interest in the other district. The majority also asserts that the configuration of the districts shows that they were drawn improperly to favor the incumbent senators from each of the districts. The majority's analysis with respect to these districts illustrates how it has cast aside the presumption of constitutionality and departed from the proper confines of our limited review.

Section 21 provides that "districts shall, where feasible, utilize existing political and geographical boundaries." Art. III, §21(b), Fla. Const. This provision does not require that the Legislature make a choice between using either political boundaries or geographical boundaries. Indeed, the text clearly contemplates that both political and geographical boundaries will be utilized. The majority, however, imposes a requirement of consistency that is designed to limit the exercise of policy judgment by the Legislature under section 21. *See* majority op. at 656, 663. This is a purely judicially created extra-constitutional requirement. It amounts to a judicial assertion that the constitution is violated if political boundaries and geographical boundaries are not utilized in a fashion that suits judicial sensibilities. It cannot be reconciled with the text of section 21.

In the context of legislative districting, compactness will necessarily be a matter of degree. It is not a standard that is subject to a neat, objective test. On the contrary, the requirement is inherently vague. (The requirement that districts be compact is akin in its vagueness to a rule of court requiring that appellate briefs be brief.) In section 21, the compactness standard is on an equal footing with the standards related to equal population and the utilization of political and geographical boundaries. The Legislature thus may exercise its policy judgment to utilize political and geographical boundaries even when doing so may result in a district that is less compact than it might otherwise be.

In the case of Senate Districts 1 and 3, the Legislature's choice to utilize certain political boundaries and geographical boundaries has resulted in the creation of districts that are less compact than many other districts in the Senate plan. It cannot be said, however, that the drawing of the district lines for Districts 1 and 3 has no rational basis related to the constitutional standards.

The majority's rejection of the Legislature's consideration of communities of interest is wholly unwarranted. Nothing in section 21 provides that the standards set forth there—along with those in section 16—are the exclusive, legitimate considerations that may be taken into account by the Legislature in drawing district lines. "[M]aintaining communities of interest" has been recognized as a "traditional districting principle[]." *Bush v. Vera*, 517 U.S. 952, 977 (1996). Although the Legislature is not constitutionally required to maintain communities of interest, nothing in the constitution precludes the Legislature from giving consideration to such a traditional districting principle. The voters adopting section 21 would have had no way of knowing—either from the text of the amendment or the ballot summary—that the proposed amendment would preclude the Legislature from considering existing communities of interest. Such a limitation on legislative authority should not be read into the constitution by implication.

Finally, the majority's conclusion that these districts were drawn with an improper intent to favor the incumbent senators is based on suspicion and surmise. It is indeed ironic that the majority relies on this factor as a ground for invalidating these districts when the only alternative Senate district map submitted to the Court reconfigures these districts but in a way that also maintains the two incumbent senators in different districts.

* * *

IV.

In the majority's analysis, the presumption that redistricting plans adopted by the Legislature are constitutional—a presumption that this Court unanimously reaffirmed ten years ago—is a quickly vanishing presumption. "As the cloud is consumed and vanisheth away,"[22] so goes the presumption of constitutionality—consumed by the majority's strict-scrutiny analysis. I dissent from this unwarranted expansion of the power of this Court.

POLSTON, J., concurs.

Commentary and Questions

In *Rucho v. Common Cause*, 139 S.Ct. 2484 (2019), the U.S. Supreme Court held that partisan gerrymandering was a non-justiciable political question under the Federal Constitution. The *Rucho* case involved partisan gerrymandering by state legislatures in North Carolina and Maryland, and illustrated that, if this issue is to be addressed, it would need to be at the state level.

As we look at *In Re SJR 1176*,

1. How did the Court define its authority to determine the validity of the apportionment plan?

2. How does the dissent evaluate the weight to be given legislative determinations on apportionment compared to the majority opinion?

League of Women Voters of Florida v. Detzner

172 So. 3d 363 (Fla. 2015)

PARIENTE, J.

In this appeal involving legal issues of first impression, we review a trial court's finding that the 2012 "redistricting process" and the "resulting map" apportioning Florida's twenty-seven congressional districts were "taint[ed]" by unconstitutional intent to favor the Republican Party and incumbent lawmakers.[23] Cognizant that this Court's role is not to select a redistricting map that performs better for one political party or another, but is instead to uphold the purposes of the constitutional provision approved by Florida voters to outlaw partisan intent in redistricting, the crux of what

---

22. [FN 71.] Job 7:9 (King James).

23. [FN 1.] This Court previously considered two issues arising out of the pre-trial discovery process—one concerning the legislative privilege and the other concerning the discovery of documents in the possession of non-party political consultants—and released three opinions while the litigation was pending. *See League of Women Voters of Fla. v. Fla. House of Representatives (Apportionment IV)*, 132 So.3d 135, 138 (Fla.2013) (addressing and largely rejecting claims of legislative privilege); *League of Women Voters of Fla. v. Data Targeting, Inc. (Apportionment V)*, 140 So.3d 510, 514 (Fla.2014) (permitting the use during trial of evidence obtained from non-party political consultants, pending further appellate review); *Bainter v. League of Women Voters of Fla. (Apportionment VI)*, 150 So.3d 1115, 1117 (Fla.2014) (upholding trial court ruling ordering production of documents in the possession of non-party political consultants).

we must decide is whether the trial court gave the appropriate legal effect to its finding that the Florida Legislature drew the state's congressional districts in violation of the Florida Constitution.

Added to the Florida Constitution in 2010, the Fair Districts Amendment sought to eliminate the age-old practice of partisan political gerrymandering—where the political party and representatives in power manipulate the district boundaries to their advantage—by forbidding the Florida Legislature from drawing a redistricting plan or an individual district with the "intent to favor or disfavor a political party or an incumbent." Art. III, § 20(a), Fla. Const. "The desire of a political party to provide its representatives with an advantage in reapportionment is not a Republican or Democratic tenet, but applies equally to both parties." *In re Senate Joint Resolution of Legislative Apportionment 1176 (Apportionment I)*, 83 So.3d 597, 615 (Fla.2012). As observed when a three-judge panel of a federal district court examined Florida's last decennial congressional redistricting plan in 2002, the "raw exercise of majority legislative power does not seem to be the best way of conducting a critical task like redistricting, but it does seem to be an unfortunate fact of political life around the country." *Martinez v. Bush*, 234 F.Supp.2d 1275, 1297 (S.D.Fla.2002).

With the voters' approval of the Fair Districts Amendment, that unfortunate fact of political life was banned in Florida. Our citizens declared that the Legislature must "redistrict in a manner that prohibits favoritism or discrimination." *Apportionment I*, 83 So.3d at 632. And the Eleventh Circuit Court of Appeals similarly declared that "[f]ar from dictat[ing] electoral outcomes, the provision seeks to maximize electoral possibilities by leveling the playing field." *Brown v. Sec'y of State of Fla.*, 668 F.3d 1271, 1285 (11th Cir.2012) (internal quotation marks omitted).

* * *

Presented in this case with a first-of-its-kind challenge under the Fair Districts Amendment, the trial court found that the Legislature's 2012 congressional redistricting plan was drawn in violation of the Florida Constitution's prohibition on partisan intent. We affirm that finding. We conclude, however, that the trial court failed to give proper legal effect to its determination that the Fair Districts Amendment was violated.

In reaching this conclusion, we recognize that the trial court had scant precedent to guide it in approaching the legal issues presented. And, we commend the trial court for the tremendous effort that was expended in deciding this novel challenge under the Fair Districts Amendment.

Nevertheless, we conclude that two legal errors significantly affected the trial court's determination of the appropriate legal effect of its finding of unconstitutional intent. First, the trial court erred in determining that there was no distinction between a challenge to the "plan as a whole"—a challenge, in effect, to the map produced from the unconstitutional "process"—and a challenge to individual districts. Second, the trial court erred in the standard of review it applied, which was improperly deferential to the Legislature's decisions after finding a violation of the Fair Districts Amendment's prohibition on partisan intent. Although it found the existence of unconstitutional intent, the trial court relied solely on objective "tier-two" constitutional indicators, such as compactness and the use of political or geographical boundaries, rather than on the direct and circumstantial evidence of "tier-one" unconstitutional intent presented at trial.

In other words, the trial court analyzed the Legislature's map as if it had not found the existence of unconstitutional intent, affording deference to the Legislature where no deference was due. Once a direct violation of the Florida Constitution's prohibition on partisan intent in redistricting was found, the burden should have shifted to the Legislature to justify its decisions in drawing the congressional district lines.

Relying on the finding of unconstitutional intent, the challengers have urged that the entire plan should be redrawn....

Based on the findings and evidence in this case, however, we ultimately reject the challengers' request that the entire plan must be redrawn or that this Court should, at this time, perform the task of redrawing the districts....

Accordingly, while we affirm the trial court's finding that the Legislature's enacted map was "taint[ed]" by unconstitutional intent, we reverse the trial court's order upholding the Legislature's remedial redistricting plan. We relinquish this case to the trial court for a period of 100 days from the date of this opinion, with directions that it require the Legislature to redraw, on an expedited basis, Congressional Districts 5, 13, 14, 21, 22, 25, 26, 27, and all other districts affected by the redrawing, pursuant to the guidelines set forth in this opinion.... Upon the completion of the redrawing of the map, the trial court shall hold a hearing where both sides shall have an opportunity to present their arguments and any evidence for or against the redrawn map, and the trial court shall then enter an order either recommending approval or disapproval of the redrawn map....

I. CHALLENGE TO TRIAL COURT'S FINDINGS

On appeal in this Court, the challengers seek affirmance of the trial court's finding of unconstitutional partisan intent in drawing the state's congressional districts—a finding that was based on both direct and circumstantial evidence. Their primary contention of error, however, is that the trial court applied an unduly deferential standard of review, thereby precluding it from imposing a more meaningful remedy for its finding of unconstitutional intent to favor the Republican Party and incumbents.[FN 3]

> FN 3. The issues raised on appeal by the challengers are: (1) the trial court erred in requiring only two districts to be redrawn after finding constitutionally improper intent in the enacted congressional redistricting plan; (2) Congressional Districts 5, 13, 14, 21, 22, 25, 26, and 27 are independently unconstitutional; (3) this Court should craft a meaningful remedy, either by adopting a constitutionally valid plan or assisting the Legislature so that it can adopt a plan that complies with the Florida Constitution; and (4) the trial court erred in rejecting the challengers' attempt to re-open the evidence to introduce additional allegations of improper partisan intent.
>
> We summarily reject the challengers' claim regarding the trial court's denial of their motion to re-open the evidence....

The Legislature, while seeking affirmance of the trial court's approval of the remedial redistricting plan, nevertheless takes issue with the trial court's finding of unconstitutional intent. In particular, the Legislature contests, first, the trial court's finding of a connection between the evidence and the Legislature itself, including the trial court's decision to ascribe the intent of a few individuals to the Legislature as a collective body. Second, the Legislature asserts that, even assuming the existence of unconstitutional intent, the trial court's finding pertains solely to the two invalidated districts and not to the broader process or map as a whole. Accordingly, the Legislature argues that any remedy that may have been necessary has already been provided through the enactment of the remedial redistricting plan.

* * *

II. THE FLORIDA CONSTITUTION'S PROHIBITION ON PARTISAN POLITICAL GERRYMANDERING

* * *

Based on the new constitutional standards that applied for the first time to the 2012 process, transparency became legally significant under the Florida Constitution. This Court explained that "if evidence exists to demonstrate that there was an entirely different, separate process that was undertaken contrary to the transparent effort in an attempt to favor a political party or an incumbent in violation of the Florida Constitution, clearly that would be important evidence in support of the claim that the Legislature thwarted the constitutional mandate." *Apportionment IV*, 132 So.3d at 149. Indeed, the challengers' principal claim in this litigation challenging the constitutional validity of the Legislature's 2012 congressional redistricting plan involved evidence of the type of "entirely different, separate process" this Court warned would be "important evidence" of a constitutional violation.

Specifically, the challengers argued that the Legislature cooperated and collaborated with partisan political operatives aligned with the Republican Party to produce a redistricting plan that was drawn in contravention of article III, section 20, with the intent to favor incumbents and the Republican Party, which was the controlling political party in the Legislature at the time of the 2012 redistricting.

* * *

Under article III, section 20, "there is no acceptable level of improper intent." *Apportionment I*, 83 So.3d at 617. The prohibition on improper partisan intent in redistricting applies, "by its express terms," to "both the apportionment plan as a whole and to each district individually" and does not "require a showing of malevolent or evil purpose." *Id.* A finding of partisan intent therefore renders the Legislature's redistricting plan constitutionally invalid, as the Florida Constitution expressly "outlaw[s] partisan political gerrymandering." *Apportionment IV*, 132 So.3d at 137....

"Florida's constitutional provision prohibits intent, not effect," which is to say that a map that has the effect or result of favoring one political party over another is not per se unconstitutional in the absence of improper intent. *Id.* at 617....

A. TRIAL COURT'S FINDING OF UNCONSTITUTIONAL INTENT

The challengers' claim of unconstitutional intent in the enacted congressional redistricting plan was that the Legislature communicated and collaborated with partisan political operatives, in the shadow of the Legislature's purportedly open and transparent redistricting process, to produce a map favoring Republicans and incumbents. After hearing all the evidence presented during a twelve-day bench trial held from late May to early June 2014, and evaluating the credibility of all the witnesses, the trial court found that the challengers had proven their case and concluded that the Florida Legislature's enacted 2012 congressional redistricting plan was drawn in violation of article III, section 20.

* * *

Specifically, the trial court stated, in pertinent part, as follows:

[The challengers'] *theory of the case regarding improper intent is that Republican leadership in the House and the Senate, their key staff members, and a small group of Republican political consultants conspired to avoid the effective application of the Fair District Amendments to the redistricting process and thereby successfully fashioned a congressional map that favors the Republican Party and its incumbents.* The strategy they came up with, according to the [challengers], was to present to the public a redistricting process that was transparent and open to the public, and free from partisan influences, but to hide from the public another secretive process. In this secretive process, the political consultants would make suggestions and submit their own partisan maps to the Legislature through that public process, but conceal their actions by using proxies, third persons who would be viewed as "concerned citizens," to speak at public forums from scripts written by the consultants and to submit proposed maps in their names to the Legislature, which were drawn by the consultants.

What is clear to me from the evidence, as described in more detail below, is that this group of Republican political consultants or operatives did in fact conspire to manipulate and influence the redistricting process. They accomplished this by writing scripts for and organizing groups of people to attend the public hearings to advocate for adoption of certain components or characteristics in the maps, and by submitting maps and partial maps through the public process, *all with the intention of obtaining enacted maps for the State House and Senate and for Congress that would favor the Republican Party.*

They made a mockery of the Legislature's proclaimed transparent and open process of redistricting by doing all of this in the shadow of that process, utilizing the access it gave them to the decision makers, but going to great lengths to conceal from the public their plan and their participation in it. *They were successful in their efforts to influence the redistricting process and the congressional plan under review here....*

The closer question is whether the Legislature in general, or the leadership and staff principally involved in drawing the maps, knowingly joined in this plan, or were duped by the operatives in the same way as the general public. The Defendants argue that if such a conspiracy existed, there is no proof that anyone in the Legislature was a part of it. If portions of the operatives' maps found their way into the enacted maps, they say, it was not because leadership or staff were told or knew they came from this group, but rather because the staff, unaware of their origins, saw the proposals as improving the draft maps they were working on.

The most compelling evidence in support of this contention of the Defendants is the testimony of the staff members who did the bulk of the actual map drawing for the Legislature. I had the ability to judge the demeanor of Alex Kelly, John Guthrie and Jason Poreda at trial and found each to be frank, straightforward and credible. I conclude that they were not a part of the conspiracy, nor directly aware of it, and that significant efforts were made by them and their bosses to insulate them from direct partisan influence. I accept that their motivation in drawing draft maps for consideration of the Legislature was to produce a final map which would comply with all the requirements of the Fair District Amendments, as their superiors had directed them.

That being said, the circumstantial evidence introduced at trial convinces me that the political operatives managed to find other avenues, other ways to infiltrate and influence the Legislature, to obtain the necessary cooperation and collaboration to ensure that their plan was realized, at least in part. They managed to taint the redistricting process and the resulting map with improper partisan intent. There is just too much circumstantial evidence of it, too many coincidences, for me to conclude otherwise.

(Emphasis supplied.)

Having reviewed the trial court's factual findings and the record, and viewing the evidence in the light most favorable to the trial court's finding of unconstitutional intent, we set forth the following relevant factual background of the case.... As we recount the facts, we emphasize that not every meeting held or every communication made was improper, illegal, or even violative of the letter of the Fair Districts Amendment. We set forth the pertinent facts in the record because, collectively, the evidence that the challengers were able to uncover after a protracted discovery process demonstrates a different scenario than the entirely open and transparent process touted by the Legislature when this Court considered the original apportionment challenges to the state Senate and House maps in *Apportionment I.* This is, indeed, what the trial court—which heard and considered all this evidence—found.

We also emphasize that since many of the e-mails were deleted or destroyed, we still may have only a partial picture of the behind-the-scenes political tactics. As the trial court found, "the Legislators and the political operatives systematically deleted almost all of their e-mails and other documentation relating to redistricting." The Legislature did so even though it had acknowledged that litigation over the redistricting plan was "a moral certainty." Indeed, if not for the production of some documents from the political consultants, including Marc Reichelderfer and Pat Bainter, there would be no record of the separate process undertaken by the consultants and no way to establish whether or not this process involved the collusion of the Legislature and ultimately affected the enacted map, as the trial court concluded.

* * *

B. EVIDENCE OF UNCONSTITUTIONAL INTENT

A month after the Florida voters approved the Fair Districts Amendment during the November 2010 general election, then-Speaker of the House Dean Cannon authorized a meeting in December 2010 at the headquarters of the Republican Party of Florida, involving Republican political consultants and legislative staffers, to discuss the upcoming redistricting process. This gathering was described by one of the consultants at trial as a meeting of "people that, prior to passage of the [new constitutional standards], would have generally been involved in the redistricting process."

[Four] key political consultants [were] in attendance.... These four consultants, along with employees of the Republican Party of Florida, met in the initial December 2010 meeting with [legislative staffers] and attorneys for the Legislature. At a second meeting the following month, in January 2011, the consultants met with Senator Gaetz, Representative Weatherford, [and two staffers].

These meetings were not open to the public and there is no record of what was discussed. As the trial court stated, "[n]o one who testified at trial about [the meetings] seemed to be able to remember much about what was discussed, though all seemed to agree that the political consultants were told that they would not have a 'seat at the table' in the redistricting process," as they had during redistricting in years past. According to the trial court, "[n]o one clearly articulated what that meant exactly, but there was testimony that they were told that they could still participate in redistricting through the public process 'just like any other citizen.'"

* * *

Ultimately, based on the evidence the challengers uncovered and presented at trial, the trial court found that there was "just too much circumstantial evidence" and "too many coincidences" to reach any conclusion other than that the political operatives had "infiltrate[d] and influence[d] the Legislature" in order to "obtain the necessary cooperation and collaboration" to "taint the redistricting process and the resulting map with improper partisan intent." While it is sometimes said that it is "hard to believe in coincidence," the trial court determined in this case that, as the saying goes, it was "even harder to believe in anything else." After reviewing all the evidence, both direct and circumstantial, the trial court thus concluded that the plan was drawn with improper partisan intent.

C. STEPS AFTER FINDING UNCONSTITUTIONAL INTENT

Despite its finding of unconstitutional partisan intent, however, the trial court invalidated only Districts 5 and 10, rejecting challenges to seven other individual districts. The trial court determined that there was no "distinction" between a challenge to the plan as a whole and a challenge to specific districts, and therefore "focused on those portions of the map" that it found to be "in need of corrective action in order to bring the entire plan into compliance with the constitution."

Its finding of unconstitutional intent notwithstanding, the trial court applied a deferential standard of review in analyzing each challenged district, "deferring to the Legislature's decision to draw a district in a certain way, so long as that decision does not violate the constitutional requirements." Believing that the "more reliable" indicators of whether the plan was drawn with the intent to favor a political party or incumbent were the tier-two constitutional measures, the trial court "first examine[d] the map for apparent failure to comply with tier-two requirements of compactness and utilization of political and geographical boundaries where feasible, then consider[ed] any additional evidence that supports the inference that such districts are also in violation of tier-one requirements."

* * *

As a remedy, the challengers urged the trial court to adopt one of their remedial plans, draw its own remedial plan, or hire an independent expert to draw a remedial plan. After a hearing, the trial court declined the challengers' suggestions and determined that the Legislature should redraw the plan.

The Legislature held a special session in August 2014 to enact a remedial redistricting plan. During this session, the chairs of the respective redistricting committees again conducted non-public meetings with staff and counsel to negotiate the features of the revised plan. The Legislature made modest changes to correct the specific tier-two deficiencies identified in Districts 5 and 10, and, after the plan was signed into law, the trial court held another hearing to consider the validity of the revised plan and whether it could be implemented in time for the 2014 elections.

Concluding that the challengers' objections to the validity of the remedial plan were without merit, the trial court approved the Legislature's remedial redistricting plan and ordered the then-impending 2014 elections to proceed under the unconstitutional 2012 plan due to time constraints, with the remedial plan to take effect for the 2016 elections. The 2016 effective date for the remedial plan has not been challenged.

The challengers appealed the trial court's initial order containing its factual findings and legal conclusions, as well as its subsequent order approving the remedial redistricting plan, and the Legislature cross-appealed, attacking certain aspects of the trial court's judgment but ultimately seeking affirmance of the order approving the remedial plan. The First District Court of Appeal then certified the trial court's judgment for direct review by this Court....

III. ISSUES OF "INTENT"

* * *

A. THE "INTENT" STANDARD

Article III, section 20, of the Florida Constitution, prohibits an apportionment plan or individual district from being "drawn" with the "intent to favor or disfavor a political party or an incumbent." Art. III, § 20(a), Fla. Const. All parties in the litigation, the trial court stated, "agreed that it is the Legislature's intent"—not the intent of, for instance, one rogue "staff member charged with actually drawing the map," or of political consultants with no influence on the Legislature—"that is at issue." But how to determine the Legislature's intent in this unique context, where the Florida Constitution contains an explicit prohibition on certain improper legislative intent in "draw[ing]" the redistricting plan, is a much more difficult proposition.

In *Apportionment I*, 83 So.3d at 617, this Court explained that "the Florida Constitution prohibits drawing *a plan or district* with the intent to favor or disfavor a political party or incumbent." (Emphasis supplied.) There is, this Court held, "no acceptable level of improper intent." *Id.* The "intent" standard "applies to both the apportionment plan *as a whole* and to each district individually." *Id.* (emphasis supplied). This Court's precedent discussing the "intent" standard in the course of prior cases during this litigation has demonstrated this principle—that improper intent, particularly if "part of a broader process to develop portions of the map," may "directly relate to whether the plan *as a whole* or any specific districts were drawn with unconstitutional intent." *Apportionment IV*, 132 So.3d at 150 (emphasis supplied).

* * *

Following this Court's precedent, which "emphasize[s] that this case is wholly unlike the traditional lawsuit challenging a statutory enactment," *id.* at 151, the trial court framed the "intent" inquiry as determining "the motive in drawing" the districts. We agree that this was the correct approach. Under this framework, the trial court appropriately concluded that "the actions and statements of legislators and staff, especially those directly involved in the map drawing process[,] would be relevant on the issue of intent."

* * *

In support of its contrary argument that "[c]ourts across the country ... refuse to impute the personal motivations of individual legislators to the legislative body as a collective whole," the Legislature offers a catalogue of citations to cases from other jurisdictions. But, as the challengers have pointed out, these cases and the arguments made by the Legislature in this case closely mirror the exact cases and arguments this Court distinguished and rejected for the same basic principle in *Apportionment IV*.

* * *

Accordingly, we hold that the trial court correctly framed the "intent" inquiry and reject the Legislature's assertion that the finding of unconstitutional intent could not be ascribed to the Legislature as a whole. Having reached the conclusion that the trial court did not err in evaluating the actions of legislators and legislative staff members in finding unconstitutional "intent," as prohibited by article III, section 20, we turn next to the legal sufficiency of the trial court's finding.

B. LEGAL SUFFICIENCY OF UNCONSTITUTIONAL INTENT

Our review of the trial court's finding of unconstitutional intent in the congressional redistricting plan takes place against the backdrop of the trial court's specific finding that the Legislature "systematically deleted almost all of their e-mails and other documentation relating to redistricting." The Legislature did so despite knowledge that litigation over the constitutionality of its redistricting plan was inevitable.

In fact, as far back as 2008, the Legislature argued to this Court that "litigation challenging reapportionment under the new standards" would increase as a result of the Fair Districts Amendment. *See Advisory Op. to Att'y Gen. re Standards for Establishing Legislative Dist. Boundaries,* 2 So.3d 161, 165 (Fla.2009). And, the Legislature informed the trial court in this case that litigation "was 'imminent' long before the days preceding the filing of" the challengers' lawsuit. From "start to finish," the Legislature asserted, the 2012 redistricting process, "more than any other, was conducted in an atmosphere charged with litigation."

To be sure, the Legislature did preserve some records related to redistricting — documents showing, for instance, the time and location of public meetings or other generally benign details of the process. But the Legislature saved virtually no communications among legislators and staff and none of the communications — which, as a result of this case, we now know to have occurred — involving the outside political consultants.

The Legislature had no specific policy requiring it to preserve communications regarding redistricting, even though it knew litigation was certain to occur, and admits that its record-retention policies applied in the same manner to redistricting as they applied to all types of legislative business. The House's policy, for example, specified that "records that are no longer needed for any purpose and that do not have sufficient administrative, legal, or fiscal significance to warrant their retention shall be disposed of systematically." Fla. H.R. Rule 14.2(b) (2010–2012).

To the extent the Legislature argues that it had no reason to know it needed to preserve these records because it could not have anticipated this Court's decision in *Apportionment IV* rejecting its broad claim of legislative privilege over communications related to redistricting, the Legislature had, according to testimony at trial, determined as early as January 2011 that no privilege would apply to any of its communications with outside political consultants....

* * *

Even in the absence of a legal duty, though, the spoliation of evidence results in an adverse inference against the party that discarded or destroyed the evidence....

The trial court was, therefore, justified in drawing an adverse inference against the Legislature in adjudicating the challengers' claim of unconstitutional partisan intent. And we too must consider the Legislature's "systematic[ ] delet[ion]" of redistricting records in evaluating whether the trial court's finding is supported by competent, substantial evidence.

Turning to the merits of the trial court's finding, we have little trouble concluding that competent, substantial evidence of unconstitutional intent exists in the record. The Legislature asserts that the trial court did not find improper intent in the plan as a whole and, in particular, contends that there was no collaboration between partisan operatives and the Legislature in drawing the congressional redistricting plan. While acknowledging that partisan operatives "sought to influence the redistricting process," the Legislature states that "at no time did the Legislature participate in their efforts." If features from the operative-created maps made it into the enacted map, the Legislature says, it is simply because those features were obvious or the similarities "superficial," and not because the operatives' "frenetic efforts to make themselves relevant" were successful. In other words, the Legislature argues that it "did not conspire with the operatives, despite the operatives' efforts."

We reject the Legislature's attempt to water down the trial court's findings and the inferences the trial court drew from the circumstantial evidence presented by pointing to an alleged lack of connection between the "parallel" process and the Legislature. The trial court found that it was "convince[d]" by the "circumstantial evidence introduced at trial" that the political operatives "obtain[ed] the necessary cooperation and collaboration" from the Legislature to ensure that the "redistricting process and the resulting map" were "taint[ed]" with "improper partisan intent." Indeed, the trial court specifically found that the operatives "were successful in their efforts to influence the redistricting process and the congressional plan under review."

* * *

There is also no doubt that the trial court's finding of unconstitutional intent pertained to the "process" of redistricting and the "enacted map" as a whole—to use the trial court's own words—rather than solely to the two specifically invalidated districts as the Legislature contends. In finding "too much circumstantial evidence" to reach any conclusion other than that the "redistricting process" and the "resulting map" were "taint[ed]" by "improper partisan intent," the trial court pointed specifically to the following evidence: the Legislature's destruction of "almost all" e-mails and "other documentation relating to redistricting"; early meetings between legislative leaders and staff with political consultants regarding the "redistricting process"; and the "continued involvement" of political consultants in the "redistricting process." None of this evidence relied on by the trial court was district-specific. The dissent's contrary interpretation of the trial court's finding of unconstitutional intent renders meaningless the trial court's extensive discussion of—and critical findings related to—this evidence.

* * *

Accordingly, for all these reasons, we affirm the trial court's finding of unconstitutional intent. We turn next to the trial court's two legal errors, which significantly affected its determination of the proper effect of its finding that the Legislature violated the Florida Constitution.

IV. TRIAL COURT'S FIRST LEGAL ERROR: FAILING TO PROPERLY ANALYZE THE CHALLENGE TO THE PLAN "AS A WHOLE"

The first legal error committed by the trial court was its determination that there was no distinction between a challenge to the redistricting plan "as a whole" and a challenge to individual districts. This error led to the trial court's failure to give any independent legal significance to its finding of unconstitutional intent when examining the challenges to individual districts.

* * *

This Court has held that "the Florida Constitution prohibits drawing a plan" with improper intent. *Apportionment I,* 83 So.3d at 617. This Court has also held that "there is no acceptable level of improper intent." *Id.* And, this Court has held that the "intent" standard "applies to … the apportionment plan as a whole." *Id.* Accordingly, under these holdings, the trial court's "general" finding of improper intent in the "process" must have some independent legal significance.

The trial court, however, failed to give effect to that finding of improper intent, in part because it never separately considered the challenge to the plan as a whole and, critically, never gave any weight to the general improper intent in analyzing the individual district challenges. The challengers correctly note that the trial court's finding of improper intent was based extensively on the existence of a "different, separate process that was undertaken contrary to the [Legislature's public] transparent [redistricting] effort in an attempt to favor a political party or an incumbent." …

In error, the trial court gave no legal weight to the existence of this separate process. The trial court's decision to invalidate District 5 was supported by numerous factors distinct from the "parallel" process, including that the district as enacted was "not compact," was "bizarrely shaped," and did not "follow traditional political boundaries as it winds from Jacksonville to Orlando," narrowing at one point to the width of a highway. The trial court found improper intent to benefit the Republican Party as to District 5 based on "the decision to increase the district to majority BVAP, which was accomplished in large part by creating [a] finger-like appendage jutting into District 7." Then, the trial court simply "buttressed" this "inference" of improper intent, based on the existence of the "oddly shaped appendage [ ]," through "the evidence of improper intent in the redistricting process generally, and as specifically related to the drawing of District 5," but did not independently rely on the "general" improper intent in any legally significant way.

* * *

The trial court's decision to invalidate District 10 is analogous.…

In rejecting challenges to seven other individual districts, the trial court never referred to the "general evidence of improper intent" that it found to exist in the "process." …

In determining that there was no distinction between a challenge to the "whole map" and a challenge to individual districts, the trial court relied on this Court's prior decision to invalidate the entire state Senate plan in *Apportionment I.* Citing this Court's decision as support, the trial court stated that this Court "invalidated the entire Senate plan but gave specific instructions as to which districts *required* corrective action."

The trial court was correct that this Court invalidated the whole Senate plan, to the extent that it determined the plan did "not pass constitutional muster" for the purposes of this Court's article III, section 16, declaratory judgment review. *Appor-*

tionment I, 83 So.3d at 683. But, unlike here, this Court in *Apportionment I* did not find a general improper intent in the state Senate plan, aside from the district numbering system that was manipulated to favor incumbents. Nor could we have, based on the nature of the limited record before us.

[.... T]his Court identified very specific deficiencies in the Senate plan—eight individual districts that were invalid, the failure to conduct a functional analysis, and the district numbering scheme. This Court did not conclude that the whole plan was unconstitutional because of improper intent in the whole plan, and this Court did not analyze—and could not have analyzed—the plan in that manner. Therefore, in relying on *Apportionment I* in this way, the trial court failed to give any actual effect to its finding in this case that the "whole plan" challenge had been proven through the direct and circumstantial evidence of improper partisan intent presented at trial.

Accordingly, for all these reasons, we conclude that the trial court erred in failing to recognize any distinction between a challenge to the redistricting plan "as a whole" and a challenge to individual districts. This error significantly affected the trial court's determination of the proper scope and legal effect of its finding of unconstitutional intent, particularly with regard to its analysis of the challenges to individual districts, and ultimately contributed to its decision to approve a remedy that was effectively no different than the remedy if there had been no finding of unconstitutional intent.

V. TRIAL COURT'S SECOND LEGAL ERROR: APPLYING A DEFERENTIAL STANDARD OF REVIEW

The trial court's error in failing to properly analyze the challenge to the plan "as a whole" was compounded by its error in the deferential standard of review it applied after finding the existence of unconstitutional intent.... This legal error in the standard of review, as with the legal error in not recognizing the independent significance of the challenge to the plan "as a whole," led to the trial court's failure to give any independent legal significance to its finding of unconstitutional intent when examining the challenges to individual districts. Once the trial court found unconstitutional intent, there was no longer any basis to apply a deferential standard of review; instead, the trial court should have shifted the burden to the Legislature to justify its decisions in drawing the congressional district lines.

The trial court's error as to the standard of review can be traced to its analysis in evaluating the challengers' claims[....] [T]he trial court began by asking whether there was any tier-two violation—whether the district was compact, and whether it followed existing political and geographical boundaries where feasible. Then, the trial court considered the direct and circumstantial evidence of tier-one improper intent only as "additional evidence" to "strengthen or weaken" an "inference of improper intent" that was identifiable from tier-two deficiencies. The trial court did so despite finding that the direct and circumstantial evidence itself had established a violation of the tier-one constitutional standards.

Although the trial court relied on *Apportionment I* as support for the standard of review it applied, the standard from that case—a facial review based on purely objective, undisputed evidence in the limited record before the Court—does not directly translate to this one—a fact-intensive challenge based on direct and circumstantial evidence developed during an adversarial trial. Discerning which aspects of the standard set forth in *Apportionment I* apply and which do not is thus of critical importance.

* * *

Although the legislative redistricting plan comes before this Court "with an initial presumption of validity," this Court explained that "the operation of this Court's process in apportionment cases is far different than the Court's review of ordinary legislative acts," including "a commensurate difference in [its] obligations." *Id.* at 606. Noting that the "new requirements" of the Fair Districts Amendment "dramatically alter[ed] the landscape with respect to redistricting," this Court held that its scope of review had "plainly increased, requiring a commensurately more expanded judicial analysis of legislative compliance." *Id.* at 607.

* * *

In this respect, the trial court was right to rely on *Apportionment I* in concluding that the nature of the legislation and the specific constitutional mandate outlawing partisan political gerrymandering require a different standard of review than applied in traditional cases challenging legislative enactments. Where the trial court erred, however, was in discounting the differences between *Apportionment I* and this case to conclude that the *same* standard must apply, even though this case involved direct and circumstantial evidence of tier-one constitutional violations that this Court had no ability to review in *Apportionment I*.

As this Court has explained, its review in *Apportionment I* was quite different than the challenge presented in this case. Unlike the fact-intensive challenge here, in which the parties had an opportunity to present extensive evidence during an adversarial trial pertaining to whether the plan and individual districts were drawn with improper intent, this Court's review in *Apportionment I* was "a facial review based on objective, undisputed evidence in the limited record before the Court." *Apportionment III*, 118 So.3d at 200.

* * *

The evidence of improper intent in this case, to the contrary, involved direct and circumstantial evidence of tier-one violations of the constitutional intent standard. Yet, despite the existence of testimony and fact-based claims regarding improper intent from a voluminous record that extended far beyond the legislative record to which this Court was constrained in *Apportionment I*, the trial court still determined that tier-two requirements—compactness and the use of political and geographical boundaries where feasible—were the "more reliable" indicators of improper intent, explaining that "a failure to comply with tier-two requirements" would "support[ ] an inference of improper intent," and that "[a]dditional direct and circumstantial evidence of intent may serve to strengthen or weaken this inference of improper intent." ...

We conclude that the trial court erred in focusing first on tier-two violations at the expense of the evidence of tier-one violations—violations it specifically found based on the evidence presented. The trial court's error was then exacerbated by its decision to apply an unduly deferential standard to its review of the map, even after finding the existence of unconstitutional partisan intent.

* * *

Once a tier-one violation of the constitutional intent standard is found, there is no basis to continue to afford deference to the Legislature....

Accordingly, after reaching the conclusion that the "redistricting process" and the "resulting map" had been "taint[ed]" by unconstitutional intent, the burden should have shifted to the Legislature to justify its decisions, and no deference should have been afforded to the Legislature's decisions regarding the drawing of the districts....

Because there are many ways in which to draw a district that complies with, for example, the constitutional requirement of compactness, which party bears the burden of establishing why a decision was made to accept or reject a particular configuration can ultimately be determinative....

Since the trial court found that the Legislature's intent was to draw a plan that benefitted the Republican Party, the burden should have been placed on the Legislature to demonstrate that its decision to choose one compact district over another compact district, or one tier-two compliant map over another tier-two compliant map, was not motivated by this improper intent....

* * *

VII. REMEDY

We now turn to the remedy. The specifically challenged districts notwithstanding, the challengers suggest that a broader remedy is required and urge this Court to invalidate the whole map and either redraw it ourselves or order the trial court to redraw it, perhaps with the assistance of an appointed expert. The Legislature counters that this Court lacks the authority to do so, because a congressional redistricting plan may be enacted only by a state legislature pursuant to article I, section 4, clause 1, of the United States Constitution, which vests exclusive authority to regulate the time, place, and manner of congressional elections in state legislatures, subject only to oversight by Congress. Although we reject the Legislature's argument that this Court has no authority to adopt a plan, if necessary, we decline the invitation to do so at this time.

... We thus conclude that the appropriate remedy at this juncture is to require the Legislature to redraw the map, based on the directions set forth by this Court.

The Legislature need not, in addition, redraw the entire map. Although we have struggled with this issue, particularly in light of the admittedly gerrymandered 2002 map that was used as a baseline for the current districts, we have ultimately determined that requiring the entire map to be redrawn is not the remedy commensurate with the constitutional violations found in this case. Further, we note that the challengers did not allege, as a separate claim, that the Legislature's reliance on the 2002 map was a basis for invalidating the whole map, nor did they identify a neutral map that showed how all of the districts could be redrawn in a manner more objectively compliant with the constitutional requirements.

We have, instead, instructed the Legislature on which districts must be redrawn — Districts 5, 13, 14, 21, 22, 25, 26, and 27 — and provided precise guidelines as to the deficiencies in these districts. Although we decline to require the whole plan to be redrawn, it follows that all adjacent districts affected by the reconfiguration of the specific districts being redrawn must also be redrawn. We have, in addition, been asked by the challengers to provide specific directives that the Legislature must follow in redrawing the districts.

* * *

We therefore set forth the following guidelines and parameters, which we urge the Legislature to consider in adopting a redrawn map that is devoid of partisan intent. First, in order to avoid the problems apparent in this case as a result of many critical decisions on where to draw the lines having been made outside of public view, we encourage the Legislature to conduct all meetings in which it makes decisions on the new map in public and to record any non-public meetings for preservation....

Second, the Legislature should provide a mechanism for the challengers and others to submit alternative maps and any testimony regarding those maps for consideration and should allow debate on the merits of the alternative maps. The Legislature should also offer an opportunity for citizens to review and offer feedback regarding any proposed legislative map before the map is finalized.

Third, the Legislature should preserve all e-mails and documents related to the redrawing of the map. In order to avoid additional, protracted discovery and litigation, the Legislature should also provide a copy of those documents to the challengers upon proper request.

Finally, we encourage the Legislature to publicly document the justifications for its chosen configurations. That will assist this Court in fulfilling its own solemn obligation to ensure compliance with the Florida Constitution in this unique context, where the trial court found the Legislature to have violated the constitutional standards during the 2012 redistricting process.

VIII. THE VOTERS SOUGHT FAIR DISTRICTS

Before we conclude, we observe that this is neither the first, nor likely the last, time this Court must confront a challenge to a redistricting plan enacted by the Legislature. In each case, we have endeavored to give meaning to the intent of the framers and voters who passed the Fair Districts Amendment to outlaw partisan political gerrymandering — no easy task given how entrenched this practice has been for years in the politics of crafting Florida's district boundaries.

A reader of Justice Canady's dissent in isolation could be forgiven for believing that this Court's decision here amounts to a creative maneuver designed to overstep its proper bounds, done in order to usurp the Legislature's role in the redistricting process. The dissent's attacks on this Court's analysis are extravagant, even when measured against prior dissenting opinions in our recent redistricting cases that have accused this Court of devising "a radical alteration in the operation of the separation of powers." *Apportionment IV,* 132 So.3d at 160 (Canady, J., dissenting).... In *Apportionment I,* the dissent repeatedly chastised this Court for "cast[ing] aside the presumption of constitutionality." *Apportionment I,* 83 So.3d at 696 (Canady, J., concurring in part and dissenting in part). In *Apportionment III,* the dissent charged that this Court had "la[id] the groundwork for the unrestrained judicial intrusion" into the redistricting process. *Apportionment III,* 118 So.3d at 218 (Canady, J., dissenting) (internal quotation omitted). And in *Apportionment IV,* the dissent hyperbolically accused this Court of "grievously violat[ing] the constitutional separation of powers." *Apportionment IV,* 132 So.3d at 156 (Canady, J., dissenting).

The dissent's position has certainly been consistent. But so too has this Court's. We pointed out in *Apportionment I* that the Fair Districts Amendment "dramatically alter[ed] the landscape with respect to redistricting," increasing the scope of judicial review and commensurately requiring "more expanded judicial analysis of legislative compliance." *Apportionment I,* 83 So.3d at 607. We emphasized in *Apportionment III* that "the framers and voters clearly desired more judicial scrutiny" of the Legislature's decisions in drawing the state's congressional and legislative districts. *Apportionment III,* 118 So.3d at 205. And we reiterated in *Apportionment IV* that there can hardly be a more compelling interest than the public interest in ensuring that the Legislature does not engage in unconstitutional partisan political gerrymandering. *Apportionment IV,* 132 So.3d at 147–48.

Far from upending the law, then, our legal analysis today adheres to our recent redistricting precedents. The dissent, to the contrary, continues its refusal to acknowledge the import of the Fair Districts Amendment. As Chief Justice Labarga eloquently stated in his concurrence in *Apportionment IV,* this Court has an "important duty" to "honor and effectuate the intent of the voters in passing Florida's groundbreaking constitutional amendment prohibiting partisan or discriminatory intent in drawing the congressional apportionment plan." 132 So.3d at 154–55 (Labarga, J., concurring). This is a responsibility we undertake with the utmost of seriousness — not because we seek to dictate a particular result, but because the people of Florida have, through their constitution, entrusted that responsibility to the judiciary.

IX. CONCLUSION

* * *

As to the remedy, we are aware that this litigation has now spanned more than three years and the qualifying period for the next congressional election of 2016 is not far away. We therefore urge that the redrawing of the map be expedited. We have chosen to relinquish this case to the trial court for a limited period of 100 days from the date of this opinion, therefore retaining jurisdiction, and we anticipate that the trial court can perform an oversight role should any disputes arise. To avoid any further delays, we have also limited the time for filing a motion for rehearing or clarification to five days from the date of this opinion and have limited the time for filing a response to such a motion to three days from the date the motion is filed.

It is so ordered.

CANADY, J., dissenting.

The circuit court properly ruled that the appellants failed to establish any basis for requiring the Legislature to further revise Florida's congressional district map. The majority's decision to reverse the circuit court and to invalidate numerous districts in the remedial congressional district plan adopted by the Legislature involves an extreme distortion of the appellate process deployed to effect a serious violation of the separation of powers. Accordingly, I dissent.

I.

The linchpin of the majority's decision is the assertion that in the final judgment the trial court "concluded that the [congressional redistricting] plan was drawn with improper partisan intent" and that the improper intent affected the entire plan.... In fact, however, the final judgment—a copy of which is appended—contains no finding whatsoever that the Legislature acted with improper intent regarding the entire congressional plan or that the "whole plan" challenge had been proven. The majority fails to identify any such finding in the final judgment. Instead, the majority puts forth a misconstruction of the trial court's ruling based on fragments from the final judgment taken out of context and creatively cobbled together. The trial court refused to draw an inference from the evidence that an improper partisan intent affected the redistricting plan in its entirety. But the majority effectively steps into the role of the trier of fact, independently reweighs the evidence, finds that the evidence supports the inference that the whole plan was affected by an improper partisan intent, imputes that broad finding of unconstitutional intent to the trial court, and then faults the trial court for not acting in accord with that fabricated finding. The upshot is a virtually revolutionary deformation of the appellate process.

The materials from which the majority fashions its misconstruction of the trial court's ruling are found largely in the trial court's findings regarding a "conspiracy" by certain Republican political consultants "to influence and manipulate the Legislature into a violation of its constitutional duty." Final Judgment at 10. But those materials are misshaped by the majority. When the trial court's ruling is considered in its full context, three essential points are clear in the trial court's findings regarding the consultants' conspiracy.

First, the consultants "managed to taint the redistricting process and the resulting map with improper partisan intent" by finding "ways to infiltrate and influence the Legislature, to obtain the necessary cooperation and collaboration to ensure that their plan was realized, *at least in part.*" Final Judgment at 22 (emphasis added). The trial court unquestionably determined that efforts of the consultants to cause partisan action by the Legislature had some success.

Second, the consultants' conspiracy was not successful in affecting the entire map drawing process. The "taint" of "improper partisan intent" attributable to the activities of the Republican consultants was limited in scope and effect. This is evident from the trial court's crucial finding that "the staff members who did the bulk of the actual map drawing for the Legislature … were not a part of the conspiracy, nor directly aware of it, and that significant efforts were made by them and their bosses to insulate them from direct partisan influence." Final Judgment at 22. The trial court specifically found that the committee staff "were insulated from the political consultants," Final Judgment at 37, and that the "motivation [of the staff] in drawing draft maps for consideration of the Legislature was to produce a final map which would comply with all the requirements of the Fair Districts Amendments, as their superiors had directed them." Final Judgment at 22.… This finding is of critical importance because of the pivotal role the committee staff indisputably had in drawing the districts the trial court refused to invalidate.

Third, the trial court found that an improper partisan intent did affect certain districts in the redistricting plan—namely, Districts 5 and 10—where there was evidence that the configuration of the districts was influenced through contact between the Republican consultants and legislative leadership or leadership staff.…

The majority simply ignores the second of these points and fabricates a broad finding of unconstitutional intent. The majority goes on to fault the trial court for failing "to give any independent legal significance to its finding of unconstitutional intent when examining the challenges to individual districts," majority op. at 393, and to assert that the trial court essentially concluded that some improper intent is acceptable. *See* majority op. at 393–94. Neither criticism of the trial court's order can withstand analysis. The trial court cannot be faulted for failing to give independent significance to a factual finding it did not make. The trial court expressly considered the question of unconstitutional intent in its analysis of the challenged individual districts. Indeed, the trial court was intently focused on the factual question of whether improper intent affected the drawing of particular districts by the Legislature. With respect to two districts, the trial court found that the districts were drawn with unconstitutional intent in the map initially adopted. With respect to the other districts, the trial court found that the appellants had failed to establish that the districts were drawn with unconstitutional intent.

At no point does the trial court indicate that it would permit some level of unconstitutional intent in the drawing of any district.… In rejecting the "whole plan" challenge, the trial court recognized the unremarkable proposition that districts that were not drawn with an unconstitutional intent and that did not otherwise violate the constitutional standards should not be invalidated.…

* * *

The majority's reading of the text of the final judgment on this point imports incoherence into the final judgment. It puts the reference to "general intent" in conflict with the trial court's reiterated conclusion that the districts now invalidated by the majority were not drawn with improper intent. But the text of the final judgment—like any other text—should be read harmoniously. The rule that "the provisions of a text should be interpreted in a way that renders them compatible, not contradictory" is a compelling rule of construction predicated on the reality that "it is invariably true that intelligent drafters do not contradict themselves." Antonin Scalia & Bryan A. Garner, *Reading Law: The Interpretation of Legal Texts* 180 (2012). There is no basis for concluding here that the trial court engaged in self-contradiction.

II.

* * *

In an opinion teeming with judicial overreaching, the invalidation of Remedial District 5 has pride of place. The basis for the majority's decision to require that this district be reoriented from its north-south configuration to an east-west configuration ultimately boils down to this: the north-south configuration must be rejected because that is the configuration chosen by the Legislature and the Legislature's choice is presumed to be unconstitutional. If the Legislature made a choice, we must begin by assuming the choice violated the constitution. This is so even though the configuration chosen by the Legislature was based on a map drawn by committee staff, who were insulated from partisan influence in selecting that configuration. The majority also suggests that the north-south configuration is somehow tainted because "the long-time incumbent of the district, Congresswoman Corrine Brown ... previously joined the leading Republicans in actively opposing the Fair Districts Amendment and redistricting reform." ...

Based on this supposed taint and the presumption of unconstitutionality, the majority treats as irrelevant the trial court's ruling that "the Plaintiffs have not offered convincing evidence that an East-West configuration is necessary in order to comply with tier-one and tier-two requirements of Article III, section 20." Order Approving Remedial Redist. Plan at 3. Under the majority's application of the presumption of unconstitutionality, an alternative suggested by the challengers is virtually guaranteed to trump any choice made by the Legislature. This vividly illustrates just how far the majority has gone in repudiating the principle that a redistricting plan should not be declared unconstitutional "unless it clearly appears beyond all reasonable doubt that, under any rational view that may be taken of the [plan], it is in positive conflict with some identified or designated provision of constitutional law." *In re Apportionment Law*, 263 So.2d 797, 805–06 (Fla.1972) (quoting *City of Jacksonville v. Bowden*, 67 Fla. 181, 64 So. 769, 772 (1914)).

* * *

With the invalidation of Remedial District 5 and other challenged districts, the ironic result is that districts drawn by professional committee staff, who were insulated from partisan influence in the drawing of the districts, are effectively displaced by districts drawn—as evidenced by deposition testimony—under the auspices of the National Democratic Redistricting Trust in cooperation with the Democratic Congressional Campaign Committee. There is something dreadfully wrong with this picture. As the Legislature argues: "To discard the work product of the Florida Legislature, which the trial court carefully considered and upheld, and substitute the partisan handiwork of the DCCC and the Democratic Trust, would be an indelible stain." Legislative Parties' Answer Brief at 91.

III.

Despite casting its disagreement with the trial court in terms of legal errors, the majority's real disagreement with the trial court is not about questions of law. It is about questions of fact. The majority thus reverses the trial court because the trial court failed to invalidate particular districts for being drawn with an unconstitutional intent when the trial court made the factual determination that those districts were not drawn with an unconstitutional intent. The majority's real problem with the trial court's ruling is that the trial court was unwilling to draw broad factual inferences concerning intent that the majority concludes should have been drawn.

* * *

It is axiomatic that determining whether a district should be invalidated based on an unconstitutional intent claim turns on the factual question of whether that district was drawn with an unconstitutional intent—a question indisputably within the province of the trier of fact. By imposing its own judgment about the factual inferences to be drawn from the evidence at trial, the majority has transgressed the boundaries of proper appellate review and invaded the province of the trier of fact. Such over-reaching by an appellate court would be a grave matter in any context, but it is doubly grave in the context of redistricting litigation, where a coordinate branch of government is a party and the constitutional authority of that branch is at issue. In a context such as this, the court has a special duty to scrupulously observe the limitations inherent in its function as an appellate court. Unfortunately, the majority has heedlessly cast those limitations aside.

The majority effectively holds that a finding of any unconstitutional intent in the drawing of congressional districts causes a presumption to arise that all the districts in the plan were drawn with an unconstitutional intent. Based on that presumption, the majority places the burden of proof on the Legislature to establish that particular districts were not drawn with an unconstitutional intent. The majority thus creates a general presumption of unconstitutionality based on a specific, narrow constitutional violation....

IV.

Having invaded the province of the trier of fact to find the factual basis for triggering the newly created presumption of unconstitutionality, the majority continues its march to dominate the redistricting process and finishes the job—at least for now—by making the factual determinations that the Legislature did not prove a lack of improper intent in the drawing of the specifically challenged districts. Marching forward, the majority eviscerates numerous factual determinations made by the trial court in its evaluation of the individual district challenges.

Under the well-established framework for appellate review, if an appellate court determines that the trier of fact has placed the burden of proof on the wrong party, the case should be remanded to the trier of fact to reevaluate the evidence in light of the correct legal rule regarding the burden of proof. The weighing of the evidence under the applicable burden of proof is the function of the trier of fact. That function should not be usurped by an appellate court. The Supreme Court has recognized as "elementary" that "'fact finding is the basic responsibility of [trial] courts, rather than appellate courts'" and "where findings are infirm because of an erroneous view of the law, a remand is the proper course unless the record permits only one resolution of the factual issue." *Pullman-Standard v. Swint*, 456 U.S. 273, 291–92 (1982) (quoting *DeMarco v. United States*, 415 U.S. 449, 450 n. (1974)). Proceedings by an appellate court contrary to these elementary principles are "incredible." *Id.* at 293.

The majority caps off its abandonment of the restraints of the appellate process by retaining jurisdiction after deciding this case, dictating the details of the proceedings in the trial court, and presuming to require that all filings submitted in the trial court shall "simultaneously be submitted to this court." This retention of jurisdiction and exercise of control of the proceedings in the trial court further vividly demonstrates the majority's aggressive determination to exercise full dominion over the redistricting process. Unlike our review of the legislative redistricting plan—over which we have original review jurisdiction under article III, section 16—our review of this case involving congressional redistricting is based on our jurisdiction to review trial court judgments that are certified by a district court under article V, section 3(b)(5). Once we have decided this case, there is no reason—other than the majority's determination to guarantee that it has the last word—that the case should not proceed like any other case that is reversed and remanded to a trial court after we have exercised our jurisdiction over a trial court judgment certified to us by a district court....

* * *

VI.

This decision causes serious damage to our constitutional structure. The proper functioning of the judicial process is deformed and the separation of powers is breached in an unprecedented manner. Since 2012, this Court's decisions concerning the redistricting process have been characterized by a repeated rewriting of the rules. The foundation for all that followed was the effective abrogation of our precedents that clothed a redistricting plan with a presumption of constitutionality. The Fair Districts Amendments—which said not a word about the alteration of the exercise of judicial power—could not bear the weight of that jettisoning of the presumption of constitutionality. And the Fair Districts Amendments certainly cannot bear the weight of today's decision, which abandons the well-established boundary between the trier of fact and a reviewing appellate court and transgresses the independence of the core function of the legislative branch in conducting the legislative process. I dissent.

POLSTON, J., concurs.

Questions

1. How does the Court evaluate intent of the Legislature?

2. Does anything other than direct statements of intent provide a basis for the Court's findings?

Article IV

Executive

Introduction

Introduction

Article IV, which describes the Executive Branch of the government, is relatively brief. Additionally, many aspects of executive authority are covered elsewhere in the Constitution. As established by the Constitution, the Governor has limited power, sharing many of her duties with the other members of the cabinet of executive officers.

The cabinet consists of an Attorney General, a Chief Financial Officer, and a Commissioner of Agriculture, in addition to the Governor. Unlike the cabinet appointed by the President of the United States, the cabinet members provided for in Florida's Constitution are elected independently in statewide elections. All the positions are elected to four-year terms and limited to two such terms. The Governor and Lieutenant Governor run in the general election as a combined ticket, much as the President and Vice President of the United States do.

It was not always this way. From 1885 through 1992, the cabinet was elected, but without term limits, while the Governor remained term-limited. An initiative on the 1992 ballot placed eight-year term limits on the cabinet members (with the clock beginning to tick at adoption, meaning every cabinet member then in office could serve another eight years). In 1998, the CRC reduced the number of elected cabinet members to the present group.

The 1885 Constitution allowed the Governor only one four-year term, and did not provide for a Lieutenant Governor at all. If the Governor died or left office, the Senate President became acting Governor until a special election could produce a new Governor. This system was tested and, in the opinion of many, failed in 1953 when newly elected Governor Dan McCarty had a heart attack early in his term and died months later. The Senate President was Charley Johns of Starke, in tiny Bradford County. Only a few thousand voters had put him in office, but he became Governor of the whole state. A member of the powerful Pork Chop Gang, Johns brought very different priorities to the position than his predecessor had; many McCarty appointees found themselves without jobs in favor of Johns's preferred appointees.

Johns lost in the 1954 special election to Tallahassee Senator LeRoy Collins. The seed, however, was planted for a new constitution — whenever one might be created — to have a Lieutenant Governor.

Article IV, Section 1(a) broadly describes the Governor's powers: "The supreme executive power shall be vested in a governor...." What, exactly, these powers are has been shaped by statutory and case law. One power that surfaces every time a hurricane threatens the state, and that became nearly ubiquitous in the COVID-19 crisis of 2020, is the Governor's power to issue executive orders. Yet nothing in the Constitution specifically enables the Governor to issue executive orders: the power is inherent in the general grant of "supreme executive power."

The power to use executive orders in emergencies is, however, described in some detail in Florida Statutes Chapter 252, which contains the State Emergency Management Act. That Act explicitly states the Governor has the power to declare emergencies, and delineates the effects and limits of that power. Though the emergency power has limitations, it is broad indeed: the Governor may "[t]ake measures concerning the conduct of civilians,"[1] which would seem to include the power to order citizens to wear masks during a pandemic, for public safety reasons.

---

1. FLA. STAT. § 252.36(5)(k).

Though this chapter is brief, and is illuminated by few cases, it presents probing questions regarding the reach of executive power.

A. Article IV, Section 1 — Governor

i. Supreme Executive Power

Kirk v. Baker
229 So. 2d 250 (Fla. 1969)

DREW, Justice.

We accept jurisdiction of this original proceeding in prohibition pursuant to the provision of the Florida Constitution which authorizes this Court to issue such writs "when questions are involved upon which a direct appeal to the supreme court is allowed as a matter of right." The case requires that we construe controlling provisions of the Florida Constitution. Hence, an appeal would come here from any final judgment that might be entered by the trial court.

The Respondent Judge has by formal order required the Governor and Gerald Mager, his subordinate and agent, to appear before him on a day certain and show cause why they should not be adjudged in contempt of Respondent's court for certain conduct set forth in an affidavit filed by Judge Baker. The Judge alleges in his order that the conduct constituted a willful, wanton and contemptuous attempt to influence him to rule in a manner contrary to the Court's conscience in presiding over the cases of *State of Florida v. Max Diamond a/k/a Mike Diamond* and *State of Florida v. Howard C. Edwards*.

The Governor asserts that the contempt order interferes with his ability as Governor to carry out the duties and responsibilities of his office under the constitution of this state and that he, as Governor, and his subordinate Gerald Mager are immune from any jurisdiction or command of said court for contempt.

Before proceeding to a consideration of the case, it is necessary to determine the scope of the inquiry. Judge Baker is Judge of the Criminal Court of Record of Dade County. He is an officer subject to removal by the Governor "for malfeasance, misfeasance, neglect of duty, drunkenness, incompetence, permanent inability to perform his official duties, or commission of a felony." The function of courts is historically limited to deciding the particular case under consideration. We are confined in our inquiry here to determining whether a judicial officer who is subject to removal by the Governor can use the processes and power of his court to adjudge the Governor in contempt. In such a determination, we must consider as a necessary implication of the contempt power the court's authority to forcibly restrain or imprison the Governor as punishment for his contemptuous conduct.

The answer to this inquiry has apparently been obvious to our forefathers, for throughout the history of the republic we find no record of a contempt proceeding ever having taken place under the particular circumstances before us. No case has been cited, and we have found none, in which any court has held a Governor in contempt for any act in furtherance of or connected with his official duties and responsibilities as Governor. In one instance the statement was made that "in extreme cases" courts have the power to restrain the Governor. But, even in that case such power was not employed.

Under our constitution the Governor is vested with the "supreme executive power." He is the commander in chief of all of the state's military forces. He must see that all laws of the state are faithfully executed, commission all state and county officers, and transact all necessary business with the officers of government. Many other duties are directly given him by the sovereign people of the state in the constitution. It is unthinkable that any inferior officer of this state could, in the guise of the exercise of judicial power, thwart the powers of the executive and thereby prevent or interfere with the full, unfettered performance of his official duties. The fact that the order names him as an individual instead of Governor is utterly of no import. To restrain the individual would be to restrain the Governor.

The discussions and conferences between the Governor and Judge Baker related to two cases pending before the Judge which had evoked great publicity in Dade County and the state at large. The Governor, in discharging his duty as Chief Executive to insure that all laws are faithfully executed, may be under a duty to suspend a judge from office for his conduct in a particular case. The Governor may have had in mind the possible exercise of this discretionary power over Judge Baker. It is only proper to assume his conferences were for the legitimate purpose of learning facts upon which to base such an exercise of his discretionary power, for it will generally be presumed that the action of the Chief Executive is in accordance with his official duty. Such an inquiry would assuredly be within the perimeter of his authority as Governor.

The charges of Judge Baker are serious accusations against the Governor, if true. But we hold that the Governor in such conduct must be cloaked with immunity. The proper forum for such charges is the House of Representatives under the provisions of Article III, Section 17, of the Constitution of 1968, or a grand jury.

Our conclusion under the facts here, that the Governor and his subordinate in his presence and under his immediate supervision are completely immune from the processes of the Criminal Court of Record of Dade County, is supported by all relevant authority we have been able to find on the subject. Unquestionably the dearth of authority is occasioned by the fact that the respective branches of government in our country have throughout our history assiduously avoided any encroachment on one another's authority. In those few instances where difficult cases have arisen, each branch has had enough foresight and respect for the orderly functioning of the governmental processes to avoid a confrontation.

It was urged upon us at oral argument that a Governor's immunity from the processes of the judiciary extended even to felonies which might be committed by him. In the narrow posture of this case we do not reach that question, and what we hold here would not be authority should such an unlikely event occur. Nor does our conclusion necessarily control a situation which might arise under a contempt order issued by a judicial officer subject only to impeachment for misdemeanors committed in office.

There has been filed in this cause a Motion for an order directing the Clerk of the Circuit Court of Dade County to make available to Judge Baker for his examination the testimony of Governor Kirk and Gerald Mager before the Dade County Grand Jury and any waivers of immunity executed by them. There is no merit to this Motion and the same is hereby denied.

Honorable Paul Baker, Judge of the Criminal Court of Record of Dade County is hereby prohibited from exercising any jurisdiction to enforce the Order to Show Cause of May 3, 1969, and should forthwith take whatever action is necessary to cancel and dismiss said charges and the Order of Contempt issued thereon.

It is so ordered.

ERVIN, C.J., and ROBERTS, ADKINS and BOYD, JJ., concur.

Women's Emergency Network v. Bush

214 F. Supp. 2d 1316, 1318 (S.D. Fla. 2002), *aff'd*,
323 F.3d 937 (11th Cir. 2003)

ORDER

MOORE, District Judge.

THIS CAUSE is before the Court upon Governor Jeb Bush's Motion to Dismiss the Amended Complaint....

Introduction

Governor Bush moves the Court ... to dismiss Plaintiffs' complaint with prejudice. In support of his motion, Governor Bush argues that he is not a proper party to this action which challenges the constitutionality of the Choose Life specialty license plate scheme, as codified at Fla. Stat. § 320.08058(30) (the "Act").

In response, Plaintiffs argue that Governor Bush is a proper party because "as head of the Department [of Highway Safety and Motor Vehicles, Governor Bush] has control over the implementation of the Act...." Governor Bush replies that Plaintiffs misrepresent that the governor is head of the Department. Instead, he argues that the "head of the Department is the Governor and Cabinet." Reply at 2 (emphasis in pleading) *citing* Fla. Stat. § 20.24. Thus, according to Governor Bush, he lacks the requisite connection with the Act and he is not a proper party.

Analysis

The primary question before the Court is whether Governor Bush is a proper party to this suit. In order to challenge the constitutionality of the Act, Plaintiffs must have brought this action against the state official or agency responsible for enforcing the allegedly unconstitutional scheme. *ACLU v. The Florida Bar*, 999 F.2d 1486, 1490–91 (11th Cir.1993). Accordingly, Plaintiffs joined as Defendants Governor Bush and

Fred Dickinson, as Executive Director of the Department. However, Governor Bush argues that he is not a proper party because the "allegations ... show no connection between the Governor and the unconstitutional conduct that is complained of...." Motion to Dismiss at 4 (emphasis in original).

Indeed a "connection" is necessary. In *Luckey v. Harris*, the Eleventh Circuit articulated the scope of the *Ex Parte Young* exception to the Eleventh Amendment. *Luckey v. Harris*, 860 F.2d 1012, 1015–16 (11th Cir.1988) *citing Ex Parte Young*, 209 U.S. 123, 157 (1908). Specifically, the Court provided:

> Personal action by defendants individually is not a necessary condition of injunctive relief against state officers in their official capacity. All that is required is that the *official be responsible for the challenged action.* As the *Young* court held, it is sufficient that the state officer sued must, 'by virtue of his office, ha[ve] some connection' with the unconstitutional act or conduct complained of. [W]hether [this connection] arises out of general law, or is specially created by the act itself, is not material so long as it exists.

Id. (Emphasis added.) Plaintiffs claim that Governor Bush has the requisite connection by virtue of his position as "head of the Department." Plaintiffs' Response to Motion to Dismiss at 3. Plaintiffs cite Florida Statute § 20.24 and Rule 15-1.001 of the Florida Administrative Code in support of this proposition. These authorities provide that "[t]he head of the Department of Highway Safety and Motor Vehicles is the Governor and Cabinet."1 Fla. Stat. § 20.24 (emphasis added). Importantly, Rule 15-1.001(3) goes on to state that "[a]n Executive Director is appointed by and serves at the pleasure of the Governor and Cabinet with the *overall duty and responsibility for the operation of the department.*" (Emphasis added.) Notably, the Governor's position as "head of the Department" is shared with six other individuals, the members of the Cabinet, and the Executive Director of the Department, who is also a party to this suit, is charged with "overall duty and responsibility" for the Department. *Id.*

Plaintiffs cite to *Luckey* and argue that it supports the notion that Governor Bush is a proper party because he has a sufficient connection with the allegedly unconstitutional Act. Instead, the Court finds that *Luckey* supports the Governor's position. In *Luckey,* the Eleventh Circuit held that Georgia Governor Joe Frank Harris was a proper party in a suit challenging deficiencies in the state's provision of indigent defense services. *Luckey,* 860 F.2d at 1013. The Court held that Governor Harris was a proper party where he: (1) was responsible for law enforcement in Georgia; (2) possessed residual power to commence criminal prosecutions; and (3) had the final authority to direct the Attorney General to "institute and prosecute" on behalf of the state. *Luckey,* 860 F.2d at 1016 *quoting* Ga. Const. Art. 5, § 2, ¶ 2. Thus, according to the Court, Governor Harris was an appropriate party where he was sufficiently responsible for the administration of the allegedly deficient indigent defense services.

On the contrary, Governor Bush's only "connection" is a position which he shares with six other individuals. Furthermore, the Executive Director of the Department is charged with "overall duty and responsibility" and even his appointment is committed to the discretion of the Governor and Cabinet. It seems undeniable that Governor Bush is not the official who is "responsible for the challenged action." *Luckey,* 860 F.2d at 1015. Indeed, Governor Bush's level of responsibility for the Act can easily be likened to that of the Commissioner of Agriculture, as a member of the Cabinet. Notably, the Act neither authorizes nor obligates the Governor to perform any duties. Instead, it empowers the Executive Director to oversee the Department and each of its sections. Rules 15-1.001(3) and 15-1.001(5), Fla. Admin. R. The Court is of the opinion that Plaintiffs' controversy is properly with the Department and the Executive Director who oversees it.

Thus, because the Governor lacks a sufficient connection to the Act in question, Plaintiffs are left to argue that Governor Bush is a proper party because he "signed into law" the Act at issue and because Article IV, § 1 of the Florida Constitution vests Governor Bush with executive power to enforce the laws of the State. Second Amended Complaint ¶¶ 14, 23. The Court is not persuaded by either of these arguments. *See e.g., Harris v. Bush,* 106 F.Supp.2d 1272, 1276 (N.D.Fla.2000) (Governor Bush was not a proper party where he possessed a general authority to enforce laws and plaintiff did not allege or suggest that he intended to enforce the statutory provision under attack); *Warden v. Pataki,* 35 F.Supp.2d 354, 358 (the well-settled doctrine of absolute legislative immunity bars actions against legislators or governors on the basis of their roles in enacting or signing legislation) *citing Supreme Court of Virginia v. Consumers Union of United States, Inc.,* 446 U.S. 719, 731–34 (1980); *Weinstein v. Edgar,* 826 F.Supp. 1165, 1167 (N.D.Ill.1993) (Governor was not a proper party; "were this court to conclude that Governor Edgar's general obligation to faithfully execute the laws is a sufficient connection to the enforcement of 105 ILCS 5/24-2, then the Illinois legislature necessarily could be challenged merely by naming the Governor as a party defendant").

In sum, the Court determines that Governor Bush does not bear a sufficient connection with the Act and, as such, the Governor's motion to dismiss is GRANTED....

This case is closed only as to Defendant Governor Jeb Bush.

Scott v. Francati

214 So. 3d 742 (Fla. 1st DCA 2017)

ROWE, J.

Governor Rick Scott petitions this Court for a writ of prohibition to bar further proceedings in the trial court because he is not a proper defendant and because no justiciable case or controversy exists. For the reasons that follow, we grant the petition.

Background

Gail Francati, a former nursing home resident, seeks a declaration regarding the constitutionality of the 2014 amendments to section 400.023, Florida Statutes. Francati argues that the amendments violate the separation of powers doctrine by creating new procedural rules singling out nursing home residents and violate her right to access to courts by limiting the parties that can be named as defendants in an action brought by a nursing home resident alleging negligence or a violation of residents' rights. She named the State of Florida and Rick Scott, in his capacity as Governor, as defendants in her complaint. Governor Scott and the State moved to dismiss the complaint on two grounds: (1) they were not proper parties to the suit; and (2) the complaint failed to state an actual case or controversy. After a hearing, the trial court granted the State's motion to dismiss but ruled that Francati's suit against Governor Scott could proceed. Governor Scott petitions this Court for a writ of prohibition to prevent further proceedings in the circuit court.

Whether the Governor is a Proper Defendant

The determination of whether a state official is a proper defendant in a declaratory action challenging the constitutionality of a statute is governed by three factors. The determination begins with ascertaining whether the named state official is charged with enforcing the statute. *Haridopolos v. Alachua Cty.*, 65 So.3d 577, 578 (Fla. 1st DCA 2011); *see also Marcus v. State Senate for the State*, 115 So.3d 448, 448 (Fla. 1st DCA 2013) (holding that state legislators were not proper parties to an action challenging a statute that preempted county and municipal regulation of firearms and ammunition because the legislators were not designated as the enforcement authority); *Walker v. President of the Senate*, 658 So.2d 1200 (Fla. 5th DCA 1995) (holding that the Senate President and Speaker of the House were not proper parties to a declaratory action challenging certain operations of the Department of Corrections). If the named official is not the enforcing authority, then courts must consider two additional factors: (1) whether the action involves a broad constitutional duty of the state implicating specific responsibilities of the state official; and (2) whether the state official has an actual, cognizable interest in the challenged action. *Atwater v. City of Weston*, 64 So.3d 701, 703 (Fla. 1st DCA 2011); *see also Coal. for Adequacy & Fairness in Sch. Funding, Inc. v. Chiles*, 680 So.2d 400, 403 (Fla. 1996) (holding that the governor was a proper party to an action challenging the failure to adequately fund the public education system due to his position as chief executive officer and chairperson of the Board of Education); *Brown v. Butterworth*, 831 So.2d 683, 689–90 (Fla. 4th DCA 2002) (holding that the attorney general and the president of the Florida Senate were proper parties to an action challenging the constitutionality of a redistricting plan). Applying these factors to Francati's complaint, we conclude that Governor Scott is not a proper defendant to her suit.

Specifically, Francati challenges the constitutionality of section 400.023(3), Florida Statutes (2015), which provides:

> (3) A cause of action may not be asserted against an individual or entity other than the licensee, the licensee's management or consulting company, the licensee's managing employees, and any direct caregivers, whether employees or contractors, unless, after a motion for leave to amend hearing, the court or an arbitration panel determines that there is sufficient evidence in the record or proffered by the claimant to establish a reasonable showing that:

(a) The individual or entity owed a duty of reasonable care to the resident and that the individual or entity breached that duty; and

(b) The breach of that duty is a legal cause of loss, injury, death, or damage to the resident.

For purposes of this subsection, if, in a proposed amended pleading, it is asserted that such cause of action arose out of the conduct, transaction, or occurrence set forth or attempted to be set forth in the original pleading, the proposed amendment relates back to the original pleading.

A review of the statute reveals that Governor Scott is not charged with enforcing the statute. Indeed, Francati never argues that Governor Scott is an enforcing authority under the statute. Neither does she allege that the nursing home pre-suit statute involves a broad constitutional duty of the state implicating specific responsibilities of Governor Scott or that Governor Scott has an actual, cognizable interest in the challenged action. Rather, Francati argues that she is not required to demonstrate any of these factors because, unlike the statutes challenged in *Marcus, Haridopolos, Atwater,* and *Walker,* the statute challenged in her declaratory action is self-executing. She posits that the Governor is a proper defendant in a suit challenging the constitutionality of a self-executing statute by virtue of his general executive duty to execute and enforce the laws of Florida. We find no merit in this argument.

While we recognize that *Atwater* involved a statute that identified a specific enforcement authority, the holding in that case is equally applicable to an action challenging the constitutionality of a self-executing statute, such as section 400.023. The question of whether a state official is a proper defendant to a suit challenging the constitutionality of a statute does not turn on whether the statute is self-executing. Rather, as our court instructed in *Atwater,* our analysis focuses on whether the named defendants have an actual interest in the outcome of the lawsuit, necessary for the court to exercise its jurisdiction to render a declaratory judgment:

> Even though the legislature has expressed its intent that the declaratory judgment act [chapter 86, Florida Statutes] should be broadly construed, there still must exist some justiciable controversy *between adverse parties* that needs to be resolved for a court to exercise its jurisdiction. Otherwise, any opinion on a statute's validity would be advisory only and improperly considered in a declaratory action.

Id. at 704–05 (quoting *Martinez v. Scanlan,* 582 So.2d 1167, 1170–71 (Fla. 1991)) (emphasis in original).

Contrary to Francati's assertion and the trial court's order, the Governor's general executive power, standing alone, does not render him a proper defendant in a challenge to the constitutionality of a self-executing statute. *Harris v. Bush,* 106 F.Supp.2d 1272, 1276–77 (N.D. Fla. 2000). Article IV, section 1 of the Florida Constitution requires Governor Scott, as Chief Executive Officer of the State, "to take care that the laws be faithfully executed." It is absurd to conclude that the Governor's general executive power under the Florida Constitution is sufficient to make him a proper defendant whenever a party seeks a declaration regarding the constitutionality of a state law. *Women's Emergency Network v. Bush*, 323 F.3d 937, 949 (11th Cir. 2003) ("If a governor's general executive power provided a sufficient connection to state law to permit jurisdiction over him, any state statute could be challenged simply by naming the governor as a defendant."). With regard to Francati's action, Governor Scott has no enforcement authority over the statute she challenges. And there is no relief the court could order Governor Scott to provide to remedy the constitutional violation alleged in the complaint. Where it is clear, as here, that the plaintiff cannot allege any proper basis for naming the Governor as a party defendant, the court should decline to assert jurisdiction.

Accordingly, we ... QUASH the order denying Governor Scott's motion to dismiss.

RAY, and M.K. THOMAS, JJ., CONCUR.

Commentary and Questions on Kirk v. Baker, Women's Emergency Network v. Bush, *and* Scott v. Francati

These cases illustrate why it can be difficult to sue the governor. In one case, the governor's "supreme executive power" placed him above the power of a judge in his state to hold him in contempt. In the other, the governor was found to have no power—in the form of a connection to the subject of litigation—to be sued. Finally, in the third case, standards for making a governor a defendant are articulated.

1. What do the justices say is the available remedy in *Kirk v. Baker* if the Governor should commit a felony? A misdemeanor?

2. Under the reasoning of *Kirk v. Baker*, can you think of any interference a governor could make in a court case that would have a legal consequence for that governor?

3. Do these opinions clarify the various roles of the Governor, Governor and Cabinet, and agency heads?

4. Does the court's reliance on case law based on the constitutions of other states make sense here?

5. What is the basis for federal jurisdiction in Women's Emergency Network v. Bush?

6. According to these cases, under what circumstances may a governor be involved in litigation?

ii. "Take Care that the Laws be Faithfully Executed"

Ayala v. Scott

224 So. 3d 755 (Fla. 2017)

LAWSON, J.

Aramis Donell Ayala, State Attorney for Florida's Ninth Judicial Circuit, petitions this Court for a writ of quo warranto, challenging Governor Rick Scott's authority

("on what authority

under section 27.14(1), Florida Statutes (2016), to reassign the prosecution of death-penalty eligible cases in the Ninth Circuit to Brad King, State Attorney for Florida's Fifth Judicial Circuit. We have jurisdiction. *See* article V, §3(b)(8), Fla. Const. For the reasons below, we deny Ayala's petition.

BACKGROUND

At a March 15, 2017, press conference, Ayala announced that she "will not be seeking [the] death penalty in the cases handled in [her] office." Several times during the same press conference, Ayala reiterated her intent to implement a blanket "policy" of not seeking the death penalty in any eligible case because, in her view, pursuing death sentences "is not in the best interest of th[e] community or in the best interest of justice," even where an individual case "absolutely deserve[s] [the] death penalty."

In response to Ayala's announcement, Governor Rick Scott issued a series of executive orders reassigning the prosecution of death-penalty eligible cases pending in the Ninth Circuit to King. In support of these orders, the Governor cited his duty as Florida's chief executive officer under article IV, section 1(a), of the Florida Constitution to "take care that the laws be faithfully executed" and his authority under section 27.14(1), Florida Statutes, to assign state attorneys to other circuits "if, for any ... good and sufficient reason, the Governor determines that the ends of justice would be best served." The reassignment orders do not direct King to pursue the death penalty in any particular case, and in a statement filed in this Court, King has sworn that the Governor made no attempt to influence his decision as to whether the circumstances of any of the reassigned cases warrant pursuing the death penalty.

After unsuccessfully seeking a stay of the reassignment orders in the Ninth Circuit, Ayala filed this petition for a writ of quo warranto challenging the Governor's authority to reassign the cases at issue to King. The record reflects that Ayala and her office have abided by the lower courts' denial of her motion and fully cooperated with King.

ANALYSIS

Ayala argues that the Governor exceeded his authority under section 27.14 by reassigning death-penalty eligible cases in the Ninth Circuit to King over her objection because article V, section 17, of the Florida Constitution makes Ayala "the prosecuting officer of all trial courts in [the Ninth] [C]ircuit." While quo warranto is the proper vehicle to challenge the Governor's authority to reassign these cases to King, ... Ayala is not entitled to relief because the Governor did not exceed his authority on the facts of this case.

As Florida's chief executive officer, the Governor is vested with the "supreme executive power" and is charged with the duty to "take care that the laws be faithfully executed." Art. IV, §1(a), Fla. Const. Florida law facilitates the Governor's discharge of this duty, among other ways, through state attorney assignments. Specifically, section 27.14(1), the constitutionality of which Ayala concedes, provides:

> If any state attorney is disqualified to represent the state in any investigation, case, or matter pending in the courts of his or her circuit or *if, for any other*

good and sufficient reason, the Governor determines that the ends of justice would be best served, the Governor may, by executive order filed with the Department of State, either order an exchange of circuits or of courts between such state attorney and any other state attorney or *order an assignment of any state attorney to discharge the duties of the state attorney with respect to one or more specified investigations, cases, or matters, specified in general in the executive order of the Governor.* Any exchange or assignment of any state attorney to a particular circuit shall expire 12 months after the date of issuance, unless an extension is approved by order of the Supreme Court upon application of the Governor showing good and sufficient cause to extend such exchange or assignment.

§ 27.14(1), Fla. Stat. (2016) (emphasis added).

This Court has previously recognized that the Governor has broad authority to assign state attorneys to other circuits pursuant to section 27.14:

> It is the duty of the Governor under Fla. Const. F.S.A., art. IV, § 1(a) in the exercise of his executive power to "take care that the laws be faithfully executed." The exercise of this power and the performance of this duty are clearly essential to the orderly conduct of government and the execution of the laws of this State. An executive order assigning a state attorney is exclusively within the orbit of authority of the Chief Executive when exercised within the bounds of the statute. *See Kirk v. Baker*, 224 So.2d 311 (Fla. 1969). The Governor is given broad authority to fulfill his duty in taking "care that the laws be faithfully executed," and he should be required to do no more than make a general recitation as to his reasons for assigning a state attorney to another circuit.

Finch v. Fitzpatrick, 254 So.2d 203, 204–05 (Fla. 1971); *see also Austin v. State ex rel. Christian*, 310 So.2d 289, 293 (Fla. 1975) ("The statutes authorizing assignments of state attorneys should be broadly and liberally construed so as to complement and implement the duty of the Governor under the Constitution of the State of Florida to 'take care that the laws be faithfully executed.'" (quoting art. IV, § 1(a), Fla. Const.)).

Accordingly, this Court reviews challenges to the Governor's exercise of his "broad discretion in determining 'good and sufficient reason' for assigning a state attorney to another circuit," *Finch*, 254 So.2d at 205, similar to the way in which it reviews exercises of discretion by the lower courts. *Compare Johns v. State*, 144 Fla. 256, 197 So. 791, 796 (1940) ("If the Governor should abuse [the assignment] power, by arbitrarily and without any reason whatsoever [for] making such an assignment, it might be that his action could be inquired into by writ of quo warranto...."); *with McFadden v. State*, 177 So.3d 562, 567 (Fla. 2015) ("Discretion is abused only when the trial court's decision is 'arbitrary, fanciful, or unreasonable.'" (quoting *Gonzalez v. State*, 990 So.2d 1017, 1033 (Fla. 2008))).

Applying this well-established standard of review to the facts of this case, the executive orders reassigning the death-penalty eligible cases in the Ninth Circuit to King fall well "within the bounds" of the Governor's "broad authority." *Finch*, 254 So.2d at 204–05. Far from being unreasoned or arbitrary, as required by section 27.14(1), the reassignments are predicated upon "good and sufficient reason," namely Ayala's blanket refusal to pursue the death penalty in any case despite Florida law establishing the death penalty as an appropriate sentence under certain circumstances. *See generally* § 921.141, Fla. Stat. (2017).

Notwithstanding the Governor's compliance with all of the requirements of section 27.14(1), however, Ayala and her amici urge this Court to invalidate the reassignment orders by viewing this case as a power struggle over prosecutorial discretion. We decline the invitation because by effectively banning the death penalty in the Ninth Circuit — as opposed to making case-specific determinations as to whether the facts of each death-penalty eligible case justify seeking the death penalty — Ayala has exercised no discretion at all. As New York's high court cogently explained, "adopting a 'blanket policy'" against the imposition of the death penalty is "in effect refusing to exercise discretion" and tantamount to a "functional[] veto" of state law authorizing prosecutors to pursue the death penalty in appropriate cases. *Johnson v. Pataki*, 91 N.Y.2d 214, 668 N.Y.S.2d 978, 691 N.E.2d 1002, 1007 (1997).

Although *Johnson* applied New York law, the standards to which this Court holds its own judicial officers establish that Ayala's actions have the same impact under Florida law. For example, our trial judges may not "*refuse* to exercise discretion" or "rely on an inflexible rule for a decision that the law places in the judge's discretion." *Barrow v. State*, 27 So.3d 211, 218 (Fla. 4th DCA 2010), *approved*, 91 So.3d 826 (Fla. 2012). Instead, exercising discretion demands an individualized determination "exercised according to the exigency of the case, upon a consideration of the attending circumstances." *Barber v. State*, 5 Fla. 199, 206 (Fla. 1853) (Thompson, J., concurring).

Thus, under Florida law, Ayala's blanket refusal to seek the death penalty in any eligible case, including a case that "absolutely deserve[s] [the] death penalty" does not reflect an exercise of prosecutorial discretion; it embodies, at best, a misunderstanding of Florida law. *Cf. Doe v. State*, 499 So.2d 13, 14 (Fla. 3d DCA 1986) (holding "the trial court failed to exercise its independent sentencing discretion" in light of its erroneous view of the law); *see also Taylor v. State*, 49 Fla. 69, 38 So. 380, 383 (1905) (recognizing that "a failure of the state's interests" occurs where "the regular state attorney is unwilling or refuses to act").

Moreover, while Ayala's blanket prohibition against the death penalty provided the Governor with "good and sufficient reason" to reassign the cases at issue to King, also important to our holding is that the Governor did not attempt to decide which cases are deserving of the death penalty. The Governor's orders do not direct King to seek the death penalty in any of the reassigned cases, and King has sworn that the Governor has not attempted to interfere with his determination as to whether to pursue the death penalty in any case. Rather, consistent with the Governor's constitutional duty, effectuated pursuant to his statutory assignment authority, the executive orders ensure the faithful execution of Florida law by guaranteeing that the death penalty —

while never mandatory—remains an option in the death-penalty eligible cases in the Ninth Circuit, but leaving it up to King, as the assigned state attorney, to determine whether to seek the death penalty on a case-by-case basis.

On these facts, the Governor has not abused his broad discretion in reassigning the cases at issue to King.

CONCLUSION

The executive orders reassigning death-penalty eligible cases in the Ninth Circuit to King do not exceed the Governor's authority on the facts of this case. Therefore, we deny Ayala's petition.

It is so ordered.

PARIENTE, J., dissenting.

This case is about the independence of duly elected State Attorneys to make lawful decisions within their respective jurisdictions as to sentencing and allocation of their offices' resources, free from interference by a Governor who disagrees with their decisions. The issue before this Court is whether a duly elected State Attorney's choice to forgo seeking one potential penalty in a class of criminal cases, in favor of seeking another penalty authorized by statute, constitutes "good and sufficient reason" for the Governor to exercise his removal power under section 27.14(1), Florida Statutes (2017). I dissent because the State Attorney's decision to prosecute first-degree murder cases but not seek the death penalty at this time does not provide a basis for the Governor to remove State Attorney Aramis Ayala.

Article V, section 17, of the Florida Constitution, which was adopted in 1972, provides for an elected state attorney "[i]n each judicial circuit," who "shall be the prosecuting officer of all trial courts in that circuit and shall perform other duties prescribed by general law." Art. V, § 17, Fla. Const. As to the role of elected State Attorneys, this Court made clear in *Austin v. State ex rel. Christian*, 310 So.2d 289 (Fla. 1975), that "the office of State Attorney is a constitutional office," stating:

> State Attorneys are *constitutional officers*, charged with the responsibility of prosecutions in the circuit in which he [or she] is elected and with the performance of such other duties as are prescribed by general law.... Being an elected official he [or she] is responsible to the electorate of [the] circuit, this being the traditional method in a democracy by which the citizenry may be assured that vast power will not be abused.... The Legislature, in its wisdom, has empowered the Governor to exchange and assign State Attorneys between judicial circuits within the confines of its enactments.

Id. at 293–94 (emphasis added). The Court also established that "[a] statute enacted by the Legislature may not constrict a right granted under the ultimate authority of the Constitution." *Id.* at 293.

Specifically at issue in this case is the decision of Aramis Ayala, the duly elected State Attorney for the Ninth Judicial Circuit, to exercise her prosecutorial discretion not to seek the death penalty in cases in which she sought and obtained indictments for first-degree murder. It is well established in our case law that "the decision to seek the death penalty," as allowed by statute, "is within the prosecutor's discretion." *Freeman v. State*, 858 So.2d 319, 322 (Fla. 2003). Nowhere in the Florida Statutes does the Legislature mandate that a prosecutor seek the death penalty in capital prosecutions. [Citations omitted.] Florida's capital sentencing scheme affords a duly elected State Attorney the discretion to pursue either of two possible sentences "[u]pon conviction or adjudication of guilt ... of a capital felony": "death or life imprisonment" without the possibility of parole. §921.141(1).

* * *

Likewise, Florida's most recently amended capital sentencing scheme further affirms that it is the prosecutor's decision whether to seek death in each capital prosecution, stating: "If the prosecutor intends to seek the death penalty, the prosecutor must give notice to the defendant and file the notice with the court within 45 days after arraignment.... The court may allow the prosecutor to amend the notice upon a showing of good cause." Ch. 2017-1, Laws of Fla., §4. Although the amicus brief of the House of Representatives asserts that the State Attorney is obligated to seek the death penalty in each prosecution where the State can prove at least one aggravating factor, the Governor disagrees with that position, acknowledging that the decision to seek death is a matter of prosecutorial discretion.

In his executive order removing State Attorney Ayala, Governor Scott referenced article IV, section 1(a), of the Florida Constitution, and section 27.14, Florida Statutes (2017). See, e.g., Exec. Order No. 17-66 (Fla. Mar. 16, 2017). Article IV, section 1(a), of the Florida Constitution, states in pertinent part: "The governor shall *take care that the laws be faithfully executed*, commission all officers of the state and counties, and transact all necessary business with the officers of government." Art. IV, §1(a), Fla. Const. (emphasis added). However, as Amici Curiae Former Judges argue, the fact that the Governor is charged to faithfully execute the laws does not supplant the constitutional authority of the independently elected State Attorney to prosecute crimes and to exercise his or her discretion in deciding what punishment to seek within the confines of the applicable laws. *See* Amici Curiae Former Judges Br. at 13 (The Governor's constitutional duty to " 'take care that the laws be faithfully executed'... cannot empower the governor, contrary to the Florida Constitution's express provision that state attorneys 'shall' be 'the' prosecutor within their circuits, to usurp prosecutorial duties." (quoting art. IV, §1(a), Fla. Const.)). Indeed, every day State Attorneys are tasked with making tough choices as to which crimes to prosecute and which penalties to pursue in consideration of their offices' limited resources. Such decisions include whether to accept a plea to a lesser degree of the charged offense, whether to prosecute certain classes of crimes, and, of course, whether to seek the death penalty in capital prosecutions.

The Governor's only constitutional authority to remove State Attorneys comes from article IV, section 7, of the Florida Constitution. That provision provides that "the governor may suspend from office any state officer not subject to impeachment ... for malfeasance, misfeasance, neglect of duty, drunkenness, incompetence, permanent inability to perform official duties, or commission of a felony." Governor Scott has not claimed that any of these grounds for exercising his constitutional removal authority applies in this case. Therefore, because Governor Scott does not have the constitutional authority to remove Ayala from her position under article IV, section 7, the Governor relies on section 27.14, Florida Statutes.

* * *

State Attorney Ayala's decision was well within the scheme created by the Legislature and within the scope of decisions State Attorneys make every day on how to allocate their offices' limited resources. Because State Attorney Ayala's decision was within the bounds of the law and her discretion, Governor Scott did not have "good and sufficient reason" to remove her from these cases.

* * *

QUINCE, J., concurs.

Questions

1. What is the standard for review of a governor's exercise of authority?

2. May a governor's act be overturned only if it is arbitrary?

3. May a governor remove an official who acts legally but in a way the governor does not approve of?

4. Does the basis for the majority decision in *Ayala v. Scott* differ from that in *Kirk v. Baker*? In what way?

iii. "Necessary Business"

This case raises multiple issues under the Florida Constitution, including the separation-of-powers issue explored in the Article II chapter. This excerpt illustrates the concept that a governor cannot justify an action by claiming that he is "faithfully execut[ing]" the law if that action, itself, actually violates the law.

Florida House of Representatives v. Crist

999 So. 2d 601 (Fla. 2008)

[Note: This case is tightly edited, as it is also treated in Articles II and V.]

CANTERO, J.

After almost sixteen years of sporadic negotiations with four governors, in November 2007 the Seminole Indian Tribe of Florida signed a gambling "compact" (a contract between two sovereigns) with Florida Governor Charles Crist. The compact significantly expands casino gambling, also known as "gaming," on tribal lands. For example, it permits card games such as blackjack and baccarat that are otherwise prohibited by law. In return, the compact promises substantial remuneration to the State.

The Florida Legislature did not authorize the Governor to negotiate the compact before it was signed and has not ratified it since. To the contrary, shortly after the compact was signed, the Florida House of Representatives and its Speaker, Marco Rubio, filed in this Court a petition for a writ of quo warranto disputing the Governor's authority to bind the State to the compact. We have exercised our discretion to consider such petitions, see art. V, § 3(b)(8), Fla. Const., and now grant it on narrow grounds. We hold that the Governor does not have the constitutional authority to bind the State to a gaming compact that clearly departs from the State's public policy by legalizing types of gaming that are illegal everywhere else in the state.

* * *

II. JURISDICTION

Before discussing the issue presented, we first address our jurisdiction. The House and Speaker Rubio have filed in this Court a petition for writ of quo warranto. The Governor contends that this Court lacks jurisdiction because the House does not seek either to remove him from office or to enjoin the future exercise of his authority. We conclude, however, that these are not the only grounds for issuing such a writ.

The Florida Constitution authorizes this Court to issue writs of quo warranto to "state officers and state agencies." Art. V, § 3(b)(8), Fla. Const. The term "quo warranto" means "by what authority." This writ historically has been used to determine whether a state officer or agency has improperly exercised a power or right derived from the State. See *Martinez v. Martinez*, 545 So.2d 1338, 1339 (Fla.1989); see also art. V, § 3(b)(8), Fla. Const. Here, the Governor is a state officer. The House challenges the Governor's authority to unilaterally execute the Compact on the State's behalf.

The Governor argues that because he already has signed the Compact, quo warranto relief is inappropriate. But the writ is not so limited. In fact, petitions for the writ historically have been filed after a public official has acted. *See, e.g., Chiles v. Phelps*, 714 So.2d 453, 455 (Fla.1998) (holding that the Legislature and its officers exceeded their authority in overriding the Governor's veto); *State ex rel. Butterworth v. Kenny*, 714 So.2d 404, 406 (Fla.1998) (issuing the writ after the Capital Collateral Regional Counsel had filed a federal civil rights suit, concluding that it had no authority to file it). The Governor's execution of the Compact does not defeat our jurisdiction.

The concurring-in-result-only opinion expresses concern that by considering a more narrow issue than the Governor's authority to execute IGRA compacts in general—that is, whether the Governor has the authority to bind the State to a compact that violates Florida law—we are expanding our quo warranto jurisdiction to include issues normally reserved for declaratory judgment actions. In prior quo warranto cases, however, we have considered separation-of-powers arguments normally reviewed in the context of declaratory judgments, such as whether the Governor's action has usurped the Legislature's power, "where the functions of government would be adversely affected absent an immediate determination by this Court." *Phelps*, 714 So.2d at 457; *see also Martinez*, 545 So.2d at 1339 (holding quo warranto appropriate to test the governor's power to call special sessions); *Orange County v. City of Orlando*,

327 So.2d 7 (Fla.1976) (holding that the legality of city's actions regarding annexation ordinances can be inquired into through quo warranto).

In this case, the Secretary has approved the Compact and, absent an immediate judicial resolution, it will be given effect. In fact, according to news reports, the Tribe already has begun offering blackjack and other games at the Seminole Hard Rock Hotel and Casino. See Amy Driscoll, "Casino Gambling: Amid glitz, blackjack's in the cards," *The Miami Herald*, June 23, 2008, at B1. Thus, if indeed the Governor has exceeded his constitutional authority, a compact that violates Florida law will, nevertheless, become effective in seven casinos located on tribal lands located in the state. As in *Phelps*, therefore, the importance and immediacy of the issue justifies our deciding this matter now rather than transferring it for resolution in a declaratory judgment action.

* * *

2. IGRA and the "Necessary Business" Clause

The Governor argues that his authority to execute the Compact derives from article IV, section 1 of the Florida Constitution. That provision states in part that "[t]he governor shall take care that the laws be faithfully executed ... and transact all necessary business with the officers of government." Art. IV, § 1(a), Fla. Const. The Governor submits that the phrase "transact all necessary business with the officers of government" includes negotiating with the Tribe and that he cannot ignore the federal directive to "negotiate"; therefore, negotiating the Compact was "necessary business" under IGRA.

* * *

We express no opinion on whether the "necessary business" clause may ever grant the governor authority to bind the State to an IGRA compact. We do conclude, however, that the clause does not authorize the governor to execute compacts contrary to the expressed public policy of the state or to create exceptions to the law. Nor does it change our conclusion that "the legislature's exclusive power encompasses questions of fundamental policy and the articulation of reasonably definite standards to be used in implementing those policies." *B.H.* [*v. State*], 645 So.2d at 993 [(Fla. 1994)].

3. Does IGRA Permit Compacts to Expand Gaming?

Contrary to Florida law, the Compact allows banked card games such as blackjack, baccarat, and chemin de fer. The House argues that the Compact therefore violates IGRA itself, which permits Class III gaming only if the state "permits 615 such gaming for any purpose by any person, organization, or entity." 25 U.S.C. § 2710(d)(1). The Governor, on the other hand, contends that, once state law permits any Class III gaming, a compact may allow all Class III gaming.

* * *

IV. CONCLUSION

We conclude that the Governor's execution of a compact authorizing types of gaming that are prohibited under Florida law violates the separation of powers. The Governor has no authority to change or amend state law. Such power falls exclusively to the Legislature. Therefore, we hold that the Governor lacked authority to bind the State to a compact that violates Florida law as this compact does.

* * *

It is so ordered.

Question

1. What is the main reason the Supreme Court of Florida found Governor Crist exceeded his authority? Is the reasoning applicable to that in the *Kirk* and *Ayala* cases?

Whiley v. Scott

79 So. 3d 702 (Fla. 2011)

PER CURIAM.

This case is before the Court on the petition of Rosalie Whiley for a writ of quo warranto seeking an order directing Respondent, the Honorable Rick Scott, Governor of the State of Florida, to demonstrate that he has not exceeded his authority, in part, by suspending rulemaking through Executive Order 11-01. We have jurisdiction. *See* art. V, § 3(b)(8), Fla. Const. In exercising our discretion to resolve this matter, we grant relief and specifically hold that the Governor impermissibly suspended agency rulemaking to the extent that Executive Orders 11-01 and 11-72 include a requirement that the Office of Fiscal Accountability and Regulatory Reform (OFARR) must first permit an agency to engage in the rulemaking which has been delegated by the Florida Legislature.[2] Absent an amendment to the Administrative Procedure Act itself or other delegation of such authority to the Governor's Office by the Florida Legislature, the Governor has overstepped his constitutional authority and violated the separation of powers. Accordingly, upon this basis we grant the petition for writ of quo warranto.

BACKGROUND

On January 4, 2011, Governor Scott issued "Executive Order Number 11-01 (Suspending Rulemaking and Establishing the Office of Fiscal Accountability and Regulatory Reform)," which created that office (OFARR) within the Executive Office of the Governor.[3] OFARR is tasked with the goal of ensuring that agency-created rules do not hinder government performance and that they are fiscally responsible. OFARR

---

2. [FN 1.] It is most unfortunate that the dissenting opinion of Justice Polston fails to comprehend the fact that parts of an executive order may be valid while other aspects are invalid. *See* Polston, J., dissenting op. at 718. Under such circumstances the executive order is unconstitutional in part. An invalid section of an executive order cannot survive constitutional scrutiny by riding on the coattails of the valid portions. Even if sections of the Governor's executive order may be valid, the provisions that are contrary to constitutional requirements simply cannot escape without analysis.

3. [FN 2.] The requisite duties of the Executive Office of the Governor are specifically identified under section 216.151, Florida Statutes (2010), and those duties pertain to state planning and budgeting.

specifically looks for rules that affect businesses, public health/safety, job growth, and indirect costs to consumers. Under Executive Order 11-01, state agencies controlled by the Governor were directed to immediately "suspend" rulemaking activities. State agencies not directly under the Governor's control were requested to "suspend" rulemaking activities. The executive order further provided that, before submitting a notice of proposed rulemaking or of amendments to existing rules pursuant to the rulemaking procedures mandated by Chapter 120, the agencies under the direction of the Governor were required to submit the complete text of the proposed rule or amendment to OFARR for review, along with any other documentation the office may require. The executive order directed each agency head to do the following: appoint an "Accountability and Regulatory Affairs Officer"; review and evaluate the agency's current policies "relating to programs and operations administered or financed by the agency and make recommendations to improve performance and fiscal accountability"; submit to the Governor a comprehensive review of existing rules and regulations, together with recommendations as to whether any such rules should be modified or eliminated; and submit a "regulatory plan" which identifies and describes any rules the agency head expects to promulgate during the following twelve-month period. The Secretary of State was ordered not to publish any rulemaking notices in the Florida Administrative Weekly absent authorization from OFARR.

A superseding, second executive order, Executive Order 11-72, also pertaining to agency rulemaking, was issued by the Governor's Office on April 8, 2011. The two executive orders are substantially the same; the primary differences are that the superseding order does not expressly use the terms "suspending" and "suspend," and that the operation of OFARR is continued rather than established.[4]

On March 28, 2011, Whiley, in her capacity as a citizen and taxpayer, filed a petition for a writ of quo warranto naming Governor Scott as the respondent. The petition challenges the authority of the Governor to issue Executive Order 11-01 as a violation of separation of powers. To the extent that Executive Order 11-01 — and superseding Executive Order 11-72 (issued subsequent to the date Whiley filed her petition) — suspend the rulemaking process established by the Florida Legislature under Chapter 120, the Florida Administrative Procedure Act (APA), we conclude that the Governor exceeded his constitutional authority.

I. JURISDICTION

Whiley seeks a writ of quo warranto, and it is clear that the Florida Constitution authorizes this Court as well as the district and circuit courts to issue writs of quo warranto. *See* art. V, §§ 3(b)(8), 4(b)(3) and 5(b), Fla. Const. The term "quo warranto" means "by what authority," and the writ is the proper means for inquiring into whether a particular individual has improperly exercised a power or right derived

---

4. [FN 3.] Apparently the act of issuing a second executive order that superseded the first executive order, excluding the word "suspend," was sufficient for one colleague to conclude that, unlike its predecessor, Executive Order 11-72 does not operate to suspend rulemaking. *See* Polston, J., dissenting op. at 719. We address what seems nothing more than a sleight of hand within our discussion of the two executive orders. *Infra* at 710.

from the State. *See Fla. House of Reps. v. Crist*, 999 So.2d 601, 607 (Fla.2008); *Martinez*, 545 So.2d at 1339. This Court "may" issue a writ of quo warranto which renders this Court's exercise of jurisdiction discretionary. Art. V, § 3(b)(8), Fla. Const. Furthermore, the Court is limited to issuing writs of quo warranto only to "state officers and state agencies." *Id.* The Governor is a state officer. See art. III, § 1(a), Fla. Const. ("The governor shall be the chief administrative officer of the state....").

Here, Whiley asserts that the Governor lacked authority to issue Executive Order 11-01 to the extent a portion of the order suspending agency rulemaking exceeds the Governor's authority and violates the doctrine of separation of powers. Thus, the petition asserts a proper basis for quo warranto relief upon which this Court may exercise its discretionary review. *See, e.g., Fla. House of Reps. v. Crist*, 999 So.2d 601, 607 (Fla.2008) (concluding that the Court had quo warranto jurisdiction where petitioners sought relief against the governor for exceeding his authority to unilaterally execute a gambling compact expanding casino gambling on tribal lands); *Martinez*, 545 So.2d at 1339 (deciding that quo warranto was the proper method to test the governor's power to call a second special session).

* * *

We find that the present case raises a serious constitutional question relating to the authority of the Governor and the Legislature respectively in rulemaking proceedings. The issue of whether the Governor has the power to suspend agency rulemaking directly and substantially affects the fundamental functions of state government. We also note that a decision from this Court on such an issue would provide important guiding principles to other state courts, and that there do not appear to be any substantial disputes of material fact. Accordingly, we exercise our discretionary jurisdiction and entertain the petition for writ of quo warranto.

II. DISCUSSION

Our precise task in this case is to decide whether the Governor has overstepped his constitutional authority by issuing executive orders which contain certain limitations and suspensions upon agencies relating to their delegated legislative rulemaking authority and the requirements related thereto. We must first consider the constitutional provision of separation of powers in the context of Florida's APA to determine the proper roles of the executive and legislative branches in that process to determine whether any portion of the executive orders interferes with that authority for the rulemaking process.

* * *

Executive Orders 11-01 and 11-72 and Agency Rulemaking

Whether some portion of the content of Executive Order 11-01 along with the superseding executive order, Executive Order 11-72, encroaches upon a function of the legislative branch of government thereby violating separation of powers raises two considerations. First, we must determine the governmental function implicated by those orders. Review of Executive Orders 11-01 and 11-72 themselves is necessary to resolve that issue. Second, we must decide which branch of government is responsible for and has authority over whatever that particular function may be. Constitutional, statutory, and decisional law controls resolution of the Court's latter consideration.

Turning first to the Governor's executive orders, Executive Order 11-01 provided in pertinent part as follows:

> *Section 1.* I hereby direct all agencies under the direction of the Governor to immediately *suspend all rulemaking.* No agency under the direction of the Governor may notice the development of proposed rules, amendment of existing rules, or adoption of new rules, except at the direction of the Office of Fiscal Accountability and Regulatory Reform (the "Office"), established herein. The Secretary of State shall not publish rulemaking notices in the Florida Administrative Weekly except at the direction of the Office.

Fla. Exec. Order No. 11-01, § 1 (January 4, 2011) (emphasis added). Though the language has been revised, Executive Order 11-72, in pertinent part, also requires the suspension of agency rulemaking until approval is obtained from OFARR:

> *Section 1.* I hereby direct all agencies under the direction of the Governor, *prior to developing new rules or amending or repealing existing rules,* to submit all proposed notices, along with the complete text of any proposed rule or amendment, to OFARR. These agencies shall also submit any other documentation required by OFARR, and no such agency may submit for publication any required notice without OFARR's approval.

Fla. Exec. Order No. 11-72, § 1 (April 8, 2011) (emphasis added). The express terms of the executive orders unequivocally reflect that the governmental function at issue is rulemaking and regulation. Observing that the first executive order, which expressly used the words "suspend" and "suspending," was superseded by the second executive order that issued after Whiley initiated this proceeding, one dissenting opinion concludes that the suspension in the first executive order has been lifted. *See* Polston, J., dissenting op. at 719. We disagree with that conclusion. Indeed, the only relevant distinction we can discern between the two orders is that Executive Order 11-01 established OFARR, while Executive Order 11-72 continues operation of OFARR. The fact that the Secretary of State is not required to seek OFARR's approval before publishing notices required by the APA, a factor identified by the dissent, fails to contemplate the corollary provision that "no such agency may submit for publication any required notice without OFARR's approval." Rather than engage in a true analysis, one comparing the language of section 1 of the two executive orders, the dissent instead hides behind a discussion of the other sections of Executive Order 11-72 — sections that do not address the issue of suspension of rulemaking. *See* Polston, J., dissenting op. at 719–20.

Turning to rulemaking, we must determine whether the branch responsible for that function is the Legislature, as Whiley asserts, or whether that function is within the executive branch.

Rulemaking is a derivative of lawmaking. An agency is empowered to adopt rules if two requirements are satisfied. First, there must be a statutory grant of rulemaking authority, and second, there must be a specific law to be implemented. § 120.536(1), Fla. Stat. (2010). "Rulemaking authority" is statutory language that explicitly authorizes or requires an agency to adopt rules. § 120.52(17), Fla. Stat. (2010). "Rules" are "statement[s] of general applicability that implement[], interpret[], or prescribe[] law or policy or describe[] the procedure or practice requirements of an agency." § 120.52(16), Fla. Stat. (2010). Accordingly, "[w]hen an agency promulgates a rule having the force of law, it acts in place of the legislature." [citation omitted.]

Moreover, the Legislature has delegated specific responsibilities to agency heads, such as the authority to determine whether to go forward with proposing, amending, repealing, or adopting rules. *See* § 120.54(3)(a)(1), Fla. Stat. (2010) (providing that, prior to the adoption, amendment, or repeal of any rule, the agency head must give approval); § 120.54(3)(e)(1), Fla. Stat. (2010) (providing that, prior to the filing of the proposed rule with the Department of State, the agency head must give approval). This authority of the agency head cannot be delegated or transferred. *See* § 120.54(1)(k), Fla. Stat. (2010). Thus, rulemaking is a legislative function. *See Sims v. State*, 754 So.2d 657, 668 (Fla.2000) ("[T]he Legislature may 'enact a law, complete in itself, designed to accomplish a general public purpose, and may expressly authorize designated officials within definite valid limitations to provide rules and regulations for the complete operation and enforcement of the law within its expressed general purpose.'") (quoting *State v. Atlantic Coast Line R.R. Co.*, 56 Fla. 617, 636–37, 47 So. 969, 976 (1908)). The Legislature delegates rulemaking authority to state agencies because they usually have expertise in a particular area for which they are charged with oversight. *See Rizov v. State, Bd. of Prof'l Eng'rs*, 979 So.2d 979, 980 (Fla. 3d DCA 2008). Accordingly, the Legislature may specifically delegate, to some extent, its rulemaking authority to the executive branch "to permit administration of legislative policy by an agency with the expertise and flexibility needed to deal with complex and fluid conditions." *Microtel, Inc. v. Fla. Pub. Serv. Comm'n.*, 464 So.2d 1189, 1191 (Fla.1985); *see also* § 120.536(1), Fla. Stat. (2010).[5]

To determine whether the executive orders encroach upon the legislative delegations of rulemaking authority, the Court must first consider the established procedure for rulemaking. When adopting rules, the agencies must specifically conform to the rule-

---

5. [FN 9.] Section 120.536 provides in pertinent part as follows:
(1) A grant of rulemaking authority is necessary but not sufficient to allow an agency to adopt a rule; a specific law to be implemented is also required. An agency may adopt only rules that implement or interpret the specific powers and duties granted by the enabling statute. No agency shall have authority to adopt a rule only because it is reasonably related to the purpose of the enabling legislation and is not arbitrary and capricious or is within the agency's class of powers and duties, nor shall an agency have the authority to implement statutory provisions setting forth general legislative intent or policy. Statutory language granting rulemaking authority or generally describing the powers and functions of an agency shall be construed to extend no further than implementing or interpreting the specific powers and duties conferred by the enabling statute.
§ 120.536(1), Fla. Stat. (2010).

making procedure enacted by the Legislature as the Florida Administrative Procedure Act in chapter 120, Florida Statutes. First, the agency must provide preliminary notice of the development of the proposed rule in the *Florida Administrative Weekly*. *See* § 120.54(2), Fla. Stat. (2010). Second, upon approval of the agency head, the agency must give a more thorough notice of the intended action in the *Florida Law Weekly*, and this notice must be published at least 28 days prior to the intended action. *See* § 120.54(3)(a), Fla. Stat. (2010). The agency must file a copy of the proposed rule with the Administrative Procedures Committee as well. *See* §§ 120.54(3)(a) 4; 120.52(4), Fla. Stat. (2010). Third, under certain circumstances and upon the request of any affected person, the agency must provide such persons the opportunity to present evidence and make arguments on all issues under consideration. *See* § 120.54(3)(c), Fla. Stat. (2010). If all of the statutory requirements are met, the rule is officially "adopted" upon filing with the Secretary of State, and the rule becomes effective twenty days after this filing. *See* § 120.54(3)(e) 6, Fla. Stat. (2010). However, if an agency finds that "an immediate danger to the public health, safety, or welfare requires emergency action," it may adopt "any rule necessitated by the immediate danger"—i.e., an emergency rule. *See* § 120.54(4), Fla. Stat. (2010). Otherwise, the agency must comply with the normal procedures for rulemaking. *See Fla. Health Care Ass'n v. Agency for Health Care Admin.*, 734 So.2d 1052, 1053–54 (Fla. 1st DCA 1998).

Both parties rely upon two 1995 executive orders issued by former Governor Lawton Chiles in support of their opposing positions with respect to whether or not Executive Orders 11-01 and 11-72 interfere with the APA. Upon review of Executive Orders 95-74 and 95-256, we conclude that the Chiles orders were clearly limited to review of agency rules and did not suspend or terminate delegated legislative rulemaking authority contrary to the Florida Administrative Procedure Act.

In Executive Order 95-74, Governor Chiles directed each agency under the supervision of the Governor to conduct a review examining the purpose, intent, and necessity of each rule. Agencies were further directed to identify any rules they felt were obsolete or unnecessary. Executive Order 95-74 mandated that the rules then be sent for analysis to the Office of Planning and Budgeting, within the Executive Office of the Governor. When completed, the rules were then to be provided to the Legislature for an opportunity to review the rules and repeal and/or amend any statutes mandating the rules so that the repeal of the rules could be effectuated. Additionally, any rules that an agency itself had discretion to repeal were also to be submitted to the Legislature for its review and comment.

Executive Order 95-256 extended that which was initially designed as a one-time review process in Executive Order 95-74 to an ongoing agency mandate to be conducted every sixty days and to be reported to the Office of the Executive. Fla. Exec. Order No. 95-256, § 2 (July 12, 1995). Executive Order 95-256 also directed agencies to review the Florida Statutes for recommendations as to legislative mandates that could be eliminated, without harm to the public health or safety, thereby reducing the operating costs of government. Fla. Exec. Order No. 5-256, § 3 (July 12, 1995). Executive Order 95-74 further instructed agencies to determine if rules were obsolete or otherwise unnecessary. Executive Order 95-256 expanded this criterion to include rules that achieved objectives that could be accomplished in a more efficient, or less expensive or intrusive manner; rules that were overly precise; or rules that duplicated other rules. Fla. Exec. Order No. 95-256, § 2 (July 12, 1995). Executive Order 95-256 also created the Governor's APA Review Commission, which was responsible for recommending changes to the APA to legislative leaders as well as the Governor.

There are limited similarities between the 1995 and 2011 executive orders not really at issue in this case. For example, both establish a review of rules promulgated by executive agencies under the direction of the Governor to take place to determine if any rules are unnecessary, and both direct that agencies pursue to repeal or amend any rule identified as unnecessary. Each also mandates that the agencies' findings be submitted to the Executive Office of the Governor on a regular basis. Aside from these review similarities, however, the 1995 executive orders and Executive Orders 11-01 and 11-72 differ in two substantial and material respects.

First, the Chiles orders did not provide for an additional review body to have authority over the decisions reached by the agencies themselves. While each of the identified executive orders mandated that agencies under the Governor's direction must review their rules and submit a report of any unnecessary rules, Governor Scott's executive orders create an office outside the agencies that has independent review power as well. Fla. Exec. Order No. 11-72, § 3 (April 8, 2011). OFARR was created to operate in the Executive Office of the Governor and has the ability to review not only existing rules to ensure they do not adversely or unreasonably affect businesses or job growth and to ensure that they do not impose unjustified overall costs on the government or consumers, but also rules to be proposed in the future. See id. In contrast, the Chiles executive orders allowed the agencies themselves to solely retain the power to review agency rules and subsequently seek the repeal of those rules.

Second, the Chiles executive orders did not change the agencies' process for proposing, amending, or repealing rules. Each Governor's action substantially and materially differs with regard to how both proposed rules, as well as established rules that are sought to be amended or repealed, are treated. Executive Order 11-72 mandates that absolutely no required notice may be published without the approval of OFARR. Fla. Exec. Order No. 11-72, § 1 (April 8, 2011). Pursuant to the APA, however, agencies are required to provide notice prior to the adoption, amendment, or repeal of any rule (other than an emergency rule). § 120.54(3)(a)(1), Fla. Stat. (2010). Executive Order 11-72 mandates that agencies receive OFARR approval before taking any of these three rulemaking actions. Significantly, Executive Order 95-256 contains no provision requiring an entity within the Executive Office of the Governor to approve rulemaking activity. Thus, under the 1995 executive orders, agencies were free to engage in the proposal, amendment, and repeal of rules without approval from a member of the Executive Office of the Governor.

Suspension

The foregoing leads the Court to conclude that the Governor's executive orders at issue here, to the extent each suspends and terminates rulemaking by precluding notice publication and other compliance with Chapter 120 absent prior approval from OFARR—contrary to the Administrative Procedure Act—infringe upon the very process of rulemaking and encroach upon the Legislature's delegation of its rulemaking power as set forth in the Florida Statutes. Whether the Governor exceeded his authority derived from state law does not turn upon the number of times the encroachment occurred or whether petitioner was personally affected by it. Issuance of Executive Order 11-72, and specifically section 1, suspends rulemaking; the precise language therein leads the Court to that inescapable conclusion. One colleague's dissent suggesting that this opinion questions the Governor's authority to issue Executive Order 11-72, see Polston, J., dissenting op. at 718, is a red herring.

Constitutional Authority

The Governor argues that his authority for establishing OFARR and the duties and responsibilities thereunder derives from the Florida Constitution, art. IV, sec. 1(a). That provision reads as follows:

> The supreme executive power shall be vested in a governor, who shall be commander-in-chief of all military forces of the state not in active service of the United States. The governor shall take care that the laws be faithfully executed, commission all officers of the state and counties, and transact all necessary business with the officers of government. The governor may require information in writing from all executive or administrative state, county or municipal officers upon any subject relating to the duties of their respective offices. The governor shall be the chief administrative officer of the state responsible for the planning and budgeting for the state.

Art. IV, § 1(a), Fla. Const.

Previously presented in an attorney general opinion dated July 8, 1981, in relevant part, was the following question: "1. Can the Governor by executive order ... give binding directions to state agencies to implement and comply with Florida's Coastal Zone Management Plan without violating the requirements of the Florida Administrative Procedure Act?" Op. Att'y Gen. Fla. 81-49, at 1 (1981). There it was opined that section 1(a) of article IV of the Florida Constitution did not confer upon the governor "any power of direct control and supervision over all state agencies...." *Id.* at 2. As explained by that opinion, "to hold otherwise, would render the plain language [Executive departments] of s. 6, Art. IV, meaningless." *Id.* The attorney general opinion addresses an issue comparable to that raised in the instant petition. Because the department heads,[6] and not the Governor, shall direct the powers, duties, and

---

6. [FN 10.] Section 20.05, Florida Statutes (2010), provides in pertinent part that "(1) Each head of a department, except as otherwise provided by law, must: ... (e) [s]ubject to the requirements of chapter 120, exercise existing authority to adopt rules pursuant and limited to the powers, duties, and functions transferred to the department;...." § 20.05(1)(e), Fla. Stat. (2010). "Department" is

functions vested in a department, the opinion stated that the Governor could not give binding directions to any state executive department to comply with a particular plan or act, or exercise rulemaking authority "in that regard over or for such executive departments, absent some specific authorization in part II of ch. 380, F.S., or other general law, which would permit such." *Id.* at 3.

Although not binding upon this Court, see *Inquiry Concerning a Judge, re Holder,* 945 So.2d 1130, 1132 (Fla.2006), we find persuasive attorney general opinion 81-49. If article IV, section 1(a) of the Florida Constitution does not authorize the Governor to direct the manner in which an executive agency shall proceed under a statutory act, we reject the proposition that that same constitutional provision authorizes the Governor to suspend, terminate, and control agency rulemaking contrary to the APA, as contrasted with review of agency rulemaking.[7]

With apparent disregard for the Court's precedent, the dissents deem the Governor all-powerful as "the supreme executive power" by virtue of article IV, section 1(a) of the Florida Constitution. *See* Canady, C.J., dissenting op. at 717; Polston, J., dissenting op. at 724. The phrase "supreme executive power" is not so expansive, however, and to grant such a reading ignores the fundamental principle that our state constitution is a limitation upon, rather than a grant of, power. *See, e.g., State ex rel. Kennedy v. Lee,* 274 So.2d 881, 882 (Fla.1973); *Bd. of Pub. Instruction v. Wright,* 76 So.2d 863, 864 (Fla.1955). Moreover, the dissents' failure to address the provisions of the APA delegating to agency heads the authority to determine whether to go forward with proposing, amending, repealing, or adopting rules—i.e., sections 120.54(3)(a)(1) and 120.54(3)(e)(1), Florida Statutes (2010)—an authority that cannot be delegated by any entity other than the Legislature, demonstrates the absence of support for the position advanced.

In support of the requirements under Executive Orders 11-01 and 11-72, the Governor also relies upon his supervisory power under article IV, section 6 of the Florida Constitution. That provision provides, in pertinent part, as follows: "The administration of each department, unless otherwise provided in this constitution, shall be placed by law under the direct supervision of the governor, ... or an officer or board appointed by and serving at the pleasure of the governor...." The Governor argues,

---

the principal administrative unit of or within the executive branch, §§ 20.03(2) and 20.04(1), and "the individual or board in charge of the department" is the "[h]ead of the department." § 20.03(4).

7. [FN 12.] The Court has carefully reviewed the arguments against application of attorney general opinion 81-49 raised by Attorney General Bondi in her amicus brief in support of the Governor. Those arguments include the following: the Governor merely established an across-the-board process by which rules and proposed rules will be reviewed; the relevance of the attorney general opinion has been lessened by the subsequently adopted administrative accountability regime, including that the Governor's powers relating to his oversight of executive agencies has been expanded, especially in light of the passage of Amendment 4 and section 20.051, Florida Statutes; and no subsequent opinion of the Attorney General has cited this particular attorney general opinion. These arguments fail to take into account the distinction between OFARR's review function, which does not run afoul of separation of powers, and OFARR's initial rulemaking role as a "gatekeeper," which does.

consequently, that he has the authority—at will—to remove agency heads who serve at his pleasure. *See* art. IV, §6, Fla. Const.

The dissents similarly give expansive interpretation to the "serving at the pleasure of the governor" phrase in article IV, section 6 of the Florida Constitution.... Apparently, the dissents believe that the Legislature only intended that the agency head not be permitted to redelegate or transfer the delegated power to approve pursuant to section 120.54(1)(k), Fla. Stat. (2010) within the agency, and that, in light of the Governor's gatekeeper role in deciding what rules would be proposed, the agency head's role pursuant to sections 120.54(3)(a)(1) and 120.54(3)(e)(1) is nothing more than that of a figurehead, whose authority is purely illusory.

We reject the Governor's and the dissents' interpretation of article IV, section 6 of the Florida Constitution; the power to remove is not analogous to the power to control. This is particularly the case where the delegated authority is a legislative function and the Legislature has expressly placed the power to act on the delegated authority in the department head, and not in the Governor or the Executive Office of the Governor. *See* §20.05(1)(a), (e), Fla. Stat. (2010). In this case, Executive Orders 11-01 and 11-72 supplant legislative delegations by redefining the terms of those delegations through binding directives to state agencies, i.e., first by suspending and terminating rulemaking, second, by requiring agencies to submit to OFARR any amendments or new rules the agency would want to propose, and then by causing OFARR to interject itself as the decisive entity as to whether and what will be proposed.

Legislative Delegation to Executive or Amendment to Chapter 120[8]

Finally, the last possible source of authority for the Governor's action in requiring prior approval by OFARR before the legislative delegation of rulemaking may occur would be by either legislative delegation or direct amendment to Chapter 120. The Legislature previously has, in specifically delineated terms and circumstances, delegated to the Executive Office of the Governor certain responsibility for the oversight of rulemaking. *See, e.g.,* §14.2015, Fla. Stat. (2010), and §288.7015, Fla. Stat. (2010). These two statutes demonstrate that the Legislature understands how to confer upon the Governor the authority to oversee agency rulemaking when it so desires. *See Cason v. Fla. Dep't of Mgmt. Servs.,* 944 So.2d 306, 315 (Fla.2006) ("In the past, we have pointed to language in other statutes to show that the Legislature 'knows how to' accomplish what it has omitted in the statute in question").[9]

---

8. [FN 13.] Although the parties did not address the potential import of legislative delegation of rulemaking authority to the Executive in their pleadings before the Court, the issue did arise at oral argument based upon a filing of supplemental authority by the Governor.

9. [FN 15.] This principle is of particular import here, as the two statutory provisions expressly provided for substantially the same goals the Governor subsequently sought through Executive Orders 11-01 and 11-72. For example,

> [t]he purpose of the Office of Tourism, Trade, and Economic Development is to assist the Governor in working with the Legislature, state agencies, business leaders, and economic development professionals to formulate and implement coherent and consistent policies and strategies designed to provide economic opportunities for all Floridians.

§14.2015(2), Fla. Stat. (2010). The "rules ombudsman" that the Governor is to appoint in the Executive

Another possible source of delegation of rulemaking authority to the Governor would be by amendment to the APA with specific provisions directed to the Executive Office of the Governor. With the enactment of section 120.745, Florida Statutes, on June 24, 2011, upon the Governor's signature of House Bill 993, see Ch. 2011–225, § 5, Laws of Fla., the Legislature essentially approved the process by which OFARR reviews agency rules that have already been promulgated. However, by its own terms, section 120.745, which pertains to legislative review of agency rules, is limited to those rules "in effect on or before November 16, 2010." Thus, the recent amendment to Chapter 120 applies to only the process by which OFARR reviews existing rules; in contrast, it does not authorize the provisions in Executive Orders 11-01 and 11-72 that suspend or terminate rulemaking.

III. CONCLUSION

We distinguish between the Governor's constitutional authority with respect to the provisions of the executive orders pertaining to review and oversight of rulemaking within the executive agencies under his control, and the Legislature's lawmaking authority under article III, section 1 of the Florida Constitution. The Legislature retains the sole right to delegate rulemaking authority to agencies, and all provisions in both Executive Order 11-01 or 11-72 that operate to suspend rulemaking contrary to the APA constitute an encroachment upon a legislative function. We grant Whiley's petition but withhold issuance of the writ of quo warranto. We trust that any provision in Executive Order 11-72 suspending agency compliance with the APA, i.e., rulemaking, will not be enforced against an agency at this time, and until such time as the Florida Legislature may amend the APA or otherwise delegate such rulemaking authority to the Executive Office of the Governor.

It is so ordered.

CANADY, C.J., dissenting.

As Justice Polston's dissent cogently explains, there is no basis for the majority's decision. I join fully in that dissent.

The petitioner strikingly has failed to show any specific action required by law that was prevented by the implementation of the executive orders at issue here. In the absence of such a showing, the majority nonetheless rules in favor of the petitioner by imposing unprecedented and unwarranted restrictions on the Governor's constitutional authority to supervise subordinate executive branch officers. In doing so, the majority's decision insulates discretionary executive policy decisions with respect to rulemaking from the constitutional structure of accountability established by the

---

Office of the Governor is to consider "the impact of agency rules on the state's citizens and businesses." § 288.7015, Fla. Stat. (2010). Specifically, the rules ombudsman is charged with, for example, reviewing "state agency rules that adversely or disproportionately impact businesses, particularly those relating to small and minority businesses," § 288.7015(2), Fla. Stat. (2010), and to "[m]ake recommendations on any existing or proposed rules to alleviate unnecessary or disproportionate adverse effects to businesses," § 288.7015(3), Fla. Stat. (2010).

people of Florida. I strongly dissent from this ill-conceived interference with the constitutional authority and responsibility of Florida's Governor.

It is elementary that the Administrative Procedure Act (APA), §§ 120.50–.891, Fla. Stat. (2011), and other pertinent statutes do not preordain the substance of all decisions made by agencies regarding rulemaking. The APA and other statutes impose certain constraints and requirements, but an area of executive policy discretion exists with respect to rulemaking. The majority's decision does not take seriously this reality that the rulemaking process involves certain discretionary policy choices by executive branch officers within the parameters established by the APA and other pertinent statutes. Nor does the majority come to terms with the absence from Florida law of any restriction on the authority of the Governor to supervise and control such policy choices made by subordinate executive branch officials with respect to rulemaking.

The Governor's right to exercise such supervision and control flows from the "supreme executive power" which is vested in the Governor by article IV, section 1(a) of the Florida Constitution, together with the Governor's power under article IV, section 6 of the Florida Constitution, to appoint executive department heads who serve at the Governor's pleasure. The Governor's "supreme executive power," of course, does not give the Governor the right to direct subordinate executive officers to disobey the requirements of law. But if "supreme executive power" means anything, it must mean that the Governor can supervise and control the policy-making choices — within the range of choices permitted by law — of the subordinate executive branch officers who serve at his pleasure.

Neither the petitioner nor the majority identify any provision of law containing an express restriction on the Governor's power to supervise and control the exercise of discretion by subordinate officers with respect to rulemaking. The majority's inference of such a restriction flies in the face of the constitutional provisions which vest "supreme executive power" in the Governor and authorize the Governor to appoint executive department heads who "serve at his pleasure." Given the constitutional structure establishing the power and responsibilities of the Governor, it is unjustified to conclude — as does the majority — that by assigning rulemaking power to agency heads, the Legislature implicitly divested the Governor of his supervisory power with respect to executive officials who serve at his pleasure.

In issuing the executive orders, the Governor acted lawfully to supervise the agency heads who are responsible to him and for whom he is responsible. The quo warranto petition should be denied.

POLSTON, J., concurs.

POLSTON, J., dissenting.

The majority improperly grants this petition for an extraordinary writ based on the hypothetical that the Governor might exceed his authority or violate the law. The majority is issuing an improper advisory opinion holding that Executive Order 11-01 and Executive Order 11-72 should not be utilized to violate Florida's Administrative

Procedure Act "to the extent" they could hypothetically be used to do so. *See* majority op. at 705, 706, 707, 713 (repeatedly employing the equivocal phrase "to the extent"). This is not a sound basis for issuing a writ of quo warranto. To the contrary, Governor Scott has the express constitutional authority to issue Executive Order 11-72 as this State's chief administrative officer charged with faithfully executing the law. *See* art. IV, § 1(a), Fla. Const.

Executive Order 11-72, which supersedes the now moot Executive Order 11-01, simply institutes a review of proposed and existing rules, a review that does not violate the separation of powers. The Petitioner has presented no evidence that this executive order violates Florida's Constitution, Florida's Administrative Procedure Act (APA), or a legislative delegation of rulemaking authority. *Cf. Fla. House of Reps. v. Crist*, 999 So.2d 601, 616 (Fla.2008) ("[T]he Governor's execution of a compact authorizing types of gaming that are prohibited under Florida law violates the separation of powers."). The Governor contends that he is exercising his authority under the Florida Constitution and has not violated the APA or altered the legislative delegation of rulemaking authority to state agencies. The Governor further contends that, if he violated the APA or altered the delegation of rulemaking authority, it would then be an unlawful act, but that issuing Executive Order 11-72 does not constitute such an act. I agree with the Governor's view. Simply put, the Governor may act according to his executive order without violating any law, and no violation has been demonstrated.

I respectfully dissent.

* * *

B. Rulemaking Overview

Rulemaking under Florida's APA is a complex process, but it is also a flexible one with room for agency discretion and public participation. *See generally* Patricia A. Dore, *Access to Florida Administrative Proceedings*, 13 Fla. St. U.L. Rev. 965, 988–1018 (1986). When an agency engages in rulemaking, it is performing a quasi-legislative function.[10] *See Adam Smith Enters., Inc. v. State Dep't of Envtl. Regulation*, 553 So.2d 1260, 1260–70 (Fla. 1st DCA 1989); *see also Gen. Tel. Co. of Fla. v. Fla. Pub. Serv. Comm'n*, 446 So.2d 1063, 1067 (Fla.1984). An agency can only engage in rulemaking if it has been granted the authority to do so from the Legislature. *See* § 120.52(17), Fla. Stat. (2010). Further, "[a] grant of rulemaking authority is necessary but not sufficient to allow an agency to adopt a rule; a specific law to be implemented is also required." § 120.536(1), Fla. Stat. (2010). And "[a]n agency may only adopt rules that implement or interpret the specific powers and duties granted by the enabling statute." *Id.*

---

10. [FN 20.] The majority misstates that agency "rulemaking is a legislative function." *See* majority op. at 710. To the contrary, when an agency engages in rulemaking pursuant to a legislative delegation of rulemaking authority, it is engaging in a quasi-legislative function. *See Askew v. Cross Key Waterways*, 372 So.2d 913, 924 (Fla.1979) ("Flexibility by an administrative agency to administer a legislatively articulated policy is essential to meet the complexities of our modern society, but flexibility in administration of a legislative program is essentially different from reposing in an administrative body the power to establish fundamental policy.")....

The rulemaking process (with the exception of emergency rules) begins in one of three ways. First, an agency on its own must initiate the process "as soon as practicable and feasible" after an agency statement becomes a rule of general applicability. § 120.54(1)(a), Fla. Stat. (2010). Second, the Legislature may require implementation of a statute by agency rules, and "such rules shall be drafted and formally proposed as provided in [the APA] within 180 days after the effective date of the act, unless the act provides otherwise." § 120.54(1)(b), Fla. Stat. (2010). Finally, the process to adopt, amend, or repeal a rule can begin upon a petition to initiate rulemaking filed by a regulated person or a person having a substantial interest in a rule. § 120.54(7), Fla. Stat. (2010). An agency must initiate the rulemaking process or deny the petition in writing no later than thirty days after the petition is filed. *Id.*

An agency must provide notice of the development of proposed rules (with the exception of an intention to repeal a rule) in the Florida Administrative Weekly. § 120.54(2)(a), Fla. Stat. (2010). However, "[t]he APA establishes no particular procedure to be followed by an agency during the original drafting of the proposed rule." *Adam Smith*, 553 So.2d at 1265 n. 4. An agency may choose to develop a proposed rule on its own, or it may choose to hold a public workshop or to utilize negotiated rulemaking between interested parties. *See* § 120.54(2)(c)–(d), Fla. Stat. (2010). However, if an affected person requests in writing a public workshop, an agency must hold one unless the agency head explains in writing why a workshop is not necessary. § 120.54(2)(c), Fla. Stat. Additionally, "[a]n agency head may delegate the authority to initiate rule development." § 120.54(1)(k), Fla. Stat. (2010).

At least twenty-eight days prior to adoption and upon the agency head's approval, a notice of the proposed rule must be published in the *Florida Administrative Weekly*, including the proposed rule's text and a reference to the statute being implemented. § 120.54(3)(a), Fla. Stat. (2010). The agency may schedule a public hearing on the proposed rule and must do so if an affected party requests a public hearing within 21 days of the publication of intended agency action. § 120.54(3)(c) 1, Fla. Stat. (2010).

As a legislative check, the agency must also file the proposed rule with the Administrative Procedures Committee. § 120.54(3)(a) 4, Fla. Stat. (2010); § 120.545(1), Fla. Stat. (2010). If the Administrative Procedures Committee objects to the proposed rule, the agency must respond. § 120.545(3), Fla. Stat. (2010). And if the agency does not initiate administrative action to address the committee's objection, the committee may recommend legislative action to address it. § 120.545(8)(a), Fla. Stat. (2010).

Additionally, the APA provides that certain matters must (or should) be considered during the rule adoption process. For instance, "all agencies must, among the alternative approaches to any regulatory objective and to the extent allowed by law, choose the alternative that does not impose regulatory costs on the regulated ... which could be reduced by the adoption of less costly alternatives that substantially accomplish the statutory objectives." § 120.54(1)(d), Fla. Stat. (2010). Moreover, prior to adoption, an agency is encouraged to prepare a statement of estimated regulatory costs and is required to do so if the proposed rule will impact small businesses. § 120.54(3)(b) 1, Fla. Stat. (2010). The statement of estimated regulatory costs must include "[a] good faith estimate of the number of individuals and entities likely to be required to comply with the rule," a good faith estimate of the cost to the agency or other government entity to implement and enforce the rule, and "[a] good faith estimate of the transactional costs likely to be incurred by individuals and entities ... to comply with the requirements of the rule." § 120.541(2), Fla. Stat. (2010). Further, the APA provides that an agency is required whenever practicable to "tier its rules to reduce disproportionate impacts on small businesses, small counties, or small cities ... that do not contribute significantly to the problem the rule is designed to address." § 120.54(3)(b) 2.a., Fla. Stat. (2010).

Within 21 days of the publication of a proposed rule notice, a substantially affected person may submit a written proposal for a lower cost alternative. § 120.541, Fla. Stat. (2010). Upon submission of a proposal, the agency must prepare a statement of estimated regulatory costs or revise its previously prepared statement. *Id.* Then, the agency must either adopt the lower cost alternative or explain its reasons for rejecting it in favor of the proposed rule. *Id.*

A substantially affected person may also "seek an administrative determination of the invalidity of the [proposed rule or an existing] rule on the ground that the rule is an invalid exercise of delegated legislative authority." § 120.56(1)(a), Fla. Stat. (2010). The APA defines an invalid exercise of delegated legislative authority to include any of the following:

(a) The agency has materially failed to follow the applicable rulemaking procedures or requirements set forth in [the APA];

(b) The agency has exceeded its grant of rulemaking authority ...;

(c) The rule enlarges, modifies, or contravenes the specific provisions of law implemented ...;

(d) The rule is vague, fails to establish adequate standards for agency decisions, or vests unbridled discretion in the agency;

(e) The rule is arbitrary and capricious....; or

(f) The rule imposes regulatory costs on the regulated person, county, or city which could be reduced by the adoption of less costly alternatives that substantially accomplish the statutory objectives.

§ 120.52(8), Fla. Stat. (2010). And an administrative law judge (ALJ) must hold a hearing on the petition challenging the rule within a specified timeframe. § 120.56(1)(c), Fla. Stat. (2010). If the ALJ determines that a proposed rule is partially or wholly invalid, the proposed rule may not be adopted unless the ALJ's determination is reversed on appeal. § 120.56(2)(b), Fla. Stat. (2010).

A proposed rule is adopted when it is filed, upon the agency head's approval, with the Department of State. § 120.54(3)(e), Fla. Stat. (2010). It cannot be filed for adoption less than 28 days or more than 90 days after the publication of the notice of proposed rulemaking, "until 14 days after the final public hearing, until 21 days after a statement of estimated regulatory costs ... or until the administrative law judge has rendered a decision" in a challenge to a proposed rule, whichever is applicable. § 120.54(3)(e) 2., Fla. Stat. (2010).

Importantly, an agency has the discretion to withdraw or modify a proposed rule after the publication of the notice of the proposed rule but before the rule is adopted. § 120.54(3)(d), Fla. Stat. (2010). An agency is required to withdraw a proposed rule if the time limits and other requirements of the APA have not been satisfied. § 120.54(3)(e) 5., Fla. Stat. (2010). Thereafter, an agency must notice its withdrawal or modification in the Florida Administrative Weekly. § 120.54(3)(d), Fla. Stat.; § 120.54(3)(e) 5., Fla. Stat. But once a rule has become effective, it can only be repealed or amended through the rulemaking process. § 120.54(3)(d) 5., Fla. Stat. (2010).

II. ANALYSIS

Under section 3(b)(8) of article V of the Florida Constitution, this Court may issue writs of quo warranto to "state officers and state agencies." "The term 'quo warranto' means 'by what authority.'" *Crist*, 999 So.2d at 607. "This writ historically has been used to determine whether a state officer or agency has improperly exercised a power or right derived from the State." *Id.* However, in exercising our jurisdiction to issue writs of quo warranto, it is important to keep in mind that they are extraordinary writs. Extraordinary writs should only be employed with great caution and under very limited circumstances. [Citations omitted.] Therefore, extraordinary writs should not be employed to address hypothetical scenarios. In fact, one cannot even seek the ordinary remedy of a declaratory judgment based upon hypothetical facts. *See Roberts v. Brown* 43 So.3d 673, 680 (Fla.2010).

Here, no one disputes that Governor Scott has the authority to issue executive orders. And Executive Order 11-72 is entirely within his constitutional authority as chief administrative officer and his constitutionally vested duty to manage, plan, and hold agencies under his charge accountable to State laws, including the APA. The actual facts before us do not demonstrate otherwise.

Article IV, section 1(a) of the Florida Constitution provides that "[t]he supreme executive power shall be vested in a governor," "[t]he governor shall take care that the laws be faithfully executed," and "[t]he governor may require information in writing from all executive or administrative state, county or municipal officers upon any subject relating to the duties of their respective offices." Section 1(a) also provides that "[t]he governor shall be the chief administrative officer of the state responsible for the planning and budgeting for the state." Section 6 of article IV states that "[t]he administration of each department, unless otherwise provided in this constitution, shall be placed by law under the direct supervision of the governor ... or an officer or board appointed by and serving at the pleasure of the governor."

Based upon these provisions, the governor of Florida has the constitutional authority to act as this State's chief administrative officer as well as the constitutional duty to faithfully execute this State's laws and to manage and hold agencies under his charge accountable to State laws, including the APA. This Court has explained that "[t]he Governor is given broad authority to fulfill his duty in taking 'care that the laws be faithfully executed.'" *In re Advisory Op. to Governor,* 290 So.2d 473, 475 (Fla.1974) (quoting *Finch v. Fitzpatrick,* 254 So.2d 203, 204 (Fla.1971)); *see also Advisory Op. to the Governor—1996 Amendment 5 (Everglades),* 706 So.2d 278, 280– 81 (Fla.1997). This Court has also recognized that that a Governor's actions are presumptively in accord with his official duties. *See Kirk v. Baker,* 229 So.2d 250, 252 (Fla.1969).

Florida law provides no specific process for carrying out the Governor's executive duties with respect to holding his executive agencies accountable in their rulemaking functions. Governor Scott has chosen to rely upon an accountability structure by which the Governor, through OFARR, reviews existing and proposed rules to ensure that the rules are in accord with the codified goals and requirements of the APA. For example, to ensure that an agency is meeting its responsibility to consider the effect of a proposed rule on small businesses as required by section 120.54(3)(b), OFARR is tasked with the responsibility of identifying rules that will have an adverse effect on businesses (particularly small businesses) and recommending actions to alleviate those effects. And to ensure that an agency is considering less costly alternatives as required by sections 120.54(1)(d) and 120.541, OFARR reviews proposed rules to determine if they impose unjustified costs and makes recommendations for simplifying the regulations.

Nothing in the APA prohibits the Governor from performing executive oversight to ensure that the rulemaking process at his agencies results in effective and efficient rules that accord with Florida law. To the contrary, a recent amendment to the APA acknowledges and implicitly approves of the Governor's oversight through OFARR. See ch. 2011–225, Laws of Fla. (providing that the required biennial review of an agency's existing rules must include a "[r]eview of each rule to determine whether the rule has been reviewed by OFARR").

Additionally, contrary to the majority's and the Petitioner's suggestions otherwise, the Governor's executive order does not violate the Legislature's delegation of rulemaking authority. Executive Order 11-72 does not impermissibly delegate or transfer the agency's or the agency head's responsibilities under the APA to OFARR. For example, the Legislature has specifically delegated to agency heads the rulemaking authority to approve notices of proposed rules and the filing of rules for adoption. *See* § 120.54(1)(k), Fla. Stat. ("An agency head may delegate the authority to initiate rule development under subsection (2); however, rulemaking responsibilities of an agency head under subparagraph (3)(a)1., subparagraph (3)(e)1., or subparagraph (3)(e)6. may not be delegated or transferred."). Under Executive Order 11-72, agency heads still must approve the notices required by section 120.54(3)(a) 1, and they still must approve the filings with the Department of State required by sections 120.54(3)(e) 1 and 120.54(3)(e) 6. However, nothing in the APA prohibits an agency from receiving OFARR's approval before an agency head authorizes the publication of notices of rulemaking activity and the filing of rules for adoption.

The Petitioner more specifically alleges that the Governor's executive orders violate the APA's time limits for adopting or withdrawing proposed rules. However, to the contrary, no provision of Executive Order 11-72 suspends the APA's time limits or requires agencies to violate them. All agencies remain subject to the APA's time limits, and the Governor remains constitutionally responsible for ensuring that Florida's laws, including the APA's time limits, are faithfully executed by the agencies under his supervision. Therefore, an agency must still initiate the rulemaking process (1) once an agency statement becomes a rule of general applicability, (2) 180 days after the effective date of the statute to be implemented, or (3) 30 days after a petition to initiate rulemaking is filed. *See* §§ 120.54(1), (7) Fla. Stat. (2010). And once the rule-making process is initiated, the agency is still responsible for abiding by the APA's other time limits. *See, e.g.,* 120.54(3)(e) 2., Fla. Stat.

Petitioner has not demonstrated in this record a single instance of the Governor's executive order causing any violation of the requirements proscribed by the APA. Moreover, if hypothetically speaking an agency violated an APA requirement due to Governor Scott's actions under the executive order, such a violation should be challenged under the remedies provided by the APA, not in an extraordinary writ proceeding before this Court. *See, e.g.,* § 120.56, Fla. Stat. (2010); § 120.68(1), Fla. Stat. (2010).

Instead of examining the facts of this case and the language of Executive Order 11-72, which is the only operative executive order at this point and therefore the only proper executive order to examine, the majority's opinion assumes that Governor Scott is incapable of acting (or unwilling to act) within the bounds of Florida law. But no provision of the Executive Order 11-72 conflicts with any Florida law. It is entirely possible for an agency to comply with all of the provisions of Executive Order 11-72 as well as all of the requirements of the APA. To get around this, the majority improperly employs the opposite of the standard used for a facial challenge. In other words, the majority construes Executive Order 11-72 (together with moot Executive Order 11-01) in a way to effect an unconstitutional outcome by coming up with a hypothetical set of circumstances under which the executive order would be invalid, rather than determining whether there is no set of circumstances under which the executive order would be valid. *Cf. Fla. Dep't of Rev. v. City of Gainesville,* 918 So.2d 250, 256 (Fla.2005) (explaining that this Court is "obligated to accord legislative acts a presumption of constitutionality and to construe challenged legislation to effect a constitutional outcome whenever possible," and that "a determination that a statute is facially unconstitutional means that no set of circumstances exists under which the statute would be valid") (quotations and citations omitted).

Specifically, the majority's decision supposes a hypothetical whereby Executive Order 11-72 (specifically the requirement that OFARR approve notices for publication) could somehow indefinitely suspend and terminate rulemaking under the APA. *See* majority op. at 706, 713, 714–15, 716–17. However, there is no evidence in this record that the order has caused any such suspension and termination. Instead, the record includes a statement from the Governor's counsel that OFARR usually completes its review of proposed rulemaking activity in less than a week and can process urgent requests even faster. The Petitioner even acknowledged during oral argument that the proposed amendment to the online application for food stamps that was of concern to her was approved by OFARR the day after it was submitted to the office by the Department of Children and Families. Accordingly, there is no evidence in this record that Executive Order 11-72 has resulted in any suspension and termination of rulemaking under the APA, and the order does not facially require it. The majority's hypothetical envisioning the contrary is improper in this extraordinary writ proceeding. *See English* [*v. McCrary*], 348 So.2d at 296 [(Fla. 1977)] (explaining that extraordinary writs should be employed cautiously and in only very limited circumstances).

III. CONCLUSION

Under article IV, section 1(a) of the Florida Constitution, Governor Scott is this State's chief administrative officer charged with faithfully executing the law and with managing and ensuring that the agencies under his control also faithfully execute the law, including the APA. Governor Scott was completely within this constitutional authority when he issued Executive Order 11-72, which institutes a review of existing and proposed rules that is consistent with the APA's requirements and goals. Therefore, instead of issuing an improper advisory opinion addressing hypothetical facts and a moot executive order, I would deny the petition for a writ of quo warranto. I respectfully dissent.

CANADY, C.J., concurs.

Commentary and Questions

This case implicates the thorny area of where the line between executive power and legislative power should be drawn. Though agencies are creations of the legislature, they are part of the executive branch. They exist to carry out laws passed by the legislature, but to do so must promulgate their own rules consistent with the Administrative Procedures Act.

1. What is the main point of this case?

2. Can governor get this involved in agency rulemaking? Is it an intrusion on legislative authority? Where does the governor's authority as head of the Executive Branch end?

3. What is the dissent saying? That the Governor's power is limitless, or something less?

4. What is the basis of each dissenting opinion in *Whiley v. Scott*? Which of the three opinions do you find most sound?

iv. "Request in Writing the Opinion of the Justices"

In re Advisory Opinion to Governor
Request of Aug. 28, 1980

388 So. 2d 554 (Fla. 1980)

August 29, 1980

The Honorable Bob Graham
Governor of the State of Florida
The Capitol
Tallahassee, Florida 32301

Dear Governor Graham:

We have your request of August 28, 1980, for our opinion affecting your executive powers and duties as follows:

"Honorable Alan C. Sundberg
Chief Justice, and the Justices of The
Supreme Court of Florida
Tallahassee, Florida

"Gentlemen:

"By virtue of the provisions of Article IV, Section 1(c), Florida Constitution, I respectfully request your written opinion as to the interpretation of a portion of the Florida Constitution affecting my executive powers and duties.

"Pursuant to Florida Appellate Rule 9.500(b)(1), the first question for the Court is whether this request is within the purview of Article IV, Section 1(c), Florida Constitution. Under Article IV, Section 1(a) of the State Constitution, I am directed to take care that the laws of this State are faithfully executed. Article IV, Section 4(e) of the State Constitution provides that the State Treasurer shall disburse no funds except upon order of the Comptroller, countersigned by the Governor. Article IV, Section 1(a) of the Constitution provides: 'The supreme executive power of the State shall be vested in a governor.' This Court has previously determined that such a question is within the purview of Article IV, Section 1(c), Florida Constitution, by responding to a similar request. *In re: Advisory Opinion to the Governor*, 60 So.2d 321 (Fla.1952).

"Dr. Ronald E. Giddens was duly qualified as a Republican candidate for membership in the Florida House of Representatives, District 81. At the close of qualifying on July 22, 1980, no other individuals had qualified as Republican candidates for district 81. (Exhibit 'A', pages 9 & 40)

"On July 29, 1980, Dr. Giddens submitted a letter of withdrawal from the race to the Secretary of State. (Exhibit 'B') On July 31, 1980, the Republican

Party requested that a Special Primary Election be called. (Exhibit 'C') The withdrawal was reaffirmed under oath on August 22, 1980, and accepted by The Secretary of State. (Exhibit 'D')

"There is an apparent ambiguity in the Florida Election Code as to whether a vacancy exists in nomination by the Republican Party for election to the Florida House of Representatives, District 81, and as to whether it is my duty to issue a special call or proclamation for a special primary of the Republican Party to fill such alleged vacancy in nomination.

"Section 100.111(3)(a), Florida Statutes, provides a method for selecting nominees of political parties when there is a 'vacancy in nomination'. Argument can be made that no vacancy in nomination can exist until after a candidate for nomination has been formally nominated at a first primary and then withdraws. However, Section 101.252, Florida Statutes, states that when only one candidate of a political party qualifies for an office, that candidate is declared to be the nominee and his name does not appear on the ballot.

"The question of whether a vacancy in nomination exists under the circumstances herein described, and whether I should call such special primary for the Republican Party involves my constitutional duty to take care that the laws of this State be faithfully executed and that I countersign no warrant for the disbursement of public funds except as may be authorized by law. Should I call a special Republican Party primary to fill a vacancy in nomination when there is no such vacancy, my act would be illegal. Should I fail to call such an election to fill a vacancy in nomination, if indeed such vacancy exists, I would have failed to perform my constitutional duty to take care that the laws of this State be faithfully executed. Should the call for a special Republican Party primary be illegal, expenditure of any public funds in connection therewith or for that purpose would also be illegal.

"In view of the doubt which exists and which has been expressed, I therefore, have the honor to request your opinion:

"I. Whether a vacancy in nomination of the Republican Party results when a candidate withdraws from the election subsequent to the close of qualifying and prior to the first primary; and,

"II. In compliance with my duty to take care that the laws be faithfully executed, is it my duty, or am I authorized under the Constitution and the laws enacted pursuant thereto, to call such a special primary election of the Republican Party to fill such a vacancy in nomination?

"Respectfully submitted,

/s/ Bob Graham

"Governor"

Pursuant to Rule 9.500(b)(1), Florida Rules of Appellate Procedure, it is incumbent upon the justices, first, to determine whether your request is within the purview of Article IV, Section 1(c), Florida Constitution. Because we do not construe your request to involve "the interpretation of any portion of (the) constitution," we conclude that the justices of this Court are without authority to render an advisory opinion regarding your responsibilities under the statutory provisions referred to in your request. Hence, we must decline your request.

Respectfully,

Alan C. Sundberg
Ben F. Overton
Arthur J. England Jr.
James E. Alderman
Parker Lee McDonald

I would answer the question posed by the Governor. *In re Advisory Opinion to the Governor*, 60 So.2d 285 (Fla.1952).

Respectfully,
JOSEPH A. BOYD, JR.

Questions

1. What part of the Constitution was Governor Graham most likely attempting to invoke?

2. What was the reasoning behind the court's refusal to find a constitutional question?

v. "Shall Fill by Appointment Any Vacancy"

An important gubernatorial duty, one with long-lasting consequences, is the duty to appoint people to fill vacancies in state positions. As this book went to press, a controversy raged over the Governor's appointment to the Supreme Court a person who had not been a member of the Florida Bar for the ten years specified as a minimum in Article V Section 8. This appointment raised both questions of when eligibility attaches and when an appointment, as opposed to a mere announcement, has been made. State Representative Geraldine Thompson sued Governor DeSantis, challenging the appointment. The situation was perhaps more charged than usual because, if allowed to take her seat as a justice, the individual would be the only Black Caribbean-American and only woman on the court. The petitioner herself is also an African-American woman; she objected to the appointment of a possibly ineligible person to the court. The case, *Thompson v. DeSantis*, is treated more fully in the Article V chapter.

B. Article IV, Section 7 — Suspensions; Filling Office During Suspensions

Israel v. DeSantis

269 So. 3d 491, 495 (Fla. 2019)

LAGOA, J.

Scott J. Israel ("Israel"), the Sheriff of Broward County, Florida, appeals the circuit court's dismissal of his petition for writ of quo warranto, challenging Governor Ron DeSantis's authority to suspend him from office in Executive Order 19-14. Israel appealed the circuit court's order to the Fourth District Court of Appeal, which certified the appeal to this Court as one of great public importance requiring immediate resolution by this Court. We have jurisdiction, *see* art. V, § 3(b)(5), Fla. Const., and affirm the circuit court's order dismissing Israel's petition.

BACKGROUND

In 2016, Israel was reelected as the Sheriff of Broward County, Florida, for a four-year term. Following Israel's reelection, two mass shootings occurred during Israel's term of office: the January 6, 2017, shooting at the Fort Lauderdale-Hollywood Airport in Broward County and the February 14, 2018, school shooting at Marjory Stoneman Douglas High School in Parkland, Florida.

On January 2, 2019, the Marjory Stoneman Douglas Public Safety Commission Report was released. Thereafter, on January 11, 2019, Governor Ron DeSantis issued Executive Order 19-14, suspending Israel from office. Executive Order 19-14 alleged that certain actions by Israel "constitute[d] neglect of duty and incompetence." In support of these grounds for Israel's suspension, Executive Order 19-14 asserts various factual allegations, based in part on the Marjory Stoneman Douglas Public Safety Commission Report and an internal investigation into the Fort Lauderdale-Hollywood Airport shooting. Executive Order 19-14 details how Israel allegedly "egregiously failed in his duties as Sheriff for Broward County," stating that two separate reports "specifically found that Sheriff Israel has not and does not provide frequent training for his deputies resulting in the deaths of twenty-two individuals and a response that is inadequate for the future safety of Broward County residents" and "specifically found that Sheriff Israel has not implemented proper protocols to provide guaranteed access to emergency services, nor proper protocols to have timely, unified command centers set up to control a crime scene leading to confusion, a lack of recognized chain-of-command, and ultimately a failure to contain the dangerous situation."

On March 7, 2019, Israel filed a petition for writ of quo warranto in the Circuit Court of the Seventeenth Judicial Circuit, alleging that Governor DeSantis exceeded his constitutional authority when suspending Israel.[11] On April 4, 2019, the circuit

---

11. [FN 1.] On January 29, 2019, Israel sought formal review on the merits of his suspension from the Florida Senate, as provided for under article IV, section 7(b) of the Florida Constitution.

court issued a written order dismissing Israel's petition. In its order, the circuit court found that "the allegations set forth in Executive Order 19-14 [were] sufficient to support the specified grounds of neglect of duty and incompetence, and therefore, [met] the jurisdictional requirements for suspension." The circuit court further found that Executive Order 19-14 "alleges facts that support and bear a reasonable relation to the stated grounds" of neglect of duty and incompetence.

On April 5, 2019, Israel appealed the circuit court's order to the Fourth District Court of Appeal. On April 9, 2019, the Fourth District certified the case for pass-through jurisdiction, finding that the appeal involved a question of great public importance that required immediate resolution by this Court.

STANDARD OF REVIEW

"Since the nature of an extraordinary writ is not of absolute right, the granting of such writ lies within the discretion of the court." *Topps v. State*, 865 So.2d 1253, 1257 (Fla. 2004). Accordingly, we generally review a circuit court's decision on a petition for writ of quo warranto for an abuse of discretion. *See Detzner v. Anstead*, 256 So.3d 820, 822 n.4 (Fla. 2018). However, because Israel's petition also concerns matters of constitutional interpretation, our review of the circuit court's constitutional interpretation is de novo. *See Zingale v. Powell*, 885 So.2d 277, 280 (Fla. 2004).

ANALYSIS

Article V, section 3(b)(8) of the Florida Constitution authorizes the judiciary to issue writs of quo warranto "to state officers and state agencies." "Quo warranto is used 'to determine whether a state officer or agency has improperly *exercised* a power or right derived from the State.'" *League of Women Voters of Fla. v. Scott*, 232 So.3d 264, 265 (Fla. 2017) (alteration in original) (quoting *Fla. House of Representatives v. Crist*, 999 So.2d 601, 607 (Fla. 2008)). The Governor is a state officer. *See Whiley v. Scott*, 79 So.3d 702, 707 (Fla. 2011).

Israel contends that the trial court erred in dismissing his petition for writ of quo warranto, arguing that Governor DeSantis lacks the authority to suspend Israel from office because Executive Order 19-14 does not provide an "objective factual predicate" to conclude Israel neglected or incompetently performed a specific "duty for which he was bound by law to perform."

We begin our analysis with the plain language of article IV, section 7(a) of the Constitution. *Zingale*, 885 So.2d at 282. Where the language of the Constitution "is clear, unambiguous, and addresses the matter in issue, then it must be enforced as written," as the "constitutional language must be allowed to 'speak for itself.'" *Fla. Soc'y of Ophthalmology v. Fla. Optometric Ass'n*, 489 So.2d 1118, 1119 (Fla. 1986); *accord Pleus v. Crist*, 14 So.3d 941, 944 (Fla. 2009) ("If that language is clear, unam-

---

The Senate scheduled a hearing on Israel's suspension for the week of April 8, 2019, but abated its review pending resolution of Israel's petition.

biguous, and addresses the matter in issue, then it must be enforced as written." (quoting *Lawnwood Med. Ctr., Inc. v. Seeger*, 990 So.2d 503, 511 (Fla. 2008))).

Article IV, section 7(a) of the Constitution provides that the Governor "may suspend from office … any county officer, for malfeasance, misfeasance, neglect of duty, drunkenness, incompetence, permanent inability to perform official duties, or commission of a felony." Once the Governor suspends a public official, the Florida Senate has the exclusive role of determining whether to remove or reinstate that suspended official. Art. IV, § 7(b), Fla. Const.

As we recently stated, the judiciary has a "limited role in reviewing the exercise of the suspension power, which the Constitution commits to the governor and which inherently involves 'judgment and discretion.'" *Jackson v. DeSantis*, No. SC19-329, 268 So.3d 662, 663, 2019 WL 1614572 (Fla. Apr. 16, 2019) (quoting *State ex rel. Hardie v. Coleman*, 115 Fla. 119, 155 So. 129, 133 (1934)). Where an executive order of suspension "names one or more of the grounds embraced in the Constitution and clothes or supports it with alleged facts sufficient to constitute the grounds or cause of suspension, it is sufficient." *Hardie*, 155 So. at 133. Similarly, the Senate's judgment of removal or reinstatement "is final and will not be reviewed by the courts," as under the constitutional process for suspension and removal, the "Senate is nothing less than a court provided to examine into and determine whether or not the Governor exercises the power of suspension in keeping with the constitutional mandate." *Id.* at 134. Assuming that the office of the suspended officer falls under one of the constitutionally enumerated categories and the Governor has filed the executive order of suspension with the custodian of records, the plain language of the Constitution excludes the judiciary from involving itself in the suspension and removal process save for a limited exception.

Turning to that exception, the Constitution requires the Governor to issue an executive order of suspension "stating the grounds" of the officer's suspension. While a suspended officer may seek judicial review of an executive order of suspension to ensure that the order satisfies that constitutional requirement, the judiciary's role is limited to determining whether the executive order, on its face, sets forth allegations of fact relating to one of the constitutionally enumerated grounds of suspension. *Id.* at 133. Thus, "[a] mere arbitrary or blank order of suspension without supporting allegations of fact, even though it named one or more of the constitutional grounds of suspension, would not meet the requirements of the Constitution." *Id.* However, where the executive order of suspension contains factual allegations relating to an enumerated ground for suspension, the Constitution prohibits the courts from examining or determining the sufficiency of the evidence supporting those facts, as the "matter of reviewing the charges and the evidence to support them is solely in the discretion of the Senate." *Id.* at 134; *see also State ex rel. Kelly v. Sullivan*, 52 So.2d 422, 425 (Fla. 1951) ("It is the function of the Senate and never that of the Courts, to review the evidence upon which the Governor suspends an officer in the event the Governor recommends his removal from office."). Therefore, the factual allegations in an executive order of suspension must satisfy only a low threshold under the judiciary's limited, facial review, and "if, on the whole, [the executive order] contains allegations that bear some reasonable relation to the charge made against the officer, it will be adjudged as sufficient." *Hardie*, 155 So. at 133.

Under this standard, Executive Order 19-14 satisfies our limited review. Executive Order 19-14 states that at the time of his suspension, Israel was serving as the Sheriff of Broward County, which is a "county officer" under article VIII, section 1(d) of the Florida Constitution. Executive Order 19-14 names the grounds for Israel's suspension—neglect of duty and incompetence—and provides various factual allegations that reasonably relate to those grounds of suspension.

Israel argues, however, that article IV, section 7(a) of the Constitution limits the grounds for suspension to a *statutory* duty prescribed to his office, which he claims Executive Order 19-14 fails to identify. "[I]n construing a constitutional provision, we are not at liberty to add words that were not placed there originally or to ignore words that were expressly placed there at the time of adoption of the provision." *Pleus*, 14 So.3d at 945. There is nothing in the plain language of article IV, section 7(a) stating that the grounds for suspending a public official are solely limited to his or her statutory duties.

Moreover, the plain and ordinary meaning of the word "duty" found in article IV, section 7(a) of the Constitution offers no support for Israel's argument. "[U]nless the text of a constitution suggests that a technical meaning is intended, words used in the constitution should be given their usual and ordinary meaning.... To this effect, 'a dictionary may provide the popular and common-sense meaning of terms....'" *Lawnwood*, 990 So.2d at 512 (quoting *Advisory Opinion to Governor—1996 Amendment 5 (Everglades)*, 706 So.2d 278, 282 (Fla. 1997)). According to *Webster's Seventh New Collegiate Dictionary* 259 (1967), "duty" is defined in part as "the action required by one's position or occupation." *See also American Heritage Dictionary* 573 (3d ed. 1992) (defining "duty" as "[a]n act or a course of action that is required of one by position, social custom, law, or religion").

Furthermore, in *Hardie*, this Court explained that with regard to the Governor's constitutional suspension power,

> Neglect of duty has reference to the neglect or failure on the part of a public officer to do and perform some duty or duties laid on him as such by virtue of his office or which is required of him by law. It is not material whether the neglect be willful, through malice, ignorance, or oversight. When such neglect is grave and the frequency of it is such as to endanger or threaten the public welfare it is gross.

155 So. at 132. "Incompetency ... has reference to any physical, moral, or intellectual quality, the lack of which incapacitates one to perform the duties of his office" and "may arise from gross ignorance of official duties or gross carelessness in the discharge of them ... [or] from lack of judgment and discretion." *Id.* at 133. A review of Executive Order 19-14 shows that it articulates factual allegations that bear a reasonable

relation to the grounds of neglect of duty and incompetence as those terms are understood in their usual and ordinary meaning.

CONCLUSION

The Constitution establishes a clear and unambiguous process for suspension and removal. The Governor may suspend for one or more of the grounds enumerated in article IV, section 7(a), and the Senate may remove or reinstate the officer pursuant to article IV, section 7(b). The Constitution reserves to the Senate the sole responsibility for reviewing the evidence supporting the Governor's executive order of suspension, and it is the constitutional role of the Senate to consider whether the suspended officer merits removal or reinstatement. Where the suspended officer falls within one of the constitutionally enumerated categories and the Governor has filed the executive order of suspension with the state custodian of records, the judiciary's sole role in this process is limited to a facial review of the executive order of suspension to determine whether it contains allegations that bear some reasonable relation to the charge made against the officer. This is "due entirely to the fact that the Constitution itself has set up its own special court to try the matter, namely the state Senate." *Hardie*, 155 So. at 136 (Davis, C.J., concurring).

Accordingly, we find that the Governor has satisfied the constitutional requirements set forth in article IV, section 7(a) of the Constitution and has the authority to suspend Israel from the office of Sheriff of Broward County. We therefore affirm the circuit court's order denying Israel's petition for writ of quo warranto.

It is so ordered.

MUÑIZ, J., concurring.

I concur in the majority opinion but write briefly to address the claim at the heart of Sheriff Israel's petition, *i.e.*, the assertion that the factual allegations underlying the suspension order are disconnected from Israel's statutory duties. Israel's view of those duties is far too narrow. Section 30.15(e), Florida Statutes (2018), makes sheriffs "in person or by deputy" the "conservators of the peace" in their respective counties. Relatedly, section 30.07, Florida Statutes (2018), authorizes sheriffs to appoint deputies and makes sheriffs responsible for the deputies' neglect in office. A sheriff's myriad day-to-day functions and responsibilities — including the development of policies and the training and supervision of employees — are the essential means of carrying out these overarching statutory obligations. And it requires no imagination to see the connection between these obligations and the significant performance deficiencies alleged in Executive Order 19-14. Of course, Israel is free to dispute the merits of the suspension order's factual allegations and to argue about the proper role of a governor in supervising local officials. But the appropriate forum for those debates is the Senate. It is not this Court's role to weigh the sufficiency of the evidence or to second-guess the governor's exercise of a discretionary function under the Constitution.

CANADY, C.J., and LAWSON and LUCK, JJ., concur.

LABARGA, J., concurring in result only.

As the circuit court correctly noted in its order, this case presents the narrow question of whether the executive order suspending Sheriff Israel alleges facts sufficient to support the suspension on the stated grounds. While I agree that Executive Order 19-14 fulfills this requirement, I write to emphasize that our review of these matters is not *pro forma*. Indeed, executive orders suspending officials pursuant to article IV, section 7(a), of the Florida Constitution must allege specific, detailed facts which support and allow for meaningful review by the Senate. This requirement, in my view, is of paramount importance when the official in question was duly elected by the voters, Furthermore, the suspension order must provide the official in question with sufficient notice of the allegations to allow the official to mount a meaningful defense.

This Court noted in *State ex rel. Hardee v. Allen*, 126 Fla. 878, 172 So. 222, 224 (1937), that "[i]t is not necessary that the allegation[s] of fact be as specific as the allegations of an indictment or information in a criminal prosecution." The allegations must, however, identify the specific instances of alleged misconduct with sufficient detail to facilitate meaningful review by the Senate, by this Court when applicable, and to allow the official to mount a defense. An executive order which presents only general or conclusory allegations will not suffice. This is not a demanding standard, but it is nonetheless a substantive requirement imposed by the Florida Constitution, and this Court is obligated to vacate any suspension which does not satisfy it.

Bruner v. State Comm'n on Ethics

384 So. 2d 1339 (Fla. 1st DCA 1980)

ORDER VACATING STAY AND DISMISSING APPEAL

McCORD, Judge.

This is an appeal brought by Raymond R. Bruner, appellant, (respondent below) from the final order and public report of appellee, State of Florida Commission on Ethics, which was the culmination of a proceeding below under Part III of Chapter 112, Florida Statutes the Code of Ethics for Public Officers and Employees. The final order made certain findings of fact and conclusions of law, and recommended a penalty. It would serve no useful purpose to here recite the details of the findings of the Commission. Suffice it to say that appellee Commission found that appellant, by his actions, violated s 112.313(6), Florida Statutes, by sexually harassing and by attempting to secure sexual favors from employees and applicants for employment of his office. The final order of appellee recommended that the Governor of the State of Florida suspend appellant from office as the Clerk of the Circuit Court of Jackson County, Florida.

On motion of appellant for a supersedeas order staying the power of the Governor to suspend appellant from office pending the disposition of the appellate proceedings, this Court, on June 27, 1980, granted the motion pursuant to s 112.3241, Florida Statutes (1979). That section provides as follows:

> Judicial review. Any final action by the commission taken pursuant to this part shall be subject to review in a District Court of Appeal upon the petition of the party against whom an adverse opinion, finding, or recommendation is made. In any case in which the Governor, upon the recommendation of the commission, has the power to suspend an officer or employee, *the court may enter a supersedeas order staying the power of the Governor to suspend pending the disposition of the appellate proceeding.* However, this section shall not be construed to limit the Governor's power to suspend a municipal official indicted for crime. (Emphasis supplied.)

On that same date, the Governor entered Executive Order No. 80-57 suspending appellant from office until further executive order, or as otherwise provided by law, and it was filed in the Office of the Secretary of State. There is conflict in the record before us as to whether or not the executive order was filed before or after this Court's order of stay. Such, however, is immaterial to the disposition of the questions before us. Subsequently on the same date, appellant filed with this Court a motion for clarification and to set aside Executive Order No. 80-57. Appellee filed a response to that motion and a motion to vacate order of supersedeas. We thereafter, on July 1, 1980, heard oral argument of the parties pursuant to show cause order by which we directed the parties to show cause why our stay order should not be vacated, and we requested counsel to direct their arguments to the constitutionality of s 112.3241, Florida Statutes (1979), insofar as it authorizes this Court to stay the exercise of the Governor's constitutional power. We further directed that the parties show cause why this appeal should not be dismissed as moot. Article IV, Section 7, of the Constitution of the State of Florida provides in pertinent part as follows:

> (a) By executive order stating the grounds and filed with the secretary of state, the governor may suspend from office any state officer not subject to impeachment, any officer of the militia not in the active service of the United States, or any county officer, for malfeasance, misfeasance, neglect of duty, drunkenness, incompetence, permanent inability to perform his official duties, or commission of a felony, and may fill the office by appointment for the period of suspension. The suspended officer may at any time before removal by reinstated by the governor.

> (b) The senate may, in proceedings prescribed by law, remove from office or reinstate the suspended official and for such purpose the senate may be convened in special session by its president or by a majority of its membership.

> (c)....

The Governor's power to suspend a public official under the Constitution is independent of, and may not be impinged upon by, a statute. While we recognize that it is the Court's duty to avoid holding a statute unconstitutional if there is a construction which may be made of the statute which would render it constitutional, the statute in question here, insofar as it authorizes the Court to enter a supersedeas order staying the exercise by the Governor of his constitutional power pending the disposition of an appellate review of Chapter 112 proceedings, collides directly with the Governor's constitutional power. Appellant argues that a court-ordered statutory stay does not conflict with the Governor's constitutional power but merely postpones it for a period of time. Such postponement, however, impinges upon the Governor's constitutional power and is, therefore, invalid. The following provision of s 112.3241, Florida Statutes (1979), is declared unconstitutional:

In any case in which the Governor, upon the recommendation of the commission, has the power to suspend an officer or employee, the court may enter a supersedeas order staying the power of the Governor to suspend pending the disposition of the appellate proceeding. However, this section shall not be construed to limit the Governor's power to suspend a municipal official indicted for crime.

Holding as we do that the legislature's grant to this Court of authority to stay the Governor's constitutional power is invalid, we next consider the question of whether or not the Governor's suspension of appellant has rendered this appeal moot. We find that it has. The order of respondent, which is before us for review, finds that grounds exist for the Governor to exercise his constitutional power to suspend appellant from office and recommends that the Governor take that action. Since the Governor now has exercised his constitutional authority by suspending appellant, the question of whether or not there was competent substantial evidence to support respondent Commission's findings and recommendations is now moot. The Governor has determined that there are sufficient grounds for him to exercise his constitutional power of suspension, and, thus, under Article IV, Section 7, of the Constitution, the question of reinstatement of appellant rests in the hands of the Governor and the Senate under the procedure outlined by s 112.41, Florida Statutes (1979) Part V. Proceedings below under Part III, Chapter 112, Florida Statutes (1979), insofar as they have terminated below with a recommendation that the Governor exercise his constitutional power to suspend appellant, were purely advisory. The Governor may suspend at any time. He may accept the Commission's recommendations for suspension when made and suspend then, or he may await the result of appellate review. The Constitution places no restrictions upon him in such regard. The Governor's suspension when made, however, shifts the forum from this Court to the Governor and the Senate. This appeal, therefore, has been rendered moot by the suspension of appellant.

The stay order entered by this Court on June 30, 1980, is vacated and the appeal is dismissed.

ROBERT P. SMITH, Jr. and BOOTH, JJ., concur.

Pizzi v. Scott

160 So. 3d 897 (Fla. 2014)

Opinion

On August 6, 2013, the United States Attorney for the Southern District of Florida filed a criminal complaint charging Petitioner Michael A. Pizzi, Jr., who was then Mayor of the Town of Miami Lakes, Florida, with multiple counts stemming from alleged actions taken in his official capacity as mayor. On the following day, Governor Rick Scott issued Executive Order Number 2013–217, which suspended Petitioner from office pursuant to section 112.51, Florida Statutes (2013). During Petitioner's suspension, the Town held a special election for mayor in accordance with the requirements of its charter. The permanent replacement mayor assumed office on October 8, 2013, and the new mayor's term will run until the next regularly scheduled election in November 2016.

Petitioner's trial commenced on July 8, 2014. The jury returned a verdict on August 14, 2014, finding Petitioner not guilty on all charges. On the following day, Petitioner requested the Governor to revoke Executive Order Number 2013–217. On the same day, the Governor's office responded by letter declining to grant Petitioner's request. On August 21, 2014, Petitioner filed a petition for writ of mandamus with this Court seeking an order compelling the Governor to revoke Executive Order Number 2013–217. The Governor filed a response opposing Petitioner's petition.

Based on a preliminary determination that the mandamus petition filed in this case demonstrates a basis for relief, on September 29, 2014, this Court issued an order that provided the Governor with the opportunity to show cause on the narrow issue of why Executive Order Number 2013–217 should not be revoked, pursuant to section 112.51(6), Florida Statutes (2013). This Court concluded that the Governor's response was warranted in light of the jury's verdict, on August 14, 2014, acquitting Petitioner of all federal felony charges. In the order to show cause, this Court stated that it was not suggesting that the Governor is required to reinstate Petitioner to his former municipal office, which has been filled by operation of a special election in accordance with the Town's charter.

The Governor timely filed a response in which he argued that because he is not required to reinstate Petitioner to his former municipal office, the Governor is not required to revoke Executive Order Number 2013–217. Petitioner timely filed a reply in which he argued that in light of his full acquittal from federal charges, the Florida Constitution requires the forthwith revocation of Executive Order Number 2013–217.

A petitioner is entitled to relief under this Court's authority to issue a writ of mandamus when: (1) the petitioner establishes a clear legal right to the performance of the requested act, (2) the respondent has an indisputable legal duty to perform that act, and (3) no other adequate remedy exists. *See Pleus v. Crist*, 14 So.3d 941, 945 (Fla.2009) (quoting *Huffman v. State*, 813 So.2d 10, 11 (Fla.2000)).

This Court has carefully considered the Governor's response to this Court's September 29, 2014, order requesting him to show cause why the petition for writ of mandamus should not be granted as to the narrow issue of why Executive Order Number 2013–217 should not be revoked, pursuant to section 112.51(6), Florida Statutes (2013). We have also considered the petitioner's reply to the Governor's response.

Under the Florida Constitution, when a municipal officer is indicted or otherwise charged with crimes, the Governor has discretion to suspend that municipal officer from office until acquitted. Art. IV, § 7(c), Fla. Const. However, upon acquittal of criminal charges, the governing statute states that the Governor has a mandatory duty to revoke the order that authorized the municipal officer's suspension. § 112.51(6), Fla. Stat. (2013).

In light of the Governor's duties set forth in section 112.51, Florida Statutes, and under article IV, section 7, Florida Constitution, the petition for writ of mandamus is hereby granted. However, because we believe that the Governor will fully comply with this order, by forthwith revoking Executive Order Number 2013–217, we withhold issuance of the writ until January 2, 2015.

It is so ordered.

CANADY, J., dissenting.

Because the Governor does not have an indisputable legal duty to revoke the executive order that suspended the Petitioner from office, the petition for writ of mandamus should be denied. Accordingly, I dissent.

The Petitioner's purported right to action by the Governor hinges on the meaning of section 112.51, Florida Statutes (2013), which provides that when a suspended municipal official is cleared of the charge on which the suspension was based "the Governor shall forthwith revoke the suspension and restore such municipal official to office."

Ordinarily, the application of this statutory provision would create an indisputable legal duty both to revoke the suspension order and to restore the suspended official to office. Here, however, the Petitioner does not suggest that the Governor has a duty to restore him to office and thus oust the Mayor elected in a special election under the charter of the municipality.

To the extent that the Governor has no indisputable legal duty to restore the Petitioner to office, the Governor likewise has no indisputable legal duty to revoke the suspension order. The statute links the act of revoking an order of suspension with the act of restoring to office. If the act of restoring to office is not required to be performed, it is not clear that the linked act of revoking the order of suspension is required. And it is not clear that the Petitioner would benefit in any way from the act of revocation unaccompanied by an act of restoration.

Given these murky legal circumstances, a proper basis for granting mandamus relief does not exist. "[A] writ of mandamus will not be allowed in a case of doubtful right" and mandamus "will not lie to compel [the] part[y] against whom it is directed to do a vain or useless thing." *State ex rel. Bergin v. Dunne*, 71 So.2d 746, 749 (Fla.1954).

POLSTON, J., concurs.

Questions

1. The Constitution grants the Governor the explicit power to suspend. How does the court limit this power, if at all?

2. Could you draft the constitutional provisions more precisely than they are?

3. What discretion does the Senate have in its grant of power to remove or reinstate a suspended official?

C. Article IV, Section 10 — Attorney General

The office of the Attorney General is created in Article IV, Section 4(a) as a member of the governor's Cabinet. Her duties are described in Section 4(b), (e), (f), and (g); she serves as the state's chief legal officer and sits as a member of the state internal improvement fund, which governs state lands and waters; as a member of the board of administration; and as a member of the head of the Florida Department of Law Enforcement. She also must, under Section 10, request the opinion of the justices of the Supreme Court of Florida as to the validity of any initiative petition. The duties of the Attorney General are further described in Articles V and VI.

D. Special Section on Executive Orders

In 2020, a historic pandemic swept the world, affecting the USA disproportionately and Florida even more disproportionately. Whether residents should be forced to wear masks to help prevent the spread of the virus became a flashpoint, with many claiming mandates to wear masks violated the U.S. Constitution and many others advising wearing masks because health officials claimed it was an effective way to prevent spread. Meanwhile, the number of new cases continued to rise steeply.

Some of the measures to try to prevent spread included executive orders by Governor Ron DeSantis. Indeed, DeSantis received criticism for orders issued, orders not issued, and orders rescinding previous orders.

The emergency nature of a pandemic seems appropriate for an executive order, as the executive can act quickly and unilaterally. It stands to reason that the same emergency nature would make courts reluctant to second-guess the executive. As the next case points out, the legislature has provided a framework for emergency actions by the governor, though the details seem to contemplate hurricanes and other natural-environment-related disasters. What is the proper extent of the Governor's power to issue executive orders? Does he have the power to force action as well as to prohibit action? When the need for an order has receded, may a Governor rescind it by issuing another order, or does some other legal avenue exist for directing residents' conduct?

Petition for Writ of Quo Warranto and Order Denying the Writ, *Abramson v. DeSantis*

Case No. SC20-646 (Fla. 2020)

In the Supreme Court of Florida

PETITION FOR WRIT OF QUO WARRANTO

Petitioner, William S. Abramson, a resident, citizen, registered voter, taxpayer, and former employee of Cucina Cabana, a restaurant located in North Palm Beach, Florida, files this petition to challenge Ronald D. Desantis' (Respondent) authority to issue and enforce Executive Orders 20-111, 20-212, dated April 29, 2020. (Exhibit A) Petitioner asserts that the issuance of these executive orders are [sic] in violation of the United States Constitution, the Florida Constitution, as well as Florida Statute 252, the cited authority to issue the above listed executive orders.

BASIS FOR INVOKING JURISDICTION

Article V, section 3(b)(8) of the Florida Constitution grants the Florida Supreme Court jurisdiction to issue writs of quo warranto to state officers and agencies. Respondent is a state officer pursuant to art V, sec 3(b)(8). *See Whiley v. Scott*, 79 So. 3d 702, 705 (Fla 2011). Quo warranto is the "proper means for inquiring into whether a particular individual has improperly exercised a power or right derived from the State." *Whiley v. Scott*, 79 So. 3d 707. Since quo warranto may be used to enforce a public right, standing [to] seek such a remedy is endowed to citizens and taxpayers. Petitioner, William S. Abramson, resides in the State of Florida, is a citizen and taxpayer. Through this instant petition, William S. Abramson, moves this Court to strike and render null and void the above listed executive orders as a violation of the Florida Constitution, as well as the improper exercise of his rights as Governor enumerated in Florida Statute 252. *See Lerman v. Scott*, 793 So. 3d (Fla 2016).

The issue before this Court is whether Respondent has the legal authority to issue the above listed executive orders. This Court has the authority to strike and render null and void the above listed executive orders. Through this petitioner, William S. Abramson seeks such action.

STATEMENT OF THE CASE

On April 29, 2020, Respondent issued Executive Orders 20-111, 112, extending the previous order, issuing a "three phase plan" to address the current "crisis." Respondent cited Article IV, section 1(a), and Florida Statute 252 as legal authority to support the issuance of Executive Orders 20-111, 20-112. Under the facts of the current situation, no such authority exists. Article IV section 1(a), merely lists the generic powers held by Respondent as Florida's chief executive. None of the powers listed in Article IV, section 1(a) gives Respondent the implicit authority to issue the above listed executive orders. If Respondent had the power to issue the above listed executive orders based on Article IV, section 1(a), he would not have cited Florida Statute 252. Respondent issued the above listed executive orders on the alleged authority granted him pursuant to Florida Statute 252.

Respondent's reliance on Florida Statute 252 is entirely misplaced. Florida Statute 252, otherwise known as "The State Emergency Management Act" (hereinafter referred to as "The Act") was enacted in 1974 and amended several times. Florida Statute 252.311, specifically addresses the legislative intent of "The Act." Florida Statute 252.311(a), states "The Legislature finds and declares that the state is vulnerable to a wide range of emergencies, including natural, technological, and manmade disasters, all of which threaten the life, health, and safety of its people; damage and destroy property; disrupt services and everyday business and recreational activities, and impede economic growth and development." Florida Statute 252.311(b) expresses the legislative intent to reduce the state's vulnerability "of the people to and property of this state, to prepare for efficient evacuation and shelter of threatened or affected persons; to provide for the rapid and orderly provision of relief to persons and for restoration of services and property; and to provide for the coordination of activities related to emergency preparedness, response, and recovery among...." Florida Statute 252.311(3) reflects the legislative intent to promote preparedness for such emergencies. Florida Statute 252.311 was enacted in 1993. No legislative history exists for this statute. [It is] a well known and accepted fact that Florida was not prepared for Hurricane Andrew, which occurred in August, 1992. The entire purpose of this statute is to facilitate the opening of the State, not closing it.

Florida Statute 252.34(8) defines "Natural emergency" as "an emergency caused by a natural event, including, but not limited to: a hurricane, a storm, a flood, severe wave action, a drought, or an earthquake." The current "emergency" is neither listed nor contemplated. There can be little doubt as the accuracy of this assertion since the Legislature nor the Division has taken any action whatsoever to prepare for the current situation. SARS and H1N1 have come and gone. If this statute was intended to cover the current situation, an emergency plan would have been developed. No such plan exists. The only conclusion is that this statute was never meant to apply to the current situation. Petitioner does not assert that every Governor, legislator, and employee of the Division, since 1993, is an abject failure. Quite the contrary. Florida's response to hurricanes since Andrew has been exemplary. Florida Statute 252 simply does not authorize Respondent to issue Executive Order 20-111 and 20-112, as well as the previous order under the facts of the current situation.

Pursuant to Florida Statute 252.35 "Emergency management powers; Division of Emergency Management" lists the powers, obligations, and responsibilities of the Division of Emergency Management ("The Division"), a state agency which is under the purview of the executive branch of the State of Florida. Respondent bears ultimate responsibility for the Division. Florida Statute 252.35(1), requires the Division to maintain "a comprehensive statewide program of emergency management." Florida Statute 252.35(2)(a), requires the plan be coordinated with the Federal Government. Florida Statute 252.35(3) requires a "post disaster response and recovery component." Florida Statute 252.35(8) requires that "The complete state comprehensive emergency plan shall be submitted to the President of the Senate, the Speaker of the House of Representatives, and the Governor on February 1 of every even-numbered years.

In essence, if an emergency were to occur, a plan must already be in place. No such plan addressing the current "emergency" exists. A cursory review of Executive Orders 20-211 and 20-212 reflect[s] the failure to address the current situation in the state's emergency management plan. Therefore, Respondent and every elected official have failed the people of the State of Florida or the statute was never intended to apply to the current situation. No other conclusion can be reached.

Further support for this conclusion comes from the following subsections of Florida Statute 252.35 that further address the Division's responsibilities to do the following:

8(3)(e)(1)	requires emergency management drills, tests, or exercises of whatever nature.
8(3)(e)(2)	requires warning signals for tests and drills, attacks, or other imminent emergencies or threats.
8(h)	Anticipate trends and promote innovations that will enhance the emergency management systems.
8(j)	create an outreach program on disaster preparedness and readiness to individuals who have limited English skills.
8(n)	Implement training programs to improve the ability of the state and local emergency management personnel to prepare and implement emergency.
8(q)	Prepare, in advance whenever possible, such executive orders, proclamations, and rules for issuance by the Governor as are necessary or appropriate for coping with emergencies and disasters.
8(t)	Maintain an inventory list of generators owned by the state … [No reference to ventilators or PPE's is mentioned].
8(w)	Report biennially to the President of the Senate, the Speaker of the House of Representatives, and the Governor, no later than February 1 of every odd-numbered year, the status of emergency management capabilities of the state and its political subdivisions.

Neither Respondent nor The Division can possibly claim that they contemplated the current situation when discharging their duties and responsibilities under Florida Statute 252.35 because there has been no compliance whatsoever with the above listed portions of Florida Statute 252. The only conclusion is that the current situation was neither contemplated nor covered under "The Act."

Further support for this assertion can be found in the failure to comply with Florida Statute 252.359(1)(2). These statutes require the Division to establish a statewide system to facilitate the transport and distribution of essential items. Essential items are defined as "goods that are consumed or used as a direct result of a declared emergency. No such action has been taken with regard to ventilators or PPE's.

Finally, if Florida Statute 252 was contemplated as giving Respondent authority to act in the current situation, Respondent has totally and completely failed to comply with the requirements of Florida Statute 252.36(3). Specifically, Respondent's executive orders fail to include any of the following:

3(a)   Activate the emergency mitigation, response, and recovery aspects of state … emergency management plan.

3(c)   Identify whether the state of emergency is due to a minor, major, or Catastrophic disaster.

Neither the constitution nor Florida Statute 252 authorizes Respondent to issue Executive Orders 20-211 and 20-212.

Even a cursory review of the remaining parts of Florida Statute 252 lend support to this Petition.

REL[IE]F SOUGHT

Therefore, Petitioner requests that this Court declare null and void Executive Orders 20-211 and 20-212. Florida Statute 252 does not authorize or even remotely contemplate Respondent's exercise of authority in this manner. In the absence of authority under Florida Statute 252, Respondent's orders must be stricken as null and void. Petitioner cannot remotely contemplate a matter that has ever been presented to this Court with greater significance.

Petitioner implores this Court to require Respondent to respond immediately. Respondent has taken great pains to issue the above executive orders. Respondent cannot possibl[y] claim he needs time to justify his actions.

CONCLUSION

Petitioner does not seek to embarrass nor subject any government official to ridicule. The sole purpose of this Petition is to restore the rights of all Floridians to live in liberty and exercise their rights as a free people, to freely assemble, and benefit from their industry. Petitioner is not unmindful of the pressure and responsibility of being Respondent. However, the rule of law must prevail. The Executive Orders have no basis in law. Respondent's unilateral and arbitrary nature determining what is "essential" and what isn't is a dangerous precedent. Florida Statute 252 was designed to facilitate the opening of the state, not closing it. Businesses are free to remain closed or require social distancing. Local school boards are vested with the authority to continue "distance learning." Major league sports can play in empty stadiums. Citizens are free to remain in their homes. If we allow Respondent to, in essence, make things up as he goes along, we have tyranny. In the words of Benjamin Franklin "Any society that will give up a little liberty to gain a little security will deserve neither and lose both."

Abramson v. Desantis

2020 Fla. LEXIS 1054, 2020 WL 3464376 (Fla. June 25, 2020)

In the Supreme Court of Florida

Thursday, June 25, 2020

Case No.: SC20-646

[Order]

Petitioner ... petitions this Court for a writ of quo warranto, arguing that Executive Orders 20-111 and 20-112, issued April 29, 2020, by Governor Ron DeSantis, are null and void because the State Emergency Management Act (the Act), §§ 252.31–.60, Fla. Stat. (2019), does not contemplate the Governor's use of his emergency powers to impose restrictions for the purpose of responding to a pandemic. We conclude that a pandemic is a "natural emergency" within the meaning of section 252.34(8). Accordingly, we further conclude that, under section 252.36(1)(b), the Governor has the authority to issue executive orders to address a pandemic in accordance with the Act. Abramson has not challenged, and we do not address, any specific provision of the executive orders at issue.

The petition for writ of quo warranto is denied.

CANADY, C.J., and POLSTON, LABARGA, LAWSON, MUÑIZ, and COURIEL, JJ., concur.

Commentary and Questions

1. The order by the Supreme Court of Florida in this case addressed only one of the issues raised by the petitioner. What do you think the reason for that was?

2. Do you agree with the petitioner's contention that because the executive orders mentioned a statutory scheme, it followed that the Order was not within the Governor's "supreme executive power"?

3. Several lawsuits were filed in response to various orders seeking to direct the actions of the public during the COVID-19 crisis of 2020. Most were filed in response to orders enacted by local authorities such as boards of city or county commissioners. What relationship do these orders have with Article IV of the Constitution of Florida?

4. An executive order may prevent behavior by citizens. May it coerce behavior by citizens as well? What, if any, constitutional provision authorizes this?

Article V

Judiciary

Introduction
A. Structure of the Court System
  i. Article V, Section 1—Courts
    1. *Laborers' International Union of North America, Local 478 v. Burroughs,* 541 So.2d 1160 (Fla. 1989).
  ii. Article V, Section 2—Administration; Practice and Procedure
    2. *State v. Johnson, Jr.,* 306 So.2d 102 (Fla. 1974).
    3. *In re Clarification of Florida Rules of Practice and Procedure (Florida Constitution, Article V, Section 2(a),* 281 So.2d 204 (Fla. 1973).
B. Administrative Duties of the Chief Justice and the Supreme Court
  i. Article V, Section(2)(b)
    4. *State ex rel. E.D. Treadwell, Jr., v. Hall,* 274 So. 2d 537 (Fla. 1973).
    5. *Payret v. Adams,* 500 So. 2d 136 (Fla. 1986).
C. Supreme Court Jurisdiction.
  i. Mandatory Jurisdiction
    a. Review of Orders Declaring Statute Invalid
      6. *D.M.T. v. T.M.H.,* 129 So. 3d 320 (Fla. 2013).
    b. Review of Proposed Amendments to the Constitution
      7. *Advisory Opinion to the Attorney General re Raising Florida's Minimum Wage,* 285 So.3d 1273 (Fla. 2019).
  ii. Discretionary Jurisdiction
    a. Conflict Jurisdiction
      8. *Jenkins v. State,* 385 So. 2d 1356 (Fla. 1980).
      9. *Dodi Publishing Co. v. Editorial America, S.A.,* 385 So. 2d 1369 (Fla. 1980).
      10. *Jollie v. State,* 405 So. 2d 418 (Fla. 1981).
      11. *Harrison v. Hyster Co.,* 515 So. 2d 1279 (Fla. 1987).
      12. *State v. Vickery,* 961 So. 2d 309 (Fla. 2007).
    b. "Bypass" Jurisdiction—Article V, Section 3(b)(5)
    c. Certified Questions
    d. Jurisdiction Based on Writs
      13. *Florida House of Representatives v. Crist,* 999 So. 2d 601 (Fla. 2008).
      14. *Detzner v. Anstead,* 256 So. 3d 820 (Fla. 2018).

Introduction

The Constitution is the fundamental law of the state. It describes the powers and limitations on all elements of Florida government. As we have seen, the Constitution defines the powers of the Legislature and the executive branch and local governments. It also defines the rights of citizens vis-a-vis government. But then who decides the meaning of the words in the Constitution and who resolves disputes about the meaning of the words? The courts do. Justice Leander Shaw once quoted from Lewis Carroll's classic, *Through the Looking Glass*, to describe the role of the courts.[1] In short, Humpty Dumpty said the meaning of words was not important. What *was* important was who got to say what the words meant: that

---

1. "When I use a word," Humpty Dumpty said, in rather a scornful tone, "it means just ~~what I~~ choose it to mean—neither more nor less. "The question is," said Alice, "whether you can make words mean so many different things."
   "The question is," said Humpty Dumpty, "which is to be master—that's all." (Emphasis added.)
   Northern Palm Beach Water Control District v. State, 604 So. 2d 440, 447 (Fla. 1992) (Shaw, J., dissenting). Justice Shaw rightfully concludes that the court is the master with regard to words in the Constitution because the Court says what words mean.

person is the master. And the master in the constitutional system is the Supreme Court. The same basic principle is established at the federal level in *Marbury v. Madison*, which established the concept of judicial review of legislative actions. The courts interpret constitutional language, statutory language and, in fact, any document that is at issue.

Article V creates the courts and describes their role and their jurisdiction.

Article V establishes a three-tier court system in Florida consisting of Trial Courts, District Courts of Appeal, and the Florida Supreme Court. The trial courts themselves are divided into two levels, so the court system is sometimes described as having four tiers. The Florida Supreme Court has the power to adopt rules for procedure and practice in state courts, and has ultimate supervision over the practice of law in Florida, including admission to the Bar, discipline of lawyers, and discipline of judges. It is interesting that, given this control over the state's legal system, the Florida Supreme Court has no power over selecting judges.

Many cases in this chapter highlight the Court's attempts to limit its own jurisdiction and maintain strict control over the administration and practice of Florida courts. The most important concepts in this chapter are determining whether a court has jurisdiction and learning how cases proceed through the Florida court system. Another concept, less explicit but worth considering, is the nature of judicial power. Article V opens: "The judicial power shall be vested in a supreme court, district courts of appeal, circuit courts and county courts." But what exactly is judicial power? What may judges do—and what may they not do? Unsurprisingly, different judges and justices see the scope of judicial power differently: some broadly, some more narrowly. As you read the cases in this chapter, think about what vision of judicial power the judges writing the opinions have.

The court system is the newest portion of the Constitution, as it was adopted in 1972, four years after the remainder of the Constitution. The reasons for this can be boiled down to the Legislature's failure to devise a plan its members, and the existing judges in the state, could agree on. The 1966–68 CRC had drafted a judicial article, but under the then existing constitution, any draft had to be approved by the Legislature. The Legislature did not approve the CRC's judicial draft, but could not devise a substitute. Therefore, the 1968 Constitution was adopted without a judicial article. For this reason, some refer to it not as the 1968 Constitution but as the 1968 revision of the 1885 Constitution.

Before 1972, the Constitution provided for a basic court structure, but also allowed the Legislature to create other courts "as it may think proper."[2] It also allowed municipalities to have judges.[3] By the time the CRC was ready to draft a proposed new

---

2. FLA. CONST. OF 1885, art. V § 18.
3. FLA. CONST. OF 1885, art. V § 34.

constitution, the court system was anything but uniform. Therefore, one feature the new judicial article had, not surprisingly, was a uniform system of courts, with no exceptions allowed.[4]

An important change after the 1972 redrafting was the 1980 amendment to limit the jurisdiction of the Supreme Court. As we will see, that amendment made the Florida Supreme Court a court of defined and limited jurisdiction. The amended article eliminated a traditional source of jurisdiction, writ of certiorari to the Supreme Court. The stated purpose of this change is an important element of understanding Florida's courts: The courts of final jurisdiction in Florida are the District Courts of Appeal. The Supreme Court is a court of limited jurisdiction by the terms of Article V § 3.

A. Structure of the Court System

i. Article V, Section 1 — Courts

Laborers' International Union of North America, Local 478 v. Burroughs

541 So. 2d 1160 (Fla. 1989)

GRIMES, Justice.

Pursuant to article V, section 3(b)(3), of the Florida Constitution, we accepted jurisdiction to review *Laborers' International Union Local 478 v. Burroughs*, 522 So.2d 852 (Fla. 3d DCA 1987), because that opinion expressly construes the Florida Constitution.

Myrtice Burroughs was hired by Local 478 as a clerk in 1982. Seventeen months later she was terminated from her employment. She then filed a complaint against the union before the Metropolitan Dade County Fair Housing and Employment Appeals Board. She alleged that she had been dismissed because she had refused the sexual advances of her immediate supervisor who was also a union officer.

After a hearing, the board found in Ms. Burroughs' favor and awarded her the following relief: back wages in the sum of $30,686.20, plus interest (back pay); so-called "front pay," i.e., future lost wages, of $8,883.00; and attorney's fees and costs of $19,178.98. The board also ordered the union to amend "its bylaws to incorporate a policy and a procedure to deal with complaints of sexual harassment."

Local 478's appeal to the circuit court was affirmed. The union then filed a petition for certiorari in the Third District Court of Appeal. In a split decision, that court denied certiorari. The court held that the ordinance creating the board was not pre-

---

4. Many judicial circuits have general magistrates and hearing officers who help alleviate judges' workloads. These positions are not considered judges; unlike judges, they are hired as courthouse staff.

empted by the Florida Human Rights Act, sections 760.01–.10, Florida Statutes (1985). The court also rejected the contention that the board was exercising judicial power prohibited under article V, section 1, of the Florida Constitution.

This case presents several issues, which we will address separately.

CONFLICT BETWEEN ORDINANCE AND STATUTE

The board derives its authority from a Dade County ordinance generally barring discriminatory employment practices. Metropolitan Dade County, Fla., Code ch. 11A, art. III, §§ 11A-2 to 11A-40 (1985). The Florida Human Rights Act of 1977 governs similar misconduct. Dade County's home rule charter specifically provides that the supremacy of state legislation must be preserved. Because section 760.02(6) limits the scope of the Human Rights Act to employers with fifteen or more employees, while the ordinance applies to employers with five or more employees, the union argues that the ordinance conflicts with the statute. In order to accept petitioner's argument we would have to conclude that the legislature intended that sexual discrimination by employers of fewer than fifteen employees was permissible. A more reasonable interpretation is that the legislature left this area open to local regulation. We agree with the following analysis of the district court of appeal:

> In the regulatory area involved in this case, the test of conflict is whether one must violate one provision in order to comply with the other. *Jordan Chapel Freewill Baptist Church v. Dade County*, 334 So.2d 661 (Fla. 3d DCA 1976).
>
> Putting it another way, a conflict exists when two legislative enactments "cannot co-exist." *E.B. Elliott Advertising Co. v. Metropolitan Dade County*, 425 F.2d 1141 (5th Cir.1970), pet. dismissed, 400 U.S. 805, 91 S.Ct. 12, 27 L.Ed.2d 12 (1970); *Metropolitan Dade County v. Santos*, 430 So.2d 506 (Fla. 3d DCA 1983), pet. for review denied, 438 So.2d 834 (Fla.1983). Neither formulation of the rule applies in a situation like this one in which the identical anti-discrimination requirements are simply imposed by the county upon a wider and broader class of entities than the state.

522 So.2d at 856.

JUDICIAL AND QUASI-JUDICIAL POWER

Article V, section 1, of the Florida Constitution, reads in pertinent part:

> The judicial power shall be vested in a supreme court, district courts of appeal, circuit courts and county courts. No other courts may be established by the state, any political subdivision or any municipality... Commissions established by law, or administrative officers or bodies may be granted quasi-judicial power in matters connected with the functions of their offices.

Thus, there is an implicit distinction between judicial power and quasi-judicial power. The issue here is how much, if any, of the jurisdiction granted to the Metropolitan Dade County Fair Housing and Employment Appeals Board's actions was proper for a quasi-judicial body. The union's attack in this area is two-pronged. It argues (A) that the board acted as a court in construing the ordinance to find that it covered the union's conduct, and (B) that in any event the board could not lawfully award the damages. We address the liability issue first.

A. Liability: Construction of the ordinance.

The Dade County ordinance provided in pertinent part:

Sec. 11A-22. Unlawful practices.

(a) It shall be unlawful employment practice for an employer:

(1) To fail or refuse to hire or to discharge any individual, or otherwise to discriminate against any individual with respect to his or her compensation, benefits, terms, conditions or privileges of employment because of such individual's race, color, religion, ancestry, national origin, age, sex, physical handicap, marital status or place of birth....

The union argues that the board improperly acted as a court in that it had to construe the ordinance to find that sexual harassment constituted employment discrimination. Only courts can construe the law, the union argues, citing no less weighty authority than *Marbury v. Madison*, 5 U.S. (1 Cranch) 137, 2 L.Ed 60 (1803). The union ignores the fact that administrative agencies are necessarily called upon to interpret statutes in order to determine the reach of their jurisdiction. Moreover, the construction of a statute by the agency charged with its administration is entitled to great weight and will not be overturned unless clearly erroneous. *Department of Ins. v. Southeast Volusia Hosp. Dist.*, 438 So.2d 815 (Fla.1983), appeal dismissed, 466 U.S. 901, 104 S.Ct. 1673, 80 L.Ed.2d 149 (1984). The board had a right to interpret the ordinance's proscription against sexual discrimination in the workplace to include sexual harassment, and that interpretation was eminently reasonable. *See Meritor Savings Bank v. Vinson*, 477 U.S. 57, 106 S.Ct. 2399, 91 L.Ed.2d 49 (1986), in which the Supreme Court of the United States held that a woman who had been sexually harassed at her job had a cause of action for employment discrimination under the analogous Title VII of the Civil Rights Act of 1964.

B. Damages

This court has considered related issues but has never squarely decided whether administrative boards created by county ordinances may assess any damages.

In *Broward County v. LaRosa*, 505 So.2d 422 (Fla.1987), we held that a Broward County human rights ordinance could not constitutionally authorize a local administrative agency to award noneconomic damages for humiliation and embarrassment. However, we made the following observation in a footnote to our opinion:

We see a significant distinction between administrative awards of quantifiable damages for such items as back rent or back wages and awards for such nonquantifiable damages as pain and suffering or humiliation and embarrassment.

Id. at 424 n. 5. A few months later, in *Metropolitan Dade County Fair Housing and Employment Appeals Board v. Sunrise Village Mobile Home Park, Inc.*, 511 So.2d 962 (Fla.1987), the Court upheld a Dade County ordinance prohibiting age discrimination in housing. Once again we also held that the enforcement agency could not constitutionally award common law damages for humiliation, embarrassment, and mental distress, emphasizing the nonquantifiable nature of such injuries. Thus, by implication we have already indicated that an administrative agency may be authorized to award quantifiable damages, and we now so hold.

* * *

CONCLUSION

We find that the Dade County ordinance in question does not constitutionally conflict with the Florida Human Rights Act. We also find that the Dade County Fair Housing and Employment Appeals Board did not usurp judicial power when it allowed Ms. Burroughs to maintain an administrative cause of action for employment discrimination based on incidents of sexual harassment. We find the board acted properly in awarding back pay and interest but had no authority to order the payment of front pay and attorney's fees.

Quasi - Judicial.
Admin. agency can interpret law that was charged with enforcing.

We approve the opinion of the district court of appeal in part, quash it in part, and remand the case for further proceedings consistent with this opinion.

It is so ordered.

OVERTON, Justice, dissenting.

I dissent. Article V, section 1, of the Florida Constitution, directs that "[t]he judicial power shall be vested in a supreme court, district courts of appeal, circuit courts and county courts" and contains the direct prohibition that "[n]o other courts may be established by the state, any political subdivision or any municipality." There are 393 municipalities, 11 chartered counties, and 56 noncharterd counties in this state. In my view, allowing these municipalities and counties to create separate bodies and rules to award damages and direct issuance of mandatory injunctions on multiple subjects is contrary to the intent and purpose of article V, section 1.

I do not condone the petitioner's conduct and am sympathetic with the respondent's position; however, I find that an award of damages and an adjudicatory determination that an injunction must be entered constitute a clear exercise of judicial power, which must be exercised within the court system of this state—not by multiple boards created by Florida's municipalities and counties.

Commentary and Questions

This case helps to define the scope of judicial authority. As with *Marbury v. Madison*, courts, to some extent, define their own role. This case, in particular, considers the role of the courts versus decisional authority of other governmental bodies.

1. What can quasi-judicial bodies to without impinging on the courts' constitutional power? Does this decision endanger the uniform-courts requirement of Article V?

2. What are the reasons to preclude governmental entities other than the courts from making certain decisions? Why are the courts a better place?

ii. Article V, Section 2 — Administration;
Practice and Procedure

Commentary

When we think of the court system, we tend, naturally, to think about which courts' judgments may be appealed to which higher courts, and what their jurisdictions are. But the picture is bigger. After all, the judiciary is one of the three branches of government. Therefore, the Supreme Court of Florida has the responsibility to run that branch. It is that court that adopts rules that prescribe how courts and cases should be run; how judges should behave; and how lawyers should behave. The Supreme Court supervises disciplinary processes for judges and lawyers and, through the Florida Board of Bar Examiners, sets the admission standards for lawyers to the Bar. The Chief Justice, then, is the head of the judicial branch of government of Florida.

The state court system is central to the balance of powers and to the fair and efficient operation of government. An interesting fact is that this critical branch accounts for only around two-thirds of one per cent of the state budget.[5] While the court controls internal procedures, the budget of the courts are a product of legislative appropriations. (*See* FLA. CONST. § 14 Funding.)

State v. Johnson, Jr.
306 So. 2d 102 (Fla. 1974)

PER CURIAM.

We review by writ of conflict certiorari a final order or judgment of the District Court of Appeal, Third District, declining to review a speedy trial order of the Circuit Court discharging Zebedee Johnson, Jr., respondent herein, because the State of Florida, which sought the review, misconceived its remedy having sought a writ of certiorari to review the speedy trial order.

The District Court concluded that any review of the speedy trial order should have been undertaken pursuant to a notice of appeal and accordingly dismissed the State's petition for writ of certiorari. Its order was final and terminated the State's effort to gain a review.

The petition for writ of certiorari was filed within 30 days after entry of the speedy trial order.

We do not believe undue elaboration is necessary in rendering our decision in this case. Under Section 2(a), Article V, Florida Constitution, this Court is mandated to adopt rules of practice and procedure in All courts which shall include "a requirement that no cause shall be dismissed because an improper remedy has been sought."

---

5. Governor's 2020–2021 Proposed State Budget, https://www.fl-counties.com/governors-2020-2021-proposed-state-budget (last visited August 15, 2020).

It is agreed that had notice of appeal been filed instead of petition for writ of certiorari, the authorizations in Section 924.07, F.S. would have allowed appellate review of the speedy trial order.

It is our view the dismissal was improper and conflicts with the rationale of *State ex rel. Scaldeferri v. Sandstrom* (Fla.), 285 So.2d 409, where we said in effect that we should entertain an appellate review or remedy which has merit "in whatever form is proper," pursuant to the mandate of said Section 2(a), Article V of the Constitution. The salutary purpose of the constitutional provision is to insure that improper or misconceived remedies which have been sought will not justify dismissal of causes or reviews where a proper remedy or review procedure is available, provided the relief sought was timely brought.

We are unable from the record before us to proceed to the point of disposing finally the merits of the speedy trial order. We quash the dismissal of the State's petition for writ of certiorari and direct the District Court to treat the petition as a notice of appeal and review the merits of the speedy trial order.

It is so ordered.

ERVIN, BOYD, DEKLE and OVERTON, JJ., concur.

ADKINS, C.J., and McCAIN, J., dissent.

Commentary

While the Legislature has the power to enact substantive laws, only the Supreme Court has authority to enact judicial rules of practice and procedure. The Legislature constitutionally may veto or repeal any rule of the Supreme Court; however, doing so requires a two-thirds approval of each house. The Legislature may not enact any law relating to practice and procedure or amend or supersede any rule the court has promulgated. The interplay between the two branches of the government has complexities in this area. The Supreme Court may promulgate rules based on statutes the Legislature has passed, as a tacit inference that a statute relating to practice and procedure signifies legislative intent. But the fact the court does adopt a statute as a rule does not vest authority in the Legislature to try to amend the court's rule by amending their own statute.

In re Clarification of Florida Rules of Practice and Procedure (Florida Constitution, Article V, Section 2(a))

281 So. 2d 204 (Fla. 1973)

PER CURIAM.

Fla. Const., art. V, § 2(a), F.S.A., contains the following provisions:

The supreme court shall adopt rules for the practice and procedure in all courts including the time for seeking appellate review, the administrative supervision of all courts, the transfer to the court having jurisdiction of any proceeding when the jurisdiction of another court has been improvidently invoked, and a requirement that no cause shall be dismissed because an improper remedy has been sought. These rules may be repealed by general law enacted by two-thirds vote of the membership of each house of the legislature.

The Legislature has the constitutional right to repeal any rule of the Supreme Court by a two-thirds vote, but it has no constitutional authority to enact any law relating to practice and procedure. *See State v. Smith and Figgers*, 260 So.2d 489 (Fla.1972). The distinction between practice and procedure, which is regulated by the Supreme Court and substantive law which is regulated by the Legislature, is discussed in a concurring opinion, *In Re: Florida Rules of Criminal Procedure*, 272 So.2d 65 (Fla.1972).

During the past session of the Legislature various laws were enacted which related to practice and procedure. This creates confusion in the judicial branch in that the laws as enacted are in conflict with or supplemental to various rules of practice and procedure. The Supreme Court has considered these laws as expressing the intent of the Legislature and has formulated rules of practice and procedure that attempts to conform with the intent of the Legislature and at the same time further the orderly procedure in the judicial branch.

We point out the provisions of Ch. 73-84, Laws of Florida. Section 2 repeals paragraph e. of Rule 3.16, Florida Appellate Rules, 32 F.S.A. This law passed by a two-thirds vote of the Legislature and was within its constitutional powers. Section 1 of this law attempts to rewrite Rule 3.16, Florida Appellate Rules. This attempted amendment is beyond the powers of the Legislature as the Supreme Court is given exclusive authority to promulgate rules of practice and procedure in the courts. In other words, under the Constitution the Legislature may veto or repeal, but it cannot amend or supersede a rule by an act of the Legislature. Rule 3.16, subd. e., Florida Appellate Rules, is amended so that it shall read in the form attached hereto.

Ch. 73-72, Laws of Florida, attempts to regulate voir dire examination during the trial by amending Fla.Stat. § 53.031, F.S.A., formerly Fla.Stat. (1965) § 54.13, F.S.A. This statute attempts to regulate practice and procedure, a matter solely within the province of the Supreme Court to regulate by rule. At the time the Civil Rules of Procedure were promulgated, there were various statutes in existence relating to procedure. The order adopting the rules (*In Re: Florida Rules of Civil Procedure 1967 Revision*, Fla., 187 So.2d 598) provided that all statutes not superseded by the rules or in conflict with the rules shall remain in effect as rules promulgated by the Supreme Court. *See Sun Insurance Office, Limited v. Clay*, 133 So.2d 735 (Fla.1961), where this Court adopted a statute as a rule.

The adoption as rules of the Court of all statutes which have not been superseded or may be in conflict with the rules is primarily a matter of convenience or administrative expediency. Such adoption avoids the question of whether a matter lies within the field of substantive law or procedural law.

The fact that this Court may adopt a statute as a rule does not vest the Legislature with any authority to amend the rule indirectly by amending the statute. In other words, an attempt by the Legislature to amend a statute which has become a part of rules of practice and procedure would be a nullity. This Court has considered Laws of Florida, Ch. 73-72, in connection with Rule 1.431(b), Florida Civil Procedure Rules, 30 F.S.A. relating to voir dire examination, and hereby amends the rule so that the same shall read in accordance with the attached amendment.

Ch. 73-27, Laws of Florida, relates to criminal procedure and authorizes the issuance of a notice to appear for certain crimes and violations. The Court has approved this procedure and appended hereto new Rule 3.125, of the Florida Criminal Procedure Rules. This rule supersedes only that portion of the statute included in the rule and the balance of the statute will remain in effect as part of the substantive law. Also, it was necessary to change the procedure set forth in the rules so as to comply with the requirements of the Florida Case Disposition Reporting System, and a suggested form is included which will enable the preparation of proper notices by the local officials. Rule 3.125 is hereby adopted.

Laws of Florida, Ch. 73-112 (Fla.Stat. (1973) §61.181, F.S.A.), creating domestic relations depository filled a great need in the judicial system. Rule 1.611, Florida Civil Rules of Procedure, 31 F.S.A. as appended hereto, is amended for the purpose of including the benefits provided in Chapter 73-112.

The Florida Rules of Practice and Procedure are hereby amended in the manner set forth in the appended rules. These amendments and changes shall take effect on the effective date of the statutes to which they are related.

It is so ordered.

CARLTON, C.J., and ROBERTS, ERVIN, ADKINS, BOYD, McCAIN and DEKLE, JJ., concur.

B. Administrative Duties of the Chief Justice and the Supreme Court

i. Article V, Section(2)(b)

Commentary

A multitude of detail on how the judicial system runs is contained in this short subsection. First, the subsection does not govern the method by which the members of the Court choose a Chief Justice, or the duration of the term of a Chief. Therefore, the details have developed as custom. The Chief customarily serves a two-year term, and with few exceptions, the Chief has been the most senior justice who has not yet served as Chief. If all have so served, the rotation begins again. Some exceptions are the renewal of Justice Jorge Labarga's term as Chief for the 2018–2020 term and the choice of former Chief Justice Charles Canady for a second term in 2020–2022, when two justices remained on the Court who had not served as Chief (but who had been on the Court only a few years at the time of the election). An effect of this rather egalitarian selection process is that no justice, no matter how long-standing, can amass power by virtue of long service as Chief.

But a much broader matter is the Chief Justice's role as chief administrative officer of the judicial branch. Obviously, one person cannot perform his judicial duties and also run an entire branch of government single-handedly, including not only the court on which she sits but also all five district courts of appeal, all twenty judicial circuits, and all sixty-seven counties. Therefore, in 1972, when Article V became the last-adopted article of the new Constitution, the Office of State Courts Administrator (OSCA) was formed. OSCA has become the main administrative office of the court system, with offices in the Supreme Court building, and also acts as a liaison to the other two branches of the government. The chief of OSCA reports to the Chief Justice. The Chief also presides over the Clerk of the Supreme Court and the Marshal, both constitutionally created offices, and over the court's Public Information Officer. Each individual justice presides over her own staff, and there is also a group of attorneys called the Central Staff, who perform needed research and writing duties in addition to those dedicated to a single justice.[6]

The next two cases examine the limits of the Chief Justice's authority to assign judges in lower courts to temporary service outside their usual work.

State ex rel. E.D. Treadwell, Jr., v. Hall

274 So. 2d 537 (Fla. 1973)

ERVIN, Justice.

We consider here suggestion for a writ of prohibition and motions to advance filed by both parties.

Relator, E. D. Treadwell, Jr. is the executor under the will of his father which estate is presently being administered in the Circuit Court of DeSoto County, Florida. Respondent is the county judge of that county 'assigned to act as a circuit judge' in that county pursuant to the order of Honorable Robert E. Hensley, Chief Judge of the Twelfth Judicial Circuit in and for DeSoto County, issued on January 2, 1973, and providing in part:

> "ORDERED that until further order the Honorable Vincent T. Hall, County Judge of DeSoto County … is hereby assigned to act as a Circuit Judge in DeSoto County in all matters of probate, guardianship, incompetency, trusts, proceedings under 'The Florida Mental Health Act' and all juvenile proceedings, dissolutions of marriage, and all uncontested civil matters in circuit court.…"

Respondent County Judge Hall has been a member of The Florida Bar for five years preceding his assignment.

Relator filed a written objection to Respondent concerning his assuming jurisdiction in the probate of his father's will.

---

6. Harry Lee Anstead, Gerald Kogan, Thomas D. Hall & Robert Craig Waters, *The Operation and Jurisdiction of the Supreme Court of Florida*, 29 Nova L. Rev. 1, 50 (2005) (hereafter Anstead, et al., *Operation and Jurisdiction*).

The issue here is whether under the provisions of revised Art. V s 2(b), Fla.Const., F.S.A., the chief judge of a judicial circuit is authorized to assign a county judge to assume jurisdiction of matters which, in the language of Section 20 of Article V (schedule) of the Constitution, are in the exclusive jurisdiction of the circuit court.

Art. V, s 2(b), State Constitution, provides in part:

"The chief justice of the supreme court shall … have the power to assign justices or judges … to temporary duty in any court for which the judge is qualified and to delegate to a chief judge of a judicial circuit the power to assign judges for duty in his respective circuit."

Art. V, s 8, State Constitution, provides in part:

… No person is eligible for the office of circuit judge unless he is, and has been for the preceding five years, a member of the bar of Florida."

Both Relator and Respondent stress the urgency of the question presented and have moved to advance the cause for final hearing. Relator states that Judge Hensley's administrative order does not allow for appeal and a declaratory decree is viewed as being too "cumbersome and time-consuming".

Unquestionably, Judge Hensley's order is presently affecting the lives and property of DeSoto County.

Florida Rules of Civil Procedure relating to court administration effective November 29, 1972, were adopted by order of the Supreme Court and appear at 269 So.2d 359. They contain Rule 1.020, 30 F.S.A. This rule was adopted to implement Revised Article V of the 1968 State Constitution. Inter alia, this rule authorizes in subsection (b)(3)(ii) thereof the chief judge of a judicial circuit to "assign any judge to temporary service for which the judge is qualified in any court in the same circuit". This Rule was designed, in part, to obviate the need for each incoming chief justice to specifically delegate to the twenty chief judges of the circuits the authority to make assignments; it also was designed to obviate the need for specific delegations when the chief judges within the circuits were re-elected or changed. Unless a chief justice indicates otherwise, his desire to continue delegation via the Rule is assumed.

It is our overall view, from a consideration of Sections 2, 5, 6, 8 and 20 of revised Article V, that county judges who have been members of the Florida Bar for five years preceding their assignment to judicial service under Section 2(b) of Article V, and who have served in such office upon or after the effective date of the revision, are qualified to be assigned as temporary circuit judges for the performance of any judicial service a circuit judge can perform.

Under revised Article V of the Florida Constitution and the procedural rules promulgated thereunder, a qualified county judge was authorized by proper assignment to discharge the judicial services described in Judge Hensley's order herein.

Since this litigation presented a question of great public importance we have granted the motions to advance, exercised our discretion to accept jurisdiction, dispensed with the issuance of the rule nisi and settled the question instanter.

Having fully considered the matter and resolved the merits as above determined, we direct that suggestion for writ of prohibition be denied.

It is so ordered.

CARLTON, C.J., and ADKINS, BOYD and DEKLE, JJ., concur.

Payret v. Adams

500 So. 2d 136 (Fla. 1986)

EHRLICH, Justice.

We have for our review *Payret v. Adams*, 475 So.2d 300 (Fla. 4th DCA 1985), wherein the district court certified the following question of great public importance:

MAY A COUNTY JUDGE BE INDEFINITELY ASSIGNED CIRCUIT COURT DUTIES IN A SPECIALLY CREATED JURY DISTRICT OF THE FIFTEENTH JUDICIAL CIRCUIT?

We have jurisdiction, article V, section 3(b)(4), Florida Constitution, and answer the question in the negative.

In order to understand the procedural history of this case and our treatment of the certified question, the current system of trying criminal cases in the Fifteenth Judicial Circuit must be examined. Of particular importance are three administrative orders issued by the chief judge of that circuit. The Glades Courthouse Annex, located in Belle Glade, is an official courthouse facility of the Fifteenth Judicial Circuit, in and for Palm Beach County. By Administrative Order 1.004, all circuit and county court matters may be heard at the Glades annex, which geographically encompasses that section of Palm Beach County lying west of a north-south line at 20-Mile Bend. Administrative Order 1.006, enacted pursuant to the authority granted the chief judge of a judicial circuit by section 40.015, Florida Statutes (1985), created the Glades jury district. Under this administrative order, where the situs of an alleged felony is within the Glades district, a felony-charged defendant may request a jury trial at the Glades annex before a jury drawn from the Glades jury district; a defendant who does not so request is tried at the main courthouse in West Palm Beach before a jury drawn from the eastern district. Administrative Order 1.003 represents a blanket authorization from the chief judge for county court judges to decide circuit court cases; assignments entered pursuant to this administrative order are for a full one-year period. This order further provides that in cases other than those in which the county court has exclusive jurisdiction, upon good cause shown a party may have a case transferred to an appropriate division of the circuit court.

Respondent is a county court judge in Palm Beach County. Pursuant to Administrative Order 1.003, respondent has been annually reassigned for the past five years to be the acting circuit court judge for the Glades district. Respondent has acknowledged that for all practical purposes, he is the circuit judge for the Glades district.

The petitioner was charged by information with a felony and the case was set for trial before the respondent, acting as circuit judge, at the Glades annex. Respondent denied petitioner's motion to transfer the case to an appropriate division of the circuit court.[7]

Following this denial, petitioner sought a writ of prohibition from the Fourth District Court of Appeal, alleging that respondent was without jurisdiction to act as a circuit court judge. The district court denied the petition stating that this Court's decision in *Crusoe v. Rowls*, 472 So.2d 1163 (Fla.1985), and our reaffirmation of *State ex rel. Treadwell v. Hall*, 274 So.2d 537 (Fla.1973), in *Crusoe* foreclosed the district court from acting. While we understand the district court's reluctance, we feel it has read *Crusoe* and *Treadwell* too broadly.

The sole issue before us sub judice is the temporal nature of respondent's assignment. The issue before us in *Treadwell* was whether the chief judge of a judicial circuit was authorized to assign duties to a county court judge which, under our constitution, are in the exclusive jurisdiction of the circuit court. 274 So.2d at 538. The extent of our holding in *Treadwell* was that those county court judges who met the qualifications for being a circuit judge under article V, section 8, were qualified to be assigned as temporary circuit judges. *Id.* at 539. The assignment in *Treadwell* stated that it was to be effective "until further order," *id.* at 538, and it is this language on which both respondent and amicus rely in support of their position that the assignment sub judice is temporary and more limited than the assignment we approved in *Treadwell*. Judging from the phrasing of the district court's opinion below, it was evidently this same open-ended language which that court found to be controlling.

In *Crusoe*, however, we explicitly stated that, "what temporary circuit judges" meant was not discussed or defined in *Treadwell*. 472 So.2d at 1165. In *Crusoe* we explained:

> "Temporary" is an antonym for "permanent." It is a comparative term. It can be said that if a duty is not permanent it is temporary. If a county judge is assigned to perform solely circuit court work, the assignment must be for a relatively short time for it to be temporary. If a county judge is assigned to spend a portion of his time performing circuit work, the assignment can be longer, but the assignment cannot usurp, supplant, or effectively deprive circuit court jurisdiction of a particular type of case on a permanent basis.

Id. (footnotes omitted). We suggested that when a county court judge is assigned to do solely circuit court work, the assignment, in order to be temporary, should be for no more than sixty days; when a county court judge is assigned to spend only

---

7. [FN*] The petitioner's motion was made pursuant to Administrative Order 1.003, which allows transfer for good cause shown. Petitioner's good cause argument was premised on the validity of respondent's nontemporary assignment as circuit court judge.

a portion of his time doing circuit court work, we suggested no more than six months.

We *suggested* these time periods because we recognized the need for giving the chief judges flexibility in order for them to effectively utilize available judicial labor, and we liberally construed the assignments in *Crusoe* with this in mind. *Id.* at 1166.

Factually, *Crusoe* dealt with successive and repetitive assignments of county court judges assigned to hear a limited class of support orders. We found these assignments valid as the county judges were assigned "to supplement and aid the circuit judges rather than to replace them." *Id.* at 1165. The facts sub judice stand in stark contrast. Respondent's assignment has been successive and repetitive, having been renewed annually for the last five years. Rather than being assigned to aid or assist the circuit judges in a limited class of cases, respondent has been assigned to hear all circuit court matters in the Glades district. Indeed, respondent has conceded that for all intents and purposes, he is the circuit judge for the Glades district.

Respondent and amicus argue that the assignment at issue is a valid temporary assignment as, facially, it is only for a one year period. We cannot simply close our eyes to the *de facto* permanency of respondent's assignment, and no exercise in liberal construction of the administrative order before us can transform this permanent assignment into a valid temporary one; such a result could only be accomplished by legerdemain.

... The only issue before us today is the validity of respondent's assignment, and constitutional provisions cannot be ignored for reasons of convenience. Article V, section 10(b), mandates that circuit judges shall be elected by vote of the qualified electors within the territorial jurisdiction of the court. Article V, section 11(b), provides that when a vacancy on a circuit court occurs, the governor shall appoint a judge to fill that vacancy. Respondent has become a permanent circuit judge not by the method mandated by the constitution, but by administrative order. This cannot be done.

Therefore, we answer the certified question in the negative, quash the decision of the district court and remand for proceedings consistent with this opinion.

It is so ordered.

OVERTON, Justice, dissenting.

The majority's decision will substantially impact on the efficient utilization of Florida's judicial manpower and is contrary to the intent and purpose of article V, section 2, of the Florida Constitution. The basic circumstances in *State ex rel. Treadwell v. Hall*, 274 So.2d 537 (Fla.1973), are identical to those in the instant case. In *Treadwell*, we approved assigning DeSoto County's county court judge to circuit court work in that county. That record reflected that the county court judge had ample time to fulfill both county court and circuit court responsibilities. The majority decision effectively overrules *Treadwell* by restricting the use of county court judges as circuit judges in rural and semi-rural counties. Further, the majority decision will require either (1) that circuit judges travel to counties where there are no resident circuit judges or (2) that qualified county court judges from other counties within the circuit periodically exchange counties to do circuit court work. As a result, judicial time will be lost in travel and other available judicial time from county court judges will be totally lost. In my view, this is poor administrative policy and clearly contrary to the intent of article V, section 2, of Florida's constitution.

The majority answers the certified question in the negative. I would answer the question in the affirmative *provided* the county court judge retains his or her county court duties. I agree with the majority, however, that a county court judge could not indefinitely be assigned exclusively to circuit court work. Consistent with *Treadwell,* I would consider the order "temporary" when the phrase "until further order of the court" is used and the judge is not relieved of county court jurisdiction.

In view of the majority's decision, article V should be amended to allow Florida to fully utilize its present judicial manpower.

McDONALD, C.J., concurs.

C. Supreme Court Jurisdiction

The Supreme Court of Florida is the highest court in the state system, but it has limited jurisdiction. It is not the court of last resort for most purposes: that distinction lies with the District Courts of Appeal. This contrast was clarified in 1980, when an overload of cases made jurisdictional reforms to limit the kinds of cases the Supreme Court could hear.[8] The Supreme Court has mandatory jurisdiction for some types of cases — cases it must hear — and permissive jurisdiction for other types of cases — cases it may hear. The Supreme Court also has original jurisdiction for some cases. Original jurisdiction means the Supreme Court is the first court in which the case is filed. In contrast, most cases must begin in a trial court and wind their way through the court system before reaching the Supreme Court.

For the Supreme Court to grant discretionary review from a District Court of Appeal decision, the court requires a ten-page jurisdictional brief to be filed. The brief must focus on legal issues rather than facts.[9] If jurisdiction is refused, the matter remains as resolved by the DCA. The decision to take jurisdiction is made by a panel of five of the justices for a period of time. If four of those justices agree to review the case, jurisdiction to hear the case is granted. If four agree to deny review, an order is entered, and the case closed. If four do not agree to either review or deny, the case goes to the other two justices.[10]

---

8. Anstead, et al., *supra* note 6, at 3–4.
9. PADOVANO, FLORIDA APPELLATE PRACTICE, § 16:14 (2020 Edition).
10. The Supreme Court of Florida Manual of Internal Operating Procedures (rev. Sept. 21, 2016), http://www.floridasupremecourt.org/pub_info/documents/IOPs.pdf (last visited Sept. 11, 2020).

The largest quantity of jurisdictional briefs deals with conflict jurisdiction. Only a minority of these are granted, and the showing of conflict is difficult. This issue is discussed below.

Jurisdiction of Fla. Sup. Ct.
Fla. Const. art. V, § 3

▶ Mandatory Jurisdiction — appeals

- ▶ Death penalty
- ▶ Constitutional invalidity
- ▶ Bond validation
- ▶ PSC
- ▶ Advisory Opinions
  - ▶ To Governor, art. IV, § 1 le)
  - ▶ To Attorney General, art. IV, § 10
- ▶ Legis. Reapportionment, art. III, § 16

▶ Inherent Jurisdiction

- ▶ Practice & Procedure
  - ▶ Court rules, art. V, § 2(a)
  - ▶ Bar admission, art. V, § 15
  - ▶ Bar discipline, art. V, § 15
  - ▶ JQC, art. V, § 12(c)

▶ Discretionary Jurisdiction — reviews

- ▶ Const. construction
- ▶ Expressly declares statute valid
- ▶ Class of Const./State officers
- ▶ Express & direct conflict with other DCA's or Sup. Ct.
- ▶ Certified Questions
  - ▶ Great public importance
  - ▶ Conflict
  - ▶ Pass-through
  - ▶ Federal appeals courts
- ▶ Writs
  - ▶ Mandamus
  - ▶ Quo Warranto
  - ▶ Prohibition
  - ▶ Habeas Corpus
  - ▶ 'all writs'

i. Mandatory Jurisdiction

a. Review of Orders Declaring Statute Invalid

D.M.T. v. T.M.H.

129 So. 3d 320 (Fla. 2013)

PARIENTE, J.

* * *

The parents in this case are two women, D.M.T. and T.M.H., who were involved in a long-term committed relationship when they agreed to jointly conceive and raise a child together as equal parental partners. Their child was conceived through the couple's use of assisted reproductive technology, with T.M.H. providing the egg and D.M.T. giving birth to the child. After the child was born, the couple gave her a hyphenation of their last names, and both T.M.H. and D.M.T. participated in raising their child until their relationship soured and D.M.T. absconded with the child. T.M.H. now seeks to establish her parental rights to the child and also to reassume parental responsibilities. D.M.T., conversely, seeks to prevent T.M.H. from doing either. D.M.T. asserts that she, and she alone, should have the fundamental right to be the parent of the child. No other individual has asserted parental rights to the child, and no party or amicus curiae in this case other than D.M.T. takes the position that T.M.H. should be denied her rights.

In *T.M.H. v. D.M.T.*, 79 So.3d 787 (Fla. 5th DCA 2011), the Fifth District Court of Appeal held that Florida's assisted reproductive technology statute—section 742.14, Florida Statutes (2008)—did not apply to T.M.H., and that the trial court's application of the statute was unconstitutional because it prevented T.M.H., who provided the egg for the couple, from asserting her parental rights to the child. Id. at 792, 798, 800. Because the Fifth District declared section 742.14 unconstitutional as applied to T.M.H., we have mandatory jurisdiction under article V, section 3(b)(1), of the Florida Constitution to review this case. In addition, the Fifth District certified a question of great public importance regarding whether the statute was unconstitutional, and we also have jurisdiction on that basis. See art. V, § 3(b)(4), Fla. Const.

We conclude that the statute is unconstitutional (1) as a violation of the Due Process Clause of the United States Constitution and separately as a violation of the Due Process Clause and privacy provision of the Florida Constitution; and (2) as a violation of the federal Equal Protection Clause and separately as a violation of the Florida Equal Protection Clause. In reaching our conclusion, we rely on long-standing constitutional law that an unwed biological father has an inchoate interest that develops into a fundamental right to be a parent protected by the Florida and United States Constitutions when he demonstrates a commitment to raising the child by assuming parental responsibilities. It is not the biological relationship per se, but rather "the assumption of the parental responsibilities which is of constitutional significance." *Matter of Adoption of Doe*, 543 So.2d 741, 748 (Fla.1989).

Because the application of section 742.14 operated to automatically deprive T.M.H. of her ability to assert her fundamental right to be a parent, we conclude, based on the circumstances of this case, that the statute is unconstitutional as applied under the Due Process Clauses of the Florida and United States Constitutions and under the privacy provision of the Florida Constitution. Further, we hold that section 742.14, in combination with the restrictive definition of the term "commissioning couple" in section 742.13(2), also violates state and federal equal protection by denying same-sex couples the statutory protection against the automatic relinquishment of parental rights that it affords to heterosexual unmarried couples seeking to utilize the identical assistance of reproductive technology.

Accordingly, we affirm the Fifth District's determination of statutory unconstitutionality and also answer the certified question in the affirmative, but we disapprove the Fifth District's holding that the statute does not apply in this situation. Our holding that T.M.H. has rights deserving of constitutional protection does not mean that D.M.T.'s parental rights are not deserving of constitutional protection—quite the opposite. Our decision does not deny D.M.T. the right to be a parent to her child, but requires only that T.M.H.'s right to be a parent of the child be constitutionally recognized. D.M.T.'s preference that she parent the child alone is sadly similar to the views of all too many parents who, after separating, prefer to exclude the other parent from the child's life. As the Fifth District wisely observed:

> [D.M.T.] suggests that because she and [T.M.H.] have separated, a choice must be made. She posits that, as the birth mother, she should have exclusive parental rights to the child and that [T.M.H.], as the biological mother, should have no rights at all. If we were to accept [D.M.T.'s] argument that a choice must be made between the two, perhaps a Solomonic approach to resolving this dispute would be preferable, but we are neither possessed of the wisdom of Solomon nor are we able to apply his particular methodology under the law as we know it today. Parental rights, which include the love and affection an individual has for his or her child, transcend the relationship between two consenting adults, and we see nothing in this record that makes either [T.M.H. or D.M.T.] an exception that places those rights in one to the exclusion of the other. It is unknown what caused these two women to cross the proverbial line between love and hate, but that is a matter between [T.M.H. and D.M.T.]. Their separation does not dissolve the parental rights of either woman to the child, nor does it dissolve the love and affection either has for the child.

T.M.H., 79 So.3d at 802–03.

We remain ever mindful that although our resolution of the constitutional issues revolves around the rights of T.M.H., the biological mother, we cannot and should not lose sight of the fact that there is a child at the center of this dispute whose best interests will ultimately determine the extent to which each parent will play a role in her life through legal rights and legal responsibilities. We therefore remand this case to the trial court to determine, based on the best interests of the child, issues such as parental time-sharing and child support, and we emphasize, as did the Fifth District, that an all-or-nothing choice between the two parents is not necessary.

FACTS AND PROCEDURAL HISTORY

The child at the center of this dispute was born on January 4, 2004. Her birth mother, D.M.T., and her biological mother, T.M.H., were in a long-term committed relationship at the time of the child's birth, and the child began her life by living with both parents. The Fifth District set forth the undisputed facts of this case as follows:

> [T.M.H.] and [D.M.T.] were involved in a committed relationship from 1995 until 2006. They lived together and owned real property as joint tenants, evidenced by a deed in the record. Additionally, both women deposited their income into a joint bank account and used those funds to pay their bills.
>
> The couple decided to have a baby that they would raise together as equal parental partners. They sought reproductive medical assistance, where they learned [D.M.T.] was infertile. [T.M.H.] and [D.M.T.], using funds from

their joint bank account, paid a reproductive doctor to withdraw ova from [T.M.H.], have them fertilized, and implant the fertilized ova into [D.M.T.]. The two women told the reproductive doctor that they intended to raise the child as a couple, and they went for counseling with a mental health professional to prepare themselves for parenthood. The in vitro fertilization procedure that was utilized proved successful, and a child was conceived.

The child was born in Brevard County on January 4, 2004. The couple gave the child a hyphenation of their last names. Although the birth certificate lists only [D.M.T.] as the mother and does not indicate a father, a maternity test revealed that there is a 99.99% certainty that [T.M.H.] is the biological mother of the child. [T.M.H.] and [D.M.T.] sent out birth announcements with both of their names declaring, "We Proudly Announce the Birth of Our Beautiful Daughter." Both women participated at their child's baptism, and they both took an active role in the child's early education.

The women separated in May 2006, and the child lived with [D.M.T.]. Initially, [T.M.H.] made regular child support payments, which [D.M.T.] accepted. [T.M.H.] ended the support payments when she and [D.M.T.] agreed to divide the child's time evenly between them. They continued to divide the costs of education.

T.M.H., 79 So.3d at 788–89.

Eventually, the couple's relationship severely deteriorated, and, as is all too commonly seen in child custody proceedings, one parent, D.M.T., unfortunately severed the other parent's, T.M.H.'s, contact with the daughter the couple had jointly planned for, conceived, and raised as a family. *Id.* Until that time, the child "did not distinguish between one [woman] being the biological or the birth parent." *Id.* at 789. Each party was simply a parent to this child up until and including the point at which D.M.T., the birth mother, absconded to an undisclosed location with the child after the parties' relationship soured. *See id.*

After finally locating the birth mother in Australia, T.M.H., the biological mother, served the birth mother with a petition to establish parental rights to the couple's child and for declaratory relief, including an adjudication of parentage pursuant to chapter 742, Florida Statutes (2008), and a declaration of statutory invalidity with respect to section 742.14, the assisted reproductive technology statute. *T.M.H.*, 79 So.3d at 789 n. 1, 799. Section 742.14 provides that, except in the case of a "commissioning couple"—defined in section 742.13 as the intended mother and father of a child who will be conceived through assisted reproductive technology using the biological material of at least one of the intended parents—and fathers who have executed a preplanned adoption agreement, an egg or sperm donor must relinquish any claim to parental rights or obligations to the donation or the resulting child. *See* §§ 742.13(2), 742.14, Fla. Stat.

In response to the biological mother's action, the birth mother filed a motion for summary judgment, alleging that the biological mother lacked parental rights as a matter of law regardless of the couple's original intent with respect to raising the child. The trial court held a hearing and granted the birth mother's summary judgment motion, explaining that it felt constrained by the current state of the law and expressing hope that an appellate court would reverse its ruling by stating as follows:

> First, let me say, I find that [the birth mother's] actions to be—this is my phraseology—morally reprehensible. I do not agree with her actions relevant to the best interest of the child. However, that is not the standard. *There is no distinction in law or recognition of rights of the biological mother verses a birth mother....*
>
> ....
>
> *Same-sex partners do not meet the definition [in section 742.13(2)] of commissioning couple.* There really is no protection for [the biological mother] under Florida law because she could not have adopted this child to prevent this current set of circumstances. I do not agree with the current state of the law, but I must uphold it....
>
> ....
>
> And, [to the biological mother], if you appeal this, I hope I'm wrong.

(Emphasis added.) The trial court therefore found both that the birth mother and the biological mother, as a same-sex couple, could not meet the definition of a "commissioning couple," as the term is defined in section 742.13(2) and used in section 742.14, to be exempt from the relinquishment of parental rights, and that Florida law does not recognize the rights of a biological mother versus a birth mother.

The biological mother appealed the trial court's ruling to the Fifth District Court of Appeal. Identifying this as a case of first impression in Florida, the Fifth District reversed the trial court's decision and held that the trial court's interpretation and application of the statute violated the biological mother's constitutional rights. *T.M.H.*, 79 So.3d at 800. Recognizing the rich body of federal and state constitutional law that would unquestionably give constitutionally protected rights to a biological father in the exact situation presented by the facts of this case, *id.* at 797–98, the Fifth District concluded that the biological mother is "entitled to constitutionally protected parental rights to the child and that the statutory relinquishment of those rights under section 742.14 is prohibited by the Federal and Florida Constitutions." *Id.* at 798.

In its analysis of the issues presented, the Fifth District reviewed the trial court's determination that the biological mother is a "donor" as that term is used in section 742.14 and that the statute therefore applies to deprive her of parental rights to her child. *Id.* at 790–91. Acknowledging that the facts in this case are undisputed, the Fifth District found that the biological mother "would not be a donor ... because she did not intend to give her ova away." *Id.* at 792. "Rather," the Fifth District explained, "she always intended to be a mother to the child born from her ova and was a mother to the child for several years after [the child's] birth." *Id.*

After concluding that section 742.14 did not apply to the biological mother, the Fifth District then addressed the birth mother's contention that the biological mother had relinquished her parental rights to the child, rejecting two aspects of this argument. First, the Fifth District explained that the biological mother's protected parental rights could not, consistent with the Florida and United States Constitutions, be extinguished through the trial court's application of section 742.14, stating as follows:

> Here, it is undisputed that [the biological mother] formed and maintained a parental relationship for several years after the child was born, and she did so as an equal parental partner with [the birth mother] who, for all that time, never suggested that [the biological mother] had relinquished her parental rights to her child. We believe that [the biological mother] has constitutionally protected rights as a genetic parent who has established a parental relationship with her genetic offspring that transcend the provisions of section 742.14.

Id. at 797.

Second, the Fifth District addressed and rejected the contention that the biological mother had relinquished her rights by signing an informed consent form in the reproductive doctor's office, concluding that the preprinted form did not constitute a waiver. *Id.* at 802. In explaining its reasoning regarding the "significant factors" that informed this conclusion, the Fifth District stated that "both women agreed to raise any child born with the ova supplied by [the biological mother] as equal parental partners and both women complied with that agreement for several years after the child was born." *Id.* at 801. The Fifth District found it "very revealing" that the birth mother "never attempted to assert this waiver claim until she decided to take the child to Australia and deprive [the biological mother] of any further contact with the child." *Id.*

Judge Monaco separately wrote a concurring opinion, which was joined by Judge Sawaya, further emphasizing the Fifth District's conclusion that section 742.14 does not apply to T.M.H. because the statute "was not designed to resolve the problem of how to treat children born by in vitro fertilization to a same-sex couple." *Id.* at 803 (Monaco, J., concurring). Judge Lawson dissented both as to the Fifth District's statutory construction and constitutional analysis, based on his belief that the birth mother is the sole legal mother of the child under established common law and Florida's statutory scheme. *Id.* at 805–06 (Lawson, J., dissenting).

ANALYSIS

With this factual and procedural background established, we now proceed to analyze the important constitutional issues presented in this case. Our analysis begins with a brief overview of the statutory provisions implicated, including our determination of whether section 742.14 is applicable to the circumstances presented. Concluding that the statute applies, we then turn to a discussion of T.M.H.'s constitutional challenges to the statute's validity. In this regard, we review the constitutional protections for parenting, determine the nature of T.M.H.'s interest, and analyze whether sections 742.13(2) and 742.14 violate the state and federal constitutional guarantees of due process, privacy, and equal protection. Finally, we address and reject D.M.T.'s argument that T.M.H. waived any interest she may have in the child by signing a standard informed consent form in the course of the couple's use of assisted reproductive technology to conceive a child.

I. Sections 742.13 and 742.14

In the decision below, the Fifth District determined that section 742.14, the assisted reproductive technology statute, did not apply to T.M.H., the biological mother, in this situation because she is not a "donor" as that term is used in the statute. We disagree with the Fifth District as to the statutory construction analysis because we conclude that the statute does, on its face, apply to T.M.H. as the provider of the egg for the couple.

Our interpretation of section 742.14 and the related provision in section 742.13 defining the term "commissioning couple," as well as our determination of the statutes' constitutionality, are pure questions of law, subject to de novo review.

* * *

Section 742.14, which is Florida's assisted reproductive technology statute, is entitled "Donation of eggs, sperm, or preembryos" and has provided as follows since 1993:

> The donor of any egg, sperm, or preembryo, *other than the commissioning couple or a father who has executed a preplanned adoption agreement* under s. 63.212, *shall relinquish all maternal or paternal rights and obligations* with respect to the donation or the resulting children. Only reasonable compensation directly related to the donation of eggs, sperm, and preembryos shall be permitted.

§ 742.14, Fla. Stat. (emphasis added). The term "commissioning couple," as used in section 742.14, is defined in section 742.13(2) as "the *intended mother and father* of a child who will be conceived by means of assisted reproductive technology using the eggs or sperm of at least one of the intended parents." § 742.13(2), Fla. Stat. (emphasis added).

The Fifth District concluded that the assisted reproductive technology statute did not apply to T.M.H. since she always intended to parent the child conceived through her provision of biological material to her partner. *T.M.H.*, 79 So.3d at 792, 803– 04. Therefore, according to the Fifth District, T.M.H. is not considered a "donor" as that term is used in the statute. *Id.*

We reject the Fifth District's construction of the assisted reproductive technology statute. The plain language of section 742.14 does not provide for the subjective intentions of someone in T.M.H.'s position to be taken into consideration in determining whether he or she is a "donor" under the terms of the statute. Rather, the statute identifies only two categories of individuals who do not relinquish parental rights as to their provision of biological material during the course of assisted reproductive technology—(1) members of a "commissioning couple"; and (2) fathers who have executed a preplanned adoption agreement. Indeed, the structure of section 742.14

designates these groups as fitting within the term "donor," and then provides that they are specifically exempted from the statutory relinquishment of parental rights. *See* § 742.14, Fla. Stat. If the statute did not apply to these groups, then they would not need to be exempted from its requirements.

In providing for these two exceptions, the Legislature expressed its intent not to allow the subjective intentions of all other individuals who provide eggs, sperm, or preembryos during the course of assisted reproductive technology to become an issue in need of litigation. *See Pro-Art Dental Lab, Inc. v. V-Strategic Group, LLC*, 986 So.2d 1244, 1258 (Fla.2008) ("Under the canon of statutory construction expressio unius est exclusio alterius, the mention of one thing implies the exclusion of another." (quoting *State v. Hearns*, 961 So.2d 211, 219 (Fla.2007))). Instead, the Legislature articulated a policy of treating all individuals who provide eggs, sperm, or preembryos as part of assisted reproductive technology as "donor[s]" bound by the terms of the statute, and then exempting two specific groups in accordance with the purpose behind the statutory enactment.

To hold that section 742.14 does not apply to T.M.H. in this case because of her subjective intention not to give her egg away would essentially create a third exception in the statute. This Court, however, is "not at liberty to add words to the statute that were not placed there by the Legislature." *Lawnwood Med. Ctr., Inc. v. Seeger*, 990 So.2d 503, 512 (Fla. 2008).

It is clear that the primary purpose behind the Legislature's enactment of the assisted reproductive technology statute was to ensure that couples taking advantage of medical advances in reproductive science to conceive a child are protected from a claim to parental rights by a third-party provider of the genetic material used for assisted reproductive technology. In this regard, we emphasize that our resolution of the constitutional issues presented in this case does not undermine the statutory protections or certainty provided to commissioning couples in any way. Rather, the specific constitutional question we address next is whether these very protections against the statutory relinquishment of parental rights can be denied to an unmarried woman who was part of a same-sex couple seeking the assistance of reproductive technology to conceive a child to jointly raise and who provided biological material to her partner with the specific intent to become a parent.

II. The Constitutionality of the Statutes

We begin our constitutional analysis of section 742.14, and the corresponding provision in section 742.13 defining the term "commissioning couple," by addressing T.M.H.'s due process and privacy arguments that application of the assisted reproductive technology statute abridges her fundamental right to be a parent. We then address the equal protection argument that section 742.14, in combination with section 742.13(2), unconstitutionally creates an unreasonable classification based on sexual orientation. We hold that section 742.14 is unconstitutional as applied on each basis under both the United States Constitution and separately under the Florida Constitution.

* * *

It is so ordered.

QUINCE, LABARGA, and PERRY, JJ., concur.

348 POLSTON, C.J., dissents with an opinion in which LEWIS and CANADY, JJ., concur.

* * *

Commentary

Note that judicial review of a decision declaring a statute invalid is mandatory, but is merely permissive when a court expressly declares a statute valid. Why does the constitution refer to "express" validation of a statute but not to "express" invalidation of one? Note that Section 3(b)(1) does not allow the court to review unelaborated per curiam DCA decisions, as they do not "declare" a statute invalid. *Jackson v. State*, 926 So. 2d 1262 (Fla. 2006).

b. Review of Proposed Amendments to the Constitution

This jurisdiction is embodied in two constitutional provisions and further informed by a statute, Florida Statutes § 101.161(3)(c).

The statute provides that courts may hear challenges to the propriety of a ballot summary or explanatory statement of constitutional amendments proposed by the Legislature or by an initiative. While it, like these constitutional provisions, deals with judicial approval of proposed constitutional amendments, it does not deal directly with Supreme Court evaluation of proposals in response to a request by the Attorney General. In addition, though the statute does not mention amendments proposed by either the Constitution Revision Commission or the Tax and Budget Reform Commission, courts, including the Florida Supreme Court, have heard challenges to proposals by those bodies, and based them on § 101.161.

Advisory Opinion to the Attorney General re Raising Florida's Minimum Wage

285 So. 3d 1273 (Fla. 2019)

PER CURIAM.

The Attorney General of Florida has petitioned this Court for an advisory opinion on the validity of a proposed citizen initiative amendment to the Florida Constitution and the corresponding financial impact statement prepared by the Financial Impact Estimating Conference (FIEC). We have jurisdiction to review the initiative petition. See art. IV, § 10; art. V, § 3(b)(10), Fla. Const. As explained below, we approve the proposed amendment titled "Raising Florida's Minimum Wage" for placement on the ballot but decline to review the financial impact statement because we lack jurisdiction to do so.

PROCEDURAL HISTORY

As required by law, the Attorney General requested an opinion from this Court addressing the validity of an initiative petition titled "Raising Florida's Minimum Wage."

Specifically, the Attorney General requested that we review the compliance of the proposed amendment with the single-subject requirement of article XI, section 3 of the Florida Constitution, and the compliance of the ballot title and summary with the substantive and technical requirements of section 101.161(1), Florida Statutes (2018).1 In addition, the Attorney General requested an opinion from this Court addressing the compliance of the corresponding financial impact statement with section 100.371, Florida Statutes (2019). We invited briefing as to the validity of the initiative petition and the financial impact statement but received none. See art. IV, § 10; Fla. R. App. P. 9.510(c)(1). Thereafter, we directed the Attorney General and all interested parties to file briefs addressing whether this Court has jurisdiction to review the financial impact statement. We received only one brief, from the Attorney General, which argues that we have jurisdiction.

LEGAL BACKGROUND

The people of Florida have the power to propose amendments to the state constitution by initiative under article XI, section 3 of the Florida Constitution. Once an initiative petition is circulated and meets certain technical requirements, *see* § 15.21, Fla. Stat. (2019), the Attorney General is constitutionally and statutorily required to seek this Court's opinion on the validity of the petition. Art. IV, § 10; § 16.061(1), Fla. Stat. (2019). The constitution directs us to "address[] issues as provided by general law" when the Attorney General invokes our jurisdiction to review initiative petitions. Art. V, § 3(b)(10), Fla. Const.

1

Under the authority provided by article V, section 3(b)(10) of the Florida Constitution, and as directed by article IV, section 10, we conduct a limited review of an initiative petition. *See Advisory Op. to Att'y Gen. re Prohib. State Spending for Experimentation that Involves Destruction of a Live Human Embryo*, 959 So. 2d 210, 212, 214 (Fla. 2007). Our review does "not address the merits or wisdom of the proposed amendment," but rather, the compliance of the petition with the requirements of the Florida constitution and statutes. *Id.* at 212 (quoting *Advisory Op. to Att'y Gen. re Fla. Marriage Prot. Amend.*, 926 So. 2d 1229, 1233 (Fla. 2006)).

Specifically, regardless of whether we receive arguments on the validity of an initiative petition, we review the petition to ensure the following: (A) that the proposed amendment "embrace[s] but one subject and matter directly connected therewith" (except when the proposed amendment limits the power of government to raise revenue), art. XI, § 3, Fla. Const., and (B) that the petition includes a ballot title and summary in compliance with the word-count, clarity, and content requirements of section 101.161(1), Florida Statutes. *See Prohib. State Spending for Experimentation that Involves Destruction of a Live Human Embryo*, 959 So. 2d at 211 n.1, 212–15.

ANALYSIS

We first address the compliance of the proposed amendment with the single-subject rule and compliance of the ballot title and summary with section 101.161(1). Then, we turn to the question of our jurisdiction to review financial impact statements.

A. Single-Subject Rule

This Court has held that, to comply with the single-subject rule, the proposed amendment must "manifest a 'logical and natural oneness of purpose'" and not "substantially alter[] or perform[] the functions of multiple branches" of government.

* * *

The proposed amendment clearly addresses only one subject, raising the minimum wage, and it does not substantially alter or perform the functions of multiple branches of government. Although it may affect contracts entered into and wages paid by each branch of government, these effects are incidental to the chief purpose of the amendment, which is not to alter or perform any governmental function

* * *

B. Ballot Title and Summary

* * *

To determine whether the ballot title and summary meet the requirements of section 101.161(1), we assess whether their language "fairly inform[s] the voter of the chief purpose of the amendment" and whether it misleads the public, keeping in mind that the ballot title and summary need to be "accurate and informative" but need not "discuss every detail or consequence of the amendment." ... We find no basis to reject the proposed ballot title and summary under section 101.161(1).

C. Financial Impact Statement

We previously concluded, in *Advisory Opinion to the Attorney General re Referenda Required for Adoption*, 963 So. 2d 210, 210 (Fla. 2007), that we have jurisdiction to review financial impact statements. We now conclude that this determination was clearly erroneous and, because we cannot exercise jurisdiction that the constitution does not provide, recede from it.

Our jurisdiction is defined in article V, section 3 of the Florida Constitution. The only provision of article V, section 3 that has been argued as providing jurisdiction to review financial impact statements is section 3(b)(10), which provides that this Court "[s]hall, when requested by the attorney general pursuant to the provisions of Section 10 of Article IV, render an advisory opinion of the justices, addressing issues as provided by general law." Because article V, section 3(b)(10) references the portion of the constitution that requires the Attorney General to seek our review of initiative petitions, art. IV, § 10, and that provision in turn references the provision of the constitution recognizing the right to file an initiative petition, art. XI, § 3, article V, section 3(b)(10) is best presented by beginning with the portion of the constitution addressing initiative petitions, proceeding to consider the portion of the constitution directing the Attorney General to seek our opinion on initiative petitions, and then reviewing the text of article V, section 3(b)(10).

* * *

Notably, none of the three [above] provisions mention financial impact statements.

Financial impact statements are addressed in a different provision of the constitution, article XI, section 5(c). Article XI, section 5(c) states, "The legislature shall provide by general law, prior to the holding of an election pursuant to this section, for the provision of a statement to the public regarding the probable financial impact of any amendment proposed by initiative pursuant to section 3 [of article XI]."

* * *

Having reached this conclusion based on the plain language of the constitution, and recognizing that this Court does not create its own jurisdiction, but rather exercises the jurisdiction provided by the constitution, we are not at liberty to adhere to our precedent Although the Legislature has the authority to revise the statutes to provide for review in a court not constrained by our constitutionally limited original jurisdiction, or perhaps to make a financial impact statement a component of an initiative petition, which would change our jurisdictional analysis, we cannot exercise subject matter jurisdiction that we do not have. To do so would be to engage in an action that is a nullity. *See Mannino v. Mannino*, 980 So. 2d 575, 577 (Fla. 2d DCA 2008); *Fedan Corp. v. Reina*, 695 So. 2d 1282, 1283 (Fla. 3d DCA 1997).

* * *

CONCLUSION

For the foregoing reasons, we conclude that the initiative petition and proposed ballot title and summary for the proposed amendment "Raising Florida's Minimum Wage" meet the legal requirements of article XI, section 3 of the Florida Constitution and section 101.161(1). Accordingly, we approve the amendment for placement on the ballot. We express no opinion on the validity of the financial impact statement.

It is so ordered.

CANADY, C.J., and POLSTON, LABARGA, LAWSON, and MUÑIZ, JJ., concur.

ii. Discretionary Jurisdiction

a. Conflict Jurisdiction

Jenkins v. State

385 So. 2d 1356 (Fla. 1980)

SUNDBERG, Justice.

We here address the question whether this Court currently has jurisdiction to review a decision of a district court of appeal which reads in its entirety "Per Curiam Affirmed" where a dissenting opinion is filed in the case. We answer the question in the negative.

Review of the decision of the District Court of Appeal, Fourth District, was sought in this cause by notice to invoke the certiorari jurisdiction of this Court filed April 11, 1980. By his application petitioner asserts that the decision of the district court is in conflict with decisions of other districts or with Supreme Court decisions upon the issue of whether uncorroborated hearsay information from a confidential informant, who had not divulged the source of his information, was sufficient to establish probable cause for a warrantless search of a vehicle. Prior to trial, petitioner moved to suppress evidence seized in a search of his vehicle. The trial court denied the motion to suppress. Petitioner subsequently entered a plea of nolo contendere preserving his right to appeal the trial court ruling. On review the district court affirmed the ruling of the trial court without opinion. One member of the three-judge panel dissented to the decision of the majority in a comprehensive opinion which recited the facts extensively and concluded that under prevailing law the search violated petitioner's fourth amendment rights.

After ratification by the people of this state at an election held on March 11, 1980, article V, section 3 of the Florida Constitution pertaining to the jurisdiction of the Supreme Court was substantially revised. In particular, section 3(b)(3) underwent a dramatic change. Prior to April 1, 1980 (the effective date of the amendment), the provisions of section 3(b)(3) relating to review of conflicting decisions read as follows:

> May review by certiorari any decision of a district court of appeal ... that is in direct conflict with a decision of any district court of appeal or of the supreme court on the same question of law....

Post April 1, 1980, that section reads with respect to review of conflicting decisions:

> May review any decision of a district court of appeal ... that expressly and directly conflicts with a decision of another district court of appeal or of the supreme court on the same question of law....

(Emphasis supplied.)

The constitutional amendment must be viewed in light of the historical development of the decisional law extant at the time of its adoption and the intent of the framers and adopters. Our inquiry must begin with the amendment to article V of the Florida Constitution occurring in 1956, whereby the district courts of appeal were created. In grappling with the significance of the revised jurisdiction of this Court, a tone was set early on. In *Ansin v. Thurston*, 101 So.2d 808, 810 (Fla.1958), speaking through Justice Drew, the Court said:

> We have heretofore pointed out that under the constitutional plan the powers of this Court to review decisions of the district courts of appeal are limited and strictly prescribed. *Diamond Berk Insurance Agency, Inc. v. Goldstein*, Fla., 100 So.2d 420; *Sinnamon v. Fowlkes*, Fla., 101 So.2d 375. It was never intended that the district courts of appeal should be intermediate courts. The revision and modernization of the Florida judicial system at the appellate level was prompted by the great volume of cases reaching the Supreme Court and the consequent delay in the administration of justice. The new article embodies throughout its terms the idea of a Supreme Court which functions as a supervisory body in the judicial system for the State, exercising appellate power in certain specified areas essential to the settlement

of issues of public importance and the preservation of uniformity of principle and practice, with review by the district courts in most instances being final and absolute.

To fail to recognize that these are courts primarily of final appellate jurisdiction and to allow such courts to become intermediate courts of appeal would result in a condition far more detrimental to the general welfare and the speedy and efficient administration of justice than that which the system was designed to remedy.

This was followed by *Lake v. Lake*, 103 So.2d 639 (Fla.1958), where Justice Thomas again reviewed the history of and purposes for the 1956 amendment to article V and held that in order to fulfill those purposes, a "per curiam" decision without opinion of a district court of appeal would not be reviewed by this Court upon petition for certiorari based on "direct conflict" jurisdiction except in those rare cases where the "restricted examination required in proceedings in certiorari (revealed) that a conflict had arisen with resulting injustice to the immediate litigant." *Id.* at 643. Some seven years later, however, in an opinion which observed that the rule of *Lake v. Lake* had been eroded *de facto* if not *de jure* by subsequent actions of the Court, a majority of the Court determined that there was jurisdictional power under section 3(b)(3) to review district court decisions rendered "per curiam" without opinion if from the "record proper" conflict with another decision could be discerned. *Foley v. Weaver Drugs, Inc.*, 177 So.2d 221 (Fla.1965).

In the interim the Court had already concluded that conflict certiorari jurisdiction could be founded on a dissenting opinion to a per curiam majority decision rendered without opinion. *Huguley v. Hall*, 157 So.2d 417 (Fla.1963). This position was adopted by a majority of the Court without discussion or rationale and has been subsequently followed without amplification of reasoning. *E.g., Autrey v. Carroll*, 240 So.2d 474 (Fla.1970); *Commerce Nat'l Bank in Lake Worth v. Safeco Ins. Co.*, 284 So.2d 205 (Fla.1973). In the *Commerce National Bank* decision, however, the impediments to relying on the factual statement contained in a dissenting opinion to establish conflict jurisdiction were observed:

> When facts and testimony are set forth in a majority opinion, they are assumed to be an accurate presentation upon which the judgment of the court is based. However, a dissent does not rise to a similar level of dignity and is not considered as precedent; note, for example, that West Publishing Company does not offer headnotes for dissents, regardless of their legal scholarship. By definition, a dissent contains information, interpretations or legal analysis which has been rejected in whole or part, by the majority. It is also possible that the majority accepts matters set forth in the dissent, but for other reasons declines to follow its line of thought. The majority is under no compulsion to respond to a dissent or to set out the measure of their reluctance to agree. The issuance of a per curiam opinion without comment or citation of authority remains the prerogative of the majority.

Id. at 207.

More recently, the wisdom of the jurisdictional policies expressed in *Foley* and *Huguley* have been brought into question by several members of this Court. [citations omitted.]

It was against this jurisprudential backdrop and in the face of a staggering case load that in November, 1979, this Court urged the legislature, meeting in special session, to enact a proposed amendment to section 3 of article V of the Florida Constitution to limit the jurisdiction of the Supreme Court. Times were not unlike the year 1956 when the challenge confronting the drafters of that amendment to the judicial article was described thus:

> The means and procedure required to accomplish the improvement were difficult, complicated, tedious and onerous.
>
> Yet the determination was not lacking for congestion in the court of last resort had become almost intolerable. The time had come when the court, working at top speed, with cases, except extremely emergent ones, set in the order of their maturity, was hearing arguments as late as fourteen months after the cases were ready for oral presentation.
>
> * * *
>
> For about eighteen months after its creation the (Judicial) Council, in periodic meetings, debated and deliberated the method which might most effectively modernize a system that by overloading had ceased to function as it should to assure litigants justice without undue, or even ruinous, delay. The words of Gladstone were often heard: "Justice delayed is justice denied."

Lake v. Lake, 103 So.2d 639, 640–41. The legislature responded through enactment of Senate Joint Resolution No. 20-C, which forms the language of the current section 3 of article V.

At hearings before the legislature and in countless meetings with representatives of The Florida Bar, The Conference of Circuit Judges of Florida, the Appellate Judges' Conference, The League of Women Voters as well as other interested organizations too numerous to recount, members of this Court represented that one of the intents and effects of the revision of section 3(b)(3) was to eliminate the jurisdiction of the Supreme Court to review for conflict purposes per curiam decisions of the district courts of appeal rendered without opinion, regardless of the existence of a concurring or dissenting opinion. These same representations were made consistently to the public at large preceding the ballot on the proposed amendment. There can be little doubt that the electorate was informed as to this matter, because opponents of the amendment broadcast from one end of this state to the other that access to the Supreme Court was being "cut off," and that the district courts of appeal would be the only and final courts of appeal in this state. With regard to review by conflict certiorari of per curiam decisions rendered without opinion, they were absolutely correct.

The pertinent language of section 3(b)(3), as amended April 1, 1980, leaves no room for doubt. This Court may only review a decision of a district court of appeal that *expressly* and directly conflicts with a decision of another district court of appeal or the Supreme Court on the same question of law. The dictionary definitions of the term "express" include: "to represent in words"; "to give expression to." "Expressly" is defined: "in an express manner." *Webster's Third New International Dictionary* (1961 ed. unabr.). The single word "affirmed" comports with none of these definitions. Furthermore, the language and expressions found in a dissenting or concurring opinion cannot support jurisdiction under section 3(b)(3) because they are not the *decision* of the district court of appeal. As stated by Justice Adkins in *Gibson v. Maloney*, 231 So.2d 823, 824 (Fla.1970), "(i)t is conflict of *decisions* not conflict of *opinions* or *reasons* that supplies jurisdiction for review by certiorari." (Emphasis in original.)

Accordingly, we hold that from and after April 1, 1980, the Supreme Court of Florida lacks jurisdiction to review per curiam decisions of the several district courts of appeal of this state rendered without opinion, regardless of whether they are accompanied by a dissenting or concurring opinion, when the basis for such review is an alleged conflict of that decision with a decision of another district court of appeal or of the Supreme Court. The application for review in the instant case having been filed subsequent to March 31, 1980, it is therefore dismissed.

ENGLAND, C. J., and BOYD, OVERTON, ALDERMAN and McDONALD, JJ., concur.

ADKINS, Justice, dissenting.

I dissent.

We are embarking on a course which limits our jurisdiction to matters concerning deep questions of law, while the great bulk of litigants are allowed to founder on rocks of uncertainty and trial judges steer their course over a chaotic reef as they attempt to apply "Per Curiam Affirmed" decisions. When the constitutional amendment is considered in light of historical development of the decisional law (as suggested by the majority), we find regression instead of progression. The majority admits that many will not obtain justice for our jurisdiction will be limited to resolving questions of importance to the public as distinguished from that of the parties. In *Ansin v. Thurston*, 101 So.2d 808, 811 (Fla.1958), cited by the majority, the Court said:

> (T)here should be developed consistent rules for limiting issuance of the writ of certiorari to "cases involving principles the settlement of which is of importance to the public, as distinguished from that of the parties, and in cases where there is a real and embarrassing conflict of opinion and authority" between decisions.

The opinion in *Ansin v. Thurston, supra* was authored by Justice Drew. This interpretation lasted for seven years and then a progressive Court adopted *Foley v. Weaver Drugs, Inc.*, 177 So.2d 221 (Fla.1965). The rule in *Ansin* had created problems which were resolved in *Foley*. In a special concurring opinion in *Foley*, Justice Drew said:

> Many problems have arisen in the interpretation of amended Article V. But there has been no dispute that under the constitutional plan for the admin-

istration of justice at the appellate level in this State the responsibility was placed in this Court to keep the law harmonious and uniform.... We must assume, in the absence of something in the record to indicate a contrary view, that an affirmance of a decision of a trial court by a decision of the District Court of Appeal makes the trial court decision the decision of the District Court. So far as the trial judge is concerned and so far as the Bench and Bar who are familiar with the decision of the trial judge are concerned, such judgment is the law of that jurisdiction. I think it would result in utter chaos in the judicial system of this State with three separate District Courts, and the possibility of a fourth in the near future, if it were impossible for this Court to maintain consistency and uniformity of the law in such cases. A different rule of law could prevail in every appellate district without the possibility of correction. The history of similar courts in this country leads to the conclusion that some of such courts have proven unsatisfactory simply because of the impossibility of maintaining uniformity in the decisional law of such state.

177 So.2d at 230.

In *Seaboard Air Lines Railroad Company v. Williams*, 199 So.2d 469, 472 (Fla.1967), Justice Drew reiterated his views, saying:

In my concurring opinion in *Foley v. Weaver Drugs*, Fla.1965, 177 So.2d 221, I observed: "I think it would result in utter chaos in the judicial system of this State with three separate District Courts, and the possibility of a fourth in the near future, if it were impossible for this Court to maintain consistency and uniformity of the law in (decisions of such district courts merely affirming without opinion) * * *." What has occurred in this case fulfills that prophecy. I, therefore, concur in the foregoing majority opinion.

Under the construction proposed by the majority we will have well-written uniform opinions, but the decisions of the five district courts of appeal will be in hopeless conflict.

The majority says there was little doubt "that the electorate was informed" and proceeds to construe a purported constitutional amendment, the terms of which were not placed on the ballot nor were they explained to the public. While discussions with some segments of the public on background and debates concerning the proposed amendment were instructive, nevertheless, what was submitted to the people for adoption was a statement on the ballot which read: "(p)roposing an amendment to the State Constitution to modify the jurisdiction of the Supreme Court." In discussing the proposed amendment, one news analyst contended:

The ballot says simply that the proposal would "modify the jurisdiction of the Supreme Court," giving the public little insight into the changes it would make in court appeals procedures.

Given the complex nature of those procedures, few voters understand the issue.

Van Gieson, *Reform Sought to Ease Court's Load*, Tallahassee Democrat, March 9, 1980 at 5b, col. 1.

A pamphlet entitled "Constitutional Amendments on Florida Supreme Court Jurisdiction ... to be Considered at March 11, 1980, Election" prepared by Manning J. Dauer and Fred Goddard discussed the content of the change in the constitution as follows:

The proposed change to Article 5 does not modify the organization of the State Supreme Court. There was a proposal from the Supreme Court to permit all justices of the State Supreme Court to be from the state at large. The legislature, however, retained subsection A of Section 3 which requires at least one of the justices to be from each of the districts in which the state is divided for district courts of appeal. In sub-section B there are a number of modifications as to the jurisdiction of the Supreme Court. The attempt has been made to retain appellate jurisdiction for the most important cases involving new point of law, the death penalty, constitutional questions, affecting the state constitution or that of the U.S., affecting the construction of new statutes passed by the legislature, *affecting disagreements among two or more district courts of appeal*, affecting bond validation, and affecting certain cases certified for review by the district courts of appeal. Also, the jurisdiction of the Supreme Court has been changed in one case category, that is, cases from administrative agencies of the state affecting rates charged to consumers or service provided by the electric utilities and gas and phone companies.

On the other hand, many other types of cases will be cut off with the appeal being exhausted at the level of the district courts of appeal. For example, cases involving life imprisonment will now be constitutionally limited to the level of the appellate district court unless the case involves a constitution question, a new statute, or a disagreement in construction among district courts. Writs of certiorari (requests for appeal) would be much more limited. Appeals from state administrative agencies' decisions would ordinarily stop at the district courts of appeal. The Supreme Court would retain, of course, the right to issue writs of certiorari, writs of habeas corpus, writs of prohibition, writs of injunction, and writs of mandamus when it entertained jurisdiction.

The aim of these and other changes is to reduce the caseload on the Supreme Court. The estimate given by the Court is that instead of handling 3000 cases per year, the changes will permit the reduction of the caseload from 3000 to 2000 or less. At the same time, the citizen will be guaranteed justice by having cases heard more quickly and by appeals being adequately considered at the district court level. Finally, in the categories of new issues, or *in case of disagreement by lower courts*, review is still available at the level of the State Supreme Court.

Dauer, *Amendment to Limit Appellate Jurisdiction of the Florida State Supreme Court*, 62 Pub.Ad. Clearing Service, Univ. of Fla. Civic Information Ser. 2, 4–5, (1980). (Emphasis supplied.)

The proposed amendment was conceived and composed by the justices of this Court. After the proposal was approved by the legislature, it was decided to place the proposed amendment on the ballot at a special election. See article XI, section 5(a), Florida Constitution. Hopefully, this special election would create interest in the voting populace because it was a special presidential primary election in which a popular homestead amendment giving tax relief would also be considered. The substance of the amendment to be placed on the ballot (section 101.151, Florida Statutes), was as follows: "An amendment to the State Constitution to modify the jurisdiction of the Supreme Court." Justices of the Court and others attempted to explain the contents of the proposed amendment to the public, and there were many discussions.

While the discussions relating to the intent of the framers, referred to by the majority, were instructive as to background, nevertheless, there was only one provision submitted to the voters for adoption: "an amendment to the state constitution to modify the jurisdiction of the supreme court." Any discussions or debate which may have taken place does not change the provision on the ballot that was approved by the voters. *See In Re Advisory Opinion*, 223 So.2d 35, 40 (Fla.1969). Construing this provision (as placed upon the ballot) under the ordinary rules of construction, the voters gave us absolute discretion in determining whether we had jurisdiction of a particular case.

Also, I disagree with the judgment of the majority that language and expressions found in a dissenting or concurring opinion cannot support jurisdiction. The effect of the 1980 amendment is to give us jurisdiction for review of a decision that expressly and directly conflicts with a decision of another district court of appeal. A "Per Curiam Affirmed" is a decision, but no decision can be rendered unless three judges of the district court of appeal participate. Art. V, §4(a), Fla.Const. (1972). A concurring or dissenting opinion is used by trial judges throughout the state in determining the effect of a "Per Curiam Affirmed" decision. We should glance through the window of our ivory tower and attempt to adjust any confusion in the law which may arise by virtue of statements made in a concurring or dissenting opinion, as it is an integral part of the decision of the district courts of appeal.

There will be occasions when a "Per Curiam Affirmed" decision will cite another case. In some instances the cited case had admittedly been in conflict with other decisions, but, because of the failure of the parties to seek our jurisdiction, the law remained unsettled. Under the construction of the present constitutional amendment, the law will remain unsettled. A heavy case load does not justify our spawning confusion in the judicial system.

The decision of the district court of appeal conflicts with other decisions and creates instability in the law. I would accept jurisdiction.

Questions

1. According to the majority, what is the role of:

    a. the District Courts of Appeal?

    b. the Florida Supreme Court?

2. According to the majority:

    a. What is the fate of Per Curiam Affirmed (PCA) decisions without opinions?

    b. Explain the Court's reasoning.

    c. What is the fate of PCAs which have a dissenting opinion, and why?

3. Distinguish between Section 3(3) and Section 3(4) of Article V.

Dodi Publishing Co. v. Editorial America, S.A.
385 So. 2d 1369 (Fla. 1980)

OVERTON, Justice.

This is a petition filed April 7, 1980, seeking review of the following per curiam opinion of the Third District Court of Appeal:

> PER CURIAM.
>
> Affirmed. See *Consolidated Electric Supply, Inc. v. Consolidated Electrical Distributors Southeast, Inc.*, 355 So.2d 853 (Fla. 3d DCA 1978).

The petitioner contends that the cited case, *Consolidated Electric Supply, Inc. v. Consolidated Electrical Distributors Southeast, Inc.*, conflicts with *Williamson v. Answer Phone of Jacksonville*, 118 So.2d 248 (Fla. 1st DCA 1960), and therefore the instant opinion conflicts with another Florida appellate decision.

The jurisdiction of this Court in this cause is controlled by section 3(b)(3) of article V of the Constitution of the State of Florida, as amended March 11, 1980, effective April 1, 1980, which provides that the Supreme Court: "May review any decision of a district court of appeal ... that expressly and directly conflicts with a decision of another district court of appeal or of the supreme court on the same question of law." A full discussion of the history and purpose of section 3 of article V, as amended, is contained in *Jenkins v. State*, No. 59,087, 385 So.2d 1356 (Fla. June 26, 1980).

We reject the assertion that we should reexamine a case cited in a per curiam decision to determine if the contents of that cited case now conflict with other appellate decisions. The issue to be decided from a petition for conflict review is whether there is express and direct conflict in the decision of the district court before us for review, not whether there is conflict in a prior written opinion which is now cited for authority.

The petition is dismissed.

SUNDBERG, C. J., and BOYD, ENGLAND, ALDERMAN and McDONALD, JJ., concur.

ADKINS, J., dissents for reasons expressed in *Jenkins*.

Jollie v. State   *one year later*
405 So. 2d 418 (Fla. 1981)

PER CURIAM.

This case involves the legal issue we recently resolved in *Tascano v. State*, 393 So.2d 540 (Fla. 1980), and a procedural issue regarding the jurisdiction of this Court which requires clarification in light of the 1980 amendment to article V, section 3, of the Florida Constitution. It is the latter issue which commands our attention here, and for which a recitation of the history of this case and of conflicting decisions on the *Tascano* issue is essential.

On January 2, 1980, the Fifth District Court of Appeal addressed a legal issue concerning requested jury instructions on which disparate views were then held among the district courts of the state. In *Murray v. State*, 378 So.2d 111 (Fla. 5th DCA 1980), a majority of the panel court concluded that this Court's rule on requested instructions was mandatory. A contrary view had been expressed by a panel of judges in the First District Court of Appeal in *Tascano v. State*, 363 So.2d 405 (Fla. 1st DCA 1978). Despite their conclusion on the mandatory nature of the rule, however, the panel majority in *Murray* affirmed his conviction on the ground that the failure to give requested instructions in his situation was harmless error. Judge Orfinger agreed with the *Tascano* judges that the Court's rule was optional, for which reason he concurred in the court's affirmance of Murray's conviction.

Other cases involving this very legal issue were pending in the Fifth District. Shortly after the *Murray* decision was published, the court entered orders summarily disposing of three of them — *Knight v. State*, 379 So.2d 1017 (Fla. 5th DCA 1980), *Allen v. State*, 380 So.2d 541 (Fla. 5th DCA 1980), and *Jollie v. State*, 381 So.2d 351 (Fla. 5th DCA 1980). Each of these dispositions read simply:

"Affirmed. See *Murray v. State* (citation)."

Petitions for certiorari were filed here in *Murray*, *Knight*, and *Allen* before April 1, 1980. A petition for review was filed in *Jollie* after that date. The intervention of the 1980 amendment placed Mr. Jollie in a different position than Messrs. Murray, Knight, or Allen with respect to the possibility of Supreme Court review. That fortuity, it will be seen, has created the procedural problem we now face.

We agreed to review the First District's *Tascano* decision, and we eventually declared that our rule regarding requested jury instructions is indeed mandatory, quashing the district court's contrary decision. *Tascano v. State*, 393 So.2d 540 (Fla. 1980). We accepted jurisdiction in *Murray* on the basis of direct jurisdictional conflict. The *Murray* decision conflicted on its face with the First District's decision in *Tascano* by holding that the rule was mandatory rather than directory and conflicted with the result we reached in *Tascano* because it negated the mandatory effect of the rule by applying the harmless error doctrine. We have consequently this day, by separate opinion, quashed the district court's opinion in *Murray* on the basis of *Tascano*, concluding that the harmless error rule should not apply. *Murray v. State*, 403 So.2d 417 (Fla. 1981). We have also accepted jurisdiction in *Knight* and *Allen* under the 1972 constitutional provision and granted relief in accordance with our decisions in *Tascano* and *Murray*. *Knight v. State*, 401 So.2d 1333 (Fla. 1981).

Petitioner Jollie's treatment by the Fifth District Court of Appeal was identical to that of Allen and Knight. Jollie, however, became the victim of happenstance, delayed processing through the district court resulting in his case reaching this Court after the effective date of the 1980 constitutional amendment limiting Supreme Court jurisdiction.

Under our interpretation of the 1980 amendment, this Court will not reexamine the case referenced in a "citation PCA" to determine whether the contents of that case now conflict with other appellate decisions. *Dodi Publishing Co. v. Editorial America, S.A.*, 385 So.2d 1369 (Fla. 1980). In a similar light, if the referenced case is a final decision and not pending review in this Court, we will not reexamine the case referenced even when the district court filed that case contemporaneously with the citation PCA. *Robles Del Mar, Inc. v. Town of Indian River Shores*, 385 So.2d 1371 (Fla. 1980). The question which we must now confront is in what posture we should place a citation PCA where the cited case is either pending review in this Court or has previously been reversed by this Court. Restated, we must decide whether Mr. Jollie should be denied relief because he was the recipient of such a decision after the effective date of the 1980 amendment.

The quartet of *Tascano*-related cases from the Fifth District Court of Appeal presents the problem in sharp focus. We here endeavor to deal with this situation in a forthright manner in order to provide clear directions for the avoidance of future difficulties in like situations. This can be done without undermining the intent and purpose of the 1980 reforms.

Justice Thomas, the father of Florida's district courts of appeal and the strongest advocate of the principle that the district courts "were meant to be courts of final appellate jurisdiction," said this Court had no authority to "dig into a record to determine whether or not a per curiam affirmance by a district court of appeal conflicts." See *Lake v. Lake*, 103 So.2d 639, 642–43 (Fla. 1958).

> If in a particular case an opinion is rendered by a district court of appeal that *prima facie* conflicts with the decision of another district court of appeal or of the Supreme Court on the same point of law, the writ of certiorari may issue, and after study, may be discharged, or the decision of the district court of appeal may be quashed or modified to the end that any conflict may be reconciled.

Id. at 643 (emphasis ours). This rule applies equally well under the 1980 amendment as it did under the amendment's 1956 predecessor.

Prior to the 1980 amendment, a PCA decision which referenced another district court decision that this Court had reversed or quashed, was prima facie grounds for conflict jurisdiction. This long-standing policy decision was in effect well before the "record proper" doctrine was conceived and adopted in *Foley v. Weaver Drugs*, 177 So.2d 221 (Fla. 1965). The reasoning behind that policy decision continues to have validity. Common sense dictates that this Court must acknowledge its own public record actions in dispensing with cases before it. We thus conclude that a district court of appeal per curiam opinion which cites as controlling authority a decision that is either pending review in or has been reversed by this Court continues to constitute prima facie express conflict and allows this Court to exercise its jurisdiction.

The situation presented in this cause ordinarily applies only to a limited class of cases. The problem arises from the practical situation which faces all appellate courts at one time or another—that is, how to dispose conveniently of multiple cases involving a single legal issue without disparately affecting the various litigants. Traditional practice in dealing with a common legal issue in multiple cases, both in district courts and here, has been to author an opinion for one case and summarily reference that opinion on all the others. Being time- and laborsaving for a court, that practice should not be discouraged.

We believe, however, that there can be improvement in the procedure through which district courts can isolate for possible review in this Court those decisions which merely reference to a lead opinion, as we now have for review, as distinguished from those per curiam opinions which merely cite counsel-advising cases such as in *Dodi Publishing*. There are two prongs to the problem, and we believe each can be treated by the judges of the district courts without undue problems.

First, we suggest the district courts add an additional sentence in each citation PCA which references a controlling contemporaneous or companion case, stating that the mandate will be withheld pending final disposition of the petition for review, if any, filed in the controlling decision. In essence, this will "pair" the citation PCA with the referenced decision in the district court until it is final without review, or if review is sought, until that review is denied or otherwise acted upon by this Court. If review of the referenced decision is requested, the parties may seek consolidation here. In any event, the district courts' withholding of the mandates will dispose of the need for separate motions to stay mandates in those courts. This simple process, moreover, can be accomplished administratively in the district courts, in the clerks' offices, without significant activity by the judges either before or after the controlling decision is filed with or acted upon by this Court.

A second aspect of the problem calls for a different approach. We recognize that no litigant can guide the district court's selection of the lead case, and that the randomness of the district court's processing would control the party's right of review unless the citation PCA is itself made eligible for review by this Court. To resolve fully this problem, we further suggest that the district courts devise one or more methods to distinguish a contemporaneous or companion case—for example, with distinguishing citation signals or by certifying that an identical point is at issue in the cited case[11]—from cases which offer a mere counsel notification citation. We have no doubt that district court judges can produce one or more methodologies to preserve the review strictures of the 1980 amendment on the one hand, while on the other eliminating the possible injustice inherent in foreclosing review to some of several equally situated litigants.

---

11. [FN*] As an example of the possibilities, see the certification on rehearing in *Griffin v. State*, 389 So.2d 261 (Fla. 4th DCA 1980), pending in this Court (No. 59,964), which states:

> (W)e certify that our affirmance in this case passed upon the same questions we certified ... in *Lawrence v. State* (388 So.2d 1250 (Fla.App.)).... The decision in this case should abide the decision in *Lawrence*.

We reaffirm that mere citation PCA decisions rendered in the traditional form will remain nonreviewable by this Court, for the reasons stated in *Dodi Publishing* and *Robles Del Mar*. The circumstances of those cases are clearly distinguishable from a district court PCA opinion which cites as controlling a case that is pending review in or has been reversed by this Court.

We grant review in this proceeding and quash the district court's decision on the basis of our decisions in *Murray v. State* and *Tascano v. State*.

It is so ordered.

SUNDBERG, C.J., and OVERTON, ENGLAND and McDONALD, JJ., concur.

BOYD, Justice, dissenting.

Invoking our discretionary jurisdiction under article V, section 3(b)(3), Florida Constitution, the petitioner seeks review of a district court of appeal decision which the court announced as follows:

Affirmed. *See Murray v. State*, 378 So.2d 111 (Fla. 5th DCA 1980).

Jollie v. State, 381 So.2d 351 (Fla. 5th DCA 1980). That portion of article V, section 3(b)(3), upon which petitioner relies in asserting that this Court has power to review the decision provides:

The supreme court:

* * *

May review any decision of a distinct court of appeal ... that expressly and directly conflicts with a decision of another district court of appeal or of the supreme court on the same question of law.

The decision of which the petitioner seeks review — an affirmance of the judgment appealed, rendered without opinion except for a citation of authority — does not, and under article V, section 3(b)(3) as amended in 1980 cannot, "expressly and directly" conflict with another decision. Therefore we lack the authority to consider the petition for review.

Prior to the amendment of April 1, 1980, this Court had the authority to consider a petition for certiorari to review a district court of appeal decision on the ground of direct conflict, even when the decision brought here for review was rendered without opinion. In order to establish that the Court had jurisdiction the petitioner had to demonstrate, by reference to the record, that a legal issue had been brought before the court on appeal, and that the decision, in passing upon the legal issue, was in direct conflict with another district court decision or a decision of the supreme court. *Foley v. Weaver Drugs, Inc.*, 177 So.2d 221 (Fla. 1965). See Note, *Conflict Certiorari Jurisdiction of the Supreme Court of Florida: The "Record Proper"*, 3 Fla.St.U.L.Rev. 409 (1975). By adopting the 1980 amendment, however, restricting that category of review to decisions that "expressly and directly" conflict, the people have taken away that authority.

The intent of the framers and the adopters of the 1980 amendment has already been addressed by this Court. The public discussion and debate that preceded the approval of the amendment "provides a frame of reference by which to ascertain the intent of the voters in adopting the amendment." *Jenkins v. State*, 385 So.2d 1356, 1363 (Fla. 1980) (England, J., concurring) (footnote omitted). During that period of public discussion, the framers of the amendment, as well as other legal and constitutional experts, told the public what effect the amendment would have if adopted:

> At hearings before the legislature and in countless meetings with representatives of The Florida Bar, The Conference of Circuit Judges of Florida, the Appellate Judges' Conference, The League of Women Voters as well as other interested organizations too numerous to recount, members of this Court represented that one of the intents and effects of the revision of section 3(b)(3) was to eliminate the jurisdiction of the Supreme Court to review for conflict purposes per curiam decisions of the district courts of appeal rendered without opinion, regardless of the existence of a concurring or dissenting opinion. These same representations were made consistently to the public at large preceding the ballot on the proposed amendment. There can be little doubt that the electorate was informed as to this matter, because opponents of the amendment broadcast from one end of this state to the other that access to the Supreme Court was being "cut off," and that the district courts of appeal would be the only and final courts of appeal in this state. With regard to review by conflict certiorari of per curiam decisions rendered without opinion, they were absolutely correct.
>
> The pertinent language of section 3(b)(3), as amended April 1, 1980, leaves no room for doubt. This Court may only review a decision of a district court of appeal that expressly and directly conflicts with a decision of another district court of appeal or the Supreme Court on the same question of law. The dictionary definitions of the term "express" include: "to represent in words"; "to give expression to." "Expressly" is defined: "in an express manner." Webster's Third New International Dictionary, (1961 ed. unabr.). The single word "affirmed" comports with none of these definitions.

Jenkins v. State, 385 So.2d 1356, 1359 (Fla. 1980).

The holding of *Jenkins* was that under the new constitutional amendment, this Court may not review, on grounds of conflict, a district court decision rendered without opinion even though a dissenting judge filed a "comprehensive opinion which recited the facts extensively and concluded that the trial court had erred." *Id.*, 385 So.2d at 1357. In *Dodi Publishing Co. v. Editorial America, S. A.*, 385 So.2d 1369, 1369 (Fla. 1980), we held that we did not have jurisdiction to review a district court decision rendered without opinion other than a citation of authority saying:

> We reject the assertion that we should reexamine a case cited in a per curiam decision to determine if the contents of that cited case now conflict with other appellate decisions. The issue to be decided from a petition for conflict review is whether there is express and direct conflict in the decision of the district court before us for review, not whether there is conflict in a prior written opinion which is now cited for authority.

Since the issue is "whether there is express and direct conflict in the decision ... before us for review," it follows that we simply cannot consider petitions for review based on conflict when the decision is not accompanied by an opinion expressing any view on a question of law. A citation of authority is not an opinion.

In *Robles Del Mar, Inc. v. Town of Indian River Shores*, 385 So.2d 1371 (Fla.1980), we again held that we lacked jurisdiction to review a district court decision rendered without opinion but with a citation of authority. We noted, however, that the case cited by the district court in issuing the decision sought to be reviewed, was filed on the same day and was "a final decision of the district court." *Id.* at 1371. By "final" we meant that the cited, contemporaneous decision was no longer subject to being reviewed by this Court. That unfortunate language, holding open the question upon which today's decision is in part predicated, was our first relapse into the much decried tendency to think of the district courts of appeal as "way stations on the road to the Supreme Court." *Lake v. Lake*, 103 So.2d 639, 642 (Fla. 1958). A decision of a district court of appeal is "final" when it has been disposed of by that court on rehearing or the time for seeking rehearing has expired. One does not have to wait and see whether supreme court review is sought before calling such decisions "final."

The 1980 amendment demonstrated an intent that the Supreme Court, in the exercise of its discretionary jurisdiction, be limited to hearing cases having important ramifications for the state's jurisprudence. The change was motivated in part by a desire to preserve the resources of the Court for the task of maintaining harmony and uniformity of decisions as legal precedents. The amendment represents an express negation of the idea of the Supreme Court, except in exercise of its appellate jurisdiction, as the court of last resort for the individual litigant in his quest for individual justice. *Jenkins v. State*, 385 So.2d 1356 (Fla. 1980); England, Hunter, and Williams, *Constitutional Jurisdiction of the Supreme Court of Florida: 1980 Reform*, 32 U.Fla.L.Rev. 147 (1980). Today's decision places an emphasis on the justice of the petitioner's cause that the constitution does not permit.

The majority opinion says that even before *Foley v. Weaver Drugs, Inc.*, a district court decision without opinion but citing a case that had been reversed by the supreme court provided prima facie ground for the exercise of conflict certiorari jurisdiction. I have been unable to find any decisional or documentary authority for that statement. The majority cites only "common sense," and refers us to Justice Thomas's formulation of conflict certiorari jurisdiction in *Lake v. Lake*, 103 So.2d 639 (Fla. 1958).

In his advocacy of the restrictive approach to conflict jurisdiction, Justice Thomas was in essence pleading for self-restraint on the part of the Court, to the end that the district courts would come to be regarded as courts of final appellate jurisdiction. By "prima facie" conflict it seems clear that he meant conflict of principles announced in opinions. But even Justice Thomas acknowledged that conceivably conflict certiorari jurisdiction might exist in the absence of an opinion. In such a case, the fact that "a conflict had arisen" would "appear from the restricted examination required in proceedings in certiorari." *Id.* at 643. What would Justice Thomas have examined in the absence of an opinion stating the legal basis for the decision? In such a context the "restricted examination required in proceedings in certiorari" must have meant examination of the "record proper" as subsequently relied upon in *Foley v. Weaver Drugs, Inc.* Thus any pre-*Foley* review of decisions without opinion would have been on the basis of conflict appearing on the "record proper."

My understanding of the effect of the 1980 amendment, based on its history, its interpretation in *Jenkins, Dodi Publishing* and *Robles Del Mar,* and on other authorities, is that by adding the word "expressly," the people intended to overrule *Foley* and, for purposes of discretionary "conflict" review jurisdiction, do away with the concept of the "record proper."

> The addition of the term "expressly" should vastly improve supreme court practice under section 3(b)(3). The much-maligned and confusing doctrine of "record proper" will have been interred, saving the justices immeasurable time and effort in locating alleged decisional conflict. The clerk's office will be able to screen petitions to ascertain if they are supported by a written opinion of a district court, and those without such support *will simply be returned to the filing attorney.* The court's review process for exercising its discretion will be expedited considerably by the district court's discussion of the point of law brought for review, enabling significantly shorter jurisdictional briefs. Moreover, where jurisdiction is accepted, the court will have a better basis for making an informed decision since the written opinions of the appellate courts will most likely analyze both sides of the same issue.

England, Hunter, and Williams, *Constitutional Jurisdiction of the Supreme Court of Florida: 1980 Reform,* 32 U.Fla.L.Rev. 147, 181 (1980) (emphasis supplied) (footnote omitted). Yet the majority today, in discussing the practical problems of the district courts' appellate processes, still speaks of the adversely affected party's "right of review" and the Court's duty to "acknowledge its own public record actions in dispensing with cases before it." Opinion of the Court at 420. Does this mean the clerk cannot simply return petitions for review of unexplained decisions to the filing attorneys? Must the Court consider every petition for review? Are the people powerless to remove a category of discretionary review jurisdiction?

I had thought that the whole point of the revision of conflict jurisdiction was to disallow petitions for review of decisions without opinion. We would thereby gradually put an end to the practice by attorneys of automatically seeking review on behalf of the adversely affected litigants. But the Court today, in making what appears to be a very narrow exception, is opening the gate the voters thought they had firmly closed. Experience teaches us that narrow classes have a tendency to expand. The Court's decision is a challenge to the ingenuity of lawyers, and prompts me to repeat the words of Justice Thornal: "If I were a practicing lawyer in Florida, I would never again accept with finality a decision of a District Court." *Foley v. Weaver Drugs, Inc.,* 177 So.2d at 234 (Thornal, J., dissenting).

Under article V, section 3(b)(3) as amended in 1980, a decision rendered without opinion other than a citation of legal authority does not establish any precedent and therefore cannot expressly and directly conflict with another decision on a question of law. The publication of such a decision announces the result to the litigants and to the public. But the report of such a decision does not reveal what principle of law was applied to the case, nor what the facts of the case were.

After 1956, when the people adopted the constitutional amendment creating the district courts of appeal and establishing the decisional conflict certiorari jurisdiction of the supreme court, there began a lively controversy that continues to the present day.

It was early recognized that the district courts of appeal were to be courts of final appellate jurisdiction and that the "conflict" basis for certiorari jurisdiction was designed to allow the supreme court the supervisory role of resolving legal conflicts among the districts and maintaining uniformity of decisions. *Lake v. Lake*, 103 So.2d 639 (Fla. 1958); *Ansin v. Thurston*, 101 So.2d 808 (Fla. 1958).

In light of the emphasis in *Ansin v. Thurston* and *Lake v. Lake* on decisions as precedents, in *Seaboard Air Line R. R. v. Branham*, 104 So.2d 356, 358 (Fla. 1958), the Court said that the term "decision" as used in the constitution "comprehends both the opinion and judgment." But a debate began on the question of whether to emphasize uniformity of written appellate court precedents or uniformity in the decisions of appellate courts.

In *Foley v. Weaver Drugs, Inc.*, 177 So.2d 221 (1965), the majority reasoned that the judgment of a case constitutes the decision, "and the opinion merely sets forth the reasons supporting the judgment...." *Id.* at 224. Justice Drew, who had espoused the restrictive decisions-as-precedents view in *Ansin v. Thurston*, concurred with the majority in *Foley*, and wrote that the Court needed to be able to review decisions rendered without opinion in order to maintain uniformity. Such decisions, he reasoned, did constitute precedents to judges and lawyers who knew what legal questions had been ruled upon by the lower court judge.

In *Gibson v. Maloney*, 231 So.2d 823 (Fla.), cert. denied, 398 U.S. 951, 90 S.Ct. 1871, 26 L.Ed.2d 291 (1970), the majority said, "It is conflict of decisions, not conflict of opinions or reasons that supplies jurisdiction.... When comparing decisions it may be necessary to consult the record to some extent." *Id.* at 824. See also *Seaboard Air Line R.R. v. Williams*, 199 So.2d 469 (Fla. 1967), *cert. denied*, 390 U.S. 920, 88 S.Ct. 851, 19 L.Ed.2d 979 (1968).

Prior to the 1980 amendment, the difficulties and ambiguities of conflict certiorari jurisdiction were such that the question of whether this Court should focus on conflict of precedents or conflict of decisions was a fairly debatable one. My predecessors, former colleagues, and present colleagues struggled with the problem and argued about it with eloquence. But the question is debatable no longer.

Being of the opinion that the Court has no jurisdiction of this case, I would deny the petition for review.

Harrison v. Hyster Co.

515 So. 2d 1279 (Fla. 1987)

PER CURIAM.

The district court of appeal in *Harrison v. Hyster Co.*, 502 So.2d 100 (Fla. 2d DCA 1987), affirmed the dismissal of petitioners' product liability action upon the authority of *Small v. Niagara Machine & Tool Works*, 502 So.2d 943 (Fla. 2d DCA 1987). The only basis upon which it could be asserted that this Court had jurisdiction to review the *Harrison* decision was the rationale of *Jollie v. State*, 405 So.2d 418 (Fla. 1981), in which we said:

> We thus conclude that a district court of appeal per curiam opinion which cites as controlling authority a decision that is either pending review in or has been reversed by this Court continues to constitute prima facie express conflict and allows this Court to exercise its jurisdiction.

Id. at 420. Since a petition for review of *Small* had been filed in this Court, we accepted jurisdiction on the petition for review filed in the instant case. Subsequently, however, this Court declined to accept jurisdiction in *Small* and denied the petition for review. *Small v. Niagara Machine & Tool Works*, 511 So.2d 999 (Fla. 1987).

The anomaly of reviewing a decision because it was decided upon the authority of another decision which was never reviewed on the merits by this Court has caused us to conclude that we should not have accepted jurisdiction of this case until it was determined to accept jurisdiction in *Small*. *Jollie*'s reference to the "controlling authority … that is … pending review" refers to a case in which the petition for jurisdictional review has been granted and the case is pending for disposition on the merits. Since *Small* never reached that status, our order accepting jurisdiction in this case was improvidently issued, and we now deny the petition for review.

It is so ordered.

McDONALD, C.J., and OVERTON, EHRLICH, SHAW, BARKETT, GRIMES and KOGAN, JJ., concur.

Questions

1. Distinguish the varying situations, which explain the different outcomes, in *Dodi Publishing Company v. Editorial America S.A.* and *Jollie v. State*.

2. Does conflict jurisdiction occur when there are two different outcomes in cases based on different facts?

Commentary

As the cases above illustrate, conflict jurisdiction can be complicated by the jurisdictional fact that opinions that state only "Per Curiam Affirmed" are not reviewable except in the very narrow exceptions described above. PCA opinions, as they are commonly known, are a source of frustration for lawyers who believe their case is not as cut-and-dried as a PCA opinion would suggest.

The Supreme Court's conflict jurisdiction takes two forms: express and direct conflict as argued by the parties in a petition for jurisdiction, and direct conflict as certified by a district court of appeal.

Conflict jurisdiction is a common issue confronting a practicing lawyer. The areas of mandatory jurisdiction are specified and limited. Otherwise taking jurisdiction is completely within the discretion of the Court. Who would review the abuse of discretion for denying jurisdiction? The Supreme Court itself?

State v. Vickery

961 So. 2d 309 (Fla. 2007)

CANTERO, J.

We review three cases in which the Fourth and Fifth District Courts of Appeal acknowledged (but did not certify) conflict with the First District Court of Appeal. These are: *Charles v. State*, 890 So.2d 542 (Fla. 4th DCA 2005), *James v. State*, 881 So.2d 85 (Fla. 5th DCA 2004), and *Vickery v. State*, 869 So.2d 623 (Fla. 5th DCA 2004). The issue is whether a claim that alleges ineffective assistance of counsel for failure to request an instruction on a lesser-included offense may be summarily denied. *See Sanders v. State*, 847 So.2d 504 (Fla. 1st DCA 2003) (en banc), approved, 946 So.2d 953 (Fla.2006). In acknowledging conflict, the Fifth District in *James* and *Vickery* cited *Sanders*, while the Fourth District in *Charles* cited *Willis v. State*, 840 So.2d 1135 (Fla. 4th DCA 2003) (on motion for rehearing and motion for certification of conflict), *quashed*, 946 So.2d 953 (Fla.2006), in which it had earlier certified conflict with *Sanders*. When the Fourth and Fifth Districts issued their respective decisions in *Charles*, *James*, and *Vickery*, both *Sanders* and *Willis* were pending review in this Court. We have jurisdiction and consolidate *Charles*, *James*, and *Vickery* for purposes of this opinion. See art. V, § 3(b)(3), Fla Const.; *Jollie v. State*, 405 So.2d 418 (Fla.1981).

JURISDICTION

Before deciding these cases, we address a jurisdictional issue. The district courts in these cases only acknowledged, but did not certify, their conflict with the First District. For purposes of our jurisdiction, this is an important distinction. While it is a district court's prerogative to acknowledge rather than certify conflict, such an approach does not give us jurisdiction under article V, section 3(b)(4) of the Florida Constitution (establishing this Court's discretionary jurisdiction to review "any decision of a district court of appeal that … is *certified* by it to be in direct conflict with a decision of another district court of appeal") (emphasis added).

As already informally recognized, "district court opinions accepted [for review as certified conflict cases under article V, section 3(b)(4) of the Florida Constitution] … almost uniformly meet two requirements: they use the word 'certify' or some variation of the root word 'certif.-' in connection with the word 'conflict;' and, they indicate a decision from another district court upon which the conflict is based." Harry Lee Anstead, Gerald Kogan, Thomas D. Hall, & Robert Craig Waters, *The Operation and Jurisdiction of the Supreme Court of Florida*, 29 Nova L.Rev. 431, 529

(2005) (footnote omitted). However, "all of the cases—with few exceptions—in which the district court has merely 'acknowledged' conflict are treated as petitions for [review based on] 'express and direct' conflict [under article V, section (3)(b)(3) of the Florida Constitution], and some are accepted for review on that basis." *Id.* at 530 (footnote omitted).

We thus hold that district court decisions that simply acknowledge, discuss, cite, suggest, or in any other way recognize conflict do not provide a proper basis for a party to seek this Court's review under our "certified conflict" jurisdiction. See art. V, § 3(b)(4), Fla. Const. To support such review, conflict must be "certified." Of course, this does not mean that we lose all jurisdiction to review the case. As occurred with the three cases here, jurisdiction may nevertheless exist under our "express and direct conflict" jurisdiction, see art. V, § 3(b)(3), Fla. Const. (granting this Court jurisdiction to review district court opinions that "expressly and directly" conflict with the decision of another district court of appeal or with a decision of the Florida Supreme Court), or on some other basis. The difference is that a certification of conflict provides us with jurisdiction per se. On the other hand, when a district court does not certify the conflict, our jurisdiction to review the case depends on whether the decision actually "expressly and directly" conflicts with the decision of another court. We therefore advise district courts that when they intend to certify conflict under article V, section 3(b)(4) of the Florida Constitution, they use the constitutional term of art "certify."

* * *

It is so ordered.

Commentary

This decision explains the difference between Supreme Court jurisdiction based on a DCA's certification of conflict and on an assertion of conflict (by either a court or a party) that is not an actual certification of conflict.

1. On what basis does the court rest its determination of whether a court has certified conflict? Do you agree with this basis?

2. What is the rationale for all of the categories of conflict jurisdiction?

b. "Bypass" Jurisdiction—Article V, Section 3(b)(5)

This source of jurisdiction allows the DCAs to fast-track cases that will end up in the Supreme Court. Though the Constitution does not mention time restraints as necessary to this jurisdiction, it does provide that the certification is "to require immediate resolution by the supreme court." Thus, it is often invoked when time is short. An example of the use of Section 3(b)(5) jurisdiction occurred in 2018, when constitutional amendments proposed by the 2017–18 Constitution Revision Commission were challenged in court. Article XI of the Constitution provides that the CRC file its proposals with the Secretary of State at least 180 days before the general election in November, but 180 days is rarely enough time for a trial court to rule, much less a DCA and the Supreme Court. In addition, the decision should be final in time for ballots to be printed accurately. Therefore, the challenges to CRC proposals that were initially filed in circuit court[12] were certified by the respective District Courts of Appeal as soon as the trial courts had ruled. *See County of Volusia v. Detzner*, 253 So. 3d 507 (Sept. 7, 2018); *Department of State v. Florida Greyhound Association, Inc.*, 253 So. 3d 513 Sept. 7, 2018); *Detzner v. League of Women Voters*, 256 So. 3d 803 (Oct. 15, Fla. 2018); *Detzner v. Anstead*, 256 So. 3d 820 (Oct. 17, 2018); *Department of State v. Hollander*, 256 So. 3d 1300 (Oct. 25, Fla. 2018). The average time from initial filing of these challenges to final disposition was eighty-nine days.[13]

c. Certified Questions

The Supreme Court also has discretionary jurisdiction to review "any decision of a district court of appeal that passes upon a question certified by it to be of great public importance." Fla. Const. Art. V, section 3(b)(4). To qualify for jurisdiction, the DCA decision must rest on the certified question and not on another legal ground.[14]

d. Jurisdiction Based on Writs

The Supreme Court is authorized to issue writs. Writs can generally be defined as a command from a court to do, or refrain from doing; the term comes from English law. Upon a party's petition, the court may issue writs of prohibition to lower courts or judges; of mandamus, forcing a state officers or agencies to perform a legal duty; of quo warranto, which challenges the authority of a party to exercise a right or privilege; and of habeas corpus, which challenges the legality of holding a person in custody. The court also has "all writs" authority, a general power meant to allow all writs necessary for the court to exercise its jurisdiction.[15]

Florida House of Representatives v. Crist

999 So. 2d 601 (Fla. 2008)

[For fuller treatment of this case, see Article II.]

CANTERO, J.

After almost sixteen years of sporadic negotiations with four governors, in November 2007 the Seminole Indian Tribe of Florida signed a gambling "compact" (a contract between two sovereigns) with Florida Governor Charles Crist. The compact significantly expands casino gambling, also known as "gaming," on tribal lands. For example, it permits card games such as blackjack and baccarat that are otherwise

---

12. Some were filed directly with the Supreme Court as quo warranto cases.

13. Adkins, Mary E, *What Florida's Constitution Revision Commission Can Teach and Learn from Those of Other States*, 71 Rutgers U. L. Rev. 1177, 1222 (2019).

14. 2 Philp J. Padovano, Florida Appellate Practice § 3:11 (West Publ., 2019).

15. *Id.* at §§ 3:14–3:18.

prohibited by law. In return, the compact promises substantial remuneration to the State.

The Florida Legislature did not authorize the Governor to negotiate the compact before it was signed and has not ratified it since. To the contrary, shortly after the compact was signed, the Florida House of Representatives and its Speaker, Marco Rubio, filed in this Court a petition for a writ of quo warranto disputing the Governor's authority to bind the State to the compact. We have exercised our discretion to consider such petitions, see art. V, § 3(b)(8), Fla. Const., and now grant it on narrow grounds. We hold that the Governor does not have the constitutional authority to bind the State to a gaming compact that clearly departs from the State's public policy by legalizing types of gaming that are illegal everywhere else in the state.

* * *

II. JURISDICTION

Before discussing the issue presented, we first address our jurisdiction. The House and Speaker Rubio have filed in this Court a petition for writ of quo warranto. The Governor contends that this Court lacks jurisdiction because the House does not seek either to remove him from office or to enjoin the future exercise of his authority. We conclude, however, that these are not the only grounds for issuing such a writ.

The Florida Constitution authorizes this Court to issue writs of quo warranto to "state officers and state agencies." Art. V, § 3(b)(8), Fla. Const. The term "quo warranto" means "by what authority." This writ historically has been used to determine whether a state officer or agency has improperly exercised a power or right derived from the State. *See Martinez v. Martinez*, 545 So.2d 1338, 1339 (Fla.1989); see also art. V, § 3(b)(8), Fla. Const. Here, the Governor is a state officer. The House challenges the Governor's authority to unilaterally execute the Compact on the State's behalf.

The Governor argues that because he already has signed the Compact, quo warranto relief is inappropriate. But the writ is not so limited. In fact, petitions for the writ historically have been filed after a public official has acted. *See, e.g., Chiles v. Phelps*, 714 So.2d 453, 455 (Fla.1998) (holding that the Legislature and its officers exceeded their authority in overriding the Governor's veto); *State ex rel. Butterworth v. Kenny*, 714 So.2d 404, 406 (Fla.1998) (issuing the writ after the Capital Collateral Regional Counsel had filed a federal civil rights suit, concluding that it had no authority to file it). The Governor's execution of the Compact does not defeat our jurisdiction.

The concurring-in-result-only opinion expresses concern that by considering a more narrow issue than the Governor's authority to execute IGRA [Indian Gaming Regulatory Act, 25 U.S.C. §§ 2701–2721 (2000)] compacts in general—that is, whether the Governor has the authority to bind the State to a compact that violates Florida law—we are expanding our quo warranto jurisdiction to include issues normally reserved for declaratory judgment actions. In prior quo warranto cases, however, we have considered separation-of-powers arguments normally reviewed in the context of declaratory judgments, such as whether the Governor's action has usurped the Legislature's power, "where the functions of government would be adversely affected absent an immediate determination by this Court." *Phelps*, 714 So.2d at 457; *see also Martinez*, 545 So.2d at 1339 (holding quo warranto appropriate to test the governor's power to call special sessions); *Orange County v. City of Orlando*, 327 So.2d 7 (Fla.1976) (holding that the legality of city's actions regarding annexation ordinances can be inquired into through quo warranto).

In this case, the Secretary has approved the Compact and, absent an immediate judicial resolution, it will be given effect. In fact, according to news reports, the Tribe already has begun offering blackjack and other games at the Seminole Hard Rock Hotel and Casino. *See* Amy Driscoll, *Casino Gambling: Amid glitz, blackjack's in the cards*, The Miami Herald, June 23, 2008, at B1. Thus, if indeed the Governor has exceeded his constitutional authority, a compact that violates Florida law will, nevertheless, become effective in seven casinos located on tribal lands located in the state. As in *Phelps*, therefore, the importance and immediacy of the issue justifies our deciding this matter now rather than transferring it for resolution in a declaratory judgment action.

* * *

3. Does IGRA Permit Compacts to Expand Gaming?

Contrary to Florida law, the Compact allows banked card games such as blackjack, baccarat, and *chemin de fer*. The House argues that the Compact therefore violates IGRA itself, which permits Class III gaming *only* if the state "permits such gaming for any purpose by any person, organization, or entity." 25 U.S.C. § 2710(d)(1). The Governor, on the other hand, contends that, once state law permits *any* Class III gaming, a compact may allow *all* Class III gaming.

* * *

Commentary

This case raises multiple issues. You have studied it in the Article II materials, where you read that the Court found the Governor's actions violated the separation of powers. It is worth noting that a basis for the Legislature's lawsuit was that the Governor violated federal law by entering the state into a compact that violated Florida's own criminal law (by allowing the Seminole Tribe to conduct forms of gambling not otherwise allowed in Florida).

Detzner v. Anstead

256 So. 3d 820 (Fla. 2018)

[For fuller treatment of this case, see Article XI.]

PER CURIAM.

Secretary of State Ken Detzner seeks review of the judgment of the Circuit Court for the Second Judicial Circuit in *Anstead v. Detzner*, No. 2018-CA-1925, 2018 WL

4868094 (Fla. 2d Cir. Ct. Sept. 5, 2018), which granted a petition for writ of quo warranto filed by Appellees, Harry Lee Anstead and Robert J. Barnas, and ordered that ballot titles and summaries of three proposed amendments to the Florida Constitution ("Amendment 7," "Amendment 9," and "Amendment 11") be stricken from the November 2018 general election ballot. The First District Court of Appeal certified the order as presenting a question of great public importance requiring immediate resolution by this Court. We have jurisdiction. See art. V, § 3(b)(5), Fla. Const. As explained below, we reverse the judgment of the circuit court.

First, there is no basis for relief in quo warranto. A writ of quo warranto is the means for determining "whether a state officer or agency has improperly exercised a power or right derived from the State." *Fla. House of Reps. v. Crist*, 999 So.2d 601, 607 (Fla. 2008) (citing *Martinez v. Martinez*, 545 So.2d 1338, 1339 (Fla. 1989)). Secretary Detzner is a state officer. See § 20.10(1), Fla. Stat. (2018) ("The head of the Department of State is the Secretary of State."). Florida law is clear that the Secretary has the authority and duty to place proposed amendments on the ballot. See § 101.161(2), Fla. Stat. (2018) (directing the Secretary to give each proposed amendment a ballot number and furnish the amendments to Florida's supervisors of elections); art. XI, §§ 2(c), 5(a), Fla. Const. (directing the Constitution Revision Commission ("CRC") to furnish its proposed amendments to the Secretary and the Secretary to deliver the proposed amendments to supervisors of elections).

Appellees do not assert or attempt to argue in the petition that Secretary Detzner improperly exercised his power or right to assign ballot positions to the challenged CRC revisions. Rather, the petition expressly concedes, consistent with Florida law, that the Secretary possessed the authority to take such action. The petition states that "[Secretary Detzner] has the power and duty to place proposals to amend the constitution on the 2018 general election ballot and to certify the results of elections."

Appellees do not demonstrate or even allege that Secretary Detzner exceeded his authority to assign ballot position to the revisions. The petition therefore fails to assert a proper basis for quo warranto relief. See *Whiley v. Scott*, 79 So. 3d 702, 707 (Fla. 2011) ("The writ [of quo warranto] is the proper means for inquiring into whether a particular individual has improperly exercised a power or right derived from the State."). The petition instead challenges the merits of the proposed amendments themselves, which is properly decided on a complaint for declaratory and injunctive relief. Accordingly, we hold that the circuit court abused its discretion in granting the petition because the standard for obtaining quo warranto relief has not been satisfied.

Moreover, the circuit court was incorrect in finding any deficiency in the proposals or ballot summaries on the merits.

* * *

It is so ordered.

PARIENTE, J., concurring in result.

* * *

iii. Jurisdiction Arising Outside Article V

The Supreme Court has jurisdiction to hear a few more kinds of cases that are not obvious from Article V, Section 3. One is apportionment cases, which arise every ten years when the Legislature must reapportion itself and Florida's congressional districts based on the most recent federal census.[16] Another is proposed amendments to the Constitution.

a. Apportionment

A "stealth" source of jurisdiction of the Supreme Court is found not in Article V but in Article III. Under Article III, Section 16(b) through (f), the Supreme Court must rule on the constitutionality of legislative apportionment plans, which are set after each federal census. Remember that the Constitution as adopted in 1968 lacked a new judicial article, which means that the "old" Supreme Court gained the obligation to rule on apportionment plans before the court system, and the obligation, were renewed under the new Article V passed in 1972.

Some have wondered why the Florida Supreme Court should rule on legislative apportionment. After all, what do judges know about such an inherently legislative and political issue? The answer can be found in the statements of the 1966 Constitution Revision Commission members themselves. It springs from the *Baker v. Carr*, 369 U.S. 186 (1962), *Reynolds v. Sims*, 377 U.S. 533 (1965), and *Swann v. Adams*, 385 U.S. 440 (1967) (Florida), apportionment cases of the early to mid-1960s. All these cases were heard in federal courts. (See the discussion in Article III, Section 16—Apportionment.) The federal courts decided Florida's *Swann v. Adams* case in three rounds that ping-ponged from the legislature to the U.S. District Court and the U.S. Supreme Court and back. The decision to have our state's Supreme Court, rather than a federal court, decide the constitutionality of apportionment plans was made explicitly to keep the federal courts out of our state's business. A conversation by two CRC members in 1966 makes this intent clear. The speakers are John E. "Jack" Mathews, Jr., a drafter and proponent of the provision, and Robert M. Ervin, also a CRC member:

> MR. ERVIN: Do you feel that that handiwork of yours will solve the problem of actual accomplishment of apportionment in the State of Florida?
>
> MR. MATHEWS: Not being a prophet or son of a prophet, all I can do is have faith and hope that it will. I hope that we get to the situation where we never have to go to court ordered apportionment again.... But if we continue, then I want our own state court to do it, rather than a federal district court.

CRC Convention Proceedings 483–85 (Nov. 28, 1966), Florida State Archives, Series 722, carton 3.

Article III, Section 16 gives the Supreme Court only thirty days to determine the constitutionality of a legislative plan, so it is limited in how deeply it can research

---

16. FLA. CONST. art. III § 16.

facts. The constitutional language states that the Court must determine the apportionment "to be valid." What does valid mean in this context? The chapter in this book that covers Article III contains examples of opinions discussing various issues the Supreme Court has had to parse in deciding the constitutionality of legislative apportionment plans.

In re Constitutionality of Senate Joint Resolution 2G, Special Apportionment Session 1992
601 So. 2d 543 (Fla. 1992)

GRIMES, Justice.

On May 13, 1992, this Court approved Senate Joint Resolution 2G apportioning the Legislature of the State of Florida. *In re Constitutionality of Senate Joint Resolution 2G*, 597 So.2d 276 (Fla.1992). On June 16, 1992, the United States Department of Justice, pursuant to its authority under section 5 of the federal Voting Rights Act objected to the Senate apportionment plan with regard to the Hillsborough County area. Because Hillsborough County is subject to the preclearance requirements of section 5, the effect of this objection was to make the Senate apportionment plan legally unenforceable in that county. As a consequence, this Court entered an order encouraging the Legislature to adopt a plan that would meet the objection of the Justice Department. However, the Court was advised that the Governor did not intend to convene the Legislature in an extraordinary apportionment session and the President of the Senate and the Speaker of the House of Representatives did not intend to convene their respective houses in an extraordinary apportionment session. Because it appeared that a legislative impasse had occurred, this Court determined to modify the Senate redistricting plan so as to resolve the objection of the Justice Department.

We acknowledge that Miguel DeGrandy, et al., have questioned this Court's jurisdiction to proceed and have asserted that jurisdiction lies in the federal district court. However, the reapportionment of state legislative bodies is not a power delegated by the Constitution of the United States to the federal government. Under the provisions of the Tenth Amendment to the United States Constitution, this is a power reserved to states. Of course, this Court is obligated to apply any applicable federal constitutional provisions and any federal statutes implementing these provisions.

The Florida Constitution places upon this Court the responsibility to review state legislative reapportionment. Art. III, § 16, Fla. Const. Pursuant to that authority, we approved the original legislative reapportionment and retained jurisdiction to entertain subsequent objections thereto. Consistent with the provisions of article III, section 16 of the Florida Constitution, we believe that it is our obligation to redraw the plan to satisfy the objection of the Justice Department now that the Legislature has declared that it is not going to do so.

A substantial number of minority persons live in the Hillsborough County area. However, the original Senate apportionment plan contained no districts in the Hillsborough County area in which the total of black and Hispanic persons constituted more than 40.1% of the voting-age population. In order to create an appreciably stronger minority district, it was evident that at the very least it would be necessary to combine minority populations in Hillsborough and Pinellas Counties. The Legislature had concluded that it was inappropriate to do this because these areas are separated by Tampa Bay and because they lack economic ties and political cohesiveness. However, the Justice Department rejected these and other legislative justifications and determined that the Senate plan with respect to the Hillsborough County area violated the Voting Rights Act. Specifically, the Justice Department pointed out that "there are no districts in which minority persons constitute a majority of the voting age population."

In order to address this problem, we permitted all interested parties to file proposed corrections to modify the Senate redistricting plan so as to resolve the objection of the Justice Department. Six corrective plans were submitted. Four of the plans created strengthened minority districts which were somewhat similar in that they combined much of the minority population of Hillsborough, Pinellas, and Manatee Counties. The voting-age populations of the strengthened minority district in these plans were as follows:

* * *

However, presumably because of their dissimilar political objectives, some of these plans differed in the manner in which they redrew the districts which adjoined the strengthened minority district.

The fifth plan, submitted by the Florida Women's Political Caucus, et al., contained a strengthened minority district with a black voting-age population of 25.8% and a Hispanic voting-age population of 18.1%. The avowed purpose of this plan was to ensure that the redrawing of district lines would not result in a defeat of incumbent women senators.

The sixth plan was submitted by Gwen Humphrey, et al., and supported by Representative Darryl Reaves, et al. The strengthened minority district in this plan encompassed not only Hillsborough, Pinellas, and Manatee Counties, but also extended into Polk County. The voting-age population statistics for this district are as follows: white 51.2%; black 45.8%; other 3.0%; and hispanic 9.4%.

None of the plans created a district with a black majority voting-age population or a Hispanic majority voting-age population, although all of the plans except that submitted by the Florida Women's Political Caucus contained a district with a combined minority majority voting-age population. While it might be possible to create a district containing a black majority voting-age population, to do so would require extending the minority district even further into other counties. We do not believe that the Voting Rights Act requires such an extreme measure. On the other hand, we are convinced that the Justice Department will not approve a plan for the Hillsborough County area which does not contain a district in which black voters have a reasonable opportunity to elect a candidate of their choice. It is for this reason that we have selected the Humphrey-Reaves plan as best suited to accomplish this result.

* * *

We recognize that the configuration of this plan is more contorted than the others because it reaches further. However, none of the plans can be considered compact because in creating a strengthened minority district it is necessary to extend fingers in several directions in order to include pockets of minority voters. The dissenters suggest that Polk County black voters have little community of interest with those in Hillsborough and Pinellas Counties other than their race. That may be so, but under the law community of interest must give way to racial and ethnic fairness.

Though the NAACP plan as well as others also created a district in which the minorities as a whole amounted to more than 50% of the voting-age population, this would not necessarily mean that a minority candidate would have a reasonable chance of being elected from such district. While statistics show that in the Hillsborough County area most blacks and Hispanics vote for Democratic candidates, there is no indication that blacks and Hispanics vote for candidates of the opposite race when they are pitted against each other.

The dissenters correctly point out that in creating a stronger minority district the influence of the minority voters in the adjoining districts is reduced. However, the Justice Department seems to interpret the Voting Rights Act as favoring the creation of more districts in which minorities have the opportunity to elect minority candidates rather than the creation of more districts in which minorities have greater influence. The Humphrey-Reaves plan gives minority voters in the Hillsborough County area the greatest opportunity to elect a senator of their choice.

The Senate apportionment plan as heretofore adopted is hereby amended to include the Humphrey-Reaves plan, all of which is set forth in the attached appendix. No motion for rehearing will be entertained.

It is so ordered.

KOGAN and HARDING, JJ., concur.

SHAW, Chief Justice, specially concurring.

Senate Joint Resolution 2G, the proposed reapportionment plan for the Florida legislature that was recently approved by a majority of this Court, has been rejected by the United States Department of Justice ("DOJ" or "the Department") under the preclearance procedure of section 5 of the Voting Rights Act of 1965, 42 U.S.C. § 1973 (the "Act"). In his rejection letter to the Florida Attorney General, Assistant United States Attorney General John Dunne stated:

> We are unable to reach the same conclusion with regard to the Senate redistricting plan. With regard to the Hillsborough County area, the state has chosen to draw its senatorial districts such that there are no districts in which minority persons constitute a majority of the voting age population. To accomplish this result, the state chose to divide the politically cohesive minority populations in the Tampa and St. Petersburg areas. Alternative plans were presented to the legislature uniting the Tampa and St. Petersburg minority

populations in order to provide minority voters an effective opportunity to elect their preferred candidate to the State Senate. Consequently, we have carefully obtained and evaluated the state's justifications for rejecting these proposals.

The state has claimed that minority voters under these alternative plans would not be able to elect a candidate of their choice in the Hillsborough area. The state further contends that even if minority voters in this area were able to elect their preferred candidate in this area, the projected influx of white population into such a district would thwart future opportunities of minority voters to elect a candidate of their choice in such a district.

We find such claims to be unsupported by the information that is before us.... [W]e have examined evidence, including evidence in the legislative record, which suggests that the state's approach to senatorial redistricting in the Hillsborough area was undertaken with an intent to protect incumbents. Such a rationale, of course, cannot justify the treatment of minority voters in this area by the State Senate plan.

In light of the considerations discussed above, I cannot conclude, as I must under the Voting Rights Act, that the state has sustained its burden in this instance. Accordingly, on behalf of the Attorney General, I must object to the 1992 redistricting plan for the Florida State Senate to the extent that it incorporates the proposed configurations for the area discussed above.

Although DOJ's review was limited to only five Florida counties (Collier, Hardee, Hendry, Hillsborough, and Monroe Counties) and to only section 5 of the Act, the Department highlighted potential problems with the proposed plan in other areas and expressly withheld overall approval:

Finally, we understand that there are challenges under Section 2 of the Voting Rights Act presently being considered.... In addition, some of the comments we received alluded to various concerns involving the adequacy of the plans in non-covered counties. Because our review of these plans is limited by law to the direct impact on geographic areas covered by Section 5, we did not undertake to assess the lawfulness of the legislative choices outside of Collier, Hardee, Hendry, Hillsborough and Monroe counties. We do note, however, that allegations have been raised regarding dilution of minority voting strength in an effort to protect Anglo incumbents in non-covered jurisdictions, for example, in the Pensacola-Escambia County area and the Dade County area. Because these and other legislative choices did not directly impact upon the five covered counties, they cannot be the basis of with-holding preclearance of either plan. Consequently, nothing in this letter should be construed as a determination by the Attorney General regarding the non-covered jurisdictions.

Because this Court's review in the present proceeding is limited in scope to DOJ's section 5 preclearance inquiry, I concur in the majority opinion. I believe the present revision in the plan meets the objection evinced in DOJ's admittedly restricted review. I write to note, however, that I still conclude that the overall plan, including the present revision, fails under section 2 of the Act because it does not provide an equal opportunity for minorities to elect representatives of their choice to the Florida legislature, as noted in my earlier dissent. See In re Constitutionality of Senate Joint Resolution 2G, No. 79,674 (Fla. May 13, 1992) (Shaw, C.J., dissenting).

OVERTON, Justice, dissenting.

I dissent. Six plans were submitted to the Court. Four of the six were very similar in addressing the Justice Department's requirements. They were the Thomas plan, which would establish a 35.5% black minority district; the Kiser plan, which would establish a 36.7% black minority district; the NAACP plan, which would establish a 36.3% black minority district; and the Wallace plan, which would establish a 35.1% black minority district. The remaining two plans are the Humphrey plan, which would establish a 45.8% black minority district and is the only plan that reaches into Polk County and into central and northern Pinellas County, and the Florida Women's Political Caucus plan, which would establish a 25.8% black minority district. The ACLU has filed a response asking that we make no changes that would adversely affect two incumbent women senators in the Tampa Bay area. Chesterfield Smith has filed a response objecting to the adoption of any new minority district. He asserts that the adoption of any of the proposed plans would "relegate blacks, hispanics, and other minorities to permanent minority status, which is the inevitable result of the Justice Department's promotion of race-based gerrymandering."

The NAACP argued that the Humphrey plan, adopted by the majority, goes too far. The NAACP expressed its objection to the Humphrey plan by stating: "This plan's proposed minority district for the Tampa Bay area lacks geographic compactness," and that it "places virtually all black residents in the four-county area into the minority district, thereby substantially diminishing the opportunity for blacks to influence elections in the surrounding districts." Chesterfield Smith expressed a similar concern, stating that establishing "a minority access district along the shores of Tampa Bay [would] 'bleach' minority voters from districts in which they have exercised some influence."

I find that the plan presented by the NAACP is an appropriate middle-ground approach to this problem. It is the fairest, given the Justice Department's demands, the geography, the community interest of the area, and the need to assure that minority interests have a voice in their local governmental entities. The Humphrey plan, adopted by the majority, effectively strips Pinellas, Hillsborough, Manatee, and Polk Counties of their black population. To illustrate, the plan will result in the three senate districts serving Pinellas County being 97.0% white, 95.9% white, and 96.9% white. The plan adopted by the majority will group so many of the minority voters into one district that the minorities in these four counties will be effectively eliminated from influencing white candidates in the other senate districts in the entire four-county area. It is also interesting to note that, while the Justice Department's section

5 preclearance jurisdiction extends only to Hillsborough County, the plan adopted by the majority will have adverse effects on Pinellas, Manatee, and Polk Counties.

Finally, this district will be so spread out and gerrymandered that it will be difficult, if not impossible, to manage constituent services. Frankly, only the senator will know where the district lines are.

McDONALD, Justice, dissenting.

I regret that I cannot concur in the plan adopted by the majority. We have now seemingly interpreted the 1982 amendment to the Voting Rights Act to require districts that can be counted on to elect a minority representative to an exclusion of all other factors. Frankly, I think that the Justice Department is erroneous in its interpretation of the 1982 Voting Rights Act and in rejecting the reapportionment plan previously approved by this Court. Assuming it to be correct, however, we need not go to the extremes we have in correcting the perceived deficiency.

* * *

I abhor discrimination. I resent it and oppose it. Discrimination is a two-way street, however, and traditional communities should not be the victims of it to afford special consideration to any segment of society. We can approve or devise a plan to accommodate the concerns of minorities and community values. We should do so.

BARKETT, Justice, dubitante.

I am loath to agree to any of the convoluted plans submitted under these hurried circumstances. It is unfortunate that the presuit delay in conjunction with the imminence of qualifying deadlines apparently makes it impossible to begin at the beginning or to further explore with the Justice Department a way to satisfy both community of interest and racial fairness. I think that both the majority and the dissenting views have merit. If I had to choose only among those presented, however, I would choose the plan submitted by the NAACP simply because this is the organization that has traditionally represented and promoted the position that advances all minority interests.

Questions

1. What is the standard the majority applies to determine which apportionment plan it approves?

2. Do you see any drawbacks to the Supreme Court of Florida having jurisdiction over legislative apportionment? On balance, is it advisable?

3. Based on the content of Justice Barkett's opinion, what does a "dubitante" opinion signify?

b. Advisory Opinions to Governor (Upon Request)

The Supreme Court has interpreted this provision, found in Article IV, rather narrowly. In 1980, the Court refused to answer a question from the Governor, finding that to do so would implicate not the Constitution but a mere statute. That letter opinion, *In re Advisory Opinion to the Governor Request of August 28, 1980*, 388 So. 2d 554 (Fla. 1980), is printed in full in the chapter covering Article IV.

D. District Courts of Appeal

State v. Creighton

469 So. 2d 735 (Fla. 1985)

BOYD, Chief Justice.

This cause is before the Court on petition for review of a decision of the District Court of Appeal, First District, *State v. Creighton*, 438 So.2d 1042 (Fla. 1st DCA 1983). The decision of which review is sought is an order dismissing an appeal brought by the state in a criminal case. The district court certified that its decision directly conflicts with *State v. W.A.M.*, 412 So.2d 49 (Fla. 5th DCA), *review denied*, 419 So.2d 1201 (Fla.1982). We have jurisdiction. Art. V, §3(b)(4), Fla. Const.

Respondent was charged in a two-count information with first-degree arson in violation of section 806.01(1)(a), Florida Statutes (1981), and failure to put out or control a fire or give a prompt fire alarm in violation of section 877.15(1), Florida Statutes (1981). The case proceeded to trial and at the close of the evidence, respondent moved for a judgment of acquittal on both counts on the ground that the evidence was insufficient to warrant convictions. *See* Fla.R.Crim.P. 3.380. The judge declined to grant judgment of acquittal at that time and submitted the case to the jury. The jury returned a verdict of not guilty on count one, arson, but a verdict of guilty on the second count, charging failure to put out or control a fire or give a prompt alarm by a person with a legal duty to do so.

Five days after the reception of the verdicts in court, the defense filed a combined motion for arrest of judgment, renewal of the motion for judgment of acquittal, and motion for new trial. The court held a hearing on the renewal of the motion for judgment of acquittal. Following the hearing, the trial judge granted judgment of acquittal on count two.

The state brought an appeal from the trial court's judgment and the district court of appeal dismissed the appeal. The issue before us is whether the state is entitled to appellate review of the trial court's order granting judgment of acquittal.

Section 924.07, Florida Statutes (1981), authorizes appeals by the state in criminal cases as follows:

The state may appeal from:

(1) An order dismissing an indictment or information or any count thereof;

(2) An order granting a new trial;

(3) An order arresting judgment;

(4) A ruling on a question of law when the defendant is convicted and appeals from the judgment;

(5) The sentence, on the ground that it is illegal;

(6) A judgment discharging a prisoner on habeas corpus;

(7) An order adjudicating a defendant insane under the Florida Rules of Criminal Procedure; or

(8) All other pretrial orders, except that it may not take more than one appeal under this subsection in any case.

Such appeal shall embody all assignments of error in each pretrial order that the state seeks to have reviewed. The state shall pay all costs of such appeal except for the defendant's attorney's fee.

A trial court's order granting a motion for judgment of acquittal is not among the rulings set out in the statute and thereby identified as appealable by the state in criminal cases.[17] In dismissing the state's appeal, the district court cited *Whidden v. State*, 159 Fla. 691, 32 So.2d 577 (1947), which held that the state's right of appeal in criminal cases is purely statutory. Thus the district court indicated that its dismissal of the appeal was based on the lack of statutory authority. The state argues, however, that it has a right to an appeal conferred not by statute, but by the Constitution of Florida.

The state relies on article V, section 4(b)(1), Florida Constitution, which provides in pertinent part that the district courts of appeal

shall have jurisdiction to hear appeals, that may be taken as a matter of right, from final judgments or orders of trial courts ... not directly appealable to the supreme court or a circuit court.

The state argues, in effect, that this provision confers upon any litigant the right to appeal a final judgment or order of a trial court. As authority for this proposition, the state relies on *State v. W.A.M.*, 412 So.2d 49 (Fla. 5th DCA), *review denied*, 419 So.2d 1201 (Fla.1982). In that decision, the district court of appeal held the state could appeal an order of speedy-trial discharge in a juvenile case, even though "no statute or rule authorize[d] it," on the ground that article V, section 4(b)(1), conferred a constitutional right of appeal. *Id.* at 50.

The district court in *W.A.M.* relied upon *Crownover v. Shannon*, 170 So.2d 299 (Fla.1964), where this Court held that the constitutional provision pertaining to the

---

17. [FN4.] Section 924.071, Florida Statutes (1981), provides additional grounds for appeal by the state in criminal cases, none of which is applicable here:

(1) The state may appeal from a pretrial order dismissing a search warrant, suppressing evidence obtained by search and seizure, or suppressing a confession or admission made by a defendant. The appeal must be taken before the trial.

(2) An appeal by the state from a pretrial order shall stay the case against each defendant upon whose application the order was made until the appeal is determined. If the trial court determines that the evidence, confession, or admission that is the subject of the order would materially assist the state in proving its case against another defendant and that the prosecuting attorney intends to use it for that purpose, the court shall stay the case of that defendant until the appeal is determined. A defendant in custody whose case is stayed either automatically or by order of the court shall be released on his own recognizance pending the appeal if he is charged with a bailable offense.

jurisdiction of the district courts of appeal did indeed confer a right to appeal final judgments of trial courts. The district court in *W.A.M.* acknowledged that *Crownover* was decided under a previous version of the constitution and that the difference in language is "substantial," but simply concluded: "we do not believe such changes were intended to eliminate the right of appeal from final judgments." 412 So.2d at 50.

The argument of the state in support of its effort to overturn the decision of the district court in the instant case requires for its proper resolution some discussion of constitutional history. In 1956, article V of the Florida Constitution was substantially revised. Among the amendments was the provision creating the district courts of appeal. Prior to the establishment of the district courts of appeal in 1957, the Supreme Court of Florida had

> appellate jurisdiction in all cases at law and in equity originating in Circuit Courts, and of appeals from the Circuit Courts in cases arising before the Judges of the County Courts in matters pertaining to their probate jurisdiction and in the management of the estates of infants, and in cases of conviction of felony in the criminal courts, and in all criminal cases originating in the circuit courts.

As can readily be seen, the Supreme Court was, under article V of the Constitution of 1885, prior to the 1956 revision, the single court of general appellate jurisdiction of major cases.[18]

In *Whidden v. State*, 159 Fla. 691, 32 So.2d 577 (1947), this Court said, "The state's right to appeal is purely statutory, and is found in Sections 924.07 and 924.08, Fla.Stat. 1941…." *Id.* at 692, 32 So.2d at 578. Applying that principle, the Court held that an order of a county judge quashing an instrument charging a criminal offense could be appealed by the state to the circuit court. The Court's opinion shows that it was accepted as obvious that the existence of statutes defining the circumstances under which the state could appeal adverse rulings in criminal cases was to be controlling. Thus it is clear that before the 1956 amendment, the state's right of appeal was purely statutory. *State v. Frear*, 155 Fla. 479, 20 So.2d 481 (1945).

In 1956 article V was revised and the district courts of appeal were created. The appellate jurisdiction of those courts was defined in pertinent part as follows:

> (3) *Jurisdiction.* Appeals from trial courts in each appellate district, and from final orders or decrees of county judge's courts pertaining to probate matters or to estates and interests of minors and incompetents, may be taken to the court of appeal of such district, as a matter of right, from all final judgments

---

18. [FN5.] The circuit courts heard appeals "in all civil and criminal cases arising in the County Court, or before the County Judge, of all misdemeanors tried in criminal Courts, of judgments or sentences of any Mayor's Courts, and of all cases arising before Justices of the Peace in counties in which there is no County Court; and supervision and appellate jurisdiction of matters arising before County Judges pertaining to their probate jurisdiction, or to the estates and interests of minors, and of such other matters as the Legislature may provide." Art. V, § 11, Fla.Const. of 1885.

or decrees except those from which appeals may be taken direct to the supreme court or to a circuit court.

The supreme court shall provide for expeditious and inexpensive procedure in appeals to the district courts of appeal, and may provide for review by such courts of interlocutory orders or decrees in matters reviewable by the district courts of appeal.

The district courts of appeal shall have such powers of direct review of administrative action as may be provided by law.

Art. V, § 5(3), Fla. Const. of 1885 (1956). The *Crownover v. Shannon* decision, relied upon by the district court in *W.A.M.* as discussed above, was an interpretation of the above-quoted language, specifically the indication that "appeals ... may be taken ... as a matter of right...." Although it had been opined that the definition of the new district courts' appellate jurisdiction was not intended to create any substantive rights not existing before, but only to re-allocate jurisdiction, see Opinion of the Attorney General 056-306 (October 16, 1956), this Court in *Crownover* said:

> The right to appeal from the final decisions of trial courts to the Supreme Court and to the District Courts of Appeal has become a part of the Constitution and is no longer dependent on statutory authority or subject to be impaired or abridged by statutory law, but of course subject to rules promulgated by the Supreme Court regulating the practice and procedure.

Crownover v. Shannon, 170 So.2d at 301. It should be noted that *Crownover* was a civil case.

Crownover stands for the legal proposition that the 1956 amendment defining the appellate jurisdiction of the district courts, by using language different from that used to define appellate jurisdiction in article V prior to the 1956 amendment, had created a constitutional right of appeal that did not exist under prior law. If indeed the 1956 change of language was intended to have such effect, then it would follow that a subsequent substantial change in the constitutional language was similarly intended to alter the effect of the jurisdictional provisions.

Where there is a significant change in the language of the constitution, it is to be presumed that the change was intentional and was intended to have a different effect from the prior language. *See, e.g., In re Advisory Opinion to the Governor*, 112 So.2d 843 (Fla.1959); *Swartz v. State*, 316 So.2d 618 (Fla. 1st DCA 1975). The 1956 language interpreted in *Crownover*, providing that "[a]ppeals ... may be taken to the court of appeal ... as a matter of right," art. V, § 5(3), Fla. Const. of 1885, was eliminated by the 1972 revision of article V. As has been stated previously the present language brought about by the 1972 revision provides that the district courts of appeal "shall have jurisdiction to hear appeals, that may be taken as a matter of right, from final judgments or orders of trial courts ... not directly appealable to the supreme court or a circuit court." Art. V, § 4(b)(1), Fla. Const. The elimination of the language found dispositive in *Crownover* must be taken as having intended to negate the interpretation given by *Crownover* that the constitution had bestowed a right of appeal, thus returning to the long-standing rule stated in *State v. Whidden* that the state's right of appeal is controlled by statute.

Principles of English usage indicate that the present language was not intended to provide that all final orders and judgments are appealable as a matter of constitutional right. The word "that" is the restrictive, or defining pronoun. It introduces matter that defines, restricts, modifies, or qualifies the matter to which it refers. On the other hand, the word "which" is the nonrestrictive or nondefining pronoun and is used to introduce a separate, independent, or additional fact about the matter referred to. W. Strunk and E.B. White, *The Elements of Style* 53 (1972). So, the clause, "that may be taken as a matter of right," restricts the term "appeals" so as to apply the grant of jurisdiction only with regard to appeals that may be taken as a matter of right. Nothing is said about the circumstances under which a litigant has the right to take an appeal. The reader is in effect told to look elsewhere to determine whether there is such a right. In order to plainly say that all final judgments may indeed be appealed as a matter of right, the constitution would have to use the clause "*which* may be taken as a matter of right." In such a context, "which" does not define or restrict such appeals but independently describes them, adding information in a way that would have independent substantive effect. *See* M. Kammer and C. Mulligan, *Writing Handbook* 117–18, 138, 151–52 (1953). If the word "which" had been used instead of "that," one could logically interpret the language to confer upon a litigant the right to appeal a final judgment or order. *See also* H.W. Fowler, *Modern English Usage* 713 (1937). But we must look at the language actually used, and that language indicates that the question of when an aggrieved litigant is entitled to an appeal is a matter to be determined by sources of authority other than the constitution.

Moreover, during the period from 1957 through 1972, when the language underlying the *Crownover* decision (a civil case) was in effect, the courts of Florida continued to operate under the assumption that the state's right of appeal in criminal cases was governed by statute. [Citations omitted.] Cases decided after the 1972 revision of article V still recognize the right of appeal as a matter of substantive law controllable by statute not only in criminal cases but in civil cases as well. [citations omitted]; *see generally* Fla.R.App.P. 9.140, Committee Note.

This understanding is in keeping with the common-law rule that a writ of error[19] would lie for the defendant but not for the state. Thus it is now generally held that, unless expressly provided for by statute, in criminal cases the state is not entitled to

---

19. [FN6.] At common law, the term "writ of error" was used to refer to the type of proceeding we now call an appeal. An appeal at common law was in the nature of a trial *de novo* in a court of superior jurisdiction while a writ of error was a means of having the judgment and record reviewed by a higher court. 4 Am.Jur.2d *Appeal and Error* §2 (1962).

The weight of authority is overwhelming, not only in this country but in England, that the writ will not lie at the instance of the State, and it is evident from the character of the legislation on the subject in this State that it has never been contemplated that the State could further pursue parties who had obtained judgment in their favor in prosecutions by indictment, whether by the judgment of the court or the verdict of a jury.

appeal adverse judgments and orders. *See United States v. Sanges*, 144 U.S. 310, 12 S.Ct. 609, 36 L.Ed. 445 (1892). The general common-law rule applied not only to judgments rendered upon verdicts of acquittal but also to determinations of questions of law. *Id.*

State v. Burns, 18 Fla. 185, 187 (1891). In view of this virtual prohibition of the common law, we can see sections 924.07 and 924.071 as strictly limited and carefully crafted exceptions designed to provide appellate review to the state in criminal cases where such is needed as a matter of policy and where it does not offend against constitutional principles.[20] The existence of these statutes and the established understanding of their purpose are incompatible with the suggestion that article V, section 4 confers a right on any litigant to appeal any adverse final judgment or order.[21]

In view of the above considerations—the fact that *Crownover* interpreted constitutional language that has been changed, that court decisions decided after the constitutional change make clear that appeals by the state are governed by statute, that *Crownover* itself was an aberration in interpretation of the pre-1973 language, that the present constitutional language merely allocates jurisdiction rather than conferring appeal rights, and that the common-law rule provides insight into the meaning and purpose of the criminal appeal statutes—we reaffirm the principle that the state's right of appeal in criminal cases depends on statutory authorization and is governed strictly by statute.

We note that the right of litigants to appeal in non-criminal cases is governed by statute as well. One would expect this as a matter of logical consistency. *See* chapter 59, Florida Statutes (1983) (appeal rights in general civil cases); § 120.68, Fla.Stat. (1983) (judicial review of administrative agency action). The rights to appeal various specific kinds of judicial and administrative acts are provided for by various specific statutes. *See, e.g.*, § 75.08, Fla.Stat. (1983) (bond validations); § 382.45, Fla.Stat. (1983) (appeals of judicial action on petition for certification of birth facts).

Having determined that the state's right of appeal is governed by statute, we now come to the remaining question of whether either section 924.07 or section 924.071 provides for an appeal by the state in the circumstances of this case. As will be recalled,

---

20. [FN7.] The common-law rule against appeals by the state after acquittal was not derived from the double jeopardy clause. In fact, the connection between the two should be stated the other way around. But until the decision in *Benton v. Maryland*, 395 U.S. 784 (1969), the constitutional rule against double jeopardy was not binding on the states. *Palko v. Connecticut*, 302 U.S. 319 (1937). Nevertheless, early in the history of the Union most states adhered to the common-law rule for the same protective reasons often mentioned as underlying the double jeopardy clause. *See, e.g., State v. Jones*, 7 Ga. 422 (1849); *State v. Johnson*, 2 Clarke 549 (Iowa 1856); *Commonwealth v. Cummings*, 3 Cushing 212 (Mass.1849); *State v. Solomons*, 6 Yerger 360 (Tenn.1834); *State v. Reynolds*, 4 Haywood 100 (Tenn.1817); *Commonwealth v. Harrison*, 2 Vir.Cas. 202 (Va.1820).

21. [FN8.] Nothing in the Bill of Rights, as made binding on the states through the fourteenth amendment, requires generally that persons convicted of criminal offenses be given the right to an appeal. Nevertheless, Florida grants such an appeal as a matter of right in section 924.06, Florida Statutes (1983). The only cases in which it might be suggested that there is a federal constitutional right of appeal are capital cases where the eighth amendment may require appellate review as a safeguard against arbitrariness. *See Proffitt v. Florida*, 428 U.S. 242 (1976).

the jury acquitted respondent of arson but convicted him of failure to control or give warning of the fire. Respondent then renewed his previously made motion for acquittal as is permitted under criminal rule 3.380. The court granted an acquittal, and it was this order that the state sought to challenge on appeal.

The respondent's request for a court-ordered judgment of acquittal was part of a combined motion which also included a motion for new trial under rule 3.600 and a motion for arrest of judgment under rule 3.610. The state may appeal an order granting a new trial by virtue of section 924.07(2) and may appeal an order in arrest of judgment under section 924.07(3). But it is clear that the court's order was in response to respondent's motion for judgment of acquittal and was in fact a judgment of acquittal. Nowhere in sections 924.07 or 924.071 is provision made for appeal by the state from an order granting a judgment of acquittal. Therefore the appeal of such an order is not authorized and is simply not available.

The suggestion that a judge's ruling on a motion for acquittal on the ground of insufficient evidence is a question of law for which an appeal could be allowed the state without running afoul of the double jeopardy clause is unavailing to the state here. If the statute were to provide such an appeal, then the constitutional question might well be raised. But the statute makes no provision for an appeal of a trial judge's judgment of acquittal either before or after the verdict so we need not reach the constitutional question.

For the foregoing reasons, the decision of the district court of appeal, dismissing the state's appeal from a judgment of acquittal, is approved.

It is so ordered.

Amendments to the Florida Rules of Appellate Procedure

696 So. 2d 1103 (Fla. 1996)

As Corrected on Denial of Rehearing Dec. 26, 1996.

Two Original Proceedings — Florida Rules of Appellate Procedure and Florida Rules of Criminal Procedure.

PER CURIAM.

We have for consideration The Florida Bar Appellate Rules Committee's (Committee) quadrennial report of proposed rule changes filed in accordance with Florida Rule of Judicial Administration 2.130(c)(3). We have jurisdiction pursuant to article V, section 2(a) of the Florida Constitution. We have consolidated the Committee's report with the file opened as a result of this Court's initiation of proposed rule amendments designed to simplify criminal appeals from guilty pleas and appeals relating to sentencing errors.

* * *

Our attention has become focused upon those portions of the Act which created section 925.051, which provides in part as follows:

(3) An appeal may not be taken from a judgment or order of a trial court unless a prejudicial error is alleged and is properly preserved or, if not properly preserved, would constitute fundamental error. A judgment or sentence may be reversed on appeal only when an appellate court determines after a review of the complete record that prejudicial error occurred and was properly preserved in the trial court or, if not properly preserved, would constitute fundamental error.

(4) If a defendant pleads nolo contendere without expressly reserving the right to appeal a legally dispositive issue, or if a defendant pleads guilty without expressly reserving the right to appeal a legally dispositive issue, the defendant may not appeal the judgment or sentence.

In their comments, the Committee as well as public defenders and others contend that the provisions of the Act are procedural in nature and cannot override this Court's Rules of Appellate Procedure. On the other hand, the Attorney General insists that the Act's provisions are substantive and, therefore, controlling.

The United States Supreme Court has consistently pointed out that there is no federal constitutional right of criminal defendants to a direct appeal. *Evitts v. Lucey*, 469 U.S. 387, 393 (1985) ("Almost a century ago the Court held that the Constitution does not require States to grant appeals as of right to criminal defendants seeking to review alleged trial court errors."). *Accord Abney v. United States*, 431 U.S. 651, 656 (1977); *Ross v. Moffitt*, 417 U.S. 600 (1974). Moreover, in *State v. Creighton*, 469 So.2d 735 (Fla.1985), this Court stated that there was no right to appeal set forth in our state's constitution. We reasoned that while our immediately preceding constitution provided that "appeals may be taken as a matter of right from all final judgments or decrees," the 1972 revision to article V eliminated the constitutional right to appeal by altering the language to authorize "appeals, that may be taken as a matter of right, from final judgments or orders."

However, the issue in *Creighton* was whether the State had a constitutional right to appeal. Furthermore, we did not consider in *Creighton* the fact that nowhere in the voluminous documents which reflect the history and intent of the 1972 revision of article V is there any suggestion that the revisers intended to remove from the constitution the right to appeal. Therefore, we now recede from *Creighton* to the extent that we construe the language of article V, section 4(b) as a constitutional protection of the right to appeal. However, we believe that the legislature may implement this constitutional right and place reasonable conditions upon it so long as they do not thwart the litigants' legitimate appellate rights.[22] Of course, this Court continues to have jurisdiction over the practice and procedure relating to appeals.

Applying this rationale to the amendment of section 924.051(3), we believe the legislature could reasonably condition the right to appeal upon the preservation of

---

22. [FN1.] As noted in *Creighton*, even during the period of 1956 to 1972 when there was no question that the right of appeal was protected by our constitution, we continued to recognize that the state's right to appeal in criminal cases was governed by statute.

a prejudicial error or the assertion of a fundamental error. Anticipating that we might reach such a conclusion, this Court on June 27, 1996, promulgated an emergency amendment designated as new Florida Rule of Criminal Procedure 3.800(b) to authorize the filing of a motion to correct a defendant's sentence within ten days. *Amendments to Florida Rule of Appellate Procedure 9.020(g) & Florida Rule of Criminal Procedure 3.800*, 675 So.2d 1374 (Fla.1996). Because many sentencing errors are not immediately apparent at sentencing, we felt that this rule would provide an avenue to preserve sentencing errors and thereby appeal them. However, since our adoption of the emergency amendment, a number of parties have expressed the view that the ten-day period is too short. They say that because of the copying process in the clerk's office or for other reasons, attorneys often do not timely receive copies of the sentencing orders. Others point out that as a result of the short time period, many public defenders are ordering expedited transcripts of the sentencing hearing at additional cost to the State. For these reasons, we have extended the time for filing motions to correct sentencing errors under rule 3.800(b) to thirty days.

The other issue immediately before us is the effect of the Act on the proposed rule on appeals from pleas of guilty or nolo contendere without reservation. In *Robinson v. State*, 373 So.2d 898 (Fla.1979), this Court addressed the validity of section 924.06(3), Florida Statutes (1977), which read:

> A defendant who pleads guilty or nolo contendere with no express reservation of the right to appeal shall have no right to a direct appeal. Such defendant shall obtain review by means of collateral attack.

The Court agreed that the statute properly foreclosed appeals from matters which took place before the defendant agreed to the judgment of conviction. However, the Court held that there was a limited class of issues which occur contemporaneously with the entry of the plea that may be the proper subject of an appeal. These included: (1) subject matter jurisdiction; (2) illegality of the sentence; (3) failure of the government to abide by a plea agreement; and (4) the voluntary intelligent character of the plea. *Robinson*, 373 So.2d at 902.

Section 924.051(b)(4) is directed to the same end but is worded slightly differently. Insofar as it says that a defendant who pleads nolo contendere or guilty without expressly reserving the right to appeal a legally dispositive issue cannot appeal the judgment, we believe that the principle of *Robinson* controls. A defendant must have the right to appeal that limited class of issues described in *Robinson*.

There remains, however, another problem. Section 924.051(b)(4) also states that a defendant pleading guilty or nolo contendere without expressly reserving the right to appeal a legally dispositive issue cannot appeal the sentence. However, a defendant has not yet been sentenced at the time of the plea. Obviously, one cannot expressly reserve a sentencing error which has not yet occurred. By any standard, this is not a reasonable condition to the right to appeal. Therefore, we construe this provision of the Act to permit a defendant who pleads guilty or nolo contendere without reserving a legally dispositive issue to nevertheless appeal a sentencing error, providing it has been timely preserved by motion to correct the sentence. *See State v. Iacovone*, 660 So.2d 1371 (Fla.1995); *Williams v. State*, 492 So.2d 1051 (Fla.1986) (statutes will not be interpreted so as to yield an absurd result).

Accordingly, we have rewritten rule 9.140 to accomplish the objectives set forth above. Consistent with the legislature's philosophy of attempting to resolve more issues at the trial court level, we are also promulgating Florida Rule of Criminal Procedure 3.170(l), which authorizes the filing of a motion to withdraw the plea after sentencing within thirty days from the rendition of the sentence, but only upon the grounds recognized by *Robinson* or otherwise provided by law. The amendments to the Florida Rules of Criminal Procedure will be included in our four-year cycle amendments to those rules. We have amended rule 9.020(h) to provide that a motion to withdraw the plea after sentencing will postpone rendition until its disposition. While we also received comments that other portions of the Act are inconsistent with the rules, we have determined to address on a case-by-case basis any of these issues which may arise.

* * *

Accordingly, the Florida Rules of Appellate Procedure are amended as reflected in the appendix to this opinion. New language is indicated by underscoring; deletions are indicated by struck-through type. The Committee Notes are offered for explanation only and are not adopted as an official part of the rules. The amendments set forth in the appendix shall become effective January 1, 1997, at 12:01 a.m.

It is so ordered.

ANSTEAD, Justice, specially concurring.

I write separately in support of our decision today to recede from the suggestion in *State v. Creighton*, 469 So.2d 735 (Fla.1985), that the citizens of Florida voted in 1972 to amend the Florida Constitution to eliminate a citizen's right to appeal from final orders and judgments.

Creighton

In *Crownover v. Shannon*, 170 So.2d 299 (Fla.1964), this Court declared:

> The right to appeal from the final decisions of trial courts to the Supreme Court and to the District Courts of Appeal has become a part of the Constitution and is no longer dependent on statutory authority or subject to be impaired or abridged by statutory law, but of course subject to rules promulgated by the Supreme Court regulating the practice and procedure.

Id. at 301.[23] That a citizen's right to appeal was protected by the Constitution was unquestioned before 1985 and the issuance of the opinion in Creighton.

---

23. [FN2.] Similarly, in *Marshall v. State*, 344 So.2d 646, 648 (Fla. 2d DCA 1977), Justice Grimes, then a district court judge, declared for an [sic] unanimous panel: "Our Florida Constitution guarantees convicted persons of the right of appeal...." See also Judge Cowart's opinion in *State v. W.A.M.*, 412 So.2d 49 (5th DCA), review denied, 419 So.2d 1201 (Fla.1982) (finding that although article V was revised in 1972, the right to appeal was not affected).

Creighton involved an issue concerning only the State's limited right to appeal.[24] The *Creighton* dicta contained no analysis of the constitutional amendment process. Nor does it address the intent of the drafters of the revisions, or the intent of the voters, or the extensive provisions concerning appeals and appellate courts set out in the Florida Constitution.[25] Rather, the entire analysis in Creighton rests on speculation as to why the legislature used the word "that" preceding its reference to the right to appeal in the constitution. This analysis is clearly flawed and inadequate.[26]

Constitutional Analysis

Unfortunately, the majority opinion in *Creighton* failed to adhere to this Court's own earlier admonitions as to the method of analysis to be applied in such a situation. Professor Levinson, in his comprehensive work on constitutional law, pointedly discusses this issue:

---

24. [FN3.] *See Crownover v. Shannon*, 170 So.2d 299, 300 (Fla.1964), holding: "Before the enactment of chapter 19554 in 1939, there was no right of appeal or writ of error by the State in criminal prosecutions."

25. [FN5.] For example, there is no explanation in *Creighton* of why the people would make such extensive provisions for a system of appeal in the constitution but leave it up to the legislature to decide if the system should ever be used. The constitution does not say that is what was contemplated.

26. [FN6.] Attorney Stephen Krosschell, in a brief filed with this Court, explains that even the "grammatical" analysis of *Creighton* is flawed:

> *Creighton* turns on the fact that Article V, Section 4(b)(1) ("District courts of appeal shall have jurisdiction to hear appeals, that may be taken as a matter of right, from final judgments or orders of trial courts....") uses the word "that" rather than "which." According to *Creighton*, "that" is a word of restriction which restricts the word "appeals" to those appeals that can be taken as a matter of right, i.e., those appeals permitted by the legislature. By contrast, if the constitution had used "which," this word would not have restricted the word "appeals," and the clause "(which) may be taken as a matter of right" would have been an independent statement of the constitutional right to appeal. 469 So.2d at 739.
>
> I doubt that, in today's usage since the turn of the century, "that" and "which" have the meanings which Creighton gave these words. These words are used interchangeably in this century, and the old grammatical distinctions no longer apply. Furthermore, the elementary (and still valid) rule of grammar applicable here in my view is that clauses separated by commas are nonrestrictive clauses intended to introduce independent concepts. The commas around the clause "that may be taken as a matter of right" in Article V, Section 4(b)(3), mean that this clause does not restrict "appeals" to those appeals permitted by the legislature. It instead is a nonrestrictive clause which independently expresses the constitutional right to appeal. Only if the commas in Article V, Section 4(b)(3), were absent would *Creighton* have been correct that this clause is a restrictive clause which restricts appeals to those permitted by the legislature.

Accordingly, this Court should recede from this reasoning in *Creighton*, which was dicta and unnecessary to the result of the case. *Creighton* involved a state appeal and was properly decided on the principle that the legislature can restrict the types of appeals which its employees (such as prosecutors) may take. *Creighton* did not need to make the further holding that the right to appeal is statutory—not only for prosecutors but for everyone else as well.

Transition from Old to New Constitution

1. REPETITION OF IDENTICAL PROVISION IN NEW AND OLD CONSTITUTIONS

If the new constitution contains a provision identical to the corresponding provision in the old, judicial interpretations of the old constitution retain their validity as interpretations of the new, since the framers or the voters are presumed to have known the old interpretations and to have intended to preserve them by repeating the same constitutional language.

2. SIMILAR BUT NOT IDENTICAL PROVISION IN NEW AND OLD CONSTITUTIONS

If the new constitution contains a provision similar but not identical to the corresponding provision in the old, the question arises whether the framers or voters intended a mere change in literary style (in which event the cases decided under the old constitution continue to govern) or a change of meaning (in which event the old cases are superseded).

In *Hayek v. Lee County* [231 So.2d 214 (Fla.1970)], the issue was whether article III, section 11(a)(1) of the 1968 constitution, on laws "pertaining to ... jurisdiction ... of [court] officers," should receive the same interpretation as had been given to the corresponding provision of the 1885 constitution about laws "regulating the jurisdiction ... of officers." The court examined the minutes of the Constitutional Revision Commission and determined, on rehearing, that the change was merely one of style and that the framers intended to preserve the meaning developed by the old cases.

L. Harold Levinson, *Florida Constitutional Law*, 28 U.Miami L.R. 551, 557 (1973).

In *Hayek*, this Court candidly declared:

Subsequent to the rendition of the original decision in this cause, November 5, 1969, from which we now recede, we have examined minutely the record of the proceedings of the Constitutional Revision Commission appointed to draft the Constitution which was adopted by the people in the General Election of 1968 and became effective January 7, 1969, and many documents relating thereto which have been collected and are now preserved in the Supreme Court Library. The revelations of these various documents and a more thorough study and comparison of the language used in each constitution convince us there was no intention to change in any way the purposes to be served by such provisions.

Had the majority in *Creighton* followed the rule of analysis set out by this Court in *Hayek* and examined the constitutional revision proceedings of 1972, it would have discovered the obvious: that there was never an intent to remove the right of appeal from article V. In fact, as the chair of the legislative committee responsible for the revisions declared at the time, the drafters of the amendments intended just the opposite—to preserve a citizen's recognized constitutional right to appeal under article V.[27]

Constitutional Revision Process of 1972

The *Creighton* dicta provides no analysis for its rather astounding conclusion that in 1972 the people of the State of Florida, without even knowing about it, affirmatively voted to take away their own right to appeal. Of course, the constitutional revision process is conducted in the Florida sunshine, and it was conducted in the sunshine in 1972. Yet, *Creighton* cites not one piece of evidence of any kind from the legislative or public process of amending the Constitution, nor any ballot summary, as informing the Florida voters that they would be doing away with their right to appeal if they approved the amendments proposed in 1972. Surely no one could seriously contend that such an important change in the Constitution would be made without disclosing this intent.

In fact, there are sixteen file folders in our own Supreme Court Library labeled "Legislative History and Intent" and brimming with letters, drafts, committee notes, and research materials—all chronicling in detail the very public 1972 article V revision process from its inception. And, there is not one word in these materials indicating that a citizen's constitutional right to appeal in article V was meant to be affected in any way by the 1972 revisions. To the contrary, those materials contain unrebutted evidence, including the House Judiciary Chairman's written expression, indicating that no change to a citizen's right to appeal was contemplated. Copies of the House summary of the proposed amendments to article V as well as the ballot summary and the League of Women Voters public information guide are footnoted here to clearly demonstrate that a citizen's right to appeal was not eliminated in 1972. There is no suggestion or hint in any of these materials that the right to appeal was affected by the proposed revisions. In fact, before the constitutional revisions of 1972 were placed on the ballot, the chairman of the House Judiciary Committee, Talbot D'Alemberte, the recognized "father" and drafter of the revisions, expressly declared that "[w]e intended to provide for the right to appeal from final judgments."

Facial Analysis of Article V, Section 4(b)(1)

In addition, even a superficial examination of the explicit provisions of article V demonstrates that the drafters clearly distinguished the jurisdiction of the district courts under article V, section 4(b)(1) "to hear appeals, that may be taken as a matter of right" from other appeals.[28] Specifically, for example, the drafters limited appeals

---

27. [FN7.] See letter of September 23, 1971, from Talbot D'Alemberte, Chairman, House Judiciary Committee, to Mallory Horton contained in materials on 1972 constitutional revisions located in the Florida Supreme Court Library; see also Talbot D'Alemberte, *Judicial Reform—Now or Never*, 46 Fla.Bar Journal 68 (1972); Talbot D'Alemberte, *The Florida State Constitution: A Reference Guide* (1991).

28. [FN10.] Article V, Section 4(b)(1) provides:

District courts of appeal shall have jurisdiction to hear appeals, that may be taken as a matter of right, from final judgments or orders of trial courts, including those entered on review of administrative action, not directly appealable to the supreme court or a circuit

in administrative matters and in circuit court to appeals "as prescribed by general law." See section 4(b)(2) (administrative appeals)[29] and section 5(b) (circuit court appellate jurisdiction).[30] There is no such limitation on the jurisdiction of the Supreme Court or the district courts of appeal. The drafters knew what the phrase "as prescribed by general law" meant and did not use it as a limitation of a citizen's right to appeal to the district courts of appeal or the Supreme Court. Instead, they used that phrase intentionally to permit the legislature to provide for appeals in administrative proceedings and in the circuit courts.

Further, after providing for appeals to the district courts as a matter of right from final judgments and orders of trial courts, the drafters provided that the Supreme Court could decide by rule what interlocutory orders could be appealed to the district courts. A plain reading of these provisions reveals that the constitution explicitly provides for appeals as a matter of right from final judgments and orders, with the Supreme Court deciding what interlocutory orders may be appealed. Otherwise, we would be left with the anomalous situation of the Supreme Court providing for interlocutory appeals in cases where the legislature may have said there shall be no appeal at all from the final outcome.

Conclusion

Whatever the method of analysis used, it is apparent that the legislature never intended and did not propose a change in article V in 1972 to eliminate a citizen's right to appeal, and Florida citizens never voted to do away with their right to appeal. By receding from the Creighton dicta, we have now set the record straight on this important right of Florida citizens.

KOGAN, C.J., and SHAW, J., concur.

State v. M.K.

786 So. 2d 24 (Fla. 1st DCA 2001)

PADOVANO, J.

This is an appeal by the state from an order denying a request to impose restitution liens in a juvenile delinquency proceeding. We conclude that we lack appellate juris-

---

court. They may review interlocutory orders in such cases to the extent provided by rules adopted by the supreme court.

29. [FN11.] Article V, Section 4(b)(2) provides:
District courts of appeal shall have the power of direct review of administrative action, as prescribed by general law.

30. [FN12.] Article V, Section 5(b) provides:
JURISDICTION.—The circuit courts shall have original jurisdiction not vested in the county courts, and jurisdiction of appeals when provided by general law. They shall have the power to issue writs of mandamus, quo warranto, certiorari, prohibition and habeas corpus, and all writs necessary or proper to the complete exercise of their jurisdiction. Jurisdiction of the circuit court shall be uniform throughout the state. They shall have the power of direct review of administrative action prescribed by general law.

diction, because there is no statute or court rule authorizing the state to appeal the order at issue. Accordingly, we dismiss the appeal.

The child, M.K., entered pleas of nolo contendere in five juvenile delinquency cases and was placed on concurrent terms of community control. In the disposition order, the trial court directed the child to make restitution in specified amounts to each of the victims. At that time, the child was seventeen and still within the jurisdiction of the juvenile court. The disposition order contains an optional clause stating that the court retains jurisdiction for enforcement or modification of restitution beyond the child's nineteenth birthday, but the trial judge did not check off this clause in the present case.

More than a year and a half after the disposition hearing, the state requested that the court impose restitution liens for the amounts remaining due to the victims. This request was considered in a hearing on July 12, 2000, about four months after the child turned nineteen. Counsel for the state argued that the trial court could impose a restitution lien without a specific reservation of jurisdiction for that purpose, but the trial court concluded that it lacked jurisdiction to enter an order enforcing restitution after the child's nineteenth birthday. Consequently, the trial court denied the state's request for the restitution liens.

The state appealed the trial court's decision to this court, but the court issued an order directing the state to show cause why the appeal should not be dismissed for lack of jurisdiction. In response, the state argued that the appeal is authorized by section 924.07(1)(k), Florida Statutes (2000), which provides that the state may appeal from "an order denying restitution under section 775.089." Counsel for the child contends that section 924.07(1)(k) applies only to appeals in adult criminal cases and that there is no comparable provision in Chapter 985 that would authorize an appeal from a restitution order in a juvenile case.

We begin with the proposition that the state's right to appeal is purely statutory. In *State v. Creighton*, 469 So.2d 735 (Fla.1985), the supreme court held that the state's right to appeal a final order in a criminal case depends on the existence of a statute authorizing the appeal. Subsequently, the court applied this same principle to orders in juvenile delinquency proceedings. See *E.N. v. State*, 484 So.2d 1210 (Fla.1986); *State v. C.C.*, 476 So.2d 144 (Fla.1985). Although the supreme court has since receded in part from *Creighton* by stating that the Florida Constitution does guarantee a citizen the right to appeal a final order, see *Amendments to Florida Rules of Appellate Procedure*, 685 So.2d 773 (Fla.1996), the court left intact its holding in *Creighton* that the state's right to appeal depends on the existence of a statute. See *State v. Allen*, 743 So.2d 532 (Fla. 1st DCA 1997). Because the Florida Constitution does not afford the state a right to appeal, the state can appeal a final order in a criminal case or a juvenile delinquency proceeding only if there is a statute authorizing the appeal.

The state contends that the appeal is authorized by section 924.071(1)(k), but this statute applies exclusively to appeals in adult criminal cases. Juvenile delinquency cases are governed by Chapter 985, which contains a separate list of orders that can be appealed by the state. *See* § 985.234(1)(b), Fla. Stat. (2000). If the Legislature meant to apply the list of appealable orders in Chapter 924 to juvenile delinquency cases as well as adult criminal cases, it would not have enacted more specific provisions in section 985.234(1)(b).

Although this case must be analyzed under the laws pertaining to juveniles, it presents a problem that once existed in adult criminal cases, as well. The history of the issue in criminal cases is helpful here. In *State v. MacLeod*, 600 So.2d 1096 (Fla.1992), the supreme court held that this court lacked jurisdiction to hear an appeal from an order denying restitution in a criminal case. At that time, Chapter 924 did not authorize an appeal by the state from a restitution order. The supreme court applied the rule in *Creighton* and other cases holding that the state's right to appeal is purely statutory, and ultimately concluded that the state's appeal was correctly dismissed for lack of jurisdiction.

Following the decision *McLeod*, the Legislature enacted section 924.071(1)(k), Florida Statutes, which authorizes the state to appeal an order denying restitution. However, the Legislature did not also add this new provision to Chapter 985 (then Chapter 39), the statute governing juvenile delinquency proceedings. Section 985.234(1)(b) identifies the kinds of orders the state can appeal in a juvenile delinquency case, and an order denying restitution is not among those orders.

The jurisdictional problem in this case could not be overcome by treating the order as a nonfinal order, because there is likewise no authority for the appeal in the applicable court rules. The jurisdiction of a district court of appeal to hear an appeal by the state from a nonfinal order depends on the existence of a court rule authorizing the appeal. *See Blore v. Fierro*, 636 So.2d 1329 (Fla.1994); *State v. Gaines*, 731 So.2d 7 (Fla. 4th DCA 1999). Rule 9.140 entitled "Appeal Proceedings in Criminal Cases" contains a provision authorizing the state to appeal an order denying restitution. *See* Fla.R.App.P. 9.140(c)(1)(L). However, there is no comparable provision in rule 9.145 entitled "Appeal Proceedings in Juvenile Delinquency Cases."

In summary, we conclude that this court lacks jurisdiction to consider the state's appeal. The state is not entitled to appeal an order in a juvenile delinquency case as a matter of right, and there is no statute authorizing the state to appeal the order at issue here.

Appeal dismissed.

BENTON and POLSTON, JJ., concur.

Commentary

The District Courts of Appeal were created in 1957, and their role was redefined in the 1980 constitutional amendments that changed Supreme Court jurisdiction. The jurisdiction of the DCAs is broad, because they are essentially the final appellate court for most cases. The jurisdiction of the DCAs is defined in Article V, Section 4(b). As the two previous cases demonstrate, interpretation of constitutional language is key. They question whether certain appeals may be taken as a matter of right, or whether the right to appeal can be limited by statute in certain circumstances. For example, a statute can limit the right of the state to appeal under the facts of the *State v. M.K.* case.

E. Binding Authority of District Courts of Appeal on Trial Courts

The Supreme Court of Florida's decisions bind all courts in Florida. But what courts are bound by the opinion of a District Court of Appeal? Is it all trial courts in Florida? Or is it only those trial courts in the geographical jurisdiction of the DCA that issued the opinion in question?

While some states provide the latter, or remain murky, Florida is fortunate enough to have an opinion from its Supreme Court clarifying the situation.

Pardo v. State
596 So. 2d 665 (Fla. 1992)

BARKETT, Justice.

We have for review *State v. Pardo*, 582 So.2d 1225 (Fla. 3d DCA 1991), in which the district court certified express and direct conflict with *Kopko v. State*, 577 So.2d 956 (Fla. 5th DCA 1991), and certified the following question of great public importance:

> Where a child victim's hearsay statements satisfy subsection 90.803(23), Florida Statutes (1989), and the child is able to testify fully at trial, must the hearsay statements be excluded solely because they are prior consistent statement by the child, or is the test for exclusion that found in section 90.403, Florida Statutes (1989)?

582 So.2d at 1228. In addition to the certified question and conflict, we also find the district court's opinion conflicts with the Fourth District's decision in *State v. Hayes*, 333 So.2d 51 (Fla. 4th DCA 1976), and our decision in *Weiman v. McHaffie*, 470 So.2d 682 (Fla.1985).

James Antonio Pardo is charged with seven counts of capital sexual battery on a child seven years of age. Pursuant to subsection 90.803(23), Florida Statutes (1989), the State filed notices of intent to rely on hearsay statements made by the child victim to nine separate individuals. After conducting a hearing as provided by the statute, the court found the statements of three witnesses sufficiently reliable to be admissible. However, the court also found that the State intended to call the child to testify at trial and that the child had the ability to testify fully concerning all the elements of the alleged crimes. The court concluded that it was required to exclude the hearsay statements under the authority of *Kopko v. State*, 577 So.2d 956, 962 (Fla. 5th DCA 1991), which held that, even though the criteria of section 90.803(23) are satisfied, where the child is able to testify fully regarding the circumstances of the alleged abuse,

Bilston rule

hearsay statements regarding the abuse are inadmissible prior consistent statements. Accordingly, the trial court ordered the hearsay statements excluded. The district court suggested that the trial court was entitled to disregard *Kopko*, and in any event, determined that the holding in *Kopko* was inconsistent with the plain language of the statute, and therefore quashed the trial court's order.

Initially, we note that the district court erred in commenting that decisions of other district courts of appeal were not binding on the trial court. This Court has stated that "[t]he decisions of the district courts of appeal represent the law of Florida unless and until they are overruled by this Court." *Stanfill v. State*, 384 So.2d 141, 143 (Fla.1980). Thus, in the absence of interdistrict conflict, district court decisions bind all Florida trial courts. *Weiman v. McHaffie*, 470 So.2d 682, 684 (Fla.1985). The purpose of this rule was explained by the Fourth District in *State v. Hayes*:

DC's bind all FL courts

(How is that even real?)

> The District Courts of Appeal are required to follow Supreme Court decisions. As an adjunct to this rule it is logical and necessary in order to preserve stability and predictability in the law that, likewise, trial courts be required to follow the holdings of higher courts — District Courts of Appeal. The proper hierarchy of decisional holdings would demand that in the event the only case on point on a district level is from a district other than the one in which the trial court is located, the trial court be required to follow that decision. Alternatively, if the district court of the district in which the trial court is located has decided the issue, the trial court is bound to follow it. Contrarily, as between District Courts of Appeal, a sister district's opinion is merely persuasive.

333 So.2d 51, 53 (Fla. 4th DCA 1976) (footnote and citations omitted). Consequently, the trial court in this case was bound by the Fifth District's decision in *Kopko*.

* * *

Accordingly, we approve in part and quash in part the opinion of the court below, disapprove the Fifth District's opinion in *Kopko*, and remand for proceedings consistent with this opinion.

It is so ordered.

SHAW, C.J., and OVERTON, McDONALD, GRIMES, KOGAN and HARDING, JJ., concur.

Questions

1. Why did the Supreme Court have to write this opinion if its holding had already been iterated in a Fourth District Court of Appeal case?

2. Does the supremacy of a DCA opinion across the entire state hold in every instance? If not, what is the exception?

F. Trial Courts

Article V, Section 5—Circuit Courts

Article V, Section 6—County Courts

Commentary

The Constitution does not prescribe the exact point at which a case at law (i.e., for money) surpasses the jurisdiction of a county court and becomes subject to the jurisdiction of a circuit court. It simply says that circuit courts "shall have original jurisdiction not vested in the county courts, and jurisdiction of appeals when provided by general law." About county courts, the Constitution provides, "There shall be a county court in each county," and leaves its jurisdiction to be "prescribed by general law." Why might something as important and basic as trial court jurisdiction be left so vague in the Constitution? The Constitution also does not prescribe any detail about the appellate jurisdiction the circuit court has. The circuit court is a trial court. Why would it have appellate jurisdiction at all? Along the same lines, a 2019 statute put into place a stepped change in county court jurisdiction and changed the court to which certain county court judgments would be appealed. FLA. STAT. § 26.012 (2019). Why would this information not be changed in the constitution?

G. Selection of Judges

Article V, Section 8—Eligibility

Article V, Section 11—Vacancies

Commentary

Before the 1972 adoption of Article V, vacancies in judicial seats were filled by the Governor. There were no particular standards and no official, consistent vetting process. But when Reubin Askew became Governor in 1970, he created judicial nominating commissions (JNCs) to select potential judges based on merit rather than political cronyism. JNCs consisted of nine individuals: three chosen by the Governor, three chosen by The Florida Bar, and three chosen by those six members. The 1972 Article V placed the JNCs in the Constitution.

However, the makeup of the JNCs was not defined in the Constitution. After Jeb Bush became Governor in 1998, Bush persuaded the Legislature to change the makeup of the JNCs, removing the three-three-and-three makeup. The new composition of the JNCs, under Florida Statute § 43.291, is four members of The Florida Bar appointed by the Governor from a list provided by The Florida Bar, which the Governor may reject and request a new list from which to choose; and five members appointed by the Governor, at least two of whom must be members of The Florida Bar. Thus, Askew's careful balance of viewpoints of JNC members has been replaced with gubernatorial approval of all nine members.

Even so, the JNCs have not always produced nominees with whom the Governor is satisfied. In *Pleus v. Crist*, which follows, the Florida Supreme Court had to resolve such a disagreement.

Pleus v. Crist

14 So. 3d 941 (Fla. 2009)

LABARGA, J.

Petitioner Robert J. Pleus, Jr., a retired judge of the Fifth District Court of Appeal, filed a petition for writ of mandamus in this Court seeking an order compelling Governor Crist to fill the vacancy created in the Fifth District Court of Appeal by the Petitioner's mandatory resignation. The issue raised by the petition concerns the extent of the Governor's authority in making judicial appointments under the Florida Constitution. Specifically, we are called upon to decide whether the Governor must fill the vacancy created by Petitioner's resignation with a judicial appointment from the list of nominees certified to him on November 6, 2008, and do so within sixty days of receiving that list. Having reviewed the parties' pleadings, as well as the briefs filed by Amici Curiae, and in consideration of the oral arguments, we conclude that the Florida Constitution mandates that the Governor appoint a judicial nominee within sixty days of the certification of nominees by the Judicial Nominating Commission for the Fifth Appellate District. We also conclude that, within this process, the Governor is not provided the authority under the constitution to reject the certified list and request that a new list be certified.

I. Background

The facts are not in dispute. Petitioner tendered his resignation as judge of the Fifth District Court of Appeal to the Governor on September 2, 2008, to become effective on January 5, 2009. Having accepted the Petitioner's letter of resignation, the Governor requested that the Judicial Nominating Commission for the Fifth Appellate District (hereinafter "JNC") provide him with a list of qualified applicants. A total of twenty-six applicants sought the appointment.

The JNC reviewed the applications and conducted interviews. On November 6, 2008, the JNC certified to the Governor a list of six nominees for appointment to the Fifth District Court of Appeal.

In a letter dated December 1, 2008, the Governor advised the JNC Chair that he was rejecting the certified list of nominees. In the interest of diversity in the courts, the Governor requested that the JNC reconvene to consider the applications of three African-Americans who had applied to fill the vacancy.

The JNC met to consider the Governor's request, and resubmitted the original list of nominees to the Governor. The Governor has not filled the vacancy to date.

II. History and Intent of Article V, Section 11(c), Florida Constitution

Article V, section 11(c), governs the time periods applicable to judicial nominating commissions in nominating judicial applicants to fill vacancies and to the governor in making judicial appointments. That provision of the constitution expressly requires the following: "The nominations shall be made within thirty days from the occurrence of a vacancy unless the period is extended by the governor for a time not to exceed thirty days. The governor shall make the appointment within sixty days after the nominations have been certified to the governor."

In the past, we have discussed at length the origin and purpose of article V, section 11, of the Florida Constitution, explaining the restraints the constitutional provision places on the Governor's appointment power:

> In the deliberations of the Florida Constitutional Revision Commission, it was proposed that judicial nominating commissions be created to screen applicants for judicial appointments within their respective jurisdictions and to nominate the three best qualified persons to the Governor for his appointment. *The commissions were to be an arm of the executive appointive power to supplant, at least in part, the Governor's so-called "patronage committee" composed of political supporters, to insure that politics would not be the only criteria in the selection of judges, and to increase generally the efficiency of the judicial appointive process.*
>
> * * *
>
> [T]he judicial nominating commissions [of the Revised Article V of the Florida Constitution, effective January 1, 1973] are elevated to constitutional stature and permanence. *The process of non-partisan selection has been strengthened even further because nominations made by the judicial nominating commissions have now been made binding upon the Governor, as he is under a constitutional mandate to appoint "one of not fewer than three persons nominated by the appropriate judicial nominating commission."* Moreover, the Governor must make the appointment within sixty days after the nominations have been certified to him. Fla. Const., art. V (Rev.), § 11(a), F.S.A. However, this same provision confers upon the Governor the express power to make the final and ultimate selection by appointment.
>
> * * *
>
> *The purpose of the judicial nominating commission is to take the judiciary out of the field of political patronage and provide a method of checking the qualifications of persons seeking the office of judge.* When the commission has completed its investigation and reached a conclusion, the persons meeting the qualifications are nominated. In this respect the commissioners act in an advisory capacity to aid the Governor in the conscientious exercise of his executive appointive power.
>
> * * *
>
> *This appointive power is diluted by the Constitution to the extent that a nomination must be made by the appropriate commission, unrestrained by the influence of the Governor.* To allow the Governor to guide the deliberations of the commissions by imposing rules of procedure could destroy its con-

stitutional independence. This does not preclude him from making recommendations concerning rules.

Seeking to remove some of the discretion of the Governor's office in the appointment of judicial officers is an apparent goal of the people which can best be attained by providing discretion to their commissions to promulgate rules of procedure for their hearings and findings, independent of any of the three standard recognized divisions of state government. While the function of the commissions is inherently executive in nature, the mandate for the commissions comes from the people and the Constitution, not from the Legislature, the Governor, or the Courts.

In re Advisory Opinion to the Governor, 276 So.2d 25, 28–30 (Fla.1973) (emphasis added) (citation omitted).

Similarly, in *Spector v. Glisson*, 305 So.2d 777 (Fla.1974), we restated the objective that underlies displacing sole executive prerogative from the judicial appointment process:

The nominating commission process in § 11 of Art. V is really a restraint upon the Governor—not a new process for removing from the people their traditional right to elect their judges as provided in the basic, preceding § 10 of Art. V. *One of the principal purposes behind the provision for a nominating commission in the appointive process was*—*not to replace the elective process*—*but to place the restraint upon the "pork barrel" procedure of purely political appointments without an overriding consideration of qualification and ability.* It was sometimes facetiously said in former years that the best qualification to become a judge was to be a friend of the Governor! The purpose of such nominating commission, then, was to eliminate that kind of selection which some people referred to as "picking a judge merely because he was a friend or political supporter of the Governor" thereby providing this desirable restraint upon such appointment and assuring a "merit selection" of judicial officers.

Id. at 783 (emphasis added).

III. Discussion

"The interpretation of the Florida Constitution is a question of law" for the Court. *Jackson-Shaw Co. v. Jacksonville Aviation Authority*, 8 So.3d 1076, 1084–85 (2008). In interpreting the constitution, our analysis is straightforward. We begin with an examination of the explicit language of article V, section 11(c). "If that language is clear, unambiguous, and addresses the matter in issue, then it must be enforced as written." *Lawnwood Med. Ctr., Inc. v. Seeger*, 990 So.2d 503, 511 (Fla.2008) (quoting *Fla. Soc'y of Ophthalmology v. Fla. Optometric Ass'n*, 489 So.2d 1118, 1119 (Fla.1986)). "Our goal in construing a constitutional provision is to ascertain and effectuate the intent of the framers and voters." *Id.* at 510. As we have previously explained:

The fundamental object to be sought in construing a constitutional provision is to ascertain the intent of the framers and the provision must be construed or interpreted in such manner as to fulfill the intent of the people, never to defeat it. Such a provision must never be construed in such manner as to make it possible for the will of the people to be frustrated or denied.

Ford v. Browning, 992 So.2d 132, 136 (quoting *Crist v. Fla. Ass'n of Crim. Defense Lawyers*, 978 So.2d 134, 140 (Fla.2008)). We remain mindful that in construing a constitutional provision, we are not at liberty to add words that were not placed there originally or to ignore words that were expressly placed there at the time of adoption of the provision. *See Lawnwood*, 990 So.2d at 512.

With these principles in mind, we turn to the language of article V, section 11(c), of the Florida Constitution:

> (c) The nominations [for judicial office] shall be made within thirty days from the occurrence of a vacancy unless the period is extended by the governor for a time not to exceed thirty days. The governor shall make the appointment within sixty days after the nominations have been certified to the governor.

Art. V, § 11(c), Fla. Const. (emphasis added). The plain language of article V, section 11(c), mandates that the Governor, upon receipt of the certified list of nominees from a judicial nominating commission, make an appointment from that list within sixty days to fill the judicial vacancy. Significantly, in addition to the mandatory language that is expressly stated in the provision, we note the absence of any language granting the Governor authority to reject the JNC's certified list of nominees or to extend the time in which the appointment for judicial office must be made. Cases such as *In re Advisory Opinion to the Governor* and *Spector* provide ample historical support for this interpretation.

We also reject the argument that mandamus does not lie because the appointment process is an executive function that is inherently discretionary. By allowing this mandamus proceeding, we do not direct the Governor's discretionary decision as to the actual appointment to fill the judicial vacancy. Rather, we simply recognize and enforce the mandate contained in article V, section 11, which requires the Governor to adhere to his duty to make an appointment within the mandated time frame from the certified list of nominees. We recognize that, in fulfilling this constitutional duty, the Governor has discretion in his selection of a nominee from the list.

Finally, we reject the argument that an action for declaratory judgment in the circuit court is an adequate legal remedy under the facts and circumstances of this case, thus requiring denial of mandamus in this Court. As the Court stated in *In re Advisory Opinion to the Governor (Judicial Vacancies)*, 600 So.2d at 462, "[v]acancies in [judicial] office are to be avoided whenever possible. We are confident that the framers of article V intended that the nominating and appointment process would be conducted in such a way as to avoid or at least minimize the time that vacancies exist." In this case, the passage of almost six months since the petitioner's resignation became effective warrants our decision, now, in this mandamus proceeding in order to effectuate the intent of the framers to avoid or minimize further delay in filling this judicial vacancy. Moreover, while we applaud the Governor's interest in achieving diversity in the judiciary—an interest we believe to be genuine and well-intentioned—the constitution does not grant the Governor the discretion to refuse or postpone making an appointment to fill the vacancy on the Fifth District Court of Appeal.

CONCLUSION

We conclude that the Governor is bound by the Florida Constitution to appoint a nominee from the JNC's certified list, within sixty days of that certification. There is no exception to that mandate. Therefore, we hold that under the undisputed facts and specific circumstances present in this case, the Governor lacks authority under the constitution to seek a new list of nominees from the JNC and has a mandatory duty to fill the vacancy created by Petitioner's retirement with an appointment from the list certified to him on November 6, 2008. Because we believe the Governor will fully comply with the dictates of this opinion, we grant the petition but withhold issuance of the writ.

It is so ordered.

QUINCE, C.J., and PARIENTE, LEWIS, CANADY, POLSTON, and PERRY, JJ., concur.

———

A 2020 case examined two intertwined issues: as two openings were pending at the Florida Supreme Court, and the Supreme Court JNC was interviewing applicants for the positions, the COVID-19 pandemic caused Governor Ron DeSantis to issue executive orders closing many of the functions of the state. He also delayed his decision to appoint people to fill the two open justice seats. Article IV, Section 1(f) and Article V, Section 11(a), (c) spell out that the Governor has sixty days to appoint a new justice from a list of persons nominated by a Judicial Nominating Commission.

When he did make appointments to fill the seats, one of the people appointed was a lawyer who, at the time (and still at the time of the order), had not been a member of The Florida Bar for the ten years required in Article V, Section 8 of the Florida Constitution. Part of the announcement of the appointment of this person was that she would take office after September 24, 2020, at which point she would have completed ten years as a member of the bar.

What follows are two orders on a challenge to the nomination and appointment of this justice on two grounds. The suit challenged both the timing in which the Governor and Judicial Nominating Commission acted to fill the vacant Supreme Court justice position and the eligibility of the person nominated by the commission and appointed by the Governor.

Thompson v. DeSantis

2020 Fla. LEXIS 1437, 2020 WL 5048539,
Case No. 20-985 (August 27, 2020)

MUÑIZ, J.

* * *

The Governor did exceed his authority in making this appointment. In a nutshell, when a governor fills by appointment a vacant judicial office, the appointee must be constitutionally eligible for that office at the time of the appointment. But that is not the end of the analysis, because the remedy Thompson seeks is legally unavailable under these circumstances. There is no legal justification for us to require a replacement appointment from a new list of candidates, rather than from the one that is already before the Governor. And the correct remedy (an appointment from the existing list of eligible nominees) would be contrary to Thompson's stated objectives in filing this case. Therefore, we hold Thompson to the remedy she requested and deny her petition.

BACKGROUND

Former Justices … resigned from this Court in November 2019…. On January 23, 2020, the JNC certified to the Governor a total of nine nominees for the two vacancies. It is undisputed that this started the clock running on the Governor's duty under Article V, Section 11(c) to fill the vacancies by appointment "within sixty days after the nominations have been certified."

Because he was focused on the COVID-19 pandemic and in light of the declared state of emergency, the Governor delayed his appointments beyond the constitutional deadline of March 23, 2020.[31] Then, on May 26, 2020, the Governor appointed John Couriel and Judge Renatha Francis to the offices of justices of the supreme court. The Couriel appointment is not at issue in this case.

* * *

In the analysis that follows, we will consider the Petitioner's claim for relief against the Governor but not against Chair Nordby. The Petitioner asserts that the JNC violated its procedural rules and the constitution by including Judge Francis on its list of nominees—an alleged defect that was immediately apparent on January 23, 2020. Nonetheless, the Petitioner waited nearly six months to bring this action. It would not be proper under these circumstances for us to entertain a challenge to the JNC's list of nominees. *See State ex. rel. Pooser v. Wester*, 170 So. 736 (Fla. 1936) (petitioner's unreasonable four-month delay precluded grant of extraordinary relief).

I. Analysis

* * *

---

31. [FN2] We express no view on whether the state of emergency made it permissible for the Governor to miss the constitutional deadline.

B. Merits

… This case requires us to decide when [the] eligibility requirement attaches in the context of a governor's appointment to fill a vacancy in judicial office under article V, section 11. The Petitioner argues that the eligibility requirement attaches at the time of appointment. The Governor responds that the eligibility requirement does not attach until the appointee actually takes the oath and assumes the duties of her office. According to the Governor, because Judge Francis does not intend to take the oath and assume office until September 24, 2020, "eligibility is not material, nor is it in question."

The plain text of article V, section 8 … does not explicitly resolve the parties' dispute. But the constitution nonetheless yields a clear answer to the question before us. That is because, "in construing multiple constitutional provisions addressing a similar subject, the provisions 'must be read in para material to ensure a consistent and logical meaning that gives effect to each provision.'" [Citations omitted.] When we read Article V, section 8 together with Article V, section 11, the only reasonable conclusion is that the Bar eligibility requirement attaches at the time of appointment.

When a vacancy arises in the officer of justice of the supreme court, article V, section 11 imposes on the governor a simple and circumscribed duty: (1) to "fill the vacancy" in office, (2) "by appointment," (3) "within sixty days after the [JNC's] nominations have been certified to the governor." Under this provision, the appointment is a means to an end — to fill the vacancy — not an end in itself. The text indicates that the appointment brings about clear legal effects: it fills the vacancy in office, and it sets the length of the appointee's term. We can also infer a legal effect from the fact that the text imposes a deadline for the appointment; if the appointment itself had no legal effect, the deadline would serve no purpose.

The most important point is that the appointment must — and does — fill the vacancy in office. And it does so immediately. Not at some time in the future, but on the effective date of the appointment itself. It necessarily follows that, in this context, any constitutional eligibility requirement "for the office" attaches at the time of appointment. Otherwise, the governor would be filling an office — again, under article V, section 11 this happens at the time of appointment — with someone whom the constitution deems ineligible for that office.

* * *

3. Remedy

It is not enough for the Petitioner to establish that the Governor exceeded his authority by appointing Judge Francis. To prevail in this action, the Petitioner also must have sought proper relief. This is where the Petitioner's case fails.

There are two insurmountable problems with the Petitioner's requested remedy. First, as we have explained, by her unexcused delay the Petitioner has forfeited any challenge to the composition of the JNC's list or to the JNC's nomination process. And second, the Petitioner has shown no reason why the irregularity of one ineligible nominee on the JNC's certified list requires discarding the whole list. As noted, that list already includes more than the minimum number of candidates that article V, section 11(a) requires. At this point, the only legally appropriate and available remedy would be to require the Governor immediately to appoint a constitutionally eligible person from the JNC's existing certified list of nominees. See *Pleus*, 14 So. 3d at 946.

Yet in her initial petition and in her reply, the Petitioner has asked for something else: that the JNC reconvene and certify a new list from the existing applicant pool, and that the Governor then be compelled to select an appointee from that new list. The Petitioner's filings characterize this as "the only remedy that complies with the Florida Constitution" and as "the only appropriate and fair remedy in this case." What the Petitioner seeks is fundamentally different from the remedy that we are authorized to grant in the circumstances presented. And more than that, the authorized remedy would defeat the Petitioner's stated objectives in filing this action.

It is not our role to impose a remedy that the Petitioner has not requested and that is inconsistent with the Petitioner's stated goals. This is the parties' case, not ours. Accordingly, we must deny the petition.

CONCLUSION

The petition is denied.

It is so ordered.

Questions

1. How does the Court's opinion regarding the Petitioner's choice of remedy square with Article V, Section 2(a), which provides: "The supreme court shall adopt rules for the practice and procedure in all courts including … a requirement that no cause shall be dismissed because an improper remedy has been sought"?

2. The Court's opinion explicitly declines (in a footnote) to address the claim that the Governor lacked authority to wait beyond the required sixty days to make his appointment. Why might this be?

———————

The Petitioner moved for rehearing on the basis that (1) Article V, Section 2(a) and the corresponding rule of court, Fla. R. App. P. 9.040(d), mandate the Court to treat a petition seeking the wrong remedy as though it had sought the correct one. (See also *State v. Johnson, Jr.* earlier in this chapter.) The Petitioner also amended her petition to alter the relief she sought by requesting that the Court order the Governor to choose from among the remaining nominees on the JNC's list. The Supreme Court denied the motion for rehearing but granted the motion to amend, citing the rule that they should allow litigants to amend to request appropriate relief. The Court then required the Governor one day to respond and the petitioner one more day to reply.

In his response, the Governor argued that he had merely announced, not appointed, the new would-be justice in May 2020; he also argued that for the Supreme Court to grant the Petitioner's request to appoint a justice from the remaining names on the original list intruded on the executive branch (which the JNC is a part of) by removing names from its list.

On September 11, 2020, the Court issued a brief final order:

Thompson v. Desantis

2020 Fla. LEXIS 1516, Case No.: SC20-985
(Fla. Sept. 11, 2020)

Before the Court is an amended petition for writ of quo warranto and writ of mandamus. We issued to the Governor an order to show cause on Tuesday, September 8, 2020. Having considered the Governor's reponse and the Petitioner's reply, we grant the amended petition for writ of mandamus.

The essentials of this case are straightforward. The resignation of former Justice Robert Luck created a vacancy in office; the constitution gave the Governor sixty days from January 23, 2020, to fill the vacancy by making an appointment from a list of certified nominees; and, at the time of the appointment the appointee necessarily needed to be constitutionally eligible for the office being filled. Not having been a member of the Florida Bar for ten years, Judge Renatha Francis was constitutionally ineligible for the office of justice of the supreme court on the expiration of the constitution's sixty-day deadline. And Judge Francis remains constitutionally ineligible now. Art. V, §§ 8, 11, Fla. Const.

The constitution's sixty-day deadline to fill this vacancy in office expired many months ago. Yet the Governor has not satisfied his legal obligation to fill the vacancy by making a constitutionally valid appointment. This is true if one views the Governor as having made a null appointment on May 26 (because Judge Francis was and is constitutionally ineligible). It is also true if, as the Governor belatedly suggests in his response to the amended petition, the May 26 "appointment" was a mere "announcement" and not really an appointment at all.[32] Either approach leads to the same conclusion: the Governor has not complied with the constitution's clear commands.

The constitution's ten-year Bar membership requirement and sixty-day appointment deadline are bright-line textual mandates that impose rules rather than standards and prioritize certainty over discretion. To some, enforcing rules like these might seem needlessly formalistic when the result is to preclude the appointment of an otherwise qualified candidate. But "formalism," as Justice Scalia observed, "is what makes a government a government of laws and not of men." Antonin Scalia, *A Matter of Interpretation: Federal Courts and the Law* 25 (rev. ed. 2018).

In these circumstances, the constitution and directly on-point precedent dictate the remedy. We hold that the constitution requires the Governor immediately to appoint and commission a constitutionally eligible nominee from among the seven remaining candidates already certified by the judicial nominating commission. *Pleus*

---

32. [FN1.] We note the inconsistency with the Governor's assertion, in his response to the initial petition in this case, that "Governor DeSantis completed his legal duty by appointing Judge Francis … to the Florida Supreme Court on May 26, 2020."

v. Crist, 14 So. 3d 941 (Fla. 2009). We reject the Governor's suggestion that this remedy somehow intrudes on the judicial nominating commission's constitutional prerogatives by "taking a red pen" to the JNC's certified list. The JNC itself made the decision to nominate a constitutionally ineligible candidate, and it is responsible for the consequences of that decision.

The Governor must fully comply with this order no later than noon on Monday, September 14, 2020. Because we believe the Governor will do so, we grant the amended petition for writ of mandamus but withhold issuance of the writ. No motion for rehearing or clarification will be entertained by this Court.

It is so ordered.

CANADY, C.J., and POLSTON, LABARGA, LAWSON, and MUÑIZ, JJ., concur. COURIEL, J., recused.

Article VI

Suffrage and Elections

Introduction

Article VI deals with voting and elections. This Article of the Florida Constitution is relatively undeveloped in Florida case law. Federal decisions provide the basis for most elections law dealing with federal offices, while state decisions deal with election to state offices. This mirrors the bifurcation within the federal Constitution: "The Times, Places and Manner of holding Elections for Senators and Representatives, shall be prescribed in each State by the Legislature thereof; but the Congress may at any time by Law make or alter such Regulations, except as to the Places of choosing Senators." U.S. Const. art. I, §4[1].

The original federal Constitution was silent on state elections for state legislatures. Four amendments have been added to the federal Constitution affecting state voting laws: the Fifteenth, the Nineteenth, the Twenty-First and the Twenty-Seventh Amendments. Within that framework, states may craft election laws. Two important Florida constitutional provisions added in 2010 provide an example of the extent to which states may control certain aspects of elections within their borders. Known as the Fair Districts Amendments, they provide strict requirements designed to minimize gerrymandering in both congressional and state legislative districting.[1]

How the Fair Districts Amendments came about illustrates the possibilities of the several ways Florida's Constitution may be amended. The genesis of the idea came

---

1. Fla. Const. art. III, §§ 20, 21 (added by initiative amendment in 2010).

from the 1997–98 CRC. At that moment in time, political power in Florida was shifting from predominant Democratic power to Republican, and the makeup of the CRC reflected that balance. By appointing authority, the CRC was nearly evenly divided among the two parties. Eighteen appointments were made by Democrat officeholders; eighteen by Republican officeholders. The Attorney General, the only automatic member, was a Democrat.[2]

This bipartisan CRC proposed that the decennial redistricting task be accomplished by an independent redistricting commission appointed to do the task free of (at least overt) political pressure. The proposal made it all the way to the full CRC and was voted to go on the ballot. Then, the legislative session started. The legislators were not willing to give up a power as important as redistricting. They succeeded in convincing the CRC to agree to a revote. This time, the proposal failed by two votes to make it on the ballot.

Participants and observers of the CRC realized that if apportionment reform could not happen in a politically balanced and collegial body, it stood even less chance in the legislative process. Former Education Secretary and President of USF Betty Castor, former CRC member Ellen Freidin, and Common Cause Florida first attempted citizens' initiatives on the 2006 ballot; after battering by a series of challenges and rule changes, the initiatives were withdrawn. Two proposals sponsored by FairDistrictsFlorida.org, still led by Freidin, eventually met all the requirements to be placed on the 2010 ballot.[3] To get there, the effort had survived a challenge by the Legislature and an intervening 2006 constitutional amendment that required all future amendments to garner sixty percent of the vote to be adopted.

Most aspects of voting are handled by the states: voting registration, polling locations, hours, days, and availability of voting; whether and on what grounds to allow mail-in voting; and when and how to conduct recounts. Florida's Constitution provides that every county have an elected supervisor of elections; that official has considerable leeway in determining exactly how the election process occurs in her county.

The federal Constitution is more specific for presidential elections, devoting the entire Twelfth Amendment to the subject. The well-known 2000 cases culminating in *Bush v. Gore*, 531 U.S. 98 (2000), dealt with federal constitutional and federal statutory issues and interpretation of Florida statutes, not the Florida Constitution.[4]

There is a historical reason for the comparative lack of state court decisions involving Article VI. Article VI was drafted by the Suffrage and Election Committee of

---

2. Mary E. Adkins, *The Same River Twice: A Brief History of How the 1968 Florida Constitution Came to Be and What It Has Become*, 18 Fla. Coastal L. Rev. 5 (Fall 2016).

3. Ellen Freidin interview with Mary E. Adkins, August 26, 2015; FairDistrictsFlorida.org (last visited August 26, 2020).

4. *See* Jon L. Mills, *Florida on Trial: Federalism in the 2000 Presidential Election*, 13 Stan. L. & Pol'y Rev. 83–99 (2002).

the Florida CRC in 1966. The debate on the committee's work concentrated on whether to lower the voting age to eighteen, which failed, and creating a citizens' initiative and recurring constitutional revision commission, which succeeded. The committee drafted Article VI to be open-ended, thus allowing the Legislature to craft the bulk of laws governing voting and elections. This was a shift from the then-existing 1885 Constitution, which contained several specific provisions controlling voting and election procedures.[5] Four of the five members on the Suffrage and Elections Committee were members of the Legislature's 1963 Interim Elections Study Committee, which proposed a comprehensive redraft of Florida's election statutes.[6]

The 1966 CRC's approach was influenced by two contemporary events: the passage of the federal 1965 Voting Rights Act and the maelstrom of Florida's legislative reapportionment. The passage of the 1965 Voting Rights Act was a capstone to the national civil rights movement in the 1960s. This legislation in pertinent part placed formerly racially repressive counties in America under a federal pre-clearance review of any changes to their electoral laws. Florida, as a former Confederate state, had fully utilized the Black Codes in the 1880s and later the Jim Crow laws to deny black citizens their civil rights. In 1966 it was unclear what the impact of pre-clearance reviews would be on state elections laws in Florida.[7] It was prudent to leave the election code open-ended to meet possible federal controls on voting.

In 1966, Florida was also in the fourth year of a five-year running battle in the federal courts over the state's extreme legislative malapportionment of federal and state voting districts. A federally mandated reapportionment of both congressional and state legislative districts was imminently expected, but how extensive the court's involvement would be on elections was still unknown. Article VI was thus drafted to be flexible towards both these developments.

A citizens' initiative added term limits to specified state and federal offices in 1992. The portion of the 1992 amendment affecting federal offices is unconstitutional but

---

5. Fla. Const. of 1885 art. VI, §§ 4, 5.

6. Interim Elections Study Committee Report dated April 8, 1965, Florida State Archives, Series 720, carton 8, folder 11. Interestingly, the CRC Suffrage and Elections Committee used the 1957 proposed draft of a revised Florida constitution as its drafting template and not the then-existing 1885 Constitution. *Revised Florida Constitution Proposed by the Legislature and Explanation of Changes.* This draft is also referred to as the "Daisy Chain" proposal. The group who created the original draft was the Florida Constitutional Advisory Committee, which is sometimes referred to as the Sturgis Committee. Mary E. Adkins, Making Modern Florida (Gainesville: University Press of Florida 2016), 22.

7. In 1965, this formula resulted in the designation of six states, but not Florida, as "covered jurisdictions." JoNel Newman, *Unfinished Business: The Case for Continuing Special Voting Rights Act Coverage in Florida*, 61 U. Miami L. Rev. 1, 7 (2006). Florida was only designated a partially covered jurisdiction in 28 C.F.R. pt. 41, app. (2012). *See* Michael Ellement, *Blocking the Ballot: Why Florida's New Voting Restrictions Demonstrate a Need for Continued Enforcement of the Voting Rights Act Pre-clearance Requirement*, 62 Cath. U. L. Rev. 541, 573 n.11 (2013) (noting that Florida counties Collier, Hardee, Hendry, Hillsborough, and Monroe are all covered under section 5 of the VRA). *See also Shelby County, Ala. v. Holder*, 570 U.S. 529 (2013).

remains in the Florida constitution.[8] The same year, a legislatively proposed amendment was adopted giving the Governor the authority to suspend or delay elections in times of emergency or "impending emergency...."[9]

The 1997–98 CRC updated significant portions of Article VI. That CRC lowered the voting age to eighteen years of age and eliminated a one-year residency requirement for voter registration, both changes made to conform to U.S. Supreme Court decisions issued after the 1968 Constitution had been adopted. The 1997–98 CRC also required the legislation of campaign funding and spending limit provisions. Significantly, the CRC added an open primary requirement allowing all voters to vote in a primary where all candidates have the same party affiliation and the winner will have no opposition in the general election. This provision, however, had an unforeseen loophole: anyone qualifying as a write-in candidate would defeat the "no opposition" requirement. This loophole, created by the courts, was contrary to the policy intent of the CRC. This open primary amendment issue was the subject of the *Brinkmann v. Francois* decision discussed later in this chapter.

Secondly, the 1997–98 CRC also placed in the Constitution a requirement that the ballot access provisions of a minor party candidate or candidate with no party affiliation not exceed those of a candidate having the largest number of registered voters. The effect of this amendment is seen in the *Reform Party v. Black* decision below.

The most significant change in the Election Article took place via citizen initiative in 2018. Motivated by the fact that Florida was one of three states that most restricted the right of convicted felons to vote, a coalition of civil rights groups drafted an amendment to restore the right to vote to persons convicted of most felonies on completion of all terms of their sentence. The change is a major shift in Florida election policy and has generated subsequent legislation and litigation over its scope. This subject will be treated in more detail in this chapter's discussion of Section 4, disqualifications on voting.

A. Article VI, Section 1 — Regulation of Elections

"Registration and elections shall, and political party functions may, be regulated by law...."

Article VI mostly leaves electoral law to be controlled by the Legislature. This encompasses who can vote, who can run for public office, and how elections are held, which includes vote counting and challenges to election results.

Section 1 states that registration of voters and elections shall be regulated by statutory law. The scope of those laws, however, is not unlimited: "[L]egislative acts that

---

8. *U.S. Term Limits, Inc. v. Thornton*, 514 U.S. 779 (1995) (term limits on federal elected offices unconstitutional); *Ray v. Mortham*, 742 So. 2d 1276 (Fla. 1999) (term limits on elected statewide offices constitutional).

9. FLA. CONST. art. VI §5(a) (added by initiative amendment in 1992).

impose unreasonable or unnecessary restraints on the elective process are prohibited." *Am. Fed'n of Labor & Cong. of Indus. Organizations v. Hood*, 885 So. 2d 373, 375–76 (Fla. 2004) (internal quotation marks omitted) (citing *Treiman v. Malmquist*, 342 So. 2d 972, 975 (Fla.1977)). The Florida Supreme Court tried to uphold a law governing qualification for office in the case of the bounced check immediately below, but concluded the law was an unreasonable restraint on the elective process.

Wright v. City of Miami Gardens

200 So. 3d 765 (Fla. 2016)

LEWIS, J.

This case is before the Court on a certified question of great public importance. . . .

In February 2016, James Barry Wright properly opened a campaign account with Wells Fargo Bank to run in the August 30, 2016, election for the office of Mayor in the City of Miami Gardens (the City). The qualifying period for this particular election commenced at 9 a.m. on May 26, 2016, and terminated at 4 p.m. on June 2, 2016.

On June 1, 2016, one day before the qualifying period ended, Wright tendered to Ronetta Taylor, the City Clerk of the City of Miami Gardens, a check issued on the Wells Fargo Bank campaign account in the amount of $620.00, which was the specifically required qualifying fee amount. The City Clerk accepted the check and issued Wright a receipt. It is undisputed that Wright's properly opened and properly maintained campaign account had ample funds to pay the qualification fee at all relevant times. Although the check was one of the first checks written by Wright after the opening of his campaign account, and therefore might be considered a starter check or "temporary" check, it bore his name, his campaign name, his campaign mailing address, and his campaign account number. Further, it is also undisputed that Wells Fargo had properly and successfully previously processed and honored six similarly formatted "temporary" checks in connection with Wright's other campaign expenses. Finally, it is undisputed that Wright met all other requirements to qualify as a candidate for the office of the Mayor of the City.

However, on June 16, 2016—more than two weeks later—the City Clerk was notified by the City's Finance Department that Wright's check had been returned to the City by its bank "because the account number on the check could not be located." Indeed, the check that was returned was stamped with the following: "UN LOCATE ACCT." Beneath that reflected "Do Not Re-deposit." To the left of the check was the following: "6/8/2016 ... This is a LEGAL COPY of your check. You can use it the same way you would use the original check. RETURN REASON—UNABLE TO LOCATE ACCOUNT."

Wright was not informed of the situation until four days later, on June 20, 2016. While the City Clerk initially informed Wright that he could still pay the filing fee (and the $45.00 returned check fee that Wells Fargo had charged the City) with a cashier's check to remain qualified, Wright later received an e-mail informing him that he had been totally disqualified. Nevertheless, Wright attempted, without success, to rectify the problem by actually tendering a cashier's check for the filing fee, as well as a separate check to pay the returned check fee.

When Wright requested an explanation as to why he could not rectify the situation which he had not created, the City Clerk referred Wright to section 99.061(7)(a) 1. of the Florida Statutes which provides:

> (7)(a) In order for a candidate to be qualified, the following items must be received by the filing officer by the end of the qualifying period:
>
>> 1. A properly executed check drawn upon the candidate's campaign account payable to the person or entity as prescribed by the filing officer in an amount not less than the fee required by s. 99.092, unless the candidate obtained the required number of signatures on petitions pursuant to s. 99.095. The filing fee for a special district candidate is not required to be drawn upon the candidate's campaign account. *If a candidate's check is returned by the bank for any reason, the filing officer shall immediately notify the candidate and the candidate shall have until the end of qualifying to pay the fee with a cashier's check purchased from funds of the campaign account. Failure to pay the fee as provided in this subparagraph shall disqualify the candidate.*

§ 99.061(7)(a) 1., Fla. Stat. (2016) (emphasis added). The City Clerk further referred Wright to the decision of the First District Court of Appeal in *Levey v. Detzner* which had held that the clear and unambiguous language of section 99.061(7)(a) 1. required disqualification under very similar circumstances:

> The statute at issue is clear and unambiguous. Although we agree with the trial court that this result is harsh, it is mandated by the clear language of the statute. If a candidate's qualifying check is returned *for any reason*, the candidate must pay the qualifying fee by cashier's check before the end of the qualifying period. Levey's check was returned, the reason for that occurring is immaterial, and she failed to cure the deficiency within the time allotted by the statute. This circumstance "shall disqualify the candidate." Courts are not at liberty to extend, modify, or limit the express and unambiguous terms of a statute. *See Hill v. Davis,* 70 So.3d 572, 575 (Fla.2011); *see also State v. Chubbuck,* 141 So.3d 1163 (Fla. 2014).
>
> The result in this case is buttressed by the fact that under an earlier version of section 99.061, if a candidate's qualifying check was returned, the candidate was allowed 48 hours after being notified of that fact by the filing officer to pay the fee by cashier's check, "the end of qualifying notwithstanding." *See* § 99.061(7)(a) 1., Fla. Stat. (2010). The operative language of the current statute, which eliminated the possibility of a post-qualifying cure period for candidates for federal, state, county, and district offices, was adopted by the Legislature in a 2011 amendment. *See* Ch. [20]11–40, § 14, at 22, Laws of Fla. It is not within a court's power to rewrite the statute or ignore this amendment, and any remedy Levey or others aggrieved by the amendment may have lies with the Legislature, not the courts.

AFFIRMED.

146 So.3d 1224, 1226 (Fla. 1st DCA 2014), *rehearing en banc denied*, Sept. 22, 2014, *review denied*, 153 So.3d 906 (Fla.2014) (footnote omitted).

On June 30, 2016, Wright sought judicial redress by filing the instant action. Wright sought declaratory and mandamus relief against the City, the City Clerk, and the Miami-Dade County Supervisor of Elections. On July 27, 2016, the trial court conducted a hearing on Wright's amended motion for temporary injunction and emergency writ of mandamus. In both counts, Wright sought to require the defendants to recognize Wright as a properly and validly qualified candidate for the office of Mayor in the August 30 election. In the alternative, Wright sought to require the defendants to reschedule the pertinent election to the general election taking place on November 9, 2016.

During the hearing on Wright's motion, the Supervisor of Elections announced that it had no objections to moving the election to the November general election if Wright were entitled to relief on the merits.

On the other hand, the City of Miami Gardens objected to consideration of this relief on the basis that it would add unnecessary expenses, create a hardship, potentially result in a separate December run-off election with low voter turnout, and affect its ability to ensure a fair election. Specifically, the City noted that Wright would be able to raise funds that other candidates would not be able to because he had not been a candidate.

Ultimately, the trial court denied both of Wright's motions on the merits. The trial court concluded that Wright was not entitled to any relief because section 99.061(7)(a) 1., Florida Statutes, explicitly required the City Clerk to disqualify Wright. The trial court further explained that it was bound by the decision of the First District Court of Appeal in *Levey*, 146 So.3d 1224, which it considered to be directly on point, absent any relevant precedent from the Third District Court of Appeal.

Wright sought review of the trial court's order in the Third District Court of Appeal. Relying on largely the same reasoning as the trial court and the First District in *Levey*, the Third District affirmed....

However, the Third District also noted that "this issue's recurrence has moved the matter from the 'mere anecdotal' column to the 'likely to recur' column" and, therefore, certified the following question to be of great public importance:

> Does section 99.061(7)(a) 1. require a candidate's disqualification when the candidate's qualifying fee check is returned by the bank after the expiration of the qualifying period due to a banking error over which the candidate has no control?

Id. [W]e accepted jurisdiction and granted a motion to expedite review. Due to the late timing, while this case was pending in this Court, the August 30 mayoral election was conducted, but voters were presented with a ballot that did not contain the name James Barry Wright.

This review follows.

ANALYSIS

I. Certified Question

The certified question is one of statutory interpretation, which is a pure question of law that we review de novo. When the Florida Election Code is at issue, we primarily rely on the same rules of statutory reading and construction that we apply to other statutes. Legislative intent is the polestar that guides our analysis. *See Knowles v. Beverly Enters.-Fla., Inc.*, 898 So.2d 1, 5 (Fla.2004).

> Florida case law contains a plethora of rules and extrinsic aids to guide courts in their efforts to discern legislative intent from ambiguously worded statutes. However, [w]hen the language of the statute is clear and unambiguous and conveys a clear and definite meaning, there is no occasion for resorting to the rules of statutory interpretation and construction; the statute must be given its plain and obvious meaning.
>
> *A.R. Douglass, Inc. v. McRainey*, 102 Fla. 1141, 137 So. 157, 159 (1931). [citation omitted] It has also been accurately stated that courts of this state are without power to construe an unambiguous statute in a way which would extend, modify, or *limit*, its express terms or its *reasonable and obvious implications*. To do so would be an abrogation of legislative power. *American Bankers Life Assurance Company of Florida v. Williams*, 212 So.2d 777, 778 (Fla. 1st DCA 1968) (emphasis added). It is also true that a literal interpretation of the language of a statute need not be given when to do so would lead to an unreasonable or ridiculous conclusion. *Johnson v. Presbyterian Homes of Synod of Florida, Inc.*, 239 So.2d 256 (Fla.1970). Such a departure from the letter of the statute, however, "is sanctioned by the courts only when there are cogent reasons for believing that the letter [of the law] does not accurately disclose the [legislative] intent." *State ex rel. Hanbury v. Tunnicliffe*, 98 Fla. 731, 124 So. 279, 281 (1929).

Holly v. Auld, 450 So.2d 217, 219 (Fla.1984). In the specific context of candidate qualification, this Court has further explained that:

> Literal and "total compliance" with statutory language which reaches hypersensitive levels and which strains the quality of justice is not required to fairly and substantially meet the statutory requirements to qualify as a candidate for public office.

State ex rel. Siegendorf v. Stone, 266 So.2d 345, 346 (Fla.1972).

* * *

Like all the other courts that have considered this language, we believe that the statute's following language is abundantly clear and unambiguous:

> If a candidate's check is returned by the bank for any reason, the filing officer shall immediately notify the candidate and the candidate shall have until the end of qualifying to pay the fee with a cashier's check purchased from funds

of the campaign account. Failure to pay the fee as provided in this subparagraph shall disqualify the candidate.

§ 99.061(7)(a) 1., Fla. Stat.

Because this language is clear and unambiguous, there is no basis or authority to apply rules of construction. *See Holly,* 450 So.2d at 219. In this case, Wright's check was returned, and although it was not due to any fault of Wright's and was exclusively due to a banking error, the statute on its face applies because it applies to returns "by the bank for any reason." Finally, although Wright was not informed of this bank error until after qualifying had ended, he only had "until the end of qualifying to pay the fee with a cashier's check purchased from funds of the campaign account." Even if we were to take issue with the draconian and irrational policy of requiring payment before notice, as was the case with the facts before us, the next sentence in the statute ends further inquiry. In no uncertain terms, the statute provides: "Failure to pay the fee as provided in this subparagraph shall disqualify the candidate."

Quite clearly, subparagraph 7(a)1. does not provide any method of paying the fee after the end of qualifying. Therefore, because the fee was not paid before the end of qualifying, under the plain language of the statute the filing officer had no choice but to disqualify Wright.

The fact that the filing officer received "[a] properly executed check drawn upon the candidate's campaign account payable to the person or entity as prescribed by the filing officer in an amount not less than the fee required" is of no moment because the statute quite clearly considers a returned check as indicating that the fee has not been paid. There could be no other explanation as to why upon a returned check, the candidate has a second opportunity "to pay the fee," albeit before "the end of qualifying."

We further agree with the district courts that have reviewed this statute in application that this law yields a most distasteful and harsh result when a candidate who did everything right is disqualified due to a banking error beyond the candidate's control. Some of the district court judges and Wright have contended that this demonstrates an absurd result that could not have been intended by the Legislature. We acknowledge that the "absurd result" doctrine is alluring on these facts, but there is no ambiguity upon which to apply that rule of construction. We are convinced that the Legislature did intend the law to effect a true bright line, and therefore, we cannot resort to a rule of construction based on "absurdity." Unlike in other cases where the absurd result doctrine has been applied to an ambiguous statute, here the Legislature specifically removed the language from the prior statute that would have avoided the result of disqualification. Specifically, the Legislature removed language that would have allowed payment of the fee within 48 hours upon notice of a returned check, "the end of qualifying notwithstanding," and added that the candidate had "until" the end of qualifying....

* * *

Furthermore, the result appears to be the product of specific intent when we note that the Legislature did not amend the identical provision that governs nonpartisan elections.... We presume that the Legislature acts purposefully when it removes language from one statute, but leaves identical language in a different statute. *See, e.g., Beach v. Great W. Bank,* 692 So.2d 146, 152 (Fla.1997); *Leisure Resorts, Inc. v. Frank J. Rooney, Inc.,* 654 So.2d 911, 914 (Fla.1995) ("When the [L]egislature has used a term, as it has here, in one section of the statute but omits it in another section of the same statute, we will not imply it where it has been excluded.").

Finally, in his *Levey* dissent, Judge Makar opined that the Legislature could not have intended this result when it could very well happen to its own members. *See Levey,* 146 So.3d at 1232 (Makar, J., dissenting from the denial of rehearing en banc). This is a thought-provoking and compelling statement. Tellingly however, in the two years following the decision in *Levey,* the law remains the same. This Court presumes that the Legislature is aware of judicial construction of its statutes. *See Dickinson v. Davis,* 224 So.2d 262, 264 (Fla.1969) (noting "[t]he Legislature is presumed to know existing law when a statute is enacted, and, also in re-enacting a statute the Legislature is presumed to be aware of constructions placed upon it by the Court.") (internal citation omitted). This suggests further that the bright line was intentional rather than an unfortunate oversight.

Therefore, because the language at issue is clear and unambiguous we are compelled to answer the certified question in the affirmative. Were we to construe the statute as allowing the payment of the fee with a cashier's check after the end of qualifying, we would literally be legislating by reinserting the language "notwithstanding the end of qualifying" after the Legislature in its wisdom removed it. This is certainly beyond our power because as a coequal branch of government with the utmost respect for the separation of powers, we can neither legislate nor question the wisdom of the Legislature. *See Holley v. Adams,* 238 So.2d 401, 404–05 (Fla.1970) ("First, it is the function of the Court to interpret the law, not to legislate. Second, courts are not concerned with the mere wisdom of the policy of the legislation ... The judiciary will not if legislative acts merely on grounds of the policy and wisdom of such act, no matter how unwise or unpolitic they might be, so long as there is no plain violation of the Constitution."). Answering the certified question in the affirmative does not end our review in this case, however, "because of the dominant force of the Constitution, an authority superior to both the Legislature and the Judiciary." *See id.* at 405.

Wright asserted his constitutional rights in his complaint, alleging that the City Clerk "further provided [Wright] with a copy of the case *Levey v. Detzner* ... upon which the City bases its untenable position to deny [Wright] his *constitutional right to run for public office.*" In addition, in his initial brief before this Court, Wright stated, "Thus, Mr. Wright implores this Court to reach a different result from the First District, and adopt the compelling dissents of Judges Benton and Makar." Init. Br. of Petitioner at 21. Before the Third District, Wright concluded his briefs by quoting and adopting Judge Makar's conclusion and reference to a case strictly concerning the constitutionality of an election qualification requirement: "Disqualifying a candidate who did everything right is both unreasonable and unnecessary." *Levey v. Det-*

zner, 146 So.3d [at 1234] (Makar, J., dissenting) (quoting *Treiman v. Malmquist*, 342 So.2d 972 (Fla.1977)).

Given the fundamental importance of free and fair elections to our republican form of government, the recurrence of these "banking errors" and their ensuing harsh consequences, as well as the strong potential that other prospective candidates have similarly been turned away, but simply declined to keep fighting, we consider this issue to be one of fundamental importance.

Our Florida Constitution opens by succinctly reaffirming a truism that is the heart of our government: "All political power is inherent in the people." Art. 1, §1 Fla. Const. This Court has long considered free and fair elections vital to ensuring that such political power is not usurped from the people.

* * *

Fundamental to our system of government is the principle that the right to be a candidate for public office is a valuable one and no one should be denied this right unless the Constitution or an applicable valid law expressly declares him to be ineligible. *cf. Vieira v. Slaughter, et al.*, 318 So.2d 490 (Fla. 1st DCA 1975). This court, in *Hurt v. Naples*, 299 So.2d 17 (Fla.1974), emphasized:

> "Discouragement of candidacy for public office should be frowned upon in the absence of express statutory disqualification. The people should have available opportunity to select their public officer from a multiple choice of candidates. Widening the field of candidates is the rule, not the exception, in Florida."
>
> To determine reasonableness of the restraint or condition placed on the right to seek public office, the nature of the right asserted by the individual must be considered in conjunction with the extent that it is necessary to restrict the assertion of the right in the interest of the public. *Jones v. Board of Control*, 131 So.2d 713 (Fla.1961).

Treiman, 342 So.2d at 975–76.

Because the disqualification involved here is due to a law expressly disqualifying Wright, our only inquiry is whether the law is a valid law. In performing this inquiry, however, we must remember that the law in question "comes to us with a presumption of validity—an extremely strong presumption in statutes regulating the conduct of elections." *Bodner* [*v. Gray*], 129 So.2d at 421. "To overcome the presumption, the invalidity must appear beyond reasonable doubt, for it must be assumed the [L]egislature intended to enact a valid law." *License Acquisitions, LLC v. Debary Real Estate Holdings, LLC*, 155 So.3d 1137, 1143 (Fla.2014) (internal quotation marks omitted).

Nevertheless, as Judge Makar and Wright have similarly concluded, we are convinced beyond a reasonable doubt that disqualifying a candidate who did everything right due to an error of a third party bank that was totally beyond the control of the candidate is both unreasonable and unnecessary, as well as plainly irrational.

* * *

For those prospective candidates who tender properly executed checks that ultimately clear because they have done all they were required to, the statute poses no problem. However, the statute effectively forecloses the candidacy of all otherwise qualified candidates who have done all they were required to do but have had their checks returned, not due to insufficient funds or some other matter within their control, but due to sheer bad luck resulting from a bank error totally beyond their control. This bright line, by turning on luck rather than conduct, is irrational and violates Wright's constitutional right to run for public office. There is no relief valve for circumstances such as these.

Moreover, a quick glance at the Florida Statutes regulating banks and checks reveals that notice that a check has been returned before the end of qualifying is essentially impossible if both the payor bank and collecting bank use all the time they are minimally entitled to under Florida law. The qualifying period for all elections by statute is only 96 hours or 4 days long. *See* §§ 99.061(1)–(3), Fla. Stat. Likewise, a collecting bank and payor bank combined are minimally entitled to at least four business days to effect notice of dishonor. *See* § 674.104(1)(j), Fla. Stat. (2016) ("In this chapter, unless the context otherwise requires, the term: (j) 'Midnight deadline' with respect to a bank is midnight on its next banking day following the banking day on which it receives the relevant item or notice or from which the time for taking action commences to run, whichever is later."); § 674.1081(2), Fla. Stat. (2016) ("An item or deposit of money received on any day after a cutoff hour so fixed or after the close of the banking day may be treated as being received at the opening of the next banking day."); § 674.1071, Fla. Stat. (2016) ("A branch or separate office of a bank is a separate bank for the purpose of computing the time within which, and determining the place at or to which, action may be taken or notices or orders must be given under this chapter and under chapter 673."); § 674.1091(2), Fla. Stat. (2016) ("Delay by a collecting bank or payor bank beyond time limits prescribed or permitted by this code or by instructions is excused if: (a) The delay is caused by interruption of communication or computer facilities, suspension of payments by another bank, war, emergency conditions, failure of equipment, or other circumstances beyond the control of the bank; and (b) The bank exercises such diligence as the circumstances require."); *see generally* § 674.202, Fla. Stat. (2016) (entitled "Responsibility for collection or return; when action timely.").

Indeed, the facts of this case demonstrate that this is more reality than theory. Here, eight days expired—twice the length of the statutory qualifying period—for Wright's check to be returned erroneously for the bank's failure to locate an account number despite the fact that his check bore his name, address, and account number. Had luck been on Wright's side, a bank official likely would have taken a proper closer look at the check and found the account, avoiding the situation presented today. However, solely because luck was not on Wright's side, he is abruptly disqualified without an opportunity to cure the error, and the citizens of Miami Gardens are deprived of an otherwise qualified candidate. Again, this is irrational. Where offering a cure would not adversely impact an election or the election process, the arbitrary disqualification is the antithesis of our democracy and the election of its officers.

In a similar manner, the bright-line rule imposed by the amendment to section 99.061(7)(a) 1. is neither reasonable nor necessary to serving any legitimate state interest we have previously considered in election cases.

* * *

It is clear that none of the other interests previously considered by this Court could possibly justify the amendment to section 99.061(7)(a) 1. The amendment does not serve to keep the ballot within manageable limits, nor does it serve to maintain party loyalty and perpetuate the party system; it does not serve to protect a candidate's right to privacy.

Therefore, we conclude that this law unconstitutionally erects a barrier that is an unnecessary restraint on one's right to seek elective office. This unnecessary and irrational barrier, which has already in the case of *Levey* completely deprived the citizens of an election, can no longer stand. Unreasonable and unnecessary restrictions on the elective process are a threat to our republican form of government. At their worst, they cloak tyranny in the garb of Democracy. *See* Thomas Paine, *Dissertation on the First Principles of Government* (1795) ("The right of voting for representatives is the primary right by which other rights are protected. To take away this right is to reduce a man to slavery, for slavery consists in being subject to the will of another, and he that has not a vote in the election of representatives is in this case.").

We therefore sever the portion of section 14 of chapter 2011–40, Laws of Florida, that amends section 99.061(7)(a) 1. of the Florida Statutes. *See* Ch. 2011–40, § 79, Laws of Fla. (2011) ("If any provision of this act or its application to any person or circumstance is held invalid, the invalidity does not affect other provisions or applications of the act which can be given effect without the invalid provision or application, and to this end the provisions of this act are severable."). Thus, the version of section 99.061(7)(a) 1. in existence prior to the 2011 amendments is revived by operation of law. *See Henderson v. Antonacci,* 62 So.2d 5, 7 (Fla.1952).

We are mindful of the impacts and burdens our decision today may have on the Legislature, the Supervisor of Elections, the other candidates, and the City of Miami Gardens. Indeed, as some of the relief requested here is at equity, these are central considerations.

However, as a Court, our first and foremost duty is to enforce our Constitution and to protect all the rights of all Floridians thereunder. In this case, an irrational, as well as unreasonable and unnecessary restriction on the elective process has tainted the entire Miami Gardens election for the office of Mayor by keeping the name of a candidate off the ballot, and therefore, beyond the reach of all the voters. This is irremediable without a new election.

CONCLUSION

We therefore quash the decision below. As the previous statute is now the law, Wright "shall, the end of qualifying notwithstanding, have 48 hours from the time such notification is received, excluding Saturdays, Sundays, and legal holidays, to pay the fee with a cashier's check purchased from funds of the campaign account." §99.061(7)(a) 1., Fla. Stat. (2010). This Court's mandate shall serve as Wright's notification. We remand for further proceedings not inconsistent with this opinion, including the invalidation of the August 30 election upon Wright's qualification.

Upon qualification, Wright's name shall be placed on the November ballot. If the parties are unable to accomplish that task, then the City will be forced into a special election for the position of Mayor of the City. [citations omitted]

No motion for rehearing will be entertained.

CANADY, J., concurring in result only.

I agree with the result reached by the majority—allowing Wright's candidacy to go forward—but I strongly disagree with the unprecedented route taken by the majority to reach that result.

Based on the arguments presented by Wright, I would decide this case as a matter of statutory interpretation along the lines advanced by Judge Makar in his dissent from the denial of rehearing en banc in *Levey v. Detzner*, 146 So.3d 1224 (Fla. 1st DCA 2014). As Judge Makar cogently explains, the critical sentence in section 99.061(7)(a) addresses only circumstances in which a check is returned before "the end of qualifying." *Id.* at 1231–32 (Makar, J., dissenting from the denial of rehearing en banc). I therefore disagree with the statutory interpretation adopted by the majority. But I agree with quashing the Third District decision and allowing Wright's candidacy to go forward.

Regarding the majority's holding that the version of section 99.061(7)(a) enacted in 2011 is unconstitutional, there is one big problem: the Petitioner has presented no argument challenging the constitutionality of the statute.[10] It is not within the

---

10. [FN 8.] The majority asserts that the constitutionality of the statute is properly at issue here because Wright "specifically claim[ed] that his constitutional rights were violated" and "has consistently asserted that the statute is unreasonable, irrational, and unnecessary." The majority's position is without any support. Wright has never sought a determination that the statute is unconstitutional. Indeed, he has never so much as suggested that the statute is constitutionally infirm. His position has consistently been that the City's position regarding application of the statute is incorrect. He has taken the position not that the statute is infirm but that the City's interpretation of the statute is unreasonable. Wright did make a reference in his complaint to the City's "untenable position to deny [Plaintiff] his constitutional right to run for public office." (quoting Petitioner's "Amended Complaint for Declaratory and Injunctive Relief, and Emergency Writ of Mandamus" at ¶ 51) (majority emphasis omitted). That is part of Wright's attack on the City's interpretation of the statute. It is by no means a challenge to the constitutionality of the statute. The majority can provide no quotations or citations to support its assertions. The vacuity of the majority's assertions on this point is highlighted by its reliance on Judge Makar's dissent from the denial of rehearing en banc in *Levey*. The majority says that Judge Makar has asserted that the "the statute is unreasonable, irrational, and unnecessary." Majority op. at 779 n. 6 (citing *Levey*, 146 So.3d at 1227). As anyone who reads Judge Makar's dissent will soon discover, the majority's characterization of his position is totally incorrect. Judge Makar's position is that the statutory interpretation adopted by the majority here is "unreasonable and unnecessary"—not that the statute is unconstitutional. *Levey*, 146 So.3d at 1234. Similarly, the majority's citation of *Holley v. Adams*, 238 So.2d 401 (Fla.1970), provides no support for the majority's consideration of an issue that has not been properly presented. Majority op. at 774. The *Holley* Court ad-

province of an appellate court to overturn the ruling of a lower court on a ground that has not been urged by the party challenging the lower court's decision. Anytime that a court does so, the basic structure of the appellate process — which depends on the presentation of issues and the marshaling of arguments by the parties — is seriously undermined. The damage is compounded when a court sua sponte — without the benefit of any argument by the parties — declares a statute unconstitutional. In such cases, injury is done not only to the appellate process but also to the separation of powers. "It is a well established principle that the courts will not declare an act of the legislature unconstitutional unless its constitutionality is challenged directly by one who demonstrates that he is, or assuredly will be, affected adversely by it.... Courts should not voluntarily pass upon constitutional questions which are not raised by the pleadings." *Henderson v. Antonacci*, 62 So.2d 5, 8 (Fla.1952); *see also State v. Turner*, 224 So.2d 290, 291 (Fla.1969) ("This Court has, on a number of occasions, held that it is not only unnecessary, but improper for a Court to pass upon the constitutionality of an act, the constitutionality of which is not challenged; that Courts are not to consider a question of constitutionality which has not been raised by the pleadings...."). Today's decision needlessly transgresses this principle.

Under our system of government, one of the most serious and consequential judgments that any court can render is a judgment that the Legislature has violated the Constitution in enacting a particular law. Here, the majority renders such a judgment without anyone suggesting — much less arguing — that such a judgment is required by the Constitution. No matter how wise and learned a court may be, the court should not strike down as unconstitutional a law adopted by the Legislature without the benefit of considering any arguments on the issue of constitutionality. As a coordinate branch of government, the Legislature is certainly entitled to have some argument in favor of constitutionality considered by a court before that court rules that a statute is unconstitutional. *See* Fla. R. Civ. P. 1.071(b) (providing that a party "drawing into question the constitutionality of a state statute" is required to serve notice on "the Attorney General or the state attorney of the judicial circuit in which the action is pending").

The potential for unanticipated and untoward consequences is manifest when the court fails to hear and consider such arguments. The majority's decision in this case provides a perfect example. Here, the majority declares the statute facially unconstitutional — rather than unconstitutional as applied — and resurrects an earlier version of the statute under which a candidate who submits a check that is properly returned by the bank for non-sufficient funds will nonetheless be given an opportunity to cure the defect. It is unfathomable that such a result could be required by the Constitution, but that result is mandated by today's ill-considered decision.

POLSTON, J., dissenting.

Section 99.061(7)(a) 1., Florida Statutes (2016) (emphasis added), clearly and unambiguously provides that "[i]f a candidate's check is returned by the bank *for any*

---

dressed the constitutional issue there because "Holley attacked the constitutionality" of the particular statute that was at issue. *Holley,* 238 So.2d at 404.

reason, the filing officer shall immediately notify the candidate and the candidate shall have until the end of the qualifying to pay the fee with a cashier's check purchased from funds of the campaign account." The same statute explains that the "[f]ailure to pay the fee as provided in this subparagraph shall disqualify the candidate." *Id.* As explained in the majority opinion, pursuant to the plain language of this subsection, Mr. Wright is disqualified as a candidate because his check was returned by the bank and he did not pay the qualifying fee with a cashier's check by the end of the qualifying period.

While this result is harsh, particularly considering that Mr. Wright did all he could possibly have done to comply with the statutory requirements, this Court does not have the constitutional authority to rewrite statutes lawfully enacted by our state's legislature by just asserting that a statute that it does not wish to enforce is unnecessary, unreasonable, and arbitrary. I agree with Justice Canady's rejection of the majority's decision to declare the statute unconstitutional. As Justice Canady explains, the petitioner here did not raise a constitutional challenge to the statute in this Court. By addressing and deciding the case based on a facial constitutional claim that was not raised or briefed by the parties, the majority becomes an advocate rather than a neutral decision maker.

Even if the petitioner had raised a facial challenge to the statute, the challenge would fail under this Court's precedent. Because section 99.061(7)(a) 1. serves the legitimate government purpose of ensuring that candidates for office lawfully pay the required qualifying fee with campaign funds, it passes the rational basis test and is, therefore, constitutional. *See Fla. High School Activities Ass'n v. Thomas,* 434 So.2d 306, 308 (Fla.1983) ("Under a 'rational basis' standard of review a court should inquire only whether it is conceivable that the regulatory classification bears some rational relationship to a legitimate state purpose.").

The majority holds that the statute is facially unconstitutional due to the circumstances involved in this case while acknowledging that "[f]or those prospective candidates who tender properly executed checks that ultimately clear because they have done all they were required to, the statute poses no problem." Majority op. at 776. This turns facial constitutional review on its head. As this Court has explained, "[f]or a statute to be held facially unconstitutional, the challenger must demonstrate that no set of circumstances exists in which the statute can be constitutionally applied." *Abdool v. Bondi,* 141 So.3d 529, 538 (Fla.2014); *cf. Accelerated Benefits Corp. v. Dep't of Ins.,* 813 So.2d 117, 120 (Fla. 1st DCA 2002) ("In considering an 'as applied' challenge, the court is to consider the facts of the case at hand."). Contrary to the majority's decision today, this Court's precedent emphasizes that an "[a]ct will not be invalidated as facially unconstitutional simply because it could operate unconstitutionally under some [] circumstances." *Abdool,* 141 So.3d at 538.

I would not foreclose the possibility of a successful as-applied constitutional challenge to this statute. However, as stated above, the petitioner did not raise any constitutional challenge to the statute in this Court, as-applied or otherwise.

I respectfully dissent.

Notes and Questions

The Court identifies two rights: the right to run for office and the right of citizens to elect persons of their choosing. The Court, however, cites only to Section 1 of Article I of the Florida Constitution as its textual authority: "All political power is inherent in the people." By contrast, the U.S. Supreme Court analyzes voting and candidacy cases through the lens of the First Amendment rights of speech and association, and equal protection. Is there any reason to not cite to the Florida Constitution's free speech, association, and equal protection provisions? The Florida Supreme Court also avoids any direct citations to the U.S. Constitution and federal decisional law in this 2016 court opinion. Is this to establish a separate and independent state basis for the opinion?

Note the extensive and unusual reliance by both the majority and separate opinions on Judge Makar's dissenting opinion in the lower appellate decision.

The majority and dissent disagree whether appellant Wright raised a constitutional objection to the statute at issue. The briefs filed and the oral argument before the Florida Supreme Court do not contain explicit reference to constitutional provisions alleged to be implicated. Normally this would bar a case from being decided upon points not argued before the Court. Should that matter in this case?

The Court used the rarely applied absurd result doctrine of statutory construction. The absurd result doctrine can override even the plain and unambiguous meaning of a statutory law. *State v. Hackley*, 95 So. 3d 92, 95 (Fla. 2012) ("In certain circumstances, the absurdity doctrine may be used to justify departures from the general rule that courts will apply a statute's plain language."). Note how the Court takes pains to find the statute is unambiguous and therefore precludes other canons of statutory interpretation. The Court therefore characterized the result of disqualification as "plainly irrational" because of the result "turning on luck rather than conduct" to exclude the candidate. *Wright*, 200 So. 3d at 776.

There are Florida constitutional restrictions on who can run for public office. The Florida Constitution bars felons and persons adjudicated mentally incompetent from running for office; prohibits dual office-holding;[11] and imposes term limits. The Constitution imposes qualification requirements, e.g., 30 years of age and 7 years residency in Florida for executive offices,[12] and qualifications for judges. There are county residency requirements for voters.[13]

A second ballot access case involved the 2004 presidential election. Some background is necessary to provide perspective on this case. In 1992, third-party presidential candidate Ross Perot ran a populist campaign, which received 18.9 percent of the nationwide vote. In 1995, Perot founded the Reform Party of the United States and ran as its presidential candidate in the 1996 presidential election. He garnered

---

11. FLA. CONST. art. II, § 5.
12. FLA. CONST. art. IV, § 5.
13. FLA. CONST. art. VI, § 2.

just 8.4 percent of the national vote this time however, which was sufficient to automatically place the Reform Party on the year 2000 state presidential ballots in many states and qualify for $12.6 million dollars in federal campaign money.

It is difficult nationwide for any minority party candidate to gain ballot access for the presidential race.[14] At the November 1998 election, Florida voters approved an amendment proposed by the 1997–98 CRC that prohibited any law that would place ballot registration requirements on independent or minor party candidates that were greater than the major political parties. Before this change, Florida had the most restrictive ballot access laws in the nation.[15] In 1999, the Florida Legislature amended Florida's ballot registration statutes to comply with the 1998 constitutional amendment.

Ross Perot chose not to run as a candidate in the 2000 presidential race. Instead, after a divisive nominating process, a former Republican party member, Pat Buchanan, was nominated as the Reform Party's candidate. Buchanan's campaign received the $12.6 million dollars of federal money, but the Reform Party lost a splinter group containing many of its voters. Buchanan gained only 0.4 percent of the national vote, and the Reform Party lost most of its automatic ballot access in the states and all its eligibility to receive federal campaign money in the 2004 race. In 2004, the consumer activist Ralph Nader ran for and was defeated as the nominee of the Green Party. Nader then began a largely unsuccessful nationwide ballot access process as an independent candidate. In Florida, however, Nader formed a minor party group that allied with a much-diminished Reform Party USA.

Reform Party of Florida v. Black

885 So. 2d 303 (Fla. 2004)

PER CURIAM.

We have for review a trial court judgment certified by the First District Court of Appeal to be of great public importance and to require immediate resolution by this Court. We have jurisdiction. *See* art. V, § 3(b)(5), Fla. Const. For the reasons explained below, we reverse the trial court's final declaratory judgment and vacate the permanent injunction that ordered Reform Party candidates Ralph Nader and Peter Camejo off the 2004 Florida presidential ballot. In making our decision in this case we are guided by the overriding constitutional principles in favor of ballot access and our recognition of the plenary authority of the Legislature to direct the manner of selecting Florida's presidential electors.

---

14. *See* Oliver Hall, *Death by A Thousand Signatures: The Rise of Restrictive Ballot Access Laws and the Decline of Electoral Competition in the United States*, 29 Seattle U.L. Rev. 407 (2005); *cf.* Ballotpedia, Ballot Access Requirements, *available online at:* https://ballotpedia.org/Ballot_access_for_presidential_ candidates (ballot access requirements) (last reviewed June 27, 2020).

15. William A Buzzett & Deborah K. Kearney, Comment to the 1998 Amendment, 26 West's Florida Statutes Annotated 146 (2018).

Procedural History

Despite the short time frame since the genesis of this case, it has a convoluted procedural history. On August 31, 2004, the Reform Party State Executive Committee submitted papers to Florida Secretary of State Glenda Hood seeking to qualify Ralph Nader and Peter Camejo as presidential and vice-presidential candidates for the Reform Party of the United States of America (Reform Party USA) on the Florida ballot for the general election scheduled for November 2, 2004, pursuant to section 103.021(4)(a), Florida Statutes (2003). Governor Jeb Bush certified the Reform Party slate of presidential electors to Secretary of State Glenda Hood, who in turn certified that the names of Nader and Camejo be placed on the 2004 Florida presidential ballot. On September 2, 2004, two separate complaints were filed in the Circuit Court for the Second Judicial Circuit, seeking a reversal of the certification and removal of Nader and Camejo's names from the ballot. One group of plaintiffs included Candice Wilson and Alan Herman, both registered members of the Reform Party, Scott Maddox, a registered member of the Democratic Party and the Chairman of the Florida Democratic Party, and the Florida Democratic Party. The second group of plaintiffs included Harriet Jane Black, a registered Republican from Pinellas County, Robert Rackleff, a registered Democrat from Leon County, William Chapman, a registered member of the Reform Party from Marion County, and Terry Anderson, a registered Independent from Miami-Dade County. Both complaints named Secretary of State Hood, the Reform Party of Florida, Ralph Nader, and Peter Camejo as defendants. The complaints alleged that Nader and Camejo are not "minor party" candidates affiliated with a national party as provided in section 103.021(4)(a), but rather are independent candidates who use the name "Reform Party of Florida" to claim affiliation with the national Reform Party where no affiliation actually exists. The plaintiffs also filed an emergency motion for injunctive relief and a memorandum of law in support of a preliminary injunction.

A status conference on the complaints was scheduled for September 7, 2004, but had to be postponed because of Hurricane Frances. When the plaintiffs received information that the Secretary of State intended to certify the Reform Party presidential slate for inclusion on the presidential ballot on Wednesday, September 8, they rescheduled the conference to include a hearing on their motion for a preliminary injunction. The new hearing, which was held on the afternoon of September 8, became a seven-hour preliminary injunction hearing.

At this hearing, the circuit court received documentary and testimonial evidence and heard argument from the parties. After the hearing, the judge issued an order preliminarily enjoining the Secretary of State from certifying Nader and Camejo as candidates for the Florida 2004 presidential ballot and from certifying the electors offered by the Reform Party of Florida. The court concluded that preliminary injunctive relief was appropriate as the plaintiffs had satisfied the four-part test under Florida law: a substantial likelihood of success on the merits; lack of an adequate remedy at law; irreparable harm absent the entry of an injunction; and that injunctive relief will serve the public interest.

The circuit court found that the plaintiffs had demonstrated a likelihood of success on the merits, finding a "substantial likelihood" that the Reform Party failed to comply with the requirements of section 103.021(4)(a). The circuit court based its conclusion on a number of findings, including that the Reform Party USA is not a "national party," candidates Nader and Camejo were not nominated in a "national convention," and the Reform Party of Florida is not affiliated with the Reform Party USA. The circuit court cited an advisory opinion issued by the Federal Election Commission as providing guidance in its determination that the Reform Party USA is not a national party. The court considered the fact that the Reform Party USA does not broadly offer or support candidates for national office, apart from its presidential and vice-presidential nominees. The circuit court noted that, rather than being nominated in a "national convention," Nader and Camejo were endorsed by the party via a conference telephone call. Further, the conference call did not follow the Reform Party USA's own definition of a "national convention." Finally, the court found that the Reform Party of Florida does not appear to be a minor party affiliated with a national party as required by the statute. The court noted that an April 2002 letter from the Chairman of the Reform Party of Florida shows that the Florida sector disaffiliated from the national party. Based on these findings, the circuit court concluded that the Reform Party of Florida would be unlikely to meet the requirements of the statute.

As to the other grounds for ordering injunctive relief, the court found that there is no adequate remedy at law because neither party's damages can be reduced to a monetary amount and the potential public harm in failing to follow the applicable legal requirements cannot be dissipated by ordinary judicial remedies. The court further found that the plaintiffs will suffer irreparable harm without the injunction. Orange County Supervisor of Elections Bill Cowles testified that the inclusion of an erroneous candidate for president on the ballot would be disastrous. Finally, the court found that the injunctive relief would serve the public interest because Florida has important interests in enforcing its election laws, ensuring that only qualified candidates appear on its ballot, protecting the integrity of the ballot and election process, and preventing voter confusion during the election.

Thus, the circuit court preliminarily enjoined Secretary Hood from certifying Ralph Nader and Peter Camejo as candidates on the 2004 Florida presidential election ballot and from certifying the electors offered by the Reform Party of Florida. As the court pointed out in its order, "time is of the essence in this dispute" in that county election supervisors are required by law to mail certain absentee ballots no later than Saturday, September 18, 2004, forty-five days prior to election day. *See* § 101.62(4)(a), Fla. Stat. (2003)....

The Reform Party of Florida, Nader, and Camejo appealed the non-final preliminary injunction to the First District Court of Appeal. They also sought a stay pending review. The district court did not rule on the stay and concluded that the case required immediate resolution by this Court, pursuant to Florida Rule of Appellate Procedure 9.125. *See Reform Party of Fla. v. Black*, No. 1D04-4050 (Fla. 1st DCA Sept. 13, 2004). In the meantime, Secretary Hood filed a notice of appeal on September 13, thereby invoking the automatic stay provision for public bodies and public officers under Florida Rule of Appellate Procedure 9.310(b)(2). This automatically stayed the circuit court's temporary injunction prohibiting the Secretary of State from certifying the names of Nader and Camejo for inclusion on the 2004 Florida presidential ballot. Simultaneously, Secretary Hood directed the supervisors of elections to include the names of Nader and Camejo on the ballot. The plaintiffs filed a motion asking the circuit court to vacate the automatic stay; they filed a similar motion in this Court.

This Court agreed to accept jurisdiction of the case, while permitting the litigation to continue in the circuit court.... This Court ordered the circuit court to proceed with its final hearing and the entry of a final order and to determine any motions relating to the automatic stay.

After receiving this Court's order on September 13, the plaintiffs contacted the trial judge, who was out of the state, and requested that he rule on their motion to vacate the automatic stay. While the judge was considering the motion, Defendants Nader, Camejo, and the Reform Party of Florida filed a petition on September 13 in the United States District Court for the Northern District of Florida to remove the case to federal court, based on a federal question. The plaintiffs responded by filing an emergency motion for remand to state court. On September 14, 2004, the United States District Court remanded the case to the state court. The federal court cited three bases for remanding the case to state court: all of the counts raised in the plaintiffs' complaint are grounded solidly in state law and thus do not raise a valid federal question sufficient to invoke the district court's jurisdiction; the defendants had not met the unanimity requirement as Secretary Hood had not consented to the removal and she is a necessary and indispensable party to the case; and the defendants waived their rights to remove the cause to federal court by invoking the jurisdiction of the Florida appellate courts and by participating in evidentiary hearings on the merits of the case.

D's filed to move to Fed courts.

Reasons the fed court remanded to state court.

The circuit court judge scheduled a hearing for 8:00 a.m. on Wednesday, September 15 to consider the plaintiffs' motion to vacate the automatic stay and their motion to modify the preliminary injunction. By early Wednesday afternoon, the circuit court issued orders vacating the automatic stay and modifying the preliminary injunction. The modified injunction ordered the Secretary of State to instruct all county supervisors of elections to mail corrected ballot forms not containing Nader and Camejo as candidates in the presidential election to all recipients who had previously been mailed ballot forms containing these names. The Secretary of State was further ordered to instruct the supervisors of elections that any corrective mailings must include clear written notice that the previous ballots did not comply with Florida law and that the corrected ballot form is the valid form. The court also ordered the plaintiffs to post a $10,000 bond to cover additional expenses that may be incurred by the supervisors of elections should this Court rule that the ballots must contain the names of Nader and Camejo.

The Secretary of State immediately filed a motion asking this Court to reinstate the automatic stay, arguing that the preservation of integrity in the election system required the circuit court's preliminary injunction to be stayed. In order to preserve the rights of the parties and the voters in anticipation of the impending disposition of this case, we granted the motion to reinstate the stay in part. However, pursuant to rule 9.310(b)(2), this Court imposed a condition that the Secretary of State instruct the county supervisors of elections to desist from mailing ballots to voters pending further order of this Court. This Court also scheduled oral argument in the case for Friday, September 17, 2004, at 8:00 a.m.

In the meantime, the circuit judge proceeded with the final hearing on the plaintiffs' complaints requesting permanent injunctive relief. During this thirteen hour evidentiary hearing, the judge heard testimonial evidence from witnesses, admitted documentary evidence, and heard argument from both sides. At the conclusion of this evidentiary hearing, the court issued a final declaratory judgment finding that Nader and Camejo are not legally qualified under Florida law to appear on the Florida ballot as candidates for president and vice-president. The court also permanently enjoined the Secretary of State from certifying Nader and Camejo on Florida's ballots, from instructing the county supervisors of elections to include their names on the ballot, and from mailing any ballots pending further order of this Court.

Based on the district court's certification of this case, we review the circuit court's declaratory judgment and order of permanent injunction. This case involves the constitutional right of individuals to associate for the advancement of political beliefs and the constitutional right of qualified voters to cast their votes effectively. *See, e.g., Munro v. Socialist Workers Party*, 479 U.S. 189, 193 (1986).... The State, however, has a "substantial state interest in encouraging compromise and political stability, in attempting to ensure that the election winner will represent a majority of the community and in providing the electorate with an understandable ballot." *Storer v. Brown*, 415 U.S. at 729 [(1974)] (citing *Williams v. Rhodes*, 393 U.S. 23, 32 (1968)). "[A]s a practical matter, there must be a substantial regulation of elections if they are to be fair and honest and if some sort of order, rather than chaos, is to accompany the democratic processes." *Storer*, 415 U.S. at 730. Thus, the United States Supreme Court has

> upheld generally applicable and evenhanded restrictions that protect the integrity and reliability of the electoral process itself. The State has the undoubted right to require candidates to make a preliminary showing of substantial support in order to qualify for a place on the ballot, because it is both wasteful and confusing to encumber the ballot with the names of frivolous candidates.

Anderson [*v. Celebrezze*], 460 U.S. at 788 n. 9 [(1983)].

Under Article II, Section 1, Clause 2 of the United States Constitution, the state legislatures are given the authority to regulate who is placed on the ballot....

As early as 1949, Florida's Legislature provided a method by which minor party candidates could access the ballot. *See* ch. 25143, Laws of Florida (1949) (allowing a candidate of a minor political party to appear on the ballot by gathering 7500 signatures with at least 25 signatures from each of 34 counties and no more than 1000 from 25 counties). In 1967 the Legislature amended the law to allow ballot access by gathering signatures from a required percentage of registered voters. *See* ch. 67-353, § 1, at 1127–28, Laws of Fla. In 1970 the Legislature added the requirement that a minor political party be affiliated with a national party holding a national convention to nominate presidential and vice-presidential candidates. *See* ch. 70-269, § 7, at 851–52, Laws of Fla. Thus, a minor party candidate was required to both gather signatures and affiliate with a national party holding a national convention in order to appear on the presidential ballot in Florida. Significant to this case is the change made to the law in 1999, when the Legislature uncoupled the requirements of gathering signatures and affiliating with a national party. *See* ch. 99-318, § 4, at 3400, Laws of Fla.[16]

This legislative history illustrates how the Florida Legislature has chosen to balance the competing interests involved in ballot access. Presidential and vice-presidential candidates who are nominated through the primary election process are entitled to have their names printed on the Florida general election ballot based on this primary election process. *See* § 101.2512(1), Fla. Stat. (2003); *see also* § 103.101, Fla. Stat. (2003) (outlining procedure for presidential preference primary). Minor party and independent candidates for president and vice-president who have not been nominated through the primary process may have their names printed on the general election ballot by complying with the statutory procedures established by the Florida Legislature. *See* § 103.021(3), (4), Fla. Stat. At issue in this case is the statute governing minor party candidates' access to the ballot, which provides:

> (a) A minor party that is affiliated with a national party holding a national convention to nominate candidates for President and Vice President of the United States may have the names of its candidates for President and Vice President of the United States printed on the general election ballot by filing with the Department of State a certificate naming the candidates for President and Vice President and listing the required number of persons to serve as electors. Notification to the Department of State under this subsection shall be made by September 1 of the year in which the election is held. When the Department of State has been so notified, it shall order the names of the candidates nominated by the minor party to be included on the ballot and shall permit the required number of persons to be certified as electors in the same manner as other party candidates.

§ 103.021(4)(a), Fla. Stat. (2003).

---

16. [FN 4.] This change was made to implement recently adopted article VI, section 1, Florida Constitution. *See* Fla. S. Comm. on Ethics & Elecs., SB 754 (1999) Staff Analysis 1 (Feb. 8, 1999) (on file with comm.) ("Senate Bill 754 implements the amendment to Article VI, section 1, Florida Constitution, which was approved by the voters in the 1998 General Election."). Article VI, section 1 provides that "the requirements for a candidate with no party affiliation or for a candidate of a minor party for placement of the candidate's name on the ballot shall be no greater than the requirements for a candidate of the party having the largest number of registered voters."

Facts

Pursuant to this statute, the Reform Party of Florida presented documents to the Secretary of State in order to have its candidates' names placed on the 2004 Florida presidential ballot. Thereafter, the plaintiffs filed two separate complaints seeking a determination of whether the Reform Party of Florida candidates should appear on the ballot and asking for an injunction. The plaintiffs alleged that the Reform Party of Florida does not meet the statutory requirements of being a "minor party that is affiliated with a national party holding a national convention to nominate candidates for President and Vice President of the United States." After a lengthy evidentiary hearing, that included receipt of documentary evidence and arguments from the parties, the trial judge issued a declaratory judgment that the Reform Party of Florida candidates are not legally qualified under Florida law to appear on the ballot because the Reform Party USA is not a national party. The trial judge also issued a permanent injunction prohibiting the Secretary of State from certifying the Reform Party of Florida candidates on Florida ballots and from instructing the county supervisors of elections from including these candidates on the ballots. This review follows.

Analysis

An order in a declaratory judgment action is generally accorded a presumption of correctness on appellate review. *See, e.g., Williams v. Gen. Ins. Co.,* 468 So.2d 1033, 1034 (Fla. 3d DCA 1985). However, to the extent that the decision rests on a question of law, the order is subject to full, or de novo, review on appeal....

As previously explained, the issue in this case is not whether the State may impose "some burden" upon the access to the ballot. The State may clearly do so. *Burdick v. Takushi,* 504 U.S. 428, 430 (1992) (concluding that Hawaii's prohibition of write-in votes did not "impermissibly burden the right to vote"). However, the rule of *Williams v. Rhodes,* 393 U.S. 23, 28–29 (1968), frames the extent of the "burden" that may be imposed:

> The State also contends that it has absolute power to put any burdens it pleases on the selection of electors because of the First Section of the Second Article of the Constitution, providing that "Each State shall appoint, in such Manner as the Legislature thereof may direct, a Number of Electors ..." to choose a President and Vice President. There, of course, can be no question but that this section does grant extensive power to the States to pass laws regulating the selection of electors. But the Constitution is filled with provisions that grant Congress or the States specific power to legislate in certain areas; these granted powers are always subject to the limitation that they may not be exercised in a way that violates other specific provisions of the Constitution.

Thus, our analysis of the specific burdens must be viewed in light of access to the ballot being constitutionally based.

The issue before us is whether the Reform Party of Florida and its presidential nominees Ralph Nader and Peter Camejo qualify for the ballot under section 103.021(4)(a). According to the statute, there must be a "certificate naming the candidates for president and vice president and listing the required number of persons to serve as electors." § 103.021(4)(a), Fla. Stat (2003). The Secretary of State asserts that her function is purely ministerial and that therefore she has no basis to look behind the certificate to determine that the party meets the statutory criteria.

The method for ballot qualification set out in section 103.021(4)(b) for a minor party *not* affiliated with a national party holding a national convention requires that a specific percentage of registered voters must petition to place the candidate on the ballot. This involves a pure question of objectively verifiable fact. However, the determination of whether the candidate qualifies under section 103.021(4)(a) by claiming to be a "minor political party that is affiliated with a national party holding a national convention to nominate candidates for President and Vice President" involves a legal determination.

We are especially mindful of the fact that this statute must be construed consistent with the important constitutional rights that are involved: "[T]he right of individuals to associate for the advancement of political beliefs, and the right of qualified voters, regardless of their political persuasion, to cast their votes effectively." *Williams v. Rhodes*, 393 U.S. at 30. As the United States Supreme Court explained in *Williams:*

> Both of these rights, of course, rank among our most precious freedoms. We have repeatedly held that freedom of association is protected by the First Amendment. And of course this freedom protected against federal encroachment by the First Amendment is entitled under the Fourteenth Amendment to the same protection from infringement by the States. Similarly, we have said with reference to the right to vote: "No right is more precious in a free country than that of having a voice in the election of those who make the laws under which, as good citizens, we must live. Other rights, even the most basic, are illusory if the right to vote is undermined."
>
> ... The right to form a party for the advancement of political goals means little if a party can be kept off the election ballot and thus denied an equal opportunity to win votes. So also, the right to vote is heavily burdened if that vote may be cast only for the one of two parties at a time when other parties are clamoring for a place on the ballot.

Id. at 30–31 (footnotes omitted) (quoting *Wesberry v. Sanders*, 376 U.S. 1, 17 (1964)). It follows that when the state imposes a burden upon access to the ballot, that burden must be clearly delineated. Thus, any doubt as to the meaning of statutory terms should be resolved broadly in favor of ballot access. As this Court recognized in the context of a challenge to a candidate's eligibility to run for governor under the Florida Constitution:

> Even if there were doubts or ambiguities as to his eligibility, they should be resolved in favor of a free expression of the people in relation to the challenged provision of the Constitution. It is the sovereign right of the people to select their own officers and the rule is against imposing disqualifications to run. The lexicon of democracy condemns all attempts to restrict one's right to

run for office. The Supreme Court of the United States has approved the support of fundamental questions of law with sound democratic precepts. Florida is committed to the general rule in this country that the right to hold office is a valuable one and should not be abridged except for unusual reason or by plain provision of law.

Ervin v. Collins, 85 So.2d 852, 858 (Fla.1956)....

In construing the statute we are also mindful that the Legislature has exclusive power to define the method of determining how the electors of the state are chosen under Article II, Section 1, Clause 2 of the United States Constitution. *See Bush v. Palm Beach County Canvassing Bd.,* 531 U.S. 70, 76 (2000). In other words, although the judiciary has the power and authority to construe statutes, it cannot construe statutes in a manner that would infringe on the direct grant of authority to the Legislature through the United States Constitution. Nevertheless, because the Legislature used terms such as "national party" and "national convention," we must assume that the Legislature intended these terms to have some meaning, especially because this method of ballot access is far less onerous than the method in section 103.021(4)(b), which requires obtaining signatures from one percent of registered voters in Florida. Thus, our ultimate question is how we should interpret these terms. We first focus on the term "national party."

The term "national party" is not defined in section 103.021(4)(a) or in any other Florida legal authority. Where there is uncertainty in the meaning to be given the words employed in a statute, "the Court must resort to canons of statutory construction in order to derive the proper meaning." *Seagrave v. State,* 802 So.2d 281, 286 (Fla.2001). Further, this Court explained that

> [o]ne of the most fundamental tenets of statutory construction requires that we give statutory language its plain and ordinary meaning, unless words are defined in the statute or by the clear intent of the legislature. When necessary, the plain and ordinary meaning of words can be ascertained by reference to a dictionary.

Nehme v. Smithkline Beecham Clinical Labs., Inc., 863 So.2d 201, 204–05 (Fla.2003) (citations and quotation marks omitted). There is no definition of "national party" in the dictionary. The dictionary definitions of "national" and "party" provide little guidance. *See Merriam Webster's Collegiate Dictionary* 773, 848 (10th ed.1998) (defining national as "of or relating to a nation"; defining party as "a group of persons organized for the purpose of directing the policies of a government"); *Black's Law Dictionary* 1144–45 (7th ed.1999) (defining "party" in the context of a legal proceeding).

In the absence of a statutory or dictionary definition, courts have relied on textbooks and legal authority from other jurisdictions. *See Smith v. State,* 80 Fla. 315, 85 So. 911 (1920) (relying on textbook definitions and courts of other jurisdictions to determine the meaning of a statutory phrase); 48A Fla. Jur.2d *Statutes* § 132 (2000). To that end, we look to how other states have defined a "national party" and how the federal government interprets this term.

[handwritten margin note: No definition of National Party]

Hawaii defines a national party as

> a party established and *admitted to the ballot in at least one state other* than Hawaii or one which is determined by the chief election officer to be making a bona fide effort to become a national party.

Haw.Rev.Stat. § 11-113(b) (1993) (emphasis added). In contrast, in order to be considered a "national political party" in Iowa, the party must

> meet[] the definition of a political party established for this state by section 43.2, and ... meet[] the statutory definition of the term "political party" or a term of like import *in at least twenty-five other states* of the United States.

Iowa Code § 68A.102(16) (2003) (emphasis added). Puerto Rico defines a national party as

> every political party that nominates and participates in the election of candidates for the offices of President and Vice-President of the United States of America.

16 P.R. Laws Ann. § 1322 (1987). Thus, there is no consensus on what constitutes a national party, even among the few states that define the term.

The Federal Election Commission (FEC) seems to have created a working definition of a "national party" in light of the elements it considers in granting national committee status to a minor political party. We glean these elements from the advisory opinions issued by the FEC. Of particular interest is FEC Advisory Opinion 1998-2, which sets forth the criteria it used to determine whether the "political party or its committees have demonstrated sufficient activity on a national level to attain national committee status." Fed. Elect. Comm. Ad. Op.1998-2. The main three factors the FEC looks to in determining whether "national committee" status exist are:

> (1) the party's nomination of candidates for various Federal offices in numerous states;
>
> (2) the party's engagement in certain activities on an ongoing basis (rather than with respect to a particular election) such as supporting voter registration and get-out-the-vote drives;
>
> (3) the party's publicization of issues of importance to the party and its adherents throughout the nation.

Id.; see also Fed. Elect. Comm. Ad. Op.1996-35.

There is no dispute that under the FEC's definition the Reform Party USA qualified as a national party up through the 2000 election. The dispute is whether the Reform Party USA subsequently lost its status as a national party because it no longer has significant support, has almost eliminated fundraising, and has candidates on the ballot for federal office other than president in only two other states.

Although the appellees have presented facts to support an argument that the Reform Party USA no longer meets the criteria set forth by the FEC, we cannot conclude that the Legislature intended to incorporate the FEC definition within the use of the term "national party." This is especially so because the FEC's interest relates to the integrity of campaign fundraising access, whereas the state's interest lies in protecting the integrity of the ballot. If we were to construe the term more narrowly than the Legislature intended, we could run afoul of Article II, Section 1, Clause 2 of the United States Constitution. This we decline to do.

Among other testimony in the record, the Reform Party presented evidence that in 1998 the FEC found it to be a national committee. Even today the Reform Party USA has affiliates remaining in several states and has placed candidates on the ballot for federal office in at least two states. While there were disputes as to whether the national convention held violated Reform Party USA's own constitution, the evidence showed that some type of meeting occurred. Additionally, while the evidence of whether the Reform Party remained affiliated with the national party was disputed, the trial court recognized that some type of affiliation continued.

The Reform Party of Florida filed its certificate for placement on the 2004 Florida presidential ballot with the Secretary of State pursuant to section 103.021(4)(a). This statute did not outline standards or definitions for the most critical terms, namely: "national party" and "national convention." Thus, the Reform Party of Florida was not on notice that these terms were to be interpreted in accordance with any specific criteria and certainly not the criteria utilized by the trial court. After a thorough review of the statute, related Florida statutes, the legislative history, statutes in other states, and federal statutes and standards, we have been unable to ascertain whether the Legislature intended for the statutory terms to have a strict or broad meaning. In the absence of more specific statutory criteria or guidance from the Legislature we are unable to conclude that a statutory violation occurred.

We therefore reverse the trial judge's declaratory judgment and vacate the permanent injunction because section 103.021(4)(a) is not sufficiently clear to put the Reform Party of Florida on notice that it could not qualify under its provisions. However, we are left with a statute that does not have its critical terms defined or standards set for ascertaining compliance with the statute. We thus urge the Legislature to revisit this important issue at its earliest opportunity.

It is so ordered.

PARIENTE, C.J., and WELLS, QUINCE, CANTERO and BELL, JJ., concur.

LEWIS, J., concurring in result only.

I cannot at all agree with the analysis and reasoning of the majority. The right to vote is a fundamental and essential part of our constitutional democracy and is subject to reasonable regulation....

Although minor political parties most certainly do have a right to be on the ballot, courts have consistently held that this right is not absolute and without restrictions.... *Libertarian Party of Fla. v. Florida*, 710 F.2d 790, 792–93 (11th Cir.1983). The states' compelling interests include maintaining fairness, honesty, and order, *see Burdick*, 504 U.S. at 433, minimizing frivolous candidacies, *see Lubin* [*v. Panish*], 415 U.S. at 715 [(1974)], and "avoiding confusion, deception, and even frustration of the democratic process," *Jenness* [*v. Fortson*], 403 U.S. at 442 [(1971)]. The United States Supreme Court has recognized that

> [a] procedure inviting or permitting every citizen to present himself to the voters on the ballot without some means of measuring the seriousness of the candidate's desire and motivation would make rational voter choices more difficult because of the size of the ballot and hence would tend to impede the electoral process.

Lubin, 415 U.S. at 715.

Florida's statutory scheme has properly enacted safeguards to protect our electoral process. Section 103.021 of the Florida Statutes (2003) requires that persons who seek to be a candidate for President on Florida's ballot must show substantial support, either by a valid signature provision, *see* § 103.021(4)(b), Fla. Stat. (2003), or by demonstrating that he or she was nominated at a national nominating convention of a minor party that is affiliated with a national party, *see* § 103.021(4)(a), Fla. Stat. (2003). The Legislature has enacted this statutory scheme to further the State's compelling interest in maintaining fairness, honesty, and order, along with minimizing frivolous candidacies to avoid confusion, deception, and frustration of the democratic process. Our system is legislatively designed so that minor parties affiliated with a national party holding a national convention, *see* § 103.021(4)(a), Fla. Stat. (2003), are treated differently than minor parties that are not affiliated with a national party holding a national convention, *see* § 103.021(4)(b), Fla. Stat. (2003). To construe subsection (4)(a) as the majority does today is nothing less than this Court basically rewriting the statute and using a judicial eraser to strip section (4)(a) of the same dignity as this Court has afforded the petition requirement in subsection (4)(b).

The present dispute has called into question the utilization of this statute by a party in connection with the current ballot....

There are no magic words or numbers to establish precisely what would qualify a party as "national." What is clear, however, is that a party labeling itself a "national party" does not make it so. Reference by the majority to the specific statutes of other states is both meaningless and a red-herring. The Florida Legislature could have selected any number of additional words or elements to impact the word "national" but it *did not do so.* Florida clearly did not include anything conceivably similar to the specific words chosen by the Legislatures of Hawaii, Iowa or Puerto Rico. Reference to these statutes certainly does not assist the analysis here and seems to be injected simply in an attempt to misdirect attention.... The facts before the trial court did not warrant the conclusion that the Reform Party is a "national" party. Instead, the evidence established and was more demonstrative of a splinter cell of what once was a "national party."

This Court must attempt to understand and apply the broad parameters of what constitutes a "national party" in light of the absence of any further specification for a definition. In devising these parameters, it is necessary to look to the traditional principles of statutory construction. "Because the statute does not define the term [national], the Court must resort to canons of statutory construction in order to derive the proper meaning." *Nehme v. Smithkline Beecham Clinical Laboratories, Inc.,* 863 So.2d 201, 204–05 (Fla.2003) (citing *Seagrave v. State,* 802 So.2d 281, 286 (Fla.2001)). "One of the most fundamental tenets of statutory construction requires that we give statutory language its plain and ordinary meaning, unless words are defined in the statute or by the clear intent of the legislature." *Id.* (citing *Green v. State,* 604 So.2d 471, 473 (Fla.1992)). "When necessary, the plain and ordinary meaning of words can be ascertained by reference to a dictionary." *Id....*

In addition, this Court must also ensure that laws are enforced with common sense; to do otherwise is to generate disrespect for the law by creating "a morass of technical regulations with no connection to human experience." *Mackey v. Household Bank, F.S.B.,* 677 So.2d 1295 (Fla. 4th DCA 1996)....

The trial court, without the benefit of a specific definition of "national," probed the parameters of what a "national party" holding a "national convention" really was intended to and actually encompassed. Expert testimony at the trial level provided attributes or characteristics of what defines a "national political party" to include but not necessarily be limited to:

> (1) the ability to recruit and run national candidates across the country;
>
> (2) the ability to stimulate interest in the political process; (3) the ability to promote, develop, and publicize issues; and (4) the ability to raise money in order to conduct political activities.

The evidence presented at the hearing below revealed that the Reform Party has no substantial funds, does not engage in substantial fundraising or party-building activities, does not actively promote its platform, is highly factionalized, and otherwise does not have a national impact and presence. Specifically, the testimony established that the Reform Party has not run any candidates in Florida since 2002, that there is currently no state activity by the Reform Party-FLA, that there has been no party building or significant fundraising in Florida since the 2000 election; and that the Reform Party filed termination of status notice with the Federal Election Commission.

If the Legislature does not define "national," we must turn to common sense and common understanding of this term. In doing so, it is proper to look to experts in the political arena in defining this term. The trial court considered the opinion testimony of experts offered by the parties in determining the parameters of the characteristics of what constitutes a "national" party in accordance with our precedent. Based on the foregoing, the trial judge had not only competent and substantial evidence to support his findings but also the only evidence presented supported the conclusion that this is not a "national party" within the purview of the controverted statute. In my view, the determinations made by the trial court are eminently correct based on the evidence and arguments presented. The majority, in my view, fails to even consider that there is a factual component as to whether one satisfies the legal criteria of a statute.

We cannot legislate or devise a specific codification of enumerated elements for this statute because that falls within the exclusive province of the Legislature not the Judiciary....

At a minimum, the parameters of what constitutes a national party, most assuredly, must be that the entity or group is an organization of voters formed to influence the government's conduct and policies by nominating and electing candidates to public office that exists throughout the nation. While the concept of "national" does not necessarily require a presence or touch in every geographical location, it certainly must require more than that which the evidence presented here has demonstrated. The facts in this case fail to rise to this level.

The majority refers to what may or may not have existed in 1998 but does not address present fact nor does it enlighten as to present circumstances. In a similar manner, the recitation of other facts by the majority in an attempt to bolster its conclusions fails to follow well established principles. The existence of other evidence is not the basis upon which a trial court's determination of factual issues is to be considered on review.

Notwithstanding that there may be various inflections of what a word may mean, an overly technical approach would result in no word ever having an acceptable or legally sufficient definite meaning or understanding. A word does not necessarily need to be defined by precise elements to have a common understanding. No matter what definition one may establish as to "national" under this statute, there would be a factual question regarding whether the entity or group satisfies that definition, which the majority summarily rejects.

Notwithstanding the foregoing, we must determine whether an appropriate remedy has been ordered in this case. Were the Court to simply affirm the injunction and deny relief to the appellants in this case, a grave inequity would result because it may be properly advanced that the appellants were not afforded adequate notice as to what constituted a "national party" under section 103.021(4)(a), Florida States (2003). It is my view that this lack of notice presents the most serious concern and due process implications that require this Court to direct that Nader and Camejo's names be placed on the November general election ballot, a remedy that has been thoughtfully considered and applied by other courts. *See Duke v. Connell*, 790 F.Supp. 50, 55–56 (D.R.I.1992); *see also Kay v. Mills*, 490 F.Supp. 844, 854–55 (E.D.Ky.1980). This is the most practicable solution, which is consistent with the competing interests to be considered. This result preserves the rights of the appellants, the rights of the public, and supports the underlying principles relating to election consideration. This remedy serves to effect a balancing of the important interests and to protect the interests of all affected, including the public.

In affording the appellants relief, it should be noted that unless section 103.021, Florida Statutes (2003), is modified to more specifically define the terms "national party" and "national convention," candidates participating in future elections should be forewarned that they must meet the criteria outlined. Those who fail to do so may be challenged and should ultimately be excluded from the ballot.

ANSTEAD, J., dissenting.

While I agree with the majority that a major impediment to judicial resolution of this case rests on the lack of a precise definition of the terms "national party" and "national convention" contained in section 103.021(4), I cannot agree that the absence of such precision compels us to ignore the requirements of section 103.021(4) altogether. I would approve the trial court's judgment because I believe it was absolutely faithful to the purpose and intent of the Legislature in enacting the provisions of section 103.021(4).

In essence, the trial court held that no matter how narrowly or broadly the terms of the statute are defined, those terms were not met here. Included in the plethora of evidence considered by the trial court of the defunct status of the Reform Party—USA and the Reform Party—Florida were actual written filings by those entities with the Federal Election Commission stating that those parties were inactive and would no longer be participating in federal elections. Of particular concern to the trial court here was the appearance that a defunct party's name was simply being used to get a candidate who was not a member of the party and had not previously been associated it, and who otherwise was not properly qualified, onto the Florida ballot. In other words, the underlying purpose of Florida's statute was being flouted. Because I conclude that the trial court's findings and legal analysis were completely faithful to the terms and especially the spirit of Florida's election laws I would approve the trial court's judgment.

When the Legislature separated the petition and national party affiliation requirements for ballot access in 1999 it clearly made access easier by providing two separate means to access the ballot rather than the more difficult dual requirements of petition and national party affiliation. Having to clear one hurdle rather than two is obviously less difficult. However, the underlying purpose of these provisions remained the same: establishing some reasonable means to assure that those seeking placement on the ballot have established their political viability and legitimacy, whether by securing a certain percentage of voters' endorsement or being associated with a viable national party....

I commend the trial court for its diligence and faithfulness to the law under extremely trying circumstances. Because I conclude that the trial court "got it right" on the facts and the law, I would approve its judgment.

Commentary and Questions

Note the frenetic pace of the litigation in *Reform Party* and its probable impact on judicial deliberation. At the trial level, an initial status conference was postponed five days after the complaints were filed because of a hurricane. The next day, a status conference—normally of fifteen minutes or less in duration—morphed into a seven-hour evidentiary hearing on a preliminary injunction. The trial court judge issued a non-final opinion on the preliminary injunction quickly, though the exact date is not provided. The Secretary of State and Reform Party appealed the non-final order on the preliminary injunction eleven days after the original complaints were filed. The Secretary's appeal automatically stayed the trial court's order.

That same day, several things happened. The First District Court of Appeal certified the appeal to the Florida Supreme Court as containing an issue of great public importance, and the Florida Supreme Court accepted jurisdiction to hear the appeal.

Using an unusual procedure, the Florida Supreme Court maintained jurisdiction but required the trial court to proceed to a final evidentiary trial and final order. The parties directly contacted the trial judge with this order. The trial judge was then outside of Florida and was obligated to return. The Reform Party filed to remove the case to federal court, and the Florida trial court had to suspend proceeding until that petition was ruled upon.

The day after that, the federal district court denied the request to remove and remanded the case to the Florida court system. The Florida Supreme Court ordered all attorneys involved to provide the court with cell phone numbers and e-mail addresses that could be accessed on a 24-hour basis. http://onlinedocketssc.flcourts.org/DocketResults/CaseByYear?CaseNumber=1755&CaseYear=2004. The day after remand from the federal court, the trial court judge held a thirteen-hour evidentiary hearing and issued a permanent injunction. Two days later, and fifteen days after the original complaints, oral argument was held before the Florida Supreme Court. The Court reversed the trial court's order in a six-to-one opinion issued the same day as the oral argument.

The concurring opinion of Justice Lewis excoriated the majority's reasoning. He agreed only that the statute failed to place candidates on notice of what requirements must be met.

1. Should the court have used a traditional void-for-vagueness analysis?

2. Can the State funnel candidates and voters toward the two major parties to simplify ballots?

The ability to run outside the two-party system is also implicated in alternate voting systems, such as ranked voting. "General elections shall be determined by a plurality of votes cast." This provision has been in all Florida constitutions since 1868.[17] The plurality rules apply only to general elections—not to primaries, caucuses, petitions, nominating conventions or executive committees. *Wagner v. Gray*, 74 So. 2d 89 (Fla. 1954). The plurality measure means a candidate does not need more than fifty percent of the votes to win in a race with three or more candidates.

This rule prevents runoff elections. The candidate receiving the most votes is the winner, even if the winning percentage is small. For example, a candidate might win with twenty-one percent of all votes in a highly fractured race of five candidates. Some commentators question whether such a winner possesses the legitimacy to govern in the name of all citizens.

Florida courts are constrained in their power over disputed elections. There are no common law or equitable rights to contest an election in Florida. The Florida Legislature prescribes any methods for protesting or contesting an election. The only fixed method to contest an election is through a writ of *quo warranto*, a writ challenging by what right a person holds an office or performs an act. That writ is limited in what it can accomplish.

---

17. D'Alemberte, Commentary, 26 West's Florida Statutes Annotated 334 (1995).

The United States Senate and House of Representatives each have the sole power to determine disputed elections to their chamber. The Florida Senate and House also have sole power to determine disputed elections to their chamber. The 1968 Constitution inserted the words "be the sole" into the provision that had been in the 1885 Constitution, changing the text from "Each house shall judge of ..." to "Each house shall be the sole judge of....".[18]

An accurate count of ballots, though, is an enforceable right:

> As is well established in this State by our contest statute, "[t]he right to a correct count of the ballots in an election is a substantial right which it is the privilege of every candidate for office to insist on, in every case where there has been a failure to make a *proper count,* call, tally, or return of the votes as required by law, and this fact has been duly established as the basis for granting such relief." *State ex rel. Millinor v. Smith,* 107 Fla. 134, 139, 144 So. 333, 335 (1932) (emphasis added)."

Gore v. Harris, 772 So. 2d 1243, 1251 (Fla. 2000), *rev'd on other grounds sub nom. Bush v. Gore,* 531 U.S. 98 (2000). In this way, Florida courts do become involved in the U.S. presidential election, elections for Florida executive department officers, and elections for local government offices. In these cases, Florida courts divide election problems into those involving intentional wrongdoing and those involving substantial noncompliance with election law through negligence or mistake.

Beckstrom v. Volusia County Canvassing Board

707 So. 2d 720 (Fla. 1998)

WELLS, Justice.

We have for review a final judgment of the Circuit Court of the Seventh Judicial Circuit in Volusia County, which judgment has been certified by the Fifth District Court of Appeal as presenting an issue of great public importance, having a great effect on the proper administration of justice throughout the state, and requiring immediate resolution by this Court. We have jurisdiction. Art. V, § 3(b)(5), Fla. Const.

This case arises out of the November 5, 1996, Volusia County election in which appellant Gus Beckstrom was an unsuccessful candidate for sheriff. On November 8, 1996, pursuant to section 102.166(11), Florida Statutes (1995), appellant filed in the circuit court a protest of the election returns. The protest was based on allegations of fraud in the counting of absentee ballots by the staff of the Volusia County Supervisor of Elections. County election officials had tabulated the votes, and appellee Volusia County Canvassing Board had subsequently certified the result to the Department of State, which declared incumbent Sheriff Robert L. Vogel, Jr. to be the winner of the election.

One month after filing the initial protest, appellant moved the court to order a manual re-count of the absentee ballots. The court granted the motion, and the clerk

---

18. FLA. CONST. OF 1885, art. III, § 6; FLA. CONST. OF 1968, art. III, § 2.

of the circuit court conducted a re-count, which was observed by representatives for both candidates. The clerk's re-count revealed that, despite miscounts in the initial ballot count, Vogel was the winner of the election. The re-count showed 79,902 total votes for Vogel and 77,012 total votes for Beckstrom.[19]

On the same day appellant filed his motion for a re-count, he filed a second amended protest and complaint, again alleging fraud and adding allegations of substantial failure on the part of Volusia County election officials to comply with the requirements of the election laws pertaining to absentee ballots. The absentee ballots were of crucial importance in the sheriff's election because, although appellant received more votes than Vogel in the precincts, Vogel received a sufficient majority in the absentee votes to overcome appellant's precinct vote margin of victory. Appellant asked the court to declare all of the absentee votes to be invalid and to declare him the winner based on the precinct vote alone. Appellant argued that absentee ballots were tampered with and modified in violation of section 101.5614(5), Florida Statutes (1995), in that at least 6500 absentee ballots contained votes which were marked over with a black felt-tip marker; and an additional 1000 absentee ballots were similarly marked, but it was impossible to determine whether they were marked over or newly marked.[20] Appellant alleged that this process of re-marking with black markers was tainted with potential fraud. The circuit court held a nonjury trial in which testimony was presented for seven days and argument of counsel was presented for one day.

The trial court thereafter entered a detailed final judgment which contained a combination of findings of fact and conclusions of law. The trial court determined that the key issue in the election contest was the re-marking procedure used by election officials on many of the absentee ballots so as to enable those ballots to be counted by an electronic scanner. The trial court found that this re-marking procedure was not in substantial compliance with section 101.5614(5), Florida Statutes (1995), because the procedure provided no reasonable substitute means of verification of the results of the election. The trial court found this noncompliance with procedures mandated by the statute to be gross negligence. The trial court found that this noncompliance created an opportunity for fraud. However, the trial court found that, although there was an opportunity for fraud, no fraud was proven.

---

19. [FN 3.] ... As appellant points out, the difference between the percentage of Vogel's precinct vote total and the percentage of his absentee vote total was 11 percentage points. However, we note that Vogel was not alone in receiving a significantly larger percentage of absentee votes than percentage of precinct votes. In the United States presidential election held the same day, another Republican Party candidate, Dole, showed a 9-percent margin between his percentage of absentee votes and percentage of precinct votes, and Republican Party congressional candidate Fields had a 15-percent margin between absentee and precinct vote percentage totals. A statistical expert who testified on behalf of Volusia County presented demographic explanations for the absentee voting percentage discrepancies.

20. [FN 5.] ... Election supervisors in three other counties (Leon, Putnam, and Monroe Counties) using this type of optical scanner testified that their procedures in respect to rejected ballots was the same as the procedure used in Volusia County.... This was the procedure recommended by the manufacturer's representative of the company that sold the optical scanners to Volusia County. The Supervisor of Elections for Leon County testified that this re-marking procedure was approved for use in processing absentee ballots by the Division of Elections of the Department of State.

The trial court applied this Court's decision in *Boardman v. Esteva,* 323 So.2d 259 (Fla.1975), to these factual findings. The trial court concluded that there was a "full and fair expression of the will of the people. Vogel won it." The court entered judgment for the defendants, thereby affirming the election of Sheriff Vogel.

Beckstrom appealed this final judgment to the Fifth District Court of Appeal. In an order certifying the case to this Court, the Fifth District stated:

> The trial judge ruled that the Canvassing Board acted with gross negligence but that there was no evidence of fraud in the process; thus the election was valid. Relying upon the analysis in *Boardman v. Esteva,* the trial court held that courts should not decide elections but should condone a "certain level of incompetence" by election officials, unless the level of incompetence, negligence or error reaches an intolerable level. Although the court found that the re-marking process used by election officials in this case irreparably harmed the sanctity and integrity of the election, attempting to apply *Boardman,* the trial court found a level of incompetence here acceptable. Further, the court found "there [was] a full and fair expression of the will of the people …" and that the will of the people was not affected by the negligence of the Canvassing Board. The trial court also found substantial compliance with absentee voting laws sufficient to make the ballots legal. The trial court then held there was an accurate count of the absentee vote and dismissed the election protest with prejudice.
>
> It is clear that the controlling authority in Florida is the *Boardman* decision and that, in *Boardman,* the supreme court intended to circumscribe the courts' involvement in the electoral process. The lower court suggested that since it was decided in 1975, the *Boardman* decision has become a "license for lawlessness by election officials." *Boardman* offers no guidance concerning the kind or degree of negligence that will warrant judicial intervention, absent fraud. This Court has found no case wherein the trial court has made a finding of gross negligence by a Canvassing Board and many technical violations of Chapter 102 by the supervisor of elections, yet validated the election. It appears that the validity of an election where there has been a finding of gross negligence, but no fraud, in the handling of absentee ballots and the use of the automatic tabulating equipment that is currently used in many counties in this state is an issue of great public importance whose resolution is required by the high court in light of the rule of *Boardman v. Esteva.*

* * *

Appellant's first and second issues encompass the issue certified to us by the district court which focuses upon our decision in *Boardman.* We begin our analysis of this issue by reiterating the statement of principle which we made in analyzing the *Boardman* election contest:

> [T]he real parties in interest here, not in the legal sense but in realistic terms, are the voters. They are possessed of the ultimate interest and it is

they whom we must give primary consideration. The contestants have direct interests certainly, but the office they seek is one of high public service and utmost importance to the people, thus subordinating their interests to that of the people. Ours is a government of, by and for the people. Our federal and state constitutions guarantee the right of the people to take an active part in the process of that government, which for most of our citizens means participation via the election process. The right to vote is the right to participate; it is also the right to speak, but more importantly the right to be heard. We must tread carefully on that right or we risk the unnecessary and unjustified muting of the public voice. By refusing to recognize an otherwise valid exercise of the right of a citizen to vote for the sake of sacred, unyielding adherence to statutory scripture, we would in effect nullify that right.

Boardman, 323 So.2d at 263.

In *Boardman*, we followed this statement with the history of cases in which we had addressed questions concerning compliance with election statutes. We then upheld the challenged election, in which an unsuccessful candidate for a judicial seat on the Second District Court of Appeal sought to be declared the winner, based solely on the precinct vote count because of alleged irregularities in the absentee ballot count. *Boardman*, 323 So.2d at 261. In upholding the election, we stated:

[R]ealizing as we do that strict compliance has been required by this Court in other cases, we now recede from that rule [and hold] to the effect that substantial compliance with the absentee voting laws is all that is required to give legality to the ballot.

Id. at 264.

We set forth in *Boardman* the following factors to be considered in determining the effect of absentee ballot irregularities:

(a) the presence or absence of fraud, *gross negligence,* or intentional wrongdoing;

(b) whether there has been substantial compliance with the essential requirements of the absentee voting law; and

(c) whether the irregularities complained of adversely affect the sanctity of the ballot and the integrity of the election.

Id. at 269 (emphasis added).

The Fifth District and appellant question whether, under our holding in *Boardman*, the trial court could find gross negligence but no fraud and still sustain the election result. We recognize that underlying this question is the direct fundamental issue as to whether a trial court can sustain a certified election result after the court has found substantial noncompliance with the election statutes, but the court has also found that this result reflects the will of the people despite the substantial noncompliance. We answer the question in the affirmative.

We stress, however, that we are *not* holding that a court lacks authority to void an election if the court has found substantial unintentional failure to comply with statutory election procedures. To the contrary, if a court finds substantial noncompliance with statutory election procedures and also makes a factual determination that reasonable doubt exists as to whether a certified election expressed the will of the voters, then the court in an election contest brought pursuant to section 102.168, Florida Statutes (1997), is to void the contested election even in the absence of fraud or intentional wrongdoing.

We hold that there is a necessary distinction between an election contest with a judicial determination of fraud and an election contest with a judicial determination of substantial noncompliance with statutory election procedures, even if the noncompliance is determined to be a result of gross negligence by election officials. Such a distinction is required in order to respect the fundamental principle upon which we based our decision in *Boardman*. As the trial court in this case recognized, the essence of our *Boardman* decision is that a trial court's factual determination that a contested certified election reliably reflects the will of the voters outweighs the court's determination of unintentional wrongdoing by election officials in order to allow the real parties in interest—the voters—to prevail. By unintentional wrongdoing, we mean noncompliance with statutorily mandated election procedures in situations in which the noncompliance results from incompetence, lack of care, or, as we find occurred in this election, the election officials' erroneous understanding of the statutory requirements. In sum, we hold that even in a situation in which a trial court finds substantial noncompliance caused by unintentional wrongdoing as we have defined it, the court is to void the election *only* if it finds that the substantial noncompliance resulted in doubt as to whether a certified election reflected the will of the voters.

In direct answer to the district court's request for "guidance concerning the kind or degree of negligence that will warrant judicial intervention, absent fraud," we clarify that the term gross negligence as used in *Boardman* is not, as in a tort action, a measurement of the degree of care by election officials. Rather, in this context, gross negligence means negligence that is so pervasive that it thwarts the will of the people.

We expressly state that our decision in *Boardman* is *not* to be read as condoning anything less than strict adherence by election officials to the statutorily mandated election procedures. Such adherence is vital to safeguarding our representative form of government, which directly depends upon election officials' faithful performance of their duties. Neither *Boardman* nor this case concerns potential sanctions for election officials who fail to faithfully perform their duties. It is for the legislature to specify what sanction should be available for enforcement against election officials who fail to faithfully perform their duties. We simply conclude that the court should not frustrate the will of the voters if the failure to perform official election duties is unintentional wrongdoing and the will of the voters can be determined.

* * *

We approve the trial court's findings in respect to fraud. We construe the trial court's finding of gross negligence in this instance to be a measurement of the culpability of the election officials but not a finding that the election failed to express the will of the voters. Therefore, we conclude that the trial court was within its discretion in determining from the evidence that the election was a "full and fair expression of the will of the people. Vogel won it."

... We do disapprove from the final judgment the statement: "I do not have jurisdiction to set aside this election." The trial court clearly had jurisdiction to consider and decide the issue presented by appellant's complaint in this election contest pursuant to sections 102.166(11) and 102.168, Florida Statutes (1995). Thus, the correct statement is that the trial court found no factual basis for requiring that the election be set aside. Accordingly, we affirm the trial court's decision.

It is so ordered.

KOGAN, C.J., OVERTON, SHAW, HARDING and ANSTEAD, JJ., and GRIMES, Senior Justice, concur.

Commentary and Questions

1. Florida is one of the states that rely on the intent of the voters as a standard. Is this a "tipsy coachman" rule?

2. Does it matter that this is an absentee ballot case? Absentee voting has traditionally been considered a privilege, not a right.

3. A plaintiff must prove that the election outcome would have been different but for the errors. That is, the plaintiff must prove enough illegal votes to overcome the margin of victory. This is a problem with the secret ballot.[21]

4. Can you think of a way around this conundrum?

B. Article VI, Section 4 — Disqualifications

"Section 4 establishes grounds for disqualification from two specific activities: voting and holding office." D'Alemberte, Commentary, 26 West's Florida Statutes Annotated 347 (1995). It also imposes term limits, wording them as a disqualification from holding office after eight consecutive years.[22] That limitation arose from a 1992 citizens' initiative, which amended the Florida Constitution to impose term limits on specified federal and state elected offices.[23] The amendments were placed on the

---

21. Justin Levitt, *Resolving Election Error: The Dynamic Assessment of Materiality*, 54 Wm. & Mary L. Rev. 83 (2012).

22. Fla. Const. art. VI, §4 (c) (added in 1992).

23. William A Buzzett & Deborah K. Kearney, Comment to the 1998 Amendment, 26 West's Florida Statutes Annotated 150–51 (2018) (discussing origin in 1992 citizen initiative).

ballot despite dissenting opinions that the change violated the federal Constitution for federal House and Senate offices.[24] The U.S. Supreme Court subsequently held unconstitutional a similar Arkansas term-limit statute on federal office.[25] The Florida Supreme Court later acknowledged this precedent for federal elective offices, but upheld the term limits on the specified Florida state-level elected offices.[26]

A strongly contested issue, at least among lawmakers, is Florida's disqualification of felons from voting. Every constitution in Florida's history has carried some form of disqualification from voting of persons convicted of a felony. Though the effect of this ban has fallen most heavily on African American men, the motivation behind its origins is murkier. When Florida's first Constitution was written in 1838, African Americans did not have the right to vote at all, so the felon disenfranchisement provision in that Constitution could not have been intended to affect African Americans.[27] The same can be said for the 1861 Constitution; as a document adopted mainly to announce Florida's secession from the Union, its racist roots are obvious, and thus, African Americans were still banned from voting completely. The 1868 Constitution, while adopted during Reconstruction and in many ways more racially fair than its predecessors, nevertheless was the product of a struggle between Radical Republicans, who supported African American voting, and native white southerners, who did not. The latter group succeeded in getting broad felon-disenfranchisement language into that Constitution.[28] After Reconstruction, when the white Southern segregationists regained power and wrote another new Constitution, they kept the broad language.[29] That Constitution, written in 1885, also authorized the Legislature to institute a poll tax, which it already had on the books, effectively disenfranchising the poor—which included many whites and most blacks.[30] That poll tax survived until 1937 in Florida.

In 1966 the CRC that drafted what would become Florida's current Constitution examined the voting provisions and discussed changes in both language and substance. As was discussed above, the suffrage and elections committee focused its attention on issues other than voter disqualification. Ultimately, the provision on voting disqualifications substantially streamlined and simplified the former constitutions' language, but kept the wholesale ban keeping felons from voting. And while the CRC members, all white, were reform-minded in many ways, there is no evidence they were thinking about racial effects either as desirable or undesirable when they passed

---

24. *Advisory Opinion to Attorney Gen.—Ltd. Political Terms in Certain Elective Offices*, 592 So. 2d 225 (Fla. 1991) (Overton, J., concurring in part and dissenting in part).

25. *U.S. Term Limits, Inc. v. Thornton*, 514 U.S. 779 (1995).

26. *See Ray v. Mortham*, 742 So. 2d 1276, 1280 (Fla. 1999) (term limits on federal offices are unenforceable), *holding modified by Cook v. City of Jacksonville*, 823 So. 2d 86 (Fla. 2002); *see also Telli v. Broward County*, 94 So. 3d 504, 513 (Fla. 2012) (term limits on countywide constitutional officer and county commissioners are enforceable under a county's home rule power).

27. "Every free white male person of the age of twenty-one years and upwards ... shall be deemed a qualified elector...." FLA. CONST. OF 1838, art. VI § 1.

28. FLA. CONST. OF 1868, art. XIV, §§ 2, 4.

29. FLA. CONST. OF 1885, art. VI, §§ 4, 5.

30. FLA. CONST. OF 1885, art. VI, § 8.

the felon-disqualification language to the Legislature. And the Legislature—newly reformed, urban, young, and liberal—but still almost completely white—kept the language when it made its tweaks to the draft constitution before putting it on the ballot. Evidence is absent to tell us what, if anything, was in the minds of the Legislators as they considered the felon-disqualification language. Then, of course, Florida's voters approved it in 1968.

In 2014, a coalition of civil rights groups united to urge an amendment that would restore the right to vote to persons convicted of most felonies on completion of all terms of their sentence. Drafters of the initiative language included one of the authors of this book. An organized coalition of former felons led by Desmond Meade, was also an effective advocacy group. The initiative language was approved by the Florida Supreme Court in 2017, gained enough signatures by January 2018 to be placed on the November 2018 ballot, and passed by more than 64% of the vote.

The cases construing this issue of felon rights restoration illustrate the interplay of initiatives, constitutional language, legislative policy, and court interpretation. Ultimately, the policy hinges on interpretation of both the state and federal Constitutions. Interestingly, the provision has been found to be self-executing by the federal courts; the Florida Supreme Court, in its initial review for ballot placement, suggested it created an automatic right to register to vote for qualifying former felons.[31] Further, supervisors of elections began registering individuals as soon as the initiative, commonly known by its ballot position as Amendment 4, was passed: prior to any legislative action.

Litigation has exposed substantial fissures in the Florida election system as it relates to former felons. The initiative contemplates that a felon becomes eligible to vote after completing the "terms of sentence." The interpretation of that phrase is key to the former felon's fate. The dispute concerns what constitutes completion.[32] An analogy was made by Howard Simon, an ACLU leader involved in drafting and passage, that when a felon had completed his debt to society, it was important that he or she be able to "graduate from college," or, in other words, participate in the society to which the felon had paid his debt.[33]

Even though the provision was self-executing, the Legislature enacted implementing legislation. Involved legislators argued that the Legislature was implementing the will of the drafters and the voters.[34] However, in one extremely significant departure from the status of the law when Amendment 4 passed, the Legislature made a major change at the last minute, one that would make qualifying to vote

---

31. *Advisory Opinion to the Attorney General Re: Voting Restoration Amendment*, 215 So. 3d 1202, 1206 (Fla. 2017).

32. The Supreme Court of Florida, in its approval of the language of the ballot title and summary, referred to completing the "terms of the sentence," not "completing the sentence." *Advisory Opinion to the Attorney General Re: Voting Restoration Amendment*, 215 So. 3d 1202, 1206 (Fla. 2017).

33. Howard Simon, conversation with Jon L. Mills.

34. Dara Kam, *Confusion surrounds felon voting rights*, SOUTH FLORIDA SUN-SENTINEL, Dec. 5, 2018, 4B.

much harder for the great majority of ex-felons. The bill declared that even criminal financial obligations that had already been converted to civil liens — a common and long-standing practice by courts to discharge financial obligations — would count as part of the "completion of the sentence." When the amendment was drafted and when it was voted on, many drafters and voters would know that many felons would have criminal financial obligations converted to civil ones and, therefore, removed from the criminal system, thus having completed their sentence under the new constitutional language. Instead, for some reason, the Legislature adopted the House version that contained this dramatic change, rather than the Senate version that did not have that limitation. Without that change, some think implementation might have gone much more smoothly.

A group of former felons sued the Governor and Secretary of State in federal court, challenging the legislation and seeking an injunction. The federal trial judge granted a temporary injunction.[35] The Eleventh Circuit Court of Appeals upheld the injunction. Trial was held remotely in April and May 2020 due to the COVID-19 pandemic. The trial judge ruled for the plaintiffs, holding that the requirement felons pay all financial obligations amounted to an equal protection violation.[36] Though the judge also held the requirement amounted to a tax, he found it was not tantamount to a poll tax.[37]

The defendants appealed, and the Governor requested a hold on registration of former felons pending the outcome of the appeal. The Eleventh Circuit granted the hold and agreed to hear the appeal en banc. Oral arguments occurred in August 2020, on primary voting day, effectively keeping many former felons, who thought they had regained voting rights well over a year earlier, from casting a vote. As this book approached deadline, the Eleventh Circuit's en banc opinion was released. A brief excerpt follows.

Jones v. DeSantis
975 F.3d 1016 (11th Cir. 2020)

* * *

A panel of this Court affirmed the preliminary injunction on interlocutory appeal. *Jones v. Governor of Fla.*, 950 F.3d 795, 800 (11th Cir. 2020). The panel held that the decision to condition reenfranchisement on the completion of "all terms of sentence" violated the Equal Protection Clause as applied to indigent felons who cannot afford to pay their fines, fees, costs, and restitution. *Id.* It reached this conclusion by applying

---

35. In the meantime, Governor Ron DeSantis sought an advisory opinion from the Florida Supreme Court, under Art. IV, Section 1(c), asking it to answer the narrow question whether "all terms of sentence" encompasses legal financial obligations. The Court answered in the affirmative. *Advisory Opinion to Governor re Implementation of Amendment 4, The Voting Restoration Amendment*, SC19-1341, 2020 WL 238556 (Fla. Jan. 16, 2020).

36. *Jones v. DeSantis*, ___ F. Supp. 3d ___, Case No. 4:19cv300-RH/MJF (May 24, 2020).

37. *Jones v. DeSantis*, ___ F. Supp. 3d ___ at *29, Case No. 4:19cv300-RH/MJF (May 24, 2020).

heightened scrutiny on the ground that Amendment 4 and Senate Bill 7066 discriminate on the basis of wealth. *Id.* at 817.

* * *

The district court certified a class and a subclass of felons for purposes of final declaratory and injunctive relief.... After a trial on the merits, the district court ruled that Amendment 4 and Senate Bill 7066 violate the Equal Protection Clause as applied to felons who cannot afford to complete their sentences. It applied heightened scrutiny to reach that conclusion based on the panel decision in the earlier appeal, and it alternatively ruled that the laws failed even rational basis review as applied to felons who are unable to pay the required amounts. The district court also ruled that Amendment 4 and Senate Bill 7066 impose a "tax" on voting by requiring felons to pay court fees and costs imposed in their sentences in violation of the Twenty-Fourth Amendment.... [The court decided the proper standard of review was rational basis.] In the earlier appeal from the preliminary injunction, the panel applied "some form of heightened scrutiny" on the ground that Amendment 4 and Senate Bill 7066 invidiously discriminate based on wealth. *Jones*, 950 F.3d at 817. That decision was wrong. To reiterate, Florida withholds the franchise from *any* felon, regardless of wealth, who has failed to complete *any* term of his criminal sentence—financial or otherwise. It does not single out the failure to complete financial terms for special treatment. And in any event, wealth is not a suspect classification. [Citation omitted.] Outside of narrow circumstances, laws that burden the indigent are subject only to rational basis review. [Citation omitted.]

* * *

MARTIN, WILSON, JORDAN, and PRYOR, JJ., dissented.

C. Article VI, Section 5 — Primary, General, and Special Elections

Interestingly, one contested area not controlled by the Constitution is political party primaries. Under the Florida Constitution, the Legislature may, but is not required to, regulate primaries by law. This provision was new to the 1968 Constitution.[38]

The 1997–98 Constitution Revision Commission proposed, and the Florida voters adopted, an amendment that specified: "If all candidates for an office have the same party affiliation and the winner will have no opposition in the general election, all qualified electors, regardless of party affiliation, may vote in the primary elections for that office." Some commentators opined the CRC added this subsection "in an effort to address the low numbers of Florida voters who participate in elections."[39]

---

38. D'Alemberte, Commentary, 26 West's Florida Statutes Annotated 334 (1995).

39. William A Buzzett & Deborah K. Kearney, Comment to the 1998 Amendment, 26 West's Florida Statutes Annotated 157 (2018).

Another perspective is that if all possible candidates for an office are contained within one party's primary roster, then all registered voters should cast votes for the person who will ultimately hold the office. The underlying tension lies between a party's right to define its membership and the ability of all eligible voters to participate in elections. Indeed, twenty years later, when a member of the 2017–18 CRC proposed an amendment that would have clarified the terms of the 1998 provision, it nearly died in committee in the face of the arguments of CRC members who believed voters should choose a party or face the consequences—inability to participate in a primary election.[40]

Brinkmann v. Francois

184 So. 3d 504 (Fla. 2016)

PERRY, J.

This case is before the Court on appeal from a decision of the Fourth District Court of Appeal, *Francois v. Brinkmann*, 147 So.3d 613, 614 (Fla. 4th DCA 2014), which declares invalid section 99.0615, Florida Statutes (2014), governing the residency requirement for write-in candidates of elections statewide. We have jurisdiction. *See* art. V, §3(b)(1), Fla. Const. For the reasons discussed below, we affirm the district court's decision.

STATEMENT OF THE CASE & FACTS

The Fourth District set forth the relevant facts and procedural history of this case as follows:

> Five candidates for Broward County Commissioner for District 2, all Democrats, qualified to have their names printed on the ballot for the August 2014 primary election. No Republican or Independent candidates filed qualifying papers. [Tyron] Francois, a sixth candidate and also a Democrat, filed qualifying paperwork to run as a write-in candidate. As a duly qualified write-in candidate, a blank space on the ballot for the November 2014 general election would have been provided to allow voters to write in Francois's name as their vote for the county commissioner to serve District 2. Francois's status as a qualified write-in candidate would constitute "opposition," as that term has been interpreted in relation to the Universal Primary Amendment (UPA), Article VI, section 5(b) of the Florida Constitution, thus re-

---

40. Ultimately, the proposal survived its substantive committees but "died in Style and Drafting," an unusual fate. The CRC's internal rules provided that proposals surviving committee votes went to the Style and Drafting Committee, which decided which proposals could be combined with others on the ballot. But also, at this stage, a proposal must survive a sixty percent vote of the full CRC before going on the ballot. The proposal had a vote of 19 yeas and 17 nays, insufficient to go forward. Constitution Revision Commission 2017–2018, Commissioner Proposals, https://crc.law.fsu.edu/Proposals/Commissioner/2017d09e.html?SearchOnlyCurrentVersion=True&IsIncludeAmendments=False&ParameterDescription=Searching%3A%20Commissioner%20Proposals&HasInputError=False&PageNumber=3&ExpandedView=False (last visited Aug. 23, 2020).

quiring that the primary election be closed. *See Telli v. Snipes,* 98 So.3d 1284 (Fla. 4th DCA 2012).

Appellee [Jennifer] Brinkmann, a resident voter, filed a complaint in the circuit court, alleging that Francois was not properly qualified to be a write-in candidate because he did not physically live within the boundaries of the district as required by section 99.0615, Florida Statutes (2014). Brinkmann also sought an order forcing the primary election to be opened to all voters pursuant to the UPA. Francois conceded below, as he does on appeal, that he did not live in the district at the time he filed papers to qualify as a write-in candidate. However, he contends that section 99.0615 is facially unconstitutional because it conflicts with the Florida Constitution and violates equal protection. After an evidentiary hearing, the circuit court found that section 99.0615 is constitutional and disqualified Francois as a write-in candidate. The circuit court also entered an injunction that opened the primary election to all registered voters.

Francois, 147 So.3d at 614.

The Fourth District reversed the circuit court's order, concluding that "section 99.0615, Florida Statutes (2014), is facially unconstitutional because the timing of its residency requirement for write-in candidates conflicts with the timing of the residency requirement for county commission candidates as established by Article VIII, section 1(e) of the Florida Constitution." *Id.* at 616. In support of its holding, the district court cited *State v. Grassi,* 532 So.2d 1055, 1056 (Fla.1988), in which this "[C]ourt construed the constitutional provision [in article VIII, section 1(e), Florida Constitution,] regarding the residency requirement for county commissioners and stated that [t]he Florida Constitution requires residency *at the time of election.*" *Id.* at 615 (internal quotation marks omitted). Given this interpretation, the Fourth District found itself "convinced beyond a reasonable doubt that the act contravenes the superior law." *Id.* at 616 (quoting *Mairs v. Peters,* 52 So.2d 793, 795 (Fla.1951)) (internal quotation marks omitted). This appeal follows.

ANALYSIS

Brinkmann ... argues that even if section 99.0615 contravenes article VIII, section 1(e), and thus Francois properly qualified as a write-in candidate, such candidates are not included within the intended meaning of "opposition" as used in a different constitutional provision, namely, article VI, section 5, Florida Constitution. Therefore, the Democratic Party's primary election should have been opened to all registered voters....

* * *

Closing of the Democratic Party's Primary Election

... Brinkmann argues that even if section 99.0615 is unconstitutional, the Fourth District still erred in closing the Democratic Party's primary election on its flawed determination that write-in candidates like Francois are "opposition" under article

VI, section 5(b), of the Florida Constitution. This issue presents a question of constitutional interpretation, also subject to de novo review. *See Graham* [*v. Haridopolos*], 108 So.3d at 603 [(Fla. 2013)].

The rules governing statutory interpretation generally apply with equal force to the interpretation of constitutional provisions. *Coastal Fla. Police Benevolent Ass'n, Inc. v. Williams,* 838 So.2d 543, 548 (Fla.2003). Accordingly,

> this Court "endeavors to construe a constitutional provision consistent with the intent of the framers and the voters." In ascertaining the intent of the voters, the Court may examine "the purpose of the provision, the evil sought to be remedied, and the circumstances leading to its inclusion in our constitutional document," with the view that a constitutional amendment must be assessed "in light of the historical development of the decisional law extant at the time of its adoption."

In re Senate Joint Resolution of Legislative Apportionment 1176, 83 So.3d 597, 614 (Fla.2012)....

* * *

Universal Primary Amendment

The Universal Primary Amendment (UPA) was passed in the 1998 general election and amended article VI, section 5, Florida Constitution, to state, "If all candidates for an office have the same party affiliation and the winner will have no opposition in the general election, all qualified electors, regardless of party affiliation, may vote in the primary elections for that office." Art. VI, § 5(b), Fla. Const.; *accord Telli v. Snipes,* 98 So.3d 1284 (Fla. 4th DCA 2012).

Two courts have determined that a write-in candidate constitutes "opposition" for purposes of opening a primary election under the UPA. *See, e.g., Lacasa v. Townsley,* 883 F.Supp.2d 1231, 1242–43 (S.D.Fla.2012). In *Telli,* three candidates were qualified to run in the Democratic Party's 2012 primary election for the Office of Broward County Commissioner. Two other candidates — one Democrat and one Republican — also qualified particularly as write-in candidates and were represented in the November 2012 general election by a blank line on the ballot. A Republican-registered voter filed suit to open the Democratic Party's primary election to all registered voters, and the trial court dismissed the suit with prejudice. *Telli,* 98 So.3d at 1285.

The Fourth District affirmed, holding "that the language of the UPA is 'unambiguous' and that write-in candidates are both 'candidates' and 'opposition' within the meaning of the UPA's unambiguous language." *Id.* at 1286. The district court found that "Florida's statutory definition of 'candidate' includes write-in candidates." *Id.* at 1286.... It further rejected the plaintiff's insistence that write-in candidates were not viable competition.

> [This] Court will not consult a crystal ball to determine when and whether a given write-in candidate constitutes "real" or mere illusory opposition. The question is not whether [the write-in candidates] *will likely* prevail in the general election over the winner of the Democratic Party (or even garner a

significant percentage of the vote), but whether, under the current framework set forth by the Florida Constitution, they *could*.

* * *

Id. at 1287.

The *Telli* court's interpretation of the UPA's plain language is consistent with the common usage of "opposition" and related terms around the time the amendment was adopted. According to dictionary definitions, "opposition" meant "a position confronting another or placing in contrast; that which is or furnishes an obstacle to some result." *Black's Law Dictionary*, 1093 (6th ed. 1990). It was also defined as an "act of opposing," a "hostile or contrary action or condition," and "something that opposes," or "a political party opposing and prepared to replace the party in power." *Merriam-Webster's Collegiate Dictionary* 816 (10th ed. 1998)....

From these definitions, it appears that the usual and ordinary meaning of "opposition" as intended by the people who adopted the UPA contemplated an individual qualified to compete against a political party's primary winner in hopes of prevailing in a contest for public office. This naturally encompasses a write-in candidate—especially considering that subsection (b) does not specify the type of "opposition" one must encounter in a general election.

Brinkmann maintains that interpreting "opposition" to include write-in candidates would not coincide with the UPA's intended purpose. Specifically, she argues that the amendment was adopted in order to allow all registered electors to vote in a primary election when the winner of that election effectively would be the person elected to office. This argument overstates the UPA's purpose. According to amendment commentary:

> The [UPA] was proposed by the Constitution Revision Commission in an effort to address the low numbers of Florida voters who participate in elections. The Commission found that, prior to the amendment, in counties where a large majority of registered voters is registered with one political party, an election was often won at the primary level. Members of the minority party, as well as members of minor parties and those with no party affiliation, would not have the opportunity to participate in the electoral process.

William A. Buzzett & Deborah K. Kearney, Commentary to 1998 Amendment, Art. VI, § 5.

The federal district court in *Lacasa* found that current election laws effectuate the UPA's purpose by giving all registered voters in a given county an opportunity to participate in the electoral process. Writing for the court, Judge Zloch explained:

> Further, Plaintiffs' argument that the write-in candidates do not constitute "opposition" justifying the closed election is inconsistent with the structure of Florida's election laws. If a candidate in a general election is unopposed, meaning that if there are no other candidates, whether write-in candidates or party-supported candidates, "the candidate [is deemed] to have voted for himself or her-

self" and thus "the names of [the] unopposed candidates shall not appear on the general election ballot." Fla. Stat. § 101.151(7). It is this type of primary that is, by definition, a *de facto* general election because there will actually be no opportunity to vote *at all* in the general election—the election for the office of Miami-Dade State's Attorney will be absent from the general election ballot.

Lacasa, 883 F.Supp.2d at 1243. Based on the record before it, the court found that

> the situation Plaintiffs decry here is much different. In the November general election, all Miami-Dade County voters will have the opportunity to vote for the [sic] either the winner of the Democratic Primary [or one of the two write-in candidates]. While Plaintiffs may claim that the write-in candidates are not "real" or legitimate candidates, their presence does not diminish Plaintiffs' and all other duly registered voters' right to cast a vote in the general election.

Id.

These passages demonstrate that, even in branding write-in candidates as "opposition" for purposes of closing a party's primary election, Florida's election laws still guarantee all registered electors meaningful opportunities to vote at the general election level. *Accord Telli*, 98 So.3d at 1287 ("Come November 6th, all duly-registered voters will have the opportunity to participate in the electoral process by voting for either the winner of the Democratic Primary or one of the write-in candidates; and the candidate receiving the most votes in the general election will be elected to the office of Broward County Commissioner."). Brinkmann simply conflates the write-in candidate's chances of winning the general election with the elector's chance to participate at all in the electoral process. *See Lacasa*, 883 F.Supp.2d at 1243 (refusing to consider the likelihood of a write-in candidate prevailing, or even garnering a significant percentage of votes, in a general election).

Brinkmann further contends that "the circumstances leading to the adoption of article VI, section 5(b) were to allow all registered voters to participate in a party primary when the minority party was fielding no candidates in the general election." And, "[b]ecause a write-in candidate is necessarily not fielded by any party" Brinkmann adds, closing a primary election "solely on the basis that a write-in candidate represented by a blank space on the general election ballot is 'opposition' ... ignores the policy behind the UPA." This position also overlooks the purpose of Florida's primary election system and, if adopted, could effectuate unintended openings of primary elections statewide.

Regarding the primary system's purpose, primary elections did not exist at common law. *Wagner v. Gray*, 74 So.2d 89, 91 (Fla.1954). Yet, article III, section 26, Florida Constitution, has historically required the Legislature "to pass laws regulating elections and prohibiting under adequate penalties all undue influence thereon from power, bribery, tumult, or other improper practice." *State ex rel. Gandy v. Page*, 125 Fla. 348, 169 So. 854, 857 (1936). In *Gandy*, this Court held that

> such section of the Constitution contemplates laws regulating primary elections as well as general elections because of the inevitable relationship of the

two classes of elections to each other. Thus, the Legislature is authorized by said section of the Constitution to enact laws designed to confine participations in party primary elections to bona fide recognized members of the political parties required by law to participate in such legally sanctioned and regulated primary elections as may be provided for by statute.

Id. Although a duly registered elector is entitled to exercise suffrage, there is a counterbalancing expectation that the elector will "comply with such other requirements of law as may be imposed upon him [or her] as a matter of policing the process by which he [or she] is authorized to cast his [or her] vote...." *Id.* at 858....

Hence, the Legislature established the primary election mechanism to permit a given political party to select a representative whom that party genuinely intended to support in a general election for public office. *See Wagner,* 74 So.2d at 91; *State ex rel. Andrews v. Gray,* 125 Fla. 1, 169 So. 501, 505 (1936)....

Additionally, federal courts have identified legitimate regulatory interests that are furthered by the closing of a primary election. In *Lacasa,* the district court accepted the State's "proposition that keeping a political party's primary election closed will preserve the party as [a] viable and identifiable interest group[ ], insuring that the results of [its] primary election, in a broad sense, accurately reflect the voting of the party members." *Lacasa,* 883 F.Supp.2d at 1239. The court further "recognize[d] the importance of ... party building efforts and the interest in maintaining party identity." *Id.* at 1240.... Next, the court agreed that "maintaining a closed primary ensures that the State's registration rolls continue to accurately reflect voters' political preferences," which in turn "encourage[s] Florida citizens to vote." *Id.*.... The court also deemed significant an "independent interest in the orderly operation of elections." *Id.* at 1240–41.... Finally, while not found to be applicable in the instant case, the court mentioned the State's interest in preventing "party raiding" and "excessive factionalism." *Id.* at 1241. We too find most, if not all, of these state interests to be prevalent in the instant case.

Further, Brinkmann's position embraces an interpretation of the UPA that would yield unintended openings of primary elections. Article VI, section 5(b) is a general law: it uniformly governs primary elections for any public office throughout the state.... Thus, under Brinkmann's theory, members of majority parties, among others, conceivably would always be permitted to participate in a given party's primary election when the minority party fields no candidate for the general election. This would be equally true "in counties where a large majority of registered voters is registered with one political party" as it would be in counties where multiple parties account for significant percentages of registered voters. Because majority parties typically influence election outcomes, it is unreasonable to conclude that the UPA was intended to create such a loophole in election laws and authorize members of a majority party to meddle in the political affairs of another party which they "have no interest in joining or in supporting." *See Lacasa,* 883 F.Supp.2d at 1238.

Based on the above, we conclude that, for purposes of opening a primary election under the UPA, the plain and obvious meaning of "opposition" includes write-in candidates. Therefore, we must determine whether the Fourth District correctly ordered the Democratic Party's primary election to be closed.

This Case

Under Florida law, a primary election for public office will not be opened to all registered voters unless two conditions are met: "(1) all candidates for the office must have the same party affiliation; and (2) the winner of the primary will have no opposition in the general election." *Telli,* 98 So.3d at 1286 (citing art. VI, §5(b), Fla. Const.). Both prongs contemplate that each candidate has met the qualification requirements set forth under Florida Statutes and thereby has been duly qualified for the office sought. *See Lacasa,* 883 F.Supp.2d at 1241.

Here, the record reflects that five candidates qualified by filing a fee or submitting a petition to run in the Democratic Party's primary election in August 2014.... The record also reflects that Francois, a sixth candidate who qualified by the write-in process, was a registered Democrat at all relevant times. Therefore, all candidates for the Office of Broward County Commissioner, District 2, shared the same party affiliation....

Nevertheless, Brinkmann cannot satisfy the second prong necessary for opening a primary election. Because we have determined today that section 99.0615, Florida Statutes, is facially unconstitutional, the fact that Francois did not live within District 2 at the close of the qualification period is not dispositive. Francois testified that he intended to move into the district if he won the general election. The parties do not otherwise dispute whether he failed to satisfy other eligibility requirements as prescribed under Florida law. Thus, the circumstances of this case are such that the primary winner was opposed by a duly qualified write-in candidate in the November 2014 general election.

Accordingly, we conclude that it was appropriate and constitutionally mandated for the Democratic Party's primary election to be closed to only Democratic-registered voters.

CONCLUSION

For the foregoing reasons, we affirm the Fourth District's decision in *Francois.*

It is so ordered.

Commentary and Questions

The court makes specific findings regarding the intent of the 1997–98 Constitution Revision Commission regarding the UPA amendment. Members of the 1997-09 CRC later stated the write-in candidate exception was an unforeseen loophole and is contrary to the intent of the UPA as proposed by the CRC.

1. Should this affect the Court's conclusions?

2. How does the Court determine the will of the voters on an amendment? In 2020, voters considered an initiative amendment proposal that would have amended Article VI, Section 5 to allow all voters to vote in primary elections regardless of political affiliation. The proposal received the approval of 57% of Florida voters, less than the 60% required under the Constitution.

Article VII

Finance and Taxation

Introduction

Article VII defines Florida's ability to raise revenue and defines ways to challenge or avoid taxation. As one may imagine, there is substantial effort focused on minimizing or avoiding taxation.

This chapter also introduces different means of raising revenue through bond issues. While the state is not authorized to deficit-spend its budget, the state as well as local government can essentially take out loans to be paid back by various methods. It is not unlike homeowners who could not afford to pay cash for a new house but anticipate revenue that would allow them to pay back a loan. The amount borrowed through bonds is substantial. For example, as of June 30, 2019, the end of Florida's fiscal year, total direct debt was $20.6 billion. Of that, $9.4 was for education facilities; $9.0 billion for transportation infrastructure; $1.2 billion in environmental bonds, such as the Florida Forever, Everglades Restoration, Florida Water Pollution Control, and Inland Protection programs; and $1.1 billion in other appropriated debts such as prisons, sports facilities and the Lee Moffit Cancer Center.[1] The legislature has established a desired ratio of yearly direct debt service obligations to yearly gross state revenues of 6% and a limit of 7%.[2] Direct debt is the only debt included in the debt to revenue ratio. Annual debt service in fiscal year 2019 was $2 billion, and the debt to revenue ratio for fiscal year 2019 was 4.64%.[3]

Also as of fiscal year 2019, Florida had an additional $8.2 billion in outstanding indirect debt. Debt classified as indirect is obligations secured by revenues not appropriated by the state or bonds issued by a separate legal entity, such as the Florida Hurricane Catastrophe Fund or Direct Support Organizations supporting universities or other state programs.[4] Indirect debt is not included in the debt-to-revenue ratio

---

1. *See* Florida Division of Bond Finance, *Debt Report*, 6–7 (December 2019). *See also*, Florida Department of Financial Services, Comprehensive Annual Report (2019), 143–53 (listing bonds payable and certificates of participation).

2. §215.98, Fla. Stat. (2020).

3. Florida Division of Bond Finance, *Debt Report*, 15, 2 (December 2019).

4. *E.g.*, Florida Hurricane Catastrophe Fund website, available at: https://www.sbafla.com/fhcf/Home.aspx (last visited August 30, 2020) ("The FHCF is structured as a tax exempt state trust fund

Understanding these terms will make it much easier to read the cases on financial topics:

1. Millage—A measure of value (1/1000).
2. Revenue bond—A bond to be paid from a source other than public funds.
3. Full faith and credit—To be paid from public funds.
4. Exemption—Excused from taxation under certain conditions.
5. Immunity—Always excused from taxation.
6. Assessment—Amount to be paid for taxes.
7. Appraisal—The valuation of property used to establish an assessment.
8. Ad valorem—Taxes based on the value of a thing.
9. Tax increment finance—Bonds repaid through tax increase increments.
10. Special assessment—Assessment made by government for an improvement.
11. Arbitrage bonds—Investment bonds paid back by interest.
12. Fees—Funds charged by government for a service or privilege. (e.g., licenses).
13. Impact fees—Type of fees charged for the impact of a development.
14. Municipal bonds—Bonds issued by a municipality.
15. Public purpose—Test for the reason bonds are issued.
16. Sales tax—Levy on a transaction.
17. Home rule—Authority delegated to local governments.
18. General revenue bond—A bond paid by taxes
19. Bond validation suit—Automatic litigation to verify legality of a bond issue.

but is tracked by credit reporting agencies due to its potential impact on Florida citizens' ability to pay all obligations.[5]

This chapter also uses many terms new to lawyers and law students who do not work on financial issues. To facilitate reading the cases in this chapter, we include a vocabulary list.

---

under the direction of the State Board of Administration."); University of Central Florida, Administration and Finance available at: https://admfin.ucf.edu/debt-and-revenue-management/dsos/ (last visited August 30, 2020) (describing the university's three direct support organizations).

5. *See* Florida Division of Bond Finance, *Debt Report*, 8 (December 2019).

Governments have three methods of raising revenue. One is direct taxation. Governments levy taxes on income, property, sales or yields from investment. The second is fees paid to government for licenses or permits. Fees are not taxes, because the person who is paying directly receives something of value. The third is issuing debt instruments. Bonds are the primary debt instrument (in this chapter, we will see that there are several types of bonds). A bond arises from a contract known as an indenture, and represents a promise to pay a sum of money at a designated maturity date, plus periodic interest at a specified rate on the face value. The types of bonds discussed in this chapter include state and local bonds pledging the full faith and credit of the government (backed by taxes), revenue bonds, and arbitrage bonds (investment revenue bonds). Full faith and credit bonds and local bonds backed by taxes must be approved by the electors of the issuing entity. Revenue bonds are so called because the interest and principal on them is paid from specified earnings, other than tax revenues. Revenue bonds may be issued by the state or its agencies and subdivisions without a vote of the electorate. Another type of bond whose use has been restricted by recent case law is the arbitrage bond. Proceeds from the sale of arbitrage bonds are used to invest in instruments paying a higher rate of interest than that being paid on the bond issue.

In Florida, once a governmental entity decides to issue bonds, the bond issue may be challenged by the state in a bond validation proceeding. The challenge is designed to ensure that the governmental entity issuing the bonds has the constitutional and statutory authority to do so. The various provisions of Article VII, which restrict Florida's governmental bodies from taxing and borrowing as they please, serve as the basis for challenging the bond issues. The Article's provisions prohibit certain types of taxes altogether, establish tax rate limits (millage) for ad valorem taxation, exempt certain property from taxation, and create procedural prerequisites for bond issues.

This chapter addresses the chief means by which state and local governments raise revenues: taxation, fees, and borrowing. The following questions are relevant when analyzing the cases in this chapter:

- Who are the actors? (Identify the governmental and private entities and their respective roles.)
- What is the basis for the issuing entity's authority to act?
- What is the basis of the challenge to the issuing entity's actions?
- What is the "test" for resolving the issue?

Many of the cases that address Article VII bond issues are part of the materials because they entail creative ways to avoid certain Article VII restrictions. Notably, lease-purchase contracts and tax increment bonds create financing arrangements that avoid the requirement that bonds pledging ad valorem taxes for payments beyond one year must be voted on by the citizens. Creative lawyers have found ways to avoid what may be perceived as the hurdle of an election.

Article VII, Finance and Taxation, and Article VIII, Local Government, are intertwined. Many of the Article VII cases are relevant to Article VIII issues. Therefore, when analyzing local government bond issues, begin by considering the additional question of the source of funds that will be used to redeem the bonds.

Although not the principal subject of the cases in this chapter, Sections 5 (dealing with the state income tax) and 6 (creating homestead exemptions) merit scrutiny. Generally, Section 5 is erroneously construed as totally banning a state income tax in Florida. Under what circumstances, however, may Florida impose a state income tax? With regard to Section 6, note the restrictions placed on homestead exemptions. The following table illustrates the types of taxes and fees authorized by the Florida Constitution, and which entity has the authority to levy them:

	State	County	Municipality
1.	Taxes authorized by statute	Taxes authorized by statute	Taxes authorized by statute
2.	Sales, excise taxes	*Ad valorem* taxes	*Ad valorem* taxes
3.	Income taxes		
4.	User fees	User fees	User fees

[handwritten margin note: Ad Valorem = VALUE]

[handwritten margin note: State cannot tax ad valorem]

History

Florida has always been a tax-allergic state. Florida has also been canny in using its tax policy to attract wealth to the state. Florida's distaste of taxes originated in its agricultural economy up through the First World War. Farmers did not need extensive public infrastructure other than roads, and education was devalued. In the 1920s, the state went through a rapid growth spurt with tourism and development. Local governments contracted extensive debt to provide services, such as streets, water, sewage, police and fire protection. Florida sought to attract the immigration of wealthy citizens by enacting prohibitions on state taxation of income and estate taxes in 1924. Florida wanted to attract wealthy citizens to encourage their use of capital to finance Florida's booming building expansion.[6] Ironically, that need disappeared when the bottom dropped out of the Florida development boom in the summer of 1926 and the state entered an economic depression.

One wealthy person who did relocate to Florida in the mid-1920s was Alfred I. duPont. Working with his brother-in-law, Edward Ball,[7] duPont quickly made large land purchases in Florida's panhandle as well as entering Florida's banking and railroad industries. Paying with cash direly needed by sellers, Edward Ball and duPont purchased large swaths of land, including ten miles of beach front totaling 34,000 acres

---

6. Tracy E. Danese, Claude Pepper and Ed Ball 35 (2000).
7. Alfred duPont characterized Edward Ball as "tenacious as a bull dog on a tramp's pants" in a letter to Alfred's brother. Kathryn Ziewitz & June Wiaz, Green Empire 38 (2004).

near Panama City in Walton and Bay Counties, followed by 12,539 acres in Bay County and another 66,000-acres in adjacent counties in the mid to late 1920s.[8] Ultimately duPont and then Ball consolidated the land into the St. Joe Paper Company, which owned 900,000 acres of land concentrated in the Florida panhandle, or three percent of all land in Florida.[9] Edward Ball began lobbying the Florida Legislature in the late 1920s to build roads through duPont's land while also cajoling local governments to issue bonds financing the road construction.[10] Ball also lobbied the Florida legislature to substitute a sales tax on merchandise for the then-existing state ad valorem tax on land.[11] Merchants opposed the switch, arguing the change was a form of class warfare designed to shift the tax burden from wealthy landowners to businesses and buyers. No change occurred for over a decade.

Many cities fell in default on their bonded debt when Florida's economy collapsed, beginning in 1926: "In the 1930s Florida had the highest number of local bond defaults in the United States."[12] Florida banks collapsed during the land bust, and homes went into foreclosure. Three years later, in 1929, the national economy entered the Great Depression. The Florida Legislature see-sawed between populist measures of relief and traditional tax curmudgeonliness in response to the financial crisis. Florida's history of bond defaults, however, left a lasting impression on public leaders and the drafters of the 1968 Constitution.

In 1934, the public adopted a legislatively proposed amendment to the Constitution that created a homestead exemption from ad valorem property tax. The tax exemption, plus an already-existing protection against forced sale by creditors, was popular with the economically-battered Florida homeowners, who voted 75% in favor of the amendment.[13] Bondholders of Florida state bonds sued and claimed the homestead exemption lessened the state's revenue and therefore imperiled repayment of its bonds.[14] The lawsuits were unsuccessful.

In 1939, the Legislature proposed a constitutional amendment prohibiting the state from imposing an ad valorem property tax on real and tangible property. The public approved the amendment at the November 1940 general election. The state was left with excise taxes, mostly on gasoline and beverage; licenses; and special taxes such as the estate tax. University of Florida political science professor Manning Dauer

---

8. Kathryn Ziewitz & June Wiaz, Green Empire 43–44.

9. Kathryn Ziewitz & June Wiaz, Green Empire 3, 6.

10. Richard Greening Hewlett, Jessie Ball duPont 73–74 (1992); Tracy E. Danese, Claude Pepper and Ed Ball 95–101 2000).

11. Allen Morris, Reconsiderations 158–59 (3d ed. 1985); Tracy E. Danese, Claude Pepper and Ed Ball 96.

12. *State v. City of Panama City Beach*, 529 So. 2d 250, 252 (Fla. 1988). *See generally* Grover C. Herring & George John Miller, *Florida Public Bond Financing—Comments on the Constitutional Aspects*, 21 U. Miami L. Rev. 1 (1966) (providing history of bond financing and defaults).

13. Allen Morris, Reconsiderations 157–58 (3d ed. 1985); Talbot D'Alemberte, The Florida State Constitution 228 (2017).

14. *Gray v. Moss*, 156 So. 262 (Fla. 1934); *Gray v. Winthrop*, 156 So. 270 (Fla. 1934).

observed that if a person drank liquor, drove, and then "cracked up on the highway and killed yourself," that would cover all Florida state taxes.[15]

In 1949, the Legislature authorized a sales tax of three percent during a special legislative session called to meet a budget deficit.[16] While it was not specifically mentioned in the Constitution, the sales tax was long opposed in the Legislature. Since it was enacted, it has been a continuous and expanded feature of Florida's taxation. It is now Florida's largest source of tax revenue.

Systemic under-valuation of real and tangible property for taxation was a persistent problem for Florida's tax system up to 1964. By 1935, the Florida Supreme Court noted that property was appraised for about fifty percent of its true value despite a constitutional requirement of assessment at just value, that is, fair market value.[17] The differences between residential property receiving the $5,000.00 homestead exemption and non-exempt residential property only magnified the discrepancy in tax impacts.[18] Florida's urbanization also complicated tax valuation, as farmland transitioned into other uses, such as residential developments. In 1964, the Florida Supreme Court ended the valuation subterfuge and required all property to be assessed at 100% of fair market value.[19] The tax shock from the increased assessments is thought to have led the 1966 CRC to include millage caps in the Constitution. The Commission also addressed valuation of farmland with a separate assessment standard tied to current use, and not the potentially higher assessment of fair market value when put to other uses.

Who Can Tax?

The Florida Constitution divides the power to tax into two parts: taxation powers granted to the state and taxation powers permitted to local governmental subdivisions such as counties, cities, and special districts. The Constitution prohibits the state from directly imposing ad valorem taxes on real estate or tangible personal property; this type of taxation is reserved for other government units. All other forms of taxation, such as sales tax, estate tax, excise taxes, are preempted to the state. FLA. CONST. art. VII, § 1(a). The Legislature may give some of its preempted taxing power

---

15. MARY E. ADKINS, MAKING MODERN FLORIDA 94 (2016). A popular jingle urged: "Bet, buy, die; Drive, drink, smoke." Gary R. Mormino, *Millard Fillmore Caldwell*, in THE GOVERNORS OF FLORIDA 454 (R. Boyd Murphree & Robert A. Taylor eds., 2020).

16. ALLEN MORRIS, RECONSIDERATIONS 159–63 (3d ed. 1985); Debbie Lelekis, *Fuller Warren*, in THE GOVERNORS OF FLORIDA 473 (R. Boyd Murphree & Robert A. Taylor eds., 2020); David R. Colburn & Richard K. Scher, *Florida Gubernatorial Politics: The Fuller Warren Years*, 53:4 FLORIDA HISTORICAL QUARTERLY 398–401 (April 1975.)

17. *Henderson v. Leatherman*, 163 So. 310 (Fla. 1935).

18. *Schleman v. Connecticut Gen. Life Ins. Co.*, 9 So. 2d 197, 199 (Fla. 1942). *See generally* George W. Ericksen & Wm. Terrell Hodges, *Assessment and Collection of Ad Valorem Property Taxes*, 13 U. FLA. L. REV. 455, 460–62 (1960) (describing effects of different valuations under the homestead exemption).

19. *McNayr v. State ex rel. Dupont Plaza Ctr., Inc.*, 166 So. 2d 142 (Fla. 1964). *See also Walter v. Schuler*, 176 So. 2d 81, 85 (Fla. 1965) (Duval County assessments in 1964 at 40% of true value; 51,000 of 96,000 homesteads fully exempt under tax roll).

to other governmental units by general law, FLA. CONST. art. VII, §§ 1(a), 9(a). The state has done this in many forms. The Legislature shares revenues and authorizes local collections. In fiscal year 2019, twenty-two revenue-sharing sources and an additional seventeen types of local revenue taxing sources were authorized.[20]

The Constitution identifies the other governmental units that can have taxing powers as counties, school districts, municipalities, and special districts. Of these, the Constitution states: "Counties, school districts, and municipalities shall, and special districts may, be authorized by law to levy ad valorem taxes and may be authorized by general law to levy other taxes, for their respective purposes...." FLA. CONST. art. VII, § 9(a) (emphasis added). The legislature granted charter and non-charter counties ad valorem taxation powers in Florida Statute 125. The legislature granted municipalities ad valorem taxation powers under the 1973 Municipal Home Rule Act. A special district is a limited form of local government created by the legislature to perform a specialized function, such as drainage, sewage, or running Disney World.[21] The Legislature creates a charter for each special district, and the Legislature specifies the taxing power of the special district in that charter, including the possible imposition of ad valorem taxes on real property and tangible personal property.

The Legislature has also authorized counties to create geographically defined Municipal Service Taxing or Benefit Units ("MSTUs") within that county's borders. MSTUs have varying tax powers and taxing limits.

Counties and municipalities also have home rule powers to impose fees and special assessments in addition to taxes. These fees and assessments must meet certain qualifications set out in the cases below to avoid classification as taxes. There is an impetus to use fees and assessments instead of taxes to avoid exhausting ad valorem millage caps and requiring a general law authorizing non-ad valorem taxes.

A. Article VII, Section 9 — Ad Valorem Taxation by Special Districts

St. Johns River Water Management District v. Deseret Ranches of Florida, Inc.

421 So. 2d 1067 (Fla. 1982)

ALDERMAN, Chief Justice.

St. Johns appeals the decision of the District Court of Appeal, Fifth District, holding chapter 77-382, Laws of Florida, which created the Greater St. Johns River

---

20. Florida Legislature's Office of Economic and Demographic Research, *2019 Local Government Financial Handbook*, 19–275 (Nov. 2019). *See also* Florida Revenue Estimating Conference, *2020 Florida Tax Handbook* (listing major state and local government revenue taxing sources).

21. Chad D. Emerson, Merging Public and Private Governance: How Disney's Reedy Creek Improvement District 'Re-Imagined' the Traditional Division of Local Regulatory Powers, 36 FLA. ST. U. L. REV. 177 (2009).

Basin, unconstitutional as a local law enacted without the notice required by article III, section 10, Florida Constitution. Deseret cross-appeals contending that the district court erred in holding that the District is not levying unconstitutional state ad valorem taxes. *Deseret Ranches of Florida, Inc. v. St. Johns River Water Management District,* 406 So.2d 1132 (Fla. 5th DCA 1981). We hold that [...] the district court properly resolved the ad valorem tax issue.

In 1979, Deseret Ranches of Florida, a landowner in Orange, Osceola, and Brevard Counties, filed suit for declaratory relief on behalf of all persons against whom ad valorem taxes and permit application fees were assessed in those counties by the St. Johns River Water Management District. Deseret contended that the Greater St. Johns River Basin, created by chapter 77-382, Laws of Florida, was unconstitutionally established, that the District is impermissibly levying state ad valorem taxes, and that the District has been improperly spending ad valorem tax revenues for its administrative and regulatory functions. Following a nonfinal order entered by the circuit court granting partial summary judgment in favor of the District and the Basin, Deseret petitioned the District Court of Appeal, Fifth District, for a writ of common law certiorari.

The district court granted certiorari and held that because chapter 77-382 does not operate uniformly throughout the state but rather applies only to those inhabitants and property owners in the District who are not within the Oklawaha Basin, it is a local law enacted in violation of article III, section 10, Florida Constitution, which requires that notice of intention to seek enactment of a special law be published in the manner provided by general law. The court also held that the District is not levying unconstitutional state ad valorem taxes and that the District, as a "special district" under the provisions of article VII, section 9(a), Florida Constitution, is authorized to levy ad valorem taxes for local purposes.

* * *

We initially address the issue of whether chapter 77-382 is unconstitutional on the basis that it was enacted without the notice required by article III, section 10, which provides:

> Special laws.—No special law shall be passed unless notice of intention to seek enactment thereof has been published in the manner provided by general law. Such notice shall not be necessary when the law, except the provision for referendum, is conditioned to become effective only upon approval by vote of the electors of the area affected.

In order to determine whether this notice was necessary, we must decide whether chapter 77-382 is a special law within the contemplation of article III, section 10. In view of the nature and history of this enactment, we hold that it is a general law rather than a special law....

In the present case, the statewide water management plan created and implemented by chapter 373 is primarily a state function serving the state's interest in protecting and managing a vital natural resource. In fact, the Fifth District in the present case took notice of the interrelationships of various areas of the state and found that water management districts further the state functions of water resource conservation, control, planning, and development. 406 So.2d at 1140.

* * *

On cross-appeal, Deseret contends that the St. Johns River Water Management District is levying state ad valorem taxes prohibited by article VII, section 1(a), Florida Constitution. We reject this contention as did the district court. Article VII, section 9, Florida Constitution, specifically authorizes the levying of ad valorem taxes for water management purposes. Section 373.503 provides the implementing legislation for ad valorem taxation to finance the works of the District. The determinative question is whether the ad valorem tax receipts are used to further a local purpose. In *Board of Public Instruction of Brevard County v. State Treasurer*, 231 So.2d 1 (Fla.1970), we upheld the constitutionality of statutes providing for local support of public junior colleges not under the control of the local school board. In finding that ad valorem taxes levied for such support are not prohibited state ad valorem taxes, we stated:

> Junior colleges serve a state function. So do the universities. So do the free public schools. Junior colleges also serve a distinctly local function.... Ad valorem taxes levied by school districts for support of such institutions are local taxes levied for local purposes.
>
> While the legislature may not circumvent the prohibition of state ad valorem taxation by any scheme or device which requires local ad valorem taxes and then channels the proceeds into essentially state functions which are not also local functions, no such situation is here presented.

231 So.2d at 4. More recently in *Sandegren v. State*, 397 So.2d 657 (Fla.1981), we upheld a comprehensive mental health plan being challenged as an improper infringement on local taxing power because it required local governments to match state funds for community health services. Citing *Board of Public Instruction of Brevard County*, we stated that "there is nothing in the state constitution which prohibits the legislature from enacting laws requiring the expenditure of local funds to support programs to the extent that such programs serve a local purpose." 397 So.2d at 659.

We likewise find that the St. Johns River Water Management District is not levying state ad valorem taxes in violation of article VII, section 1(a), Florida Constitution, because, as the district court properly found:

> The fact that water resource conservation, control, planning and development are state functions does not make them exclusively so. The availability of adequate fresh water supplies is of critical local interest. The interrelations of various areas of the state mandates supervision of the various water management districts to assure that they do not operate at cross purposes. It is clear that simply because a water management district furthers a state function, policy, or purpose does not prevent it from levying ad valorem taxes where the local function, policy, or purpose is similarly vital to the local district area.

406 So.2d at 1140.

Accordingly, the decision of the District Court of Appeal, Fifth District, is affirmed in part and reversed in part.

It is so ordered.

Commentary and Questions

A commentary provides a brief history of the five water management districts in addition to that given in the above opinion:

> The language relating to millage caps for water management purposes was added by the 1976 amendment. Prior to the amendment, there existed two special districts created for water management purposes which had taxing authority established by general law: (1) the Central & Southern Florida Flood Control District and (2) the Southwest Florida Water Management District. Pursuant to Article VII, Section 9(b) of the 1968 Constitution, special districts could impose taxes only if authorized by law *and* by referendum. The Central & Southern Flood Control District and the Southwest Florida Water Management District, however, could impose taxes without referendum and this authority was grandfathered-in by Article XII, Section 15 of the 1968 Constitution.
>
> In the early 1970's, it became clear that a comprehensive, statewide system of managing the state's water resources was necessary, whereupon the legislature divided the state into five regional water management districts. Adjustments were made to the boundaries of the pre-existing districts. It was concluded that any change to the geographical jurisdiction of the two pre-existing districts would jeopardize their ability to impose taxes without referendum. The 1976 amendment, therefore, allowed the continuance of taxing authority for the Southwest Florida Water Management District and the Central & Southern Florida Flood Control District (later the South Florida Water Management District). The amendment also, for the first time, authorized the newer water management districts to impose taxes without voter referendum. These districts had previously been funded from state General Revenue.

FLA. CONST. art. VII, §9 (Fla. Stat. Ann., William A. Buzzett & Deborah K. Kearney, Commentary to 1976 Amendment).

Did the Court reason in two directions? First, it found the basin law is a general law, not a local special law, because it fit within a pre-existing statutory scheme for statewide water management. The Court analogized to river tributaries and railway systems to demonstrate the interconnection between the particular St. Johns basin and general Florida water resources. The Court then reasoned in the other direction to find the legislation serves a "vital" local purpose, plus a general statewide purpose. The Court concluded it is the vital local purpose that saves the tax from being a state-imposed ad valorem tax.

Why does the statewide characteristic predominate for being a general law but the local characteristic predominate sufficiently to avoid state-mandated taxation?[22]

---

22. The distinction between special laws and general laws is also treated in the Article III chapter.

The Constitution caps the ad valorem tax rate millage for water management districts. FLA. CONST. art. VII, §9(b). The Legislature, however, specifies the millage rate under that cap for each of the five water management districts. Does the Legislature's control of the millage rate affect the Court's reasoning this is a locally-imposed tax?

This case addresses where the state might try to carry out a prohibited state ad valorem tax through a local unit of government. The Court cites to two precedent cases where local governments could be compelled to contribute funds toward statewide goals of junior colleges and state mental health facilities. In 1990, an amendment was added to the Constitution that limits the Legislature's ability to impose funding requirements on local governments without also granting additional revenue sources. FLA. CONST. art. VII, §18.[23]

An earlier case involving a special district involved Disney World.

State v. Reedy Creek Improvement District

216 So. 2d 202 (Fla. 1968)

ERVIN, Justice.

We review on appeal a final judgment of the Circuit Court for Osceola County validating two series of drainage revenue bonds sought to be issued by Reedy Creek Improvement District, within Orange and Osceola Counties, in the aggregate principal amount not to exceed $12,000.000.

Chapter 67-764, Laws of Florida, Special Acts 1967, provides for the establishment, powers and functions of the Reedy Creek Improvement District. The act specifically grants the power to the District Board of Supervisors to adopt a plan of drainage and reclamation of wet and submerged lands within the District and the placing of such lands under a system of water control, and authorizes the District to issue revenue bonds to finance the cost of same.

The District, by resolution duly adopted by its Board of Supervisors on January 31, 1968 (hereinafter called the Board), divided the District into two areas, designated Subdistricts One and Two, so that the facilities and services of such drainage improvements can be furnished on the basis of subdistricts as provided by the act.

The Board adopted on May 6, 1968 a resolution authorizing Drainage Revenue Bonds, Series A and B, in the aggregate principal amount of not exceeding $12,000,000 for the purpose of paying the cost of providing for the drainage and reclamation of wet and submerged lands within Subdistrict One and the placing of such lands under a system of water control....

The bonds shall be payable as to both principal and interest solely from the net revenues derived from the services and facilities of the project. The bonds will not constitute general obligations of the District and no holder shall have the right to compel the exercise of the taxing power of the District or taxation in any form upon

---

23. *See also* Talbot D'Alemberte, The Florida State Constitution 245–47 (2017).

any real property therein to pay the cost of the operation and maintenance of the project or to pay such bonds or the interest thereon. Said bonds and the interest thereon shall not constitute a lien upon any property of or in the District, but only a lien upon the revenues derived from the services and facilities of the project.

After entry of an order to show cause and the submission of an answer to the complaint on behalf of the State, a hearing was held after which the Circuit Court entered its final judgment determining, inter alia, that the bonds are not "bonds" within the meaning of Section 6, Article IX, State Constitution, F.S.A., and are not required by the Constitution and Statutes to be approved at an election by the qualified electors who are freeholders residing in Orange and Osceola counties. The court also found that the primary purpose of the project funded by the bonds is public and that such benefit to private enterprise, if any, from the construction of the project is purely incidental to the primary purpose. Finally, the court found the District had been lawfully created and that the enabling act, Chapter 67-764, did not violate any provisions of the Constitution of Florida.

The State challenges the final judgment of the Circuit Court on several grounds.

The first challenge against validation of the bonds is that their issuance will constitute the employment of public funds or the pledging of public credit for private purposes in violation of Section 10, Article IX, State Constitution. The basis for the State's contention in this regard is that [Walt Disney World Company] is the largest landowner in the District and that therefore the contemplated reclamation and water control improvements are oriented to serve primarily the benefit of that particular private enterprise. We find this contention untenable.

In enacting Ch. 67-764, the Legislature found that the general welfare and continued prosperity of Florida depends in a large measure upon tourism, recreation and the conservation of natural resources. The Legislature further determined that fostering such programs are valid public purposes and that through the creation and operation of the instant special improvement district such desirable objectives will be furthered to the extent of the District's ability. While the legislative finding that development of the proposed district would serve a valid public purpose is not conclusive, it should not be disturbed absent a showing that it is arbitrary and unfounded. *State v. Daytona Beach Racing & Rec. Fac. Dist.*, 89 So. 2d 34 (Fla. 1956). At this juncture we need not belabor the numerous authorities in this jurisdiction sustaining the promotion and development of tourism and recreation as valid public purposes.

In the present case we are convinced that the measures and improvements contemplated by the District are designed to encourage and develop those purposes spelled out in the enabling act. Successful completion and operation of the District no doubt will greatly aid the Disney interest and its contemplated Disneyworld project. However, it is obvious that to a lesser degree the contemplated benefits of the District will inure to numerous inhabitants of the District in addition to persons in the Disney complex.

The proposed improvements also embrace measures designed to develop improved sanitation and pest control conditions as well as aiding the conservation of natural resources. Besides the public benefit derived by inhabitants of the District from such measures, we conclude that the integrated plan or workings of the District and its related improvements are essentially and primarily directed toward encouraging and developing tourism and recreation for the benefit of citizens of the state and visitors to the state generally. Accordingly, we find no reason for disturbing the Circuit Court's finding that the primary purpose of the project funded by the bonds is public and that any benefit to private enterprise from construction of the project is purely incidental to the primary purpose.

[W]e reject the State's argument that the powers granted the District are commensurate in scope with those characteristic of a local municipal government rendering the enabling act a mere subterfuge to avoid the creation of a municipality. Nor can we accept the view advanced by the State that the enabling act embraces an unlawful attempt to delegate the taxing power of the state or that the same is tantamount to a gross abuse of legislative authority. The taxing provisions contained in Ch. 67-764 contain sufficient limitations to absolve them from the charge that they are unlawful delegations of authority.

* * *

Chapter 67-764 specifically empowers the District to issue general obligation bonds, revenue bonds, assessment bonds or any other bonds or obligations, or any combination of the foregoing, to pay all or part of the cost of construction, operation and maintenance of the projects of the District, and for the retirement or refunding of any obligations issued for such purposes. Pursuant to such power, the Board, in the exercise of its delegated discretion, determined that the project best could be financed by the issuance of revenue bonds. Subsection 17.D of the resolution authorizing the bonds in question contains a covenant on the part of the District that the fees charged will be sufficient to provide (1) for operation and maintenance of the facilities, (2) for debt service on the bonds, and (3) for other payments required by the resolution. In this respect, the resolution complies with the requirements set out in Section 18 of the enabling act pertaining to the sufficiency of the fees to be charged for services of the facilities operated by the District. The resolution imposing fees for the use of the facilities provides that the fees will be revised from time to time in order to be sufficient to meet the requirements of Section 18 of the act and Section 17.D of the bond resolution. The rates imposed by this resolution are based directly on the amount of rainfall in the District. A minimum charge is fixed to meet the requirements as set out in the act and bond resolution and in addition provision is made for a surcharge based upon excessive rainfall to cover the cost of protecting lands in the District against flooding. The users of the facilities are classified pursuant to a zoning system with a relative runoff factor assigned to each class. The District Engineer testified that the rates, fees and charges were based directly upon the value of the services to be provided by the project and that the method adopted by the Board was reasonable. We conclude from the record evidence that the charges and fees under the system set up by the Board have a direct and reasonable relationship to the beneficial use of the District's facilities and accordingly are not arbitrary, unfair or inequitable as asserted by the State. Compare *State v. City of Miami,* 157 Fla. 726, 27 So. 2d 118 (1946); *State v. City of Daytona Beach,* 160 Fla. 204, 34 So. 2d 309 (1948).

No error having been made to appear, the final judgment of validation is affirmed.

* * *

[Concurring opinion omitted.]

Commentary and Questions

Although the validity of proposed bonds was before the Court, "[t]he court's unanimous decision also upheld the broad array of powers delegated to the District by chapter 67-764, through what some ... might consider dicta."[24] Why then does the majority opinion undertake that excursion?

Regarding public purpose, the Court concludes the promotion of tourism supports the special district, and the Court finds: "[I]t is obvious that to a lesser degree the contemplated benefits of the District will inure to numerous inhabitants of the District in addition to persons in the Disney complex."

Like the *Deseret Ranches* case above, operations within the special district impact the larger public: "[T]he integrated plan or workings of the District and its related improvements are essentially and primarily directed toward encouraging and developing tourism and recreation for the benefit of citizens of the state and visitors to the state generally."

The majority ruled, "[W]e reject the State's argument that the powers granted the District are commensurate in scope with those characteristic of a local municipal government rendering the enabling act a mere subterfuge to avoid the creation of a municipality." This special district is unlike a municipality as its residents do not vote on a one-person, one-vote basis and access is restricted within the special district.[25]

B. Article VII, Section 9(a) — Local Government — Other Taxes than Ad Valorem: The General Law Requirement for Ad Valorem Taxes

Alachua County v. Adams

702 So. 2d 1253 (Fla. 1997)

GRIMES, Senior Justice.

This is an appeal from a decision of the First District Court of Appeal holding chapter 94-487, Laws of Florida, to be an unconstitutional special act. *Alachua County*

---

24. Kent Wetherell, *Florida Law Because of and According to Mickey: The "Top 5" Florida Cases and Statutes Involving Walt Disney World,* 4 Fla. Coastal L.J. 1, 6 (2002).

25. *Id.* at 4 (voting); *See generally* Chad D. Emerson, *supra* note 21, at 177 (history of enacting the Reedy Creek special district); Nadav Shoked, *Quasi-Cities,* 93 B.U.L. Rev. 1971 (2013) (special districts assuming municipal status, including the Ave Maria special district in Florida).

v. Adams, 677 So.2d 396 (Fla. 1st DCA 1996). We have jurisdiction under article V, section 3(b)(1) of the Florida Constitution.

There are two provisions of the Florida Constitution relevant to the determination of this case.

> SECTION 1. Taxation; appropriations; state expenses; state revenue limitation.—
>
> (a) No tax shall be levied except in pursuance of law. No state ad valorem taxes shall be levied upon real estate or tangible personal property. *All other forms of taxation shall be preempted to the state except as provided by general law.*

Art. VII, § 1(a), Fla. Const. (emphasis added).

> SECTION 9. Local taxes.—
>
> (a) *Counties*, school districts, and municipalities shall, and special districts may, be authorized by law to levy ad valorem taxes and *may be authorized by general law to levy other taxes, for their respective purposes,* except ad valorem taxes on intangible personal property and taxes prohibited by this constitution.

Art. VII, § 9(a), Fla. Const. (emphasis added).

As authorized by these constitutional provisions, the legislature has enacted the following general law:

> 212.055 Discretionary sales surtaxes; legislative intent; authorization and use of proceeds.—
>
> ....
>
> (2) LOCAL GOVERNMENT INFRASTRUCTURE SURTAX.—
>
> (a)1. The governing authority in each county may levy a discretionary sales surtax of 0.5 percent or 1 percent....
>
> ....
>
> (d)1. The proceeds of the surtax authorized by this subjection ... shall be expended ... to finance, plan, and construct infrastructure.... *Neither the proceeds nor any interest accrued thereto shall be used for operational expenses of any infrastructure....*
>
> 2. For the purposes of this paragraph, "infrastructure" means:
>
> a. Any fixed capital expenditure or fixed capital outlay associated with the construction, reconstruction, or improvement of public facilities which have a life expectancy of 5 or more years and any land acquisition, land improvement, design, and engineering costs related thereto.

§ 212.055, Fla. Stat. (1995) (emphasis added).

However, in 1994 the legislature enacted chapter 94-487, Laws of Florida. This special law, applicable only to Alachua County, stated in pertinent part:

Section 1. *In addition to the uses authorized by s. 212.055(2), Florida Statutes,* the board of county commissioners of Alachua County and the municipalities of Alachua County may use local government infrastructure surtax revenues for *operation and maintenance of parks and recreation programs and facilities established with the proceeds of the surtax.*

Ch. 94-487, Laws of Fla. (emphasis added).

Thereafter, Alachua County and all of the municipalities within the county entered into an interlocal agreement specifying that the surtax proceeds be used to operate and maintain a county-wide recreational program. Dwight Adams, a citizen and taxpayer of the county, disputed the constitutionality of chapter 94-487 and threatened legal action to enjoin the pending referendum on the surtax. Consequently, Alachua County and the City of Gainesville filed a declaratory judgment action, seeking a declaration of the legality of the surtax and the interlocal agreement. The trial judge held that chapter 94-487, Laws of Florida, was an unlawful special act which purported to amend the county's power to levy the local government infrastructure surtax in violation of article VII, section 1(a) of the Florida Constitution. This judgment was affirmed by the First District Court of Appeal. *Adams,* 677 So.2d 396.

Appellants point out that article VII, section 1(a), by its express language, relates only to the "forms of taxation." They suggest that the "form" of the tax authorized by section 212.055 is a sales tax, whereas the special act relates only to the purposes for which the revenues may be spent. Thus, they posit that while the county's authorization to impose a surtax must be based on general law, the uses for which the proceeds may be expended can be changed by special law.

To this argument, the court below stated:

Appellants' distinction between taxing and spending in this case is unpersuasive and largely semantic. As the Florida Supreme Court recently held in a different context, "the power of a municipality to tax should not be broadened by semantics...." *State v. City of Port Orange,* 650 So.2d 1, 3 (Fla.1994).

Adams, 677 So.2d at 398. We agree.

The "form of taxation" rationale misconstrues article VII, section (1)(a). The overriding purpose of this article is to make a constitutional division of tax revenues between those available for state uses and those reserved for local government. The phrase "all other forms of taxation" obviously refers to any tax other than those previously designated ad valorem taxes on real property and tangible personal property. This provision is designed to prevent the legislature from undermining non-ad valorem tax sources needed to support state government by the enactment of special laws authorizing local governments to impose non-ad valorem taxes for local purposes.

Moreover, appellants ignore article VII, section (9)(a), which does not contain the phrase "all other forms of taxation." This provision permits the legislature to authorize counties to levy non-ad valorem taxes, of whatever form or description, but only by general law. A determination that a special law may allow a county to redirect the tax proceeds in a manner explicitly contrary to the general law which authorized the tax in the first place would clearly undercut the purpose of article VII, section 9(a).

Appellants' reliance upon *Rowe v. Pinellas Sports Authority*, 461 So.2d 72 (Fla.1984), is misplaced. Significantly, neither section (1)(a) nor section (9)(a) of article VII of the constitution was ever mentioned in that opinion. Further, there was no argument that the tax revenues could not be pledged to pay off the bonds which would raise the money to be used to build a stadium. Rather, the point discussed was whether a special act could properly authorize these bonds to be issued by the Pinellas County Sports Authority rather than the county itself. The special act simply changed the manner in which the money would be borrowed. The tax authorized by the general law was not altered because the tax revenues were still to be used for the purpose of allowing the stadium to be built. The cases of *Wilson v. Hillsborough County Aviation Authority*, 138 So.2d 65 (Fla.1962), and *Kirkland v. Phillips*, 106 So.2d 909 (Fla.1958), do not bear on the issue before us because they were decided prior to 1968 when the pertinent constitutional provisions were different from those in our present constitution.

Section 212.055(2) is a general law that authorizes counties to levy an infrastructure tax under precisely defined conditions. These conditions prescribe the rates of taxes, the uses for the revenue raised by the taxes, and the procedure to be followed for approving the taxes. To permit chapter 94-487 to stand would convert subsection 212.055(2) into a general grant of sales tax authority to counties, subject only to the enactment of special law. If Alachua County can be authorized to levy the sales tax surcharge to fund operations and maintenance of facilities, then some other county can be authorized by special law to fund general governmental operations. This is the exact consequence that sections (1)(a) and (9)(a) of article VII of the Florida Constitution were intended to prevent.

Chapter 94-487, which is a special act relating only to Alachua County, purports to amend section 212.055(2), a general taxing statute, to levy the surtax for uses that are not only not permitted to any other county but are also positively prohibited to all counties. In the face of the unambiguous restrictions imposed by article VII, section 1(a) and article VII, section 9(a) of the Florida Constitution, we declare chapter 94-487 to be unconstitutional.

We affirm the decision of the court below.

It is so ordered.

OVERTON, Justice, dissenting.

The majority, through its construction of our constitution, has restricted the ability of citizens of local governmental entities to vote to impose an authorized tax upon themselves and to use the tax revenue for purposes specifically identified by special law. The majority opinion not only restricts the power of the people to provide wanted services for themselves, but also restricts the power of the legislature to provide the people with a means to have the desired local governmental services. This majority opinion is directly contrary to prior decisions of this Court that allowed special laws to be used in the manner desired by Alachua County in this instance. The majority summarily dismisses those cases by saying they were decided before the 1968 constitution was adopted. Interestingly, the majority's interpretation of the 1968 constitution makes its provisions more restrictive of local governments' authority than the 1885 constitution when, in fact, the philosophy of the 1968 constitution was to "broaden" local governments' control of the tax structure.

The issue in this case is whether our present constitution prohibits the legislature from expanding or contracting by special law the class of permitted uses for the proceeds of a discretionary sales surtax set out by general law. Article VII, section 1(a), of the Florida Constitution plainly states that only the "form of taxation" must be authorized by general law. Article VII, section 9, states that counties may be authorized by general law to levy various forms of taxes. Pursuant to these provisions, the legislature enacted section 212.055(2), Florida Statutes (1995), *authorizing* the levy of a sales surtax. The statute also sets forth how the tax revenue must be used. The special law in issue set forth in chapter 94-487, Laws of Florida, simply expanded the permitted *uses* of the sales surtax revenues in Alachua County. Consistent with our prior decisions, this special law does not violate the Florida Constitution. In my view, the decision of the majority is contrary to the mandate of this Court to "interpret statutes in such a manner as to uphold their constitutionality." *Capital City Country Club, Inc. v. Tucker*, 613 So.2d 448, 452 (Fla.1993).

* * *

The majority's interpretation of the 1968 constitution makes its provisions more restrictive of local governmental control of the tax structure than the provisions under the 1885 constitution. In fact, the philosophy of the 1968 constitution was to give local governments more control, not less. For example, an analysis by the Legislative Reference Bureau of the 1968 constitutional revisions explains that article VII, section 9, governing local taxes, was intentionally "broadened" from its form under the 1885 constitution.

In conclusion, the majority finds that the provisions of article VII now require that both the tax itself and the use of the tax revenues be authorized by general law. As explained above, this is contrary to prior decisions of this Court that separate the form of taxation from the allocation of the revenue. To be intellectually correct, the majority should merely state that it is overruling these prior decisions.

The people in local governmental entities lose by this decision, and the Constitution Revision Commission should develop a means for the people in a particular geographical area to enact a tax upon themselves for specific uses applicable to their community.

ANSTEAD, J., concurs.

Commentary and Questions

This decision states the rule that the form of tax and use of tax must be authorized by general, not special law: "[Subsection 9(a)] permits the legislature to authorize counties to levy non-ad valorem taxes, of whatever form or description, but only by general law."

The Court notes that subsection 1(a) "is designed to prevent the legislature from undermining non-ad valorem tax sources needed to support state government by the enactment of special laws authorizing local governments to impose non-ad valorem taxes for local purposes." Contrast this with the concern in the *Deseret Ranches* case above where the state might require local governments to exhaust their ad valorem millage caps funding state functions.

C. Article VII — How Much Can They Tax?

There are many limits on taxation in Florida. At the state level, the Constitution requires the Legislature to produce a balanced budget each year.[26] There is, however, a constitutional limit on increases in state government revenues, which was approved in 1994.[27] Budgeted revenues for the fiscal year (July 1st to June 30th) may be increased only by the average annual growth in Florida personal income over the past twenty quarters (five years). The Legislature should set aside at least five percent of net revenues into the budget stabilization fund, a "rainy day" account, until the fund's principal balance equals a cap of ten percent of net revenues in the past fiscal year.[28] State revenues exceeding the cap must be returned to the taxpayers. "State revenues" is defined within this constitutional subsection.[29] This limitation can be overcome only with a two-thirds vote of the membership in both legislative chambers in a separate bill containing no other subject and after a seventy-two-hour cooling off period after the final bill reading.

Every Florida Constitution since 1868 has contained a balanced budget requirement.[30] Nationwide at least forty-six states have some form of balanced budget requirement.[31] Florida's type of mandatory balanced budget is classified as the most inflexible. Commentators have criticized the inflexible, annual balancing as destructive during rapid economic downfalls, such as the 2008 recession or the 2020 coronavirus pandemic. Legislators are left with no alternative to meet plunging tax revenues than to cut expenses and terminate state workers, which in turn exacerbates the state's economic slump by accelerating unemployment and decreasing incomes and sales purchases that generate tax revenue. Some states utilize a multiyear balancing window, such as three years, in which the budget must be balanced. This, in theory, gives law-

---

26. FLA. CONST. art. VII, § 1(d).

27. FLA. CONST. art. VII, § (1)(e); *see also* D'ALEMBERTE, *supra* note 13, at 212.

28. FLA. CONST. art. VII, § (1)(e); art. III, § 19(g).

29. FLA. CONST. art. VII, § (1)(e).

30. *See* FLA. CONST. OF 1868, art. XII, § 2; FLA. CONST. OF 1885, art. IX, § 2. Earlier constitutional versions provided: "No other or greater amount of Tax, or Revenue, shall at any time be levied, than may be required for the necessary expenses of Government." FLA. CONST. OF 1838, art. 8, § 2. Identical passages were contained in the 1861 and 1865 Constitutions.

31. National Conference of State Legislatures, NCSL Fiscal Brief: State Balanced Budget Provisions, 2 (Oct. 2010).

makers flexibility to run temporary budget deficits during recessions and to make up those deficits as the economy improves.

Florida voters amended the constitution in 1924 to restrict the taxation of personal income and inheritance or estates. The restriction made Florida an attractive state for the wealthy to reside in. By a 1930 amendment, the state was permitted to enact laws taxing personal income and inheritances or estates up to "the aggregate of amounts which may be allowed to be credited upon or deducted from any similar tax levied by the United States or any state."[32] Florida levied estate taxes up to 2004 when federal law completed a phase-out of the federal tax credit; Florida now collects no estate taxes.[33] Florida remains one of eight states nationally that does not have a personal income tax.[34]

Corporate income tax is limited to five percent of net income unless sixty percent of the membership of each chamber authorizes a higher amount.[35] Five thousand dollars of net income would be exempt. The corporate income tax rate is currently 5.5%, but the exempt amount was increased to $50,000.00 in 2012.[36]

In 1996, voters adopted a citizens' initiative which required any future constitutional amendments that increase taxes or fees to pass by a popular vote of 67%.[37] This is slightly greater than the 60% passage rate required for all other amendments of the Constitution.[38]

The most important amendment restricting state revenues was approved by the voters at the 2018 election.[39] This amendment requires legislative supermajorities to create new or raise existing taxes or fees. The amendment explicitly "does not apply to any tax or fee imposed by, or authorized to be imposed by, a county, municipality, school board, or special district."[40] The voters approved the amendment by 65.73% in the 2018 election.[41] The combination of this restriction and the balanced budget requirement during an economic downturn is still unknown.

The Florida Constitution limits ad valorem tax levies by governmental units below state level at ten mills each for county purposes, municipal purposes, and school purposes.[42] The millage caps were new with the 1968 Constitution. D'Alemberte suggests the caps were created by the 1966 CRC to meet a fear of escalating tax demands following then-recent Florida Supreme Court decisions mandating true uniformity

---

32. Fla. Const. art. VII, § 5(a).

33. Robert M. Jarvis, Florida Constitutional Law in a Nutshell 580 (West Academic Publishing 2020).

34. See id. at 582.

35. Fla. Const. art. VII, § 5(b).

36. See Jarvis, supra note 33, at 583.

37. Fla. Const. art. XI, § 7.

38. Fla. Const. art. XI, § 5(e).

39. Fla. Const. art. VII, § 19.

40. Fla. Const. art. VII, § 19(1)(c).

41. See Fla. Div. of Elections, available at: https://dos.elections.myflorida.com/initiatives/initdetail.asp?account=10&seqnum=97 (last accessed August 10, 2020).

42. Fla. Const. art. VII, § 9(b).

for ad valorem tax valuations.[43] Water management districts also have millage caps that differ depending on the area of the state.

The Florida Supreme Court has also interpreted Section 9(b) to limit counties to 20 mills maximum if the county seeks to levy taxes in addition to those a municipality has already levied.[44]

The Constitution also specifies that certain tangible property can only be assessed a license fee and is not subject to ad valorem taxes. This includes motor vehicles, boats, airplanes, trailers, trailer coaches and mobile homes.[45]

Finally, the Constitution sets forth exemptions as a limit on taxation. It is these exemptions, and attempts to enlarge or avoid them, that create the bulk of litigation.

i. Article VII — Exemptions

"[A]ll property is subject to ad valorem taxation unless it is constitutionally exempted." *Colding v. Herzog*, 467 So. 2d 980, 982 (Fla. 1985). As noted by D'Alemberte, exemptions from ad valorem taxation can be subdivided between the exemptions themselves (Sections 3, 4, 6), permitted departures from the principles of just valuation (Section 4), and departures from a uniform rate of taxation (Section 2). Some exemptions are mandatory, some permissive.[46]

Article VII contains six exemptions from tangible property taxation.[47] The first $25,000.00 of personal property is exempted from tangible tax.[48] There is included a specific exemption of household goods and personal effects of not less than $1,000.00 to the head of a household.[49]

Restrictions are also imposed on assessing property for ad valorem taxation in Section 4. Section 4 begins: "By general law regulations shall be prescribed which shall secure a just value of all property for ad valorem taxation. . . ." Just value is equated with the fair market value of the property.[50] Section 4 also specifies that certain land, such as land used for high water recharge to aquifers, agricultural, and noncommercial recreational purposes, may be assessed on the more lenient basis of character or use.[51] Specified working waterfront properties receive a lenient assessment based on current use, not highest and best use.[52] Section 4 contains other specific permissible lenient valuations for land. Homestead assessment, amplified

---

43. D'Alemberte, *supra* note 13, at 224, 233–34.

44. *State ex rel. Dade City v. Dickinson*, 230 So. 2d 130, 131 (Fla. 1969); D'Alemberte, *supra* note 13, at 234.

45. Fla. Const. art. VII, § 1(b).

46. D'Alemberte, *supra* note 13, at 217.

47. Jarvis, *supra* note 33 at 588–90.

48. Fla. Const. art. VII, § 3(e).

49. Fla. Const. art. VII, § 3(b).

50. *Smith v. Krosschell*, 937 So. 2d 658, 662 (Fla. 2006).

51. Fla. Const. art. VII, § 4(a).

52. Fla. Const. art. VII, § 4(j).

by the Save Our Homes and portability amendments, are the best known protections from ad valorem taxes.

ii. Article VII, Section 6(a) — Homestead

"[T]he most confusing aspect of ad valorem taxes is the treatment accorded 'homestead taxes.'"[53] Homestead issues have also appeared repeatedly as essay questions on the Florida Bar Examination. Homestead encompasses three facets: tax exemption, protection from forced sale, and limitations on devise. *Snyder v. Davis*, 699 So. 2d 999, 1001 (Fla. 1997). This part focuses only on tax exemption.

In the following case, the taxpayers, citizens of Honduras, purchased a condominium in Key Biscayne, Florida, in 2003, which they occupied with their three minor children, ages 7, 12, and 14. *De La Mora v. Andonie*, 51 So. 3d 517, 518–19 (Fla. 3d DCA 2010), *aff'd sub nom. Garcia v. Andonie*, 101 So. 3d 339 (Fla. 2012). By the time the 2012 Florida Supreme Court opinion was issued, two children had emancipated under Florida law, being 21 and 23 years of age. A 16-year-old minor remained in the home.

Garcia v. Andonie

101 So. 3d 339 (Fla. 2012)

LABARGA, J.

This case is before the Court on the Miami-Dade Property Appraiser's (Property Appraiser) appeal of the Third District Court of Appeal's decision in *De La Mora v. Andonie*, 51 So.3d 517 (Fla. 3d DCA 2010). In *Andonie*, the Third District affirmed a circuit court's grant of an ad valorem homestead tax exemption to David and Ana Andonie (the Taxpayers), and declared a portion of section 196.031(1), Florida Statutes (2006), invalid and unenforceable because the statutory provision limits the class of property owners otherwise eligible for ad valorem tax relief under article VII, section 6(a), of the Florida Constitution. This Court has jurisdiction....

Overview

In this appeal, the Property Appraiser argues that the Third District erred by concluding that a portion of section 196.031(1) is invalid and unenforceable. The Property Appraiser also argues that the record evidence in this case is insufficient to establish the Taxpayers' entitlement to the ad valorem tax exemption provided for in article VII, section 6(a), of the Florida Constitution. Accordingly, the Property Appraiser argues that the Third District erred in affirming the circuit court's judgment that grants the Taxpayers the ad valorem tax exemption provided for in article VII, section 6(a), of the Florida Constitution. In this opinion, we discuss two separate issues relating to a property owner's entitlement to the ad valorem tax exemption provided for in article VII, section 6(a), of the Florida Constitution.

---

53. Jarvis, *supra* note 33 at 603.

First, we address the legal elements that must be proven to establish entitlement to this constitutional tax exemption. Relative to this issue of law, we hold that the express language of the Florida Constitution, as amended in 1968, creates the right for every person who owns Florida real property to receive a prescribed reduction in the taxable value of that property where the owner maintains on the property *either* (1) the permanent residence of the owner *or* (2) the permanent residence of another legally or naturally dependent on the owner — provided the individual for whom the permanent residence is maintained has no legal impediment to residing on the property on a permanent basis. Based on this conclusion, we hold consistent with the Third District's decision in *Andonie* that section 196.031(1), Florida Statutes (2006), is invalid and unenforceable to the extent that it imposes a substantive requirement for entitlement not contained in the Constitution and thereby materially limits the class of taxpayers entitled to ad valorem tax relief under the Florida Constitution.

* * *

We first examine the legal elements of entitlement that must be established by an owner of Florida property to obtain the ad valorem tax relief that is guaranteed to owners of Florida property as a matter of constitutional right.

The Legal Elements of Entitlement for the Constitutional Homestead Tax Exemption

The determination of a statute's constitutionality and the interpretation of a constitutional provision are both questions of law reviewed de novo. *See Zingale v. Powell*, 885 So.2d 277, 280 (Fla.2004).... If the language in the constitution is clear, there is no need to resort to other tools of construction. *Lawnwood Med. Ctr., Inc. v. Seeger*, 990 So.2d 503, 510 (Fla.2008).... Based on the foregoing authority, we first examine the plain language of the constitutional provision that creates the right to an ad valorem tax exemption for owners of Florida property.

The Florida Constitution provides *every* owner of Florida real property the right to apply for and receive a reduction in the assessed value of real property for ad valorem tax purposes, under specified circumstances. *See* art. VII, § 6(a), Fla. Const. Before the Florida Constitution was amended by the people of Florida in 1968, an owner of real property seeking to establish entitlement to a homestead tax exemption was required to both "reside" on the property in question *and* make the property either (1) his or her permanent home or (2) the permanent home of others legally or naturally dependent upon the owner.[54] When the Florida Constitution was amended

---

54. [FN 5.] ... When article X, section 7 of the Florida Constitution was originally adopted in 1934, the class of individuals eligible for the homestead tax exemption was [] narrow, and available to only "every head of a family who is a citizen of and resides in the State of Florida." Fla. HJR 20 (1933) (proposed Fla. Const. art. X, § 7). *See also Smith v. Voight*, 158 Fla. 366, 28 So.2d 426, 426 (1946). This language was removed by constitutional revision approved by the voters in a general election in 1938, effective for the tax year of 1939. SJR 21 (1937) (proposed Fla. Const. art. X, § 7). *See also Smith*, 28 So.2d at 427. Because of the elimination of the citizenship requirement, this Court has held that citizenship is no longer a requirement to establish the right to the ad valorem tax ex-

in 1968, the homestead tax exemption provision was renumbered and the requirement that the property owner reside on the property was removed. *See* art. VII, § 6(a), Fla. Const. Article VII, Section 6(a), of the Florida Constitution, as amended in 1968, states in relevant part:

> *Every person who has* the legal or equitable *title to real estate and maintains thereon the permanent residence of* the owner, or *another legally or naturally dependent upon the owner, shall be exempt from taxation* thereon ... upon establishment of right thereto in the manner prescribed by law.

Homestead now [handwritten]

Art. VII, § 6(a), Fla. Const. (emphasis added). Thus, the plain language of the Florida Constitution, as amended in 1968, requires that the property owner maintain on the property either (1) the permanent residence of the owner; *or* (2) the permanent residence of another legally or naturally dependent upon the owner. Accordingly, under the Florida Constitution there are two separate and independent means by which a property owner's entitlement to the homestead tax exemption may be accomplished. And, where a property owner claims a homestead tax exemption based on the owner's act of maintaining the permanent residence of his or her dependents on the property, the owner need not also prove that he or she is residing on the property, permanently or otherwise, because the two textual means by which entitlement to the exemption may be established under the constitution are stated independently and as alternatives to one another. *See* art. VII, § 6(a), Fla. Const.; *see also* § 196.031(6), Fla. Stat. (2006) (explaining permanent resident of state other than Florida who is receiving tax exemption in that state is not precluded from also obtaining homestead tax exemption in Florida where owner maintains the permanent residence of dependents on Florida property); *see generally Matter of Cooke*, 412 So.2d 340, 341 (Fla.1982)....

Notwithstanding the specific elements of entitlement to the ad valorem tax exemption contained in article VII, section 6(a), of the Florida Constitution (1968), section 196.031(1), a legislative enactment intended to implement the constitutional tax exemption contains a substantive element of entitlement that is no longer required by the Constitution:

> Every person who, on January 1, has the legal title or beneficial title in equity to real property in this state and *who resides thereon* and in good faith makes the same his or her permanent residence, or the permanent residence of another or others legally or naturally dependent upon such person, is entitled to an exemption ... as defined in s. 6, Art. VII of the State Constitution.

§ 196.031(1), Fla. Stat. (2006) (emphasis added). Under the requirements of section 196.031(1), every property owner seeking the constitutional ad valorem tax exemption must establish that he is residing on the Florida property, regardless of whether the tax exemption is being claimed because the property is being maintained as the permanent residence of the property owner or as the permanent residence of the owner's depend-

emption, and the right is available to aliens and other non-citizens who otherwise meet the criteria set forth in the constitution....

ents. *See* § 196.031(1), Fla. Stat. (2006). Accordingly, the "and who resides thereon" element of entitlement set forth in section 196.031(1)—although accurately reflecting the requirements contained in the Florida Constitution as it existed before the 1968 revisions—is inconsistent with the requirements of the constitution as amended in 1968.

We have held that although the Legislature is permitted to enact laws regulating "the manner" of establishing the right to the constitutional homestead tax exemption, it cannot substantively alter or materially limit the class of individuals entitled to the exemption under the plain language of the constitution. *See Sparkman v. State*, 58 So.2d 431, 432 (Fla.1952) (declaring invalid statute that imposed one-year residence requirement for entitlement to homestead tax exemption, even though constitutional provision in question authorized Legislature to "prescribe appropriate and reasonable laws regulating the manner of establishing the right to [the] exemption"). Because the plain language of article VII, section 6(a), of the Florida Constitution permits an owner of Florida property to obtain the exemption based on the act of maintaining the permanent residence of his or her natural or legal dependents on the property—irrespective of the owner's citizenship or place of residence, requirements that were removed from the Constitution—the additional "and who resides thereon" requirement imposed by section 196.031(1) substantively limits and narrows the class of property owners and taxpayers eligible for the ad valorem tax exemption under the plain language of the Florida Constitution.[55] Accordingly, we hold, consistent with the result reached by the Third District in *Andonie*, that the "and who resides thereon" criterion contained in section 196.031(1) is invalid and unenforceable as a legal element of entitlement[56] for the ad valorem tax exemption as provided for under the plain language of article VII, section 6.[57]

We note that the Department of Revenue, the agency with statewide control over the administration of ad valorem taxation, is a respondent before this Court. The

---

55. [FN 7.] We also note that the extra-constitutional "and who resides thereon" requirement imposed by section 196.031(1) is seemingly at odds with section 196.031(6), Florida Statutes. The text of section 196.031(6) acknowledges that a permanent resident of a state other than Florida can receive a homestead tax exemption in both Florida and the property owner's home state, where the non-resident property owner maintains the permanent residence of dependents on Florida property. *See* § 196.031(6), Florida Statutes (2006).

56. [FN 8.] Because the issue of whether a piece of property is being used as the true permanent residence of either the property owner or his dependents is generally an issue of fact to be determined on a totality of circumstances, see section 196.015, Florida Statutes (2006), we do not hold that the property owner's place of residence is irrelevant to factual determinations that might turn on such considerations. The case before us, however, does not turn on factual considerations.

57. [FN 9.] In *Andonie*, the Third District provided a detailed history regarding the Florida constitutional homestead tax exemption and its implementing statutes, and commented that the "and who resides thereon" language in section 196.031(1) was likely a vestige of prior implementing statutes that was inadvertently not removed by the statutory draftsmen, "as clearly should have occurred." 51 So.3d at 523–24. Nevertheless, because the Legislature is without the authority to substantively limit the class of taxpayers eligible for the constitutional ad valorem tax exemption, we conclude that it matters not whether the Legislature's inclusion of the "and who resides thereon" language was inadvertent or otherwise.

Department argues that the Third District's decision in *Andonie* is consistent with the Florida Constitution, Florida statutes, and the public policy that governs homestead tax exemption. Further, in its brief, the Department maintains that the plain language of article VII, section 6(a), and the record before us permits the taxpayers here to establish entitlement to the ad valorem tax exemption. Accordingly, the Department of Revenue, the agency with the legal duty of prescribing rules and regulations for the collection of taxes, properly acknowledges the supremacy of the constitution over any administrative rule or statute that might limit the class of individuals eligible for the exemption under the plain language of the constitution. *See* § 195.027(1), Fla. Stat. (2006) (providing Department of Revenue shall prescribe rules for assessing and collecting taxes that are in compliance with the constitution). Thus, the Department, through its arguments to this Court, properly recognizes that although it has the authority to prescribe procedural rules for the collection and assessment of taxes, it is without the authority to impose substantive rules or elements of entitlement that limit the class of property owners and taxpayers otherwise eligible to receive the tax exemption under the Constitution. *See generally, Dep't of Prof'l Regulation v. Florida Soc'y of Prof'l Land Surveyors*, 475 So.2d 939, 942 (Fla. 1st DCA 1985) (explaining all rulemaking authority is limited by statute that confers such power); *see also Sparkman*, 58 So.2d at 432 (stating, "Express or implied provisions of the Constitution cannot be altered, contracted or enlarged by legislative enactments.") (quoting *State ex rel. West v. Butler*, 70 Fla. 102, 69 So. 771, 777 (1915)). Based on the foregoing, we conclude that the legal elements of entitlement to the constitutional homestead exemption require a property owner to establish that the owner is maintaining on Florida real property *either* (1) the permanent residence of the owner *or* (2) the permanent residence of another legally or naturally dependent on the owner. And the additional element of entitlement contained in section 196.031(1) requiring all property owners to demonstrate that they reside on the property is therefore invalid and unenforceable to the extent it limits the class of individuals eligible for the constitutional tax exemption.

We next turn to the appropriate legal standards to be used to determine whether a piece of property is being used as the "permanent residence" of either a property owner or the property owner's dependents. Section 196.012(18), Florida Statutes (2006), defines "permanent residence" for ad valorem taxation purposes and states that the inquiry to be made in determining whether one's property qualifies as a "permanent residence" is whether the property in question is being used as the "true" permanent home of the individual:

> "Permanent residence" means that place where a person has his or her true, fixed, and permanent home and principal establishment to which, whenever absent, he or she has the intention of returning....

§ 196.012(18), Fla. Stat. (2006). Accordingly, because the legislative definition of "permanent residence," consistent with the constitutional context from which it emerges, requires a determination as to whether the property is being used as the true permanent home or residence of the owner or his dependents, most determinations regarding whether a permanent residence is being maintained on Florida property will involve some level of factual inquiry regarding the actual use of the residential property in question. Indeed, section 196.015 states that "[i]ntention to establish a permanent residence in this state is a factual determination," *see* § 196.015, Fla. Stat. (2006), not an issue of law. Although section 196.015 contains a number of relevant discretionary factors that "may" be considered to make the factual determination as to whether the applicant for the tax exemption has the requisite intent to establish a permanent residence on his or her Florida property, this provision also cautions that no one factor is "conclusive" on this issue of fact. *Id.*

Thus, in most instances, an individual's intent to establish a permanent residence on a piece of Florida real property will present an issue of fact. We have held, however, that some individuals—those who do not possess the legal right to permanently reside in Florida—cannot, as a matter of law, establish that their permanent residence is being maintained on Florida real property. *See Juarrero v. McNayr*, 157 So.2d 79, 81 (Fla.1963) (holding non-citizen in the United States under temporary visa "cannot 'legally,' 'rightfully,' or in 'good faith' make or declare" a "permanent home" of this state for purposes of establishing entitlement to homestead tax exemption).

In *Juarrero* we concluded that citizenship is not a prerequisite for eligibility to the constitutional ad valorem tax exemption. *Id.* at 81. Nevertheless, we also held in *Juarrero* that where a non-citizen possesses only a temporary visa, he cannot legally form the intent to reside on Florida property permanently because he has no assurance that he can continue to reside in good faith for any fixed period of time in this country. *Id.* Hence, the rationale of *Juarrero* instructs that those without limitations or legal impediments on their right to live permanently on Florida property are included in the class of individuals for whom a permanent residence may be maintained on Florida property. And conversely, those who do not possess the legal right to reside permanently in Florida cannot be included in the class of individuals for whom a permanent residence may be maintained on Florida property. Thus, in a given case, the question of whether a property owner has maintained a permanent residence on Florida property—whether for the owner or another dependent upon the owner—will present a mixed question of fact and law. The question of fact centers upon whether the Florida property is being used and maintained as the "true" and actual permanent home of either the owner or the owner's dependents, to be governed by the definition of permanent residence contained in section 196.012(18) and the factors set forth in section 196.015. And the legal question presented is whether the individual for whom the permanent residence is being maintained has a legal impediment to or restriction from living permanently on the Florida property. Accordingly, we affirm the decision of the Third District in *Andonie*, which reaches a consistent result.

Having defined the legal elements of entitlement that must be met for an owner of Florida property to establish entitlement to the constitutional tax exemption provided for in article VII, section 6(a), we now turn to the facts and the procedural history of this case.

This Case

The Taxpayers are a husband and wife, both citizens of Honduras, who are residing lawfully in the United States under a temporary (E-2) visa issued by the United States Department of Homeland Security. The Taxpayers have three minor children—ages seven, twelve, and fourteen—who, unlike their parents, are citizens of the United States and the State of Florida. The Taxpayers own a residential condominium in Key Biscayne, Florida, and live on the property with their three minor children. The record before this Court contains no evidence that suggests that the Taxpayers' children have ever lived outside of Florida, nor is there an indication that the children have a legal impediment to residing in Florida on a permanent basis. For the 2006 tax year, the Taxpayers submitted to the Property Appraiser a timely application for a reduction in the assessed taxable value of their Florida property as provided for in article VII, section 6(a), of the Florida Constitution. On the sworn application form generated by the Property Appraiser, the Taxpayers averred that their Florida property was being maintained as the permanent residence of their minor children, each of whom is a citizen of the United States and naturally and legally dependent on the Taxpayers. The Taxpayers did not seek to establish that the property was being used as their own permanent residence.

The Property Appraiser administratively denied the Taxpayers' application for the ad valorem tax exemption for the stated reason that the Taxpayers are not permanent residents of Florida. The Taxpayers, as permitted by section 194.011(3), Florida Statutes (2006), petitioned the Miami-Dade County Value Adjustment Board to challenge the Property Appraiser's denial.

After conducting a hearing on the Taxpayers' petition, the Miami-Dade Value Adjustment Board granted the Taxpayers' ad valorem tax exemption and, in so doing, overturned the Property Appraiser's administrative denial of the exemption. The Property Appraiser then appealed the decision of the Value Adjustment Board to the circuit court. *See* § 194.036(1), Fla. Stat. (2006) ... ; *see also* § 194.036(3), Fla. Stat. (2006).... The Property Appraiser alleged in the circuit court that the Taxpayers were not entitled to the ad valorem tax exemption provided for in article VII, section 6(a), because the Taxpayers could not establish that the Florida property was being used as the Taxpayers' permanent residence. The Property Appraiser also alleged that the exemption granted to the Taxpayers by the Value Adjustment Board violated the Florida Constitution and, for this reason, the Department of Revenue became a party plaintiff to the circuit court action as permitted by section 194.181(5), Fla. Stat. (2007).

In the circuit court, the Property Appraiser moved for summary judgment and alleged that because the Taxpayers were residing in the United States on a temporary visa, they were legally prohibited from obtaining the constitutional tax exemption at issue. Significantly, the Property Appraiser—the party that bore the burden of proof in the circuit court proceeding—did not introduce any evidence so as to establish that the Taxpayers' minor children were not living on the property or that the children had a legal or factual impediment to living permanently on the Florida property—

nor did the Property Appraiser prove to any degree that the Taxpayers' children are legally permitted to live anywhere other than the United States. To the contrary, the Property Appraiser introduced evidence establishing that each of the Taxpayers' three children was a citizen of the United States and was residing on the Taxpayers' property, and at the hearing on the Property Appraiser's motion for summary judgment, counsel for the Property Appraiser informed the circuit court that "this has nothing to do with whether the children are allowed to reside in the United States or reside in the residence they want."

In response to the Property Appraiser's motion for summary judgment, the Taxpayers submitted a sworn affidavit that affirmatively avers that the Taxpayers' residential property is, in fact, being used as the permanent residence of the three minor children, and that the children have a legal right to live in Florida, the United States, and on the property, permanently. Further, the Taxpayers' affidavit established that it was the Taxpayers' intent as parents that their children remain permanently in the United States, a place where the children had the right to live. In the circuit court proceeding, the Property Appraiser raised no objection and made no challenge to the Taxpayers' affidavit or the averments of facts contained therein. Based on the arguments made by the Property Appraiser in the circuit court, the Taxpayers filed a cross motion for summary judgment on the basis that the uncontroverted facts established that the Florida property was being used as the permanent residence of their minor children who were legally and naturally dependent on the Taxpayers and had the legal right to live on the property permanently consistent with their parents' intent.

In accordance with the respective positions taken by the parties, the circuit court entered an order granting the Taxpayers an ad valorem tax exemption for the 2006 tax year on the bases that there was no dispute in the facts and that the Taxpayers, by maintaining the permanent residence of their legally dependent children on the property, established entitlement to the exemption under the plain language of article VII, section 6(a), of the Florida Constitution. The Property Appraiser then appealed the circuit court's order granting the tax exemption to the Third District Court of Appeal. This appeal was the foundation of the Third District's opinion in *Andonie*.

In *Andonie*, the Third District affirmed the circuit court's order granting the Taxpayers' motion for summary judgment. In its opinion, the Third District referred to the definition of "permanent residence" contained in section 196.012(18) and concluded that the Taxpayers' affidavit, which established that the true and actual permanent residence of the minor children was on the Florida property, went uncontested and sufficiently established that the Taxpayers' property was used as the children's permanent residence. The Third District also concluded in *Andonie* that the "and who resides thereon" criterion contained in section 196.031(1) is unenforceable; based on this ruling, the Property Appraiser appealed the Third District's decision to this Court under the authority of article V, section 3(b)(1), of the Florida Constitution.

In this Court, the Property Appraiser argues that the evidence introduced by the Taxpayers in the circuit court is "self-serving" and insufficient to establish that the Taxpayers' Florida property is in fact being used as the minor children's permanent residence. The Property Appraiser's arguments regarding the sufficiency of the evidence are unavailing for several reasons.

The Property Appraiser's Factual Arguments

In the circuit court action that gave rise to this appeal, the Property Appraiser failed to raise any arguments regarding the sufficiency of the evidence introduced by the Taxpayers. Nor did the Property Appraiser seek to refute or contest the uncontradicted evidence submitted by the Taxpayers. To the contrary, the Property Appraiser assured the circuit court that there was no material dispute in the facts and that its argument had "nothing to do with" whether the children could legally live on the property permanently. Accordingly, the Property Appraiser's arguments raised in this appeal regarding the sufficiency of the evidence submitted by the Taxpayers were not properly preserved and are, thus, waived. *See Aills v. Boemi,* 29 So.3d 1105, 1108–09 (Fla.2010)....

* * *

Conclusion

The plain language of article VII, section 6(a), permits every owner of Florida real property to apply for and receive ad valorem tax relief where it is sufficiently demonstrated that the owner has maintained on that property the permanent residence of another legally or naturally dependent on the owner. We therefore affirm the decision of the Third District in *Andonie* that holds as much. We conclude that here the Property Appraiser failed to sufficiently preserve for appellate review any argument regarding the sufficiency of the evidence introduced in the circuit court below, and the record here sufficiently demonstrates that the Taxpayers maintained on their Florida property the permanent residence of their minor children, each of whom is legally and naturally dependent on the Taxpayers. We emphasize that the result we reach in this case is dependent on the fact that it was demonstrated that the property is being used as the permanent residence of the owners' dependent, minor children, and the evidence establishes that the minor children for whom the permanent residence was maintained have no impediment, legal or otherwise, to residing permanently on the property in accordance with their parents' intent. We therefore affirm the decision of the Third District in *Andonie* to the extent it is consistent with our holding here today.

It is so ordered.

POLSTON, C.J., and PARIENTE, LEWIS, QUINCE, CANADY, LABARGA, and PERRY, JJ., concur.

Commentary and Questions

The Court notes and quickly dismisses whether the combination of citizenships can create a "family unit" for the homestead exemption. Originally added to the section in the 1968 Constitution, the concept of "family unit" continues to evolve.

A husband and wife living apart were considered separate family units; one spouse could claim the Florida homestead exemption while the other spouse maintained an out-of-state exemption.[58]

The court states in footnote 9 that the statute in conflict with the 1968 homestead provision was overlooked when conforming the laws to the 1968 constitutional change. Why would the property appraiser urge applying the obsolete statute?

iii. Article VII, Section 4(d) — Save Our Homes

B.S.

"Democratic philosophy mandates that every taxpayer be treated consistently, and that everyone contribute his fair share, no more and no less, to the tax revenues." *ITT Cmty. Dev. Corp. v. Seay*, 347 So. 2d 1024, 1028 (Fla. 1977).

A significant exception to the principle of uniform taxation contained in Section 2 is the 1992 amendment popularly named "Save Our Homes." The amendment caps ad valorem tax assessments of homesteads to the lesser of three percent or the percentage change in the Consumer Price Index.[59] The voters approved an enhancement to the Save Our Homes amendment at a special election called by the Legislature in 2008 that allowed qualifying taxpayers to carry a portion of accrued assessment reductions to a new home. This amendment was called the "Portability of Save Our Homes." In 2020, the voters adopted an amendment extending portability from two years to three.

Zingale v. Powell
885 So. 2d 277 (Fla. 2004)

PARIENTE, C.J.

Basically a lens/cleaner or property tax

In this case, we construe article VII, section 4(c) of the Florida Constitution, known as the "Save Our Homes" amendment, which limits the annual change in property tax assessments on homestead exempt property to three percent of the previous assessment or the change in the Consumer Price Index, whichever is less. We must decide whether a homeowner qualifies for the provision's limit on increases in property tax assessments immediately upon meeting the ownership and residency requirements for a homestead exemption, or instead only upon being granted the homestead exemption. We conclude that the cap is tied to the grant of a homestead exemption, and therefore quash the decision below, in which the Fourth District

---

58. *Wells v. Haldeos*, 48 So. 3d 85 (Fla. 2d DCA 2010); *see generally*, Michael A. Sneeringer & Joshua M. Bialek, *Only One Can Win? Property Tax Exemptions Based on Residency Under Florida Law*, Fla. B.J., September/October 2018, at 78 (surveying cases allowing two homestead exemptions); Amanda S. Coffey, *Pillow Talk and Property Taxes: Florida's Family Unit Requirement for Homestead Exemption and the Modern Marriage*, 41 Stetson L. Rev. 401 (2012) (same).

59. Fla. Const. art. VII, §4(d)(8); The Consumer Price Index is as reported by the U.S. Department of Labor, Bureau of Labor Statistics.

Court of Appeal reached a contrary conclusion. *See Powell v. Markham,* 847 So.2d 1105, 1106 (Fla. 4th DCA 2003).

I. FACTS AND PROCEDURAL HISTORY

Robert and Ann Powell purchased a home in Fort Lauderdale in 1990. They have continuously used the home as their primary residence since its purchase, but did not apply for a homestead exemption until September 2001, after the Broward County Property Appraiser notified them of an increase of almost $40,000 in their ad valorem property taxes. The steep rise in the Powells' property taxes resulted from a correspondingly large increase in the assessed value of their home, from $2.3 million to almost $3.9 million. In addition to filing for a homestead exemption in 2001, the Powells also sought to have the Save Our Homes cap applied to limit the increase in their assessment from 2000 to 2001. Their homestead exemption application was approved for 2001, but the property appraiser did not reduce the 2001 assessment to the limits of the Save Our Homes cap for that year. The Powells subsequently filed suit to challenge Broward County's refusal to apply the Save Our Homes cap to the increase in the assessed value of their home from 2000 to 2001. The trial court granted judgment on the pleadings in favor of the defendants. The trial court concluded that "[b]ecause the Powells' property did not 'receive' the Homestead Exemption until 2001, that is their base year, one year after which commences their entitlement to the assessment limitations of the Constitution." The Powells appealed.

The Fourth District reversed the trial court order, concluding that the cap applied to homeowners who qualified for the exemption, not just to those who applied for it. Therefore, the Fourth District held that the cap applied to the increase in the assessed value of the Powells' home from 2000 to 2001. *See Powell,* 847 So.2d at 1106–07. In dissent, Judge Stone concluded that because the Powells had not timely applied for a homestead exemption for 2000, they were not entitled to application of the cap on increases in value based on an assessment for 2000. *See id.* at 1107 (Stone, J., dissenting). Zingale, Executive Director of the State Department of Revenue, seeks review of the Fourth District's decision.

II. ANALYSIS

Like the Fourth District before us, we must determine the meaning of the language in article VII, section 4(c) of the Florida Constitution. This provision took its place in the Florida Constitution after the voters of this State approved a citizens' initiative on November 3, 1992. Although we take into consideration the district court's analysis on the issue, constitutional interpretation, like statutory interpretation, is performed *de novo. Cf. BellSouth Telecomm., Inc. v. Meeks,* 863 So.2d 287, 289 (Fla.2003) ("Statutory interpretation is a question of law subject to *de novo* review.")

Article VII, section 4(c) provides:

> (c) All persons entitled to a homestead exemption under Section 6 of this Article shall have their homestead assessed at just value as of January 1 of the year following the effective date of this amendment. This assessment shall change only as provided herein.

(1) Assessments subject to this provision shall be changed annually on January 1st of each year; but those changes in assessments shall not exceed the lower of the following:

   a. Three percent (3%) of the assessment for the prior year.

   b. The percent change in the Consumer Price Index for all urban consumers, U.S. City Average, all items 1967=100, or successor reports for the preceding calendar year as initially reported by the United States Department of Labor, Bureau of Labor Statistics.

(2) No assessment shall exceed just value.

(3) After any change of ownership, as provided by general law, homestead property shall be assessed at just value as of January 1 of the following year. Thereafter, the homestead shall be assessed as provided herein.

(4) New homestead property shall be assessed at just value as of January 1st of the year following the establishment of the homestead. That assessment shall only change as provided herein.

(5) Changes, additions, reductions, or improvements to homestead property shall be assessed as provided for by general law; provided, however, after the adjustment for any change, addition, reduction, or improvement, the property shall be assessed as provided herein.

(6) In the event of a termination of homestead status, the property shall be assessed as provided by general law.

(7) The provisions of this amendment are severable. If any of the provisions of this amendment shall be held unconstitutional by any court of competent jurisdiction, the decision of such court shall not affect or impair any remaining provisions of this amendment.

Article VII, section 6, which is referred to in subsection 4(c), provides in pertinent part:

(a) Every person who has the legal or equitable title to real estate and maintains thereon the permanent residence of the owner, or another legally or naturally dependent upon the owner, shall be exempt from taxation thereon, except assessments for special benefits, up to the assessed valuation of five thousand dollars, upon establishment of right thereto in the manner prescribed by law.

Both constitutional provisions reduce the tax burden on homestead property. The First District Court of Appeal has succinctly stated:

The purpose of the amendment is to encourage the preservation of homestead property in the face of ever increasing opportunities for real estate development, and rising property values and assessments. The amendment supports the public policy of this state favoring preservation of homesteads. Similar policy considerations are the basis for the constitutional provisions relating to homestead tax exemption (Article VII, Section 6, Florida Constitution), exemption from forced sale (Article X, Section 4(a), Florida Constitution), and the inheritance and alienation of homestead (Article X, Section 4(c), Florida Constitution).

Smith v. Welton, 710 So.2d 135, 137 (Fla. 1st DCA 1998) (footnote omitted); *see also* Op. Att'y Gen. Fla. 02-28 (2002).

Zingale and the county property appraisers appearing as amici in this case assert that a homeowner's entitlement to the benefits of the cap in article VII, section 4(c) is dependent upon establishing the right to a homestead exemption under article VII, section 6 "in the manner prescribed by law," i.e., by timely application for a homestead exemption. In *Horne v. Markham*, 288 So.2d 196, 199 (Fla.1973), this Court held that article VII, section 6 does not create an absolute right to a homestead exemption but instead requires that taxpayers establish the right thereto by following the procedures required by law. As stated in *Horne* and still the case today, these procedures include a timely application under chapter 196, Florida Statutes. Zingale and his amici claim that without a requirement that a homeowner obtain a homestead exemption to qualify for the cap, the property appraiser cannot ascertain whether property is in fact homestead property and thus eligible for the limit on the increase in the assessed value of the homestead property.

The Powells contend that a homeowner becomes entitled to the benefits of the cap upon meeting the ownership and eligibility requirements for homestead status, and that article VII, section 4(c) does not require that the property be granted a homestead exemption in order to trigger the cap's protection. They maintain that the requirements in article VII, section 6 for establishing a homestead exemption do not apply to obtaining the benefit of the cap in article VII, section 4(c). They also assert that subsection 4(c)(4) supports this construction because it requires an assessment of new homestead property at just value for the "year following the establishment of the homestead," rather than the year following the establishment of the homestead exemption. Thus, according to the Powells, they are entitled to the benefits of the cap based upon demonstrating their eligibility to receive the homestead exemption rather than upon demonstrating that they have received the homestead exemption. However, Zingale asserts that "establishment of the homestead" in subsection 4(c)(4) in fact means successfully applying for the homestead exemption.

Our task in this case of constitutional interpretation follows principles parallel to those of statutory interpretation. *See Coastal Fla. Police Benev. Ass'n v. Williams*, 838 So.2d 543, 548 (Fla.2003) ("The rules which govern the construction of statutes are generally applicable to the construction of constitutional provisions."). In a recent case concerning construction of another constitutional provision enacted by referendum on a ballot initiative, we explained the principles to be applied when interpreting constitutional provisions:

> We agree with the petitioners that "[a]ny inquiry into the proper interpretation of a constitutional provision must begin with an examination of that provision's explicit language." *Florida Society of Ophthalmology v. Florida Op-*

tometric Assn., 489 So.2d 1118, 1119 (Fla.1986). Likewise, this Court endeavors to construe a constitutional provision consistent with the intent of the framers and the voters.... Moreover, in construing multiple constitutional provisions addressing a similar subject, the provisions "must be read in pari materia to ensure a consistent and logical meaning that gives effect to each provision." *Advisory Opinion to the Governor — 1996 Amendment 5 (Everglades),* 706 So.2d 278, 281 (Fla.1997).

Caribbean Conservation Corp. v. Florida Fish & Wildlife Conservation Comm'n, 838 So.2d 492, 501 (Fla.2003) (footnote omitted).

We thus begin with the actual language used. The first paragraph of subsection 4(c) provides that "[a]ll persons *entitled* to a *homestead exemption* ... shall have their homestead assessed at just value as of January 1 of the year following the effective date of this amendment." (Emphasis supplied.) In its decision below, the Fourth District, focusing on the word "entitled," concluded that persons who owned property eligible for a homestead exemption should receive the benefit of the cap. *See Powell,* 847 So.2d at 1106–07. The majority rejected Judge Stone's dissenting view that a timely application for a homestead exemption was necessary to establish entitlement to the benefits of the cap, concluding that the Powells were seeking the assessment cap, rather than a homestead exemption, for the year 2000. *See id.* at 1107.

We conclude that the Fourth District's focus on the word "entitled" in the first paragraph of subsection 4(c) is misplaced. Under the plain language of this provision, the entitlement to a baseline just value assessment applies solely to the initial assessment required by the provision. We have already determined that the initial year for the baseline assessment was January 1, 1994. *See Fuchs v. Wilkinson,* 630 So.2d 1044, 1045–46 (Fla.1994) ("[F]rom the plain reading of the amendment, January 1, 1994 (the year following the effective date of the amendment), is the date homestead property is to be 'assessed at just value.'"). Thus, the provision that the Powells and the Fourth District rely on is not applicable to them because they did not seek to invoke the baseline assessment of January 1, 1994. In fact, the Powells do not contend that January 1, 1994 is the date for the baseline assessment but rather claim that date as January 1, 2000, more than a year before they applied for a homestead exemption.

The Fourth District's resolution of the issue is also contrary to the implementing legislation for article VII, section 4(c). Section 193.155, Florida Statutes (2001), provides:

> Homestead property shall be assessed at just value as of January 1, 1994. Property receiving the homestead exemption after January 1, 1994, shall be assessed at just value as of January 1 of the year in which the property receives the exemption.

Section 193.155(6) specifies that "[o]nly property that receives a homestead exemption is subject to this section." Therefore, under the implementing statute, the initial baseline assessment would be in 2001, the year in which the Powells obtained the homestead exemption. Because the first paragraph of article VII, section 4(c) applies only to the initial, January 1, 1994, assessment, we reject the Powells' suggestion that the reference in section 193.155 to property that receives the homestead exemption after January 1, 1994, places the statute in conflict with the constitutional provision.

In fact, section 193.155 is consistent with another provision of the cap, article VII, section 4(c)(4), which provides that "new homestead property shall be assessed at just value as of January 1st of the year following the establishment of the homestead."[60] There is no definition in article VII, section 4(c) of "new homestead property"; however, since subsection 4(c)(3) deals with assessments following changes in ownership, it is logical to construe "new homestead property" as property newly receiving the homestead exemption, and "establishment of the homestead" as a successful application for the exemption independent of any ownership change. This construction would then allow homeowners who had not received a homestead exemption entitling them to the January 1, 1994, baseline assessment, or whose property did not previously qualify for an exemption, to obtain the baseline assessment upon receiving a homestead exemption.

This construction of the first paragraph of subsection 4(c), when considered in conjunction with the other provisions of article VII, section 4(c), allows every homeowner who receives a homestead exemption to receive the benefit of the cap with the only variation being when the baseline year is established. For those homeowners whose property had already received a homestead exemption under article VII, section 6 as of the effective date of the amendment, the baseline year pursuant to the first paragraph of subsection 4(c) would be January 1, 1994. For property in which ownership has changed, subsection 4(c)(3) provides that homestead property would be assessed at a baseline the year following the change of ownership. Lastly, subsection 4(c)(4) allows any homeowner who obtains a homestead exemption to have a baseline assessment in the year following the "establishment" of the homestead.

Conversely, if article VII, section 4(c)(4) is construed to mean that "new homestead property" is established when the ownership and residency requirements are met without regard to a successful homestead application, there is no identifiable starting point for the cap in the case of a homeowner who had not obtained a homestead exemption before January 1, 1994. The Powells assert that the January 1, 2000, assessment is their baseline, but their position appears to rest solely on the fact that they are challenging the increased assessment for 2001 rather than on the inherent operation of subsection 4(c). Their interpretation thus relies more on the timing of their assertion of the right to the cap than on the starting point for their legal entitlement thereto.

---

60. [FN 5.] Section 193.155(1) requires the baseline assessment as of January 1 of the year in which the property receives the exemption, while article IV, section 4(c)(4) requires the baseline assessment "as of January 1st of the year following the establishment of the homestead." In this case, Zingale acknowledges that the baseline assessment was on January 1, 2001, consistent with the statute, rather than January 1, 2002, the year following the grant of the homestead exemption. Therefore, we need not address the different baseline assessments in the constitutional provision and the statute.

Construing the reference in subsection 4(c)(4) to "new homestead property" as property newly obtaining a homestead exemption is also consistent with article VII, section 6, which conditions the exemption "upon establishment of the right thereto in the manner prescribed by law." *Horne*, 288 So.2d at 199 (quoting art. VII, § 6, Fla. Const.). As Judge Stone observed below, section 196.011(1)(a), which implements the homestead exemption, requires a timely application, by March 1, to obtain the exemption for that year. The provision further specifies that failure to timely file results in waiver for that year. See *Powell*, 847 So.2d at 1107 (Stone, J., dissenting).

Although subsection 4(c) establishes a constitutional right to receive the benefit of the cap on increases in valuation, and section 6 establishes a constitutional right to an exemption of part of a property's value from taxation, both provisions are parts of a coordinated constitutional scheme relating to taxation and have as their underlying purpose the protection and preservation of homestead property.[61] Therefore, we conclude that subsection 4(c) and section 6 should be read *in pari materia* so that only those homeowners who have applied for and received the homestead exemption are entitled to the benefits of either constitutional provision. Under an *in pari materia* construction, a successful application for a homestead application is necessary both to obtain the exemption and to qualify for the cap.

Additionally, this construction facilitates a logical, orderly scheme that is entirely consistent with the purpose of the amendment. Although taxpayers have a right to the constitutional cap, the right is not self-executing. Requiring a timely filing for a homestead exemption imposes only a slight burden on the taxpayer in comparison to the tax benefit received. At the same time, this requirement prevents substantial uncertainty in taxing authorities' annual taxing and budgeting process. By allowing only homeowners who have received a homestead exemption to qualify for the cap, property appraisers will be able to ascertain who is eligible for the benefits of the cap simply by checking the tax roll. Without this requirement, there would be no reliable way to determine which taxpayers might qualify for the cap. In this orderly scheme, taxing authorities drawing up annual budgets will also be able to rely on the list of properties for which there is a homestead exemption in determining the limits on tax revenue imposed by the cap, rather than having to ascertain which properties *might* be eligible *if* the property owner applied for the cap.

III. CONCLUSION

Applied to the facts of this case, our conclusion that the grant of a homestead exemption is necessary for a homeowner to obtain the baseline assessment for the Save Our Homes cap in article VII, subsection 4(c) precludes the [Powells] from benefiting from the cap for the increase in their property taxes from 2000 to 2001. Under sub-

---

61. [FN 6.] The link between article VII, sections 4 and 6 is demonstrated not only by the reference to section 6 in subsection 4(c), but also by subsection 6(d), which provides that the increase in the homestead exemption "shall stand repealed on the effective date of any amendment to section 4 which provides for the assessment of homestead property at a specified percentage of its just value." Before the adoption of subsection 4(c), this Court held that the provision would not trigger the repealer in subsection 6(d). See *Florida League of Cities* [*v. Smith*], 607 So.2d at 401 [(1992)].

section 4(c)(4), the Powells' successful application for the exemption in 2001 constituted an "establishment of the homestead," which triggered the baseline assessment for the Save Our Homes cap. Under section 193.155, their baseline year is 2001, and thereafter they will receive the benefits of the cap. Any change in their assessment from 2001 to 2002 and for every year thereafter should be limited to the lesser of 3 percent or the change in the Consumer Price Index.

WELLS, ANSTEAD, LEWIS, QUINCE, CANTERO and BELL, JJ., concur.

Commentary and Questions

"[W]hen a new homeowner moves to an established neighborhood he is 'welcome' by the longer term neighbors who know that the new homeowner will contribute a larger percentage of support for local government. This is the 'Welcome Stranger' effect, which terminology was originally coined in California."[62]

The Court recites the amendment's purpose as preserving homesteads against rapidly rising real estate prices and corresponding increases in ad valorem tax assessments. The countervailing issues are the reductions in local ad valorem tax revenue collections and the disparity of accrued savings realized by high-value homesteads proportionally to other homesteads. The Florida Department of Revenue found in 2019 that the Save Our Homes reduction has removed $306.87 billion out of Florida's total $2.955 trillion just value assessments, or 10.4% of taxable property.[63] The standard $25,000.00 homestead exemption removed another $114.86 billion, or 3.9% of assessed value.

The portability of tax assessment savings has even reached marital law as a potential asset for equitable division during a divorce.[64]

iv. Article VII, Section 3 — Municipal Property

The general rule is that "all property is subject to taxation unless expressly exempt and such exemptions are strictly construed against the party claiming them."[65]

Article VII, Section 3 mandatorily and permissively exempts municipal property from ad valorem taxation. First, for municipal property to be mandatorily exempt under subsection 3(a), the property must be owned by the municipality, exclusively used by the municipality, and serve a municipal or public purpose.[66] Second, a municipality owning property outside the municipality may be permissibly exempt unless a general law requires its taxation. In 2019, the Department of Revenue reported

---

62. Richard S. Franklin & Roi E. Baugher III, *Protecting and Preserving the Save Our Homes Cap,* FLA. B.J., October 2003, at 34, 37.

63. Florida Department of Revenue, *County Just, Assessed & Taxable Value,* available at: https://floridarevenue.com/property/Documents/jat.pdf (last accessed August 18, 2020)).

64. *See* Ronald H. Kauffman, *Underwater Treasure: Equitable Distribution of the "Save Our Homes" Limitation,* FLA. B.J., February 2011, at 34.

65. *Sebring Airport Auth. v. McIntyre,* 642 So. 2d 1072, 1073 (Fla. 1994) (citation omitted).

66. *See* D'ALEMBERTE, *supra* note 13 at 218 (citing *Sebring Airport Auth. v. McIntyre,* 783 So. 2d 238 (Fla. 2001)).

governmental tax exemptions totaled $180.56 billion or 6% of the total just value of all property.[67]

Cases where a municipality pairs with a private business are the most contentious under the Florida Constitution. There are concerns about lost local government tax revenues and skewed tax equities when one project not paying local ad valorem taxes competes with a similarly situated non-exempt project that pays tax, and indeed, possibly a higher tax to make up for the portion of the lost tax revenue caused by the exempt project.[68]

The *Sebring* case below is the second appearance of the Sebring Airport Authority before the Florida Supreme Court. The following additional facts about the case appear in the first decision denying the airport authority a tax exemption:

> Sebring Airport Authority is a legislatively-created public instrumentality. Ch. 67-2070, §2, at 4238, Laws of Fla. From the late 1970s to 1991, the Authority promoted and operated an automobile race, the "Twelve Hours of Sebring" (Race), on real property it owns in Highlands County, Florida. In 1991, to alleviate financial difficulties and continue the race, the Authority entered into a lease agreement with Sebring International Raceway (Raceway), a for-profit corporation. The agreement required Raceway to assume the Authority's promotion and operation of the Race. During the 1991 tax year, the Highlands County Property Appraiser assessed and levied an ad valorem real estate tax on the real property and improvements leased by Raceway from the Authority.

Sebring Airport Auth. v. McIntyre, 642 So. 2d 1072, 1072–73 (Fla. 1994). The following decision followed the Legislature's attempt to craft a new definition of public purpose.

Sebring Airport Authority v. McIntyre

783 So. 2d 238 (Fla. 2001)

LEWIS, J.

We have on appeal the decision of the Second District Court of Appeal in *Sebring Airport Authority v. McIntyre*, 718 So.2d 296, 297 (Fla. 2d DCA 1998) ("*Sebring III*"), which declared a portion of section 196.012(6), Florida Statutes (Supp.1994), to be unconstitutional. The invalidated provision would have created an ad valorem tax exemption for situations where private enterprise leases governmental property to be utilized for profit-making endeavors such as convention and visitor centers, sports facilities, concert halls, arenas and stadiums, parks or beaches. The exemption for these ventures was to be accomplished by statutorily defining these types of activities

---

67. Florida Department of Revenue, *County Just, Assessed & Taxable Value*, available at: https://floridarevenue.com/property/Documents/jat.pdf (last accessed August 18, 2020)).

68. *See* David M. Hudson, *Governmental Immunity and Taxation in Florida*, 9 U. Fla. J.L. & Pub. Pol'y 221 (1998) (cited with approval by unanimous Court in *Sebring Airport Auth. v. McIntyre*, 783 So. 2d 238 (Fla. 2001)).

as serving "a governmental, municipal, or public purpose or function." We have jurisdiction. Art. V, §3(b)(1), Fla. Const.

The primary premise advanced in support of the constitutional validity of this legislative scheme of exemptions is that these types of activities have traditionally been recognized to serve or be a "public purpose" in connection with bond validation proceedings, an approach which involves an analysis of the nexus between governmental financing and private profit making ventures pursuant to article VII, section 10 (pledging credit) of the Florida Constitution. A fundamental flaw in virtually all of the arguments submitted in support of the constitutionality of this legislation is that one cannot adopt and apply the phrase or concept of "public purpose" from decisions concerning issues other than ad valorem taxation exemptions in this ad valorem taxation context. The bond validation concept simply cannot be superimposed upon or commingled with the constitutional ad valorem taxation exemption analysis. For example, article VII, section 10, which is directly implicated in bond validation matters, itself undermines the theory advanced to support the validity of the exemption, in the provision related to the issuance and sale of certain revenue bonds which provides:

> If any project so financed, or any part thereof, is occupied or operated by any private corporation, association, partnership or person pursuant to contract or lease with the issuing body, the property interest created by such contract or lease *shall be subject to taxation* to the same extent as other privately owned property.

Art. VII, §10I, Fla. Const.

The 1994 amendment under consideration here attempts to create an ad valorem tax exemption for private, profit-making ventures conducted upon property leased from a governmental entity—a result which the Florida Constitution does not allow. Therefore, we agree with the Second District to the extent that it held the 1994 amendment to be unconstitutional, and affirm the result below.

The broad question posed here is not new: we must address the source and the constitutionally derived limitations upon provisions establishing and creating exemptions from ad valorem taxation. The issue is not the popularity of such activities, nor the pleasure derived from such operations. We certainly understand, acknowledge and respect the legislative direction involved here, but we are compelled to review and address the issue from a specific constitutional perspective.

The activities of the appellants—the Sebring Airport Authority and Sebring International Raceway (collectively, "Raceway")—have received prior scrutiny by this Court, and are conceded to be unchanged since our last review. As observed by the trial court, "[t]he factual uses of the subject property include the operation of a racetrack by the lessee for profit and attendant functions, such as food stands, drink stands, souvenirs, all of which are, per se, proprietary activities."

We first addressed Raceway's activities, as measured against the "public purpose" requirement for mandatory tax exemptions, in *Sebring Airport Authority v. McIntyre*, 642 So.2d 1072 (Fla.1994) ("*Sebring II*"). In that case, Raceway asserted that the subject property was being used to further a public purpose, and it was therefore entitled to an exemption from ad valorem taxation under section 196.199(2)(a), Florida Statutes (1991). That section provided, in pertinent part, that "[p]roperty owned by the following governmental units but used by nongovernmental lessees shall only be exempt from taxation ... when the lessee serves or performs a governmental, municipal, or public purpose or function, as defined in s. 196.012(6)." Section 196.012(6), in turn, provided:

> (6) Governmental, municipal, or public purpose or function shall be deemed to be served or performed when the lessee under any leasehold interest created in property of the United States, the state or any of its political subdivisions, or any municipality, agency, authority, or other public body corporate of the state is demonstrated to perform a function or serve a governmental purpose which could properly be performed or served by an appropriate governmental unit or which is demonstrated to perform a function or serve a purpose which would otherwise be a valid subject for the allocation of public funds.

The trial court denied the exemption, and entered summary judgment for the county. The district court affirmed. *Sebring Airport Authority v. McIntyre*, 623 So.2d 541 (Fla. 2d DCA 1993) ("*Sebring I*"). Asserting conflict with *Page v. Fernandina Harbor Joint Venture*, 608 So.2d 520 (Fla. 1st DCA 1992), Raceway then sought to have this Court review the denial of the exemption.

In asserting entitlement to an exemption, Raceway did not dispute its status as a for-profit corporation. Rather, Raceway argued that "a governmental lease to a nongovernmental lessee is exempt from ad valorem taxation if the lessee serves a public purpose, regardless of the for-profit motive." *Sebring II*, 642 So.2d at 1073. This Court disagreed:

> A governmental-proprietary function occurs when a nongovernmental lessee utilizes governmental property for-proprietary and for-profit aims.[69] [We have no doubt that Raceway's operation of the racetrack serves the public, but such service does not fit within the definition of a public purpose as defined by section 196.012(6). Raceway's operating of the race for profit is a governmental-proprietary function; therefore, a tax exemption is not allowed under section 196.199(2)(a).

Id. at 1074. In approving the Second District's decision denying Raceway an exemption, the Court "disapprove[d] *Page v. Fernandina Harbor Joint Venture*, 608 So.2d 520 (Fla. 1st DCA 1992), to the extent that it may be read to grant ad valorem tax exemption to a nongovernmental lessee of governmental property that uses such property for governmental-proprietary purposes." *Id.* at 1074.

---

69. [FN 2.] In a footnote, this Court explained that "[p]roprietary functions promote the comfort, convenience, safety and happiness of citizens, whereas government functions concern the administration of some phase of government," citing *Black's Law Dictionary* 1219 (6th ed.1990). *Sebring II*, 642 So.2d at 1074 n. 1.

Following the outcome in *Sebring II,* the Legislature amended section 196.012(6) ("the 1994 amendment"). *See* ch. 94-353, §59, at 2566, Laws of Fla. That amendment—which is the subject of this appeal—provides, in pertinent part:

> The use by a lessee, licensee, or management company of real property or a portion thereof as a convention center, visitor center, sports facility with permanent seating, concert hall, arena, stadium, park, or beach is deemed a use that serves a governmental, municipal, or public purpose or function when access to the property is open to the general public with or without a charge for admission.

Once again, appellants sought a tax exemption for the subject property. This time, appellants cited the 1994 amendment to support their argument that they qualified for an exemption.

Based upon Raceway's "proprietary-governmental" activities, the trial court again determined that appellants were not entitled to a tax exemption. Relying on the "guiding principles" set forth in *Williams v. Jones,* 326 So.2d 425 (Fla.1975), and *Volusia County v. Daytona Beach Racing & Recreational Facilities Dist.,* 341 So.2d 498 (Fla.1976), the court rejected Raceway's argument that the definition of "public purpose," as contained in the statutory amendment, was determinative.

Rather, the court observed that the principles established in *Williams* and *Volusia County* were "premised on a constitutional foundation that all privately used property must bear the proper tax burden." Applying what it thus perceived to be a *constitutional limitation* on the Legislature's ability to define "public purpose," the trial court declared the 1994 amendment to be "unconstitutional as an attempt to create an exemption not permitted in the Florida Constitution."

On appeal, the Second District affirmed. It agreed with the trial court "that the language quoted above is an impermissible attempt by the Legislature to create a tax exemption that is not authorized by the Florida Constitution." 718 So.2d at 297. Thus, the lower appellate court also held the 1994 amendment to be unconstitutional "[t]o the extent that [it] attempts to exempt from taxation municipal property used for a proprietary purpose." *Id.* at 298.

The thrust of Raceway's argument here is that the Florida Constitution is a fluid document, and the concepts contained therein should be responsive to changing times. Appellants contend that this Court should, in the context of a mandatory tax exemption analysis, defer to the Legislature in its determination of what constitutes a modern-day "public purpose." They argue that, unless the legislative definition is "patently erroneous" when measured against common usage, the Court should parallel its interpretation of the constitutional limitation contained in article VII, section 3(a), to comport with the legislative definition. However, because it is the constitution itself, rather than "common usage," which is the touchstone against which the Legislature's enactments are to be judicially measured, this somewhat circuitous argument is a classic example of the proverbial tail wagging the dog. Additionally, the current popularity of any particular endeavor is not the constitutional prism through which this issue must be seen. Issues concerning funding or the construction of entertainment facilities are not interchangeable with those involved in ad valorem taxation or exemptions.

This Court has consistently recognized that the judiciary has an obligation, pursuant to the separation of powers contained in article II, section 3 of the Florida Constitution, to construe statutory pronouncements in strict accord with the legislative will, so long as the statute does not violate organic principles of constitutional law. *See In re Apportionment Law, Senate Joint Resolution No. 1305*, 263 So.2d 797 (Fla.1972)....

Later, in *In re Apportionment Law*, while cognizant that "[t]he propriety and wisdom of legislation are exclusively matters for legislative determination," we also recognized that the Legislature's authority was not unbridled. Thus, we observed there that, although "this Court, in accordance with the doctrine of separation of powers, will not seek to substitute its judgment for that of another coordinate branch of the government," pursuant to that same constitutional doctrine, the Court is responsible for measuring legislative acts "with the yardstick of the Constitution." 263 So.2d at 806. The specific provisions against which the amendment in this case is to be measured are article VII, section 4, and article VII, section 3(a), of the Florida Constitution, and with recognition of some aspects of the provisions of article VII, section 10(c). Article VII, section 4, contains the overarching provision that "[b]y general law regulations shall be prescribed which shall secure a just valuation of all property for ad valorem taxation." Article VII, section 3(a), sets forth the mandatory and permissive exemptions from this constitutional admonition regarding ad valorem taxation.[70] [FN 8] It provides:

> All property owned by a municipality and used exclusively by it for municipal or public purposes shall be exempt from taxation. A municipality, owning property outside the municipality, may be required by general law to make payment to the taxing unit in which the property is located. Such portions of property as are used predominantly for educational, literary, scientific, religious or charitable purposes may be exempted by general law from taxation.

Here, we are required to interpret the application of article VII, section 3(a), to private, for-profit uses of leased, governmental property having absolutely nothing whatsoever to do with educational, literary, scientific, religious, or charitable activities.

As this Court, in *Volusia County*, expressly recognized, the language presently contained in the first sentence of article VII, section 3(a), reflects a marked change from its counterpart in the 1885 Constitution:

> The Constitution of 1885 provided that property owned by corporations "shall be subject to taxation unless ... used exclusively for religious, scientific, municipal, educational, literary or charitable purposes." Article 16, Section 16, Florida Constitution 1885. The phrase "municipal ... purposes" was

---

70. [FN 8.] "Immunity and exemption differ in that immunity connotes an absence of the power to tax while exemption presupposes the existence of that power." *Canaveral Port Authority v. Department of Revenue*, 690 So.2d 1226, 1234 n. 7 (Fla.1996).

broadly interpreted to include any "public" purpose; under the Constitution of 1885, this Court decided that simply holding a proprietary interest in "a community recreational asset and business stimulant," *Daytona Beach Racing & Rec. Fac. Dist. v. Paul*, 179 So.2d 349, 353 (Fla.1965), like the speedway served a "municipal purpose." *Id.* Perceiving decisions of this kind as creating inequities in the tax structure, the draftsmen of the Constitution of 1968 limited the municipal purpose exemption to "property owned by a municipality and used exclusively by it for municipal or public purposes." Article VII, Section 3(a), Florida Constitution 1968.

341 So.2d at 502. Pursuant to the adopted changes which resulted in the 1968 Constitution, the 1971 Legislature enacted a "sweeping reform" of chapters 192 and 196, Florida Statutes, *see* ch. 71-133, Laws of Fla. (commonly known as the "tax reform act"):

> The legislature repealed all the statutory provisions, both general laws and special acts, relevant to leasehold taxation and exemption. In their place, the legislature substituted a provision stating that all leasehold interests in governmental property were taxable unless expressly exempted by law. The lawmakers provided an express exemption to leaseholds "only when the lessee serves or performs a governmental, municipal, or public purpose or function...." Governmental, municipal, or public purpose or function was defined as a use which is "demonstrated to perform a function or serve a governmental purpose which could properly be performed or served by an appropriate governmental unit, or which is demonstrated to perform a function or serve a purpose which would otherwise be a valid subject for the allocation of public funds."

Bonnie Roberts, *Ad Valorem Taxation of Leasehold Interests in Governmentally Owned Property*, 6 Fla. St. U.L.Rev. 1085, 1092 (1978). "When read together, the provisions of article VII, section 3(a) of the 1968 constitution and the 1971 statutory modifications substantially tighten[ed] the requirements of an exemption." *Id.*

However, it was not until this Court's decisions in *Williams* and *Volusia County* that the substantial changes in article VII, section 3(a) of the 1968 Constitution were finally given effect....

In *Williams,* the Court first enunciated the current "governmental-governmental" standard for determining "public purpose" in the ad valorem tax exemption context. The *Williams* opinion reflected that this standard was constitutionally required:

> The operation of the commercial establishments represented by Raceway's cases is purely proprietary and for profit. They are not governmental functions. If such a commercial establishment operated for profit on Panama City Beach, Miami Beach, Daytona Beach, or St. Petersburg Beach is not exempt from tax, then why should such an establishment operated for profit on Santa Rosa Island Beach be exempt? No rational basis exists for such a distinction. The exemptions contemplated under Sections 196.012(5) and

196.199(2)(a), Florida Statutes, relate to "governmental-governmental" functions as opposed to "governmental-proprietary" functions. With the exemption being so interpreted all property used by private persons and commercial enterprises is subjected to taxation either *directly* or *indirectly* through taxation on the leasehold. Thus all privately used property bears a tax burden in some manner and this is what the Constitution mandates.

326 So.2d at 433.

Williams heralded a "judicial abandonment of the broad exemption theory articulated in Pan American." Roberts, *supra,* at 1096. As one commentator (writing in 1978) observed:

> If one were to accept the statutory definitions of public purpose as the sole basis for the decision in *Volusia County,* one might conclude that some legislative tinkering with the appropriate statutes could once again render a profit-oriented lease tax-exempt. This conclusion, however, would be erroneous because of that seemingly innocuous statement in *Straughn v. Camp* that leasehold interests used for private purposes must be taxed by virtue of the 1968 constitution. Should the legislature attempt to amend the statutory definition of public purpose to include private uses for profit, the supreme court might strike the amendment as unconstitutional on the ground that the private use under the 1968 constitution must be subjected to ad valorem taxation.

Id. at 1098. Indeed, in *Archer v. Marshall,* 355 So.2d 781 (Fla.1978), the prediction of the commentator came to pass. In *Marshall,* the Legislature had enacted a special act, the primary effect of which was to require that all rentals due to the Santa Rosa Island Authority on leases dated on or before December 1, 1975, be reduced each year by the amount of ad valorem taxes for county and school purposes paid on the leasehold interests for the preceding year. This legislation reflected an attempt to undo, with respect to the Santa Rosa Island commercial and residential leaseholders, what had previously been done pursuant to the tax reform act. In the predecessor to *Marshall,* the Court, in *Williams* (relying on *Straughn*), had upheld the Legislature's prior decision (reflected in the tax reform act) to subject the leaseholds to ad valorem tax.

Thereafter, the Legislature, through a special act, purported to grant the leaseholders relief from ad valorem taxation. This Court, relying on *Williams* and *Straughn,* struck what it perceived to be "an indirect exemption from taxation on property not authorized by the state constitution." 355 So.2d at 783. In so doing, the Court stated:

> The Legislature is without authority to grant an exemption from taxes where the exemption has no constitutional basis. *Presbyterian Homes of the Synod of Florida v. Wood,* 297 So.2d 556 (Fla.1974). Regardless of the term used to describe the set-off, the reduction in rent afforded the leaseholders has the effect of a tax exemption and as such is unconstitutional since such exemption is not within the provisions of our present state constitution. *Williams v. Jones,* 326 So.2d 425 (Fla.1975); *Straughn v. Camp,* 293 So.2d 689

(Fla.1974). It is fundamentally unfair for the Legislature to statutorily manipulate assessment standards and criteria to favor certain taxpayers over others. *Interlachen Lakes Estates, v. Snyder*, 304 So.2d 433 (Fla.1974 [1973]).

Accordingly, we hold that Chapter 76-361, Florida Statutes, Special Acts, 1976, violates Article VII, Section 3, Florida Constitution (1968), and is invalid.

Archer v. Marshall, 355 So.2d 781, 785 (Fla.1978).

Thus, it has long been clear that, based upon the amendments which resulted in the 1968 Constitution, the "public purpose" standard applicable in tax exemption cases is the "governmental-governmental" standard first established in *Williams*, later confirmed in *Volusia County*, and consistently applied in subsequent cases involving claimed tax exemptions for private leasehold interests. [citations omitted] Pursuant to this "governmental-governmental" standard, article VII, section 3(a) does not permit municipal property leased to private entities for governmental-proprietary activities to be tax exempt; rather, article VII, section 4, requires property so used to be subject to ad valorem tax.[71]

Here, however, Raceway asks that a dramatically different standard be applied to determine whether its activities constitute a "public purpose" use of municipally owned property. In so doing, it places significant reliance on two bond validation cases recently decided by this Court, *Poe v. Hillsborough County*, 695 So.2d 672 (Fla.1997), and *State v. Osceola County*, 752 So.2d 530 (Fla.1999).13

[handwritten margin note: Raceway wants a diff standard applied. Based on 2 cases.]

---

71. [FN 10.] In *Williams*, in upholding legislation imposing ad valorem tax on the Santa Rosa Island leaseholds, the Court—alluding to the language contained in article VII, section 4—observed that, in being subjected to the tax, the leaseholders paid their fair share of fire, police, and education services provided by the county in which they were situated:

> The result obtained through application of Sections 196.001(2) and 196.199, Florida Statutes, is to require that the leasehold interests defined therein shall be taxed at a just valuation like "all other property" in the state. To accept the appellants' contention that the Legislature is without power to so classify such leasehold interests as real property would not only result in such leasehold interests being taxed on the reduced intangible personal property ad valorem rate but would also deprive the political subdivisions wherein the leaseholds are situated from raising revenues from such sources in order to defray the costs of the services supplied to the users thereof, services which include, especially, the education of the children of such users. The holder of a lease on Santa Rosa Island requires no less police protection, fire protection or education of his or her children than does his or her neighbor in the county who occupies under a fee simple title. But if appellants' argument is accepted the revenues derived from the tax of a leasehold as intangible personal property must constitutionally be paid into the coffers of the state rather than the local political subdivision. See Article VII, Sections 1 and 9. The Legislature clearly has the power to classify so that all property devoted to private use is treated on a parity and, therefore, there is an equitable distribution of the tax burden. Basically, the appellants contend for a constitutional exemption from ad valorem real estate taxation where none exists and, if it did, such an exemption would undoubtedly be discriminatory and violative of the equal protection provisions of the Florida and United States Constitutions.

Williams, 326 So.2d at 431–32.

In *Poe* and *Osceola County,* the Court considered, respectively, whether a community stadium (leased upon lucrative terms—from the lessee's perspective—to a local football team) and a convention center (to be built and operated by the prospective lessee) served a "paramount public purpose." However, the "public purpose" (for non-recourse bonds) or "paramount public purpose" analysis (for recourse bonds) undertaken in a bond validation case implicates a provision of the Florida Constitution far different from that which governs in a tax exemption case.

In bond validation cases, the scope of this Court's review is limited to the following issues: "(1) whether the public body has the authority to issue bonds; (2) whether the purpose of the obligation is legal; and (3) whether the bond issuance complies with the requirements of the law." *Osceola County,* 752 So.2d at 533. It is the second prong of this analysis—whether the purpose of the obligation is legal—which implicates article VII, section 10 of the Florida Constitution. That section provides, in pertinent part:

> Neither the state nor any county, school district, municipality, special district, or agency of any of them, shall become a joint owner with, or stockholder of, or give, lend or use its taxing power or credit to aid any corporation, association, partnership or person. . . .

Therefore, it is the constitutional prohibition against lending "its taxing power or credit" to aid private entities which compels an analysis historically described as "public purpose" in bond validation cases. The Second District distinguished Raceway's reliance on the bond cases, stating:

> The airport authority and the raceway argue that the supreme court's decision in *Poe v. Hillsborough County,* 695 So.2d 672 (Fla.1997), supports the argument that the legislature properly construed the term "governmental, municipal or public purpose or function." We disagree. The *Poe* case involves the court's determination of a proposed bond issue by Hillsborough County and the City of Tampa for a community stadium. The court was concerned with whether or not a particular clause in a stadium lease, which granted the local football team the first $2 million dollars in net revenues from non-football events, would change the purpose of the project. It was in this context that the court validated the proposed bond issue.

Sebring III, 718 So.2d at 299. *See also Dade County v. Pan American World Airways, Inc.,* 275 So.2d 505, 515 (Fla.1973) (Ervin, J., dissenting) ("It is also important to recognize that the concept of 'public purpose' justifying the issuance of revenue bonds, does not in itself require exemption from taxation."); *cf. Volusia County,* 341 So.2d at 501 (observing that, under article VII, section 10I, where a municipal project financed by revenue bonds "is occupied or operated by any private corporation . . . pursuant to . . . lease . . . the property interest created by such . . . lease shall be subject to taxation to the same extent as other privately owned property").

Bond validation cases such as *Poe* and *Osceola County* are not analogous to tax exemption cases, and the legal theories cannot be used interchangeably. They involve not only very different constitutional provisions, but also significantly different fiscal implications. In bond validation cases involving projects such as the stadium or the convention center, specifically targeted tourist development tax revenues (rather than ad valorem taxes) may have been used in acquiring or constructing the subject facilities. Further, the revenue stream generated by the project itself may be calculated to repay any bond indebtedness which a local government guarantees.

Thus, in bond validation cases, a shift in the ad valorem tax burden to other taxpayers is not anticipated. In tax exemption cases, in contrast, any newly-created tax exemption necessarily involves a direct shift in tax burden from the exempt property to other, non-exempt properties.[72]

It is perhaps both confusing and unfortunate, then, that the same term—"public purpose"[73]—has traditionally been used in both of these analytical contexts. At least in tax exemption cases, however, it has been clearly established that the "governmental-governmental" public purpose standard governs. The 1994 amendment simply does not comport with this standard or the constitutional requirements.

Additionally, Raceway's argument predicated upon bond validation cases falls far short of complete analysis and fails to accommodate other constitutional provisions. As previously noted, the Florida Constitution expressly contemplates that, even when it is determined in the bond validation context that a particular project is appropriate under the standards of article VII, section 10, when certain projects are occupied or operated privately pursuant to contract or lease, the property interest *shall be subject to taxation to the same extent as other privately owned property. See* art. VII, § 10I.

Even the Senate Staff Analysis and Economic Impact Statement which accompanied the proposed 1994 amendment disclosed a candid awareness that the revision would be contrary to the current of established law. In fact, each of the cases cited in support of the amendment has since been either reversed or disapproved by this Court; all those cited as being inconsistent with the amendment have either been approved or affirmed.

---

72. [FN 14.] The Senate Staff Analysis and Economic Impact Statement accompanying the 1994 amendment acknowledged this significant shift in tax burden:

V. *ECONOMIC IMPACT AND FISCAL NOTE:*

A. Tax/Fee Issues:

While it cannot be accurately estimated at this time how much local governments' property tax base would be reduced by this broadened exemption, it is anticipated to be significant. Consequently, the resulting shift in the property tax burden to other taxpayers will be significant.

Fla. S. Comm. on Fin., Tax'n & Claims, CS for SBs 162 & 1558 (1994) Staff Analysis 5 (Mar. 17, 1994).

73. [FN 15.] The "public purpose" analysis is constitutionally derived in the tax exemption context; however, as applied to the bond validation context, in contrast, the phrase "public purpose" does not appear in the governing constitutional provision. *Compare* art. VII, § 3(a), Fla. Const. (providing that "[a]ll property owned by a municipality and used exclusively by it for municipal or *public purposes* shall be exempt from taxation") (emphasis supplied), *with* art. VII, § 10, Fla. Const. (providing that no municipality "shall become a joint owner with, or stockholder of, or give, lend or use its taxing power or credit to aid any corporation, association, partnership or person").

Nonetheless, Raceway urges that the Legislature "used the normal and ordinary meaning of the constitutional term 'public purposes' when it included in § 196.012(6) the types of for-profit-operated facilities which are recognized ... to promote the general welfare by stimulating tourism and economic development." The Second District determined otherwise, reasoning that "[t]he legislature's redefinition of the term in this instance must fail because the redefined term conflicts with the 'normal and ordinary meaning' of the phrase 'governmental, municipal or public purpose or function.'" *Sebring III*, 718 So.2d at 298.

Commentators have suggested that this 1994 amendment has attempted to convert the entire nature of permitted exemptions into that never envisioned by constitutional concepts. *See* David M. Hudson, *Governmental Immunity and Taxation in Florida*, 9 U. Fla. J.L. & Pub. Pol'y 221, 250 (1998). When viewed through the lens of the constitution, this amendment's approach cannot meet with success because mere labeling does not and cannot effectuate a transformation of constitutional acceptance. "[L]egislatively deeming a governmental-proprietary purpose to be a 'governmental-governmental' purpose does not change its true nature and does not result in the constitutional awarding of a tax exemption where, absent the legislation, there clearly could be no exemption." *Id.*

As we stated in *Volusia County*, 341 So.2d at 502, "Operating an automobile racetrack for profit is not even arguably the performance of a 'governmental-governmental' function." The time has not come to construe the Florida Constitution to provide otherwise.[74] We certainly understand that there is enormous competition to secure professional athletic teams and other forms of entertainment and economic development which benefit Florida citizens. We also recognize the tremendous economic forces and implications that become involved in this type of issue and the good faith legislative attempts to balance these concerns. However, as long as the people of Florida maintain the constitution in the form we are required to apply today, neither we nor the Legislature may expand the permissible exemptions based on this type of argument. The people of Florida have spoken in the organic law and we honor that voice.... [W]e affirm the decision below and approve the Second District's opinion only to the extent it is consistent with this opinion.

It is so ordered.

WELLS, C.J., and SHAW, HARDING and ANSTEAD, JJ., concur.

QUINCE, J., recused.

Commentary and Questions

The opinion emphasizes that a shift in exempt municipal property occurred in the 1968 Constitution. This opinion finds the 1968 limits are more restrictive than

---

74. [FN 19.] We add, parenthetically, however, that the time *may* be ripe to adopt a new phraseology for use in bond validation cases—such as "in the public interest" and "in the paramount public interest"—to avoid confusion between an article VII, section 10 analysis in bond validation cases, and an article VII, section 3(a) analysis in tax exemption cases.

under the 1885 Constitution. The Court cites the earlier opinion, *Volusia County v. Daytona Beach Racing & Recreational Facilities Dist.*, 341 So. 2d 498, 501 (Fla. 1976), which found the 1968 Constitution was correcting tax inequities.

Are legislative attempts to authorize public and private partnerships in jeopardy due to constitutional restraints?

The issue in this case was the imposition of ad valorem taxes on real property and improvements. The lease between the airport authority and raceway is apparently not contested as exempt. Article VII, Section 10I expressly provides in pertinent part that where any project financed by revenue bonds "is occupied or operated by any private corporation ... pursuant to ... lease ... the property interest created by such ... lease shall be subject to taxation to the same extent as other privately owned property."

Justice Lewis, writing for a unanimous Court, distinguishes between "public purpose" for tax exemption purposes and for bond validations. He notes the difference in part is:

> [I]n bond validation cases, a shift in the ad valorem tax burden to other taxpayers is not anticipated. In tax exemption cases, in contrast, any newly-created tax exemption necessarily involves a direct shift in tax burden from the exempt property to other, non-exempt properties.

He also observes in footnote 15 that "public purpose" appears in the language of subsection 3(a) but is an imported judicial gloss for bond validations under Article VII, Section 10. Justice Lewis will repeat this distinction in cases printed below on bond validation and the necessity of public referendums for bonds, but now his opinions are always in dissent.

Does Justice Lewis's use of the distinction between municipal tax exemptions and bond validation work consistently across all the cases?

The Court draws the permissible public-to-private arrangement as one that is "government-to-government." This mirrors the traditional distinction between municipalities providing both government services and proprietary services. The government-proprietary distinction can be amorphous.[75] Is the difference subjective? Four years after the 2001 *Sebring* decision, the Court held that two-way telecommunications equipment owned by the City of Gainesville was not tax exempt as city property under subsection 3(a). Unlike the constitutional change in 1968 regarding use of governmental property by a private company, the Court found there was no comparable change for municipal property: "There is nothing in the language of article VII, section 3(a) that evinces an intent to create a more restrictive definition of 'municipal or public purposes' for property that is owned and used exclusively by

---

75. § 10:5. Classifications and descriptions of municipal powers—Governmental and private, 2A McQuillin Mun. Corp. § 10:5 (3d ed.) ("No hard and fast rule satisfactorily distinguishing the one capacity from the other for general application has been announced."). *See generally*, Hugh D. Spitzer, *Realigning the Governmental/Proprietary Distinction in Municipal Law*, 40 Seattle U.L. Rev. 173 (2016); Janice C. Griffith, *Local Government Contracts: Escaping from the Governmental/Proprietary Maze*, 75 Iowa L. Rev. 277 (1990).

the municipality than the definition applied to 'municipal purposes' under the 1885 Constitution...."[76] The Court, however, concluded the telecommunications service was not an "essential" governmental function because other private providers already offered telecommunications service.[77] Twelve years later, the Court upheld a municipally owned public marina as exempt, distinguishing the *Gainesville* decision as "no more than a passing wave in the vast ocean of ad valorem taxation precedent."[78] The Court held a public marina historically provided transportation needs as well as allowing free access to the water. The Court added a third public purpose of providing recreational opportunities: "Landlocked citizens may break free from the confines of their yards or apartment complexes and enjoy the magnificent Florida waters through public marinas."[79]

Given these differences, is the *Sebring* Court premature in rejecting Raceway's argument that the Constitution is "is a fluid document" and that the concept of an essential governmental service should evolve with time? Does the Court's rejection of adaptability add an unnecessary restriction on the governmental provision of new, non-traditional services such as high-speed broadband internet connections or online library services?

The opinion acknowledges the "enormous competition" and "tremendous economic forces" at work to pass these projects. Is the Court referring to the Legislature in passing statutes like the one abnegated here or local governments in pushing these projects, or both?

v. Article VIII, Section 1(h) —
The Real and Substantial Benefit Requirement for
County Services Within a City

Article VIII, Section 1(h), in the chapter on local government, imposes a restriction on counties levying taxes within a municipality for services that will have no connection with the municipality. This was a new restriction included in the 1968 Constitution. The subsection restricts only how the tax revenue is spent; it does not directly correlate with the amount of tax collected. The intent of subsection 1(h) is to prevent taxpayers living in cities from paying for the same services twice or for paying for services that do not benefit them. In the 1970 lead case of *City of St. Petersburg v. Briley, Wild & Associates, Inc.*, 239 So. 2d 817 (Fla. 1970), the Florida Supreme Court held the connection between the county project and the city need

---

76. *Florida Dept. of Revenue v. City of Gainesville*, 918 So. 2d 250, 263 (Fla. 2005).

77. *Id.* at 265. The case also turns in significant measure on the city's challenge to the relevant statute as facially unconstitutional, meaning the city must prove there was not set of circumstances in which the statute could be constitutional. *See also* E. Kelly Bittick, Jr., *Department of Revenue v. City of Gainesville: The Florida Supreme Court Attempts to Define the Scope of Municipal Exemption from Ad Valorem Taxation*, 36 Stetson L. Rev. 457 (2007).

78. *Treasure Coast Marina, LC v. City of Fort Pierce*, 219 So. 3d 793, 795 (Fla. 2017).

79. *Id.* at 800.

not be direct or primary but only have "a real and substantial" connection. Perhaps predictably, what "real and substantial" entails is nebulous.

In a later case, equally well known for its holding on the testimony of expert witnesses, the *Town of Palm Beach* expands on "real and substantial" connections necessary for county taxes within a municipality.

Town of Palm Beach v. Palm Beach County

460 So. 2d 879 (Fla. 1985)

ADKINS, Justice.

This cause comes before us on petition for discretionary review of a question certified to be of great public importance by the Florida District Court of Appeal, Fourth District. *Palm Beach County v. Town of Palm Beach*, 426 So.2d 1063 (Fla. 4th DCA 1983). We have jurisdiction. Art. V, § 3(b)(4), Fla. Const.

The petitioners, four municipalities situated within Palm Beach County, allege that they have been subjected to "double taxation" in contravention of article VIII, section 1(h), Florida Constitution, which provides:

> Property situate within municipalities shall not be subject to taxation for services rendered by the county exclusively for the benefit of the property or residents in unincorporated areas.

Each of the petitioners challenges the use of property taxes collected by Palm Beach County which support the Palm Beach County Sheriff's road patrol and detective divisions, and also challenges the use of county-wide revenues to finance the maintenance and construction of local "nonclassified" roads in the unincorporated sections of the county. Additionally, two of the petitioners, the Town of Palm Beach and the City of West Palm Beach, dispute the use of their county-collected property taxes for the maintenance of neighborhood parks.

The trial court resolved each issue adversely to the county and held that the four challenged services do not provide a "real and substantial benefit" to the municipalities' residents or property. The Fourth District Court of Appeal reversed, finding a lack of competent substantial evidence to support the trial court's ruling and concluded that each of the services do substantially benefit the petitioners. Recognizing the need for "equitable and fair and uniform treatment under the taxing statutes," the district court certified the following question to this Court:

> Whether the "real and substantial benefits" test established by *City of St. Petersburg v. Briley, Wild & Associates*, 239 So.2d 817 (Fla.1970) has been correctly interpreted and appropriately applied in this case?

426 So.2d at 1072.

The issue of county taxation of municipalities for services accruing primarily to the benefit of unincorporated areas is not one of equity and fairness. The constitutional proscription against "double taxation," article VIII, section 1(h), Florida Constitution, and indeed, the statutory prohibition, section 125.08, Florida Statutes (1981), are not framed in terms of proportionality. Each merely requires that the municipality and its residents receive a benefit which must achieve a magnitude described as "real and substantial." *Briley, Wild*, 239 So.2d at 823. As we have stated in the past, substantial is not necessarily a quantifiable term and a benefit may achieve substantiality without being direct or primary. All that is required is a minimum level of benefit which is not illusory, ephemeral or inconsequential. *Id.; Burke v. Charlotte County*, 286 So.2d 199 (Fla.1973).... To meet this test, it is incumbent upon the petitioners to prove a negative—that a service provided by the county and funded by county-wide revenues does not provide a real and substantial benefit to the particular municipality. *Briley, Wild*, 239 So.2d at 823. In any given case this will be a heavy burden, but it is by no means impossible to prove or "automatic" in the sense that the constitutional test can never be met. *See, e.g., Manatee County v. Town of Longboat Key*, 352 So.2d 869 (Fla. 2d DCA 1977), *rev'd in part on other grounds*, 365 So.2d 143 (Fla.1978).

In the present case, the facts are essentially undisputed. Although petitioners contend that there was highly conflicting lay and expert testimony, a review of the disputed factual issues pointed to by petitioners demonstrates that it is not the facts which are contravened, but rather the legal conclusions to be drawn therefrom. For example, the petitioners state that evidence of the benefit derived by the municipality from the sheriff's backup or standby capacity was in conflict at trial. It is clear to us, however, that the existence and availability of standby assistance is not disputed, nor is there any question that the backup capacity has not been widely used in the past. What is at issue is the legal conclusion to be drawn from this fact. As this Court has consistently stated, where the facts are essentially undisputed, the legal effect of the evidence will be a question of law. *Uhrig v. Redding*, 150 Fla. 480, 8 So.2d 4 (1942); *Florida East Coast Railway v. Thompson*, 93 Fla. 30, 111 So. 525 (1927).

* * *

As the district court has previously noted, any decision concerning article VIII, section 1(h) "is limited to the facts, taxable years, and circumstances of [the] particular case...." *Alsdorf v. Broward County*, 373 So.2d 695, 701 (Fla. 4th DCA 1979), *cert. denied*, 385 So.2d 754 (Fla.1980). Accordingly, any decisions concerning the dual taxation issue must be carefully scrutinized to ascertain the facts existing in the individual county.

At trial, petitioners presented several statistical reports and other quantifiable evidence to demonstrate that the sheriff's road patrol and detective divisions do not provide a substantial benefit to the municipalities' citizens. The reports, garnered from the sheriff's computer records, expressed in percentage form the actual assists to the city by the road patrol and detective divisions as a proportion of overall municipal police activity. The only other evidence presented by petitioners was opinion testimony that the use of sheriff's patrol cars by off-duty deputies does not provide any crime-deterrence benefit to the municipalities in which the deputies reside.

Even though it is the petitioners' burden to demonstrate the absence of real and substantial benefit, and not the respondents' burden to prove the presence of any requisite benefit, the respondents presented numerous former and present police officers who testified to benefits which are extant but non-quantifiable. For instance, the respondents presented evidence that reduction of crime in the urban unincorporated corridor between the turnpike and the municipalities' boundaries will necessarily have some spillover effect by curtailing the movement of crime into the cities. Testimony was presented concerning the ever-present standby capability of the sheriff's department, which is available to assist any municipality in times of emergency or when requested. Municipal residents often travel in the unincorporated areas and thereby temporarily fall within the protective jurisdiction of the sheriff. Whenever called upon by a municipality, though historically infrequently, the sheriff's patrol and detective divisions have responded.

In addition, it is undisputed that the assist chart prepared by petitioners reflects only the minimum number of times a deputy-sheriff has entered a municipality to give aid or assistance to municipal residents. The sheriff stated that many noncrime municipal assists are likely to be unreported by deputies. The petitioners concede that the assist chart does not reflect time, money or effort expended in each assist. The evidence at trial was substantial that the majority of reported intermunicipality assists involved nonroutine matters requiring above average expenditures of deputy time, money and expertise. Finally, the quantified assist chart failed to fully account for assists such as the recovery by the sheriff's office of property stolen in a municipality.

Of course, as petitioners note, even allowing a margin of error of 100 per cent in the assist chart's numerical data, the number of assists would still remain minimal when stated as a percentage of police activity. However, the relative number of assists is not the sole issue. The constitutional question is whether the municipal residents substantially benefit from the challenged programs, and not whether the county provides proportionally significant services.

Taken independently, each of the above benefits would not be constitutionally substantial. We are, however, constrained to review the benefits delivered by the challenged services as a composite. In doing so, we find that the sheriff's road patrol and detective divisions provide not only a minimal level of direct benefit, but also a substantial degree of indirect benefit. That benefit, as a matter of law, given the geographic makeup of Palm Beach County, is sufficient to withstand the petitioners' heavy burden of proving a lack of substantial benefit. It is evident from the trial court's written decision that the trial judge did not discuss and consider many of the above benefits and failed to accord proper weight to the evidence of unquantifiable indirect and potential benefits. Whereas the constitutional test does not rest solely on quantitative benefits, the district court has correctly applied the holding of *Briley, Wild* to the instant case and we approve its decision on this point.

Respondent, Palm Beach County, pursuant to section 337.03, Florida Statutes (1981), has responsibility for all minor arterial roads within the county not on the state highway system, all collector roads, whether located in the municipal or unincorporated area of the county, and all local or nonclassified roads located within the unincorporated areas of the county. The petitioners challenge the use of their county-collected taxes to fund maintenance and construction of the nonclassified roads.

The entire substance of petitioners' evidence concerning these roads was that categorically a nonclassified road, because of its description and unincorporated area location, could not possibly be of real and substantial benefit to the municipal residents. The expert who presented this generalized characterization testified that he did not know who used the roads, did not know the volume of traffic on any of the roads, and did not know whether property abutting the nonclassified roads was commercial or residential. The record reflects that petitioners merely identified the total road system of the county and separated it into two components — classified and nonclassified.

Palm Beach County identified at least thirteen nonclassified roads which have traffic volumes comparable to roads on the classified road system. It was stipulated that the thirteen identified roads were not intended to be all-inclusive. Although the county did not present evidence of who used the roads, it did note that the roads were not subdivision streets or shell-rock as petitioners had described all nonclassified roads. We reiterate that the petitioners must bear the burden here. The respondents are not required to prove that the existing benefits are substantial. The petitioners must prove the nonexistence or nonsubstantiality of benefits.

From the foregoing, it is clear in this uncontested factual record that the petitioners presented a paucity of evidence and failed to carry the burden of proving that local nonclassified roads do not provide a real and substantial benefit to municipal residents.

We disapprove, however, the district court's statement that a municipal petitioner must identify all roads which do not provide a substantial benefit. *Palm Beach County,* 426 So.2d at 1070....

* * *

The trial court ruled that any benefits enjoyed by the municipalities' residents from county operated neighborhood parks were at best illusory. We agree. As the trial judge noted in his written judgment, the Town of Palm Beach is an island, connected to the mainland only by several bridges. Each of these bridges leads into West Palm Beach. Therefore, in order to take advantage of a neighborhood park, a resident of Palm Beach would have to leave the town, pass through a large city which has no county-funded neighborhood parks, and arrive at an ultimate destination surely not within walking distance....

As to the City of West Palm Beach, an analogous situation arises. West Palm Beach has several large county operated nonneighborhood parks within its boundaries and maintains its own local parks. Although there may be county funded neighborhood parks in municipalities adjoining West Palm Beach, these are not within walking distance of West Palm Beach residents. In order to actively and intentionally use a county operated neighborhood park, a resident of West Palm Beach would have to ignore his or her own city's local parks and bypass nearby large nonneighborhood parks with extensive recreational facilities. The few residents doing so would not raise the level of use to one of real and substantial benefit.

We find that the district court improperly required a showing of "statistical data as to park attendance, residence of park users or other relevant factors...." *Palm Beach County*, 426 So.2d at 1070. *Briley, Wild* requires only that a municipality challenging a county levied tax prove the absence of a real and substantial benefit. Although this is a difficult burden, not every case will require extensive and costly studies. It remains for the individual petitioner to determine what evidence will be presented to the trier of fact. In the instant case, national park standards and the location of the many parks in Palm Beach County demonstrate the insignificant possibility that residents of West Palm Beach and Palm Beach will use parks that are not maintained for their benefit....

We recognize that a city resident may visit a neighboring municipality or outlying unincorporated area and use a neighborhood park, inasmuch as such parks are available to the general public without restriction. We find, from the geographical makeup of Palm Beach County and the locations of the numerous parks, neighborhood and otherwise, that use of neighborhood parks by these two petitioners' residents is illusory, ephemeral and inconsequential, and does not rise to the magnitude required by the real and substantial benefits test.

On this point alone, we find that the district court has misapplied the test enunciated in *Briley, Wild*. We therefore quash the district court's determination that the petitioners did not meet their burden of proving lack of substantial benefit.

* * *

For the foregoing reasons, the certified question is answered in the affirmative as to the sheriff's road patrol, detective divisions, and nonclassified roads, and answered in the negative as to the neighborhood parks. We remand this cause to the district court with instruction that it be further remanded to the trial court for proceedings consistent with this opinion.

It is so ordered.

OVERTON, McDONALD, EHRLICH and SHAW, JJ., concur.

BOYD, C.J., concurs in part and dissents in part with an opinion, in which ALDERMAN, J., concurs.

BOYD, Chief Justice, concurring in part and dissenting in part.

I concur with those portions of the majority opinion that reject the argument of the municipalities that certain county services, financed by county-wide taxation, are benefitting only residents in the unincorporated areas of the county. I dissent from that portion of the majority opinion that holds that certain county-financed "neighborhood parks" in unincorporated locations benefit only the residents of unincorporated areas in violation of the state constitutional right of residents of municipalities in the county.

The sheriff of a county in Florida is the sheriff for all the people of the county. The fact that municipalities may organize police forces to provide their residents with additional law enforcement services does not relieve municipal residents of the obligation of paying county taxes to finance the operation of the sheriff's office. The sheriff is accountable to the voters for the use of the resources entrusted to the office. Similarly, county-maintained roads in unincorporated areas are available for use by everyone. Favoritism toward one area of the county at the expense of another can be remedied through the political process.

Regarding the issue of "neighborhood parks," I believe the record shows that such parks are available for use and enjoyment by anyone who happens to be in the area, including county residents, city residents, and travellers from other areas. They are an amenity provided by the whole county community for use by the whole county community. Even if, as the majority finds, it is unlikely that city residents would use the neighborhood parks in question, their existence and maintenance in those neighborhoods serves the interest of and benefits all the residents of the entire county, both in and out of the incorporated areas. Palm Beach County is a metropolitan community in which the need for urban services and amenities serving the whole community does not stop at municipal boundary lines.

I would answer the certified question in the affirmative as to all issues and approve the district court decision in its entirety.

ALDERMAN, J., concurs.

Commentary and Questions

This section limits the power of counties only to expend ad valorem taxes, not other non-ad valorem county revenues. *Manatee County v. Town of Longboat Key*, 365 So. 2d 143 (Fla. 1978). Also, no constitutional provision prohibits the taxation of unincorporated parts of the county for the benefit of areas in a municipality. *McLeod v. Orange County*, 645 So. 2d 411 (Fla. 1994). The Legislature has also enacted the Florida Governmental Conflict Resolution Act, in Chapter 164, that may reduce the future appearances of county and city taxing conflicts.[80]

The majority finds the sheriff road patrols and detective divisions provide indirect benefits to all four municipalities, including the island Town of Palm Beach which connects only to the city of West Palm Beach and not directly to the unincorporated county areas. The majority finds indirect benefits in the "spillover effect" of curtailing crime, the standby capacity of sheriffs to assist city officers, the sheriff's assistance with non-crime incidents such as traffic control during accidents, recovery of stolen property, and the temporary travel of city residents through the sheriff's jurisdiction in unincorporated areas.

For a municipality abutting another county, why wouldn't the same arguments favor tax allocations to the abutting county?

---

80. *See* David G. Tucker, *A Primer on Counties and Municipalities, Part 2*, FLA. B.J., April 2007, at 70.

Justice Boyd in his dissent points to the constitutional office of the sheriff as an embedded feature of county government. Is Justice Boyd's argument about the sheriff strengthened by the need to financially support other countywide, constitutional officers, such as supervisor of elections, property appraiser, and tax collector? Art. VIII, § 1(d). In 2018 the voters amended Article VIII to require all counties to maintain the constitutional county officers and fill those offices only by election.[81] Does this make any difference to Justice Boyd's argument that "favoritism" or poor allocation of funds within the county can be solved through the political process? Is it realistic that the Town of Palm Beach can politically influence the countywide allocation of resources?

Is it the difficulty of picking and choosing individual programs within an office, such as sheriff road patrols as one function of the sheriff's office, which underlies the difficult burden of proof imposed on the challengers? The rule of real and substantial connection between taxes and services to an incorporated area is not based on proportionality. Is this to avoid arguments on who gets how much?

D. Fees and Assessments

There is a significant interest in fees and special assessments as local governments approach ad valorem millage caps, or as they seek to target costs directly against those causing those costs. Judicial and statutory controls have evolved over both fees and assessments, depending on the type of charge. Fees and assessments for counties and municipalities may legislatively originate in either statute or home rule authority. The late Robert Nabors succinctly wrote the analysis as:

> The judicial inquiry, when a county or municipality home rule revenue source is imposed by ordinance, is whether the charge meets the legal sufficiency test for a valid fee or assessment. If not, the charge is a tax and general law authorization is required under the tax presumption provisions of Article VII, section 1, Florida Constitution. If not a tax under Florida case law, the imposition of the fee or assessment by ordinance, in absence of a legislative or charter preemption, is within the constitutional and statutory home rule power of municipalities and counties.[82]

Fees are sometimes distinguished in case law as either regulatory fees, user fees, or impact fees. In a 2018 constitutional amendment, fees were given an inclusive constitutional definition: "'Fee' means any charge or payment required by law, including any fee for service, fee or cost for licenses, and charge for service."[83]

The following case, *City of Dunedin*, is an early statement on the legal standards for fees, and addresses an impact fee. Note the opinion's reliance on legal precedents

---

81. Division of Elections, available at: https://dos.elections.myflorida.com/initiatives/fulltext/pdf/11-24.pdf (last accessed August 10, 2020).
82. Robert L. Nabors, Florida Home Rule Green Book, § 13.01, p. 171 (2d ed. 2014).
83. Fla. Const. art. VII, § 19(d)(1); *see also* Jarvis, *supra* note 33 at 616.

from outside Florida and utility rate-making concepts, such as allocation of costs among customer classes, as the Court attempts to create a standard in this state.

Contractors and Builders Association of Pinellas County v. City of Dunedin

329 So. 2d 314 (Fla. 1976)

HATCHETT, Justice.

In an action for declaratory judgment, brought against the City of Dunedin in Circuit Court, provisions of certain ordinances were adjudged defective, as being an *ultra vires* attempt by the city to impose taxes; and the city was enjoined from collecting fees the ordinances required as a precondition for municipal water and sewerage service. In addition, the Circuit Court ordered the City to refund the fees, but only to persons who had paid under protest. On appeal to the District Court of Appeal, Second District, that court reversed the circuit court judgment, *City of Dunedin, Florida v. Contractors and Builders Association of Pinellas County, etc. et al.*, 312 So.2d 763; and, on June 10, 1975, certified that its decision passed upon a question of great public interest. As is customary in cases where such certificates have been entered, we exercise our discretion to review on its merits the decision below. *E.g., Grant v. State*, 316 So.2d 282 (Fla.1975); *Winston v. State*, 308 So.2d 40 (Fla.1974) (*reh. den.* 1975). See Fla.Const. art. V, s 3(b)(3).

Plaintiffs in the trial court, petitioners here, are building contractors, an incorporated association of contractors, and owners of land situated within the city limits of Dunedin.[84] They do not complain of all the fees Dunedin requires to be collected upon issuance of building permits,[85] but contend that monies which the city collects and earmarks for "capital improvements to the (water and sewerage) system as a whole" ... constitute taxes, which a municipality is forbidden to impose, in the absence of enabling legislation. It is agreed on all sides that "a municipality cannot impose a tax, other than ad valorem taxes, unless authorized by general law," 312 So.2d at 766, and that no general law gives such authorization here. Respondent contends that these fees are not taxes, but user charges analogous to fees collected by privately owned utilities for services rendered. For the reasons stated in Judge Grimes' scholarly opinion, we accept this analogy, but we decline to uphold a revenue gen-

---

84. [FN 2.] Petitioners take the position that the ordinance is bad, if for no other reason, then [sic] because it denies equal protection of the laws to new residents of Dunedin. There is a substantial question whether petitioners here have standing to assert new residents' rights. *Construction Industry Association of Sonoma County v. City of Petaluma*, 522 F.2d 897 (9th Cir., 1975). Assuming standing arguendo, the ordinance easily meets the rational basis test, see *post*, pp. 319–320, and no right to travel interstate is affected, contrary to petitioners' assertion. *Cf.* Annot., 63 A.L.R.3d 1184 (1975). In *Shapiro v. Thompson*, 394 U.S. 618 (1969), welfare recipients were disqualified as such for one year by moving into Connecticut. Under Dunedin's ordinance, a joint water and sewer connection costs approximately $800.00, regardless of whether the new user comes from Dunedin, elsewhere in Florida, or from another state or country.

85. [FN 3.] In the event of connection to an existing structure, the fees are payable 'when the permits for water or sewer connections are issued.' Dunedin, Fla.Code s 25-71(d). The complaint here did not allege existing structures on the plaintiffs' land, however.

erating ordinance that omits provisions we deem crucial to its validity. We are unpersuaded, moreover, that the limitations, which the city has in fact placed on fees collected pursuant to Dunedin, Fla., Code ss 25-31, 25-71(c) and (d), can suffice to make those fees "just and equitable", within the meaning of Fla.Stat. s 180.13(2) (1973). In principle, however, we see nothing wrong with transferring to the new user of a municipally owned water or sewer system a fair share of the costs new use of the system involves.

Petitioners contend that Dunedin has imposed a tax under the guise of setting charges for water and sewer connections, relying on *Broward County v. Janis Development Corp.*, 311 So.2d 371 (Fla.4th Dist.1975) *aff'g Janis Development Corp. v. City of Sunrise*, 40 Fla.Supp. 41 (17th Cir. 1973); *Pizza Palace of Miami v. City of Hialeah*, 242 So.2d 203 (Fla.3d Dist.1972); and *Venditti-Siraro, Inc. v. City of Hollywood*, 39 Fla.Supp. 121 (17th Cir. 1973). The *Pizza Palace* case is wholly inapposite, and the others are readily distinguishable....

[T]he fees in *Janis Development* and *Venditti-Siraro* bore no relationship to (and were greatly in excess of) the costs of the regulation which was supposed to justify their collection. In each case, the fees were required to be paid as a condition for issuance of building permits. In the *Janis Development* case, $200.00 per dwelling unit built was put into a fund for road maintenance. In *Venditti-Siraro*, one percent of estimated construction costs went into a fund for parks. Because the surcharges were collected for purposes extraneous to the enforcement of the building code, the courts concluded that the surcharges amounted in law to taxes, which the municipalities had not been authorized to impose. In contrast, evidence was adduced here that the connection fees were less than costs Dunedin was destined to incur in accommodating new users of its water and sewer systems. We join many other courts in rejecting the contention that such connection fees are taxes. [citations omitted.]

The avowed purpose of the ordinance in the present case is to raise money in order to expand the water and sewerage systems, so as to meet the increased demand which additional connections to the system create. The municipality seeks to shift to the user expenses incurred on his account. A private utility in the same circumstances would presumably do the same thing, in which event surely even petitioners would not suggest that the private corporation was attempting to levy a tax on its customers.[86]

---

86. [FN 5.] Petitioners contend that utility revenues constitute taxes, to the extent such revenues are expended for purposes unrelated to the utility. Nothing prohibits a municipality's "making a modest return of its utility operation or certain portions thereof, providing the rate is not unreasonable." *Pinellas Apartment Ass'n v. City of St. Petersburg*, 294 So.2d 676, 678 (Fla.2d Dist. 1974); *Mitchell v. Mobile*, 244 Ala. 442, 13 So.2d 664 (1943). *Contra, Madera v. Black*, 181 Cal. 306, 184 P. 397 (1919). Augmenting general revenues is a natural use for such profits, and general revenues are expended for the whole range of municipal purposes. Privately held utilities also apply a modest portion of revenues to public or charitable purposes, and such charitable contributions are counted as operating expenses, when rates and charges are calculated. [citations omitted] Just as a modest surplus over costs of regulation does not invalidate regulatory fees, *State ex rel. Harkow v. McCarthy*, 126 Fla. 433, 171 So. 314 (1936) (parking meters permissible unless "city was making inordinate and unjustified profits", at 317), so a modest profit from operation of a public utility does not transform user charges into

Under the constitution, Dunedin, as the corporate proprietor of its water and sewer systems, can exercise the powers of any other such proprietor (except as Fla.Stat. ss 180.01 Et seq., or statutes enacted hereafter, may otherwise provide.)[87] Municipal corporations have "governmental, corporate and proprietary powers" and "may exercise any power for municipal purposes, except as otherwise provided by law." Fla.Const. art. VIII, s 2(b); *City of Miami Beach v. Fleetwood Hotel, Inc.*, 261 So.2d 801 (Fla.1972).[88] "Implicit in the power to provide municipal services is the power to construct, maintain and operate the necessary facilities." *Cooksey v. Utilities Commission*, 261 So.2d 129, 130 (Fla.1972). There are no provisions in Chapter 180, Florida Statutes, expressly governing capital acquisition other than through deficit financing,[89] but it is provided that the "legislative body of the municipality ... may establish just and equitable rates or charges" for water and sewerage. Fla.Stat. s 180.13(2) (1973). *See generally* Annot., 61 A.L.R.3d 1236, 1248–1259 (1975).

When a municipality sells debentures as a means of financing the extension or enlargement of a public utility, the indebtedness thus incurred is eventually made good with utility revenues; and anticipated revenues "may be pledged to secure moneys advanced for the ... improvement." Fla.Stat. s 180.07(2) (1973). When money for capital outlay is borrowed, water and sewer rates are set with a view towards raising the money necessary to repay the loan. *State v. City of Tampa*, 137 Fla. 29, 187 So. 604, 609 (1939); *State v. City of Miami*, 113 Fla. 280, 152 So. 6 (1933) (*reh. den.* 1934) ("certificates of indebtedness ... are payable as to both principal and interest solely out of a special fund to be created ... out of the net earnings", at 13).

Water and sewer rates and charges do not, therefore, cease to be "just and equitable" merely because they are set high enough to meet the system's capital requirements, as well as to defray operating expenses. *State v. City of Tampa, supra; State v. City of Miami, supra.* We see no reason to require that a municipality resort to deficit financing, in order to raise capital by means of utility rates and charges. On the contrary, sound public policy militates against any such inflexibility. It may be a simpler technical task to amortize a known outlay, than to predict population trends and the other variables necessary to arrive at an accurate forecast of future

---

taxes. *Pinellas Apartment Ass'n v. City of St. Petersburg, supra.* On the other hand, unreasonable reliance on utility revenues does amount to "imposing upon (ratepayers) unfair tax burdens." *Mitchell v. Mobile*, 13 So.2d at 667. *Cf. City of Panama City v. State*, 60 So.2d 658 (Fla.1952)....

87. [FN 6.] Chapter 180 was enacted before the 1968 Constitution was adopted, and some language in the chapter is anachronistic. The statutes refer to "powers granted by this chapter," Fla.Stat. ss 180.03(1), .21 (1973), whereas, under the 1968 Constitution, the provisions of Chapter 180 are restrictions on the exercise of power the constitution itself confers, rather than the grant of powers these statutory provisions formerly constituted.

88. [FN 7.] But a municipality's power to tax is subject to the restrictions enumerated in Fla.Const. art. VII s 9 including the restriction discussed above. *City of Tampa v. Birdsong Motors, Inc.*, 261 So.2d 1 (Fla.1972).

89. [FN 8.] Special assessments are another common means of financing sewer construction. Fla.Stat. s 170.01 (1973). The fees in controversy here are not special assessments. They are charges for use of water and sewer facilities; the property owner who does not use the facilities does not pay the fee. Under no circumstances would the fees constitute a lien on realty.

capital needs. But raising capital for future use by means of rates and charges may permit a municipality to take advantage of favorable conditions, which would alter before money could be raised through issuance of debt securities; and the day may not be far distant when municipalities cannot compete successfully with other borrowers for needed capital. The weight of authority supports the view that raising capital for future outlay is a legitimate consideration in setting rates and charges [citations omitted].

It is also established that differential utility rates and charges may be "just and equitable". Fla.Stat. s 180.13(2) (1973); *Hayes v. City of Albany*, [7 Or.App. 277, 490 P.2d 1018 (1971)], notwithstanding the differential. In *Brandel v. Civil City of Lawrenceburg*, 249 Ind. 47, 230 N.E.2d 778 (1967), the court upheld an ordinance setting differential connection charges where two distinct sewerage systems had been engineered in the same political entity. The user connecting to the more expensive system paid a higher connection charge. Another common type of differential charge makes the character of the user determinative of utility rates:

> In determining reasonable rate relationships, a municipality may sometimes take into account the purpose for which a customer receives the service.... Courts have recognized that differences in sewer use rates for residential customers and various other customers may be reasonable. Some customers may be subject to a flat rate while other customers are subject to rates based on water consumption or type and number of receptacles. *Rutherford v. City of Omaha*, 183 Neb. 398, 160 N.W.2d 223, 228 (1968) (authorities omitted).

Dunedin distinguishes between residential and commercial users, on one hand, and industrial users, on the other. See *ante*, pp. 316–317 n. 1, and petitioners do not question this distinction. Here the issue is whether differential connection charges are "just and equitable", when they vary depending on the time at which the connection to the utility system is made.

Raising expansion capital by setting connection charges, which do not exceed a *pro rata* share of reasonably anticipated costs of expansion, is permissible where expansion is reasonably required, *if use of the money collected is limited to meeting the costs of expansion*. Users "who benefit expecially [sic], not from the maintenance of the system, but by the extension of the system ... should bear the cost of that extension." *Hartman v. Aurora Sanitary District, supra*, 177 N.E.2d at 218 [(Ill. 1961)]. On the other hand, it is not "just and equitable" for a municipally owned utility to impose the entire burden of capital expenditures, included replacement of existing plant, on persons connecting to a water and sewer system after an arbitrarily chosen time certain.

The cost of new facilities should be borne by new users to the extent new use requires new facilities, but only to that extent. When new facilities must be built in any event, looking only to new users for necessary capital gives old users a windfall at the expense of new users.

When certificates of indebtedness are outstanding, new users, like old users, pay rates which include the costs of retiring the certificates, which represent original capitalization. *State v. City of Miami, supra.* New users thus share with old users the cost of original facilities. For purposes of allocating the cost of replacing original facilities, it is arbitrary and irrational to distinguish between old and new users, all of whom bear the expense of the old plant and all of whom will use the new plant.[90] The limitation on use of the funds, shown to exist *de facto* in the present case, has the effect of placing the whole burden of supplementary capitalization, including replacement of fully depreciated assets, on a class chosen arbitrarily for that purpose.

In *Hayes v. City of Albany, supra,* the situation was very much like the situation here. An existing system faced the imminent prospect of expansion and, as of a date certain, residential connection fees climbed from $25 to $255. (An hypothetical industrial user's charges soared from $200 to a prohibitive $400,000.) These charges were to be deposited in a fund restricted as follows:

> All monies received from the Sewer Connection Charges plus interest, if any, shall be deposited in the Sanitary Sewer Capital Reserve Fund ... and shall be expended from that fund only for the purpose of making major emergency repairs, extending or oversizing, separating, or constructing new additions to the treatment plant or collection and interceptor systems, 490 P.2d at 1020.

If the ordinance in the present case had so restricted use of the fees which it required to be collected, there would be little question as to its validity. We conclude that the ordinance in the present case cannot stand as it is written.

The same considerations which underlie statutes of frauds require that a revenue producing ordinance explicitly set forth restrictions on revenues it generates, where such restrictions are essential to its validity. As between private parties, a contract "that is not to be performed within the space one year", Fla.Stat. s 725.01 (1973), or which is "for the sale of goods for the price of $500 or more", Fla.Stat. s 672.201 (1973), is unenforceable unless reduced to writing, with certain exceptions not pertinent here. Counsel for respondent has represented that the fees collected under the ordinance exceed $196,000.00. Brief for Respondent at 53. Nothing in the record indicates that capital outlay for expansion will be completed within a year's time.

The failure to include necessary restrictions on the use of the fund is bound to result in confusion, at best. City personnel may come and go before the fund is exhausted, yet there is nothing in writing to guide their use of these moneys, although certain uses, even within the water and sewer systems, would undercut the legal basis for the fund's existence. There is no justification for such casual handling of public moneys, and we therefore hold that the ordinance is defective for failure to

---

90. [FN 11.] There is authority to the contrary. *Hartman v. Aurgora Sanitary District, supra*; *Home Builders Ass'n of Greater Salt Lake v. Provo City*, [28 Utah 2d 402, 503 P.2d 451 (1972)]. In *Provo City*, an ordinance like Dunedin's was upheld even though the fees were used for "general operating expenses." 503 P.2d at 451. We reject the view these cases represent.

spell out necessary restrictions on the use of fees it authorizes to be collected.[91] Nothing we decide, however, prevents Dunedin from adopting another sewer connection charge ordinance, incorporating appropriate restrictions on use of the revenues it produces. Dunedin is at liberty, moreover, to adopt an ordinance restricting the use of moneys already collected. We pretermit any discussion of refunds for that reason.

The decision of the District Court of Appeal is quashed and this case is remanded to the District Court with directions that the District Court dispose of the question of costs; and that the District Court thereafter remand for further proceedings in the trial court not inconsistent with this opinion. In the trial court's consideration *de novo* of the question of refunds the chancellor is at liberty to take into account all pertinent developments since entry of his original decree.

It is so ordered.

ADKINS, C.J., and ROBERTS, OVERTON and ENGLAND, JJ., concur.

Commentary and Questions

The Court distinguishes fees that "underwrite the administrative costs" of issuing or enforcing a regulation as permissible and as not being at issue in this case. Such fees are sometimes referred to as regulatory fees. Regulatory fees are imposed under police power of local government and require fee proceeds to be applied to provide for the cost of the regulatory activity.[92] Examples of regulatory fees are building permits and inspection fees. The Court notes in this case that the fees cannot be "excessive" and must relate to the regulatory activity.

The Court refers to the Dunedin municipal water and sewer system as a proprietary activity. The Court finds the City of Dunedin has authority under its home rule powers conferred in Chapter 180, Florida Statutes, to impose a fee. In footnote 8, the court states: "The fees in controversy here ... are charges for use of water and sewer facilities; the property owner who does not use the facilities does not pay the fee. Under no circumstances would the fees constitute a lien on realty." Sometimes user fees are imposed by local government in the exercise of a proprietary activity and, as the *Dunedin* Court notes, these fees can generate a reasonable profit. Examples are admission fees, utility fees, franchise fees and traditional user fees.[93] User fees do not create a lien on real property; impact fees, however, may create a lien against the assessed property. User fees are the subject of the following *City of Port Orange* case.

---

91. [FN 12.] If subsection c were excised from Dunedin, Fla.Code s 25-71, the ordinance would be unobjectionable, because reasonable meter connection charges may permissibly furnish utility revenues for unrestricted use within the utility system. The validity of such charges does not depend on limitation of their use.

92. ROBERT L. NABORS, FLORIDA HOME RULE GREEN BOOK § 14.02 (2d ed. 2014).

93. *Id.* § 14.03, p. 176.

The Court is confronting in *Dunedin* what is now termed an impact fee. Dunedin is charging new users a portion of the added capital expansion costs the system incurs as it adds new customers. The Court states an early standard for impact fees that covers both the amount and how the charges are distributed among the different types of new customers: "Raising expansion capital by setting connection charges, which do not exceed a *pro rata* share of reasonably anticipated costs of expansion, is permissible where expansion is reasonably required, *if use of the money collected is limited to meeting the costs of expansion*." (Emphasis in original.) The Court holds: "The cost of new facilities should be borne by new users to the extent new use requires new facilities, but only to that extent."

The problem with the Dunedin ordinance was its failure to separate costs caused only by new customers from those distinct costs of replacing existing utility assets. For example, the addition of new customers to the end of an existing water or sewer main might require resizing the entire pipe to handle more capacity. As the Court notes, the cost of the existing pipe is already being recaptured through the utility rates charged existing customers. New customers will pay those rates and therefore also pay for the cost of the old pipe. A new, larger pipe will last longer than the old pipe and thus benefit both existing and new customers with added life. The Dunedin ordinance lumps the new connection fee into a single category of replacing the pipe with no cost allocation between existing needs and the new demand needs. The Court returned the case to the lower court to allow this allocation to happen.

Though not explicit in the opinion, the Court is effectively separating tax from fee. Taxes are imposed over all like taxpayers and can be used for all governmental purposes. Fees are collected only from those payers using the system, are limited in amount to the costs actually incurred, and can be used only to pay for those costs. Imposition of a local tax requires a general law enacted by the Florida Legislature; a fee only requires enactment by the local government.

Interestingly, the Court notes in footnote 8 that Dunedin might have used a special assessment to accomplish the same purpose as the impact fee. Special assessments by local governments have a long history in the United States and are discussed later in this chapter.

The evolution and sophistication of user fees is seen eighteen years after the *City of Dunedin* case.

State v. City of Port Orange

650 So. 2d 1 (Fla. 1994)

WELLS, Justice.

We have on appeal a decision of the trial court declaring that a proposed bond issue is valid. We have jurisdiction....

Judicial inquiry in bond validation proceedings is limited. Specifically, courts should: (1) determine if a public body has the authority to issue the subject bonds;

(2) determine if the purpose of the obligation is legal; and (3) ensure that the authorization of the obligation complies with the requirements of law. *Taylor v. Lee County*, 498 So.2d 424, 425 (Fla.1986) (citing *Wohl v. State*, 480 So.2d 639 (Fla.1985)).

The City of Port Orange (the City) enacted a "Transportation Utility Ordinance," City of Port Orange Ordinance No. 1992-11, creating a "Transportation Utility" of the City and adopting a "transportation utility fee" relating to the use of city roads. The fee is imposed upon the owners and occupants of developed properties within the City. No fees are imposed on undeveloped property. Any unpaid fee becomes a lien upon the property until such fee is paid. The costs to be defrayed by the fee are the City's expenses relating to the operation, maintenance, and improvement of the local road system. The circuit court limited these costs to capital projects.

The ordinance requires that city-maintained roads be classified as arterial, collector, or local roads, and the cost of constructing and maintaining such roads be allocated separately. Because arterial and collector roads provide mobility and facilitate traffic movement to and from all properties, the ordinance requires that costs incurred by the City on those roads be allocated to all developed properties within the city.

The function of local roads, it was determined, is to provide access to abutting properties. The ordinance requires the City to allocate costs incurred on local roads to developed properties fronting those roads. None of the costs of local roads are allocated to properties fronting private subdivision roads.

The City is required by the ordinance to estimate the amount of usage of the local roads by the owners and occupiers of developed properties through a mixture of actual traffic counts and the use of a "Trip Generation Manual" developed by the Institute of Traffic Engineers. The City allocates the costs for each class of roads to the users of that class of road in proportion to the number of trips generated by each user. The ordinance states that the fees collected from any property need not be in close proximity to such property or provide a special benefit to such property that is different in type or degree from benefits provided to the community as a whole.

The City further authorized the issuance of Transportation Utility Bonds, City of Port Orange Ordinance No. 1992-28, to finance the costs of constructing, renovating, expanding, and improving certain city transportation facilities. Such bonds are to be paid by a pledge of the transportation utility fees.

Subsumed within the inquiry as to whether the public body has the authority to issue the subject bond is the legality of the financing agreement upon which the bond is secured. *GRW Corp. v. Department of Corrections*, 642 So.2d 718 (Fla.1994). Integral to the financing agreement here under review is the pledge of what the bond ordinance labels "transportation utility fees." Thus, we must determine whether the pledge of the transportation utility fees is a pledge of tax revenue or is a pledge of user charges or fees. Because a tax must be authorized by general law, the City agrees that if the transportation utility fee is a tax, even broad home rule powers granted to municipalities do not authorize it.

The circuit court ruled that the transportation utility fee is a valid user fee, not a tax, and the City is authorized under municipal home rule powers to impose and collect the fee. We do not agree. We reverse the decision of the circuit court. We hold that what is designated in the bond ordinance as a transportation utility fee is a tax which must be authorized by general law.

This Court has held that taxation by a city must be expressly authorized either by the Florida Constitution or grant of the Florida Legislature. "Doubt as to the powers sought to be exercised must be resolved against the municipality and in favor of the general public." *City of Tampa v. Birdsong Motors, Inc.,* 261 So.2d 1, 3 (Fla.1972). It is our view that the power of a municipality to tax should not be broadened by semantics which would be the effect of labeling what the City is here collecting a fee rather than a tax.

In *City of Boca Raton v. State,* 595 So.2d 25 (Fla.1992), this court noted that a tax is an enforced burden imposed by sovereign right for the support of the government, the administration of law, and the exercise of various functions the sovereign is called on to perform. *Klemm v. Davenport,* 100 Fla. 627, 631, 129 So. 904, 907 (1930). Funding for the maintenance and improvement of an existing municipal road system, even when limited to capital projects as the circuit court did here, is revenue for exercise of a sovereign function contemplated within this definition of a tax.

User fees are charges based upon the proprietary right of the governing body permitting the use of the instrumentality involved. Such fees share common traits that distinguish them from taxes: they are charged in exchange for a particular governmental service which benefits the party paying the fee in a manner not shared by other members of society, *National Cable Television Assn. v. United States,* 415 U.S. 336, 341 (1974); and they are paid by choice, in that the party paying the fee has the option of not utilizing the governmental service and thereby avoiding the charge. *Emerson College v. City of Boston,* 391 Mass. 415, 462 N.E.2d 1098, 1105 (1984) (citing *City of Vanceburg v. Federal Energy Regulatory Comm'n,* 571 F.2d 630, 644 n. 48 (D.C.Cir.1977), *cert. denied,* 439 U.S. 818 (1978)). The above concept of user fees was approved by this Court in *City of Daytona Beach Shores v. State,* 483 So.2d 405 (Fla.1985). The City's transportation utility fee falls within our definition of a tax, not our definition of a user fee.

The circuit court found this transportation utility fee to be similar to the concept of impact fees which this Court has approved. Impact fees imposed by a municipality were upheld in *Contractors and Builders Association v. City of Dunedin,* 329 So.2d 314 (Fla.1976). However, in that case, impact fees were clearly limited:

> Raising expansion capital by setting connection charges, which do not exceed a *pro rata* share of reasonably anticipated costs of expansion, is permissible where expansion is reasonably required, *if use of the money collected is limited to meeting the costs of expansion.* Users "who benefit expecially [sic],

not from the maintenance of the system, but by the extension of the system ... should bear the cost of that extension." *Hartman v. Aurora Sanitary District*, [23 Ill.2d 109, 177 N.E.2d 214, 218 (Ill.1961)]. On the other hand, it is not "just and equitable" for a municipally owned utility to impose the entire burden of capital expenditures, including replacement of existing plant, on persons connecting to a water and sewer system after an arbitrarily chosen time certain.

The cost of new facilities should be borne by new users to the extent new use requires new facilities, but only to that extent. When new facilities must be built in any event, looking only to new users for necessary capital gives old users a windfall at the expense of new users.

Id. at 320–21 (footnote omitted).

Thus, the impact fee in *Contractors and Builders Association v. City of Dunedin* was a valid user fee because it involved a voluntary choice to connect into an existing instrumentality of the municipality. The Port Orange fee, unlike Dunedin's impact fee, is a mandatory charge imposed upon those whose only choice is owning developed property within the boundaries of the municipality.

The circuit court cites to storm-water utility fees as being analogous to the transportation utility fee. However, storm-water utility fees are expressly authorized by section 403.031, Florida Statutes (1993). Similarly, various municipal public works and charges for their use are authorized by chapter 180, Florida Statutes (1993). However, the City's transportation utility fee is not authorized by chapter 180, Florida Statutes.

What the City's transportation utility fee does is convert the roads and the municipality into a toll road system, with only owners of developed property in the city required to pay the tolls. We find no statutory or constitutional authority for such tolls by a municipality.

Finally we recognize the revenue pressures upon the municipalities and all levels of government in Florida. We understand that this is a creative effort in response to the need for revenue. However, in Florida's Constitution, the voters have placed a limit on ad valorem millage available to municipalities, art. VII, § 9, Fla. Const.; made homesteads exempt from taxation up to minimum limits, art. VII, § 9, Fla. Const.; and exempted from levy those homesteads specifically delineated in article X, section 4 of the Florida Constitution. These constitutional provisions cannot be circumvented by such creativity.

The issuance by the City of transportation utility revenue bonds in an aggregate principal amount not to exceed $500,000, pursuant to Ordinance No. 1992-28, is not authorized and is hereby invalidated. The circuit court's judgment is reversed.

It is so ordered.

GRIMES, C.J., and OVERTON, SHAW, KOGAN, HARDING and ANSTEAD, JJ., concur.

Commentary and Questions

The Court identifies a prime differentiating feature of user fees: they are paid by choice. The option to pay a user fee entitles to person paying to a particular benefit not shared by everyone else:

> User fees are charges based upon the proprietary right of the governing body permitting the use of the instrumentality involved. Such fees share common traits that distinguish them from taxes: they are charged in exchange for a particular governmental service which benefits the party paying the fee in a manner not shared by other members of society.

A similar definition appears in the U.S. Supreme Court case cited by this Court:

> A fee, however, is incident to a voluntary act, e.g., a request that a public agency permit an applicant to practice law or medicine or construct a house or run a broadcast station. The public agency performing those services normally may exact a fee for a grant which, presumably, bestows a benefit on the applicant, not shared by other members of society.

Nat'l Cable Television Ass'n, Inc. v. United States, 415 U.S. 336, 340–41 (1974).

The Court makes a distinction between traditional governmental powers, identified as including a road system, with governmental-proprietary functions that offer non-essential benefits for which the government can demand a user fee, like admission to a public auditorium event. Is the distinction between governmental and proprietary functions of a municipality either necessary or useful to this case? Or is the real concern compulsion, that property owners abutting a local road must pay the fee?

The Court writes: "What the City's transportation utility fee does is convert the roads and the municipality into a toll road system, with only owners of developed property in the city required to pay the tolls. We find no statutory or constitutional authority for such tolls by a municipality." What if the city chose to build a toll road, or even an express lane on an existing road, accessed only by drivers using the road? Is the on-ramp access payment a tax or permissible user fee?

The Court compares the *Port Orange* fee to an impact fee and states loosely that "the impact fee in *Contractors and Builders Association v. City of Dunedin* was a valid user fee because it involved a voluntary choice to connect into an existing instrumentality of the municipality." While arguably a person could decline to connect to a water and sewer system, bothersome points on the allocation of charges like *City of Dunedin* may have influenced the decision. Private subdivisions encompassing many homes and road trips pay no charge, undeveloped land pays no charges, and charges from property fronting the local road can be spent anywhere in the system. How do these allocations compare to those in *City of Dunedin*?

Finally, the Court states a rule of construction that appears in later cases: "It is our view that the power of a municipality to tax should not be broadened by semantics which would be the effect of labeling what the City is here collecting a fee rather than a tax."

Collier County v. State

733 So. 2d 1012 (Fla. 1999)

PARIENTE, J.

We have on appeal the final judgment of the trial court refusing to validate revenue certificates authorized by county ordinance. We have jurisdiction....

Collier County filed a complaint for validation of revenue certificates, which the County intended to issue pursuant to Ordinance 98-25, entitled "Interim Governmental Services Fee Ordinance" (ordinance). Because the revenue certificates were to be repaid from the collection of a fee authorized by the ordinance, the trial court's decision whether to validate the revenue certificates focused on the validity of the fee.

After a hearing, the trial court denied the complaint for validation, concluding that the fee was actually an unauthorized tax. We affirm the final judgment of the trial court for two reasons. First, we agree that the "Interim Governmental Services Fee" is not a valid special assessment or fee, but an impermissible tax. Second, we conclude that the ordinance conflicts with the ad valorem taxation scheme enacted by the Legislature.

An overview of the extent of the local government's authority to levy taxes is essential to a proper understanding of the issues in this case and to provide the backdrop for the reasons the County passed the ordinance. The power of state and local governments to levy taxes is governed by the constitution. Article VII, section 1(a), Florida Constitution, provides that:

> No tax shall be levied except in pursuance of law. No state ad valorem taxes shall be levied upon real estate or tangible personal property. All other forms of taxation shall be preempted to the state except as provided by general law.

Article VII, section 9(a) further provides that:

> Counties, school districts, and municipalities shall, and special districts may, be authorized by law to levy ad valorem taxes and may be authorized by general law to levy other taxes, for their respective purposes, except ad valorem taxes on intangible personal property and taxes prohibited by the constitution.

Thus, the constitution *mandates* that the state pass general laws authorizing local governments to levy ad valorem taxes on real estate and tangible personal property, subject to the millage rate limitations of article VII, section 9(b). All other forms of taxation are preempted to the state, unless authorized by general law. The constitution further *allows* the Legislature to authorize counties to levy other taxes. Therefore, local governments have no other authority to levy taxes, other than ad valorem taxes, except as provided by general law. The County does, however, possess authority to impose special assessments and user fees. *See generally* art. VIII, § 1(f), Fla. Const.; § 125.01(1)(r), Fla. Stat. (1997)....

The County does not contend that the additional revenue it seeks to collect pursuant to its ordinance is specifically authorized by general law. Accordingly, if the "Interim Governmental Services Fee" constitutes a tax, rather than a special assessment or a valid fee, the assessment is unconstitutional.

The County passed the ordinance in question because it contends that the general law governing ad valorem taxation creates a "windfall" for certain property owners. Chapter 192, Florida Statutes (1997), entitled "Taxation: General Provisions," implements, in part, the mandate of article VII, section 9(a) that the Legislature authorize counties to levy ad valorem taxes. Chapter 192 includes provisions requiring all property to be assessed, except inventories, *see* section 192.011, and, as pertinent here, provisions regarding the date that "[a]ll property shall be assessed according to its just value." § 192.042.

Section 192.042(1) provides that real property is to be assessed on January 1 of each year and that "[i]mprovements or portions not substantially completed on January 1 *shall have no value placed thereon*." (Emphasis supplied.) Therefore, if improvements are not substantially completed by January 1, there will be no tax liability on the value of the improvements until the following fiscal year. Further, section 197.333 provides that all taxes are due and payable on November 1, but those taxes do not become delinquent until April 1 following the year in which they are assessed. As a result of the valuation scheme enacted by the Legislature, there can be a delay in payment of taxes on improvements of up to twenty-seven months after substantial completion.

In addition, the Legislature requires the County's fiscal year to begin on October 1. *See* § 129.04, Fla. Stat. (1997). However, because of the valuation scheme imposed by the Legislature, property improvements substantially completed after October 1 incur no ad valorem taxes on the improved value for the balance of the fiscal year.

The County does not challenge the constitutionality of the statutory valuation scheme, but asserts that the statutory scheme is unfair because the County is required to provide services to the improved property without a corresponding payment of taxes on the improvements for up to twenty-seven months. The County described the situation in its ordinance:

> Immediately upon the substantial completion and availability for lawful occupancy of any improvements to real property ... the County is required to provide full government services to the occupant or user of such property, for the duration of the fiscal year in progress at the time of such completion or acquisition, but the owner of such property is not required to pay ad valorem taxes with respect to such property for that fiscal year.

The purpose of the fee is to provide the equivalent of a partial year assessment of ad valorem taxes on improvements to property substantially completed after January 1 that would not otherwise be subject to ad valorem taxation at its new increased value. However, the County stresses that the assessment is not based on the value of the property, but rather on the increased cost of providing certain "growth-sensitive" services as a result of the improvement.

The County's methodology identified certain government services that the experts maintained are growth sensitive. According to the expert who testified at the hearing, these growth-sensitive County services experience an increase in demand corresponding to the improvement of property. Through a complicated set of calculations, the County arrived at a fee for the improvements to properties substantially completed after January 1 "equivalent to the [pro rata] cost of governmental services otherwise funded by that portion of the County General Fund ... derived from ad valorem taxation." The County's methodology calls for the calculation of the fee to be based on the conversion of a per capita cost for increased services to a per home cost in the case of residential property, and a per employee cost to a per square foot cost in the case of nonresidential uses.

The fee is assessed only for the number of weeks between the time the improvements on the property are "substantially completed," and the next January 1 assessment. The ordinance provides that the fee will be collected by the uniform method for collection of non-ad valorem assessments established by section 197.3632, thus, as a special assessment on the ad valorem tax bill. A credit is given for the taxes that are payable and the value of the homestead exemption.

The government growth-sensitive services funded by the fee are: (1) the Office of the Sheriff; (2) elections; (3) code enforcement; (4) courts and related agencies; (5) animal control; (6) libraries; (7) parks and recreation; (8) public health; (9) medical examiner; (10) public works; and (11) support services. The County admits that these are the exact services funded through the general revenue fund from ad valorem taxes that all property tax payers are required to support.

The trial court explained its reasoning in concluding that the proposed fee to fund the revenue certificates was in fact a tax, which the County is prohibited from imposing:

> The purpose of the [Interim Governmental Services Fee] was to provide the equivalent of a partial year's assessment of ad valorem taxation on property which had been improved or put into service after January 1 of a given year. That improved property would not have been otherwise eligible for ad valorem taxation at its new value until the subsequent calendar year. *As pointed out by the County, this situation created a windfall to certain citizens which was unfair to those taxpayers who did not receive the same advantage.* It is axiomatic that the Government must provide all citizens of the County such general public services as police, courts, libraries, and fire protection. These basic services are provided whether the property is fully inhabited, vacant or under construction. Ad valorem taxpayers who are assessed at full value pay their proportionate share of these services based upon the millage rate established by the County. *Those who are not assessed at full value obviously pay less than their proportionate share.... It was the County's desire to recapture this lost revenue which created the impetus for the Fee.*
>
> ....
>
> ... [However] the Fee in this case is to be used to pay for law enforcement, courts, libraries, Supervisor of Election services, code enforcement, public health and many other general support services. These are the types of ben-

efits the supreme court has clearly stated do not meet the standard for special assessments.

We agree with the trial court's analysis.

THE "INTERIM GOVERNMENTAL SERVICES FEE" IS A NOT A VALID SPECIAL ASSESSMENT

Although the County argues that the "Interim Governmental Services Fee" is a valid special assessment, we find that the "fee" has all the indicia of a tax. In *City of Boca Raton v. State*, 595 So.2d 25 (Fla.1992), we explained the distinction between special assessments and taxes:

> [A] legally imposed special assessment is not a tax. Taxes and special assessments are distinguishable in that, while both are mandatory, there is no requirement that taxes provide any specific benefit to the property; instead, they may be levied throughout the particular taxing unit for the general benefit of residents and property. *On the other hand, special assessments must confer a specific benefit upon the land burdened by the assessment....*
>
> A tax is an enforced burden of contribution imposed by sovereign right for the support of the government, the administration of the law, and to execute the various functions the sovereign is called on to perform. *A special assessment* is like a tax in that it is an enforced contribution from the property owner, it may possess other points of similarity to a tax but it is inherently different and governed by entirely different principles. *It is imposed upon the theory that that portion of the community which is required to bear it receives some special or peculiar benefit in the enhancement of value of the property against which it is imposed as a result of the improvement made with the proceeds of the special assessment.* It is limited to the property benefitted, is not governed by uniformity and may be determined legislatively or judicially.

Id. at 29 (quoting *Klemm v. Davenport*, 100 Fla. 627, 631–32, 129 So. 904, 907–08 (1930)) (emphasis supplied). In *City of Boca Raton*, this Court found that an assessment to be levied against downtown property owners to revitalize the downtown area was a valid assessment under these criteria. 595 So.2d at 31....

In *Lake County v. Water Oak Management Corp.*, 695 So.2d 667 (Fla.1997), we recited the two-pronged test an assessment must satisfy in order to be considered a valid special assessment, rather than a tax. The two prongs are: (1) the property burdened by the assessment must derive a "special benefit" from the service provided by the assessment; and (2) the assessment for the services must be properly apportioned. *Id.* at 668 (citing *City of Boca Raton*, 595 So.2d at 30).

The assessment in this case fails because it does not satisfy the first prong of the test. Contrary to the County's contention, the first prong of the test is not satisfied by establishing that the assessment is rationally related to an increased demand for county services. If that were the test, the distinction between taxes and special assessments would be forever obliterated.

We explained in *Water Oak Management* that the first prong requires that the services funded by the special assessment provide a "direct, special benefit" to the real property burdened. 695 So.2d at 670. A majority of this Court concluded that the fire services funded by the assessment in *Water Oak Management* met this requirement by providing for lower insurance premiums and enhancing the value of property. *Id.* at 669. In rejecting the criticism that our decision in *Water Oak Management* would open the flood-gates for municipalities and counties to impose improper taxes labeled as special assessments, we made clear that

> *services such as general law enforcement activities, the provision of courts, and indigent health care are,* like fire protection services, *functions required for an organized society.* However, unlike fire protection services, those services provide no direct, special benefit to real property. *Thus, such services cannot be the subject of a special assessment.*

Id. at 670 (citation omitted) (emphasis supplied).

The County concedes that the services funded by the assessment in this case are the same general police-power services the County provides to all county residents for their general benefit, funded from ad valorem taxes, including: sheriff services; libraries; parks; election services; public health services; and public works. Thus, the fee in this case has the indicia of a tax because it is proposed to support many of the general sovereign functions contemplated within the definition of a tax. *See City of Port Orange,* 650 So.2d at 3.

[We] reject the County's argument that the time period after January 1, during which the taxpayer incurs no increased ad valorem tax liability on the improved property, constitutes a "special benefit," satisfying the first prong of the special assessment analysis. A special benefit to the property, as set forth in this Court's case law, does not occur because the property is not subject to taxation for a period of time as a result of an explicit legislative scheme. We reject the County's suggestion that simply because a lien for unpaid taxes attaches to the property, the benefit inures to the property, as opposed to the taxpayer. While the delay certainly may benefit the taxpayer, it is only that—a benefit to the taxpayer, and not the property.

THE "INTERIM GOVERNMENTAL SERVICES FEE" IS NOT A VALID USER OR IMPACT FEE

The County's ordinance includes a "savings clause" providing for the collection of the same amount of money as a fee upon the issuance of the certificate of occupancy, if the uniform method of collection is declared invalid. However, a change in the method of collection will not convert a prohibited tax into a valid fee. As we stated in *City of Port Orange,* the power "to tax should not be broadened by semantics which would be the effect of labeling what the City is here [attempting to collect] a fee rather than a tax." 650 So.2d at 3.

[U]ser fees are similar to special assessments, in that the fee must result in a benefit not shared by persons not required to pay the fee.

Similarly, the fee cannot be authorized as a valid impact fee. *See St. Johns County v. Northeast Florida Builders Ass'n*, 583 So.2d 635 (Fla.1991). In *St. Johns*, the County enacted an ordinance requiring that no new building permits could be issued except upon payment of an impact fee. *See id.* at 636. The collected fees were to be placed in a trust fund to be spent to "acquire, construct, expand and equip" educational sites and facilities "necessitated by new development." *Id.* at 637.

We observed that impact fees had become an accepted method of paying for "*public improvements*" to serve new growth. *Id.* at 638 (emphasis supplied). We found the fee to be invalid because it was imposed only on those *outside* a municipality, with limited exceptions. *See id.* at 639. Those residing in a municipality were not required to pay the fee. However, there was nothing in the ordinance restricting the use of the funds to build schools that would *only* benefit those outside municipalities, who were the ones paying the fee. *See St. Johns County*, 583 So.2d at 639. Thus, like the invalid fee in *City of Port Orange*, the fee in *St. Johns County* was invalid because it did not provide a unique benefit to those paying the fee. *See also Contractors & Builders Ass'n v. City of Dunedin*, 329 So.2d 314, 320 (Fla.1976) ("Users who benefit *especially* ... by the extension of [sewer] system ... should bear the cost of that extension.") (ellipses in original).

[T]he services to be funded by the "Interim Government Services Fee" provide no direct benefit to the property. Those paying the fee are not benefitted by the services provided in a manner not shared by those *not* paying the fee. Instead, the services to be funded by the fee are the same general police-power services provided to all County residents. Moreover, the fee would not provide the source for any capital improvements to the County's existing facilities, but instead would defray the operating costs for the County to exercise its sovereign functions. Just as the fee fails to meet the requirements of a special assessment, so does it fail to qualify as a valid fee.

THE ORDINANCE CONFLICTS WITH THE LEGISLATURE'S AD VALOREM TAXATION SCHEME

The County has been candid in admitting that the purpose of the ordinance is to recoup the losses in ad valorem taxation caused by the legislative scheme for valuing property for ad valorem tax purposes. In fact, the County specifically intends the ordinance to substitute for the legislatively prohibited partial year assessment. However, as explained previously, the County has no inherent power to tax, but obtains that authority only from the constitution and general law. *See Whitney v. Hillsborough County*, 99 Fla. 628, 643, 127 So. 486, 492 (1930). Thus, special acts or local ordinances that impose taxes that are unauthorized by general law are unconstitutional. *See Alachua County v. Adams*, 702 So.2d 1253, 1255 (Fla.1997).

The constitution requires the Legislature to enact the general law regarding the collection of ad valorem taxes, and the Legislature has established a *specific* statutory scheme for the timing of the valuation and assessment. Section 192.042(1) makes clear that partial year assessments are not authorized for improvements to real property substantially completed after January 1, which "shall have no value placed thereon." There is no ambiguity in the statute. It appears that any benefit to taxpayers was specifically contemplated by the legislative scheme. Therefore, the ordinance, which attempts to rectify what the County terms a "glitch" in the present general statutory law, conflicts with the method and timing for valuation of property for ad valorem purposes established by the Legislature by general statutory law.

If there is a windfall created by the current statutory scheme, as the County claims, the County's redress lies with the Legislature. While we do not know why the Legislature has declined to act, as observed by the trial court in this case: "We clearly have able and competent legislators who are obligated to do the right thing."

To achieve the relief sought, the counties must persuade the Legislature to provide the cure, not the courts. Accordingly, the trial court's decision is hereby affirmed.

It is so ordered.

HARDING, C.J., and SHAW, WELLS, ANSTEAD, LEWIS and QUINCE, JJ., concur.

Commentary and Questions

This opinion provides many of the rules governing fees.[94] It begins with "an overview" that encapsulates the constitutional powers of exacting money: "[T]he constitution *mandates* that the state pass general laws authorizing local governments to levy ad valorem taxes on real estate and tangible personal property, subject to the millage rate limitations of article VII, section 9(b).[95] All other forms of taxation are preempted to the state, unless authorized by general law. The constitution further *allows* the Legislature to authorize counties to levy other taxes. Therefore, local governments have no other authority to levy taxes, other than ad valorem taxes, except as provided by general law. The County does, however, possess authority to impose special assessments and user fees." (Emphasis in original.)

The Court re-emphasized, "the two-pronged test for an assessment must satisfy in order to be considered a valid special assessment, rather than a tax. The two prongs are: (1) the property burdened by the assessment must derive a 'special benefit' from the service provided by the assessment; and (2) the assessment for the services must be properly apportioned."

The Court acknowledged the criticism from an earlier case that the "special benefit" test would "open the flood-gates" on using special assessments, but stated the benefit

---

94. *See generally* Susan Churuti, Chris Roe, Ellie Neiberger, Tyler Egbert & Zach Lombardo, *The Line Between Special Assessments and Ad Valorem Taxes: Morris v. City of Cape Coral*, 45 STETSON L. REV. 471 (2016) (discussing the *Morris* decision).

95. The Court stated: "[T]he constitution *mandates* that the state pass general laws authorizing local governments to levy ad valorem taxes on real estate and tangible personal property, subject to the millage rate limitations of article VII, section 9(b)." The 1966 Constitutional Revision Commission did debate and amend the proposed draft of Section 9(a) to change "may be authorized" to "shall be authorized." The amendment proponent stated: "it makes the Legislature more conscious of the fact that it's got to make provisions for the finances of our local governments." Transcript of the 1966 Constitutional Revision Commission, 1094, Dec. 2, 1966. *See also* ROBERT L. NABORS, FLORIDA HOME RULE GREEN BOOK § 11.07 (2d ed. 2014) (opining that the 1968 constitutional revision provided direct grant to counties and municipalities to levy ad valorem taxes).

must be a "direct, special benefit" not provided by normal governmental police-power services. The Court identified government police-power services as "the same general police-power services the County provides to all county residents for their general benefit, funded from ad valorem taxes, including: sheriff services; libraries; parks; election services; public health services; and public works." Of note, the Court specifically rejected the county's assertion that only a rational relationship must exist between imposition of the special assessment fee and its benefit.

The Court likewise found the fee did not qualify as an impact fee, because it did not provide a unique benefit to the property assessed the taxes.

Admittedly the special assessment in this case was an effort to recapture ad valorem taxes lost due to a timing difference between receipt of services and payment of ad valorem taxes for the services. The Court directed the county to change the law: "If there is a windfall created by the current statutory scheme, as the County claims, the County's redress lies with the Legislature. While we do not know why the Legislature has declined to act, as observed by the trial court in this case: 'We clearly have able and competent legislators who are obligated to do the right thing.' " How else might the county overcome the timing? Must the county provide the accelerated services and existing taxpayers pay the deficit?

In the following case, *Morris v. City of Cape Coral*, the Court returned to how direct and special the benefit conferred by a special assessment must be. Is this a retreat from *Collier County*?

Morris v. City of Cape Coral
163 So. 3d 1174 (Fla. 2015)

PERRY, J.

This case arises from a final judgment validating the City of Cape Coral's special assessment to provide fire protection services. We have jurisdiction.... The City of Cape Coral ("City" or "Cape Coral") passed an ordinance levying a special assessment against all real property in the city, both developed and undeveloped. The assessment has two tiers—one for all property and a second that applies only to developed property. Scott Morris and other property owners (collectively referred to as either "Morris" or "Property Owners") appeal the validation, arguing that the two-tier methodology is arbitrary [and] that the assessment violates existing law.... Because we find that Cape Coral properly exercised its authority to issue a special assessment to fund fire protection services and that the assessment does not violate existing law, we affirm the order of validation.

FACTS

In April 2013, Cape Coral authorized its city manager to hire Burton & Associates ("Burton") to prepare a study relating to a non-ad valorem assessment to fund the City's fire protection services. Burton presented its findings in a report dated June 10, 2013, which the City accepted. The report recommended a two-tier assessment, reasoning that all parcels in the city benefited from fire protection services and that developed property received an added benefit of protection from losses. Burton calculated the costs to maintain the facilities, equipment, and personnel necessary to provide fire protection services on a 24-hour-per-day, 365-days-per-year basis to all parcels in the city (exclusive of Emergency Medical Services costs). These costs represented seventy percent of the total fire protection services cost and were to be evenly distributed among all parcels. The costs for fuel, equipment maintenance, actual response to a fire, and other related operations were associated with protection from loss of structures.

At a June 10, 2013, public meeting, the City read and approved an Assessment Ordinance, which was again read and approved at the July 15, 2013, meeting. The City also passed a Note Ordinance at the same meeting. Thereafter, the Initial Assessment Resolution was adopted on July 29, 2013, and the Final Assessment Resolution was adopted on August 26, 2013. On August 28, 2013, the City filed its complaint to validate the debt under Chapter 75, Florida Statutes. The trial court issued an Order to Show Cause on September 11, 2013, which provided the time and date of the hearing. The Order to Show Cause was published in the local newspaper twenty days prior to the hearing and again the following week.

The trial court held the Show Cause hearing on October 7, 2013. Eight property owners appeared in opposition to the special assessment. The hearing was initially scheduled to last an hour, with each party given three minutes to present its argument. The trial court realized this was insufficient time and extended the hearing for two additional days.

On the second day, October 8, 2013, the Property Owners moved for a continuance in order to seek discovery. The trial court denied the motion; instead, the court permitted all parties to submit post-hearing legal memoranda which were due within twenty days of the Show Cause hearing. On the day the memoranda were due, Talan Corporation, which did not appear at the Show Cause hearing, filed a Motion to Intervene and an objection to the validation.

The trial court held a hearing on Talan's motion on November 27, 2013, but did not reopen evidence. Talan argued that the City had miscalculated some parcels, and the City attempted to demonstrate that it had corrected the error. Ultimately, the trial court denied Talan's motion.

On December 11, 2013, the trial court entered its final judgment of validation. The judgment found, in pertinent part:

> (1) that the City of Cape Coral has the legal authority to issue the bond and assess properties within its jurisdiction as requested, (2) that the intended purpose of the bond is legal, to wit, it shall provide a continuation or provision of fire safety related service for all affected parcels, and (3) that the issuance of the bond and its related process comply with all essential elements and requirements of law, including reasonable apportionment.

Morris, joined by three other property owners, filed a Notice of Appeal with this Court on February 18, 2014.

STANDARD OF REVIEW

This Court's scope of review is limited to: (1) whether the municipality has the authority to issue the assessment; (2) whether the purpose of the assessment is legal; and (3) whether the assessment complies with the requirements of the law. *See City of Winter Springs v. State*, 776 So.2d 255, 257 (Fla.2001) (citations omitted).

"[A] valid special assessment must meet two requirements: (1) the property assessed must derive a special benefit from the service provided; and (2) the assessment must be fairly and reasonably apportioned according to the benefits received." *Sarasota Cnty. v. Sarasota Church of Christ*, 667 So.2d 180, 183 (Fla.1995) (citing *City of Boca Raton v. State*, 595 So.2d 25, 30 (Fla.1992)). "These two prongs both constitute questions of fact for a legislative body rather than the judiciary." *Id.* at 183. The standard to be applied to both prongs is that the legislative findings should be upheld unless the determination is arbitrary. *Id.* at 184....

ANALYSIS

The Property Owners raise several issues, which at their core attack the correctness of the trial court's determination that the City's special assessment is valid. In response, the City argues that it passed the special assessment under its home rule authority and not chapter 170 of the Florida Statutes. Further, the City argues that the Property Owners have waived any right to challenge the trial court's determination that the City properly exercised its authority by failing to raise it as a discrete issue.

The authority to issue special assessments under a municipality's home rule powers was addressed by this Court in *Boca Raton*. In *Boca Raton*, after providing a history of home rule authority, we determined that

> a municipality may now exercise any governmental, corporate, or proprietary power for a municipal purpose except when expressly prohibited by law, and a municipality may legislate on any subject matter on which the legislature may act [with exceptions].... Therefore, it would appear that the City of Boca Raton can levy its special assessment unless it is expressly prohibited....

Boca Raton, 595 So.2d at 28. Then, addressing whether chapter 170 expressly prohibited a municipality from exercising its home rule authority to issue a special assessment, we determined, "it is evident that chapter 170 is not the only method by which municipalities may levy a special assessment." *Id.* at 29. Accordingly, irrespective of whether the Property Owners have waived any right to raise the issue, there is no question that the City had the legal authority to levy the special assessment.

Further, we have previously upheld the validity of special assessments to fund fire protection services. *See, e.g., Lake Cnty. v. Water Oak Mgmt. Corp.*, 695 So.2d 667 (Fla.1997)....

The Property Owners allege that the benefit from the fire protection services is a general one, and not a specific benefit. To support their argument, the Property Owners rely on our decision in *St. Lucie County—Fort Pierce Fire Prevention & Control District v. Higgs*, 141 So.2d 744 (Fla.1962), for their contention that assessments levied on property for maintenance and operation of fire prevention services constitutes a tax. *See Higgs*, 141 So.2d at 746. In *Higgs*, this Court agreed with the circuit court's finding that a particular assessment to fund fire services was invalid because "no parcel of land was *specially* or peculiarly benefited in proportion to its value...." *Id.*

However, in 1997, we held that solid waste disposal and fire protection services funded by a special assessment did provide a special benefit. *Water Oak Mgmt.*, 695 So.2d at 668. Therein, the Fifth District Court of Appeal had found Lake County's assessment invalid under this Court's decision in *Higgs* because everyone in the county had access to fire protection services and so was not a special benefit. We found that the Fifth District had misconstrued our decision in *Higgs*, stating:

> In evaluating whether a special benefit is conferred to property by the services for which the assessment is imposed, the test is not whether the services confer a "unique" benefit or are different in type or degree from the benefit provided to the community as a whole; rather, the test is whether there is a "logical relationship" between the services provided and the benefit to real property.

Water Oak Mgmt., 695 So.2d at 669 (citing *Whisnant v. Stringfellow*, 50 So.2d 885 (Fla.1951) (footnote omitted); *Crowder v. Phillips*, 146 Fla. 440, 1 So.2d 629 (1941)). Noting our decision in *Fire District No. 1* [*v. Jenkins*, 221 So. 2d 740 (Fla. 1969)], we found that "fire protection services do, at a minimum, specially benefit real property by providing for lower insurance premiums and enhancing the value of the property. Thus, there is a 'logical relationship' between the services provided and the benefit to real property." *Water Oak Mgmt.*, 695 So.2d at 669. We then clarified that our decision in *Higgs* turned not on the benefit prong, but on the apportionment prong. *Id.* at 670.

In this case, Cape Coral has established that the assessed property receives a special benefit. In the Assessment Ordinance, the City made the following statement:

> **Legislative Determinations of Special Benefit.** It is hereby ascertained and declared that the Fire Protection services, facilities, and programs provide a special benefit to property because Fire Protection services possess a logical relationship to the use and enjoyment of property by: (1) protecting the value and integrity of the improvements, structures, and unimproved land through the provision of available Fire Protection services; (2) protecting the life and safety of intended occupants in the use and enjoyment of property; (3) lowering the cost of fire insurance by the presence of a professional and comprehensive Fire Protection program within the City and limiting the potential financial liability for uninsured or underinsured properties; and (4) containing and extinguishing the spread of fire incidents occurring on property, including but not limited to unimproved property, with the potential to spread and endanger the structures and occupants of property.

Likewise, the experts retained by Cape Coral determined that all parcels in the City received a special benefit from the City's fire protection services and facilities.... These findings are similar to the reasons we accepted in *Water Oak Mgmt. Water Oak Mgmt.*, 695 So.2d at 669 ("[F]ire protection services do, at a minimum, specially benefit real property by providing for lower insurance premiums and enhancing the value of the property."). Thus, the facts of the present case lie squarely within the facts of *Water Oak Mgmt.* Only the methodology differs.

The Property Owners question the validity of Tier 1 and Tier 2 of the assessment. In short, the Property Owners argue that the assessment is not properly apportioned. We have instructed:

> To be legal, special assessments must be directly proportionate to the benefits to the property upon which they are levied and this may not be inferred from a situation where all property in a district is assessed for the benefit of the whole on the theory that individual parcels are peculiarly benefited in the ratio that the assessed value of each bears to the total value of all property in the district.

Higgs, 141 So.2d at 746.... And, the proportional benefits cannot be calculated by the ratio of the value of the assessed property against the value of all property. *See Water Oak Mgmt.*, 695 So.2d at 670 (explaining that the decision in *Higgs* turned on whether the land was benefitted in proportion to its value, stating: "the assessment in that case was actually a tax because it had been wrongfully apportioned based on the assessed value of the properties rather than on the special benefits provided to the properties."). However, this Court has also held that "[t]he mere fact that some property is assessed on an area basis, and other property is assessed at a flat rate basis, does not in itself establish the invalidity of the special assessment." *S. Trail Fire Control Dist.* [*v. State*], 273 So. 2d at 384 [(Fla. 1973)].

To this end, the Property Owners allege that Tier 1 of the assessment is invalid because it equally assesses all property and therefore is not proportional. The Property Owners further argue that Tier 2 of the assessment, being based on the value of any structures and improvements on a parcel, amounts to nothing more than a tax. In other words, the Property Owners allege that the City's chosen methodology is arbitrary and does not properly apportion the costs. We find that the City's methodology is not arbitrary. *See Sarasota Church of Christ*, 667 So.2d at 184....

In the present case, the City contracted for a study to determine the best method to apportion the costs of fire services. By adopting the approach recommended in the study, the City has attempted to apportion the costs based on both the general availability of fire protection services to everyone (Tier 1) and the additional benefit of improved property owners of protecting structures from damage (Tier 2). We have not previously addressed a bifurcated approach to fire service assessments. However, this sort of approach closely resembles the approach we approved in *Sarasota Church of Christ*.

In *Sarasota Church of Christ*, we considered the validity of special assessments against developed property for stormwater management services. There, undeveloped property was not assessed at all, residential property was assessed at a flat rate per number of individual dwelling units on the property, and non-residential property was assessed based on a formula. Specifically, "[t]his method for apportionment focuse[d] on the projected stormwater discharge from developed parcels based on the amount of 'horizontal impervious area' assumed for each parcel and divide[d] the contributions based on varying property usage." This Court held that "this method of apportioning the costs of the stormwater services is not arbitrary and bears a reasonable relationship to the benefits received by the individual developed properties...." *Sarasota Church of Christ*, 667 So.2d at 186.

... [L]ike that of Sarasota County, the City's [Tier 2] methodology reasonably relates to the additional benefits received by improved properties. The formula contemplates that each improved parcel benefits differently because the cost to replace the respective structure differs. The use of the property appraiser's structure value is reasonable because the property appraiser is statutorily required to use a replacement cost to determine this value. *See* § 193.011(5), Fla. Stat. (2014). We find that this is a reasonable approach to apportionment and not arbitrary.

* * *

The methodology at issue here was found by the trial court to be "valid, non-arbitrary and considered established insofar as the [opposing parties] failed to present any competent, persuasive evidence to dispute or call into reasonable question [the court's] findings and determinations." A review of the record supports the trial court's determination.

* * *

CONCLUSION

For the foregoing reasons, we affirm the final judgment of validation.

It is so ordered.

Commentary and Questions

The Court begins this decision by confirming the home rule authority to impose a special assessment. The Court reiterates that the property assessed must derive a special benefit and the assessment must be fairly apportioned, that is, "the assessment cannot be in excess of the proportional benefits."

Both *Collier County* and this case cite to the earlier decision *Lake County. v. Water Oak Management. Corp.*, 695 So. 2d 667 (Fla.1997), as authority. The Court here repeats from *Lake County* that:

> In evaluating whether a special benefit is conferred to property by the services for which the assessment is imposed, the test is not whether the services confer a "unique" benefit or are different in type or degree from the benefit provided to the community as a whole; rather, the test is whether there is a "logical relationship" between the services provided and the benefit to real property.

How does the "logical relationship" test compare to the rejected "rational relationship" test in the *Collier County* decision?

The Court stresses past cases involving firefighting special districts that were valid special assessment areas. Are firefighting special districts *sui generis*? Do such districts benefit from clear and quantifiable benefits, such as reduced insurance premiums and response times to disasters, unlike other special districts? In *Collier County*, the Court noted that a special assessment for general police-power services such as law enforcement is an indicia that the fee is a disguised tax. Is firefighting a boutique-type, proprietary service selectively offered by governments and therefore unlike law enforcement? Is the *Collier County* distinction between services offered through a police-power classification and other services a useful difference?

Lastly, the Court approves the rule from *Sarasota Church of Christ, Inc.* that announced legislative findings are presumptively persuasive unless arbitrary. How difficult is the announced legislative finding to overcome, especially in this case, when drafted by experts and adopted by a governing board?

A broad array of funding options is available to local governments. Three funding options are Lease Financing, Payment-in-Lieu-of-Taxes (PILOT) agreements, and Tax Increment Financing (TIF).

Two methods evolved to avoid the public referendum requirements for local bonds. Tax-increment financing is discussed later in this chapter in the *Strand* case. The next case involves a second method, lease financing. As noted in a 2012 law review article: "[L]ease financings exploit an important distinction that the Florida Supreme Court drew between using ad valorem-tax revenues to pay debt service and pledging ad valorem-tax power to support debt obligations."[96] Lease financing proceeds as follows:

> In a typical school-district, lease-financing transaction, the school district first leases land to a related not-for-profit financing corporation through one or more ground leases. The land-owning school district generally creates or controls the financing corporation for the purpose of facilitating the overall lease-financing transaction. Once the financing corporation has acquired an interest in the land through the ground lease, it arranges the construction of the desired school facilities on the land and borrows funds for this purpose, often in the public-finance market. The financing corporation leases the newly-constructed school's facilities back to the school district and uses the lease revenues to repay the money borrowed for the school facilities' construction. To help secure the repayment of the borrowed funds, the financing corporation assigns its interest in the ground lease and the facilities lease to a corporate trustee; the corporation's interest includes, importantly, its rights to receive the rental revenues as well as its rights to exercise eviction remedies. The trustee collects the rent revenues from the school district and uses them to repay the lenders who provided financing for the construction of the school facilities. The trustee acts on behalf of the lender, the creditors, or both, in

---

96. E. Lamar Taylor, *Florida's School-District Lease Financing: Cross Collateralization, Path Dependency, and Their Implications*, 41 STETSON L. REV. 349, 361 (2012).

SALE LEASEBACK

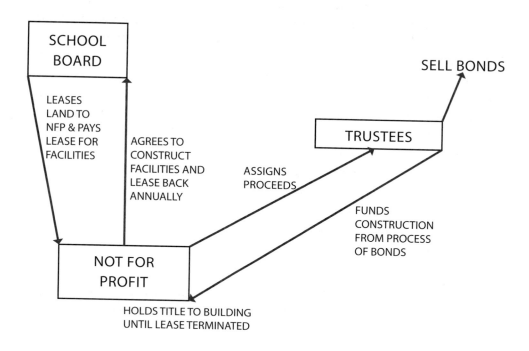

collecting rental payments and transmitting them to the creditors in case the school district defaults in paying rent.[97]

State v. School Board of Sarasota County

561 So. 2d 549 (Fla. 1990)

CORRECTED OPINION

PER CURIAM.

We review three final judgments validating certain obligations pursuant to chapter 75, Florida Statutes (1989). We have jurisdiction.... We affirm the final judgments.

Pursuant to resolutions, the School Boards of Sarasota, Collier and Orange Counties (boards) entered into agreements supporting the bonds and certificates of participation (bonds) under review. These agreements provide for the lease of public land owned by the boards to not-for-profit entities (by way of ground leases), the construction or improvement of public educational facilities upon the leased lands and the annual leaseback of the facilities to the respective school boards (by way of facilities leases), and the conveyance of the lease rights of the not-for-profit entities to trustees (by way

97. *Id.* at 354–56 (footnotes omitted).

of trust agreements). The trustees are to market the bonds and disburse funds to finance construction of the facilities. Title to the public lands remains in the respective school boards. Title to the facilities constructed with the proceeds of the bonds passes to the respective school boards at the end of the term of the ground lease. In the cases of Sarasota County and Collier County, the ground-lease term is up to thirty years. In the case of Orange County, the ground-lease term is fifteen years.

Money from several sources, including ad valorem taxation, will be used to make the annual facilities' lease payments.[98] If, in any year, a board does not appropriate money to pay the lease, the board's obligations terminate without penalty and it cannot be compelled to make payments.[99] The board then has two options. It may purchase the facilities and terminate the ground lease. Alternatively, it may surrender possession of the facilities and lands for the remainder of the ground-lease term and is free to substitute other facilities for those surrendered. The trustee may relet the facilities for the remainder of the leases' term or sell its interest in the leases to generate revenue to pay bondholders. As an additional precaution, insurance has been purchased for the benefit of bondholders to cover the risk of insufficient revenue. Amounts received in excess of that owed to bondholders must be paid to the board as ground rent.

We are presented with two basic issues: whether the agreements at issue here may be validated pursuant to chapter 75, Florida Statutes (1989), and, if so, whether article VII, section 12, Florida Constitution (1968), requires referendum approval for the bonds' validation.

Section 75.02 provides that a political subdivision of the state may determine its authority to incur bonded debt by filing a complaint in circuit court. In *State v. City of Daytona Beach,* 431 So.2d 981 (Fla.1983), we held that the city's complaint to validate an "interlocal agreement"[100] pursuant to chapter 75 was proper because the agreement was evidence of the city's indebtedness to pay designated revenues to assist in servicing bonds which the interlocal agreement supported. In the instant cases, likewise, the supporting agreements—the facilities and ground leases and the trust agreements—are evidence of the boards' indebtedness. They constitute obligations

---

98. [FN 3.] The boards have identified four revenue sources for lease payments: (1) monies paid to them from Florida's Educational Finance Program; (2) monies derived from the Public Education Capital Outlay and Debt Service Trust Fund; (3) monies received from the local government infrastructure sales surtax levied pursuant to section 212.055(2)(1989), Florida Statutes (1989); and (4) to the extent not paid from the foregoing sources, up to one-half of the boards' *receipts from the levy of up to two mills of capital outlay millage,* authorized by section 236.25(2), Florida Statutes (1989), to pay lease-purchase obligations. The first three sources are non-ad valorem sources; the fourth is from ad valorem taxes.

99. [FN 4.] For a discussion of the "nonappropriation mechanism" as a device to permit financing of essential governmental functions consistent with constitutional debt limitations, see Note, *State and Municipal Lease-Purchase Agreements: A Reassessment,* 7 Harv.J.L. & Pub.Pol'y 521 (1984) (authored by Reuven Mark Bisk).

100. [FN 6.] The interlocal agreement provided that the city guaranteed to the county certain payments each fiscal year in order to support county revenue bonds. The bonds that the agreement supported had been validated in a separate earlier proceeding.

of the boards, so long as funds are appropriated, to pay the designated revenues to the trustees to assist in servicing the bonds. *Id.* at 982.

Appellant argues that the benefits of chapter 75 validation proceedings are conferred on political subdivisions of the state, not private parties. The state asserts that it is the not-for-profit entities and trustees, rather than the school boards, who are employing chapter 75 procedures to impress the court's imprimatur upon this type of "creative" bond financing. We rejected this argument in *State v. Brevard County,* 539 So.2d 461 (Fla.1989). We accordingly find that the boards are proper plaintiffs within the meaning of section 75.02.

Regarding the bonds' validity, the issue presented is whether a referendum is required by article VII, section 12 of the Florida Constitution (1968). We conclude that because these obligations are not supported by the pledge of ad valorem taxation, they are not "payable from ad valorem taxation" within the meaning of article VII, section 12, and referendum approval is not required.

In *State v. Miami Beach Redevelopment Agency,* 392 So.2d 875 (Fla.1980), we interpreted the words "payable from ad valorem taxation" in article VII, section 12 and held that a referendum is not required when there is no direct pledge of the ad valorem taxing power. We noted that although contributions may come from ad valorem tax revenues: "What is critical to the constitutionality of the bonds is that, after the sale of the bonds, a bondholder would have no right, if [funds] were insufficient to meet the bond obligations … to compel by judicial action the levy of ad valorem taxation.… [T]he governing bodies are not obliged nor can they be compelled to levy any ad valorem taxes in any year." *Id.* at 898–99. The agreements here, as in *Miami Beach,* although supported in part by ad valorem revenues, expressly provide that neither the bondholders nor anyone else can compel use of the ad valorem taxing power to service the bonds.

In *State v. Brevard County,* 539 So.2d 461 (Fla.1989), we interpreted the "maturing more than twelve months after issuance" language of article VII, section 12. The *Brevard* agreements provided traditional lease remedies and preserved the county's right, in adopting its annual budget, to terminate the lease without further obligation. We held that article VII, section 12 was not violated. As in *Brevard,* the agreements here give the boards freedom to decide anew each year, burdened only by lease penalties, whether to appropriate funds for the lease payments.

The state's fall-back position is that if an approving referendum is not constitutionally required, section 230.23(9)(b) 5., Florida Statutes (1989), mandates a referendum in this instance. We disagree. The pertinent statutory section is a general grant of power to school boards with a proviso that if "the rental is to be paid from funds received from ad valorem taxation and the agreement is for a period greater than 12 months, an approving referendum must be held." We view the referendum requirement in this section as no more than a codification of the referendum requirement set forth in the constitution.

The state contends that *County of Volusia v. State,* 417 So.2d 968 (Fla.1982), precludes validation in this instance. We disagree. In *Volusia,* the obligations were supported by the pledge of all legally available unencumbered revenues other than ad valorem taxation, along with a promise to fully maintain the programs and services which generated the non-ad valorem revenue. We held that referendum approval was required because the interrelated promises "in effect constitutes a promise to levy ad valorem taxes." *Id.* at 971. The instant case is not analogous. We have here no interrelated promises which will inevitably lead to an increase in ad valorem taxation.

The state in addition argues that validation is precluded by *Nohrr v. Brevard County Educational Facilities Authority,* 247 So.2d 304 (Fla.1971). In *Nohrr,* we held that a bond-supporting agreement which granted a mortgage with right of foreclosure violated the predecessor to article VII, section 12, absent an approving referendum. The rationale of *Nohrr* does not apply to the instant case. There is no mortgage with right of foreclosure. Here the bondholders are limited to lease remedies and the annual renewal option preserves the boards' full budgetary flexibility.

Appellees, in addition to asking us to validate these bonds, invite us to reinstitute the "essential governmental function" referendum-exception first enunciated in *Tapers v. Pichard,* 124 Fla. 549, 169 So. 39 (1936). We rejected the exception in *State v. County of Dade,* 234 So.2d 651 (Fla.1970), and decline to reinstate it here.

Our approval of these financing arrangements does not constitute an endorsement of the bonds and certificates of indebtedness to be issued. Questions of business policy and judgment are beyond the scope of judicial interference and are the responsibility of the issuing governmental units. *Town of Medley v. State,* 162 So.2d 257 (Fla.1964).

We affirm the judgments of validation.

McDONALD, Justice, dissenting.

Today the Court approves form over substance. The financial schemes employed in these cases are the equivalent to the issuance of bonds and pledging ad valorem taxes to support them. Thus, I totally disagree that the bonds in question can be approved without a referendum from the owners of freeholds as required by article VII, section 12 of the Florida Constitution. I believe it pure sophistry to say that "these obligations are not supported by the pledge of ad valorem taxation." Majority at 552. If ad valorem taxes are not levied and paid each year for the duration of the agreements the school boards default not only all interest acquired under the agreement for the remainder of the agreement, but they also lose the right to use the preowned property for the remainder of the agreement. Never before have we approved a nonreferendum bond where ad valorem taxes have been involved to the extent they are involved in these cases. By approving these financing agreements we have approved a method of nullifying the provisions of article VII, section 12, Florida Constitution.

It is true that in *State v. Miami Beach Redevelopment Agency,* 392 So.2d 875 (Fla.1980), we approved a bond supported in part by ad valorem taxes. I hasten to point out, however, that the extent of that pledge was the *tax increment* created by the development. These bonds, on the other hand, come from existing ad valorem tax sources, and the schools do not increase the tax base. *State v. Miami Beach Redevelopment* stated:

> What is critical to the constitutionality of the bonds is that, after the sale of bonds, a bondholder would have no right, if the redevelopment trust fund were insufficient to meet the bond obligations and the available resources of the county or city were insufficient to allow for the promised contributions, to compel by judicial action the levy of ad valorem taxation.

392 So.2d at 898. That same court in the same opinion, however, also said:

> On the other hand, when a project is financed by the sale of bonds to be repaid with revenues produced by the project supplemented by governmental funds derived from ad valorem taxation, an approving vote of the electorate is required.

> [I]n no instance has this Court upheld the pledge of gross revenue of a facility coupled with a supporting pledge of ad valorem taxes. When gross revenues have been pledged with collateral support for operating the facility, the supporting revenues pledged have always been derived from sources other than ad valorem levies. [internal citation omitted]

Id. at 897–98.

These financing schemes are secured by a pledge of ad valorem taxes, at least on a year-by-year basis. This contrasts with the financing plan approved in *State v. Brevard County*, 539 So.2d 461 (Fla.1989), where ad valorem taxes were not a part of the financing agreement. If certificates are secured by a pledge of ad valorem taxes, they are bonds and must be approved by the voters. *Klein v. City of New Smyrna Beach*, 152 So.2d 466 (Fla.1963).

In practical effect a school board must levy, collect, and pay ad valorem taxes or forfeit its ability to supply a school plant. No school board will do that. When this circumstance exists, the realities of the situation should supersede the technical inability to require the levy of ad valorem taxes. As we did in *Volusia County v. State*, 417 So.2d 968 (Fla.1982), we should require approval of the affected ad valorem taxpayers before these financial arrangements obtain approval from this Court.

OVERTON, J., concurs.

Commentary and Questions

The Court noted the school board has two options if it chooses to end the annual payments: "It may purchase the facilities and terminate the ground lease. Alternatively, it may surrender possession of the facilities and lands for the remainder of the ground-lease term and is free to substitute other facilities for those surrendered."

The majority declined the school board's request to allow an exception under the 1885 Constitution to referendums: "Appellees, in addition to asking us to validate these bonds, invite us to reinstitute the 'essential governmental function' referendum-exception first enunciated in *Tapers v. Pichard*, 124 Fla. 549, 169 So. 39 (1936). We rejected the exception in *State v. County of Dade*, 234 So.2d 651 (Fla.1970), and decline to reinstate it here." In *County of Dade*, the Court held that the 1968 Constitution changed the requirements for local bonds and now required a referendum: "The present Constitution is clearly more restrictive and expresses the will of the people that financial arrangements of the type formerly upheld in the *Tapers v. Pichard* line of cases be no longer permitted."[101] The Court, therefore, recognized the intent of the 1968 Constitution to impose new referendum requirements. Why has it allowed that requirement to escape enforcement?

The dissent wrote: "I believe it pure sophistry to say that 'these obligations are not supported by the pledge of ad valorem taxation.'" *School Bd. of Sarasota Cnty.*, 561 So. 2d at 554 (McDonald, J., dissenting). The dissent noted the school board will forfeit future interest, a loss not mentioned in the majority opinion unless contained in the phrase "the usual lease penalties." Also, these are not tax increment bonds. "These financing schemes are secured by a pledge of ad valorem taxes, at least on a year-by-year basis." How realistic is the walk-away option? The dissent noted: "In practical effect a school board must levy, collect, and pay ad valorem taxes or forfeit its ability to supply a school plant. No school board will do that."

PILOT agreements normally involve an agreement between a non-profit organization otherwise exempt from ad valorem taxes and a local government. The tax-exempt non-profit agrees to some type of payment to the local government and receives some benefit in return.

The 2017 *City of Largo* decision below involves a PILOT agreement under which a tax-exempt affordable housing development agreed to pay the equivalent amount of ad valorem taxes to the city in return for the city sponsoring tax-exempt bonds to finance the development.

City of Largo v. AHF-Bay Fund, LLC
215 So. 3d 10 (Fla. 2017)

QUINCE, J.

This case is before the Court for review of the decision of the Second District Court of Appeal in *AHF-Bay Fund, LLC v. City of Largo*, 169 So.3d 133 (Fla. 2d DCA 2015). In its decision, the district court ruled upon the following question, which the court certified to be of great public importance:

> DO PILOT AGREEMENTS THAT REQUIRE PAYMENTS EQUALING THE AD VALOREM TAXES THAT WOULD OTHERWISE BE DUE BUT FOR A STATUTORY TAX EXEMPTION VIOLATE SECTION 196.1978, FLORIDA STATUTES (2000), AND ARTICLE VII, § 9(a) OF THE FLORIDA CONSTITUTION?

---

101. *State v. Dade County*, 234 So. 2d 651, 653 (Fla. 1970).

Id. at 138. We have jurisdiction.... For the reasons that follow, we answer the certified question in the negative and quash the decision of the Second District.

FACTS

AHF-Bay Fund, LLC (AHF) appealed a judgment awarding $695,158.23 in damages and prejudgment interest to the City of Largo, Florida (City) for AHF's failure to make payments pursuant to an agreement for payment in lieu of taxes (PILOT agreement) between the City and RHF-Brittany Bay (RHF), AHF's predecessor in interest. *AHF-Bay Fund*, 169 So.3d at 135. Under the agreement, AHF was required to make payments that equaled the ad valorem taxes that would have otherwise been due but for the statutory tax exemption found in section 196.1978, Florida Statutes (2000). *Id.* The facts that prompted the filing of suit are as follows:

In December 2000, RHF acquired the subject property. RHF was a tax exempt 501(c)(3) organization as defined by the Internal Revenue Code. See 26 U.S.C. § 501(c)(3) (2000). RHF planned to develop the property to provide affordable housing for persons with low to moderate income pursuant to chapter 420, Florida Statutes. As set forth in section 196.1978, Florida Statutes (2000), affordable housing projects owned by a 501(c)(3) organization are exempt from ad valorem taxation.

To finance the project, RHF reached an agreement with the City wherein the City would arrange for the issuance of tax-exempt bonds that carried a considerably lower interest rate than RHF could have obtained using traditional bank financing. In exchange for the issuance of the bonds, RHF entered into the PILOT agreement, thereby agreeing to make annual payments to the City "in an amount equal to the portion of ad valorem taxes to which the City would otherwise be entitled to receive for the [p]roperty as if the [p]roject were fully taxable in accordance with standard taxing procedures." The PILOT agreement provided that the amount of the payments would be determined by multiplying the property's assessed value by the millage rate established by the City each year. The PILOT agreement also provided that "the City has and will provide services to [RHF] as a result of [RHF's] status as a tax-exempt entity."

The PILOT agreement specified that it was binding on any subsequent owners of the subject property as long as certain conditions were met, though it made no mention of a covenant running with the land. The PILOT agreement was not recorded in the official public records. However, simultaneously with the execution of the PILOT agreement, the parties executed a memorandum of agreement that was recorded in the public records. The memorandum indicated that the PILOT agreement was available for inspection in the city clerk's office and that it imposed certain covenants running with the land.

RHF made the payments as required by the PILOT agreement for the years 2001 through 2005. AHF, also a nonprofit affordable housing provider, acquired the property in November 2005. AHF has continued to own and operate the property as an affordable housing community since the purchase. However, when the City did not receive the annual payment that was due on December 31, 2006, it contacted AHF. AHF denied knowledge of either the PILOT agreement or the memorandum of agreement, asserting that neither had been shown to be an exception to coverage in its title insurance policy and that neither had been referenced in the special warranty deed by which AHF took title.

Based upon AHF's refusal to make payments under the PILOT agreement, the City filed suit in 2010. The City sought a summary judgment and the trial court granted the motion in part. Ultimately, the trial court entered a final judgment in favor of the City, awarding $695,158.23 in damages and prejudgment interest.

Id. at 134–35 (alterations in original) (footnote omitted). On appeal, the Second District reversed the trial court, finding that the PILOT agreement at issue "violates the public policy of promoting the provision of affordable housing for low to moderate income families and is therefore void." *Id.* at 138. The court reasoned that the PILOT payments are the substantive equivalent of taxes because the payments are equal to the amount of taxes that would be due if the property were not tax-exempt. *Id.*

ANALYSIS

The certified question presents two issues: (1) whether the PILOT agreement violates section 196.1978, Florida Statutes (2000), and (2) whether the PILOT agreement violates article VII, section 9(a) of the Florida Constitution. Each will be addressed in turn. Because the issues before this Court on the certified question involve pure questions of law that arise from undisputed facts, they are reviewed de novo....

* * *

The Second District also invalidated the PILOT agreement on the ground that it violated article VII, section 9(a) of the Florida Constitution. Article VII, section 9(a) of the Florida Constitution provides in relevant part:

> Counties, school districts, and municipalities shall, and special districts may, be authorized by law to levy ad valorem taxes and may be authorized by general law to levy other taxes, for their respective purposes, except ad valorem taxes on intangible personal property and taxes prohibited by this constitution.

Art. VII, § 9(a), Fla. Const. In its decision, the district court concluded that the payments under the PILOT agreement are, in substance, disguised ad valorem taxes, and the City did not have the authority to impose taxes in circumvention of the affordable housing tax exemption. *AHF-Bay Fund*, 169 So.3d at 137. Thus, the court held that the PILOT agreement violated article VII, section 9(a) of the Florida Constitution, which provides that cities may only impose taxes as permitted by law. *Id.*

What constitutes a "tax" has been well established by Florida courts. A tax is an enforced burden imposed by a sovereign right for the support of the government, the administration of law, and the exercise of various functions the sovereign is called on to perform. [citations omitted.] Thus, there are two factors that exist when taxes are imposed: (1) the government acts unilaterally by sovereign right, and (2) the government acts in order to support routine government functions.

Neither of the two factors are present here. First, the City did not act by sovereign right in entering into the agreement with RHF. Local governments operate in several different capacities, including proprietary (i.e., as a party to a contract), and governmental (i.e., by sovereign right). *E.g., Daly v. Stokell*, 63 So.2d 644, 645 (Fla. 1953); *Commercial Carrier Corp. v. Indian River Cty.*, 371 So.2d 1010 (Fla. 1979). Here, the City's decision to accept RHF's offer and enter into the PILOT Agreement was a proprietary one. *See Daly*, 63 So.2d at 645....

The City did not exercise any element of sovereignty by entering into the PILOT Agreement. When a city enters into an express, written contract it waives sovereign immunity. *Pan-Am Tobacco Corp. v. Dep't of Corr.*, 471 So.2d 4 (Fla. 1984).

In its decision, the Second District relied on our decision in *State v. City of Port Orange*, 650 So.2d 1 (Fla. 1994), to conclude that the payments were ad valorem taxes disguised under another name and that the power to tax cannot be broadened by semantics. The issue in *Port Orange* was whether a "user fee" unilaterally imposed on all developed property for improving roads was really a "tax." *Id.* at 3. However, in this case, the City did not unilaterally impose any obligations, and the payments were not used for routine government functions, such as roads. The City and RHF negotiated the method to calculate the consideration for the City's authorization of the tax-exempt bonds. The City performed this non routine service specifically for RHF.

Furthermore, the obligation under the PILOT agreement was not citywide. Instead, the payments were offered to the City by RHF to induce the City to exercise its proprietary capacity to contract with the Capital Trust Agency for the sole benefit of RHF. Respondent argues that the City used the PILOT payments as general revenue. However, Respondent fails to provide any evidence in support of this argument, and instead appears to take issue with the value of the City's service compared to its perceived benefit. Nonetheless, the PILOT agreement was consideration for the City to authorize the tax-exempt bonds. That authorization facilitated the conversion of the property to affordable housing.

Therefore, because the City did not act unilaterally by sovereign right for the purpose of supporting government functions, the payments negotiated by the City and RHF are not taxes and do not implicate article VII, section 9(a). Consequently, the agreement does not violate the Florida Constitution.

CONCLUSION

Because the PILOT agreement does not violate section 196.1978, Florida Statutes (2000), or article VII, section 9(a) of the Florida Constitution, we answer the certified question in the negative and quash the decision of the Second District. We do not address Respondent's argument concerning whether the PILOT agreement at issue is a covenant with the land, as that issue is beyond the scope of the certified question. [citation omitted.]

It is so ordered.

Commentary and Questions

The Second District Court of Appeal held that the PILOT agreement was a disguised ad valorem tax following the precedent of *City of Port Orange* case reprinted above. *AHF-Bay Fund, LLC v. City of Largo*, 169 So. 3d 133 (Fla. 2d DCA 2015). The Florida Supreme Court on review repeated verbatim the Second District's recitation of the facts, "The facts that prompted the filing of suit are as follows...," and reached an opposite result. The Second District ignored the fact that the non-profit corporation voluntarily entered into the PILOT agreement and undoubtedly received extremely favorable bond financing through the city-sponsored tax-exempt bonds. There is no law in any jurisdiction requiring a nonprofit to enter into a PILOT agreement.[102]

Why did the Second District ignore the contract?

The Florida Supreme Court again used the distinction between governmental powers and propriety powers. The Court gave a novel summation for the governmental power to impose taxes, that "there are two factors that exist when taxes are imposed: (1) the government acts unilaterally by sovereign right, and (2) the government acts in order to support routine government functions." Using Occam's razor, is there reason to associate the power to enter into a PILOT agreement with a type of proprietary local government power in this case? Is it sufficient to state local governments have ad valorem taxing powers specified in the Constitution and home rule powers that encompass contractual agreements?

The *Strand v. Escambia County* case, which follows, is interesting on many levels. It involves ad valorem tax increments, a relatively new form of financing that swept the country, starting with community redevelopment projects.[103] Tax increment financing occurs where improvements are made to a specifically identified territorial area within a local government, and the increased ad valorem taxes presumably resulting from higher assessments on the improved property are dedicated to repaying bonds financing the improvements.

Strand also occupies a rare status of starting out as a unanimous opinion, only to be withdrawn on a motion for rehearing and reissued with a diametrically opposite

---

102. Alan S. Zimmet et al., *Pilot Agreements Have Liftoff: City of Largo v. Ahf-Bay Fund, LLC*, 47 STETSON L. REV. 405, 407 (2018).

103. Richard Briffault, *The Most Popular Tool: Tax Increment Financing and the Political Economy of Local Government*, 77 U. CHI. L. REV. 65, 65 (2010) ("Tax increment financing (TIF) is the most widely used local government program for financing economic development in the United States"); Harry M. Hipler, *Tax Increment Financing in Florida: A Tool for Local Government Revitalization, Renewal, and Redevelopment*, FLA. B.J., July/August 2007, at 66.

result.[104] This sequence of decisions shows that the stability of judicial precedent is perhaps second in importance to the stability of bond legal opinion letters. The original Court opinion held the tax increment required a public referendum and explicitly overruled a prior court opinion, *Miami Beach*, on that point.[105] Escambia County filed a motion for rehearing and clarification that asserted Standard & Poor's had placed a negative outlook on Florida Tax Increment Financing and Certificate of Participation bonds, jeopardizing $13 billion in financing.[106] Six amici curiae also filed motions on the same day. Three days later, the Court issued an order granting the Attorney General's motion as amicus and grouping the other amici curiae into two interest groups and setting a schedule for oral argument on the motion for rehearing.[107] In the meantime, the Court revised its opinion to withdraw the reversal of *Miami Beach* precedent and hold that its *Strand* opinion was not retroactive.[108] However, that still was not enough. Only after a full re-briefing was conducted and oral argument held did the new *Strand* opinion, printed below, issue.

The opinion is also notable for a dissent by Justice Lewis that echoes his concerns first voiced in the *Sebring* opinion, and which he later repeated in court decisions over bonding, arguing that public consent through a referendum is needed.

Finally, the *Strand* decision also serves as a bridge to the next section on financing and bonds, where the Constitution requires a public referendum to issue a local bond backed by ad valorem taxes.

Strand v. Escambia County

992 So. 2d 150 (Fla. 2008)

WELLS, J.

We have before us an appeal from a final judgment validating a proposed bond issue from the Circuit Court of the First Judicial Circuit, in and for Escambia County, Florida. We have jurisdiction. *See* art. V, § 3(b)(2), Fla. Const. Upon consideration of appellee Escambia County's motion for rehearing, we withdraw our revised opinion, filed on September 28, 2007, and substitute the following opinion. We affirm the circuit court's final judgment.

---

104. *See generally* Robert C. Reid & Jason M. Breth, *Miami Beach: Receded, Revised, and Reaffirmed*, FLA. B.J., February 2009, at 18 (giving history of the case).

105. *Strand v. Escambia County*, 32 Fla. L. Weekly S500 (Fla. Sept. 6, 2007).

106. Appellee's [Escambia County] Motion for Rehearing and Clarification, Sept. 6, 2007, No. SC 06-1894 (available at Florida Supreme Court Online Docket, http://onlinedocketssc.flcourts.org/DocketResults/CaseDocket?Searchtype=Case+Number&CaseTypeSelected=All&CaseYear=2006&CaseNumber=1894) (last visited August 23, 2020).

107. *Strand v. Escambia County*, Order Amicus Curiae Granted, Order Oral Argument Schedule, Sept. 20, 2007, No. SC 06-1894. The September 20, 2007 order on oral argument was subsequently vacated and a plenary oral argument order issued. *Strand v. Escambia County*, Order on Oral Argument, Sept. 28, 2007, No. SC 06-1894; *Strand v. Escambia County*, 32 Fla. L. Weekly S587, S587 (Fla. Sept. 28, 2007).

108. *Strand v. Escambia County*, 32 Fla. L. Weekly S587 (Fla. Sept. 28, 2007).

I. FACTUAL AND PROCEDURAL BACKGROUND

On May 4, 2006, Escambia County (County) adopted Ordinance 2006-38 (Ordinance). The Ordinance establishes the Southwest Escambia Improvement District (District) in the southwest portion of the County, running to the peninsula known as Perdido Key. The Ordinance also establishes the Southwest Escambia Improvement Trust Fund (Trust Fund), which will be used to finance or refinance infrastructure improvements in the District, and authorizes the use of tax increment financing to fund the Trust Fund. In conjunction with the adoption of the Ordinance, the County adopted Resolution R2006-96 (Resolution) on May 4, 2006, authorizing the County to issue bonds not exceeding $135,000,000 for the District. The stated purpose of these bonds is to finance a four-lane road-widening project in the District to improve economic development within that area and alleviate traffic congestion. The bonds are to reach maturity no later than the thirty-fifth year after revenues are first deposited into the Trust Fund.

The Ordinance provides that the bonds are to be "payable out of revenues pledged to and received by the County and deposited to its Southwest Escambia Improvement Trust Fund." Ordinance §4(4). The Ordinance requires the County to appropriate to the Trust Fund by February 1 of each year an amount equal to the "Tax Increment"[109] so long as any applicable indebtedness is outstanding. *Id.* §4(1)–(3). The funds equaling the Tax Increment that are placed into the trust are known as "Tax Increment Revenues." *Id.* §2.

The Resolution employs the term "Trust Fund Revenues," which are the moneys other than "Supplemental Revenues"[110] deposited in the Trust Fund pursuant to the provisions of the Ordinance. Resolution art. I, §101 (May 4, 2006). The Resolution provides that the bonds shall be repaid from "Pledged Funds," which are the funds deposited in the Trust Fund including the Trust Fund Revenues and the Supplemental Revenues. *Id.* art. III, §301. The Resolution does require that if necessary, the County shall appropriate in its annual budget non-ad valorem revenues if available as Supplemental Revenues sufficient to secure the indebtedness in each fiscal year. However, the Resolution expressly states that the County does not covenant to maintain any

---

109. [FN 1.] The Ordinance defines "Tax Increment" as:

[T]he amount equal to the lesser of (a) the amount by which (i) the tax revenues that would have been generated at the millage rate in effect for the current Fiscal Year at the current Assessed Valuation exceeds (ii) the tax revenues that would have been generated at the millage rate in effect for the current Fiscal Year at the Base Assessed Valuation and (b) an amount equal to the sum of (i) 110% of the debt service of any outstanding indebtedness secured by the Tax Increment Revenues coming due in such Fiscal Year and (ii) an amount sufficient to restore any deficiencies in payment of debt service for such indebtedness for prior periods and to fund any planned expenditures described in Section 4(6) hereof.

Ordinance §2.

110. [FN 2.] "Supplemental Revenues" are County revenues derived from a source other than ad valorem taxation on real and personal property that are appropriated and deposited into the Trust Fund in the event that the Trust Fund Revenues are not sufficient to pay the debt service on the bonds. Resolution art. I, §101; art. III, §304.

services or programs now provided which generate non-ad valorem tax revenues. *Id.* §304(m).

The Ordinance and the Resolution dictate that the bonds do not pledge the full faith and credit or taxing power of the County, the State, or any political divisions thereof. Section 4 of the Ordinance states as follows:

> (4) The revenue Bonds and notes of every issue under this part are payable out of revenues pledged to and received by the County and deposited to its Southwest Escambia Improvement Trust Fund. The lien created by such bonds, notes or other forms of indebtedness shall not attach until the revenues referred to herein are deposited in the Southwest Escambia Improvement Trust Fund at the times, and to the extent that, such Tax Increment Revenues accrue. The holders of such bonds, notes or other forms of indebtedness have no right to require the imposition of any tax or the establishment of any rate of taxation in order to obtain the amounts necessary to pay and retire such bonds, notes or other forms of indebtedness.

> (5) Revenue Bonds issued under the provisions of this part shall not be deemed to constitute ... a pledge of the faith and credit of the County or the state or any political subdivision thereof, but shall be payable solely from the revenues provided therefor.

Ordinance §4(4)–(5). Section 103(i) of the Resolution reiterates that the bonds are payable solely from the Pledged Funds and "shall not constitute an indebtedness, liability, general or moral obligation, or a pledge of the faith, credit or taxing power of the Issuer, the State, or any political subdivision thereof." Section 301 adds that no bondholder

> shall ever have the right to compel the exercise of the ad valorem taxing power of the Issuer, the State or any political subdivision thereof, or taxation in any form of any real or personal property therein, or the application of any funds of the Issuer, the State or any political subdivision thereof ... other than the Pledged Funds as provided in this Resolution.

Section 302 explains that the bonds "shall not constitute a lien upon any property owned by or situated within the corporate territory of the Issuer, but shall constitute a lien only on the Pledged Funds." Accordingly, no lien created by the bonds shall attach until the revenues are deposited in the Trust Fund. Finally, the Resolution includes a finding that "[t]he estimated Pledged Funds will be sufficient to pay all principal of and interest on the [bonds]." Resolution art. I, §103(h).

On May 16, 2006, the County filed a complaint for validation in the Escambia County Circuit Court, seeking validation of the bond issuance. The state attorney [answered], and Dr. Gregory Strand intervened.... Dr. Strand argued that the bond issuance was distinguishable from the bond issuance approved by this Court in *State v. Miami Beach Redevelopment Agency*, 392 So.2d 875 (Fla.1980), and therefore required a referendum pursuant to the requirement of article VII, section 12 of the Florida Constitution.

On August 18, 2006, the circuit court entered the final judgment validating the bond issuance. The circuit court concluded that the County had the authority to issue the bonds and that the bonds were not subject to referendum pursuant to article VII, section 12. The circuit court cited to our decisions in *Miami Beach* and *Penn v. Florida Defense Finance & Accounting Service Center Authority*, 623 So.2d 459 (Fla.1993). Dr. Strand, the intervenor, appeals that final judgment.

II. STANDARD OF REVIEW

In *City of Gainesville v. State*, 863 So.2d 138, 143 (Fla.2003), this Court explained the scope of a bond validation proceeding as follows:

> We have previously explained the scope of a bond validation proceeding: "[C]ourts should: (1) determine if a public body has the authority to issue the subject bonds; (2) determine if the purpose of the obligation is legal; and (3) ensure that the authorization of the obligation complies with the requirements of law." *State v. City of Port Orange*, 650 So.2d 1, 2 (Fla.1994).

This Court reviews the "trial court's findings of fact for substantial competent evidence and its conclusions of law de novo." [citations omitted.] The final judgment of validation comes to this Court clothed with a presumption of correctness. *Wohl v. State*, 480 So.2d 639, 641 (Fla.1985).

III. ANALYSIS

Dr. Strand raises three issues in his appeal: (A) whether the circuit court abused its discretion in denying his motion for continuance; (B) whether the circuit court's final judgment is supported by competent, substantial evidence; and (C) whether the bonds required a referendum pursuant to the requirement of article VII, section 12 of the Florida Constitution.

* * *

B. Competent, Substantial Evidence

* * *

Dr. Strand next argues that the findings of fact contained in the circuit court's final judgment are not supported by competent, substantial evidence in the record. Specifically, Dr. Strand challenges the circuit court's findings that the District project is necessary and serves a public purpose; that there is a sufficient nexus between the property within the District and the benefits of the project to be financed by the bonds; and that the public improvements to be financed by the revenue bonds are necessary. Dr. Strand's argument is without merit.

In this case, the County offered into evidence the Ordinance and the Resolution, and presented testimony concerning the purpose of the project and the tax increment financing mechanism. In its final judgment, the circuit court relied primarily on the legislative findings contained in the Ordinance and the Resolution. This Court has held that "legislative declarations of public purpose are presumed valid and should be considered correct unless patently erroneous." *Boschen v. City of Clearwater*, 777 So.2d 958, 966 (Fla.2001) (quoting *State v. Housing Fin. Auth. of Pinellas County*,

506 So.2d 397, 399 (Fla.1987)). The findings in the Ordinance and the Resolution must be accorded great deference by the trial court, and Dr. Strand has not demonstrated the findings to be clearly erroneous. Moreover, this Court has recognized that the admission of a resolution may be sufficient evidence justifying a bond validation....

Likewise in this case, the legislative findings are competent, substantial evidence sufficient to support the final judgment.

C. Legal Authority to Issue Bonds Without a Referendum

The circuit court determined that the bonds could be validated without the referendum required by article VII, section 12, Florida Constitution, because the bonds to be issued under the Ordinance and the Resolution do not constitute an indebtedness, liability, or pledge of the faith, credit, or taxing power of the County. On appeal, Dr. Strand argues that the bonds should not have been validated because the County did not comply with the Community Redevelopment Act, chapter 163, Florida Statutes. The County responds that chapter 163 does not apply to the County's issuance of the bonds. Rather, the County intends to issue the bonds based upon the powers granted to the County by section 125.01, Florida Statutes (2006). We agree with the County. We find that this issue is controlled by our decision in *Penn*, in which we previously affirmed the Escambia County Circuit Court's validation of bonds issued under a similar tax ordinance and resolution and issuance structure.[111]

Dr. Strand further argues, as the appellant in *Penn* contended, that this financing mechanism violates article VII, section 12 of the Florida Constitution, which requires a referendum for bonds payable from ad valorem taxation and maturing more than twelve months after issuance. We rejected this argument in *Penn* because we found the financing mechanism in that case indistinguishable from the financing mechanism that we approved in *Miami Beach*. Likewise, we find that the financing mechanism in the instant case is not distinguishable from that which we approved in the *Miami Beach* case. Thus, we reject Dr. Strand's argument that the bonds in this case require a referendum.

On rehearing, Dr. Strand argues, and the dissenters to our present opinion agree, that we should recede from our decision in *Miami Beach*. In *Miami Beach*, we reviewed a judgment of the Circuit Court for Dade County which validated bonds issued pursuant to sections 163.385 and 163.387, Florida Statutes (1977), which

---

111. [FN 6.] In *Penn* we stated:

Under the ordinances, the bonds will be secured by lease payments from the city and county, which in turn are secured by tax increment revenues measured in part by future increases in ad valorem tax receipts. Any shortfall will be made whole by non-ad valorem revenues, but the bondholders' lien attaches only to monies actually deposited in the trust funds.

623 So.2d at 461.

authorized the issuance of bonds utilizing tax increment financing to finance redevelopment projects.

In *Miami Beach,* the opponents of the bond issuance contended that the bonds were payable from ad valorem taxation and therefore required a referendum. The opponents maintained that the bonds were payable from ad valorem taxation because the required contributions of Dade County and the City of Miami Beach to the repayment fund were to be derived from taxes levied on the real property in the redevelopment area. In response, the Miami Beach Redevelopment Agency (Agency) argued that the bonds did not come within the referendum requirement because there was no pledge of the ad valorem taxing power of the county and city. *Miami Beach,* 392 So.2d at 893–94. In its brief, the Agency maintained that "[t]he crux of the matter is that there is no pledge of the ad valorem taxing power to which bondholders may look, and which they may legally enforce, as a source of funds to pay the bonds." Answer Brief to Initial Brief of Appellant at 32, *State v. Miami Beach Redev. Agency,* 392 So.2d 875 (Fla.1980) (No. 57997).

In our *Miami Beach* opinion, we decided the issue in favor of the Agency stating:

> The Agency contends in effect that where there is no direct pledge of ad valorem tax revenues, but merely a requirement of an annual appropriation from any available funds, the referendum provision of article VII, section 12 is not involved. We agree with this view....

392 So.2d at 894. We thereafter delineated the history of judicial precedents which led to our conclusion and held:

> The bonds in the instant case are payable from a trust fund, and the fund will receive revenue from two sources. One source is the money the Agency receives from sales, leases, and charges for the use of, redeveloped property. This source is analogous to revenues generated by a utility or facility. The other source is the money to be contributed each year by the county and city, measured by the tax increment. The source of this revenue is not limited to any specific governmental revenue. That the statutory duty to make the annual contributions would become a contractual duty, part of the obligation of the bonds, does not mean, however, that these bonds are payable from ad valorem taxation, in the constitutional sense of the term.

> The Agency notes that even though the money the county and city will use to make the contributions may come from ad valorem tax revenues, we have indicated this does not bring the bonds within the referendum requirement. *Tucker v. Underdown,* 356 So.2d 251 (Fla.1978). In that case, county bonds previously issued without referendum to finance a solid waste disposal system had been validated as payable from user charges, giving bondholders no power to compel the levy of ad valorem taxes for operating expenses or debt service. The subsequent lawsuit concerned whether the county had violated the covenants of the earlier bond issue by levying and spending ad valorem taxes for these purposes. The Court held that it had not.

Tucker v. Underdown supports the argument that there is nothing in the constitution to prevent a county or city from using ad valorem tax revenues where they are required to compute and set aside a prescribed amount, when available, for a discreet [sic] purpose. The purpose of the constitutional limitation is unaffected by the legal commitment; the taxing power of the governmental units is unimpaired. *What is critical to the constitutionality of the bonds is that, after the sale of bonds, a bondholder would have no right, if the redevelopment trust fund were insufficient to meet the bond obligations and the available resources of the county or city were insufficient to allow for the promised contributions, to compel by judicial action the levy of ad valorem taxation.* Under the statute authorizing this bond financing the governing bodies are not obliged nor can they be compelled to levy any ad valorem taxes in any year. The only obligation is to appropriate a sum equal to any tax increment generated in a particular year from the ordinary, general levy of ad valorem taxes otherwise made in the city and county that year. Issuance of these bonds without approval of the voters of Dade County and the City of Miami Beach, consequently, does not transgress article VII, section 12.

Miami Beach, 392 So.2d at 898–99 (emphasis added). Two members of the Court dissented from this conclusion. In his concurring in part and dissenting in part opinion, Justice Boyd specifically expressed the view that the promised annual contributions to the trust fund based on the tax increment revenues constituted a pledge by the county and the city of their general revenue and made the bonds general obligation bonds, which were payable from ad valorem taxation. *Id.* at 900 (Boyd, J., concurring in part and dissenting in part). Thus, the arguments advocated here by Dr. Strand and the present dissenters were previously advanced in *Miami Beach* and rejected by this Court.

In 1990, we reinforced our holding in *Miami Beach* in our decision in *State v. School Board of Sarasota County*, 561 So.2d 549 (Fla.1990). We stated:

Regarding the bonds' validity, the issue presented is whether a referendum is required by article VII, section 12 of the Florida Constitution (1968). We conclude that because these obligations are not supported by the pledge of ad valorem taxation, they are not "payable from ad valorem taxation" within the meaning of article VII, section 12, and referendum approval is not required.

In *State v. Miami Beach Redevelopment Agency*, 392 So.2d 875 (Fla.1980), we interpreted the words "payable from ad valorem taxation" in article VII, section 12 and held that a referendum is not required when there is no direct pledge of the ad valorem taxing power. We noted that although contributions may come from ad valorem tax revenues: "What is critical to the constitutionality of the bonds is that, after the sale of the bonds, a bondholder would have no right, if [funds] were insufficient to meet the bond obligations ... to compel by judicial action the levy of ad valorem taxation.... [T]he governing bodies are not obliged nor can they be compelled to levy any ad valorem taxes in any year." *Id.* at 898–99. The agreements here, as in *Miami Beach*, although supported in part by ad valorem revenues, expressly provide that neither the bondholders nor anyone else can compel use of the ad valorem taxing power to service the bonds.

Id. at 552 (footnote omitted) (alterations in original). Again, the majority's decision was met by a dissent, which maintained that the financing mechanism employed in those cases were equivalent to issuing bonds and pledging ad valorem taxation to support them. Again, the dissenters' view was rejected by the Court.

* * *

We have stated that we are committed to the doctrine of stare decisis. *N. Fla. Women's Health & Counseling Services, Inc. v. State*, 866 So.2d 612, 637 (Fla.2003). In that case, we ... set forth the questions to be considered when asked to recede from precedent, expressly stating that the presumption in favor of precedent is strong. The questions to be asked are:

> (1) Has the prior decision proved unworkable due to reliance on an impractical legal "fiction"? (2) Can the rule of law announced in the decision be reversed without serious injustice to those who have relied on it and without serious disruption in the stability of the law? And (3) have the factual premises underlying the decision changed so drastically as to leave the decision's central holding utterly without legal justification?

N. Fla. Women's Health, 866 So.2d at 637. In the instant case, we do not find that the answers to these questions overcome the presumption in favor of stare decisis.

In answer to the first question, we have not been presented with evidence showing that the *Miami Beach* decision has proven unworkable due to reliance on a legal fiction. Rather, we find that the holding of the majority in *Miami Beach* was scrutinized and tested by the dissenters in *Miami Beach* and later in the *School Board of Sarasota County* decision, and determined by the Court's majority to be developed from seasoned historic precedent.

In answer to several questions, we conclude that for the past twenty-seven years there has been widespread reliance upon the *Miami Beach* decision in the issuance of bond financing by local government authorities, including school boards, enabling the financing of many public works that have enhanced the quality of life in our State. Tax increment financing and the undergirding principles of our *Miami Beach* decision have been inextricably woven into the financial fabric of our State. We conclude that receding from the precedent of *Miami Beach* would cause serious disruption to the governmental authorities that have relied upon that precedent for planning public works that are in various stages of development and approval.

Finally, we do not find that any changes have occurred since the *Miami Beach* decision that affect that decision. There have in fact been no changes which would affect our construction of the applicability of article VII, section 12, to bond issues using the tax increment financing structure determined to be valid in *Miami Beach*—article VII, section 12 of the Florida Constitution has not been amended....

Alternatively, Dr. Strand contends that if we do not recede from *Miami Beach* and its progeny, we should find that it does not control the decision in this case. Dr. Strand argues that, instead, this case should be controlled by this Court's decision in *County of Volusia v. State*, 417 So.2d 968 (Fla.1982). In that case, we affirmed the Volusia County Circuit Court's denial of validation of a bond issue in part because the circuit court found that Volusia County's pledge of all legally available revenues other than ad valorem taxes would have the effect of requiring the levy of increased ad valorem taxation so that, under article VII, section 12, the bonds could not be issued without a referendum. In *County of Volusia*, we specifically affirmed the circuit court....

In the present case, the County argues that *County of Volusia* is distinguishable because section 304(m)(1) of the Resolution expressly does not covenant to maintain any services or programs now provided or maintained by the County which generate non-ad valorem revenues. The County further points out that we approved a similar financing mechanism in *Murphy v. City of Port St. Lucie*, 666 So.2d 879 (Fla.1995).

We agree that as in *City of Port St. Lucie*, the instant Ordinance and Resolution differ from those in *County of Volusia* in that non-ad valorem revenues here are to be used only as a supplemental source of funding in the event that the Trust Fund revenues are insufficient for debt service and in that the County expressly does not covenant to maintain services or programs for the purpose of generating income to repay the bonds. *See City of Port St. Lucie*, 666 So.2d at 881.

IV. CONCLUSION

For the reasons stated above, we affirm the final judgment of validation of the Escambia County Circuit Court.

It is so ordered.

LEWIS, J., dissenting.

In my view, the decision of Escambia County to issue tax-increment-financed bonds to fund a road-construction project without first obtaining approval through a constitutionally mandated referendum is contrary to the clear and plain words of article VII, section 12 of the Florida Constitution. Here, without consulting the electorate, the County seeks to pledge thirty-five years' worth of ad valorem tax revenue as the *primary* funding source for a typical "capital project." Conversely, article VII, section 12 was clearly designed to address the expanding capital needs of local government, but was tempered by the inclusion of democratic control with regard to the decision to finance "capital projects" with long-term debt "payable from ad valorem taxation." Art. VII, § 12, Fla. Const. In this road-construction context, the majority's avoidance of this clear command perpetuates and expands a distortion of our fundamental organic law, leads us far beyond our prior precedent, and denies the voters of this State their constitutional right to determine whether their local governments should issue long-term debt that is "payable from ad valorem taxation," as that phrase is understood through its "usual and obvious meaning." [Citation omitted.] With regard to typical "capital projects," such as Escambia County's road-expansion plan, the Constitution unmistakably communicates that entities of local government are required to use a referendum to obtain voter approval when a pledge of ad valorem tax revenue or ad valorem taxing authority is a source of payment for relevant forms of long-term debt. *See* art. VII, § 12, Fla. Const.

I write separately in this road-construction context to emphasize two additional points that, in my view, demonstrate the violence that expansion of the legal fiction of *State v. Miami Beach Redevelopment Agency*, 392 So.2d 875 (Fla.1980), visits upon the plain text and manifest intent of article VII, section 12. First, much of our case law in this area has been opaque and counterintuitive due to its complete divorce from the text of this constitutional provision. *Cf.* [*City of Jacksonville v.*] *Cont'l Can Co.*, 151 So. at 490 [(Fla.1933)] ("Constitutions import the utmost discrimination in the use of language, *that which the words declare is the meaning of the instrument.*" (emphasis supplied)). Here, the Court should not expand prior decisions from different contexts to advance a movement away from the text of article VII, section 12. The decision of the majority to do so today is contrary to a primary tenet of constitutional interpretation: Begin with the plain and clear meaning of the text. The original decision of this Court on September 6, 2007, which receded from the fundamentally erroneous "pledge of taxing power only" premise of *Miami Beach* within the context of typical capital projects (e.g., road construction), was a proper return to the constitutional mandate. *See Strand v. Escambia County*, 32 Fla. L. Weekly S587, S590–91 (Fla. Sept. 6, 2007), *as revised*, No. SC06-1894, 992 So.2d 150 (2007). Relatedly, the motions for rehearing and clarification filed by Escambia County and the amici have not added anything of substance to the cogent legal analysis contained within this Court's *unanimous, context-specific* decision to recede from the flawed premise of *Miami Beach*. Instead, these motions have impermissibly used rehearing as a means to reargue and attack the merits of this Court's decision, which we have previously considered and determined. *Cf., e.g., Brennan v. State*, 754 So.2d 1, 6 n. 4 (Fla.1999) ("Motions for rehearing may only be used to apprise a court of 'the points of law or fact that the court has overlooked or misapprehended.'" (quoting Fla. R.App. P. 9.330(a))); *Jacobs v. Wainwright*, 450 So.2d 200, 201 (Fla.1984) ("A motion for rehearing shall not reargue the merits of the Court's order."). Nothing has changed in this case and nothing has been overlooked; the county and the amici calling for rehearing have simply pandered, postured, and expressed a self-serving desire to thwart the democratic voice of Florida's citizens contrary to the text of the Florida Constitution.

Second, article VII, section 10 of the Florida Constitution ("Pledging Credit") further undermines application of the "pledge of taxing power only" premise of *Miami Beach* in the road-construction context presented here. This separate, distinct constitutional provision demonstrates that the framers of our Constitution were aware of, *and intended a textual distinction between,* an entity of local government "*giv[ing], lend[ing] or us[ing] its taxing power or credit,*" as addressed in that constitutional provision, and an entity of local government issuing "bonds, certificates of indebtedness or any form of tax anticipation certificates, *payable from ad valorem taxation,*" as addressed in article VII, section 12. (Emphasis supplied.) If the framers had truly intended for article VII, sections 10 and 12 to each only address *pledges of the taxing power* of local government, then these constitutional drafters would have used similar language in section 12; however, they did *not* do so. Thus, the faulty premise of *Miami Beach* accomplishes that which we are proscribed from doing as judicial officers who have sworn to support, protect, and defend our state Constitution: It amends article VII, section 12 through judicial fiat by removing and rendering meaningless the phrase "payable from ad valorem taxation" and replacing it with materially different language drawn from a separate, distinct constitutional provision (i.e., article VII, section 10). *Cf., e.g., Burnsed v. Seaboard Coastline R.R.*, 290 So.2d 13, 16 (Fla.1974) ("It is a fundamental rule of construction of our [C]onstitution that a construction ... which renders superfluous, meaningless or inoperative any of its provisions should not be adopted by the courts.").

The People and the Legislature need not resort to the amendment procedures of article XI to overturn *Miami Beach* because the plain text of article VII, section 12 already unambiguously conveys a clear meaning. Like the hapless protagonist in "Groundhog Day," this Court will be forced to continuously relive this controversy until we "get it right" because the constitutional provision at issue simply does not support the gloss placed upon it by *Miami Beach* (which the majority erroneously expands to this road-construction context) and related, distinguishable decisions. Sooner or later we must recognize that the faulty expansion of *Miami Beach* to far different cases involving typical capital projects unjustifiably perpetuates an obvious legal error and deprives Florida's citizens of a clear constitutional right. *Cf. Puryear v. State*, 810 So.2d 901, 905 (Fla.2002) ("Our adherence to stare decisis ... is not unwavering. The doctrine of stare decisis bends ... where there has been an error in legal analysis.").

When faced with a typical capital project, such as the road-expansion plan involved in this case, I would interpret and enforce article VII, section 12 as written and would also salvage and apply a long-forgotten portion of our *Miami Beach* decision: "The Court looks at the *substance* and *not the form* of the proposed bonds" to determine whether the entity of local government has complied with the Constitution. 392 So.2d at 894 (emphasis supplied). Where, as here, the bond-financing plan will inevitably lead to diverting funds from ad valorem tax revenue to pay for or "service" the associated long-term debt for a non-revenue producing capital project, the Constitution requires a referendum. *See* art. VII, § 12, Fla. Const; [citations omitted.] Political expediency cannot alter the text of the Florida Constitution nor should it be used to thwart the will of the voters of this State.

Consequently, I believe that expansion of the "pledge of taxing power only" premise of *Miami Beach* to typical capital projects violates article VII, section 12, and that any associated local-government bond-financing plan that will inevitably lead to diverting funds from ad valorem tax revenue to service related long-term debt requires a referendum under our state Constitution. Thus, even if we uphold *Miami Beach*, Escambia County's tax-increment-financing scheme for this road-construction project nevertheless violates article VII, section 12. Unlike *Miami Beach*, which involved a redevelopment project under the auspices of the Community Redevelopment Act (part III of chapter 163, Florida Statutes (1975)), this case only involves a typical "capital project" within the meaning of article VII, section 12 (widening a county road). Furthermore, in contrast to *Miami Beach*—where ad valorem tax revenue was only a *contingent source* from which the city planned to service the associated debt if the primary source proved insufficient—here, ad valorem tax revenue is the *primary source* from which Escambia County will service the debt created by these bonds. This distinction brings the instant case squarely within the rule and rationale of *County of Volusia* and *Magaha*: Escambia County cannot circumvent the referendum requirement because its bond-financing scheme inevitably requires that it pay for its debt with ad valorem tax revenue.

The local-government shell game, which is played to avoid the Florida voter, should not be sanctioned by this tribunal. Unfortunately, we have done so today by improperly expanding this game to the very "capital projects" addressed in article VII, section 12. For these reasons, I join my colleague in dissenting from the majority's unjustifiable expansion of a fundamentally flawed principle, which operates to circumvent voter participation in a decision that requires popular approval under the Florida Constitution.

QUINCE, C.J., concurs.

Commentary and Questions

The Court states: "Tax increment financing and the undergirding principles of our *Miami Beach* decision have been inextricably woven into the financial fabric of our State." Unlike other areas of the law, bond financing law relies on strong consistency or well-telegraphed, minor changes. Reversals in financing law affect past bond issues still being repaid, current attempts to issue bonds, and the future attractiveness of bonds issued from Florida local governments. The Florida Supreme Court has mandatory jurisdiction to hear bond validation cases. Art. V, § 3(b)(2), Fla. Const.

Should the Court develop a separate doctrine of *stare decisis* for bond validations?

The Court gives a firm legal basis for authority of tax increment financing: "[T]here is nothing in the constitution to prevent a county or city from using ad valorem tax revenues where they are required to compute and set aside a prescribed amount, when available, for a discreet [sic] purpose." The core issue for the Court is that bondholders cannot compel the diversion of ad valorem taxes to pay the bonds. However, how clear is the local government's authority to pledge other sources of revenue to sweeten the security of bond repayment to potential bond buyers? The Court states that pledging to continue all programs that generate revenue is permissible while the government "does not covenant to maintain any services...." Is the difference that the government collects and diverts the revenue from other services and then terminates the other services due to lack of funding? Is the majority's argument persuasive?

Tax increment financing is a use of ad valorem taxes caused by higher assessments to repay bonds. What if higher assessments do not occur or assessments fall within the specific project? Should the pledge of any ad valorem taxes, incremental or not, be subject to a referendum?

Justice Lewis writes in his dissent: "The local-government shell game, which is played to avoid the Florida voter, should not be sanctioned by this tribunal." The only issue is whether to trigger a referendum. What's the problem? Is it a worry the voters will refuse a referendum? Bond financing requires many preparatory and expensive steps to reach the stage where the definite terms on which the bond will issue are known.[112] What changes might be made to the Constitution to advance referendum approval to a point before this work is fully completed, underwriting obligations are fixed, and bond issuance costs incurred?

Two cases cited in *Strand* show the evolution of "some but not all" doctrine of pledging non-ad valorem taxes.

County of Volusia v. State

417 So. 2d 968 (Fla. 1982)

BOYD, Justice.

This cause is before the Court on appeal from a judgment of the circuit court denying the complaint of the County of Volusia for validation of capital improvement bonds in the amount of $40,000,000. We have jurisdiction. [citation omitted.]

The county seeks to issue the bonds to finance construction of a jail to be located on Indian Lake Road eleven miles from DeLand, the county seat. The payment of the bonds is to be secured by the county's pledge of all legally available, unencumbered sources of county revenue including all money derived from regulatory fees and user charges assessed by the county. The county also covenants to do all things necessary to continue receiving the various revenues pledged.

The trial court found the proposed bond issue to be unlawful on three grounds. ... Second, the court found that the pledge of all legally available revenues other than ad valorem taxation would have the effect of requiring the levy of increased ad valorem taxation so that, under article VII, section 12, Florida Constitution, the bonds may not be issued without approval of the eligible voters by referendum. ...

The County of Volusia argues that the trial court was wrong on all three counts and asks that we reverse and order the bonds validated so that it can proceed with construction of the much-needed jail. We affirm the trial court's judgment denying validation. We hold that the pledge of all the legally available, unencumbered revenues of the county other than ad valorem taxation, along with a covenant to do all things necessary to continue receiving the revenues, as security for the bonds, will have the effect of requiring increased ad valorem taxation so that a referendum is required. Our disposition of the case on this ground makes it unnecessary to reach and settle

---

112. Robert L. Nabors, Florida Home Rule Green Book § 17.08 (2d ed. 2014).

the questions of whether the various non-ad valorem revenues may be pledged to the financing of a jail facility....

* * *

We discuss now the dispositive issue and hold that the pledge of *all* legally available, unencumbered revenues—*i.e.*, all revenues, other than ad valorem taxation, which the governing body has the authority to spend or pledge at its discretion—calls into play the referendum requirement of article VII, section 12 because it in effect constitutes a promise to levy ad valorem taxes. The county correctly states that this Court has approved pledges of various local government revenue sources without referendum even though the encumbrance of the funds would have an incidental effect on the exercise of the ad valorem taxing power. *State v. Alachua County*, 335 So.2d 554 (Fla.1976); *Town of Medley v. State*, 162 So.2d 257 (Fla.1964). In *Town of Medley v. State*, 162 So.2d 257 (Fla.1964), a municipality proposed to construct a water supply system and building together with storm sewers and streets and to finance these improvements by the sale of revenue bonds. As security for the payment of the bonds, the town pledged to their retirement the revenues to be earned by the water system, together with revenues from the following four specific sources: the proceeds from cigarette taxes, a municipal utility franchise tax, utilities taxes, and occupational license taxes. The bond issue was challenged on the ground that diverting these revenues from the town's general operating fund would require increased ad valorem taxes in order to replace those funds, and that such a result required approval by referendum. This Court responded:

> Only bonds or certificates of indebtedness which directly obligate the ad valorem taxing power are encompassed by [the constitutional referendum requirement]. The incidental effect on use of the ad valorem taxing power occasioned by the pledging of other sources of revenue does not subject such bonds or certificates to that constitutional requirement.

162 So.2d at 258. The Court said that to hold otherwise would prevent a local government from pledging non-ad valorem funds previously used for general operating expenses without a referendum, a result not required in light of the purpose of the constitutional requirement.

In *State v. Alachua County*, 335 So.2d 554 (Fla.1976), we held that the county's pledge of its annual revenue sharing funds and its annual share of state race track funds to the repayment of bonds issued to finance various capital projects and public improvements without referendum did not violate article VII, section 12. Citing *Town of Medley v. State* as authority, we again held that only a direct pledge of, and not indirect impact on, the ad valorem taxing power required referendum approval.

The present case differs from both *Town of Medley v. State* and *State v. Alachua County.* One point of distinction is that here the county has attempted to pledge all legally available revenue sources other than ad valorem taxation, rather than several specific sources. Secondly, here the county has further promised to fully maintain the programs and services which generate the service fees and user charges. To maintain all of the programs that produce the revenues, while devoting the revenues themselves to the retirement of the bonds, will inevitably require that ad valorem taxes be increased so that the county will have sufficient operating revenue to maintain the programs and services that generate the pledged revenues.

* * *

That which may not be done directly may not be done indirectly. *See, e.g., State v. Halifax Hospital District*, 159 So.2d 231 (Fla.1963). While the county has not directly pledged ad valorem taxes to the payment of the bonds, its pledge of all other available revenues, together with its promise to do all things necessary to continue to receive the various revenues, will inevitably lead to higher ad valorem taxes during the life of the bonds, which amounts to the same thing. We find in this case that the pledge of all available revenues, together with a promise to maintain the programs entitling the county to receive the various revenues, will have a substantial impact on the future exercise of ad valorem taxing power and brings this case within the rule of *Halifax Hospital District*. The taxpayers of Volusia County must have an opportunity to vote on the bond issue.

* * *

Accordingly, the order denying validation is affirmed.

ALDERMAN, Justice, dissenting.

I would reverse the trial court and remand with directions that these bonds be validated.

* * *

I disagree, however, with the majority's conclusion that these bonds require referendum approval under article VII, section 12, Florida Constitution. This Court has repeatedly upheld the validity of pledges of local non-ad valorem revenue sources without referendum approval. In *State v. Tampa Sports Authority*, 188 So.2d 795 (Fla.1966), we affirmed the trial court's validation of bonds to be issued for the development and maintenance of a sports facility where the city and county agreed that repayment of the bonds should be from available moneys derived from sources other than the proceeds of ad valorem taxation. Citing *State v. City of Jacksonville*, 53 So.2d 306 (Fla.1951), we said:

> We have repeatedly held that when certificates of indebtedness are for an authorized public purpose and are payable solely from revenues derived from utilities service, excise taxes, licenses or some other source than ad valorem taxes, they may be issued without an approving vote of the freeholders as required by Section 6, Article IX of the Constitution.

188 So.2d at 797. *See also State v. Monroe County*, 81 So.2d 522 (Fla.1955).

We have upheld such pledges by local governments even though ad valorem taxes probably would be affected. In *Town of Medley v. State*, 162 So.2d 257 (Fla.1964), the trial court denied validation of public improvement revenue bonds which were to be repaid with revenues from a proposed water system, proceeds of the cigarette tax, franchise taxes on electric power, utility taxes, and occupational license taxes. Although no ad valorem taxes were pledged and the ordinance authorizing the bond issue specifically provided that the town would not be obligated to levy ad valorem taxes for repayment of the bonds, the trial court concluded that validation of the bonds would result in an increase in real property taxes without vote of the freeholders. In reversing the order denying validation, this Court held:

> In any instance in which a municipality has been using funds from special non-ad valorem sources of revenue to meet its operating costs and then diverts those funds by pledging them to payment of a specific indebtedness as done here, the result will probably be that ad valorem taxes will have to be increased to make up the deficiency in funds available for operating expenses.

> Nevertheless, this result does not make the revenue bonds or certificates subject to the provisions of Section 6, Article IX, of our State Constitution, F.S.A. A contrary holding would mean that any pledging of non-ad valorem revenues previously used for the general operating expenses of a municipality would require approval by vote of the freeholders and such was never the purpose of the cited constitutional provision.

> Only bonds or certificates of indebtedness which directly obligate the ad valorem taxing power are encompassed by Section 6, Article IX, Fla.Const. The incidental effect on use of the ad valorem taxing power occasioned by the pledging of other sources of revenue does not subject such bonds or certificates to that constitutional requirement.

162 So.2d at 258. More recently, we reaffirmed this position in *State v. Alachua County*, 335 So.2d 554 (Fla.1976).

This issue is not governed by *State v. Halifax Hospital District*, 159 So.2d 231 (Fla.1963), wherein we declined to affirm validation of hospital improvement bonds to be repaid from gross revenues of the hospital. In that case, we held that the hospital's pledge of all gross revenues *coupled with its pledge not to reduce during the life of the bonds the currently assessed ad valorem tax levy for maintenance and operation of the hospital* required referendum approval. We found that the hospital's pledge of ad valorem taxes was as much an obligation of the bond resolution as was the pledge of the gross revenues. Volusia County, unlike the Halifax Hospital District, has not expressly pledged ad valorem taxes to continue the operation of those governmental functions needed to generate the revenues to repay the bonds.

In the present case, as in *Town of Medley* and *Alachua County*, the authorizing documents specifically state that the ad valorem taxing power is not directly pledged to repayment of the bonds and such repayment cannot be compelled by the bondholders. The pledge of non-ad valorem funds results in a diversion of funds from the county's general revenue and probably will require ad valorem taxes to be increased to make up the deficiency in funds available for operating expenses, but I would hold, as we did in *Town of Medley* and *Alachua County*, that such an incidental effect on Volusia County's ad valorem taxing power does not require referendum approval pursuant to article VII, section 12 of the Florida Constitution.

* * *

Accordingly, I would reverse the trial court's order and remand with directions that these bonds be validated.

ADKINS and OVERTON, JJ., concur.

Questions and Comments

The four-to-three majority sets forth the distinguishing facts that: "While the county has not directly pledged ad valorem taxes to the payment of the bonds, its pledge of all other available revenues, together with its promise to do all things necessary to continue to receive the various revenues, will inevitably lead to higher ad valorem taxes during the life of the bonds, which amounts to the same thing." Is it the combination of "all legally available, unencumbered sources of county revenue," and the commitment to do "all things necessary" to maintain the revenue stream that leads the majority to conclude that ad valorem taxes will be used, or raised, to plug a bond repayment gap?

Both the majority and dissent rely on the same cases of *Town of Medley v. State*, 162 So. 2d 257 (Fla. 1964), and *State v. Alachua County*, 335 So. 2d 554 (Fla. 1976). The *Town of Medley* case, of course, was decided before the adoption of the 1968 Constitution. The majority notes that in *Alachua County*, the county only pledged "its annual revenue sharing funds and its annual share of state race track funds" for the bonds, a fairly delimited commitment. How are the majority and dissent reaching such divergent interpretations based on the same cases?

As the ink on the *County of Volusia* case dried, the Florida Supreme Court issued a second opinion the next year softening the *County of Volusia* holding.

City of Palatka v. State
440 So. 2d 1271 (Fla. 1983)

ADKINS, Justice.

This cause is before the Court on direct appeal from a final judgment in a bond validation proceeding in Putnam County. We have jurisdiction. Art. V, § 3(b)(2), Fla. Const.

The City of Palatka owns and operates a water and sewer system. The city has financed the construction and acquisition of its existing facilities in part through the issuance of revenue bonds, some of which are outstanding. The city now seeks to issue the bonds which are the subject of this proceeding for two purposes: 1) to refund the prior bonds which are outstanding in order to defease the city's contractual obligations to the holders of those prior bonds; and 2) to finance construction of a new sewage treatment plant. The city will accomplish the refunding of previously issued bonds by depositing proceeds of the proposed bonds in an irrevocable escrow for the benefit of the holders of the refunded bonds. The escrowed funds are to be invested in obligations of the United States government which are specifically designed to facilitate and implement refinancing of state and local government obligations.

In the validation proceeding the circuit court found that the revenues pledged to the repayment of the bonds by the City of Palatka constituted approximately eighty percent of the total revenues available to the city from all sources other than ad valorem tax revenues. Concluding that this would have more than an incidental effect on the exercise of the ad valorem taxing power, the court held that a referendum was required under article VII, section 12, of the Florida Constitution. . . .

The City of Palatka argues that the lower court's finding that eighty percent of all revenues available to the city from sources other than ad valorem taxes have been pledged for payment of the bonds is erroneous. The city asserts that the correct figure is forty-nine percent and the appellee has conceded in its brief and at oral argument that this figure is correct. The city challenges the court's holding that the issuance of the bonds would have more than a mere incidental effect on the exercise of the ad valorem taxing power. The city contends that the court mistakenly relied on *County of Volusia v. State*, 417 So.2d 968 (Fla.1982), to support its holding.

We agree that the court's reliance on the *County of Volusia* case is misplaced. In *County of Volusia* this Court dealt with the validity of a bond issue which was secured by a pledge of all legally available unencumbered sources of county revenue, including all monies derived from regulatory fees and user charges. Volusia County had also covenanted to do all things necessary to continue receiving the various user fees pledged. The facts of the present case are easily distinguishable from *County of Volusia*. In this case only two specific revenue sources are pledged—water and sewer revenues and utility taxes—not *all* available revenues. In addition, the City of Palatka has covenanted only to maintain water and sewer rates and utility taxes at levels sufficient to pay the bonds. These limited covenants do not place a potential burden on ad valorem taxes. . . .

This Court's decision in *Jacksonville Shipyards, Inc. v. Jacksonville Electric Authority*, 419 So.2d 1092 (Fla.1982), made a clear distinction between the holding in *County of Volusia* and revenue bond issues similar to the instant case. In that case, only a specific revenue source, the City of Jacksonville's annual contribution from the Jacksonville Electric Authority of electric system revenues, was pledged for payment of the bonds. We held that the possibility that the city would not receive the annual contribution would have, at the very most, a merely incidental effect on the city's exercise of its ad valorem taxing power. . . .

We hold that the issuance of these bonds will have no more than an incidental effect on the taxing power of the City of Palatka. The city manager testified that none of the water and sewer utility revenues are used for other branches of city government. There simply has been no showing that ad valorem taxes will be affected by this bond issue.

* * *

Accordingly, we reverse the order of the circuit court and remand for entry of a final judgment validating the bonds.

It is so ordered.

ALDERMAN, C.J., and BOYD, OVERTON, McDONALD, EHRLICH and SHAW, JJ., concur.

Commentary and Questions

The Court notes that the city "has covenanted only to maintain water and sewer rates and utility taxes at levels sufficient to pay the bonds." Presumably, the sewer rates to sustain bond payments will be in addition to the ordinary expenses to operate the system. What if the rates become exorbitant and there is an ordinance requiring hookup to the city system within the city boundaries to eliminate groundwater contamination from septic tanks? Is this an indirect tax?

Is the Court using an arbitrary legal standard when a fact-specific finding is required to prove that the other revenue sources might become insufficient and ad valorem taxes are necessary? Here the Court writes only: "There simply has been no showing that ad valorem taxes will be affected by this bond issue." Should the Court require a sensitivity analysis to prove under different conditions, such as a sharp economic recession reducing fees, that ad valorem taxes are unnecessary?

E. How Can They Tax?

i. Tax Rates

"All ad valorem taxation shall be at a uniform rate within each taxing unit, except the taxes on intangible personal property may be at different rates...." FLA. CONST. art. VII, §2.

In the 1978 case *Gallant v. Stephens*, 358 So. 2d 536 (Fla. 1978), the issue was raised whether Pinellas County could create a Municipal Service Taxing or Benefit Unit ("MSTU") covering all of the unincorporated land in the county and tax the MSTU property at a higher millage rate than property within Pinellas County cities. The Florida Supreme Court answered yes and agreed with the prevailing party that "the uniformity clause [applies] to the objects of taxation[—]subjects within the unit actually being taxed[—]rather than to the taxing authority itself."[113]

The 1968 Constitution capped taxes on intangible personal property, such as stock certificates, at two mills of the assessed value.[114]

ii. Tax Assessments and Valuations

While Section 4 generally prescribes just value as the assessment standard, Section 4 also contains many different, permissive, property assessment classifications burnt into the Constitution for tax policy reasons. For example, some of these provisions permit the Legislature to set by general law property assessment standards based on

---

113. *Gallant v. Stephens*, 358 So. 2d 536, 541 (Fla. 1978).
114. FLA. CONST. art. VII, §2.

character and use of the land instead of just value. Character and use recognize the land may have a lower value than fair market value because of a special use. Agricultural land, high-aquifer recharge land, and land used for only noncommercial recreational uses may be assessed on character and use.[115] Conservation land may likewise be assessed by character and use.[116] Subsection 4(j) requires certain marine related land, including for example such uses as marinas and boat drystacks, to be assessed based on their current uses with conditions set by the legislature.[117]

Section 4 also contains many other exceptions limiting assessments based on change of use or a reduction based on other specialized uses, such as reconversion of property to accommodate parents or grandparents in the home.[118]

Straughn v. GAC Properties, Inc.

360 So. 2d 385 (Fla. 1978)

ENGLAND, Justice.

We granted certiorari to review the decision of the Fourth District Court of Appeal in *GAC Properties, Inc. v. Lanier*, 345 So.2d 812 (Fla. 4th DCA 1977), on the basis of an asserted conflict with *Spooner v. Askew*, 345 So.2d 1055 (Fla.1976), and *Armstrong v. State ex rel. Beaty*, 69 So.2d 319 (Fla.1954). The general proposition of law addressed in all these decisions is whether real property in one county of the state may be valued and assessed for ad valorem tax purposes by reference to the valuation of real property in another county. The narrow question presented in this case is whether a cause of action lies against the Department of Revenue to compel equalization of ad valorem tax valuations where real property situated in one county is assessed on the basis of a higher value than that assigned to allegedly identical property located in another county.

GAC Properties owns a large tract of undeveloped land on both sides of the Osceola-Polk County line. The Polk County tax appraiser valued that portion of the property in his jurisdiction for 1975 at $300 per lot, while the Osceola County appraiser valued the lands in his domain at $560 per lot. GAC Properties sued to reduce the Osceola County tax assessment, charging in Count II of its complaint that the discrepancy violates the "just valuation" requirement of Article VII, Section 4, Florida Constitution, and that the Department of Revenue has the responsibility to correct the imbalance....

The *Spooner* and *Armstrong* decisions quite clearly state that inter-county assessment uniformity is not required by the Constitution, and that variations even between adjacent counties are not a basis for lowering tax assessments which are neither greater than 100% of fair market value nor unequally or improperly determined in relation

---

115. FLA. CONST. art. VII, §4(a).

116. FLA. CONST. art. VII, §4(b).

117. FLA. CONST. art. VII, §4(j).

118. FLA. CONST. art. VII, §4(8)(f) (county may reduce assessed value for parents or grandparents); *see generally* FLA. CONST. art. VII, §4 (detailing other exceptions from fair value).

to other properties within the same county. These principles flow from the constitutional directive that Florida's counties each have their own tax appraiser. We recognized in *Spooner*, of course, that the legislature has in recent years endeavored to equalize real property tax assessments among the counties by developing statewide valuation standards, and by superimposing the department as a monitoring force in an effort to achieve uniformity in procedures and equalization of results. We carefully noted the limits on the department's authority, however, and observed that in the last analysis the ability of the legislature to harmonize tax assessments throughout the state

> "must remain conditioned by the Constitution's directive that a class of county officers are assigned the primary responsibility to perform assessment functions. At best the legislative goal can be achieved only incrementally through cooperative efforts of the assessors and the Department, and by the development of procedures which will accommodate the responsibilities of both."[119] [FN 4]

We decline to hold, merely on the basis of an allegation that different values have been assigned to adjacent properties of like character in different counties, that a taxpayer can claim a violation of the "just valuation" requirement or that the department can be compelled to equalize the values. The trial court properly dismissed that count of the complaint which sought relief from the department.

The decision of the court below is quashed, and the case is remanded for the district court to reinstate the trial court's order of dismissal.

OVERTON, C. J., and BOYD, SUNDBERG and HATCHETT, JJ., concur.

Commentary and Questions

Article VII, Section 4 begins: "By general law regulations shall be prescribed which shall secure a just valuation of all property for ad valorem taxation...." Just valuation is fair market value, "established by the classic formula that it is the amount a 'purchaser willing but not obliged to buy, would pay to one willing but not obliged to sell.'" *Walter v. Schuler*, 176 So. 2d 81, 85–86 (Fla. 1965).

The core issue presented here is how a contiguous piece of real estate be can valued so differently, almost 190% per lot, by two different tax appraisers using the same yardstick of fair market value. The Court ducks the issue and rephrases it as a question of power: "The narrow question presented in this case is whether a cause of action lies against the Department of Revenue to compel equalization of ad valorem tax val-

---

119. [FN 4.] 345 So.2d at 1059–60. In also noting that the relatively new procedures for improving statewide uniformity had not seasoned in 1973 to the point of "flawless harmony" (*Id.* at 1060), we did not intend to imply that they would ever eradicate all inter-county variations. Infinite variations in the subjects of tax assessment, as well as the nature of the assessment process, preclude any serious prospect of ever achieving an assessment of each parcel of property within the state that is in complete and harmonious uniformity with every other parcel. All possible efforts toward the goal of uniformity should be pursued vigorously, but reasonable efforts short of the goal must always be tolerated.

uations...." The Court answers, no. There are sixty-seven property appraisers in the state, one in each county, and each assesses property within their county. Each is elected in a countywide election, so is beholden to no one other than the electorate. The result in *Straughn* is the court will not pit one against the other. In the *Spooner* case, cited and quoted in this opinion, the court held that:

> The mandate of "just valuation" derives from the Constitution. The requirement of statewide uniformity derives from statute. The latter is more a goal than a compellable right, and it would be naive to have expected instant statewide uniformity (assuming it can ever be achieved) merely because that goal had been announced by law. The Legislature commendably desired to create uniformity of assessments in Florida, but its ability to do so must remain conditioned by the Constitution's directive that a class of county officers are assigned the primary responsibility to perform assessment functions.

Spooner v. Askew, 345 So. 2d 1055, 1059 (Fla. 1976) (footnote omitted). The effort to coordinate between property appraisers and the Florida Department of Revenue continues four decades later.[120]

The Court also builds some flexibility into its standard in the *Spooner* quotation immediately above and in footnote 4 of the *Straughn* opinion: "Infinite variations in the subjects of tax assessment, as well as the nature of the assessment process, preclude any serious prospect of ever achieving an assessment of each parcel of property within the state that is in complete and harmonious uniformity with every other parcel." Compare this doubt of achieving uniformity with the assessments in the following case.

Southern Bell Telephone and Telegraph Company v. County of Dade

275 So. 2d 4 (Fla. 1973)

PER CURIAM.

By petition for certiorari, we have for review a decision of the District Court of Appeal, Third District (234 So.2d 135) on grounds of conflict with both prior decisions of this Court and different District Courts of Appeal of this State on the same points of law. Fla.Const., Art. V, s 4, F.S.A....

Petitioner sought relief from the 1967 assessment of its tangible personal property in Dade County, alleging that its property was assessed at a substantially higher percentage of market value than that which the tax assessor had systematically assessed the property of other taxpayers. Petitioner contended that (1) although its property was assessed at full market value, the assessor had generally assessed real property at a ratio of approximately 80% of its market value, and (2) the assessor's systematic

---

120. Florida Department of Revenue, Property Oversight Program, https://floridarevenue.com/property/Pages/Cofficial_MOI.aspx (last visited August 24, 2020) (providing manuals and guidelines).

use of net book value to assess tangible personal property resulted in the personal property of other taxpayers being assessed at a level substantially lower than that of the petitioner's property.

Respondents admitted the petitioner's property had been assessed at its full market value thereby reducing the basic issue for trial to the proof and effect of other property in the county being assessed at a lower level.

In a very lengthy opinion detailing the testimony and exhibits received, the trial judge denied petitioner's requested relief. On appeal, the District Court quoted extensively from the judgment, added its own language and affirmed denial of relief. See *Foley v. Weaver Drugs, Inc.*, Fla.1965, 177 So.2d 221.

To prove the assessment level of real property in the county, petitioner introduced evidence of three assessment sales ratio studies.

First, assessment sales ratio studies were described by two expert witnesses, Weil and Ekeblad, which established that an assessment sales ratio study is a scientific comparison of the assessments of properties with the sales prices of a statistically reliable sample of properties that are actually sold in the taxing jurisdiction. These experts confirmed that sales ratio studies give as objective measure of the level of assessment as can possibly be obtained, that they are widely used in other states, and that the generally accepted method of conducting them is outlined in a Guide for Assessment-Sales Ratio Studies published by the National Association of Tax Administrators....

The experts' actual experience in other states demonstrated that in such a study documentary stamps were reliable evidence of sales prices. Dr. Weil's studies disclosed that understamping was as prevalent as overstamping and that with the relatively large number of transactions utilized in sales ratio studies, any inaccuracies that creep in tend to offset one another with the result that studies based on documentary stamps are quite reliable.

Dr. Ekeblad, who made the statistical computations, demonstrated that in 1967 the best single estimate of the median level of assessment of all real properties was 81.37% of market value, with only 99 chances in 100 that the median level of assessment was no lower than 80.58% or higher than 82.17%.

Second, the next sales ratio study introduced by petitioner covered all Dade County sales transactions handled from July 1, 1966, to June 30, 1967, by the Keyes Company, one of the largest real estate firms in Florida. This study included only transactions in which a sales commission had been paid by one of the parties to Keyes. Therefore, there was no doubt that all of them involved actual sales price. Documentary stamps were not relied on to determine sales prices in this study. The prices were determined from the records of Keyes. As in the first study the tax roll was examined, the actual sales prices were compared with the assessments and a ratio of the sales price to the assessment of each property was computed. The resulting ratios were analyzed by the same process used in the Weil-Ekeblad study and disclosed a median assessment ratio of 82.01%. The similarity in the results of this study with those of the Weil-Ekeblad study supported the conclusions given by Weil and Ekeblad that a detailed investigation of each and every sale of record was unnecessary.

The Third, and final study introduced was made by the U.S. Bureau of Census, which considered sales of non-farm residential properties for the last six months of 1966. This study disclosed a median ratio of 83.2%.

Even though the three studies used samples selected in different ways, they reached remarkably similar results, ranging from a low of 81.37% to a high of 83.2%, with a variation of only 1.83%.

To show that the tangible personal property of other taxpayers had been assessed at a substantially lower level than the level at which petitioner's property was assessed, petitioner established (1) that the assessor had generally assessed personal property at its book value, (2) that under regulations of the Florida Public Service Commission and the Federal Communications Commission, petitioner is required to include in the cost of its property for accounting purposes certain items not generally capitalized by unregulated taxpayers, and (3) petitioner is required to use the straight line method of taking depreciation while other taxpayers may use various kinds of accelerated depreciation. On this point petitioner established that if other taxpayers were taking advantage of the accounting options available to them the book value of their property would range from 21% to 61% lower than the book value of similar property owned by petitioner. However, petitioner was unable to establish the extent to which other taxpayers actually were taking advantage of these options.

Respondents did not offer any evidence that sales ratio studies of the type introduced by petitioner are not a reliable and reasonable means of determining the assessment level in a taxing jurisdiction or that the studies introduced by petitioner had not been conducted according to generally accepted standards for conducting sales ratio studies, or that real property in the county was assessed at a level higher than the level disclosed by the studies. Instead, respondents opined that sales price is only one of the eight (formerly seven) factors which must be considered under Section 193.011 (formerly 193.021) Fla.Stat., F.S.A. in arriving at just valuation of property. They further opined that even if the price at which real property is sold is good evidence of its market value, that price may not be inferred from documentary stamps. They contended finally that the court should not accept a sales ratio study as reliable unless an investigation of each transaction is made to determine the sales price, whether the transaction was in fact at arm's length and, if so, whether the parties were fully informed when they agreed on the price.

Confronted with the foregoing, the Circuit Court denied relief, and the Third District Court of Appeal affirmed, holding that sales prices in the context of the studies introduced were not prima facie evidence of market value. Quoting in pertinent part from the judgment and opinion under review, we find these statements:

> "In spite of the fact that the Telephone Company's personal property was admittedly assessed at full market value, the Telephone Company would be

entitled to relief if it could prove that the County systematically assessed real property at some lesser percentage of fair market value....

"... To reach the result desired by the Telephone Company, it would then be necessary to again infer that the true consideration represents the true market value. This does not necessarily follow. The sale price of property does not even in itself conclusively or even prima facia reflect true market value...."

In *Dade County v. Salter*, Fla.1966, 194 So.2d 587, we recognized that the constitutional rights of a taxpayer are infringed if his property is assessed at a percentage of value substantially higher than the percentage at which other property in the county is generally assessed even though his assessment is not above fair market value. *Cf. Sioux City Bridge Co. v. Dakota County*, 260 U.S. 441; *Township of Hillsborough v. Cromwell*, 326 U.S. 620. Since the tax base includes both real and personal property and the total base largely determines the millage rate, it makes no difference whether it is real or personal property that is undervalued. [citations omitted].

The *Salter* case was decided on the pleadings. It held simply that the allegations of discrimination in the complaint stated a cause of action. It did not consider all the factual circumstances that may give a right to relief or how those facts must be proved. It did, however, establish one overriding principle: a taxpayer is entitled to a practical means of obtaining relief from discrimination. This case must be considered in light of that principle. In *Salter*, we held:

"... A taxpayer ... should not be precluded from relief because the sworn official has not performed the duty requiring him to assess all property at its full cash value. Nor does the granting of relief to these taxpayers in any respect affect or impair or be in any way inconsistent with the recent decisions of this Court holding that all real property in this State should be assessed at its full cash value.... The Supreme Court of the United States many years ago dealt with the identical problems in *Sioux City Bridge Co. v. Dakota County*, 260 U.S. 441, where Mr. Chief Justice Taft, speaking for the Court said:

'... This Court holds that the right of the taxpayer whose property alone is taxed at 100 per cent of its true value is to have his assessment reduced to the percentage of that value at which others are taxed even though this is a departure from the requirement of statute. The conclusion is based on the principle that where it is impossible to secure both the standards of the true value, and the uniformity and equality required by law, the latter requirement is to be preferred as the just and ultimate purpose of the law.'

"The Court then observed that to deny relief to the taxpayer would uphold the violation of the Fourteenth Amendment to the injury of the taxpayer in that litigation....

"To adhere to the opinion which has been filed would require these taxpayers, and other taxpayers who might find themselves in the same position in any of the sixty-seven counties in this State, to successfully institute and prosecute proceedings to require the assessor to raise all other properties in the county to the statutory valuation, a burden which in most instances would amount to depriving the taxpayer of any remedy whatever, in order to obtain relief...."

The "just valuation" at which property must be assessed under the Constitution and Section 193.011 (formerly 193.021) Fla. Stat. is synonymous with fair market value, i.e., the amount a purchaser willing but not obliged to buy would pay to a seller who is willing but not obliged to sell. *Walter v. Schuler*, Fla.1965, 176 So.2d 81. When no actual sale has occurred, Section 193.011 Fla.Stat., F.S.A. requires the assessor to place himself in the position of the parties to a hypothetical sale of the property, to consider all of the factors they would regard as important in fixing the price of the property and to arrive at an opinion of value.

When a sale has actually occurred each party to the transaction has prima facie made his own appraisal of the individual property based on his needs, his ability to pay, the price at which like properties are offered and other relevant factors. Each party has backed up his appraisal by paying or receiving the price finally negotiated. In reaching an agreement the parties influence the price negotiations of later buyers and sellers of similar properties. Therefore, in this context the price at which property is sold as indicated by documentary stamps on the instrument is prima facie evidence of its value. *See* Fla.Stat., ss 201.01 and 201.02, F.S.A.

In *Kelly v. Threlkeld*, [193 So. 2d 7 (Fla. App. 1966), citing *Florida Moss Products Co. v. City of Leesburg*, [93 Fla. 656, 112 So. 572 (Fla. 1927)], the Fourth District Court of Appeal held that documentary stamps can be prima facie evidence of consideration paid....

In *City of Tampa v. Colgan, supra,* our Court stated, among other things:

"... If similar property is commonly bought and sold, the price which it brings is the best test of the value of the land under consideration and the assessors need look no further ..."

* * *

Of course, sale price is not conclusive evidence of value in every case. The sale may not have been at arm's length. The parties may not have been fully informed. One party may have taken unfair advantage of the other. A full investigation of every sale might well reveal that many took place under other than ideal conditions, and departures from the ideal exist in any market, even the stock market. However, unusual transactions do not prevent the market as a whole from being good evidence of value.

Sub judice it is clear that, although in a limited number of cases where factors may exist that detract from the reliability of an individual transaction as evidence, taken as a whole, sales prices are acceptable indicators of value. Certainly, when a large number of sales are considered, the factors which detract from the reliability of individual sales tend to offset one another, and the overall result is highly dependable. This is especially true when steps have been taken to eliminate transactions which appear on their face not to be at arm's length.

Sales ratio studies are intended to provide a statistically reliable method of relating assessments to sales prices. They have been recognized and accepted by the courts of our state, *Burns v. Butscher*, [187 So.2d 594 (Fla. 1966)], and *Dickinson v. Geraci*, [190 So.2d 368 (Fla. App. 1966)], as well as having been recognized by the courts of other states as a reliable means of determining an assessment level. [citations omitted].

… In this case the evidence as established by the judgment's findings was uncontradicted that at least the Weil-Ekeblad study was conducted according to generally accepted principles for conducting sales ratio studies. In holding that the studies were not reliable, the courts below substituted their own views for the undisputed evidence.

Although the sales ratio studies in this case revealed the median assessment level of real property to be approximately 82% they also disclosed that the property of other taxpayers had not been assessed at any particular uniform level. A graph of the ratios reveals a bell-shaped curve with a few assessments at very low levels, the largest in the five percentage point range between 80% and 85%, and a few assessments at very high levels. The Courts below held that because the percentage range from 80% to 85% contained less than 50% of the ratios, petitioner was not entitled to relief. This holding runs contrary to the decisions of all the other courts that have considered this question. These decisions recognize that a taxpayer whose property is assessed at a level substantially higher than the average level of assessment suffers the same injury as he would suffer (1) if the property of every other taxpayer were assessed at a uniform level, and (2) if a taxpayer is denied relief either because other taxpayers are not treated uniformly or because they also suffer from discrimination, the assessor can make himself immune from suit by his discriminatory conduct. [citations omitted].

* * *

The courts below, having held that petitioner was not entitled to any relief, did not have occasion to consider how relief should be measured. This question is admittedly complicated, i.e., determining petitioner's fair share of the tax burden based upon a calculation of the ad valorem taxes petitioner would have been required to pay if the tax roll had been at full value, considering the established level of real property assessment and considering the level at which personal property had been assessed. Since the trial court did not consider or pass on this issue, the case should be remanded for an opportunity to do so.

For the reasons outlined above, the decision below is reversed and the cause remanded for further proceedings consistent herewith.

It is so ordered.

ERVIN, Judge (dissenting):

I feel I would be remiss if I did not briefly discuss why I think the petition for rehearing should be granted. The County points out in its petition that the Court majority herein at the appellate level has factually used sales ratio statistics of Real property transactions in Dade County as the basis for a factual finding concluding Southern Bell is entitled to assessment over-valuation relief, while Southern Bell's suit for relief is for alleged discriminatory overassessment of its Tangible personal property above the assessment of the property of other Dade County taxpayers.

The County points out in its petition for rehearing that

> "the record indicates ... that the County assessed tangible personal property in 1967 on the basis of its net book value, which was its original cost less depreciation.... Personalty valuations which were based on net book values that began with original costs, rather than present day replacement costs, did not take increasing values produced by inflationary trends into account...."

The majority opinion used an improper yardstick to compare the alleged systematic assessment discrimination between Southern Bell's tangible personal property assessment and other Dade County taxpayers' tangible personal property assessments. It used sales ratio statistics of real estate transactions to factually determine there existed discrimination in tangible personal property tax assessments.

It is quite apparent the majority predicates its decision in F.S. Section 193.011, F.S.A., which has primary reference to real property assessments under Section 4, Article VII of the State Constitution, F.S.A. Tangible personal property valuation obviously does not include many of the eight factors of F.S. Section 193.011, F.S.A., therefore it follows sales ratio statistics of real estate transactions (market value) are inapplicable as a basis for comparison in order to determine if there was a systematic discrimination.

It is obvious that the majority decision with its patently incorrect criterion for determining systematic discrimination plays havoc with Petitioner's admitted tax liability of $5,080,571.91, less the statutory discount. This disturbing result allows a basis for an even greater tax reduction than Southern Bell claimed in its complaint.

I fail to see any basis for conflict with the decisions of the trial court or District Court of Appeal. Those decisions represent findings of fact based upon evidentiary considerations. There is no departure by these lower courts from any rule of decisional law in the area of tax assessment. I think the majority has merely substituted its evidentiary findings for those of the lower tribunals is a conflict case.

I would have discharged the writ.

Commentary and Questions

The Court holds that a taxpayer is harmed if the taxpayer's property is assessed at a higher rate than others. The Court reasons: "A taxpayer whose property is assessed at a level substantially higher than the average level is required to contribute substantially more than his proportionate share of the tax burden. Therefore, the fact that other taxpayers are not assessed at a uniform level or that a few of them are also discriminated against does not bar a taxpayer from obtaining relief."

In establishing the taxpayer's rights in this case, note that the Court cites to United States Supreme Court decisions. The Court is establishing a federal rights case.

Note the unusual nature of the business being assessed. Southern Bell was regulated at state and federal levels, which mandated some important accounting practices, such as capitalization of assets and straight-line depreciation. Southern Bell's complaint regarding the tangible personal property assessment is that the county appraiser relied on net book value, that is, original cost less accrued depreciation. Southern Bell objected that it was forced by regulatory agencies to add some cost items when capitalizing its assets that non-regulated companies would not. This would result in a higher original cost of those assets, and hence, a higher original tax basis. Also, straight-line depreciation results in a higher net book value of tangible property when compared to accelerated depreciation, because the asset is depreciated at a slower rate with straight-line depreciation. Both practices are required of a regulated utility to minimize utility rates. A utility will only earn a modest rate of return on its assets while its utility rates recapture depreciation on a dollar-for-dollar basis. The utility is entitled to recapture depreciation as an expense in its rates, and the greater the depreciation expense, the higher the utility rates. Southern Bell is thus being hammered two ways on higher-capitalized assets and straight-line depreciation: it can only charge lower utility rates while paying higher tax rates based on net book value of its tangible assets. Is this the tax (property) appraiser's problem? The appraiser has been consistent in the use of net book value as its assessment measure. Is this a complaint that Southern Bell should take to its regulators—that their rules are causing the utility to pay higher taxes and therefore the ratepayers must pay higher utility rates for those taxes?

The Court relies on fair market value and elaborates on the concept of a willing seller and buyer: "When a sale has actually occurred each party to the transaction has prima facie made his own appraisal of the individual property based on his needs, his ability to pay, the price at which like properties are offered and other relevant factors. Each party has backed up his appraisal by paying or receiving the price finally negotiated." Is this a good measure for a regulated utility?

Finally, the Court confidently concludes that Southern Bell was assessed at a higher rate. How does this compare with its skepticism about the possibility of achieving uniform assessments expressed in the *Straughn* opinion above?

F. Bonds

"Borrowing money is a form of taxing the future, especially so far as governments are concerned."[121] A tension between the ease of issuing bonds and the accountability to those repaying the bonds runs through the following Court decisions. The tension appears in the restrictions imposed on general obligation bonds pledging the full faith and credit of the state to repay versus bonds repaid through other sources, such as revenue bonds. General obligation bonds are restricted and therefore more difficult to issue. The tension also appears in whether public approval is required to issue the

---

121. Joseph W. Little, *The Historical Development of Constitutional Restraints on the Power of Florida Governmental Bodies to Borrow Money*, 20 STETSON L. REV. 647, 650 (1991).

bonds. There is a strong inclination to avoid having to seek public approval on issuing bonds, because that approval is sometimes denied.

The 1968 Constitution established a conservative position on state and local bonds. The 1968 Constitution divided state bonding into two categories: pledges of the state's full faith and credit, and revenue bonds. The 1968 Constitution was the first real constitutional release on the use of revenue bonds. Full faith and credit bonds issued by the state were limited to financing or refinancing state fixed capital outlay projects which had been authorized by law. Full faith and credit bonds required a vote of the electors approving the issuance. Total full faith and credit bond amounts were further limited to 50% or less of the total tax revenue for the preceding two fiscal years, exclusive of revenue held under trust provisions otherwise appearing in the Constitution.[122] Full faith and credit bonds could be used without a vote of the electors to refund already-outstanding bonds if the full faith and credit bonds were at a lower net average interest rate.[123] The most recent years have exclusively seen full faith and credit bond reissues and no new fixed capital outlay bonds.

The 1968 Constitution authorized revenue bonds without a vote of the electorate to repay fixed capital outlay bonds. The revenue bonds were required to be payable solely from funds directly derived from sources other than state tax revenues.[124] The Legislature was required to first approve by appropriation or general law any project, building, or facility financed by revenue bonds.[125]

The 1968 Constitution authorized counties, school districts, municipalities, special districts, and other local government entities with taxing power to issue bonds, certificates of indebtedness, or any form of tax anticipation certificates. Bonds payable from ad valorem taxes and maturing more than twelve months after issue could only be issued: (1) for financing or refinancing capital projects authorized by law, and (2) when approved by the electors.[126] Municipal bonds refunding other outstanding bonds at a lower net average interest rate could be issued without voter approval.[127]

Subsequent constitutional amendments have seen a progressive loosening of restrictions. In 1970, pollution control and other water facility bonds were added. These permitted pledges of full faith and credit without an election. They were required, however, to be primarily payable from project revenues, and the project required authorization by general law.[128] Their total could not exceed 50% of the prior two years' tax revenue, and a state agency had to determine that the annual debt service was less than 75% of all pledged revenues when including other bonds secured by the same revenue source.[129]

---

122. FLA. CONST. art. VII, § 11(a),
123. FLA. CONST. art. VII, § 11(a).
124. FLA. CONST. art. VII, § 11(d).
125. FLA. CONST. art. VII, § 11(f).
126. FLA. CONST. art. VII, § 12.
127. FLA. CONST. art. VII, § 12.
128. FLA. CONST. art. VII, § 14.
129. FLA. CONST. art. VII, § 14.

In 1972, revenue bonds were authorized to fund student scholarship loans. The revenue bonds were to be secured by and primarily payable from the loan repayment proceeds.[130] No approving election is contained in this section.

In 1980, revenue bonds issued without an approving election were added to the Constitution for housing and related facilities.[131] The bonds were secured by and primarily payable from the financing, operation and sale of facilities, including mortgage and loan payments and other non-ad valorem taxation and other sources.[132] A state agency must certify that pledged revenues will exceed, in each fiscal year, the debt service of the bonds.[133]

Finally, in 1988, an amendment was added permitting bonds issued with the full faith and credit of the state without an approving election for transportation rights-of-way and bridges. The bonds are secured by and primarily payable from motor fuel and special fuel taxes, except those specified in Article VII, subsection 9(c). A state agency must certify that the bond service in each fiscal year is less than 90% of the same source of pledged revenues that year.[134]

The following decision is a comprehensive opinion, including the dissent, on bond financing. The financing mechanism in the case involves certificates of participation purchased by buyers.

Miccosukee Tribe of Indians of Florida v. South Florida Water Management District

48 So. 3d 811 (Fla. 2010)

QUINCE, J.

This case is before the Court on appeal from a circuit court judgment validating a proposed bond issue. We have jurisdiction. [citation omitted.] For the reasons expressed below, we affirm in part and reverse in part the circuit court's judgment.

FACTUAL AND PROCEDURAL HISTORY

In October 2008, the South Florida Water Management District (the District), filed a complaint in the Fifteenth Judicial Circuit seeking validation of certificates of participation (COPs), pursuant to Chapter 75 of the Florida Statutes, in order to purchase land owned by the United States Sugar Corporation for the purpose of Everglades restoration. The court issued a notice and order to show cause and scheduled a hearing for December 12, 2008.... The parties appeared before the court on December 12 and the court granted the District's motion to continue the hearing. The court subsequently [rescheduled] the bond validation proceeding for February 6, 2009.

* * *

---

130. FLA. CONST. art. VII, § 15.
131. FLA. CONST. art. VII, § 16(a).
132. FLA. CONST. art. VII, § 16(b).
133. FLA. CONST. art. VII, § 16(c).
134. FLA. CONST. art. VII, § 17.

The validation hearing was held over a number of days in February, March, July, and August of 2009. Counsel appeared on behalf of the District, New Hope, the Tribe, the state attorneys, Concerned Citizens of Glades, the Audubon Society, Nathaniel P. Reid, and U.S. Sugar. In the midst of these proceedings, various parties filed motions to abate the proceedings and reopen them for the court to consider new evidence regarding a modification of the transaction, which the court granted. The parties engaged in more expedited discovery and filed more motions during this time.

On August 26, 2009, the circuit court issued its final judgment, validating the COPs in the amount of $650 million, an amount sufficient to purchase 73,000 acres of property from U.S. Sugar. The order contained eight pages of factual findings and sixteen pages of legal conclusions. The court found that the District's responsibilities include restoring and cleaning up the Everglades ecosystem; the District's Governing Board had adopted resolutions amending the District's five-year plan to include acquisition of the U.S. Sugar lands, establishing a master lease-purchase program, and authorizing the issuance of COPs to finance these transactions; all of the meetings related to this matter had been open, public, and duly noticed. The court also found that under the master lease-purchase agreement, the District will purchase the property and ground lease the property to a nonprofit Leasing Corporation. In turn, the Leasing Corporation will lease back the property to the District, which will manage the property and make improvements to it. Under the agreement, the District must determine annually whether to appropriate funds to pay the Leasing Corporation for the annual rental of the property, and the District regains possession of the property at the end of the ground lease. Additionally, a Master Trust Agreement was executed to issue COPs and to hold the proceeds from the COPs in trust to pay the costs of acquiring, constructing, and installing facilities on the sites. The COPs are secured by the lease payments. The court concluded that the District has the legal authority to issue the COPs, that the COPs will serve a legal purpose (water storage and treatment), and that the issuance of the COPs complies with the requirements of law.

In June 2009, pursuant to sections 120.569 and 120.57, Florida Statutes (2009), and rule 28-106.201 of the Florida Administrative Code, New Hope requested a formal administrative hearing challenging the District's purchase of land from U.S. Sugar. Later, the Tribe filed a similar request. The District consolidated the parties' separate petitions for administrative hearing and dismissed them with prejudice for lack of standing. Both New Hope and the Tribe filed notices of administrative appeal, requesting that the district court grant them a formal hearing for their administrative law claim. The District filed an all-writs petition, asking this Court to transfer the administrative appeals cases from the district court because the cases deal with the same issues presented in the bond validation proceedings. We granted the petition and transferred [and consolidated] the cases.

In September 2009, the Tribe and New Hope filed separate notices of appeal regarding the bond validation proceeding. We granted the District's unopposed motion to consolidate the two bond validation appeals. We heard oral argument from the parties in April 2010.

ISSUES AND ANALYSIS

* * *

Judicial inquiry in a bond validation proceeding, both at the trial court and this Court, is limited to determining: (1) whether a public body has the authority to issue the subject bonds; (2) whether the purpose of the obligation is legal; and (3) whether the authorization of the obligation complies with the requirements of law. *See City of Gainesville v. State*, 863 So.2d 138, 143 (Fla.2003). This Court reviews the "trial court's findings of fact for substantial competent evidence and its conclusions of law de novo." *Id.* . . . The final judgment of validation comes to this Court clothed with a presumption of correctness. *See Strand v. Escambia County*, 992 So.2d 150, 154 (Fla.2008). Moreover, the appellants have the burden of demonstrating that the record and evidence fail to support the lower court's conclusions. *See Wohl v. State*, 480 So.2d 639, 641 (Fla.1985). We consider the issues raised within this legal framework.

Issue [handwritten annotation]

1. Findings of Fact and Economic Feasibility

The Tribe and New Hope argue that the factual findings made by the trial court in its order of final judgment are incomplete because the trial court failed to consider the economic feasibility of the project and because the court failed to recognize that the proceeds of the COPs will be used to purchase 73,000 acres from U.S. Sugar and not to finance infrastructure projects on the land.

In its conclusions of law in the final judgment, the trial court recognized that "the economic feasibility of the project is outside of its scope of review." The court acknowledged that the Tribe and New Hope had made strong arguments that the project is economically impossible. The court also questioned the wisdom of seeking this large amount of COPs during the current economic times. However, the court stated that it was "bound by precedent which instructs that economic feasibility is collateral to bond validation proceedings" and cited a number of previous decisions by this Court that stand for this proposition. Ultimately, the court stated that it "cannot and does not base its decision on whether the District will have the financing to actually complete a project of this magnitude."

Court said project is economically impossible but it was bound by precedent [handwritten annotation]

This Court has repeatedly explained that

the fiscal feasibility of a revenue project is an administrative decision to be concluded by the business judgment of the issuing agency. Such problems as the advisability of the project and its income potential, must be resolved at the executive or administrative level. They are beyond the scope of judicial review in a validation proceeding.

State v. Manatee County Port Auth., 171 So.2d 169, 171 (Fla.1965). In *Town of Medley v. State*, 162 So.2d 257, 258–59 (Fla.1964), we explained that the reasonableness and economic feasibility of the financing plan were "the responsibility and prerogative of the governing body of the governmental unit in the absence of fraud or violation of legal duty." ...

This Court has adhered to these limitations over the years. For example, in *State v. School Board of Sarasota County*, 561 So.2d 549, 553 (Fla.1990), we stated that "[q]uestions of business policy and judgment are beyond the scope of judicial interference and are responsibility of the issuing governmental units." Similarly, in *State v. City of Daytona Beach*, 431 So.2d 981, 983 (Fla.1983), we stated that "questions concerning the financial and economic feasibility of a proposed plan are to be resolved at the executive or administrative level and are beyond the scope of judicial review in a validation proceeding."

The rationale that underlies the limited judicial review in bond validation cases was explained by this Court in *Town of Medley*, 162 So.2d at 259:

> [T]he courts do not have the authority to substitute their judgment for that of officials who have determined that revenue certificates should be issued for a purpose deemed by them to be in the best interest of those whom they represent. ...
>
> A contrary holding would [give] the courts ... power in matters such as this to determine what in their opinion was good or bad for a city and its inhabitants thereby depriving the inhabitants of the right to make such decisions for themselves as is intended under our system of government.

Indeed, "[t]he function of a validation proceeding is merely to settle the basic validity of the securities and the power of the issuing agency to act in the premises. Its objective is to put in repose any question of law or fact affecting the validity of the bonds." [*State v.*] *Manatee County Port Auth.*, 171 So.2d at 171 [(Fla. 1965)].

[T]he Governing Board passed three separate resolutions authorizing this project, argued the merits of the project at various board meetings, and heard reports by District staff at a number of meetings and workshops. A reviewing court cannot go behind the resolutions of the Governing Board which authorized this project. Thus, we agree with the trial court's conclusion that economic feasibility is beyond the scope of judicial review in a bond validation proceeding.

2. Public Purpose

The Tribe and New Hope argue that the purpose of the obligation is not legal because the proceeds of the COPs will not be used for the purposes delineated by the District, but merely to buy land. They also argue that the public purpose cannot be discerned here because the District does not have specific projects planned for the various parcels of land to be acquired.

"This Court has held that 'legislative declarations of public purpose are presumed valid and should be considered correct unless patently erroneous.'" *Strand v. Escambia County*, 992 So.2d 150, 156 (Fla.2008) (quoting *Boschen v. City of Clearwater*, 777 So.2d 958, 966 (Fla.2001)). In its resolution approving the purchase of the land from U.S. Sugar and the issuance of the COPs, the District's Governing Board stated that the acquisition of the land will serve a public purpose by increasing the water storage capability of the District to reduce harmful freshwater discharges from Lake Okeechobee to Florida coastal rivers and estuaries; improving the timing and quality of delivery of cleaner water to the Everglades ecosystem; preventing phosphorous from entering the Everglades ecosystem; eliminating the need for "back-pumping" water into Lake Okeechobee and improving the sustainability of agriculture and green energy....

Additionally, the Legislature has declared that it is "necessary for the public health and welfare that water and water-related resources be conserved and protected" and that the "acquisition of real property for this objective shall constitute a public purpose for which public funds may be expended." § 373.139(1), Fla. Stat. (2008). The Legislature has also given water management districts the authority to "issue revenue bonds to finance the undertaking of any capital or other project for the purposes permitted by the State Constitution" and "to pay the costs and expenses incurred in carrying out the purposes of this chapter." § 373.584(1), Fla. Stat. (2008). In fact, the Legislature has provided that

[t]he powers and authority of districts to issue revenue bonds ... shall be coextensive with the powers and authority of municipalities to issue bonds under state law. The provisions of this section constitute full and complete authority for the issuance of revenue bonds and shall be liberally construed to effectuate its purpose.

§ 373.584(2), Fla. Stat. (2008).

For purposes of section 373.584, the definition of a project is broadly defined as

a governmental undertaking approved by the governing body of a water management district and includes all property rights, easements, and franchises relating thereto and deemed necessary or convenient for the construction, acquisition, or operation thereof, and embraces any capital expenditure which the governing body of a water management district shall deem to be made for a public purpose, including the refunding of any bonded indebtedness which may be outstanding on any existing project.

§ 373.584(4)(b), Fla. Stat. (2008). "Works of the district" are also broadly defined in chapter 373 as "those projects and works, including, but not limited to, structures, impoundments, wells, streams, and other watercourses, together with the appurtenant facilities and accompanying lands, which have been officially adopted by the governing board of the district as works of the district." § 373.019(26), Fla. Stat. (2008).

Thus, the District has authority to acquire lands to further the objective of conserving and protecting water and water-related resources. This objective has been deemed a "public purpose" by the Legislature. The District can also issue revenue bonds to finance the costs of carrying out its responsibilities and projects under chapter 373. Its authority to issue such bonds is coextensive with that of municipalities and is to be liberally construed so that it can serve its purpose. The lands upon which the District's projects reside are part of its statutorily defined works. In fact, it would be impossible for the District to construct its projects without first acquiring the accompanying lands. These statutes provide ample evidence to satisfy the first prong of our review, i.e., whether the District has the authority to issue the subject bonds. *See City of Gainesville,* 863 So.2d at 143.

The Appellants cite this Court's decision in *State v. Suwannee County Development Authority,* 122 So.2d 190 (Fla.1960), in support of their argument that no public purpose has been proven. In *Suwannee County,* the Development Authority sought validation of revenue certificates for the purchase of land and construction of buildings that would be leased to private businesses. *Id.* at 191. There were no definite plans as to what land would be purchased with the proceeds from the sale of the certificates, what buildings would be constructed, or what firms would lease the buildings. *Id.* The Development Authority intended to devise the program after the validation. *Id.* On review, this Court explained that in order to determine whether an agency may lawfully expend the bond proceeds for the contemplated purpose, the issuing governmental agency should set forth in the petition for validation "a description of the purpose for which the proceeds are to be used, which description should be sufficiently detailed to enable a member of the public and the state to determine whether the issuing agency can lawfully expend public monies therefor." *Id.* at 193. Thus, "petitions for validation of bonds and revenue certificates should set forth in reasonable detail the purpose or purposes which will be accomplished with the proceeds." *Id.* at 194.

The complaint for validation and two supplements to the complaint that were filed in this case describe the land to be acquired with the proceeds of the COPs and the structure of the financing agreement. The complaint also states that the land will be used to further the District's mandate to restore natural resources. Exhibits filed with the complaint include the Governing Board's resolutions which authorize the land purchase, the issuance of COPs, and the financing structure; a report detailing the benefits to be derived from the land acquisition; a number of reports relating to the District's projects and the Everglades restoration; and copies of the master lease-purchase agreement, the master trust agreement, the ground leases to be used for the leases between the District and the Leasing Corporation, the assignment agreement between the Leasing Corporation and the named trustee, and the COPs to be issued. In all, well over 500 pages of exhibits were filed with the complaint for validation.

This is a far cry from the *Suwannee County* case, where the complaint did not specify what land would be purchased, what buildings would be constructed, and to whom the buildings would be leased. Here, the 73,000 acres have been identified. The land will be leased back to U.S. Sugar, which will be required to maintain the land as specified in the ground lease and to use best practices in its farming. The land will eventually house various water storage and treatment projects. At the July 13, 2009, evidentiary hearing, the District's Executive Director specified the various projects and uses for each parcel of the 73,000 acres. In fact, it was the lack of such projects or planned uses for the remaining 107,000 acres that caused the trial court to deny validation of COPs for the purchase of those additional acres.

This Court addressed a similar challenge based on the fact that "plans and specifications of the proposed improvements were not offered in evidence by" the governmental entity seeking validation in *Rianhard v. Port of Palm Beach District*, 186 So.2d 503, 505 (Fla.1966). In that case, we concluded that the introduction of the supporting resolution, which "sufficiently describe[d] the purposes for which the funds derived from the sale of the certificates [would] be expended," was "all that was necessary to justify validation." *Id.* We reiterated this holding in *Strand*, when we stated that "the admission of a resolution may be sufficient evidence justifying a bond validation." *Strand*, 992 So.2d at 156. There, the County offered into evidence its ordinance and resolution authorizing bonds for a road construction project and presented testimony concerning the purpose of the project and the financing mechanism. *See id.* at 155. We concluded that these legislative findings were "competent, substantial evidence sufficient to support the final judgment." *Id.* at 156.

The same can be said in the instant case, where the trial court conducted nine days of evidentiary hearings resulting in thousands of pages of transcripts, heard testimony from numerous expert witnesses, and considered numerous evidentiary materials. The transcript contains numerous passages in which the trial judge questions witnesses to gain more information and asks the parties to clarify various issues. The trial court's order of final judgment is comprehensive and well-documented. The arguments by the Appellants here do not meet the burden of "demonstrat[ing] from the record the failure of the evidence to support the [government body's] and the trial court's conclusions." *Wohl v. State*, 480 So.2d 639, 641 (Fla.1985). The trial court's final judgment of validation comes to this Court "clothed with a presumption of correctness." *Strand*, 992 So.2d at 154 (citing *Wohl*, 480 So.2d at 641). We conclude that there is competent substantial evidence in the record to support the finding of a public purpose.

3. Constitutional Challenges

The Tribe and New Hope argue that the transaction is not valid because it does not comply with several provisions of the Florida Constitution. These include the prohibition in article VII, section 10 against using the state's taxing power or credit to aid a private entity or person; the requirement of article VII, section 12 that voters must approve bonds or COPs which are payable from ad valorem taxation and mature more than twelve months after issuance; and the requirement in article VII, section 11 that bonds issued by the state or its agencies must first be approved by the Legislature through an act relating to appropriations or by general law. For the reasons explained below, we conclude that the instant transaction does not violate any of these constitutional provisions.

a. Public Purpose Test of Article VII, Section 10

Article VII, section 10 of the Florida Constitution provides in pertinent part: "Neither the state nor any county, school district, municipality, special district, or agency of any of them, shall ... give, lend or use its taxing power or credit to aid any corporation, association, partnership or person....” The Appellants contend that the land acquisition in this case violates this constitutional provision because the District is buying lands that will then be leased back to U.S. Sugar for a number of years, therefore not meeting the paramount public purpose test.

The basic test for determining whether an expenditure of public funds violates this section of the Florida Constitution is whether such expenditure is made to accomplish a public purpose. If the District has used either its taxing power or pledge of credit to support issuance of bonds, the purpose of the obligation must serve a paramount public purpose and any benefits to a private party must be incidental. *See State v. JEA*, 789 So.2d 268, 272 (Fla.2001) [citations omitted].

As used in article VII, section 10, “credit” means “the imposition of some new financial liability upon the State or a political subdivision which in effect results in the creation of a State or political subdivision debt for the benefit of private enterprise.” *Jackson-Shaw Co. v. Jacksonville Aviation Auth.*, 8 So.3d 1076, 1095 (Fla.2008) (quoting *Nohrr v. Brevard County Educ. Facilities Auth.*, 247 So.2d 304, 309 (Fla.1971)). This Court has explained that the lending of credit means:

> [T]he assumption by the public body of some degree of direct or indirect obligation to pay a debt of the third party. Where there is no direct or indirect undertaking by the public body to pay the obligation from public funds, and no public property is placed in jeopardy by a default of the third party, there is no lending of public credit.

Id. (quoting *State v. Housing Fin. Auth.*, 376 So.2d 1158, 1160 (Fla.1979)). Under this definition, we conclude that the COPs in this case do not contemplate a pledge of the District’s credit, and that only a public purpose, not a paramount public purpose, need be shown.

In its final judgment, the trial court concluded that the acquisition of the land would serve the public purpose of water storage and treatment. The trial court noted that the Governing Board had voted to approve the acquisition after much debate and that District witnesses had outlined, parcel by parcel, the immediate and future benefits to be gained by the land acquisition. The court found that the following benefits would be achieved: storage and treatment of water before it is pumped into Lake Okeechobee; additional storage and treatment facilities that will work in conjunction with Comprehensive Everglades Restoration Projects basins; and land that will be valuable for future land swaps.

* * *

In the instant case, the District will retain title to the lands acquired. The land will be leased back to the seller U.S. Sugar to continue its agricultural operations, which will generate revenues and maintain the land until the District can construct the infrastructure projects required for water storage and treatment for Everglades restoration. Because we conclude that the purchase of the property serves the public purposes of furthering Everglades restoration and the management of water resources, the requirements of article VII, section 10 are satisfied.

b. Voter Referendum Requirement of Article VII, Section 12

Article VII, section 12 of the Florida Constitution, provides:

> Local bonds.—Counties, school districts, municipalities, special districts and local governmental bodies with taxing powers may issue bonds, certificates of indebtedness or any form of tax anticipation certificates, payable from ad valorem taxation and maturing more than twelve months after issuance only:
>
> (a) to finance or refinance capital projects authorized by law and only when approved by vote of the electors who are owners of freeholds therein, not wholly exempt from taxation; or
>
> (b) to refund outstanding bonds and interest and redemption premium thereon at a lower net average interest cost rate.

The trial court concluded that the referendum requirement of article VII, section 12 does not apply in this case because the District's obligation to make the lease payments is an annual obligation that does not extend more than twelve months and the lease payments are not payable from ad valorem taxation within the meaning of the constitutional provision. The trial court found that the arguments advanced by the Tribe and New Hope ignored the plain language of the Florida Constitution, the relevant Florida Statutes, the governing resolution and agreements, and this Court's recent decision in *Strand v. Escambia County*, 992 So.2d 150, 157–59 (Fla.2008), in which this Court reaffirmed its long-held distinction between pledges of ad valorem *taxing power* and the use of ad valorem tax *revenues*. We agree.

In *State v. Miami Beach Redevelopment Agency*, 392 So.2d 875 (Fla.1980), we explained that a referendum is not required by article VII, section 12 when there is no direct pledge of the ad valorem taxing power. Although contributions may come from ad valorem tax revenues, "[w]hat is critical to the constitutionality of the bonds is that, after the sale of the bonds, a bondholder would have no right, if [funds] were insufficient to meet the bond obligations ... to compel by judicial action the levy of ad valorem taxation." *Id.* at 898. Where a governing body is not obliged and cannot be compelled to levy any ad valorem taxes, then the obligation is not "payable from ad valorem taxation" for purposes of article VII, section 12, and referendum approval is not required. *Id.* [citations omitted.]

The trial court found that the District has not pledged its ad valorem taxing powers to pay any sum under the lease agreement or any of the leases, cannot be compelled to levy any ad valorem tax to pay the lease payments, and cannot be compelled to pay any lease payments beyond one year. We agree. Under the terms of the Master Lease Purchase Agreement, the basic lease payments are payable only from funds appropriated by the Governing Board and are not payable "from any source of taxation." The District has not pledged its "full faith and credit ... for payment of such sums." Further, the agreement provides that "[n]either the [Leasing] Corporation, the Trustee, nor any certificate holder may compel the levy of ad valorem taxes by the Governing Board to pay the lease payments." The District's Chief Financial Officer also testified that the way the deal was structured, none of the certificate holders could ever compel the District to levy ad valorem taxes in order to pay the District's obligations. Under the nonappropriation clause of the agreement, the obligations and liabilities are dependent upon appropriations being made by the Governing Board. Additionally, the Governing Board is free to terminate the lease annually without further obligation and the certificate holders are limited to lease remedies. The failure of the Governing Board to appropriate the sufficient funds for lease payments does not constitute a default, does not require payment of a penalty, and does not limit the District's right to purchase or use facilities similar in function. Instead, the nonappropriation of the funds results in the termination of the lease, requiring the District to surrender possession of the facilities to the trustee for the remainder of the term of the ground lease. However, the fee title to the property remains in the name of the Governing Board. Thus, the terms of the agreement maintain the District's "full budgetary flexibility." *State v. Brevard County*, 539 So.2d 461, 464 (Fla.1989) [citations omitted].

The Tribe and New Hope assert that this nonappropriation clause is illusory because the District cannot practically walk away from its obligation. They cite *Frankenmuth Mutual Insurance Co. v. Magaha*, 769 So.2d 1012 (Fla.2000), and *Volusia County v. State*, 417 So.2d 968, 969 (Fla.1982), in support of this argument. However, we find both cases to be distinguishable from the instant case.

Frankenmuth involved a master lease agreement for computer equipment to be used for county payroll and central data processing for the county offices. In addition to a nonappropriation clause that terminated the lease if the funding authority failed to appropriate funds to make the lease payments, the agreement also contained a nonsubstitution clause, providing that the county could not purchase or rent substitute computer equipment for two years in the event of nonappropriation. *See Frankenmuth*, 769 So.2d at 1014–18. Although the agreement stated that there was no pledge of ad valorem taxes by the county and the county could not be compelled to appropriate funds to make the lease payments, we concluded that the nonsubstitution clause rendered the nonappropriation clause illusory.... *See id.* at 1024. Thus, the county was "morally compel[led] ... to pledge ad valorem taxes to fulfill the obligations of the lease." *Id.* at 1026.

Similarly, in *Volusia County*, 417 So.2d at 972, the county pledged all available revenues and covenanted "to do all things necessary to continue receiving the various revenues" pledged in bonds for the construction of a new jail. We concluded that these two pledges would "inevitably lead to higher ad valorem taxes during the life of the bonds, which amounts to the same thing." *Id.*

Here, the master lease agreement contains a nonappropriation clause that gives the District the right to terminate the lease on an annual basis if the Governing Board should decide not to appropriate the funds for the lease.... Unlike *Volusia County*, there are no further pledges as to the source of revenues or efforts to maintain revenues. Unlike *Frankenmuth*, the only the penalties for nonappropriation are normal lease penalties, i.e., the District loses possessory interest for the term of the lease and this interest may be re-leased for the benefit of the certificate holders. At the termination of the lease, the District regains possession and it always retains title to the land. We conclude that this structure maintains the District's budgetary flexibility and thus does not require a referendum under article VII, section 12.

* * *

c. Legislative Approval under Article VII, Section 11(f)

Article VII, section 11 of the Florida Constitution governs state bonds and revenue bonds. Subsection (f) provides that "[e]ach project, building, or facility to be financed or refinanced with revenue bonds issued under this section shall first be approved by the Legislature by an act relating to appropriations or by general law." This provision applies to bonds issued by "the state or its agencies." Art. VII, § 11(d), Fla. Const. The trial court concluded that the legislative approval was not required in this case because the District was not a state agency for purposes of article VII of the Florida Constitution. The trial court based this conclusion on the fact that article VII, section 1(a) of the Florida Constitution prohibits the state and its agencies from levying ad valorem taxes, while article VII, section 9(b) authorizes the levy of ad valorem taxes "for water management purposes" and for "all other special districts." The court reasoned that because the District can and does levy ad valorem taxes, it cannot be deemed a "state agency" under article VII.

Water management districts have an "amorphous nature" in Florida law, being deemed state agencies or arms of the state for some purposes, but not for other purposes. *Compare Fla. Sugar Cane League, Inc. v. South Fla. Water Mgmt. Dist.*, 617 So.2d 1065, 1066 (Fla. 4th DCA 1993) (explaining that the district is a "regulatory state agency" subject to Florida's Administrative Procedure Act), *with Martinez v. South Fla. Water Mgmt. Dist.*, 705 So.2d 611 (Fla. 4th DCA 1997) (determining that the District was not subject to the provisions of the Drug-Free Workplace Act because it was not a state agency). In this case the dispositive question is whether the District is a "state agency" for purposes of article VII, section 11(f), which would require legislative approval through general law or an appropriations act before the District could issue revenue bonds. In the past, we have concluded that water management districts are not included in the prohibition against state ad valorem taxation in article VII, section 1(a) of the Florida Constitution. *See St. Johns River Water Mgmt. Dist. v. Deseret Ranches of Florida, Inc.*, 421 So.2d 1067, 1070 (Fla.1982) (concluding that ad valorem taxes levied by the district did not violate the constitutional prohibition against state ad valorem taxes because article VII, section 9 "specifically authorizes the levying of ad valorem taxes for water management purposes," and section 373.503 of the Florida Statutes "provides the implementing legislation for ad valorem taxation to finance the works of the District")....

Accordingly, we agree with the trial court's conclusion that legislative approval is not required before the District can issue these certificates of participation.

* * *

5. Purchase of Land Option

The purchase agreement between U.S. Sugar and the District contains an "Option to Purchase Real Property," which gives the District an exclusive option to purchase an additional 107,000 acres for a period of three years after the closing date of the sale at a fixed price of $7400 per acre. During the following seven years, the provision gives the District a nonexclusive option to purchase the land at the appraisal value and the right of first refusal if U.S. Sugar sells the option land. There is no mention of a cost for this option in this section of the purchase agreement, only a listing of the cost per acre should the option be exercised. The parties disagree on whether the price to be paid for the 73,000 acres includes a cost for the option to purchase the additional 107,000 acres of U.S. Sugar land. Additionally, the District asserts that this issue was not raised below by the Appellants and thus is not preserved for review by this Court.

The order of final judgment states that the District is "initially acquiring approximately 73,000 acres for approximately $536 million, with a $50 million option to acquire the remaining 107,000 acres later in time." The record of the proceedings below is replete with evidence to support the trial court's factual determination that the option to purchase the additional acreage will cost the District $50 million. The record also indicates that the Appellants raised the issue of the cost of the option during the hearing.

In various written responses and throughout the validation hearing, the Appellants asserted that the option to purchase the additional 107,000 acres would cost the District $50 million. The District never directly contradicted these assertions and, in fact, the testimony of several District witnesses tends to support the assertions. On redirect questioning, the District's Deputy Executive Director in Charge of Everglades Restoration testified that the $50 million value of the option had been presented to the Governing Board. On cross-examination, the District's Budget Director admitted that the $536 million purchase price "appeared" to include payment for the option. Although the District's Executive Director would not assign a monetary value to the option, she admitted on cross-examination that an expert appraiser had "blended [the value of the option and the value of the land] together in a very intricate way." Additionally, the District never disagreed with the judge's characterization of the option as costing $50 million.

The record of the May 2009 Governing Board meeting also supports the conclusion that $50 million was being paid for the option. The District's Director of Land Acquisitions testified that "the exclusive three-year option has a value the appraisers put in the marketplace of $50 million." When asked by a Board member whether the $50 million would be credited to the land cost if the option were exercised, the Director responded no and explained that the $50 million had to be paid to U.S. Sugar at the closing. She further explained that "the $50 million is part of the acquisition price, the 536."

The record of the bond validation hearing also negates the District's assertion that the Appellants never raised the issue of whether COPs can be used to purchase a land option. Counsel for both Appellants challenged the public purpose of the $50 million in COPs that would be spent on the option. The Tribe's counsel argued that the option money would not be spent on anything tangible, that there was no public benefit because the District was merely buying an opportunity, and that the taxpayers would be responsible for the $50 million debt even if the District never exercised the option. New Hope's counsel made a similar argument in closing, questioning the public purpose of the $50 million option.

Based on the portions of the record described above, we find competent, substantial evidence to support the circuit court's conclusion that the purchase agreement includes a $50 million cost for the option to purchase the remaining 107,000 acres of U.S. Sugar land. We also conclude that the issue of whether the option serves a public purpose was presented to the circuit court below and thus was properly preserved for our review. The circuit court found the record "essentially devoid of any information discussing how the remaining 107,000 acres (if acquired) would be utilized" and thus the legality of the bond validation as to that acreage could not be determined. Because no public purpose has been proven as to the land that is the subject of the option, no public purpose has been shown for the option either. Thus, we reverse that part of the circuit court's order validating $50 million in COPs related to the land option.

6. Conveyance of Land to Municipalities

The Tribe argues that the transaction is illegal because the District plans to convey some of the acquired lands to local communities for economic development. The Tribe contends that the District does not have the legal authority to purchase land with the express purpose of conveying it to a local governmental entity and that a purchase for this purpose exceeds the District's statutory authority to purchase land so that "water-related resources [may] be conserved and protected." § 373.139(1), Fla. Stat. (2008). We find no merit to this argument.

The Legislature has given the District authority to convey land to a governmental entity. The statute specifically provides as follows:

> Any water management district within this chapter shall have authority to convey or lease to any governmental entity, other agency described herein or to the United States Government, including its agencies, land or rights in land owned by such district not required for its purposes under such terms and conditions as the governing board of such district may determine.

§ 373.056(4), Fla. Stat. (2008). Additionally, section 373.089(1), Florida Statutes (2008), authorizes the District to sell lands that the Governing Board has determined to be surplus. Thus, there is no question that the District has the authority to convey land to local communities. Moreover, the statutory authorization to dispose of *surplus* land clearly indicates that water management districts may acquire more land than is ultimately required for a project. *Cf. Dep't of Transp. v. Fortune Fed. Sav. & Loan Ass'n*, 532 So.2d 1267, 1269–70 (Fla.1988) (explaining that the state may take more property than necessary for a contemplated project when it would save money by doing so).

CONCLUSION

With the exceptions stated above, we conclude that the District has the authority to issue the certificates of participation for the purchase of the 73,000 acres from U.S.

Sugar, that this obligation serves the public purpose of conserving and protecting water and water-related resources, and that the authorization of the obligation complies with the requirements of law. *See City of Gainesville v. State*, 863 So.2d 138, 143 (Fla.2003). However, because the purchase of the option does not serve a public purpose, COPs may not be issued to cover this expense. Further, to the extent that the substitution of other lands may implicate a pledge of the District's ad valorem taxing power, such lands may not be substituted.

Accordingly, we affirm in part and reverse in part the circuit court's order of final judgment validating $650 million in certificates of participation to finance the land acquisition.

It is so ordered.

LEWIS, J., concurring in result only.

Restoration of the Everglades and environmental protection are topics of both great public concern and importance. Water quality, flood control, water supply, and ecosystem protection are critical concerns in Florida. The wisdom and desirability of positive steps to restore and protect our environment are beyond dispute. Governor Charlie Crist has proposed a bold vision for the future, and those involved in this work and movement should be commended. However, the wisdom, desirability, and vision of the underlying project are not considerations in the legal analysis of the validity of the proposed bond issue here. [citation omitted] I do recognize and acknowledge that my reading of Florida constitutional requirements and restrictions on long-term public debt payable from ad valorem taxation is not currently the majority view of this Court and, therefore, I must concur in result only.

The plan here is just another variety of the attempted devices to circumvent the Florida Constitution, as established by Florida citizens, and contains highly questionable aspects, such as the creation of an excess land "real property slush fund" referred to in the final judgment below as "valuable for future land swaps." Additionally, the substance of this bond issue falls within article VII, section 12 of the Florida Constitution, which requires the approval of the voters in a referendum.

First, the final judgment below addressed, and oral argument confirmed, that a portion of the proposed project includes "land that will be valuable for future land swaps" without any attempt to define or disclose anything further for the purpose of that land in this bond issue. While flexibility and economic considerations may favor this type of undisclosed "slush fund" of real property, considerations for legal validity do not allow this nebulous "pot of land." Not only does the law require more details or parameters, this "land swap" concept without boundaries is certainly subject to abuse and mischief. The law of Florida with regard to public debt requires at least some detail with regard to all of the property purchased with the bond proceeds and, most certainly, more detail than just a "pot" of land for "future land swaps." *See State v. Suwannee Cnty. Dev. Auth.*, 122 So.2d 190, 193–94 (Fla.1960). While this is not fatal for the entire project, the real property in the "slush fund" for "land swaps" should not be approved. This is not sufficiently detailed to allow the public or the

State to legitimately determine whether the future undisclosed and indeterminate "land swaps" are proper expenditures of public monies.

Second, and importantly, article VII, section 12, of the Florida Constitution requires that any long-term public financing payable from ad valorem taxes and maturing more than twelve months after issue be approved through referendum:

> Counties … *special districts* and local governmental bodies with taxing powers may issue bonds [and] certificates of indebtedness … *payable from ad valorem taxation* and maturing more than twelve months after issuance only:
>
> (a) to finance or refinance capital projects authorized by law and *only when approved by vote of the electors.…*

Art. VII, § 12(a), Fla. Const. (emphasis added).

The finding by the trial court and the bond argument advanced by the bond proponents here that the obligation to make payments under the proposed structure is *only* an annual obligation and does not extend more than twelve months is fantasy at the highest level. This phantom and illusory "walk away" argument is built on a foundation of straw. Those who seek public money, but to avoid public approval, have developed a variety of devices that create a "theoretical" illusion that there is a legitimate escape from the obligation to continue payments beyond twelve months. This "phantom" escape argument has been rejected by this Court in *Frankenmuth Mutual Insurance Co. v. Magaha*, 769 So.2d 1012 (Fla.2000). This Court has understood the necessity to look beyond the self-serving language and disclaimers of any long-term obligations to analyze the effect of the documents as applied and as a matter of practical reality.…

In a similar manner, this non-income producing plan depends on ad valorem taxes to repay bondholders. The uncontradicted evidence from the Water Management District established that with the proposed involvement of federal funds and the integrated nature of the proposed expansive water restoration work, the Water Management District would not and could not simply "walk away" from this land purchase. In my view, the decision to issue bonds to fund a project without first obtaining approval through a constitutionally mandated referendum is contrary to the clear and plain words of article VII, section 12, of the Florida Constitution. Article VII, section 12, was clearly designed to address the expanding capital needs of local government, but was tempered by the inclusion of democratic control with regard to the decision to finance "capital projects" with long-term debt "payable from ad valorem taxation." Art. VII, § 12, Fla. Const. In this context, the majority's avoidance of this clear command perpetuates and expands a distortion of our fundamental organic law, leads us beyond our prior precedent, and denies the voters of this State their constitutional right to determine whether their local governments should issue long-term debt that is "payable from ad valorem taxation," as that phrase is understood through its "usual and obvious meaning." *City of Jacksonville v. Cont'l Can Co.*, 113 Fla. 168, 151 So. 488, 489–90 (Fla.1933).…

I write separately in this context to emphasize two additional points that, in my view, demonstrate the violence that expansion of the legal fiction of *State v. Miami*

Beach Redevelopment Agency, 392 So.2d 875 (Fla.1980), visits upon the plain text and manifest intent of article VII, section 12. First, much of our case law in this area has been opaque and counterintuitive due to its complete divorce from the text of this constitutional provision. *Cf. Cont'l Can Co.*, 151 So. at 490 ("Constitutions import the utmost discrimination in the use of language, *that which the words declare is the meaning of the instrument*" (emphasis added)). Here, the Court should not expand prior decisions from different contexts to advance a movement away from the text of article VII, section 12.

Second, article VII, section 10, of the Florida Constitution ("Pledging Credit") further undermines application of the "pledge of taxing power only" premise of *Miami Beach* in the context presented here. This separate, distinct constitutional provision demonstrates that the framers of our Constitution were aware of, *and intended a textual distinction between,* an entity of local government "*giv[ing], lend[ing] or us[ing] its taxing power or credit,*" as addressed in that constitutional provision, and an entity of local government issuing "bonds, certificates of indebtedness or any form of tax anticipation certificates, payable from ad valorem taxation," as addressed in article VII, section 12. (Emphasis added.) If the framers had truly intended for article VII, sections 10 and 12, to each only address *pledges of the taxing power* of local government, then these constitutional drafters would have used similar language in section 12; however, they did *not* do so. Thus, the faulty premise of *Miami Beach* accomplishes that which we are proscribed from doing as judicial officers who have sworn to support, protect, and defend our state Constitution: It amends article VII, section 12, through judicial fiat by removing and rendering meaningless the phrase "payable from ad valorem taxation" and replacing it with materially different language drawn from a separate, distinct constitutional provision (i.e., article VII, section 10)....

When faced with a typical capital project, such as the land-purchase plan involved in this case, I would interpret and enforce article VII, section 12, as written and would also salvage and apply a long-forgotten portion of our *Miami Beach* decision: "The Court looks at the *substance* and *not the form* of the proposed bonds" to determine whether the entity of local government has complied with the Constitution. 392 So.2d at 894 (emphasis added). Where, as here, the bond-financing plan will inevitably lead to diverting funds from ad valorem tax revenue to pay for or "service" the associated long-term debt for a non-revenue producing capital project, the Constitution requires a referendum [citations omitted]. Political expediency cannot alter the text of the Florida Constitution nor should it be used to thwart the will of the voters of this State.

* * *

Even good or great ideas that require long-term public debt payable from ad valorem taxation must follow constitutional requirements. For these reasons, I can join in the result only, but reject the unjustifiable expansion of a fundamentally flawed principle, which operates to circumvent voter participation in a decision that requires popular vote approval under the Florida Constitution.

Commentary and Questions

The Court first confronts whether the project is economically feasible by noting that the trial "court acknowledged that the [opponents] had made strong arguments that the project is economically impossible." The Court demurs on assessing feasibility, however, and says, "[t]he function of a validation proceeding is merely to settle the basic validity of the securities and the power of the issuing agency to act in the premises. Its objective is to put in repose any question of law or fact affecting the validity of the bonds."[135] How does this relate to the Court's following rules on deciding a public purpose?

The Court begins its analysis of public purpose by reiterating: "This Court has held that 'legislative declarations of public purpose are presumed valid and should be considered correct unless patently erroneous.' *Strand v. Escambia County*, 992 So. 2d 150, 156 (Fla. 2008) (quoting *Boschen v. City of Clearwater*, 777 So. 2d 958, 966 (Fla. 2001))."

The Court then gives the explanation for determining public purpose:

> The basic test for determining whether an expenditure of public funds violates [Article VII, section 10] of the Florida Constitution is whether such expenditure is made to accomplish a public purpose. If the District has used either its taxing power or pledge of credit to support issuance of bonds, the purpose of the obligation must serve a paramount public purpose and any benefits to a private party must be incidental. If the District has not exercised its taxing power or pledged its credit to support the bond obligation, the obligation is valid if it serves a public purpose. Incidental private benefit from a public revenue bond issue is not sufficient to negate the public character of the project (internal citations omitted).

As stated, either the use of taxing power or the pledge of credit triggers the need to serve a paramount public purpose where private benefit can be only incidental.

---

135. *See also* Little, supra note 121, at 654-55 (footnote citations omitted):
Florida is one of a few states that permits the bona fides of the borrowing governmental entity's authority to issue and sell any form of debt to be tested by adjudication in advance of the sale. As Florida lawyers and financiers know, a final judgment validating a borrower's authority is thereafter "forever conclusive" against it and "shall never be called into question in any court by any person or party." This power, created to eliminate any uncertainties of the government's legal capacity to issue a particular debt, confers substantial advantage upon both the governmental borrower and the private lender who supplies the money to the government by purchasing the bonds. The lender gets advance assurance that the bonds are "valid," which means any subsequent legal action brought to enforce the provisions of the bonding agreement cannot be defeated by the defense that the borrowing governmental entity had no power to borrow money or acted ultra vires. The borrowing government gets a better deal in the loan agreement (probably a lower rate of interest) by virtue of the ironclad assurance that the lending governmental entity has the power to incur the debt.

The obvious clash within the Court opinion is whether the bonds must be put to a public referendum. The Court majority concludes no, because the annual lease payments can be terminated at twelve months, and no ad valorem tax powers are pledged under the *Strand* analysis. Justice Lewis disagrees and follows his contention that originated in *Strand*, characterizing the twelve-month, terminable lease as "fantasy at the highest level." Justice Lewis bluntly observes: "Those who seek public money, but to avoid public approval, have developed a variety of devices that create a 'theoretical' illusion that there is a legitimate escape from the obligation to continue payments beyond twelve months." Grounding his objection in public control, he writes: "Article VII, section 12, was clearly designed to address the expanding capital needs of local government, but was tempered by the inclusion of democratic control with regard to the decision to finance 'capital projects' with long-term debt 'payable from ad valorem taxation.'" Who is right? Recall Professor Little's remark at the beginning of this book section on bonding that: "Borrowing money is a form of taxing the future, especially so far as governments are concerned."[136]

The Court notes at the beginning of the opinion that the bonds are being issued "in order to purchase land owned by the United States Sugar Corporation for the purpose of Everglades restoration." Are South Florida River Water Management District taxpayers in effect paying for an Everglades clean-up project? Is this the problem encountered in *Town of Palm Beach v. Palm Beach County*, but on a much larger scale, where ad valorem taxpayers are funding benefits realized outside their taxing district?

The Court warns the District away from including by substitution any land acquired through a pledge of ad valorem taxes. Is this restriction necessary if the remaining indebtedness on those bonds is refinanced by money obtained through this financing?

The Court also notes that the water management district's authority "to issue such bonds is coextensive with that of municipalities and is to be liberally construed so that it can serve its purpose." Note this is an explicit, precedential statement establishing a water management district's bonding power. Is this accurate? Do the home rule powers of counties and municipalities to tax for bond funding and the issuance of the bonds differ from the powers of special districts?

The following decision is identified as a corrected memorandum opinion based solely on two typographical errors in the original opinion.[137] This four-to-three opinion closely divides on whether a pledge of state credit has been extended to private use. Note that the majority opinion and the dissenting opinion offer differing statements of facts.

---

136. *Id.* at 650.

137. Florida Supreme Court online docket, West Correspondence, 6/19/92, No. 77098, available at: http://onlinedocketssc.flcourts.org/DocketResults/CaseByYear?CaseNumber=77098&CaseYear= 1960 (last visited August 23, 2020).

Northern Palm Beach County Water Control District v. State

604 So. 2d 440 (Fla. 1992) (corrected opinion)

PER CURIAM.

This is an appeal from a final judgment which declined to validate water control and improvement bonds proposed to be issued by the Northern Palm Beach Water Control District (District). We have jurisdiction pursuant to article V, section 3(b)(2) of the Florida Constitution, and chapter 75, Florida Statutes (1989).

The District is a drainage district organized and existing under chapter 59-994, Laws of Florida, as amended and supplemented by chapter 89-462, Laws of Florida, and the applicable provisions of chapter 298, Florida Statutes (1989). The District sought validation of water control and improvement bonds to finance on-site road improvements in Unit of Development No. 31 (Unit 31), a unit of the District created for the purpose of draining and reclaiming the land located within the unit. The Unit 31 site, also known as Ballen Isles of the JDM Country Club, is being developed by Hansen-Florida II, Inc., and will include single family residences, multifamily housing, park areas, and three golf courses.

The Circuit Court of the Fifteenth Judicial Circuit appointed three commissioners to prepare a report regarding the District's water management plan for Unit 31. The commissioners' report determined that the estimated cost of the improvements would be less than the benefits assessed against the lands in Unit 31. The report distinguished between two separate components of the planned improvements. The first component improvements, consisting of the water management system, the water and sewer facilities, and exterior road improvements, are not at issue here. The Program Two improvements, which are the subject of this appeal, include interior or on-site road improvements such as paving, striping, signs, landscaping, irrigation, bridges, an overpass, culverts, street lighting, security gatehouses, and a secondary drainage system consisting of storm drain pipes, inlets, manholes and surface drainage. The commissioners' report assessed the benefits of the Program Two improvements to be $18,125,000. The circuit court entered an order approving and confirming the report.

In December 1989, the Board of Supervisors of the District adopted a general bond resolution which authorized the issuance of Water Control and Improvement Bonds, Unit of Development No. 31, Program Two, in a principal amount not to exceed $16,312,500. The bond resolution provided that the bonds "shall not be general obligations or indebtedness" of the District, but instead are "special obligations payable solely" from, and secured by, a first lien and pledge of the proceeds of the drainage tax levied on the lands in Unit 31. In March 1990, the Board of Supervisors adopted a resolution levying a $42,625,000 drainage tax on the lands in Unit 31 in proportion to the benefits to be derived from the construction of the Program Two improvements. The amount levied consisted of an initial assessment of $18,125,000, plus the $24,500,000 interest estimated to accrue on the bonds.

After the bond validation hearing, the circuit court entered a final judgment which declined to validate the bonds because "[t]he intended use of the proceeds of this bond issue serves no valid public purpose." The final judgment also stated that the District failed to comply with its enabling legislation because it "did not meet the requirements of the Safe Neighborhoods Act, as enumerated in Sections 163.501–163.522, Florida Statutes."

... Only two questions are presented for our consideration here: 1) whether the revenue bond proceeds will be used for a valid public purpose, and 2) whether the District has complied with the requirements of its enabling legislation in issuing the bonds.

As to the first issue, the State contends that these bonds violate article VII, section 10 of the Florida Constitution, which prohibits the District from using its taxing power or pledging public credit to aid private enterprise, and that no valid public purpose can be served by financing the construction of roadways within a private development where public access will be limited by security gatehouses. The District asserts that in enacting chapters 59-994 and 89-462 the legislature found a public purpose in designating roads for the exclusive use and benefit of a unit of development and its residents.

Article VII, section 10 of the Florida Constitution prohibits the state and its subdivisions, including special districts such as this water control district, from using its taxing power or pledging public credit to aid any private person or entity. However, if the project falls within one of the four subsections of article VII, section 10, then no constitutional prohibition is involved. *See Linscott v. Orange County Indus. Dev. Auth.*, 443 So.2d 97 (Fla.1983). The on-site road improvements planned for Unit 31 do not fall within these four subsections. Thus, in order to determine if the bonds run afoul of the constitution, we must first determine whether the District's taxing power or pledge of credit is involved. If either is involved, then the improvements must serve a paramount public purpose. *See Orange County Indus. Dev. Auth. v. State*, 427 So.2d 174 (Fla.1983). However, if we conclude that neither is involved, then the paramount public purpose test is not applicable and "it is enough to show only that a public purpose is served." *Linscott*, 443 So.2d at 101.

Section 298.36(1), Florida Statutes (1989), authorizes the board of supervisors of a water control district to "levy a tax" in proportion to the benefits to be derived from the works and improvements of the district. The District's resolution also refers to the assessment as a "drainage tax." However, we find that a special assessment rather than a tax is at issue in this case. *See Lake Howell Water & Reclamation Dist. v. State*, 268 So.2d 897 (Fla.1972). As this Court explained in *City of Boca Raton v. State*, 595 So.2d 25, 29 (Fla.1992), "there is no requirement that taxes provide any specific benefit to the property.... [But] special assessments must confer a specific benefit upon the land burdened by the assessment." We also noted that special assessments must be "reasonably apportioned among the properties that receive the special benefit." *Id.* Because this is a special assessment, rather than a tax, no use of the District's taxing power is involved. Moreover, the general bond resolution provides that the District cannot be compelled to exercise its taxing power in order to pay the bonds.

The resolution further provides that the bonds "shall be special obligations payable solely" from the drainage assessments to the landowners for the Program Two improvements, and that the bonds "shall not constitute a lien upon any of the facilities or properties" of the District. "Where there is no direct or indirect undertaking by the public body to pay the obligation from public funds, and no public property is placed in jeopardy by a default of the third party, there is no lending of public credit." *State v. Housing Fin. Auth.*, 376 So.2d 1158, 1160 (Fla.1979); *see also Nohrr v. Brevard County Educ. Facilities Auth.*, 247 So.2d 304 (Fla.1971). Thus, the bonds do not contemplate a pledge of the District's credit. Because neither the District's taxing power nor a pledge of its credit is involved here, the bonds need only serve a public purpose rather than a paramount public purpose. *See Linscott*, 443 So.2d 97.

Chapter 59-994 created the District and imbued it with a number of powers, including the authority to "issue negotiable or other bonds" and "to construct, improve, pave and maintain roadways and roads" needed to access and develop those areas which are made suitable for settlement and development as a result of the operations of the District. Ch. 59-994, §3, Laws of Fla. Chapter 89-462 empowered the District to construct roads "for the exclusive use and benefit of a unit of development and its landowners, [and] residents," to "finance and maintain said roads and their associated elements as part of a water management plan," and to "construct and maintain security structures to control the use of said roads." Ch. 89-462, §6, Laws of Fla. Chapter 298, Florida Statutes (1989), also authorizes water control districts to issue bonds to pay for the costs of proposed improvements. *See, e.g.,* §§298.36(2), 298.47, Fla.Stat. (1989).[138] This enabling legislation evidences a clear legislative expression that the on-site controlled-access roads at issue in this case serve a valid public purpose. In addition, the District's Board of Supervisors adopted a resolution stating that the designation of roads for the exclusive use and benefit of Unit 31 is a public purpose "in the best interest of the health, safety, and general welfare of these areas and their inhabitants, visitors, property owners and workers." This Court has stated that a legislative declaration of public purpose is presumed to be valid, and should be deemed correct unless so clearly erroneous as to be beyond the power of the legislature. *Nohrr*, 247 So.2d 304. Although these legislative expressions of public purpose are not controlling, they are "entitled to great weight." *State v. Leon County*, 400 So.2d 949, 951 (Fla.1981).

As to the public purposes actually served by these bonds, we note that the roadway improvements at issue will provide access to the water management facilities and aid in the development of the reclaimed lands. However, the fact that public access to the roads will be limited raises a question of whether the stated public purposes are

---

138. [FN 2.] The District's enabling legislation provides in pertinent part:
  It is to the benefit of the land in the district and its ultimate users and residents to include provision in a water management plan *pursuant to and in furtherance of the Safe Neighborhoods Act, ss. 163.501–163.522, Florida Statutes,* for roads for the exclusive use and benefit of a unit of development and its residents.
Ch. 89-462, §6, Laws of Fla. (emphasis added).

only incidental to a primary private purpose, the development of Unit 31 by Hansen-Florida II, Inc. "A broad, general public purpose … will not constitutionally sustain a project that in terms of direct, actual use, is purely a private enterprise." *Orange County*, 427 So.2d at 179. In *Orange County*, the Court found that the expansion of a television station's broadcast facilities did not serve a paramount public purpose even though the public would receive a number of benefits from the proposed expansion. However, the Court also noted that the presence of public ownership would be a significant factor in a finding of public purpose. *Id.*

In this case, the District will retain ownership of the roadways in question. This public ownership coupled with the legislative declaration of public purpose contained in the District's enabling legislation leads us to the conclusion that the on-site road improvements serve a public purpose. Thus, the proposed water control and improvement bonds are not prohibited by article VII, section 10 of the Florida Constitution.

* * *

Accordingly, we reverse the final judgment and remand with directions that the bond issue be approved....

It is so ordered.

SHAW, C.J., dissenting.

The majority opinion trips lightly over the matter of how public financing of the construction and beautification of a private country club roadway serves a valid public purpose within the purview of article VII, section 10, Florida Constitution. I would affirm the trial court's judgment invalidating the bonds.

I. FACTS

A. Private Country Club

The Northern Palm Beach Water Control District ("District"), a public drainage district of the State of Florida, proposes to issue $16,312,500 in government revenue bonds to pay for the construction and maintenance of approximately 24,000 feet of roadway [4.5 miles] within Unit of Development No. 31, otherwise known as the JDM Country Club ("Club"), a planned 1,313-acre private golf and tennis club. The District's Board of Supervisors ("Board") adopted a formal Water Management Plan ("Plan") for the Club, which provides in part:

> The Unit 31 site, known as JDM Country Club, is being developed as a Planned Community District under the procedures and requirements of the City of Palm Beach Gardens Code of Ordinances. The development will include [2,384 single family dwelling units], park areas and three golf courses.

The homes within the Club will occupy prime residential sites abutting, or lying in close proximity to, the fairways and greens of the three golf courses and, according to Paul Urschalitz, the District's security expert, will vary in price from a quarter-million to over a million dollars apiece:

Q. Would you anticipate looking at the type homes—did you have a chance to get an idea of what type of homes they're going to put in there?

A. Yes.

Q. What type of price range homes did you look at?

A. I think they're listed in this document, two hundred and fifty thousand to over a million. . . .

In addition to the roadway itself, the District will pay for extensive roadway improvements within the Club. Tracy Bennett, the District's engineer, testified:

The onsite roadway improvements include paving of the roadways, the striping, the signage, landscaping with the roadways, irrigation to maintain the landscaping and sodding, bridges, an overpass, culverts, street lighting, security gatehouses, and secondary drainage system consisting of storm drainage pipes, inlets, manholes and surface drainage.

B. *"Caribbean Island" Motif*

The District's Plan calls for extensive roadside landscaping paid for by the District to enhance the private Club's "Caribbean Island" theme.

Extensive landscaping within the onsite roadway rights-of-way system is planned. . . . The overall theme of the development is to provide a Caribbean Island effect. Strong emphasis in the roadway planting will be on various palm species 20 to 30 feet high with a full-canopied backdrop, accented with dwarf palms and a wide variety of blooming groundcover plants. . . .

According to the Plan, the initial cost to the District of this garden-like landscaping is vast. The Plan states:

Estimated Costs of Improvements for Unit of Development No. 31	
. . . .	
III. Roadway Improvements	
A. Onsite [Roads]	$5,705,000
B. Landscaping Onsite Roads	$5,803,000

Thus, the District, a public entity, will pay nearly six million dollars in initial roadside landscaping costs—more than the cost of the entire roadway itself—to promote the private Club's "Caribbean Island" motif. This amounts to almost *one and one-half million dollars of landscaping per mile of proposed roadway* for the private Club.

C. *Security Gatehouses*

In addition to the "Caribbean Island" landscaping and other improvements noted above, the District will also pay for the construction and maintenance of three gatehouses to be staffed by security personnel to block all public access to the private Club. The District's official Plan provides:

In addition, the Board of Supervisors has the power to provide, control ingress and egress, and maintain roads for the exclusive use and benefit of a Unit of Development and its landowners, residents and invitees.

....

The onsite roadway system [is] planned for the exclusive use and benefit of [the Club] and its landowners, residents, and invitees....

* * *

[A]ll on-site improvements within the Club—including the landscaping and roadway itself—that are paid for by the public District will be closed to the general public.

D. *Financing*

To pay for the District's proposed on-site improvements within the Club, the Board adopted a general bond resolution that authorizes issuance of Water Control and Improvement Bonds in a principal amount not to exceed $16,312,500. The resolution provides that the bonds shall not be general obligations or indebtedness of the District, but shall instead be special obligations payable solely from, and secured by, a first lien and pledge of the proceeds of a drainage tax levied on the lands of the Club. The Board subsequently adopted a resolution levying a $42,625,000 drainage tax on the lands of the Club in proportion to the benefits to be derived from the construction of the improvements. The tax, which consists of an initial assessment of $18,125,000 plus $24,500,000 interest expected to accrue on the bonds, will be paid solely by the landowners within the Club. The landowners will thus ultimately foot the bill for the District's proposed roadway improvements within the Club.

The bonds will be issued in the denomination of $5,000, or multiples thereof, will mature within 30 years, and significantly, will pay interest periodically (twice a year) from the District to bondholders at a rate to be determined later. In paying this interest, the Board covenants that it will comply with specific requirements of the federal tax code concerning the tax status of certain government bonds. These provisions, which are designed to stimulate funding for public projects, specify that interest payments by state and local governments to their investors may be tax-exempt for the investors. The Board's bond resolution states:

> Section 4.08. *Compliance with Tax Requirements.* The Issuer hereby covenants and agrees, for the benefit of the Owners from time to time of the Bonds, to comply with the requirements applicable to it contained in Section 103 and Part IV of Subchapter B of Chapter 1 of the Code and to the extent necessary to preserve the exclusion of interest on the Bonds from gross income for federal income tax purposes.

Because the District's interest payments to bondholders will be tax-exempt for the holders, the bonds will be readily marketable even though the District may offer the bonds at an interest rate substantially below that of privately-issued, taxable securities. This reduced interest rate will minimize the District's financial obligations to bondholders and the resulting tax obligations of the Club's landowners.

II. THE APPLICABLE LAW

* * *

In the present case, we are concerned primarily with whether the purpose of the District's bonds is legal.

Article VII, section 10, Florida Constitution, bars governments within Florida from using their taxing power or credit to aid private corporations or persons:

> SECTION 10. Pledging credit. — Neither the state nor any county, school district, municipality, special district, or agency of any of them, shall become a joint owner with, or stockholder of, or give, lend or use its taxing power or credit to aid any corporation, association, partnership or person....

The purpose of section 10 is to prevent state government from using its vast resources to monopolize, or otherwise "destroy," a segment of private enterprise, and also "to protect public funds and resources from being exploited in assisting or promoting private ventures when the public would be at most only incidentally benefited." *Bannon v. Port of Palm Beach Dist.*, 246 So.2d 737, 741 (Fla.1971). To pass constitutional muster, a government bond issue must serve a truly public purpose, i.e., it must bestow a benefit on society exceeding that which is normally attendant to any successful business venture.[139]

During the pendency of the present case and immediately prior to oral argument before this Court, the legislature amended chapter 89-462, section 6, Laws of Florida, which concerns the Northern Palm Beach County Water Control District, to provide that restricted roadways serve a public purpose.

> Section 6. Roads for exclusive use and benefit of a unit of development and its residents. — It is hereby found and declared that among the many causes of deterioration in residential neighborhoods are the proliferation of crime, excessive automobile flow, and excessive noise levels from automobile traffic. It is to the benefit of the land in the district and its ultimate users and residents and it is hereby declared to be a public purpose to include provision in a water management plan for roads for the exclusive use and benefit of a unit of development and its residents. Therefore ... the district has the power to adopt by resolution, a water management plan for a unit of development, that will permit the district to exercise the following powers:

---

139. [FN. 7] This Court has used a myriad of terms in assessing the sufficiency of public purpose in revenue bond proceedings. *See, e.g., State v. City of Orlando*, 576 So. 2d 1315, 1317 (Fla. 1991) ("a paramount public purpose," and "a valid [public] purpose"); *State v. City of Panama City Beach*, 529 So. 2d 250, 256 (Fla. 1988) ("valid [public] purposes"), *receded from on other grounds*, 576 So. 2d 1315 (Fla. 1991); *Linscott v. Orange County Indus. Dev. Auth.*, 443 So. 2d 97, 101 (Fla. 1983) ("a public purpose"); *Orange County Indus. Dev. Auth. v. State*, 427 So. 2d 174, 179 (Fla. 1983) ("paramount public purpose"); *State v. Miami Beach Redevelopment Agency*, 392 So. 2d 875, 886 (Fla. 1980) ("some substantial benefit to the public"); *State v. Housing Fin. Auth.*, 376 So. 2d 1158, 1160 (Fla. 1979) ("if the public interest, even though indirect, is present and sufficiently strong," and "a reasonable and adequate public interest"); *Nohrr v. Brevard County Educ. Facilities Auth.*, 247 So. 2d 304, 309 (Fla. 1971) ("a public purpose").

(1) To provide roads for the exclusive use and benefit of a unit of development and its landowners, residents and invitees to control ingress and egress.

. . . .

(3) To construct and maintain security structures to control the use of said roads.

Ch. 91-408, § 2, Laws of Florida (emphasis and strike-through omitted).

III. CONCLUSION

Simply designating a project "public" by legislative fiat does not necessarily make it so, especially where uncontroverted facts attest otherwise. A quote from Lewis Carroll makes the point:

> "I don't know what you mean by 'glory,'" Alice said.
>
> Humpty Dumpty smiled contemptuously. "Of course you don't—till I tell you. I meant 'there's a nice knock-down argument for you!'"
>
> "But 'glory' doesn't mean 'a nice knock-down argument,'" Alice objected.
>
> "When I use a word," Humpty Dumpty said, in rather a scornful tone, "it means just what I choose it to mean—neither more nor less."
>
> "The question is," said Alice, "whether you can make words mean so many different things."
>
> "The question is," said Humpty Dumpty, "which is to be master—that's all."

Lewis Carroll, *Through the Looking Glass* 113 (Dial Books for Young Readers, NAL Penguin, Inc. 1988) (1872). Under our constitutional system of government in Florida, courts, not legislators or water control districts, are the ultimate "masters" of the constitutional meaning of such terms as "public purpose" in judicial proceedings.

While a restricted roadway may serve a valid public purpose under certain circumstances, I conclude that no reasonable and sufficient public purpose is served by issuance of government bonds to finance the construction and landscaping of roadways within the private JDM Country Club. The extraordinarily expensive roadside landscaping to enhance the "Caribbean Island" motif of the private residences and golf courses within the Club would serve virtually no reasonable public purpose even if the Club were to be open to the general public. The fact that security gatehouses will be erected for the sole purpose of barring the public from the premises renders any alleged benefit to the public from the landscaping or roadway moot.

It is perfectly clear to me that the District's bond project serves a simple, very private, purpose. It allows the owners of the proposed 2,384 residences within the Club to capitalize on a massive tax-break, intended for public projects, in financing the construction of a luxurious environment for their own private use. The undertaking smacks of state-sponsored, economic apartheid. I can conceive of few more private projects.

Rather than relying on an eleventh hour legislative declaration of public purpose and this Court's own examination of a cold record, I would place great weight on the reasoned judgment of the respected trial judge, for he alone had the opportunity to personally observe—on both direct and cross-examination—the demeanor of many of the Club's main functionaries, and he is far more familiar with the local circumstances surrounding this issue. Sufficient competent evidence supports his ruling.

I would affirm the trial court's judgment invalidating the bonds.

Commentary and Questions

Note the unusual feature that the dissent supplies an alternative recitation of the facts. For example, the dissent alone points out that one-half of the bond is devoted to "Caribbean" landscaping and the enactment of a late-arriving legislative change in the law while the litigation was pending. If all the recitation of facts by the majority and dissent were conjoined, would it change how the majority could write its opinion?

This is a specialized form of special district, a drainage district, which was recognized in Florida law long before the 1968 Constitution. The imposition of a "drainage tax" is against the land based on the property's character, more like a special assessment, and the Court accordingly finds "that a special assessment rather than a tax is at issue in this case."[140] Also, "the general bond resolution provides that the District cannot be compelled to exercise its taxing power in order to pay the bonds." The Court therefore concludes "no use of the District's taxing power is involved." The District is able to pledge and give a lien on the drainage tax proceeds, not on property owned by the District. The Court concludes "that the bonds shall not constitute a lien upon any of the facilities or properties of the District. Where there is no direct or indirect undertaking by the public body to pay the obligation from public funds, and no public property is placed in jeopardy by a default of the third party, there is no lending of public credit." (Internal quotation marks omitted; citations omitted.) The Court concludes that neither the District's taxing power nor a pledge of credit is involved, and therefore, a paramount showing of public purpose is not necessary. Is the District free to stop the special assessment and default on the bonds after purchase with no adverse effects to the District?

At issue is whether there is a public purpose at all. The majority concludes legislative findings plus public ownership of the roads, if not use, is sufficient to ground a public purpose. There is a benefit to the private developer. The bondholders receive the benefit of tax-free interest; the bond issuers presumably receive the benefit of marketability and faster bond marketability plus a lower interest rate. Dissenting Justice Shaw observes in footnote 7 that the Court "has used a myriad of terms in assessing the sufficiency of public purpose in revenue bond proceedings." For this case, Justice Shaw proposes that a public purpose "must bestow a benefit on society exceeding that which is normally attendant to any successful business venture." Would this higher standard for assessing public interest still attract public-private ventures such as affordable housing?

---

140. The court identified the District's statutory authority to tax. It did not identify its authority to levy special assessments.

Is the core concern here class-based? This is a high-value housing development with multiple golf courses and facilities, specialized landscaping, and no public access or use. Is the development's strongest argument that here is a knock-on benefit of higher ad valorem taxes, like tax increment financing, to another governmental body but not the drainage district?

Article VIII

Local Government

H. Article VIII, Section 1(d) — County Officers
19. *Brock v. Board of County Commissioners of Collier County*, 21 So. 3d 844 (2d DCA 2009), *rev. dismissed*, 48 So. 3d 810 (Fla. 2010).
20. *Demings v. Orange County Citizens Review Board*, 15 So. 3d 604 (Fla. 5th DCA 2009).

Introduction: Basis of Local Government Authority in Florida

The issues addressed by local government are complex and critical. A local government attorney may be dealing with a bond issue worth hundreds of millions of dollars one day and the next day be dealing with a bitter dispute about free exercise of religion in a municipal park.

The police power allows a state to legislate on any matter affecting public health, safety, morals, or welfare so long as the state does not impinge upon rights protected by the federal Constitution or usurp a function exclusively federal in nature.[1] States have delegated this power to local governments, both counties and cities. Although both counties and municipalities exercise powers that are similar in many ways, there are important distinctions between them. The Florida Constitution describes counties as "subdivisions" of the state.[2] Municipalities, on the other hand, are creations of the state.[3] Earlier in our exploration of local taxation, we noticed one significant distinction between counties and cities when we learned that county-owned property is immune from local ad valorem taxation, while municipally owned property may only be exempt from taxation.[4] The logic of that designation is that the state is immune, and therefore, a subdivision of the state is immune as well.

As the following cases show, the Florida Constitution gives Florida municipalities broad home rule powers.[5] Under this authority, Florida municipalities may act in

---

1. *See, e.g., Lawton v. Steele*, 152 U.S. 133 (1894); *Coca-Cola Co., Food Div., Polk Cty. v. Department of Citrus*, 406 So. 2d 1079 (Fla. 1981), *appeal dismissed*, 456 U.S. 1002 (1982) (state may regulate in protected areas where there is a reasonable relationship to public safety, health, morals and the general welfare); *Hav-A-Tampa Cigar Co. v. Johnson*, 5 So. 2d 433, 437 (Fla. 1942) (private property rights are subject to the sovereign police power of the state to protect the safety, health, morals and general welfare of the public).

2. Fla. Const. art. VIII, § 1; *see City of Miami v. Lewis*, 104 So. 2d 70, 73 (Fla. 3d DCA 1958) (quoting *City of Miami v. Rosen*, 151 Fla. 677, 10 So. 2d 307, 309 (1942)).

3. *See City of Miami v. Lewis*, 104 So. 2d at 72.

4. *See, e.g., Dickinson v. City of Tallahassee*, 325 So. 2d 1, 3 (Fla. 1975); *Park-N-Shop, Inc. v. Sparkman*, 99 So. 2d 571, 573–74 (Fla. 1957).

5. Fla. Const. art. VIII, § 2. Municipalities. —
    (b) POWERS. Municipalities shall have governmental, corporate and proprietary powers to enable them to conduct municipal government, perform municipal functions and render municipal services, and may exercise any power for municipal purposes except as otherwise provided by law. Each municipal legislative body shall be elective.

any area where they are not forbidden to act by state law.[6] However, as the cases below show, it may not be clear whether the state has preempted the field.

Florida counties are either charter or non-charter counties. Charter counties "have all powers of local self-government not inconsistent with general law, or with special law approved by vote of the electors. The governing body of a county operating under a charter may enact county ordinances not inconsistent with general law." FLA. CONST. art. VIII, § 1(g). Non-charter counties have "such power of self-government as is provided by general or special law." FLA. CONST. art. VIII, § 1(f) (2019). In many cases, the distinction between charter and non-charter counties is an academic one, for Florida law clearly gives cities and both charter and non-charter counties similar powers.[7] One significant distinction between charter and non-charter counties is the status of county ordinances within incorporated municipalities inside the county. In a non-charter county, a conflicting municipal ordinance will prevail over a county ordinance within the municipality. FLA. CONST. art. VIII, § 1(f) (2019). However, as

---

6. Section 166.021, Florida Statutes, provides in relevant part:
(1) As provided in s. 2(b), Art. VIII of the State Constitution, municipalities shall have the governmental, corporate, and proprietary powers to enable them to conduct municipal government, perform municipal functions, and render municipal services, and may exercise any power for municipal purposes, except when expressly prohibited by law.
Cf. Boca Raton v. State, 595 So. 2d 25 (Fla. 1992) (municipalities may exercise any government or proprietary power for municipal purpose except those prohibited by law, and municipalities may legislate on any matter appropriate, except for those specifically excluded by the Municipal Home Rule Act); Ocala v. Nye, 608 So. 2d 15 (Fla. 1992) (broad authorization for cities to legislate on any "valid municipal purpose"); Miami Beach v. Forte Towers, Inc., 305 So. 2d 764, 766 (Fla. 1974) (Chapter 166 of the Florida Statutes is a "broad grant of power to municipalities in recognition and implementation of Art. VIII, § 2(b), Fla. Const."); Lakeland v. State ex rel. Harris, 197 So. 470 (Fla. 1940) ("municipal functions" are those granted for benefit of the community which promote comfort, convenience, safety, and happiness of citizens of the municipality, including proper care of streets, parks and public places, erection and maintenance of public utilities and improvements); cf. Florida Dept. of Revenue v. City of Gainesville, 918 So. 2d 250, 262–63 (Fla. 2005) (distinguishing "municipal purpose" under Article VIII, § 2(b) from the term as used in the tax provisions under Article VII, § 3(a)).
7. For example, § 125.01(1), Florida Statutes, delegates broad powers to all county governments regardless of charter status. The act states:
The legislative and governing body of a county shall have the power to carry on county government. To the extent not inconsistent with general or special law, this power includes, but is not restricted to, the power to:

* * *

(f) Provide parks, preserves, playgrounds, recreation areas, libraries, museums, historical commissions, and other recreation and cultural facilities programs.
(g) Prepare and enforce comprehensive plans for the development of the county.
(h) Establish, coordinate, and enforce zoning and such business regulations as are necessary for the protection of the public.
(i) Adopt, by reference or in full, and enforce building, housing, and related technical codes and regulations.
The Florida Supreme Court, in Speer v. Olson, 367 So. 2d 207, 211–13 (Fla. 1978), suggested, in the face of lower court precedent to the contrary, that Chapter 125, Florida Statutes, operated as a complete grant of power to non-charter counties in the area of taxation. The Local Government Comprehensive Planning Act (FLA. STAT. §§ 163.3161–.3217) also empowers local governments to enact land use regulations within the context of Florida's comprehensive planning structure.

we will see, in a charter county, the county charter may specify that the ordinances of the county prevail in the event of a conflict with a municipal ordinance. Fla. Const. art. VIII, § 1(g) (2019). This additional authority for charter counties is critical in resolving conflicts between cities and counties. Keep in mind there are some counties where the population is concentrated in one or two cities. Therefore, those cities may in fact have differing interests from the county and may resent or oppose attempts by a county to control or supersede city policies.

The cases in this chapter will focus on Sections 1, 2 and 4. Section 1 sets forth the limitations on the power of the state's political subdivisions and establishes guidelines for the interplay between counties and municipalities. In this Section, note which powers are exclusive to chartered counties, and how these powers affect municipal government. Section 2 deals with municipalities: establishment, powers, and annexation. One of the most important issues in Section 2 is the implication of the "Municipal Home Rule Powers Act," which allows a municipality to exercise any power for municipal services except when expressly prohibited by law. Section 3, "Consolidation," and Section 4, "Transfer of Powers," present two constitutional options for restructuring local government. Since these two provisions occasionally overlap with powers of charter counties under Section 1(g), the cases for Section 1 will also address Sections 3 and 4.

Finally, Article VIII also identifies county officers, a group of local officials who are elected by county voters: 1) sheriff; 2) tax collector; 3) property appraiser; 4) supervisor of elections; and 5) clerk of the court. The cases provided explore some of the interplay between these independently elected officials and the county commissions.

A. Article VIII, Section 1 — Counties

State ex rel. Volusia County v. Dickinson

269 So. 2d 9 (Fla. 1972)

ERVIN, Justice.

We have for consideration an alternative writ of mandamus issued on Petition of the Relator, Volusia County, a charter county under the State Constitution, directed to Respondents, the State Comptroller and the Director of the State Beverage Department.

We have accepted jurisdiction because this cause clearly raises questions of constitutional construction and is an important public controversy, as will hereinafter appear. The pertinent question raised is as follows:

Did Volusia County, as a charter county, have the power in 1971 to levy an excise tax upon the sale of cigarettes in the unincorporated areas of the county and have said tax collected by the Director of the Department of Business Regulation and have the proceeds so collected returned to the County by the State Comptroller in accordance with the procedures under the provisions of Section 210.20(2)(c), F.S.?

Our answer to the question is in the affirmative.

Volusia County became a home rule charter government pursuant to the authority of Section 1(c), Article VIII, State Constitution, F.S.A., by the enactment of a special act of the Legislature establishing its county charter, Chapter 70-966, which was ratified by a referendum vote of the electors. In Section 202 thereof it is expressly provided the county shall have such municipal powers as may be required to fulfill the intent of the charter.

Respondents deny the Legislature by general law has expressly given charter counties similar authority as municipalities have been given to adopt a cigarette tax levy, relying upon *City of Tampa v. Birdsong Motors, Inc.*, Fla., 261 So.2d 1. Birdsong Motors notes that under Section 9(a), Article VII, State Constitution, counties and municipalities may be authorized by general law to levy "other taxes" for their respective purposes.

When Section 1(g), Article VIII and Section 9(a), Article VII are read together, it will be noted that charter counties and municipalities are placed in the same category for all practical purposes. That upon a county becoming a charter county it automatically becomes a metropolitan entity for self-government purposes. This is so because Section 1(g) of Article VIII provides a charter county "shall have all powers of local self-government not inconsistent with general law.... The governing body of a county operating under a charter may enact county ordinances not inconsistent with general law." This all inclusive language unquestionably vests in a charter county the authority to levy any tax not inconsistent with general or special law as is permitted municipalities.

Read together, Sections 9(a), Article VII and 1(g), Article VIII, clearly connote the principle that unless precluded by general or special law, a charter county may without more under authority of existing general law impose by ordinance any tax in the area of its tax jurisdiction a municipality may impose.

The issue here is quite analogous in principle to the one considered by us in *State ex rel. Dade County v. Brautigam*, Fla., 224 So.2d 688. There, specific constitutional home rule authority was found to be reposed in Dade County to adopt a cigarette tax levy to apply in the county's unincorporated area. The Dade County home rule amendment provided "Dade County may exercise all the powers conferred now or hereafter by general law upon municipalities." Section 6(f), Article VIII, State Constitution. As we have noted, similar authority is logically reposed in any county becoming a home rule charter county by the all-inclusive language of Article VIII of the 1968 Revised Constitution. Non-charter counties, on the other hand, shall only have the power of self-government as is provided by general or special law. Section 1(f), Article VIII, State Constitution.

The foregoing considered, it is ordered that peremptory writ issue directed to the Respondents granting the relief sought.

It is so ordered.

CARLTON, ADKINS, BOYD and DREW (Retired), JJ., concur.

Questions

1. What are the necessary steps for establishing a chartered county?

2. Why would residents of a county wish to gain "chartered" status?

3. Why does Volusia County have the power to levy the cigarette tax at issue here?

4. What does "not inconsistent with general law" actually mean?

B. Article VIII, Section 4 — Transfer of Powers (from Municipalities to Counties)

Sarasota County v. Town of Longboat Key

355 So. 2d 1197 (Fla. 1978)

ENGLAND, Justice.

The Sarasota County Commission adopted an ordinance proposing five amendments to the county charter which would transfer the responsibilities for performing five distinct governmental functions from four Sarasota County cities to the county.[8] Four of the affected cities challenged the proposed amendments in court before they could be voted on by the residents of Sarasota County, and in due course they obtained from the Twelfth Judicial Circuit Court a permanent injunction prohibiting the referendum on the dual grounds that the ordinance attempts an unconstitutional "consolidation" in violation of Article VIII, Section 3 of the Florida Constitution, and is unconstitutionally vague. Inasmuch as the trial court construed a provision of the Constitution, appeal of the trial court's ruling to this Court is appropriate.

The five proposed amendments adopted by the County Commission are identical in their terminology except for the delineation of the different services and functions in each. The first reads:

> "Section 1.4: Consolidation of Air and Water Pollution Control Services and Functions.

Notwithstanding any other provision of this Charter, all municipal air and water pollution control services and functions and all county air and water pollution control services and functions shall be consolidated and provided by this county government. The Board of County Commissioners shall have power to carry out and enforce this section by appropriate ordinances which, notwithstanding any other provision of this Charter, shall prevail over any municipal ordinances in conflict therewith."

Significant principles of local government autonomy are at stake in this proceeding. The cities seek to enjoin a voter referendum on these amendments out of a general concern that municipalities could be effectively abolished if a county government

---

8. [FN1.] The functions to be transferred are air and water pollution control, parks and recreation, roads and bridges, planning and zoning, and police.

were free to propose for county-wide voter approval, and without the separate approval of the affected municipality's voters, the transfer of city functions to the county level of government. The respective concerns of the cities and the county quite naturally implicate several provisions of the Florida Constitution.

At the heart of this controversy is Article VIII, Section 3 of the Florida Constitution, entitled "Consolidation", which describes the manner in which the governments of counties and municipalities may be consolidated. Of equal importance in our consideration of the issues presented is Article VIII, Section 4 of the Florida Constitution, entitled "Transfer of powers", which specifies the method by which any function or power of a county or municipality may be transferred to or performed by another governmental unit. Also relevant to these proceedings are subsections 1(f) and 1(g) of Article VIII, Florida Constitution, which define the limit of powers for non-charter and charter governments, respectively.

The major contentions of the parties are more easily understood if each is discussed separately.

1. Does the ordinance propose a "consolidation" under Article VIII, Section 3?

The trial judge enjoined a county-wide voter referendum of the five amendments on the grounds that a "consolidation" of municipal services into the county would result, and that the amendments obviously do not comport with the requirement of Article VIII, Section 3 to the effect that consolidation must be proposed by "special law". We disagree with the trial court's premise, for despite their denomination by the Sarasota County Commission as "consolidation" amendments, it is apparent that the proposed amendments do not effect a consolidation within the meaning of Article VIII, Section 3. The process provided in that provision is the unification of the government of a county and the government of one or more municipalities "into a single government", which would then exercise the powers previously held by both or all of the consolidated units. This provision of the Constitution applies only when one or more of the underlying governments disappears or is merged into the government of the surviving unit.

2. Is the ordinance unconstitutionally vague?

The trial judge specifically held that the proposed charter amendments were vague, in that they did not specify the manner in which property, services or functions would be transferred from the cities to the county. Although it is true that the proposed amendments provide no roadmap for the assignment of functions or the transfer of property or monies as between the municipalities and the county, we do not find that omission to be a basis to strike them as unconstitutionally vague. The amendments are not self-executing. They specifically provide that additional ordinances will be adopted to implement the proposal when and if the voters of the county approve the transfers. We think it is permissible to proceed in this fashion, and that the orderly processes of government initially require no more than a determination of the proper place for the functions to be assigned. To require that details be precisely defined before the voters may approve a transfer of functions would burden county commissions with potentially unnecessary minutiae which, even at the approval stage, might require additional litigation. The amendments are not "clearly and conclusively defective" by reason of vagueness.

3. Does the ordinance constitute an attempted transfer of powers under Article VIII, Section 4?

The trial judge did not expressly rule on the cities' contention that the County Commission has essentially proposed a transfer of powers, a procedure governed by Article VIII, Section 4 of the Constitution. The municipalities, joined by the Florida League of Cities, reassert that argument here. None of the parties seriously disputes the notion that this proceeding really involves a proposed transfer of functions between different units of government. The cities simply claim that the county's ordinance does not comply with Article VIII, Section 4 since it was initiated neither "by law" nor by resolution of all affected governments. Sarasota County suggests that charter counties are excluded from Article VIII, Section 4 by reason of Article VIII, Section 1(g), or alternately that the transfer requirements of Article VIII, Section 4 are met by Section 125.86(7) Florida Statutes (1975).[9] For the following reasons we conclude that the cities' position is the correct one.

The county suggests that because it operates under a charter form of government, Section 1(g) of Article VIII alone governs its powers. We do not agree. Section 4 of Article VIII refers to "counties", without distinction. The same term is used throughout the Constitution to refer both to charter and to non-charter counties. Where there has been an intent to distinguish the two forms of county government, it has been done explicitly. Not only are we disinclined to read into Section 4 something that is not expressly provided, but we are all the more reluctant to elevate the general provisions of Article VIII, Section 1(g) to a dominant position over the specific provisions of Article VIII, Section 4. We hold that Section 4 applies both to charter and non-charter counties.

We also reject the county's assertion that Article VIII, Section 4 contemplates a law of general applicability such as Section 125.86(7), by which counties may accomplish the transfer of municipal functions by county resolution. A plain reading of Article VIII, Section 4 reflects that a transfer of governmental powers requires distinctive procedures for the initiation of a transfer, that is, "by law or by resolution of the governing bodies of each of the governments affected." We think it clear from the specificity of the procedure in Section 4 that the "by law" reference connotes the need for a separate legislative act addressed to a specific transfer, in the same manner that two or more resolutions of the affected governments would address

---

9. [FN12.] This section grants the board of county commissioners the power to:
"Adopt pursuant to the provisions of the charter, such ordinances of county-wide force and effect as are necessary for the health, safety, and welfare of the residents. It is the specific legislative intent to recognize that a county charter may properly determine that certain governmental areas are more conducive to uniform county-wide enforcement and may provide the county government powers in relation to those areas as recognized and as may be amended from time to time by the people of that county(.)"

a specific transfer. Section 125.86(7), in contrast, does no more than provide general authority for county commissions to exercise police powers. It in no way provides "by law" the procedures necessary to initiate the transfer of governmental functions or powers.

We conclude, therefore, that Sarasota County's five proposed amendments constitute attempts to transfer powers and functions from the cities to the county within Article VIII, Section 4, but because the procedure by which the transfers have been proposed does not comport with the requirements of that Section, the county's resolution is ineffective for that purpose.

We affirm the order of the Circuit Court of Sarasota County permanently enjoining a referendum on the five proposed amendments.

It is so ordered.

OVERTON, C. J., and BOYD, SUNDBERG, HATCHETT and DREW (Retired), JJ., concur.

Questions

1. What type of county is Sarasota County?

2. What were the arguments advanced by Sarasota County?

3. How did the Supreme Court respond to these arguments?

4. According to the Court, why is Section 3 inapplicable to this case?

5. What is the meaning of the term "transfer"?

6. Why are the provisions of Section 4 so critical to the cities involved in this case?

7. Does Section 4 control all counties?

C. Article VIII, Section 1(g) — Charter County Preemption of Municipal Authority

Broward County v. City of Fort Lauderdale

480 So. 2d 631 (Fla. 1985)

EHRLICH, Justice.

This case is before us to answer a question certified by a district court to be of great public importance. We have jurisdiction. Art. V, §3(b)(4), Fla. Const.

The Broward County Commission sought to regulate certain aspects of the sale of handguns in the county. In pursuing this goal, the commission held a county-wide referendum to amend the county charter. Pursuant to article VIII, section 1(g) of the Florida Constitution, the charter provided that, with two exceptions, municipal ordinances would prevail when conflict arose with county ordinances. The amendments added a third exception providing that county ordinances relating to handgun control would prevail.[10] The amendments were approved, and the commission enacted a handgun ordinance.

The city unsuccessfully sought an injunction to stop the referendum. It argued that article VIII, section 4 of the Florida Constitution required a city-wide as well as county-wide referendum. Section 4 requires dual referenda whenever there is a transfer of any function or power from one governmental entity to another. The district court agreed with the city, reversed the trial court, and certified the following question:

> WHETHER, IN A CHARTER COUNTY, A TRANSFER OF POWER OCCURS, THEREBY INVOKING THE PROVISIONS OF ARTICLE VIII, SECTION 4 OF THE CONSTITUTION OF THE STATE OF FLORIDA, WHERE, PURSUANT TO CHARTER AMENDMENT, A COUNTY ORDINANCE RELATING TO HANDGUN MANAGEMENT PREVAILS OVER A MUNICIPAL ORDINANCE RELATING TO THE SAME SUBJECT MATTER TO THE EXTENT OF ANY CONFLICT.

City of Fort Lauderdale v. Broward County, 458 So.2d 783, 786 (Fla. 4th DCA 1984). We answer the question in the negative and quash the decision below.

The problem arises because of the seemingly conflicting provisions of sections 1(g) and 4. If we construe "any function or power" in section 4 to give full effect to the all-encompassing adjective "any," then, assuming that virtually all ordinances constitute exercise of governmental power, all county preemptions pursuant to section 1(g) will be "transfers of power."

---

10. [FN 2.] The language sought to be added to the county charter consisted of the following underscored provisions:

> Section 8.04 CONFLICT OF COUNTY ORDINANCES WITH MUNICIPAL ORDINANCES. Notwithstanding any other provisions of this Charter, any county ordinance in conflict with a municipal ordinance shall not be effective within the municipality to the extent of such conflict regardless of whether such municipal ordinance was adopted or enacted before or after the County ordinance, provided that the county ordinance shall prevail over municipal ordinances whenever the County shall set minimum standards protecting the environment by prohibiting or regulating air or water pollution, or the destruction of the resources of the County belonging to the general public within the parameters set forth in Section 8.17 of this Charter. As set forth in this Charter, a county ordinance shall also prevail over a municipal ordinance in the area of land use planning. *A County ordinance shall also prevail over a municipal ordinance in matters relating to Handgun Management within the parameters set forth in Section 8.19 of this Charter.* In the event a county ordinance and a municipal ordinance shall cover the same subject matter without conflict, both the municipal ordinance and the county ordinance shall be effective, each being deemed supplemental, one to the other.
>
> Section 8.19 HANDGUN MANAGEMENT.
>
> *The County Commission may adopt a countywide ordinance relating to Handgun Management which may provide for law enforcement authorities to make criminal history checks for handgun purchasers prior to the delivery of a handgun not to exceed ten (10) days, exclusive of Saturdays, Sundays, and Holidays, and to provide standards for transfers of handguns and licensing of handgun dealers.*

458 So.2d at 784, n. 3.

The circumstances of this case are the obverse of those in *Sarasota County v. Town of Longboat Key*, 355 So.2d 1197 (Fla.1978), wherein we rejected the county's attempt to completely preempt five essential municipal functions under section 1(g) without the dual referenda required by section 4. We held that section 1(g) did not exempt a charter county from application of section 4: "We are … reluctant to elevate the general provisions of Article VIII, Section 1(g) to a dominant position over the specific provisions of Article VIII, Section 4." *Id.* at 1201. In the case sub judice, to construe section 4 as having the breadth seemingly dictated by the troublesome adjective "any" would eviscerate section 1(g) and elevate section 4 to a dominant position. This we must not do.

It is a fundamental rule of construction of our constitution that a construction of the constitution which renders superfluous, meaningless or inoperative any of its provisions should not be adopted by the courts. Where a constitutional provision will bear two constructions, one of which is consistent and the other which is inconsistent with another section of the constitution, the former must be adopted so that both provisions may stand and have effect. Construction of the constitution is favored which gives effect to every clause and every part thereof. Unless a different interest is clearly manifested, constitutional provisions are to be interpreted in reference to their relation to each other, that is in pari materia, since every provision was inserted with a definite purpose.

Burnsed v. Seaboard Coastline Railroad, 290 So.2d 13, 16 (Fla.1974) (citations deleted).

Our task herein, then, must be to glean the intent of the framers and strike the balance necessary to give both provisions the effect intended.

Dean D'Alemberte's commentaries on the sections at issue offer an indication of intent. As to section 1(g):

This entirely new subsection provides for the broadest extent of county self-government or "home rule" as it is commonly described. It was taken with only editorial changes from the Revision Commission recommendation.

Under subsection (c) of this section [Art. VIII, § 1], charter governments may be established, amended or repealed only be general or special act which is approved by a vote of the electors of the county at a special election called for that purpose.

As a result of the provisions of subsections [sic] (f) of this section (non-charter government), the power which may be granted to county governments under a charter is the power to have county ordinances take precedence over municipal ordinances. Also, where the non-charter government may be empowered by the legislature to adopt ordinances as long as they are not inconsistent with general or special law, the charter counties may adopt ordinances as long as they are not inconsistent with general law.

Commentary to Art. VIII, § 1, Fla. Const., 26A Fla. Stat. Ann. (West 1970). As to section 4:

This section was taken from the Revision Commission recommendation. It is an entirely new section which gives to the legislature and to the various local governing units, special districts included, the authority to transfer powers. Such transfers under the 1885 Constitution, when not provided by the general power of the legislature over municipalities and counties, was accomplished by special constitutional amendment (see Article VIII, Section 10(a), Sections 12–21, and Article XX, Section 1). All of these specific provisions related to the assessment and collection of municipal taxes. In 1954, the 1885 Constitution was amended by a general provision (Article VIII, Section 22, House Joint Resolution 851, 1953, adopted in 1954) providing that the tax assessor and the county tax collector may by special or general act, with the approval of the electors of a municipality, be authorized to assess and collect municipal taxes.

Commentary to Art. VIII, §4, Fla. Const., 26A Fla. Stat. Ann. (West 1970).

Section 1(g), as we conclude both from the commentary and an understanding of the constitutional scheme vis-a-vis charter counties, was intended to specifically give charter counties two powers unavailable to non-charter counties: the power to preempt conflicting municipal ordinances, and the power to avoid intervention of the legislature by special laws. The power to preempt is the power to exercise county power to the exclusion of municipal power. Preemption is a transfer of power, from exclusive municipal authority or concurrent authority, to exclusive county authority. It is clear from reading the transcripts of the Florida Constitution Revision Commission's discussion of preliminary versions of what would become section 1(g), that the preemption power was specifically included to eliminate the necessity of most if not all special laws when a charter county sought to preempt city ordinances in such areas as speed limits and other regulatory matters. Transcripts of Florida Constitution Revision Committee, Vol. 50 (1966) (available in Florida Supreme Court library). Section 4, on the other hand, was intended to provide for a more convenient procedure whereby local governments could transfer functions and powers without the cumbersome procedure of seeking a special law or constitutional amendment.

Thus, on the one hand the constitution has a provision intended to expand the power of charter counties, while on the other hand it includes a provision to expand the shared power of governmental units to transfer powers and functions. Both were intended to reduce the need for special laws and constitutional amendments. The conflict arises when the expansive power of a charter county collides with the requirements of section 4. But section 4 did not contemplate giving municipalities veto power over a charter county's preemptive power. Rather, section 4 contemplated situations where a law authorizes dual referenda or where the city and county mutually desire to shift a function or power of the type which required special law or constitutional amendment under the 1885 constitution.

A line must be drawn between these overlapping provisions. We hold that section 1(g) permits regulatory preemption by counties, while section 4 requires dual referenda to transfer functions or powers relating to *services*. A charter county may preempt a municipal regulatory power in such areas as handgun sales when county-wide uniformity will best further the ends of government. §125.86(7), Fla. Stat. (1983). Dual referenda are necessary when the preemption goes beyond regulation and intrudes upon a municipality's provision of services.

The case law on point reflects the underlying principle we now adopt. In *Sarasota County*, the county sought to preempt municipal control of air and water pollution control services and functions, parks and recreation, roads and bridges, planning and zoning, and police. The opinion includes the language from only one of the proposed charter amendments, relating to air and water pollution. It is clear from the language of that amendment that the county sought to consolidate all pollution control and enforcement under county authority. Presumably, the remaining amendments also sought to preempt broad control and enforcement powers. The wholesale assumption of the burden of providing what had been municipal services, going far beyond regulatory preemption, required dual referenda under section 4.

In *City of Palm Beach Gardens v. Barnes*, 390 So.2d 1188 (Fla.1980), the issue of preemption under section 1(g) was not raised. However, the question of whether dual referenda were required under section 4 was at issue. The city in that case contracted with the county sheriff to provide police services to the city. This Court held that contracting for services, without divesting ultimate authority to supervise and control, did not constitute a transfer of powers vis-a-vis section 4. Thus, provision of services may be transferred without section 4 implications if the ultimate responsibility for supervising those services is not transferred.

In *Miama [sic] Dolphins, Ltd. v. Metropolitan Dade County*, 394 So.2d 981 (Fla.1981), opponents to a tourist development tax plan challenged a provision that would allocate some of the funds raised by the county to renovation of the city-owned Orange Bowl stadium. This Court rejected the argument that the plan was an unconstitutional transfer of powers since jurisdiction over the stadium would not be transferred. Instead, the county merely planned to make funds available to the city for the renovation. Again, control over municipal services was not transferred.

We believe the distinction between regulatory preemption, and transfer of functions and powers relating to services, achieves the balance between sections 1(g) and 4 intended by the framers of the 1968 constitution.

Accordingly, the decision of the district court is quashed. We remand for action consistent with this opinion.

It is so ordered.

BOYD, C.J., and ADKINS, OVERTON, McDONALD and SHAW, JJ., concur.

Questions

1. How does the Court strike a balance between Section 1(g) and Section 4?

2. What is the language in Section 4 which creates the problem discussed in this case?

3. Under Section 1(g), which two powers are granted exclusively to chartered counties?

4. What is the difference between a regulation and transfer?

City of Coconut Creek v.
Broward County Board of County Commissioners

430 So. 2d 959 (Fla. 1983)

ANSTEAD, Judge.

This is an appeal by twenty municipalities located in Broward County from a final summary judgment upholding the validity of provisions of the Broward County Land Development Code which vest final authority for plat approval of development projects, within and without the municipalities, in the county. We affirm.

Broward County acquired charter county status on March 1, 1975. Article VI of the Broward County Charter deals with land use planning. Section 6.05(D) of Article VI, amended in November, 1976, sets forth the requirement of a county land use plan to be adopted by the Board and provides that local governments may submit plans for certification also. In November, 1976, section 6.12 was amended to provide:

The legislative body of each municipality within Broward County and the County Commission for the unincorporated area shall, within six (6) months after the effective date of this Charter, create a mandatory plat ordinance.

No plat of lands lying within Broward County, either in the incorporated or unincorporated areas, may be recorded in the Official Records prior to approval by the County Commission. The County Commission shall enact an ordinance establishing standards, procedures and minimum requirements to regulate and control the platting of lands within the incorporated and unincorporated areas of Broward County. The governing body of each municipality may enact an ordinance establishing additional standards, procedures and requirements as may be necessary to regulate and control the platting of lands within its boundaries.

The County has implemented its land use plan by adoption of Ordinance 81-16, the Broward County Land Development Code, effective April 3, 1981. Division 4 of the Ordinance delineates platting procedures and requirements in municipal areas. Section 5-197 of Division 4 deals with the procedural requirements; section 5-198 outlines the substantive requirements for final plat approval by the Board. Briefly summarized, the substantive factors for independent review include:

(a) adequacy of regional transportation network,

(b) dedication of right-of-way for major roads,

(c) access to trafficways,

(d) adequacy of water management,

(e) adequacy of potable water service,

(f) adequacy of wastewater treatment and disposal services,

(g) adequacy of solid waste disposal sites and facilities,

(h) adequacy of regional parks and recreation facilities,

(i) consideration of impact on environmentally sensitive lands,

(j) consideration of toxic waste disposal sites and impact on air quality, and

(k) adequacy of school sites and school buildings.

In November, 1977, the Board adopted the Broward County Land Use Plan. Article IV contains the following pertinent sections:

Section 2: *GENERAL REQUIREMENTS OF THE COUNTY LAND USE PLAN*

2.01 The County Land Use Plan shall be implemented by the adoption and enforcement of appropriate local regulations on the development of lands and waters within the jurisdiction of each unit of local government and no public or private development may be permitted except in compliance with the County Land Use Plan or a certified land use plan.

Section 3: *CERTIFICATION OF LOCAL LAND USE PLANS*

3.01 Each unit of local government may prepare, in conformance with the requirements of the County Land Use Plan and the Planning Act, a local land use plan for submittal to the Planning Council. The local land use plan shall be certified by the Planning Council prior to its final adoption by a unit of local government, in conformance with the Planning Act.

. . . .

Section 5: *DEVELOPMENT REVIEW REQUIREMENTS*

5.01 After the effective date of the County Land Use Plan, a unit of local government may grant an application for a development permit consistent with the County Land Use Plan or a certified land use plan when it has determined that the following requirements are met;. . . .

The development review requirements of Section 5 pertain to:

(a) adequacy of potable water service,

(b) adequacy of wastewater treatment and disposal services,

(c) adequacy of solid waste disposal service,

(d) adequacy of drainage,

(e) adequacy of the regional transportation network,

(f) adequacy of local streets and roads,

(g) adequacy of fire protection service,

(h) adequacy of police protection service,

(i) adequacy of parks and recreation facilities, and

(j) adequacy of school sites and school buildings.

The municipalities qualify as units of local government under this plan. Eighteen of twenty have certified land use plans; fourteen have plat laws; only eight have adopted development review regulations.

The municipalities claim that the Board lacked the authority to adopt section 5-198; that the criteria of 5-198 duplicate those in section 5.01 of the County Land Use Plan; and that the Board's independent review of these criteria usurps the home rule powers of the municipalities. The municipalities do not challenge the authority of the County to certify local land use plans, to approve plats for recordation in the public record or the procedural requirements for plat approval and recordation set forth in section 5-197. Rather, they dispute the right of the Board to impose the substantive requirements contained therein. They assert that independent review of these factors for final plat approval improperly gives the Board a veto power over any prior approval given by the municipality and, therefore, usurps its home rule powers and conflicts with the land use planning scheme authorized by the legislature and adopted by the County. The County, on the other hand, contends that such veto power is necessary to insure consideration of countywide problems each time a development project is approved, and that ordinarily that is at the time of plat approval. The County also points out that it only retains the authority to veto, and does not have the authority to approve a plat request turned down by the municipality.

All of the municipalities in this action possess home rule powers. Home rule power of the municipalities is derived from article VIII of the Florida Constitution of 1968. Section 2(b) grants to each municipality the authority to conduct municipal government, perform municipal functions, render municipal services and exercise any power for municipal purposes, unless expressly prohibited by the constitution, general or special law or county charter. *See* § 166.021(4), Fla. Stat. (1981), and *State v. City of Sunrise*, 354 So.2d 1206, 1209 (Fla.1978). However, Article VIII, section 1(g) of the constitution grants the following powers to charter counties:

> Counties operating under county charters shall have all powers of local self-government not inconsistent with general law or with special law approved by vote of the electors. The governing body of a county operating under a charter may enact county ordinances not inconsistent with general law. The charter shall provide which shall prevail in the event of conflict between county and municipal ordinances.

Thus, the question of whether the county has usurped the power of the municipalities can ordinarily be answered by examining the charter and the general law.

Article VIII, General Provisions, section 8.04 of the Broward County Charter specifically deals with the problem of conflict, if any, of county ordinances with municipal ordinances. The charter declares:

> Notwithstanding any other provisions of this Charter, any county ordinance in conflict with a municipal ordinance shall not be effective within the municipality to the extent of such conflict regardless of whether such municipal ordinance was adopted or enacted before or after the County ordinance provided that the county ordinance shall prevail over municipal ordinances whenever the County shall set minimum standards protecting the environment by prohibiting or regulating air or water pollution, or the destruction of the resources of the County belonging to the general public within the parameters set forth in Section 8.17 of this Charter. *As set forth in this Charter, a county ordinance shall also prevail over a municipal ordinance in the area of*

land use planning. In the event a county ordinance and a municipal ordinance shall cover the same subject matter without conflict, both the municipal ordinance and the county ordinance shall be effective, each being deemed supplemental, one to the other.

(Emphasis supplied.) The challenged provisions of Section 5-198 deal, of course, with land use planning. In addition, section 125.86(7), Florida Statutes (1981), provides that charter counties have the power to:

Adopt, pursuant to the provisions of the charter, such ordinances of countywide force and effect as are necessary for the health, safety, and welfare of the residents. It is the specific legislative intent to recognize that a county charter may properly determine that certain governmental areas are more conducive to uniform countywide enforcement and may provide the county government powers in relation to those areas as recognized and as may be amended from time to time by the people of that county....

That land use planning is necessary for the health, safety, and welfare of all county residents is clear from another Florida statute, the Local Government Comprehensive Planning Act of 1975. Section 163.3161(3) of the Act declares:

It is the intent of this act that its adoption is necessary so that local governments can preserve and enhance present advantages; encourage the most appropriate use of land, water, and resources, consistent with the public interest; overcome present handicaps; and deal effectively with future problems that may result from the use and development of land within their jurisdictions. Through the process of comprehensive planning, it is intended that units of local government can preserve, promote, protect, and improve the public health, safety, comfort, good order, appearance, convenience, law enforcement and fire prevention, and general welfare; prevent the overcrowding of land and avoid undue concentration of population; facilitate the adequate and efficient provision of transportation, water, sewerage, schools, parks, recreational facilities, housing, and other requirements and services; and conserve, develop, utilize, and protect natural resources within their jurisdictions.

It is apparent that the Broward County Land Use Plan was the County's response to this legislative mandate; Ordinance 81-16, which includes section 5-198, merely implements the plan. An even more specific indication that the county's authority is paramount in the area of land use planning is contained in Section 163.3174(1)(b) of the Act which declares:

In the case of chartered counties, the planning responsibility between the county and the several municipalities therein shall be as stipulated in the charter.

Another legislative pronouncement, section 177.071(1)(a), Florida Statutes, provides that the municipality has exclusive jurisdiction to approve plats; however, section 177.071(2) states that if any provision in a county charter or ordinance is inconsistent with any provision in this section, the county charter shall prevail.

The net result of this analysis of the relevant provisions of the constitution, statutes, charter and ordinances is that, with regard to land use planning in general and to plat approval in particular, the county's authority is supreme.

The municipalities also suggest that the county should be limited to setting technical requirements for a plat as a map or delineated representation of the subdivision of lands. § 177.031(14), Fla. Stat. (1981). They construe the provision in section 6.12 of the county charter that the Board "shall enact an ordinance establishing standards, procedures and minimum requirements to regulate platting of lands" within the county to have reference to technical requirements only. They further assert that the only purpose of recording plats is "to serve to establish the identity of all lands shown, section 177.021, Florida Statutes (1981); and to inform the public, especially innocent purchasers, of facts regarding the property." *Coffman v. James*, 177 So.2d 25, 30 (Fla. 1st DCA 1965). However, this view fails to take into account the rest of the statutory definition, "being a complete exact representation of the subdivision of and other information in compliance with the requirement of all applicable sections of this chapter and of any local ordinances...." § 177.031(14). Section 177.011 states that the platting statute establishes only minimum requirements to regulate and control the platting of lands and "does not exclude additional provisions or regulations by local ordinance, laws or regulations." The municipalities rely for their view on the Plat Act of 1953 which was superseded, to the extent of any inconsistencies, by the Broward County Charter in 1975. It also appears that the municipalities' narrow construction of the purpose of platting requirements was implicitly rejected in *Kass v. Lewin*, 104 So.2d 572, 579 (Fla.1958), when the supreme court acknowledged that the legislature intended the plat act "to promote community planning."

... In our view, the challenged provisions deal not merely with the technical requirements for plats, but with the requirements for plat approval and all of its attendant development consequences. The substantive requirements are consistent with the objectives of the constitution, the platting act, and chapters 163 and 177; thus, such requirements are authorized by the county charter. More importantly, it is clear that the county is vested with the substantive authority to retain veto power over the municipalities platting decisions to insure that development within the county is consistent with the overall scheme set out in the county's land use plan. To hold otherwise would be to deny the county effective, coordinated control over development within the entire county including the municipalities located therein. Without some overall supervision the municipalities would be free to make development decisions without consideration of their effect on adjacent communities. While the Planning Council exercises some authority to insure that local land use plans are enacted in conformance with the county-wide land use plan and that only local development projects consistent with the overall plan are permitted, its supervisory authority is still limited. It appears, for instance, that the Council exercises no control over platting. The County's authority fills this void.

Finally, we believe this case is covered by the provision "where a municipal ordinance and a county ordinance cover the same subject matter without conflict they shall be deemed supplemental and both shall be effective." Broward County Charter § 8.04. In two recent decisions this court has rejected challenges to the County's authority similar to those raised herein. *Kane Homes, Inc. v. City of North Lauderdale,* 418 So.2d 451 (Fla. 4th DCA 1982) and *Hollywood, Inc. v. Broward County,* 431 So.2d 606 (Fla. 4th DCA 1983). Both of these decisions recognized the extensive authority that has been vested in a charter county in the realm of land use planning. A comparison of section 5-198 of Ordinance 81-16, the Broward County Land Development Code and section 5.01 of the Broward County Land Use Plan reveals immediately the lack of any substantial conflict. The criteria for final plat approval in the former are far more broad in scope than the criteria for development review in the latter. Any concern that the substantive requirements of section 5-198 are intended to refer only to matters of countywide concern should also be dispelled by a reading of section 5-199 of the county ordinances which specifies that such concerns as garbage collection, fire and police protection and local parks and recreational facilities shall not be the subject of independent review. Clearly, these are local concerns for which "the County shall rely on municipal review." In our view the county and municipal ordinances are supplemental and section 5-198 does not improperly infringe upon any right of the municipalities. Of course, even if there were a conflict with a municipal ordinance, under the legal analysis set out above, the county ordinance would prevail.

Accordingly, the judgment of the trial court is affirmed.

DOWNEY and HURLEY, JJ., concur.

Questions

1. Why does the county ordinance prevail?

2. What is the wording of the county ordinance that controls?

D. Article VIII, Section 1(h) — Limitation of Taxing Authority Over County Property

City of St. Petersburg v. Briley, Wild & Associates, Inc.

239 So. 2d 817 (Fla. 1970)

MASON, Circuit Judge.

This is an appeal from a decision of the Circuit Court of Pinellas County initially construing Article VIII, Section 1(h) of the 1968 Constitution of Florida, F.S.A., which is as follows:

"(h) Taxes; Limitation. Property situate within municipalities shall not be subject to taxation for services rendered by the County exclusively for the benefit of the property or residents in unincorporated areas."

We have jurisdiction under the provisions of Article V, Section 4(2).

This suit is one brought by the plaintiff, Briley, Wild & Associates, Inc., consulting engineers, against the defendant, Pinellas County, Florida, to recover payment of the sum of $100,381.73 allegedly due the plaintiff from the defendant for engineering services rendered under a contract between the parties by the terms of which the County employed the plaintiff as consulting engineers in connection with a proposed construction and expansion of sanitary sewage facilities in Pinellas County. The contract between the plaintiff and defendant County provided that the plaintiff would furnish all sanitary engineering work for the County in connection with said project. The over-all plan called for the ultimate cost to the County of approximately $50,000,000.00 to be divided into several phases. The beginning phase is calculated to cost $2,500,000.00, and it is for services rendered by plaintiff in connection with this phase of the project that this suit was instituted. This particular phase of the work contemplates the construction of a master sewage treatment plant in an unincorporated area of the county, together with the construction of transmission lines and lift stations, in accordance with the plans and specifications prepared by the plaintiff.

The defendant County included in its 1969–70 budget as an item in the General Fund Capital Outlay Reserve Account the sum of $2,500,000.00 estimated to defray the costs of this phase one construction. This sum is now in the General Fund of the County and was raised from ad valorem taxes levied upon all properties situated in the county, both in the incorporated and in the unincorporated areas. When the plaintiff presented its bill for payment for services to date the same was questioned by the Clerk of the Circuit Court, acting as County Auditor, it being his contention that the provisions of Article VIII, Section 1(h), supra, prohibit the use of monies raised by general ad valorem taxation to defray the costs of sewage facilities to be constructed in unincorporated areas of the county. The defendant County wants to pay the plaintiff, and, therefore, this lawsuit was begun as a friendly suit to determine its authority to do so. By way of counterclaim the defendant County sought a declaratory judgment of the trial court to construe the effect of the above constitutional provision upon its authority to pay not only the plaintiff for its services rendered to date, but also to use general county ad valorem taxes to defray this particular phase of the contemplated project and future phases thereof. The City of St. Petersburg, the Clerk of the Circuit Court of Pinellas County, the City of Safety Harbor, the City of Belleair Beach and the McGonegals, as taxpayers, intervened to contest the authority of the County to spend funds derived from general ad valorem taxes for the purposes heretofore stated. Thus, a suit which started out as a friendly lawsuit concluded as a bitterly contested one, primarily between the County of Pinellas and the City of St. Petersburg and the McGonegals, as residents and taxpayers of the City of Safety Harbor.

The suit went to trial upon the complaint of the plaintiff, the answer and counterclaim of the defendant County and the pleadings of the intervenors. The trial judge held that the contract sued upon was a valid and binding contract between the County and the plaintiff, that the amount sued for was properly due and owing from the County to the plaintiff under the contract, that the County was entitled to a declaratory judgment as to its authority to pay such sum to the plaintiff, that the Board of County Commissioners of the County proceeded properly under Special Act 69-1479 in approving and initiating the implementation of the master sewage facilities plan of the County, in accordance with the plan prepared by the plaintiff, for the purpose of eliminating pollution for the benefit of all areas of the County, both incorporated and unincorporated.

The record upon which the trial judge based his findings establishes that the population of the County is increasing rapidly in many of the unincorporated areas which are urban in nature and already densely populated; that the City of St. Petersburg located in the southeast portion of the county composes about one-fourth of the county area and has approximately 222,885 people and 58 square miles; that the city millage rate in that city is 16.25 mills; that the county millage rate is 10 mills countywide; that St. Petersburg, through its own resources plus a federal grant, has built and operated its own sewer treatment facility and renders quality sewerage services to its residents estimated to be adequate for its own area until 1985; that the urbanized areas of the County with few exceptions have shown no desire to incorporate; that over a period of years the County has attempted to solve the sewage pollution problem of the county as a whole by acquisition and construction of sewer systems through the use of special sewer districts created pursuant to the provisions of Chapter 153, Part II, F.S., financing such systems by revenue certificates issued against prospective service fees charged to the people served and/or assessed against their property; that the County purchased the sewer system serving the municipality of Kenneth City with the proceeds of such revenue certificates, and has purchased several other small existing systems by using available general funds of the County; that there exists an admitted present need in the County for upgrading its sewer plants and for providing additional sewage treatment facilities for the districts and for the other fast-growing urban areas of the County; two of the existing municipal systems have inadequate treatment facilities and are now being operated beneath State Health standards and have been cited by State Health authorities for failure to bring their plants up to proper standards. Because of these problems the County sought and obtained a special act of the Legislature in 1969 (Chapter 69-1479) which would authorize it to consolidate the various sewer districts as a first step to embark on a county-wide sewerage system plan pursuant to the general act, Chapter 153, F.S., and in accordance with a master plan prepared by consulting engineers; that this master plan called for as the first phase of the overall plan of sewerage control the construction of a master sewage treatment plant to be located in the southwestern portion of the County which would permit and call for the elimination of several smaller plants in some of the municipalities and unincorporated areas of the county; such master treatment plant is to be constructed adjacent to the existing treatment plant of the South Cross Bayou Sanitary District located in an unincorporated area of the county; that the existing plant now treats sewage from the City of Kenneth City and from parts of the cities of Pinellas Park and Largo; that it is proposed that such new master treatment plant (including the existing South Cross plant) will treat the sewage of the incorporated areas of Madeira Beach, Redington Beach, North Redington Beach and Redington

Shores immediately upon its completion, and contracts have been entered into with those cities by the County for such purpose.

The Board of County Commissioners of the County in implementing the special act of the Legislature (Chapter 69-1479, Special Laws of Florida) adopted the master plan as prepared by the plaintiff consulting engineers and by resolution determined that there was a need for master pollution control facilities of sanitary sewerage in the County; that inadequate sewage treatment is presently polluting the rivers, streams, and bays throughout the County; that the implementation of the master sewerage facilities plan prepared by the plaintiff will tend to eliminate such pollution, and that the results will be beneficial to all residents of the County, including those in the incorporated as well as in the unincorporated areas.

The trial Court entered judgment against the County and in favor of the plaintiff in the sum sued for and adjudged that the County may proceed to construct and legally pay for from the General Fund of the County the facilities called for in such plans and specifications.

Two questions are raised by the appellants. First, whether all necessary parties were before the Court below to enable it to enter a proper declaratory judgment and, second, whether the facts before the chancellor justified him in concluding that the services proposed to be rendered by the County by the use of county-wide levied taxes would not be "exclusively for the benefit of property and residents in the unincorporated areas," but would benefit the residents and property of all areas of the County, both incorporated and unincorporated.

As to the first question, we find that all parties necessary for the trial court to enter its declaratory judgment were before the Court. Such parties were the plaintiff, who was suing to recover for its engineering services, the County, who was sued for such services, and the Clerk of the Circuit Court, who, acting as County Auditor, had refused to pay the bill and who intervened for the purpose of raising the question of the authority of the County to use monies raised from county-wide levied taxes for the project contemplated by the over-all plan prepared by the plaintiff engineering company, under its contract with the County.

The critical question in this case is whether the expenditure of county-wide levied tax monies is authorized for the proposed project. Article VIII, Section 1(h), proscribes the use of tax monies received from taxes levied upon property situate within municipalities "for services rendered by the County, exclusively for the benefit of the property or residents in unincorporated areas." The record discloses that Pinellas County is composed of unincorporated areas, plus approximately twenty-three cities and towns. It is conceded by the appellees that the fund from which it is proposed to pay the plaintiff's bill and to construct the proposed sewer expansion was created by the receipts from ad valorem taxes levied by the County upon property situate within the municipalities of the County, as well as upon property lying within the unincorporated areas of the County. Therefore, if the services proposed to be rendered by the County and to be paid from such fund are services "exclusively for the benefit of property and residents in the unincorporated areas" the County may not use such county-wide levied tax monies for such purpose. We are called upon to decide first what is proscribed by the language "exclusively for the benefit of property and residents in the unincorporated areas" as used in Article VIII, Section 1(h) of the 1968 Florida Constitution, and second, whether or not the record herein supports the findings of the trial judge that the proposed project is not for such proscribed services, but will benefit the property and residents of the municipalities as well as those of the unincorporated areas.

This is a case of first impression in Florida since the constitutional provision construed by the trial court is new in the 1968 Constitution, neither it nor a similar one being incorporated in the Constitution of 1885. In reviewing his construction of the provision we are called upon to decide what is meant by the language which says that "property situate within municipalities shall not be subject to taxation for services rendered by the County *exclusively for the benefit of the property or residents in unincorporated areas.*" (Emphasis supplied). The key phrase to be interpreted is the phrase "exclusively for the benefit of the property or residents in unincorporated areas," for the proscription here is against the taxation of municipally-situated property to pay for services rendered exclusively for the benefit of the unincorporated areas of the County. It is evident from this language of proscription that the cost of services rendered by the County which are not rendered "exclusively for the benefit of the property or residents in unincorporated areas", but which benefit property situate in incorporated areas may be taxed against municipally-situate property as well as that outside of cities. We must determine what is meant by the term "exclusively for the benefit of" as here used by the framers of this provision, and as understood by the people at the time they adopted it in the General Election of 1968. We are obligated to give effect to this language according to its meaning and what the people must have understood it to mean when they approved it. *Advisory Opinion to the Governor*, 156 Fla. 48, 22 So.2d 398 (1945); *In Re Advisory Opinion to the Governor*, Fla., 223 So.2d 35 (1969). If the language is clear and not entirely unreasonable or illogical in its operation we have no power to go outside the bounds of the constitutional provision in search of excuses to give a different meaning to words used therein. *Vocelle v. Knight Bros. Paper Co.*, Fla. App., 118 So.2d 664; *Cassady v. Consolidated Naval Stores Co.*, Fla., 119 So.2d 35. The term "exclusive", which is the adjective from which the adverb "exclusively" is derived, is defined in Webster's New International Dictionary as "single", "sole"; "as an exclusive agent"; also "singly devoted", "undivided"; "limiting or limited to possession, control, or use by a single individual, organization, etc.," "as the exclusive privileges of the citizens of a country." If we give the phrase this literal interpretation it would be to hold that if the service proposed to be rendered by the County would be of the slightest benefit to property located in a particular municipality, however minute in quantity or quality, such service could not be said to be "exclusively for the benefit" of the unincorporated areas of the County, and it would, therefore, subject such municipal property to county taxation for such service. But, there is another and cardinal rule of statutory construction applicable to the construction of constitutional provisions and that is that the fundamental object is to ascertain and give effect to the intent of the framers and adopters thereof, and constitutional provisions must be interpreted in such a manner as to fulfill this intention, rather than to defeat it. 6 Fla. Jur. 281. Furthermore, constitutional interpretation is actuated by the rule of reason, and unreasonable or absurd consequences should, if possible, be avoided. *Florida Dry Cleaning & Laundry Board v. Everglades Laundry*, 137 Fla. 290, 188 So. 380. A literal interpretation should not be accorded if it leads to an unreasonable conclusion or to a result not intended by the lawmakers. *Lanier v. Tyson*, Fla. App. (1962), 147 So.2d 365.

To prevent an interpretation of this language which would lead to an unreasonable conclusion, or to one such as was not intended by the framers, we are privileged to look to the historical background of this particular provision. *In Re Advisory Opinion to the Governor*, Fla., 223 So.2d 35 (1969). When this particular proposal was before the Revisory Commission which framed the 1968 Constitution, there was considerable debate as to its meaning and purpose, as reflected by the minutes of such Revisory Commission. Also, when this proposal was considered by the Committee of the Whole of the House of Representatives, further debate reflected the purpose and intent of the proposal. An examination of the minutes of both bodies leads us to conclude that the purpose of the Revisory Commission in drafting this provision, and the House of Representatives in accepting it as so drafted, is to prevent double taxation of municipally-situated property for a single benefit. That the framers of the provision, and the people in adopting it, intended to prevent future taxation by counties of city-located property for services from which the owners of said property received no real or substantial benefit. We, therefore, hold that Article VIII, Section 1(h) of the 1968 Constitution of Florida prohibits the taxation of municipally-situate property by the County for any services rendered by the County where no real or substantial benefit accrues to city property from such services. Conversely, this provision permits such taxation where such service is found to be of real and substantial benefit to such property.

We have examined the record to determine whether the proposed project will render any real or substantial benefits to property situate within the various municipalities of Pinellas County. It is conceded that the sewage from the City of St. Petersburg will not be treated in the proposed [system. Under] the express provision of Chapter 69-1479, Special Acts of 1969, it is not permissible for the county system to enter into an incorporated city without the express permission of the latter. The record does disclose that the existing county system treats sewage from the City of Kenneth City and from parts of the Cities of Pinellas Park and Largo. It is proposed that the master treatment plant will treat the sewage of the incorporated areas of Madeira Beach, Redington Beach, North Redington Beach and Redington Shores, under contracts with those municipalities. But, the larger municipalities of the county will not actually use these facilities. This is particularly true of St. Petersburg and Clearwater.

But, there is undisputed testimony in the record to the effect that now substandard treated sewage is being discharged at points close to the City of St. Petersburg, the Madeira Beach outfall area and the outfall of the lower county system. Also, the County Sanitary Engineer testified that there is a serious possibility of disease spilling over and spreading from the county areas to the city areas, particularly into St. Petersburg, if the present situation is not remedied. The witnesses appearing before the trial judge testified that indirect benefit would result to all of the property and residents of the entire county by the elimination of pollution from the waters surrounding the county. There is testimony in the record to the effect that at present there are some one hundred forty-eight sewage outlets discharging effluent into the streams, waters and soils of the county, and that such discharge creates a county-wide pollution problem. The record reflects that the purpose of the proposed construction and expansion is to remedy this situation by reducing the number of septic tanks now discharging waste and improving the treatment of raw sewage now emptying into the soils, streams and waters of the county, with the ultimate goal of reducing pollution to acceptable standards promulgated by the State of Florida.

The trial court held that the proposed project had as its purpose the remedying of the situation outlined above and that it would result in such benefits to properties located in the municipalities of Pinellas County so as to authorize county taxation of such property for this particular service proposed to be rendered by the County. We agree. It is true that the benefits may not be direct in the sense that the owners of city-located property will physically use the expanded treatment plant, lines and lift stations. But we reject the argument of appellants that in order to avoid the proscription of Article VIII, Section 1(h) it is necessary that any benefit to municipalities be direct and primary. We hold that the proper interpretation of the language of this section of the Constitution does not require a direct and primary use benefit from a particular service to city-located property in order to remove the same from the proscription of the constitutional provision. It is sufficient to authorize county taxation of such property if the benefits accruing to the municipal areas are found to be real and substantial and not merely illusory, ephemeral and inconsequential. That it was not the intent of the framers of this provision of the Constitution to require a direct benefit to city-located property in order to avoid the proscription is evidenced by the fact that attempts to amend the provision to substitute the words "directly" and "primarily" for the word "exclusively" were defeated before the proposition was submitted to the people for approval.

Water pollution and the attendant diseases and ills to human habitation that flow therefrom know no city or county lines. The evidence before the trial court indicates that the contamination of the waters of Pinellas County which occurs in the unincorporated areas contaminates waters located in the incorporated areas through the natural process of flow. Disease originating in the unincorporated areas resulting from improperly-treated sewage can and will readily spread throughout the county. Protection against such contamination and disease is not merely an incidental or collateral benefit which would result to the incorporated areas of the county by the correction of the problem in the unincorporated areas. This Court takes judicial knowledge of the fact that Pinellas County, with its numerous bays and streams, some of which are within the County and others contiguous thereto, is one of the finest recreation areas devoted to boating, fishing and swimming, in the entire south-eastern portion of the nation. We are now living in a time when our citizenry is pollution conscious.

It is impossible to separate as between the various areas of the county the deleterious effect upon the public health of contamination and pollution occurring in a particular area. It is unrealistic to say that the elimination of pollution and contamination of the soils, waters and streams of the unincorporated areas of Pinellas County will not be of substantial benefit, healthwise and recreation-wise, to the incorporated areas.

We can conceive of services sought to be rendered by a county within a particular unincorporated area which would have no consequential benefits to the municipalities of the county such as, for instance, a library set up in an unincorporated area for the use and benefit of the area residents or, perhaps, a park or recreation facility for the residents of such area. Even the establishment of fire fighting facilities in a particular unincorporated area may not reasonably be said to be of consequential benefit to the incorporated areas. But, in the field of public health a different situation may readily exist. We believe that the record before the trial judge amply substantiates his conclusion that the proposed project would be of beneficial use to and in the best interest of the present and future welfare and well-being of the residents of all areas of Pinellas County, and that, therefore, the proscription of Article VIII, Section 1(h) is not applicable to the particular project involved in this suit.

We conclude that the judgment below is without error and should be affirmed:

It is so ordered.

ERVIN, C.J., and DREW, CARLTON and BOYD, JJ., concur.

Questions

1. According to the Court, what was the purpose of the 1968 revision of Section 1(h)?

2 a. How does the Court define "exclusively for the benefit ..."?

  b. How helpful is this definition?

  c. How is the Court's definition "used" in this case?

3. Note the examples of services cited by the Court in the final paragraph. Which of these services would fail under the Court's test? Why would they not provide the exclusive benefit required?

Alsdorf v. Broward County

333 So. 2d 457 (Fla. 1976)

ENGLAND, Justice.

This matter was brought to us by direct appeal from a final judgment rendered by the Broward County Circuit Court, construing Article VIII, Section 1(h) of the 1968 Florida Constitution as being inherently too vague to be self-executing. We have jurisdiction to review that judgment under Article V, Section 3(b)(1) of the Florida Constitution.

This lawsuit began as a class action by twenty-four mayors of Florida municipalities, in their governmental capacities and as citizen-taxpayers, seeking declaratory and other forms of relief against Broward County in connection with the County's 1973–74 budget. The mayors' lawsuit challenges Broward County's expenditure of various sums raised by property tax levies from residents within municipal boundaries, in the light of Article VIII, Section 1(h) of the Florida Constitution, which provides:

> "(h) Taxes; limitation. Property situate within municipalities shall not be subject to taxation for services rendered by the county exclusively for the benefit of the property or residents in unincorporated areas."

Following a four day non-jury trial, the trial court entered final judgment against the mayors and dismissed their lawsuit, finding

> "... that Article VIII, Sec. 1(h) of the Florida Constitution (1968), is too vague by itself to be workable. There are no standards, no guidelines by which to aide the municipalities and counties in their attempt to work within the Constitutional provision. This Court feels that it is the legislature's duty to supply the necessary standards so as to make the provision workable."

The mayors attack that judgment here.

We previously construed the language of this constitutional provision in *City of St. Petersburg v. Briley, Wild & Assocs., Inc.*, 239 So.2d 817 (Fla.1970). In that case we held that the term "exclusively" could not be read literally, and that county taxation of municipal properties is barred only when county services bring to municipal property owners no "real or substantial benefit". We there held, on the facts of that case, that tax-supported expenditures for a county sewage treatment plant benefited the residents of intra-county municipalities by preserving their health, even though no lines, mains, pumping stations or other physical facilities were constructed within city boundaries.[11]

Other Florida appellate decisions have upheld the use of city-derived property tax revenues for a county fire department, for county sewer facilities, and for county roads, canals and related improvements.

Unlike previous litigants who have challenged individual county expenditures, the mayors in this lawsuit challenge an array of county expenditures, asserting that each provides no "real and substantial benefit" to city dwellers within the county. The trial court analyzed these assertions and found from the evidence adduced at trial that, while "some of the items listed in the plaintiffs' lawsuit clearly benefit all citizens of

---

11. [FN3.] The Court also suggested, although it was not germane to the controversy, that county parks, libraries, and perhaps even fire-fighting equipment, might be services for which the county could not tax municipal properties.

the County ... numerous other items benefit only the residents of the unincorporated areas and, therefore, must necessarily come within the purview of this lawsuit." Nonetheless, the court dismissed the mayors' lawsuit on the ground that legislative guidelines were needed to make the constitutional provision work. We disagree.

Both appellant and appellee support their positions here with our decision in *Gray v. Bryant*, 125 So.2d 846 (Fla.1960). Appellant cites several portions of that decision for support and points out that the constitutional provision at issue there was held to require no legislative implementation for its effectiveness. Appellee finds support for its position in the Court's language on page 851, to the effect that:

> "The basic guide, or test, in determining whether a constitutional provision should be construed to be self-executing, or not self-executing, is whether or not the provision lays down a sufficient rule by means of which the right or purpose which it gives or is intended to accomplish may be determined, enjoyed, or protected without the aid of legislative enactment."

From this appellee argues that the complexity of financing, budgeting and conducting a variety of necessary governmental activities in a county which contains multiple municipalities, coupled with the ever present factual uncertainty of what is and what is not of "real and substantial benefit" to particular municipal residents, requires an affirmation of the trial court's conclusion.

We recognize the logic of appellee's argument. We concede, in fact, that the practical consequences of holding for the mayors may pose such horrendous fiscal problems for the administration of 67 counties that their governmental operations may be virtually incapacitated by uncertainty and lawsuits. If there were any practical way to avoid that result consistent with the Constitution, we would readily adopt it. But neither party here has offered such a solution, and we can conceive of none.[12] We simply cannot abdicate our responsibility to follow the will of the people as expressed in the Constitution, on the grounds of administrative complexity.

The mandate against city taxation for exclusive county activities is absolute and unequivocal. The people appear to have directed this consequence despite the fact that extensive judicial labor is required to separate the permissible from the impermissible. Indeed, we fail to see any way in which legislative intervention would lessen that labor.

Our view of the self-executing nature of this constitutional position has three bases.

(1) The language of the Constitution is reasonably straightforward and unambiguous. The intent of this tax limitation provision is both obvious and understandable. Practical considerations aside, there is no reason that the

---

12. [FN8.] It has been suggested that we recede from *Briley* by adopting a literal view of "exclusively", and by so doing leave the area for operation of this provision so narrow as to be inconsequential and unenforceable. Tempting as this appears, this solution merely offers an absurd result in place of an impractical one. 239 So.2d at 822.

words cannot be applied to mean precisely what they say (with the gloss previously given the term "exclusively" in *Briley*).

(2) The format of the particular provision is not unique to our Constitution. The identical mandatory negative "shall not" or its equivalent appears in numerous other provisions as a direct check on governmental and nongovernmental acts, some of which also bar ad valorem taxation on various subjects.[13] We are not willing to lessen the negative directive in this provision in light of the implications which that action could have in other areas.

(3) The trial court found as a fact that several of the county expenditures enumerated in the mayors' complaint are of no real or substantial benefit to municipal residents.[14] Neither party has challenged the trial court's findings as being without factual support in the record. This appears to prove appellants' point that the Constitution can operate without legislative clarification.

We conclude, therefore, that Article VIII, Section 1(h) of the Florida Constitution is self-executing, and that with or without legislative interpretation the courts will be required to draw the lines between acceptable and prohibited municipal taxation. We must, therefore, reverse the trial court's decision and remand this proceeding for further action by the trial court in light of our opinion.

We recognize, however, that the fiscal effect of our decision may significantly affect Broward County and that neither it nor the Legislature has provided revenue for this eventuality. Under these circumstances, we direct the trial court to exercise

---

13. [FN11.] See, for example, Article I, Sections 3 ("There shall be no law respecting the establishment of religion...."), 4 ("No law shall be passed to restrain or abridge the liberty of speech or of the press."), 6 ("The right of employees ... to bargain collectively shall not be denied or abridged.") and 10 ("No bill of attainder, ex post facto law or law impairing the obligation of contracts shall be passed."); Article VII, Sections 1(b) ("Motor vehicles, boats (etc) ... shall not be subject to ad valorem taxes.") and 9(b) ("Ad valorem taxes ... shall not be levied in excess of the following millages...."); Article VIII, Section 3 ("Consolidation shall not extend the territorial scope of taxation for the payment of pre-existing debt...."); Article X, Sections 1 ("The legislature shall not take action on any proposed amendment to the constitution of the United States unless a majority of the members thereof have been elected after the proposed amendment has been submitted for ratification."), 4(c) ("The homestead shall not be subject to devise if the owner is survived by spouse or minor child...."), and 9 ("Repeal or amendment of a criminal statute shall not affect prosecution or punishment for any crime previously committed."). Cf., *Dade County Classroom Teachers Ass'n, Inc. v. Florida Legislature*, 269 So.2d 684 (Fla.1972).

14. [FN12.] The trial court identified four categories of services and facilities in Broward County, listing some items believed to be within each category. One category involves items from which all cities receive benefits all of the time, such as the county commission. Another involves items from which all cities receive benefits some of the time, such as the sheriff's office and the personnel office. Items in these categories were found to be properly taxable to city residents. As to the necessary extent of real and substantial benefit, see *Dressel v. Dade County*, 219 So.2d 716 (3d DCA Fla.1969). Another category involves items from which some but not all municipalities benefit, such as emergency medical services available only in West Broward County and the county library. Items in this category would require an identification and allocation of revenues and expenditures. The last category involves items from which no city benefits, such as the building and zoning department.

its inherent equitable powers to fashion a suitable remedy for the resolution of this controversy.

"In a changing world marked by the ebb and flow of social and economic shifts, new conditions constantly arise which make it necessary, that no right be without a remedy, to extend the old and tried remedies. It is the function of courts to do this. It may be done by working old fields, but, when it becomes necessary, they should not hesitate to 'break new ground' to do so." *State ex rel. Watkins v. Fernandez*, 106 Fla. 779, 143 So. 638, 641 (1932).

The parties may be able to agree among themselves on an arrangement which recognizes the rights of municipal taxpayers and the obligations incurred by county government. If such a settlement is now possible, the courts should not intervene. Otherwise, the plaintiffs are entitled to remedial orders which take into account the equities on both sides.

The decision of the circuit court is reversed and this case is remanded for further action consistent with this opinion.

OVERTON, C.J., and ADKINS, SUNDBERG and HATCHETT, JJ., concur.

BOYD, J., dissents with an opinion.

ROBERTS, J., dissents and concurs with BOYD, J.

BOYD, Justice (dissenting).

I respectfully dissent to the majority opinion.

This Court should be fully aware that Broward is one of Florida's largest and perhaps the fastest growing counties in the Nation. It has many municipalities and unincorporated areas which appear to be the same with no major differences in public services offered in such areas. To require the County to separate tax dollars expended based upon municipal boundaries imposes an unrealistic and impossible task.

As we stated in *City of St. Petersburg v. Briley, Wild and Associates*, 239 So.2d 817 (Fla.1970), and *Burke v. Charlotte Co.*, 286 So.2d 199 (Fla.1973), there is no requirement that funds expended by counties outside of municipalities be "direct and primary," but "real and substantial" to the benefit of municipal residents. It is hard to imagine any expenditure which could be made in populous Broward County which could benefit only persons in the unincorporated areas without real and substantial benefits to at least some of those residents of incorporated areas.

Such a division stated in the constitutional provision construed by the majority opinion could only be accomplished in those rural areas of the state having small municipalities wherein the services furnished in the towns or cities can be clearly identified as separate in nature from rural benefits provided for agricultural and similar purposes.

I would adopt the trial court's judgment except that I would hold that under *Gray v. Bryant*, 125 So.2d 846 (Fla.1960), the constitutional provision is self-executing in rural or semi-rural areas in which municipal limits clearly distinguish between city and rural areas. The separation of tax dollars as stated in the Constitution cannot be accomplished in the vast metropolitan complex of Broward County.

ROBERTS, J., concurs.

Questions

1. What is the dissent's argument? To what extent is this a practical, as opposed to a legal, argument? What is the task for the trial court based on this opinion?

2. See also *County of Volusia v. State*, 417 So. 2d 968 (Fla. 1982) (discussing Article VIII, Section 1(k)).

E. Article VIII, Section 2 — Municipalities

City of Miami Beach v. Forte Towers, Inc.

305 So. 2d 764 (Fla. 1974)

PER CURIAM.

Jurisdiction of this direct appeal from the Circuit Court of Dade County vests under Art. V, s 3(b)(1), Fla. Const., the trial court having expressly held unconstitutional F.S. s 166.021 relating to municipal home rule (a portion of Ch. 73-129, Laws of Florida, 1973).

It is the unanimous opinion of this Court that F.S. s 166.021 is constitutionally valid, as more fully set forth in the special concurring opinion of the Mr. Justice Dekle. A majority of this Court also concurs in the trial court's holding that insufficient evidence was presented at trial to overcome the city council's finding that an emergency existed (at the time it was passed) to support enactment of the rent control ordinance at that time, although Justices Roberts and Boyd expressly dissent on this point.

However, a majority of this Court holds that this particular rent control ordinance is constitutionally defective in its attempted delegation of the legislative powers of the city to the rent control administrator without prescribing sufficient objective guidelines, as is more fully set forth in Mr. Justice Dekle's specially concurring opinion, with which (on this point) Justices Roberts, Boyd and Overton join.

Accordingly, the opinion of the trial court is reversed insofar as it holds F.S. s 166.021 to be unconstitutional and holds that Ch. 73-129 does not authorize the city to enact a rent control ordinance; to the extent that the trial court found the provisions of the ordinance to be invalid as to guidelines and standards, it is affirmed.

Affirmed in part; reversed in part.

DEKLE, J., concurring specially with opinion with which OVERTON, J., concurs.

OVERTON, J., concurring specially with opinion.

ROBERTS, J., concurring in part and dissenting in part with opinion with which BOYD, J., concurs.

ERVIN, J., concurring in part and dissenting in part with opinion with which AD-KINS, C.J., and McCAIN, J., concur.

DEKLE, Justice (concurring specially):

Following the enactment of Ch. 73-129, also known as the Municipal Home Rule Powers Act, the City of Miami Beach (hereafter referred to as "the city") adopted a rent control ordinance which included a finding of public emergency due to a housing shortage and abnormal rent increases. Thereafter, the instant suit was filed seeking a declaratory judgment and injunctive relief on the ground that the rent control ordinance was invalid for numerous reasons. Following trial, the circuit court held F.S. s 166.021 invalid to the extent that it authorized municipal rent control laws, and struck down the ordinance on the basis that it conflicted with certain general laws of the state and that it unlawfully delegated the city's legislative authority without establishing sufficient guidelines. The able trial judge also effectively settled certain issues when he specifically ruled that insufficient evidence had been presented, (1) to overcome the city council's finding that an emergency existed, (2) to established that the ordinance was improperly enacted, (3) to establish that the ordinance was ambiguous, and (4) to establish that the ordinance was discriminatory.

This is not the initial appearance of a rent control ordinance before this Court. We dealt with a prior rent control ordinance of the city in *City of Miami Beach v. Fleetwood Hotel, Inc.*, 261 So.2d 801 (Fla.1972); there we affirmed a trial court order invalidating that ordinance. In so doing, we stated that a municipality has no power to enact a rent control ordinance "absent a legislative enactment authorizing the exercise of such a power by a municipality"; that the ordinance then under consideration contained provisions amounting to an unlawful delegation of the legislative authority of the city without appropriate guidelines, and that the ordinance then in question conflicted with certain general laws regulating landlord and tenant relationships.

First, therefore, we must consider whether the municipality now has the power to enact such an ordinance; that is, whether the enactment of Ch. 73-129 after our decision in *Fleetwood Hotel* necessitates a change in the result there reached. I believe that it does, and that municipalities now are empowered to enact such ordinances by virtue of new Ch. 73-129.

Ch. 73-129 is a broad grant of power to municipalities in recognition and implementation of the provisions of Art. VIII, s 2(b), Fla. Const.[15] [FN1] It should be so construed as to effectuate that purpose where possible. It provides, in new F.S. s 166.021(1), that municipalities shall have the governmental, corporate and proprietary powers to enable them to conduct municipal government, perform municipal functions and render municipal services; it further enables them to exercise any power for municipal services, except when expressly prohibited by law.

---

15. [FN1.] Contrary to appellee's assertion, this statute is not "a mere delegation of the police power," which would not carry with it the power to enact rent control ordinances.

Appellee contends that the broad definition of municipal purposes contained in Ch. 73-129 does not grant the city the power to enact rent control ordinances, since the determination of what constitutes a proper municipal purpose is for the judiciary. *City of Miami Beach v. Seacoast Towers-Miami Beach, Inc.*, 156 So.2d 528 (Fla.App.3d 1963). This argument misses the mark. It is not the definition of municipal purposes found in new F.S. s 166.021(2) that grants power to the municipality to enact such an ordinance, but rather the provision of new F.S. s 166.021(1) which expressly empowers municipalities to "exercise any power for municipal purposes, except when expressly prohibited by law." As we noted in *In re Apportionment Law*, 281 So.2d 484 (Fla.1973), the intent of this chapter was largely to eliminate the "local bill evil" by implementing the provisions of Art. VIII, s 2, Fla. Const. The power to enact rent control ordinances in appropriate circumstances is contained in new F.S. s 166.021(1), and is not dependent upon the definitional provision of new F.S. s 166.021(2).

If we must deal with an application of "municipal purposes" in F.S. s 166.021(2) under appellee's challenge and determine whether rent control constitutes a proper municipal purpose, then it presents no judicial problem, for rent control under appropriate circumstances clearly falls within the general category of "municipal purposes." Such a finding has ample support in the authorities. The question apparently has never been determined before in this state, but there is authority for the enactment of rent control ordinances in appropriate circumstances as a proper municipal purpose in *Warren v. City of Philadelphia*, 382 Pa. 380, 115 A.2d 218 (1955); *Inganamort v. Borough of Fort Lee*, 120 N.J. Super. 286, 293 A.2d 720 (1972); McQuillen or Municipal Corporations, s 24.563(d).

The enactment of rent control ordinances, given sufficient justifying Conditions, is a proper municipal purpose. It is not "expressly prohibited by law" and therefore comes within the grant of power contained in new F.S. s 166.021(1). We need not, therefore, reach the general question of overbroadness of the definitional portion of the act at s 166.021(2).

That the power to enact rent control laws was intended to be included in the broad grant of power to municipalities in Ch. 73-129 can be seen from the legislature's rejection of a proposed amendment to Ch. 73-129 during debate which would have expressly excluded the power to enact such ordinances from the broad grant of power contained in that chapter. Additionally, note the conclusion of the Attorney General in his Opinion 073-267 that Ch. 73-129 empowers a municipality to enact rent control ordinances. I conclude that it was the legislative intent to include in this broad grant of powers the power to enact rent control ordinances in appropriate circumstances, thereby providing the missing authority required by *Fleetwood Hotel*.

The trial court also ruled that Ch. 73-129 is invalid in that it attempts unlawfully to delegate the State's legislative power to deal in matters reserved to the State, including landlord-tenant relationships and the regulation of decedents' estates. In so doing, the trial court failed to apply the rule that statutes will be so construed as to uphold their constitutional validity whenever possible. And here the statute may be upheld, for F.S. s 166.021(3)(c) expressly excludes from the grant of power to municipalities "any subject expressly preempted to state or county government by the constitution or by general law." Thus, even if a rent control ordinance which was passed under the authority of Ch. 73-129 should seek to regulate such a matter preempted by the State, it would be invalid to that extent under the terms of the authorizing statute itself. While a provision of that nature would require the invalidating of such a provision of the statute, it does not necessitate or even justify a finding that the total statute is invalid.

It has also been contended that Ch. 73-129 is inapplicable to Miami Beach due to the provisions of Art. VIII, s 6(e), Fla. Const., and F.S., s 166.021(3)(d), which exempt from the broad grant of powers any subject preempted to a county pursuant to a county charter adopted under authority of Art. VIII, s 6(e). That constitutional provision states that all provisions of the Metropolitan Dade County Home Rule Charter shall be valid if authorized under Art. VIII, s 11 of our constitution of 1885, and that Art. VIII, s 11, of the former constitution (the Dade County Home Rule Charter provision), shall remain in full force and effect as it Art. VIII of the new constitution had not been adopted. It is contended that the only method by which the power to enact rent control ordinances may be conferred on a municipality in Dade County is by amendment to the municipal charter, as provided in s 5.03 of the County Charter.

It is true that s 5.03 provides the only way in which a city charter may be *amended* in Dade County. *Andrews v. Linden*, 284 So.2d 398 (Fla.App.3d 1973). But amendment to the city charter is not the only means by which *additional* powers may be *conferred* on a Dade County municipality. The Metro County Charter s 5.02 provides that each municipality shall have the authority to exercise all powers relating to its local affairs not Inconsistent with the charter. Section 5.01 reserves the right of municipal self-determination except as otherwise provided by the charter. So long as the additional power does not conflict with the provisions of the charter—and the power to enact rent control ordinances does not so conflict—there is no reason why the Legislature may not confer such additional power on a Dade County municipality. Nor has the power to control rents been preempted by Dade County pursuant to its charter, so as to bring into play the exemption provision of new F.S. s 166.021(3)(d). Accordingly, I conclude that Ch. 73-129, at least insofar as it allows municipalities to enact rent control ordinances, is applicable to municipalities in Dade County.

Having determined that Ch. 73-129 is not an improper delegation of the State's legislative authority, that it provides the legislative authorization to enact rent control ordinances lacking in Fleetwood Hotel, and that its provisions are applicable, insofar as they authorize enactment of rent control ordinances to municipalities in Dade County, despite the provisions of new F.S. s 166.021(3)(d), now let us turn to the validity of the ordinance itself. The trial court found the ordinance invalid both for unlawful delegation of the city's legislative authority without sufficient objective guidelines and for conflict with the Florida Residential Landlord and Tenant Act (specifically, F.S. ss 83.46, 83.57, 83.58, and 83.59) and F.S. Ch. 731 (Florida Probate Law).

I too find difficulty with the guidelines set forth in the ordinance, both on the question of whether it is by its fixed terms confiscatory and therefore unconstitutional in its results, and also on the charge that the ordinance is arbitrary and unreasonable and therefore unconstitutional.[16] Each aspect of the ordinance in question must be reviewed to determine whether or not it rationally attempts to relieve the critical shortage of residential housing and accommodations which justify rent control in order to promote a return to a more nearly normal basis.[17] The purpose of rent control legislation has always been to stabilize rentals in emergency areas and under emergency conditions in order to prevent extortionate increases in rent resulting from housing shortages, and at the same time to allow landlords a fair and equitable return upon their investments. *Foti v. Heller*, 48 N.J. Super. 57, 137 A.2d 10 (N.J.App.1957).

If the guidelines in our ordinance here were predicated on the criteria of the authorities mentioned above, such guidelines would probably meet with approval on the constitutional grounds raised. I am impelled by these precedents, however, to find that the standards and guidelines for the rent administrator are so fixed and arbitrary in this particular ordinance and in such exact percentages and amounts and terms as to prevent the administrator, even if he desired, from allowing a fair rate of return in certain situations which demanded it in order to avoid being confiscatory. This remains the result despite an attempt in other language of the ordinance to allow the administrator leeway in specified instances. Perhaps the city council has been overly conscientious in its efforts to spell out everything but in so doing it has run afoul of the buoys in the constitutional channel.

The various guidelines and standards have been closely evaluated to bring them into harmony with constitutional requirements but I am simply unable to do so, short of a virtual judicial rewrite of these provisions of the ordinance. This we are not authorized to do within our judicial limitations.

For example, a "freeze" date is set as of October 1, 1973, and despite limited authorizations in specified cases for some latitude to be granted, these provisions remain so restrictive that the continuing spiraling costs since that date, of which we must take judicial notice, would preclude an administrator from allowing, even if he wanted, a rate of return that would be less than confiscatory at least in part. Needed in such an ordinance is a greater flexibility to take such matters into account so that the ultimate goals earlier expressed in the authorities of a fair rate of return and yet an avoidance of unfair rents would be more likely to be attained. They cannot be reached with provisions in the ordinance like Section 4(c)(4)(v) which allows an adjustment in rent where, "it is established that the earned income from the property does not result in a net annual return of 6% Of the assessed evaluation of the property in effect as of October 1, 1973." The same provision then states:

---

16. [FN 4.] *Nebbia v. People of State of New York*, 291 U.S. 502, 539 (1934); *Nashville, C. & St. L. Ry. v. Walters*, 294 U.S. 405, 415 (1935); *Rivera v. R. Cobian Chinea & Co.*, 181 F.2d 974, 978 (1st Cir. 1950); *Mora v. Mejias*, 223 F.2d 814, 816 (1st Cir. 1955); *Kress, Dunlap & Lane, Ltd. v. Downing*, 193 F. Supp. 874 (D.V.I.1961).

17. [FN 5.] *Russell v. Treasurer & Receiver General*, 331 Mass. 501, 509, 120 N.E.2d 388 (1954); *Nayor v. Rent Board of Town of Brookline*, 334 Mass. 132, 134 N.E.2d 419 (S.Jud.Ct.1956).

"For the purposes of this paragraph, net annual return shall be the amount by which the earned income exceeds the operating expenses of the property, excluding mortgage interest, amortization, depreciation and debt service."

For one thing, the assessed valuation of property is not necessarily the proper basis for a fair return. Despite the requirement for 100% Assessed valuation for purposes of taxation in Florida, this is not always current and such values do not coincide with the anniversary tax date. For example, the expert testimony in this cause is that in Miami Beach it approximates 75% Of the fair market value on apartment buildings which would in reality compute out to a 4.5% return instead of the 6% provided, even if that should be found to be a fair return. Mortgage interest is expressly excluded as an operating expense and when this is calculated in the "return" it becomes a negative one of minus 4.25% under this provision of the ordinance. Obviously, this becomes confiscatory and the administrator is not allowed under these guidelines to make a sufficient adjustment to avoid confiscation and a deprivation of the landlord's property without due process of law.

Testimony revealed that each of the plaintiff corporations in this cause is operating at an actual loss before depreciation and yet under the ordinance's formula it had a "profit" and a "rate of return" of 10.46%. The expert observed that in order to qualify for an "increase" under the ordinance's formula, the owner would have to increase his losses to $183,000! As to the fair market value in relation to the assessment, the testimony reflected the value of one large apartment unit at $7 million which had been its purchase price in 1971 and yet its assessed value during the interim of increasing property values never did exceed $5 million; that competition had kept its rental increases during the 3-year period to an average of less than 5% And with an overall loss of $36,000 in the first 11 months of 1973, meaning, again, that to qualify for rent increase under the formula in the ordinance would require an increased Loss up to $150,000 before an "increase" could be granted. These results simply do not square with the requirements of due process; they would constitute confiscation beyond the control of the Administrator under the tools he is given to work with. The council will simply have to try again.

The ordinance is unconstitutional in its present form, in my view, in that its provisions and guidelines are arbitrary and unreasonable and would be confiscatory and a denial of due process.

Having found the ordinance to be deficient for these reasons, the other grounds asserted as invalidating the ordinance need not be considered.

Accordingly, I concur in the majority opinion of the Court for the reasons set forth herein.

OVERTON, J., concurs.

OVERTON, Justice (concurring specially).

I agree that Section 166.021, Florida Statutes, is constitutional and that the City of Miami Beach has the constitutional authority to enact a rent control ordinance upon a finding that an emergency exists.

The finding of the trial judge that the city council properly determined that an emergency does exist, because of "the extraordinary, unusual and unique factual situation existing in the south beach area" of Miami Beach, is proper.

The ordinance adopted by the City is deficient in that it lacks proper standards and guidelines for its enforcement. The opinion by Mr. Justice Dekle sets forth with particularity many of its deficiencies, which in effect make it confiscatory. I am concerned that the holding that certain standards and guidelines are so fixed as to make the ordinance confiscatory raises an inference that this situation could be corrected by giving the administrator even broader discretionary authority. It would be clearly improper to delegate broad discretionary powers to the administrator, although he could be authorized to promulgate rules and regulations that relate to the implementation of the act and are strictly procedural in nature. The correction must be in the standards and guidelines.

I concur with the majority judgment entered herein.

ROBERTS, Justice (concurring in part, dissenting in part):

I concur with the majority's holding that Sections 4(b)(1), 4(b)(4), and 9 of the questioned ordinance constitute *City of Miami Beach v. Forte Towers, Inc.* an unlawful delegation of legislative powers without sufficient objective guidelines, and, therefore, render the ordinance invalid. For emphasis, we restate the following excerpt from *City of Miami Beach v. Fleetwood Hotel, Inc.*, 261 So.2d 801 (Fla.1972):

> "The same restrictions which apply to the Legislature's delegation of legislative authority also apply to the enactment of municipal ordinances under the general police power by municipalities in that city ordinances must not constitute an improper delegation of legislative, executive or administrative power. *Blitch v. City of Ocala*, 142 Fla. 612, 195 So. 406 (1940). It has been previously held by this Court in *Smith v. Portante*, 212 So.2d 298, 299 (Fla.1968), that:
>
> > 'No matter how laudable a piece of legislation may be in the minds of its sponsors, *objective guidelines and standards should appear expressly* in the act or be within the realm of reasonable inference from the language of the act where a delegation of power is involved and especially so where the legislation contemplates a delegation of power to intrude into the privacy of citizens.' (italics added).
>
> "The rent control Ordinance at issue in the instant case does not contain objective guidelines and standards for its enforcement by the City Rent Agency nor can such be reasonably inferred from the language of the Ordinance.
>
> "Unrestricted discretion in the application of a law without appropriate guidelines and determining its meaning may not be delegated by the City Council to an agency or to one person. (cases cited)"

However, rent control is a drastic measure to be utilized with the greatest caution and only in extreme situations. As the Court previously stated in Fleetwood, supra, in the area of rent control legislation in general, the Supreme Court of the United States has placed severe limitations on the power of state and municipal governments. When such legislation is enacted, deprivation of rights under the Fifth and Fourteenth Amendments to the Constitution and Section 9 of Article I, the Declaration of Rights of the Constitution of Florida, and freedom to contract are endangered. In Fleetwood, supra, this Court further explicated:

> "The only justification for the utilization of such legislation found by the U.S. Supreme Court is an emergency. *Marcus Brown Co. v. Feldman*, 256 U.S. 170 (1921), *Lincoln Building Association v. Barr*, 1 N.Y.2d 413, 153 N.Y.S.2d 633, 135 N.E.2d 801. *Appeal dismissed* 355 U.S. 12. Emergency has been narrowly defined. An increase in the cost of living (an inflationary spiral) alone is not a justification for rent control legislation which limits the amount of rent which a tenant may be required to pay. *Chastleton Corporation, et al. v. Sinclair, et al.*, 264 U.S. 543 (1924). Explicitly designating the type of emergency which would be a viable basis for such legislation, the United States Supreme Court has held in *Levy Leasing Co. v. Siegel*, 258 U.S. 242, at 245.
>
>> 'The warrant for this legislative resort to the police power was the conviction on the part of the state legislators that there existed in the larger cities of the state a social emergency, caused by an insufficient supply of dwelling houses and apartments, so *grave that it constituted a serious menace to the health, morality, comfort, and even to the peace of a large part of the people of the state.* That such an emergency, if it really existed, would sustain a resort, otherwise valid, to the police power for the purpose of dealing with it cannot be doubted, for unless relieved, the public welfare would suffer in respects which constitute the primary and undisputed, as well as the most usual basis and justification for the exercise of that power.'" (emphasis supplied)

As explained by Bernard Frielander and Anthony Curreri in their treatise on Rent Control, which was published in 1948, shortly after the close of World War II, rent control arose as a war-time government control because of the grave situation in housing posed by both the First and Second World War. In their forward to their treatise, the authors explained:

> "The origin of the conditions of which these controls are an outgrowth may be traced back almost twenty years to the beginning of the depression. When that economic cataclysm engulfed the nation, construction of new homes and business buildings dwindled to insignificant proportions. Before the building industry could show signs of revival, we were at war, and a virtual moratorium on construction was imposed. The cessation of hostilities has been followed by an upsurge of new construction, but soaring costs and other factors have seriously retarded the creation of additional residential accommodations and business space. During the entire period while construction lagged behind the nation's requirements, the population grew steadily. Both factors combined to produce a large deficit in housing facilities

of which we became acutely aware when millions of veterans returned from the war and sought to establish homes for their existing or newly founded families.

* * *

"The American people dislike government regulation of their business affairs and tolerate it only when they believe it to be justified by compelling considerations of public good. Accordingly, there is general agreement that the landlord tenant relationship should be freed from rent controls at all government levels at the earliest time consistent with the public welfare."

The mere inability by a group of tenants to meet rent payments is not such an emergency as to justify government controls which are suitable to that group of tenants but which would render investments in housing projects far less attractive and in some instances lead to bankruptcy. The right to invest capital and expect it to earn a fair return is a basic civil right and one which should not be destroyed merely for the convenience of tenants who are living in accommodations apparently beyond their financial ability. I do not believe that such an emergency as would warrant the questioned rent control ordinance existed in the instant cause. The shortage of housing units throughout this nation and particularly in Florida today is a matter of grave concern to all our people and certainly one which commands the attention and consideration of all responsible echelons of government. It is also a great challenge to the free enterprise system. Nevertheless, the housing crisis which we have allowed to creep upon us is not good and sufficient reason to confiscate the profits from investments in housing units which have been made in good faith. Unless government is to assume the total responsibility for low cost housing, private investors should be Encouraged and not discouraged in making investments in additional housing units.

BOYD, J., concurs.

ERVIN, Justice (concurring in part and dissenting in part):

I concur in all of the opinion insofar as it upholds Ch. 73-129, but emphatically dissent to the remainder of the opinion striking down the City of Miami Beach's rent control ordinance. I find no rational basis in the majority opinion for now invalidating the ordinance. I perceive nothing in the ordinance itself which is contrary to Ch. 73-129 or to the Constitution, or to *City of Miami Beach v. Fleetwood Hotel, Inc.*, Fla.1972, 261 So.2d 801. The majority view is all quite puzzling to me in view of the aftermath of City of Miami Beach v. Fleetwood Hotel, Inc., and all that has been done by the Legislature and the City of Miami Beach to comply with the guidelines implicit in that decision.

It does not appear that the ordinance is substantially different from rent control ordinances or legislation enacted in other jurisdictions. See citations of cases upholding same in the dissent in the Fleetwood Hotel case, 261 So.2d, text 808.

The majority misconceives the import and impact of such provisions in the ordinance that relate to "net annual return," "assessed evaluation of property," and "operating expenses of the property," by contending they are universally confiscatory ab initio. On the contrary, all operating expenses of a rental property except debt service and depreciation are to be computed in the rental rates before a net annual return of 6 per cent is calculated on the assessed evaluation of the rental property. Taxes payable on a rental property are to be figured as operational costs. Rents are to be adjusted from time to time in keeping with the assessed valuation of the rental property at the rate of 6 per cent per annum of such valuation over and above said operating expenses. Even if return by the taxpayer can bring a property up to 100 per cent valuation against which the 6 per cent rate will be applied. Debt service requirements will vary among rental properties. To draw a flat conclusion that the rate will universally be 4.5 per cent as to all rental property and confiscatory is logically insupportable. There are further provisions in the ordinance which permit the administrator reasonable latitude to relieve particular landlords in hardship situations and, of course, court review affording due process against confiscation is stipulated.

Since the beginning date of operation of the ordinance and its freeze of rents on October 1, 1973 were rendered inoperative by the present litigation, it will be necessary that the beginning operational date of rent control be judicially readjusted in keeping with the intendment of the ordinance.

It is hardly judicial to conclude blanketly that confiscation will ensue as to *all* rental properties in advance of any conclusive evidentiary demonstration to that effect as to any rental property or properties pursuant to an administrative hearing or court review.

ADKINS, C.J., and McCAIN, J., concur.

Questions

1. What has changed since the Court's earlier decision in *Fleetwood Hotel* that explains the result in this case?

2. What becomes of Chapter 83 in the Court's "new" analysis?

3. What is the delegation issue in this case, and how is it resolved?

4. What segment of the Court makes a determination on Chapter 166 and why is that important?

City of Ocala v. Nye

608 So. 2d 15 (Fla. 1992)

PER CURIAM.

We have for review *Nye v. City of Ocala*, 559 So.2d 360 (Fla. 5th DCA 1990), in which the Fifth District Court of Appeal construed article VIII, section 2(b) of the Florida Constitution. We have jurisdiction pursuant to article V, section 3(b)(3), Florida Constitution, and quash the decision below.

This case involves the question of whether a municipality has the power of eminent domain to acquire an entire tract of land when only a portion of the tract is needed for a municipal purpose. This issue is important because by acquiring the whole tract a business damage claim can be avoided, thus making the acquisition cost less expensive than when acquiring only a portion of the tract.

The City of Ocala (the City) sought to condemn property in order to widen a city street. In the resolution attached to the eminent domain petition, the City showed the requirements for only a partial taking of the property. In their answer to the City's petition, the tenants on the property, O.J. and Carolyn Nye (the Nyes), asserted a claim for special damages to their business. The City amended its petition to seek a total taking of the property in order to eliminate the business damage claim. The trial court ultimately entered a judgment allowing the City to take the entire tract of land. On appeal, the Fifth District Court of Appeal reversed the trial court "by holding that a municipality ... does not have the power of eminent domain to acquire an entire tract when only a portion of the tract is needed for a municipal purpose merely because the cost to acquire a portion of the tract is more than the cost of acquiring the entire tract." *Nye,* 559 So.2d at 362.

The City contends that under its home rule powers, article VIII, section 2(b), Florida Constitution, and section 166.021, Florida Statutes (1989),[18] it may exercise any power for a municipal purpose except when expressly prohibited by law. The City argues that because the Department of Transportation (DOT) and counties, as political subdivisions of the state, are expressly permitted by statute to condemn more property than is necessary where they would save money by doing so,[19] the City may likewise do so pursuant to its home rule powers. We agree.

The power of eminent domain is an attribute of the sovereign which is circumscribed by, rather than conferred by, constitution or statute. *Peavy-Wilson Lumber Co. v. Brevard County,* 159 Fla. 311, 31 So.2d 483 (1947). This power can only be exercised by counties and state agencies if the state delegates that power to those political

---

18. [FN 3.] Section 166.021, Florida Statutes (1989), provides, in pertinent part:

(1) As provided in Art. VIII, s.2(b) of the State Constitution, municipalities ... may exercise any power for municipal purposes, except when expressly prohibited by law.

(2) "Municipal Purpose" means any activity or power which may be exercised by the state or its political subdivisions.

(3) ....

(4) The provisions of this section shall be so construed as to secure for municipalities the broad exercise of home rule powers granted by the constitution. It is the further intent of the Legislature to extend to municipalities the exercise of powers for municipal governmental, corporate, or proprietary purposes not expressly prohibited by the constitution, general or special law, or county charter and to remove any limitations, judicially imposed or otherwise, on the exercise of home rule powers other than those so expressly prohibited.

19. [FN 4.] Section 337.27(2), Florida Statutes (1989), authorizes the DOT to acquire an entire tract of land if the acquisition costs will be equal to or less than the costs of acquiring a portion of the property. This subsection further provides that "this means of limiting the rising costs to the state of property acquisition is a public purpose." Section 127.01(1)(b), Florida Statutes (1989), grants this same power to the counties.

subdivisions. Furthermore, "when the sovereign delegates the power [of eminent domain] to a political unit or agency a strict construction will be given against the agency asserting the power." 159 Fla. at 314, 31 So.2d at 485. Thus, it is only through another specific legislative grant that the DOT and the counties are authorized to acquire land in its entirety in order to reduce acquisition costs. Section 337.27(1), Florida Statutes (1989), vests in the DOT the power of eminent domain to secure transportation rights-of-way, while section 337.27(2) authorizes the DOT to acquire the land in its entirety if by doing so the acquisition cost will be less than the cost of acquiring only a portion of the property. The legislature granted these same powers to counties by expressly authorizing counties to exercise those powers granted to the DOT under subsections 337.27(1) and (2). *See* § 127.01(1)(b), Fla. Stat. (1989). Thus, the legislature expressly granted to the DOT and counties the power to take more property than necessary for a particular project.

Article VIII, section 2, Florida Constitution, expressly grants to every municipality the authority to conduct municipal government, perform municipal functions, and render municipal services. The only constitutional limitation placed on the municipalities' authority is that such powers be exercised for valid "municipal purposes." *State v. City of Sunrise*, 354 So.2d 1206 (Fla.1978). The "Municipal Home Rule Powers Act," enacted by the legislature in 1973, states that as provided by the Florida Constitution municipalities "may exercise any power for municipal purposes, except when expressly prohibited by law." § 166.021(1), Fla. Stat. (1989). Thus, municipalities are not dependent upon the legislature for further authorization, and legislative statutes are relevant only to determine limitations of authority. *City of Sunrise*, 354 So.2d at 1209. Although section 166.401, Florida Statutes (1989),[20] purports to authorize municipalities to exercise eminent domain powers, municipalities could exercise those powers for a valid municipal purpose without any such "grant" of authority. If the state has the power to take particular land for public purposes, then a municipality may also exercise that power unless it is "expressly prohibited." Although section 166.401(2) does not expressly grant the taking of an entire parcel by a municipality to save money, it also does not expressly prohibit a municipality from doing so.

---

20. [FN 6.] Section 166.401, Florida Statutes (1989), provides:

(1) All municipalities in the state may exercise the right and power of eminent domain; that is, the right to appropriate property within the state, except state or federal property, for the uses or purposes authorized pursuant to this part. The absolute fee simple title to all property so taken and acquired shall vest in such municipal corporation unless the municipality seeks to condemn a particular right or estate in such property.

(2) Each municipality is further authorized to exercise the eminent domain powers granted to the Department of Transportation in s. 337.27(1) and the transportation corridor protection provisions of s. 337.273.

The legislature has since amended the municipal eminent domain statute to expressly permit municipalities to exercise those powers granted the DOT under section 337.27(2). *See* § 166.401(2), Fla. Stat. (Supp.1990).

With regard to the taking of an entire parcel to avoid business damages, this Court has stated that "the purpose of cutting acquisition costs to expand the financial base for further public projects constitutes a valid public purpose." *Department of Transp. v. Fortune Fed. Sav. & Loan Ass'n*, 532 So.2d 1267, 1270 (Fla.1988). If it is a public purpose to save state and county money in road acquisition costs by taking an entire parcel rather than part of a parcel of land, then it is also a public purpose for municipalities to save taxpayers' money for the same type of acquisition.

We find that the taking in this instance is a municipal purpose that has not been expressly prohibited by law, and the district court erred in finding that the City did not have the power to acquire the Nyes' entire property when only a portion was needed for a municipal purpose. Because we find that the City was authorized to acquire the entire tract of land, we need not address the issue of whether this taking constituted a constructive total taking.

Accordingly, we quash the decision of the district court and remand with directions to affirm the trial court's judgment.

It is so ordered.

BARKETT, C.J., and OVERTON, McDONALD, SHAW, GRIMES and HARDING, JJ., concur.

KOGAN, J., dissents.

Questions

1. What is the limitation or meaning of "valid municipal purpose"? What is an example of an action that would not be a valid municipal purpose?

2. What is the meaning of "expressly prohibited by law"?

Lake Worth Utilities Authority v. City of Lake Worth

468 So. 2d 215 (Fla. 1985)

EHRLICH, Justice.

The Lake Worth Utilities Authority was created by special law adopted by referendum in 1969. In 1984, the City of Lake Worth by ordinance dissolved the Authority, terminating three of its employees, including the director, changed the locks on the doors, changed the signatories on the Authority bank accounts, terminated the services of the Authority's attorneys, and sued the Authority.

The Authority filed a counter-complaint for declaratory and injunctive relief, contending that the City had exceeded its power and could not dissolve by ordinance that which the legislature had created by special act.

The City filed a motion to dismiss, asserting that the Authority was unconstitutional from its inception and that it was empowered to act as it did by the Municipal Home Rule Powers Act, Chapter 166, Florida Statutes (1983). The City extended its argument to assert that all similar utility authorities or commissions in the state were unconstitutional.

The trial court granted the City's motion and dismissed the Authority's complaint with prejudice, holding the Authority to be unconstitutionally created.

Appeal was taken by the Authority, and the Fourth District Court of Appeal certified the issue as one of great public importance requiring immediate resolution by this Court. For the following reasons we reverse the order of the circuit court.

The circuit court phrased the central issues as follows:

> Whether Chapter 69-1215 is unconstitutional because it attempts to transfer from the City, municipal powers mandated to it by Article VIII, Section 2(b) of the Florida Constitution (1968), and attempts to create a local governmental agency having municipal legislative powers which are exercised by non-elected officials in violation of the same constitutional article.

In ruling that Chapter 69-1215 did unconstitutionally transfer municipal powers to the Authority, the court focused on the last part of the first sentence of article VIII, section 2(b), Florida Constitution:

> (b) Powers. Municipalities shall have governmental, corporate and proprietary powers to enable them to conduct municipal government, perform municipal functions and render municipal services, *and may exercise any power for municipal purposes except as otherwise provided by law.* Each municipal legislative body shall be elective.

(Emphasis supplied.) The court held that the limiting prepositional phrase, "except as otherwise provided by law," modifies only the clause, "and may exercise any power for municipal purposes." To read the words of limitation otherwise, the court held, would nullify the change represented by the 1968 constitutional revision and return the municipalities to their pre-1968 dependence on the legislature for grants of power. "Each time municipal authority, or change in municipal authority, was sought, it would be necessary to approach the legislative branch of government," the court reasoned.

Such an interpretation misapprehends the import of the 1968 revision and unduly denigrates the supremacy of the legislature as a state policy-making body. Before the adoption of article VIII, section 2(b) in 1968, municipalities were creatures of legislative grace. Article VIII, section 8, Florida Constitution of 1885, provided, in pertinent part, "The Legislature shall have power to establish, and to abolish, municipalities to provide for their government, to prescribe their jurisdiction and powers, and to alter or amend the same at any time." Thus, the municipalities were inherently powerless, absent a specific grant of power from the legislature. The noblest municipal ordinance, enacted to serve the most compelling municipal purpose, was void, absent authorization found in some general or special law.

The clear purpose of the 1968 revision embodied in article VIII, section 2 was to give the municipalities inherent power to meet municipal needs. But "inherent" is not to be confused with "absolute" or even with "supreme" in this context. The legislature's retained power is now one of limitation rather than one of grace, but it remains an all-pervasive power, nonetheless.

Thus, the words "except as otherwise provided by law" must be read as modifying the entire sentence preceding it. Such a reading is supported by historical analysis, grammatical precepts, and common sense. It finds further support in the commentary to the 1968 Florida Constitution provided by the reporter for the Constitutional Revision Commission, Talbot "Sandy" D'Alemberte:

> The provisions in the subsection were new with the Revision Commission proposal, but the 1885 Constitution granted the power to the legislature to prescribe the jurisdiction and powers of municipalities by law in Article VIII, Section 8. *The apparent difference is that under the new language, all municipalities have governmental, corporate and proprietary powers unless provided otherwise by law,* whereas under the 1885 Constitution, municipalities had only those powers expressly granted by law.

(Emphasis supplied.)

We therefore hold that the enactment of Chapter 69-1215 was a constitutional exercise of power specifically reserved to the legislature in article VIII, section 2(b).

Turning to the second allegation of unconstitutionality, that the Authority was a non-elected legislative body, in contravention of the last sentence of section 2(b), we find this issue is controlled by our decision in *Cooksey v. Utilities Commission,* 261 So.2d 129 (Fla.1972). There we held that the proprietarial powers and duties vested in the Utility Commission of New Smyrna Beach did not constitute an improper delegation of legislative duties. We find nothing in Chapter 69-1215 which would require a different result here.

We therefore reverse the decision of the circuit court and remand with orders that the Authority's demand for injunctive relief be granted and that ordinances 84-12 through 84-15 of the City Commission of the City of Lake Worth be declared void as violative of section 166.021, Florida Statutes (1983). The Authority's petition for attorney's fees is denied.

It is so ordered.

BOYD, C.J., and ADKINS, OVERTON, ALDERMAN, McDONALD and SHAW, JJ., concur.

i. Annexation by Municipality

City of Long Beach Resort v. Collins

261 So. 2d 498 (Fla. 1972)

PER CURIAM.

This is a direct appeal from the 14th Judicial Circuit Court which inherently passed upon the constitutionality of a state statute by its order of dismissal for failure to state a cause of action; we accordingly have jurisdiction under Fla. Const. art. V, s 4, F.S.A. and *Evans v. Carroll,* 104 So.2d 375 (Fla.1958); *Harrell's Candy Kitchen, Inc. v. Sarasota-Manatee Airport Authority,* 111 So.2d 439 (Fla.1959); and *Milliken v. State,* 131 So.2d 889 (Fla.1961).

The statute in question is House Bill No. 5288, which was passed by the Legislature in 1970. It provides for merging the several cities along the western Gulf resort area of Panama City, Florida. (Petitioner suggests that the real attempt is at "consolidation" rather than a "merger" citing Fla. Const. art. VIII, s 3 (1968).) Among the grounds recited for unconstitutionality of the act are that it constitutes:

(a) A denial of equal protection under the Federal and State Constitutions in not allowing residents within these municipalities to vote on the proposed merger or consolidation, whereas the residents of the surrounding unincorporated areas were permitted to vote on the issue (it passed by such vote of only the unincorporated area residents).

(b) A deprivation of property rights without due process under both constitutions.

(c) Denial of franchise or referendum to the residents in the city.

(d) An unconstitutional delegation of power to the new municipality sought to be created.

(e) It constitutes class legislation favoring the residents of unincorporated areas over those dwelling within the city limits.

Intervenor-petitioner City of Long Beach Resort, Florida, a municipality, urges additionally that:

(a) Intervenor City which holds a franchise for the sale and distribution of water within its city and also to existing Panama City Beach, has issued water revenue bonds which have an outstanding balance plus accrued interest; and that to abolish Intervenor City and said City of Panama City Beach would jeopardize said bonds and properties in that no provision is made by the new act for the protection of the bond holders.

(b) Intervenor would be deprived of its property without due process of law contrary to the U.S. and Florida Constitutions.

(c) That the act's provision for payment of debts from revenues collected ONLY within respective former municipalities would deny intervenor city-water supplier that portion of its income from water distribution into Panama City Beach and thus lose income therefrom to pay said bonds.

Petitioners brought proceedings both in quo warranto and for declaratory decree as to said House Bill No. 5288. The entire complaints in both causes were dismissed by the trial judge.

During appellate proceedings there has been a tender as reflected by motions filed before this Court to pay the Long Beach Resort bonds in full with interest pursuant to a call of said bonds by the City of Panama City Beach, in accordance with their terms. The tender has been refused on the ground that "information regarding the source of funds used to make the tender of payment of bonds" has not been furnished and that appellees "refuse to allow a certified public accountant employed by appellant access to the books and records of the City of Panama City Beach pertaining to the Long Beach Resort Water System, thereby preventing evaluation that the tender of funds for payment of the bonds was made from 'net revenues derived from the operation of the water system of the City of Long Beach Resort', as required by bond provisions."

Such a call of the bonds and tender, supported by affidavit before this court, render moot the above additional questions raised by intervenor. Accordingly, the motion to dismiss intervenor's appeal is granted and is remanded to the trial court for disposition as may be indicated solely on the two objections raised regarding, (1) the providing of information as to the source of funds for tender of payment, and (2) access to the records of the old City of Panama City Beach, so as to afford evaluation, if necessary, that the tender meets requirements of the bond issue.

We revert now to the basic question here regarding the constitutionality of House Bill No. 5288, particularly in regard to the denial of the vote to city residents while granting it to adjoining unincorporated area residents in voting on the consolidation of the several municipalities along the famous "Miracle Strip" and its adjoining areas West of the resort City of Panama City, Florida.

The Legislature, by various special acts, created the Town of Edgewater Gulf Beach (1953), the City of West Panama City Beach (1967), the City of Long Beach Resort (1953) and the City of Panama City Beach (1953), all located along the glittering white sand beaches west of Panama City, Florida. Then, in 1970, the Legislature passed a sequence of bills which would have the effect of consolidating the four municipalities, together with five adjoining unincorporated areas, into a single governmental entity.

The first five of these special acts designated unincorporated areas contiguous to the several existing municipalities and granted the residents of each of these unincorporated areas the right of referendum to determine whether or not they would be joined with the consolidated, new City of Panama City Beach created by the final one of this series of Acts, House Bill 5288 (Ch. 70-874). None of the residents and citizens of the former municipalities was granted the right of referendum on the issue of consolidation ("merger"). (It is into the corporate entity of existing City of West Panama City Beach that all are to be "merged." That city is then to become a new City of Panama City Beach.)

This was the prerogative of the Legislature which has life and death powers over municipalities which are created, modified and can be abolished by the Legislature. *Saunders v. City of Jacksonville*, 157 Fla. 240, 25 So.2d 648 (Fla.1946); *State ex rel. Landis v. Town of Lake Placid*, 117 Fla. 874, 158 So. 497 (1935); *State v. Town of Boynton Beach*, 140 Fla. 327, 156 So. 539 (1934); *Smith v. Treadwell*, 161 So.2d 49 (1st DCA Fla.1964).

There is no doubt of the Legislature's power to annex territory to an existing municipality. *MacGuyer v. City of Tampa*, 89 Fla. 138, 103 So. 418 (1925).

Town of San Mateo City v. State, 117 Fla. 546, 158 So. 112 (1935), upheld a statute which submitted a referendum vote to freeholders only. The Legislature may make its acts effective upon the happening of a contingency, which includes the approval of the affected citizens or a class of the affected citizens. *San Mateo*, supra, and *State ex rel. Cheyney v. Sammons*, 62 Fla. 303, 57 So. 196 (1911).

No constitutional infirmity having been demonstrated, the trial court's orders dismissing the amended petitions, and the final judgments entered for appellees, are accordingly.

Affirmed.

It is so ordered.

ROBERTS, C.J., ERVIN, CARLTON, ADKINS and BOYD, JJ., and SPECTOR, Circuit Judge, concur.

DEKLE, J., dissents with Opinion. [omitted]

Questions

1. What are the limits of authority of the Legislature when dealing with municipalities?

2. Can municipalities be abolished? Can counties be abolished?

Capella v. City of Gainesville

377 So. 2d 658 (Fla. 1979)

ALDERMAN, Justice.

By direct appeal, the plaintiff in the trial court, Joseph A. Capella, seeks reversal of the final order of the Circuit Court of Alachua County, upholding the constitutionality of chapter 77-557, Laws of Florida (1977), and granting summary judgment in favor of the defendants, City of Gainesville and Gainesville Corporate Limits Council, in a suit protesting annexation of certain land to the City of Gainesville. We affirm the decision of the trial court.

An annexation referendum was held by the City of Gainesville in November 1976, pursuant to the provisions of chapter 76-378, Laws of Florida (1976). The proposed annexation was defeated. Then in 1977, the legislature enacted chapter 77-557, Laws of Florida (1977), which created the Gainesville Corporate Limits Council and defined its authority and responsibility to make studies, to hold public hearings, and to make recommendations to the City of Gainesville on the enlargement of the City's corporate limits. The act authorizes the Council to recommend annexation of land contiguous to the City's corporate limits upon a majority vote of its five city commission members and a majority vote of its five county commission members. The act further provides that upon such recommendation and upon approval of a majority of the qualified electors participating in a referendum, the city commission may enlarge the City's limits to include such additional land. Those qualified to participate in the referendum are the electors residing in the area to be annexed, together with the electors residing within the corporate limits of the City. The lands sought to be annexed must meet all the standards specified in section 171.043, Florida Statutes (Supp.1976). Chapter 77-557 also states that all laws or parts of laws in conflict with it are superseded to the extent of the conflict.

The Gainesville Corporate Limits Council, on March 21, 1978, by resolution, recommended that certain described land be annexed. The land described was a part of that which previously had been included in the November 2, 1976, annexation referendum and included Capella's residence. On April 17, 1978, pursuant to this resolution, the City of Gainesville adopted an ordinance, extending the corporate limits to include the contiguous lands described in the resolution. This ordinance was to be effective if a majority of those voting in the election called on the question of extending the corporate limits on May 2, 1978, voted in favor of such extension. At this election, a majority of the qualified electors participating approved the annexation.

Capella claims that the effect of the ordinance was to subject a portion of the area previously the object of the November 1976, annexation referendum to a second annexation referendum within a two-year period in violation of section 171.0413(2)(e), Florida Statutes (1977). The City and Council respond that this section does not apply because it was superseded by chapter 77-557 and additionally because the language of that statute does not encompass the particular facts of this controversy. We hold that section 171.0413(2)(e) has not been superseded by chapter 77-557 since a reading of the special act in conjunction with the general act reveals no inconsistency, but we do find that the two-year requirement of section 171.0413(2)(e) does not apply in this case.

Section 171.0413(2)(e) provides:

> If there is a separate majority vote for annexation in the annexing municipality and in the area proposed to be annexed, the ordinance of annexation shall become effective on the effective date specified therein. If there is a majority vote against annexation in either the annexing municipality or in the area proposed to be annexed, or in both, the ordinance shall not become effective, and *the area proposed to be annexed* shall not be the subject of an annexation ordinance by the annexing municipality for a period of 2 years from the date of the referendum on annexation. (Emphasis added.)

Its predecessor, section 171.0415(9), Florida Statutes (Supp.1974), provided:

> A majority vote "Against annexation" shall prevent *any part of the area proposed for annexation* from being the subject of an annexation ordinance by the same municipality for a period of 2 years from the date of the referendum election. (Emphasis added.)

We find significant the difference in language between section 171.0413(2)(e), Florida Statutes (1977), and section 171.0415(9), Florida Statutes (Supp.1974). The predecessor statute proscribed "any part of the area proposed for annexation" from being the subject of an annexation ordinance within two years and had a much broader scope than the present statute which only proscribes "the area proposed to be annexed."

When the legislature amends a statute by omitting words, we presume it intends the statute to have a different meaning than that accorded it before the amendment. *Carlisle v. Game and Fresh Water Fish Commission*, 354 So.2d 362 (Fla.1977); *Arnold v. Shumpert*, 217 So.2d 116 (Fla.1968). Accordingly, we agree with the trial court that the change in language is indicative of the legislature's intent to change the meaning of this statutory provision to proscribe only the attempt to annex the identical area of property described in a previous annexation ordinance defeated within a period of two years. In the present case, the City sought to annex only "a part of the area" originally proposed for annexation, not the identical area.

Having concluded that section 171.0413(2)(e) does not preclude the annexation and that the ordinance is valid, we now consider the constitutional challenge to chapter 77-557.[21] Capella asserts that although the majority of qualified electors in the area proposed to be annexed voted against annexation, the annexation was still approved because a majority of all those voting in the referendum voted in favor of annexation. He argues that chapter 77-557 violates the equal protection clause of the Florida and federal constitutions because it allows the voting power of those residing in the area to be annexed to be debased and diluted where the voters in the area to be annexed are substantially fewer in number than those residing within the City's corporate limits. This argument was properly rejected by the trial court.

In *City of Long Beach Resort v. Collins*, 261 So.2d 498 (Fla.1972), a legislative enactment providing for the merger of several cities along the western Gulf resort area of Panama City was challenged on the basis that it denied equal protection under the Florida and federal constitutions in not allowing residents within these municipalities to vote on the proposed merger or consolidation while the residents of the surrounding unincorporated areas were permitted to vote on the issue. We held that there was no constitutional infirmity in the act and said:

> There is no doubt of the Legislature's power to annex territory to an existing municipality. *MacGuyer v. City of Tampa*, 89 Fla. 138, 103 So. 418 (1925).

261 So.2d at 500–501. There is no absolute right to vote on proposed alteration of municipal boundaries. *North Ridge General Hospital, Inc. v. City of Oakland Park*, 374 So.2d 461 (Fla.1979); *Sailors v. Board of Education*, 387 U.S. 105 (1967); *Hunter v. City of Pittsburgh*, 207 U.S. 161 (1907). The legislature can cause annexation to occur with or without any vote or by a single majority vote of all those affected. In the present case each affected qualified elector was afforded the right to vote, and, in addition, those residing in the area to be annexed had the initial protection of a majority vote of the five county commission members of the council, which was

---

21. [FN 1.] Section 5, chapter 77-557, Laws of Florida (1977), provides:
    Upon recommendation for enlargement of the corporate limits of the City of Gainesville, as set forth above, the city commission may, upon approval of a majority of those qualified electors participating in a referendum, enlarge the corporate limits of the City of Gainesville to include such additional lands within the City. The participants in such referendum shall include those qualified electors residing in the area to be annexed, together with those qualified electors residing within the corporate limits of the city.

a prerequisite to the Council's recommendation to the City that certain lands be annexed.

Accordingly, having found that chapter 77-557 is constitutional, that section 171.0413(2)(e) is not applicable, and that the ordinance and referendum were valid, we affirm the judgment of the trial court.

It is so ordered.

ENGLAND, C.J., and ADKINS, BOYD and OVERTON, JJ., concur.

SUNDBERG, J., concurs in result only.

ii. Preemption by State of Local Government Authority

City of Palm Bay v. Wells Fargo Bank, N.A.

114 So. 3d 924 (Fla. 2013)

CANADY, J.

In this case we consider whether a municipal ordinance may validly establish superpriority status for municipal code enforcement liens. In *City of Palm Bay v. Wells Fargo Bank, N.A.*, 57 So.3d 226 (Fla. 5th DCA 2011), the Fifth District Court of Appeal concluded that such an ordinance superpriority provision is invalid because it conflicts with a state statute and that the City's lien accordingly did not have priority over the lien of Wells Fargo's mortgage that was recorded before the City's lien was recorded. Palm Bay sought review, and we accepted jurisdiction based on the Fifth District's certification of the following question of great public importance:

> Whether under Article VIII, section 2(b), Florida Constitution, section 166.021, Florida Statutes and Chapter 162, Florida Statutes, a municipality has the authority to enact an ordinance stating that its code enforcement liens, created pursuant to a code enforcement board order and recorded in the public records of the applicable county, shall be superior in dignity to prior recorded mortgages?

City of Palm Bay v. Wells Fargo Bank, N.A., 67 So.3d 271, 271 (Fla. 5th DCA 2011) (mem.).

On appeal, the City argues that the ordinance superpriority provision is within the "broad home rule powers" of the City. The City contends that because the Legislature has made certain exceptions to the general rules governing the priority of liens, municipalities have the power to likewise make exceptions. For the reasons we explain, we conclude that the Fifth District correctly decided that the ordinance superpriority provision is invalid. Accordingly, we answer the certified question in the negative.

I. BACKGROUND

City of Palm Bay Ordinance 97-07 provides for the operation of the City's Code Enforcement Board and contains the following superpriority provision:

> Liens created pursuant to a Board order and recorded in the public record shall remain liens coequal with the liens of all state[,] county[,] district [,] and municipal taxes, superior in dignity to all other liens[,] titles [,] and claims until paid, and shall bear interest annually at a rate not to exceed the legal rate allowed for such liens and maybe foreclosed pursuant to the procedures set forth in Florida Statutes, Chapter 173.

City of Palm Bay, Ordinance No. 97-07, § 1 (1997).

Chapter 162, Florida Statutes (2004), contains the Local Government Code Enforcement Boards Act. Section 162.03, Florida Statutes (2004), authorizes municipalities to establish by ordinance local code enforcement boards. Section 162.09(3), Florida Statutes (2004), provides that "[a] certified copy of [a code enforcement] order imposing a fine, or a fine plus repair costs, may be recorded in the public records and thereafter shall constitute a lien against the land on which the violation exists and upon any other real or personal property owned by the violator." The Act contains no provision expressly authorizing municipalities to establish superpriority for such liens.

Article VIII, section 2(b), Florida Constitution, contains a general provision relating to the exercise of municipal powers: "Municipalities shall have governmental, corporate and proprietary powers to enable them to conduct municipal government, perform municipal functions and render municipal services, and may exercise any power for municipal purposes *except as otherwise provided by law.*" (Emphasis added). Section 166.021, Florida Statutes (2004), contains general provisions governing the exercise of municipal powers under the framework established in article VIII, section 2(b). Section 166.021(1) states: "As provided in s. 2(b), Art. VIII of the State Constitution, municipalities shall have the governmental, corporate, and proprietary powers to enable them to conduct municipal government, perform municipal functions, and render municipal services, and may exercise any power for municipal purposes, except when expressly prohibited by law." Section 166.021(3) provides in pertinent part as follows:

> The Legislature recognizes that pursuant to the grant of power set forth in section 2(b), Art. VIII of the State Constitution, the legislative body of each municipality has the power to enact legislation concerning any subject matter upon which the state Legislature may act, except:
>
> ....
>
> (c) Any subject expressly preempted to state or county government by the constitution or by general law....

The priority of interests in real estate under Florida law is generally determined by the operation of three statutes. Section 28.222(2), Florida Statutes (2004), requires the clerk of the circuit court to record instruments in the official records and to "keep a register in which he or she shall enter at the time of filing the filing number of each instrument filed for record, the date and hour of filing, the kind of instrument, and the names of the parties to the instrument." Section 695.11, Florida

Statutes (2004), provides that "[t]he sequence of [official register numbers required under section 28.222] shall determine the priority of recordation" so that "[a]n instrument bearing the lower number in the then-current series of numbers shall have priority over any instrument bearing a higher number in the same series." The legal significance of priority of recordation comes into play in the context of the rule established in section 695.01(1), Florida Statutes (2004), which provides as follows: "No conveyance, transfer, or mortgage of real property, or of any interest therein … shall be good and effectual in law or equity against creditors or subsequent purchasers for a valuable consideration and without notice, unless the same be recorded according to law."

The Legislature has, however, provided separately for the priority of certain liens over the priority established under chapter 695. For example, section 197.122(1), Florida Statutes (2004), provides that "[a]ll taxes imposed pursuant to the State Constitution and laws of this state shall be a first lien, superior to all other liens." Similarly, section 170.09, Florida Statutes (2004), provides that special assessment liens are "coequal with the lien of all state, county, district, and municipal taxes, superior in dignity to all other liens, titles, and claims, until paid."

II. ANALYSIS

Based on the provisions of article VIII, section 2(b), Florida Constitution, and the related provisions in section 166.021, we have acknowledged that "[i]n Florida, a municipality is given broad authority to enact ordinances under its municipal home rule powers." *City of Hollywood v. Mulligan*, 934 So.2d 1238, 1243 (Fla.2006). We have also stated that—as is recognized in section 166.021—"a municipality may legislate concurrently with the Legislature on any subject which has not been expressly preempted to the State." *Hollywood*, 934 So.2d at 1243. But we have never interpreted either the constitutional or statutory provisions relating to the legislative preemption of municipal home rule powers to require that the Legislature specifically state that the exercise of municipal power on a particular subject is precluded. Instead, we have held that "[t]he preemption need not be explicit so long as it is clear that the legislature has clearly preempted local regulation of the subject." *Barragan v. City of Miami*, 545 So.2d 252, 254 (Fla.1989). We have also recognized that where concurrent state and municipal regulation is permitted because the state has not preemptively occupied a regulatory field, "a municipality's concurrent legislation must not conflict with state law." *Thomas v. State*, 614 So.2d 468, 470 (Fla.1993).

The critical phrase of article VIII, section 2(b)—"except as otherwise provided by law"—establishes the constitutional superiority of the Legislature's power over municipal power. Accordingly, "[m]unicipal ordinances are inferior to laws of the state and must not conflict with any controlling provision of a statute." *Thomas*, 614 So.2d at 470. When a municipal "ordinance flies in the face of state law"—that is, cannot be reconciled with state law—the ordinance "cannot be sustained." *Barragan*, 545 So.2d at 255. Such "conflict preemption" comes into play "where the local enactment irreconcilably conflicts with or stands as an obstacle to the execution of the full purposes of the statute." 5 McQuillin Mun. Corp. §15:16 (3d ed. 2012).

[handwritten margin notes: "The Legislature has provided otherwise"; "The court acknowledges that municipalities are granted certain powers."; "Municipal ordinances are inferior to state law."]

The Palm Bay ordinance conflicts with the state law.

Here, it is undisputed that the Palm Bay ordinance provision establishes a priority that is inconsistent with the priority established by the pertinent provisions of chapter 695. In those statutory provisions, the Legislature has created a general scheme for priority of rights with respect to interest in real property. Giving effect to the ordinance superpriority provision would allow a municipality to displace the policy judgment reflected in the Legislature's enactment of the statutory provisions. And it would allow the municipality to destroy rights that the Legislature established by state law. A more direct conflict with a statute is hard to imagine.

We categorically reject the City's argument that the legislative enactment of exceptions to a statutory scheme provides justification for municipalities to enact exceptions to the statutory scheme. No authority supports this argument. Although municipalities generally have "the power to enact legislation concerning any subject matter upon which the state Legislature may act," § 166.021(3), Fla. Stat. (2004), in exercising their power within that scope municipalities are precluded from taking any action that conflicts with a state statute. In this context, concurrent power does not mean equal power.

III. CONCLUSION

The Fifth District correctly concluded that the superpriority provision of the Palm Bay ordinance is invalid because it conflicts with state law. We approve that determination and answer the certified question in the negative.

It is so ordered.

POLSTON, C.J., and LEWIS, QUINCE, and LABARGA, JJ., concur.

PERRY, J., dissents with an opinion, in which PARIENTE, J., concurs.

PERRY, J., dissenting.

The majority holds that the City of Palm Bay's home rule authority does not provide it with the authority to enact an ordinance providing code enforcement liens superior priority over prior recorded mortgages. Because I disagree that the ordinance irreconcilably conflicts with the mechanical recording statute provided in section 162.09, Florida Statutes (2004), or that the Florida Legislature has expressed a scheme "so pervasive as to evidence an intent to preempt the particular area," I would find that the city's ordinance was properly enacted. Accordingly, I dissent.

Wrong test to determine whether a municipality overstepped.

The majority reasons that section 162.09(3) "contains no provision expressly authorizing municipalities to establish special priority for such liens." Maj. op. at 927. However, this is not the appropriate test to determine whether a municipality has exceeded its powers. The City of Palm Bay does not require the Legislature's express permission to act under its home rule powers. Section 166.021(1) states in relevant part that "municipalities ... may exercise any power for municipal purposes, except when expressly prohibited by law." Further, section 166.021(3)(c) provides that the municipality has the power to enact legislation concerning any subject matter upon which the Legislature may act except "[a]ny subject *expressly* preempted to state or county government by the constitution or by general law...." (Emphasis added).

Thus, it is not whether the Legislature has expressly authorized municipal power, but whether such power has been expressly prohibited. Here, there has been no express preemption that would prohibit the City's action.

Because the language contained in sections 162.09, 695.11, and related provisions does not expressly conflict with the ordinance, the City was within its authority to enact the ordinance. The majority avoids this outcome by relying on a single line from this Court's decision in *Barragan v. City of Miami*, 545 So.2d 252, 254 (Fla.1989), stating, "[t]he preemption need not be explicit so long as it is clear that the legislature has clearly preempted local regulation of the subject." Maj. op. at 928. The majority's reliance on *Barragan* here is misguided and misleading.

Barragan concerned an ordinance that permitted the City to deduct workers' compensation benefits from an employee's pension benefits in contradiction to the provisions of section 440.21, Florida Statutes (1987). Because the workers' compensation scheme outlined in chapter 440 explicitly applied to every employer and employee working in the state, the City's ordinance was expressly preempted by the statute. *See Barragan*, 545 So.2d at 254 (citing § 440.03, Fla. Stat. (1987)). Clearly there is no express preemption of the subject matter concerning the City's ordinance. Yet, the majority maintains that "the Palm Bay ordinance is invalid because it conflicts with state law." Again, the majority applies the improper test.

[handwritten margin note: This case differs from the case the court relies on.]

Express preemption is not the same as implied preemption or conflict—this Court has previously distinguished between these concepts. *See Sarasota Alliance for Fair Elections, Inc. v. Browning*, 28 So.3d 880, 886, 888 (Fla.2010) (defining implied preemption as "when the legislative scheme is so pervasive as to evidence an intent to preempt the particular area, and where strong public policy reasons exist for finding such an area to be preempted by the Legislature" and conflict as "when two legislative enactments cannot coexist"); *see also Phantom of Brevard Inc. v. Brevard Cnty.*, 3 So.3d 309, 314 (Fla.2008); *City of Hollywood v. Mulligan*, 934 So.2d 1238, 1243, 1246–47 (Fla.2006) (internal quotations omitted). Here, section 166.021 provides that the City may act except where expressly preempted, not impliedly preempted or in conflict. These are distinct tests that should not be conflated. However, no matter the test applied here, there is no preemption evident in the statutes, neither explicit nor implicit.

While the majority recognizes that municipalities can legislate concurrently with the Legislature, *see* Maj. op. at 928 (citing *City of Hollywood*, 934 So.2d at 1243), the majority nevertheless "categorically reject[s] the City's argument that the legislative enactment of exceptions to a statutory scheme provides justification for municipalities to enact exceptions to the statutory scheme." Maj. op. at 929. To read the statute and ordinance as unable to coexist ignores that the Legislature has not previously regarded the mechanical recording statute as a pervasive scheme without exemptions. *See* § 170.09, Fla. Stat. (2004) (providing lien priority and superiority for non-home rule municipality special assessments); § 197.552, Fla. Stat. (2004) (providing superiority for tax deeds except to municipal liens); § 718.116(5)(a), Fla. Stat. (2004) (providing superior lien priority for condominium assessments); § 713.07(2), Fla. Stat. (2004) (providing lien priority for construction liens). Additionally, lien priority can be altered by contract. Likewise, courts have recognized liens with superior priority despite their inferior filing dates. In *Gailey v. Robertson*, 98 Fla. 176, 123 So. 692 (Fla.1929), this Court found that a "mortgagee has no greater vested right ... than the fee simple owner and the rights of both must yield alike to the sovereign power when exercised to impose proper and lawful taxes." *Id.* at 179, 123 So. 692. The Court accordingly found that the mortgage held by Gailey was not prior in dignity to the lien claimed by the city of Winter Haven, despite its prior recording date. *Id.* at 177, 123 So. 692.

I would find that the Legislature has therefore not expressed a pervasive scheme—the statutes on the issue are scattered and separately enacted. Because the Legislature has provided several exemptions to the "first in time" rule, the City may likewise legislate such a rule under its home rule authority.

I would likewise find that there is nothing in section 695.11 that expressly preempts the City of Palm Bay's ordinance. Because there is no express limitation by section 695.11, The City of Palm Bay had authority under section 166.021 to enact the ordinance. Accordingly, I dissent.

PARIENTE, J., concurs.

Barragan v. City of Miami

545 So. 2d 252 (Fla. 1989)

GRIMES, Judge.

These cases, which involve the same issue, are consolidated for our consideration. In both cases, the First District Court of Appeal certified the following question as one of great public importance:

> DOES THE EMPLOYER'S REDUCTION OF CLAIMANT'S PENSION BENEFITS, PURSUANT TO CONTRACTUAL PROVISION FOR OFFSET OF WORKER'S COMPENSATION, PERMIT THE DEPUTY'S APPLICATION OF SECTION 440.21, FLORIDA STATUTES, TO AWARD COMPENSATION BENEFITS TO CLAIMANT "AT HIS COMBINED MAXIMUM MONTHLY WAGE"?

The facts of these cases are very similar. Both Barragan and Giordano were Miami police officers who suffered permanent, work-related injuries. In both cases they were granted workers' compensation benefits and disability pension benefits. In both cases the city, in conformity with a city ordinance, reduced the disability pension benefits by the amount of workers' compensation benefits.

The deputy commissioner found Barragan entitled to combined disability pension and workers' compensation benefits up to his average monthly wage. The First District Court of Appeal reversed on the authority of *City of Miami v. Knight*, 510 So.2d 1069 (Fla. 1st DCA), *review denied*, 518 So.2d 1276 (Fla.1987). *City of Miami v. Barragan*, 517 So.2d 99 (Fla. 1st DCA 1987). In Giordano's case the deputy commissioner originally held the offset to be impermissible. The First District Court of Appeal affirmed this ruling without opinion in *City of Miami v. Giordano*, 488

So.2d 538 (Fla. 1st DCA 1986). However, when the city continued to deduct from Giordano's pension a sum equal to his workers' compensation, Giordano sought a comparable increase in his workers' compensation. The deputy commissioner denied this claim on the premise that even though the city had made deductions from the pension benefits, it had fulfilled its obligations under the workers' compensation laws. Notwithstanding its prior decision, the First District Court of Appeal also affirmed that ruling. *Giordano v. City of Miami*, 526 So.2d 737 (Fla. 1st DCA 1988) (relying on *Knight*).

The city asserts in each case that the deputy commissioner did not have jurisdiction to decide whether the city could reduce its pension benefits to the extent of workers' compensation payments. However, case law supports the view that a deputy commissioner may properly increase the amount of workers' compensation to offset illegal deductions made on the account of the payment of workers' compensation benefits. *Marion Correctional Inst. v. Kriegel*, 522 So.2d 45 (Fla. 5th DCA), *review denied*, 531 So.2d 1354 (Fla.1988); *Chancey v. Florida Pub. Utils.*, 426 So.2d 1140 (Fla. 1st DCA 1983); *see Jewel Tea Co. v. Florida Ind. Comm'n*, 235 So.2d 289 (Fla.1969).

Section 440.21, Florida Statutes (1987), an integral part of the workers' compensation law, states:

> 440.21 Invalid agreements; penalty.—
>
> (1) No agreement by an employee to pay any portion of premium paid by his employer to a carrier or to contribute to a benefit fund or department maintained by such employer for the purpose of providing compensation or medical services and supplies as required by this chapter shall be valid, and any employer who makes a deduction for such purpose from the pay of any employee entitled to the benefits of this chapter shall be guilty of a misdemeanor of the second degree, punishable as provided in s. 775.083.
>
> (2) No agreement by an employee to waive his right to compensation under this chapter shall be valid.

In *Jewel Tea Co. v. Florida Industrial Commission*, 235 So.2d 289 (Fla.1969), the Court held that this statute prevented a private employer from deducting group health insurance benefits from an injured claimant's workers' compensation benefits. In pointing out that the employer could not accomplish the same result by deducting the compensation payments from the insurance benefits, the Court said:

> Regardless of whether you say the workmen's compensation benefits reduce the group insurance benefits or visa [sic] versa, the result violates the Statute. Claimant is entitled to workmen's compensation in addition to any benefits under an insurance plan to which he contributed.

Id. at 291. The same rule was followed with respect to sick leave benefits, *Brown v. S.S. Kresge Co.*, 305 So.2d 191 (Fla.1974), and pension benefits, regardless of whether the employee contributed to the funding of these benefits. *Domutz v. Southern Bell Tel. & Tel. Co.*, 339 So.2d 636 (Fla.1976). However, the total benefits from all sources cannot exceed the employee's weekly wage. *Domutz; Brown.*

Originally, the rule was different with respect to public employees. In *City of Miami v. Graham*, 138 So.2d 751 (Fla.1962), the Court held that where an employee of the City of Miami had received pension benefits in excess of the amount of workers' compensation benefits to which he would have otherwise been entitled, the city was not obligated to pay him any workers' compensation benefits. The Court based its holding on section 440.09(4), Florida Statutes (1957), which provided that any workers' compensation benefits payable to injured public employees should be reduced by the amount of pension benefits which were also payable.

In 1973, the legislature repealed section 440.09(4). Thereafter, there was no state statute on this subject which authorized public employees to be treated any differently than private employees. However, the City of Miami has maintained an ordinance since 1973 which provides for the offset of pension benefits against workers' compensation benefits. In *Hoffkins v. City of Miami*, 339 So.2d 1145 (Fla. 3d DCA 1976), the district court of appeal upheld the deduction of workers' compensation benefits from the pension check of a City of Miami employee based on this ordinance. The court reasoned that if section 440.09(4) was valid before its repeal, the ordinance which was enacted under the city's home rule power must also be valid. It is this decision which was wrong and which misled the district court of appeal in this case.

Section 166.021(3)(c), Florida Statutes (1987), which is part of the municipal home rule powers act, limits cities from legislating on any subject expressly preempted to state government by general law. The preemption need not be explicit so long as it is clear that the legislature has clearly preempted local regulation of the subject. *Tribune Co. v. Cannella*, 458 So.2d 1075 (Fla.1984), *appeal dismissed*, 471 U.S. 1096 (1985). There can be no doubt that chapter 440 has preempted local regulation on the subject of workers' compensation. Section 440.03, Florida Statutes (1987), states that every "employer" and "employee" as defined in section 440.02 shall be bound by the provisions of chapter 440. The definition of "employer" in section 440.02(12), Florida Statutes (1987), includes all political subdivisions of the state. Section 440.10, Florida Statutes (1987), requires *every* employer coming within the provisions of the workers' compensation law to provide the compensation set forth therein.

Under state law, section 440.21 prohibits an employer from deducting workers' compensation benefits from an employee's pension benefits. Yet, the City of Miami has passed an ordinance which permits this to be done. The ordinance flies in the face of state law and cannot be sustained.

The employer may not offset workers' compensation payments against an employee's pension benefits except to the extent that the total of the two exceeds the employee's average monthly wage. We answer the certified question in the affirmative and disapprove the opinions in *City of Miami v. Knight* and *Hoffkins v. City of Miami*. We quash the decisions of the district court of appeal in *Barragan* and *Giordano* and remand for proceedings consistent with this opinion.

It is so ordered.

OVERTON, SHAW and BARKETT, JJ., concur.

EHRLICH, C.J., concurs in result only, with an opinion [omitted].

McDONALD, J., dissents with an opinion.

KOGAN, J., did not participate in this case.

McDONALD, Justice, dissenting.

The decision of the district court of appeal should be approved and the certified question answered in the negative.

The claimants' workers' compensation benefits are not, and have not been, reduced in the slightest; the claimants are not contributing to their workers' compensation benefits contrary to section 440.21, Florida Statutes (1987). What is involved here is the calculation of disability pension benefits, which are paid in addition to workers' compensation benefits. The majority opinion requires the city, absent a direct statutory or contractual basis therefor, to pay an amount of pension benefits greater than that for which the city bargained.

Workers' compensation benefits are mandated by statute for injuries and disability flowing therefrom as a result of an accident occurring on the job. Disability pension benefits are not statutorily required. Yet the city, as a part of its employment package, has agreed to pay its employees a disability pension if the employee becomes disabled while working for the city. It does not matter whether the disability was caused by a work-related accident or not. As a part of that bargain, however, the parties agreed that if the disability was covered by workers' compensation benefits, then the disability pension benefits shall be reduced by the amount of workers' compensation benefits. In all events the total of the two would never be less than that called for in the agreement for disability pension benefits. It is true that a small sum is deducted from each employee's wages to go into the disability pension funds, but this contribution is always less than the disability pension benefits paid even when workers' compensation benefits are paid and deducted from what the disability payments would have been had the disability been nonjob-related. This contribution is to the pension fund and not to benefits required under chapter 440, Florida Statutes, which is what section 440.21 prohibits.

I cannot see how such a contractual agreement can be construed to be in violation of section 440.21.

City of Hollywood v. Mulligan

934 So. 2d 1238 (Fla. 2006)

BELL, J.

The Fourth District Court of Appeal has certified the following question to us as one of great public importance:

Does the Florida Contraband Forfeiture Act preempt local governments from adopting ordinances imposing forfeiture of personal property for misdemeanor offenses?

Mulligan v. City of Hollywood, 871 So.2d 249, 257 (Fla. 4th DCA 2003). The Fourth District answered this question in the affirmative. We rephrase the question as follows:

Does the Florida Contraband Forfeiture Act (FCFA), sections 932.701–.707, Florida Statutes (2002), preempt a municipality from adopting an ordinance that authorizes the seizure and impoundment of vehicles used in the commission of certain misdemeanor offenses?

We answer this rephrased question in the negative. We hold that the FCFA does not preempt a municipality from using its home rule powers to enact such an ordinance. Therefore, we quash the decision of the Fourth District and remand this case for further proceedings consistent with this opinion.

I. FACTS

This case arose from a suit brought by Colon Bernard Mulligan (Mulligan) against the City of Hollywood (City) challenging the validity of the City's vehicle impoundment ordinance, section 101.46, Hollywood, Florida, Code of Ordinances (1999). Mulligan was arrested by City police officers for soliciting a prostitute in violation of section 796.07, Florida Statutes (2000), a misdemeanor offense. Because Mulligan was in his vehicle at the time of the solicitation, the police officers seized and impounded his vehicle pursuant to the City's ordinance.

As provided by the ordinance, Mulligan appeared before a special master and argued that the seizure was not supported by probable cause. The special master disagreed. Finding probable cause to support the seizure, the special master imposed the sanction as provided for in the ordinance. The special master ordered Mulligan to either pay a $500 administrative fine or forfeit the bond he had previously posted. Mulligan paid the administrative fine, and the vehicle was returned to him.

Mulligan then brought suit against the City seeking a declaratory judgment that the ordinance is invalid. The action was certified as a class action, and Mulligan was named class representative. Mulligan and the City filed cross-motions for summary judgment. The trial court granted the City's motion for summary judgment.

On appeal, the Fourth District reversed. Finding that the ordinance "effects a criminal forfeiture" of the vehicles seized and is therefore "a forfeiture scheme," *Mulligan*, 871 So.2d at 252, the Fourth District held the ordinance is preempted by or, in the alternative, is in conflict with the FCFA. *Id.* at 256.

II. ANALYSIS

A. The FCFA Does not Preempt the Adoption of Municipal Ordinances Authorizing the Seizure and Impoundment of Vehicles

In analyzing the preemption question, we (1) describe the City's ordinance; (2) highlight the law of preemption; (3) discuss the FCFA; and, finally, (4) apply the law of preemption to the ordinance and the FCFA. As for our standard of review, the Fourth District's ruling on the validity of the ordinance is a question of law subject to de novo review by this Court. *See State v. J.P.*, 907 So.2d 1101, 1107 (Fla.2004) (finding that rulings on the constitutionality of several ordinances should be reviewed de novo) (citing *City of Miami v. McGrath*, 824 So.2d 143, 146 (Fla.2002)).

1. The City's Ordinance

Section 101.46 of the Hollywood, Florida, Code of Ordinances is entitled "Vehicle Impoundment." This ordinance was enacted on May 5, 1999, as part of ordinance 0-99-12. Its purpose is to aid the City's law enforcement in deterring crimes related to drugs and prostitution. The ordinance authorizes the seizure and impoundment of motor vehicles whenever a police officer has probable cause to believe that the vehicle (1) contains cannabis or a controlled substance under chapter 893 of the Florida Statutes; (2) was used to purchase or attempt to purchase cannabis or a controlled substance; or (3) was used to facilitate the commission of an act of prostitution, assignation, or lewdness pursuant to section 796.07, Florida Statutes. § 101.46(A), Ord. Significantly, each of the offenses enumerated in the ordinance is a misdemeanor crime, and, by its express terms, the ordinance does not apply when a vehicle is subject to seizure under the FCFA. § 101.46(C), Ord.

The ordinance requires that upon seizing and impounding a vehicle for one or more of the enumerated misdemeanor offenses, the City's police officers must follow a number of procedures. The officer must provide written notice to the owner of the vehicle or the person in control of the vehicle that the vehicle is being impounded by the City of Hollywood Police Department and that there is a right to request a preliminary hearing. § 101.46(B), (D), Ord. This notice must be delivered either by hand or, if the owner or operator is not available, by certified mail within five days. *Id.* An owner or operator may request a preliminary hearing, and, if requested, the hearing must be held within ninety-six hours. This preliminary hearing is held before a code enforcement official called a special master who, according to the City, is appointed pursuant to chapter 162, Florida Statutes, in lieu of appointing a local government code enforcement board. *See* § 162.03, Fla. Stat. (1999). The City bears the burden of showing that the seizure was supported by probable cause. § 101.46(D), Ord. If probable cause is shown, the owner can regain possession of the vehicle only by paying an administrative fee of up to $500 plus towing and storage costs or by posting a bond in the same amount. *Id.* If probable cause is not shown, the vehicle is released, and the vehicle owner is not liable for any costs. *Id.*

If the owner does not request a preliminary hearing, or if the special master finds probable cause for the seizure at the preliminary hearing, the City schedules a final hearing and notifies the vehicle owner. § 101.46(E), Ord. The final hearing must occur no later than forty-five days after the date that the vehicle is impounded. *Id.* At the final hearing, the City must establish by a preponderance of the evidence that the vehicle was (1) properly impounded pursuant to the ordinance and (2) that the owner of the vehicle either knew or should have known that the vehicle was used or was likely to be used in violation of the ordinance. *Id.* If the City fails to establish either of these elements, the vehicle is returned to the owner without penalty. *Id.* If the special master finds that the vehicle is subject to impoundment, an order is then entered finding the record owner of the vehicle civilly liable to the City for an administrative fee, not to exceed $500, as well as towing and storage costs. *Id.* The vehicle remains impounded until the administrative fees are satisfied. The funds recovered are allocated, first, as reimbursement to the police department for costs incurred in enforcing the ordinance (towing and storage), and second, as surplus to the City's general fund. § 101.46(G), Ord. Unclaimed vehicles are subject to Florida's provisions for the disposition of lost or abandoned property contained in chapter 705, Florida Statutes (1999). § 101.46(F), Ord.

2. The Law of Preemption

In Florida, a municipality is given broad authority to enact ordinances under its municipal home rule powers. Art. VIII, § 2(b), Fla. Const.; § 166.021(1), (3)(c), (4), Fla. Stat. (1999). Under its broad home rule powers, a municipality may legislate concurrently with the Legislature on any subject which has not been expressly preempted to the State. *Wyche v. State*, 619 So.2d 231, 237–38 (Fla.1993) (citing *City of Miami Beach v. Rocio Corp.*, 404 So.2d 1066, 1069 (Fla. 3d DCA 1981)); *see also Barragan v. City of Miami*, 545 So.2d 252, 254 (Fla.1989) (stating that the municipal home rule powers act "limits cities from legislating on any subject expressly preempted to state government by general law"). "Preemption essentially takes a topic or a field in which local government might otherwise establish appropriate local laws and reserves that topic for regulation exclusively by the legislature." *Phantom of Clearwater, Inc. v. Pinellas County*, 894 So.2d 1011, 1018 (Fla. 2d DCA 2005). "Express pre-emption requires a specific statement; the pre-emption cannot be made by implication nor by inference." *Fla. League of Cities, Inc. v. Dep't of Ins. & Treasurer*, 540 So.2d 850, 856 (Fla. 1st DCA 1989) (quoting *Bd. of Trs. v. Dulje*, 453 So.2d 177, 178 (Fla. 2d DCA 1984)). However, "[t]he preemption need not be explicit so long as it is clear that the legislature has clearly preempted local regulation of the subject." *Barragan*, 545 So.2d at 254 (citing *Tribune Co. v. Cannella*, 458 So.2d 1075 (Fla.1984)).

The Fourth District held that the City's ordinance is preempted by the FCFA. It based this holding upon the language of the FCFA's policy statement as found in section 932.704, Florida Statutes (1995). We examine this holding by looking at the history and language of the FCFA, in particular section 932.704.

3. The Florida Contraband Forfeiture Act

In 1974, one year after the adoption of the Municipal Home Rule Powers Act, the Legislature adopted the Florida Uniform Contraband Transportation Act. Ch. 74-385, §§ 1–4, Laws of Fla., codified at §§ 943.41–.44, Fla. Stat. (1975). In 1980, the name of this act was changed to the Florida Contraband Forfeiture Act (FCFA). The FCFA was later renumbered to sections 932.701–.704; and, in 1992, section 932.704 was amended to include a policy statement. In 1995, this policy statement was amended to its current form:

> It is the policy of this state that law enforcement agencies *shall utilize* the provisions of the Florida Contraband Forfeiture Act to deter and prevent the continued use of *contraband articles* for *criminal purposes* while protecting

the proprietary interests of innocent owners and lienholders and to authorize such law enforcement agencies to use the proceeds collected under the Florida Contraband Forfeiture Act as supplemental funding for authorized purposes. The potential for obtaining revenues from forfeitures must not override fundamental considerations such as public safety, the safety of law enforcement officers, or the investigation and prosecution of criminal activity. It is also the policy of this state that law enforcement agencies ensure that, in all seizures *made under* the Florida Contraband Forfeiture Act, their officers adhere to federal and state constitutional limitations regarding an individual's right to be free from unreasonable searches and seizures, including, but not limited to, the illegal use of stops based on a pretext, coercive-consent searches, or a search based solely upon an individual's race or ethnicity.

§ 932.704(1), Fla. Stat. (2005) (emphasis added).

Relying on this policy statement in section 932.704, the Fourth District held that the City's ordinance is expressly preempted by the FCFA. Specifically, the Fourth District reasoned that because section 932.704 provides that law enforcement agencies "shall utilize" the provisions of the FCFA when forfeiting contraband articles used for criminal purposes, the Legislature had expressly preempted "municipal criminal contraband forfeiture laws" to the State. 871 So.2d at 256. The Fourth District further found that under section 932.701(2)(a)(5) of the FCFA, the Legislature had expressly limited the forfeiture of vehicles to felony offenses. *Id.*

In her special concurrence, Judge May disagreed with this finding. She opined that because the FCFA is limited to felonies, the FCFA does not expressly preempt a municipality from legislating with regard to misdemeanors under its municipal home rule powers. *Id.* at 257 (May, J., concurring specially). We agree with Judge May on this point.

4. Application of Law of Preemption to the FCFA and the Ordinance

Contrary to the Fourth District's findings, the words "shall utilize" alone do not express preemption. This phrase should be read in context and with an eye toward its plain meaning. "We have recognized as 'axiomatic' the principle that 'all parts of a statute must be read together in order to achieve a consistent whole.' When possible, we 'must give full effect to all statutory provisions and construe related statutory provisions in harmony with one another.'" *Clines v. State*, 912 So.2d 550, 557 (Fla.2005) (citation omitted) (quoting *Forsythe v. Longboat Key Beach Erosion Control Dist.*, 604 So.2d 452, 455 (Fla.1992)).

In section 932.704(1), the Legislature provides that "[i]t is the policy of this state that law enforcement agencies shall utilize the provisions of the Florida Contraband Forfeiture Act to deter and prevent the continued use of contraband articles for criminal purposes." The term "contraband" is a defined term under the FCFA. In pertinent part, the FCFA defines contraband as

[a]ny personal property, including ... any ... vehicle of any kind ... which was used or was attempted to be used as an instrumentality in the commission

of, or in aiding or abetting in the commission of, *any felony,* whether or not comprising an element of the felony....

§ 932.701(2)(a)(5), Fla. Stat. (2002) (emphasis added). When this statutory definition of contraband is placed in the FCFA's policy statement, that statement reads as follows:

> It is the policy of this state that law enforcement agencies *shall utilize* the provisions of the [FCFA] to deter and prevent the continued use of contraband articles [i.e., any personal property, including ... any ... vehicle of any kind ... which was used or was attempted to be used as an instrumentality *in the commission of,* or in aiding or abetting in the commission of, *any felony,* whether or not comprising an element of the felony] for criminal purposes.

§§ 932.701(2)(a)(5), .704(1), Fla. Stat. (emphasis added). Read in this manner, the FCFA's policy statement refers to contraband articles, such as vehicles, as those articles that are connected with the commission of felony offenses. Stated otherwise, for purposes of preemption, when the statutory definition of contraband is applied to the policy statement in section 932.704(1), the FCFA does *not* express any intent to preempt seizure and forfeiture in the context of nonfelony offenses.

Furthermore, when the FCFA and the question of preemption are considered in light of the Municipal Home Rule Powers Act, the absence of an express legislative intent to preempt the field of forfeiture in enacting the FCFA becomes more significant. As of 1941, the law in Florida was that the subject of forfeiture is a field preempted to the Legislature, and a municipality had to expressly be given the authority to legislate in that field. *City of Miami v. Miller,* 148 Fla. 349, 4 So.2d 369, 370 (1941). However, a change in this law occurred in 1973 when the Municipal Home Rule Powers Act was enacted. This act removed all general limitations on a municipality's power to legislate in a particular field. *See* § 166.021, Fla. Stat. (2002). Passed the year before the original version of the FCFA, the Municipal Home Rule Powers Act does not reserve to the Legislature the power to legislate in the field of forfeiture. One cannot lightly disregard this omission because the Legislature did retain field preemption in other areas. For example, in chapter 166 itself, the Legislature preempted the field in regard to ammunition sales. *See* § 166.044, Fla. Stat. (2002) ("No municipality may adopt any ordinance relating to the possession or sale of ammunition."). And since 1973, the Legislature has continued to use similar preemptive language in other contexts. For instance, regarding the lottery, the Legislature stated that "[a]ll matters relating to the operation of the state lottery are preempted to the state, and no county, municipality, or other political subdivision of the state shall enact any ordinance relating to the operation of the lottery authorized by this act." § 24.122(3), Fla. Stat. (2005); *see also* § 320.8249(11), Fla. Stat. (2005) ("The regulation of manufactured homes installers or mobile home installers is preempted to the state....").

Given the forgoing analysis, we determine that the FCFA does not preempt to the Legislature the field of vehicle seizure and forfeiture, much less impoundment, for misdemeanor offenses. Accordingly, in answering the certified question as rephrased, we hold that the FCFA does not preempt a municipality from adopting an ordinance that authorizes the seizure and impoundment of vehicles used in the commission of certain misdemeanors.

B. The Ordinance is Not in Conflict with the FCFA

As an alternative basis for its decision, the Fourth District held that even if the ordinance is not preempted by the FCFA, the ordinance is in conflict with the FCFA because it does not meet the procedural due process requirements of the FCFA. 871 So.2d at 256 (citing *Dep't of Law Enforcement v. Real Prop.*, 588 So.2d 957 (Fla.1991)). We disagree. In addition to the absence of preemption, there is no conflict between the FCFA and the ordinance. The statute and the ordinance can coexist.

Certainly, "[m]unicipal ordinances are inferior to laws of the state and must not conflict with any controlling provision of a statute." *Thomas v. State*, 614 So.2d 468, 470 (Fla.1993). In other words, "[a] municipality cannot forbid what the legislature has expressly licensed, authorized or required, nor may it authorize what the legislature has expressly forbidden." *Id.* (quoting *Rinzler v. Carson*, 262 So.2d 661, 668 (Fla.1972)). "[A]n ordinance penalty may not exceed the penalty imposed by the state"; however, "a municipality may provide a penalty less severe than that imposed by a state statute." *Id.* (citing *Edwards* [*v. State*], 422 So.2d 84 [(Fla. 2d DCA 1982)]).

The FCFA and the ordinance do not conflict because they authorize different remedies for different criminal conduct. The FCFA allows for the forfeiture of vehicles used in the commission of a felony. *See* § 932.701(2)(a)(5), Fla. Stat. (2002). The ordinance authorizes the impoundment of vehicles used in the commission of a misdemeanor. *See* § 101.46(A)–(C), Ord. Additionally, the ordinance expressly does not apply when the vehicle is subject to seizure under the FCFA. The fact that the FCFA and the ordinance employ differing procedures to achieve their purposes does not amount to an improper "conflict" necessitating the invalidation of the ordinance. Therefore, the FCFA and the ordinance can coexist.

Although we find that the differing procedures employed by the FCFA and the ordinance do not create a conflict necessitating the invalidation of the ordinance, we agree with the Fourth District that the ordinance's procedures raise serious constitutional concerns. However, we do not address these concerns because (1) these constitutional concerns are independent of whether the FCFA and the ordinance are in conflict with each other, and (2) no constitutional issues were raised before us. The Fourth District is free to address these issues on remand, if appropriate.

C. The Impoundment Ordinance is Not a Forfeiture Scheme

Finally, we note that although impoundment and forfeiture are related concepts in the context of government seizure of personal property, they are not synonymous terms. Essentially, an impoundment is the temporary taking of tangible, personal property; a forfeiture is the permanent taking of real or personal property (tangible or intangible). For example, forfeiture has been defined as a permanent governmental taking of title and all rights to and in property that has been condemned for its role in a criminal violation. *See United States v. Ursery*, 518 U.S. 267, 284

(1996) ("Forfeitures serve a variety of purposes, but are designed primarily to confiscate property used in violation of the law, and to require disgorgement of the fruits of illegal conduct."). On the other hand, impoundment is defined as "to place (something, such as a car or other personal property) in the custody of the police or the court, often with the understanding that it will be returned intact at the end of the proceeding." *Black's Law Dictionary* 760 (7th ed.1999). The Virginia Court of Appeals noted the essential difference in the nature of the deprivation imposed by an impoundment as opposed to a forfeiture in *Wilson v. Commonwealth*, 23 Va.App. 443, 477 S.E.2d 765, 768 (1996): "A temporary impoundment of a vehicle is not a forfeiture, although it has characteristics of a forfeiture. Being temporarily deprived of one's vehicle until one pays a fee to release it also resembles a civil penalty."

Based on the foregoing definitions, contrary to the Fourth District's conclusion, the ordinance does not "effect a forfeiture." It does not seek to permanently divest the owner of all right and title to the vehicle. Rather, the ordinance authorizes the temporary deprivation of access to one's vehicle when it is used in the commission of a drug- or prostitution-related misdemeanor. Although the ordinance requires that the vehicle owner be temporarily deprived of the vehicle and requires that the owner pay a fee in exchange for the return of the vehicle, these requirements do not transform the impoundment ordinance into a "forfeiture scheme." The vehicle owner is never permanently deprived of the vehicle; rather, the vehicle's return is simply conditioned upon payment of an administrative fee and incidental costs. If a vehicle owner fails to pay the administrative fee and other costs, the vehicle is not "forfeited" as in the FCFA. Instead, the vehicle is disposed of as if it were lost or abandoned property under chapter 705, Florida Statutes (2005). § 101.46(F), Ord. Under chapter 705, the vehicle is sold. The money due the City is taken from the sale proceeds, and the balance is held in an account for the owner for up to one year.

III. CONCLUSION

For the foregoing reasons, we conclude that the FCFA does not preempt a municipality such as the City of Hollywood from adopting an ordinance that authorizes the seizure and impoundment of vehicles used in the commission of certain misdemeanor offenses. Furthermore, though its procedures raise serious constitutional concerns, the ordinance is not in conflict with any provision of the FCFA. Accordingly, we quash the decision of the Fourth District Court of Appeal and remand for further consideration consistent with this opinion.

It is so ordered.

LEWIS, C.J., and WELLS, ANSTEAD, PARIENTE, QUINCE, and CANTERO, JJ., concur.

F. Article VIII, Section 3 — Consolidation

Albury v. City of Jacksonville Beach

295 So. 2d 297 (Fla. 1974)

BOYD, Justice.

This is an appeal from an opinion and order of the District Court of Appeal, First District, (Case No. S-448, opinion filed November 8, 1973, not yet reported). We have jurisdiction by virtue of Article V, Section 3(b)(1).

Plaintiffs, Beaches and Baldwin, in their amended complaint, sought a declaration as to their legal status and relationship to the Defendant-City under the new charter adopted in 1967. Further, Beaches and Baldwin sought to determine whether they might levy municipal occupational license taxes on persons engaging in occupations in their jurisdictions, as well as whether they have a right to receive directly from the state and federal agencies revenues designated under general law to be distributed to municipalities. In the Consolidated Government's counterclaim, it and its Tax Collector sought different declarations as to many of the same points, plus further judicial clarification of its authority to enact ordinances pre-empting ordinances of the Beaches and Baldwin. The trial court granted substantially the relief sought by the Consolidated Government, holding the Beaches and Baldwin to subordinate urban services districts and no longer entitled to levy occupational license taxes or to otherwise assert legal standing as incorporated municipalities. On appeal, the District Court of Appeal, First District, reversed on the authority of this Court's opinion in *Jackson v. Consolidated Government of the City of Jacksonville*, 225 So.2d 497 (Fla.1969); it held that the Beaches and Baldwin continue to exist as quasi-municipal corporations; that, as such, they are empowered to exercise all municipal functions which they were permitted to perform under their original municipal charters and the general laws of the State immediately prior to consolidation; and, that they are corporate entities having the same rights as duly constituted municipal corporations to share in, receive, and expend revenues allocable to municipal corporations by both the federal and state governments. We agree.

An examination of pertinent legislative history shows that, prior to 1967, the Plaintiffs were created by special acts of the Legislature in accordance with the existing constitution. In 1967, pursuant to the constitutional authority vested in the Legislature by Article VIII, Sections 8 and 9, the Legislature adopted Chapter 67-1320, Laws of Florida, 1967, by which the present City of Jacksonville was created. Four days later another statute (Chapter 67-1535, Laws of Florida, 1967) was introduced which altered materially the original charter act; this amendatory act was passed by the Legislature. Thereafter, there was passed Chapter 67-1547, Laws of Florida, 1967, also amending the basic act. All three acts, which together comprise the present charter of the consolidated City of Jacksonville, were subject to a referendum held in Duval County and were approved.

According to the original act, Chapter 67-1320, a single government was created (Section 1.01) which had any and all powers of the cities, county, or any former government (Section 3.01) including the power to levy occupational license tax (Section 3.02). By the terms of Chapter 67-1320, the corporate municipal structures of the Beaches and Baldwin were effectively abolished, becoming a part of urban services districts whose sole function was to act in accordance with such power and authority as might be delegated to them by the Consolidated Government for convenience in administering municipal functions. Under Chapter 67-1320, the Consolidated Government was empowered to levy both an occupational license tax against all businesses and professions in the county in the exercise of its county function, and to levy a second occupational license tax against all businesses and professions operating within the urban services districts of the City in the exercise of its municipal function. Since there is no authority in Chapter 67-1320 for the urban services districts to levy or collect occupational license taxes, if there had been no amendments to that chapter, it would be clear that only the Consolidated Government would be entitled to levy occupational license taxes against businesses and professions operating in the county at large and in the urban services districts.

We note, however, that Chapter 67-1535 was enacted within days after the original charter act. This act effectively restored to the Beaches and Baldwin the powers which the first act took away. Since it was adopted by the Legislature subsequent to the prior act divesting them of authority, and since the last expression of the Legislature will prevail in cases of conflicting statutes,[22] and since all three were approved by referendum, the modifications became effective simultaneously with the original act. Therefore, we must conclude that the intent of the Legislature and the people was to preserve the powers formerly granted to the municipal governments of the Beaches and Baldwin including the power to tax and authority to receive federal and state grants.

This Court has held in *Jackson, supra,* that the legislative intent was to preserve the smaller governmental entities of the Beaches and Baldwin as quasi-municipalities. If that is not what the people and the Legislature intended or presently desire, appropriate changes should be made by them and not by this Court.

Concerning the authority of the consolidated government to collect occupational license taxes in the quasi-municipalities, we observe that the opinion of the District Court of Appeal herein reviewed correctly finds each quasi-municipality to be authorized to collect such a tax. No challenge is made against payment of a county-wide occupational tax to what was formerly Duval County. The record and admissions of counsel show that business and professional persons in other parts of old Duval County are now required by ordinance to pay two license taxes, one being a municipal tax paid to the Consolidated Government and the other being to the same entity of government in place of the old Duval County occupational license.

A careful examination of the Constitution and Statutes of Florida leads us to the conclusion that whenever any one of the small quasi-municipalities is collecting oc-

---

22. [FN 1.] *DeConingh v. City of Daytona Beach,* 103 So.2d 233 (Fla.App.1958).

cupational license taxes, the consolidated government can collect only that tax which would have been payable to old Duval County had consolidation never occurred.

To require business and professional persons in the small quasi-municipalities to pay three such license taxes (one to the quasi-municipality and two to the Consolidated Government—one "county" and one "municipal"), while their neighbors would pay only the latter two, would be unconstitutionally discriminatory and a denial of due process of law unless it should be clearly shown that a higher quality of governmental services was being furnished them than in other parts of the Consolidated Government. No such justification is shown by this record.

Accordingly, we affirm the decision of the District Court of Appeal, and since the case is disposed of as an appeal, the petition for certiorari is denied.

It is so ordered.

ADKINS, C.J., and ERVIN, MCCAIN, DEKLE and OVERTON, JJ., concur.

ROBERTS, J., specially concurring with opinion. [omitted]

Question

1. Do cities exist within the Consolidated City of Jacksonville?

Town of Baldwin v. Consolidated City of Jacksonville

610 So. 2d 95 (Fla. 1st DCA 1992)

SHIVERS, Judge.

This appeal is from a final order granting summary judgment and declaring annexation ordinances passed by the Town of Baldwin unconstitutional. We affirm.

Fred Miller and A.G. Ambrose each own land in Duval County. The two parcels total approximately 57 acres and adjoin the Town of Baldwin, which is also in Duval County. In April and September 1990, at the petition of Miller and Ambrose, Baldwin's town council passed ordinances annexing the two parcels into its incorporated area.

In October 1990 Jacksonville filed an amended complaint seeking declaratory and injunctive relief. The complaint alleges that the annexed land "is located entirely within the boundary of the corporate limits of the Consolidated City of Jacksonville." The complaint also alleges that the boundary of the corporate limits of Jacksonville is coextensive with the territorial boundary of Duval County; with the exceptions of Baldwin and three beach cities, "there have been no unincorporated areas located within the territorial boundaries of Duval County." Accordingly, Jacksonville sought an adjudication that Baldwin's annexation ordinances are unconstitutional.

Baldwin answered the complaint and denied that (1) the annexed property is located within the boundary of the corporate limits of the Consolidated City of Jacksonville, and (2) there have been no unincorporated areas located within the territorial boundaries of Duval County.

Both parties moved for summary judgment. As background, Baldwin quotes from *City of Jacksonville Beach v. Albury*, 291 So.2d 82 (Fla. 1st DCA 1973), *aff'd*, 295 So.2d 297 (Fla.1974):

> [The Beach Cities' and Baldwin's] freedom to function as independent corporate entities is restricted only by the right of the consolidated government of the City of Jacksonville to adopt ordinances in the exercise of its county governmental functions binding on the territory and inhabitants of those urban service districts comprising the Beaches and Baldwin only to the extent as would have been permitted by Duval County prior to consolidation.
>
> ....
>
> [The Beach Cities and Baldwin] are empowered to exercise all municipal functions, powers, duties, and authority normally possessed and exercised by other duly chartered municipal corporations in this state.

Id. at 89–90. Baldwin argued that it thus has the same power to annex as any municipality.

Jacksonville also moved for summary judgment. It argued that Chapter 78-536, Laws of Florida, states that the consolidated governments of the City of Jacksonville and Duval County "shall ... extend territorially throughout Duval County ... and shall have jurisdiction as a municipality throughout Duval County except in ... the Town of Baldwin." All lands are incorporated as either the municipal corporation of Jacksonville or several 'quasi municipal' corporations, such as Baldwin. Therefore, there are no unincorporated lands within the boundaries of Duval County. Section 171.043, Florida Statutes, prohibits annexation of an area "included within the boundary of another incorporated municipality." Further, pursuant to section 2.06 of Jacksonville's Charter, only the legislature can expand the territory of Baldwin unless the Charter itself provides otherwise; the Charter does not provide otherwise.

The trial court entered a final order granting Jacksonville's motion for summary judgment, denying Baldwin's motion for summary judgment, and declaring Baldwin's annexation ordinances unconstitutional and void ab initio. The order states, "Within the boundaries of Duval County there is no unincorporated land."

We affirm the trial court's order. Article VIII, section 9, of the 1885 Florida Constitution, as preserved by Article VIII, section 6(e), of the 1968 constitution, empowered the legislature to establish

> a Municipal corporation to be known as the City of Jacksonville extending throughout the present limits of Duval County, in the place of any or all county ... and local governments.... Such municipality may exercise all the powers of a municipal corporation ... which would accrue to it if it were a county. All property of Duval County and of the municipalities in said county shall vest in such municipal corporation when established....

The legislature divided the City of Jacksonville into a general services district (Duval County) and five urban services districts: #1) the former city limits of Jacksonville,

#2) Jacksonville Beach, #3) Atlantic Beach, #4) Neptune Beach, and #5) the Town of Baldwin. The first Charter of the City of Jacksonville states that all the governments in Duval County

> are hereby consolidated into a single body politic and corporate.... The consolidated government shall ... succeed to and possess all the properties ... of the former governments.... The consolidated government shall have jurisdiction, and extend territorially throughout the present limits of Duval County.

Ch. 67-1320, §§ 1.01 and 1.02, Laws of Fla. (1967). In 1978 the Charter was amended to clarify that Jacksonville's municipal powers extended throughout the county, except for the Beach Cities and Baldwin.

The conflict in this case is between (1) Baldwin's right as a quasi-municipal corporation to exercise municipal functions (such as annexation of unincorporated land) just as any other municipal corporation in Florida pursuant to *Albury,* and (2) the right of any incorporated municipality (such as the City of Jacksonville) to be protected from annexation of land within its boundaries by another municipality pursuant to section 171.043(1). Appellee correctly states, "The essence of the issue in this case is whether the area in Jacksonville designated as 'general services district' is part of the [incorporated] City of Jacksonville."

Chapter 67-1320, Laws of Florida (1967), consolidated all of Duval County into "a single body politic and corporate." The consolidation was initiated "pursuant to the power granted by section 9 of article VIII of the [Florida] Constitution." Section 9 states, "The Legislature shall have power to establish, alter or abolish, *a Municipal corporation* to be known as the City of Jacksonville, extending territorially throughout the present limits of Duval County...." (emphasis added). Therefore, according to the Florida Constitution, the Consolidated City of Jacksonville is a municipal corporation extending throughout Duval County; there is no unincorporated land in Duval County.

The 1967 legislature amended Chapter 1320 in Chapter 1535, the intent of which was to "preserve for the people residing in the (second through fourth) urban districts the same local governmental structure ... and laws which existed in those areas prior to the effective date of this charter." Ch. 67-1535, § 2A.01, Laws of Fla. The second through fourth urban districts also (1) retained use of its property and the entitlement to "own, acquire, encumber and transfer property in its own name," and (2) remained subject to all special and general laws which applied to their former governments "as if the municipal charters of those former governments were still in full force and effect." Ch. 67-1535, §§ 2A.05 and 2A.06, Laws of Fla. Accordingly, the supreme court held in *Jackson v. Consolidated Government of the City of Jacksonville,* 225 So.2d 497 (Fla.1969), that the consolidated city "will extend throughout the territory, but that one or more municipal or local governments in the territory may continue in existence [as] quasi municipal corporations." *Id.* at 503.

Baldwin argues that because *Albury* classifies it as a "duly constituted municipal corporation," which is empowered to exercise all municipal functions that they were permitted to perform under state law prior to consolidation, they can annex as freely as any municipality.

However, "[m]unicipal annexation of unincorporated territory, merger of municipalities, and exercise of extraterritorial powers by municipalities shall be as provided by general or special law." Art. VIII, §2(c), Fla. Const. Regardless of whether Baldwin is relying on section 171.04(1), Florida Statutes (1965), or section 171.043(1), Florida Statutes (1989), general law provides that no municipality can annex land "within the boundary of another incorporated municipality."

Because (1) according to the Florida Constitution there is no unincorporated land in Duval County, (2) the land annexed by Baldwin is in Duval County, and (3) no municipality can unilaterally annex incorporated land, the trial court correctly ruled that Baldwin's attempted annexation of land within Duval County is unconstitutional.

AFFIRMED.

SMITH and KAHN, JJ., concur.

G. Article VIII, Section 6 — Schedule to Article VIII

Article VIII, Section 6 contains several provisions of the 1885 Constitution which have been incorporated by reference into the current Florida Constitution. These include provisions relating to charter government for Duval, Monroe, Miami-Dade, and Hillsborough Counties. *See* FLA. CONST. art. VIII, §6(e) (incorporating by reference Article VIII, Sections 9, 10, 11 & 24, Florida Constitution of 1885). For those counties listed in the Schedule which had not yet adopted charters, the Schedule is not the exclusive means of establishing a charter government. *See* Op. Att'y Gen. Fla. 81-07 (1981). Thus, Hillsborough County adopted its county charter under the provisions of Article VIII, Section 1(g). *See* HILLSBOROUGH COUNTY CHARTER art. I, §1.01. Jacksonville's consolidation with Duval County was made under the 1885 Constitution, so this provision remains relevant for that consolidated government. *See* DUVAL COUNTY CHARTER art. 1, §1.101; *cf. Jackson v. Consolidated Govt. of City of Jacksonville*, 225 So. 2d 497, 500–01 (Fla. 1969) (discussing the history of Jacksonville's consolidation with Duval County).

The next two cases look at the impact of Miami-Dade County's Charter, originally adopted under the Article VIII, Section 11, Florida Constitution of 1885.

Metropolitan Dade County v. City of Miami
396 So. 2d 144 (Fla. 1980)

McDONALD, Justice.

Dade County appeals a judgment invalidating a county ordinance regulating taxicabs throughout Dade County, including the cities of Miami and Miami Beach. The trial judge based his ruling on a declaration that article VIII, section 4, Florida Constitution prevails over article VIII, section 6(e), Florida Constitution. We have jurisdiction pursuant to article V, section 3(b)(1), Florida Constitution (1972).

In 1974 the legislature transferred all of the Public Service Commission's existing authority to regulate taxicabs to those charter counties which wished to accept that responsibility. The voters of Dade County amended their home rule charter in 1976 to expand the county's authority to regulate taxicabs to include the entire county. In 1979 the county enacted an ordinance designed to provide comprehensive countywide regulation of taxicabs. For many years prior thereto, however, the cities of Miami and Miami Beach had regulated taxicabs within their respective city limits. These cities filed suit contending that the county exceeded its authority in enacting such a comprehensive ordinance. To support their contention, the cities relied on section 323.052(3), Florida Statutes,[23] which provides that cities regulating for-hire vehicles on July 1, 1974 would continue to do so "unless such authority is transferred to the county by a majority vote of the governing body of the municipality." Neither city relinquished its authority by means of this statutory procedure or by any other method.

The trial court determined that two provisions of the state constitution pertain to the transfer of powers between counties and municipalities: Article VIII, section 4; and article VIII, section 11(1)(d), 1885 Constitution,[24] which is incorporated into the 1968 Constitution by article VIII, section 6(e). The trial court first found the challenged ordinance to have been properly enacted pursuant to section 11(1)(d)

---

23. [FN 4.] s 323.052(1), Fla. Stat., which reads as follows:

(1) Notwithstanding any other provisions of this part to the contrary, any chartered county may regulate and license for-hire passenger motor vehicles in the unincorporated area of the county and in those municipalities that do not regulate such vehicles on July 1, 1974, or that do not adopt regulations at least as strict as those initially adopted by the county, by filing with the Public Service Commission a written resolution that the county will be assuming regulatory jurisdiction of for-hire passenger motor vehicles throughout said county. Said resolution shall not become effective sooner than 90 days from the date the resolution is received by the commission. When said date arrives, the county that has filed its intent to regulate and license shall have exclusive jurisdiction to regulate and license for-hire passenger motor vehicles in the unincorporated area of said county and those municipalities specified above, and no other body shall have jurisdiction to regulate and license such for-hire passenger motor vehicles in such areas. This subsection shall be authority for the chartered counties of the state, solely within the areas herein defined and upon the election set forth herein, to exercise all powers and functions of regulation, including, but not limited to, permits, areas of operation, rates and charges, inspection, and any other powers presently held by the Public Service Commission. Any chartered county making the election set forth herein shall adopt by ordinance, after holding public hearings, a complete set of rules and regulations which shall apply to all regulatory aspects within the areas herein defined.

24. [FN 5.] SECTION 11. Dade County, home rule charter.—(1) The electors of Dade County, Florida, are granted power to adopt, revise, and amend from time to time a home rule charter of government for Dade County, Florida, under which the Board of County Commissioners of Dade County shall be the governing body. This charter:

(d) May provide a method by which any and all of the functions or powers of any municipal corporation or other governmental unit in Dade County may be transferred to the Board of County Commissioners of Dade County.

and the county home rule charter. The court also found, however, that section 4 controls over section 6(e). According to the trial court, therefore, the "or as otherwise provided by law" language in section 4 means that the general law provision in section 323.052(3) should prevail over the home rule provisions in sections 6(e) and 11(1)(d), the county home rule charter, and the case law interpreting those provisions. Since the statutory procedure had not been followed, the court invalidated the ordinance, and this appeal followed.

To support its finding that section 4 prevails over section 6(e), the trial court relied on *Sarasota County v. Town of Longboat Key*, 355 So.2d 1197 (Fla.1978). That reliance is misplaced. *Sarasota County*, stands for the proposition, inter alia, that both charter and noncharter counties are subject to the provisions of section 4. The instant case, on the other hand, presents the question of whether section 4 prevails over the explicit savings clause in section 6(e).

The main purpose in construing constitutional provisions is to ascertain the intent of the framers and to effectuate the object designed to be accomplished. *State ex rel. Dade County v. Dickinson*, 230 So.2d 130 (Fla.1969); *State ex rel. West v. Gray*, 74 So.2d 114 (Fla.1954); *Amos v. Mathews*, 99 Fla. 1, 126 So. 308 (1930); *Mugge v. Warnell Lumber & Veneer Co.*, 58 Fla. 318, 50 So. 645 (1909). Section 6(e) is a clear and unambiguous statement of intent by the state's electors. That section provides that the Dade County Home Rule Amendment (section 11, article VIII, 1885 Constitution) "shall remain in full force and effect ... as if this article (VIII, 1968 Constitution) had not been adopted." To hold that section 4 prevails over this direct savings clause would go against the intent expressed in section 6(e) and would thwart the objective of preserving Dade County's constitutional home rule amendment. We hold, therefore, that section 6(e) controls over section 4 and that the trial court erred in finding otherwise.

Because of its finding that section 4 prevails over section 6(e), the trial court saw no necessity to rule on the conflict between the county ordinance and section 323.052(3). Due to our holding above, however, that question must now be considered.

This Court has noted that the metropolitan government of Dade County is unique in this state due to its constitutional home rule amendment. *See McNayr v. Kelly*, 184 So.2d 428 (Fla.1966). That amendment gives Dade County numerous powers which set Dade apart from the state's other counties. One such difference is Dade County's power to enact ordinances, when expressly authorized by the home rule amendment, which conflict with the state constitution or with state law.[25]

---

25. [FN 6.] Art. VIII, s 11(5), Fla. Const. (1885), which reads as follows:
(5) Nothing in this section shall limit or restrict the power of the Legislature to enact general laws which shall relate to Dade County and any other one or more counties in the state of Florida or to any municipality in Dade County and any other one or more municipalities of the State of Florida, and *the home rule charter provided for therein shall not conflict with any provision of this Constitution nor of any applicable general laws non applying to Dade County and any other one or more counties of the State of Florida except as expressly authorized in this section nor shall any ordinance enacted in pursuance to said home rule charter conflict with this Constitution or any such applicable general law except as expressly authorized herein,*

Numerous decisions have invalidated Dade County ordinances and parts of the Dade County Charter, however, because of impermissible, unauthorized conflict with the state constitution or with general state law. In *State ex rel. Dade County v. Dickinson*, 230 So.2d 130 (Fla.1969), this Court held that nothing in the Dade County Home Rule Amendment allowed that county to exceed the ten-mill constitutional cap on county taxes. This Court has also found nothing in section 11 which would permit Dade County cities to abrogate the statutory debt limit imposed on cities. *Seminole Rock Prods., Inc. v. Town of Medley*, 180 So.2d 457 (Fla.1965). Since state law recognized fortunetelling and similar occupations, a Dade County ordinance prohibiting engaging in such occupations was invalidated because the home rule amendment did not expressly reserve such power in the county. *Board of County Comm'rs of Dade County v. Boswell*, 167 So.2d 866 (Fla.1964). In *Kaulakis v. Boyd*, 138 So.2d 505 (Fla.1962), this Court struck down a section of the county charter which waived the county's tort immunity. Nothing in section 11 permitted such waiver, and the constitution specifically prohibited it. The Court also invalidated Dade County's 1958 taxicab ordinance as creating impermissible conflict with state law. *Dade County v. Mercury Radio Serv., Inc.*, 134 So.2d 791 (Fla.1961). Finally, in *Dade County v. Kelly*, 99 So.2d 856 (Fla.1957), the Court held that Dade could not make piecemeal transfers of the sheriff's duties, in contravention of the governor's constitutional power to remove constitutional officers, without abolishing the office of sheriff.

The Third District Court of Appeal has also considered whether Dade County ordinances can conflict with general laws and with the state constitution. That court struck down Dade's requirement that claims against the county be filed within sixty days as being in unauthorized conflict with the statutory three-year notice period. *Scavella v. Fernandez*, 371 So.2d 535 (Fla. 3d DCA 1979). Likewise, the four-year statute of limitations on filing suit against a county was found to prevail over Dade's reduction of that time to one year. *Dade County v. Lambert*, 334 So.2d 844 (Fla. 3d DCA 1976).

In the above-cited cases, the conflict has been in areas not specifically authorized by section 11. In several cases, on the other hand, either authorized, permissible conflict, or no conflict, has been found, resulting in the validation of numerous county ordinances and portions of the county charter.[26] Such cases are not controlling in the

---

nor shall the charter of any municipality in Dade County conflict with this Constitution or any such applicable general law except as expressly authorized herein, provided however that said charter and said ordinances enacted in pursuance thereof may conflict with, modify or nullify any existing local, special or general law applicable only to Dade County. (emphasis supplied)

26. [FN 8.] *Buckress Land Co. v. Metropolitan Dade County*, 232 So.2d 384 (Fla.1970); *Dade County v. Kelly*, 153 So.2d 822 (Fla.1963); *In re Advisory Opinion to the Governor*, 116 So.2d 425 (Fla.1959); *Miami Shores Village v. Cowart*, 108 So.2d 468 (Fla.1958); *Dade County v. Young Democratic Club of Dade County*, 104 So.2d 636 (Fla.1958); *City of Sweetwater v. Dade County*, 343 So.2d 953 (Fla. 3d DCA 1977); *Jordan Chapel Freewill Baptist Church v. Dade County*, 334 So.2d 661 (Fla. 3d DCA 1976); *City of North Miami Beach v. Metropolitan Dade County*, 317 So.2d 110 (Fla. 3d DCA 1975); *State ex rel. Lehman v. Buchanan*, 190 So.2d 594 (Fla. 3d DCA 1966); *Carol City Utils., Inc. v. Dade County*, 183 So.2d 227 (Fla. 3d DCA 1966); *City of Miami v. Benitez*, 116 So.2d 463 (Fla. 3d DCA 1959). *See*

instant case, however, because we hold that the ordinance in question is not expressly authorized by section 11.

The Dade County Home Rule Charter Amendment specifically provides that Dade County can do nothing to limit or restrict the power and jurisdiction of the Public Service Commission.[27] Prior to the 1974 amendment which prompted the instant case, chapter 323 provided that the power to regulate taxicabs resided solely with the Public Service Commission and with the state's municipalities. Counties, whether chartered or not, shared none of this power. Thus, this Court struck down Dade County's 1958 attempt to regulate taxicabs in the county's unincorporated areas, regardless of an original charter provision permitting such regulation. *Dade County v. Mercury Radio Serv., Inc.*, 134 So.2d 791 (Fla.1961).

By passing the amendment allowing charter counties to regulate taxicabs, the legislature has acknowledged that thereafter such regulation is a function subject to countywide control. If that amendment had said no more, the ordinance in question would be valid. *See Miami Shores Village v. Cowart*, 108 So.2d 468 (Fla.1958).

The legislature's grant of authority to charter counties to regulate taxicabs, an authority the counties did not previously have, however, is a limited grant. It includes a proviso allowing municipalities to continue such regulation unless they formally and affirmatively accede to their counties' authority. The appellee cities in the instant case did not give up their power to regulate taxicabs in the manner specified by statute. Since the transfer of powers proviso is such an integral part of the total amendment, there is no way to separate that limitation on a charter county's power from the grant of power to charter counties.

Although the Dade County Home Rule Amendment allows that county to enact ordinances which conflict with state law, it can do so only when such conflict is in areas specifically authorized in the home rule amendment. Art. VIII, s 11(5), Fla. Const. (1885). We can find no provision in section 11 that expressly authorizes Dade County to contravene the method of transferring power set out in section 323.052(3). We have kept in mind the home rule amendment's admonishment that section 11 is to be liberally construed in order to effectuate the purpose of giving home rule to Dade County. Art. VIII, s 11(9), Fla. Const. (1885). Section 11 also provides, however, that, if conflict is not expressly authorized, general state law must prevail. Art. VIII,

---

also In re Advisory Opinion of the Governor, 313 So.2d 697 (Fla.1975) (recognizing that, although the Dade County Commission has the power to fill vacant offices, the governor has the power to fill offices during a period of suspension).

27. [FN 9.] Art. VIII, s 11(7), Fla. Const. (1885), which reads as follows:

(7) Nothing in this section shall be construed to limit or restrict the power and jurisdiction of the Railroad and Public Utilities Commission or of any other state agency, bureau or commission now or hereafter provided for in this Constitution or by general law and said state agencies, bureaus and commissions shall have the same powers in Dade County as shall be conferred upon them in regard to other counties.

s 11(6), Fla. Const. (1885). Indeed, if unauthorized conflict is found, we are instructed that section 11 is to "be strictly construed to maintain ... (the) supremacy of this Constitution and of the Legislature in the enactment of general laws pursuant to this Constitution." Art. VIII, s 11(9), Fla. Const. (1885).

We hold, therefore, that the ordinance in question is in unauthorized conflict with state law because Dade County did not follow the statutory method for transferring power.[28] The ordinance is invalid to the extent that the county seeks to regulate taxicabs in Miami and Miami Beach. Unless the cities of Miami and Miami Beach accede to regulation by the county, Dade County does not have the authority to usurp the regulation of taxicabs within the city limits of those municipalities. We thus affirm the judgment of the trial court, but for different reasons.

It is so ordered.

SUNDBERG, C.J., and ADKINS, OVERTON, ENGLAND and ALDERMAN, JJ., concur.

BOYD, J., dissents.

Board of County Commissioners of Dade County v. Wilson

386 So. 2d 556 (Fla. 1980)

SUNDBERG, Chief Justice.

Section 7.01 of the Dade County Home Rule Charter provides that any county elector may seek the passage of an ordinance by means of initiative and referendum. An elector attempting to invoke the charter provision must submit his proposed ordinance to the Board of County Commissioners (the Board) in the form of a petition. Approval by the Board of the petition's form is a prerequisite to the circulation of the petition for a specified number of signatures. If sufficient signatures are obtained, the Board must either adopt the petition or submit the matter to the electorate for a referendum.

Pursuant to the dictates of this charter provision, Harry L. Wilson requested that the Board "approve as to form" his initiative petition designed to set county millage for the 1980–81 fiscal year at four mills.[29] The Board disapproved the form of Mr.

---

28. [FN 13.] Ch. 76-168, s 3, Laws of Fla., as amended by ch. 77-457, s 1, Laws of Fla., repealed ch. 323, Fla. Stat., in its entirety, effective July 1, 1980. Thus, s 323.052(3) was of no force and effect on the original publication date of this opinion. In its motion for rehearing, Dade County contends that lack of conflict (due to the repeal of ch. 323) on the date of publication requires our approval of the ordinance in question. The ordinance, however, was invalid as to Miami and Miami Beach when passed. Repeal of a statute does not validate an ordinance which is void at its inception.

29. [FN 1.] The proposed ordinance provides:

Be it ordained by the people of Dade County, Florida:

Section 1. The county millage for the 1980–81 fiscal year shall be 4.00 mills on all property subject to ad valorem tax in Dade County, Florida, as the millage fixed and determined to be levied for all county operating purposes.

Section 2. This ordinance does not determine the millage for county bonded debt service,

Wilson's petition, finding that the ordinance proposed in the petition was violative of the Florida Constitution. Mr. Wilson applied to the circuit court for a writ of mandamus and, finding that the proposed ordinance was not facially unconstitutional, the court issued the writ. Pursuant to this judicial action, which has not been stayed, the petition has been circulated, the requisite number of signatures obtained and a referendum election scheduled for September 9, 1980.

On appeal, the District Court of Appeal, Third District, determined that the proposed ordinance was not unconstitutional on its face and affirmed the trial court but, recognizing the issue as a persistent one, certified its decision to us as passing upon a question of great public importance. *Board of County Commissioners v. Wilson*, 382 So.2d 431 (Fla.3d DCA 1980). We have jurisdiction. Art. V, s 3(b)(4) Fla. Const. (1980).

The question certified by the district court is as follows:

> Whether the courts may pass upon the validity of an ordinance, fixing the millage rate of the county's operating budget, prior to its adoption by the voters through the initiative and referendum process.

Mr. Wilson argues that this issue was raised in *Wilson v. Dade County* (*Wilson I*), 369 So.2d 1002 (Fla.3d DCA 1979), *cert. denied*, 373 So.2d 457 (Fla.1979), wherein the validity of a similar proposed ordinance was challenged by the Board. The district court's decision in *Wilson I*, Mr. Wilson asserts, is dispositive of the present proceeding. We disagree. Courts may consider the constitutional validity of proposed ordinances. While recognizing this authority, the district court specifically stated that only the statutory validity of the ordinance was at issue. Courts may not rule upon the validity of a proposed ordinance challenged solely on nonconstitutional grounds. Since the Board is here challenging the constitutionality of Wilson's proposed ordinance, we have the authority to inquire further into the validity of the ordinance.

In the present proceeding, the district court concluded that article VII, section 1(a), Florida Constitution, does not pose a constitutional impediment to a proposed ordinance designed to establish the millage rate for county taxation. We agree that the constitutional provision does not, in itself, prescribe the method and means by which taxes are to be imposed.[30] As a consequence, where there is no legislative directive relating to a specific method or means of taxation, that procedure may be controlled by ordinance.

We find it unnecessary to decide whether an ordinance which is in direct conflict with a legislatively prescribed method of taxation would violate article VII, section 1(a). Rather, we turn our attention to the requirements of article VIII, section 6 of

---

or the library district fund, or other special district millages.

Section 3. This ordinance shall be included in the Dade County Code.

Section 4. This ordinance shall take effect at the beginning of the fiscal year commencing on October 1, 1980.

30. [FN 4.] For examples of instances in which we have determined that the Florida Constitution does provide the exclusive manner of performing an act, see *Sullivan v. Askew*, 348 So.2d 312 (Fla.1977), and *Weinberger v. Board of Public Instruction*, 93 Fla. 470, 112 So. 253 (1927).

the 1968 Constitution relating to Dade County home rule. Article VIII, section 11 of the Constitution of 1885 authorized the creation of a metropolitan government for Dade County and granted to the electors of that county the power to adopt a home rule charter. Pursuant to this authority, the voters of Dade County adopted a home rule charter for the metropolitan government of the county. Article VIII, section 6(e) of the 1968 Constitution provides that article VIII, section 11 of the 1885 Constitution is to remain in full force and effect, and that:

> All provisions of the Metropolitan Dade County Home Rule Charter, heretofore or hereafter adopted by the electors of Dade County pursuant to Article VIII, Section 11, of the Constitution of 1885, as amended, shall be valid, and any amendments to such charter shall be valid; *provided that the said provisions of such charter and the said amendments thereto are authorized under said Article VIII, Section 11, of the Constitution of 1885, as amended.*

(Emphasis supplied, footnotes omitted.) Hence the authorizing amendment of the former constitution has been incorporated by reference into the 1968 Constitution. The Dade County Charter has been given constitutional approval, but only to the extent that it is consistent with the former article VIII, section 11 (now in article VIII, section 6). If any provision of the Dade County Charter, or any action taken pursuant to the Charter, contravenes the limitations or prescriptions of article VIII, section 6 of the 1968 Constitution, it is necessarily unconstitutional and void. *See State ex rel. Dade County v. Nuzum,* 372 So.2d 441 (Fla.1979); *Gray v. Golden,* 89 So.2d 785 (Fla.1956).

The focus thus narrows to whether the proposed ordinance is authorized by the enabling constitutional language.[31] Article VIII, section 11(1)(b) of the 1885 Constitution states that the charter "(m)ay grant full power and authority to the Board of County Commissioners of Dade County ... to levy and collect such taxes as may be authorized by general law and no other taxes...." The authority granted under the enabling section is circumscribed by subsections (5) and (6) of section 11:

> (5) (T)he home rule charter provided for herein shall not conflict with any provision of this Constitution nor of any applicable general laws now applying to Dade County and any other one or more counties of the State of Florida except as expressly authorized in this section nor shall any ordinance enacted in pursuance to said home rule charter conflict with this Constitution or any such applicable general law except as expressly authorized herein....

> (6) Nothing in this section shall be construed to limit or restrict the power of the Legislature to enact general laws which shall relate to Dade County and

---

31. [FN 5.] We will accept, without deciding, the district court's conclusion that the proposed ordinance is authorized by the Dade County Charter. See s 7.01(6)(a), Home Rule Charter of Metropolitan Dade County.

any other one or more counties of the state of Florida or to any municipality in Dade County and any other one or more municipalities of the State of Florida relating to county or municipal affairs and all such general laws shall apply to Dade County and to all municipalities therein to the same extent as if this section had not been adopted and such general laws shall supersede any part or portion of the home rule charter provided for herein in conflict therewith and shall supersede any provision of any ordinance enacted pursuant to said charter and in conflict therewith, and shall supersede any provision of any charter of any municipality in Dade County in conflict therewith.

Moreover, in subsection (9) of section 11 it is declared to be the intent of the legislature and the electors of Florida that

the provisions of this Constitution and general laws which shall relate to Dade County ... shall be the supreme law in Dade County, Florida, except as expressly provided herein and this section shall be strictly construed to maintain such supremacy of this Constitution and of the Legislature in the enactment of general laws pursuant to this Constitution.

Clearly then, the provisions of the Home Rule Charter and the ordinances adopted pursuant thereto must be in accordance with general law unless there is express constitutional authorization otherwise.

Despite the above-quoted constitutional provisions, Mr. Wilson contends that this Court's decision in *Dade County v. Young Democratic Club*, 104 So.2d 636 (Fla.1958), requires that we find the present ordinance to be valid. In Young Democratic Club, however, this Court found that, even though in conflict with general election laws, Dade County charter provisions dealing with the method of electing county commissioners were specifically authorized by the Constitution. Therefore, the charter provisions were constitutionally valid. There is, however, no similar constitutional authorization for the citizens or governing body of Dade County to devise its own method for levying taxes or establishing millage rates. As a consequence, the proposed ordinance at issue here will withstand constitutional scrutiny only if it does not conflict with general law. See *Buckress Land Co. v. Metropolitan Dade County*, 232 So.2d 384 (Fla.1970); *Gray v. Golden, supra*.

Applying the preceding analysis, we conclude that the proposed ordinance is unconstitutional. An ordinance will be declared unconstitutional because in conflict with general law if the ordinance and the legislative provision cannot coexist. *State ex rel. Dade County v. Brautigam*, 224 So.2d 688 (Fla.1969). Petitioner cites as conflicting a number of legislative provisions which delineate the manner in which a county commission is to determine the appropriate millage rate for ad valorem taxation purposes. In particular, section 200.191(1)(a)–(c) authorizes three categories of countywide millage rates:

200.191 Millages; definitions.

(1) County millages shall be composed of three categories of countywide millage rates, as follows:

(a) General county millage, which shall be that nonvoted millage rate set by the governing body of the county.

(b) County debt service millage, which shall be that millage rate necessary to raise taxes for debt service as authorized by a vote of the electors pursuant to s. 12, Art. VII of the State Constitution.

(c) County voted millage, which shall be that millage rate set by the governing body of the county as authorized by a vote of the electors pursuant to s. 9(b), Art. VII of the State Constitution.

The rates are to be set under subsections (a) and (c) by the governing body of the county, and under (b) by the vote of the electors pursuant to article VII, Section 12, Florida Constitution (1968). We read these subsections to comprise the exclusive manner by which to set countywide millage rates. The proposed ordinance, which would set the millage rate through the initiative petition process, is thus in direct conflict with section 200.191.

Moreover, subsequent to the filing of this cause in the Supreme Court, petitioner brought to our attention a law passed by the 1980 session of the Florida Legislature which is in direct conflict with the present proposed ordinance. Section 27 of chapter 80-274, Laws of Florida, adding subsection (6) to 200.191, Florida Statutes, states:

(6) Millages shall be fixed only by resolution of the governing body of the taxing authority in the manner specifically provided by general law or by special act.

Section 64(1) of chapter 80-274 provides that the above section shall be effective for taxes levied for 1980 and each year thereafter, thus it applies to the proposed ordinance before us. And because the proposed ordinance, if approved by a majority of voters in the referendum election, would become law without the necessity of a resolution passed by the Dade County Commission, it flies directly in the face of general law as enunciated in section 27.

Respondent attempts to avoid the effect of section 27 by asserting first that section 27 is superseded by the Dade County Home Rule Charter, and second that the portion of the title of chapter 80-274 pertaining to the amendment of section 200.191, Florida Statutes, is constitutionally defective. His assertions are unpersuasive. As noted previously, subsection 6 of section 11, article VIII of the 1885 Constitution mandates that general laws enacted subsequent to the adoption of the Home Rule Charter "shall apply to Dade County and to all municipalities therein to the same extent as if this section had not been adopted and such general laws shall supersede any part or portion of the home rule charter provided for herein in conflict therewith and shall supersede any provision of any ordinance enacted pursuant to said charter and in conflict therewith...." Hence, it is the general law which supersedes the Home Rule Charter. With regard to respondent's second argument, we believe that the portion of the title to chapter 80-274 with which we are here concerned does not mislead a person of average intelligence as to the scope of the enactment and is sufficient to put that person on notice and cause him to inquire into the body of the statute itself. *See Williams v. State*, 370 So.2d 1143 (Fla.1979) and cases cited therein.

Accordingly, the certified question is answered in the affirmative but the decision of the District Court of Appeal, Third District, is quashed. This cause is remanded to the district court with directions to remand to the trial court for entry of a judgment consistent with this opinion. Due to the exigent circumstances presented by the budgeting process of Dade County for the fiscal year 1980–81, no petition for rehearing will be entertained in this cause.

Respondent's petition for attorney's fees is denied.

It is so ordered.

ADKINS, BOYD, OVERTON and ALDERMAN, JJ., concur.

H. Article VIII, Section 1(d) — County Officers

This provision provides constitutional status to a group of local officials who are elected by county voters. These county officers include the sheriff, tax collector, property appraiser, supervisor of elections, and the clerk of the circuit court. The role of these independent elected officials with their own constitutional mandates has engendered some friction with county commissioners. The following cases discuss conflicts over the role of clerk of court as county auditor and regarding the county sheriff's role as chief law enforcement officer of each county.

Prior to 2018, counties were able to abolish these county offices by charter or by special law. As of that date, Volusia County had abolished all independent county officer positions, making them subordinate offices under the county manager. *See* VOLUSIA COUNTY CHARTER art. VI, § 601.1 (2018). Likewise, Broward County had abolished the independently elected tax collector position, folding its duties into a Department of Finance and Administrative Services under the county administrator. *See* BROWARD COUNTY CHARTER art. III, § 3.06 (2018). In 2018, the Constitution Revision Commission proposed Amendment 10 which, among other things, amended Article VIII, Section 1(d) to require that all of these county officers be elected. Broward, Miami-Dade and Volusia Counties tried to have Amendment 10 struck from the ballot alleging that it was confusing to voters, but the Supreme Court upheld the proposal, and it was approved by some 63% of Florida voters. *See County of Volusia v. Detzner*, 253 So. 2d 507 (Fla. 2018). In 2019, subsequent to passage of the amendment, Broward and Volusia Counties again challenged the retroactive application of the amendment to those counties. The circuit court found, and the First District Court of Appeal affirmed, that the amendment applied prospectively to the counties in question. *See County of Volusia v. DeSantis*, 302 So. 3d 1001 (Fla. 1st DCA 2020).

Brock v. Board of County
Commissioners of Collier County

21 So. 3d 844 (2d DCA 2009), *rev. dismissed*,
48 So. 3d 810 (Fla. 2010)

CANADY, Associate Judge.

In this case involving a dispute between appellant, the Clerk of the Circuit Court of Collier County (Clerk), and appellee, the Board of County Commissioners of Collier County, we consider questions concerning the scope of the powers exercised by the Clerk acting in his capacity as county auditor and custodian of all county funds.

The establishment by county employees of a checking account for a fire district controlled by the county precipitated the dispute underlying this litigation. Although the funds in the fire district checking account were ultimately surrendered to the Clerk, the litigation of a declaratory judgment action instituted by the Clerk and quo warranto proceedings instituted by the county moved forward. In the declaratory judgment action, the Clerk sought a determination that it was appropriate for him to make inquiries regarding an account such as the fire district account and to obtain custody of the funds contained in the account. In addition, the Clerk sought a determination that certain other actions were within the scope of his powers with respect to the county's fiscal affairs. In the quo warranto proceedings, the county sought a judgment limiting the Clerk's activities related to the county's fiscal affairs.

In the consolidated declaratory judgment and quo warranto proceedings, the circuit court entered summary judgment in favor of the county. On appeal, the Clerk challenges the circuit court's ruling on three issues. First, the Clerk challenges the ruling that the Clerk has no authority to investigate the status of county funds which were not in the actual custody of the Clerk. Second, the Clerk challenges the ruling that the Clerk is not authorized to conduct postpayment internal audits concerning county expenditures. Third, the Clerk challenges the ruling that the Clerk does not have independent authority to prepare the county's financial statements.

... We affirm the trial court's ruling on [the third] issue [because the Clerk's authority to prepare financial statements for the County is derived from a delegation of authority by the Board of County Commissioners]. With respect to the other two issues, however, we reverse the trial court's ruling for the reasons we explain below.

... Article 8, section 1(d) of the Florida Constitution provides that "[w]hen not otherwise provided by county charter or special law approved by vote of the electors, the clerk of the circuit court shall be ex officio clerk of the board of county commissioners, auditor, recorder and custodian of all county funds." There is no special law or charter provision divesting the Clerk of the duties specified in this constitutional provision. As is the case with other state and county officers, the powers and duties of the clerk of the circuit court "shall be fixed by law." Art. II, § 5(c), Fla. Const. Section 28.12, Florida Statutes (2007), provides that the "clerk of the circuit court shall be clerk and accountant of the board of county commissioners," and that the

Clerk "shall keep the minutes and accounts and perform such other duties as provided by law." Section 136.08, Florida Statutes (2007), provides that the "accounts of each and every board and the county accounts of each and every depository ... shall at all times be subject to the inspection and examination by the County auditor." Section 136.06(1) requires that checks or warrants drawn on county accounts shall be "attested by the clerk." Section 129.09, Florida Statutes (2007), imposes both personal civil liability and criminal liability on any clerk of the circuit court acting as county auditor who signs a warrant for any illegal or unauthorized payment of county funds.

"A statutory grant of power or right carries with it by implication everything necessary to carry out the power or right and make it effectual and complete." *Deltona Corp. v. Fla. Pub. Serv. Comm'n*, 220 So.2d 905, 907 (Fla.1969).

> It is the well settled rule in this state that if a statute imposes a duty upon a public officer to accomplish a stated governmental purpose, it also confers by implication every particular power necessary or proper for complete exercise or performance of the duty, that is not in violation of law or public policy.

Peters v. Hansen, 157 So.2d 103, 105 (Fla. 2d DCA 1963); *see also Bailey v. Van Pelt*, 78 Fla. 337, 82 So. 789, 792 (1919).

We conclude that the trial court's ruling prohibiting the Clerk from investigating county funds that have not been placed in his custody unduly limits the Clerk's ability to carry out his responsibilities as the custodian of all county funds. A public officer with the right and responsibility to maintain custody of public funds necessarily has the authority both to investigate circumstances in which public funds have wrongfully been withheld from the officer's custody and to seek to obtain custody of the withheld funds. Restricting the Clerk's authority to do so is inconsistent with the goal of protecting public funds from misappropriation, and it is inconsistent with the effectual and complete exercise of the Clerk's authority as custodian of all county funds. We make no comment on the availability of any specific legal processes that the Clerk may seek to utilize in investigating county funds that have been withheld from his custody.

Similarly, we conclude that the trial court's ruling prohibiting postpayment audits is inconsistent with the Clerk's statutory power to inspect and examine all county accounts at all times and with the Clerk's statutory duty to ensure that all payments of county funds comply with applicable legal requirements. Postpayment audits to verify the legality of payments that have been made are necessary to effectively carry out the Clerk's duty to ensure that county funds are expended only as authorized by law. Verification of the legality of payments already made—a process which tests the soundness of existing internal controls—is directly related to ensuring that future payments are legal. To deny the Clerk the ability to conduct such postpayment audits would compromise the Clerk's duty and power to guard against the illegal use of county funds. Such audits are distinct from the "financial audits" of financial statements defined in sections 11.45(1)(c) and 218.31(17), Florida Statutes (2007).

Affirmed in part; and reversed in part.

FULMER, J., Concurs.

SILBERMAN, J., Concurring in part, dissenting in part, with opinion. [omitted]

Demings v.
Orange County Citizens Review Board
15 So. 3d 604 (Fla. 5th DCA 2009)

LAWSON, J.

Orange County Sheriff Jerry Demings ("Sheriff") and Deputy Steven Jenny ("Jenny") appeal from an amended final summary judgment in favor of Orange County ("County") and the Orange County Citizen's Review Board ("CRB"). In that order, the trial court upheld sections of the Orange County charter and ordinances establishing the CRB and authorizing it to review and investigate citizen complaints of excessive force and abuse of power. Particularly at issue is the CRB's power to compel the Sheriff's deputies to appear and testify in CRB investigations by subpoena. We agree with Sheriff Demings and Jenny that the county charter and ordinance provisions creating the CRB and authorizing it to investigate citizen complaints against the Sheriff's deputies are unconstitutional, and reverse the order on appeal.

Jurisdiction and Standard of Review

Jurisdiction exists under Florida Rule of Appellate Procedure 9.030(b)(1)(A). The issues were preserved below, and the *de novo* standard of review applies.

Background and Relevant Facts

Under Florida's Constitution, the state is divided into political subdivisions called counties, Article VIII, Section 1(a), Florida Constitution, so that much of the state's "police power" can be controlled and exercised at the community level.[32] Generally, the constitution provides for non-charter counties, which are permitted to exercise only those powers expressly authorized by the Legislature through general or special laws, Article VIII, Section 1(f), Florida Constitution, and charter counties, which are broadly granted "all powers of local self-government" not inconsistent with general or special law. Art. VIII, § 1(g), Fla. Const. Additionally, under Florida's constitution, certain responsibilities of local governance are separately entrusted to independent constitutional officers who, at least in non-charter counties, are not accountable to the county's governing board, but derive their power directly from the state. Art. VIII, § 1(d), Fla. Const. These officers are independently accountable to the electorate unless otherwise provided by law. *Id.*

In charter counties, the electorate has an option of either maintaining these independent constitutional offices or abolishing them and transferring their responsibilities to the board of the charter county or to local offices created by the charter.

---

32. [FN 2.] *See also City of Miami v. Lewis*, 104 So.2d 70, 72 (Fla. 3d DCA 1958) ("counties derive their status as political subdivisions of the state through constitutional designation whereas the cities or municipalities are creatures of the statutes"); *City of Miami v. Rosen*, 151 Fla. 677, 10 So.2d 307, 309 (1942) ("Municipalities in Florida are not subdivisions of the state as are counties.").

Id. However, the constitution does not allow for the piecemeal transfer of responsibilities from an independent constitutional officer. *Id.; Cook v. City of Jacksonville,* 823 So.2d 86 (Fla.2002); *Dade County v. Kelly,* 99 So.2d 856 (Fla.1958). Therefore, if the electorate wants to transfer any responsibility from a constitutional officer to the county's governing board, it can do so only by abolishing the constitutional office altogether. *Id.*

On November 4, 1986, a majority of Orange County's electorate approved a charter form of government for the County, which left the independent constitutional office of sheriff intact.

On November 3, 1992, a majority of the County's voters then approved a charter amendment abolishing the constitutional office of sheriff and creating a sheriff's department headed by a county charter office of sheriff. At the same time, the electorate added a charter provision creating the CRB to investigate citizen complaints against the deputies working in the new county department, and to review the sheriff's internal departmental investigations into those complaints. Art. VIII, §801, Orange County Charter. The charter provides for a CRB composed of seven to eleven members, and requires the sheriff to appoint two of the members. The remaining members are appointed by the board of county commissioners. To aid the CRB in "conducting [its] investigations," the charter grants it the power to "subpoena witnesses, administer oaths, take testimony and require production of evidence." *Id.* By ordinance, the board has set the number of CRB members at nine, and confirmed the CRB's "duty" to "review citizen complaints ... regarding the alleged use of excessive force or abuse of power by any officer or employee of the office of sheriff." Ch. 2, Art. V, Div. 6, §§2-193, 2-196, Orange County Code.

On November 5, 1996, a majority of the County's voters approved a charter amendment abolishing the charter office of sheriff, re-establishing the Sheriff as an independent constitutional officer, but leaving the CRB intact. This structure still exists, as it did when the events arose which relate to deputy Jenny, on May 7, 2004. On that day, Jenny was on duty, assigned to the Sheriff's Juvenile Arrest and Monitor Unit. He was investigating a complaint that J.M., a seventeen-year-old juvenile male on probation for aggravated assault with a deadly weapon, was in violation of his court-ordered curfew. Jenny ultimately arrested J.M. for the curfew violation, and J.M. later filed a complaint alleging that Jenny had used excessive force during the arrest. The Sheriff's Professional Standards Division investigated the complaint and determined that J.M.'s complaint was meritless.

After completion of the Sheriff's internal investigation, the CRB initiated its own independent investigation, issuing a subpoena to Jenny and ordering him to appear before the CRB for questioning by the entire board. Jenny contested the validity of the subpoena, filing a petition for emergency writ of prohibition or alternative petition for writ of certiorari and contending that the CRB lacked the power to subpoena him as a matter of law. This petition was rejected on procedural grounds, and the CRB served Jenny with a second subpoena. Jenny's counsel then appeared at the CRB hearing, again objecting to issuance of the subpoena and refusing to subject Jenny to questioning by the CRB. In response, the CRB filed an action in circuit court seeking to enforce its subpoena.

Independently, the Sheriff filed a complaint for declaratory judgment and supplemental relief, also challenging the CRB's authority to independently investigate J.M.'s complaint against Jenny. The two cases were consolidated, and decided on summary judgment in the order on appeal, which held that the CRB was authorized to independently investigate J.M.'s complaint against Jenny. This appeal followed.

Relevant Statutes

Pursuant to the Orange County Career Service Act, chapter 89-507, Laws of Florida, the Sheriff possesses the authority to receive, investigate, and dispose of complaints against his personnel. Section 30.53, Florida Statutes, also preserves the Sheriff's independence in selecting, retaining, or firing personnel and setting salaries. Finally, section 112.533 requires the Sheriff to establish and operate a system for receiving and investigating complaints against his deputies that fully complies with the procedures set forth in section 112.532, Florida Statutes. These latter statutes, together with the other provisions in part VI of chapter 112, are commonly referred to as the Law Enforcement Officer Bill of Rights. *Hinn v. Beary*, 701 So.2d 579, 580 (Fla. 5th DCA 1997).

Enacted in 1974, section 112.533 was amended in chapter 2003-149, Laws of Florida, which explains in the title that the procedure set forth in these statutes "shall be the *exclusive procedure* used by law enforcement and correctional agencies for investigation of complaints against law enforcement … officers." *Id.* (emphasis added). The amendment clarified that a law enforcement agency's internal investigation "shall be *the* procedure for investigating a complaint against a law enforcement and correctional officer and for determining whether to proceed with disciplinary action or to file disciplinary charges, *notwithstanding any other law or ordinance to the contrary*." § 112.533(1)(a), Fla. Stat. (2008) (emphasis added).[33]

In 2007, the statute was further amended to require "[a]ny political subdivision that initiates or receives a complaint against a law enforcement officer or correctional officer" to "forward the complaint to the employing agency of the officer who is the subject of the complaint for review or investigation" within five business days of initiating or receiving the complaint. Ch. 2007-110, Laws of Fla.; § 112.533(1)(b) 1., Fla. Stat. (2008). "Political subdivision" is expressly defined to include counties and any board, commission or other "agency or unit of local government created or established by law or ordinance" by a local government. § 112.533(1)(b) 2., Fla. Stat. (2008).

---

33. [FN 3.] The statute does, however, provide an express exception authorizing investigation by the Criminal Justice Standards and Training Commission. § 112.533(1)(a), Fla. Stat. (2008). In addition, the Florida Police Benevolent Association notes that allegations of excessive force and abuse or power against Florida law enforcement officers are subject to possible investigation by the state attorney's office, state grand jury, state criminal courts, Florida Department of Law Enforcement, Criminal Justice Standards and Training Commission, Federal Bureau of Investigations, United States Department of Justice, federal grand jury and federal criminal courts.

Legal Analysis

A. *Plain Meaning of Section 112.533, Florida Statutes.*

"[I]n construing a statute, the courts must 'look first to the statute's plain meaning.'" *Hennis v. City Tropics Bistro, Inc.*, 1 So.3d 1152, 1156 (Fla. 5th DCA 2009) (quoting *Moonlit Waters Apartments, Inc. v. Cauley*, 666 So.2d 898, 900 (Fla.1996))....

Section 112.533, as amended in 2003 and 2007, is unambiguous. It conveys a clear and definite directive that when a complaint is registered against a law enforcement officer, the employing agency is the only local governmental entity authorized to investigate that complaint. This is clear from: (1) the title language of chapter 2003-149, designating the investigation required by chapter 112 as the "exclusive procedure" for investigation; (2) the language added to section 112.533 in 2003, mandating that the investigation authorized by chapter 112 "shall be *the* procedure" for investigating complaints against local law enforcement "notwithstanding any other law or ordinance to the contrary;" and (3) the language added to section 112.533 in 2007, directing any local governmental entity that receives or initiates a complaint against a local law enforcement officer to forward it to the employing agency for investigation in accordance with chapter 112.

B. *Constitutional Limitation on the County's Authority.*

As previously noted, as a charter county, Orange County is constitutionally granted "all powers of local self government not inconsistent with general law," and may only enact ordinances "not inconsistent with general law." Art. VIII, Section 1(g), Fla. Const. The County is also prohibited from transferring any of the Sheriff's powers or duties to another county office, department or board, without abolishing the constitutional office of sheriff by charter. Art. VIII, § 1(d), Fla. Const.; *Kelly*, 99 So.2d at 858–59.

Based on these constitutional provisions, the question presented is whether the County charter and ordinance creating and authorizing an independent board to review citizen complaints against the Sheriff's deputies, without first abolishing the constitutional office of sheriff, is "inconsistent" with general law.[34] The answer seems clear to us in light of the plain language of section 112.533, Florida Statutes. Because section 112.533 limits the investigation of complaints against law enforcement officers by local government to the employing agency's investigation, the charter provisions and ordinance that establish an additional procedure for investigating these complaints necessarily and directly conflict with the statute.[35]

We have also considered the County's citation to *Timoney v. City of Miami Civilian Investigative Panel*, 990 So.2d 614 (Fla. 3d DCA 2008), and find that case equally unhelpful. *Timoney* dealt with a city police chief, a law enforcement officer expressly

---

34. [FN 5.] County charters and ordinances may be inconsistent with general law in two ways. "First, a county cannot legislate in a field if the subject area has been preempted to the State.... Second, in a field where both the State and local government can legislate concurrently, a county cannot enact an ordinance that directly conflicts with a state statute." *Phantom of Brevard, Inc. v. Brevard County*, 3 So.3d 309, 314 (Fla.2008).

35. [FN 6.] Based on our finding that the charter and ordinance directly conflict with the plain language of section 112.533, we need not conduct a separate preemption analysis.

exempted from the chapter 112 investigation. *See* § 112.531(1), Fla. Stat. (2008). Accordingly, from our reading of *Timoney,* it seems clear that the local board's authority to investigate a complaint in light of section 112.533 was never raised as an issue in that case. In fact, section 112.533 is neither cited nor discussed in *Timoney.*[36]

Finally, we note that the CRB's argument in defense of its authority merits no serious analysis. The CRB's argument is simply that it does not investigate complaints against the Sheriff's deputies. This argument completely ignores the record before us, as well as the CRB's own organic documents. Article VIII, section 801A, Orange County Charter, expressly charges the CRB with "*reviewing citizen complaints* and departmental investigations thereof *regarding the use of force or abuse of power by any officer or employee of the office of sheriff.*" (Emphasis added.) And, section 801B grants the CRB with subpoena and other powers for the express "purpose of conducting investigations pursuant to this section...."

C. *Other Problems with the CRB Charter Provision and Implementing Ordinances.*

As an independent constitutional officer, the Sheriff does not derive his authority from the County's charter or the board of county commissioners, and is neither generally accountable to the Board for his conduct in office nor subject to the board's direction in the fulfillment of his duties. Art. VIII, § 1(d), Fla. Const. In the event of misconduct or misfeasance by the Sheriff, it is Florida's governor who is authorized to suspend the Sheriff from office — and not the County's governing board. Art. IV, § 7(a), Fla. Const.[37] And, ultimately, the Sheriff is independently accountable to the electorate of Orange County. Art. VIII, § 1(d), Fla. Const.; *State v. Sheats,* 78 Fla. 583, 83 So. 508 (1919) (explaining that the term "office" as used in the Florida Constitution "implies a delegation of a portion of the sovereign power to, and the possession of it by, the person filling the office" or "independent authority of a governmental nature"). Given this constitutional framework, we also find that the County cannot interfere with the Sheriff's independent exercise of his duty to investigate misconduct by his deputies either by forcing him to appoint members to the CRB or by mandating his participation in CRB proceedings, either in person or through his deputies or employees. Therefore, we agree with the Sheriff that the basic structure or composition of the CRB is constitutionally infirm, and with Jenny that those provisions of the charter and ordinance authorizing the CRB to compel the attendance of Sheriff's employees to appear for questioning by the CRB, or to produce documents, are also unconstitutional.

---

36. [FN 8.] *Timoney* does contain language suggesting that nothing in chapter 112 prohibits an "independent, external investigation" by a local governing board of a complaint against a law enforcement officer. If this was an intended conclusion in *Timoney,* we believe it to be in error — as inconsistent with the plain language of section 112.533. Again, however, the argument based upon section 112.533 does not appear to have been made in *Timoney.* Additionally, *Timoney* did not involve the relationship between a local governmental body and an independent constitutional officer. Rather, that case involved a city's authority to investigate its own employee.

37. [FN 9.] The Senate is authorized to remove a suspended county officer from office. Art. IV, § 7(b), Fla. Const.

D. *Doctrine of Severance and Relief Required.*

"Severability is a judicial doctrine recognizing the obligation of the judiciary to uphold the constitutionality of legislative enactments where it is possible to strike only the unconstitutional portions." *Ray v. Mortham*, 742 So.2d 1276, 1280 (Fla.1999). In this case, we have carefully considered the four-part test applied to determine whether portions of a statute or ordinance that have been declared unconstitutional may be severed from the rest. *See Cramp v. Bd. of Pub. Instruction of Orange County*, 137 So.2d 828, 830 (Fla.1962). Given the number of significant constitutional infirmities with the charter provision creating the CRB, and the ordinance implementing that provision, we simply see no practical way to sever out any part of the provision — and therefore declare article VIII, section 801 of the Orange County Charter, along with the ordinance implementing this charter provision, to be void as violative of article VIII, sections (1)(d) and (1)(g) of the Florida Constitution.

Our conclusion that no part of the charter provision at issue can be salvaged is also influenced by the fact that article VIII, section 801 was added to the charter in tandem with the charter amendment abolishing the constitutional office of sheriff and creating a department of sheriff as part of the charter government. As previously discussed, that department was subsequently abolished by the voters of Orange County when they restored the constitutional office of Sheriff. Therefore, the department referred to in article VIII, section 801 — whose investigations the CRB is authorized to review — no longer exists. However, we note that we see no reason why a county cannot comment upon a sheriff's exercise of any constitutional duty affecting the county's citizens, either through its board or with input from an independent board or commission. Nor do we see any constitutional impediment that would prohibit a county board from reviewing public records or considering testimony from anyone volunteering to appear and discuss issues related to the discharge of any responsibility entrusted to a constitutional sheriff by law. Therefore, in theory, we see no reason why the County could not create a board with more limited power to review and comment upon internal investigations conducted by the Sheriff. But, we will not speculate, in a vacuum, about how such a board might work, or the extent of the powers it could be granted without unconstitutionally interfering with the Sheriff's independent authority. In this case, it suffices to say that the charter provision before us so far exceeds the scope of that allowed by current law that it cannot stand.

Conclusion

For the reasons set forth above, we reverse the order on appeal and remand for entry of judgment consistent with this opinion.

REVERSED.

GRIFFIN and EVANDER, JJ., concur.

Article IX

Education

Introduction

Article IX outlines the structure and lines of authority in Florida's vast public education system. The state has the obligation to maintain free public schools available to the citizens of Florida. Local school boards then operate the public schools. At the top of the system, a board of governors directs the state university system to which university trustees report.

Each of Florida's six constitutions has featured some provision related to education.[1] As the following cases discuss, the Constitutions of 1838, 1861 and 1865 did not con-

---

1. *See* FLA. CONST. OF 1838, art. X, §§ 1, 2; FLA. CONST. OF 1861, art. X, §§ 1, 2; FLA. CONST. OF 1865, art. 10, §§ 1, 2; FLA. CONST. OF 1868, art. VIII, §§ 1, 2; FLA. CONST. OF 1885, art. XII, § 1; FLA. CONST. OF 1968, art. IX, § 1; *see also* TALBOT D'ALEMBERTE, THE FLORIDA STATE CONSTITUTION: A REFERENCE GUIDE (1991).

tain any constitutional standards or requirements, but focused on funding schools using proceeds of lands dedicated by Congress to support public education. The 1868 Constitution, however, greatly expanded the education article and included a declaration in Article VIII, Section 1, that it was the "paramount duty of the State to make ample provision for education." The 1868 Constitution also introduced the requirement for a "uniform system of common schools."[2] The 1885 Constitution abolished the "paramount duty" language, but retained the uniform system requirement.[3] In full, the 1885 section provided: "The Legislature shall provide for a uniform system of public free schools, and shall provide for the liberal maintenance of the same."[4]

When the 1968 Constitution was first adopted, the "uniform system" requirement was included along with the requirement that "adequate provision be made by law" for its support. The following cases explore the meaning of the terms "uniform system" and "adequate provision" as used in Article IX, Section 1.

A. Article IX, Section 1 — Public Education

i. Uniformity

Early education litigation in Florida focused on the meaning and extent of the "uniform system" requirement in the Education Article. The first case to do so, *State ex rel. Clark v. Henderson*, 137 Fla. 666, 188 So. 351 (1939), examined the Education Clause under the 1885 Constitution, and found that the "uniform system" requirement required public schools that were "established upon principles that are of uniform operation throughout the state and that such system be liberally maintained." *Id.* at 352. The Supreme Court noted in *Henderson* that "the purpose intended to be accomplished in establishing" the uniform system of free public schools was "to advance and maintain proper standards of enlightened citizenship." *Id.* at 353. In the 1970s, a series of cases involving the levy of local discretionary millage came before the Court which implicated the "uniform system" of public schools. In one of these, *School Bd. of Escambia County v. State*, 353 So. 2d 834, 838 (Fla. 1977), the Supreme Court expanded its definition of uniformity, holding that "by definition ... a uniform system results when the constituent parts, although unequal in number, operate subject to a common plan or serve a common purpose."

The following case further explores the uniform system requirement, and also addresses the question of whether local school boards may provide additional funding for public education.

---

2. FLA. CONST. OF 1868, art. VIII, § 2.
3. FLA. CONST. OF 1885, art. XII, § 1.
4. *Id.*

St. Johns County v. Northeast Florida Builders Ass'n

583 So. 2d 635 (Fla. 1991)

GRIMES, Justice.

We review *St. Johns County v. Northeast Florida Builders Association*, 559 So.2d 363 (Fla. 5th DCA 1990), in which the district court of appeal certified as a question of great public importance the question of whether St. Johns County could impose an impact fee on new residential construction to be used for new school facilities. We have jurisdiction under article V, section 3(b)(4) of the Florida Constitution.

In 1986, St. Johns County initiated a comprehensive study of whether to impose impact fees to finance additional infrastructure required to serve new growth and development. At the request of the St. Johns County School Board, the county included educational facilities impact fees within the scope of the study. In August of 1987, the county's consultant, Dr. James Nicholas, submitted a methodology report setting forth what action the county could take to maintain an acceptable level of service for public facilities. The report calculated the cost of educational facilities needed to provide sufficient school capacity to serve the estimated new growth and development and suggested a method of allocating that cost to each unit of new residential development. As a consequence, on October 20, 1987, the county enacted the St. Johns County Educational Facilities Impact Fee Ordinance.

The ordinance specifies that no new building permits[5] will be issued except upon the payment of an impact fee. The fees are to be placed in a trust fund to be spent by the school board solely to "acquire, construct, expand and equip the educational sites and educational capital facilities necessitated by new development." St. Johns County, Fla., Ordinance 87-60, § 10(B) (Oct. 20, 1987). Any funds not expended within six years, together with interest, will be returned to the current landowner upon application. The ordinance also provides credits to feepayers for land dedications and construction of educational facilities. The ordinance recites that it is applicable in both unincorporated and incorporated areas of the county, except that it is not effective within the boundaries of any municipality until the municipality enters into an interlocal agreement with the county to collect the impact fees.

The Northeast Florida Builders Association together with a private developer (builders) filed suit against the county and its county administrator (county) seeking a declaratory judgment that the ordinance was unconstitutional. The opposing sides each filed a motion for summary judgment. The trial court entered summary judgment for the builders, declaring the ordinance to be unconstitutional on a variety of grounds. In a split decision, the district court of appeal affirmed, holding that the ordinance violated the constitutional mandate for a uniform system of free public schools.

---

5. [FN1.] The ordinance applies to residential building permits, permits for residential mobile home installations, and permits to make improvements to land reasonably expected to place additional students in St. Johns County public schools.

This Court upheld the imposition of impact fees to pay for the expansion of water and sewer facilities in *Contractors & Builders Association v. City of Dunedin*, 329 So.2d 314 (Fla.1976). We stated:

> Raising expansion capital by setting connection charges, which do not exceed a pro rata share of reasonably anticipated costs of expansion, is permissible where expansion is reasonably required, if use of the money collected is limited to meeting the costs of expansion.

Id. at 320. In essence, we approved the imposition of impact fees that meet the requirements of the dual rational nexus test adopted by other courts in evaluating impact fees. *See* Juergensmeyer & Blake, *Impact Fees: An Answer to Local Governments' Capital Funding Dilemma*, 9 Fla. St. U. L. Rev. 415 (1981). This test was explained in *Hollywood, Inc. v. Broward County*, 431 So.2d 606, 611–12 (Fla. 4th DCA), *review denied*, 440 So.2d 352 (Fla.1983), as follows:

> In order to satisfy these requirements, the local government must demonstrate a reasonable connection, or rational nexus, between the need for additional capital facilities and the growth in population generated by the subdivision. In addition, the government must show a reasonable connection, or rational nexus, between the expenditures of the funds collected and the benefits accruing to the subdivision. In order to satisfy this latter requirement, the ordinance must specifically earmark the funds collected for use in acquiring capital facilities to benefit the new residents.

The use of impact fees has become an accepted method of paying for public improvements that must be constructed to serve new growth. *See Home Builders & Contractors Ass'n v. Board of County Comm'rs*, 446 So.2d 140 (Fla. 4th DCA 1983) (road impact fees upheld), *review denied*, 451 So.2d 848 (Fla.), *appeal dismissed*, 469 U.S. 976 (1984); *Hollywood, Inc. v. Broward County*, 431 So.2d at 606 (park impact fees upheld). However, the propriety of imposing impact fees to finance new schools is an issue of first impression in Florida.

[The Court first found that the impact fee failed the dual rational nexus test, because a substantial portion of the county was not subject to the fee.]

The builders also contend that the ordinance violates article IX, section 1 of the Florida Constitution, which provides:

> SECTION 1. System of public education.—Adequate provision shall be made by law for a uniform system of free public schools and for the establishment, maintenance and operation of institutions of higher learning and other public education programs that the needs of the people may require.

Insofar as the constitution provides for "free public schools," it is clear that no student may be required to pay tuition as a condition of being admitted into school. Of course, this does not mean that the students' parents are exempt from paying any of the costs of maintaining the school system. Obviously, property owners who have children pay ad valorem taxes, portions of which pay for schools. The mandate of free public schools insures that students' access to public schools is not dependent upon the payment of any fees or charges. Under the schedule of charges in the St.

Johns County ordinance, the payment of the impact fees is unrelated to school attendance. Thus, to the extent that the impact fee is imposed upon each dwelling unit,
we see no violation of the constitutional imperative of free schools.

The builders point out, however, that the feepayer is given an alternative to paying
the impact fee set forth in the uniform schedule of fees. Thus, section 7 of the ordinance provides in part:

> B. If a feepayer opts not to have the impact fee determined according to para-
> graph (A) of this section, then the feepayer shall prepare and submit to the
> St. Johns County School Board an independent fee calculation study for the
> land development activity for which a building permit or permit for mobile
> home installation is sought. The student generation and/or educational im-
> pact documentation submitted shall show the basis upon which the inde-
> pendent fee calculation was made. The St. Johns County School Board may
> adjust the educational facilities impact fee to that deemed to be appropriate
> given the documentation submitted by the fee payer. The County Adminis-
> trator shall make the appropriate modification upon notice of such adjust-
> ment from the School Board.

St. Johns County, Fla., Ordinance 87-60 (Oct. 20, 1987). Dr. Nicholas stated that
under section 7(B), the developer of an adult retirement living facility could avoid
the payment of the impact fee because no children would be living in the facility. He
also said that property owners who warranted that their children would attend private
school could be exempt upon the understanding that if a school child later occupied
the home, the fee would have to be paid. He acknowledged that childless couples
could also obtain an exemption under the same warranty. Thus, in a very real way
the alternative mechanism of determining the impact fee under section 7(B) permits
households that do not contain public school children to avoid paying the fee. This
means that the impact fees have the potential of being user fees that will be paid primarily by those households that do contain public school children, thereby colliding
with the constitutional requirement of free public schools.

The county asks that if we conclude that section 7(B) has the effect of converting
the educational facilities impact fee into a user fee, the offending section be severed
in order to preserve the validity of the balance of the ordinance. The ordinance contains a severability clause. A legislatively expressed preference for severability of voided
clauses, although not binding, is highly persuasive. *State v. Champe*, 373 So.2d 874,
880 (Fla. 1978). Severance of section 7(B) will not impair the operation or effectiveness
of the ordinance. Further, the severance of section 7(B) will not affect the stated purpose or intent of the ordinance, which reads:

> *Section Three: Intents and Purposes*
>
> A. This ordinance is intended to assist in the implementation of the St. Johns
> County Comprehensive Plan.
>
> B. The purpose of this ordinance is to regulate the use and development of
> land so as to assure that new development bears a proportionate share of the

cost of capital expenditures necessary to provide public educational sites and facilities in St. Johns County.

St. Johns County, Fla., Ordinance 87-60 (Oct. 20, 1987). We believe the ordinance, absent section 7(B), constitutes a workable scheme within the legislative intent.[6] *See Eastern Air Lines, Inc. v. Department of Revenue*, 455 So.2d 311, 317 (Fla.1984) (severance appropriate if legislative intent can be accomplished absent invalid portions and if remainder of law is not rendered incomplete by severance), *appeal dismissed*, 474 U.S. 892 (1985); *State ex rel. Boyd v. Green*, 355 So.2d 789 (Fla.1978) (test for severability is whether portion to be stricken is of such import that remainder would be incomplete or would cause results not contemplated by the legislative body).

The builders further contend that the ordinance conflicts with the requirement of a "uniform system" of public schools contained in article IX, section 1 of the Florida Constitution. In *School Board v. State*, 353 So.2d 834 (Fla.1977), this Court rejected the thought that the constitutional provision required uniformity in physical plant or curriculum from county to county. To the contrary, the Court said:

> By definition, then, a uniform system results when the constituent parts ... operate subject to a common plan or serve a common purpose.

Id. at 838. We see nothing in this section of the constitution that mandates uniform sources of school funding among the several counties. In fact, it could be argued that educational facilities impact fees are themselves a vehicle for achieving a uniform system of free public schools because in rapidly growing counties ordinary funding sources may not be sufficient to meet the demand for new facilities. We further note that the legislature must contemplate that the uniform system of free public schools may be funded by a variety of sources, including county funds because section 236.24(1), Florida Statutes (1989), provides:

> (1) The district school fund shall consist of funds derived from the district school tax levy; state appropriations; *appropriations by county commissioners*; local, state, and federal school food service funds; any and all other sources for school purposes; national forest trust funds and other federal sources; and gifts and other sources.

(Emphasis added.) Sections 236.012(4) and 236.35, Florida Statutes (1989), also suggest that the legislature did not intend to limit the financing alternatives available to individual school districts or counties.

The builders' reliance upon *Brown v. City of Lakeland*, 61 Fla. 508, 54 So. 716 (1911), is misplaced. This case held that the legislature could not authorize municipalities to issue bonds for the purpose of erecting schools that would be paid by a municipal tax levy. However, the provisions of the 1885 constitution upon which the Court predicated its decision have not been carried forward into our present constitution.

---

6. [FN6.] We would not find objectionable a provision that exempted from the payment of an impact fee permits to build adult facilities in which, because of land use restrictions, minors could not reside. *See White Egret Condominium, Inc. v. Franklin*, 379 So.2d 346 (Fla.1979).

The Florida Constitution only requires that a system be provided that gives every student an equal chance to achieve basic educational goals prescribed by the legislature. The constitutional mandate is not that every school district in the state must receive equal funding nor that each educational program must be equivalent. Inherent inequities, such as varying revenues because of higher or lower property values or differences in millage assessments, will always favor or disfavor some districts. We hold that the ordinance does not violate the requirement of a uniform system of public schools. *See Penn v. Pensacola-Escambia Governmental Center Auth.*, 311 So.2d 97 (Fla.1975) (even if city or county funds benefitted the capital needs of the school board, there would be no violation of article IX).

We also reject the builders' contention that the county is preempted by the constitution and by state law from enacting the ordinance. The builders' argument is twofold. First, they claim that the ordinance interjects the county into an area in which school boards have been given exclusive authority by constitution and by statute. Because school boards have the authority to tax under article IX, section 4(b) of the Florida Constitution, the builders reason, counties and school boards must be fiscally independent of each other. They also assert that under section 230.23(10)(a), Florida Statutes (1989) (School Boards shall "arrange for the levying of district school taxes necessary to provide the amount needed from district sources."), school boards have exclusive authority to secure financing of public schools through appropriate channels. Second, the builders argue that the pervasive legislative control of various aspects of school financing evinces an intent that the legislative scheme be the sole mechanism for funding school construction.

We do not agree. Article VIII, section 1(f), provides:

The board of county commissioners of a county not operating under a charter may enact, in a manner prescribed by general law, county ordinances not inconsistent with general or special law....

(Emphasis added.) The implementing statute, section 125.01(1), Florida Statutes (1989), provides the governing body of a county with home-rule power, unless the legislature has preempted a particular subject by general or special law. *Speer v. Olson*, 367 So.2d 207, 210–11 (Fla.1979). The provisions of section 125.01 are to be liberally construed "in order to ... secure for the counties the broad exercise of home rule powers authorized by the State Constitution." Section 125.01(3)(b), Fla. Stat. (1989).

We do not find the ordinance inconsistent with the constitutional and statutory provisions cited by the builders. First, article IX, section 4(b) is only a grant of taxing authority to the school boards. It does not limit the imposition of a fee such as the one at issue here. Nor does that provision in any way limit county involvement in school financing. Further, section 230.23 does not place the exclusive duty to secure adequate public school financing with school boards. Finally, nothing in the legislative scheme regarding education finance suggests a legislative intent to preempt county involvement in the financing of public schools. To the contrary, various statutes make clear that the legislature contemplated county involvement in educational funding. *See* §§ 236.012(4), 236.24(1), 236.35, Fla. Stat. (1989). Even the Local Government Comprehensive Planning and Land Development Regulation Act contemplates that counties should become involved in facilitating the adequate and efficient provision of schools. Section 163.3161(3), Fla. Stat. (1989).

Finally, we conclude that the ordinance does not create an unlawful delegation of power. The county determines the amount of the fees and collects them. The money is placed in a separate trust fund. The school board may only spend the funds for the new educational facilities prescribed by the ordinance. The school board must make annual accountings of its expenditure of the funds to the county. There has been no unlawful delegation of power because the fundamental policy decisions have been made by the county, and the discretion of the school board has been sufficiently limited. *See Brown v. Apalachee Regional Planning Council*, 560 So.2d 782 (Fla.1990).

We quash the decision below and uphold the validity of the ordinance upon the severance of section 7(B) therefrom. However, no impact fee may be collected under the ordinance until the second prong of the dual rational nexus test has been met.

It is so ordered.

SHAW, C.J., and OVERTON, McDONALD, BARKETT, KOGAN and HARDING, JJ., concur.

Questions

1. a. How does the term "free public schools" restrict the collection of monies for education?

   b. Why did the Court conclude that section 7B of the ordinance was unconstitutional?

2. a. How can the state meet the requirement of providing a "uniform system" of public schools?

   b. Is this standard quantifiable? If so, how?

3. According to the Court, in which instances would an impact fee be an effective way to promote a uniform system of free public schools?

In 1993, the Court revisited Article IX, Section 1's uniform system requirement in *Department of Education v. Glasser*, 622 So. 2d 944 (Fla. 1993). *Glasser* involved an attempt by a school board to increase discretionary ad valorem taxes without legislative authorization. *Id.* at 946–47. The legislature had set the maximum amount of discretionary millage that school districts could levy under the state's Florida Education Finance Program. *Id.* at 948. The Court found that the school board violated Article VII, Section 9(a), Florida Constitution, which requires legislative authorization for the imposition of any new taxes. *Id.* at 946–47. The Court also rejected arguments that its decision in *Northeast Florida Builders* allowed school boards to provide any level of support as long as legislatively adopted education goals were met. *Id.* at 947. The Court stated that it was not required to explicitly define "a uniform system of free public schools," as used in Article IX, Section 1, but that this was for the Legislature to do. *Id.* In support of the Florida Education Finance Program, the court added:

The right to education is basic in a democracy. Without it, neither the student nor the state has a future. Our legislature annually implements a complicated formula to fund this basic right. We find that the legislation at issue here, which is part of the overall funding formula, is in harmony with the Florida Constitution.

Id. at 948–49 (citation omitted). The result of these two decisions, according to Justice Kogan, concurring specially in *Glasser*, is that:

Florida law now is clear that the uniformity clause will not be construed as tightly restrictive, but merely establishing a larger framework in which a broad degree of variation is possible.... [V]ariance from county to county is permissible so long as no district suffers a disadvantage in the basic educational opportunities available to its students, as compared to the basic educational opportunities available to students of other Florida districts.

Id. at 950 (Kogan, J., concurring). Justice Kogan went on to state that differences among districts in the ability to offer "Latin or painting classes" would not create "lack of uniformity," but the inability of a district to fund any language or mathematics classes would indeed amount to lack of uniformity. *Id.* at 951 (Kogan, J., concurring) ("The Legislature cannot allow students in one district to be deprived of basic educational opportunities while students in other districts do not suffer the same."). The uniformity requirement of Article IX, Section 1, thus does not require public schools to deliver equal service to each student or to spend equally. Rather, because "uniform" has been defined as a "common plan or purpose," the duty to each student is a substantially equal chance at an education.

ii. Adequacy

The other focus of litigation in Article IX, Section 1 has been the requirement that the Legislature make "adequate provision" for the system of public education in Florida. The first case, *Coalition for Adequacy & Fairness in School Funding v. Chiles*, 680 So. 2d 400 (Fla. 1996), involved a challenge to the overall adequacy of the state education system. In *Coalition*, the Court was looking at the original wording of Article IX, Section 1 (prior to the CRC amendment in 1998). Note the result in this case. Note also the division of the judges as to whether the question of adequacy is even justiciable by the courts.

Coalition for Adequacy & Fairness in School Funding v. Chiles
680 So. 2d 400 (Fla. 1996)

PER CURIAM.

In a one-count complaint, appellants sought declaratory relief against the appellees and asked the trial court to declare that an adequate education is a fundamental right under the Florida Constitution, and that the State has failed to provide its students that fundamental right by failing to allocate adequate resources for a uniform system of free public schools as provided for in the Florida Constitution. In support of their action, appellants alleged: (1) Certain students are not receiving adequate programs to permit them to gain proficiency in the English language; (2) Economically deprived students are not receiving adequate education for their greater educational needs; (3) Gifted, disabled, and mentally handicapped children are not receiving adequate special programs; (4) Students in property-poor counties are not receiving an adequate education; (5) Education capital outlay needs are not adequately provided for; and (6) School districts are unable to perform their constitutional duties because of the legislative imposition of noneducational and quasi-educational burdens.

The trial court dismissed the complaint with prejudice.[7] Upon appeal, all parties filed a joint suggestion that the First District certify this case to be one of great public importance requiring immediate resolution by this Court. The First District certified this case to this Court and we granted jurisdiction pursuant to the provisions of article V, section 3(b)(5) of the Florida Constitution. While not agreeing with all of the reasons advanced by the trial court, we affirm the order of dismissal.

PARTIES AND STANDING

Appellants assert that the trial court erred in ruling that they had not sufficiently alleged a jurisdictional basis for an action against the defendants in this suit. We agree. See Florida Dep't of Educ. v. Glasser, 622 So.2d 944, 948 (Fla.1993)(declaratory action relating to State's role in education should join "all persons who have an actual, present, adverse, and antagonistic interest in the subject matter"). With the exception of the Governor who, with the consent of appellants, did not file a response in the trial court, all of the named appellees have either taken a present, adverse, and antagonistic position to that espoused by appellants or would be necessary parties to an action to determine the State's responsibility under the controlling constitutional provision. We agree that the Governor, both in his position as chief executive officer and as chairperson of the Board of Education, is an appropriate party because of the nature of the action.

---

7. [FN2.] In denying appellants relief, the trial court made the following findings: (1) To grant relief, the trial court would have to usurp or intrude upon the appropriation power exclusively reserved to the legislature; (2) The instant claim presents a non-justiciable political question; (3) Adequate provision as expressed under article IX, section 1, of the Florida Constitution cannot refer to "adequate" funding; (4) The alleged facts do not show a substantial inequality of education funding among school districts; (5) The appellant coalition and the school boards are not "persons" protected under article I, section 9 of the Florida Constitution; (6) The school children have not shown that the funding formula is not rationally related either to the charge of providing a uniform system of free public education or to the general health, safety, and welfare of Florida citizens; (7) Florida's Constitution does not create a fundamental right to a particular level of funding; (8) There are no allegations which indicate discrimination of a suspect class which would justify reviewing the legislature's education policy under a strict scrutiny test; (9) Appellants have failed to state a claim under article IX, section 6 of the Florida Constitution; (10) Appellants have failed to state a claim under article X, section 15 of the Florida Constitution; (11) Appellants have failed to state a claim against the Speaker of the House and President of the Senate.

We also agree that the Florida Senate and the Florida House of Representatives, acting through their respective presiding officers, are proper parties.... We find no jurisdictional flaw in appellants' joining the House and Senate by including the presiding officers of those bodies in their respective capacities. Even if the House and Senate were required to be joined in some other manner, this would not be a basis for a dismissal with prejudice.

The trial court also questioned the standing of appellants to bring this action. This Court has held that "a citizen and taxpayer can challenge the constitutional validity of an exercise of the legislature's taxing and spending power without having to demonstrate a special injury." *Chiles v. Children A, B, C, D, E & F*, 589 So.2d 260, 262 n. 5 (Fla.1991). Furthermore, in Florida, unlike the federal system, the doctrine of standing has not been rigidly followed. *Department of Revenue v. Kuhnlein*, 646 So.2d 717, 720 (Fla.1994), *cert. denied*, 515 U.S. 1158 (1995). Based on the allegations in this complaint, we conclude that all of the appellants have standing.[8]

DECLARATORY RELIEF

Appellants' request for declaratory judgment is fully consistent with several recent decisions of this Court. *See, e.g., Chiles v. Children A, B, C, D, E, & F*, 589 So.2d 260 (Fla.1991) (accepting jurisdiction over complaint for declaratory relief by children seeking to declare certain provisions of budgetary scheme unconstitutional); *Martinez v. Scanlan*, 582 So.2d 1167 (Fla.1991) (accepting jurisdiction in declaratory action to resolve dispute between various groups and Governor over validity of workers' compensation laws); *Department of Revenue v. Kuhnlein*, 646 So.2d 717 (Fla.1994) (granting declaratory relief in action brought by residents alleging that rights under Commerce Clause were being infringed by illegal impact fee), *cert. denied*, 515 U.S. 1158 (1995).

As we recently explained in *Santa Rosa County v. Administration Commission, Division of Administrative Hearings*, "[t]he purpose of a declaratory judgment is to afford parties relief from insecurity and uncertainty with respect to rights, status, and other equitable or legal relations." 661 So.2d 1190, 1192 (Fla.1995)....

---

8. [FN4.] The trial court found that neither the school boards nor the coalition are "'natural persons' within the meaning of [article 1, section 2 of the Florida Constitution] ... [and] [w]hile the plaintiff school children and parents of school children are natural persons, they allege no facts showing that they have been deprived of any right guaranteed them by law because of race, religion or physical handicap; nor any facts showing that they are in a class treated differently from other classes without rational relationship to legitimate state goals."

There is no question that this case involves a controversy that would have a direct impact on Florida children. The eleven public school students have alleged that they are suffering a continuing injury as a result of being denied an adequate education. We also recognize their parents' standing as natural parents and guardians of the students.

The school boards claim standing to challenge a constitutional violation which renders them unable to adequately discharge their duties. In *Reid v. Kirk* we said, "standing is allowed when a public official is willing to perform his duties, but is prevented from doing so by others." 257 So.2d 3, 4 (Fla.1972). Because the school boards are allegedly prevented from carrying out their statutory duties, we agree that they have standing to litigate this matter. While we question the standing of the coalition, we need not discuss that issue because of the standing of the other plaintiffs.

Applying these legal principles to this case, we conclude that the instant case properly seeks declaratory relief.

OTHER JURISDICTIONS

Appellants urge us to examine cases from jurisdictions which have considered allegations of failure to ensure constitutional rights to adequate education and have defined adequacy in particular factual contexts. Appellants cite a number of cases where courts have rejected the notion that the judiciary lacks jurisdiction to perform any inquiry into state funding of education. Some have held that the state had failed to meet the constitutional requirements imposed by that state's constitution, while others have rejected such attacks.[9] While the views of other courts are always helpful, we conclude that the dispute here must be resolved on the basis of Florida constitutional law and the relevant provisions of the Florida Constitution.

---

9. FN5. For example, in *Washakie County School District v. Herschler*, 606 P.2d 310, 314 (Wyo.), *cert. denied*, 449 U.S. 824 (1980), the school districts, school board members, and students brought an action seeking declaratory judgment that the state system of financing public education was unconstitutional because state funding was conditioned upon the wealth of the taxpaying ability of the local school district. *Id.* at 321. Since this system created a wealth-based classification, the court reviewed the matter under a strict-scrutiny standard. *Id.* at 333. After applying the strict-scrutiny test, the court held that the Wyoming system of funding education failed to meet this standard. *Id.* Thus, the *Washakie* court found the state educational funding system unconstitutional because it violated that state's equal protection provision. *Id.* at 334.

On the other hand, the Supreme Court of Kentucky found the state's school system unconstitutional, not on equal protection grounds, but because it violated Kentucky's constitutional requirement for an efficient system of common schools. *Rose v. Council for Better Educ.*, 790 S.W.2d 186, 212 (Ky.1989). In finding that the Kentucky school system fell short of the constitutionally mandated standard of an "efficient" school system, the court looked at evidence which revealed that Kentucky's school system was underfunded, inadequate, and fraught with inequalities and inequities. *Id.* at 196. Likewise, the Alabama Supreme Court found that Alabama's system of elementary and secondary education was unconstitutional because it violated both the equal protection clause and the education article of Alabama's constitution. *Opinion of the Justices*, 624 So.2d 107, 110 (Ala.1993). In several other jurisdictions, courts have reversed dismissals and remanded for lower courts to determine whether the states' educational systems were constitutional. For example, in Idaho the supreme court reversed a dismissal in a lower court because the plaintiffs (citizens/taxpayers, school districts, superintendents, and superintendents' association) had "stated a valid cause of action in alleging that the current funding system did not provide a thorough education." *Idaho Schools for Equal Educ. Opportunity v. Evans*, 123 Idaho 573, 850 P.2d 724, 734 (1993); *see also Claremont School Dist. v. Governor*, 138 N.H. 183, 635 A.2d 1375 (1993); *Pauley v. Kelly*, 162 W.Va. 672, 255 S.E.2d 859 (1979).

In contrast, in Ohio, the court upheld the constitutionality of its school system. *Board of Educ. v. Walter*, 58 Ohio St.2d 368, 390 N.E.2d 813 (1979), *cert. denied*, 444 U.S. 1015 (1980). In so doing, the Supreme Court of Ohio found that the rational basis standard applied because "the case is more directly connected with the way in which Ohio has decided to collect and spend state and local taxes than it is a challenge to the way in which Ohio educates its children." *Id.* 390 N.E.2d at 818. The Court found that local control was a rational basis that supported Ohio's school financing system, and the system therefore withstood the challenge and was declared constitutional. *Id.* 390 N.E.2d at 819. Similarly, North Carolina courts have rejected attacks on its school system under the education article of the North Carolina constitution. *Leandro v. North Carolina Bd. of Educ.*, 468 S.E.2d 543 (N.C. 1996).

EDUCATION ARTICLE

This dispute turns on the meaning of the education article of the Florida Constitution and the respective roles of each branch of government in carrying out the mandate of that article. Article IX, section 1 of the Florida Constitution provides:

Adequate provision shall be made by law for a uniform system of free public schools and for the establishment, maintenance and operation of institutions of higher learning and other public education programs that the needs of the people may require.

(Emphasis added). We must analyze the plain meaning of the term "adequacy" by reviewing the historical evolution of Florida's education article. The constitutions of 1838, 1861, and 1865 all contained almost identical education articles.[10] It was not until 1868 that the legislature significantly expanded this constitutional provision. In 1868, the constitution was amended to provide in article VIII, sections 1 and 2:

It is the *paramount* duty of the State to make ample provision for the education of all the children residing within its borders, without distinction or preference.

The Legislature shall provide a uniform system of Common schools, and a University, and shall provide for the liberal maintenance of the same. Instruction in them shall be free.

(Emphasis added.) By this change, education became the "paramount duty of the State" and required the State to make "ample provision for the education of all the children."[11] In 1885, the phrase "paramount duty" was deleted from the education article. Subsequently, in 1968, the education article underwent another revision.

---

10. [FN6.] In its entirety the education article of the 1838 constitution stated:

1. The proceeds of all lands that have been, or may hereafter be, granted by the United States for the use of schools, and a seminary or seminaries of learning, shall be and remain a perpetual fund, the interest of which, together with all moneys derived from any other source applicable to the same object, shall be inviolably appropriated to the use of schools and seminaries of learning respectively, and to no other purpose.

2. The general assembly shall take such measures as may be necessary to preserve from waste or damage all land so granted and appropriated to the purpose of education.

Art. X, Fla. Const. (1838). The education provisions of the 1861 and 1865 constitutions were substantially the same. Art. X, Fla. Const. (1865); Art. X, Fla. Const. (1861).

11. [FN7.] In order to understand the significance of this change, we must first determine the level of duty imposed on the legislative branch by the use of these words. Several scholars, who have analyzed state education clauses, have developed a four-category system. By using this category system, they attempt to measure the level of duty imposed on the state legislature. For instance, a Category I clause merely requires that a system of "free public schools" be provided. A Category II clause imposes some minimum standard of quality that the State must provide. A Category III clause requires "stronger and more specific education mandate[s] and purpose preambles." And, a Category IV clause imposes a maximum duty on the State to provide for education. Barbara J. Staros, *School Finance Litigation in Florida: A Historical Analysis*, 23 Stetson L. Rev. 497, 498–99 (1994). Using this rating system, Florida's education clause in 1868 imposed a Category IV duty on the legislature—a maximum duty on the State to provide for education. In addition, it also imposed a duty on the legislature to

Still unanswered is the level of duty the present education clause places upon the legislature to ensure a certain quality of education in Florida. As the trial court correctly noted, "[t]here is no textually demonstrable guidance in Article IX, section 1, by which the courts may decide, a priori, whether a given overall level of state funds is 'adequate,' in the abstract." Although the term "adequate provision" has not been defined, several Florida cases have attempted to define the second phrase in this clause, "uniform system of free public education."

The earliest case to define "uniform system" under the education article of the 1885 constitution was *State ex rel. Clark v. Henderson*, 137 Fla. 666, 188 So. 351 (1939), where we said:

> [A uniform system] ... means that a system of public free schools, as distinguished from the authorized State educational institutions, shall be established upon principles that are of uniform operation throughout the State and that such system shall be liberally maintained.

Id. 188 So. at 352. Subsequently, in *School Board of Escambia County v. State*, 353 So.2d 834 (Fla.1977), this Court defined "uniform system" as one where "the constituent parts, although unequal in number, operate subject to a common plan or serve a common purpose." *Id.* at 837. We also noted that nothing within this constitutional phrase required that all school districts have an equal number of board members or uniformity in physical plant or curriculum from county to county.

In *St. Johns County v. Northeast Florida Builders Ass'n*, 583 So.2d 635 (Fla.1991), this Court again reviewed the education article. In that case, a builders' association and a private developer brought a suit against St. Johns County claiming that an ordinance which imposed an impact fee on new residential construction for new school facilities violated the education article. In rejecting this claim, our opinion declared:

> The Florida Constitution only requires that a system be provided that gives every student an equal chance to achieve basic educational goals prescribed by the legislature. The constitutional mandate is not that every school district in the state must receive equal funding nor that each educational program must be equivalent. Inherent inequities, such as varying revenues because of higher or lower property values or difference in millage assessments, will always favor or disfavor some districts.

Id. at 641. More recently, in *Florida Department of Education v. Glasser*, 622 So.2d 944 (Fla.1993), we declined to more specifically define "a uniform system of free public schools." In so doing, we reasoned that the legislature should be the one to

---

provide for a uniform system of education. Under the same system, Florida's present educational clause would be a Category II. That is, in Florida, the legislature is required to provide some minimum level of quality in education. *Id.* at 498.

initially give this phrase its meaning. *Id.* at 947. Justice Kogan's concurring opinion summarized the education uniformity clause under this framework:

> The uniformity clause is not and never was intended to require that each school district be a mirror image of every other one. Such a goal is clearly impossible on a practical level, and the constitution should not be read to require an impossibility.
>
> Moreover, Florida law now is clear that the uniformity clause will not be construed as tightly restrictive, but merely as establishing a larger framework in which a broad degree of variation is possible.

Id. at 950. As Justice Kogan's concurring opinion explained in *Glasser*, uniformity is a complicated question "involving the special expertise of the Legislature, its staff, its advisers on public finance, and the Department of Education." *Id.* at 951. Further, as these cases illustrate, each time the education article has been challenged, the challenging party made an objection to some specific funding issue. In contrast, in this case appellants have made a blanket assertion that the entire system is constitutionally inadequate....

SEPARATION OF POWERS

Appellants, on the other hand, claim that they have not asked the court to usurp the legislative appropriation power but simply to declare that appellees' constitutional obligations have not been met. Although appellants recognize that the judiciary's broad grant of jurisdiction is subject to the separation of powers doctrine, they believe that the separation of powers doctrine is subject to an exception in the area of constitutionally guaranteed or protected rights. *See Dade County Classroom Teachers Ass'n v. Legislature*, 269 So.2d 684, 686 (Fla.1972). Appellants assert that they are simply asking the court to declare that adequate provision has not been made for the present system of free public education.

Appellees contend that the trial court correctly held that granting appellants relief would violate the separation of powers doctrine. Appellees maintain that what appellants want is for the trial court to order the appropriation of more money for education. This means that the judiciary would be intruding into the legislative power of appropriations. The trial court agreed with appellees and found that adjudicating appellants' claims was beyond its power because the claims presented a "non-justiciable political question."

Appellees further argue that we must consider this issue in the context that appropriations are textually and constitutionally committed to the legislature. Any judicial involvement would involve usurping the legislature's power to appropriate funds for education. The judiciary must defer to the wisdom of those who have carefully evaluated and studied the social, economic, and political ramifications of this complex issue—the legislature. Ultimately, appellees suggest, it is up to the lawmakers and the citizens of this State to determine how much to appropriate for education.

We conclude that here, especially in view of our obligation to respect the separation of powers doctrine, an insufficient showing has been made to justify judicial intrusion.

Article II, section 3 of the Florida Constitution expressly sets forth the separation of powers doctrine:

> The powers of the state government shall be divided into legislative, executive and judicial branches. No person belonging to one branch shall exercise any powers appertaining to either of the other branches unless expressly provided herein.

As this text demonstrates, each branch of government has certain delineated powers that the other branches of government may not intrude upon. For instance, the power to appropriate state funds is expressly reserved to the legislative branch. More specifically, article VII, section 1(c) provides: "No money shall be drawn from the treasury except in pursuance of appropriation made by law." Thus, it is well settled that the power to appropriate state funds is assigned to the legislature. *See Chiles v. Children A, B, C, D, E, and F*, 589 So.2d 260, 264 (Fla.1991) (holding that power to appropriate is legislative).

In conjunction with their position on the separation of powers doctrine, appellees claim that appellants have raised a political question which is outside the scope of the judiciary's jurisdiction. The United States Supreme Court in *Baker v. Carr*, 369 U.S. 186, 209 (1962), set forth six criteria to gauge whether a case involves a political question: (1) a textually demonstrable commitment of the issue to a coordinate political department; (2) a lack of judicially discoverable and manageable standards for resolving it; (3) the impossibility of deciding without an initial policy determination of a kind clearly for nonjudicial discretion; (4) the impossibility of a court's undertaking independent resolution without expressing lack of the respect due coordinate branches of government; (5) an unusual need for unquestioning adherence to a political decision already made; and lastly (6) the potentiality of embarrassment from multifarious pronouncements by various departments on one question.

Appellees claim that at least the first two of these criteria mandate affirmance here. Appellees suggest that the constitution has committed the determination of "adequacy" to the legislature, and that there is a "lack of judicially discoverable and manageable standards" to apply to the question of "adequacy." That is, appellees assert that there are no judicially manageable standards available to determine adequacy. In contrast, they note that the phrase "uniform" has manageable standards because by definition this word means a lack of substantial variation. By contrast, appellees contend, "adequacy" simply does not have such straightforward content.[12] We agree.

While we stop short of saying "never," appellants have failed to demonstrate in their allegations, or in their arguments on appeal, an appropriate standard for determining "adequacy" that would not present a substantial risk of judicial intrusion into the powers and responsibilities assigned to the legislature, both generally (in de-

---

12. [FN8.] The dictionary defines adequate as "enough or good enough for what is required or needed; sufficient; suitable." *Webster's New World Dictionary* 16 (2d ed.1978).

termining appropriations) and specifically (in providing *by law* for an adequate and uniform system of education).

CONCLUSION

We hold that the legislature has been vested with enormous discretion by the Florida Constitution to determine what provision to make for an adequate and uniform system of free public schools. Appellants have failed to demonstrate in their allegations a violation of the legislature's duties under the Florida Constitution.

For all of the foregoing reasons, we affirm the trial court's order of dismissal.

It is so ordered.

GRIMES, HARDING and WELLS, JJ., concur.

OVERTON, J., concurs with an opinion.

ANSTEAD, J., dissents in part with an opinion, in which KOGAN, C.J., and SHAW, J., concur.

OVERTON, Justice, concurring.

I concur with the majority that an insufficient showing has been made by the appellants to justify a judicial intrusion under the circumstances of this case.

I write to emphasize the importance of the education provision contained in article IX, section 1, of the Florida Constitution, and to explain that, in my view, our holding today does not mean that the judiciary should not be involved in the enforcement of this constitutional provision.

This education provision was placed in our constitution in recognition of the fact that education is absolutely essential to a free society under our governmental structure. As the majority notes, provisions similar to the current education provision have been contained in our constitution since the early history of this state.

The authors of our United States Constitution and our general governmental structure have acknowledged the importance of education as well. As James Madison said:

> Knowledge will forever govern ignorance; and a people who mean to be their own governours must arm themselves with the power that knowledge gives.... Learned institutions ought to be favorite objects with every free people. They throw that light over the public mind which is the best security against crafty and dangerous encroachments on the public liberty.

Robert S. Peck, The Constitution and American Values, in *The Blessings of Liberty: Bicentennial Lectures at The National Archives* 133 (Robert S. Peck & Ralph S. Pollock eds., 1989). Thomas Jefferson said it even more succinctly: "If a nation expects to be ignorant and free ... it expects what never was and never will be." Letter from Thomas Jefferson to Colonel Charles Yancey (Jan. 6, 1816). Further, in one of the most important cases ever decided by the United States Supreme Court, *Brown v. Board of Education*, 347 U.S. 483, 493 (1954), the Court stated that education is important "to our democratic society. It is required in the performance of our most basic public responsibilities.... It is the very foundation of good citizenship."

These quotes emphasize the need for education and knowledge in a democratic free society. There have been many examples in the world where, when tyrannical individuals or entities seize power, their first action is to eliminate, imprison, or exile the educated and take control of the educational process. Our forefathers intended that our state constitutions would protect our basic fundamental rights and that local governments would provide education for our citizens. Education has never been a responsibility of the federal government. The basic responsibility for education has always been with the states. The drafters of Florida's constitution recognized this fact and, accordingly, included the education provision to guarantee that a system of free public education be established for the citizens of Florida.

While I agree with Justice Kogan's view in *Glasser* that we should not give the constitution a stilted reading by requiring absolute uniformity among school districts, such a position does not preclude the treatment of education as an essential, fundamental right. In my view, this Court can recognize the basic need for the right to an adequate provision of educational opportunities without engaging in micro-management and without offending the separation-of-powers doctrine. There seems to be a belief that a fundamental right will be interpreted as guaranteeing a perfect or ideal education under this provision. Such a view ignores, however, the nature and purpose of our education provision. In my view, the intent of this provision, which mandates that adequate provision shall be made by law for a uniform system of free public schools, is to require the establishment of an educational system that fulfills the basic educational needs of the citizens of this state to provide for a literate, knowledgeable population. When a significant segment of our population is illiterate, our freedom can be easily threatened. I fully recognize that this provision does not ensure a perfect system. While "adequate" may be difficult to quantify, certainly a minimum threshold exists below which the funding provided by the legislature would be considered "inadequate." For example, were a complaint to assert that a county in this state has a thirty percent illiteracy rate, I would suggest that such a complaint has at least stated a cause of action under our education provision. To say otherwise would have the effect of eliminating the education provision from our constitution and relegating it to the position occupied by statutes. As noted, however, I agree with the majority that a proper showing of inadequacy has not been made in this case.

In conclusion, I emphasize that education is the key to unlocking the door to freedom and keeping it open and that this constitutional provision was intended to do just that. Consequently, I believe that the right to an adequate education is a fundamental right for the citizens of Florida under our Florida Constitution.

ANSTEAD, Justice, dissenting in part.

I would reverse the dismissal of this action and remand for further proceedings so that a factual context can be established for determining whether the legislature has complied with the mandate of the people of Florida to make adequate provision for a uniform system of free public schools. By our action today, we have reduced to empty words a constitutional promise to provide an adequate educational system for our children.

By approving the dismissal of this case without any further factual inquiry, this Court has failed to carry out its duty to ensure that the legislature has performed its constitutional mandate to make "[a]dequate provision ... for a uniform system of free public schools." *See* Art. IX, § 1, Fla. Const. While the legislature may be vested with considerable leeway in carrying out this mandate, we cannot determine in a factual vacuum, without abrogating our own responsibility, that the mandate has been met. Indeed, the courts in other states have not hesitated to accept this fundamental and essential responsibility to give life and meaning to similar provisions in their state constitutions.[13] Justice Overton demonstrates this point in a very concrete way when he asserts that a claim of a thirty percent illiteracy rate in a county could demonstrate a constitutional violation.[14] Under the comprehensive allegations of inadequacies set out in appellants' complaint, it is entirely possible that they may be able to submit proof of such poor literacy rates if given the opportunity at an evidentiary hearing. Of course, low literacy rates constitute just one form of proof of an inadequate educational system.

Justice Overton has also made an eloquent case for the importance of education in our society. Indeed, that case stands unrebutted. In a society founded upon the principle of equal opportunity, education is the key. Surely all would agree that education is a fundamental value in our society. The question remains as to how we have recognized that value in Florida. The most obvious and effective way to recognize a value as fundamental and of the highest importance and priority is to make provision for that value in our society's supreme and basic charter, our constitution. We did that in Florida. The people of Florida recognized the fundamental value of education by making express provision for education in our constitution.

Of course, the people of Florida have gone much further than merely recognizing education as a fundamental value. They have mandated, in an express, direct way, that our legislature make adequate provision for an education system for our children, who are the obvious intended beneficiaries of the education article in the constitution. The legislature has been given no discretion or choice as to whether to act. Rather,

---

13. [FN9.] *See, e.g., Alabama Coalition for Equity, Inc. v. Hunt,* Nos. CV-90-883-R, CV-91-0117 (Ala.Cir.Ct., Montg.Cty., 1993), included as appendix to *Opinion of the Justices,* 624 So.2d 107 (Ala.1993); *Roosevelt Elementary Sch. Dist. No. 66 v. Bishop,* 179 Ariz. 233, 877 P.2d 806 (1994); *Rose v. Council for Better Educ., Inc.,* 790 S.W.2d 186 (Ky.1989); *McDuffy v. Secretary of Exec. Office of Educ.,* 415 Mass. 545, 615 N.E.2d 516 (1993); *Helena Elementary Sch. Dist. No. 1 v. State,* 236 Mont. 44, 769 P.2d 684 (1989), *opinion amended by,* 236 Mont. 44, 784 P.2d 412 (1990); *Robinson v. Cahill,* 62 N.J. 473, 303 A.2d 273 (1973); *Bismarck Pub. Sch. Dist. No. 1 v. State,* 511 N.W.2d 247 (N.D.1994); *City of Pawtucket v. Sundlun,* 662 A.2d 40 (R.I.1995); *Tennessee Small Sch. Sys. v. McWherter,* 851 S.W.2d 139 (Tenn.1993); *Carrollton-Farmers Branch Indep. Sch. Dist. v. Edgewood Indep. School,* 826 S.W.2d 489 (Tex.1992); *Seattle Sch. Dist. No. 1 v. State,* 90 Wash.2d 476, 585 P.2d 71 (1978); *Washakie County Sch. Dist. No. 1 v. Herschler,* 606 P.2d 310 (Wyo.), *cert. denied,* 449 U.S. 824 (1980).

14. [FN10.] The appellants, of course, have the option of filing another action if they can allege and demonstrate inadequacies sufficient to meet the requirements set out in the various opinions of the judges of this Court filed in this case.

the legislature has been "ordered" by the people to act, and the intent of the people is clear: to provide our children with an adequate system of education.

There are two other arguments advanced in support of the trial court's dismissal that lack merit. First, I find it to be pure sophistry to suggest that by including a "uniformity" requirement within its terms, the education article is concerned only that whatever provision is made for education, the system be uniform. The major purpose of the education article is to provide for education, not to merely provide for uniformity. Hence, I reject the view that the education article contemplates an inadequate, but uniform, education system. Such a view does a great disservice to the citizens of this state who historically and repeatedly have insisted that provision for education be made in the constitution.

Second, I also reject the view that our education article allows any lesser system of education because it uses the word "adequate" as opposed to some superlative like "terrific" or "first class," etc. It would be redundant, and totally unnecessary, having directed that adequate provision be made for a system to educate our children, to add "puffing" words to suggest the quality of the system contemplated. "Adequate" does the job. It also would be insulting to prior generations of Floridians to suggest that, by utilizing the word "adequate" in the education article, they intended a lower quality system of education. What is obvious is that Floridians have recognized the value of education for well over a hundred years and have "put their money where their mouths are" by providing for education in the state constitution.

Further proceedings below may ultimately end in the same result as the dismissal here. Indeed, based upon a sufficient factual predicate, it may well be determined that the Florida legislature has made adequate provision for the education of Florida's children. But those who had the wisdom to provide for education in our constitution are at least entitled to know that we took them at their word and held the legislature accountable for the responsibility and trust placed in it to provide for Florida's children.

KOGAN, C.J., and SHAW, J., concur.

Questions

1. What is the division in this case on whether the Education Clause is justiciable with regard to adequacy? Where does Justice Overton fit in this division?

2. Why did Justice Overton concur with the majority in the result of this case?

3. Why did the majority view the issue of adequacy as an inherently political question?

––––––––––––

In 1998, Florida voters approved an amendment to Article IX, Section 1 proposed by the Constitution Revision Commission. The following two cases explore the revised Article IX, Section 1, and specifically whether the revised constitutional provision sets forth a justiciable standard that can be applied by the courts in the context of an adequacy challenge.

Bush v. Holmes

919 So. 2d 392 (Fla. 2006)

PARIENTE, C.J.

Because a state statute was declared unconstitutional by the First District Court of Appeal, this Court is required by the Florida Constitution to hear this appeal. *See* art. V, §3(b)(1), Fla. Const. The issue we decide is whether the State of Florida is prohibited by the Florida Constitution from expending public funds to allow students to obtain a private school education in kindergarten through grade twelve, as an alternative to a public school education. The law in question, now codified at section 1002.38, Florida Statutes (2005), authorizes a system of school vouchers and is known as the Opportunity Scholarship Program (OSP).

Under the OSP, a student from a public school that fails to meet certain minimum state standards has two options. The first is to move to another public school with a satisfactory record under the state standards. The second option is to receive funds from the public treasury, which would otherwise have gone to the student's school district, to pay the student's tuition at a private school. The narrow question we address is whether the second option violates a part of the Florida Constitution requiring the state to both provide for "the education of all children residing within its borders" and provide "by law for a uniform, efficient, safe, secure, and high quality system of free public schools that allows students to obtain a high quality education." Art. IX, §1(a), Fla. Const.

As a general rule, courts may not reweigh the competing policy concerns underlying a legislative enactment. The arguments of public policy supporting both sides in this dispute have obvious merit, and the Legislature with the Governor's assent has resolved the ensuing debate in favor of the proponents of the program. In most cases, that would be the end of the matter. However, as is equally self-evident, the usual deference given to the Legislature's resolution of public policy issues is at all times circumscribed by the Constitution. Acting within its constitutional limits, the Legislature's power to resolve issues of civic debate receives great deference. Beyond those limits, the Constitution must prevail over any enactment contrary to it.

Thus, in reviewing the issue before us, the justices emphatically are not examining whether the public policy decision made by the other branches is wise or unwise, desirable or undesirable. Nor are we examining whether the Legislature intended to supplant or replace the public school system to any greater or lesser extent. Indeed, we acknowledge, as does the dissent, that the statute at issue here is limited in the number of students it affects. However, the question we face today does not turn on the soundness of the legislation or the relatively small numbers of students affected. Rather, the issue is what limits the Constitution imposes on the Legislature. We make no distinction between a small violation of the Constitution and a large one. Both are equally invalid. Indeed, in the system of government envisioned by the Founding Fathers, we abhor the small violation precisely because it is precedent for the larger one.

Our inquiry begins with the plain language of the second and third sentences of article IX, section 1(a) of the Constitution. The relevant words are these: "It is ... a paramount duty of the state to make adequate provision for the education of all children residing within its borders." Using the same term, "adequate provision," article IX, section 1(a) further states: "Adequate provision shall be made by law for a uniform, efficient, safe, secure, and high quality system of free public schools." For reasons expressed more fully below, we find that the OSP violates this language. It diverts public dollars into separate private systems parallel to and in competition with the free public schools that are the sole means set out in the Constitution for the state to provide for the education of Florida's children. This diversion not only reduces money available to the free schools, but also funds private schools that are not "uniform" when compared with each other or the public system. Many standards imposed by law on the public schools are inapplicable to the private schools receiving public monies. In sum, through the OSP the state is fostering plural, nonuniform systems of education in direct violation of the constitutional mandate for a uniform system of free public schools. Because we determine that the OSP is unconstitutional as a violation of article IX, section 1(a), we find it unnecessary to address whether the OSP is a violation of the "no aid" provision in article I, section 3 of the Constitution, as held by the First District.

PROCEDURAL HISTORY

Various parents of children in Florida elementary and secondary schools and several organizations (hereinafter collectively referred to as the plaintiffs) filed complaints in the circuit court challenging the constitutionality of the OSP under article I, section 3, article IX, section 1, and article IX, section 6 of the Florida Constitution, as well as under the Establishment Clause of the First Amendment to the United States Constitution. The trial court found that the OSP was facially unconstitutional under article IX, section 1 of the Florida Constitution. On appeal, a panel of the First District reversed, concluding that "nothing in article IX, section 1 clearly prohibits the Legislature from allowing the well-delineated use of public funds for private school education, particularly in circumstances where the Legislature finds such use is necessary." *Bush v. Holmes*, 767 So.2d 668, 675 (Fla. 1st DCA 2000) (*Holmes I*) (footnote omitted). The First District declined to address the other constitutional issues raised and remanded for further proceedings. *See id.* at 677. This Court denied discretionary review. *See Holmes v. Bush*, 790 So.2d 1104 (Fla.2001).

While the case was pending on remand, the United States Supreme Court held that the Ohio Pilot Project Scholarship Program, a voucher program similar to the OSP, was constitutional under the Establishment Clause. *See Zelman v. Simmons-Harris*, 536 U.S. 639 (2002). The plaintiffs in this case then voluntarily dismissed their challenges under the Establishment Clause,[15] leaving undecided only the issue

---

15. [FN1.] The plaintiffs also dismissed their separate claim under article IX, section 6 of the Florida Constitution, which provides:

State school fund. — The income derived from the state school fund shall, and the principal of the fund may, be appropriated, but only to the support and maintenance of free public schools.

of whether the OSP was facially constitutional under article I, section 3 of the Florida Constitution.[16]

The circuit court entered final summary judgment in favor of the plaintiffs, declaring the OSP unconstitutional. The trial court found that the OSP violated the last sentence of article I, section 3, referred to as the "no aid" provision. A divided panel of the First District affirmed the trial court's order. *See Bush v. Holmes*, 29 Fla. L. Weekly D1877 (Fla. 1st DCA Aug. 16, 2004). The district court subsequently withdrew the panel opinion and issued an en banc decision in which a majority of the First District again affirmed the trial court's order. *See Bush v. Holmes*, 886 So.2d 340, 366 (Fla. 1st DCA 2004) (*Holmes II*). In a separate concurring opinion in which four other judges concurred, Judge Benton suggested that he would also have found the OSP unconstitutional under article IX, section 1. *See Bush*, 886 So.2d at 377 (Benton, J., concurring).

ANALYSIS

Because both issues are questions of law, we review both the First District's interpretation of article IX, section 1(a) and its determination that the OSP violates the constitutional provision de novo, without deference to the decision below. *See Zingale v. Powell*, 885 So.2d 277, 280 (Fla. 2004) ("[C]onstitutional interpretation ... is performed *de novo*."); *D'Angelo v. Fitzmaurice*, 863 So.2d 311, 314 (Fla. 2003) (stating that in a de novo review, "no deference is given to the judgment of the lower courts"). In interpreting article IX, section 1(a), we follow principles parallel to those guiding statutory construction. *See Zingale*, 885 So.2d at 282; *Coastal Fla. Police Benevolent Ass'n v. Williams*, 838 So.2d 543, 548 (Fla. 2003).

In the analysis that follows, we first examine the operation of section 1002.38, Florida Statutes, which authorizes the OSP, then explore both the language and history of article IX, section 1(a). We then explain our conclusion that the OSP violates article IX, section 1(a).

I. The Opportunity Scholarship Program

The OSP provides that a student who attends or is assigned to attend a failing public school may attend a higher performing public school or use a scholarship provided by the state to attend a participating private school. *See* § 1002.38(2)(a), (3), Fla. Stat. (2005). In re-authorizing this program in 2002, the Legislature stated:

(1) FINDINGS AND INTENT. — The purpose of this section is to provide enhanced opportunity for students in this state to gain the knowledge and skills necessary for postsecondary education, a career education, or the world of work. The Legislature recognizes that the voters of the State of

---

16. [FN2.] Article I, section 3 provides:

Religious freedom. — There shall be no law respecting the establishment of religion or prohibiting or penalizing the free exercise thereof. Religious freedom shall not justify practices inconsistent with public morals, peace or safety. No revenue of the state or any political subdivision or agency thereof shall ever be taken from the public treasury directly or indirectly in aid of any church, sect, or religious denomination or in aid of any sectarian institution.

Florida, in the November 1998 general election, amended s. 1, Art. IX of the Florida Constitution so as to make education a paramount duty of the state. The Legislature finds that the State Constitution requires the state to provide a uniform, safe, secure, efficient, and high-quality system which allows the opportunity to obtain a high-quality education. The Legislature further finds that a student should not be compelled, against the wishes of the student's parent, to remain in a school found by the state to be failing for 2 years in a 4-year period. The Legislature shall make available opportunity scholarships in order to give parents the opportunity for their children to attend a public school that is performing satisfactorily or to attend an eligible private school when the parent chooses to apply the equivalent of the public education funds generated by his or her child to the cost of tuition in the eligible private school as provided in paragraph (6)(a). Eligibility of a private school shall include the control and accountability requirements that, coupled with the exercise of parental choice, are reasonably necessary to secure the educational public purpose, as delineated in subsection (4).

§ 1002.38(1), Fla. Stat. (2005).

Section 1002.38(4), Florida Statutes (2005), which sets forth the eligibility requirements for private schools accepting OSP students, provides that these schools "may be sectarian or nonsectarian," and must:

(a) Demonstrate fiscal soundness....

(b) Notify the Department of Education and the school district in whose service area the school is located of its intent to participate in the program under this section....

(c) Comply with the antidiscrimination provisions of 42 U.S.C. s. 2000d.

(d) Meet state and local health and safety laws and codes.

(e) Accept scholarship students on an entirely random and religious-neutral basis without regard to the student's past academic history; however, the private school may give preference in accepting applications to siblings of students who have already been accepted on a random and religious-neutral basis.

(f) Be subject to the instruction, curriculum, and attendance criteria adopted by an appropriate nonpublic school accrediting body and be academically accountable to the parent for meeting the educational needs of the student. The private school must furnish a school profile which includes student performance.

(g) Employ or contract with teachers who hold a baccalaureate or higher degree, or have at least 3 years of teaching experience in public or private schools, or have special skills, knowledge, or expertise that qualifies them to provide instruction in subjects taught.

(h) Comply with all state statutes relating to private schools.

(i) Accept as full tuition and fees the amount provided by the state for each student.

(j) Agree not to compel any student attending the private school on an opportunity scholarship to profess a specific ideological belief, to pray, or to worship.

(k) Adhere to the tenets of its published disciplinary procedures prior to the expulsion of any opportunity scholarship student.

§ 1002.38(4)(a)–(k), Fla. Stat (2005).

The OSP also places obligations on students participating in the program and their parents. *See* § 1002.38(5), Fla. Stat. (2005). In addition to requiring the student to remain in attendance at the private school throughout the school year and the parent to comply with the private school's parental involvement requirements, section 1002.38(5) also requires the parent to ensure that the participating student "takes all statewide assessments required pursuant to s. 1008.22." § 1002.38(5)(c), Fla. Stat. (2005).[17] A failure to comply with any of these requirements results in a forfeiture of the scholarship. *See* § 1002.38(5)(d), Fla. Stat. (2005). However, unless forfeited, the scholarship "remain[s] in force until the student returns to a public school or, if the students chooses to attend a private school the highest grade of which is grade 8, until the student matriculates to high school and the public high school to which the student is assigned is an accredited school with a performance grade category designation of 'C' or better." § 1002.38(2)(b), Fla. Stat. (2005). In other words, the OSP allows the student to remain in the private school of his or her choice, and even switch private schools, regardless of whether the student's assigned public school improves its grade in the interim. The only circumstance in which a student who has elected to attend a private school must return to a public school is if the private school ends at grade eight and the public high school to which the student is assigned has received a grade of C or better.

Section 1002.38(6), Florida Statutes (2005), provides the method for funding and payment of opportunity scholarships. The maximum amount of an opportunity scholarship is "equivalent to the base student allocation in the Florida Education Finance Program multiplied by the appropriate cost factor for the educational program that would have been provided for the student in the district school to which he or she was assigned, multiplied by the district cost differential." § 1002.38(6)(a), Fla. Stat. (2005). This amount includes "the per-student share of instructional materials

---

17. [FN4.] Section 1008.22, Florida Statutes (2005), is titled "Student assessment program for public schools," and requires the Commissioner of Education to, among other things, develop and implement the Florida Comprehensive Assessment Test ("FCAT"). *See* § 1008.22(3)(c), Fla. Stat. (2005).

funds, technology funds, and other categorical funds as provided for this purpose in the General Appropriations Act." *Id.* The funds for the opportunity scholarship are transferred "from each school district's appropriated funds ... to a separate account for the Opportunity Scholarship Program." § 1002.38(6)(f), Fla. Stat. (2005). Accordingly, the payment of the scholarships results in a reduction in the amount of funds available to the affected school district. The scholarship is made payable to the parent of the student who is then required to "restrictively endorse the warrant to the private school." § 1002.38(6)(g), Fla. Stat. (2005).

II. Language and History of Florida's Education Articles

The Florida Constitution has contained an education article since its inception in 1838. *See* art. X, Fla. Const. (1838). The original education article contained only two brief sections that dealt almost exclusively with the preservation of public lands granted by the United States for the use of schools. In 1849, the Legislature provided for a system of schools by authorizing the establishment of "common schools." *See* ch. 229, Laws of Fla. (1848).[18] The education article remained substantially the same in the 1861 and 1865 Constitutions. *See* art. X, Fla. Const. (1861); art. X, Fla. Const. (1865).

In 1868, the education article was significantly expanded, *see* art. VIII, §§ 1–9, Fla. Const. (1868), and included the first requirement that the state provide a system of free public schools for all Florida children:

> Section 1. It is the paramount duty of the State to make ample provision for the education of all the children residing within its borders, without distinction or preference.

> Section 2. The Legislature shall provide a uniform system of Common Schools, and a University, and shall provide for the liberal maintenance of the same. Instruction in them shall be free.

As this Court explained in *Coalition for Adequacy & Fairness in School Funding, Inc. v. Chiles*, 680 So.2d 400, 405 (Fla.1996), "[b]y this change, education became the 'paramount duty of the State' and required the State to make 'ample provision for the education of all the children.'"

In 1885, the education provisions were moved to article XII and the provision imposing a "paramount duty" on "the State to make ample provision for the education of all the children" was deleted. *See* art. XII, § 1, Fla. Const. (1885). Section 1 of article XII simply provided that "[t]he Legislature shall provide for a uniform system of public free schools, and shall provide for the liberal maintenance of the same."[19]

---

18. [FN7.] This first public system of schools was open only to white children between the ages of five and eighteen. *See* ch. 229, art. I, § 3, Laws of Fla. (1848–49).

19. [FN8.] Although not confirmed by the written record of the 1885 constitution, some commentators have suggested that the removal of the "paramount duty" provision along with the addition of a section explicitly requiring racial segregation (article XII, section 12, Florida Constitution (1885)) may indicate that the "drafters of the 1885 Constitution wished to prevent both mixed-race schooling and any real 'equality' requirement for the supposedly 'separate but equal' schools established for African-American children." Jon Mills & Timothy McLendon, *Setting a New Standard for Public Ed-*

The adoption of the 1968 Constitution saw another substantial revision of the education article, with section 1 of article IX providing that

> [a]dequate provision shall be made by law for a uniform system of free public schools and for the establishment, maintenance and operation of institutions of higher learning and other public education programs that the needs of the people may require.

Art. IX, § 1, Fla. Const. (1968). The new reference to "other public education programs" referred "to the existing systems of junior colleges, adult education, etc., which are not strictly within the general conception of free public schools or institutions of higher learning." *Bd. of Pub. Instruction v. State Treasurer*, 231 So.2d 1, 2 (Fla.1970). The effect of the addition of the phrase "adequate provision" was analyzed in *Coalition for Adequacy & Fairness*, in which we ultimately concluded that it is the Legislature, not the Court, that is vested with the power to decide what funding is "adequate." *See* 680 So.2d at 406–07.

In 1998, in response in part to *Coalition for Adequacy & Fairness*, the Constitutional Revision Commission proposed and the citizens of this state approved an amendment to article IX, section 1 to make clear that education is a "fundamental value" and "a paramount duty of the state," and to provide standards by which to measure the adequacy of the public school education provided by the state:

> *The education of children is a fundamental value of the people of the State of Florida. It is, therefore, a paramount duty of the state to make adequate provision for the education of all children residing within its borders.* Adequate provision shall be made by law for a *uniform, efficient, safe, secure, and high quality* system of free public schools that allows students to obtain a high quality education and for the establishment, maintenance, and operation of institutions of higher learning and other public education programs that the needs of the people may require.

Art. IX, § 1(a), Fla. Const. (emphasis supplied).

A commentary on the 1998 amendment by the Executive Director and the General Counsel of the Constitution Revision Commission explained that the amendment revised section 1 by

> (1) making education a "fundamental value," (2) making it a paramount duty of the state to make adequate provision for the education of children, and (3) defining "adequate provisions" by requiring that the public school system be "efficient, safe, secure, and high quality."

The "fundamental value" language, new to the constitution, was codified from the language taken from the Florida Supreme Court decision in *Coalition for Adequacy and Fairness in School Funding, Inc. v. Chiles*, 680 So.2d 400 (Fla.1996). Early proposals presented before the Constitution Revision Com-

---

ucation: Revision 6 Increases the Duty of the State to Make "Adequate Provision" for Florida Schools, 52 Fla. L. Rev. 329, 349 n. 98 (2000).

mission framed education in terms of being a "fundamental right." In response to concerns of commissioners that the state might become liable for every individual's dissatisfaction with the education system, the term "fundamental value" was substituted.

The "paramount duty" language represents a return to the 1868 Constitution, which provided that "[i]t is the paramount duty of the State to make ample provisions for the education of all children residing within its borders, without distinction or preference."....

The addition of "efficient, safe, secure, and high quality" represents an attempt by the 1997–98 Constitution Revision Commission to provide constitutional standards to measure the "adequacy" provision found in the second sentence of section 1. The action of the commission was in direct response to recent court actions seeking a declaration that Article IX, section 1 created a fundamental right to an adequate education, which the state had arguably violated by failing to provide sufficient resources to public education.

William A. Buzzett and Deborah K. Kearney, *Commentary*, art. IX, § 1, 26A Fla. Stat. Annot. (West Supp.2006) (first alteration in original).

In reviewing article IX, section 1 in *Coalition for Adequacy & Fairness*, the Court recognized a four-category system for analyzing state education clauses to ascertain the level of duty imposed on the state legislature by language in the Constitution:

[A] Category I clause merely requires that a system of "free public schools" be provided. A Category II clause imposes some minimum standard of quality that the State must provide. A Category III clause requires "stronger and more specific education mandate[s] and purpose preambles." And, a Category IV clause imposes a maximum duty on the State to provide for education. Barbara J. Staros, *School Finance Litigation in Florida: A Historical Analysis*, 23 Stetson L.Rev. 497, 498–99 (1994). Using this rating system, Florida's education clause in 1868 imposed a Category IV duty on the legislature—a maximum duty on the State to provide for education. In addition, it also imposed a duty on the legislature to provide for a uniform system of education.

680 So.2d at 405 n. 7. After the 1998 revision restoring the "paramount duty" language, Florida's education article is again classified as a Category IV clause, imposing a maximum duty on the state to provide for public education that is uniform and of high quality.

Continuing concern over the quality of the education provided by the public schools led the citizens of this state to adopt a constitutional amendment in 2002 mandating maximum class sizes. *See* art. IX, § 1(a), Fla. Const.; *Advisory Opinion to Attorney Gen. re Florida's Amendment to Reduce Class Size*, 816 So.2d 580, 586 (Fla.2002) (approving the proposed amendment for placement on the ballot).[20] In

---

20. [FN9.] Article IX, section 1 was renumbered as section 1(a) and modified to include the class size amendment.

this same election, the citizens of this state also approved a constitutional amendment requiring the state to provide "a high quality pre-kindergarten learning opportunity." Art. IX, § 1(b)–(c), Fla. Const.; *see also Advisory Opinion to Attorney Gen. re Voluntary Universal Pre-Kindergarten Education*, 824 So.2d 161, 167 (Fla.2002) (approving the proposed amendment for placement on the ballot).

III. Constitutionality of the Opportunity Scholarship Program

In our review of the constitutionality of the OSP, "[t]he political motivations of the legislature, if any, in enacting [this legislation] are not a proper matter of inquiry for this Court. We are limited to measuring the Act against the dictates of the Constitution." *School Bd. of Escambia County v. State*, 353 So.2d 834, 839 (Fla.1977). We are also mindful that statutes come to the Court "clothed with a presumption of constitutionality," *City of Miami v. McGrath*, 824 So.2d 143, 146 (Fla.2002) (quoting *Dep't of Legal Affairs v. Sanford-Orlando Kennel Club, Inc.*, 434 So.2d 879, 881 (Fla.1983)), and that the Court should give a statute a constitutional construction where such a construction is reasonably possible. *See Tyne v. Time Warner Entertainment Co.*, 901 So.2d 802, 810 (Fla.2005). However, in this case we conclude that the OSP is in direct conflict with the mandate in article IX, section 1(a) that it is the state's "paramount duty" to make adequate provision for education and that the manner in which this mandate must be carried out is "by law for a uniform, efficient, safe, secure, and high quality system of free public schools."

A. The State's Obligation Under Article IX, Section 1(a)

This Court has long recognized the constitutional obligation that Florida's education article places upon the Legislature:

> Article XII, section 1, constitution [the predecessor to article IX, section 1] commands that the Legislature shall provide for a uniform system of public free schools and for the liberal maintenance of such system of free schools. This means that a system of public free schools … shall be established upon principles that are of uniform operation throughout the State and that such system shall be liberally maintained.

State ex rel. Clark v. Henderson, 137 Fla. 666, 188 So. 351, 352 (1939). Currently, article IX, section 1(a), which is stronger than the provision discussed in *Henderson*, contains three critical components with regard to public education. The provision (1) declares that the "education of children is a fundamental value of the people of the State of Florida," (2) sets forth an education mandate that provides that it is "a paramount duty of the state to make adequate provision for the education of all children residing within its borders," and (3) sets forth *how* the state is to carry out this education mandate, specifically, that "[a]dequate provision shall be made by law for a *uniform*, efficient, safe, secure, and *high quality system of free public schools*." (Emphasis supplied.)

Justice Overton explained in his concurring opinion in *Coalition for Adequacy & Fairness* that "[t]his education provision was placed in our constitution in recognition of the fact that education is absolutely essential to a free society under our governmental structure." 680 So.2d at 409. Justice Overton also noted that

[t]he authors of our United States Constitution and our general governmental structure have acknowledged the importance of education as well. As James Madison said:

> Knowledge will forever govern ignorance; and a people who mean to be their own governours must arm themselves with the power that knowledge gives.... Learned institutions ought to be favorite objects with every free people. They throw that light over the public mind which is the best security against crafty and dangerous encroachments on the public liberty.

Robert S. Peck, The Constitution and American Values, in *The Blessings of Liberty: Bicentennial Lectures at the National Archives* 133 (Robert S. Peck & Ralph S. Pollock eds., 1989). Thomas Jefferson said it even more succinctly: "If a nation expects to be ignorant and free ... it expects what never was and never will be." Letter from Thomas Jefferson to Colonel Charles Yancey (Jan. 6, 1816). Further, in one of the most important cases ever decided by the United States Supreme Court, *Brown v. Board of Education*, 347 U.S. 483, 493 (1954), the Court stated that education is important "to our democratic society. It is required in the performance of our most basic public responsibilities.... It is the very foundation of good citizenship."

Id. (alterations in original).

B. Article IX, Section 1(a): A Mandate with a Restriction

In the 1999 legislation creating the OSP, the Legislature recognized its heightened obligation regarding public education imposed by the 1998 amendment to article IX, section 1:

> (1) FINDINGS AND INTENT. — The Legislature recognizes that the voters of the State of Florida, in the November 1998 general election, amended s. 1, Art. IX of the Florida Constitution so as to make education a paramount duty of the state. The Legislature finds that the State Constitution requires the state to provide the opportunity to obtain a high-quality education.

§ 229.0537(1), Fla. Stat. (1999). In 2002 legislation that renumbered the statutory provisions dealing with education, the Legislature made essentially the same finding in language that more closely tracked the language of article IX, section 1(a):

> The Legislature finds that the State Constitution requires the state to provide a uniform, safe, secure, efficient, and high-quality system which allows the opportunity to obtain a high-quality education.

§ 1002.38(1), Fla. Stat. (2005). Although these statements purport to fulfill the constitutional mandate, the legislative findings omit critical language in the constitutional provision. In neither the 1999 nor the 2002 version of the OSP legislation is there an acknowledgment by the Legislature that the state's constitutional obligation under article IX, section 1(a) is to provide a uniform efficient, safe, secure, and high quality *system of free public schools*." (Emphasis supplied.)

The constitutional language omitted from the legislative findings is crucial. This language acts as a limitation on legislative power. *See generally Savage v. Bd. of Pub. Instruction*, 101 Fla. 1362, 133 So. 341, 344 (1931) ("The Constitution of this state is not a grant of power to the Legislature, but a limitation only upon legislative power...."). Absent a constitutional limitation, the Legislature's "discretion reasonably exercised is the sole brake on the enactment of legislation." *State v. Bd. of Pub. Instruction*, 126 Fla. 142, 170 So. 602, 606 (1936).

Article IX, section 1(a) is a limitation on the Legislature's power because it provides both a mandate to provide for children's education and a restriction on the execution of that mandate. The second and third sentences must be read *in pari materia,* rather than as distinct and unrelated obligations. This principle of statutory construction is equally applicable to constitutional provisions. As we stated in construing a different constitutional amendment, the provision should "be construed as a whole in order to ascertain the general purpose and meaning of each part; each subsection, sentence, and clause must be read in light of the others to form a congruous whole." *Dep't of Envtl. Prot. v. Millender*, 666 So.2d 882, 886 (Fla.1996); *see also Physicians Healthcare Plans, Inc. v. Pfeifler*, 846 So.2d 1129, 1134 (Fla.2003).

The second sentence of article IX, section 1(a) provides that it is the "paramount duty of the state to make adequate provision for the education of all children residing within its borders." The third sentence of article IX, section 1(a) provides a restriction on the exercise of this mandate by specifying that the adequate provision required in the second sentence "shall be made by law for a uniform, efficient, safe, secure and high quality system of *free public schools.*" (Emphasis supplied.) The OSP violates this provision by devoting the state's resources to the education of children within our state through means other than a system of free public schools.[21]

The principle of construction, "*expressio unius est exclusio alterius*," or "the expression of one thing implies the exclusion of another," leads us to the same conclusion. This Court has stated:

> [W]here the Constitution expressly provides the manner of doing a thing, it impliedly forbids its being done in a substantially different manner. Even though the Constitution does not in terms prohibit the doing of a thing in another manner, the fact that it has prescribed the manner in which the thing shall be done is itself a prohibition against a different manner of doing it. Therefore, when the Constitution prescribes the manner of doing an act, the manner prescribed is exclusive, and it is beyond the power of the Legis-

---

21. [FN10.] In *Davis v. Grover*, 480 N.W.2d 460 (Wis. 1992), which is cited by the dissent, the Wisconsin Supreme Court in a four-to-three decision upheld a program providing public funds to children from low-income families to attend nonsectarian schools against several constitutional challenges, including one resting on language similar to the third sentence in article IX, section 1(a) of the Florida Constitution. *See id.* at 473–74. However, the education article of the Wisconsin Constitution construed in *Davis, see* Wis. Const., art. X, does not contain language analogous to the statement in article IX, section 1(a) that it is "a paramount duty of the state to make adequate provision for the education of all children residing within its borders."

lature to enact a statute that would defeat the purpose of the constitutional provision.

Weinberger v. Bd. of Pub. Instruction, 93 Fla. 470, 112 So. 253, 256 (1927) (citations omitted); *see also S & J Transp., Inc. v. Gordon,* 176 So.2d 69, 71 (Fla.1965) (providing that "where one method or means of exercising a power is prescribed in a constitution it excludes its exercise in other ways"). We agree with the trial court that article IX, section 1(a) "mandates that a system of free public schools is the manner in which the State is to provide a free education to the children of Florida" and that "providing a free education ... by paying tuition ... to attend private schools is a 'a substantially different manner' of providing a publicly funded education than ... the one prescribed by the Constitution." *Holmes v. Bush,* No. CV99-3370 at 10, 2000 WL 526364 (2nd Cir. Ct. order filed March 14, 2000) (citation omitted).

In reaching this conclusion, we distinguish *Taylor v. Dorsey,* 155 Fla. 305, 19 So.2d 876, 882 (1944), in which the Court declined to apply the "*expressio unius est exclusio alterius*" maxim based on its determination that the statute at issue did not conflict with the primary purpose of the relevant constitutional provision. In *Taylor,* the Court considered whether a law that allowed married women to manage and control their separate property by, *inter alia,* suing or being sued over the property conflicted with a constitutional provision allowing a married woman's separate property to be charged in equity to satisfy claims related to that property. *See id.* at 880. The Court concluded that "it was not the primary purpose of [the constitutional provision] to effect the adjudication in equity of all claims against married women, but to require positive action on the part of the legislature to insure enforcement in equity against their separate property of claims having equitable qualities because they represented money traceable into the property." *Id.* at 882. Unlike the constitutional provision at issue in *Taylor,* which had a narrow primary purpose, article IX, section 1(a) provides a comprehensive statement of the state's responsibilities regarding the education of its children.

The dissent considers our use of rules of construction such as "*in pari materia*" and "*expressio unius*" unnecessary to discern the meaning of a provision that the dissent considers clear and unambiguous. "Ambiguity suggests that reasonable persons can find different meanings in the same language." *Forsythe v. Longboat Key Beach Erosion Control Dist.,* 604 So.2d 452, 455 (Fla.1992). It is precisely because the amendment is not clear and unambiguous regarding public funding of private schools that we look to accepted standards of construction applicable to constitutional provisions. *See Joshua v. City of Gainesville,* 768 So.2d 432, 435 (Fla.2000) (stating that "if the language of the statute is unclear, then rules of statutory construction control"); *Zingale,* 885 So.2d at 282, 285 (applying rules of statutory construction, including "*in pari materia,*" to constitutional provisions); *Caribbean Conservation Corp. v. Florida Fish & Wildlife Conservation Comm'n,* 838 So.2d 492, 501 (Fla.2003) (same). "*In pari materia*" and "*expressio unius*" are objective principles to apply in our analysis.

Although parents certainly have the right to choose how to educate their children,[22] article IX, section (1)(a) does not, as the Attorney General asserts, establish a "floor" of what the state can do to provide for the education of Florida's children. The provision mandates that the state's obligation is to provide for the education of Florida's children, specifies that the manner of fulfilling this obligation is by providing a uniform, high quality system of free public education, and does not authorize additional equivalent alternatives.

C. Diversion of Funds from the Public Schools

The Constitution prohibits the state from using public monies to fund a private alternative to the public school system, which is what the OSP does. Specifically, the OSP transfers tax money earmarked for public education to private schools that provide the same service—basic primary education. Thus, contrary to the defendants' arguments, the OSP does not supplement the public education system. Instead, the OSP diverts funds that would otherwise be provided to the system of free public schools that is the exclusive means set out in the Constitution for the Legislature to make adequate provision for the education of children.

Section 1002.38(6)(f), Florida Statutes (2005), specifically requires the Department of Education to "transfer from each school district's appropriated funds the calculated amount from the Florida Education Finance Program and authorized categorical accounts to a separate account for the Opportunity Scholarship Program." Even if the tuition paid to the private school is less than the amount transferred from the school district's funds and therefore does not result in a dollar-for-dollar reduction, as the dissent asserts, it is of no significance to the constitutionality of public funding of private schools as a means to making adequate provision for the education of children.

Although opportunity scholarships are not now widely in use, if the dissent is correct as to their constitutionality, the potential scale of programs of this nature is unlimited. Under the dissent's view of the Legislature's authority in this area, the state could fund a private school system of indefinite size and scope as long as the state also continued to fund the public schools at a level that kept them "uniform, efficient, safe, secure, and high quality." However, because voucher payments reduce funding for the public education system, the OSP by its very nature undermines the system of "high quality" free public schools that are the sole authorized means of fulfilling the constitutional mandate to provide for the education of all children residing in Florida.[23] The systematic diversion of public funds to private schools on either a small or large scale is incompatible with article IX, section 1(a).

---

22. [FN11.] *See Pierce v. Soc'y of Sisters*, 268 U.S. 510, 534–35 (1925) (holding that a law that prohibited parents from choosing private education over public schooling for their children "unreasonably interfere[d] with the liberty of parents … to direct the upbringing and education of [their] children"); *Beagle v. Beagle*, 678 So.2d 1271, 1276 (Fla.1996) ("[T]he State may not intrude upon the parents' fundamental right to raise their children except in cases where the child is threatened with harm.").

23. [FN12.] Further, as the dissent acknowledges, students become eligible for opportunity scholarships only if a public school has repeatedly failed to meet the Legislature's standards for a "high

D. Exemption from Public School Uniformity

In addition to specifying that a system of free public schools is the means for complying with the mandate to provide for the education of Florida's children, article IX, section 1(a) also requires that this system be "uniform." The OSP makes no provision to ensure that the private school alternative to the public school system meets the criterion of uniformity. In fact, in a provision directing the Department of Education to establish and maintain a database of private schools, the Legislature expressly states that it does not intend "to regulate, control, approve, or accredit private educational institutions." § 1002.42(2)(h), Fla. Stat. (2005). This lack of oversight is also evident in section 1001.21, which creates the Office of Private Schools and Home Education Programs within the Department of Education but provides that this office "ha[s] no authority over the institutions or students served." § 1001.21(1), Fla. Stat. (2005).

Further, although the parent of a student participating in the OSP must ensure that the student "takes all statewide assessments" required of a public school student, § 1002.38(5)(c), the private school's curriculum and teachers are not subject to the same standards as those in force in public schools. For example, only teachers possessing bachelor's degrees are eligible to teach at public schools, but private schools may hire teachers without bachelor's degrees if they have "at least 3 years of teaching experience in public or private schools, or have special skills, knowledge, or expertise that qualifies them to provide instruction in subjects taught." § 1002.38(4)(g), Fla. Stat. (2005).

In addition, public school teachers must be certified by the state. *See* § 1012.55(1), Fla. Stat. (2005). To obtain this certification, teachers must meet certain requirements that include having "attained at least a 2.5 overall grade point average on a 4.0 scale in the applicant's major field of study" and having demonstrated a mastery of general knowledge, subject area knowledge, and professional preparation and education competence. *See* § 1012.56(2)(c), (g)–(i), Fla. Stat. (2005).

Public teacher certification also requires the applicant to submit to a background screening. *See* § 1012.56(2)(d), Fla. Stat. (2005). Indeed, all school district personnel hired to fill positions that require direct contact with students must undergo a background check. *See* § 1012.32(2)(a), Fla. Stat. (2005). This screening is not required of private school employees. *See* § 1002.42(2)(c)(3), Fla. Stat. (2005) (providing that owners of private schools *may* require employees to file fingerprints with the Department of Law Enforcement).

Regarding curriculum, public education instruction is based on the "Sunshine State Standards" that have been "adopted by the State Board of Education and delineate the academic achievement of students, for which the state will hold schools accountable." § 1003.41, Fla. Stat. (2005). Public schools are required to teach all basic subjects

---

quality education." Dissenting op. at —n. 11. Similarly, Judge Benton noted below that the only circumstances in which opportunity scholarships are available "are antithetical to and forbidden by" the constitutional requirement that the state provide a "high quality system of free public schools." *Bush*, 886 So.2d at 370–71 (Benton, J., concurring).

as well as a number of other diverse subjects, among them the contents of the Declaration of Independence, the essentials of the United States Constitution, the elements of civil government, Florida state history, African-American history, the history of the Holocaust, and the study of Hispanic and women's contributions to the United States. *See* § 1003.42(2)(a), Fla. Stat. (2005). Eligible private schools are not required to teach any of these subjects.

In addition to being "academically accountable to the parent," a private school participating in the OSP is subject only "to the ... curriculum ... criteria adopted by an appropriate nonpublic school accrediting body." § 1002.38(4)(f), Fla. Stat. (2005). There are numerous nonpublic school accrediting bodies that have "widely variant quality standards and program requirements." Florida Department of Education, *Private School Accreditation*, http://www.floridaschoolchoice.org/Information/Private_Schools/accreditation.asp (last visited Jan. 3, 2005). Thus, curriculum standards of eligible private schools may vary greatly depending on the accrediting body, and these standards may not be equivalent to those required for Florida public schools.

In all these respects, the alternative system of private schools funded by the OSP cannot be deemed uniform in accordance with the mandate in article IX, section 1(a).

E. Other Provisions of Article IX

Reinforcing our determination that the state's use of public funds to support an alternative system of education is in violation of article IX, section 1(a) is the limitation of the use of monies from the State School Fund set forth in article IX, section 6. That provision states that income and interest from the State School Fund may be appropriated "only to the support and maintenance of free public schools." Art. IX, § 6, Fla. Const. It is well established that "[e]very provision of [the constitution] was inserted with a definite purpose and all sections and provisions of it must be construed together, that is, in pari materia, in order to determine its meaning, effect, restraints, and prohibitions." *Thomas v. State ex rel. Cobb*, 58 So.2d 173, 174 (Fla.1952); *see also Caribbean Conservation Corp.*, 838 So.2d at 501 ("[I]n construing multiple constitutional provisions addressing a similar subject, the provisions 'must be read in pari materia to ensure a consistent and logical meaning that gives effect to each provision.'") (quoting *Advisory Opinion to the Governor—1996 Amendment 5 (Everglades)*, 706 So.2d 278, 281 (Fla.1997)). Reading sections 1(a) and 6 of article IX in *pari materia* evinces the clear intent that public funds be used to support the public school system, not to support a duplicative, competitive private system.

Further, in reading article IX as a whole, we note the clear difference between the language of section 1(a) and that of section 1(b), which was adopted in 2002 and provides in full:

> Every four-year old child in Florida *shall be provided by the State a high quality pre-kindergarten learning opportunity in the form of an early childhood development and education program which shall be voluntary, high quality, free, and delivered according to professionally accepted standards.* An early childhood development and education program means an organized program designed

to address and enhance each child's ability to make age appropriate progress in an appropriate range of settings in the development of language and cognitive capabilities and emotional, social, regulatory and moral capacities through education in basic skills and such other skills as the Legislature may determine to be appropriate.

(Emphasis supplied.) Although this provision requires that the pre-kindergarten learning opportunity must be free and delivered according to professionally accepted standards, noticeably absent is a requirement that the state provide this opportunity by a particular means. Thus, in contrast to the Legislature's obligation under section 1(a) to make adequate provision for kindergarten through grade twelve education through a system of free public schools, the Legislature is free under section 1(b) to provide for pre-kindergarten education in any manner it desires, consistent with other applicable constitutional provisions.

We reject the argument that the OSP falls within the state's responsibility under article IX, section 1(a) to make "[a]dequate provision ... for ... other public education programs that the needs of the people may require." As this Court explained in *Board of Public Instruction*, the reference to "other public education programs" added in 1968 "obviously applies to the existing systems of junior colleges, adult education, etc., which are not strictly within the general conception of free public schools or institutions of higher learning." 231 So.2d at 2. The OSP is limited to kindergarten through grade twelve education.

F. Other Programs Unaffected

The OSP is distinguishable from the program at issue in *Scavella v. School Board of Dade County*, 363 So.2d 1095 (Fla.1978), under which exceptional students could attend "private schools because of the lack of *special* services" in their school district. *Id.* at 1097 (emphasis supplied). The program allowed a school board to use state funds to pay for a private school education if the public school did "not have the *special* facilities or instructional personnel to provide an adequate educational opportunity" for certain exceptional students, specifically physically disabled students. *See id.* at 1098 (emphasis supplied). Further, it was not the program itself that was challenged in *Scavella* but a subsequent amendment to the program that placed a cap on the amount of money a school district could pay to a private institution. *See id.* at 1097. The issue was whether the cap violated the students' right to equal protection under article I, section 2, Florida Constitution, which expressly provided that "[n]o person shall be deprived of any right because of ... physical handicap." *See id.* at 1097. The Court held that "the statute requires the school districts to establish a maximum amount that would not deprive any student of a right to a free education," and that so interpreted the statute did "not deny anyone of equal protection before the law." *Id.* at 1099. We conclude that the First District erred in relying on *Scavella* to support its determination that the OSP does not violate article IX, section 1(a).[24]

---

24. [FN14.] The dissent notes that Florida funded private schools until the early Twentieth Century, which is of merely historical interest because the practice ended long before the adoption of the 1998

We reject the suggestion by the State and amici that other publicly funded educational and welfare programs would necessarily be affected by our decision. Other educational programs, such as the program for exceptional students at issue in *Scavella*, are structurally different from the OSP, which provides a systematic private school alternative to the public school system mandated by our constitution. Nor are public welfare programs implicated by our decision, which rests solely on our interpretation of the provisions of article IX, the education article of the Florida Constitution. Other legislatively authorized programs may also be distinguishable in ways not fully explored or readily apparent at this stage. The effect of our decision on those programs would be mere speculation.

CONCLUSION

In sum, article IX, section 1(a) provides for the manner in which the state is to fulfill its mandate to make adequate provision for the education of Florida's children—through a system of public education. The OSP contravenes this constitutional provision because it allows some children to receive a publicly funded education through an alternative system of private schools that are not subject to the uniformity requirements of the public school system. The diversion of money not only reduces public funds for a public education but also uses public funds to provide an alternative education in private schools that are not subject to the "uniformity" requirements for public schools. Thus, in two significant respects, the OSP violates the mandate set forth in article IX, section 1(a).

We do not question the basic right of parents to educate their children as they see fit. We recognize that the proponents of vouchers have a strongly held view that students should have choices. Our decision does not deny parents recourse to either public or private school alternatives to a failing school. Only when the private school option depends upon public funding is choice limited. This limit is necessitated by the constitutional mandate in article IX, section 1(a), which sets out the state's responsibilities in a manner that does not allow the use of state monies to fund a private school education. As we recently explained, "[w]hat is in the Constitution always must prevail over emotion. Our oaths as judges require that this principle is our polestar, and it alone." *Bush v. Schiavo*, 885 So.2d 321, 336 (Fla.2004).

Because we conclude that section 1002.38 violates article IX, section 1(a) of the Florida Constitution, we disapprove the First District's decision in *Holmes I*. We affirm the First District's decision finding section 1002.38 unconstitutional in *Holmes II*, but neither approve nor disapprove the First District's determination that the OSP violates the "no aid" provision in article I, section 3 of the Florida Constitution, an issue we decline to reach. In order not to disrupt the education of students who are receiving vouchers for the current school year, our decision shall have prospective application to commence at the conclusion of the current school year.

---

constitutional amendment we construe and apply today. The dissent cites no authority suggesting that the constitutional validity of these allocations was ever challenged as an unconstitutional public funding of private schools under Florida's education article.

It is so ordered.

WELLS, ANSTEAD, LEWIS, and QUINCE, concur.

BELL, J., dissents with an opinion, in which CANTERO, J., concurs.

BELL, J., dissenting.

"[N]othing in article IX, section 1 clearly prohibits the Legislature from allowing the well-delineated use of public funds for private school education, particularly in circumstances where the Legislature finds such use is necessary." *Bush v. Holmes*, 767 So.2d 668, 675 (Fla. 1st DCA 2000) (footnote omitted). This conclusion, written by Judge Charles Kahn for a unanimous panel of the First District Court of Appeal, is the only answer this Court is empowered to give to the constitutional question the majority has decided to answer. Therefore, I dissent.

In its construction of this constitutional provision, the majority asserts that it "follow[s] principles parallel to those guiding statutory construction," yet its reasoning fails to adhere to the most fundamental of these principles. Majority op. at 400. It fails to evince any presumption that the OSP is constitutional or any effort to resolve every doubt in favor of its constitutionality. Therefore, I begin this dissent by stating the fundamental principles that should direct any determination of whether the OSP violates article IX, section 1. Next, I address the text of article IX, section 1. I will show that this text is plain and unambiguous. Because article IX is unambiguous, it needs no interpretation, and it is inappropriate to use maxims of statutory construction to justify an exclusivity not in the text. Finally, I find no record support for the majority's presumption that the OSP prevents the State from fulfilling its mandate to make adequate provision for a uniform system of free public schools.

I. Fundamental Principles of State Constitutional Jurisprudence

This Court has long proclaimed that courts "have the power to declare laws unconstitutional only as a matter of imperative and unavoidable necessity," *State ex rel. Crim v. Juvenal*, 118 Fla. 487, 159 So. 663, 664 (1935), and are "bound 'to resolve all doubts as to the validity of [a] statute in favor of its constitutionality, provided the statute may be given a fair construction that is consistent with the federal and state constitutions as well as with the legislative intent.'" *Caple v. Tuttle's Design-Build, Inc.*, 753 So.2d 49, 51 (Fla.2000) (quoting *State v. Stalder*, 630 So.2d 1072, 1076 (Fla.1994)). Indeed, "[w]hen a legislative enactment is challenged the court should be liberal in its interpretation; every doubt should be resolved in favor of the constitutionality of the law, and the law should not be held invalid unless clearly unconstitutional beyond a reasonable doubt." *Taylor v. Dorsey*, 155 Fla. 305, 19 So.2d 876, 882 (1944).

This judicial deference to duly enacted legislation is derived from three "first principles" of state constitutional jurisprudence. First, the people are the ultimate sovereign. *Rivera-Cruz v. Gray*, 104 So.2d 501, 506 (Fla.1958) (Terrell, C.J., concurring) (recognizing that "[t]he Constitution is the people's document.... As said by George Mason in the Virginia Declaration of Rights, adopted June 12, 1776: 'all power is vested in, and consequently derived from, the people; [therefore,] [m]agistrates are their trustees and servants, and at all times amenable to them'"). Second, unlike the federal constitution, our state constitution is a limitation upon the power of government rather than a grant of that power. *Chiles v. Phelps*, 714 So.2d 453, 458 (Fla.1998) (citing *Savage v. Board of Public Instruction*, 101 Fla. 1362, 133 So. 341, 344 (1931), for the proposition that "[t]he Constitution of this state is not a grant of power to the Legislature, but a limitation only upon legislative power, and unless legislation be clearly contrary to some express or necessarily implied prohibition found in the Constitution, the courts are without authority to declare legislative [a]cts invalid"). This means that the Legislature has general legislative or policy-making power over such issues as the education of Florida's children except as those powers are specifically limited by the constitution. *Id.* (recognizing that "[t]he legislature's power is inherent, though it may be limited by the constitution"); *see also State ex rel. Green v. Pearson*, 153 Fla. 314, 14 So.2d 565, 567 (1943) ("It is a familiarly accepted doctrine of constitutional law that the power of the Legislature is inherent.... The legislative branch looks to the Constitution not for sources of power but for limitations upon power."). Third, because general legislative or policy-making power is vested in the legislature, the power of judicial review over legislative enactments is strictly limited. Specifically, when a legislative enactment is challenged under the state constitution, courts are without authority to invalidate the enactment unless it is clearly contrary to an express or necessarily implied prohibition within the constitution. *Chapman v. Reddick*, 41 Fla. 120, 25 So. 673, 677 (1899) ("[U]nless legislation duly passed be clearly contrary to some express or implied prohibition contained [in the constitution], the courts have no authority to pronounce it invalid.").

Because of these three "first principles," statutes like the OSP come to courts with a strong presumption of constitutionality. *State v. Jefferson*, 758 So.2d 661, 664 (Fla.2000) ("[w]henever possible, statutes should be construed in such a manner so as to avoid an unconstitutional result"); *see also State ex rel. Shevin v. Metz Const. Co., Inc.*, 285 So.2d 598, 600 (Fla.1973) ("It is elementary that a statute is clothed with a presumption of constitutional validity"). And, as we will see from the text of article IX, section 1, when read in light of these fundamental principles, the OSP does not violate any express or necessarily implied provision of article IX, section 1(a) of the Florida Constitution.

II. Article IX, Section 1 and the OSP

The text of article IX, section 1 is plain and unambiguous. In its third sentence, it clearly mandates that the State make adequate provision for a system of free public schools. But, contrary to the majority's conclusion, it does not preclude the Legislature from using its general legislative powers to provide a private school scholarship to a finite number of parents who have a child in one of Florida's relatively few "failing" public schools. Even if the text of article IX, section 1 could be considered ambiguous on this issue, there is absolutely no evidence that the voters or drafters ever intended any such proscription. Given these irrefutable facts, it is wholly inappropriate for a court to use a statutory maxim such as *expressio unius est exclusio alterius* to imply such a proscription.

A. The Plain Meaning of Article IX, Section 1

The majority ... states that the public school system is "the exclusive means set out in the constitution for the Legislature to make adequate provision for the education of children." Majority op. at 409. It reads article IX, section 1(a) as "a limitation on the Legislature's power because it provides both a mandate to provide for children's education and a restriction on the execution of that mandate." Majority op. at 406. Therefore, the majority concludes that "[t]he OSP violates [article IX, section 1] by devoting the state's resources to the education of children within our state through means other than a system of free public schools." Majority op. at 407.

The majority's reading of article IX, section 1 is flawed. There is no language of exclusion in the text. Nothing in either the second or third sentence of article IX, section 1 requires that public schools be the sole means by which the State fulfills its duty to provide for the education of children. And there is no basis to imply such a proscription.

The meaning of this clause, especially if read in light of the presumptions and "first principles" discussed above, is plain. The people of Florida declare in the first sentence that they consider the education of children a core value. In the second sentence, they establish that it is a primary duty of their government to see that this value is fulfilled. These two sentences state:

> The education of children is a fundamental value of the people of the State of Florida. It is, therefore, a paramount duty of the state to make adequate provision for the education of all children residing within its borders.

Having laid this foundation, the people specify exactly what they demand of their government in regards to this duty to make adequate provision for the education of Florida's children. They specify three things; however, only the first mandate is at issue in this case. This first mandate requires the Legislature to make adequate provision by law *for* a system of free public schools, institutions of higher learning and other educational programs. Specifically, the mandate states:

> Adequate provision shall be made by law *for* a uniform, efficient, safe, secure, and high quality system of free public schools that allows students to obtain a high quality education and for the establishment, maintenance, and operation of institutions of higher learning and other public education programs that the needs of the people may require.

(Emphasis added.) This mandate is to make adequate provision *for* a public school system. The text does not provide that the government's provision for education shall be "by" or "through" a system of free public schools. Without language of exclusion or preclusion, there is no support for the majority's finding that public schools are the exclusive means by or through which the government may fulfill its duty to make adequate provision for the education of every child in Florida.

As the ultimate sovereign, if the people of Florida had wanted to mandate this exclusivity, they could have very easily written article IX to include such a proscription. Ten other states have constitutional provisions that expressly prohibit the allocation of public education funds to private schools.[25] *Compare* art. IX, Fla. Const., *with, e.g.,* Miss. Const. art. 8, §208 ("[N]or shall any funds be appropriated toward the support of any sectarian school, or to any school that at the time of receiving such appropriation is not conducted as a free school."), *and* S.C. Const. art. XI, §4 ("No money shall be paid from public funds nor shall the credit of the State or any of its political subdivisions be used for the direct benefit of any religious or other private educational institution."). However, the people of Florida have not included such a proscription in article IX, section 1 of the Florida Constitution. Therefore, without any express or necessarily implied proscription in article IX, section 1 of Florida's Constitution, this Court has no authority to declare the OSP unconstitutional as violative of article IX, section 1.

B. The History of Article IX: Discerning the Voters' and Drafters' Intent

Because the plain language of article IX, section 1 is wholly sufficient to conclude that this provision does not prohibit a program such as the OSP, it is unnecessary and improper to go beyond the text by citing to the intent of the voters and drafters.[26] However, I include it here because the majority asserts that article IX, section 1 is "not clear and unambiguous regarding public funding of private schools," majority op. at 408, and a majority of this Court has found legislative history persuasive in the past—at least in regard to statutory interpretation. *See Am. Home Assur. Co. v. Plaza Materials Corp.*, 908 So.2d 360 (Fla.2005). Moreover, the history of article IX helps to highlight why the majority's use of the *expressio unius* maxim, in particular, is improper because this history provides no support for the majority's implied exclusivity.

1. The 1998 Amendments to Article IX, Section 1

My criticism of the majority's interpretation of article IX, section 1 is confirmed by looking at how the amendments to article IX were presented to the voters in 1998. Consistent with the plain meaning of the text, the ballot summary reveals that: (1) the first sentence was added as a declaration of the value of education; (2) the second sentence was added to "establish adequate provision for education as a paramount duty of the state"; and (3) the third sentence was modified to expand the terms of the existing mandate relative to public schools. Nowhere in this ballot summary were the voters informed that by adopting the amendments, they would be mandating

---

25. [FN17.] In addition to Mississippi and South Carolina, Alaska, California, Hawaii, Kansas, Michigan, Nebraska, New Mexico, and Wyoming also prohibit public education funds from going to any private school in their state constitutions. *See* Alaska Const. art. VII, §1; Cal. Const. art. IX, §8; Haw. Const. art. 10, §1; Kan. Const. art. 6, §6(c); Mich. Const. art. VII, §2; Neb. Const. art VII, §11; N.M. Const. art. VII, §2; Wyo. Const. art. VII, §4.

26. [FN19.] Courts should not use legislative history to depart from the text's plain meaning. It is dangerous to attempt to divine the intent behind a statutory or constitutional provision from the statements of individuals involved in the process. *See Am. Home Assur. Co. v. Plaza Materials Corp.*, 908 So.2d 360, 371 (Fla.2005) (Cantero, J., concurring in part and dissenting in part). Nonetheless, a majority of this Court apparently finds legislative history persuasive, at least when interpreting statutory text. *Id.* at 368–69. Therefore, I include the history of article IX here not because I would rely on it in upholding the OSP program, but because it demonstrates that there is no refuge for the majority's finding the OSP is unconstitutional.

that the public school system would become the exclusive means by which the State could fulfill its duty to provide for education.

The [ballot summary] of the 1998 amendment read as follows

BALLOT SUMMARY

Declares the education of children to be a fundamental value to the people of Florida; establishes adequate provision for education as a paramount duty of the state; expands constitutional mandate requiring the state to make adequate provision for a uniform system of free public schools by also requiring the state to make adequate provision for an efficient, safe, secure and high quality system.

Significantly, the *only* reference to a mandate in the ballot summary is in regard to the preexisting third sentence, and this reference only speaks of "expand[ing] the constitutional mandate requiring the State to make adequate provision for" the public school system. It does not refer to the second sentence as a mandate. And it certainly does not describe this amendment as mandating that the public school system be the exclusive means for carrying out the State's duty to provide education under article IX, section 1.

2. The Constitution Revision Commission

The majority will also find no support for its interpretation of article IX, section 1 in the history behind the drafting of the 1998 amendments. There is no evidence that this clause was intended to place "a limitation on the Legislature's power because it provides both a mandate to provide for children's education and a restriction on the execution of that mandate." Majority op. at 406. Instead, the evidence from the 1997–98 Constitution Revision Commission supports the textual understanding I described above.

According to a prominent member of this Commission, the sole purpose for amending article IX, section 1 was to emphasize the importance of education and to provide a standard for defining "adequate provision." Jon Mills & Timothy McClendon, *Setting a New Standard for Public Education: Revision 6 Increases the Duty of the State to Make "Adequate Provision" for Florida Schools*, 52 Fla. L.Rev. 329, 331 (2000) (stating that "The Constitution Revision Commission's clear goal [when revising article IX] was to increase the state's constitutional duty and raise the constitutional standard for adequate education, and in fact to make the standard high quality"). There was no intent to make public schools the exclusive manner by which the Legislature could make provision for educating children.

A review of the minutes of the meetings of the Commission reveals a finding that a proposal to preclude educational vouchers was actually presented to the Commission by the public, but never accepted. When the Constitution Revision Commission convened to draft the language for the 1998 amendments, the issue of whether the state should be allowed to fund education at private schools was clearly before them. The debate over education vouchers had been a matter of nationwide public debate since at least the early 1990s. For example, in 1992 the Wisconsin Supreme Court upheld a program similar to the OSP under an education article that also required the state legislature to provide by law for the establishment of a uniform public school system. *Davis v. Grover*, 480 N.W.2d 460 (Wis. 1992). And opportunity scholarships were a central part of Florida's hotly contested 1998 gubernatorial campaign. Peter Wallsten & Tim Nickens, *Governor's Race is Set; Education is the Issue*, St. Petersburg Times, July 7, 1998, at 1A, *available at* http://www.sptimes.com (search Archives for "governor's race is set"). Indeed, the citizens of Florida raised this very issue at the Commission's public hearings.... Despite this intense public debate, the Commission offered no amendments related to educational vouchers.

Again, the Commission's goal, as stated by Commissioner Jon Mills, was "to increase the State's constitutional duty and raise the constitutional standard for education." As another commissioner explained:

> Now I want to point out clearly and for purposes of intent that as the education of our children in the state move in various directions, whether it be charter schools, private schools, public schools, and whatever preference you have as to how our children are educated, this amendment [to article IX] does not address that.

> What this amendment does is says that as we move off in those directions ... this amendment is going to ensure everyone moves together, that every child is ensured an education: the poor, the black, the whites, the Asians, the Hispanics. Every one will be ensured this fundamental right, no matter what direction this State takes.

Florida Constitution Revision Commission, Meeting Proceedings for January 15, 1998, Transcript at 265–66, http://www.law.fsu.edu/crc/minutes.html [hereinafter CRC Jan. 15 Transcript] (statement of Commissioner Brochin). A number of other commissioners affirmed this position, voicing their convictions that the amendments to article IX should not limit the Legislature's authority to determine the best method for providing education in Florida. *See, e.g.*, CRC Jan. 15 Transcript at 296–97 (statement of Commissioner Thompson expressing a desire to ensure the Legislature retains the freedom to determine how best to provide education); *see also* Florida Constitution Revision Commission, Meeting Proceedings for February 26, 1998, at 55, http://www.law.fsu.edu/crc/minutes.html (statement of Commissioner Evans conveying fear that the heightened importance of education in article IX would transfer power from the voters to the courts); *see also* CRC Jan. 15 Transcript at 269 (statement of Commissioner Langley expressing concern that the heightened importance of education in article IX would transform the Florida Supreme Court into the State Board of Education).

C. The Maxims of Statutory Construction

As established above, there is no textual or historical support for the majority's reading of article IX, section 1 as a prohibition on the Legislature's authority to provide any public funds to private schools. Given this complete absence of textual or historical support, I strongly disagree with the majority's use of maxims of statutory construction to imply such a prohibition. *See Holly v. Auld*, 450 So.2d 217 (Fla.1984), where this Court held, "'[w]hen the language of the statute is clear and unambiguous and conveys a definite meaning, there is no occasion for resorting to the rules of statutory interpretation and construction; the statute must be given its plain and obvious meaning.'" *Id.* at 219 (quoting *A.R. Douglass, Inc. v. McRainey*, 102 Fla. 1141, 137 So. 157, 159 (1931)). In particular, the use of *expressio unius* in this case significantly expands this Court's case law in a way that illustrates the danger of liberally applying this maxim.

It is generally agreed in courts across this nation that *expressio unius* is a maxim of statutory construction that should rarely be used when interpreting constitutional provisions and, then, only with great caution. *See generally State ex rel. Jackman v. Court of Common Pleas of Cuyahoga County*, 9 Ohio St.2d 159, 224 N.E.2d 906, 910 (1967) (recognizing that the *expressio unius* maxim "should be applied with caution to [constitutional] provisions ... relating to the legislative branch of government, since [the maxim] cannot be made to restrict the plenary power of the legislature") (citing 16 C.J.S. *Constitutional Law* § 21); 16 Am.Jur.2d *Constitutional Law* § 69 (2005) (stating "the maxim 'expressio unius est exclusio alterius' does not apply with the same force to a constitution as to a statute ..., and it should be used sparingly"); *see also, e.g., Reale v. Bd. of Real Estate Appraisers*, 880 P.2d 1205, 1213 (Colo.1994) (finding the *expressio unius* maxim "inapt" when used to imply a limitation in a state constitution because the "powers not specifically limited [in the constitution] are presumptively retained by the people's representatives").

This Court has employed *expressio unius* in addressing constitutional questions, but only rarely. As Judge Kahn aptly noted in his 2000 opinion, the question of whether article IX proscribes a program such as the OSP is clearly distinguishable from other cases in which we have applied this maxim:

> In *Weinberger,* and the other cases relied upon by the trial court, ... the *expressio unius* principle found its way into the analysis only because the constitution forbade any action other than that specified in the constitution, and the action taken by the Legislature defeated the purpose of the constitutional provision.

> In contrast, in this case, nothing in article IX, section 1 clearly prohibits the Legislature from allowing the well-delineated use of public funds for private school education, particularly in circumstances where the Legislature finds such use is necessary.

Bush, 767 So.2d at 674 (citations and footnote omitted). I agree with this analysis. Article IX, section 1 does not forbid the Legislature from enacting a well-delineated program such as the OSP.

In accord with courts across this nation, this Court has long recognized that the *expressio unius* maxim should not be used to imply a limitation on the Legislature's power unless this limitation is absolutely necessary to carry out the purpose of the constitutional provision. *Marasso v. Van Pelt*, 77 Fla. 432, 81 So. 529, 530 (1919). We have repeatedly refused to apply this maxim in situations where the statute at issue bore a "real relation to the subject and object" of the constitutional provision, *id.* at 532, or did not violate the primary purpose behind the constitutional provision. *Taylor v. Dorsey*, 155 Fla. 305, 19 So.2d 876, 882 (1944). The majority's use of this maxim violates both restrictions.

The principles stated in *Marasso* and *Taylor* restricting the application of the *expressio unius* maxim in constitutional interpretation apply in this case. The OSP bears a "real relation to the subject and object" of article IX. The primary objective of article IX is to ensure that the Legislature makes adequate provision for a public school system. It does not require that this system be the exclusive means. And, as I have said earlier and will elaborate in more detail below, there is no evidence that the OSP prevents the Legislature from making adequate provision for a public school system that is available to every child in Florida. Because it is not absolutely necessary to imply such a limitation upon the Legislature's power in order to carry out the purpose of article IX, section 1, it is improper for this court to use *expressio unius* as the basis for doing so. *Marasso v. Van Pelt*, 77 Fla. 432, 81 So. 529, 530 (1919).

Likewise, the majority's reading of article IX, section 1 *in pari materia* with article IX, section 6 certainly supports the importance of the public school system in this State. However, it does not imply an absolute prohibition against the use of public funds to provide parents with children in a public school that is not properly educating their child with the option of placing that child in a private school. In fact, in the more than 150 years that section 6 has been a part of Florida's Constitution, it has never been interpreted as preventing the State from using public funds to provide education through private schools. Historical records indicate that Florida provided public funds to private schools until, at least, 1917. *See, e.g.,* Thomas Everette Cochran, *History of Public-School Education in Florida* 25 (1921) (indicating the State provided $3,964 to private academies in 1860); Nita Katharine Pyburn, *Documentary History of Education in Florida: 1822–1860* 27 (1951) (recognizing that it was relatively common for the State to fund private academies, the "accepted form of secondary education" through general revenues); Richard J. Gabel, *Public Funds for Church and Private Schools* 638, 639 n. 3 (May 1937) (Ph.D. dissertation, Catholic University of America) (relying on historical documents to find that Florida use public funds to provide private education until at least 1917). In addition, a commentary on the proposed 1958 constitutional revision described the education article as "authoriz[ing] a system of uniform free public schools, and also permit[ting] the legislature to provide assistance for 'other non-sectarian schools.'" Manning J. Dauer, *The Proposed New Florida Constitution: An Analysis* 16 (1958). When the Florida House of Representatives considered language for the 1968 constitution, it rejected a proposal to add a section to article IX that would have limited the Legislature's use of education funds by preventing any state money from going to sectarian schools. *See 3 Minutes: Committee of the Whole House, Constitutional Revision* 34 (1967) (proposed art. IX, §7, Fla. Const). Consequently, I can find no justification for the majority's assertion that reading article IX, section 1 in pari materia with article IX, section 6 justifies its conclusion that article IX, section 1 must be interpreted to restrict the Legislature from applying public funds to private schools.

II. No Evidence That the OSP Prevents the Legislature from Fulfilling its Article IX Mandate

Given the fact that neither the text nor the history of article IX supports the majority's reading of this provision as "mandat(ing) that 'adequate provision for the education of all children' shall be by a ... system of free public schools," the only other basis for concluding that the OSP violates article IX is to establish that the program prevents the Legislature from fulfilling its duty to make adequate provision by law for the public school system. The majority does not cite, nor can I find, any evidence in the record before us to support such a finding. In this facial challenge to the OSP, there is absolutely no evidence that the Legislature has either failed to make adequate provision for a statewide system of free public schools or that this system is not available to every child in Florida.

To support its position, the majority critiques the Legislature's failure to recognize its duty to provide a system of free public schools in the statute authorizing the OSP. Majority op. at 406–07. While the Legislature may not have recited the language of article IX verbatim in the statute authorizing the OSP, I find no competent, substantial evidence that the OSP was enacted to somehow escape article IX's mandate to make adequate provision for a system of free public schools, or that this program, in fact, results in an inadequate provision by law for the public school system.

Indeed, the statute authorizing the OSP presents the public school system as the first option for parents with children in a public school that has twice failed to meet the Legislature's educational standards. § 1002.38, Fla. Stat. (2004). It requires school districts to notify parents whose children attend a school qualifying for an opportunity scholarship of the right to attend a higher-performing public school either within or outside of their district. §§ 1002.38(3)(a)(2), 1002.38(3)(b), Fla. Stat. (2004). In addition, the legislative history surrounding the OSP indicates that the purpose behind the program was to improve the public school system by increasing accountability in education. In fact, around the time the OSP was enacted, the Senate rejected a bill authorizing a pilot program that would have provided education vouchers without regard to the public school's performance. See Fla. SB 100 (1999).

Moreover, there is absolutely no evidence that the OSP prevents the Legislature from making adequate provision for a public school system. Opportunity scholarships are available on a very limited basis—only to students whose public school has repeatedly failed to meet the Legislature's minimum standard for a "high quality education." While the scholarships are taken from public moneys allocated to public education, the amount of money removed from the public schools is not a dollar-for-dollar reduction because the opportunity scholarships are capped at the nonpublic school's tuition. On average, this is apparently less than the per-pupil allocation to public schools. Furthermore, the program is part of a broader education initiative that provides additional assistance to failing schools. Schools that receive an "F" must file school improvement plans, and studies show that these schools actually receive, on average, $800 more in per-pupil funding than "A" schools, even after accounting for the financial rewards given to high performing schools. Governor's Office Initiatives: A+ Plan, Opportunity Scholarships, http://www.myflorida.com/myflorida/government/governorinitiatives/aplusplan/opportunityScholarships.html (Aug. 17, 2005). Therefore, the omission of the phrase "uniform public school system" in the legislative findings in the statute authorizing the OSP provides no justification for the majority's conclusion that the OSP violates article IX.

Just as there is no textual or historical support for the majority's finding that article IX, section 1 mandates that the Legislature must make adequate provision for the education of Florida's children exclusively through the public school system, there is absolutely no support for the alternative finding that the OSP somehow prevents the Legislature from fulfilling its article IX mandate.

Conclusion

Our position as justices vests us with the right and the responsibility to declare a legislative enactment invalid—but only when such a declaration is an "imperative and unavoidable necessity." *State ex rel. Crim*, 159 So. at 664. No such necessity is evident in this case. Nothing in the plain language or history of article IX requires a finding that the Opportunity Scholarship Program is unconstitutional. The clear purpose behind article IX is to ensure that every child in Florida has the opportunity to receive a high-quality education and to ensure access to such an education by requiring the Legislature to make adequate provision for a uniform system of free public schools. There is absolutely no evidence before this Court that this mandate is not being fulfilled.... The Opportunity Scholarship Program does not violate article IX, section 1 of Florida's Constitution.

CANTERO, J., concurs.

Questions

1. How did the 1998 revision to Article IX, Section 1 change the nature of the Education Clause? Why did this change mandate the result in this case with regard to vouchers?

2. How does the dissent see the role of the Legislature in providing for public education? What constraints are placed upon the Legislature by the Education Clause?

Citizens for Strong Schools v. State Board of Education

262 So. 3d 127 (Fla. 2019)

PER CURIAM.

This case involves a nearly ten-year attempt by Petitioners to have the State of Florida's K-12 public education system declared unconstitutional due to the State's alleged failure to comply with article IX, section 1(a) of the Florida Constitution, which provides in relevant part as follows:

> (a) The education of children is a fundamental value of the people of the State of Florida. It is, therefore, a paramount duty of the state to make adequate provision for the education of all children residing within its borders. Adequate provision shall be made by law for a uniform, efficient, safe, secure, and high quality system of free public schools that allows students to obtain a high quality education. . . .

Art. IX, § 1(a), Fla. Const. Specifically, Petitioners seek a declaration that the State is breaching its "paramount duty to make adequate provision for a uniform, efficient, safe, secure, and high quality system of free public schools that allows students to obtain a high quality education." And Petitioners request the courts to order the State "to establish a remedial plan that . . . includes necessary studies to determine what resources and standards are necessary to provide a high quality education to Florida students."

The language in article IX, section 1(a) regarding "fundamental value," "paramount duty of the state," and "efficient, safe, secure, and high quality system of free public schools that allows students to obtain a high quality education" was added in 1998, after the changes were proposed by the Constitution Revision Commission (CRC) and approved by the voters. Prior to 1998, article IX, section 1 provided in relevant part as follows:

> Adequate provision shall be made by law for a uniform system of free public schools. . . .

The 1998 amendments were in part in response to *Coalition for Adequacy & Fairness in School Funding, Inc. v. Chiles* (*Coalition*), 680 So. 2d 400 (Fla. 1996), in which this Court upheld the trial court's dismissal with prejudice of a complaint that "asked the trial court to declare that an adequate education is a fundamental right . . . and that the State has failed to provide its students that fundamental right by failing to allocate adequate resources for a uniform system of free public schools." *Id.* at 402. The allegations in *Coalition*—made in the context of "a blanket assertion that the entire system is constitutionally inadequate," *id.* at 406—focused on purported inadequacies in funding and disparities relating to certain subgroups of students, including "[e]conomically deprived students," disabled students, and "[s]tudents in property-poor counties." *Id.* at 402. This Court upheld the dismissal with prejudice because the appellants made "an insufficient showing" "to justify" "judicial intrusion" into the Legislature's powers and responsibilities. *Id.* at 407; *see id.* at 408 (Overton, J., concurring).

Here, Petitioners' blanket challenge bears a striking resemblance to that in *Coalition*, namely in its focus on purportedly inadequate funding and on disparities relating to certain subgroups of students. The trial court, relying on *Coalition* and dismissing the relevance of the 1998 amendments, rejected Petitioners' challenge. The First District Court of Appeal affirmed.

We have for review *Citizens for Strong Schools, Inc. v. Florida State Board of Education* (*Citizens*), 232 So. 3d 1163 (Fla. 1st DCA 2017), in which the First District concluded that the 1998 amendments—namely, the words "efficient" and "high quality"—do not provide sufficiently manageable standards to overcome the political question and separation of powers concerns that were determinative in *Coalition*. We have jurisdiction. *See* art. V, §3(b)(3), Fla. Const.

We conclude that *Coalition* defeats Petitioners' claim because Petitioners—like the appellants in *Coalition*—fail to present any manageable standard by which to avoid judicial intrusion into the powers of the other branches of government. Accordingly, we approve the result reached by the First District. Before explaining our decision, we review the lengthy procedural history of this case.

I. BACKGROUND

This case began in November 2009—in the wake of the Great Recession—when certain public school students, parents, and citizen organizations (collectively, Petitioners) filed suit against the State Board of Education, the President of the Florida Senate, the Speaker of the Florida House of Representatives, and the Florida Commissioner of Education (collectively, Respondents) seeking a declaration that the State is breaching its paramount duty under article IX, section 1(a). Or as the First District later described it, Petitioners' claim is "that the State's entire K-12 public education system—which includes 67 school districts, approximately 2.7 million students, 170,000 teachers, 150,000 staff members, and 4,000 schools—is in violation of the Florida Constitution." *Citizens*, 232 So. 3d at 1165.

In their complaint, Petitioners cited the 1998 amendments to article IX, section 1 and asserted that "adequate provision" and "high quality" are to be "measured by both the enumerated characteristics of and inputs into the system itself as well as the outcome results of that system." Petitioners largely focused on purported inadequacies in funding and alleged that the "2009 Appropriations Act for K-12 education violates the Education Clause of the Florida Constitution." Petitioners also criticized, among other things, the State's "current accountability policy," "misus[e]" of standardized test results, inadequate graduation rates, and achievement test results. Petitioners further alleged that the State's alleged "failure to provide a high quality education disproportionately impacts minority, low income and students with disabilities." In the end, Petitioners requested that the trial court order Respondents "to establish a remedial plan that conforms with the Florida Constitution." Petitioners later amended their complaint to request that the remedial plan "include[] necessary studies to determine what resources and standards are necessary to provide a high quality education to Florida students."

Respondents' Motion to Dismiss

Respondents moved to dismiss Petitioners' complaint, principally on the basis that Petitioners' claim "alleges a non-justiciable political question" and was similar to the blanket challenge rejected in *Coalition*. The trial court denied Respondents' motion, distinguishing *Coalition* as "no longer binding authority" because the allegations there were less comprehensive and were "based on a prior and weaker version of the current article IX, Section 1." The trial court instead relied on this Court's 2006 decision in

Bush v. Holmes, 919 So. 2d 392 (Fla. 2006), which interpreted the post-1998 article IX, section 1 in the context of a challenge to a voucher program. The trial court pointed to language in *Holmes* that noted that the 1998 amendments had been drafted "to provide *standards* by which to measure the adequacy of the public school education provided by the state." (Quoting *Holmes*, 919 So. 2d at 403.) The trial court thus permitted Petitioners' claim "seek[ing] system-wide declaratory and supplemental relief" to proceed.

Respondents' Petition for a Writ of Prohibition

Respondents—continuing to rely on *Coalition*—next petitioned the First District for a writ of prohibition, asserting that the trial court lacked jurisdiction to adjudicate the political questions presented by the case. *Haridopolos v. Citizens for Strong Sch., Inc.*, 81 So. 3d 465, 470 (Fla. 1st DCA 2011). The First District sitting en banc denied the petition but noted that Respondents' arguments regarding the political question doctrine would remain available on appeal. *Id.* at 471. The First District also certified the following as a question of great public importance:

> DOES ARTICLE IX, SECTION 1(A), FLORIDA CONSTITUTION, SET FORTH JUDICIALLY ASCERTAINABLE STANDARDS THAT CAN BE USED TO DETERMINE THE ADEQUACY, EFFICIENCY, SAFETY, SECURITY, AND HIGH QUALITY OF PUBLIC EDUCATION ON A STATEWIDE BASIS, SO AS TO PERMIT A COURT TO DECIDE CLAIMS FOR DECLARATORY JUDGMENT (AND SUPPLEMENTAL RELIEF) ALLEGING NONCOMPLIANCE WITH ARTICLE IX, SECTION 1(A) OF THE FLORIDA CONSTITUTION?

Id. at 473. Judge Roberts and six other judges dissented, arguing that the petition should be granted. *Id.* at 481 (Roberts, J., dissenting). Judge Roberts examined *Coalition* and concluded that the 1998 amendments were "ultimately irrelevant":

> Whether the [Constitution Revision] Commission intended to create a justiciable standard is ultimately irrelevant. The test is whether an enforceable standard was actually created by the text of the amendment itself. Because the terms "efficient ... and high quality" are no more susceptible to judicial enforcement than the term "adequate," this claim cannot be enforced by the courts.

Id. at 478 (Roberts, J., dissenting).

This Court declined to exercise jurisdiction. *Haridopolos v. Citizens for Strong Sch., Inc.*, 103 So. 3d 140 (Fla. 2012) (table).

Petitioners' Second Amended Complaint

In May 2014—nearly 4.5 years after their original complaint challenging the "2009 Appropriations Act"—Petitioners filed a Second Amended Complaint. Petitioners again focused on funding, including alleged failures of the State both to provide an adequate "overall level of funding" and to "conduct[] a cost analysis in order to determine the amount of funding required to institute a high quality education system."

Petitioners also alleged that the State had failed to provide "a 'uniform' system of free public schools," was instead "systematically diverting public funds to private schools," and had "created a parallel system of schools." To support their uniformity argument, Petitioners described two choice programs—the Florida Tax Credit Scholarship Program (FTC) and the McKay Scholarship for Students with Disabilities Program (McKay). Petitioners also alleged for the first time that the State had failed to provide an "efficient system of free public schools," claiming that the State's various reforms and programs had "wasted millions of dollars without producing the desired effect of a high quality public school system." Petitioners reiterated their allegation that the State had failed to produce a "high quality" system, and they again requested an order directing Respondents "to establish a remedial plan that ... includes necessary studies to determine what resources and standards are necessary to provide a high quality education to Florida students."

FTC/McKay Intervenors

In the wake of Petitioners' factual allegations regarding the FTC and McKay programs, the trial court permitted certain parents whose children were beneficiaries of those programs to intervene (Intervenors). Petitioners later filed a Motion for Partial Summary Judgment seeking a declaratory judgment that the FTC and McKay programs violate the uniformity requirement of article IX, section 1(a). The Intervenors opposed and submitted their own Motion for Partial Judgment on the Pleadings.

The trial court eventually ruled that the Second Amended Complaint did not contain any "claim that either program violates the Florida Constitution" and did not include any request for declaratory relief with respect to either program. The trial court also ruled that Petitioners lacked standing to challenge the FTC program. The trial court nevertheless permitted Petitioners—consistent with the pleadings—to present evidence "regarding the impact of each program on the uniformity and funding of the overall public education system."

The Trial Court's Final Judgment

After years of substantial discovery, the case proceeded to trial in 2016. After a nearly four-week bench trial involving dozens of witnesses and more than 5,000 exhibits, the trial court—a different trial judge than the one who originally denied Respondents' motion to dismiss—entered Final Judgment against Petitioners "on all claims." The trial court did so after making extensive and detailed findings. Indeed, the Final Judgment includes a 175-page appendix of findings of fact.

The trial court early on noted that "Florida's system of education is structurally complicated," in part because each county has its own school board with constitutional duties and authority. The trial court thus explained that variability necessarily exists between school districts, even among those with equivalent funding, given "variations in how the local districts allocate their resources." And the trial court concluded that the school districts, who were not parties to the suit, were "indispensable parties" to the extent Petitioners "seek relief for decisions that Florida law entrusts to local school districts—including decisions on hiring, staffing, and the allocation of resources among schools within a particular district."

The trial court went on to address the issue of justiciability anew, concluding that Petitioners presented a nonjusticiable "blanket" challenge to the adequacy of the entire education system and that, despite the 1998 amendments, the "new adjectives ...— 'efficient and high quality'—do not give judicially manageable content to the adequacy standard that was held non-justiciable in the *Coalition* case." In other words, the issues remained "political questions best resolved in the political arena." The trial court noted for example that "many of Florida's education policies and programs are subject to ongoing debate without any definitive consensus." The trial court also held that Petitioners' claim fails because of "Florida's strict separation-of-powers doctrine."

Nevertheless, given the lack of a final appellate ruling on the justiciability issue, the trial court—at great length—addressed the evidence. After determining that the burden was on Petitioners to show that Respondents' actions "are irrational or un-constitutional beyond a reasonable doubt," the trial court repeatedly discussed the "weight of the evidence" and what the evidence showed for each of Petitioners' major subdivisions of allegations. For example, the trial court concluded:

> The weight of the evidence shows that the State has made education a top priority both in terms of implementation of research-based education policies and reforms, as well as education funding. The State has an accountability and assessment system that is rated among the best in the nation, resulting in more "A" graded schools over time. The State has also adopted rigorous teacher certification, training and evaluation standards, resulting in over 94% of courses being taught by teachers who are "highly qualified" under federal standards.

Regarding funding, the trial court found, "based on the evidence presented, that there is not a constitutional level lack of resources available in Florida schools." More specifically, the trial court observed:

> With respect to funding, the evidence indicates that over the past twenty years, K-12 education has been the single largest component of the state general revenue budget. Even during the recent, severe economic downturn, the State ensured that education funding was less impacted than other government services and functions. In the current school year, the State funds education at the highest level in Florida history. Since the 1997–98 school year, education funding has outpaced inflation. The State has made efforts to equalize its funding and considers education costs for different student programs and cost-of-living differences across the state. It also is significant that the State has provided sufficient funding for schools to meet the class size requirements set forth in Article IX [under a 2002 amendment to the provision].

The trial court also found that the State's "complex funding formula"—the Florida Education Finance Program—"is generally recognized as one of the most equalizing school funding formulas in the nation." The trial court also determined that "all of the school districts in Florida have excess capacity for generating revenue through local property taxes or sales surtaxes" and that "many" of the district witnesses cited "political" reasons for not doing so.

The trial court also addressed Petitioners' arguments regarding graduation rates, test results, and disparities among certain subgroups. After determining that the "most appropriate" examination of student performance is one that views that performance "over time and in context," the trial court described substantial, dramatic, and sustained improvements that have taken place in Florida since the late 1990's, including that "the high school graduation rate has increased by over 25 points, with more students of all racial, ethnic, and socioeconomic backgrounds graduating than ever before." The trial court also cited "dramatic" and sustained improvement on test results as measured by "a variety of measures, including national and international assessments." Regarding achievement and performance gaps, the trial court found that these gaps unfortunately "exist throughout the country," but that "Florida's gaps are smaller than the national gaps, and Florida has *outpaced the nation in closing these gaps*." (Emphasis added.) As one example, the trial court found that "Florida's students eligible for free-and-reduced-price lunch ranked first in the nation, outperforming similar economically disadvantaged students in all other states." As another example, the trial court found that during the relevant period, Florida was "the only state in the nation to narrow the achievement gap between White and Black/African-American students in both reading and mathematics in the fourth and eighth grades." And as it relates to Petitioners' theory of the case—that is, the "need for more resources" argument—the trial court specifically found that Petitioners "*failed to establish any causal relationship* between any alleged low student performance and a lack of resources." (Emphasis added.) In the end, the trial court described an education system that is not perfect but that is working very well overall and has been "a top priority" of the State.

Finally, regarding the FTC and McKay programs, the trial court reiterated its prior rulings and found "no negative effect on the uniformity or efficiency of the State system of public schools due to these choice programs."

The First District's Decision

On appeal, the First District affirmed in all respects. *Citizens*, 232 So. 3d at 1174. The First District agreed with the trial court that Petitioners' arguments "raise political questions not subject to judicial review, because the relevant constitutional text does not contain judicially discoverable standards by which a court can decide whether the State has complied with organic law." *Id.* at 1165. The First District also agreed that Florida's "strict separation of powers ... requires judicial deference to the legislative and executive branches to adopt and execute educational policies those branches deem necessary and appropriate to enable students to obtain a 'high quality' education." *Id.* at 1165–66. According to the First District, article IX, section 1(a) does not "empower judges to order the enactment of educational policies regarding teaching methods and accountability, the appropriate funding of public schools, the proper allowance of charter schools and school choice, the best methods of student account-ability and school accountability, and related funding priorities." *Id.* at 1166.

The First District began by examining *Coalition* and its reference to the Supreme Court's analysis of the political question doctrine in *Baker v. Carr*, 369 U.S. 186 (1962). *Citizens*, 232 So. 3d at 1168. The First District explained how the instant case fell within *Baker's* "dominant considerations" of "attributing finality to the action of the political departments and also the lack of satisfactory criteria for a judicial de-termination.'" *Id.* (quoting *Baker*, 369 U.S. at 210). Indeed, the First District noted that this case "consume[d] years in the court system ... over the meaning of subjective and undefined phrases that might function to give guidance to political decision mak-ers as laudable goals, but cannot guide judges in deciding whether a state or local government has in fact complied with the text." *Id.* at 1169.

The First District then explained how *Coalition* rejected a similar "blanket challenge to the adequacy of the education system." *Id.* at 1169–70. The First District noted that the plaintiffs in *Coalition* "failed to demonstrate any manageable standards that could be applied without 'a substantial risk of judicial intrusion into the powers and responsibilities assigned to the legislature.'" *Id.* at 1170 (quoting *Coalition*, 680 So. 2d at 408). The First District agreed with the trial court that "'efficient' and 'high quality' are no more susceptible to judicial interpretation than 'adequate' was under the prior version of the education provision." *Id.*

The First District concluded that its holding was supported "by Florida's strict sep-aration of powers doctrine and by the language of the amended constitutional article itself." *Id.* On the latter point, the First District noted that the 1998 amendments re-tained the language that "adequate provision shall be made by law," *id.* at 1171 (quoting art. IX, § 1(a), Fla. Const.), leading the First District to conclude "that the constitution continues to commit education policy determinations to the legislative and executive branches," *id.*

The First District "recognize[d] that courts in other states have sometimes purported to define" similar concepts in their education articles, but the First District concluded that those decisions were "insufficiently deferential to the fundamental principle of separation of powers ... and the practical reality that educational policies and goals must evolve to meet ever changing public conditions." *Id.* at 1172. The First District instead agreed with other courts that have declined to impose upon the legislature the court's view of "adequacy, efficiency, and quality." *Id.*[27]

Lastly, the First District affirmed the trial court's rejection of Petitioners' arguments regarding uniformity and the FTC and McKay programs. *Id.* at 1173–74.

---

27. [FN 3.] The First District specifically noted its agreement with the Pennsylvania Supreme Court's decision in *Marrero v. Commonwealth*, 739 A.2d 110, 112 (Pa. 1999). However, as Petitioners point out, the Pennsylvania Supreme Court had distanced itself from *Marrero* prior to the First District's decision. *See William Penn Sch. Dist. v. Pennsylvania Dep't of Educ.*, 642 Pa. 236, 170 A.3d 414, 457 (Pa. 2017) ("We find irreconcilable deficiencies in the rigor, clarity, and consistency of the line of cases that culminated in [*Marrero*].").

II. ANALYSIS

This Court is being asked to determine whether in this case we have been presented with a manageable standard for assessing—in the context of a blanket challenge to the constitutionality of the K-12 education system—whether the State has made "adequate provision" for an "efficient" and "high quality" system of education "that allows students to obtain a high quality education" under article IX, section 1(a) of the Florida Constitution. The trial court and the First District both held in the negative, relying on the reasoning in Coalition. This question presents a pure issue of law that is subject to de novo review. *W. Fla. Reg'l Med. Ctr., Inc. v. See*, 79 So. 3d 1, 8 (Fla. 2012) "Statutory and constitutional construction are questions of law subject to a de novo review."). We decline to address the other issues raised by Petitioners.

We agree with the lower courts that Petitioners' blanket challenge does not survive the reasoning in Coalition, notwithstanding the 1998 amendments to article IX, section 1(a). Although we do not necessarily agree with what appears to be the district court's conclusion that an article IX challenge could never be justiciable, see *Coalition*, 680 So. 2d at 408 (declining to say "never"), we need not decide that issue. Instead, this case turns in part on Petitioners' failure to present the courts with any roadmap by which to avoid intruding into the powers of the other branches of government.

At the outset, we strongly reject any suggestion in the dissenting opinions that those of us agreeing to approve the result reached by the First District are shirking a constitutional duty or somehow care less than the dissenting justices about the education of Florida's children. Indeed, the refusal to recognize both the blanket nature of Petitioners' challenge and that this case amounts to a request for the courts to determine the appropriate amount of education funding explains in large part the asserted struggle to understand the "judicial universe" in which this case is being decided. Dissenting op. at 42, 64 (Pariente, J.).[28]

This suit began nearly a decade ago in what largely resembled a funding challenge to the "2009 Appropriations Act." Since then, not only has that appropriations act come and gone, but so too have many subsequent appropriations acts. Moreover, in that same time span, the Legislature has revised—on more than one occasion—the standards and assessments complained of by Petitioners. And the trial court explained how the State's process for developing, administering, scoring, and reporting is "an inclusive process involving Florida educators all along the way." The point being, the

---

28. [FN 5.] The dissent disputes the notion that Petitioners' claim is a "'blanket challenge' to the entire state education system." Dissenting op. at 46 (Pariente, J.). But the blanket nature of Petitioners' claim is not reasonably in dispute. The original trial judge recognized that Petitioners sought "system-wide declaratory and supplemental relief." The trial judge who later rendered Final Judgment recognized that Petitioners "have 'made a blanket assertion that the entire system is constitutionally inadequate.'" (Quoting *Coalition*, 680 So. 2d at 406.) And the First District recognized that Petitioners "assert[ed] that the State's entire K-12 public education system ... is in violation of the Florida Constitution." *Citizens*, 232 So. 3d at 1165. The attempt by the dissenters to recharacterize this case is totally at odds with the way this case has been presented by Petitioners.

education system—and education policy itself—does not remain static and is instead continually being shaped by various interested parties. Thus, Petitioners' challenge is fundamentally different than a challenge to a specific program or a specific funding issue. In effect, Petitioners ask this Court to declare the current educational system unconstitutional based on years-old evidence.

In any event, to explain why we approve the result reached by the First District, we begin by reviewing this Court's 1996 decision in *Coalition*. We then examine certain subsequent amendments to and failed attempts to amend article IX, section 1, including the adopted 1998 amendments at issue. We then examine this Court's more recent decision in *Holmes*. We conclude by explaining why Petitioners fail to overcome *Coalition*. As this Court did in *Coalition*, we decline to look to other jurisdictions. *Coalition*, 680 So. 2d at 404–05. Instead, we look to the language of the Florida Constitution and this Court's decisions.

Coalition

In *Coalition*, this Court addressed a similar challenge to the "adequacy" of the entire school system, but one brought under the pre-1998 article IX, section 1. *Coalition*, 680 So. 2d 400. The appellants in *Coalition* sought a declaration "that an adequate education is a fundamental right under the Florida Constitution, and that the State has failed to provide its students that fundamental right by failing to allocate adequate resources for a uniform system of free public schools." *Id.* at 402. Among other things, the allegations focused on purported inadequacies relating to certain subgroups of students. *Id.* The trial court dismissed the complaint with prejudice, and this Court affirmed. *Id.*

Coalition began by exploring the history of Florida's education article, noting among other things that the Constitution was amended in 1868 to provide that it was "the *paramount* duty of the State to make ample provision for the education of all the children," and that the "paramount duty" language was subsequently deleted in 1885. *Id.* at 405. *Coalition* then examined the language of the present education article, noting that "adequate provision" had not been defined but that this Court had on numerous occasions "attempted to define" the phrase "uniform system of free public education." *Id.* at 406. In doing so, this Court noted that those prior cases all involved "an objection to some specific funding issue," as opposed to "a blanket assertion" against the adequacy of "the entire [education] system." *Id.* Recognizing the nature of the case as a challenge to the Legislature's overall funding of education, this Court ultimately agreed with the trial court that "the courts cannot decide whether the Legislature's appropriation of funds is adequate in the abstract, divorced from the required uniformity" because doing so "would necessarily" require the courts "to subjectively evaluate the Legislature's value judgments as to the spending priorities to be assigned to the state's many needs, education being one among them." *Id.* at 406–07 (quoting trial court's order). This Court further agreed that "if the Court were to declare present funding levels 'inadequate,' presumably the Plaintiffs would expect the Court to evaluate, and either affirm or set aside, future appropriations decisions." *Id.* at 407 (quoting trial court's order).

Coalition then more directly addressed the separation of powers doctrine, explaining that the appellants' funding challenge implicated constitutional provisions other than just article IX. Indeed, after noting that the separation of powers doctrine was "expressly set[] forth" in article II, section 3 and that article VII, section 1(c) "expressly reserve[s] to the legislative branch" the power to appropriate funds, this Court concluded that "an insufficient showing has been made to justify judicial intrusion" into the Legislature's appropriations power. *Id.* at 407–08. This Court further concluded that, unlike the term "uniform," the term " 'adequacy' simply does not have such straightforward content." *Id.* at 408. This Court thus agreed with the appellees' reliance on] *Baker*, in which the Supreme Court "set forth six criteria to gauge whether a case involves a political question," including "(1) a textually demonstrable commitment of the issue to a coordinate political department; [and] (2) a lack of judicially discoverable and manageable standards for resolving it." *Id.*.... In doing so, this Court stated "that the legislature has been vested with *enormous discretion* by the Florida Constitution to determine what provision to make for an adequate and uniform system of free public schools." *Id.* (emphasis added).

In a concurring opinion, Justice Overton agreed with the majority that an insufficient showing had been made to justify judicial intrusion but wrote separately to express his view that the majority's holding does not preclude the judiciary from being involved in the enforcement of article IX, section 1. *Id.* at 408 (Overton, J., concurring). Justice Overton opined that although the education article "does not ensure a perfect system" or "guarantee[] a perfect or ideal education," it also "does not preclude the treatment of education as an essential, fundamental right." *Id.* at 409 (Overton, J., concurring). And Justice Overton suggested that the term "adequate" must have some "minimum threshold ... below which the funding provided by the legislature would be considered 'inadequate.' " *Id.* As an example, Justice Overton suggested that an allegation of "a thirty percent illiteracy rate" in a county would "at least state[] a cause of action." *Id.*[29]

In a dissenting-in-part opinion joined by two other justices, Justice Anstead argued that, given the "comprehensive allegations of inadequacies set out in appellants' complaint," the appellants should have been permitted to establish a factual context and that this Court had "failed to carry out its duty to ensure that the legislature has performed its constitutional mandate." *Id.* at 410 (Anstead, J., dissenting in part). Justice Anstead also emphasized the importance of education, positing that "[s]urely all would agree that education is a fundamental value in our society." *Id.* In Justice Anstead's view, the education article "recognized the fundamental value of education," and there was no need "to add 'puffing' words to suggest the quality of the system contemplated." *Id.* at 410–11 (Anstead, J., dissenting in part).

The 1998 Amendments to Article IX

In 1998, the CRC proposed and the voters approved the changes to article IX, section 1 at issue here. The 1998 amendments did not adopt Justice Overton's view in

---

29. [FN 7.] The trial court here directly addressed Justice Overton's "excellent example of why the judicial branch should never say never," finding that "[t]his case is not about a significant level of illiteracy."

Coalition and declare education to be a "fundamental right." *Coalition*, 680 So. 2d at 409 (Overton, J., concurring). Instead, the amendments stated that education of children is "a fundamental value of the people," tracking some of the language in Justice Anstead's dissenting-in-part opinion in *Coalition*. *See id.* at 410 (Anstead, J., dissenting in part). The 1998 amendments also returned the "paramount duty" language to the education article, although the amendments ... described the State's duty to make adequate provision as "a paramount duty," whereas the 1868 Constitution described the duty as "the paramount duty." Finally, the 1998 amendments added words such as "efficient" and "high quality" to describe the contemplated system of free public schools.

Members of the 1998 CRC submitted competing amicus briefs in this case. On the one hand, some of the members assert that one of the goals of the 1998 amendments was "to provide a judicially-enforceable right to a public school system that is 'uniform, efficient, safe, secure, and high quality.'" On the other hand, other members argue that "common sense" indicates that "the ambiguous terms 'high quality' and 'efficient'" were used to "set forth aspirational goals" and "to avoid litigation of the type brought in this case."

2002 Amendment to Article IX—Class Size Reduction

In 2002—before any judicial interpretation of the term "high quality"—article IX, section 1(a) was amended by initiative petition. The 2002 amendment set a maximum number of students per classroom for various grade levels. *See Advisory Op. to the Att'y Gen. re Florida's Amend. to Reduce Class Size*, 816 So. 2d 580, 581–82 (Fla. 2002). The 2002 amendment also established a phase-in period and expressly provided that the costs associated with meeting the class size reductions were to be borne by "the legislature"—i.e., "the state"—as opposed to the "local school districts." *Id.* at 581. The 2002 amendment also directly referenced the term "high quality" added to article IX, section 1(a) in 1998:

> *To assure that children attending public schools obtain a high quality education, the legislature shall make adequate provision* to ensure that ... there are a sufficient number of classrooms....

(Emphasis added.) This Court upheld the validity of the initiative petition. *Id.* at 585–86.

Here, there is no suggestion that the Legislature failed to "make adequate provision" for the reduction of classroom sizes. On the contrary, the trial court found it "significant that the State has provided sufficient funding for schools to meet the class size requirements set forth in Article IX." In arguing to this Court that "high quality" is a judicially manageable standard for measuring the State's compliance with article IX, Petitioners make no mention of the 2002 amendment and the fact that the citizens constitutionalized a specific statewide policy with funding mandate "[t]o assure that children attending public schools obtain a high quality education." *See Holmes*, 919 So. 2d at 407 ("[W]hen the Constitution prescribes the manner of doing an act, the manner prescribed is exclusive...." (quoting *Weinberger v. Bd. of Pub. Instruction*, 93

Fla. 470, 112 So. 253, 256 (Fla. 1927))). And in effectively urging the adoption of Petitioners' argument, the dissent references "basic rules of statutory construction," dissenting op. at 60 (Pariente, J.), and yet—like Petitioners—ignores the language added to article IX in 2002. We are unaware of any principle of statutory construction that supports Petitioners' and the dissent's approach.

Holmes

In 2006, this Court in *Holmes* addressed article IX, section 1(a) but not in the context of a blanket challenge to the K-12 system. Rather, *Holmes* involved a challenge to a specific voucher program known as the Opportunity Scholarship Program (OSP), under which any student from a "fail[ing]" public school could either move to a different, non-failing public school or "receive funds from the public treasury, which would otherwise have gone to the student's school district, to pay the student's tuition at a private school." *Holmes*, 919 So. 2d at 397. The "narrow question" in *Holmes* was whether that second option involving the use of public funds was prohibited by article IX, section 1(a). *Id.* at 397–98. *Holmes* answered in the affirmative, concluding that the OSP "diverts public dollars into separate private systems parallel to and in competition with the free public schools that are the sole means set out in the Constitution for the state to provide for the education of Florida's children" and that the OSP "funds private schools that are not 'uniform' when compared with each other or the public system." *Id.* at 398.

As *Coalition* did previously, *Holmes* examined the history of Florida's education article. In doing so, *Holmes* noted that the 1998 amendments were made "in response in part to *Coalition* … to make clear that education is a 'fundamental value' and 'a paramount duty of the state,' and to provide standards by which to measure the adequacy of the public school education provided by the state." *Id.* at 403. *Holmes* also cited certain commentary from individuals involved with the 1998 CRC explaining that the 1998 amendments represented "an attempt" to provide measurable standards. *Id.* at 404. *Holmes* later recognized the 1998 amendments as "imposing a maximum duty on the state to provide for public education that is uniform and of high quality." *Id.* And *Holmes* later described article IX, section 1(a) as "provid[ing] a comprehensive statement of the state's responsibilities regarding the education of its children." *Id.* at 408.

Although *Holmes* recognized the usual framework of the presumptive constitutionality of statutes, *Holmes* ultimately invalidated the OSP because it was "in direct conflict with the mandate in article IX, section 1(a)." *Id.* at 405. *Holmes* explained that article IX, section 1(a) contained not just a mandate to make adequate provision for the education of all children, but also a restriction that the mandate be fulfilled solely by means of a system of free public schools. *Id.* at 407. In other words, the constitutional provision "does not authorize additional equivalent alternatives." *Id.* at 408.

The Reasoning and Result in *Coalition* Defeat Petitioners' Challenge

In *Coalition*, this Court upheld a dismissal with prejudice of a blanket challenge to the "adequacy" of the entire K-12 system—a challenge that bears a close resemblance to the challenge here. 680 So. 2d at 402. This Court rejected the challenge in part because the phrase "adequate provision" did not have "straightforward content." *Id.* at 408. In doing so, this Court explained that previous cases attempting to interpret the education article all involved some "specific" challenge. *Id.* at 406. This Court thus balked at the possibility of intruding into the powers of the other branches, including possibly being expected "to evaluate, and either affirm or set aside, future appropriations decisions." *Id.* at 407 (quoting trial court's order). However, this Court refused to say "never." *Id.* at 408. Rather, the case turned on the challengers' "fail[ure] to demonstrate ... an appropriate standard ... that would not present a substantial risk of judicial intrusion." *Id.*

In his concurring opinion, Justice Overton agreed with the majority "that an insufficient showing has been made by the appellants to justify a judicial intrusion under the circumstances of this case." *Id.* at 408 (Overton, J., concurring). He went on to add that, in his view, the holding of the Court "does not mean that the judiciary should not be involved in the enforcement of this constitutional provision." *Id.*

In sum, although recognizing the possibility that some future case might present a justiciable claim under article IX, section 1, a majority of the Court determined that the *Coalition* appellants had not presented such a claim. There is no basis for concluding that Petitioners here have been any more successful in framing a claim that is justiciable.

The 1998 amendments to article IX, section 1 undoubtedly heightened the Legislature's mandate to "a paramount duty." But the fact that the Legislature's duty to make "adequate provision" was heightened does not in and of itself provide the courts with "an appropriate standard for determining 'adequacy.'" *Coalition*, 680 So. 2d at 408. Rather, the primary issue here is whether the term "high quality" provides such a standard. Although *Holmes* spoke of the 1998 amendments as "provid[ing] standards by which to measure the adequacy of the public school education provided by the state," 919 So. 2d at 403, that language has no relevance here. *Holmes* did not involve a blanket "adequacy" challenge and did not remotely address the issue of whether the entire K-12 system was "efficient" or of "high quality." Instead, *Holmes* addressed a "narrow question," *id.* at 397, involving a specific voucher program and turned on other language in article IX, primarily "system of free public schools." In other words, *Holmes* in no way answers the question presented.[30]

Looking to the language of article IX, section 1(a), we conclude that the term "high quality" in and of itself does not have "straightforward content," *Coalition*, 680 So. 2d at 408, at least in the context of a blanket challenge to the adequacy of the entire K-12 system. Indeed, "high quality" can reasonably be viewed as "puffing." *Id.* at 411 (Anstead, J., dissenting in part). It is thus hardly surprising that article IX,

---

30. [FN 8.] We disagree with the dissent's suggestion that the reasoning of *Holmes* was intended to and should apply to the type of blanket challenge brought in this case. Dissenting op. at 51 (Pariente, J.). Not only did *Holmes* expressly note the "narrow" scope of the issue presented in that case, *Holmes*, 919 So. 2d at 397, but *Holmes* turned on language in article IX that long predated the 1998 amendments.

section 1(a) was subsequently amended in 2002 to constitutionalize a *specific statewide policy*—a classroom-size policy—along with a funding directive to "assure that children attending public schools obtain a high quality education." Art IX, § 1(a), Fla. Const.; *see Reduce Class Size*, 816 So. 2d 580.

Putting aside the class size amendment, Petitioners simply cannot overcome this Court's reasoning and the result in *Coalition*. As in *Coalition*, they have failed to present the courts with any manageable standard by which to avoid judicial intrusion into the powers of the Legislature. Moreover, we find that the standard actually proposed by Petitioners for measuring the Legislature's compliance with article IX, section 1(a) is foundationally flawed.

Petitioners' argument largely is that the constitutional test "for measuring whether the State is providing an opportunity for a high quality education" should be based solely on the assessment results that measure whether students have learned the core content standards established by the Legislature. In other words, Petitioners do not ask this Court to define "high quality." Rather, they assert that the Legislature itself has already defined "high quality" and how to measure it.

They thus allege that the educational system is constitutionally inadequate because the "assessment results show low achievement and wide disparities," particularly "for children experiencing poverty or attending school in poorer school districts."

Petitioners essentially ask this Court to constitutionalize the Legislature's own standards, which in part serve as goals. We reject that argument. In effect, Petitioners' argument is that a "high quality" system is whatever the Legislature says it is, so long as some acceptable—yet unknown—percentage of all subgroups of students achieve a satisfactory level of "3" on the assessment. Nothing in the language of article IX, section 1(a) supports Petitioners' argument. Nor does this Court's case law. Moreover, as amicus Foundation for Excellence in Education logically points out, "adopting State standards as constitutional minima would have the perverse effect of encouraging the *weakening* of curriculum standards in order to achieve higher passage rates and to satisfy court-imposed requirements." *See* Br. of Amicus Foundation for Excellence in Education in Support of Respondents, at 13–14 (explaining how this phenomenon occurred in the wake of the federal No Child Left Behind Act of 2001).

Not only do Petitioners conflate constitutional requirements with legislative standards, they also ignore—as do the dissenters—that in the years since this suit was first filed, the Legislature has revised the complained-of standards and assessments on more than one occasion. Moreover, Petitioners' argument flies in the face of the trial court's detailed findings, none of which Petitioners challenge for lacking a basis in the record. As just a few examples, the trial court found that: "Florida has been a national leader in education reform"; Florida *intentionally* adopted rigorous standards and set cut scores at a level that places the majority of students below the satisfactory level; scoring a "Level 1 or 2" on the assessment "is not an indication that a student 'can't read' or is illiterate"; the State's "high performance standards ... have led to improvement over time"; and Florida "has outpaced the nation in closing" achievement and performance gaps that "exist throughout the country."

While Petitioners' proposed standard is problematic in and of itself, Petitioners' own pleadings expose the flaws in their arguments and highlight why *Coalition* requires that we approve the result reached by the First District. Indeed, what Petitioners seek is for the courts to order Respondents "to establish a remedial plan that … includes *necessary studies to determine what resources and standards are necessary* to provide a high quality education to Florida students." (Emphasis added.) In other words, Petitioners do not know what a "high quality system" looks like, how it can be achieved, or what resources and standards are necessary. Instead, they—and presumably the courts—will know an "efficient" and "high quality" system, as well as an "adequate" level of overall funding, when they see a study that shows what it is. Petitioners invite this Court to not only intrude into the Legislature's appropriations power, *see Coalition*, 680 So. 2d at 407 ("[P]resumably the Plaintiffs would expect the Court to evaluate, and either affirm or set aside, future appropriations decisions.…"), but to inject itself into education policy making and oversight. We decline the invitation for the courts to overstep their bounds.

Even if we were inclined to accept all of Petitioners' arguments regarding justiciability and separation of powers, on the record presented here Petitioners still could not prevail. At bottom, Petitioners' blanket challenge to the educational system is a funding challenge, one rooted in the notion that the Legislature is not providing an adequate overall level of funding and that the lack of funding has resulted in disproportionate outcomes for certain students. That is clear from Petitioners' allegations, Petitioners' specific request for relief, and the rest of the record. Indeed, the trial court noted, among other things, that "[t]he primary thrust of [Petitioners'] complaint is that there is a crisis … caused by the State of Florida's inadequate funding of education," that Petitioners "asserted that more resources were clearly needed to address the problems they identified in their complaint," and "that the evidence was focusing on [Petitioners'] 'need for more resources' argument." But the trial court's express findings doom Petitioners' funding challenge and theory of the case. Not only did the trial court find that Petitioners "failed to establish any causal relationship between any alleged low student performance and a lack of resources," but the trial court found that "the weight of the evidence … establishes a *lack* of any causal relationship between additional financial resources and improved student outcomes." Petitioners' failure to establish such a causal relationship provides an independent basis for rejection of their claims.

III. CONCLUSION

Given the blanket nature of Petitioners' challenge, the trial court's extensive and detailed findings after Petitioners were permitted to establish a factual record, and the failure of Petitioners to provide any manageable standard to support their challenge to the adequacy of the funding of the entire K-12 education system, we approve the result reached by the First District in affirming the trial court's rejection of Petitioners' challenge.

It is so ordered.

CANADY, C.J., and LAWSON, J., and EDWARD C. LaROSE, Associate Justice, concur.

CANADY, C.J., concurs with an opinion, in which LAWSON, J., and EDWARD C. LaROSE, Associate Justice, concur.

LABARGA, J., concurs in result only.

PARIENTE, J., dissents with an opinion, in which LEWIS and QUINCE, JJ., concur.

LEWIS, J., dissents with an opinion, in which PARIENTE and QUINCE, JJ., concur.

POLSTON, J., recused.

NO MOTION FOR REHEARING WILL BE ALLOWED.

CANADY, C.J., concurring.

The manifest goal of the Petitioners and the dissenting justices is to put educational funding and educational policy firmly under the control of the judiciary. That is the only possible path forward once a judicial decision is made that "the State has failed to ensure that its allocations are the best use of funding," that "the State is not funding schools in an efficient manner," and that the State has not "allocate[d] resources in a productive manner and without waste." Dissenting op. at 58–59 (Pariente, J.). The response to such a judicial decision would involve judicial control of educational funding levels and judicial control of how educational funds are used. There is no reason to believe that the judiciary is competent to make these complex and difficult policy choices. And there is every reason to believe that arrogating such policy choices to the judiciary would do great violence to the separation of powers established in our Constitution.

Contrary to the position of the Petitioners and the dissenters, the addition to the Constitution of the capaciously vague terms "efficient" and "high quality" cannot be understood to have wrought a revolution in the separation of powers. I therefore fully concur with the plurality opinion's view that going down the path charted by the Petitioners and the dissenters would be inconsistent with this Court's precedent in *Coalition for Adequacy & Fairness in School Funding, Inc. v. Chiles*, 680 So. 2d 400 (Fla. 1996), that requires judicially manageable standards in order for the judiciary to intervene.

In striking down a delegation of legislative power to the executive, we previously held that "[t]he legislative responsibility to set fiscal priorities through appropriations is totally abandoned when the power to reduce, nullify, or change those priorities is given over to the total discretion of another branch of government." *Chiles v. Children A, B, C, D, E, & F*, 589 So. 2d 260, 265 (Fla. 1991). We recognized the fundamental point that "[u]nder any working system of government, one of the branches must be able to exercise the power of the purse, and in our system it is the legislature, as representative of the people and maker of laws, including laws pertaining to appropriations, to whom that power is constitutionally assigned." *Id.* at 267. We emphasized the importance of this unique role played by the Legislature in controlling state spending:

The constitution specifically provides for the legislature alone to have the power to appropriate state funds. More importantly, only the legislature, as the voice of the people, may determine and weigh the multitude of needs and fiscal priorities of the State of Florida. The legislature must carry out its constitutional duty to establish fiscal priorities in light of the financial resources it has provided.

Id.

Of course, this does not mean that the judiciary in adjudicating individual constitutional claims can never make decisions that have an impact on state spending. But it does mean that the judiciary cannot take over the appropriations process and policymaking concerning the use of state funds for the public school system. If the judiciary does so, it strikes a grievous blow against the constitutional separation of powers. And that is exactly what the Petitioners and the dissenters would have us do. This is not a case in which a constitutional attack is made on specific identified actions of the government that have violated the Constitution. Instead, it is a challenge based on particular conditions that allegedly offend the Constitution and that are assumed to result from a complex series of deficient actions of the State — involving appropriations and the use of appropriated funds — that remains unidentified.

At its core, this is a case in search of a remedy. Or more to the point, it is a case in search of a remediator. In brief, the Petitioners and the dissenters take the position that educational funding and policy in Florida are not working as well as they should, and that the judiciary should figure out how funding and policy can work better. The judiciary is very good at making certain types of decisions — that is, judicial decisions. But it lacks the institutional competence — or the constitutional authority — to make the monumental funding and policy decisions that the Petitioners and the dissenters seek to shift to the judicial branch. And there is not a hint of any manageable judicial standards to apply in making those decisions. Instead, if the Petitioners and the dissenters had their way, judges would simply apply their own policy preferences. This collides with the basic principle of our constitutional structure that "[t]he judicial power of the state extends" only to "controversies justiciable in their nature." *Burnett v. Greene*, 97 Fla. 1007, 122 So. 570, 575 (Fla. 1929).

LAWSON, J., and EDWARD C. LaROSE, Associate Justice, concur.

PARIENTE, J., dissenting.

I dissent. With its decision today, the majority of this Court fails to provide any judicial remedy for the students who are at the center of this lawsuit — African-American students, Hispanic students, economically disadvantaged students, and students who attend school in poorer school districts or attend persistently low-performing schools. The majority of this Court eviscerates article IX, section 1, of the Florida Constitution, contrary to the clear intent of the voters, and abdicates its responsibility to interpret this critical provision and construe the terms "uniform," "efficient," and "high quality," enshrined in that provision. Today, even more emphatically than before the 1998 amendment to article IX, section 1, I echo the words of Justice Anstead, joined by Justices Kogan and Shaw: "By [the Court's] action today, we have reduced to empty words a constitutional promise to provide an adequate educational system for our children." *Coalition for Adequacy & Fairness in Sch. Funding, Inc. v. Chiles*, 680 So. 2d 400, 410 (Fla. 1996) (Anstead, J., dissenting).

Article IX, section 1 became one of the strongest education provisions in the country when, in 1998, the voters of this State approved an amendment, which designated the education of children "a fundamental value of the people of the State of Florida" and placed "a paramount duty [on] the state" to provide a "uniform, efficient, safe, secure, and high quality system of free public schools" for Florida's students. Art. IX, § 1(a), Fla. Const. That amendment, a product of the 1998 Constitution Revision Commission, was intended to remedy the Court's 1996 opinion in *Coalition*, which held that article IX, section 1 did not provide judicially manageable standards for the courts to adjudicate claims brought under the provision. 680 So. 2d at 407–08.

In this case, Petitioners—a group of public school parents, students, and citizen organizations—brought a declaratory action against the State, alleging that the State is violating its constitutional obligation to provide all students with a uniform, efficient, and high quality education system. The trial court held a four-week long bench trial, at which evidence was presented that, in 2014, only 58% of Florida students across all grades scored on grade level on statewide reading assessments; that number was only 56% for statewide math assessments. Petrs.' Initial Br. at 4. To properly understand these statistics, "grade level" means only that a student's performance is at least "satisfactory;" which also signifies that the student "may need additional support for the next grade/course." These figures are on average lower for African-American students, Hispanic students, and economically disadvantaged students.

In what judicial universe do the facts presented demonstrate that the State is fulfilling its constitutional obligation to provide a "uniform," "efficient," and "high quality" education? By holding that a claim like Petitioners'—which alleged wide disparities in performance among certain subgroups of students and persistently low-performing schools—cannot be adjudicated by the courts, the majority of this Court renders article IX, section 1, a "hollow phrase[] of nothingness." Dissenting op. at 79 (Lewis, J.). Indeed, the effect of the plurality's holding is to deny Petitioners the opportunity to establish in a court of law that the State has failed to live up to its paramount constitutional obligation set forth in article IX, section 1.[31]

---

31. [FN 15.] The plurality refuses to look at the jurisprudence of other state supreme courts addressing similar constitutional provisions. And, while Florida's education system should not necessarily be compared to other states, it is worth noting that, as of February of this year, Florida's education system ranks 29th in the country. Stebbins & Frohlich, [*Geographic Disparity: States with the Best (and Worst) Schools*, USA Today (Feb. 8, 2018), https://www.usatoday.com/story/money/economy/2018/02/08/geographic-disparity-states-best-and-worst-schools/1079181001/]. This ranking is based in part on the fact that "Florida's public schools receive some of the lowest funding of any state school system in the country." *Id.* In fact, Florida's per-pupil spending falls well below the national average.

For these and all the reasons that follow, I dissent from the conclusion of the majority of this Court that the claim raised by Petitioners in this case is not justiciable. I also concur with Justice Lewis's excellent explanation of justiciability and why this particular controversy is justiciable. *See generally* dissenting op. (Lewis, J.).

Petitioners' Claim

The plurality opinion is premised on a basic mischaracterization of Petitioners' claim as one to "have the State of Florida's K-12 public education system declared unconstitutional." Plurality op. at 1. This mischaracterization sets the stage for the rest of the plurality's opinion, including its conclusion that Petitioners' claim is non-justiciable.

Contrary to the plurality's contention, Petitioners' claim is not "a blanket challenge to the constitutionality of the K-12 education system." Plurality op. at 16. Rather, Petitioners allege that the State has violated its constitutional obligation under article IX, section 1 in specific ways. Most notably, Petitioners allege that the State has failed to address wide disparities in performance among certain subgroups of students—specifically, African-American students, Hispanic students, students experiencing poverty, and students attending school in poorer school districts—as well as persistently low-performing schools. In support of their claim, Petitioners set forth detailed statistics, which show, for example, "disparities in reading achievement by subgroup as only 38% of Black students passed reading; 54% of Hispanic students; 19% of English Language Learners (ELL); 47% of students receiving Free-Reduced Lunch (FRL) (a proxy for poverty); and 37% of homeless students." Petrs.' Initial Br. at 4 (footnotes omitted). These statistics demonstrate that disparities do not just exist among certain subgroups of students, but also between school districts. For example:

> The statewide average passing rate for reading for third graders is 56%, and 55% for tenth graders. In St. Johns, 76% of third graders and 75% of tenth graders passed reading. Hamilton has the lowest overall reading passing rate for third graders at 35% of students. The lowest reading rate for tenth graders was Gadsden with 26%. Thus, the difference in reading rates among districts in third grade is 41 percentage points, and 49 in tenth grade.

> On the 8th grade math assessment, Bradford had the lowest passing rate at 5% overall, 0% for Black students, 6% for FRL, and 0% for students with disabilities.

> In 2015, Franklin had the lowest graduation rate at 49%, and three other school districts were below 60%. In contrast, St. Johns and three other dis-

---

Map: Per-Pupil Spending, State-by-State, Educ. Week (June 6, 2018), https://www.edweek.org/ew/collections/quality-counts-2018-state-finance/map-per-pupil-spending-state-by-state.html. Indeed, the national average is $12,256 per student, while Florida spends a mere $9,737 per student.

tricts had graduation rates over 90%, and Dixie had the highest at 96.9%. The difference in graduation rates between Franklin and Dixie was almost 48 percentage points. One of the State's measures of college readiness shows a statewide average of 27%, with disparities ranging from St. Johns at 55% versus Hamilton with 1%.

Id. at 5 (footnotes omitted). The accuracy of these statistics are not challenged.

Further, Petitioners set forth statistics showing that, among other things, "28 schools (all serving high poverty students) ... are persistently low-performing (5 or more years as F)." *Id.* at 6. In fact, despite concluding that Petitioners' claim was non-justiciable, the trial court in this case expressed particular concern about the issue of persistently low-performing schools:

> [T]he Court must note that it was surprised at how long a school could re-main in "F" status pursuant to the enactments of the legislature. If there is one area that this Court was most concerned about based on the evidence heard, it is in the area of Differentiated Accountability. There can be little doubt that allowing a school to remain in F status for an extended period of time raises serious issue regarding the constitutional acceptance of such an event.... To bring the matter to a point, I would raise the following question. How many people would want a judge deciding or presiding over their lawsuit in a Circuit that had been rated by the Supreme Court with an "F" as to judicial performance for many years? Similarly, parents do not want their children attending a school that continues to receive an "F" based on its performance rating. The evidence presented, while not rising to the level of a constitutional violation, should serve as a warning not to be com-placent about a local districts [sic] failure to address long term "F" schools. This is especially true since the Defendants [sic] own evidence shows that an "F" school can be turned around without additional resources being provided.

Final J. at 13–14.

The trial court also expressed concern over the State's "handling of local School Districts [sic] failure to address the problem of long term 'F' schools at the local level," stating that "[a]t some point in time the State Board should do more if the local School District will not." Findings of Fact at 70. Thus, contrary to the plurality's con-tention, Petitioners' claim is not a "blanket challenge" to the entire state education system but, rather, a claim that the State is violating its constitutional obligation in specific ways—most significantly, by failing to address wide disparities in performance among certain subgroups of students and schools.

Petitioners' Claim Brought Under Article IX, Section 1 Is Justiciable

I completely agree with Justice Lewis that this Court "ha[s] a responsibility to in-terpret and apply the rights and principles set forth in the Constitution, including article IX, section 1(a)." Dissenting op. at 69 (Lewis, J.). This responsibility includes adjudicating controversies brought under article IX, section 1.

To conclude that the claim presented is not capable of judicial resolution would "reduce to empty words a constitutional promise to provide an adequate educational system for our children." *Coalition*, 680 So. 2d at 410 (Anstead, J., dissenting). While deference to the Legislature and separation of powers are clearly important constitutional principles, this Court cannot use those principles to escape its obligation to interpret provisions of the Florida Constitution and enforce the rights it grants to the citizens of this state. *See League of Women Voters v. Detzner*, 172 So. 3d 363, 400 (Fla. 2015) ("While the Legislature is generally entitled to deference as a result of its role in the redistricting process, that deference applies only 'so long as [its redistricting] decision[s] do[] not violate the constitutional requirements." (alterations in original) (quoting *In re Senate Joint Res. of Legislative Apportionment 1176*, 83 So. 3d 597, 599 (Fla. 2012) (*Apportionment I*))).

In 2012, for example, this Court was tasked with defining for the first time the new standards set forth in the Fair Districts Amendment, which had been approved by voters two years earlier. *See generally Apportionment I*, 83 So. 3d 597. This Court did not shy away from the task, but rather recognized its "extremely weighty responsibility" entrusted to it "by the citizens of this state through the Florida Constitution to interpret the constitutional standards and to apply those standards to the legislative apportionment plans." *Id.* at 599. Just as the Court was able to define the terms in the Fair Districts Amendment, it is equally able to define the terms in article IX, section 1.

In concluding that Petitioners' claim is not justiciable, the First District Court of Appeal "respectfully disagree[d]" with other state supreme courts that have found similar claims justiciable. *Citizens for Strong Sch., Inc. v. Fla. State Bd. of Educ.*, 232 So. 3d 1163, 1172 (Fla. 1st DCA 2017). Instead, the First District relied on *Marrero v. Commonwealth*, 739 A.2d 110, 112–13 (Pa. 1999), where the Pennsylvania Supreme Court held that such a claim was non-justiciable. *See Citizens for Strong Sch.*, 232 So. 3d at 1172. Three months before the First District's decision, however, the Pennsylvania Supreme Court declined to follow its decision in *Marrero* and held that Petitioner's challenge to the education system based on the state constitution *was* justiciable. *William Penn Sch. Dist. v. Pa. Dep't of Educ.*, 642 Pa. 236, 170 A.3d 414, 457 (Pa. 2017). In declining to follow *Marrero*, the Pennsylvania Supreme Court explained:

> To the extent that our prior cases have suggested, if murkily, that a court cannot devise a judicially discoverable and manageable standard for Education Clause compliance that does not entail making a policy determination inappropriate for judicial discretion, or that we may only deploy a rubber stamp in a hollow mockery of judicial review, we underscore that we are not bound to follow precedent when it cannot bear scrutiny, either on its own terms or in light of subsequent developments.

Id. at 456. Thus, in holding that article IX, section 1 of our state constitution does not provide judicially manageable standards, the First District relied on outdated and overruled precedent, to the exclusion of the majority of other state supreme courts.

Although the plurality does not go so far as to say that a claim under article IX, section 1 could *never* be justiciable, it nevertheless concludes that Petitioners' claim in this case is not justiciable. *See* plurality op. at 17. In reaching this conclusion, the plurality, without explanation—like the First District—declines to consider other jurisdictions that have found similar claims justiciable. *See id.* at 19. Instead, the plurality limits itself "to the language of the Florida Constitution and this Court's decisions," ignoring the reasoning of the majority of other state supreme courts that have held that similar claims under their respective state constitutions are justiciable. *Id.*[32] Indeed, those courts adjudicated similar claims even though many of the education constitutional provisions in their state constitutions are less detailed than ours.

In concluding that a claim similar to Petitioners' in this case was justiciable, the Supreme Court of Kentucky wrote: "The judiciary has the ultimate power, and the duty, to apply, interpret, define, construe all words, phrases, sentences and sections of the ... Constitution as necessitated by the controversies before it. It is *solely* the function of the judiciary to so do." *Rose*, 790 S.W.2d at 209. Likewise, in declining to follow its earlier precedent, the Supreme Court of Pennsylvania explained the importance of the court's judicial review function:

> Two decades after *Marbury* [*v. Madison*, 5 U.S. 137 (1803)], in another paean to the importance of judicial review, Chief Justice Marshall cautioned that "[t]he judiciary cannot, as the legislature may, avoid a measure because it approaches the confines of the [C]onstitution. We cannot pass it by because it is doubtful. With whatever doubts, with whatever difficulties, a case may be attended, we must decide it, if it be brought before us." *Cohens v. Virginia*, 19 U.S. 264, 404 (1821). The spirit of Chief Justice Marshall's cautionary refrain has informed the clear majority of state courts that have held it their judicial duty to construe interpretation—begging state education

---

32. [FN 16.] *See, e.g., Lobato v. State*, 304 P.3d 1132, 1137 (Colo. 2013) ("Plaintiffs presented a justiciable claim because 'determin[ing] whether the state's public school financing system is rationally related to the constitutional mandate that the General Assembly provide a "thorough and uniform" system of public education' does not 'unduly infring[e] on the legislature's policymaking authority.'" (quoting *Lobato v. State*, 218 P.3d 358, 363 (Colo. 2008))); *Conn. Coalition for Justice in Educ. Funding, Inc. v. Rell*, 990 A.2d 206, 210 (Conn. 2010) ("[T]his court has a role in ensuring that our state's public school students receive th[e] fundamental guarantee" provided in the state constitution.); *Rose v. Council for Better Educ. Inc.*, 790 S.W.2d 186, 189 (Ky. 1989); *Cruz-Guzman v. State*, 916 N.W.2d 1, 9 (Minn. 2018) ("Although specific determinations of educational policy are matters for the Legislature, it does not follow that the judiciary cannot adjudicate whether the Legislature has satisfied its constitutional duty under the Education Clause."); *Columbia Falls Elementary Sch. Dist. No. 6 v. State*, 109 P.3d 257, 261 (Mont. 2005) ("As the final guardian and protector of the right to education, it is incumbent upon the court to assure that the system enacted by the Legislature enforces, protects and fulfills the right. We conclude this issue is justiciable."); *Leandro v. State*, 488 S.E.2d 249, 253 (N.C. 1997) ("It has long been understood that it is the duty of the courts to determine the meaning of the requirements of our Constitution."); *McCleary v. State*, 269 P.3d 227, 231 (Wash. 2012) ("The judiciary has the primary responsibility for interpreting [the constitution] to give it meaning and legal effect."); *see also, e.g., Hoke Cty. Bd. of Educ. v. State*, 599 S.E.2d 365 (N.C. 2004).

clauses like ours to ensure legislative compliance with their constitutional mandates, no matter the difficulties invited or, in many cases, confronted. We hold that our Education Clause, viewed in the overarching context of our cases taking up the question of abstention from political questions, compels the same result.

William Penn, 170 A.3d at 463.

In support of its conclusion in this case, the plurality attempts to distinguish this Court's precedent in *Bush v. Holmes*, 919 So. 2d 392 (Fla. 2006), reasoning that *Holmes* addressed a narrow question involving a specific voucher program. *See* plurality op. at 27. However, nothing in *Holmes* suggests that its reasoning applies only to specific education program challenges. In fact, in *Holmes*, we clearly stated that the entire purpose of the 1998 amendment to article IX, section 1 was to "provide standards by which to measure the adequacy of the public school education provided by the state." 919 So. 2d at 403. And it was because the 1998 amendment added judicially manageable standards that this Court was able to determine whether the program at issue in *Holmes* violated article IX, section 1. *Id.* at 409. Just as in *Holmes*, a court can use the judicially manageable standards added to article IX, section 1 in 1998 to determine whether the State has violated its obligation in the context of Petitioners' claim in this case.

As an additional justification for concluding that Petitioners' claim is not justiciable, the plurality reasons that the claim "does not survive the reasoning in *Coalition*." Plurality op. at 17. But this ignores the purpose of the 1998 amendment, which was to provide judicially manageable standards so that, in the future, courts would be equipped to evaluate alleged constitutional violations. *See Holmes*, 919 So. 2d at 403.

The plurality's main contention with Petitioners' claim appears to be that they failed to present a judicially manageable standard that would allow this Court to consider their claim in a way that avoids judicial intrusion into the functions of the legislative and executive branches. *See* plurality op. at 30–31. This misunderstands Petitioners' claim as well as the judiciary's role. Petitioners do not ask the judiciary to recreate Florida's education system. Rather, they ask the judiciary to adjudicate whether, in light of the performance statistics they have presented and the State's statutory standards, the State has violated its constitutional obligation under article IX, section 1.

Article IX, Section 1 Provides Judicially Manageable Standards

As this Court stated almost ninety years ago, "[t]he object of constitutional construction is to ascertain and effectuate the intention and purpose of the people in adopting it." *Amos v. Mathews*, 126 So. 308, 316, 99 Fla. 1 (Fla. 1930). This Court has reiterated that principle on multiple occasions. *See, e.g., Apportionment I*, 83 So. 3d at 599 ("When interpreting constitutional provisions, this Court endeavors to ascertain the will of the people in passing the amendment."); *Pleus v. Crist*, 14 So. 3d 941, 944–45 (Fla. 2009).

Indeed, in asserting that the State has violated its constitutional obligation, Petitioners explain that the State has already determined what a high quality education is and how to measure it. They cite, for example, section 1003.41, Florida Statutes (2017), which sets forth the "core content knowledge and skills that K-12 public school students are expected to acquire." § 1003.41, Fla. Stat. (2017). In conjunction with the core content students are expected to learn, the Legislature has tasked the Commissioner of Education with "design[ing] and implent[ing] a statewide, standardized assessment program aligned to the core curricular content" established in section 1003.41. *Id.* § 1008.22(3). The State Board of Education then sets "a passing score for each statewide, standardized assessment." *Id.* § 1008.22(3)(e)(2).

Further, Petitioners cite section 1000.03(5)(d), which prioritizes that "[a]cademic standards for every level of the K-20 education system are aligned, and education financial resources are aligned with student performance expectations at each level of the K-20 education system." *Id.* § 1000.03(5)(d). However, Petitioners argue that "[n]either the Legislature nor the Department of Education has ensured that education financial resources are aligned with student performance expectations as required by statute." Petrs.' Initial Br., at 9 (citing § 1000.03(5)(d)). This claim is very different than simply asking that the State allocate additional funding; rather, it is about the "efficient" use of the resources provided based on evidence-based practices that is critical to the success of *all* students. Thus, Petitioners do not ask the judiciary to re-create the state education system, but only to determine whether the State has complied with its constitutional obligation under its own standards in light of the fact that many students — particularly certain subgroups of students — are failing to meet the standards set by the State.

The plurality contends that Petitioners' reliance on the State's own standards is "foundationally flawed" because "adopting State standards as constitutional minima would have the perverse effect of encouraging the weakening of curriculum standards in order to achieve higher passage rates and to satisfy court-imposed requirements." Plurality op. at 31–32 (quoting Br. of Amicus Foundation for Excellence in Educ. in Support of Resps., at 13–14). The reasoning is faulty. If the State were to intentionally adopt low standards to achieve higher pass rates, those standards could be challenged as a violation of the State's constitutional obligation to provide a "high quality" education. Simply because Petitioners in this case do not challenge the standards set by the State does not render their claim non-justiciable.

In my view, using the State's own standards, a court could evaluate Petitioners' claim by construing the judicially manageable terms set forth in article IX, section 1, as other state supreme courts have done with their respective state constitutions. *See, e.g., Rose,* 790 S.W.2d at 211; *Davis v. State,* 804 N.W.2d 618, 623–24 (S.D. 2011); *Campbell Cty. Sch. Dist. v. State,* 907 P.2d 1238, 1259 (Wyo. 1995). And, while the definitions set forth below could generally apply to any claim brought under article IX, section 1 they are construed here in the context of Petitioners' claim, which does not include a challenge to the constitutionality of the State's standards.

Uniformity

When defining constitutional terms, it is appropriate to utilize dictionary definitions. *See Apportionment I*, 83 So. 3d at 632; *see also, e.g., Lobato*, 218 P.3d at 375; *Davis*, 804 N.W.2d at 624. "Uniform" is defined as "having always the same form, manner, or degree: not varying or variable" or "consistent in conduct or opinion." *Merriam-Webster*, https://www.merriam-webster.com/dictionary/uniform (last visited Dec. 17, 2018).

In 1997, construing the 1968 version of article IX, section 1, this Court concluded that a "uniform" system is one that "operate[s] subject to a common plan or serve[s] a common purpose." *Sch. Bd. of Escambia Cty. v. State*, 353 So. 2d 834, 838 (Fla. 1977) (emphasis added). Thereafter, we explained that "uniformity," as used in article IX, section 1, "requires that a system be provided that gives every student an equal chance to achieve basic educational goals prescribed by the legislature." *St. Johns Cty. v. Ne. Fla. Builders Ass'n*, 583 So. 2d 635, 641 (Fla. 1991); *see also Rose*, 790 S.W.2d at 211 ("Each child … must be provided with an equal opportunity to have an adequate education.").

Significantly, in defending against the plaintiffs' claim in *Coalition*, the State conceded in this Court that "the phrase 'uniform' has manageable standards because by definition this word means a lack of substantial variation." 680 So. 2d at 408. Further construing this term in *Holmes*, this Court concluded that the Opportunity Scholarship Program at issue violated article IX, section 1 because it "reduce[d] money available to the free schools" and "fund[ed] private schools that [we]re not '*uniform*' when compared with each other or the public system." 919 So. 2d at 398 (emphasis added).

Importantly, as Justice Kogan explained, the uniformity requirement of article IX, section 1 "is not and never was intended to require that each school district be a mirror image of every other one." *Fla. Dep't of Educ. v. Glasser*, 622 So. 2d 944, 950 (Fla. 1993) (Kogan, J., specially concurring). Rather, "variance from county to county is permissible *so long as* no district suffers a disadvantage in the basic educational opportunities available to its students, as compared to the basic educational opportunities available to students of other Florida districts." *Id.* (emphasis added). Other state supreme courts have expressed similar understandings of the term "uniform," as used in this context. *E.g., Lobato*, 304 P.3d at 1138 (defining "thorough and uniform" in the state's constitution as "a free public school system that is of a quality marked by completeness, is comprehensive, and is consistent across the state"); *Leandro*, 488 S.E.2d at 258 (concluding that the right ensures that all children enjoy the right but does not require equal funding among the school districts).

These definitions provide a workable standard by which courts can determine whether the State has fulfilled its paramount duty under article IX, section 1. In this case, a court could apply these definitions and determine whether, in the context of Petitioners' claim, the State has violated its constitutional obligation under article IX, section 1.

Efficient

"Efficient" is defined as "productive of desired effects." *Merriam-Webster*, https://www.merriam-webster.com/dictionary/efficient (last visited Dec. 17, 2018). Also looking to dictionary definitions, the Supreme Court of Wyoming defined "efficient" in this context as "productive without waste." *Campbell*, 907 P.2d at 1258–59 (quoting *Webster's Collegiate Dictionary* (10th ed. 1994)); *see also Edgewood Independent Sch. Dist. v. Kirby*, 777 S.W.2d 391, 395 (Tex. 1989) (defining "efficient" as "the use of resources so as to produce results with little waste"). The Supreme Court of Kentucky went further, defining "efficient," as used in its state constitution, as a system that is not only "operated with no waste, no duplication, no mismanagement, and with no political influence," but also, "provide[s] funding which is sufficient to provide each child in Kentucky an adequate education." *Rose*, 790 S.W.2d at 212–13.

Currently, the State uses a complex funding formula—the Florida Education Finance Program (FEFP)—that includes both state and local funds and considers many factors, including but not limited to economic disparity, cost of living, and population, to determine how much money to allocate to each school district. *See generally* § 1011.62, Fla. Stat. (2018). Petitioners do not challenge the amount of funding but, rather, assert that the State has failed to ensure that its allocations are the best use of funding. Petitioners allege that the State is not funding schools in an efficient manner, as required by article IX, section 1. *See* Second Am. Complaint at 19 ("Many of the State's reforms and programs ... have wasted millions of dollars without producing the desired effect of a high quality public school system, and are thus not efficient.").

Accordingly, "efficient," as used in article IX, section 1 should be defined to mean that the State must allocate resources in a productive manner and without waste. In this case, a court could apply this definition of "efficient," and determine whether, in the context of Petitioners' claim, the State has violated its constitutional obligation under article IX, section 1.

High Quality

Finally, perhaps the most critical term in article IX, section 1 must be construed. "Quality" is defined as "degree of excellence." *Merriam-Webster*, https://www.merriam-webster.com/dictionary/quality (last visited Dec. 17, 2018). "High," of course, modifies the word "quality" to demand something more than average quality. In defining this term, we are cognizant of the fact that the term "high quality" is used twice in article IX, section 1. "Adequate provision shall be made by law for a uniform, efficient, safe, secure, and *high quality* system of free public schools that allows students to obtain a *high quality* education...." Art. IX, § 1, Fla. Const. (emphasis added). The plain language of the provision requires the State to not only provide a high quality *system*, but also allow students to obtain a high equality *education*.

As the Supreme Court of North Carolina has explained, courts may look to "[e]ducational goals and standards" set forth by the Legislature for determining whether the State has met its constitutional obligation. *Leandro*, 488 S.E.2d at 259. Indeed, the Florida Legislature has already defined "high quality" by providing substantive content standards for students. As an example, the State prioritizes students' preparation for postsecondary education without remediation. § 1000.03(5)(a), Fla. Stat. (2018). The State also prioritizes students' preparation "to become civically engaged and knowledgeable adults who make positive contributions to their communities." *Id.* § 1000.03(5)(c).

Accordingly, for purposes of the controversy before us, "high quality" means an education system that allows all students an equal opportunity to learn the core content knowledge set by the State and become knowledgeable and engaged adults. In this case, a court could apply this definition of "high quality" and determine whether, in the context of Petitioners' claim, the State has violated its constitutional obligation under article IX, section 1.

Thus, contrary to the plurality's contentions, using basic rules of statutory construction—including looking to the dictionary to determine plain meaning—the terms in article IX, section 1 are fully capable of being construed by the courts. Reading these definitions together, a court would be perfectly capable of determining whether, under the facts presented, the State has fulfilled its "paramount" constitutional duty to make "adequate provision" for a "uniform, efficient ... and high quality system of free public schools" for Florida's children. Art. IX, § 1, Fla. Const. In this case, because the trial court concluded that article IX, section 1 did not provide judicially manageable standards and used the wrong evidentiary standard for evaluating the petitioners' claim, I would remand the case back to the trial court to reconsider the evidence and Petitioners' claim in light of these definitions.

No Independent Basis Exists for Rejecting Petitioners' Claim

As an "independent basis" for rejecting Petitioners' claim, the plurality concludes that "on the record presented here the Petitioners still could not prevail." Plurality op. at 34. In support of this conclusion, the plurality notes the trial court's finding that Petitioners "failed to establish any causal relationship between any alleged low student performance and a lack of resources," and that "the weight of the evidence ... establishes a *lack* of any causal relationship between additional financial resources and improved student outcomes." *Id.* at 35. However, even though the trial court used the phrase "weight of the evidence," it made clear that, to prevail, Petitioners would have to show that the State's actions "are irrational or unconstitutional beyond a reasonable doubt." Final J. at 24.

Although the trial court ultimately concluded that Petitioners failed to establish causation, significant evidence was presented, indicating that when additional resources were allocated to low-performing schools, those schools improved. In fact, the State's own expert agreed with Petitioners that more resources are needed to educate African-American students, Hispanic students, and students in poverty. That very expert has written articles on the fact that state education systems "should ... effectively use more resources for poor kids." The State's expert further agreed with Petitioners' contention that money matters when it is spent efficiently, testifying: "Effective use by management, the funds will be effective." This is logical given that the students who perform the lowest on statewide assessments generally attend schools in poorer school districts.

Indeed, only 5% of 8th graders in Bradford County passed the statewide mathematics assessment, with a pass rate of 0% among African-American students. Petrs.'

Initial Br. at 5. That's correct: Zero. None. And only 26% of the 10th graders in Gadsden County passed the statewide reading assessment. *Id.* On the other hand, in St. Johns County, one of the State's wealthier school districts, 76% of 3rd graders and 75% of 10th graders passed the statewide reading assessment. *Id.*

Additionally, the trial court reached its conclusion on causation only after determining that the terms in article IX, section 1, were not capable of judicial construction. In other words, the trial court's conclusion on causation is based on a flawed premise — that article IX, section 1 does not provide judicially manageable standards — and an improper evidentiary standard, beyond a reasonable doubt. Thus, because the trial court's findings on the merits were made in a constitutional vacuum, they are not entitled to deference.

Based on the evidence presented, Petitioners have made a strong showing that the State has failed to provide a "high quality" and "efficient" education to all of Florida's students. Thus, we cannot presume that if this case were remanded to the trial court to reconsider the evidence and Petitioners' claim using these definitions and the proper evidentiary standard, the trial court would reach the same conclusion. Accordingly, I disagree that the trial court's finding that Petitioners' "failure to establish such a causal relationship provides an independent basis for rejection of their claims." Plurality op. at 35.

We Should Remand this Case to the Trial Court to Reconsider the Evidence and Petitioners' Claim in Light of These Definitions

In concluding that the State has not violated its constitutional obligation, the trial court observed that in 2014, 58% of students across grades 3 through 10 scored at or above grade level in reading, "a two percentage point improvement over 2011." Findings of Fact at 81. The trial court further found that, in 2001, only 47% of students were reading at or above grade level. *Id.* at 80. The trial court also devoted eight pages to comparing Florida's results to other states' results. *See id.* at 71–79. However, in my view, "adequate provision," as used in article IX, section 1, is an objective standard that does not consider improvements that have been made or what other states are doing. Further, it is hard to understand how objectively Florida compares to other states that might not even have the "high quality" education mandate in their constitutions when it ranks 29th overall in education and its per-pupil spending falls well below the national average. *See supra* note 15.

Instead of focusing on improvements over the years or state-by-state comparisons, the trial court should have considered the statewide deficits on achievement in reading and math.[33] While it cannot be disputed that Florida has made improvements, the evidence, as found by the trial court, still shows that only a bare majority of Florida's children are reading at grade level; 42% are below grade level. Again, I must ask: In what judicial universe does the set of facts presented demonstrate that the State is

---

33. [FN 20.] *See, e.g., Leandro*, 488 S.E.2d at 259 ("Another factor which may properly be considered in this determination is the level of performance of the children of the state and its various districts on standard achievement tests.").

fulfilling its constitutional obligation to provide a "uniform," "efficient," and "high quality" education?

Using the definitions provided and the State's own standards as a measuring stick, the trial court could very well have concluded on remand that the State has violated its constitutional obligation under article IX, section 1 thereby entitling Petitioners to a declaratory judgment. The trial court could then have heard arguments on the appropriate remedy.[34]

Certainly, I recognize that the task of making adequate provision for a high quality education is primarily for the Legislature. We are not legislators. We are justices charged with enforcing the rights set forth in Florida's Constitution. That is why with article IX, section 1 the citizens of this State intended for compliance—or noncompliance—with that provision to be adjudicated by the judiciary when properly brought to the court. Indeed, the task of construing the constitution and determining whether the State is fulfilling its express obligations required by the constitution—and the citizens of this State who approved the relevant constitutional language—is solely the judiciary's task. "This duty must be exercised even when such action serves as a check on the activities of another branch of government or when the court's view of the constitution is contrary to that of other branches, or even that of the public." *Rose*, 790 S.W.2d at 209.

CONCLUSION

The significance of education both to the success of our children and to a functioning democracy cannot be overstated. The drafters of Florida's Constitution recognized this fact "and, accordingly, included the education provision to guarantee that a system of free public education be established for the citizens of Florida." *Coalition*, 680 So. 2d at 409 (Overton, J., concurring). That guarantee means nothing, however, without a judicial branch willing to perform its constitutional duty.

With its decision today, "this Court has failed to carry out its duty to ensure that the legislature" and the executive branch have complied with their constitutional obligation under article IX, section 1. *Id.* at 410 (Anstead, J., dissenting). The plurality has abdicated its responsibility to interpret the constitution and eviscerated article IX, section 1 contrary to the clear intent of the voters. And, at the center of this dispute are the students who are at the greatest risk of failing—African-American students, Hispanic students, economically disadvantaged students and school districts, and students attending persistently low-performing schools.

---

34. [FN 21.] *See, e.g., Idaho Schs. for Equal Educ. Opportunity v. State*, 976 P.2d 913, 922 (Idaho 1998) ("We do not express any opinion at this time about the appropriate relief that should be granted if the trial court decides that Plaintiffs are entitled to relief."); *Leandro*, 488 S.E.2d at 261 (stating that if, on remand, the trial court finds a violation "it will then be the duty of the court to enter a judgment granting declaratory relief and such other relief as needed to correct the wrong while minimizing the encroachment on the other branches of government").

Because I would conclude that Petitioners' claim is justiciable and would allow them the opportunity to establish that the State is violating its constitutional obligation, I dissent.

LEWIS and QUINCE, JJ., concur.

LEWIS, J., dissenting.

My friends and colleagues in the majority make a very grave and harmful mistake today. Although I understand their good-faith and well-intentioned approach, only time will truly reveal the depth of the injury inflicted upon Florida's children. The words describing the right to a high quality education and the constitutional concept of protecting that right ring hollow without a remedy to protect the right.

The Florida Constitution guarantees each child the right to a high quality education. Art. IX, § 1(a), Fla. Const.; *Scavella v. School Bd. of Dade Cty.*, 363 So. 2d 1095, 1098 (Fla. 1978) ("[A]ll Florida residents have the right to attend this public school system for free."). When that right is infringed upon by the Legislature, the Department of Education, a county school board, or some other entity, our children must have the opportunity to seek a remedy in the courts. Art. I, § 21, Fla. Const. ("The courts shall be open to every person for redress of any injury, and justice shall be administered without sale, denial or delay.").... Here the majority now places Florida among the very few other states which are in disagreement with regard to whether these educational type claims are justiciable. In my view, article IX, section 1(a) clearly presents many justiciable questions that Florida courts can and should decide. This Court has already decided that article IX, section 1(a), Florida Constitution, is justiciable, and most other states which have addressed the issue have held the same. I write separately, however, to emphasize the propriety of Florida courts addressing these claims.

Our Florida Constitution is a principled document, constructed with principled words, which produces principled concepts that our citizens have asserted as the organic law of our society. It is a dereliction of our duty as the ultimate arbiter of Florida constitutional law to conclude that the interpretation of that text is beyond our grasp and solely within the realm of legislative whims. We have a responsibility to interpret and apply the rights and principles set forth in the Constitution, including article IX, section 1(a). *Dade Cty. Classroom Teachers Ass'n v. Legislature of Fla.*, 269 So. 2d 684, 686 (Fla. 1972) ("When the people have spoken through their organic law concerning their basic rights, it is primarily the duty of the legislative body to provide the ways and means of enforcing such rights; however, in the absence of appropriate legislative action, it is the responsibility of the courts to do so.").... Therefore, the onus falls on this Court to ensure that the principles enshrined by Floridians in our Constitution have meaning and a field of operation, including the right to a high quality education. *See Zivotofsky v. Clinton*, 566 U.S. 189, 194–95 (2012) ("In general, the Judiciary has a responsibility to decide cases properly before it, even those it 'would gladly avoid.'" (quoting *Cohens v. Virginia*, 19 U.S. (6 Wheat.) 264, 404 (1821))).

A "narrow exception" to the rule of judicial review is made for nonjusticiable political questions. *Id.* To be sure, the doctrine of nonjusticiability is proper in some cases under certain circumstances: for instance, when "there is 'a textually demonstrable constitutional commitment of the issue to a coordinate political department; or a lack of judicially discoverable and manageable standards for resolving it.'" *Nixon v. United States*, 506 U.S. 224, 228 (1993) (quoting *Baker v. Carr*, 369 U.S. 186, 217 (1962)).[35] Yet, in my view, neither of those elements are present here.

Preliminarily, "courts must, in the first instance, interpret the text in question and determine whether and to what extent the issue is textually committed." *Nixon*, 506 U.S. at 228. Both the First District Court of Appeal below and the Respondents argue that the inclusion of the phrase "by law" in article IX, section 1(a) somehow places the entire field of education as within the exclusive, unreviewable province of the legislative and executive branches. That logic is flawed. "By law" is a common phrase in our Constitution—used on 155 occasions—simply to signify that some legislation in the area is either permissible or necessary. *See Ison v. Zimmerman*, 372 So. 2d 431, 434 (Fla. 1979); *Fla. Carry, Inc. v. City of Tallahassee*, 212 So. 3d 452, 460 (Fla. 1st DCA 2017). Perhaps nowhere is the fallacy of this reasoning more apparent than as it pertains to Florida's constitutional right to bear arms—article I, section 8(a), Florida Constitution. That provision guarantees the "right of the people to keep and bear arms," "except that the manner of bearing arms may be regulated *by law*." *Id.* (emphasis added). Surely, neither the First District nor the Respondents could argue with a straight face that Florida's right to bear arms is a nonjusticiable political question, despite it being a hot-button political issue and including the phrase "by law." Gun owners regularly challenge gun laws and courts concomitantly adjudicate those challenges as justiciable. *See Norman v. State*, 215 So. 3d 18 (Fla. 2017). Therefore, nothing in the language of article IX, section 1(a) so much as hints at the notion that the definition of a right to education is exclusively a legislative and executive prerogative.

Next, courts look to whether there are "judicially discoverable and manageable standards." *Vieth*, 541 U.S. at 278 (quoting *Baker*, 369 U.S. at 217). Article IX, section 1(a) expressly includes the standard for determining the "adequate provision" for education: the public system must be "uniform, efficient, safe, secure, and high quality." Art. IX, § 1(a). One of these requirements, uniformity, we have already construed and adjudicated. *Bush v. Holmes*, 919 So. 2d 392, 412–13 (Fla. 2006). Two of the other requirements, safe and secure, are certainly subject to judicial review—as the trial court concluded in the final order. Final Order at 19 ("The terms in Article IX relating to "safe" and "secure" are subject to judicially manageable standards.... Florida's trial courts deal with issues related to safety and security all day long."). That leaves two of the five requirements, which are the two at issue here, efficient and high quality. Both of those terms are capable of interpretation.[36] Therefore, there

---

35. [FN 22.] Although there are six *Baker* factors, the Supreme Court places most emphasis on the first two, which are listed here. *See Zivotofsky*, 566 U.S. at 194–95; *see also Vieth v. Jubelirer*, 541 U.S. 267, 278 (2004) (plurality opinion).

36. [FN 23.] Other courts have defined an efficient school system. *E.g.*, *DeRolph v. State*, 89 Ohio St. 3d 1, 2000-Ohio 437, 728 N.E.2d 993, 997–98 (Ohio 2000); *Neeley v. West Orange-Cove Consol. Indep. Sch. Dist.*, 176 SW.3d 746, 752–53 (Tex. 2005); *Pauley v. Kelly*, 162 W. Va. 672, 255 S.E.2d 859,

are clearly judicial standards to guide courts—those that the people of Florida specifically chose to include in article IX, section 1(a).

The process of interpreting and defining those terms may be somewhat challenging, but nonjusticiability is simply not the appropriate solution. Judges occasionally throw up justiciability barricades only to avoid the difficult or complex cases, taking the easy way out by using excuses to defer the decision of a case to a legislative body. But if our standard is to avoid difficult questions simply because they may implicate some attenuated political concern, then the Legislature has carte blanche to do as it pleases without any constitutional oversight or protection. The Legislature is composed of politicians; so, by definition, everything that the Legislature does is political in the abstract. Moreover, almost every statute that the Legislature passes involves appropriations to some extent. Therefore, it should be with severe caution that judges decide an entire constitutional provision is nonjusticiable on the basis that it touches upon politics or the spending of money. I understand and recognize that separation of powers is certainly a foundational principle of our system of government, art. II, § 3, Fla. Const.; however, that proposition is as much about delineating a department's proper exercise of power as it is about establishing a system of checks and balances to prevent the accumulation of power in any one branch.... The history of our constitutional experiment is riddled with examples of courts struggling with difficult and complex questions—and providing eloquent answers—to the extent and meaning of broadly phrased constitutional protections, even when answering arguably political questions. There are far too many illustrations to list here, so a few examples must suffice.

First, courts have wrangled with the meaning of due process since the inception of this country. *See, e.g., Mathews v. Eldridge,* 424 U.S. 319, 332–35 (1976); *Dent v. West Virginia,* 129 U.S. 114, 122–24 (1889). Well over 100 years ago, the United States Supreme Court concluded that "it may be difficult, if not impossible, to give to the terms 'due process of law' a definition which will embrace every permissible exertion of power affecting private rights." *Dent,* 129 U.S. at 123. Despite the impossibility of any bright-line judicial standard, here we are today still deciding the meaning and extent of guaranteed due process rights. *E.g., Jennings v. State,* 265 So. 3d 460 (Fla. Oct. 4, 2018) (concluding that a defendant's due process rights were not violated). Correspondingly, courts regularly wrestle with the rubik's cube of due process to determine the extent of constitutional protections despite those protections virtually always implicating appropriations. For instance, in *Goldberg v. Kelly,* 397 U.S. 254 (1970), the Supreme Court held that due process requires states to provide public-aid recipients with a hearing before terminating their benefits. *Id.* at 261–66. Although hearings necessitate funding and welfare benefits are a politically charged issue, the Court properly decided the case on due process grounds without mention of justi-

---

865–67 (W. Va. 1979). Although high quality may be more difficult to define, it is not beyond a precise definition. *Contra Comm. for Educ. Rights v. Edgar,* 672 N.E.2d 1178, 1191–93 (Ill. 1996) (holding that "high quality" cannot be judicially ascertained based on the Illinois Constitution).

ciability. Thus, for as long as courts are trying to define the precisely undefinable, such as due process, they should be expected to apply express constitutional principles, like those announced in article IX, section 1(a).

Second, judges determine the meaning of equal protection, which regularly implicates political, policy, and appropriations issues without absolute or exactingly clear judicial standards. It is fitting to use *Brown v. Board of Education*, 347 U.S. 483 (1954), as an example. The Court there held that segregated schools are "inherently unequal" and, therefore, violate equal protection. *Id.* at 495. Of course, *Brown* had wide-ranging effects on appropriations by Congress and state legislatures across the country. Moreover, the case settled an abhorrent political debate. But, in ordering desegregation, the Court could not set out exactingly detailed judicial standards on how the process would occur—that was left for state school officials, legislatures, and courts to sort out. *Brown v. Bd. of Educ.* (*Brown II*), 349 U.S. 294, 299–300 (1955). The Court understood that there was no one-size-fits-all judicial standard on the most effective manner of desegregation, so it ordered state courts to supervise that process—which most certainly entailed many policy decisions—to determine compliance. *Brown II*, 349 U.S. at 299–300. A similar circumstance exists here. Petitioners ask this Court to review certain actions, performances, and conduct of the school system to decide whether it is within constitutional parameters. They do not ask us to make any of the myriad policy decisions that go into the operation of a school system; rather, they seek review of the system itself to determine if it meets constitutional muster. Thus, any suggestion that the express Florida constitutional right to an education is nonjusticiable cannot in my view withstand scrutiny.

Third, courts draw lines every day on unreasonable searches and seizures regardless of the fact that constantly changing circumstances make a final resolution of Fourth Amendment protections with mathematical precision impossible. For example, whether interpreting privacy rights in invoices for cases of glass, *Boyd v. United States*, 116 U.S. 616 (1886), or cell phone location data, *Carpenter v. United States*, 138 S. Ct. 2206 (2018), the Supreme Court has interpreted the same words to elucidate their meaning throughout the ages in vastly different areas. Just because those standards will most assuredly change over time does not portend that legislative actions are free from judicial review. With regard to justiciability, it is also of no importance that court interpretations of the Fourth Amendment will always remain behind the cutting edge of technology. Judges will continue to interpret that language to determine the protections guaranteed for as long as our system exists. The same should be true of the express right to an education in Florida.

Finally, courts have interpreted the implicit constitutional right to marriage. In *Obergefell v. Hodges*, 135 S. Ct. 2584 (2015), the Supreme Court held that same-sex couples have a fundamental right to marriage, which states cannot abridge. *Id.* at 2604–05. Despite the fact that there is no express constitutional right to marriage and *Obergefell* concerned a divisive political issue, the Court decided the case. Tellingly for our purposes, however, not even the various dissenting opinions there disputed the justiciability of that question. *Id.* at 2611–43. If implied constitutional rights are justiciable, then surely expressly stated constitutional rights with parameters are—thus article IX, section 1(a) presents a justiciable question.

The point of these examples is to simply illustrate that courts regularly define and interpret broad, principled constitutional language on politically sensitive issues, regardless of appropriations and policy concerns, even in the absence of bright-line mathematically precise standards. The instant dispute is not about whether the education system is adequate; rather, we face the threshold question of whether that issue can even be considered and ruled upon by Florida courts. Our school system may or may not be adequate, but we will never know if the Court categorically relegates the question to an unreviewable status. In my view, justiciability is an excuse here to avoid a tough case in these education adequacy challenges, rather than sound legal reasoning based on a valid separation of powers analysis. And, when the risk is that a nonjusticiability label could render nugatory our children's constitutional right to an education, dodging our duty will not suffice. . . .

The importance of education to the people of this State and to the State itself cannot be overstated. Education and educational opportunities are not only foundational for the State of Florida but are part of the essential building blocks for a free and open society. Letter from James Madison to W.T. Barry (Aug. 4, 1822), *in* 9 *The Writings of James Madison* 103 (Gaillard Hunt ed. 1910) ("Knowledge will forever govern ignorance: And a people who mean to be their own Governors, must arm themselves with the power which knowledge gives."). The life of a strong and vibrant republic has and always will have a direct connection to the quality of the educational status of our people.

While the substantive concept of education generally has grown to become both vast and complex, it does not always lend itself to fastidious description with absolute and complete mathematical, formal precision. The politicians do not own our government nor do they have the power to ignore specific rights placed in our Constitution by our citizens. Art. I, § 1, Fla. Const. ("All political power is inherent in the people."). The protections our citizens have demanded are merely hollow phrases of nothingness if there is no remedy or actual access to the protections listed.

For these reasons, I would conclude that the rights enshrined in article IX, section 1(a) are justiciable.

PARIENTE and QUINCE, JJ., concur.

Questions

1. Why does the majority consider Article IX, Section 1, as amended in 1998, to be non-justiciable?

2. Why do the dissenting judges disagree with this conclusion about the ability of judges to discover meaningful standards to enforce Article IX, Section 1?

3. How do the majority and the dissent view the role of the judiciary differently? And how does that affect the result in this case?

4. Does it appear that the 2019 majority reaches a narrower definition of justiciability than the plurality of the Adequacy Court?

Notes

The Supreme Court's decision in *Citizens for Strong Schools* brought to an end a decade of litigation attempting to enforce the terms of the Education Clause of the Florida Constitution. At this point, notwithstanding the high language from *Bush v. Holmes* about Florida being a "Category IV" state with regard to its state constitution, it is difficult to imagine any case succeeding that would give meaning to the terms "adequate provision", "efficient", or "high quality," as used in Article IX, Section 1. The CRC drafters of the revision to Article IX, Section 1 attempted to use constitutional terminology when trying to add meaningful standards to the provision. Although they used terms that had been applied in other states, the majority in *Citizens for Strong Schools* still found the terms non-justiciable. Interestingly, the drafters of the Class Size Initiative felt no obligation to use constitutional-sounding language in their 2002 initiative. Instead, they linked the term "high quality" in Article IX, Section 1 to specific numbers and specific dates. The result in Article IX, Section 1(a) was an enforceable standard, though at the cost of inserting code-type language into the relatively inflexible Constitution.

The 2020–2021 COVID-19 pandemic has brought renewed attention to the Education Clause in the form of a challenge by a group of teachers to the Education Commissioner's Order that Florida public schools include a "brick and mortar" component to their reopening plans that would allow an option for public school students to be physically present at schools for fall 2020. In August, days before most schools began, a circuit judge in Leon County issued an injunction against this Order finding it to be an unconstitutional violation of the requirement in Article IX, Section 1(a) that the public education system be "safe" and "secure." *See Florida Education Ass'n v. DeSantis*, Order Granting Motion for Temporary Injunction, Case No. 2020-CA-001450 (Fla. Cir. Ct., Aug. 24, 2020). The trial judge found that these terms have judicially manageable standards. *Id.* However, the First District Court of Appeal, in an Order Reinstating the Emergency Stay that the trial judge had vacated, called into question whether these terms are indeed justiciable. *See DeSantis v. Fla. Educ. Ass'n*, Order on Emergency Motion to Reinstate Automatic Stay, Case No. 1D20-2470 (Fla. 1st DCA, Aug. 31, 2020) (also noting the highly political nature of these pandemic-related executive orders). On appeal, the First District Court of Appeal ultimately reversed the lower court and vacated the temporary injunction for violating separation of powers and as involving non-justiciable political decisions. *See DeSantis v. Fla. Educ. Ass'n*, Case No. 1D20-2470, 2020 WL 5988207 (Fla. 1st DCA, Oct. 9, 2020).

B. Article IX, Section 4 — School Districts, School Boards

Article IX, Section 1 gives the state the primary responsibility for the public education system, while Article IX, Section 2 creates the State Board of Education with "such supervision of the free public education as is provided by law." Article IX,

Section 4 provides for local, elected school boards in each county which are empowered to "operate, control and supervise all free schools within each school district and determine the rate of school district taxes" within certain limits. Thus, the governance of public schools is shared between the state, including the Legislature and the State Board of Education, and local school boards. The exact parameters of this shared authority are constantly evolving and have been the subject of controversy and litigation. Charter schools have been one recent area of controversy. The Constitution and statutes provide for charter schools, and they are an integral part of the public education system. However, the unique nature of their creation provides ample area for state authorities and local school boards to clash. The following charter school case explores this tension between the statewide oversight of public education and the local control vested in the school boards.

Duval County School Board v. State Board of Education

998 So. 2d 641 (Fla. 1st DCA 2008)

BARFIELD, J.

The Duval County School Board challenges the constitutionality of section 1002.335, Florida Statutes (2006), alleging it violates article IX of the Florida Constitution. We conclude that section 1002.335 is facially unconstitutional.

In 2006, the Florida legislature enacted section 1002.335, Florida Statutes, which established the "Florida Schools of Excellence Commission" as an independent, state-level entity with the power to authorize charter schools throughout the State of Florida. Prior to the enactment of section 1002.335, only district school boards could authorize charter schools. Under section 1002.335, the district school boards may exercise that exclusive authority only if the State Board of Education grants them such power within their district. The statute became effective for the 2007–2008 fiscal year.

Multiple school boards filed resolutions with the State Board of Education seeking to retain exclusive authority to authorize charter schools in their respective districts. After conducting hearings, the Board of Education allowed only three school boards (Orange County, Polk County, and Sarasota County) to retain their exclusive authority. The resolutions of the remaining 28 school boards were denied. Several school boards then filed notices of appeal, challenging the constitutionality of section 1002.335.

Article IX of the Florida constitution sets forth provisions regarding education. Article IX, section 4 provides:

SECTION 4. School districts; school boards.—

(a) Each county shall constitute a school district; provided, two or more contiguous counties, upon vote of the electors of each county pursuant to law, may be combined into one school district. In each school district there shall be a school board composed of five or more members chosen by vote of the electors in a nonpartisan election for appropriately staggered terms of four years, as provided by law.

(b) The school board shall operate, control and supervise all free public schools within the school district and determine the rate of school district taxes within the limits prescribed herein. Two or more school districts may operate and finance joint educational programs.

A "determination that a statute is facially unconstitutional means that no set of circumstances exists under which the statute would be valid." *Fla. Dep't of Revenue v. City of Gainesville*, 918 So.2d 250, 256 (Fla.2005). A facial challenge considers only the text of the statute, not its application to a particular set of circumstances, and the challenger must demonstrate that the statute's provisions pose a present total and fatal conflict with applicable constitutional standards. *Ogborn v. Zingale*, 988 So.2d 56, 59 (Fla. 1st DCA 2008); *Cashatt v. State*, 873 So.2d 430 (Fla. 1st DCA 2004).

Section 1002.335 provides for the creation of charter schools throughout Florida. This statute permits and encourages[37] the creation of a parallel system of free public education escaping the operation and control of local elected school boards. It vests in an "Excellence Commission" of seven people appointed by the State Board of Education from recommendations of the Governor, President of the Senate and Speaker of the House of Representatives, all the powers of operation, control and supervision of free public education specifically reserved in article IX, section 4(b) of the Florida Constitution, to locally elected school boards, with regard to charter schools sponsored by the Commission.

The State Board of Education argues that section 1002.335 was enacted to further the explicit constitutional goals of systemic uniformity and efficiency, and that state-level involvement promotes the fair treatment of charter schools. The State Board also argues that district school boards "will continue to operate and control the overwhelming majority of Florida's public schools, excluding just a small percentage of schools," and that section 1002.335 will have a modest impact limited to the narrow charter school sphere....

The further arguments that the statute authorizes the Department of Education to permit the districts to retain exclusive control over the chartering of schools and permits districts to retain control over charter schools sponsored by district boards provide no salvation as the statute also provides the vehicles to remove that authority, relegating local boards to essentially ministerial functions. *See* § 1002.335(5)(e), (10)(a), Fla. Stat. (2006). At the time of the filing of this appeal, only three school boards had been allowed to retain "control" over local chartered schools. All other applications had been rejected, including those from district boards which had never had an opportunity to demonstrate ability to operate such schools as they had never had an application for a charter school.

---

37. [FN 2.] Florida Statutes, section 1002.335(2)(a), provides that it is the intent of the Legislature that "[t]here be established an independent, state-level commission whose primary focus is the development and support of charter schools."

The provisions of section 1002.335, Florida Statutes (2006), pose a present total and fatal conflict with article IX, section 4 of the Florida Constitution. We therefore hold that section 1002.335, Florida Statutes (2006), is facially unconstitutional.

BROWNING, C.J., and KAHN, J., concur.

School Board of Collier County v. Florida Department of Education

279 So. 3d 281 (Fla. 1st DCA 2019)

LEWIS, J.

Appellants/Cross-Appellees, several Florida school boards, appeal a final judgment entered in favor of Appellees, the Florida Department of Education, the State Board of Education, the Florida Commissioner of Education, and the Chair of the State Board of Education, seeking review of the trial court's rejection of their facial constitutional challenge to several provisions contained in Chapter 17-116, Laws of Florida, also known as House Bill 7069 ("HB 7069"), pertaining to charter schools, including the new "schools of hope." The school boards contend, as they did below, that the challenged provisions violate their right to "operate, control and supervise all free public schools" in Florida pursuant to Article IX, section 4(b) of the Florida Constitution, that certain provisions violate the uniformity requirement contained in Article IX, section (1)(a), and that HB 7069's capital millage provisions violate Article VII, section 1 by permitting the State to levy ad valorem taxes. On cross-appeal, Cross-Appellants/Appellees challenge the trial court's rejection of their defenses of lack of standing, estoppel, and failure to exhaust administrative remedies. For the reasons that follow, we conclude that the school boards have standing to challenge only those provisions of HB 7069 that address capital millage and federal Title I funds. However, because we find the school boards' challenge to those provisions unavailing on the merits, we affirm the Final Judgment.

FACTUAL BACKGROUND

In October 2017, the school boards filed a Complaint for Declaratory and Injunctive Relief against Appellees, alleging that HB 7069 unconstitutionally: (1) mandates that they share a portion of their discretionary capital outlay millage revenues with charter schools; (2) allows for the creation of charter schools called "schools of hope" that would be allowed to operate outside of any meaningful control or supervision by the school boards and create dual or even multiple systems of public education; (3) allows schools of hope and authorized charter school systems to serve as local education agencies; (4) strips the school boards of their ability to supervise and control charter schools by requiring them to enter into a standard charter contract with charter school operators; (5) restricts the authority of the school boards to effectively use federal Title I funds to operate, supervise, and control public schools in their district; and (6) divests the school boards of their authority and responsibility to decide how best to improve a public school that the State has identified as low-performing.

With respect to capital millage, the school boards claimed that before HB 7069 was passed, they had full discretion as to whether to use any portion of their capital millage for charter schools. They also challenged the fact that HB 7069 prescribed a specific formula for the Florida Department of Education to use and directed that each district distribute funds to charter schools according to the formula. They alleged that the distribution of funds would severely impact their ability to build new and necessary schools and to adequately maintain the facilities they currently operated. As to federal Title I funding, the school boards alleged that HB 7069 restricted their authority to use the funds for purposes they deemed to be the most educationally beneficial and most likely to effectively address the educational needs of low-income students.

The undisputed facts common to all of the school boards' claims, as set forth by the trial court, are as follows:

> The parties agree that "constitutional authority over public education in Florida is shared among the State and local district school boards." ... Article IX, section 1(a) of the Florida Constitution provides that the State shall make "adequate provision ... by law for a uniform, efficient, safe, secure, and high quality system of free public schools that allows students to obtain a high quality education." Article IX, section 2 of the Florida Constitution gives the State Board of Education "such supervision of the system of free public education as is provided by law." And article IX, section 4(b) provides that the local "school board shall operate, control and supervise all free public schools within the school district."

> This shared authority is reflected in Florida's long-standing system of free public schools and education finance. "Public education is a cooperative function of the state and local educational authorities," and "[t]he state retains responsibility for establishing a system of public education through laws, standards, and rules." § 1000.03(3), Fla. Stat. In addition, "[t]he district school system shall be considered as a part of the state system of public education. All actions of district school officials shall be consistent and in harmony with state laws and with rules and minimum standards of the state board." ... Florida's charter schools are likewise "part of the state's program of public education," and "[a]ll charter schools in Florida are public schools." § 1002.33(1), Fla. Stat.

> The Local Boards do not challenge the overall structure of Florida's system of public schools or its primary funding mechanism, the Florida Education Finance Program ("FEFP"), and Florida courts have repeatedly acknowledged the constitutionality of Florida's basic funding formula for public education....

> Nor do the Local Boards challenge the underlying constitutionality of public charter schools or the State's authority to require local boards to approve an application to open a charter school—both of which also have been upheld by Florida courts....

> Under these presumptively constitutional laws, local school boards are responsible for considering and approving applications to open a charter school

(including "[t]he facilities to be used and their location") and for monitoring and reviewing any charter schools that they approve or "sponsor." ... The Local Boards thus "monitor the revenues and expenditures of [each] charter school" and may terminate or nonrenew a charter for a variety of reasons, including "failure to meet the requirements for student performance stated in the charter" and "[f]ailure to meet generally accepted standards of fiscal management." ... Since the creation of public charter schools in 1996, Florida's charter-school laws have also required local school boards to "make timely and efficient payment and reimbursement to charter schools" based on a statutory funding formula that includes "gross state and local funds, discretionary lottery funds, and funds from the school district's current operating discretionary millage levy." ... For example, during the 2016–2017 school year, 12 of the Local Boards (excluding the school boards for Hamilton and Collier counties) distributed nearly $780 million in FEFP funding to charter schools—including over $330 million in locally generated ad valorem tax revenues....

The parties filed cross-motions for summary judgment. Appellees challenged the school boards' standing to raise all but their capital millage claim. Following the summary judgment hearing, the trial court entered its Final Order and Judgment ... in favor of Appellees. This appeal and cross-appeal followed.

ANALYSIS

Standing

Cross-Appellants/Appellees contend on cross-appeal that the trial court erred in rejecting their arguments that the school boards lacked standing to raise all but their capital millage claim, that they should be estopped from raising their claims, and that they failed to exhaust their administrative remedies. We reject the latter two arguments without comment. As to the standing argument, we review the issue de novo. *Cartwright v. LJL Mortg. Pool, LLC*, 185 So. 3d 614, 615 (Fla. 4th DCA 2016).

In rejecting the standing argument, the trial court cited section 86.021, Florida Statutes, which permits any person whose rights may be in doubt to "obtain a declaration of rights, status, or other equitable or legal relations thereunder." The trial court determined that because the school boards alleged that the "statutes at issue" affected their rights, they had standing to seek declaratory relief. We hold, however, that the public official standing doctrine controls the issue of standing in this case, not the declaratory judgment statute.

The doctrine, which we recently addressed and which is grounded in the separation of powers, "recognizes that public officials are obligated to obey the legislature's duly enacted statute until the judiciary passes on its constitutionality." *Sch. Dist. of Escambia Cty. v. Santa Rosa Dunes Owners Ass'n*, 274 So. 3d 492, 494 (Fla. 1st DCA 2019). It is for that reason that a public official's "'[di]sagreement with a constitutional or statutory duty, or the means by which it is to be carried out, does not create a justiciable controversy or provide an occasion to give an advisory judicial opinion.'" *Id.* (quoting *Dep't of Revenue v. Markham*, 396 So. 2d 1120, 1121 (Fla. 1981), *superseded by statute as recognized in Crossings at Fleming Island Cmty. Dev. Dist. v. Echeverri*, 991 So. 2d 793, 802–03 (Fla. 2008)). The prohibition against public officials attacking the constitutionality of a statute is not limited to those public officials charged with a duty under the challenged law, but also extends to public officials whose duties are affected by the challenged law. *Id.* at 495; *see also Echeverri*, 991 So. 2d at 794–803 (holding that a property appraiser acting in his or her official capacity lacks standing to raise the constitutionality of a statute as a defense in an action by a taxpayer and finding its earlier holding in *State ex rel. Atlantic Coast Line Railway Co. v. State Board of Equalizers*, 84 Fla. 592, 94 So. 681 (1922), that a public official may not challenge the constitutionality of the statute as "promot[ing] an important public policy of ensuring the orderly and uniform application of state law"); *Dep't of Educ. v. Lewis*, 416 So. 2d 455, 458 (Fla. 1982) ("State officers and agencies must presume legislation affecting their duties to be valid, and do not have standing to initiate litigation for the purpose of determining otherwise."); *Island Resorts Invs., Inc. v. Jones*, 189 So. 3d 917, 922 (Fla. 1st DCA 2016) (holding that the property appraiser and tax collector lacked standing to raise the constitutionality of the statute at issue based upon the public official standing doctrine).

The school boards' constitutional challenge to HB 7069's provisions represents their disagreement with new statutory duties enacted by the Legislature. As the foregoing authority makes clear, however, the school boards must presume that the provisions at issue are constitutional. In reaching our determination on standing, we reject the school boards' argument that this case is governed by the rule that standing is allowed where a public official is willing to perform his or her duties but is prevented from doing so by others. *See Reid v. Kirk*, 257 So. 2d 3, 4 (Fla. 1972) (recognizing that standing is permitted when a public official is prevented "by others" from performing the duties that he or she is willing to perform). While the school boards rely upon the supreme court's determination in *Coalition for Adequacy & Fairness in School Funding, Inc. v. Chiles*, 680 So. 2d 400, 411 n.4 (Fla. 1996), that the schools boards in that case had standing under the "prevention of duties" doctrine to challenge "a constitutional violation which renders them unable to adequately discharge their duties," the plaintiffs in that case, which included private plaintiffs as well as school boards, sought a declaration that the State failed to provide Florida students an adequate education by failing to allocate adequate resources for a uniform system of free public schools. It was not a situation where the school boards were claiming that a statute was unconstitutional, as is the case here. *See Markham*, 396 So. 2d at 1121 ("For important policy reasons, courts have developed special rules concerning the standing of governmental officials to bring a declaratory judgment action questioning a law those officials are duty-bound to apply. As a general rule, a public official may only seek a declaratory judgment when he is 'willing to perform his duties, but … prevented from doing so by others.' *Reid v. Kirk*, 257 So.2d 3, 4 (Fla.1972). Disagreement with a constitutional or statutory duty, or the means by which it is to be carried out, does not create a justiciable controversy or provide an occasion to give an advisory judicial opinion.").

Based upon the foregoing, the school boards lack standing to challenge the constitutionality of HB 7069's provisions pertaining to the schools of hope, the charter school standard contract, and the charter school "turnaround" provisions. As for the school boards' claims regarding capital millage and federal Title I funds, we find that the public funds exception, which allows for standing to challenge the constitutionality of a law providing for the expenditure of public funds, confers standing upon the school boards to raise those claims. *See Echeverri*, 991 So. 2d at 797 (recognizing the public funds exception); *Branca v. City of Miramar*, 634 So. 2d 604, 606 (Fla. 1994) (same); *Island Resorts Invs, Inc.*, 189 So. 3d at 922 (same). As such, we will address the school boards' constitutional claims as to those provisions on the merits.

Constitutional Claims

The determination of whether a statute is constitutional is a pure question of law reviewable de novo. *Scott v. Williams*, 107 So. 3d 379, 384 (Fla. 2013). The same standard applies to a summary judgment ruling where there is no genuine issue of material fact. *Id.* "As a general rule, courts may not reweigh the competing policy concerns underlying a legislative enactment." *Bush v. Holmes*, 919 So. 2d 392, 398 (Fla. 2006). When the Legislature acts within its constitutional limits, its power to resolve issues of civic debate is to receive great deference. *Id.* A facial constitutional challenge considers only the text of the statute, not its application to a particular set of circumstances. *Duval Cty. Sch. Bd. v. State, Bd. of Educ.*, 998 So. 2d 641, 643 (Fla. 1st DCA 2008). A determination that a statute is facially unconstitutional means that no set of circumstances exists under which the statute would be valid. *Id.* The party claiming that a statute is facially unconstitutional must demonstrate that the statute's provisions pose a present total and fatal conflict with applicable constitutional standards. *Id.*

As for the State's constitutional authority for education, article IX, section 1(a) of the Florida Constitution provides in part:

> The education of children is a fundamental value of the people of the State of Florida. It is, therefore, a paramount duty of the state to make adequate provision for the education of all children residing within its borders. Adequate provision shall be made by law for a uniform, efficient, safe, secure, and high quality system of free public schools that allows students to obtain a high quality education and for the establishment, maintenance, and operation of institutions of higher learning and other public education programs that the needs of the people may require.

Article IX, section 2 provides that the "state board of education shall be a body corporate and have such supervision of the system of free public education as is provided by law." With respect to the school boards' constitutional authority, article IX, section 4 provides in part:

> (b) The school board shall operate, control and supervise all free public schools within the school district and determine the rate of school district

taxes within the limits prescribed herein. Two or more school districts may operate and finance joint educational programs.

Article IX, Section 4 Claims

The school boards contend that HB 7069 removes their discretion over financial decisions by imposing strict limits on how they can spend the tax dollars they raise and, therefore, violates their constitutional right to operate, control, and supervise the schools in their districts. Prior to the passage of HB 7069, section 1011.71(2), Florida Statutes (2016), read, "In addition to the maximum millage levy as provided in subsection (1), each school board may levy not more than 1.5 mills against the taxable value for school purposes for district schools, including charter schools at the discretion of the school board" to fund certain enumerated expenses and projects. HB 7069 amended the provision and removed "at the discretion of the school board." Ch. 17-116, § 29, Laws of Fla. (codified at § 1011.71(2), Fla. Stat. (2017)). Prior to the passage of HB 7069, section 1013.62(1), Florida Statutes (2016), set forth, "In each year in which funds are appropriated for charter school capital outlay purposes, the Commissioner of Education shall allocate the funds among eligible charter schools as specified in this section." That provision was deleted in HB 7069, and the following was added in its place: "Charter school capital outlay funding shall consist of revenue resulting from the discretionary millage authorized in s. 1011.71(2) and state funds when such funds are appropriated in the General Appropriations Act." Ch. 17-116, § 31, Laws of Fla. (codified at § 1013.62(1), Fla. Stat. (2017)). The Legislature also added, "The department shall use the following calculation methodology to allocate state funds appropriated in the General Appropriations Act to eligible charter schools." Id. (codified at § 1013.62(2), Fla. Stat. (2017)). The Legislature added as well, "If the school board levies the discretionary millage authorized in s. 1011.71(2), the department shall use the following calculation methodology to determine the amount of revenue that a school district must distribute to each eligible charter school...." Id. (codified at § 1013.62(3), Fla. Stat. (2017)).[38]

The school boards claim that they are not attacking the formula chosen by the State or the concept that charter schools must be funded. Their "narrow complaint" is that the Florida Constitution requires the funding decisions to be made by local elected officials, not by state employees far removed from local needs and concerns.

---

38. [FN *] As the parties point out, the Legislature amended section 1013.62 in 2018 by providing that charter school capital outlay funding would consist of only state funds rather than state funds and revenue resulting from discretionary millage. Ch. 18-6, § 45, Laws of Fla. The Legislature added, "Beginning in fiscal year 2019–2010, charter school capital outlay funding shall consist of state funds when such funds are appropriated in the General Appropriations Act and revenue resulting from the discretionary millage authored in s. 1011.71(2)...." The school boards contend that even with this postponement of the implementation of the capital millage provision to 2019–20, they "still must plan for this diversion of revenue in their long-term budgeting plans."

In rejecting their argument, the trial court reasoned in part that the school boards failed to explain how the Florida Constitution could preclude the State from imposing conditions on a discretionary capital millage tax that can be levied only with legislative authorization. The school boards have failed to show any error on the trial court's part. Appellees are correct that what the Legislature has done with respect to the capital millage provisions is exercise its supervisory power under article IX, section 1(a) to ensure adequate provision be made for the "free public schools" in Florida. While charter schools are statutorily considered to be public schools, the reality is that they do compete with the traditional public schools in their districts. Indeed, section 1002.33(2)(c)2., Florida Statutes (2017), sets forth that one of the purposes of charter schools is to "[p]rovide rigorous competition within the public school district to stimulate continual improvement in all public schools." Given such, the State's constitutional duty to make adequate provision for Florida's public schools must be interpreted to mean that the State has a duty to ensure that charter schools are not neglected by the school boards. By requiring that charter schools receive a certain portion of capital millage funds, the State is not violating article IX, section 4, but is fulfilling the purpose of article IX, section 1. As the Fourth District has reasoned:

> The Florida Constitution therefore creates a hierarchy under which a school board has local control, but the State Board supervises the system as a whole. This broader supervisory authority may at times infringe on a school board's local powers, but such infringement is expressly contemplated — and in fact encouraged by the very nature of supervision — by the Florida Constitution.

Sch. Bd. of Palm Beach Cty. v. Fla. Charter Educ. Found. Inc., 213 So. 3d 356, 360 (Fla. 4th DCA 2017). Moreover, as Appellees contend, section 1013.62(4) is very detailed as to what charter schools may spend capital outlay funds on, and subsection (5) of that statute provides that if a charter school is nonrenewed or terminated, any unencumbered funds and all equipment and property purchased with school board funds revert to the boards' ownership. We, therefore, reject the school boards' constitutional challenge to the capital millage provisions under article IX, section 4.

Turning to Title I, the federal program that helps fund the needs of low-income students, HB 7069 added the following language to section 1011.69, Florida Statutes:

> After providing Title I, Part A, Basic funds to schools above the 75 percent poverty threshold, school districts shall provide any remaining Title I, Part A, Basic funds directly to all eligible schools as provided in this subsection. For purposes of this subsection, an eligible school is a school that is eligible to receive Title I funds, including a charter school....

Ch. 17-116, §45, Laws of Fla. (codified at §1011.69(5), Fla. Stat. (2017)). The school boards contend that prior to the enactment of HB 7069, they could use a portion of the Title I funds to fund district-wide programs, such as summer school, after-hours programs, district-wide science and technology initiatives, or a transportation system to ensure that low-income students could take advantage of the programs. They claim that the foregoing provision unconstitutionally divested them of their right to decide how to spend federal Title I funds. In rejecting this claim, the trial court correctly recognized that the school boards do not have any constitutional right to federal Title I funds. Moreover, as is the case with capital millage, we find that the Title I issue is governed by the State's constitutional authority under article IX, section 1 to ensure the adequate provision of education for all children in Florida. Ensuring that students in charter schools receive the federal funds that they are entitled to without relying upon the school boards' discretion on how to allocate those funds does not violate Florida's Constitution.

Article VII Claim

The school boards also challenge HB 7069 by contending that the Legislature imposed forbidden state ad valorem taxation by adding the capital millage provisions. Article VII, section 1(a) of the Florida Constitution provides in part that "[n]o tax shall be levied except in pursuance of law" and "[n]o state ad valorem taxes shall be levied upon real estate or tangible personal property." Article VII, section 9(a), which addresses "[l]ocal taxes," sets forth in part that "[c]ounties, school districts, and municipalities shall, and special districts may, be authorized by law to levy ad valorem taxes and may be authorized by general law to levy other taxes, for their respective purposes...." As the supreme court has explained, article VII, section 9(a) requires legislative authorization before the entities named therein may levy ad valorem taxes. *Fla. Dep't of Educ. v. Glasser*, 622 So. 2d 944, 946–47 (Fla. 1993).

In rejecting the school boards' capital millage argument under article VII, the trial court relied upon *Board of Public Instruction of Brevard County v. State Treasurer of Florida*, 231 So. 2d 1 (Fla. 1970). There, the issue was whether two 1967 statutes, sections 230.0111(2) and 230.0117(7), which provided "for the support of junior colleges by county (now district) boards of public instruction," were constitutional. *Id.* at 2. According to the trial court's judgment, which the supreme court adopted as its decision, it was the appellant board's position that it had the power and duty to operate, control, and supervise all free public schools within the school district under article IX, section 4(b) of the 1968 Florida Constitution, that the control and supervision of junior colleges were placed under officers, and that if junior colleges were no longer part of the free public school system, they could not be supported by funds of the county or district boards. *Id.* The trial court, in citing article VII, section 9, which placed a limit of ten mills on taxes "for all school purposes," set forth, "'All school purposes' is certainly broader than 'free public schools.' This would seem to imply that while the local board must determine the rate of all school district taxes, some of the taxes ... can properly be used for local school purposes other than the support of the free public school...." *Id.* The opinion further set forth, "Nor is there anything in the constitution which requires that all taxes levied by a county-wide school district be appropriated exclusively to free public schools or that requires that no part of such funds may be appropriated for other school purposes and administered by other officers." *Id.* The opinion also provided in part:

But it [the appellant] takes the position that once the junior college ceases to be a part of the system of free public schools (and thus is removed from its control) any local financing of the junior college becomes unconstitutional. Nothing in the constitution justifies this conclusion. Subject to the power of the legislature to establish a Uniform system of free public schools the control of the free public schools in each district is vested in the local school board. This does not prohibit the legislature from placing upon the local school districts the duty to render financial support to junior colleges which are not under the control of the local school boards but which have been established at their request.

Plaintiff finally asserts that the whole legislative plan is to establish junior colleges as state institutions and to require their support by local ad valorem taxes, thus circumventing the provision section 1 article VII which prohibits state ad valorem taxes. Junior colleges serve a state function. So do the universities. So do the free public schools. Junior colleges also serve a distinctly local function. The law requires that the plan of each junior college "contain provisions for serving all eligible students in the junior college district." The court knows what everybody knows. One of the major reasons for establishing a junior college is to bring this level of education within commuting distance of large numbers of students who could not otherwise attend college. The local board must recognize the need and request its establishment before it can be authorized. Ad valorem taxes levied by school districts for support of such institutions are local taxes levied for local purposes.

While the legislature may not circumvent the prohibition of state ad valorem taxation by any scheme or device which requires local ad valorem taxes and then channels the proceeds into essentially state functions which are not also local functions, no such situation is here presented.

Id. at 4; *see also Sandegren v. State, Sarasota Cty. Pub. Hosp. Bd.*, 397 So. 2d 657, 659 (Fla. 1981) (citing Brevard County in support of its conclusion that there was nothing in the state constitution that prohibited the Legislature from enacting laws requiring the expenditure of local funds to support programs, such as mental health service programs, that served a local purpose).

The trial court properly rejected the school boards' arguments that *Brevard County* is a highly fact-specific case that does not address the funding of the system of free public schools that are under their operation, control, and supervision and that HB 7069's mandate is completely different because it tells them how to spend capital dollars on schools. As the trial court reasoned, if local tax revenues could be used in *Brevard County* to support junior colleges that were not even under the local board's control, "surely those funds can be used to support local public charter schools that will in turn use the funds to house and educate local schoolchildren." While the school boards also contend that *Brevard County* is distinguishable because there "was no evidence that local dollars were spent on state priorities," education, whether it be at the K-12 level or at the college level, is not only a state or legislative interest, nor should it be. The school boards' assertion that "when the State determines how local taxes are being spent, and mandates that these taxes be spent to satisfy State priorities, these taxes can no longer be considered local taxes" ignores the fact that charter schools serve their local communities. While charter schools may indeed be considered a legislative or state priority in Florida, their primary purpose is the education of children, which is unquestionably a local priority. Given such, the use of local taxes to fund charter schools does not, as the school boards assert, convert or transform those local taxes into something else. Moreover, while the school boards argue that "local management makes all the difference" in its attempt to distinguish *Brevard County*, the local boards in that case no longer had control over the junior colleges, which was a point clearly made in the opinion. The fact that the school boards in Florida continue to have a role in the operation of charter schools supports our conclusion that HB 7069's capital millage provisions are constitutional.

CONCLUSION

For the reasons set forth herein, we hold that the school boards lacked standing to raise all but their capital millage and federal Title I funding constitutional claims. Because those claims fail on the merits, the Final Judgment is affirmed.

AFFIRMED.

OSTERHAUS and M.K. THOMAS, JJ. concur.

C. Article IX, Section 7 — State University System

Article IX, Section 7 was added by an initiative amendment in 2002. The amendment creates a statewide Board of Governors responsible for operating the State University System, with each state university being administered by its own Board of Trustees. The following case explores the authority of the constitutionally created Board of Governors with respect to tuition and fees raised by the various universities of the state university system.

Graham v. Haridopolos

108 So. 3d 597 (Fla. 2013)

PARIENTE, J.

The issue presented to the Court in this case is one of constitutional construction: whether the Legislature or the constitutionally created Board of Governors has the power to control the setting of and appropriating for the expenditure of tuition and fees for the Florida university system under article IX, section 7(d), of the Florida Constitution. In 2007, the Legislature passed several statutes and included a provision in the 2007–2008 General Appropriations Act that exerted control over the setting of and appropriating for the expenditure of tuition and fees.[39] The Petitioners challenge these statutes as unconstitutional, contending that the 2002 constitutional amendment creating the Board of Governors transferred the authority over tuition and fees to the Board, divesting the Legislature of any power over these funds.

S.O.P issue

Although the question in this case is whether the challenged statutes are constitutional, the answer hinges on our interpretation of the Florida Constitution. Specifically, we address whether the 2002 amendment to the Florida Constitution creating the Board of Governors and transferring to the Board the power to "operate, regulate, control, and be fully responsible for the management of the whole university system," art. IX, §7(d), Fla. Const., carried with it the power to control tuition and fees and thereby divested the Legislature of that authority. The First District Court of Appeal held that this constitutional amendment did not transfer to the Board the authority to set and appropriate for the expenditure of tuition and fees and, therefore, that the challenged statutes were valid. *Graham v. Haridopolos*, 75 So. 3d 315, 321 (Fla. 1st DCA 2011). Because the district court expressly declared a state statute valid, this Court has jurisdiction.

For the reasons more fully explained below, we hold that the constitutional source of the Legislature's control over the setting of and appropriating for the expenditure of tuition and fees derives from its power under article VII, sections 1(c) and (d), of the Florida Constitution to raise revenue and appropriate for the expenditure of state funds. The language of the 2002 amendment, now contained in article IX, section 7, is devoid of any indication of an intent to transfer this power to the Board of Governors. Accordingly, we conclude that the challenged statutes by which the Legislature has exercised control over these funds are facially constitutional and approve the First District's decision.

FACTS AND BACKGROUND

Prior to 2001, the Board of Regents, a statutorily created entity, managed the state university system under the control and supervision of the State Board of Education. The Board of Regents was abolished as of July 1, 2001, by the Legislature and its powers were transferred to a new entity known as the Florida Board of Education.[40]

In apparent response to the Legislature's actions, a constitutional amendment was proposed by citizen initiative that "sought to amend the Florida Constitution to create a system of governance for the state university system." *In re Advisory Op. to Atty. Gen. ex rel. Local Trustees*, 819 So. 2d 725, 727 (Fla. 2002). In November 2002, the

---

39. [FN 1.] *See* §§ 1011.41, 1011.4106, and 1011.91, Fla. Stat. (2007); ch. 2007-72, § 2, subsection 156, Laws of Fla.

40. [FN 3.] *See* ch. 2002-387, § 3(5)(a), Laws of Fla. ("Effective July 1, 2001: 1. The Board of Regents is abolished. 2. All of the powers, duties, functions, records, personnel, and property; unexpended balances of appropriations, allocations, and other funds; administrative authority; administrative rules; pending issues; and existing contracts of the Board of Regents are transferred by a type two transfer, pursuant to s. 20.06(2), to the Florida Board of Education.").

voters approved the proposed amendment to article IX of the Florida Constitution, establishing "a system of governance for the state university system of Florida" and creating the Board of Governors to "operate, regulate, control, and be fully responsible for the management of the whole university system." *See* art. IX, § 7(a), (d), Fla. Const. The amendment, which had been proposed by a citizen initiative petition and is now contained in article IX, section 7, of the Florida Constitution, provided in pertinent part as follows:

SECTION 7. State University System. —

(a) PURPOSES. In order to achieve excellence through teaching students, advancing research and providing public service for the benefit of Florida's citizens, their communities and economies, the people hereby establish a system of governance for the state university system of Florida.

(b) STATE UNIVERSITY SYSTEM. There shall be a single state university system comprised of all public universities. A board of trustees shall administer each public university and a board of governors shall govern the state university system.

. . . .

(d) STATEWIDE BOARD OF GOVERNORS. The board of governors shall be a body corporate consisting of seventeen members. The board shall operate, regulate, control, and be fully responsible for the management of the whole university system. These responsibilities shall include, but not be limited to, defining the distinctive mission of each constituent university and its articulation with free public schools and community colleges, ensuring the well-planned coordination and operation of the system, and avoiding wasteful duplication of facilities or programs. The board's management shall be subject to the powers of the legislature to appropriate for the expenditure of funds, and the board shall account for such expenditures as provided by law. . . .

Art. IX, § 7, Fla. Const.

In 2007, the Legislature enacted the challenged statutory provisions involving tuition and fees. *See* § 1011.41, Fla. Stat. (2007) (stating that funds provided to state universities in the General Appropriations Act were contingent upon each university complying with tuition and fee policies established by the Legislature); § 1011.4106, Fla. Stat. (2007) (stating that any appropriations provided in the General Appropriations Act from the Education/General Student and Other Fees Trust Fund are the only budget authority for the universities to expend tuition and out-of-state fees and that the expenditure of tuition and fee revenues from local accounts by each university shall not exceed the authority provided in the General Appropriations Act unless otherwise approved); § 1011.91, Fla. Stat. (2007) (stating that except as otherwise provided in the General Appropriations Act, all monies received by universities from, among other things, student fees authorized in section 1009.24 are appropriated to the use of the universities collecting the same, to be expended by the university board of trustees pursuant to detailed budgets filed with the Board of Governors). In addition, the Legislature included similar language in the 2007–2008 General Appropriations Act.

Shortly thereafter, the Petitioners in this case, as individually named plaintiffs in their capacity as citizens and taxpayers, sought a declaratory judgment that the above-referenced statutes were unconstitutional because they violated article IX, section 7, of the Florida Constitution. The Board of Governors itself is not a party to this case. The Petitioners do not allege that any of the specific tuition and fee policies set by the Legislature are unconstitutional as applied, but rather broadly assert that the Legislature no longer has the power to control tuition and fees. In other words, the Petitioners contend that while the Legislature retains appropriations authority over the portion of university funding derived from general revenue, the Legislature was divested of authority over the funding stream generated by tuition and fees.

The trial court granted summary judgment in favor of the Legislature, ruling that the statutes in question were constitutional because article IX, section 7, of the Florida Constitution "does not reveal an intent to remove the Legislature's historic revenue-raising and appropriations authority over tuition and fees at public universities granted in Article VII, Section 1, and Article IX, Section 1, of the Constitution."

On appeal, the First District Court of Appeal affirmed, holding that the statutes were constitutional. The First District rejected the Petitioners' attempt to "draw a distinction between general revenue funds, which they concede still fall within the Legislature's constitutional appropriation power, and tuition and fees, which they categorize as 'agency' funds within the Board's exclusive control." *Graham*, 75 So. 3d at 317. The First District reasoned that "[t]he legislative power to raise funds is not limited to the imposition of taxes; it includes the power to impose fees necessary to offset the costs of using state government services. Likewise, the power of appropriation is not limited to certain types of funds; it extends to all funds in the State Treasury from whatever source." *Id.* at 318. With respect to university tuition and fees, the First District held that they "are unquestionably state funds; they are collected by state universities for the use of their services and the monies collected are deposited into the State Treasury." *Id.*

The First District therefore framed the issue as whether the constitutional amendment establishing the Board divested the Legislature of its "power of the purse" over state tuition and fees by vesting that authority in the Board. *Id.* at 319. [T]he First District concluded that article IX, section 7(d), did "not grant the Board authority to set and appropriate tuition and fees; rather, as it was prior to the adoption of [the amendment], that power is vested exclusively in the Legislature" under the Legislature's appropriations power. *Id.* at 321.

ANALYSIS

In analyzing the issue presented in this case, it is important to be clear at the outset as to what this case is *not* about. This case is not about an as-applied challenge to a specific tuition and fee policy or a contingency attached to an appropriation that would encroach on the Board's constitutional responsibility to manage the state university system. Although the attorney for the Legislature stated in oral argument that the appropriations power includes the authority to attach contingencies to the appropriation of funds, relying on *Florida Department of Education v. Glasser*, 622 So. 2d 944, 948 (Fla. 1993), we emphasize that such authority is not without limits. The question of determining the limits on attaching contingencies with respect to the Board, however, is not before the Court in this case. Nor is this case about which entity has control over monies from federal grants or private donations to universities.

The sole issue presented in this case is whether the 2002 constitutional amendment creating the Board of Governors transferred authority over the setting of and appropriating for the expenditure of tuition and fees from the Legislature to the Board, and whether the challenged statutes exercising control over tuition and fees are therefore facially unconstitutional. "Because the issue before the Court involves the determination of a statute's constitutionality and the interpretation of a provision of the Florida Constitution, it is a question of law subject to de novo review." *Crist v. Fla. Ass'n of Criminal Def. Lawyers, Inc. (FACDL)*, 978 So. 2d 134, 139 (Fla. 2008). Although the Court's review is de novo, "statutes come clothed with a presumption of constitutionality and must be construed whenever possible to effect a constitutional outcome." *Id.*

"When reviewing constitutional provisions, this Court follows principles parallel to those of statutory interpretation. First and foremost, this Court must examine the actual language used in the Constitution. If that language is clear, unambiguous, and addresses the matter in issue, then it must be enforced as written." *Id.* at 139–40 (internal quotation marks and citations omitted). "When interpreting constitutional provisions, this Court endeavors to ascertain the will of the people in passing the amendment." *In re Senate Joint Resolution of Legislative Apportionment 1176*, 83 So. 3d 597, 599 (Fla. 2012). "In accord with those tenets of constitutional construction, this Court 'endeavors to construe a constitutional provision consistent with the intent of the framers and the voters.'" *Id.* at 614 (quoting *Zingale v. Powell*, 885 So. 2d 277, 282 (Fla. 2004)). "Moreover, in construing multiple constitutional provisions addressing a similar subject, the provisions 'must be read in pari materia to ensure a consistent and logical meaning that gives effect to each provision.'" *Caribbean Conservation Corp. v. Fla. Fish & Wildlife Conservation Comm'n*, 838 So. 2d 492, 501 (Fla. 2003) (quoting *Advisory Op. to the Gov.—1996 Amend. 5 (Everglades)*, 706 So. 2d 278, 281 (Fla. 1997)).

Both parties agree that the amendment at issue did not alter the Legislature's article VII, section 1, appropriations power. "Appropriation" is defined as a "legal authorization to make expenditures for specific purposes within the amounts authorized by law." §216.011, Fla. Stat. (2007). The Florida Constitution in article VII, section 1, vests in the Legislature the constitutional duty and power to raise and appropriate state funds:

> (c) No money shall be drawn from the treasury except in pursuance of appropriation made by law.

(d) Provision shall be made by law for raising sufficient revenue to defray the expenses of the state for each fiscal period.

Art. VII, § 1, Fla. Const.; *see also Chiles v. Children A, B, C, D, E, & F*, 589 So. 2d 260, 265 (Fla. 1991) (stating that based on article VII, sections 1(c) and 1(d), "this Court has long held that the power to appropriate state funds is legislative and is to be exercised only through duly enacted statutes"). Article VII, section 1(c), of the Florida Constitution gives the Legislature "the exclusive power of deciding how, when, and for what purpose the public funds shall be applied in carrying on the government." *Republican Party of Fla. v. Smith*, 638 So. 2d 26, 28 (Fla. 1994) (quoting *State ex rel. Kurz v. Lee*, 121 Fla. 360, 384, 163 So. 859, 868 (1935)).

The legislative authority over public funds has been referred to as the "power of the purse." *Children A, B, C, D, E, & F*, 589 So. 2d at 267. As this Court has explained:

> Under any working system of government, one of the branches must be able to exercise the power of the purse, and in our system it is the legislature, as representative of the people and maker of laws, including laws pertaining to appropriations, to whom that power is constitutionally assigned....
>
> ....
>
> The constitution specifically provides for the legislature alone to have the power to appropriate state funds. More importantly, only the legislature, as the voice of the people, may determine and weigh the multitude of needs and fiscal priorities of the State of Florida. The legislature must carry out its constitutional duty to establish fiscal priorities in light of the financial resources it has provided.

Id.

The Legislature has been given further responsibility and authority with respect to funding universities in article IX, section 1(a), of the Florida Constitution, which provides that the Legislature must make adequate provision for the establishment, maintenance, and operation of Florida's universities. See art. IX, § 1(a), Fla. Const. ("Adequate provision shall be made by law ... for the establishment, maintenance, and operation of institutions of higher learning and other public education programs that the needs of the people may require."). Unquestionably, this legislative obligation was not altered by the amendment.

Because the issue presented in this case involves constitutional construction, we begin with the actual language of the constitutional provision. *Caribbean Conservation Corp.*, 838 So. 2d at 501 ("[A]ny inquiry into the proper interpretation of a constitutional provision must begin with an examination of that provision's explicit language." (citation and internal quotation marks omitted)). Article IX, section 7, of the Florida Constitution states that its purpose is to "establish a system of governance for the state university system of Florida." Art. IX, § 7(a), Fla. Const. It provides for the Board of Governors, which "shall operate, regulate, control, and be fully responsible for the management of the whole university system." Art. IX, § 7(d), Fla. Const. The provision then lists examples: "These responsibilities shall include, but not be limited to, defining the distinctive mission of each constituent university and its articulation with free public schools and community colleges, ensuring the well-planned coordination and operation of the system, and avoiding wasteful duplication of facilities or programs." *Id.* The provision also expressly states that the Board's "management shall be subject to the powers of the legislature to appropriate for the expenditure of funds, and the board shall account for such expenditures as provided by law." *Id.*

The Petitioners contend that the language of the amendment constituted an "all-inclusive" transfer of power to the Board, transferring control over every aspect of universities, with the exception of the Legislature's power of appropriations over the general revenue portion of university funding. However, contrary to the Petitioners' position, the language of article IX, section 7, does not plainly transfer to the Board the Legislature's control over tuition and fees, but instead grants to the Board the responsibility to "operate," "regulate," "control," and "be fully responsible for the management of the whole university system." Art. IX, § 7(d), Fla. Const. Nothing within the language of article IX, section 7, indicates that it was intended to transfer power over tuition and fees to the Board. Simply put, the language of article IX, section 7, is not "clear" or "unambiguous" and does not expressly "address the matter in issue." *FACDL,* 978 So. 2d at 140. We therefore turn to principles of construction, always endeavoring to construe the constitutional provision "in a manner consistent with the intent of the framers and voters." *W. Fla. Reg'l Med. Ctr., Inc. v. See,* 79 So. 3d 1, 9 (Fla. 2012); *FACDL,* 978 So. 2d at 140.

The canon of construction known as *ejusdem generis* is instructive in construing the meaning of "operate, regulate, control, and be fully responsible for the management of the whole university system." Art. IX, § 7(d), Fla. Const. Under this canon, "when a general phrase follows a list of specifics, the general phrase will be interpreted to include only items of the same type as those listed." *State v. Hearns,* 961 So. 2d 211, 219 (Fla. 2007). Employing this canon of constitutional construction, the Board's responsibilities in operating, regulating, controlling, and being responsible for the management of the university system include responsibilities that are executive and administrative in nature, such as "defining the distinctive mission of each constituent university" and "avoiding wasteful duplication of facilities or programs." Art. IX, § 7(d), Fla. Const. The ability to set and appropriate for the expenditure of tuition and fees is of a wholly different nature than the executive and administrative functions delineated in the constitutional provision and therefore is not included in the meaning of "operate, regulate, control, and be fully responsible for the management of the whole university system." Art. IX, § 7(d), Fla. Const.

We also review the ballot summary, because it is indicative of voter intent. *See Benjamin v. Tandem Healthcare, Inc.,* 998 So. 2d 566, 570 n.3 (Fla. 2008) ("[B]allot materials are one source from which the voters' intent and the purpose of the amendment can be ascertained."). Here, the ballot summary that accompanied the amendment and appeared on the ballot also indicated a grant of power that appears to be executive and administrative in nature. The ballot title and summary provided as follows:

> *Ballot title*: Local trustees and statewide *governing board to manage* Florida's university system
>
> *Ballot summary*: A local board of trustees shall administer each state university. Each board shall have thirteen members dedicated to excellence in teaching, research, and service to community. A statewide governing board of seventeen members shall be responsible for the *coordinated and accountable operation* of the whole university system. *Wasteful duplication of facilities or programs is to be avoided.* Provides procedures for selection and confirmation of board members, including one student and one faculty representative per board.

In re Advisory Op. to Atty. Gen. ex rel. Local Trs., 819 So. 2d at 727–28 (emphasis added). Nowhere in the ballot title or ballot summary does it indicate that the voters or framers intended for the Board of Governors to have authority over the setting of and appropriating for the expenditure of tuition and fees.

When this Court approved the amendment for placement on the ballot, we concluded that

> the sole purpose of the proposed amendment is to create a governance of the state university system. The enumeration of the duties and responsibilities of the statewide board of governors and the local university boards of trustees is a necessary component of a single dominant plan that complies with the single-subject requirement. While the proposed amendment may affect more than one branch of government, we cannot say it substantially alters or performs the functions of multiple branches of government....

Id. at 730. This Court also concluded that the amendment did not "substantially affect or change" article IX, section 1, of the Florida Constitution, *id.*, which provides that the Legislature must make adequate provision for the establishment, maintenance, and operation of Florida's universities. *See* art. IX, § 1(a), Fla. Const. ("Adequate provision shall be made by law ... for the establishment, maintenance, and operation of institutions of higher learning and other public education programs that the needs of the people may require."). Accordingly, this Court concluded that the amendment did not violate the single-subject requirement. *See In re Advisory Op. to Atty. Gen. ex rel. Local Trs.*, 819 So. 2d at 730 ("Even though the proposed amendment interacts with [article IX, sections 1 and 3] by providing a two-tier governing system specifically for the state university system, it does not substantially affect or change either one.... We therefore conclude that the only subject embraced in the proposed amendment is the two-tier system of governance of the state university system."). If the framers intended that the Board would have expansive authority over the setting of and appropriating for the expenditure of tuition and fees, neither the ballot summary nor the title indicated such an intent.

The Petitioners contend, however, that university funding has a dual nature: (1) tuition and fees from article III revenue paid by the recipients of education services; and

(2) the state subsidy from article VII general revenue paid by taxpayers. The Petitioners therefore argue that the Legislature's prior authority to control tuition and fees emanated solely from its article III authority to legislate and when voters passed the constitutional amendment creating the Board, this article III authority was necessarily transferred to the Board as a part of its power to "operate, regulate, control, and be fully responsible for the management of the whole university system." Art. IX, § 7(d), Fla. Const.

In support, the Petitioners point to article III, section 1, of the Florida Constitution as having been the prior source of the legislative authority to control the setting and expenditure of university tuition and fees, rather than article VII. However, article III, section 1, entitled "Composition," states only that the "legislative power of the state shall be vested in a legislature." Moreover, article VII, sections 1(c) and 1(d), do not limit the Legislature's power to raise revenue and make appropriations to monies raised by taxes, nor does the constitution indicate that fees for use of a state service fall outside of the Legislature's power to raise revenue and appropriate funds. Further, this Court's decisions regarding revenue and appropriations do not include this distinction. *See, e.g., Children A, B, C, D, E, & F*, 589 So. 2d at 265 (stating that based on article VII, sections 1(c) and 1(d), "this Court has long held that the power to appropriate *state funds* is legislative and is to be exercised only through duly enacted statutes" (emphasis added)).

Rather, it has been long-established that the Florida Constitution "requires legislative appropriation or authorization for the use of any funds from whatever source by a public agency or official for a public purpose." *Advisory Op. to the Governor*, 200 So. 2d 534, 536 (Fla. 1967). Although that statement was made with respect to provisions in the 1885 Florida Constitution, similar provisions, including an identical appropriations provision, appear in the current 1968 Florida Constitution. *Id.* (citing art. IV, § 24[41] and art. IX, § 4,[42] Fla. Const. (1885), now art. IV, § 4(c),[43] and art. VII, § 1(c),[44] Fla. Const. (1968)). As cogently explained by the First District, "[u]niversity tuition and fees are unquestionably state funds; they are collected by state universities for the use of their services and the monies collected are deposited into the State Treasury." *Graham*, 75 So. 3d at 318 (citing § 215.31, Fla. Stat. (2007)).

---

41. [FN 7.] Art. IV, § 24, Fla. Const. (1885) ("The Treasurer shall receive and keep all funds, bonds, and other securities, in such manner as may be prescribed by law, and shall disburse no funds, nor issue bonds, or other securities, except upon the order of the Comptroller countersigned by the Governor, in such manner as shall be prescribed by law.").

42. [FN 8.] Art. IV, § 24, Fla. Const. (1885) ("The Treasurer shall receive and keep all funds, bonds, and other securities, in such manner as may be prescribed by law, and shall disburse no funds, nor issue bonds, or other securities, except upon the order of the Comptroller countersigned by the Governor, in such manner as shall be prescribed by law.").

43. [FN 9.] Art. IV, § 4(c), Fla. Const. (1968) ("The chief financial officer shall serve as the chief fiscal officer of the state, and shall settle and approve accounts against the state, and shall keep all state funds and securities.").

44. [FN 10.] Art. VII, § 1(c), Fla. Const. (1968) ("No money shall be drawn from the treasury except in pursuance of appropriation made by law.").

The Petitioners rely in part upon the fact that tuition and fees were deposited in a trust fund, stating that the "Legislature correctly 'segregated' the Article III funds from the Article VII funds throughout the legislative process," including requiring the monies in the Education and General Student and Other Fees Trust Fund to be "segregated for a purpose authorized by law." This distinction has no bearing on the nature of the funds or the Legislature's constitutional authority over them, because, as explained by the First District below, "a trust fund is, at its essence, nothing more than an accounting tool used to segregate monies within the State Treasury." *Graham*, 75 So. 3d at 318–319 (citing § 215.32, Fla. Stat. (2007); *Mortham v. Milligan*, 704 So. 2d 152, 158 (Fla. 1st DCA 1997)). We therefore conclude that the Legislature's pre-amendment control over the setting of and appropriating for the expenditure of tuition and fees derived from its article VII, section 1, revenue-raising and appropriations power.

Finally, we reject the Petitioners' reliance on the constitutional systems of governance of universities established in other states, particularly Michigan, Minnesota, and California, as evidence of what the amendment at issue was intended to accomplish. The constitutional systems of university governance in Michigan,[45] Minnesota,[46] and California[47] are clearly different than that in Florida.

CONCLUSION

For the foregoing reasons, we hold that the constitutional source of the Legislature's authority to set and appropriate for the expenditure of tuition and fees derives from its power to raise revenue and appropriate for the expenditure of state funds. Nothing within the language of article IX, section 7, of the Florida Constitution indicates an intent to transfer this quintessentially legislative power to the Board of Governors. Accordingly, we conclude that the challenged statutes by which the Legislature has exercised control over these funds are facially constitutional and approve the First District's decision.

It is so ordered.

QUINCE, LABARGA, and PERRY, JJ., concur.

---

45. [FN 11.] *See* Mich. Const. art. VIII, § 5 (expressly giving each board of regents "general supervision of its institution and the control and direction of all expenditures from the institution's funds").

46. [FN 12.] *See* Minn. Const. art. XIII, § 3 (providing that "[a]ll the rights, immunities, franchises and endowments heretofore granted or conferred upon the University of Minnesota are perpetuated unto the university"); *Minnesota v. Chase*, 220 N.W. 951, 954 (Minn. 1928) (explaining that under this provision, "the University, in respect to its corporate status and government, *was put beyond the power of the Legislature by paramount law*, the right to amend or repeal which exists only in the people themselves" (emphasis added)).

47. [FN 13.] *See* Cal. Const. art. 9, § 9(a) (providing that the University of California "shall constitute a public trust, to be administered by the existing corporation known as 'The Regents of the University of California,' with full powers of organization and government, *subject only to such legislative control as may be necessary to insure the security of its funds and compliance with the terms of the endowments of the university and such competitive bidding procedures as may be made applicable* to the university by statute for the letting of construction contracts, sales of real property, and purchasing of materials, goods, and services" (emphasis added)).

LABARGA, J., concurs with an opinion.

POLSTON, C.J., and LEWIS and CANADY, JJ., concur in result.

LABARGA, J., concurring.

I concur with the majority that the challenged statutes by which the Legislature has exercised control over the setting of and appropriation of tuition and fees are *facially* constitutional. I write, however, to re-emphasize that our opinion does not address an *as-applied* challenge to a specific tuition and fee policy. Furthermore, our opinion does not address the question of the legality of any contingency attached to an appropriation that would encroach on the Board's constitutional responsibility for management of the university system. The power to attach contingencies to funds appropriated to the university system may not be employed to impair the constitutional authority of the Board to operate and manage the university system. Article IX, section 7(d), makes clear that it is the Board of Governors that "shall operate, regulate, control, and be fully responsible for the management of the whole university system." This constitutional grant of power is not insignificant. As aptly noted by the majority, the appropriations authority of the Legislature to attach contingencies to the appropriation of funds is not without limits. Majority op. at 9. I note that this same caution would apply equally to other budgetary functions historically assigned to the Legislature. With these caveats, I concur.

Commentary

Article IX, Section 7 was an initiative amendment. The sponsors of the initiative intended to restore the autonomy of the state university system which had been diminished when the Legislature abolished the former Board of Regents in 2001. After adoption of Article IX, Section 7, the Board of Governors was initially placed under the supervision of the State Board of Education. A declaratory judgment action followed resulting in a mediated agreement recognizing the autonomy of the Board of Governors and the State University System within the Executive branch. *See Floridians for Constitutional Integrity, Inc. v. State Board of Education*, Case No. 04-CA-3040, Order Ratifying Mediation Agreement (Fla. Cir. Ct., Mar. 17, 2006).

One area not addressed by the amendment creating the Board of Governors involved the system of community colleges. In 2018, voters approved an amendment proposed by the CRC for the State College System. See Fla. Const. art. IX, §8. However, the new amendment places the State College System under the supervision of the State Board of Education. *See* FLA. CONST. art. IX, §8(d).

Article X

Miscellaneous and Article II General Provisions

Introduction
A. Original Miscellaneous Provisions
   i. Article X, Section 4—Homestead Exemptions
      1. *In re Estate of McGinty*, 258 So. 2d 450 (Fla. 1971).
      2. *Public Health Trust of Dade County v. Lopez*, 531 So. 2d 946 (Fla. 1988).
      3. *McKean v. Warburton*, 919 So. 2d 341 (Fla. 2005).
      4. *In re Estate of Scholtz*, 543 So. 2d 219 (Fla. 1989).
      5. *Butterworth v. Caggiano*, 605 So. 2d 56 (Fla. 1992).
   ii. Article X, Section 6—Eminent Domain
      6. *Seadade Industries, Inc. v. Florida Power & Light Co.*, 245 So. 2d 209 (Fla. 1971).
      7. *System Components Corp. v. Florida Department of Transportation*, 14 So. 3d 967 (Fla. 2009).
      8. *Flatt v. City of Brooksville*, 368 So. 2d 631 (Fla. 2d DCA 1979).
B. Environmental Provisions
   i. Article X, Section 11—Sovereignty Lands.
      9. *Coastal Petroleum Co. v. American Cyanamid Co.*, 492 So. 2d 339 (Fla. 1986), *cert. denied sub. nom. Mobil Oil Co. v. Board of Trustees of Internal Improvement Trust Fund*, 479 U.S. 1065 (1987).
      10. *Walton County v. Stop Beach Renourishment, Inc.*, 998 So. 2d 1102 (Fla. 2008), *aff'd*, 560 U.S. 702 (2010).
   ii. Article X, Section 16—Limited Marine Net Fishing
      11. *Lane v. Chiles*, 698 So. 2d 260 (Fla. 1997).
   iii. Article II, Section 7—Natural Resources and Scenic Beauty
      12. *Advisory Opinion to the Governor—1996 Amendment 5 (Everglades)*, 706 So. 2d 278 (Fla. 1997).
      13. *Barley v. South Florida Water Management District*, 823 So. 2d 73 (Fla. 2002).
   iv. Article X, Section 28—Land Acquisition Trust Fund
      14. *Oliva v. Florida Wildlife Federation, Inc.*, 281 So. 3d 531 (1st DCA 2019), *rev. denied*, 2020 WL 3525953 (Fla., Jun. 29, 2020).
C. Other Initiative Amendments
   i. Article X, Section 29—Medical Marijuana Production, Possession, and Use

15. *Forest v. State*, 257 So. 2d 603 (Fla. 1st DCA 2018).

16. *Florida Department of Health v. Florigrown, LLC*, 2019 WL 2943329
(1st DCA, July 19, 2019), *rev. granted*, 2019 WL 5208142
(Fla., Oct. 16, 2019).

Introduction

Article II of the Florida Constitution is entitled "General Provisions," while Article X is entitled "Miscellaneous." Both Article II and Article X contain original material relating to how the State and its government are organized, and how that government relates to its citizens.[1] Many of these provisions were part of previous Florida Constitutions.[2] However, the miscellaneous sections of earlier Constitutions also included provisions that would be unconscionable today.[3] We have already encountered Article

---

1. The first part of Article II contains provisions dealing with the State Boundaries (Section 1), the Seat of Government (Section 2), and the State Seal and Flag (Section 4). Article II, Section 5 deals with Public Officers, including a prohibition on dual office-holding by public officials, while Section 6 allows for emergency measures to continue government in the event of enemy attack. We will look at the Natural Resources provision, Article II, Section 7, later in this section along with other environmental provisions.

Likewise, Article X originally included provisions dealing with: 1) Amendments to the U.S. Constitution (Section 1); 2) the Militia (Section 2); 3) Vacancy in office of public officials (Section 3); 4) Homestead (Section 4); 5) a requirement that married men and women be treated the same with regard to property rights (Section 5); 6) Eminent Domain (Section 6); 7) a prohibition on lotteries (Section 7); 8) a recognition of the U.S. Census as the official census for Florida (Section 8); 9) a provision that repeal of criminal statutes does not affect prosecution for crimes committed prior to the repeal (Section 9); 10) a definition of "felony" for criminal statutes (Section 10); 11) a requirement that sovereignty lands under navigable waters are held in trust and cannot be sold or leased except when in the public interest (Section 11, amended by legislative amendment in 1970); 12) Rules of construction (Section 12); and a provision allowing lawsuits against the State (Section 13). In addition, a 1976 legislative amendment requires that any increases to public pensions must be funded. *See* FLA. CONST. art. X, § 14.

2. The 1838, 1861, and 1865 Constitutions each contained a "General Provisions" article. Both the 1868 and 1885 Constitutions contained a "Miscellaneous" article. The current Constitution contains both.

3. Thus, the 1838 and 1861 Constitutions prohibited the Legislature from emancipating slaves, and it likewise allowed the Legislature to prevent the immigration of free black persons to Florida. *See* FLA. CONST. OF 1838 art. XVI, § 1-2; FLA. CONST. OF 1861, art. XV, § 1-2. The 1865 Constitution recognized the fact of emancipation. *See* FLA. CONST. OF 1865 art. 16, § 1. That provision provides:

> Whereas, slavery has been destroyed in this State by the Government of the United States; therefore, neither slavery nor involuntary servitude shall in future exist in this State, except as a punishment for crimes, whereof the party shall have been convicted by the courts of the State, and all the inhabitants of the State, without distinction of color, are free, and shall enjoy the rights of person and property without distinction of color.

Id. However, the 1865 Constitution excluded the testimony of black citizens from any trial involving white person. *See* FLA. CONST. OF 1865, art. 16, § 2. Article 16, Section 3 also provided that only white men could sit on juries.

The 1868 Constitution did not include any of these overtly discriminatory provisions. The 1868 Constitution did include provisions forbidding citizens who had held civil or military office under

II, Section 3 when we discussed the important principle of Separation of Powers. Because of their miscellaneous scope, both Article II and especially Article X have been the receiving ground for many newer amendments, especially initiative amendments. The first such initiative was the Ethics in Government initiative, originally approved by voters in 1976, which added Article II, Section 8.[4] In 1988, voters approved the English Language initiative as Article II, Section 9. We will discuss later the environmental provisions added to Article II, Section 7, which have been modified three times: once by initiative in 1996 (Article II, Section 7(b)), then by the 1998 Constitution Revision Commission (Article II, Section 7(a)), and finally as part of a 2018 Constitution Revision Commission proposal (Article II, Section 7(c)). In Article X, three provisions were added by Constitution Revision Commission proposals.[5] Article X, Section 22 ("Parental Notice of Termination of a Minor's Pregnancy") is the only recent legislative proposal, and was added in 2004.[6] The remaining provisions of Article X were all added via initiative amendment.[7]

In this chapter, we will also look at the Homestead Exemption in Article X, Section 4 and the provision governing Eminent Domain in Article X, Section 6. Then we will look at some of the environmental provisions of the Florida Constitution, including conflicts that have arisen surrounding a couple of initiative amendments. Finally, we will look at the issues surrounding implementation of the recent Medical Marijuana initiative amendment, Article X, Section 29.

---

the Confederacy during the Civil War from holding office unless the U.S. Congress removed that disability. *See* FLA. CONST. OF 1868, art. XVI, § 1. The 1868 Constitution also allowed anyone who had property seized and taken by the Confederate or Florida governments as enemy aliens to recover damages. *See* FLA. CONST. OF 1868, art. XVI, § 27. The post-Reconstruction 1885 Constitution removed any disabilities due to wartime service under the Confederacy. The 1885 Constitution also inserted a provision prohibiting interracial marriage. *See* FLA. CONST. OF 1885, art. XVI, § 24.

4. This amendment was itself amended by the 2018 Constitution Revision Commission. Revision 7 tightened rules on lobbying and expanded restrictions on lobbying by former public officials. Part of this Revision was the creation of Article II, Section 8(h)(2) forbidding public officers or employees from abusing their position "in order to obtain a disproportionate benefit for [the official, family members, or business associates]."

5. Article X, Section 18 was added in 1998 as part of Revision 5 ("Conservation of Natural Resources and Creation of Fish & Wildlife Conservation Commission"). Article X, Section 31 was added in 2018 as part of Revision 2 ("First Responder and Military Member Survivor Benefits; Public Colleges and Universities"). Article X, Section 32 was added in 2018 as part of Revision 8 ("Ends Dog Racing").

6. We examined this provision briefly when we looked at Article I, Section 23 and the constitutional right to privacy.

7. These include the State Lottery (Section 15, added in 1986), the Net Ban (Section 16, added in 1994), the Everglades Trust Fund (Section 17, added in 1996), the Bullet Train (Section 19, added in 2000, repealed by a separate initiative amendment in 2004), the Prohibition on Workplace Smoking (Section 20, added in 2002), the provision protecting pregnant pigs (Section 21, added in 2002), local referenda to allow slot machines in Dade and Broward Counties (Section 23, added in 2004), the Minimum Wage (Section 24, added in 2004), patient's right to know about adverse medical incidents (Section 25, added in 2004), prohibition of medical licenses after repeated medical malpractice (Section 26, added in 2004), tobacco education and prevention (Section 27, added in 2006), the Land Acquisition Trust Fund (Section 28, added in 2014), Medical Marijuana (Section 29, added in 2016), and Restrictions on Casino Gambling (Section 30, added in 2018).

A. Original Miscellaneous Provisions

i. Article X, Section 4 — Homestead Exemptions

We looked first at the Homestead Exemption in our discussion of Article VII, Section 6(a). That Homestead Exemption removes a certain assessed value of homestead property from liability for ad valorem taxes to local governments.[8] The Homestead Exemption in Article X, Section 4 provides an additional benefit for homestead property in the form of a relief from forced sale. It also provides limits on alienation of homestead property where the owner is survived by a spouse or minor child. Florida law first protected homestead property in 1845, originally protecting 40 acres of homestead property.[9] The 1868 Constitution was the first to mandate the protection of homestead property.[10] The exemption likewise appeared in the 1885 Constitution.[11] The cases below explore the boundaries of the homestead exemption in the context of limits on devise and whether it can protect homestead property from the operation of forfeiture laws.

In re Estate of McGinty

258 So. 2d 450 (Fla. 1971)

BOYD, Justice.

This cause is before us on appeal from the County Judge's Court, Palm Beach County. The judgment sought to be reviewed directly passes on the validity of a Florida Statute, giving this Court jurisdiction of the cause under s 4, Article V, of the Florida Constitution, F.S.A.

The basic issue presented is whether the purported devise by Thomas J. McGinty, deceased, of his residence in Palm Beach County, Florida, to his daughter, Patricia, is valid. The trial court held that the property was homestead and not subject to devise because the decedent was survived by lineal descendants. In reaching this result, the trial court held that the provisions of s 4(c), Article X, of the Florida Constitution, that a homestead is not subject to devise "if the owner is survived by spouse

---

8. For a practical explanation of Florida's Homestead provision, see, e.g., Rohan Kelley, *Homestead Made Easy*, Fla. B.J., Mar. 1991, at 17; Rohan Kelley, *Homestead Made Easy, Part II*, Fla. B.J., April 1991, at 19.

9. *See generally* Paul Goodman, *The Emergence of Homestead Exemption in the United States: Accommodation & Resistance to the Market Revolution*, 80 J. Am. Hist. 470, 471–72 (1993) (discussing the adoption of homestead protection by states in the aftermath of the 1837 economic panic); *see also* Dennis J. Wall, *Homestead and the Process of History: The Proposed Changes in Article X, Section 4*, 6 Fla. St. Univ. L. Rev. 877, 895–904 (1978) (discussing the history of Florida's protection of homestead).

10. *See* Fla. Const. of 1868 art. IX (protecting 160 acres). The provision made clear that it did not apply to prevent forced sale in the case of debts incurred to purchase the property itself or for the payment of taxes. *See id.* art. IX, § 2. The restriction of this protection to "head of a family" first appeared in the 1868 Constitution. *Id.* art. IX, § 1.

11. *See* Fla. Const. of 1885 art. X. A 1934 amendment added Section 7 to Article X, and raised the value of personal property included in the homestead exemption from $1,000 to $5,000.

or minor child"[12] was not in conflict and did not repeal Florida Statutes s 731.05(1), F.S.A., which provides:

> "Any property, real or personal, held by any title, legal or equitable, with or without actual seisin, may be devised or bequeathed by will; provided, however, that whenever a person who is head of a family, residing in this state and having a homestead therein, dies and leaves either a widow or lineal descendants, or both surviving him, the homestead shall not be the subject of devise, but shall descend as otherwise provided in this law for the descent of homesteads."

The foregoing statute has remained substantially unchanged since 1933.

The Constitution of Florida, as adopted in 1968, adds the requirement of minority as regards the surviving children of a deceased homestead owner. The Constitution of 1885, s 4, Article X, in effect at the time Florida Statutes s 731.05(1), F.S.A. was adopted simply provided:

> "Nothing in this Article shall be construed to prevent the holder of a homestead from alienating his or her homestead so exempted by deed or mortgage duly executed by himself or herself, and by husband and wife, if such relation exists; nor if the holder be without children to prevent him or her from disposing of his or her homestead by will in a manner prescribed by law."

The class of persons designated as "minor children" is substantially different from and inconsistent with, "lineal descendants." We hold, therefore, that the requirements of Article X, s 4 of our present Constitution, adopted in 1968, controls and repeals the inconsistent provision of Florida Statutes s 731.05(1). The restraint on the right of an individual to devise his property at death should not be extended beyond that expressly allowed by the Constitution.

In the instant case, the four children of Thomas J. McGinty, widower, who survived him were not minors. All were over twenty-one years of age at the time of McGinty's death. We hold, therefore, that McGinty's devise of his residence to his daughter, Patricia Ann McGinty, is valid. Because of our decision on this controlling point, it is unnecessary to consider the correctness of the trial court's findings regarding the dependency of the testator's adult children and the contiguous nature of the property in question.

Accordingly, the judgment of the trial court is reversed and the cause remanded for further proceedings consistent herewith.

It is so ordered.

ROBERTS, C.J., and ERVIN, CARLTON, McCAIN and DEKLE, JJ., concur.

ADKINS, J., dissents with opinion.

ADKINS, Justice (dissenting):

I must respectfully dissent.

---

12. [FN 1.] Fla.Con. s 4(c), Art. X: "The homestead shall not be subject to devise if the owner is survived by spouse or minor child."

The majority opinion takes the position that a restraint on the right of an individual to devise his property at death should not be extended beyond that expressly *allowed* by the Constitution.

It is well settled that the State Constitution is not a grant of power but a limitation upon power. Unless legislation duly passed be clearly contrary to some express or implied prohibition contained in the Constitution, the courts have no authority to pronounce it invalid. *Harry E. Prettyman, Inc. v. Florida Real Estate Commission*, 92 Fla. 515, 109 So. 442 (1926); *State ex rel. Jones v. Wiseheart*, 245 So.2d 849 (Fla.1971).

The right to inherit is controlled by legislative fiat, and devolution is a matter of legislative discretion. It is the sole province of the Legislature to designate heirs and to infuse inheritable blood into those who are to inherit the property of a decedent. See 10 Fla.Jur., Descent and Distribution, s 11, p. 243, citing *Christopher v. Mungen*, 61 Fla. 513, 55 So. 273, *reh. den.* 61 Fla. 534, 55 So. 281 (1911); *Coral Gables First National Bank v. Hart*, 155 Fla. 482, 20 So.2d 647 (1945). See also 7 F.L.P., Descent and Distribution, s 3, p. 520.

The Legislature is empowered to determine the law of succession as long as such laws are not in conflict with the Constitution and additional legislative restrictions should be held valid. In other words, the Legislature may prescribe any method for succession of homestead or devise of homestead subject only to the prohibition that a homestead is not subject to devise "if the owner is survived by spouse or Minor child." This provision is not in conflict with Fla.Stat. s 731.05(1).

The majority opinion can be justified only if we overlook the basic principle that the Constitution is a limitation upon power, not a grant of power.

Questions

1. Under the majority's reasoning, how does Section 4 limit the Legislature's power in dealing with the devise of homestead property?

2. How does Justice Adkins' reasoning differ as expressed in his dissent?

Public Health Trust of Dade County v. Lopez

531 So. 2d 946 (Fla. 1988)

BARKETT, Justice.

We review the conflicting decisions of *Lopez v. Public Health Trust of Dade County*, 509 So.2d 1286 (Fla. 3d DCA 1987), and *In re Estate of Taylor*, 516 So.2d 322 (Fla. 2d DCA 1987). In so doing, we answer in the affirmative the following question posed in *Lopez*:

> Whether article X, section 4 of the Constitution of Florida, as amended, serves to exempt a decedent's homestead property from forced sale for the benefit of the decedent's creditors, where the decedent is not survived by a dependent spouse or children?

We have jurisdiction. Art. V, §§ 3(b)(3) and (4), Fla. Const.

The principal facts are not in dispute. In *Lopez,* the decedent homeowner, Nereida Lopez, at the time of her death, was residing in the home with her three adult children. The decedent's personal representatives petitioned the probate court to have the property set aside as homestead under article X, section 4 of the Florida Constitution. The petition was opposed by Public Health Trust, to whom the decedent was indebted. The trial court denied the petition based upon its finding that the decedent's heirs, her three adult children, were not dependent on her at the time of her death.

Similarly, in *Hines,* the home owner, Helen Taylor, at the time of her death, was single and residing in the home she had acquired from her divorced husband. She died intestate, survived by four adult, nondependent children who lived elsewhere. Here, too, the probate court denied the personal representatives' petition to have the home set aside as exempt from the decedent's creditors, Gessler Clinic and Winter Haven Hospital.

On appeal, the Third District reversed in *Lopez,* concluding that the homestead exemption inures to the benefit of the decedent's heirs whether or not the heirs were dependent on the decedent. Conversely, in *Hines,* the Second District affirmed the lower court, holding that the residence of a single person who is not survived by a spouse or dependent family members is *not* exempt from the decedent's creditors.

On this appeal, Public Health Trust, Gessler Clinic, and Winter Haven Hospital ("creditors") argue that article X, section 4(b), extending the homestead exemption to the "surviving spouse or heirs of the owner," must be construed to apply only to minor or dependent heirs. To support this interpretation, the creditors assert that under prior case law, Florida's homestead exemption was not available to adult heirs of a decedent unless the heirs had been dependent on the decedent. They point to the history of the 1985 amendment as evidence that the legislature never intended to eliminate this requirement. The creditors also argue that a literal interpretation of section 4(b) would provide a windfall for financially independent heirs at the expense of the decedent's creditors, distorting the historical purpose of homestead laws to protect dependents in need of shelter.

In addition, Public Health Trust questions whether the amended provision protects the homes of all single persons and suggests that it applies only to those single persons who are surviving widows or divorced parents.

The personal representatives, on the other hand, argue that the language of the homestead exemption is clear and unambiguous; that the cases relied upon by the creditors are inapposite; and that the precise question presented already has been answered in their favor in *Miller v. Finegan,* 26 Fla. 29, 7 So. 140 (1890); *Scull v. Beatty,* 27 Fla. 426, 9 So. 4 (1891); and *Cumberland & Liberty Mills v. Keggin,* 139 Fla. 133, 190 So. 492 (1939).

For the reasons advanced by the personal representatives, we reject the creditors' position. For over a century, Florida has by constitutional provision made the homeplace exempt from the claims of creditors. *See Baker v. State*, 17 Fla. 406 (1879) (construing homestead provision of the Florida Constitution of 1868). As a matter of public policy, the purpose of the homestead exemption is to promote the stability and welfare of the state by securing to the householder a home, so that the homeowner and his or her heirs may live beyond the reach of financial misfortune and the demands of creditors who have given credit under such law. *See Bigelow v. Dunphe*, 143 Fla. 603, 197 So. 328 (1940).

Until 1985, the homestead protection was limited to those persons who qualified under the constitutionally designated term "head of a family." *See* art. X, §4, Fla. Const. (1983). In 1984, however, the people of Florida approved an amendment changing the term "head of a family" to "a natural person." The amendment thus expanded the class of persons who can take advantage of the homestead provision and its protections.

As an initial matter, we reject Public Health Trust's suggestion that "natural person," when applied to single persons, means only widows and divorced parents. Such an interpretation is contrary to the language, logic and history of the amendment. As Representative Hawkins, who sponsored the amendment in the House of Representatives, explained, the purpose of the revision was "to give protection against forced sale for the homestead of a single person, a divorced person, any person who has a homestead, rather than just a head of a family." House Judiciary Full Committee Meeting, March 29, 1983.

The 1985 amendment thus made the homestead protection available to *any* natural person. Accordingly, the property and residences in question clearly fit within the definition of "homestead" under section 4(a)(1), as amended.

We turn then to the principal issue before us, the meaning and application of article X, section 4(b). The language of this provision is indeed plain and unambiguous....

As the creditors themselves point out, legislative intent controls construction of statutes in Florida.[13] Moreover, "that intent is determined primarily from the language of the statute [and] ... [t]he plain meaning of the statutory language is the first consideration." *St. Petersburg Bank and Trust Co. v. Hamm*, 414 So.2d 1071, 1073 (Fla.1982) (citation omitted). This Court consistently has adhered to the plain meaning rule in applying statutory and constitutional provisions. *See Holly v. Auld*, 450 So.2d 217, 219 (Fla.1984)....

The constitutional provision at issue is clear, reasonable and logical in its operation. Section 4(b) states, without any qualification, that the benefits "inure to the surviving spouse or heirs of the owner." There are no words suggesting that the heirs or surviving spouse had to have been dependent on the homeowner to enjoy this protection. Consequently, the creditors are not asking us merely to construe or interpret the amendment but rather to graft onto it something that is not there. This we cannot do. We

---

13. [FN 4.] The principles governing construction of statutes are generally applicable to the construction of constitutions. *City of Jacksonville v. Continental Can Co.*, 113 Fla. 168, 171, 151 So. 488, 489 (1933); *State ex rel. Moodie v. Bryan*, 50 Fla. 293, 385, 39 So. 929, 958 (1905).

are not permitted to attribute to the legislature an intent beyond that expressed, *see Bill Smith, Inc. v. Cox,* 166 So.2d 497, 498 (Fla. 2d DCA 1964), or to speculate about what should have been intended. *Tropical Coach Line v. Carter,* 121 So.2d 779, 782 (1960). Nor may we insert words or phrases in a constitutional provision, or supply an omission that was not in the minds of the people when the law was enacted. *See Brooks v. Anastasia Mosquito Control Dist.,* 148 So.2d 64, 66 (Fla. 1st DCA 1963). The legislature, and in this case, the people who adopted the amendment, must be held to have intended what was so plainly expressed.

We are fortified in our conclusion by the legislative history of the amendment. We have examined the materials submitted by the parties and find nothing in them even remotely suggesting that the legislature intended "surviving spouse or heirs" to mean "dependent spouse or heirs." Nor can we say that the people of Florida had any such limitation in mind. The Ballot Summary upon which the people voted said:

> EXEMPTION OF HOMESTEAD AND PERSONAL PROPERTY FROM FORCED SALE—Provides that the exemption of a homestead and of personal property to the value of $1,000 from forced sale and certain liens shall extend to any natural person, not just head of a family.

We conclude that neither the language nor the legislative history of the amendment supports the creditors' position.

Nor does prior case law. Contrary to the creditors' assertion, homestead property always has descended to the heirs free of creditor's liens without regard to whether the heirs were dependents.

The creditors have confused the issue by relying on cases that did not apply section 4(b), but only answered the threshold question of whether the property qualified as homestead. That threshold question required a factual finding that the decedent, at the time of his death, had been, in the words of the old constitution, the "head of a family." That term was construed to mean someone who either had a legal duty of support arising out of a family relationship or lived with at least one other as a family and was regarded as the "head" of that "family." *Whidden v. Abbott,* 124 Fla. 293, 294–95, 168 So. 253, 254 (1936). In each case cited by the creditors, ... the court decided the owner was not the head of a family at the time of his death, and thus never reached the question of whether the property, had it been homestead, would have passed to the heirs exempt from the claims of the decedent's creditors. *E.g., Brown* [*v. Hutch*], 156 So.2d at 686 [(Fla. 2d DCA 1963)] (at time of Brown's death, property in question was not homestead property); *In re Wilder's Estate,* 240 So.2d 514 (Fla. 1st DCA 1970) (where son or daughter becomes head of his or her own family, that child not also considered member of parent's family of which parent is considered head).

Miller and *Scull,* in contrast, are on all fours with the cases before us and we adhere to the reasoning there expressed. In *Miller,* the heirs were adults, and this Court stated:

> This exemption is from liability for the debts of the ancestor, and it is given to whoever may be heirs without reference to whether they be infants

or adults. No such condition is to be found in the Constitution, but according to its plain language and meaning, the heirs, if they be all adult, take the exemption with the land in the same way that infant heirs do.

. . . .

It may be said, however, that to permit adult heirs to enjoy the benefit of the exemption is inconsistent with the general idea or purpose of a homestead, and that this is more prominently so when such adults have not lived under the home roof and been a part of the family it protects. The answer to this is found in the very provision of the Constitution that the exemption shall accrue to the heirs of the party having enjoyed it. That property which creditors could not take from the head of the family when he was living, they cannot take from his heirs after his death. This is what the Constitution plainly said to any one who might become a creditor.

26 Fla. at 36–37, 7 So. at 142.

And in *Scull*, the Court again rejected the argument that the protection should not be extended to a homesteader's nonresident adult children, finding instead that homestead property accrues to the heirs without regard to their residence or ages. 27 Fla. at 436–37, 9 So. at 6 (1891). . . .

Lastly, we reject the creditors' argument that a literal interpretation of section 4(b) will provide a windfall for financially independent heirs at the expense of the just demands of creditors. Even if we were free to ignore the plain language of the constitution, we would not be persuaded by this argument. The homestead protection has never been based upon principles of equity, *see Bigelow*, but always has been extended to the homesteader and, after his or her death, to the heirs whether the homestead was a twenty-two room mansion or a two-room hut and whether the heirs were rich or poor.

In sum, we conclude that the homestead exemption formerly only enjoyed by a head of a family can now be enjoyed by any natural person. The exemption continues after the homesteader's death without regard to whether the heirs were dependent on the homestead owner. Thus, the homestead descends directly to the spouse or heirs[14] free and clear of creditor's claims.

Accordingly, we approve *Lopez* but disapprove *Hines* and remand it to the Second District Court of Appeal for proceedings consistent with this opinion.

It is so ordered.

OVERTON, EHRLICH, SHAW and KOGAN, JJ., concur.

McDONALD, C.J., concurs in part and dissents in part with an opinion.

McDONALD, Chief Justice, concurring in part and dissenting in part.

I would approve both *Lopez v. Public Health Trust of Dade County*, 509 So.2d 1286 (Fla. 3d DCA 1987), and *In re Estate of Taylor*, 516 So.2d 322 (Fla. 2d DCA 1987).

---

14. [FN 6.] The term "heirs" is defined by section 731.201(18), Florida Statutes (1985), as those persons entitled to the decedent's property under the statutes of intestate succession.

There is a critical factual distinction between these two cases. In *Lopez* the adult children lived with their mother. Her home was their principal place of abode and their home. In *Taylor* the children lived apart from their deceased mother. They had their own separate and distinct place of abode, did not share the home with their mother, and did not claim it to be their home.

The reasoning of the majority opinion, and its interpretation of article X, section 4(a)(2), (b), Florida Constitution, is sound and within the intent of the 1984 amendment to protect the home, when it is a home, from creditors. This Court, however, has always said that a person can claim but one homestead. If a party has a separate home it has all the protection of article X, section 4. Under these circumstances, however, there is no need, and no public purpose, for continuing to protect the house or property of one who dies leaving a house which is no longer a home for the children or heirs of the decedent.

I would therefore approve extending the protection of article X, section 4 to the property in *Lopez,* but disallow it as to the property in *Taylor.*

Questions

1. a. What is the purpose of the homestead provision in Section 4?

   b. Note that the protection from "creditors" is not absolute.

2. What did Appellant argue?

3. How did the Court respond to Appellant's arguments?

McKean v. Warburton

919 So. 2d 341 (Fla. 2005)

QUINCE, J.

We have for review a decision of the Fourth District Court of Appeal which certified the following question to be of great public importance:

> WHERE A DECEDENT IS NOT SURVIVED BY A SPOUSE OR ANY MINOR CHILDREN, DOES DECEDENT'S HOMESTEAD PROPERTY, WHEN NOT SPECIFICALLY DEVISED, PASS TO GENERAL DEVISEES BEFORE RESIDUARY DEVISEES IN ACCORDANCE WITH SECTION 733.805, FLORIDA STATUTES?

Warburton v. McKean, 877 So.2d 50, 53 (Fla. 4th DCA 2004). We have jurisdiction. *See* art. V, § 3(b)(4), Fla. Const. For the reasons discussed below, we answer the certified question in the negative, and hold that where a decedent is not survived by a spouse or minor children, the decedent's homestead property passes to the residuary devisees, not the general devisees, unless there is a specific testamentary disposition ordering the property to be sold and the proceeds made a part of the general estate.

FACTS

Henry Pratt McKean II died testate and was not survived by a spouse or minor child. When he died, McKean owned a condominium which was his homestead. The condominium was sold and netted $141,000. McKean also had nominal assets valued at approximately $10,000. The estate's liabilities amounted to $14,000, plus personal representative's fees and attorney's fees.

McKean's will states in pertinent part as follows:

ARTICLE III

I hereby give, devise and bequeath the following amounts of money to the following named individuals, per capita:

Russell Cappelen, Jr. of Vero Beach, Florida $20,000.00;

and

Peter Warburton of Hamilton, Massachusetts . . . . $150,000.00.

ARTICLE IV

I hereby give, devise and bequeath the automobile which I own at the time of my death to Glenn Van Hest of Vero Beach, Florida.

ARTICLE V

I hereby give, devise and bequeath to my half-brother ROBERT McKEAN, all of the oil interest I own and royalties due me in Exxon Well, Webster Field.

. . . .

ARTICLE VII

All the rest, residue and remainder of my property which I may own at the time of my death, real, personal or mixed, tangible or intangible, of whatsoever nature and wheresoever situate, including all property which I may acquire or be given title to after the execution of this Will, including all lapsed legacies and devises or gifts made by this Will which fail for any reason, including all insurance(s) on my life payable to my estate or receivable by my Personal Representative, and including any property over or concerning which I may have any power of appointment, I give, devise and bequeath to my half-brothers, THOMAS McKEAN, JOHN W. McKEAN, ROBERT McKEAN and DAVID McKEAN, in equal shares, share and share alike, per stirpes.

Absent the homestead proceeds, the estate assets are insufficient to satisfy any creditor's claims and the cash bequests. Peter Warburton, McKean's nephew, argues that the assets from the homestead property should be used to fund the cash gift to him, free from creditor's claims, as preresiduary property. McKean's half brothers argue that the homestead property passes through the residuary clause of the will to them.

LAW AND ANALYSIS

The issue before this Court is who is entitled to homestead property that is not specifically devised in a testator's will when the testator does not have a surviving spouse or minor children. Although section 731.201, Florida Statutes (2004), does not define homestead, it defines "protected homestead" as that property described in the Florida Constitution "on which at the death of the owner the exemption inures to the owner's surviving spouse or heirs." § 731.201(29), Fla. Stat. (2004). The Florida Constitution defines and protects homesteads in three distinct ways: it provides homesteads with an exemption from taxes; it protects homesteads from forced sale by creditors; and it places certain restrictions on a homestead owner from alienating or devising the homestead property. *See Snyder v. Davis*, 699 So.2d 999, 1001 (Fla.1997). The public policy furthered by a homestead exemption is to "promote the stability and welfare of the state by securing to the householder a home, so that the homeowner and his or her heirs may live beyond the reach of financial misfortune and the demands of creditors who have given credit under such law." *Public Health Trust v. Lopez*, 531 So.2d 946, 948 (Fla.1988). To that end, issues of homestead protections have been interpreted broadly by the courts. *See Snyder*, 699 So.2d at 1002; *Tramel v. Stewart*, 697 So.2d 821 (Fla.1997) (liberally construing the homestead provision in the face of an attempted forfeiture action against homestead property). It is with these policy considerations that we consider the issue in this case.

The parties agree that McKean's property was protected homestead property. Because McKean had no surviving spouse or minor child at the time of his death, the devise of his homestead property to certain family members was protected from creditors. *See Snyder v. Davis*, 699 So.2d 999, 1005 (Fla.1997). Florida's intestacy statute, section 732.103, Florida Statutes (2004), includes the following family members: the surviving spouse, the lineal descendants, the decedent's mother or father or both, the decedent's brothers and sisters, and then the descendents of the brothers and sisters. Petitioners are McKean's half brothers. Section 732.105, Florida Statutes (2004), provides:

> When property descends to the collateral kindred of the intestate and part of the collateral kindred are of the whole blood to the intestate and the other part of the half blood, those of the half blood shall inherit only half as much as those of the whole blood; but if all of the half blood they shall have whole parts.

Thus, McKean's half brothers and his nephew are "heirs" pursuant to Florida's intestacy statute.

It is an elementary principle that a person can dispose of his or her property by will as he or she pleases so long as that person's intent is not contrary to any principle of law or public policy. *See, e.g., Mosgrove v. Mach*, 133 Fla. 459, 182 So. 786, 790–91 (1938). Moreover, once the intent of the testator is ascertained, the entire will should be considered and construed liberally to effectuate the testator's intent. *See Marshall v. Hewett*, 156 Fla. 645, 24 So.2d 1, 2 (1945). The primary objective in construing a will is the intent of the testator. *Id.*

When McKean died, he had approximately $10,000 in assets, plus his homestead condominium. The condominium was sold and netted approximately $141,000.00.[15]

---

15. [FN 3.] The constitutional provision protects homestead property from forced sale to satisfy creditors. The protected homestead may be voluntarily sold, however, and the funds will be protected so long as they are not commingled and are held for the sole purpose of acquiring another home within a reasonable period of time. *See Orange Brevard Plumbing & Heating Co. v. La Croix*, 137 So.2d

The estate's liabilities included funeral expenses, credit card debt, the personal representative's fees, and the attorney's fees. The $10,000 in assets was insufficient to settle the liabilities and the specific cash gifts. Warburton, one of the general devisees, seeks to have the $141,000.00 in proceeds from the sale of the homestead satisfy his cash gift, and as an "heir," he seeks to have the cash gift satisfied with protected homestead assets free from all creditor's claims. The Fourth District agreed with Warburton and considered the proceeds from the sale of the protected homestead as part of the general assets of the estate and available to satisfy specific and general devises under the will. Relying on section 733.805, Florida Statutes (2004),[16] the Fourth District concluded that residuary gifts abate or fail before general or specific devises. It then applied the estate assets, including the $141,000, in accordance with section 733.805 and found that the residuary gift abated or failed.

While it is true that a decedent may devise protected homestead property in his or her will if there is no surviving spouse or minor child, the property may only pass as a general asset of the estate by a specific devise. In the absence of a specific devise, the property may pass through the residuary, which is a sufficiently precise indicator of testamentary intent to pass protected homestead property. *See Estate of Murphy*, 340 So.2d 107 (Fla.1976) (finding that a specific devise of homestead property is preferred, but the general language of a residuary clause is a sufficiently precise indicator of testamentary intent). In this case, the will did not specifically devise the protected homestead property to Warburton, and therefore the homestead passed under the residuary clause to the four half brothers.

... Likewise, in this case, the homestead property was not specifically devised. It therefore passes through the residuary clause to McKean's heirs and is protected from forced sale to satisfy the cash devise to Warburton. A contrary result creates an apparent conflict because the same factual situation has resulted in different outcomes. *See* art. V, § 3(b)(3), Fla. Const.

... Florida's statutory scheme and cases from other Florida district courts of appeal support the result we reach today. Section 733.607, Florida Statutes (2004), provides that the personal representative takes possession or control of the decedent's property, except for protected homestead. The personal representative is then charged with the duty to protect the estate until distribution. Nothing in the statutes indicates that the protected homestead should be distributed as part of the decedent's estate, as Warburton contends. Florida's case law supports this conclusion.

---

201 (Fla.1962). The proceeds can be used to pay off an existing mortgage. *See Suntrust Bank/Miami, N.A., v. Papadopolous*, 740 So.2d 594 (Fla. 3d DCA 1999).

16. [FN. 4] Section 733.805(1), Florida Statutes (2004), provides that funds of the estate shall be used to pay debts, charges, expenses, and devises, and that if the property is insufficient to cover all of those, gifts under the will shall lapse in the following order: property passing by intestacy; property devised to the residuary devisee or devisees; property not specifically or demonstratively devised; and property specifically or demonstratively devised.

In *Clifton v. Clifton*, 553 So.2d 192, 194 n. 3 (Fla. 5th DCA 1989), the court held that "[h]omestead property, whether devised or not, passes outside of the probate estate. Personal representatives have no jurisdiction over nor title to homestead, and it is not an asset of the testatory estate." *See also Cavanaugh v. Cavanaugh*, 542 So.2d 1345, 1352 (Fla. 1st DCA 1989) (holding that the transfer of probate jurisdiction to the circuit court did not change the law that the homestead is not an asset of the probate estate). It is only when the testator specifies in the will that the homestead is to be sold and the proceeds are to be divided that the homestead loses its "protected" status. *See Knadle v. Estate of Knadle*, 686 So.2d 631, 632 (Fla. 1st DCA 1996).... Thus, where the will directs that the homestead be sold and the proceeds added to the estate, those proceeds are applied to satisfy the specific, general, and residual devises, in that order. *See also Elmowitz v. Estate of Zimmerman*, 647 So.2d 1064 (Fla. 3d DCA 1994). In fact, the Second District has stated that "[t]he best, and perhaps the only, recognized exception to the general rule occurs when the will specifically orders that the property be sold and the proceeds be divided among the heirs." *In re Estate of Hamel*, 821 So.2d 1276, 1279 (Fla. 2d DCA 2002).

Because the law is clear that the protected homestead is not a part of the decedent's estate for purposes of distribution, the accepted way the $141,000 in proceeds could be applied to the general devises in this case is if McKean had ordered the sale of his protected homestead and ordered that the proceeds be made a part of his general estate. It is clear that McKean's will did not direct that the protected homestead be sold for this purpose.

We therefore answer the certified question in the negative and hold that where a decedent is not survived by a spouse or minor children, the decedent's homestead property passes to the residuary devisees, not the general devisees, unless there is a specific testamentary disposition ordering the property to be sold and the proceeds made a part of the general estate. Accordingly, the decision of the district court of appeal is quashed and the case is remanded for further proceedings consistent with this opinion.

It is so ordered.

PARIENTE, C.J., and WELLS, ANSTEAD, LEWIS, CANTERO, and BELL, JJ., concur.

In re Estate of Scholtz

543 So. 2d 219 (Fla. 1989)

GRIMES, Justice.

We review *In re Estate of Scholtz*, 525 So.2d 516 (Fla. 4th DCA 1988), in which the district court of appeal certified a question to be of great public importance. Our jurisdiction is predicated upon article V, section 3(b)(4), of the Florida Constitution.

John and Alice Scholtz were married in 1928. In 1956 they separated and have lived apart ever since. During their separation, John bought a piece of residential property which was titled solely in his name. He lived there until he moved to a nursing home shortly before his death. John left surviving his wife and one daughter. The trial court determined that the residential property was John's homestead. Relying upon its prior decision of *In re Estate of Boyd*, 519 So.2d 692 (Fla. 4th DCA), *review dismissed*, 525 So.2d 876 (Fla.1988), the district court of appeal affirmed and certified the following question to this Court:

> IS THE CONCEPT OF ABANDONMENT AS SET OUT IN BARLOW V. BARLOW STILL VIABLE IN VIEW OF THE 1985 AMENDMENT OF THE HOMESTEAD PROVISIONS OF THE FLORIDA CONSTITUTION?

525 So.2d at 517.

Article X, section 4, of the Florida Constitution, dealing with homestead, reads as follows:

> SECTION 4. Homestead; exemptions.—
>
> (a) There shall be exempt from forced sale under process of any court, and no judgment, decree or execution shall be a lien thereon, except for the payment of taxes and assessments thereon, obligations contracted for the purchase, improvement or repair thereof, or obligations contracted for house, field or other labor performed on the realty, the following property owned by *a natural person:*
>
>> (1) a homestead, if located outside a municipality, to the extent of one hundred sixty acres of contiguous land and improvements thereon, which shall not be reduced without the owner's consent by reason of subsequent inclusion in a municipality; or if located within a municipality, to the extent of one-half acre of contiguous land, upon which the exemption shall be limited to the residence of the owner or his family;
>>
>> (2) personal property to the value of one thousand dollars.
>
> (b) These exemptions shall inure to the surviving spouse or heirs of the owner.
>
> (c) The homestead shall not be subject to devise if the owner is survived by spouse or minor child, except the homestead may be devised to the owner's spouse if there be no minor child. The owner of homestead real estate, joined by the spouse if married, may alienate the homestead by mortgage, sale or gift and, if married, may by deed transfer the title to an estate by the entirety with the spouse. If the owner or spouse is incompetent, the method of alienation or encumbrance shall be as provided by law.

(Emphasis added.) Before the 1985 amendment referred to in the certified question, the words "a natural person," which are italicized above, read "the head of a family."

Prior to the 1985 amendment, Florida courts had held that under certain circumstances the surviving spouse would be deemed to have abandoned the homestead, thereby permitting the owner to devise the property despite the constitutional proscription. Thus, in *Barlow v. Barlow*, 156 Fla. 458, 23 So.2d 723 (1945), the wife left the home that was owned by her husband while his death was imminent. At the time she left, she told others that she had no intention of returning. After leaving she engaged counsel to procure a divorce. This Court held that the wife had abandoned the homestead and could not make a claim against it after her husband had died. The question before us is whether the concept of abandonment has survived the elim-   *Issue* ination of the head of the family language in article X, section 4.

In *Public Health Trust v. Lopez*, 531 So.2d 946 (Fla.1988), this Court addressed the effect of the 1985 amendment on the exemption of the homestead from forced sale provided in article X, section 4(a). The creditors argued that under case law prior to the amendment, the homestead exemption was not available to the adult heirs of a decedent unless the heirs were dependent upon the decedent. The creditors contended that a literal interpretation of the constitution would provide a windfall for financially independent heirs at the expense of the decedent's creditors, thereby distorting the historical purpose of the homestead laws to protect dependents in need of shelter. This Court ruled against the creditors, finding that the constitutional provision at issue was clear, reasonable, and logical in its operation. The Court said that it was fortified in its conclusion by the legislative history of the amendment. Finally, we concluded that homestead property always descended free of the claims of creditors without regard to whether the heirs were dependents. The Court pointed out that the cases relied upon by the creditors were ones in which it had been decided that the owner was not the head of the family at the time of his death.

Unlike the situation in *Lopez*, there is no legislative history surrounding the amendment to illustrate what its proponents had in mind with respect to the devise of homesteads. However, it is significant that effective upon the adoption of the 1985 amendment, the legislature repealed section 222.19(1), Florida Statutes (1983), which had provided that it was the declared intention of the legislature that the purpose of the constitutional exemption of the homestead was to shelter the family and the surviving spouse. At the same time, section 732.401, Florida Statutes (1985), which provides the means by which homesteads shall descend, remained unchanged.

Notwithstanding, the petitioner, who is the decedent's nephew, argues that the rationale for the prohibition against the devise of homestead property is for the protection of the surviving family and that when the family no longer resides together in the household, the reason for the prohibition no longer exists. Thus, petitioner argues that the concept of abandonment remains applicable despite the 1985 amendment. In response to such a contention, the district court of appeal in *In re Estate of Boyd* stated:

> It appears that the abandonment concept set out in *Barlow* and other cases was inextricably tied to the "head of household" requirement of the prior constitutional homestead scheme. The abandonment concept appears to be predicated on two possible bases. The first is that a homeowner whose spouse abandons him and sets up her own residence elsewhere with no intent of returning cannot be a "head of household" because there is no longer a family residing with him in the home. In that case, the property loses its homestead status by definition and the surviving spouse has no claim simply because there is no homestead. A second possible basis for *Barlow*'s holding is the

court's concern that it would be inequitable to allow a spouse who has "abandoned" the homestead to come back and claim it when her spouse dies. This equitable concern would also appear to be tied to the family unit definition of homestead. Even if it is not, however, we do not believe the courts have the authority to act upon such concerns no matter what the equities may be, in view of the clear and unequivocal language to the contrary in the constitutional and statutory homestead scheme.

519 So.2d at 692 (footnotes omitted).

We are compelled to agree with the district court of appeal. The concepts of abandonment and inequity that were part of the cases predating the 1985 amendment all related to the definition of homestead which contemplated a "head of the family." The constitution no longer contains these words and refers only to ownership of the property by a natural person.

Article X, section 4, must be read in its entirety. This Court has previously rejected the argument that the term homestead should be given a different definition under subparagraph (c) than that under subparagraphs (a) and (b). *Holden v. Estate of Gardner*, 420 So.2d 1082 (Fla.1982). While we may have some doubt about whether the proponents of the amendment considered its effect as related to the prohibition against the devise of homesteads, we are unable to state with any certainty that they did not intend the surviving spouse and the children to receive the homestead regardless of whether the family unit continued to exist at the time of the owner's death. In any event, the language of article X, section 4, is clear and unambiguous. The homestead may not be devised if the owner is survived by a spouse or minor child. Because John Scholtz died leaving a spouse, the descent of his property is controlled by section 732.401(1), Florida Statutes (1987).

We approve the decision of the district court of appeal.

It is so ordered.

SHAW, BARKETT and KOGAN, JJ., concur.

McDONALD, J., concurs specially with an opinion. [omitted]

EHRLICH, C.J., dissents with an opinion, in which OVERTON, J., concurs.

EHRLICH, Chief Justice, dissenting.

I am of the opinion that the concept of abandonment survived the elimination of the "head of household" language in article X, section 4, of the Florida Constitution.

Historically, the purpose of the homestead provision was to protect the family. *See generally Barlow v. Barlow*, 156 Fla. 458, 23 So.2d 723 (1945). I agree with the dissent of Judge Walden in *In re Estate of Boyd*, 519 So.2d 692, 693 (Fla. 4th DCA) (Walden, J., concurring in part, dissenting in part), *review dismissed*, 525 So.2d 879 (Fla.1988), and with the dissent of Judge Stone below, *In re Estate of Scholtz*, 525 So.2d 516, 517 (Fla. 4th DCA 1988) (Stone, J., concurring in part, dissenting in part). It is clear from the constitutional provisions prohibiting devise of homestead property if the owner is survived by a *spouse or minor child*, that the concern for protection of the family still underlies the homestead provision. Without that concern there would be no compelling reason to restrict the ability to devise in this manner. The amendment substituting "a natural person" for "a head of household" did not eliminate the underlying concern for family protection from the homestead provision. Rather, the amendment effectively broadened the category of families protected by the homestead provision to include those not covered by the traditional definition of "head of household." For example, prior to the 1985 amendment, where a husband and wife lived together on property owned solely by the wife, and the husband was found to be the head of the household, the property would not be homestead, i.e., not owned by the "head of household," and could be devised by the wife without restriction. *Holden v. Estate of Gardner*, 420 So.2d 1082 (Fla.1982). That type of family was not protected by the homestead provision. After the 1985 amendment, however, the property need only be owned by "a natural person" to be homestead; the property in the above example would qualify and could not have been devised by the wife because she is survived by a spouse.

Where there has been an abandonment and the surviving spouse has severed all family ties, no real family remains to be protected. It is therefore inconsistent with the purpose of the homestead provision to restrict devise of the property where there has been an abandonment....

OVERTON, J., concurs.

Questions

1. Why does the majority reason that the doctrine of abandonment does not survive the 1985 amendment of Section 4?

2. What is Justice Ehrlich's reason for retaining the doctrine?

Butterworth v. Caggiano
605 So. 2d 56 (Fla. 1992)

BARKETT, Chief Justice.

We have for review *Caggiano v. Butterworth*, 583 So.2d 347, 348 (Fla. 2d DCA 1991), in which the district court certified the following question of great public importance:

Whether forfeiture of homestead under the RICO Act is forbidden by article X, section 4 of the Florida Constitution?

We answer the certified question in the affirmative and approve the decision below.

Caggiano was convicted in 1986 of one count of racketeering in violation of the Florida Racketeer Influenced and Corrupt Organization Act (Florida RICO Act), chapter 895, Florida Statutes (1983 & Supp.1984), and fifteen counts of bookmaking in violation of chapter 849, Florida Statutes (1983 & Supp.1984). Three of the bookmaking incidents occurred at Caggiano's personal residence. The State later sought forfeiture of the residence in separate civil proceedings under the Florida RICO Act on the grounds that the property was "used" in the course of racketeering activity in violation of section 895.05(2)(a), Florida Statutes (1989). The trial court, relying on *DeRuyter v. State*, 521 So.2d 135 (Fla. 5th DCA 1988), found that the homestead exemption in article X, section 4 of the Florida Constitution did not protect Caggiano's residence against RICO forfeiture, and entered final summary judgment for the State. Caggiano appealed to the Second District Court of Appeal, which reversed the trial court's entry of summary judgment and held that homestead property is not subject to forfeiture under the Florida RICO Act. The Second District noted conflict with *DeRuyter* and certified the question to this Court. The State seeks review of the Second District's decision.

The "civil remedies" section of the Florida RICO Act provides:

> All property, real or personal, including money, used in the course of, intended for use in the course of, derived from, or realized through conduct in violation of a provision of ss. 895.01–895.05 is subject to civil forfeiture to the state.

§ 895.05(2)(a), Fla.Stat. (1989). "Real property" is defined as "any real property or any interest in such real property, including, but not limited to, any lease of or mortgage upon such real property." § 895.02(9), Fla.Stat. (1989).

In *DeRuyter* the Fifth District Court of Appeal held that constitutional homestead property was not exempt from RICO forfeiture. The court reasoned:

> No appellate decisions on this question have been cited and none have been found by our research. However, we view forfeiture of property due to its use in a criminal enterprise, to be entirely different from the "forced sale" language in the constitution. The purpose of the constitutional provision is to protect homestead property from forced sale for debts of the owner. *Tullis v. Tullis*, 360 So.2d 375 (Fla.1978). Forfeiture here is not predicated upon debts incurred by the owner but rather is based solely on the illegal uses to which the property is being put. Article X, section 4, Florida Constitution, was simply not designed to immunize real property for use in a criminal enterprise.

521 So.2d at 138.

The State argues that a forfeiture is not a "forced sale" and that the homestead exemption was not intended to apply outside the debtor context, and urges that, like the Fifth District, we interpret the constitutional provision as inapplicable to forfeiture. In light of the purpose and language of the provision, we are unable to do so.

A settled rule of constitutional interpretation is that:

> The words and terms of a Constitution are to be interpreted in their most usual and obvious meaning, unless the text suggests that they have been used in a technical sense. The presumption is in favor of the natural and popular meaning in which the words are usually understood by the people who have adopted them.

City of Jacksonville v. Continental Can Co., 113 Fla. 168, 172, 151 So. 488, 489–90 (1933); *see also Wilson v. Crews*, 160 Fla. 169, 175, 34 So.2d 114, 118 (1948); *City of Jacksonville v. Glidden Co.*, 124 Fla. 690, 692–93, 169 So. 216, 217 (1936).

Additionally, Florida courts have consistently held that the homestead exemption in article X, section 4 must be liberally construed. *E.g., Graham v. Azar*, 204 So.2d 193, 195 (Fla.1967); *Hill v. First Nat'l Bank*, 79 Fla. 391, 401, 84 So. 190, 193 (1920). A liberal construction of the homestead exemption is particularly appropriate in the context of forfeiture. Forfeitures are considered harsh penalties that are historically disfavored in law and equity, and courts have long followed a policy of strictly construing such statutes. *Department of Law Enforcement v. Real Property*, 588 So.2d 957, 961 (Fla.1991); *General Motors Acceptance Corp. v. State*, 152 Fla. 297, 302, 11 So.2d 482, 484 (1943); *see* Michael Paul Austern Cohen, Note, *The Constitutional Infirmity of RICO Forfeiture*, 46 Wash. & Lee.L.Rev. 937, 939 (1989).

Applying these principles, we first note that all property forfeited under the Florida RICO Act is required by statute to be sold at a state auction. Section 895.05(2)(c), Florida Statutes (1989), provides:

> The state shall dispose of all forfeited property as soon as commercially feasible. If property is not exercisable or transferable for value by the state, it shall expire. All forfeitures or dispositions under this section shall be made with due provision for the rights of innocent persons. The proceeds realized from such forfeiture and disposition shall be promptly distributed in accordance with the provisions of s. 895.09.

In any event, there is no indication that the word "sale" in article X, section 4 is being used in its technical, legal sense in isolation from the surrounding language. To the contrary, it appears that the homestead exemption uses broad, nonlegal terminology that was intended simply to guarantee that the homestead would be preserved against any involuntary divestiture by the courts, without regard to the technicalities of how that divestiture would be accomplished.

… Contrary to the State's assertion, the plain import of the constitutional language of article X, section 4 is not limited to the debtor-creditor context. The language of the provision refers to "forced sales," not "forced sales arising from debts." The purpose of the homestead exemption has been described broadly as being to protect the family, and to provide for it a refuge from misfortune, without any requirement that the misfortune arise from a financial debt. *See, e.g., Collins v. Collins*, 150 Fla. 374, 377, 7 So.2d 443, 444 (1942) ("The purpose of the homestead is to shelter the family and provide it a refuge from the stresses and strains of misfortune.").

Most significantly, article X, section 4 expressly provides for three exceptions to the homestead exemption. Forfeiture is not one of them. According to the plain and unambiguous wording of article X, section 4, a homestead is *only* subject to forced sale for (1) the payment of taxes and assessments thereon; (2) obligations contracted for the purchase, improvement or repair thereof; or (3) obligations contracted for house, field or other labor performed on the realty. Under the rule "*expressio unius est exclusio alterious"*—the expression of one thing is the exclusion of another—forfeitures are not excluded from the homestead exemption because they are not mentioned, either expressly or by reasonable implication, in the three exceptions that are expressly stated.

It makes no difference that the attempted divestiture in this case was an adjunct to a criminal proceeding. As the Supreme Court of Kansas declared in construing its state's constitutional homestead exemption:

> The homestead provision of our Constitution sets forth the exceptions and provides the method of waiving the homestead rights attached to the residence. *These exceptions are unqualified. They create no personal qualifications touching the moral character of the resident nor do they undertake to exclude the vicious, the criminal, or the immoral from the benefits so provided.* The law provides for punishment of persons convicted of illegal acts, but the forfeiture of homestead rights guaranteed by our Constitution is not part of the punishment.

State ex rel. Apt v. Mitchell, 399 P.2d 556, 558 (Kan.1965) (emphasis added). Florida law likewise prohibits the implication of exceptions or limitations to article X, section 4. In *Olesky v. Nicholas,* 82 So.2d 510, 513 (Fla.1955), this Court noted:

> We find no difficulty in holding that *the Florida constitutional exemption of homesteads protects the homestead against every type of claim and judgment except those specifically mentioned in the constitutional provision itself* and that, therefore, the claim of homestead is good against the demands of a judgment grounded on a malicious tort.

(Emphasis added.) *See also Graham v. Azar,* 204 So.2d at 195. The Florida homestead provision clearly contains no exception for criminal activity. Neither the legislature nor this Court has the power to create one.[17] *See, e.g., Henderson v. State,* 155 Fla.

---

17. [FN 5.] The State cites a number of cases for the proposition that Florida courts have refused to allow the homestead exemption to shield property where there is fraud or other "reprehensible conduct." In particular, the State cites cases where the courts have imposed equitable liens on homesteads. *See, e.g., Bessemer v. Gersten,* 381 So.2d 1344 (Fla.1980); *La Mar v. Lechlider,* 135 Fla. 703, 185 So. 833 (1939); *Jetton Lumber Co. v. Hall,* 67 Fla. 61, 64 So. 440 (1914); *Milton v. Milton,* 63 Fla. 533, 58 So. 718 (1912). Thus, the State argues that a constitutional provision that does not shield fraud or other "reprehensible conduct" cannot logically shield property where there is a pattern of criminal conduct involved.

All of the cases cited by the State where a court has actually imposed a lien on the homestead in question, however, are either factually or legally inapposite. Virtually all of the relevant cases involve situations that fell within one of the three stated exceptions to the homestead provision. Most of those cases involve equitable liens that were imposed where proceeds from fraud or reprehensible conduct were used to invest in, purchase, or improve the homestead. *See, e.g., Jones v. Carpenter,* 90 Fla. 407, 415, 106 So. 127, 130 (1925); *La Mar,* 135 Fla. 703, 711, 185 So. 833, 836. Other relevant cases cited involve situations where an equitable lien was necessary to secure to an owner the benefit of his or her interest in the property. *See, e.g., Tullis v. Tullis,* 360 So.2d 375, 377 (Fla.1978) ("We hold, with the First District, that our constitutional provisions allow the partition and forced sale of homestead property upon suit by one of the owners of that property, if such partition and forced sale is necessary to protect the beneficial enjoyment of the owners in common to the extent of their interest in the property."). In particular, *Tullis* involved a marital situation with joint homestead property. In no other case has this Court imposed a lien on a homestead beyond one of the three stated

487, 491, 20 So.2d 649, 651 (1945); *Crawford v. Gilchrist,* 64 Fla. 41, 54, 59 So. 963, 968 (1912).

Consequently, in light of the historical prejudice against forfeiture, the constitutional sanctity of the home, and the rules of construction requiring a liberal, non-technical interpretation of the homestead exemption and a strict construction of the exceptions to that exemption, we hold that article X, section 4 of the Florida Constitution prohibits civil or criminal forfeiture of homestead property.

Accordingly, we answer the certified question in the affirmative, disapprove *DeRuyter,* and approve the decision of the court below.

It is so ordered.

OVERTON, McDONALD, SHAW, KOGAN and HARDING, JJ., concur.

GRIMES, J., dissents with an opinion.

GRIMES, Justice, dissenting.

Article X, section 4(a) of the Florida Constitution, provides that homesteads "shall be exempt from forced sale under process of any court, and no judgment, decree or execution shall be a lien thereon," except those arising from certain obligations not relevant to this case. RICO forfeitures do not come within the literal language of this exemption because they do not involve a forced sale and there is no judgment, decree, or execution which purports to be a lien on the property. Therefore, the question becomes whether or not it reasonably can be said that RICO forfeitures fall within the intent of this constitutional exemption.

From the time the homestead exemption was first placed in our constitution, Florida courts have consistently pointed out that its purpose was to protect the home from loss occasioned by economic misfortune. *Bigelow v. Dunphe,* 143 Fla. 603, 197 So. 328 (1940); *Hill v. First Nat'l Bank,* 79 Fla. 391, 84 So. 190 (1920); *Vandiver v. Vincent,* 139 So.2d 704 (Fla. 2d DCA 1962). After the adoption of our 1968 constitution, we reaffirmed this principle in *Tullis v. Tullis,* 360 So.2d 375, 377 (Fla.1978), when we stated:

> The purpose of the homestead exemption provision in our state constitution is to protect the family home from forced sale for the debts of the owner and head of the family.

While the homestead exemption is to be liberally construed, the law should not be applied to make it an instrument of fraud or imposition upon creditors. *Milton v. Milton,* 63 Fla. 533, 58 So. 718 (1912). Thus, Florida courts have not hesitated to impose equitable liens on homesteads to provide relief from fraud or other reprehensible conduct. *Jones v. Carpenter,* 90 Fla. 407, 106 So. 127 (1925); *Gepfrich v.*

---

exceptions in the constitutional provision. The Court in *Bessemer* specifically did not address the issue of whether the lien came within one of the stated exceptions to the homestead exemption. 381 So.2d at 1347 n. 1.

The factual situations involved in the cited cases are not present here. It is undisputed that no illicit proceeds were used to purchase, acquire, or improve Caggiano's property.

Gepfrich, 582 So.2d 743 (Fla. 4th DCA 1991). In *La Mar v. Lechlider*, 135 Fla. 703, 711, 185 So. 833, 837 (1939), we reasoned:

> To say that a lien could not be decreed against the homestead under the facts in this case would be to make the homestead an instrument of fraud.

If the courts are unwilling to permit the homestead exemption to protect a home which has been used as an instrument of fraud, it seems obvious that the homestead exemption should not be applied to protect a home that has been an instrument of crime....

RICO forfeitures were unknown until the 1970 enactment of the federal RICO statute. Constitutional provisions should be construed in light of the reasonable meanings according to the subject matter, but in the framework of contemporary societal needs and structure. *In re Advisory Opinion to Governor*, 276 So.2d 25 (Fla.1973). Can it seriously be argued that the homestead exemption would have been intended to protect the forfeiture of a home when the home itself was an instrumentality of a criminal enterprise?

Under the forfeiture statute, the interests of innocent persons are protected. Here, however, Caggiano does not even have a family to protect. Under the majority opinion, a building which is used for the manufacture of illegal drugs is immune from forfeiture so long as the owner lives on the premises. Such a ruling is against the public policy of the state as expressed by the legislature in the enactment of laws which forfeit property used in the commission of crimes. While the majority refers to the "historical prejudice against forfeiture," I suggest that there is an even greater historical prejudice against crime.

I respectfully dissent.

ii. Article X, Section 6 — Eminent Domain

The power of the sovereign to take property by eminent domain is a traditional aspect of sovereignty.[18] The current Florida Constitution is the first to include a provision directed specifically at the use of eminent domain.[19] Article X, Section 6 was

---

18. *See Daniels v. State Road Dept.*, 170 So. 2d 846, 878 (Fla. 1964) (citing *Spafford v. Brevard County*, 92 Fla. 617, 110 So. 451, 458 (1926)); *Peavy-Wilson Lumber Co. v. Brevard County*, 159 Fla. 311, 31 So. 2d 483, 485 (1947). When local governments and quasi-public entities exercise delegated eminent domain authority, this is an attribute of the police power and must relate to the power "to legislate in behalf of public health, public morals and public safety." *Peavy-Wilson*, 159 Fla. 311, 31 So. 2d at 486.

19. Earlier constitutions only included the protection in the Declaration of Rights against taking property without paying compensation. *See* FLA. CONST. OF 1838, art. I, § 14 ("That private property shall not be taken, or applied to public use; unless just compensation be made therefor."); FLA. CONST. OF 1861, art. I, § 14; FLA. CONST. OF 1865, art. I, § 14; FLA. CONST. OF 1868, Declaration of Rights, § 8; FLA. CONST. OF 1885, Declaration of Rights, § 12 ("nor shall private property be taken without just compensation").

amended in the aftermath of the decision by the U.S. Supreme Court in *Kelo v. City of New London*, 545 U.S. 469 (2005). In that case, the U.S. Supreme Court found that the City of New London's plans to take private property by eminent domain and transfer it to private developers did not violate the Fifth Amendment's prohibition on taking property except for a public purpose. In *Kelo*, the Court found that, where the property had been declared "distressed" or "blighted" and where this taking was in accordance with a comprehensive development plan, it could be considered a public purpose, and thus constitutional under the Fifth Amendment. *Id.* at 488–89.

Widespread concern at the implications of this decision prompted numerous reform efforts at the state level. In Florida, although there are considerable procedural protections provided by the statutory rights to jury trial and attorney fees in eminent domain cases,[20] there were also fears that local governments could call property blighted and target it for transfer to private developers via eminent domain.[21] The response was Article X, Section 6(c), approved by 69% of the voters in 2006, and implemented by § 73.013, Florida Statutes.[22]

Article X, Section 6, together with Article I, Section 2, also protects citizens by providing for "inverse condemnation" claims in the case of regulatory takings, physical invasion takings or other uncompensated takings by government and quasi-government entities. Regulatory takings occur when government so restricts the use of the property as to effectively amount to an expropriation. When considering inverse condemnation claims, Florida courts have followed the test employed by the federal courts for takings cases under the Fifth Amendment.[23]

---

20. Please note, however, that many of these procedural protections in Florida's eminent domain process, including the right to a jury trial and attorney's fees, are provided by statute. *See* Fla. Stat. ch. 73 & 74; *see generally* Florida Eminent Domain Practice & Procedure (9th ed., 2014).

21. For example, a circuit court in Volusia County upheld the taking of private property in the Daytona Beach Boardwalk and found that its subsequent transfer to a private party did not affect its public purpose. *See City of Daytona Beach v. Mathas*, Case No. 2004-31846-CICI (Fla. Cir. Ct. Aug. 19, 2005) (upholding the taking of property even though the designation of the property as "blighted" was 24 years old). Even more egregious was publicity surrounding a plan by the City of Riviera Beach through its Community Redevelopment Agency to condemn some 1700 units and displace more than 5,000 residents in order to make way for a large marina development. *See generally* Nicholas M. Gieseler & Steven G. Gieseler, *Strict Scrutiny and Eminent Domain after Kelo*, 25 J. Land Use 191, 215–21 (2010). *But see* Ann Marie Cavazos, *Beware of Wooden Nickels: The Paradox of Florida's Legislative Overreaction in the Wake of Kelo*, 13 U. Pa. J. Bus. L. 685, 705–11 (2010) (criticizing Florida's approach as overly restrictive on local governments).

22. Section 73.013, Florida Statutes, generally forbids the state or any subdivision from conveying land taken by eminent domain to a private entity for a period of ten years except for purposes of common carrier services, roads or transportation purposes, public utilities, or for public infrastructure.

23. *See, e.g., Teitelbaum v. South Fla. Water Mgmt. Dist.*, 176 So. 3d 998 (3d DCA 2015), *rev. denied*, 2016 WL 1065552, Case No. SC15-1994 (Fla., Mar. 16, 2016) (using the federal test for ad hoc regulatory takings) (citing *Penn Central Transp. Co. v. City of New York*, 438 U.S. 104, 124 (1978)); *Alachua Land Investors, LLC v. City of Gainesville*, 107 So. 3d 1154, 1159 (Fla. 1st DCA 2013); *Martin County. v. Section 28 Partnership, Ltd.*, 676 So. 2d 532, 537 (4th DCA), *rev. denied*, 686 So. 2d 581 (Fla. 1996), *cert. denied*, 520 U.S. 1196 (1997). For more generally on inverse condemnation claims in Florida, see S. William Moore, *Inverse Condemnation, in* Florida Eminent Domain Practice &

In *City of Ocala v. Nye*, 608 So. 2d 15 (Fla. 1992), included in our discussion of Article VIII, the Court addressed the eminent domain powers of a municipality. The following cases focus on the exercise of eminent domain authority by other governmental entities.

Seadade Industries, Inc. v. Florida Power & Light Co.

245 So. 2d 210 (Fla. 1971)

CARLTON, Justice.

This eminent domain case involves the authority of a Utility to secure condemnation of adjacent lands prior to gaining ultimate approval by appropriate authorities of the project for which the land is to be condemned. Circuit Court, Dade County, entered an Order of Taking in behalf of the Utility, Florida Power & Light Company, granting to it a fee simple interest in properties neighboring its Turkey Point facilities for the purpose of constructing and maintaining a discharge water drainage canal 4.5 miles in length and, including access and related areas, 660 feet in width.

On petition for writ of certiorari addressed to that Order, the District Court of Appeal, Third District, affirmed the taking, but required modification of the quality of the title for approximately 430 of the 660 feet width given in fee simple. See 232 So.2d 46 (3rd D.C.A. Fla.1970). We have taken jurisdiction in order to resolve a conflict between the District Court's opinion and our previous decision in *Robertson v. Brooksville & Inverness Railway*, 100 Fla. 195, 129 So. 582 (1930). See Article V, Section 4(2), Florida Constitution, F.S.A.

The District Court's opinion sets out the multiple issues operative in this cause. These issues will not be detailed or discussed here save to the extent appropriate to our treatment of the case. Briefly, stated, the situation is as follows. The Utility operates electrical generating facilities just north of petitioner Seadade's unimproved marshland fronting to the East on lower Biscayne Bay and Card Sound. The Utility proposes to cool two new generators by drawing water from Biscayne Bay, circulating the waters through the generating facilities, and then discharging the waters through a canal into Card Sound. The canal would cut through Seadade's property for a distance of 4.5 miles. Seadade had attempted to resist the taking on numerous grounds, all of which center on the related propositions that the canal project does not comport with public interest, and that condemnation constitutes a gross abuse of discretion by the Utility.

Turning now to a close examination of Seadade's position, we find that it concedes the Utility has the power and authority to condemn land for a proper purpose under Fla.Stat. s 361.01, F.S.A., and our decision in *Demeter Land Co. v. Florida Public Service Co.*, 99 Fla. 954, 128 So. 402 (1930). But it argues that the Utility has failed to show any necessity of valid public purpose for the taking in question. Fundamental to Seadade's position is its contention that the discharge project must be approved by Federal, State and local authorities before any discharge can begin. Because of thermal pollution aspects, Seadade maintains that there is so imminent a likelihood that these authorities will reject the project, or require substantial modification of it, that condemnation is premature, and that the Utility is grossly abusing the discretion vested in it by seeking condemnation. We quote from Seadade's Answer filed in response to the Utility's Summons to Show Cause:

"Petitioner's proposed canal project would be contrary to the public interest in that it would provide for the discharge of heated water into the waters of Biscayne Bay opposite this Defendant's upland property and would cause great damage to the ecology of Biscayne Bay and would cause the death and destruction of marine life, both plant and animal, in Biscayne Bay. Petitioner's proposed canal project would also be contrary to the public interest in that it would concentrate the effects of the alteration in water conditions caused by the Plant in the Card Sound area of Biscayne Bay which is known to be a body of water not subject to tidal flushing, and would cause a residual build up of all adverse factors created by the plant effluent. The plant effluent which would be discharged from the canal into Biscayne would also contain harmful radio-active material from the nuclear powered generating plant proposed by Petitioner at Turkey Point as well as other harmful effluents from said plant.

"The facts are well established that such discharge of heated effluent from the canal into Biscayne Bay would violate the ordinances of Dade County, Laws of the State of Florida, and the Rules and Regulations of the U.S. Department of the Interior, and would seriously adversely affect the flood control program and salt water intrusion prevention program of the Central and Southern Florida Flood Control District. Before the proposed canal project could be undertaken, the Petitioner must obtain approval for the program and the discharge of the effluent into the water of Biscayne Bay from the following Agencies and Boards:

a. The U.S. Atomic Energy Commission

b. The U.S. Department of the Interior

c. The Florida Anti-Pollution Control Board

d. Dade County Anti-Pollution Control

e. Central and Southern Florida Flood Control District

"Petitioner has not been granted approval, permit or license by any of the above-named Agencies and Boards, and in fact has been specifically denied approval by some of the above-named Agencies, and, therefore, is not in a position to undertake the proposed canal project."

Seadade points out that in the case of *Robertson v. Brooksville & Inverness Railway, supra,* this Court held that a railroad was not entitled to pursue condemnation proceedings leading to a taking of land over which a pipeline to a waterhole was to be constructed, when it had not secured the right to use the waterhole....

Seadade also relies upon a recent case decided by the Third District Court of Appeal a few days after its Seadade decision; in *City of Miami Beach v. Manilow*, 232 So.2d 759 (3rd D.C.A.Fla.1970), the District Court held that a City was not entitled to bring condemnation proceedings for the taking of property for a road when it had failed to secure permission of the State Road Department in advance. From the holdings in *Robertson* and *Manilow*, Seadade draws the conclusion that the Utility was not entitled to bring condemnation proceedings before obtaining approval for its discharge project.

The Utility's response is three-fold. First, it asserts that the canal is necessary to its operation of the Turkey Point facilities. The Utility currently operates two gas and oil-fired power generators at Turkey Point, a site located about 25 miles south of the City of Miami on the lower reaches of Biscayne Bay. These generators are the prime source of electric power for Dade County. According to the Utility, it has been unable to keep pace with power demands since 1960. In 1960, the peak load in Dade County approximated 800,000 KW, whereas the Utility only had a generating capacity of 500,000 KW. As of 1969, the Utility was sustaining a 2,000,000 KW load whereas its generating capacity was limited to 1,300,000 KW. The difference is made up by bringing into the County power generated elsewhere a practice that involves economic penalties and problems of reliability. To avoid these penalties and problems, and meet its responsibilities, the Utility constructed its existing facilities consisting of two generating units of 432,000 KW each at Turkey Point; similarly, this is why it is now constructing two 760,000 KW nuclear-fueled units due for operation in 1971.

The Utility informs us that every power plant has a cooling and circulating water system for the condenser cooling system which is necessary to the process of generating electricity. The Utility has had to consider precisely what type of system would be appropriate for its new generating facilities; these would require a circulation of 1,800,000 gallons of water per minute, and the heat transfer involved would raise the temperature of this water by as much as 15 Fahrenheit. The existing facilities use water taken directly from Biscayne Bay; after circulation through the system, this water is discharged back into the Bay at a point fairly close to the point of intake. It was realized that it would not be desirable, either from an engineering or an environmental standpoint, to use the present intake-discharge cooling system for the new facilities. Were this done, more heated water would be circulated into the Bay than the Bay could handle; that is to say, the Bay temperature would rise progressively without there being sufficient heat transfer throughout the Bay to cool the discharge waters before they were brought back into the system. This cumulative temperature rise would reduce the efficiency of the plant and at the same time endanger the marine life in the Bay.

Alternative methods of securing cooling were examined. Cooling towers, cooling ponds, spray ponds, ocean outfall, deep wells and closed circuit air cooling systems were all rejected for one or more of the following reasons: (1) excessive costs; (2) existing technology was insufficient; (3) no experience was available as to reliability or maintenance at scale required; (4) danger of salt intrusion into underlying fresh water; (5) severe operational difficulties. The one viable solution, one which was expected to achieve desirable results while avoiding the problems of the other alternatives, was to modify the existing intake-discharge system by utilizing the waters of Biscayne Bay for intake and the waters of Card Sound for discharge. This would eliminate the temperature cumulation problem of direct discharge into Biscayne Bay.... The Canal route fell across Seadade's lands, and so condemnation proceedings were commenced by the Utility.

Second, the Utility asserts that it has conformed to all statutory requirements regarding condemnation and taking. Fla.Stat. Stat. s 361.01, F.S.A. provides that the president and directors of a utility may appropriate lands necessary to the business contemplated by the charter. Following determination that the canal was essential and necessary, these corporate officers of the Utility adopted formal resolutions ordering that proceedings be begun. Subsequently, a petition in condemnation was filed under Fla.Stat. s 73.021(1), F.S.A., setting forth the Utility's authority, the use of the property to be condemned, and the necessity of the use; the petition included the statement of good faith intention to construct the project as required by Fla.Stat. s 73.021(2), F.S.A. Seadade was summoned under Fla.Stat. s 73.031 to show cause why the canal land should not be taken. Concurrently, the Utility sought possession in advance of judgment as provided for by Fla.Stat. s 74.011, F.S.A.; a Declaration of Taking was filed pursuant to Fla.Stat. s 74.031, F.S.A. Hearings on the Declaration were entertained by the Circuit Court, Dade County, in accord with Fla.Stat. s 74.051, F.S.A., and subsequently, by Order of that Court, upon payment of proper deposit, title of the condemned land vested in the Utility under Fla.Stat. s 74.061, F.S.A.

Third, the Utility maintains that the condemnation process may not be disturbed unless the landowner can demonstrate fraud, bad faith or gross abuse of discretion. *Adams v. Housing Authority of Daytona Beach*, 60 So.2d 663 (Fla.1952); *Inland Waterway Development Co. v. Jacksonville*, 38 So.2d 676 (Fla.1948); *Wilton v. St. John's County*, 98 Fla. 26, 123 So. 527 (1929). According to the Utility, Seadade has failed to demonstrate the existence of any of these conditions.

The District Court, 232 So.2d 46 (3rd D.C.A.Fla.1970), held that the Circuit Court had properly entered its Order of Taking; that the Utility demonstrated both necessity, and that its taking was for a valid public purpose; that the fact that the Utility needed to secure permission from various agencies before it could put its project into operation, and use the canal it sought to condemn, was not significant so far as the condemnation proceedings were concerned; and that fee simple was an appropriate quality of title for the canal and its access roads, but that an easement or term of years was appropriate for the remainder.

We agree with the District Court's rulings on all of these issues, except for the holding that the necessity for the approval of the cooling system project was not significant in condemnation proceedings. We have consistently held that even though statutory requirements regarding condemnation and taking appear to have been satisfied, the action will be overthrown or prohibited if a gross abuse of discretion is apparent (*Wilton v. St. Johns County, supra*; *Robertson v. Brooksville & Inverness Ry., supra*), or if it can be shown that because of the passage of time and changed conditions, the public interest will be impaired (*Zabel v. Pinellas County Water & Nav. Con. Auth.*, 171 So.2d 376 (Fla.1965)). A utility does not have within the discretion accorded to it, the right to act in violation of the public interest. Similarly, it does not have within the discretion accorded to it the right to act precipitously when the public interest has not been ascertained.

Article II, Section 7, Florida Constitution, F.S.A., contains a declaration that the protection of our natural resources shall be the policy of the State. The protection of resources, being a policy of the State, is an appropriate matter for consideration in condemnation cases. We think it logically follows that if taking and condemnation is sought in furtherance of a condemning authority's project affecting natural resources, and independent authorities guarding the public interest must approve the project before it can be put into operation, it is within the discretionary power of the judiciary to require that safeguarding of the public interest be demonstrated by the condemning authority. This is in keeping with traditional doctrine recently reannounced by this Court in *Canal Authority of State of Florida v. Miller*, 243 So.2d 131, filed December 16, 1970:

> "In order to insure the property rights of the citizens of the State against abuse of the condemning authority's power it is imperative that the Necessity for the exercise of the eminent domain power be ascertained and established. This is ultimately a judicial question to be decided in a court of competent jurisdiction. *Wilton v. St. Johns County, supra*; *Spafford v. Brevard County*, 92 Fla. 617, 110 So. 451 (1926); *Robertson v. Brooksville & I. Ry.*, 100 Fla. 195, 129 So. 582 (1930)."

In a proper case, the judiciary may require, first, that the condemning authority reasonably demonstrate that the regulations and requirements of the independent authorities can and will be met; second, that condemnation and taking in advance of project approval will not result in irreparable damage to natural resources and environment, should the independent authorities decline to approve the proposed project.

The reasoning behind these requirements becomes apparent when the following factors are considered in this case. The Utility seeks to secure condemnation of a considerable portion of land for use "in the public interest"; specifically, it seeks to excavate and construct a discharge canal. But if, for ecological reasons, the various agencies concerned, or any one of them, should decide that discharge into the Sound is not "in the public interest," then there is the possibility that the canal cannot be utilized if the adverse decision is upheld by a court of competent jurisdiction. This leaves the Utility in the awkward position of having to demonstrate "necessity" without really being able to show "necessity" until it has secured the required approvals of the agencies. On the other hand, as the nuclear-powered facilities approach completion, the need for a cooling system becomes urgent. It would be unreasonable to allow canal construction to begin only after all permissions have been granted since this would needlessly postpone the benefits of the completed facilities, which would stand idle and untested until completion of the canal. A rational balance must be struck between protection of the public interest in our natural resources under Article II, Section 7, Florida Constitution, and the completion of public works which are also in the public interest.

This balance is struck through our decision today. By requiring that the Utility, as a condemning authority, reasonably demonstrate that the regulations and requirements of the appropriate agencies can and will be met, the public interest is safeguarded while a rational scheme of construction and development is allowed. Further, by requiring a demonstration by the Utility that condemnation in advance of project approval will not lead to irreparable damage to natural resources should approval be denied, the public interest is again safeguarded. A reasonable demonstration by the Utility, and any condemning authority, that it can satisfy these two requirements will not be overturned unless the adverse party meets the burden of presenting "strong and convincing evidence" to the contrary as required under *Rott v. City of Miami*, 94 So.2d 168 (Fla.1957).

In the instant case, Seadade has contended that, if carried through, the proposed project will harm the Card Sound ecology. The contention has merit in that it cannot be denied that a disruption of the indigenous biota is inevitable when immense amounts of heated waters are constantly flushed into the Sound. But the prime ecological issue is the *extent* of the disruption, not whether disruption is to occur or not. See *United States v. Florida Power & Light Company*, 311 F.Supp. 1391 (S.D.Fla.1970), in which the United States District Court having jurisdiction over the Sound denied a motion for a preliminary injunction to halt discharge from the Utility's present operations; the District Court recognized that some harm occurs, but held that no irreparable damage was demonstrated. The local, State and Federal authorities ultimately concerned with the Utility's nuclear project are still in the process of determining the permissible temperature levels for discharge waters, but from testimony and exhibits contained in the record, it does not appear likely that the concept of water circulation and discharge itself will fall from favor.

In our view, through the proceedings below the Utility has demonstrated sufficiently that it can adjust its discharge temperatures by various means if necessary, so that even if its proposed discharge temperatures are found to be unacceptable, adjustments are possible, and compliance will be forthcoming....

As was noted earlier, the conflict giving rise to our jurisdiction stems from a clash between the District Court's holding that consent or approval of a condemning authority's project by outside authorities is not an issue in condemnation proceedings, and this Court's holding in *Robertson v. Brooksville & Inverness Ry.*, *supra*, to the effect that a condemning authority cannot proceed without a right of use. We now resolve these conflicting decisions by holding that where independent governmental agencies charged with safeguarding natural resources must ultimately approve a project involving condemnation, the condemning authority must demonstrate a reasonable probability of obtaining approval, and it must also demonstrate that the condemnation will not result in irreparable harm should the approvals be denied. Cases of this nature are to be distinguished from those cases akin to *Carlor Co. v. City of Miami*, 62 So.2d 897 (Fla.1953), wherein it was said:

> "It is not necessary that a political subdivision of the state have money on hand, plans and specifications prepared and all other preparations necessary for immediate construction before it can determine the necessity for taking private property for a public purpose." 62 So.2d at 902.

Carlor was concerned with the progress of the condemning authority's preparations in advance of condemnation, a matter *solely* within the responsibility of the condemning authority. Here, instead, we are concerned with condemnation powers in connection with projects having a direct effect upon our natural resources, which cannot succeed, or have any practical value, save if the proposed project receives the approval of authorities charged with safeguarding the public interest, and which are external to and independent of the condemning authority.

We find upon consideration of the exhibits and testimony adduced below that the Utility has successfully met the requirements announced in this opinion. Because the District Court in effect reached the result we have come to today, and because we concur in all other aspects of the District Court's opinion save as modified by this opinion, the writ heretofore issued in this cause must now be discharged.

It is so ordered.

ROBERTS, C.J., ADKINS and DREW (Retired), JJ., and HODGES, Circuit Judge, concur.

ERVIN, J., concurs specially with opinion. [omitted]

ERVIN, Justice (specially concurring):

If Florida Power is in fact denied the required described governmental permits, signifying there are pollution or ecological hazards, and is unable to go forward with its proposed canal plan, it will own a strip of land in fee simple through the middle of Seadade's property which it cannot devote to the use originally contemplated and for which purpose only eminent domain was authorized to be brought by Florida Power. This would create a problem unnecessarily disadvantaging to condemnee and inimical to its future use of its tract of land considered as a whole. On the other hand, condemnor would own title to lands which it could not devote to the use for which it was condemned. Moreover, in any event, in order to protect the public interest, consummation of the right to excavate the canal ought to be held in abeyance in these proceedings until the described permits are secured.

This potential problem can be readily and easily avoided if this Court were to hold, as I feel it should, that the fee simple title to the condemned land taken by the condemnor is a defeasible fee unless and until the required permits are granted to condemnor. The condemned unexcavated canal land and other lands taken would then return to the condemnee if the condemning body were unable to obtain the necessary authorizations (described in the majority opinion) from pollution control agencies. In the event this were to occur, the condemnee should be required to return all the condemnation money awarded that it received from the condemnor within a short period of time, perhaps within thirty days from the date the described necessary permits were unquestionably and irrevocably denied; otherwise, title absolute in the condemned land would vest in condemnor.

... The object of this special opinion is not to suggest any delay in the affirmance of these proceedings for the condemnation of the subject lands for the canal use, etc., or to in anywise thwart realization of the condemnor's project, but only to do equity by stipulating conditions rendering title to the condemned land defeasible in the event the project fails because required permits relating to subjects of pollution and ecological hazards are irrevocably denied.

Except as herein otherwise suggested, I agree to the conclusion reached by the majority.

CARLTON and ADKINS, JJ., concur.

Commentary and Questions

In *Seadade*, the petitioner had challenged the taking as harmful to the environment. The Court found that the Natural Resources clause of Article II, Section 7 provided a basis to gauge whether a proposed condemnation was in the public interest. The Court also had to consider whether to allow the condemnation for a project for which required permits and approvals had not yet been secured.

1. According to the Petitioner:

    a. Is Florida Statutes § 361.01 unconstitutional?

    b. What was the critical element lacking in this condemnation proceeding?

    c. How did the utility "jump the gun"?

2. Under § 361.01, what is the underlying premise for the taking of land by the utility?

3. According to the Court, when a condemnation order is challenged, what are the two prerequisites to be established by the utility, and what is the standard of proof?

4. What standard of proof is placed on the challenger of the "taking"?

5. Why does the Court dedicate a substantial portion of the opinion to discussing the "environmental impact"?

6. What is Justice Ervin's solution to the problem of condemnation prior to project approval?

7. Why do the statute and the Court allow the condemnation to take place before permits and plans are approved?

———————

In the following case, the Florida Supreme Court looks at the elements of statutory business damages and other types of damages that may be considered in an eminent domain action.

System Components Corp. v.
Florida Department of Transportation

14 So. 3d 967 (Fla. 2009)

LEWIS, J.

In this case, we review *System Components Corp. v. Department of Transportation*, 985 So.2d 687 (Fla. 5th DCA 2008), in which the Fifth District Court of Appeal certified that its decision directly conflicts with the decision of the Fourth District Court of Appeal in *State Department of Transportation v. Tire Centers, LLC*, 895 So.2d 1110 (Fla. 4th DCA 2005). We thus possess and exercise our discretionary jurisdiction to resolve this conflict. *See* art. V, §3(b)(4), Fla. Const. Here, we must consider whether an award of business damages in an eminent-domain action under section 73.071(3)(b), Florida Statutes (2004), should include and account for the actual economic realities of the business's operations given its relocation following a partial taking. As more fully explained in our analysis, we approve the Fifth District's decision in *System Components* and disapprove the Fourth District's decision in *Tire Centers* because we agree that the *actual* extent of harm suffered by an affected business is the "*sine qua non*" of any eminent-domain business damages awarded pursuant to section 73.071(3)(b). *Sys. Components*, 985 So.2d at 693.[24] Due to the inherent nature of "damages" in this context, business damages "are not intended to be a windfall unconnected with any out-of-pocket loss." *Id.* at 690. For these reasons, when a qualified partial taking destroys a business at its prior location, and the land/business owner chooses to relocate, the resulting business damages are measured by the "probable" financial impact "reasonably" suffered as a result of the taking. §73.071(3)(b), Fla. Stat. (2004); *see also Sys. Components*, 985 So.2d at 689–93. Under the circumstances presented here, we therefore conclude that *if an affected business chooses to relocate*, its business damages must be determined in light of its continued existence at its new location.

BACKGROUND

The Condemned Property and the Affected Business

On May 13, 2004, the Florida Department of Transportation ("FDOT") filed an eminent-domain petition pursuant to chapters 73 and 74, Florida Statutes (2004). The petition involved several parcels, which FDOT requested permission to condemn for purposes of expanding a road right-of-way. The overall taking was necessary to widen a portion of West State Road 40 from S.W. 85th Avenue to and including the intersection located at 52nd Avenue in Ocala, Florida.

A tract of real property labeled parcel 130 (6750 West State Road 40, Ocala, Florida) was part of this proposed taking and belonged to the petitioner, System Components Corporation. The Fifth District accurately described System Components as "a wholesale distributor of fluid purification control and instrumentation…, [which] has exclusive Florida distributor arrangements with a number of manufacturers and service

---

24. [FN 1.] *See also Black's Law Dictionary* 1418 (8th ed.2004) ("*sine qua non*. An indispensable condition or thing; something on which something else necessarily depends.").

customers in food processing, drug manufacturing, municipal water and other related areas." *Sys. Components*, 985 So.2d at 688 n. 1. System Components receives fluid-purification component parts from manufacturers and then assembles, repackages, and ships completed systems to its Florida customers. There is virtually no walk-in business; instead, System Components' physical location simply functions as a point of assembly and distribution. Prior to the taking, parcel 130 consisted of 1.774 acres and contained a 5000-square-foot, single-story building, from which System Components conducted its distribution and service business. The building included front-office and warehouse areas. Additionally, parcel 130 provided System Components sufficient land to accommodate future expansion. In contrast, the eventual taking and demolition bisected System Components' building and reduced parcel 130 to .648 acres, which the parties agreed rendered the remaining land unusable and of nominal value due to required setback lines that precluded rebuilding.

FDOT proceeded under the quick-take procedures provided in chapter 74, Florida Statutes. *See* § 74.011, Fla. Stat. (2004) ("In any eminent domain action, properly instituted by and in the name of . . . the Department of Transportation . . . , the petitioner may avail itself of the provisions of this chapter *to take possession and title in advance of the entry of final judgment*" (emphasis supplied)). Pursuant to section 74.051(2) and a stipulated order of taking entered on July 13, 2004, FDOT deposited into the circuit-court registry a good-faith estimate of the "full compensation" due to System Components under article X, section 6 of the Florida Constitution (i.e., compensation for (1) the value of the land, (2) associated appurtenances and improvements, and (3) severance damages).[25] The deposited amount agreed to by both parties was $348,300 ($88,300 for the value of the condemned land, $109,400 for appurtenances and improvements, $130,900 for severance damages, and $19,700 to demolish a portion of the building left standing on the remainder).

The taking occurred on July 22, 2004, and System Components sought and obtained FDOT's permission to remain on the property pending demolition. FDOT and System Components entered into a lease agreement through which System Components leased back its prior property at $2000 per month for a five-month term ending in December 2004. Subsequently, System Components entered into an agreement with a third party to lease separate warehouse space in another area of Ocala for $2068 per month for a one-year term (October 1, 2004 through September 30, 2005), which System Components was later forced to extend due to the delayed construction of its new facility ($3000 per month for an additional three months). During this time, George Kirkland, System Components' principal, sought to continue the business while also obtaining a permanent relocation site. As part of this process, Kirkland (1) consulted commercial real-estate brokers to obtain a suitable relocation site; (2) hired an architect and an engineer to design and prepare the replacement

---

25. [FN 3.] *See Black's Law Dictionary* 419 (8th ed.2004) ("*severance damages.* In a condemnation case, damages awarded to a property owner for diminution in the fair market value of land as a result of severance from the land of the property actually condemned; compensation awarded to a landowner for the loss in value of the tract that remains after a partial taking of the land.").

site and building (as required by Marion County); and (3) rehired a former employee to accomplish the eventual move to the relocation site. To finance these efforts, Kirkland and System Components were forced to incur additional debt.

On October 5, 2004, System Components purchased new land in an area of Ocala approximately eleven miles from its prior location. Kirkland testified that land near his prior location had become scarce and more expensive, so he decided to move the business further from the I-75 corridor to a location where land was more plentiful and less expensive. On December 23, 2005, the new building was completed, and System Components relocated from its temporary, leased location.

The Business-Damages Trial

Prior to trial, the parties agreed that System Components qualified for statutory business damages under section 73.071(3)(b), Florida Statutes (2004), which are *not* part of the "full compensation" guaranteed by the Florida Constitution. *See, e.g., Tampa-Hillsborough County Expressway Auth. v. K.E. Morris Alignment Serv., Inc.,* 444 So.2d 926, 928–29 (Fla.1983). The only remaining issue involved the proper measure of business damages in light of System Components' relocation and continued existence. As the Fifth District later explained:

> During the litigation, relying on section 73.071(3)(b), Florida Statutes, and *Florida Department of Transportation v. Tire Centers, LLC,* 895 So.2d 1110 (Fla. 4th DCA 2005), System Components filed a motion in limine seeking to exclude all evidence of what it terms "off-site cure," i.e., that Systems Components was continuing to operate in another location. The trial court denied the motion, expressing disagreement with the *Tire Centers* decision and undertaking to distinguish it.

Sys. Components, 985 So.2d at 689.

Specifically, System Components maintained that eminent-domain proceedings are solely concerned with the land taken and the resulting damages to the condemnee. Therefore, in the view of System Components, it was entitled to the "total-take" value of its business as though it had ceased to exist on the date of taking. This position was consistent with the decision of the Fourth District in *Tire Centers,* which was decided on substantially similar facts and held:

> Eminent domain law focuses only on the land taken, notwithstanding that in a case such as this a substantial portion of lost goodwill may possibly be recaptured by way of a nearby relocation. As such, the taking of the specific property at issue is the sole focus of business damages under section 73.071(3)(b). If the legislature had intended business damages to be subject to mitigation by an off-site cure, it could have easily done so. Consequently, we find that the trial court did not err by excluding any consideration of mitigated business damages by way of an off-site cure.

Tire Centers, 895 So.2d at 1113. FDOT resisted the application of *Tire Centers* and asserted that it was the constitutional duty of the trial court not to apply this precedent because, in FDOT's view, the Fourth District had erroneously "legislated" and thereby exceeded its authority to construe section 73.071(3)(b).[26] The trial court eventually refused to follow *Tire Centers* and, correspondingly, denied the motion in limine.

During trial, which lasted from February 13, 2006, until February 24, 2006, the court permitted each side to present expert testimony concerning the extent of the business damages sustained by System Components and, further, charged the jury that it was to determine (1) the total value of the business on the date of taking; and (2) the business damages sustained by System Components in light of its relocation and continued existence. In response, the jury returned a verdict determining each valuation based upon the testimony presented by System Components' experts: (1) the business's total value derived from an income-based approach — $2,394,964[27]; and (2) System Components' business damages in light of its relocation and continued existence — $1,347,911.[28]

On July 14, 2006, the trial court entered a final judgment, which awarded System Components the latter figure and deducted the value of the good-faith registry deposit to avoid the award of duplicative damages. *Cf., e.g., Glessner v. Duval County*, 203 So.2d 330, 335 (Fla. 1st DCA 1967) (explaining that there may be some overlap between severance and business damages; if so, the condemnee is not entitled to double recovery). The remaining balance of business damages awarded to System Components totaled $999,611. System Components later sought review of this judgment in the appropriate district court of appeal.

The Appeal to the Fifth District

On appeal, System Components asserted that the trial court erred by not following *Tire Centers*, which was then-binding precedent for all Florida trial courts. *See, e.g., Pardo*, 596 So.2d at 666. System Components offered two basic claims to support its contention that it was entitled to the "total-take" value of its business: (1) eminent-domain cases are *in rem* proceedings, which exclusively concern the land subject to taking and any remainder (i.e., the "parent tract"); and (2) the trial court impermissibly altered the text of section 73.071(3)(b), Florida Statutes, by reading in a duty to mitigate damages beyond the boundaries of the parent tract. *See* Appellant's Initial Brief at 5–15, *Sys. Components Corp. v. Fla. Dep't of Transp.*, 985 So.2d 687 (Fla. 5th DCA 2008) (No.

---

26. [FN 4.] We agree with the Fifth District that FDOT's contentions in this regard were totally improper. *See Sys. Components*, 985 So.2d at 689 n. 3. In the absence of inter-district conflict or contrary precedent from this Court, it is absolutely clear that the decision of a district court of appeal is binding precedent *throughout Florida*. *See, e.g., Pardo v. State*, 596 So.2d 665, 666 (Fla.1992). Consequently, a trial court may not overrule or recede from the controlling decision of a district court.

27. [FN 5.] *See* American Society of Appraisers, *Business Valuation Standards Glossary, available at* www.bvappraisers.org/glossary/glossary.pdf ("[A] general way of determining a value indication of a business … using one or more methods that convert anticipated economic benefits into a present single amount."); Jeffrey M. Risius, *Business Valuation: A Primer For The Legal Professional* 65 (2007) ("The general theory behind the Income Approach is that the value of the business is equal to the present value of the cash flows expected to be generated by that business in the future into perpetuity.").

28. [FN 6.] The record reflects that this latter amount included damages for (a) loss of value due to altered capital structure (i.e., increased debt); (b) moving expenses and rent; (c) costs associated with obtaining a replacement property; (d) costs associated with constructing a replacement facility; and (e) down-time productivity losses.

5D06-2864). Conversely, FDOT asserted that the trial court was not required to follow *Tire Centers* because, in that decision, the Fourth District usurped the role of the Legislature by excluding evidence of off-site mitigation even though section 73.071(3)(b) is silent with regard to this issue. *See* Answer Brief of Appellee at 9–23, *Sys. Components Corp. v. Fla. Dep't of Transp.*, 985 So.2d 687 (Fla. 5th DCA 2008) (No. 5D06-2864).

In a well-reasoned opinion, the Fifth District refused to adopt the extreme positions advanced by either party. First, the district court rejected the position of System Components that the Legislature intended section 73.071(3)(b) to compensate a fully functioning, relocated business by awarding it the total value of its operations as though it had ceased to exist on the date of taking:

> Application of the analysis in *Tire Centers* would mean that a fully functioning business would receive a windfall of over a million dollars for damages it did not suffer. Rather than recover its business damages, it would recover something else, a form of compensation for the taking of part of its property measured by the full value of the business, as though it had ceased to exist. We conclude that this is not what section 73.071 says or intends.

Sys. Components, 985 So.2d at 689–90. Second, the district court rejected FDOT's contention that the doctrine of avoidable consequences (i.e., the "duty to mitigate" damages) requires off-site relocation whenever necessary and possible:

> Although the statute *does not require* relocation *or* a damage calculation based on what damages would be if the business were to hypothetically relocate, if a business *does* elect to relocate and to continue in existence, the business can only recover its *damages*—i.e., the amount of harm to its business resulting from the taking of its location. *Where,* as here, *the business has elected to continue in business in a different location,* the business should be *fully compensated for all damages done to the business caused by the taking,* but it should *not* be compensated based *on the fiction that it has been entirely lost.*

Id. at 692–93 (some emphasis supplied). Supported by this rationale, the Fifth District affirmed the award of business damages as determined by the trial court and certified conflict with *Tire Centers. See Sys. Components*, 985 So.2d at 693.

We subsequently accepted jurisdiction and now resolve this certified conflict. *See Sys. Components Corp. v. Fla. Dep't of Transp.*, 990 So.2d 1060 (Fla.2008) (table).

ANALYSIS

This case presents a question of statutory interpretation, which is subject to *de novo* review. *See, e.g., Fla. Dep't of Envtl. Prot. v. ContractPoint Fla. Parks, LLC*, 986 So.2d 1260, 1264 (Fla.2008). In particular, we must determine whether an award of business damages in an eminent-domain action under section 73.071(3)(b), Florida Statutes (2004), may take into consideration only the actual damages sustained by the affected business when there is a relocation following a partial taking. After reviewing the plain text of the statute and considering pertinent precedent and legal commentary, we hold that a qualifying business that chooses to relocate must receive a business-damages award based upon its continued existence and the true economic realities of the given case.

Relevant Eminent-Domain Doctrine and an Overview of Statutory Business Damages

Eminent Domain and "Full Compensation"

The power of eminent domain is an inherent aspect of sovereignty vested in the government of Florida, "which is circumscribed by, rather than conferred by, constitution or statute." *City of Ocala v. Nye*, 608 So.2d 15, 17 (Fla.1992) (citing *Peavy-Wilson Lumber Co. v. Brevard County*, 159 Fla. 311, 31 So.2d 483 (1947)). While it remains "[t]he central policy of eminent domain ... that owners of property taken by a governmental entity [must] receive full and fair compensation," both this Court and the United States Supreme Court have very clearly held that business damages are *not* a constitutionally required component of "just" or "full" compensation. *See, e.g., Tampa-Hillsborough County Expressway Auth. v. K.E. Morris Alignment Serv., Inc.,* 444 So.2d 926, 928 (Fla.1983) ("Business damages ... fall in the category where compensation is not constitutionally required but depends on legislative authorization."); *Jamesson v. Downtown Dev. Auth. of Fort Lauderdale*, 322 So.2d 510, 511 (Fla.1975) ("The right to business damages is a matter of legislative grace, not constitutional imperative. Lost profits and business damages are intangibles which generally do not constitute 'property' in the constitutional sense." (footnote omitted)). Thus, the "full compensation" mandated by article X, section 6 of the Florida Constitution is restricted to (1) the value of the condemned land,[29] (2) the value of associated appurtenances and improvements, and (3) damages to the remaining land (i.e., severance damages). *See, e.g., State Road Dep't v. Bramlett*, 189 So.2d 481, 484 (Fla.1966); *cf. United States v. Bodcaw Co.*, 440 U.S. 202, 204 (1979) ("Perhaps it would be fair or efficient to compensate a landowner for all the costs he incurs as a result of a condemnation action.... But such compensation is a matter of legislative grace rather than constitutional command."). Conversely, when a governmental entity actually "takes" or appropriates *the business* for its proprietary use, the government is constitutionally required to compensate the business owner(s) for the reasonable value of the appropriated business. *See generally Kimball Laundry Co. v. United States*, 338 U.S. 1 (1949) (involving the U.S. Army's wartime acquisition of a well-established, profitable laundry business).

Statutory Business Damages

Despite the general eminent-domain rule that business damages are intangible, consequential injuries, which the government is not constitutionally required to com-

---

29. [FN 11.] The concept of "highest and best use" applies to the valuation of condemned land and severance damages:

> An owner of lands sought to be condemned is entitled to their "market value fairly determined." *United States v. Miller*, 317 U.S. 369. That value may reflect not only the use to which the property is presently devoted but also that use to which it may be readily converted. [*Mississippi & Rum River*] *Boom Co. v. Patterson*, 98 U.S. 403 [(1878)]; *McCandless v. United States*, 298 U.S. 342. In that connection the value may be determined in light of the special or higher use of the land....

United States ex rel. TVA v. Powelson, 319 U.S. 266, 275 (1943); *see also Black's Law Dictionary* 1577 (8th ed. 2004) ("In valuing property, the use that will generate the most profit. This standard is used esp[ecially] to determine the fair market value of property subject to eminent domain.").

pensate, Florida has elected to provide such compensation through statute since 1933. *See* ch. 15927, Laws of Fla. (1933); Martha L. Koval & Andrew B. Sasso, *The Bottom Line on Eminent Domain Business Damages*, Fla. B.J., June 1986, at 59. However, this statutory allowance is *narrow*, and the condemnee bears the burden of specifically pleading and satisfying each of the requirements provided in the business-damages statute, which is currently codified at section 73.071(3)(b), Florida Statutes. *See K.E. Morris*, 444 So.2d at 929 ("[A]ny ambiguity in section 73.071(3)(b) should be construed against the claim of business damages, and such damages should be awarded only when such an award appears clearly consistent with legislative intent."); *City of Fort Lauderdale v. Casino Realty, Inc.*, 313 So.2d 649, 652 (Fla.1975) (Overton, J., specially concurring; adopted as majority) (holding that the condemnee bears the burden of proving the existence and extent of business damages); Fla. R. Civ. P. 1.120(g) ("When items of special damage are claimed, they shall be specifically stated.").

Section 73.071(3)(b), Florida Statutes (2004), provides as follows (our bracketed numerals and altered formatting separately indicate each statutory requirement):

(3) *The jury* shall determine solely the amount of compensation to be paid, which compensation shall include:

. . . .

(b) Where

[1] *less than the entire property is sought to be appropriated,* any damages to the remainder caused by the taking [i.e., severance damages], *including,*

[2] when the action is by the *Department of Transportation*, county, municipality, board, district or other public body for

[3] the *condemnation of a right-of-way,* and

[4] the effect of the taking of the property involved may *damage or destroy* an *established business* of *more than 4 years' standing* before January 1, 2005, *or* the effect of the taking of the property involved may *damage or destroy* an established business of *more than 5 years' standing* on or after January 1, 2005,

[5] *owned by the party whose lands are being so taken,*

[6] *located upon adjoining lands* owned or held by such party, the *probable damages* to such business which the *denial of the use of the property* so taken may *reasonably cause;*

[7] any person claiming the right to recover such special damages shall *set forth in his or her written defenses the nature and extent of such damages.*

(emphasis supplied) (formatting altered); *see also Florida Eminent Domain, supra,* § 9.46, at 9-62–9-63; *Koval & Sasso, supra,* at 60–61. This statute implements the constitutional requirement of compensating severance damages *and* provides for business damages under specified circumstances. *See Fla. Dep't of Transp. v. Ness Trailer Park, Inc.*, 489 So.2d 1172, 1180–81 (Fla. 4th DCA 1986).

Severance and business damages are both available in appropriate cases, but they should not be confused. *Severance damages* are part of the constitutional guarantee of "full compensation" and reimburse the owner for the reduction in value the taking causes to any remaining land, while *business damages* are a creature of statute and compensate the owner for "probable" reductions in business value, business losses, or increased business expenses "reasonably cause[d]" by the taking. § 73.071(3)(b), Fla. Stat. (2004); *see Sys. Components*, 985 So.2d at 690–91 (citing *Blockbuster*, 714 So.2d at 1224); *Ness Trailer*, 489 So.2d at 1181; *Florida Eminent Domain, supra*, §§ 9.34, 9.35, at 9-46–9-47. Where the two forms of damages overlap, double recovery is prohibited. *See Mulkey v. Fla. Div. of Admin.*, 448 So.2d 1062, 1066 (Fla. 2d DCA 1984). Business damages are not part of the "full compensation" guaranteed by the Florida Constitution, and the State is not required to pay interest on these damages or to include these damages as part of its "good faith" registry deposit. *See Behm v. Div. of Admin.*, 383 So.2d 216, 219 (Fla.1980) (citing *Div. of Admin. v. Pink Pussy Cat, Inc.*, 314 So.2d 192 (Fla. 1st DCA 1975)); *State Road Dep't v. Abel Inv. Co.*, 165 So.2d 832, 833–34 (Fla. 2d DCA 1964).

In more informal terms, the business-damages portion of the statute has been suggested to generally *apply if, and only if*:

(1) a partial taking occurs;

(2) the condemnor is a state or local "public body";

(3) the land is taken to construct or expand a right-of-way;

(4) the taking damages or destroys an established business, which has existed on the parent tract for the specified number of years;

(5) the business owner owns the condemned and adjoining land (lessees may qualify);

(6) business was conducted on the condemned land and the adjoining remainder; and

(7) the condemnee specifically pleads and proves (1)–(6).

See § 73.071(3)(b), Fla. Stat. (2004); Carlos A. Kelly, *Eminent Domain: Identifying Issues in Damages for the General Practitioner*, Fla. B.J., May 2009, at 52. The statute is thus limited in scope and completely exempts the award of business damages in total-taking cases. In fact, the Legislature formerly permitted FDOT to totally condemn a parcel to avoid the imposition of business damages if the total taking (as opposed to a partial taking) resulted in a lower bottom line. *See Dep't of Transp. v. Fortune Fed. Sav. & Loan Ass'n*, 532 So.2d 1267, 1270 (Fla.1988) (upholding the constitutionality of section 337.27(3), Florida Statutes (1985)). In 1999, the Legislature rescinded this authority, thereby prohibiting this type of total taking, which had become known as "*Fortune Federal* takings." *See* ch. 99-385, § 64, at 3882, Laws of Fla.; Fla. H.R. Comm. on Transp., HB 591 (1999) Staff Analysis 2, 18, 24, 28 (final July 16, 1999) (on file with State Archives); Paul D. Bain, *1999 Amendments to Florida's Eminent Domain Statutes*, Fla. B.J., Nov. 1999, at 68, 70.

Notwithstanding the narrow nature of the business-damages statute, Florida precedent maintains:

> The purpose of section 73.071(3)(b) is to mitigate the hardship that may result when the state exercises the power of eminent domain paying only the constitutionally required full compensation for the property actually taken. The legislature in doing so has recognized that a business location may be an asset of considerable value....

K.E. Morris, 444 So.2d at 929. However, section 73.071(3)(b) does not compensate land owners for business damages when (i) a total taking occurs, (ii) the condemnor is not a "public body" (the Legislature has vested some private parties, e.g., utilities, with eminent-domain powers), *or* (iii) the land is taken for some purpose other than building or expanding a right-of-way. *Cf. Fortune Fed.*, 532 So.2d at 1270 ("[T]he legislature has created a right to business damages, so it may also limit that right.").

The Legislature has not specifically defined what may constitute compensable "business damages." However, this Court has held:

> [S]ection 73.071(3)(b) ... *does not* require the calculation of business damages by one mechanically applied, one-size-fits-all formula which would not produce proper results. *For an ongoing business,* ... business damages are *inherently fact-intensive....* Ultimately, it is for the fact-finder to calculate the damages.

Murray v. Dep't of Transp., 687 So.2d 825, 827 (Fla.1997) (emphasis supplied). Further, the Fourth District, in a widely cited opinion, explained:

> The Legislature did not define or otherwise elaborate upon what constitutes "business damages," but there is absolutely no indication that it intended this statute to be construed as allowing business damages for lost profits only. The statutory language, which authorizes compensation for "the probable damages to such business which the denial of the use of the property so taken may reasonably cause," simply does not warrant this restrictive interpretation.

Matthews v. Div. of Admin., 324 So.2d 664, 666 (Fla. 4th DCA 1975)....

Case law has specifically identified at least three types of business damages — (1) lost profits, (2) moving/relocation expenses, and (3) loss of goodwill — but section 73.071(3)(b)'s plain text is *not* so limited. Rather, it simply states that the land/business owner is entitled to receive "the *probable damages* to such business which the *denial of the use of the property* so taken may *reasonably cause.*" § 73.071(3)(b), Fla. Stat. (2004) (emphasis supplied). Each party is thus entitled to approach the "inherently fact-intensive" task of business-damage valuation by presenting the opinions of qualified experts "based upon *generally accepted accounting principles* as to what should be included in the jury's calculation." *Murray*, 687 So.2d at 827 (emphasis supplied). Expert valuation testimony must be consistent with the law and "is impermissible if based merely on speculation or groundless prognostication, but can be admitted where necessary to explain previously admitted factual evidence tending to prove or disprove the existence of a reasonable probability." *Broward County v. Patel*, 641 So.2d 40, 43 (Fla.1994). Business damages determined by the fact-finder must fall within the range of expert valuations presented by the parties. *See Patel*, 641 So.2d at 43 n. 5. A business-damages award based on the total cost and damages associated with relocation may *not* exceed the total value of the business as measured by the appropriate valuation method—whether an income-based approach (i.e., value based on current and future revenue stream discounted to a total present value), market-based approach (i.e., value based on comparison to comparable businesses existing in the particular market adjusted for the individual characteristics and risks associated with the specific business), or asset-based approach (i.e., value based on total assets net liabilities; typically used when the business is not profitable). *See* § 73.071(3)(b), Fla. Stat. (2004); Jeffrey M. Risius, *Business Valuation: A Primer For The Legal Professional* chs. 8, 10, 12 (2007); American Society of Appraisers, *Business Valuation Standards Glossary*, *available at* www.bvappraisers.org/glossary/glossary.pdf.

System Components' Business Damages

Before trial, the parties stipulated that System Components satisfied each statutory requirement for business damages. Their remaining dispute centered on the significance of the statutory command that the land/business owner receive "the *probable damages* to such business which the *denial of the use of the property* so taken may *reasonably cause*." § 73.071(3)(b), Fla. Stat. (2004) (emphasis supplied). System Components correctly highlights that section 73.071(2), Florida Statutes (2004), states:

> The amount of such compensation shall be determined *as of the date of trial, or the date upon which title passes, whichever shall occur first.*

(Emphasis supplied.) Based on this subsection, System Components contends that its business-damages compensation should be determined *as of the date of the taking,* July 22, 2004, which occurred prior to trial, and further contends that all of its *subsequent* relocation efforts should not impact the result that the taking completely destroyed the business at its prior location.

Unfortunately, this contention ignores several important facts and a significant point of law. First, System Components continued in business at its prior location *post-taking* with FDOT's assent. System Components (a) leased back the condemned parcel for a five-month term ending in December 2004, (b) later transferred to a temporary facility, and (c) finally moved to its new, permanent location on December 23, 2005, approximately 1.5 months before the business-damages trial occurred during mid-February 2006. Second, with regard to the ignored point of law, Florida's appellate courts have not mechanically applied the timing requirement of section 73.071(2) when addressing business damages. For example, in *Malone v. Division of Administration*, 438 So.2d 857 (Fla. 3d DCA 1983), a case involving an established type of business damages (i.e., moving expenses), the Third District recognized—consistent with this Court's precedent—that "Florida law requires ... courts [to] take into account *all facts and circumstances bearing a reasonable relationship to the loss occasioned* an owner by virtue of his property being taken," *id.* at 863, and held that "[t]he [business-damages] award should be based on the allowable costs incurred *or* that will be incurred *as long as the move is undertaken seasonably." Id.* at 861 (emphasis supplied). Hence, the Third District refused to strictly adhere to section 73.071(2) when doing so would have produced an absurd result. *Cf. K.E. Morris,* 444 So.2d at 929 ("[I]t is axiomatic that courts should … avoid giving [a statute] an interpretation that will lead to an absurd result."). Instead, the district court permitted a valuation of business damages based on the actual damages suffered by the condemnee following the taking—which were later established at trial. The court did so because the condemnee had relocated.

A similar situation exists here. System Components relocated and never ceased operations. Therefore, the jury calculated these business damages with reference to the "probable" damages "reasonably" suffered as a result of "the denial of the use of the property so taken." §73.071(3)(b), Fla. Stat. (2004). Based upon the record, System Components received nothing more and nothing less. As both the Fourth and Fifth Districts have held, business damages "are not intended to be a windfall unconnected with any out-of-pocket loss." *Sys. Components,* 985 So.2d at 690 (citing *Tire Centers,* 895 So.2d at 1112). In this case, the jury awarded System Components business damages for (a) loss of value due to an altered capital structure (i.e., increased debt), (b) moving expenses and rent, (c) costs associated with obtaining a replacement property, (d) costs associated with constructing a replacement facility, and (e) downtime productivity losses, and the trial court subsequently deducted the amount of FDOT's good-faith deposit to avoid double recovery. System Components did not lose any goodwill and its witnesses could not identify any specific loss of sales. The company did not cease to exist on the date of taking. Consequently, System Components received the "probable" business damages "reasonably" suffered as a result of the taking. §73.071(3)(b), Fla. Stat. (2004).

As we will more fully explain, the decision of the Fourth District in *Tire Centers,* which awarded the total value of the affected business—rather than awarding actual business damages—was based upon an understandable misconception of Florida law.

The Doctrine of Avoidable Consequences Does *Not* Require Courts to Ignore the Actual Business Damages Caused by a Taking in Light of Business Relocation

The doctrine of avoidable consequences, which is also somewhat inaccurately identified as the "duty to mitigate" damages, commonly applies in contract and tort actions. *See generally* 17 Fla. Jur.2d, *Damages,* §§ 103–04 (2004). There is no actual "duty to mitigate," because the injured party is not compelled to undertake any ameliorative efforts. The doctrine simply "prevents a party from recovering those damages inflicted by a wrongdoer that the injured party *could have* reasonably avoided." The Florida Bar, *Florida Civil Practice Damages* § 2.43, at 2–30 (6th ed.2005) (emphasis supplied) (citing *Sharick v. SE. Univ. of Health Scis., Inc.,* 780 So.2d 136 (Fla. 3d DCA 2000); *Graphic Assocs., Inc. v. Riviana Rest. Corp.,* 461 So.2d 1011 (Fla. 4th DCA 1984)). The doctrine does not permit damage reduction based on what "could have been avoided" through Herculean efforts. *See, e.g., Thompson v. Fla. Drum Co.,* 651 So.2d 180, 182 (Fla. 1st DCA 1995) ("Extraordinary efforts on the part of a plaintiff to mitigate are not required."), *approved,* 668 So.2d 192 (Fla.1996). Rather, the injured party is only accountable for those hypothetical ameliorative actions that could have been accomplished through "ordinary and reasonable care," without requiring undue effort or expense. *Graphic Assocs.*, 461 So.2d at 1014 (the doctrine "prevents a party from recovering those damages inflicted by a wrongdoer which the injured party 'could have avoided *without undue risk, burden, or humiliation.*'" (emphasis supplied) (quoting Restatement (Second) of Contracts § 305(1) (1979))); *Royal Trust Bank of Orlando v. All Fla. Fleets, Inc.*, 431 So.2d 1043, 1045 (Fla. 5th DCA 1983) (substantially similar).

In Florida eminent-domain cases, severance damages are subject to the doctrine of avoidable consequences through a valuation concept known as the "cost to cure":

> [T]he "cost to cure" is the cost of an attempt to ameliorate the damage to value sustained by the [remaining] property as a result of the partial taking by the government. The theory is that it is more economical to spend additional money on a "cure" to restore value to the remaining property because the "cure" will restore more lost value than its "cost."

Fla. Dep't of Transp. v. Armadillo Partners, Inc., 849 So.2d 279, 285 (Fla.2003). The plain text of section 73.071(3)(b), Florida Statutes (2004), conveys that the Legislature views business damages as an otherwise noncompensable subtype of severance damages:

> Where less than the entire property is sought to be appropriated, *any damages to the remainder* [i.e., severance damages] caused by the taking, *including, … the probable damages to such business* which the denial of the use of the property so taken may reasonably cause.…

(Emphasis supplied.) *See also Pro-Art Dental Lab, Inc. v. V-Strategic Group, LLC*, 986 So.2d 1244, 1257 (Fla.2008) ("[T]he term 'including' is not one of all-embracing definition, but connotes simply an illustrative application of the general principle." (emphasis omitted) (quoting *Fed. Land Bank of St. Paul v. Bismarck Lumber Co.*, 314 U.S. 95, 100 (1941))). Therefore, the doctrine of avoidable consequences/cost-to-cure approach may similarly apply to business damages *when limited to a proposed, reasonably feasible restoration of the business on the parent tract. See Mulkey*, 448 So.2d at 1066–67 (holding that the doctrine of avoidable consequences/cost-to-cure approach is limited to *the parent tract*). However, this recognition does not alter the fact that true severance damages are a constitutionally required component of "full compensation," whereas business damages are not. *See Florida Eminent Domain, supra,* §§ 9.34, 9.35, at 9-46–9-47. In addition, as stated above, severance and business damages fulfill substantively distinct roles: *Severance damages* reimburse the owner for the reduction in value the taking causes to any remaining land, while *business damages* compensate the owner for probable reductions in business value, business losses, or increased business expenses reasonably caused by the taking. *See* § 73.071(3)(b), Fla. Stat. (2004); *Sys. Components*, 985 So.2d at 690–91 (citing *Blockbuster*, 714 So.2d at 1224); *Ness Trailer*, 489 So.2d at 1181; *Florida Eminent Domain, supra,* §§ 9.34, 9.35, at 9-46–9-47.

In *Tire Centers*, the Fourth District erroneously (but understandably) relied on Florida's historical limitation of the "cost to cure" to the parent tract and overlooked the *actual damages* suffered by the condemnee. Instead, the Fourth District awarded the total value of the condemnee's business ($1,738,235) as though it had ceased to exist on the date of taking. *See* 895 So.2d at 1112–13. In reality, the tire business simply relocated within the same general vicinity and continued its business unabated (much the same as System Components in the case at bar). *See id.* at 1111. *Tire Centers* thus misstates and misapplies the doctrine of avoidable consequences, which involves *hypothetical* ameliorative efforts.[30] It is true that Florida precedent limits *the cost to cure* to the parent tract. *See Mulkey*, 448 So.2d at 1066–67.[31] Nevertheless, it is equally true that the cost-to-cure approach is *not* an independent measure of damages; it is simply a means through which the condemnee's damages may be reduced by pleading and proving reasonably implemented, *hypothetical* ameliorative efforts that are limited to *the parent tract. See Armadillo Partners*, 849 So.2d at 285 ("[W]hile the cost to cure may be relevant evidence on the issue of damages, it is not a measure of damages to be separately assessed without reference to" other germane evidence concerning the actual damages suffered by the condemnee.).

In contrast, the relocation efforts of Tire Centers and System Components were *not* hypothetical but, rather, were probative of the *actual damages* sustained by these businesses in light of their relocation and continued operation. *Cf. Malone*, 438 So.2d at 860–63 (permitting valuation based on actual business damages suffered post-taking); *Mulkey*, 448 So.2d at 1067 (same). To ignore planned, executed business relocations in interpreting section 73.071(3)(b) would lead to an absurd result (i.e., overcompensating businesses as though they ceased to exist on the date of taking), which this Court must seek to avoid. *Cf. K.E. Morris*, 444 So.2d at 929. The Legislature has authorized the award of "probable damages ... which the denial of the use of the property so taken may reasonably cause," and we must properly construe the statute and only award compensation when clearly consistent with legislative intent. *See K.E. Morris*, 444 So.2d at 929.

---

30. [FN 23.] However, we do agree with the Fourth District that goodwill is often uniquely associated with a particular site (especially a retail storefront), and that such a location may provide much of a business's intrinsic, intangible value. *See Matthews*, 324 So.2d at 667 ("[C]ommon experience teaches us that where the 'effect of the taking' is to totally destroy an established neighborhood-retail business, there is, or at least well may be, a substantial loss ... of customer goodwill."); *see also Black's Law Dictionary* 715 (8th ed.2004) ("*goodwill.* A business's reputation, patronage, and other intangible assets that are considered when appraising the business, esp[ecially] for purchase; the ability to earn income in excess of the income that would be expected from the business viewed as a mere collection of assets."); American Society of Appraisers, *Business Valuation Standards Glossary, available at* www.bvappraisers.org/glossary/glossary.pdf ("*Goodwill*—that intangible asset arising as a result of name, reputation, customer loyalty, location, products, and similar factors not separately identified."). Here, due to the nature of its wholesale-distribution business, System Components could not establish that it lost any goodwill following its relocation.

31. [FN 24.] The *Florida Eminent Domain Practice and Procedure* treatise explains this rule as follows:

> Evidence of a cure to the remainder must show that the cure can be constructed on the premises. A cure cannot be admitted if it would require an owner to go outside the premises, to property over which the owner has no ownership interest, to effect the cure.

Id. § 9.42, at 9–55 (citing *Mulkey*, 448 So.2d 1062); *see also* Kelly, *supra*, at 54 (discussing *Mulkey*).

Section 73.071(3)(b) is thus intended to compensate "probable" business damages in light of actual events. However, the statute is *completely silent* with regard to imposing an affirmative duty to relocate, which FDOT contends should be the rule despite the absence of any explicit statutory command. In other words, if the destroyed business chooses not to relocate and, instead, to close up shop, FDOT requests the ability to reduce the business's damages through the doctrine of avoidable consequences (i.e., introducing relocation hypotheticals beyond the boundaries of the parent tract to reduce business damages). While such a rule might provide an economic incentive to force the reestablishment of businesses following condemnation, imposing an affirmative duty to relocate is a legislative, rather than judicial, function. This is particularly true given that Florida eminent-domain precedent has limited the doctrine of avoidable consequences to *the parent tract,* and the Legislature has been operating under this assumption for a number of years, during which time it has amended Florida's eminent-domain statutes without imposing an affirmative duty to relocate. *See, e.g., Essex Ins. Co. v. Zota,* 985 So.2d 1036, 1043 (Fla.2008) ("[T]he legislature is presumed to know the judicial constructions of a law when enacting a new version of that law and ... is presumed to have adopted prior judicial constructions of a law unless a contrary intention is expressed in the new version." (internal quotation marks omitted) (quoting *Jones v. ETS of New Orleans, Inc.,* 793 So.2d 912, 917 (Fla.2001))); *see generally* ch. 99-385, Laws of Fla. (making several changes to Florida's eminent-domain statutes). If the Legislature wishes to impose this type of affirmative duty, it remains free to do so. *Cf.* Idaho Code Ann. § 7-711(2)(b) (Supp.2007) (imposing an affirmative duty to relocate under reasonable circumstances).

This case does not involve a hypothetical relocation, and both the Fourth and Fifth Districts have recognized that section 73.071(3)(b) does not directly impose an affirmative or hypothetical duty to relocate. *See Sys. Components,* 985 So.2d at 692; *Tire Centers,* 895 So.2d at 1112–13. Accordingly, we defer to the Legislature concerning the question of whether affected businesses should be required to relocate to mitigate their business damages while, at the same time, we recognize that under the applicable statute no such requirement exists.

CONCLUSION

For the reasons provided in our analysis, we approve the decision of the Fifth District Court of Appeal in *System Components Corp. v. Department of Transportation,* 985 So.2d 687 (Fla. 5th DCA 2008), and disapprove the decision of the Fourth District in *State Department of Transportation v. Tire Centers, LLC,* 895 So.2d 1110 (Fla. 4th DCA 2005). In resolving this conflict, we conclude that when a qualified partial taking destroys a business at its prior location, and the land/business owner chooses to relocate, the resulting business damages must be measured by the probable financial impact reasonably suffered as a result of the taking. Therefore, these business damages must be determined in light of the true economic realities of the given case, which, here, involved a relocated business's continued existence at its new location.

It is so ordered.

QUINCE, C.J., and PARIENTE, POLSTON, and LABARGA, JJ., concur.

CANADY, J., concurs in result only.

PERRY, J., did not participate.

Questions

1. Is there a constitutional right to business damages?

2. Is a business owner in Florida entitled to business damages if the entire parcel is taken?

In the following case, the court explores inverse condemnation claims.

Flatt v. City of Brooksville

368 So. 2d 631 (Fla. 2d DCA 1979)

SCHEB, Judge.

Appellants challenge the trial court's holding that they were not entitled to recover compensation for damage to their personal property occurring as a result of a "taking" by appellee City. We reverse.

Appellants/plaintiffs instituted inverse condemnation proceedings against appellee City to recover for damage to their home and personal property.[32] Appellants alleged that a drainage system constructed by the City caused surface water to flood their land and home. The trial court determined that there had been a taking by the City, and we affirmed. *City of Brooksville v. Flatt*, 345 So.2d 433 (Fla. 2d DCA 1977).

A jury trial was then conducted to determine how much compensation appellants were entitled to. Appellants sought to introduce evidence of the value of their personal property destroyed by the flooding. The court declined to receive such evidence, and entered a final order holding that damage to personal property was not recoverable "under the eminent domain provision of the Florida Constitution and applicable Florida Statute."

Article X, s 6(a), Fla.Const. provides, "No private property shall be taken except for a public purpose and with full compensation therefor...." Thus, no apparent distinction is made between real and personal property. This constitutional provision does not require enabling legislation to be effective, *Jacksonville Expressway Authority v. Henry G. DuPree Co.*, 108 So.2d 289, 294 (Fla.1958), so it is immaterial that there is no statute specifically authorizing recovery for loss of personal property. Only by allowing such recovery can a property owner receive his constitutional entitlement to "full compensation" for his loss.

---

32. [FN 1.] A public body is, of course, liable to the same extent in an inverse condemnation action as it would be if it were a petitioner in a direct condemnation action. *State Road Department v. Lewis*, 190 So.2d 598 (Fla. 1st DCA 1966).

We agree with the general principle stated in *Kirkpatrick v. City of Jacksonville*, 312 So.2d 487, 489 (Fla. 1st DCA 1975), where the court said:

> (A)n aggrieved property owner whose Real or personal property has been destroyed by unwarranted governmental action may institute a proceeding to compel the governmental body to exercise its power of eminent domain and award just compensation to the owner. (Emphasis supplied.)

Accordingly, the order of the trial court is reversed and this cause remanded for a trial on the issue of the value of appellants' personal property damaged or destroyed as a result of the City's taking.

HOBSON, Acting C. J., and BOARDMAN, J., concur.

Questions

1. What constitutes an "inverse condemnation"?

2. According to the Second District, why can a "condemnee" receive compensation for loss of personal property?

B. Environmental Provisions

There are several constitutional provisions which govern or mandate the protection of the environment, through establishment of policy, governmental structure, tax incentives, and finance.[33] Most of these provisions are contained in Article II and Article X and have evolved through amendments proposed by the Legislature, Constitution Revision Commissions, and initiative.

The 1968 Constitution contains the Natural Resources Clause that sets forth "the policy of the state to conserve and protect its natural resources." As we saw in *Seadade Industries, Inc. v. Florida Power & Light Co.*, this clause can be used to place limits on other governmental action, including the exercise of eminent domain. The first environmental provisions were amendments to the 1885 Constitution. A 1942 amendment created the Game and Fresh Water Fish Commission as an independent agency to manage and conserve birds, game and fresh water fish.[34] Another 1942 amendment authorized the Legislature to provide for the protection of salt water fish.[35] In 1998, voters ratified a proposal from the Constitution Revision Commission that combined both provisions into a new agency called the Fish and Wildlife Conservation Com-

---

33. For more on the environmental protections mandated by the Florida Constitution, see generally Clay Henderson, *The Greening of the Florida Constitution*, 49 STETSON L. REV. 575 (2020).

34. *See* FLA. CONST. OF 1885, art. IV, § 30 (effective in 1943). Article IV, Section 9 of the 1968 Constitution continued the regulation of game and freshwater fish by this independent agency.

35. *See* FLA. CONST. OF 1885, art. XVI, § 32 (effective in 1943). The Legislature created the Marine Fisheries Commission endowing it with regulatory authority by statute. This amendment was not carried forward in the 1968 Constitution, and this resulted in differential treatment for marine fisheries, regulated by the statutory Marine Fisheries Commission, from game and freshwater fish, which had their own independent regulatory agency.

mission with jurisdiction over wild animal life plus fresh and salt water fishing. Another amendment to the 1885 Constitution had authorized the issuance of state bonds for "outdoor recreation and natural resources conservation" for a period of 50 years.[36] This provision was incorporated into the 1968 Constitution with an authorization for bonds for environmentally endangered lands.[37] A 1998 Constitution Revision Commission proposed amendment ended the 50-year limitation,[38] and a 2014 initiative dedicated funds for conservation purposes.

Access to public beaches and waterways is a fundamental aspect of Florida life based upon the Public Trust Doctrine that holds that certain lands and waters are held in trust for the public. The 1885 Constitution made no reference to this, as it was accepted that the Public Trust Doctrine was part of established common law.[39] However, the 1968 Constitution included Article X, Section 11, entitled "sovereignty lands," which essentially placed the common law Public Trust Doctrine into the organic law. Given Florida's lengthy history of land sales, the Legislature in 1970 proposed an amendment to Section 11 to make clear that "beaches below mean high water" are held "in trust for all the people" and may only be disposed of after an affirmative showing that the sale was "in the public interest." The *Coastal Petroleum Co. v. American Cyanamid Co.* case which follows deals with the applicability of the Florida Marketable Record Title Act to sovereignty lands.

In 1994, the first environmental initiative amendment was approved by Florida voters. The Net Ban in Article X, Section 16, applied to both recreational and commercial fishing in "nearshore and inshore Florida waters." Intended to prevent overfishing, it had a heavy impact on small fishing communities along the Gulf Coast.[40] The *Lane v. Chiles* case below is typical of the many challenges to this initiative amendment.

The Net Ban was followed by an attempt to force the sugar industry to pay for Everglades restoration. However, the Florida Supreme Court struck the Save Our Everglades initiative amendment from the ballot, finding that it exercised multiple government functions in contravention of Article XI, Section 3, and that it employed misleading rhetoric in its title and summary.[41] In 1996, the sponsors of the failed

---

36. *See* FLA. CONST. OF 1885 art. IX, § 17. This provision was incorporated by reference into Article XII, Section 1 of the 1968 Constitution.

37. *See* FLA. CONST. art. XII, § 9(a)(1), incorporating by reference Article IX, Section 17 of the 1885 Constitution.

38. *See* FLA. CONST. art. VII, § 11(e).

39. For more on the history of the public trust doctrine in Florida, see, e.g., Sidney F. Ansbacher & Joe Knetsch, *The Public Trust Doctrine & Sovereignty Lands in Florida: A Legal & Historical Analysis*, 4 J. LAND USE & ENVT'L L. 337 (1989); Henderson, *supra* note 33, at 631–34.

40. Many Gulf Coast fishermen also objected to the disparate treatment under the Net Ban amendment where "nearshore and inshore Florida waters" was defined as "all Florida waters inside a line three miles seaward of the coastline along the Gulf of Mexico and inside a line one mile seaward of the coastline along the Atlantic Ocean." FLA. CONST. art. X, § 16(c)(5). The Supreme Court considered this distinction as part of the challenge to the amendment in *Lane v. Chiles*, 698 So. 2d 260 (Fla. 1997), which will be discussed later in this chapter.

41. *See In re Advisory Opinion to the Atty. Gen'l—Save Our Everglades*, 636 So. 2d 1336 (Fla. 1994).

Save Our Everglades initiative returned with a package of three separate initiatives that would: 1) impose a fee on sugar for Everglades protection; 2) create a trust fund to receive and expend the funds raised; and 3) impose a standard of liability for polluters in the Everglades.[42] Although all of these initiatives were approved by the Court, the sugar fee amendment was defeated by Florida voters. The Everglades Trust Fund was adopted as Article X, Section 17, but without any constitutional source of funds. In addition, the "Responsibility for Paying Costs of Water Pollution Abatement in the Everglades" initiative was adopted as Article II, Section 7(b). One of the two cases dealing with that amendment arose as an Advisory Opinion to Governor Chiles about the impact of the newly adopted Article II, Section 7(b) on existing Everglades restoration legislation.[43] The *Barley v. South Florida Management* case that follows that Advisory Opinion illustrates the difficulties involved in implementing this amendment to the Florida Constitution.

In 1998, the Constitution Revision Commission proposed Revision 5, which included four bundled provisions. One portion of the proposal created the Fish and Wildlife Conservation Commission in Article IV, Section 9 (in succession to the Game and Fresh Water Fish Commission and the statutory Marine Fisheries Commission). Revision 5 also created Article VII, Section 11(e), which allowed the state to issue bonds to finance acquisition of land for conservation purposes and created Article X, Section 18 to restrict the disposition of state lands that have been designated for conservation purposes. Finally, the 1998 CRC expanded the natural resources clause of Article II, Section 7(a) to include "the conservation and protection of natural resources."[44]

In 2014, an initiative amendment created Article X, Section 28 which requires 33% of funds raised from the excise tax on documents to be placed in the Land Acquisition Trust fund and expended for certain environmental and conservation purposes. The *Oliva v. Florida Wildlife Federation* case which follows again illustrates the challenge in forcing the Legislature and executive agencies to implement a new constitutional provision.

The 2018 Constitution Revision Commission proposed the most recent environmental amendment. Adopted by the voters as Article II, Section 7(c), the new provision bans drilling for oil or natural gas in state waters.[45]

---

42. See *Advisory Opinion to the Atty. Gen'l—Fee on the Everglades Sugar Prod.*, 681 So. 2d 1124 (Fla. 1996).

43. See *Advisory Opinion to the Governor—1996 Amendment 5 (Everglades)*, 706 So. 2d 278 (Fla. 1997).

44. For more on the 1998 CRC's Revision 5, see Henderson, *supra* note 33 at 590–92 (discussing the CRC amendment to the natural resources clause of Article II, Section 7(a)), 596–611 (Land Acquisition Trust Fund and Fish & Wildlife Conservation Commission), 623–24 (state bonding for environmental purposes), 636–37 (disposition of conservation lands).

45. This amendment may be of limited significance due to the definition of state boundaries, including state waters, in Article II, Section 1. This definition is different from other coastal states, and Florida is unique in having one definition for the Atlantic coast and another for the Gulf coast. *See* Fla. Const. art. II, § 1.

i. Article X, Section 11 — Sovereignty Lands

Coastal Petroleum Co. v. American Cyanamid Co.

492 So. 2d 339 (Fla. 1986), *cert. denied sub. nom. Mobil Oil Co. v. Board of Trustees of Internal Improvement Trust Fund*, 479 U.S. 1065 (1987).

SHAW, Justice.

These consolidated cases are before us on petitions to review decisions of the Second District Court of Appeal reported as *Coastal Petroleum Co. v. American Cyanamid Co.*, 454 So.2d 6 (Fla. 2d DCA 1984), and *Board of Trustees of the Internal Improvement Trust Fund v. Mobil Oil Corp.*, 455 So.2d 412 (Fla. 2d DCA 1984), in which the following questions were certified as being of great public importance:

> I. Do the 1883 swamp and overflowed lands deeds issued by the trustees include sovereignty lands below the ordinary high-water mark of navigable rivers?
>
> II. Does the doctrine of legal estoppel or estoppel by deed apply to 1883 swamp and overflowed deeds barring the trustees' assertion of title to sovereignty lands?
>
> III. Does the marketable record title act, chapter 712, Florida Statutes, operate to divest the trustees of title to sovereignty lands below the ordinary high-water mark of navigable rivers?

American Cyanamid Co., 454 So.2d 6, 9–10. We have jurisdiction pursuant to article V, section 3(b)(4), Florida Constitution, and answer all three questions in the negative.

In 1982 and 1983, respondents filed separate quiet title actions in Polk County Circuit Court against petitioners claiming fee simple title to portions of the beds of the Peace and Alafia rivers. In each case, petitioners moved to dismiss the suits to quiet title based on *Mabie v. Garden Street Management Corp.*, 397 So.2d 920 (Fla.1981). The trial court denied the motions. Respondents then moved for summary judgments in their respective cases. The trial court granted said motions.

The Second District Court of Appeal affirmed the summary judgments in separate opinions filed on July 13, 1984. 454 So.2d 6; 455 So.2d 412. In *American Cyanamid*, the district court held that under section 197.228(2), Florida Statutes (1981), this state's unconditional conveyance of land to private individuals without reservation of public rights contemplated a finding that the land is not sovereignty land; that the Trustees were barred from asserting a sovereignty title claim by the doctrine of legal estoppel; and, that Florida's Marketable Record Title Act barred any otherwise valid sovereignty title claim. 454 So.2d at 8, 9. Recognizing, however, the significant impact of its decision on the riverbeds at issue, the district court certified to this Court the aforementioned three questions as being of great public importance. *Id.*

In *Mobil Oil*, the district court held that the Polk County Circuit Court did not err in denying petitioner Trustees' motion in the alternative because the Leon County

Circuit Court lacked jurisdiction over the subject matter of respondent Mobil's reply counterclaim for the reason that the counterclaim is *in rem* in nature and local to Polk County Circuit Court. 455 So.2d at 416. The district court further noted that the substantive issues raised by petitioner Trustees were decided adversely to the Trustees in *American Cyanamid. Id.* By order of September 4, 1984, the district court certified to this Court the same three questions certified in *American Cyanamid.*

The first certified question is premised on the uncontroverted legal proposition that Florida received title to all lands beneath navigable waters, up to the ordinary high water mark, as an incident of sovereignty, when it became a state in 1845. No patents or surveys were required to delineate the boundaries of such sovereignty lands and title vested in the state to be held as a public trust. Thereafter, the federal government did not hold title to such sovereignty lands and had no power to convey them to either the state or other parties. Moreover, any surveys run by the federal government establishing meander lines were not conclusive against the state as the boundary lines between state sovereignty lands and federal uplands. *Borax Consolidated Ltd. v. City of Los Angeles*, 296 U.S. 10 (1935); *Martin v. Busch*, 93 Fla. 535, 112 So. 274 (1927).

In contrast to state sovereignty lands, the title to non-navigable swamp and overflowed lands, and other federal uplands, continued to reside in the federal government after 1845. However, in the 1850s, Congress exercised its power by conveying swamp and overflow uplands to the state. Surveys were conducted and patents issued whereby Florida received approximately twenty million acres of such lands. It is important to recognize that Congress had no intent or power to convey state sovereignty lands through such acts or patents and that land surveys conducted in connection with these conveyances of swamp and overflowed lands are not conclusive against the state as to the meandered boundaries of state sovereignty lands. *See Borax Consolidated, Ltd.*, 296 U.S. at 16, citing to and relying on *Donnelly v. United States*, 228 U.S. 243 (1913); *Mobile Transportation Co. v. City of Mobile*, 187 U.S. 479 (1903); *Shively v. Bowlby*, 152 U.S. 1 (1894); *Goodtitle ex dem. Pollard v. Kibbe*, 50 U.S. (9 How.) 471 (1850); and *Pollard v. Hagan*, 44 U.S. (3 How.) 212 (1845). The title to swamp and overflowed lands which Florida received in the 1850s and thereafter was vested in the Board of Trustees for the Internal Improvement Fund of Florida by the legislature. The title to sovereignty lands at this point remained in the legislature as a public trust. *Illinois Central Railroad v. Illinois*, 146 U.S. 387 (1892); *Broward v. Mabry*, 58 Fla. 298, 50 So. 826 (1909); *State v. Black River Phosphate Co.*, 32 Fla. 82, 13 So. 640 (1893). These lands differ from other state lands. Sovereignty lands are for public use, "not for the purpose of sale or conversion into other values, or reduction into several or individual ownership." *State v. Gerbing*, 56 Fla. 603, 608, 47 So. 353, 355 (1908). Even after title to sovereignty lands was subsequently assigned to the Trustees, their authority to dispose of the land was rigidly circumscribed by court decisions and was separate and distinct from their authority to dispose of swamp and overflowed lands. We answered the first certified question in the negative when we held in *Martin*, 93 Fla. at 573, 112 So. at 286–87 that:

> The State Trustee defendants cannot, by allegation, averment or admission
> in pleadings or otherwise affect the legal status of or the State's title to sov-

ereignty, swamp and overflowed or other lands held by the Trustees under different statutes for distinct and definite State purposes.... The subsequent vesting of title to sovereignty lands in the Trustees for State purposes under the Acts of 1919 or other statutes does not make the title to sovereignty land inure to claimants under a previous conveyance of swamp and overflowed lands by the State Trustees who then had no authority to convey such sovereignty lands and did not attempt or intend to convey sovereignty lands.

Further,

[i]f by mistake or otherwise sales or conveyances are made by the Trustees of the Internal Improvement Fund of sovereignty lands, such as lands under navigable waters in the State or tide lands, or if such Trustees make sales and conveyances of State School lands, as and for swamp and overflowed lands, under the authority given such Trustees to convey swamp and overflowed lands, such sales and conveyances are ineffectual for lack of authority from the state.

Id. at 569, 112 So. at 285 (citations omitted).

The court below relied in part on the provisions of section 197.228(2), Florida Statutes (1981), which provides:

(2) Navigable waters in this state shall not be held to extend to any permanent or transient waters in the form of so-called lakes, ponds, swamps or overflowed lands, lying over and upon areas which have heretofore been conveyed to private individuals by the United States or by the state without reservation of public rights in and to said waters.

We do not agree that this section is pertinent to the issues at hand. We are dealing with navigable rivers not "so-called lakes, ponds, swamps, or overflowed lands." We are not persuaded that the legislature intended by this statute to divest the state of title to navigable waters which were not, or could not be, conveyed to private owners. To accept this position would mean, inter alia, that if a navigable river gradually and imperceptibly changed its course onto previously conveyed lands, the navigable river would become private property and the public would retain the dry river bed. The high and low water marks of navigable waters change over time, but these natural changes do not divest the public of ownership of the navigable waters. *Bonelli Cattle Co. v. Arizona*, 414 U.S. 313 (1973); *Municipal Liquidators, Inc. v. Tench*, 153 So.2d 728 (Fla. 2d DCA), *cert. denied*, 157 So.2d 817 (Fla.1963).

The second certified question pertains to the effect of the Trustees' later acquisition of legal title to sovereignty lands encompassed within previously conveyed swamp and overflowed lands. This question was also addressed and answered in *Martin*, as the quotations above show. Not only is there no legal estoppel to the Trustees' claim of ownership in sovereignty lands, but the Trustees are prohibited by case law from surrendering state title to sovereignty lands based on a prior conveyance of swamp and overflowed lands. Sovereignty lands cannot be conveyed without clear intent and authority, and conveyances, where authorized and intended, must retain public use of the waters. *Martin, Mabry.* The fact that a deed of swamp and overflowed lands does not explicitly exempt sovereignty lands from the conveyance does not show that the Trustees intended to convey sovereignty lands encompassed within the swamp and overflowed lands being conveyed. Further, because grantees of swamp and overflowed lands took with notice that such grants did not convey sovereignty lands, neither they nor their successors have any moral or legal claim to these lands. *Martin*, 93 Fla. at 569–73, 112 So. at 285–87.

The final certified question is whether the Marketable Record Title Act (MRTA), chapter 712, Florida Statutes, operates to divest the state of title to sovereignty lands. Respondents and the courts below rely on *Odom v. Deltona Corp.*, 341 So.2d 977 (Fla.1976), for the proposition that the state's title to navigable water beds previously conveyed as swamp and overflowed lands is extinguished by MRTA. This reliance is misplaced. In *Odom* we rejected the state's argument that the notice of navigability concept applied to the grantees of swamp and overflowed lands under certain trustees' deeds because "it seems absurd to apply this test to small, non-meandered lakes and ponds of less than 140 acres and, in many cases, less than 50 acres in surface." *Id.* at 988. The ground on which *Odom* rests is this factual determination that the small lakes and ponds at issue were non-navigable, non-sovereignty lands. Unfortunately, even though this factual determination controlled and resolved the case, we went on to answer irrelevant arguments put to us by the parties and in answering one such argument concluded that MRTA was applicable to sovereignty lands encompassed within conveyances of swamp and overflowed lands and that the claims of trustees "to beds underlying navigable waters previously conveyed are extinguished by the Act." *Id.* at 989. The statements concerning the effect of MRTA on navigable waterbeds were dicta and are non-binding in the instant case inasmuch as there were no navigable waterbeds at issue in *Odom*....

The issue of whether MRTA is applicable to sovereignty lands is squarely presented here. The issue has two prongs. The first is whether the legislature intended to overturn the well-established law that prior conveyances to private interests did not convey sovereignty lands encompassed within swamp and overflowed lands being conveyed. We must assume that the legislature knew this well-established law when it enacted MRTA. We are persuaded that had the legislature intended to revoke the public trust doctrine by making MRTA applicable to sovereignty lands, it would have, by special reference to sovereignty lands, given some indication that it recognized the epochal nature of such revocation. We see nothing in the act itself or the legislative history presented to us suggesting that the legislature intended to casually dispose of irreplaceable public assets. The legislative purpose of simplifying and facilitating land title transactions does not require that the title to navigable waters be vested in private interests....

In summary, we hold that conveyances of swamp and overflowed lands do not convey sovereignty lands encompassed therein, that such conveyances without exemption of sovereignty lands do not legally estop the state from asserting title to sovereignty lands, and that MRTA, as originally enacted and subsequently amended in 1978, is not applicable to sovereignty lands.

We approve the portion of *Mobil Oil* holding that jurisdiction rested in Polk County and quash the remainder. We quash entirely *Coastal Petroleum v. American Cyanamid.* The cases are remanded for further proceedings consistent with this opinion.

It is so ordered.

ADKINS, OVERTON and EHRLICH, JJ., concur.

BOYD, C.J., dissents with an opinion, in which McDONALD, J., concurs in part and dissents in part with an opinion. [omitted]

BOYD, Chief Justice, dissenting.

Because I find that the circuit court and the district court were correct in their resolution of these quiet-title lawsuits, I must respectfully dissent. I can find no basis for holding that the deeds to the lands in question in these cases, which were duly executed by authorized public officials over one hundred years ago, may now be called into question under the public-trust doctrine or any other theory. I would approve the decisions of the district court of appeal.

The petitioners argue that the lands at issue in these quiet title actions, or some portions of them, lie below the high water marks of and thus constitute parts of the beds of certain rivers and streams that are in fact navigable and are therefore the property of the state by virtue of the public trust doctrine. The petitioners assert that the Trustees of the Internal Improvement Fund did not have authority to alienate lands underlying the waters of inland rivers and streams at the time of the execution of the Trustees' deeds forming the origins of the chains of title under which the various respondents claim ownership of the lands in question.

The essential fact upon which this case turns is that the lands were conveyed into private ownership without reservation of those portions underlying navigable waters. The legal descriptions in the deeds constituting the origins of the chains of title under which the respondents claim encompassed the lands in question. These deeds described the property to be conveyed by reference to the official government survey. These government surveys were made for the purpose of determining the proper classification of public lands in Florida, including a determination of what lands were swamp and overflowed lands and where navigable rivers and other bodies of water were located. The official surveys made in Florida were used by state and federal land officials as the basis for selecting the parcels to be patented to the state by the United States government as swamp and overflowed lands. *South Florida Farms Co. v. Goodno*, 84 Fla. 532, 94 So. 672 (1922). The original United States government surveyors were instructed to locate and meander all navigable rivers and other bodies of water. *Lopez v. Smith*, 145 So.2d 509 (Fla. 2d DCA 1962). The official surveys containing no meandering showing navigable rivers, the federal patents issued pursuant to congressional authorization under the Swamp and Overflowed Lands Act of 1850, the official state requests for such patents, and the Trustees' deeds of the lands in question as swamp and overflowed lands, taken together, constitute official, contemporaneous determinations that the lands in question were swamp and overflowed lands and that any waters lying thereon were not navigable. The Trustees' determination that land is of a character that gives them the authority to sell it is not subject to collateral attack. *Pembroke v. Peninsular Terminal Co.*, 108 Fla. 46, 146 So. 249 (1933).

The cases upon which the petitioners place their principal reliance are *Martin v. Busch*, 93 Fla. 535, 112 So. 274 (1927); *Broward v. Mabry*, 58 Fla. 398, 50 So. 826 (1909); and *State ex rel. Ellis v. Gerbing*, 56 Fla. 603, 47 So. 353 (1908). However, many of the principles of law stated in these cases have been modified or at least qualified by later decisions. Moreover, these cases are factually distinguishable from the present case. At the least it can readily be said that none of these cases supports the proposition that land underlying a navigable river or stream simply cannot, as a matter of law, be conveyed into private ownership. To the contrary, the cited cases recognize that such lands, notwithstanding the fact that the state may have obtained title by virtue of its sovereignty, may be conveyed when the authority and intention to do so are clear. As has already been shown, there was authority and intent to convey the lands in question.

Numerous cases recognize that the state may convey the title to submerged sovereignty lands into private ownership, so long as the public trust safeguarding the rights of the public to the use and benefit of the waters is not violated. *See, e.g.,* *Gies v. Fischer*, 146 So.2d 361 (Fla.1962); *Holland v. Fort Pierce Financing & Construction Co.*, 157 Fla. 649, 27 So.2d 76 (1946); *Pembroke v. Peninsular Terminal Co.*, 108 Fla. 46, 146 So. 249 (1933); *Tampa N.R.R. v. City of Tampa*, 104 Fla. 481, 140 So. 311 (1932); *State ex rel. Buford v. City of Tampa*, 88 Fla. 196, 102 So. 336 (1924). The right of the public to the use of the water is the inalienable portion of sovereign ownership under the public trust doctrine. Florida law has long recognized that it is not necessary for the state to retain absolute ownership of the bed of a river in order to retain the control of the use of the surface waters for the benefit of the public.

The petitioners argue that the trial court should have allowed them to present evidence that the lands in question are under waters that were in fact navigable at the time of the original deeds from the state. Such evidence, they argue, would overcome the presumption of non-navigability arising from the lack of meandering in the survey. The fact of navigability at that time, they argue, would establish that the trustees had no authority to deed the river beds and would establish the sovereignty land reservation which they say exists as a matter of law. However, summary judgment without receiving such evidence was proper.

The title to land should rest upon a grant, not upon an evidentiary fact. *Pembroke v. Peninsular Terminal Co.* As I have stated above, the Trustees in making the deeds from which the respondents' titles derive made official determinations of the character of the lands and those determinations are not now subject to question. The petitioners have cited the noted treatise by Dean Maloney and others[46] for the proposition that the early official surveyors encountered difficulties which may account for the lack of meandering of rivers later known to be navigable in fact. Actually, the cited work

---

46. [FN 2.] F. Maloney, S. Plager, and F. Baldwin, *Water Law and Administration: The Florida Experience* (1968).

offered this historical observation as a possible explanation for the fact that so many of Florida's inland lakes were not shown on the surveys. It is highly unlikely that the surveyors would have allowed the problems of swampy shorelines, snakes, and other hazards to deter them from noting the presence of an obviously navigable river. Thus it is appropriate to apply the concept stated in *Odom v. Deltona Corp.*, 341 So.2d 977, 988 (Fla.1977), that we should presume that the official surveyors did their work correctly, conscientiously, and as instructed.

The majority accepts the petitioners' argument that the trial court's judgment quieting title to the lands in question in the respondents violates the public trust doctrine by divesting the public of its common-law rights to the use and benefit of navigable waters. However, there is no such divestment of the public rights of use and benefit of the waters.

Contrary to the assertions of the petitioners and as discussed above with citations of authority, a determination that the bed of a river or stream is in private ownership does not divest the public of its rights in the use and benefit of the water for purposes such as transport, fishing, floating, and swimming if the river or stream is in fact useful for such purposes. When a riparian owner holds title to the land between high-water mark and the thread of the stream (or owns both banks and the bed from high-water mark to high-water mark), such title is held subject to a servitude in favor of the public to pass over the water in boats if such use of the water is possible. Moreover, this public right does not depend on the river being in fact navigable in the sense of being useful for navigation for commercial purposes. Thus, to the extent that the original Trustees' deeds are taken as a determination that the rivers were not navigable, any such determination has no effect on public rights in the waters today if the waters are now in fact useful for navigational purposes. The Trustees deeded away only the proprietary interest in the submerged land. The right to the use of the overlying waters was inalienable under the public trust doctrine. Even if a river or stream is not navigable in the commercial sense but is used or useful for lesser degrees of navigation by small vessels, such as boats, canoes, and rafts, commonly employed in the recreational uses of rivers and streams, then the public retains the right to the use of the waters for such purposes. *See, e.g., Elder v. Delcour*, 364 Mo. 835, 269 S.W.2d 17 (1954).

Even were I to agree that the Trustees needed and lacked specific legislative authority to execute the deeds in question on the ground that the properties were sovereignty lands rather than swamp and overflowed lands, I believe that the doctrine of estoppel would support the lower courts' declaration of respondents' ownership. Florida law recognizes that where a grantor conveys land by mistake, he is estopped to later deny that he intended the conveyance as expressed in the deed.... Moreover, a deed will be held valid if the grantor, lacking authority to make the deed at the time, later acquires title or acquires the authority to alienate the property. That situation also obtains here.

The circumstances of these cases show that the doctrine of estoppel is properly applied here; these are classic cases for application of the doctrine of estoppel. The deeds were executed in 1883. At various times following that date, the respondents or their predecessors in title engaged in acts evincing the intent to exercise dominion and control over the lands in question. Some of the respondents or their predecessors in title have engaged in mining operations on the lands in question. If the Trustees disputed the respondents' title, they should have taken action to enjoin such operations and to evict the respondents long before this. The law should not come to the aid of one who is not diligent in asserting his own rights.

The respondents' "sovereignty-lands" argument fails for another reason. In 1819, the territorial legislature of Florida adopted a statute declaring the common law of England to be of force in Florida. The statute, in modified form but unchanged as to substance, is still in effect and is now codified as section 2.01, Florida Statutes (1985), and provides as follows:

> The common and statute laws of England which are of a general and not a local nature, with the exception hereinafter mentioned, down to the 4th day of July, 1776, are declared to be of force in this state; provided, the said statutes and common law be not inconsistent with the Constitution and laws of the United States and the acts of the Legislature of this state.

Thus English common-law rules concerning land ownership and land transfers, as they developed up until July 4, 1776, were, have been, and continue to be the law in Florida unless and until modified by statute or court decision.

Even if we accept, as the majority does, the proposition that title to lands underlying navigable rivers was vested in the state upon admission into the Union, this does not compel acceptance of the further proposition that such lands were then inalienable under the public trust doctrine. From medieval times right on through the eighteenth century, the common law of England recognized land grants and land deeds vesting title to land underlying non-tidal but navigable rivers in private riparian owners. *See Hardin v. Jordan*, 140 U.S. 371 (1891). Therefore, at the time of Florida's admission into the Union, there was no impediment to the execution of deeds of such lands into private ownership. The fact that in other American jurisdictions, courts modified the English common law by imposing a public trust on the state's ownership of such lands, *see, e.g., Illinois Central R.R. v. Illinois*, 146 U.S. 387 (1892), could not have affected the land law of Florida, which still followed the English common-law rules. The earliest Florida court decision the majority is able to cite in support of the existence of the public trust doctrine is *State v. Black River Phosphate Co.*, 32 Fla. 82, 13 So. 640 (1893), which was not decided until *after* the execution of the deeds in question in these cases.

In addition to the common-law rule allowing for grants of river bottom land to riparian owners, notice should also be taken of the effect of chapter 791, Laws of Florida (1856), in which the state expressly divested itself of and granted to riparian landowners "all right title and interest to all lands covered by water, lying in front of any tract or land ... lying upon any navigable stream ... as far as the edge of the channel, and hereby vest the full title to the same in and unto the riparian proprietors." Sixty-five years later, the legislature amended the statute to provide that the title would not vest unless and until such a riparian owner had filled in or permanently improved such submerged land. Ch. 8536, Laws of Fla. (1921). But in the meantime, many riparian proprietors, in reliance on the 1856 legislation, had exercised dominion and control over various lands underlying navigable waters, for purposes other than the building of wharves and so forth, as envisioned when the 1856 legislation was passed. Decisions of this Court construing the 1856 act recognized that the state could grant the proprietary interest in the submerged lands without violating the public trust for protection of public rights in the use of the waters. *See, e.g., Alden v. Pinney*, 12 Fla. 348 (1869); *Geiger v. Filor*, 8 Fla. 325 (1859).

The decisions of The Florida Supreme Court from 1856 up until 1893 demonstrate that Florida followed the English common-law rules that land under navigable tide waters was titled in the sovereign, but could be alienated subject to public rights of navigation and fishing; and that the title to land underlying navigable inland rivers could be held in private hands subject to similar public rights. *See State v. Black River Phosphate Co.*, 27 Fla. 276, 9 So. 205 (1891); *Bucki v. Cone*, 25 Fla. 1, 6 So. 160 (1889); *Sullivan v. Moreno*, 19 Fla. 200 (1882); *Rivas v. Solary*, 18 Fla. 122 (1881).

As the foregoing discussion of legal authorities shows, the suggestion that the state must hold title to all lands underlying navigable rivers and streams in order to protect the rights of the public to the use and enjoyment of the waters is based on a misconception. As in many other areas of property law, the law recognizes various degrees of legal rights and interests in the same property and does not demand that one person hold the entire "bundle of sticks." The sovereign trust in favor of the public to use navigable waters for fishing, navigation, and recreation can be preserved inviolate even though the beds of such rivers and streams be titled in private owners.

Some of the petitioners and *amici curiae* in these cases, as well as observers in the communications media and among the public generally, have inaccurately suggested that the state must have title in order to protect wetlands from environmental damage. However, the legal proposition that parts of the lands underlying rivers or streams are in private ownership has nothing whatsoever to do with the plenary power of the legislature to regulate the use of such property for the purpose of protecting the natural environment. The scope of that regulatory authority is very broad and fully adequate to the purpose of protecting Florida's environment against harmful activities. *See, e.g., Atlantic International Investment Corp. v. State*, 478 So.2d 805 (Fla.1985); *Graham v. Estuary Properties, Inc.*, 399 So.2d 1374 (Fla.1981), *cert. denied*, 454 U.S. 1083 (1982).

… Much has been written and spoken, in the communications media and elsewhere, concerning the legal issues in this case and the related political issues. Many have suggested that the courts are being asked to give away state-owned lands. The truth is that the lands in question here, as well as other lands, were legally conveyed by authorized state officials. It may very well be the case that in doing so, public officials failed to exercise care and diligence on behalf of the public. But the fact that decisions of former officials were unwise is no reason to now penalize innocent purchasers who paid market value and relied upon state officers' authority to sell. I can see no constitutionally permissible basis for the state to recover such lands except by purchase or by eminent domain based on a public purpose and the payment of just compensation.

There has also been much public discussion of the effect of the Marketable Record Title Act. I agree with the district court's holding that MRTA applies with the same force to land claims of the state as to those of private claimants. The law was intended to apply and should apply to all real estate claims without an exception for those of the state. Under MRTA, the claims of the state in these cases are asserted too late and cannot be revived. If private claimants were to seek to call into question the deeds of an ancestor given over one hundred years ago, based on mistakes, reservations or infirmities not preserved by re-recording under the statute, such claims would be barred under MRTA. The same rule should apply against the state because of the overriding interest in the stability and marketability of land titles.

Constitutional protection of private property rights is an essential feature of our form of government and our society. Whenever the awesome power of government is used to extract from people their lives, liberties, or property, their only refuge is in the courts. The circuit court orders in these cases correctly preserved the vested rights of real property owners against attempted state confiscation. The district court was in my view correct in affirming those circuit court judgments. I would approve the district court decisions. I therefore respectfully dissent.

Commentary and Questions

In *Coastal Petroleum*, the Supreme Court affirmed the importance of the public trust doctrine. The Court recognized limits on when sovereignty lands can be conveyed.

   1. a. What are "sovereignty lands"?

      b. How do "swamp and overflowed lands" differ from sovereignty lands?

      c. Who holds title to sovereignty and swamp lands, and who controls the lands?

   2. Can sovereignty lands be conveyed (as opposed to swamp lands)? If so, by whom?

   3. According to the majority, what happens when conveyances of swamp lands later implicate sovereignty lands?

   4. Why did Justice Boyd dissent in this case?

Walton County v. Stop Beach Renourishment, Inc.

998 So. 2d 1102 (Fla. 2008), *aff'd*, 560 U.S. 702 (2010)

[In *Walton County v. Stop Beach Renourishment, Inc.*, the Supreme Court upheld Florida's Beach Renourishment Act against challenges by littoral landowners. The Court elaborated on the extent of the sovereignty lands on the coast and the impact of the Public Trust Doctrine on these lands:]

A. The Relationship at Common Law between the Public and Upland Owners

Since the vast development of Florida's beaches, there has been a relative paucity of opinions from this Court that describe the nature of the relationship at common law between the public and upland owners in regard to Florida's beaches. It is important that we outline this relationship prior to resolving the specific issues in this case.

(1) The Public and Florida's Beaches

Under both the Florida Constitution and the common law, the State holds the lands seaward of the MHWL, including the beaches between the mean high and low water lines, in trust for the public for the purposes of bathing, fishing, and navigation. *See* art. X, §11, Fla. Const. ("The title to lands under navigable waters, within the boundaries of the state, which have not been alienated, including beaches below mean high water lines, is held by the state, by virtue of its sovereignty, in trust for all the people."); *White v. Hughes*, 139 Fla. 54, 190 So. 446, 449 (1939) ("The State holds the fore-shore in trust for its people for the purposes of navigation, fishing and bathing."); *see also Clement v. Watson*, 63 Fla. 109, 58 So. 25, 26 (1912).

As we explained in *Brickell v. Trammell*, 77 Fla. 544, 82 So. 221 (1919), this public trust doctrine has its origins in English common law:

Under the common law of England the crown in its sovereign capacity held the title to the beds of navigable or tide waters, including the shore or the space between high and low water marks, in trust for the people of the realm who had rights of navigation, commerce, fishing, bathing, and other easements allowed by law in the waters. This rule of the common law was applicable in the English colonies of America.

After the Revolution resulting in the independence of the American states, title to the beds of all waters, navigable in fact, whether tide or fresh, was held by the states in which they were located, in trust for all the people of the states respectively.

When the Constitution of the United States became operative, the several states continued to hold the title to the beds of all waters within their respective borders that were navigable in fact without reference to the tides of the sea, not for purposes of disposition to individual ownerships, but such title was held in trust for all the people of the state respectively, for the uses afforded by the waters as allowed by the express or implied provisions of law, subject to the rights surrendered by the states under the federal Constitution.

The rights of the people of the states in the navigable waters and the lands thereunder, including the shore or space between ordinary high and low waters marks, relate to navigation, commerce, fishing, bathing, and other easements allowed by law. These rights are designed to promote the general welfare and are subject to lawful regulation by the states, and such regulation is subordinate to the powers of Congress as to interstate commerce, navigation, post roads, etc., and to the constitutional guaranties of private property rights.

The trust in which the title to the lands under navigable waters is held is governmental in its nature and cannot be wholly alienated by the states. For the purpose of enhancing the rights and interests of the whole people, the states may by appropriate means grant to individuals limited privileges in the lands under navigable waters, but not so as to divert them or the waters thereon from their proper uses for the public welfare, or so as to relieve the states respectively of the control and regulation of the uses afforded by the land and the waters, or so as to interfere with the lawful authority of Congress. *See* 62 Fla. 549, 57 So. 428; *Clement v. Watson*, 63 Fla. 109, 58 So. 25.

New states, including Florida, admitted "into the Union on equal footing with the original states, in all respects whatsoever," have the same rights, prerogatives, and duties with respect to the navigable waters and the lands thereunder within their borders as have the original 13 states of the American Union. Among these prerogatives are the right and duty of the states to own and hold the lands under navigable waters for the benefit of the people....

Id. at 226 (parallel citations omitted); *see also Hayes v. Bowman*, 91 So.2d 795, 799 (Fla.1957); *State v. Gerbing*, 56 Fla. 603, 47 So. 353, 355–56 (1908).

In addition to its duties under the public trust doctrine, the State has an obligation to conserve and protect Florida's beaches as important natural resources. As article II, section 7(a) of the Florida Constitution states,

[i]t shall be the policy of the state to conserve and protect its natural resources and scenic beauty. Adequate provision shall be made by law for the abatement of air and water pollution and of excessive and unnecessary noise and for the conservation and protection of natural resources.

Concisely put, the State has a constitutional duty to protect Florida's beaches, part of which it holds "in trust for all the people." Art. X, § 11, Fla. Const.

[The Court went on to consider the dynamic nature of these boundaries in the context of accretion or avulsion caused by a hurricane:]

(3) Dealing with a Dynamic Boundary

The boundary between public or sovereignty lands and private uplands is a dynamic boundary, which is located on a shoreline that, by its very nature, frequently changes. Florida's common law attempts to bring order and certainty to this dynamic boundary in a manner that reasonably balances the affected parties' interests.

Before detailing the common law rules that are intended to balance public and private interests in the changing shoreline, it is helpful to review several common law definitions. "Erosion" is the gradual and imperceptible wearing away of land from the shore or bank. *See generally Black's Law Dictionary* (8th ed.2004). And, as we have explained,

"[a]ccretion" means the gradual and imperceptible accumulation of land along the shore or bank of a body of water. "Reliction" or "dereliction" is an increase of the land by a gradual and imperceptible withdrawal of any body of water. "Avulsion" is the sudden or perceptible loss of or addition to land by the action of the water or a sudden change in the bed of a lake or the course of a stream. "Gradual and imperceptible" means that, although witnesses may periodically perceive changes in the waterfront, they could not observe them occurring. *See generally* Black's Law Dictionary (5th ed.1979);

F. Maloney, S. Plager & F. Baldwin, *Water Law and Administration — The Florida Experience* 385–92 (1968); 65 C.J.S. *Navigable Waters* §§ 81, 86, 93 (1966).

[*Bd. of Trs. of the Internal Improvement Trust Fund v. Sand Key Assocs., Ltd.*], 512 So.2d at 936 [(Fla. 1987)]. Moreover, "alluvion" describes the actual deposit of land that is added to the shore or bank. *See* Mark S. Dennison, *Proof of Accretion or Avulsion in Title Boundary Disputes Over Additions to Riparian Land*, 73 Am.Jur. Proof of Facts 3d 167, § 2, at 180 (2003).

The boundary between public lands and private uplands is the MHWL, which represents an average over a nineteen-year period. *Kruse v. Grokap, Inc.*, 349 So.2d 788, 789–90 (Fla. 2d DCA 1977) (citing *Borax Consolidated, Ltd. v. City of Los Angeles*, 296 U.S. 10 (1935). This nineteen-year period for determining the MHWL is codified in section 177.27, Florida Statutes (2007), a provision of the Florida Coastal Mapping Act of 1974. *See id.* at 790 n. 8 (citing § 177.27(15), Fla. Stat. (1975)).

Under Florida common law, the legal effect of changes to the shoreline on the boundary between public lands and uplands varies depending upon whether the shoreline changes gradually and imperceptibly or whether it changes suddenly and perceptibly. [As the current law summarizes:]

> [t]he principal significance of the distinction between erosion[, reliction,] and accretion on the one hand, and avulsion on the other, is that the owner of the [upland] loses title to land that is lost by erosion and ordinarily becomes the owner of land that is added to his land by accretion [or reliction], whereas if an avulsion has occurred, the boundary line remains the same regardless of the change in the ... shoreline.

73 Am.Jur. Proof of Facts 3d 167, § 3, at 182; *see also* 1 *Water and Water Rights* § 6.03(b)(2), at 189 (Robert E. Beck ed., 1991); 78 Am.Jur.2d *Waters* § 315 (2002).

Accordingly, under the doctrines of erosion, reliction, and accretion, the boundary between public and private land is altered to reflect gradual and imperceptible losses or additions to the shoreline. *See, e.g., Sand Key*, 512 So.2d 934. In contrast, under the doctrine of avulsion, the boundary between public and private land remains the MHWL as it existed before the avulsive event led to sudden and perceptible losses or additions to the shoreline. *See, e.g., Bryant v. Peppe*, 238 So.2d 836, 838 (Fla.1970).

These common law doctrines reflect an attempt to balance the interests of the parties affected by inevitable changes in the shoreline. For instance, as the Second District explained in *Board of Trustees of the Internal Improvement Trust Fund v. Medeira Beach Nominee, Inc.*, 272 So.2d 209, 212–13 (Fla. 2d DCA 1973), "[t]here are four reasons for the doctrine of accretion:"

> (1) *[D]e minimis non curat lex;* (2) he who sustains the burden of losses and of repairs imposed by the contiguity of waters ought to receive whatever benefits they may bring by accretion; (3) it is in the interest of the community that all land have an owner and, for convenience, the riparian is the chosen one; (4) the necessity for preserving the riparian right of access to the water. *See St.*

Clair County v. Lovingston, 90 U.S. (23 Wall.) 46, 67 (1874); Maloney, Plager and Baldwin, *Water Law and Administration: The Florida Experience*, 386 (1968).

Id. 212–13 (parallel citations omitted). These same reasons explain the doctrine of reliction. And, as for the rationale underlying the doctrine of avulsion, it has been argued that there is a need to mitigate the hardship of drastic shifts in title that would result if the doctrines of accretion, erosion, and reliction were applied to sudden and unexpected changes in the shoreline.

While our common law has developed these specific rules that are intended to balance the interests in our ever-changing shoreline, Florida's common law has never fully addressed how public-sponsored beach restoration affects the interests of the public and the interests of the upland owners. We now turn to the legislative attempt to deal with this subject.

B. The Beach and Shore Preservation Act's Balancing of Public and Private Interests

As explained earlier, the State has a constitutional duty to protect Florida's beaches, part of which it holds in trust for public use. The Beach and Shore Preservation Act effectuates this constitutional duty when the State is faced with critically eroded, storm-damaged beaches.

Like the common law, the Act seeks a careful balance between the interests of the public and the interests of the private upland owners. By authorizing the addition of sand to sovereignty lands, the Act prevents further loss of public beaches, protects existing structures, and repairs prior damage. In doing so, the Act promotes the public's economic, ecological, recreational, and aesthetic interests in the shoreline. On the other hand, the Act benefits private upland owners by restoring beach already lost and by protecting their property from future storm damage and erosion. Moreover, the Act expressly preserves the upland owners' rights to access, use, and view, including the rights of ingress and egress. *See* § 161.201. The Act also protects the upland owners' rights to boating, bathing, and fishing. *See id.* Furthermore, the Act protects the upland owners' view by prohibiting the State from erecting structures on the new beach except those necessary to prevent erosion. *See id.* Thus, although the Act provides that the State may retain title to the newly created dry land directly adjacent to the water, upland owners may continue to access, use, and view the beach and water as they did prior to beach restoration. As a result, at least facially, there is no material or substantial impairment of these littoral rights under the Act. *See Duval*, 77 So.2d at 434 (finding no taking when there was no material or substantial impairment of littoral rights to access and view).

Finally, the Act provides for the cancellation of the ECL if (1) the beach restoration is not commenced within two years; (2) restoration is halted in excess of a six-month period; or (3) the authorities do not maintain the restored beach. *See* § 161.211. Therefore, in the event the beach restoration is not completed and maintained, the rights of the respective parties revert to the status quo ante.

To summarize, the Act effectuates the State's constitutional duty to protect Florida's beaches in a way that reasonably balances public and private interests. Without the beach renourishment provided for under the Act, the public would lose vital economic and natural resources. As for the upland owners, the beach renourishment protects their property from future storm damage and erosion while preserving their littoral rights to access, use, and view. Consequently, just as with the common law, the Act facially achieves a reasonable balance of interests and rights to uniquely valuable and volatile property interests.

* * *

III. CONCLUSION

In light of the above, we find that the Act, on its face, does not unconstitutionally deprive upland owners of littoral rights without just compensation. Consequently, we answer the rephrased certified question in the negative and quash the decision of the First District. And we again emphasize that our decision in this case is strictly limited to the context of restoring critically eroded beaches under the Beach and Shore Preservation Act.

It is so ordered.

QUINCE, C.J., ANSTEAD and PARIENTE, JJ., and CANTERO, Senior Justice, concur.

WELLS [omitted] and LEWIS, JJ., dissent with opinions [omitted].

ii. Article X, Section 16— Limited Marine Net Fishing

Lane v. Chiles

698 So. 2d 260 (Fla. 1997)

PER CURIAM.

We have for review a final summary judgment of the Circuit Court in Leon County, upholding the constitutionality of article X, section 16, of the Florida Constitution, limiting marine net fishing. The First District Court of Appeal certified the trial court order to be of great public importance, requiring immediate resolution by this Court. We have jurisdiction. Art. V, Sec. 3(b)(5), Fla. Const. We affirm.

In November 1994, article X, section 16, known as the "net ban" amendment, was adopted through an initiative petition. Eight months after the amendment was passed, but immediately prior to its effective date, Cecil Lane and four other individuals engaged in the business of commercial net fishing brought an action in circuit court challenging its validity on both procedural and substantive grounds. On cross motions for summary judgment, the trial court applied the rational basis test in analyzing Lane's claims, finding there were no fundamental rights or suspect classes involved. The trial court found that the amendment does not violate Lane's rights under the due process, equal protection, or impairment of contract clauses of the Florida or Federal Constitutions; that there is no legal restraint on the subject matter of a constitutional amendment in Florida except for the single-subject rule; that the time had passed for Lane to challenge the sufficiency of the ballot summary; and that the ballot summary meets the requirements of Florida law.

Lane argues that the trial court erred in applying the rational basis test rather than the strict scrutiny standard to review the amendment's validity. We disagree.... In most cases the rational basis standard is used to test the constitutional validity of a state statute. *Lite v. State*, 617 So.2d 1058, 1059–60 (Fla.1993). It follows logically that the same test would be used to determine the validity of a constitutional amendment adopted through the initiative process. In exceptional cases, where actions by the state abridge some fundamental right or adversely affect a suspect class, the strict scrutiny standard should be applied. *Lite*, 617 So.2d at 1060 n. 2. Because fishing is not a fundamental right, and commercial fishermen do not constitute a suspect class, the rational basis test rather than the strict scrutiny standard applies in the instant case. Thus, article X, section 16, must be upheld if it bears a reasonable relationship to a permissible governmental objective, and is not discriminatory, arbitrary, or oppressive. *See* 617 So.2d at 1059–60.

Lane also claims that the amendment constitutes special interest legislation and is improper subject matter for inclusion in the Florida Constitution. We disagree. This Court has stated that

> the people can by initiative amend any "portion or portions" of the Constitution *in any way that they see fit,* provided that the amendment brought to vote by an initiative petition confines itself to a single subject matter.

Smathers v. Smith, 338 So.2d 825, 827 (Fla.1976) (emphasis added). There is no limitation on matters which can be the subject of a constitutional amendment in Florida; thus, Lane's claim is without merit.

Lane next argues that the amendment is unconstitutional because it deprives him of his right to due process of law. He claims that he and other fishermen have been deprived of a fundamental liberty interest [right to engage in a lawful occupation] and property interest [right to possess and enjoy private property, i.e. fishing nets] and that his personal property has been taken without just compensation [i.e. fishing nets]. We find no merit to these claims. To comply with the constitutional guarantee of due process under the rational basis standard, the amendment must bear a reasonable relationship to a permissible governmental objective. *See Lite*, 617 So.2d at 1059. We hold that the net ban amendment seeks to protect the state's natural resources which is a valid state objective, and the amendment's limitation on the types and sizes of nets that can be used to fish in Florida waters is rationally related to that goal and does not constitute a taking.

As to Lane's assertion that he has been deprived of his right to due process in a liberty or property interest, we disagree and approve of the trial court's analysis and conclusion:

> [A] state regulation violates a protected liberty interest if it completely interferes with the right to engage in a lawful occupation. *Fraternal Order of Police*

v. Department of State, 392 So.2d 1296 (Fla.1980). However, that is not the case with respect to Article X Section 16. The amendment satisfies the rational basis test in that it serves to accomplish a legitimate governmental objective. The amendment is designed to conserve marine resources and it attempts to meet that objective by a reasonable regulation on commercial fishing. While citizens of differing views could argue the wisdom of the amendment, it would be hard to say that the amendment is without any rational basis.

Moreover, the amendment does not completely prevent the plaintiffs from engaging in their chosen occupation. Commercial fishermen can still fish with nets beyond the territorial limits set by the amendment and they can still fish with nets of a smaller size within the territorial limits. Article X, Section 16 is widely known as the "net ban amendment" but despite this reference the amendment does not actually ban all net fishing. It is more accurate to say the amendment restricts certain methods of net fishing.

... Article X, Section 16 is a valid exercise of the police power and it operates uniformly to prohibit all persons from using certain kinds of fishing equipment in certain areas of the State waters. It does not set arbitrary restrictions that apply only to some persons or classes of persons and not others.

Furthermore, the amendment does not prohibit all possible uses for the property and equipment in question. State statutes that limit fishing seasons, restrict permitted gear, and define certain zones for particular activities have been upheld. *See State v. Perkins*, 436 So.2d 150 (Fla. 2d DCA 1983). The State clearly has an interest in preserving and protecting the resources of the State, which are commonly owned by the people, and restrictions on the harvest of marine fish does not constitute a taking of property from particular individuals.

We also reject Lane's contention that the amendment is unconstitutional on equal protection grounds. Lane argues that the amendment unequally burdens him and the other fishermen by making an irrational distinction between commercial fishermen and sport fishermen. We again agree with the trial court's analysis and conclusion:

The amendment does not seek to punish anyone nor does it seek to single out particular kinds of fishermen. Rather, the restriction established by the amendment relates only to particular kinds of fishing equipment.

Likewise, the distinction between the east coast of Florida and west coast does not render the law unconstitutional. This distinction can be explained by the difference in the extent of sovereign waters on the differing coasts. Therefore, the court concludes that Article X, Section 16 does not violate the plaintiff's rights to equal protection under the laws.

Finally, Lane challenges article X, section 16, on the grounds that the ballot summary did not properly inform the citizens of the effect of the amendment....

We find this claim to be untimely and without merit. In addition to the fact that this Court specifically approved the ballot summary,[47] the general rule is that a challenge to the form of a proposed amendment must be made before the amendment is adopted. *Sylvester v. Tindall*, 154 Fla. 663, 18 So.2d 892 (1944). Lane filed this challenge on June 20, 1995, eight months after the amendment was adopted by a vote of the people and less than two weeks before the amendment was to be effective on July 1, 1995.

Accordingly, we affirm the judgment of the trial court and hold that article X, section 16, is constitutional.

It is so ordered.

OVERTON, SHAW, GRIMES, HARDING and ANSTEAD, JJ., concur.

WELLS, J., concurs in result only.

Questions

1. Are there any subject areas that may not be addressed by the Florida Constitution?

2. What standard of review does a court use when dealing with a challenge to a newly adopted constitutional amendment?

iii. Article II, Section 7 — Natural Resources and Scenic Beauty

Advisory Opinion to the Governor — 1996 Amendment 5 (Everglades)

706 So. 2d 278 (Fla. 1997)

The Honorable Lawton Chiles
Governor, State of Florida
The Capitol
Tallahassee, Florida 32301

Dear Governor Chiles:

We acknowledge receipt of your communication of March 6, 1997, requesting our advice pursuant to section 1(c), article IV of the Florida Constitution. Omitting the formal parts, your letter reads as follows:

Pursuant to Article IV, Section 1(c) of the Constitution of the State of Florida, your opinion is requested as to the interpretation of my executive

---

47. [FN 7.] *Advisory Opinion to the Attorney General—Limited Marine Net Fishing*, 620 So.2d 997, 999 (Fla.1993).

duties and responsibilities as chief executive under Article IV, Section 1(a), Article III, s.19(h), and Article II, Section 7(b), of the Constitution of the State of Florida.

... As background, it should be noted that the "Everglades Forever Act" was enacted after many years of litigation involving the United States of America, the State of Florida, the South Florida Water Management District, the Department of Environmental Protection, and certain large agricultural interests to determine how and at whose expense pollution of the Everglades should be abated. s. 373.4592, Fla. Stat.

The Everglades Forever Act established two funding sources for pollution abatement in the Everglades Agricultural Area (EAA); that is, the Everglades agricultural privilege tax, and the levy of a 0.1 mill ad valorem tax on property within the Okeechobee Basin. Ss. 373.4592(6) and (4)(a). Therefore, the law in effect at the time of the adoption of Amendment 5 was designed to divide the burden of the costs of pollution abatement on the public by the 0.1 mill tax and the agricultural users by the privilege tax of $24.89 per acre.

I.

Prior to the time that the debate on these issues rose to the current pitch, the Attorney General opined that Amendment 5 was self-executing. Op. Att'y Gen. Fla. 96-92 (1996). Other government entities have suggested an opinion that the amendment is not self-executing; that too many policy determinations remain unanswered. These entities question any agency's ability to determine rights and responsibilities, the purposes intended to be accomplished, and the means by which the purposes may be accomplished.

Due to the uncertainty created by the unclear language of Amendment 5, the South Florida Water Management District and the Department of Environmental Protection, the governmental entities charged with enforcing the Everglades pollution abatement initiatives, are unable to move forward to enforce this amendment without a clear interpretation as to its meaning and effect. As Governor, I am responsible for providing these executive agencies with direction as to their enforcement responsibilities, to see that the law is faithfully executed, and to report on the state's progress in restoring the Everglades System.

II.

Several divergent interpretations have been suggested by interested parties as to the meaning of "primarily responsible." Some government agencies believe that "primarily responsible" could mean something in excess of fifty percent. Therefore, polluters within the EAA are chiefly, but not totally, responsible for the costs of abatement. They also believe that whether these costs are to be apportioned according to the amount of pollution contributed, and whether and to what extent other entities not described in Amendment

5 are responsible for pollution abatement costs, is not clear from the text of Amendment 5 and is subject to clarification.

Proponents of Amendment 5 have opined that the amendment imposes the entire cost of abatement on polluters within the EAA. Only upon failure of the primarily responsible parties to satisfy the costs of abatement would a secondarily responsible party (the public) be called upon to satisfy the obligation.

As the state's chief administrative officer responsible for planning and budgeting, I am in doubt as to my duties in seeing that Amendment 5 is being faithfully executed.

CONCLUSION

The consequences of these determinations are substantial and of immense importance to the well-being of the state and of the future of the Florida Everglades. Years of litigation have transpired, which has delayed implementation of the necessary steps to clean up this international treasure. The lack of clarity in Amendment 5 promises to engender further litigation absent an expeditious resolution of the questions I am posing.

For the foregoing reasons, I respectfully request the opinion of the Justices of the Supreme Court on the following questions affecting my executive duties and responsibilities:

> 1. Is the 1996 Amendment 5 to the Florida Constitution self-executing, not requiring any legislative action considering the existing Everglades Forever Act? Or is the Legislature required to enact implementing legislation in order to determine how to carry out its intended purposes and defining any rights intended to be determined, enjoyed, or protected?

> 2. What does the term "primarily responsible" as used in 1996 Amendment 5 to the Florida Constitution, mean? Does it mean responsible for more than half of the costs of abatement, or responsible for a substantial part of the costs of abatement, or responsible for the entire costs of the abatement, or does it mean something different not suggested here?

In accordance with our rules, we made a preliminary determination that your request is properly within the purview of article IV, section 1(c), in that Amendment 5 directly affects your duty as governor to see that the law is faithfully executed (by providing the South Florida Water Management District and the Department of Environmental Protection with direction as to their enforcement responsibilities) and to report on the state's progress in restoring the Everglades System. To ensure full and fair consideration of the issues raised, we permitted interested persons to file briefs and to present oral argument before the Court.

The 1996 Amendment 5, also known as "polluter pays," amended article II, section 7 of the Florida Constitution by adding section 7(b), and as amended, section 7 provides:

SECTION 7. Natural resources and scenic beauty.—

(a) It shall be the policy of the state to conserve and protect its natural resources and scenic beauty. Adequate provision shall be made by law for the abatement of air and water pollution and of excessive and unnecessary noise.

(b) Those in the Everglades Agricultural Area [EAA] who cause water pollution within the Everglades Protection Area [EPA] or the Everglades Agricultural Area shall be primarily responsible for paying the costs of the abatement of that pollution. For purposes of this subsection, the terms "Everglades Protection Area" and "Everglades Agricultural Area" shall have the meanings as defined in statutes in effect on January 1, 1996.

As to your first question, that is, whether Amendment 5 is self-executing, we are guided by the test set forth in *Gray v. Bryant*, 125 So.2d 846 (Fla.1960), which states that

whether a constitutional provision should be construed to be self-executing, or not self-executing, is whether or not the provision lays down a sufficient rule by means of which the right or purpose which it gives or is intended to accomplish may be determined, enjoyed, or protected without the aid of legislative enactment.

Id. at 851. Applying the aforementioned test, we conclude that Amendment 5 is not self-executing and cannot be implemented without the aid of legislative enactment because it fails to lay down a sufficient rule for accomplishing its purpose. As you suggest in your letter, "too many policy determinations remain unanswered ... [such as the various] rights and responsibilities, the purposes intended to be accomplished, and the means by which the purposes may be accomplished." Amendment 5 raises a number of questions such as what constitutes "water pollution"; how will one be adjudged a polluter; how will the cost of pollution abatement be assessed; and by whom might such a claim be asserted.

In addition, Amendment 5 does not exist in isolation; it was incorporated into an existing section and employs key terms of that provision, now article II, section 7(a). Where the constitution contains multiple provisions on the same subject, they must be read *in pari materia* to ensure a consistent and logical meaning that gives effect to each provision. *In re Advisory Opinion of Governor Appointment of County Comm'rs*, 313 So.2d 697, 701 (Fla.1975). Article II, section 7(a) establishes the state's policy "to conserve and protect its natural resources" and directs the legislature to provide by statute for the "abatement of air and water pollution." Thus, we answer the first part of your first question in the negative.

The second part of your first question asks whether legislative action is required in light of the pre-existing Everglades Forever Act. We answer in the affirmative. In cases where the constitutional provision is not self-executing, such as the instant case, "all existing statutes which are consistent with the amended Constitution will remain in effect until repealed by the Legislature." *In re Advisory Opinion to the Governor*, 132 So.2d 163, 169 (Fla.1961). We find no inconsistency between the Everglades Forever Act and Amendment **5**. As you noted in your letter, the "Everglades Forever Act was enacted … to determine how and at whose expense pollution of the Everglades should be abated." Amendment 5 was adopted for a similar purpose—to require polluters to pay for the abatement of their pollution. Notwithstanding the mutuality of subject matter, we do not construe the Everglades Forever Act to be the enabling legislation for Amendment 5.

Based on our review of the pre-election publicity and promotion, most of which focused on Amendment 4, the "sugar tax" amendment,[48] and some of which included discussion of the Everglades Forever Act, we conclude that the voters intended to defeat the penny per pound sugar tax and adopt Amendment 5, which requires polluters to pay "the costs of abatement of that pollution." We believe the voters adopted Amendment 5 to effect a change, and construing the Everglades Forever Act as Amendment 5's implementing legislation would effect no change, nullify the Amendment, and frustrate the will of the people. We therefore glean that in adopting Amendment 5, the voters expected the legislature to enact supplementary legislation to make it effective, to carry out its intended purposes, and to define any rights intended to be determined, enjoyed, or protected.

Your second question asks us to construe the phrase "primarily responsible" as used in Amendment 5. The touchstone for determining the meaning of a constitutional amendment adopted by initiative is the intent of the voters who adopted it, and it is well settled that

> [t]he words and terms of a Constitution are to be interpreted in their most usual and obvious meaning, unless the text suggests that they have been used in a technical sense. The presumption is in favor of the natural and popular meaning in which the words are usually understood by the people who have adopted them.

City of Jacksonville v. Continental Can Co., 113 Fla. 168, 172, 151 So. 488, 489–90 (1933). In general, a dictionary may provide the popular and common-sense meaning of terms presented to the voters. *Myers v. Hawkins*, 362 So.2d 926, 930 n.10 (Fla.1978). [Webster's Third New International D]ictionary defines the word "responsible" to mean "liable" or "answerable," and the word "primarily" is intended to qualify or limit the word "responsible." The question then becomes to what extent does the word "primarily" qualify or limit the word "responsible." The word "primarily" is defined to mean "fundamentally," "in the first place," "for the most part," "chiefly," "principally," or "mainly." The dictionary does not restrict the word "primarily" to "entirely" or "substantially" or "more than half," as you suggest in your question; thus we conclude that the voters did not attach such limited meanings. In the context of the amendment, we find that the voters contemplated the phrase "primarily responsible" to be a recognition that no one person or entity is responsible

---

48. [FN 6.] *See Advisory Opinion to Attorney General Fee on Everglades Sugar Production*, 681 So.2d 1124, 1127–28 (Fla.1996) (approving place on ballot for proposed amendment imposing a levy of a penny per pound on raw sugar).

for 100% of the pollution in the Everglades Agricultural Area (EAA) or the Everglades Protection Area (EPA),[49] but those within the EAA who are determined to be responsible must pay their share of the costs of abating that pollution. Voters reading the ballot summary or the entire amendment would most likely understand that the words "primarily responsible" would be applied in accordance with their ordinary meaning to require that individual polluters, while not bearing the total burden, would bear their share of the costs of abating the pollution found to be attributable to them.[50]

In conclusion, we answer your inquiries by finding that (1) Amendment 5 is not self-executing; (2) the amendment requires implementing legislation, notwithstanding the existence of the Everglades Forever Act; and (3) the words "primarily responsible" require those in the EAA who cause water pollution in the EPA or EAA to bear the costs of abating that pollution.

Respectfully,

/s/ Justice Gerald Kogan
/s/ Chief Justice Ben F. Overton
/s/ Justice Leander J. Shaw, Jr.
/s/ Justice Major B. Harding
/s/ Justice Charles T. Wells
/s/ Justice Harry Lee Anstead
/s/ Senior Justice Stephen H. Grimes

Questions

1. What does it mean for a constitutional provision to be self-executing?

2. When will a constitutional provision be considered self-executing?

3. What hints does the Court in this case give as to the meaning of the "primarily responsible" standard included in the newly adopted "Polluter Pays" amendment?

Barley v. South Florida Water Management District

823 So. 2d 73 (Fla. 2002)

PER CURIAM.

We have for review *Barley v. South Florida Water Management District*, 766 So.2d 433 (Fla. 5th DCA 2000), a decision of the Fifth District Court of Appeal which expressly declared a Florida statute valid and expressly construed a provision of the Florida Constitution. We have jurisdiction. *See* art. V, § 3(b)(3), Fla. Const.

---

49. [FN 11.] The causes of such pollution run the gamut from lawn run-off to pollution from cattle ranching and the growing of sugar cane.

50. [FN 12.] We recognize, of course, that not all of the water pollution within the EPA and the EAA may be caused by polluters within the EAA. Therefore, while polluters within the EAA as a group must pay for 100% of the cost to abate the pollution they cause, Amendment 5 does not require them to pay for the abatement of such portion of the pollution they do not cause.

Petitioners are property owners within an area designated by section 373.0693(10), Florida Statutes (1993), as the Okeechobee Basin. This basin is within an area regulated by respondent South Florida Water Management District (District). Respondent is authorized under article VII, section 9 of the Florida Constitution and sections 373.503 and 373.0697, Florida Statutes (1993), to levy ad valorem taxes on property within the District.

Section 373.4592, Florida Statutes (Supp.1994), is known as the Everglades Forever Act (EFA). [The EFA defines the Everglades Agricultural Area (EAA) and the Everglades Protection Area (EPA). The Everglades Construction Project (ECP) is a project described in the EFA.]

[The EFA] provides for implementation of the ECP. This section also provides: "The district shall not levy ad valorem taxes in excess of 0.1 mill within the Okeechobee Basin for the purpose of the design, construction, and acquisition of the Everglades Construction Project." *Id.* [The EFA] provides for the imposition of an annual Everglades Agricultural Privilege Tax....

Petitioners filed an action in the Circuit Court of the Ninth Judicial Circuit in and for Orange County. That action sought a declaration that respondent's levy of a 0.1 mill ad valorem tax [under the EFA] to abate pollution in the EAA and the additional ad valorem taxes levied under respondent's ad valorem taxing authority for other pollution abatement costs attributable to polluters in the EAA violate article II, section 7(b), Florida Constitution, as applied to petitioners and other similarly situated property owners within the Okeechobee Basin. The petitioners alleged that they were non-polluters and that the polluters within the EAA were not at that time paying for 100 percent of the costs of abating the pollution they caused. Petitioners also sought a declaration that [the EFA] violates article II, section 7(b), [to the extent that it] prohibited respondent from raising additional revenues from EAA polluters who were not paying for 100 percent of the costs of abating the pollution they caused.

This case presents to us the issue of the application of the EFA-authorized 0.1 mill ad valorem tax subsequent to the adoption by the voters of the initiative known as Amendment 5, which is now article II, section 7(b), Florida Constitution. Our review begins with the history of the EFA and of article II, section 7(b).

HISTORY

The EFA was passed by the Legislature in its regular session in 1994.... The goal of the EFA includes reducing pollution flowing from the EAA into the EPA....

In 1996, this Court had for review three separate initiative petitions concerning the Everglades, which we addressed in one opinion. *See Advisory Opinion to Attorney Gen.—Fee on Everglades Sugar Prod.*, 681 So.2d 1124 (Fla.1996). The title and summary for the first petition concerning the proposed fee was:

TITLE: FEE ON EVERGLADES SUGAR PRODUCTION

SUMMARY: Provides that the South Florida Water Management District shall levy an Everglades Sugar Fee of 1 [cent] per pound on raw sugar grown in the Everglades Agricultural Area to raise funds to be used, consistent with statutory law, for purposes of conservation and protection of natural resources and abatement of water pollution in the Everglades. The fee is imposed for twenty-five years.

Id. at 1127. The title and summary for the second petition concerning the Trust Fund was:

TITLE: EVERGLADES TRUST FUND

SUMMARY: Establishes an Everglades Trust Fund to be administered by the South Florida Water Management District for purposes of conservation and protection of natural resources and abatement of water pollution in the Everglades. The Everglades Trust Fund may be funded through any source, including gifts and state or federal funds.

Id. at 1129. The title and summary for the third petition, concerning the proposed responsibility amendment, was:

TITLE: RESPONSIBILITY FOR PAYING COSTS OF WATER POLLUTION ABATEMENT IN THE EVERGLADES

SUMMARY: The Constitution currently provides the authority for the abatement of water pollution. This proposal adds a provision to provide that those in the Everglades Agricultural Area who cause water pollution within the Everglades Protection Area or the Everglades Agricultural Area shall be primarily responsible for paying the costs of the abatement of that pollution.

Id. at 1130.

Again, the two issues before this Court were whether the amendments addressed but a single subject and whether the amendments' titles and summaries were sufficiently clear. In this 1996 decision, we held that each of the initiatives met these requirements, and the initiatives proceeded to the ballot.

Regarding the Fee on Everglades Sugar Production initiative, we held that the initiative proposed a clear, single question to the voters: "Should the sugar industry pay a penny a pound towards Everglades restoration?" *Id.* at 1128.

Regarding the Everglades Trust Fund initiative, we held that the initiative had "a single, limited purpose: the creation of a trust to receive and disperse funds for Everglades conservation." *Id.* at 1130.

We likewise upheld the Responsibility for Paying Costs of Water Pollution Abatement in the Everglades initiative against the contention that the initiative violated the single subject requirement. We stated:

The initiative has a limited and focused objective: Those who cause water pollution within the Everglades Protection Area or the Everglades Agricultural Area shall be primarily responsible for paying the costs of the abatement of that pollution. We also conclude that the ballot title and summary are not misleading. The Responsibility initiative makes clear that those in the Everglades Protection Area or the Everglades Agricultural Area who cause water pollution will pay for their pollution.

Id. at 1130–31 (emphasis added).

The three initiatives were on the ballot in the general election in 1996. The fee initiative was not approved by the voters. The trust fund initiative was approved and is now article X, section 17, Florida Constitution. The responsibility initiative was approved and is now article II, section 7(b), which we consider here.

The adopted article II, section 7(b), was, in March 1997, the subject of a request from the Governor for an advisory opinion pursuant to article IV, section 1(c). We responded to the Governor in *Advisory Opinion to the Governor—1996 Amendment 5 (Everglades)*, 706 So.2d 278 (Fla.1997) (hereinafter *1997 Advisory Opinion*)....

Before answering the Governor's questions, "To ensure full and fair consideration of the issues raised, we permitted interested persons to file briefs and to present oral argument before the Court." *Id.* at 281. We then specifically answered the questions the Governor presented to us:

> ... In conclusion, we answer your inquiries by finding that (1) Amendment 5 is not self-executing; (2) the amendment requires implementing legislation, notwithstanding the existence of the Everglades Forever Act; and (3) the words "primarily responsible" require those in the EAA who cause water pollution in the EPA or EAA to bear the costs of abating that pollution.

Advisory Opinion to the Governor—1996 Amendment 5 (Everglades), 706 So.2d 278, 281–83 (Fla.1997) (emphasis added) (second alteration and first and third omissions in original) (some footnotes omitted).

THE INSTANT CASE

In the circuit court, respondent answered the petitioner's amended complaint and thereafter moved for a judgment on the pleadings. The circuit court granted respondent's motion and held the following in its order:

> 10. In the Florida Supreme Court's advisory opinion to Florida's Governor on Amendment 5, *Advisory Opinion to the Governor—1996 Amendment 5 (Everglades)*, 706 So.2d 278 (Fla.1997) ("*Advisory Opinion-Amendment 5*"), the supreme court addressed three questions posed by the Governor: (1) is Amendment 5 self-executing or does it require enabling legislation?; (2) assuming Amendment 5 is not self-executing, is legislative action required to make it effective in light of the pre-existing Everglades Forever Act?; and (3) what is the meaning of "primarily responsible" as used in Amendment 5? In summary, the supreme court ultimately determined that Amendment 5 is not self-executing, that legislative action is required to implement Amendment 5 and that the Act could not be deemed the implementing legislation, and that "primarily responsible" in Amendment 5 should be given its ordinary meaning, to wit: "individual polluters, while not bearing the total burden,

would bear their share of the costs abating the pollution found to be attributable to them." *Id.* at 283.

11. Specifically relevant to the instant motion, the Florida Supreme Court considered the *consistency* between Amendment 5 and the Act in question. In discussing whether legislative action was required in light of the pre-existing Everglades Forever Act, the court reaffirmed its earlier holding in *In re Advisory Opinion to the Governor*, 132 So.2d 163 (Fla.1961), and expressly found that there was no inconsistency between the Everglades Forever Act and Amendment 5. While the court then noted the similarity in purpose between the Everglades Forever Act and Amendment 5, it is obvious that the court reviewed the totality of the Act to determine that the Act was not the enabling legislation for Amendment 5.

12. Based on the standard for reviewing the impact of non self-executing constitutional provisions and the Florida Supreme Court's discussion of the consistency of the Everglades Forever Act and Amendment 5 in *Advisory Opinion to the Governor—1996 Amendment 5 (Everglades)*, 706 So.2d 278 (Fla.1997), this Court finds that a cause of action would not be established by proving plaintiff's allegations.

Barley v. South Florida Water Mgmt. Dist., No. CI97-10228, order at 5–6 (Fla. 9th Cir. Ct. order filed Oct. 22, 1998).

Petitioners appealed the circuit court's order granting the respondent's motion for judgment on the pleadings. In a divided decision, the Fifth District affirmed the circuit court's order. *See Barley v. South Florida Water Mgmt. Dist.*, 766 So.2d 433 (Fla. 5th DCA 2000). The Fifth District determined that in *1997 Advisory Opinion*, this Court answered the issues presented by the petitioner's petition for declaratory judgment. *See id.*

Before us, petitioners argue that this is not *1997 Advisory Opinion* revisited. Petitioners contend that, unlike the issues of facial consistency with the EFA and article II, section 7(b), which were considered in *1997 Advisory Opinion*, the instant case presents factual issues and an as-applied constitutional challenge to the respondent's discretionary 0.1 mill tax levy on the owners of property within the Okeechobee Basin who are non-polluters. Petitioners claim that since *1997 Advisory Opinion* held that the meaning of primarily responsible in article II, section 7(b), was that polluters are to pay the costs related to the pollution the polluters cause, it necessarily follows that non-polluters are constitutionally protected from paying any of the costs of pollution abatement. Thus, petitioners contend that this Court's interpretation of article II, section 7(b), in *1997 Advisory Opinion* establishes an implied right to not have to contribute for pollution abatement in the EPA or EAA. We disagree.

We agree with the Fifth District that our *1997 Advisory Opinion* has answered the fundamental issues in this case and that the circuit court's following our *1997 Advisory Opinion* is to be affirmed. We have consistently stated that "[w]hile advisory opinions to the Governor are not binding judicial precedents, they are frequently very persuasive and usually adhered to." *Lee v. Dowda*, 155 Fla. 68, 19 So.2d 570, 572 (1944). Regarding advisory opinions concerning initiative opinions, we recently reiterated in *Ray v. Mortham*, 742 So.2d 1276, 1285 (Fla.1999), that "although our advisory opinions are not strictly binding precedent in the most technical sense, only under *extraordinary* circumstances will we revisit an issue decided in our earlier advisory opinions." Regarding article II, section 7(b), we have issued an advisory opinion regarding the validity of the initiative which resulted in article II, section 7(b), being placed on the ballot, and we have issued an advisory opinion to the Governor regarding the consistency between the EFA and article II, section 7(b), after the initiative was approved by the voters.

In *1997 Advisory Opinion*, we specifically determined that article II, section 7(b), is not self-executing and then expressly reiterated our precedent:

> In cases where the constitutional provision is not self-executing, such as the instant case, "all existing statutes which are consistent with the amended Constitution will remain in effect until repealed by the Legislature." *In re Advisory Opinion to the Governor*, 132 So.2d 163, 169 (Fla.1961).

1997 Advisory Opinion, 706 So.2d at 281–82. We then expressly found "no inconsistency between the Everglades Forever Act and Amendment 5." *Id.* at 282.... Thus, the need for the *1997 Advisory Opinion* contemplated the issues that are now presented in the framework of the instant case.

Additionally, there is no express language in Amendment 5 creating for the petitioners a prohibition against being required to contribute for pollution abatement in the EPA or EAA. Although the *1997 Advisory Opinion* stated that "the words 'primarily responsible' require those in the EAA who cause water pollution in the EPA or EAA to bear the costs of abating that pollution," we further stated that the words "primarily responsible" would be applied within their ordinary meaning, which includes a recognition that individual polluters would not bear "the total burden." *Id.* at 283. The corollary to this is that other persons or entities continue to have responsibility for EPA or EAA pollution abatement. The lack of guiding principles in Amendment 5 concerning this division of responsibility is precisely why we held that legislative action was needed. *See id.* at 282.

Therefore, we again hold that the EFA remains in effect. Respondent's levy of 0.1 mill tax and other ad valorem taxes in conformity with the EFA is not unconstitutional as applied to petitioners. The decision of the district court of appeal is approved.

It is so ordered.

WELLS, C.J., and SHAW, HARDING, and ANSTEAD, JJ., concur.

WELLS, C.J., concurs with an opinion.

LEWIS, J., concurs in result only.

PARIENTE, J., dissents with an opinion, in which QUINCE, J., concurs.

WELLS, C.J., concurring.

I concur with the majority decision that our decision in *Advisory Opinion to the Governor—1996 Amendment 5 (Everglades)*, 706 So.2d 278 (Fla.1997) (hereinafter *1997 Advisory Opinion*), compels us to affirm the circuit court's ruling below.

I write to explain that I believe this decision is also consistent with the history of the amendment which resulted in article II, section 7(b) of the Florida Constitution. The majority's setting out in detail this Court's cases concerning the Everglades initiatives is helpful in putting article II, section 7(b), in proper context. What the history shows is that this section was presented to this Court and to the voters as part of a comprehensive plan to establish a trust fund to be used for restoration and protection of the Everglades against pollution. The proponents of the initiatives intended that the trust fund be funded by a fee imposed on sugar growers in the Everglades Agricultural Area (EAA). The responsibility amendment was to lend support to the application of the fee to those who were doing the polluting. But, of course, what happened along the way was that the fee amendment was defeated while the other two amendments passed.

It must be noted that nothing in either the 1994 initiative, which was struck by this Court, or in the 1996 responsibility initiative, which was allowed by this Court to proceed, limited in any way or even referred to the ad valorem taxes which the South Florida Water Management District is authorized by the Constitution and general law to levy. To the contrary, this Court specifically stated that the responsibility initiative had a limited and focused objective, which was to have those who cause water pollution within the Everglades Protection Area (EPA) or the EAA pay the cost of the abatement of that pollution. *See Advisory Opinion to Attorney Gen.—Fee on Everglades Sugar Prod.*, 681 So.2d 1124, 1130 (Fla.1996). Fixing primary responsibility for these payments is *not* an express limitation on the government's power to levy a tax on property within the area.

... Further, I would be very concerned about the effect that a judicially imposed limitation on the Everglades Forever Act's (EFA) 0.1 mill levy would have on the present restoration plan of the EFA. I recognize that the petitioners seek for this Court to declare that "the Everglades Construction Project ... be permitted to continue while the Legislature is granted 'a reasonable period of time' to reallocate the relative contribution by innocent ad valorem taxpayers and EAA polluters" and, if the Legislature does not act by the conclusion of the next legislative session, that this Court should provide for that reallocation. However, I agree with the Fifth District that the courts have no authority to do this. *See Barley v. South Florida Water Mgmt. Dist.*, 766 So.2d 433, 434 (Fla. 5th DCA 2000).

I do conclude that the Legislature is under a constitutional mandate to pass legislation implementing Amendment 5. In our *1997 Advisory Opinion*, we noted this by stating that "the voters expected the legislature to enact supplementary legislation to make it effective, to carry out its intended purpose, and to define any rights intended to be determined, enjoyed, or protected." *1997 Advisory Opinion*, 706 So.2d at 282. I urge the Legislature to carry out the will of the voters.

PARIENTE, J., dissenting.

Although I agree with the majority that the enactment of article VII, section 9, of the Florida Constitution did not render the EFA unconstitutional on its face, I would quash the Fifth District's decision because I conclude that the portion of the declaratory judgment action seeking a determination that the EFA is unconstitutional as applied would not be prohibited.[51] Thus, I agree with Judge Harris's dissenting opinion that the amendment represents a clear mandate from the citizens of our State protecting non-polluters within the EAA and EPA from paying polluters' clean-up costs. *See Barley v. South Florida Mgmt. Dist.*, 766 So.2d 433, 435–36 (Fla. 5th DCA 2000) (Harris, J., dissenting). As Judge Harris explained:

> Appellants argue that even though the legislature has failed to enact legislation defining water pollution and determining what constitutes a polluter and hence may not be in a position to carry out the mandate of the amendment by making the polluters pay, this does not affect their rights as non-polluters, also granted by the amendment, not to pay any of the costs of abating pollution caused by others since the amendment. This portion of the amendment, they urge, is self executing. No legislative action is necessary to implement the constitutional right to be free from paying a tax to abate others' pollution. This is a current, organic right granted by the people. I agree. The legislature cannot by inaction repeal the will of the people.

Id. (footnote omitted).

In fact, in defining the phrase "primarily responsible" as used in the amendment, we concluded in *Advisory Opinion to the Governor*, 706 So.2d 278, 283 (Fla.1997), that the phrase "require[s] those in the EAA *who cause water pollution in the EPA or EAA to bear the costs of abating that pollution.*" (Emphasis supplied.) If non-polluters in the EPA or EAA are paying for the costs of the abatement of water pollution within the EPA and the EAA, this would violate the clear language of the amendment. No additional legislation is necessary to effectuate non-polluters' rights to be free from the clean-up costs associated with polluters-as opposed to the necessity for legislation to ensure that polluters pay the cost of the abatement of water pollution that they cause. Thus, I conclude that this constitutional amendment vests certain rights that can be enforced through a declaratory judgment action. Accordingly, I would quash the Fifth District's decision.

QUINCE, J., concurs.

---

51. [FN 6.] For example, the petitioners' prayer for relief included the following:

2. Declaring that the 0.1 mill ad valorem tax levied by the SFWMD pursuant to section 373.4592(4)(a), Florida Statutes (1994) of the EFA to abate EAA pollution and the additional ad valorem taxes levied under the SFWMD's general ad valorem taxing authority for other pollution abatement costs attributable to EAA polluters, violate the Polluter Pays Amendment as applied to the Plaintiffs and other ad valorem taxpayers within the Okeechobee Basin because the polluters within the EAA as a group are not presently not paying for 100% of the costs to abate the pollution they cause, thereby resulting in non-EAA ad valorem taxpayers paying a significant portion of the EAA polluters' clean-up costs.

Questions

1. How did the Supreme Court's earlier decision in the 1997 Advisory Opinion to the Governor that the Polluter Pays amendment is not self-executing impact this challenge to the funding scheme in the Everglades Forever Act?

2. What is the precedential value of an advisory opinion in a subsequent "as-applied" challenge?

iv. Article X, Section 28 — Land Acquisition Trust Fund

This provision was added by an initiative amendment in 2014. The initiative sought to dedicate some 33% of documentary stamp tax revenues "to finance or refinance the acquisition and improvement" of conservation lands, and for debt service on such land acquisitions.[52] The case that follows examines how much discretion was left by the amendment to the Legislature in spending these stamp tax funds.[53]

Oliva v. Florida Wildlife Federation, Inc.

281 So. 3d 531 (1st DCA 2019), *rev. denied*,
2020 WL 3525953 (Fla., Jun. 29, 2020)

BILBREY, J.

In 2014, the voters of Florida overwhelmingly approved a ballot measure to amend the Florida Constitution. That ballot measure became section 28 of Article X of the Florida Constitution. Since then, two separate suits were filed by various plaintiffs against various state actors alleging that certain appropriations were contrary to section 28; those suits were consolidated. A final summary judgment was thereafter entered holding that the legislature had not complied with section 28 and that judgment is now before us. As explained below, we reverse the summary judgment and remand for further proceedings.

BACKGROUND

In 2014, the voters of Florida approved adding Article X, section 28 to the Florida Constitution. . . .

In 2015, a complaint for declaratory and supplemental relief was filed by the Florida Wildlife Federation (FWF) and several other plaintiffs. . . . The gravamen of the complaint was that certain appropriations which utilized revenue from the Land Acquisition Trust Fund (LATF) were not permissible under that provision and hence were unconstitutional. After several amendments to the complaint, FWF moved for summary judgment.

---

52. *See* Fla. Const. art. X, §28(b)(1).

53. For more on the implementation of this amendment and this litigation, see Henderson, *supra* note 33, at 639–41.

In a separate proceeding, the Florida Defenders of the Environment, Inc., and other individual plaintiffs (collectively "FDE") filed suit against the Florida Secretary of State, the Florida Commissioner of Agriculture, the Director of the Florida Fish and Wildlife Commission, and the Secretary of the Florida Department of Environmental Protection. By that complaint, later amended, FDE sought a declaration that certain expenditures made by the defendant agencies were violative of LATF. FDE also moved for summary judgment.

The separate proceedings were consolidated. Certain affidavits and other matters were attached to the various pleadings filed by plaintiffs and defendants. A hearing was then held on the pending motions for summary judgment.

… In its judgment on the consolidated case, the trial court found that the "plain meaning" of section 28 is that "funds in the Land Acquisition Trust Fund can be expended only for the (1) acquisition of conservation lands, and (2) the improvement, management, restoration and enhancement of public access and enjoyment of those conservation lands purchased **after the effective date of the amendment**" in 2015. (Emphasis added).

In so finding, the trial court noted that the title of the amendment ("Land Acquisition Trust Fund") is "an important part of what makes the language [of section 28] so unambiguous." The purpose of section 28 is for the acquisition of land, per the title, the trial court reasoned.

The trial court further explained its reasoning by noting that a long list is given in subsection (b) of types of conservations lands which may be acquired by LATF expenditures. At the end of the long list of types of conservation lands is the phrase "together with management, restoration of natural systems, and the enhancement of public access or recreational enjoyment of conservation lands." The phrase "together with" is an important one, as the trial court explained:

> The connecting words "together with" does more than add one group to the list — it also attaches it to the clauses preceding it. After conservation lands are first acquired, they then may be managed or restored so that public enjoyment of them is enhanced. This is the plain meaning of the text, and it is the only reading of that subsection that gives effect to all the words, the grammar and punctuation.

Besides the title of the provision and the plain meaning of the words of the provision, the trial court considered the ballot title and summary put before the voters. That ballot title was: "Water and Land Conservation — Dedicates Funds to Acquire and Restore Florida Conservation and Recreation Lands."

As for the ballot summary, it provided: "Funds the Land Acquisition Trust Fund to acquire, restore, improve, and manage conservation lands." The trial court observed that the summary then listed those conservation lands that "can be acquired and then restored, improved, and managed." The Florida Supreme Court, in its review of the ballot initiative, held the title and summary were "straightforward and accurate." *Advisory Op. to Att'y Gen. re Water & Land Conservation — Dedicates Funds* to *Acquire and Restore Fla. Conservation and Recreation Lands*, 123 So. 3d 47, 52 (Fla. 2013).

The trial court reviewed the history of the LATF, which was originally added to the Florida statutes as part of the Outdoor Recreation and Conservation Act of 1963. Ch. 63-36, § 1, Laws of Fla. The LATF was then made a part of the 1885 Florida Constitution by amendment in 1965. *See* Art. IX, § 17, Fla. Const. (1965). That amendment, however, was by its own terms to last only 50 years. The 2014 amendment, which became Article X, section 28 of the Florida Constitution, was intended to replace the expired version.

The trial court noted that the Legislature and State agencies commingled LATF funds with other appropriations despite the lack of constitutional authorization for such co-mingling. In fact, subsection (c) of Article X, section 28 specifically forbids co-mingling of LATF revenue with general revenue. The trial court found that the Legislature and other defendants admitted that "no existing programs could have been shifted from other funding sources to the Land Acquisition Trust Fund."

Given all the above, the trial court concluded that the "clear intent was to create a trust fund to purchase new conservation lands and take care of them. The conservation lands the State already owned were to be taken care of, certainly, but from non-trust money." Thus, the trial court held that Article X, section 28:

1. creates a fund for the acquisition of conservation lands and property interests the State did not own prior to the effective date of the amendment and for the improvement, management, restoration, and enhancement of those newly acquired lands;

2. forbids LATF revenue to be used on land acquired before the effective date of the amendment;

3. prohibits commingling of LATF revenue with general revenue.

The trial court held further that agencies must track expenditures from the LATF to ensure LATF compliance. Finally, the trial court declared some 100 appropriations unconstitutional.

Following entry of this final summary judgment, the defendants moved for rehearing. A motion to disqualify the trial judge was also filed by the legislative defendants. All of these motions were denied. Appellants then brought this appeal.

ANALYSIS

A final summary judgment is reviewed de novo. *Treasure Coast Marina, LC v. City of Fort Pierce*, 219 So. 3d 793 (Fla. 2017); *Volusia Cty. v. Aberdeen at Ormond Beach, L.P.*, 760 So. 2d 126 (Fla. 2000). A question of constitutional law is also reviewed de novo. *Treasure Coast*; *Lewis v. Leon Cty.*, 73 So. 3d 151 (Fla. 2011). A court's task in "constitutional interpretation follows principles parallel to those of statutory interpretation." *Zingale v. Powell*, 885 So. 2d 277, 282 (Fla. 2004); *Coastal Fla. Police Benev. Ass'n, Inc. v. Williams*, 838 So. 2d 543, 548 (Fla. 2003) ("The rules which govern the construction of statutes are generally applicable to the construction of constitutional provisions."). Therefore, a reviewing court's analysis begins with the plain text of the constitution. *See Benjamin v. Tandem Healthcare, Inc.*, 998 So. 2d 566 (Fla. 2008); *Florida Soc'y of Ophthalmology v. Fla. Optometric Ass'n*, 489 So. 2d 1118 (Fla. 1986). "The words of the constitution 'are to be interpreted in their most usual and obvious meaning, unless the text suggests that they have been used in a technical sense.'" *Lewis*, 73 So. 3d at 153 (quoting *Wilson v. Crews*, 160 Fla. 169, 34 So. 2d 114, 118 (1948)). If the language of a constitutional provision "is clear, unambiguous, and addresses the matter in issue, then it must be enforced as written." *Florida Soc'y of Ophthalmology*, 489 So. 2d at 1119 (Fla.1986).

A reviewing court should also construe the text in a manner consistent with the intent of the framers and voters. *See Caribbean Conservation Corp., Inc. v. Fla. Fish & Wildlife Conservation Comm'n*, 838 So. 2d 492 (Fla. 2003). Voter intent is discerned through the plain meaning of the text. "We are obligated to give effect to [the] language [of a Constitutional amendment] according to its meaning and what the people must have understood it to mean when they approved it." *City of St. Petersburg v. Briley, Wild & Assocs., Inc.*, 239 So. 2d 817, 822 (Fla.1970); *see Benjamin*, 998 So. 2d at 570.

While the trial court purported to construe the plain meaning of the constitutional text, that provision does not plainly restrict the use of LATF revenue to improvement, management, restoration, or enhancement of lands only acquired after 2015. Subsection (b) of the amendment subsection authorizes LATF revenue to be used to finance the acquisition of land, water areas, easements, and the like. The subsection also authorizes refinancing. That the text specifically authorizes refinancing suggests that property for which the State already owns title is within the purview of permissible LATF activities.

The subsection further authorizes LATF revenue to finance the improvement of land, water areas, easements, and the like. There is no explicit limitation in the text that restoration activities must be on State owned lands. Indeed, the text indicates that restoration can occur on "working farms and ranches," which presumably would not be owned by the State.

Further still, the text does not plainly limit the improvement of property to those properties only recently acquired. Instead, the plain words of the subsection, as well as the placement of the only colon in subsection (b), indicate that acquisition and improvement are separate but coequal activities for LATF revenue.

As for the phrase "together with management, restoration of natural systems, and the enhancement of public access or recreational enjoyment of conservation lands" at the end of the subsection, it would be grammatically incorrect to assume, as the trial court did, that this phrase modifies all which comes before it in subsection (b). As noted in the friend of the court brief of Florida Conservation Voters, Inc., the successor to the sponsor of the citizen's initiative that became Article X, section 28, the phrase "together with" generally means "in addition to" or "in association with." *See Merriam-Webster's Dictionary* https://www.merriam-webster.com/dictionary/together%20with (last visited Aug. 6, 2019). The plain words "management," "restoration," and "enhancement" authorize expenditure of LATF funds on activities not expressly concerned with acquisition or improvement per se. Thus, management of an existing natural resource, which is already owned by the State and which is not in immediate need of improvement, is apparently authorized by subsection (b).

It should be noted that when the Florida Supreme Court considered the ballot initiative, it did not determine how LATF revenue could be spent. Instead, its inquiry was three-fold. First, it considered whether the proposed amendment satisfied the single-subject requirement of Article XI, section 3 of the Florida constitution and found it did. *Advisory Op. to Att'y Gen. re Water & Land Conservation*, 123 So. 3d at 51.

Second, the Supreme Court considered whether the financial impact statement prepared for the ballot measure was clear, unambiguous, no more than seventy-five words, and addressed only estimated increases or decreases in revenues or costs to state and local governments. *Id.* at 52. The Supreme Court found that the financial impact statement satisfied these requirements. *Id.*

Third, and importantly for our purposes, the Supreme Court considered, as required by section 101.161(1), Florida Statutes (2012), whether the ballot title and summary fairly informed the voters of the chief purpose of the amendment and was not misleading. The Supreme Court observed that both

> the title and summary state that the prosed amendment will dedicate documentary tax revenue to the Land Acquisition Trust Fund. The title includes the language "Dedicates Funds to Acquire and Restore Florida Conservation and Recreation Lands," and the summary begins with the clause "Funds the Land Acquisition Trust Fund," describes the uses of the Fund, and explains that the funds will be obtained "by dedicating 33 percent of net revenues from the existing excise tax on documents for 20 years." The title and summary are straightforward and accurate.

Advisory Op. to Att'y Gen. re Water & Land Conservation, 123 So. 3d at 52. There was no comment by the Supreme Court as to whether revenue from the LATF could only be spent on acquisition and then maintenance of new resources. As discussed above, we hold that the trial court so ruling was error.

Because we must overturn the trial court's unsupportable reading of Article X, section 28, the trial court's declaration that multiple appropriations are unconstitutional must necessarily be overturned as well as the declaration was premised on the trial court's view of the amendment. Also, the trial court's order that agencies must provide an accounting of its use of LATF revenue is reversed as well as such an order was premised on an erroneous reading of the amendment.

Finally, we find no error in the trial court's denial of the Appellants' motions to disqualify and affirm as to that issue. The grounds raised in the motion for disqualification pertain to the scope and nature of the adverse ruling on FDE's motion for summary judgment. An adverse ruling is not a legally sufficient ground for disqualification. *See Thompson v. State*, 759 So. 2d 650 (Fla. 2000).

By our ruling we do not speak to the legality of the appropriations since enactment of Article X, section 28, a question which remains pending. We hold only that LATF revenue is not restricted to use on land purchased by the State after 2015. Accordingly, the final summary is reversed, and the cause is remanded to the circuit court for further proceedings.

AFFIRMED in part, REVERSED in part, and REMANDED.

LEWIS and MAKAR, JJ., concur.

C. Other Initiative Amendments

i. Article X, Section 29 — Medical Marijuana Production, Possession, and Use

This amendment, adopted by initiative in 2016,[54] once more provides an opportunity for illustrating the challenge of dealing with implementation by an unwilling Legislature and executive agency. The cases that follow are among several involving the medical marijuana amendment. The first case deals with its possible impact on criminal law. The second case deals with a challenge to the implementing legislation, § 381.986, Florida Statutes,[55] and specifically the question of who may be registered by the Department of Health as a medical marijuana treatment center.

Forest v. State
257 So. 3d 603 (Fla. 1st DCA 2018)

PER CURIAM.

Appellant challenges his criminal judgment and sentence for possession of more than 20 grams of a controlled substance, cannabis. Appellant contends that he could not have committed the charged crime because Florida's criminal code, which classifies cannabis as a substance that "has no current medical use," is in direct conflict with the recent amendment to the Florida Constitution regarding the production, possession, and use of medical marijuana. We disagree.

A "controlled substance" is "any substance named or described in Schedules I–V of s. 893.03." § 893.02(4), Fla. Stat. (2016). Cannabis, or marijuana, is statutorily

---

54. A similar initiative was brought to the voters in 2014, but failed to meet the constitutional 60% threshold for approval.

55. Earlier litigation dealt with an attempt by the Legislature to impose an absolute prohibition on smoking as an approved delivery device for medical marijuana. *See People United for Medical Marijuana v. Fla. Dept. of Health*, Case No. 2017-CA-1394, Order & Final Judgment (Fla. 2nd Cir. Ct., May 5, 2018). In 2019, the Legislature amended § 381.986 to allow for the use of smoking as a delivery device for medical marijuana, subject to certain restrictions. *See* 2019 Fla. Laws ch. 2019-1. Thereafter, the parties agreed to dismiss the appeal as moot, and the First District Court instructed the trial court to dismiss the case. *See Florida Dept. of Health v. People United for Medical Marijuana*, Case No. 1D18-2206, Order Dismissing Appeal (Fla. 1st DCA, Mar. 20, 2019).

defined as a Schedule I controlled substance. § 893.03(1)(c) 7., Fla. Stat. (2016). A Schedule I substance is one that "has a high potential for abuse and has no currently accepted medical use in treatment in the United States and in its use under medical supervision does not meet accepted safety standards." § 893.03(1), Fla. Stat.

Article X, section 29 of the Florida Constitution, which was approved by voters in 2016, provides for the production, possession, and use of medical marijuana. However, the amendment specifically states "[n]othing in this section allows for a violation of any law other than for conduct in compliance with the provisions of this section" and "[n]othing in this section shall affect or repeal laws relating to non-medical use, possession, production, or sale of marijuana." Art. X, § 29(c)(1)–(2), Fla. Const. Accordingly, nothing in the amendment expressly repeals section 893.03(1)(c) 7.

Florida courts have long held that "[a] statute valid when enacted, and made effective, is not invalidated by a subsequent amendment to the Constitution, unless the amendment is designed to have that effect." *Neisel v. Moran*, 80 Fla. 98, 85 So. 346, 360 (1919) (on rehearing); *see also Graham v. Haridopolos*, 108 So.3d 597 (Fla. 2013) (holding that a constitutional amendment creating the Board of Governors did not prohibit the Legislature from enacting statutes that exerted control over the setting of an appropriation for the expenditure of tuition and fees because the amendment did not expressly transfer the Legislature's authority to raise revenue and appropriate for the expenditure of state funds).

As such, we find section 893.03(1)(c) 7., Florida Statutes, constitutional, and we affirm appellant's judgment and sentence.

AFFIRMED.

WOLF, LEWIS, and ROWE, JJ., concur.

Florida Department of Health v. Florigrown, LLC

2019 WL 2943329 (1st DCA, July 9, 2019), *rev. granted*,
2019 WL 5208142 (Fla., Oct. 16, 2019)

PER CURIAM.

The Department of Health (Department) challenges the trial court's entry of a temporary injunction which [(1) enjoined the Department from registering or licensing any Medical Marijuana Treatment Centers under the unconstitutional legislative scheme set forth in § 381.986, Fla. Stat., (2) required the Department to commence registering MMTC's in accordance with the plain language of the Medical Marijuana Amendment, and (3) required the Department to register Florigrown as an MMTC by 5:00 PM Friday, October 19, 2018.].

We determine that certain aspects of the injunction are overbroad and unsupported by the evidence and factual findings. We, however, uphold the injunction to the extent it requires the Department to consider Florigrown's request for licensure without applying the portions of the statutory scheme which this opinion identifies as being unconstitutional.

PROCEDURAL HISTORY

In 2016, voters amended the Florida Constitution to protect the production, possession, and use of medical marijuana. Art. X, §29, Fla. Const. The amendment went into effect on January 3, 2017, and states, in relevant part:

> (b)(5) "Medical Marijuana Treatment Center" (MMTC) means an entity that acquires, cultivates, possesses, processes (including development of related products such as food, tinctures, aerosols, oils, or ointments), transfers, transports, sells, distributes, dispenses, or administers marijuana, products containing marijuana, related supplies, or educational materials to qualifying patients or their caregivers and is registered by the Department.
>
> ....
>
> (d) The Department shall issue reasonable regulations necessary for the implementation and enforcement of this section. The purpose of the regulations is to ensure the availability and safe use of medical marijuana by qualifying patients. It is the duty of the Department to promulgate regulations in a timely fashion.
>
> (1) Implementing Regulations. In order to allow the Department sufficient time after passage of this section, the following regulations shall be promulgated no later than six (6) months after the effective date of this section:
>
> ....
>
> (3) If the Department does not issue regulations, or if the Department does not begin issuing identification cards and registering MMTCs within the time limits set in this section, any Florida citizen shall have standing to seek judicial relief to compel compliance with the Department's constitutional duties.

Art. X, §29(b)(5) and (d)(1), (3), Fla. Const.

Two weeks after the amendment went into effect, appellee sent the Department a letter seeking to register as an MMTC. The Department denied the request because it had not yet promulgated any regulations pursuant to the amendment.

In June 2017, the Legislature passed a bill later signed by the governor amending section 381.986, Florida Statutes, which set forth a statutory framework for the registration of MMTCs by:

- Directing the Department to convert the existing licenses of low-THC and medical cannabis dispensing organizations into MMTC licenses so long as the organizations still maintained all of the criteria set forth in section 381.986(8)(a) 1., Florida Statutes.

- Providing for ten additional MMTC licenses for applicants that were (1) previously denied a dispensing organization license under the prior version of section 381.986 so long as the organization had a pending a judicial or administrative challenge pending as of January 1, 2017, or had a final ranking within one point of the highest final ranking in its region; (2) in compliance with the requirements of the amended statute; and (3) able to provide the Department with documentation that they could begin cultivating marijuana within 30 days of registration as an MMTC. *See* § 381.986(8)(a) 2., Fla. Stat.

• Stating that a licensed medical marijuana treatment center shall cultivate, process, transport, and dispense marijuana for medical use. *See* § 381.986(8)(e), Fla. Stat.

• Requiring the Department to adopt rules to establish a procedure for issuing MMTC licenses in accordance with the amended statute. *See* § 381.986(8)(b), Fla. Stat.

In December 2017, appellee filed suit requesting a declaratory judgment and a permanent injunction declaring these provisions unconstitutional and mandating the Department register appellee as an MMTC.

During this suit, appellee filed a motion for a temporary injunction. The trial court initially denied appellee's motion without prejudice despite finding that appellee had a substantial likelihood of success on the merits, because it found that appellee could not prove irreparable harm or that a temporary injunction would be in the public's best interests.

Three months later, appellee filed a renewed motion for a temporary injunction. The trial court granted this motion, finding that the Department's unwillingness to draft rules for registering MMTCs in accordance with the plain language of the amendment in the three months since it denied appellee's original motion for a temporary injunction required a different result and incorporating the findings of its earlier order.

STANDARD OF REVIEW

We review a trial court's order on a request for temporary injunction in a hybrid format: "The court's factual findings are reviewed for an abuse of discretion, whereas its legal conclusions are reviewed de novo." *State, Dep't of Health v. Bayfront HMA Med. Ctr., LLC*, 236 So. 3d 466, 471 (Fla. 1st DCA 2018) (citing *Gainesville Woman Care, LLC v. State*, 210 So. 3d 1243, 1258 (Fla. 2017)).

ANALYSIS

To obtain a temporary injunction, a party must provide specific facts establishing four elements: "(1) a substantial likelihood of success on the merits, (2) a lack of an adequate remedy at law, (3) the likelihood of irreparable harm absent the entry of an injunction, and (4) that injunctive relief will serve the public interest." *Id.* at 472 (citing *Sch. Bd. of Hernando Cty. v. Rhea*, 213 So. 3d 1032, 1040 (Fla. 1st DCA 2017)).

SUBSTANTIAL LIKELIHOOD OF SUCCESS ON THE MERITS

A statute enacted by the legislature may not restrict a right granted under the constitution and, to the extent that a statute conflicts with express or implied mandates of the constitution, the statute must fall. *Notami Hosp. of Florida, Inc. v. Bowen*, 927 So. 2d 139, 142 (Fla. 1st DCA 2006), *aff'd sub nom. Florida Hosp. Waterman, Inc. v.*

Buster, 984 So. 2d 478 (Fla. 2008). Similarly, the State is not permitted to alter the definition or meaning of a term laid out in the constitution. See *Dep't of Envtl. Prot. v. Millender*, 666 So. 2d 882 (Fla. 1996).

The Department contends that appellee did not prove it had a substantial likelihood of success on the merits because section 381.986 does not conflict with the amendment, and the amendment does not prohibit the legislature from placing a cap on the number of MMTCs the Department may register. We disagree.

The amendment defines a Medical Marijuana Treatment Center as:

an entity that acquires, cultivates, possesses, processes (including development of related products such as food, tinctures, aerosols, oils, or ointments), transfers, transports, sells, distributes, dispenses, *or* administers marijuana, products containing marijuana, related supplies, or educational materials to qualifying patients or their caregivers and is registered by the Department.

Art. X, § 29(b)(5) Fla. Const. (emphasis added).

Meanwhile section 381.986(8)(e), Florida Statutes, states, in pertinent part, "A licensed medical marijuana treatment center shall cultivate, process, transport, *and* dispense marijuana for medical use." (emphasis added).

Section 381.986(8)(e) thus creates a vertically integrated business model which amends the constitutional definition of MMTC by requiring an entity to undertake several of the activities described in the amendment before the Department can license it. Under the statute, an entity must conform to a more restricted definition than is provided in the amendment; therefore, all MMTCs under the statute would qualify as MMTCs under the constitutional amendment, but the reverse is not true.

We thus find the statutory language directly conflicts with the constitutional amendment, and appellee has demonstrated a substantial likelihood of success in procuring a judgment declaring section 381.986(8)(e) unconstitutional. *See Notami Hosp.*, 927 So. 2d at 142.

As a direct result, we are constrained to find that appellee has also established a substantial likelihood of success in its challenge to the statutory cap of MMTCs under section 381.986(8)(a) 1.–2., 4., Florida Statutes.

The State may not regulate an industry governed by a constitutional amendment in such a manner that would severely restrict or diminish the industry. *Millender*, 666 So. 2d at 887. Here, the amendment requires the Department to issue "reasonable regulations necessary for the implementation and enforcement of this section. The purpose of the regulations is to ensure the availability and safe use of medical marijuana by qualifying patients." Art. X, § 29(d), Fla. Const. The statute provides for the registration of seventeen MMTCs in the entire state, with a requirement that within six months of an additional 100,000 patients registering with the Department another four MMTCs shall be licensed. § 381.986(8)(a) 1.–2., 4., Fla. Stat.

Our ruling that the vertically integrated system conflicts with the constitutional amendment thus renders the statutory cap on the number of facilities in section 381.986(8)(a) unreasonable. It is therefore unnecessary for us to address the Department's authority to establish any caps.

IRREPARABLE HARM AND INADEQUATE REMEDY AT LAW

A trial court is required to provide specific reasons for entering a temporary injunction which must be supported by specific factual findings. Fla. R. Civ. P. 1.610(c); *Milin v. Nw. Florida Land, L.C.*, 870 So. 2d 135, 136 (Fla. 1st DCA 2003). We find that the trial court made sufficient findings supported by the record to establish that appellee will suffer irreparable harm without injunctive relief and that appellee has no adequate remedy at law.

The irreparable harm and inadequate remedy at law prongs are established by the fact that appellee is being unconstitutionally prevented from participating in the process for obtaining a license to operate as an MMTC. The amendment itself recognizes there is no adequate remedy at law where, as here, a state agency or actor refuses to abide by its express duties mandated under the constitution. The amendment specifically provides a cause of action to seek to "compel compliance with the Department's constitutional duties." Art. X, § 29(d)(3), Fla. Const.

Even if there were a remedy at law, the law recognizes that a continuing constitutional violation, in and of itself, constitutes irreparable harm. The law also recognizes that implementation of an unconstitutional statute for which no adequate remedy at law exists leads to irreparable harm, which is the case here. *Gainesville Woman Care, LLC v. State*, 210 So. 3d 1243, 1264 (Fla. 2017). And where time is of the essence, as the Medical Marijuana amendment clearly provides, "[i]t truly can be said in this type of litigation that relief delayed is relief denied." *Capraro v. Lanier Bus. Products, Inc.*, 466 So. 2d 212, 213 (Fla. 1985)....

PUBLIC INTEREST

To sustain a temporary injunction a party must also establish that injunctive relief will serve the public interest. *Bayfront HMA Med. Ctr., LLC*, 236 So. 3d at 472.

The trial court's temporary injunction requires the Department to undertake three specific actions previously discussed. We determine that the trial court's factual findings support the conclusion that it is in the public interest to require the Department to registering or license MMTCs without applying the unconstitutional statutory provisions which appellee has challenged. However, the public interest does not support requiring the Department to immediately begin registering MMTCs or registering appellee at this stage of the proceedings. The amendment specifically directs the Department to establish "standards [for MMTCs] to ensure proper security, record keeping, testing, labeling, inspection, and safety." Art. X, § 29(d)(1)c., Fla. Const.

While it is in the public interest for the Department to promulgates rules that do not thwart the purpose of the amendment, it is also clear that the public interest would not be served by requiring the Department to register MMTCs pursuant to a preliminary injunction without applying other regulations to uphold the safety of the public.

We thus AFFIRM that portion of the injunction that precludes appellants from enforcing the unconstitutional provisions but allows the Department a reasonable period of time to exercise its duties under the constitutional amendment.

WOLF, J., concurs; MAKAR, J., concurs with opinion [omitted]; WETHERELL, J., concurs in part and dissents in part with opinion.

WETHERELL, J., concurring in part and dissenting in part.

I agree with the majority opinion insofar as it quashes the portions of the preliminary injunction requiring the Department to immediately register Appellees—and potentially others—as medical marijuana treatment centers (MMTCs). However, I respectfully dissent from the remainder of the opinion because, in my view, Appellees failed to establish that the portion of the injunction affirmed by the majority is in the public interest.

The purpose of a preliminary injunction is to preserve the status quo pending the final disposition of the case. *See City of Jacksonville v. Naegele Outdoor Advertising Co.*, 634 So. 2d 750, 754 (Fla. 1st DCA 1994) (quoting *Ladner v. Plaza Del Prado Condo. Ass'n*, 423 So. 2d 927, 929 (Fla. 3d DCA 1982)). The issuance of a preliminary injunction is "an extraordinary remedy which should be granted sparingly." *Id.* at 752 (quoting *Thompson v. Planning Comm'n of Jacksonville*, 464 So. 2d 1231, 1236 (Fla. 1st DCA 1985)). This is especially true where, as here, the act being enjoined is an act of a co-equal branch of government.

The Medical Marijuana Amendment provides immunity from criminal sanctions and civil liability for the medical use of marijuana, but only when it is used "in compliance with [the Amendment]." Art. X, §29(a), Fla. Const.; *see also Fla. Dep't of Health v. Redner*, ___ So.3d ___, ___, 2019 WL 1466883, at *2 (Fla. 1st DCA Apr. 3, 2019). The Amendment authorizes the Department to adopt regulations to "ensure the availability and safe use of medical marijuana by qualifying patients," art. X, §29(d), Fla. Const., and it also authorizes the Legislature to "enact[ ] laws consistent with [the Amendment]," *id.* at §29(e). The Amendment specifically contemplates the adoption of regulations pertaining to the registration and operation of MMTCs. *See id.* at §29(d)(1)c.

The medical marijuana industry is unique in that its product is *illegal* to possess, sell, and use, both under federal law and for non-medical purposes under Florida law. Because of this, the state has a compelling interest in ensuring that the industry is highly-regulated and operating within the narrow bounds established by the Medical Marijuana Amendment. However, that compelling interest cannot justify the enactment of statutes or regulations that contravene the plain language of the Amendment.

The primary issue in this case is whether the statute requiring MMTCs to be "vertically integrated" and perform all activities in the medical marijuana supply chain from cultivation to distribution is consistent with the definition of MMTC in the

Medical Marijuana Amendment.[56] Appellees contend that the statute is inconsistent with the Amendment because, unlike the statute, the constitutional definition expressly contemplates that an entity can be engaged in as little as one aspect of the medical marijuana supply chain and still be an MMTC. *Compare* § 381.986(8)(e), Fla. Stat. ("A licensed medical marijuana treatment center shall cultivate, process, transport, *__and__* dispense marijuana for medical use.") (emphasis added) *with* Art. X, § 29(a)(5), Fla. Const. ("[MMTC] means an entity that acquires, cultivates, possesses, processes…, transfers, transports, sells, distributes, dispenses, __*or*__ administers marijuana….") (emphasis added). The Department responds that because the constitutional definition "in no way speaks to how the supply chain of medical marijuana must be structured," the Legislature had the constitutional authority to determine as a policy matter which supply-chain structure best ensures not only the availability of medical marijuana but also its safety and security.

Although there may be sound policy reasons for requiring MMTCs to be vertically integrated, I agree with Appellees (and the majority) that the statute likely contravenes the constitutional definition of MMTC because an entity that meets the constitutional definition by performing one or more—but not all—of the activities in the medical marijuana supply chain cannot be registered and operate as an MMTC under the statute. Accordingly, I agree with the majority that Appellees have shown a substantial likelihood of success on the merits of their claim that the statute contravenes the constitutional definition of MMTC and, thus, is unconstitutional.

A substantial likelihood of success on the merits is not, however, enough to obtain a preliminary injunction. The movant must also establish that it will likely suffer irreparable harm absent an injunction, that the movant does not have an adequate remedy at law, and that the injunction would serve the public interest. *See City of Jacksonville*, 634 So. 2d at 752 (quoting *Thompson*, 464 So. 2d at 1236). Here, unlike the majority, I am not persuaded that any portion of the preliminary injunction entered by the trial court is in the public interest.

The portion of the injunction affirmed by the majority will effectively mandate an immediate change in the entire structure of the medical marijuana industry in Florida. Although such a change may ultimately be warranted, the trial court did not articulate—and Appellees did not show—how the public interest would be served by mandating this change through a preliminary injunction…. The court did not explain how an injunction was now in the public interest, but rather simply stated that "[t]he public interest was clearly stated with the passage of the Constitution's Medical Marijuana Amendment by over 70% of Florida voters."

The trial court's focus on the popularity of the Medical Marijuana Amendment misses the mark because the Amendment contemplated a highly-regulated medical

---

56. [FN 3.] Appellees also challenge the statute capping the number of MMTCs, see § 381.986(8)(a), Fla. Stat., but the merit of that claim was not addressed by the trial court. Moreover, at this stage of the litigation, the challenge to the caps is largely derivative of Appellees' challenge to the statute requiring vertical integration because if the vertical integration requirement is invalid, then the caps are clearly indefensible.

marijuana industry, not unlimited availability and unrestricted access to medical marijuana. To that end, the statutory scheme put in place by the Legislature—and implemented by the Department—appears to be serving the public interest because, despite the limited number of vertically-integrated MMTCs currently in operation, it is undisputed that medical marijuana is being produced and sold to qualifying patients. Additionally, Appellees failed to show how the preliminary injunction requiring the wholesale restructuring of the medical marijuana industry in Florida would be in the public interest, and on that issue, I agree with the Department that the confusion and uncertainty that the change would inject into the fledgling industry is not in the public interest....

Accordingly, for the reasons stated above, I would quash the preliminary injunction in its entirety and let the litigation play out below. This would, among other things, allow the existing MMTCs to join the fray because it is their golden geese that may be killed—or at least be devalued—if the oligopolistic statutory scheme established by the Legislature to implement the Medical Marijuana Amendment is ultimately invalidated.

Article XI

Amendments

Introduction

State constitutions are much easier to amend than the federal Constitution, and the Florida Constitution is no exception to this rule. In fact, the Florida Constitution has more methods to amend than any other state's constitution, including two methods unique to Florida. State constitutions are generally easier to amend than the U.S. Constitution for a reason: states must be nimble and responsive to the needs of their people. Florida's Constitution is easy to amend for another reason, though, and it harks back to the governmental changes Florida was beginning to experience in the middle of the twentieth century.

At that time, Florida's Constitution could be amended in only two ways: by a constitutional convention, which no one wanted to invoke, or by the Legislature placing a proposed amendment on the ballot for voter approval. Florida's 1885 Constitution, which was in effect until 1968, had been amended well over a hundred times, but the amendments reflected only the priorities of the Legislature, which did not always align with those of the voting public.

This was because the Legislature did not accurately represent the population of Florida. As the introductory chapter of this book mentioned, the legislative districts were drawn accurately for the population patterns of 1885, and the terms of that Constitution made it hard to redraw the lines to accommodate large and radical population changes. But large and radical changes are exactly what happened to Florida's population between 1885, when the population of the whole state was around 300,000, most of it in the north, and 1960, when the population of Dade County alone was more than 900,000, and the north had experienced little to no growth. The result was that the many rural counties of the north had most of the legislative districts — and, thus, legislators — and the populous counties of the south had few districts and legislators. Thus, the needs of the newly urban parts of Florida were not met with sympathy by the rural majority in the Legislature.

And the Constitution's strictures on changing legislative districts made meaningful reapportionment impossible. The Constitution would have to be amended to make these changes possible. But the only way to change the Constitution was through the Legislature — the very people who would lose their jobs through reapportionment.

This self-interest was one major example of the lack of alignment between the Legislature's interest and the population's.

Even when the Legislature finally passed a bill enabling a Constitution Revision Commission (CRC), it held all the cards: whatever the CRC proposed would have to pass the Legislature or die. It is probably through a remarkable fluke of timing that the CRC's progressive new Constitution ever made it to the people for a vote. That accident was the U.S. Supreme Court's decision, on the very day the Legislature was supposed to take up the CRC's draft Constitution, holding the Legislature was illegally apportioned and must adjourn until the federal district court could draw its own, fair, apportionment plan.

As this book's first chapter explains in more detail, the reapportioned Legislature did pass a draft constitution very similar to the CRC's and placed it on the ballot, where the people adopted it. And that Constitution contained the many amendment methods that the CRC members had included. The CRC created so many ways to amend the Constitution with the explicit purpose of taking sole power to amend from the Legislature and sharing it with the people.[1]

Therefore, one can read Article XI of this Constitution as a reaction to the amendment provisions of the 1885 Constitution. Instead of excluding the people's voices,

---

1. Mary E. Adkins, Making Modern Florida (Gainesville: University Press of Florida 2016), 149.

it provided two ways to include them: through a citizens' initiative process, then relatively new but not unheard-of, and through an every-twenty-year CRC, a process both new and unheard-of.

It would not be until nearly thirty years later that the fifth method of amending the Constitution, the Taxation and Budget Reform Commission, became part of the Constitution. This body, like the CRC, consists of individuals nominated by governmental leaders. Like the CRC members, the TBRC members are technically beholden to no political person; once appointed, they cannot be removed from the commission. They sit for a limited period of time and consider what budget- and tax-related changes may be beneficial for the Constitution.

Currently, the Florida Constitution can be amended by:

1) Joint resolution of three-fifths of each house of the Legislature;

2) the CRC, which meets every twenty years to examine the whole Constitution and propose amendments;

3) the Taxation & Budget Reform Commission, which also meets every twenty years and has a more limited examination of the state budget and revenue structure;

4) Citizen initiatives, where citizens gather sufficient signatures to put an amendment on the ballot; and

5) a constitutional convention.

Voters must approve any changes to the Constitution. *See* FLA. CONST. art. XI, § 5(a). All of these methods, except the constitutional convention, have been used to submit amendments to the voters. Between 1978 and 2018, the Florida Legislature proposed some 83 amendments, of which 62 were approved by the voters. Another 25 amendments were proposed by the three CRCs, of which 16 were approved. Some 11 amendments were proposed by the Taxation and Budget Reform Commission, of which 5 were approved. Finally, some 38 initiative amendments appeared on the ballot, of which 30 were approved by the voters. *See generally* Database of Initiatives, Amendments & Revisions maintained by the Florida Division of Elections, available online at: https://dos.elections.myflorida.com/initiatives/.

A. Article XI, Section 3 — Initiatives

However, these ballot numbers do not tell the full story. Although citizens may propose amendments by initiative, the number of signatures required (8% of votes in last presidential election in at least half the state's congressional districts) is high, and most initiatives cannot make the ballot for this reason. In 1986, Article IV, Section 10 was introduced which provided for the Attorney General to seek an advisory opinion from the Florida Supreme Court for proposed initiatives which have gathered 10% of the signatures needed to put the proposal on the ballot. As we shall see in the cases below, the Court reviews initiative proposals under Article XI, Section 3 to determine whether they present a "single subject" to the voters. The Court also reviews the ballot title and summary under § 101.161, Florida Statutes. In recent years, the Court has also reviewed amendments proposed by other means for compliance with the ballot title and summary requirements.

Notwithstanding its attraction, the initiative process has become more difficult in recent years. In 2006, Article XI, Section 5(e) was amended to require 60% of voters voting on a measure to approve an amendment. (That amendment passed with 57.8% of the vote, enough to pass then but not enough to pass under the standard it created.) All amendments must be approved for the ballot by February 1 in the year in which a general election takes place.[2] Before 2011, signatures gathered for an initiative amendment were valid for four years, allowing them to cover two elections. However, since 2011, initiative signatures are valid for only two years.

As we saw with the many initiative amendments placed in Article X, some initiatives fit awkwardly with the traditional theory that the state Constitution is a "limitation on legislative power." With initiatives like the Net Ban, Pregnant Pigs, or Prohibits Indoor Smoking, the Florida Constitution has begun to target the behavior of citizens. Furthermore, many initiatives deal with matters which are not traditionally constitutional in nature. However, because no statutory initiative exists, the constitutional initiative is the only mechanism available for citizens frustrated by legislative inaction on a favored issue.

The following cases illustrate how the Florida Supreme Court has reviewed initiative proposals. Note the use of the advisory opinion process for the later cases. It is worth mentioning that no specific jurisdiction is provided in the Florida Constitution for Supreme Court review of CRC or TBRC proposals, yet when they were challenged, the Supreme Court accepted jurisdiction without comment.

Fine v. Firestone
448 So. 2d 984 (Fla. 1984)

OVERTON, Justice.

Petitioner, Martin Fine, sought an extraordinary writ from the First District Court of Appeal directing the secretary of state to remove from the 1984 general election ballot a proposed constitutional amendment identified as Citizens' Choice on Government Revenue. In an opinion reported as *Fine v. Firestone*, 443 So.2d 253 (Fla. 1st DCA 1983), the district court declined to issue the extraordinary writ but certified the following questions to this Court:

WHETHER IN THE CIRCUMSTANCES PRESENTED THE PROPOSED CONSTITUTIONAL AMENDMENT IS SUSCEPTIBLE TO CONSTITUTIONAL CHALLENGE BY PETITION FOR AN EXTRAORDINARY WRIT, AND IF SO:

---

2. Fla. Const. art. XI, § 5(b).

WHETHER THE PROPOSED REVENUE LIMITATION AMENDMENT INVOLVED IN THIS CASE COMPORTS WITH ARTICLE XI, SECTION 3, FLORIDA CONSTITUTION, AND IF SO:

WHETHER THE PROPOSED REVENUE LIMITATION AMENDMENT INVOLVED IN THIS CASE IS PRESENTLY SUSCEPTIBLE TO A DUE PROCESS CHALLENGE UNDER THE FEDERAL CONSTITUTION.

Id. at 257. We have jurisdiction, article V, section 3(b)(4), Florida Constitution.

In summary, we find that the extraordinary writ of mandamus is a proper means for resolving the strictly legal issue of whether the Citizens' Choice proposal addresses more than one subject in violation of article XI, section 3 of the Florida Constitution. We therefore answer the first certified question in the affirmative.

We hold that the Citizens' Choice proposal clearly violates the single-subject requirement of the Florida Constitution. We find that the proposal includes at least three subjects, each of which affects a separate existing function of government. First, it limits how governments can tax, thereby affecting the general operation of state and local government. Second, it restricts all government user-fee operations, such as garbage collection, water, electric, gas, and transportation services which are paid for by the users of the services. Third, it affects the funding of capital improvements through revenue bonds, which are financed from revenue generated by the capital improvements. Accordingly, the second certified question is answered in the negative.

Having so answered the second certified question, it is unnecessary for this Court to address the third certified question. The reasons for our holdings are fully expressed below.

Factual History

The proposed amendment originated with an initiative petition for a constitutional amendment entitled "Citizens' Choice on Government Revenue." The initiative petition ... was approved by the secretary of state for inclusion on the 1984 general election ballot as Amendment One. The ballot summary and full language of the proposed constitutional provision read as follows:

Ballot title and summary:

CITIZENS' CHOICE ON GOVERNMENT REVENUE

Limits the state and each taxing unit to 1980–81 revenue dollars plus ad valorem taxes on subsequent new construction and annual adjustments of two-thirds of the Consumer Price Index percentage change; however, the maximum annual adjustment increase for ad valorem taxes is five percent. Revenue limits may be exceeded only with voter approval, for specified purposes, amounts and periods. Enforcement is by setting aside excess revenue, reduction of rates and taxpayer suits. Includes related provisions.

The following new section is added to Article VII of the Florida Constitution:

CITIZENS' CHOICE ON GOVERNMENT REVENUE:

(a) Revenue received by the state and by each taxing unit for each fiscal period shall be limited to the revenue limit for the preceeding [sic] fiscal period plus the annual adjustment and any ad valorem taxes on improvements due to new construction subject to assessment for the first time.

(b) For purposes of this section:

(1) revenue includes ad valorem taxes, other taxes and all other receipts, but excludes receipts from the United States government and its instrumentalities, bonds issued, loans received and the cost of investments sold. Receipts of agencies and instrumentalities and propriatary and trust funds shall be included in the revenue of the state or other taxing unit as appropriate.

(2) the annual adjustment for each fiscal period shall be the revenue limit of the preceeding [sic] fiscal period times two-thirds of the percentage change in the Consumer Price Index for All Urban Consumers, U.S. City Average, All Items, 1967 = 100, or successor reports, for the preceeding [sic] calendar year, as initially reported by the United States Department of Labor, Bureau of Labor Statistics; however for ad valorem taxes no annual adjustment increase shall exceed five percent of the ad valorem taxes of preceeding [sic] fiscal period.

(3) each fiscal period shall be twelve months[.]

(4) the initial revenue limit, for the first fiscal period beginning after the effective date of this section, shall be calculated by using the revenue in the fiscal period beginning in 1980, plus subsequent changes due to annual adjustments and ad valorem taxes on new construction, as if this section had been in effect.

(c) Revenue collected in excess of a revenue limit shall be placed in escrow until the following fiscal period, in which period it shall be deemed revenue received, and applicable rates shall be reduced in an amount reasonably calculated to comply with the revenue limits of this section.

(d) When authorized by vote of the electors of a taxing jurisdiction:

(1) revenue limits may be exceeded for specified purposes and amounts, for not longer than two fiscal periods;

(2) revenue limits may be exceeded to provide for principal and interest payments on designated bonds for specified purposes.

(3) a taxing unit may use its first fiscal period, in lieu of one beginning in 1980, for determining initial revenue limits.

(e) Revenue limits may be exceeded to the extent necessary to avoid impairment of obligations of contracts and bonds existing on the effective date of this section.

(f) Any taxpayer of the state shall have standing to bring suit to enforce this section and, if successful, shall recover costs and attorney fees from the taxing jurisdiction.

Fine instituted this action claiming that the proposed amendment violates both the single-subject rule of the Florida Constitution and the due process clause of the federal constitution. He sought, in the First District Court of Appeal, to have the amendment removed from the ballot by an extraordinary writ. In denying relief, the district court first held that petitioner's assertions required fact-finding and that there was an available remedy by declaratory judgment or injunction in the circuit court. The district court, however, then proceeded to address the merits of the petition. On the merits, the district court, relying primarily on this Court's decisions in *Floridians Against Casino Takeover v. Let's Help Florida,* 363 So.2d 337 (Fla.1978), and *Weber v. Smathers,* 338 So.2d 819 (Fla.1976), found that "the proposed amendment in this case contains various elements within the ambit of the single subject of revenue limitation, and that petitioner has not established that the proposal is 'clearly and conclusively defective' within the purview of Article XI, Section 3, Florida Constitution." 443 So.2d at 257. The district court also rejected petitioner's contention that the proposal violates the due process clause of the federal constitution. The court then certified the previously quoted questions.

* * *

The Single-Subject Requirement of an Initiative Proposal to Revise or Amend the Constitution

The primary question before this Court is whether there is more than one subject contained in the Citizens' Choice proposal. Article XI, section 3 of the Florida Constitution authorizes changes in our constitution by initiative petition and provides that:

> [t]he power to propose the revision or amendment of any portion or portions of this constitution by initiative is reserved to the people, *provided that, any such revision or amendment shall embrace but one subject and matter directly connected therewith.*

(Emphasis added.) The single-subject requirement in the proviso language of this section is a rule of restraint. It was placed in the constitution by the people to allow the citizens, by initiative petition, to propose and vote on singular changes in the functions of our governmental structure....

It is apparent that the authors of article XI realized that the initiative method did not provide a filtering legislative process for the drafting of any specific proposed constitutional amendment or revision. The legislative, revision commission, and constitutional convention processes of sections 1, 2 and 4 all afford an opportunity for public hearing and debate not only on the proposal itself but also in the drafting of any constitutional proposal. That opportunity for input in the drafting of a proposal is not present under the initiative process and this is one of the reasons the initiative process is restricted to single-subject changes in the state constitution. The single-subject requirement in article XI, section 3, mandates that the electorate's attention be directed to a change regarding one specific subject of government to protect against multiple precipitous changes in our state constitution. This requirement avoids voters having to accept part of an initiative proposal which they oppose in order to obtain a change in the constitution which they support. An initiative proposal with multiple subjects, in which the public has had no representative interest in drafting, places voters with different views on the subjects contained in the proposal in the position of having to choose which subject they feel most strongly about.

We recognize that there is a similar one-subject restriction contained in article III, section 6 of the Florida Constitution regarding laws enacted by the legislature. The purpose of this provision is to prohibit the aggregation of dissimilar provisions in one law in order to attract the support of diverse groups to assure its passage. In legislative parlance, article III, section 6, prohibits what is known as "logrolling." *See Brown v. Firestone*, 382 So.2d 654 (Fla.1980); *Green v. Rawls*, 122 So.2d 10 (Fla.1960). We recognize that we have taken a broad view of this legislative restriction but only to the extent that the contents of the legislation must be reasonably related. *See Chenoweth v. Kemp*, 396 So.2d 1122 (Fla.1981); *State v. Lee*, 356 So.2d 276 (Fla.1978). We recede from our prior language in *Floridians* that expressed the view that there is no difference between the legislative one-subject restriction and the initiative constitutional proposal one-subject limitation. We find it is proper to distinguish between the two. First, we find that the language "shall embrace but one subject and matter *properly connected* therewith" in article III, section 6, regarding statutory change by the legislature is broader than the language "shall embrace but one subject and matter *directly connected* therewith," in article XI, section 3, regarding constitutional change by initiative. (Emphasis added.) Second, we find that we should take a broader view of the legislative provision because any proposed law must proceed through legislative debate and public hearing. Such a process allows change in the content of any law before its adoption. This process is, in itself, a restriction on the drafting of a proposal which is not applicable to the scheme for constitutional revision or amendment by initiative. Third, and most important, we find that we should require strict compliance with the single-subject rule in the initiative process for constitutional change because our constitution is the basic document that controls our governmental functions, including the adoption of any laws by the legislature.

In our view, the single-subject restraint on constitutional change by initiative proposals is intended to direct the electorate's attention to one change which may affect only one subject and matters directly connected therewith, and that includes an understanding by the electorate of the specific changes in the existing constitution proposed by any initiative proposal.

In *Adams v. Gunter*, 238 So.2d 824 (Fla.1970), this Court found, under a more restrictive constitutional provision, that a proposal to create a unicameral legislature violated the single-section requirement of article XI, section 3. Under the prior constitutional provision, the initiative process was limited to the amendment of "any section" of the constitution. After our decision in *Adams*, the constitutional initiative provision was broadened to allow the revision or amendment of "any portion or portions" of the constitution. In *Adams* this Court expressed concern that the proposal neither identified the sections amended nor specified how they would be amended. We have the same concerns in this cause.

Although an initiative petition under the present constitution may amend multiple sections of the constitution as long as the proposal contains a single subject, an initiative proposal should identify the articles or sections of the constitution substantially affected. This is necessary for the public to be able to comprehend the contemplated changes in the constitution and to avoid leaving to this Court the responsibility of interpreting the initiative proposal to determine what sections and articles are substantially affected by the proposal. The problem of conflicting provisions resulting from the adoption of an initiative proposal cannot be satisfactorily addressed by the application of the principle of constitutional construction that the most recent amendment necessarily supersedes any existing provisions which are in conflict. We recede from *Floridians* to the extent that it conflicts with this view. Reliance on the application of this principle of constitutional construction in these circumstances would grant to this Court broad discretionary authority in determining the effect of a proposed amendment or revision on the existing constitution. No official record of legislative history or debate would be available to aid this Court in the construction of an amendment resulting from an initiative proposal. We do not believe it was the intent of the authors of the initiative-amendment provision, nor the intent of the electorate in adopting it, that the Supreme Court should be placed in the position of redrafting substantial portions of the constitution by judicial construction. This, in our view, would be a dangerous precedent.

* * *

In *Floridians* we held that the legalization of casino gambling, its taxation, and the distribution of the taxes collected, constituted a single subject. In rejecting the assertion that the proposed amendment contained more than one subject, we reaffirmed a part of the test expressed in *City of Coral Gables v. Gray*, 154 Fla. 881, 19 So.2d 318 (1944), that in determining whether a proposal addresses a single subject the test is whether it "may be logically viewed as having a natural relation and connection as component parts or aspects of a single dominant plan or scheme. Unity of object and plan is the universal test...." *Id.* at 883–84, 19 So.2d at 320. We also emphasized in *Floridians* that, under the present constitutional provision, the test should include a determination of whether the proposal affects a function of government as opposed to whether the proposal affects a section of the constitution.... In *Floridians* we also held that the question of whether an initiative proposal conflicted with other articles or sections of the constitution had "no place in assessing the legitimacy of an initiative proposal." 363 So.2d at 341. We recede from that language and find that how an initiative proposal affects other articles or sections of the constitution is an appropriate factor to be considered in determining whether there is more than one subject included in an initiative proposal.

The supporters of the Citizens' Choice proposal contend that all of its provisions deal with government revenue and are of a common and consistent theme. They contend that each provision of the amendment promotes the single object of limiting government revenue in a slightly different way. We reject the contention that the proposal necessarily affects only one function of government and contains only one subject. There is no question but that this proposal addresses at least three subjects which affect separate, distinct functions of the existing governmental structure of Florida, and substantially affects multiple sections and articles of our present constitution which are not in any way identified to the electorate.

First, we find that the proposal clearly restricts all types of taxation utilized for general governmental operations, including ad valorem real property taxes, personal property taxes, sales and use taxes, excise taxes on cigarettes, liquor and gasoline, corporate income taxes, and estate and inheritance taxes....

The second distinct subject which we find in the Citizens' Choice proposal involves the restriction on the operation and expansion of all user-fee services. User-fee services are those services, ordinarily utilities, which are primarily paid for by the users of the services. These include garbage collection, water, electricity, gas, and transportation services.... The intent of the proposal is to limit all "receipts of agencies and instrumentalities and proprietary and trust funds," which includes all revenue generated by government-operated utilities and other user-fee services.

* * *

All of these services would be substantially affected by this proposal. The proposal limits the expansion or growth of any user-fee service operated by a governmental entity. We conclude that the effect on these types of user-fee services is a separate subject that is readily distinguishable from the subject of taxation for general governmental operations....

The third distinct subject which we find in the Citizens' Choice proposal is the substantial effect it has on the constitutional scheme for the funding of capital improvements with revenue bonds. Under article VII of the Florida Constitution, there are a number of provisions which allow governmental entities to finance the construction of capital improvements with funds from government bonds without the necessity of an election. These bonds are generally repaid from revenue generated by the capital improvement rather than from general tax revenue....

We find that this is a distinct subject that is not connected to the limitation on tax revenue for general governmental operations.

Finally, we reject respondent's argument that the severability language contained on the petition form operates to cure any violation of the single-subject requirement. The language reads:

> If any portion of this ballot title, summary and amendment is found to be invalid, the remaining portions shall not be invalidated. If this amendment is found to contain multiple subjects, all references to such additional subjects, found after the first subject, shall be invalid, but the remaining portions of the amendment shall not be invalidated.

This language is not part of the amendment and would not appear on the ballot. Further, such language cannot circumvent this Court's responsibility to determine whether the proposed amendment may constitutionally be placed before the voters.

Conclusion

We conclude that the Citizens' Choice proposal contains at least three subjects. It limits the way in which governmental entities can tax; it limits what government can provide in services which are paid for by the users of such services; and it changes how governments can finance the construction of capital improvements with revenue bonds that are paid for from revenue generated by the improvements.

* * *

SHAW, Justice, concurring in result only.

Prior to 1972 article XI, section 3, Florida Constitution, provided that the people could amend any section of the constitution by an initiative petition. In *Adams v. Gunter*, 238 So.2d 824 (Fla.1970), we concluded that the initiative power included "only the power to amend any section in such a manner that such amendment if approved would be complete within itself, relate to one subject and not substantially affect any other section or article of the Constitution or require further amendments to the Constitution to accomplish its purpose." *Id.* at 831.

In *Weber v. Smathers*, 338 So.2d 819 (Fla.1976), and *Floridians Against Casino Takeover v. Let's Help Florida*, 363 So.2d 337 (Fla.1978), we addressed the effect of the 1972 amendment to article XI, section 3, which expanded the scope of initiative petitions by providing that they could be used to revise or amend any portion or portions of the constitution if such revisions or amendments embraced but one subject and matter directly connected therewith. In *Weber*, the Court was presented with a choice of diametrically opposed views concerning the standard of review to be applied to such citizen initiatives. In his concurring opinion, Justice England took a liberal and expansive view which had the effect of transferring the largest part of the responsibility for analyzing such initiatives to the citizenry and of minimizing the role of the courts in such analysis. In his dissenting opinion, Justice Roberts took a more conservative view which placed greater responsibility on the courts. In *Floridians* we adopted and expanded the more liberal views expressed in the *Weber* concurrence. In my opinion, if we were to review the present initiative using the standard of review which we announced in *Weber* and *Floridians*, we could only hold that the initiative meets the provisions of article XI, section 3 and affirm the decision of the district court, *Fine v. Firestone*, 443 So.2d 253 (Fla. 1st DCA 1983).

The standard of review established in *Weber* and *Floridians* consisted of ten principles which I summarize as follows:

1. The 1972 amendment enlarged the right to amend or revise the constitution by initiative.

2. The burden is on a challenger to establish that the initiative proposal is clearly and conclusively defective.

3. The one subject limitation places a functional, as opposed to a locational, restraint on the range of authorized amendments.

4. The wisdom of the proposed initiative is not a matter for judicial review.

5. The one subject limitation should be viewed broadly rather than narrowly.

6. A parallel should be drawn between the one subject restraints placed on the citizens' initiative process and the legislative enactment of laws process. More specifically, the judicial gloss placed on legislative enactments which permit widely divergent rights and requirements in statutes covering a single subject are applicable to citizen-initiative amendments or revisions. . . .

7. The quality of the initiative draftmanship is not a matter for judicial review.

8. The substantial effect of the initiative proposal upon any other section or article of the constitution is irrelevant.

9. Conflicts between the initiative and existing articles of the constitution afford no logical basis for invalidating an initiative proposal.

10. When the newly-adopted amendment or revision conflicts with preexisting constitutional provisions, the newly-adopted provisions necessarily supersede the previous provisions.

While the first four principles are appropriate for appellate review of challenged initiatives, they do not furnish answers to the general question of how far the 1972 amendment enlarged the scope of permissible initiatives or the more specific question of what constitutes one subject under article XI, section 3. Principles five through ten, by contrast, are much more specific and result oriented. Their cumulative effect, in my opinion, is to largely nullify the one subject limitation by forswearing appellate review of the very factors which distinguish multi-subject initiatives from one-subject initiatives. In *Floridians* the initiative to legalize casino gambling and earmark tax proceeds was relatively narrow from a constitutional viewpoint. It could be described as the camel's nose under the tent. By contrast, the present initiative is extremely broad and brings the entire camel into the tent. . . .

* * *

Principles six through ten compound the difficulties presented by a broad view of the one-subject limitation. Each year, hundreds of laws are passed, amended, or repealed. Amendment or revision of the constitution is a far more serious matter. Suggesting that the two are analogous, as principle six does, is to blur the distinction. Principle seven is also flawed. An ineptly drawn initiative is a legitimate matter for judicial review for three reasons. First, it may be difficult, perhaps impossible, for a court to determine whether such an initiative meets the one-subject limitation. Second, an ineptly drawn initiative may not present the voters with an understandable proposition. Third, if adopted, the amendment or revision may present formidable difficulties to the three branches of government which have to obey it and may have to implement it. Such an "empty vessel," as the majority opinion recognizes, serves to transfer power to the judiciary, for example, which is directly contrary to the underlying purpose of citizen initiatives. This is not to suggest that citizen initiatives should be thrown out because they are not crystal clear or exactingly precise. If challenged, it may be that a contemporary interpretation can be placed on the initiative which preserves its constitutionality and serves to inform both the voters and the branches of government.

Principles eight and nine are closely related. Examination of the initiative to determine its substantial effect and whether it conflicts with existing provisions of the constitution is highly pertinent to the questions of whether it encompasses only one subject and whether its meaning is clear to the citizenry. This does not mean that an initiative is per se unconstitutional because it has a substantial effect and conflicts with preexisting provisions of the constitution. It does mean that when the initiative petition is challenged the judiciary must examine these factors in order to carry out its constitutional duty.

As to principle ten, it may be that a *newly adopted* amendment, which cannot be reconciled with older provisions of the constitution, will supersede these older provisions. This is not to say, however, that we should simply dismiss the conflict as irrelevant to the question of the one-subject limitation.

In sum, *Weber* and *Floridians* attempted to establish a standard of review for citizens' initiatives which facilitated the citizens' right to amend the constitution by initiative proposals. Unfortunately, in our desire not to unnecessarily impede the initiative process, we forswore the full use of relevant factors which would aid us in determining whether the initiative was limited to one subject. We should recede from the unrealistic standard of review in *Weber* and *Floridians*.

I see the one-subject limitation on initiative petitions as serving two purposes:

1. Ensuring that initiatives are sufficiently clear so that the reader, whether layman or judge, can understand what it purports to do and perceive its limits.

2. Ensuring that there is a logical and natural unity of purpose in the initiative so that a vote for or against the initiative is an unequivocal expression of approval or disapproval of the entire initiative.

When the two purposes above are examined, I conclude that the initiative fails on both prongs. The limits of the initiative are not clear and the scope of the single word "revenue" is so broad that citizens might well approve of limitations on one source of revenue while contrarily disapproving of limitations on other sources.

* * *

Questions

1. Note the difference accorded by the majority to the "single subject" requirement of Article III and the "single subject" requirement in Article XI.

2. According to the majority, what is the purpose behind the "single subject" requirement in Article XI?

3. How does the majority determine the number of subjects affected by the proposed amendment and what are those distinct subjects?

4. In what way does the majority recede from *Floridians*?

5. According to Justice Shaw, what are the purposes of the "single subject" requirement?

Advisory Opinion to the Attorney General re: Standards for Establishing Legislative District Boundaries

2 So. 3d 175 (Fla. 2009)

LEWIS, J.

The Attorney General of Florida has requested an opinion from this Court with regard to the validity of two initiative petitions sponsored by FairDistrictsFlorida.org, a political committee. We have jurisdiction. *See* art. IV, § 10, art. V, § 3(b)(10), Fla. Const. We conclude that the proposed amendments comply with the single-subject requirement of article XI, section 3 of the Florida Constitution, and that the ballot titles and summaries comply with section 101.161(1), Florida Statutes (2008).

I. THE PROPOSED AMENDMENTS

The two amendments and their respective ballot titles and summaries are nearly identical except for references to legislative versus congressional boundaries. The full text of the proposed amendment that governs *legislative-district* boundaries states:

Section 21. Add a new Section 21 to Article III

STANDARDS FOR ESTABLISHING LEGISLATIVE DISTRICT BOUNDARIES

In establishing Legislative district boundaries:

(1) No apportionment plan or individual district shall be drawn with the intent to favor or disfavor a political party or an incumbent; and districts shall not be drawn with the intent or result of denying or abridging the equal opportunity of racial or language minorities to participate in the political process or to diminish their ability to elect representatives of their choice; and districts shall consist of contiguous territory.

(2) Unless compliance with the standards in this subsection conflicts with the standards in subsection (1) or with federal law, districts shall be as nearly equal in population as is practicable; districts shall be compact; and districts shall, where feasible, utilize existing political and geographical boundaries.

(3) The order in which the standards within sub-sections (1) and (2) of this section are set forth shall not be read to establish any priority of one standard over the other within that subsection.

The ballot title for this proposed initiative is:

STANDARDS FOR LEGISLATURE TO FOLLOW IN LEGISLATIVE REDIS-TRICTING.

The ballot summary provides:

Legislative districts or districting plans may not be drawn to favor or disfavor an incumbent or political party. Districts shall not be drawn to deny racial or language minorities the equal opportunity to participate in the political process and elect representatives of their choice. Districts must be contiguous. Unless otherwise required, districts must be compact, as equal in population as feasible, and where feasible must make use of existing city, county and geographical boundaries.

The full text of the proposed amendment that governs *congressional-district* boundaries states:

Add a new Section 20 to Article III

Section 20. STANDARDS FOR ESTABLISHING CONGRESSIONAL DISTRICT BOUNDARIES

In establishing Congressional district boundaries:

(1) No apportionment plan or individual district shall be drawn with the intent to favor or disfavor a political party or an incumbent; and districts shall not be drawn with the intent or result of denying or abridging the equal opportunity of racial or language minorities to participate in the political process or to diminish their ability to elect representatives of their choice; and districts shall consist of contiguous territory.

(2) Unless compliance with the standards in this subsection conflicts with the standards in subsection (1) or with federal law, districts shall be as nearly equal in population as is practicable; districts shall be compact; and districts shall, where feasible, utilize existing political and geographical boundaries.

(3) The order in which the standards within sub-sections (1) and (2) of this section are set forth shall not be read to establish any priority of one standard over the other within that subsection.

The ballot title for this proposal is:

STANDARDS FOR LEGISLATURE TO FOLLOW IN CONGRESSIONAL REDISTRICTING.

The ballot summary provides:

Congressional districts or districting plans may not be drawn to favor or disfavor an incumbent or political party. Districts shall not be drawn to deny racial or language minorities the equal opportunity to participate in the political process and elect representatives of their choice. Districts must be contiguous. Unless otherwise required, districts must be compact, as equal in population as feasible, and where feasible must make use of existing city, county and geographical boundaries.

II. ANALYSIS

A. Single-Subject Requirement

Article XI, section 3 of the Florida Constitution provides: "The power to propose the revision or amendment of any portion or portions of this constitution by initiative is reserved to the people, provided that, any such revision or amendment, except for those limiting the power of government to raise revenue, *shall embrace but one subject and matter directly connected therewith.*" (Emphasis supplied.) This Court has previously explained the rationale behind the single-subject requirement:

The single-subject limitation exists because the initiative process does not provide the opportunity for public hearing and debate that accompanies the other methods of proposing amendments. Consequently, "[the] single-subject provision is a rule of restraint designed to insulate Florida's organic law from precipitous and cataclysmic change." This Court requires "strict compliance with the single-subject rule in the initiative process for constitutional change because our constitution is the basic document that controls our governmental functions, including the adoption of any laws by the legislature." The single-subject requirement also prevents logrolling, a practice that combines separate issues into a single proposal to secure passage of an unpopular issue. Thus, voters are protected by the single-subject requirement because they are not forced to "accept part of an initiative proposal which they oppose in order to obtain a change in the constitution which they support."

Advisory Op. to Att'y Gen. re Amendment to Bar Gov't From Treating People Differently Based on Race in Pub. Educ., 778 So.2d 888, 891 (Fla.2000).... To determine whether a proposed amendment addresses a single subject, this Court must evaluate whether the proposal "may be logically viewed as having a natural relation and connection as component parts or aspects of a single dominant plan or scheme." *Advisory Op. to Att'y Gen. re Patients' Right to Know About Adverse Med. Incidents,* 880 So.2d 617, 620 (Fla.2004) (quoting *Fine v. Firestone,* 448 So.2d 984, 990 (Fla.1984)).

A proposed amendment is not invalid merely because it affects more than one branch of government or may interact with other provisions of the Florida Constitution. *See Advisory Op. to Att'y Gen. re Limited Casinos,* 644 So.2d 71, 74 (Fla.1994) ("[W]e find it difficult to conceive of a constitutional amendment that would not affect other aspects of government to some extent."). We have further explained that "the fact that [a] branch of government is required to comply with a provision of the Florida Constitution does not necessarily constitute the usurpation of the branch's function within the meaning of the single-subject rule." *Advisory Op. to Att'y Gen. re Protect People, Especially Youth, From Addiction, Disease, & Other Health Hazards of Using Tobacco,* 926 So.2d 1186, 1192 (Fla.2006). Rather, "it is when a proposal substantially alters or performs the functions of multiple branches that it violates the single-subject test." *Patients' Right to Know,* 880 So.2d at 620. Finally, speculation about possible impacts of a proposed amendment on other branches of government is premature when determining whether a proposed amendment, *on its face,* meets the single-subject requirement. [citation omitted.]

With regard to reapportionment, article III, section 16(a) of the Florida Constitution currently provides, in relevant part:

(a) SENATORIAL AND REPRESENTATIVE DISTRICTS. The legislature at its regular session in the second year following each decennial census, by joint resolution, shall apportion the state in accordance with the constitution of the state and of the United States into not less than thirty nor more than forty consecutively numbered senatorial districts of either contiguous, overlapping or identical territory, and into not less than eighty nor more than one hundred twenty consecutively numbered representative districts of either contiguous, overlapping or identical territory.

We conclude that the proposed amendments (1) encompass a single subject, (2) do not engage in logrolling, and (3) do not substantially alter the functions of multiple branches of government. The proposed amendments address a single function of a single branch of government—establishing additional guidelines for the Legislature to apply when it redistricts legislative and congressional boundaries. This Court has previously stated that under the state and federal Constitutions, the only requirements for a redistricting plan are: (1) compliance with the equal protection standard of one-person, one-vote—i.e., that "legislatures be apportioned in such a way that each person's vote carries the same weight"; and (2) that districts consist of contiguous, overlapping, or identical territory. *In re Constitutionality of House Joint Resolution 1987*, 817 So.2d 819, 824–25 (Fla.2002) (quoting *In re Constitutionality of Senate Joint Resolution 2G*, 597 So.2d 276, 278 (Fla.1992)).

Logrolling—Although the Legislature contends that the proposals violate the single-subject rule because they implement multiple reapportionment standards, such an interpretation of the rule is far too narrow. The overall goal of the proposed amendments is to require the Legislature to redistrict in a manner that prohibits favoritism or discrimination, while respecting geographic considerations. Although the proposed amendments delineate a number of guidelines, we conclude that these components possess "a natural relation and connection as component parts or aspects of a single dominant plan or scheme." *Patients' Right to Know*, 880 So.2d at 620 (quoting *Fine*, 448 So.2d at 990).

The instant case is distinguishable from others in which this Court has determined that proposals have violated the single-subject requirement. For example, in *In re Advisory Opinion to Attorney General—Restricts Laws Related to Discrimination*, 632 So.2d 1018, 1019 (Fla.1994) (*Discrimination*), the proposed amendment sought to prohibit discrimination based on ten separate classifications—race, color, religion, sex, national origin, age, handicap, ethnic background, marital status, and familial status. While the sponsor contended that the amendment addressed the single subject of discrimination, we rejected this contention and instead concluded that the proposal "enfold[ed] disparate subjects within the cloak of a broad generality" in violation of the single-subject requirement. *Id.* at 1020 (quoting *Evans v. Firestone*, 457 So.2d 1351, 1353 (Fla.1984))....

Unlike the provision in *Discrimination*, the proposals in the instant cases do not group multiple subjects under the cloak of "redistricting." Rather, they address *solely* the *guidelines* to be applied in legislative and congressional reapportionment. Thus, the instant proposals are also distinguishable from the proposed amendment in *Advisory Opinion to Attorney General re Independent Nonpartisan Commission to Apportion Legislative & Congressional Districts Which Replaces Apportionment by Legislature*, 926 So.2d 1218 (Fla.2006) (*Nonpartisan*), which we determined to be in violation of the single-subject requirement. The proposal in *Nonpartisan* sought not only to implement redistricting standards, *but to also create an entirely new commission* to replace the

Legislature as the entity responsible for reapportionment in Florida. *See id.* at 1225. The proposed amendments here do *not* encompass two such disparate functions.

The proposed amendments here are more similar to proposals we have previously approved because they encompassed a single plan and merely enumerated various elements necessary to accomplish that plan. In *Health Hazards of Using Tobacco,* 926 So.2d at 1189, this Court approved for placement on the ballot a proposed amendment that would create a comprehensive statewide tobacco education and prevention program. The program was designed to encompass an advertising campaign, the creation of programs to educate youth about tobacco, enforcement of laws against the sale of tobacco to minors, and annual evaluations of the effectiveness of the program. *See id.* Further, the proposal included a provision which required that the Legislature appropriate fifteen percent of the gross funds collected from a tobacco settlement to the program. *See id.* This Court held that despite the various components, the proposal did not engage in logrolling:

> It addresses a single comprehensive plan for the education of youth about the health hazards related to tobacco. Although this plan includes a list of components such as advertising, school curricula, and law enforcement, all of these components are related to the single unifying purpose. It does not "combine subjects in such a manner as to force voters to accept one proposition they might not support in order to vote for one they favor." *Advisory Op. to Att'y Gen. re Fla.'s Amendment to Reduce Class Size,* 816 So.2d 580, 583 (Fla.2002)....

Id. at 1191–92. Similarly, here, the various components within the proposed amendments are directed to the single unified purpose of establishing standards by which legislative and congressional districts are to be drawn. Accordingly, we hold that the proposed amendments address a single subject.

Multiple Government Functions—The Legislature next asserts that the proposals will essentially shift the duty of reapportionment to the judiciary and, therefore, the proposals impact multiple branches of government in violation of the single-subject rule. This contention is without merit. Under the Florida Constitution, after the Legislature drafts a reapportionment plan, the attorney general files a request with this Court for a "declaratory judgment" with regard to the validity of the plan. Art. III, § 16(c), Fla. Const. If this Court rejects the plan, the Governor must reconvene the Legislature for an "extraordinary apportionment session," during which the Legislature must adopt a joint resolution that conforms to this Court's judgment. *Id.* § 16(d). If the extraordinary session fails to produce a resolution of apportionment, or if this Court holds that the subsequent apportionment is invalid, the Court "shall, not later than sixty days after receiving the petition of the attorney general, file with the custodian of state records an order making such apportionment." *Id.* § 16(f).

* * *

The proposed amendments do not alter the functions of the judiciary. They merely change the standard of review to be applied when either the attorney general seeks a "declaratory judgment" with regard to the validity of a legislative apportionment, or a redistricting plan is challenged. This effect of the proposed amendments does not constitute a substantial alteration of the functions of the judicial branch....

The contention of the Legislature that a redistricting plan can never comply with the amendment guidelines and, therefore, the role of reapportionment will always fall upon the courts—thereby substantially changing a function of the courts—is speculative argument. There is no basis that the judiciary will reject any redistricting plan that the Legislature adopts for failure to comply with the guidelines. We must assume the Legislature will comply with the law at the time an apportionment plan is adopted. Moreover, such speculation with regard to a possible impact of the proposals on the judicial branch is premature because we need only determine at this time whether the proposed amendments, *on their face,* satisfy the single-subject requirement. *See [In re Advisory Op. to Att'y Gen. re] English—The Official Language,* 520 So.2d at 13 [(Fla. 1988)].

In light of the foregoing, we hold that the proposed amendments comply with article XI, section 3 of the Florida Constitution.

B. Ballot Title and Summary

The requirement that a ballot title and summary comply with section 101.161(1), Florida Statutes (2008), was recently explained by this Court as follows:

> [A]ny proposed constitutional amendment must be "accurately represented on the ballot; otherwise, voter approval would be a nullity." *Armstrong v. Harris,* 773 So.2d 7, 12 (Fla.2000). Section 101.161(1), Florida Statutes (2007), codifies this principle:
>
> Whenever a constitutional amendment or other public measure is submitted to the vote of the people, the substance of such amendment or other public measure shall be printed in *clear and unambiguous language* on the ballot.... Except for amendments and ballot language proposed by joint resolution, the substance of the amendment or other public measure shall be an explanatory statement, not exceeding 75 words in length, of the chief purpose of the measure.... The ballot title shall consist of a caption, not exceeding 15 words in length, by which the measure is commonly referred to or spoken of.

(Emphasis supplied.)

* * *

... This Court has recognized that it must exercise extreme caution and restraint before removing a constitutional amendment from Florida voters. *See Advisory Opinion to Attorney Gen. re Fla. Marriage Prot. Amendment,* 926 So.2d 1229, 1233 (Fla.2006). We have further noted that we have no authority to inject this Court into the process, unless the laws governing the process have been "clearly and conclusively" violated. *Advisory Opinion to the Attorney Gen. re Right to Treatment & Rehab. for Non-Violent Drug Offenses,* 818 So.2d 491, 498–99 (Fla.2002).

Fla. Dep't of Rev. v. Slough, 992 So.2d 142, 146–47 (Fla.2008). Despite these various requirements, we have also noted that even though a ballot summary could have better explained the text of the amendment, that fact alone does *not* require a proposal to be struck:

> There is no requirement that the referendum question set forth the [text] verbatim nor explain its complete terms at great and undue length. Such [requirements] would hamper instead of aiding the intelligent exercise of the privilege of voting. Under our system of free elections, the voter must acquaint himself with the details of a proposed ordinance on a referendum together with the pros and cons thereon before he enters the voting booth....

Advisory Op. to Att'y Gen. re Right to Treatment & Rehab. for Non-Violent Drug Offenses, 818 So.2d 491, 498 (Fla.2002) (quoting *Metro. Dade County v. Shiver,* 365 So.2d 210, 213 (Fla. 3d DCA 1978), *aff'd sub nom. Miami Dolphins v. Metro. Dade County,* 394 So.2d 981 (Fla.1981)). Moreover, inadvertent use of different but clearly synonymous terms in the proposed amendment and the summary will *not* render a ballot summary fatally defective where "[t]he differing use of terminology could not reasonably mislead the voters." *English — The Official Language,* 520 So.2d at 13 (use of the phrase "to *implement* this *article*" in the ballot summary not misleading where the text of the proposed amendment actually provided "to *enforce* this *section*" (alteration in original)).

The Legislature presents multiple claims that the ballot titles and summaries for the proposed amendments are misleading. We address each of those arguments.

Ballot title — The Legislature first asserts that the titles are misleading because they indicate that only the Legislature must comply with the new redistricting standards where, in fact, the judiciary will be similarly obligated to apply these standards when a legislative attempt at reapportionment fails and the courts are required to redraw the districts. We conclude that this challenge is without merit.

* * *

"Drawn to favor" vs. *"Drawn with the intent to favor"* — The amendment summaries provide that redistricting plans "shall not be drawn to favor or disfavor an incumbent or political party"; however, the body of the proposals provide that districting plans "shall not be drawn *with the intent* to favor or disfavor an incumbent or political party." (Emphasis supplied.) According to the Legislature, the summaries indicate that the *effect* of a reapportionment plan cannot be to favor or disfavor anyone or any party; however, under the proposed amendments, proof of *intent* to favor an incumbent or party must be demonstrated before a reapportionment plan will be rejected for noncompliance. The Legislature contends that the summaries are misleading because voters will believe that the proposals prohibit reapportionment plans whose *effect* is to favor a party or incumbent, while the amendments actually permit districts that favor a party or incumbent, provided that the district lines were drawn without intending that result.

We reject this assertion. The ballot summaries are currently seventy-four words in length. Hence, to add the words "with the intent" to the ballot summaries would exceed the statutory word limit. Thus, at issue in this case is whether the omission of these three words from the summaries (likely in an attempt to comply with the statutory word limit) causes them to be fatally misleading. As previously noted, a ballot summary need not (and because of the statutory word limit, often cannot) explain "at great and undue length" the complete details of a proposed amendment, and some onus falls upon voters to educate themselves about the substance of the proposed amendment....

Additionally, such an intent requirement has been historically applied with regard to allegations of gerrymandering in reapportionment. For example, this Court has held that a discriminatory *effect* is not sufficient to prove racial discrimination in redistricting; rather, a discriminatory *intent* must be demonstrated:

> This invidious intent or purpose of racial discrimination, the Supreme Court explained, cannot be proved by merely showing that the group discriminated against has not elected representatives in proportion to its numbers. Disproportionate effects alone will not establish a claim of unconstitutional racial vote dilution. Rather, "[a] plaintiff must prove that the disputed plan was conceived or operated as a purposeful device to further racial discrimination." Proof of a discriminatory effect is not sufficient.

Milton v. Smathers, 389 So.2d 978, 981–82 (Fla.1980)....

While ideal summaries for these amendments might have included the words "with the intent," we conclude that—given the strict word limits—the failure of the summaries to include these three words does not render them so misleading as to clearly and conclusively violate section 101.161, Florida Statutes. *See Right to Treatment & Rehabilitation,* 818 So.2d at 498 (holding that failure of ballot summary to explain that proposed amendment is self-effectuating did not render the summary misleading and noting that "imperfection is not necessarily fatal given the seventy-five word statutory maximum").

Shift of Authority—The Legislature next contends that the summaries are misleading because they fail to mention that the proposed amendments divest the Legislature of its responsibility to draw legislative and congressional districts and transfer this role to the judiciary. However, we have already concluded that the proposed amendments do not substantially alter the functions of multiple branches of government....

"City/County" boundaries vs. "Political" Boundaries—The ballot summaries state that district boundaries shall, where feasible, utilize existing "city, county and geographical boundaries"; however, the body of the amendments provide that districts must use "existing *political* and geographical boundaries." (Emphasis supplied.) The Legislature asserts that the term "political boundaries" encompasses more than city or county boundaries, and under the Florida Statutes, this State has many special districts—such as voting precincts and water-management districts—the borders of which would constitute "political boundaries." Thus, to the extent that the summaries use language inconsistent with that of the proposed amendments, the Legislature contends that they are misleading.

Although the phrase "political and geographical boundaries" used in the proposed amendments may be technically broader than the "city, county, and geographical boundaries" phrase used in the summaries, we conclude that this differing use of terminology could not reasonably mislead voters....

The And/Or Distinction—Under this challenge, the Legislature contends that the summaries are misleading because while they provide that "[d]istricts shall not be drawn to deny racial or language minorities the equal opportunity to participate in the political process *and* elect representatives of their choice," the proposed amendments provide that "districts shall not be drawn with the intent or result of denying or abridging the equal opportunity of racial or language minorities to participate in the political process *or* to diminish their ability to elect representatives of their choice." (Emphasis supplied.) According to the Legislature, the "or" in the proposals demonstrates that an apportionment plan need satisfy *only one* of the two conditions to comply with the amendment—either districts must not be drawn to deny racial or language minorities the equal opportunity to participate in the political process *or* districts must not be drawn to diminish the ability of racial or language minorities to elect representatives of their choice. According to the Legislature, both standards need not be accomplished. Conversely, the Legislature posits that use of the word "and" in the summary indicates that *both* standards must be satisfied to comply with the amendments—thus, the summaries are misleading because they promise more than is required under the proposed amendments.

We conclude that the logic of the Legislature is faulty. In support of its assertion, the Legislature relies upon the case *Armstrong v. Harris*, 773 So.2d 7, 16 (Fla.2000), in which this Court held that a ballot title which read "United States Supreme Court Interpretation of Cruel and Unusual Punishment" and a summary which provided that the proposed amendment "[r]equires construction of the prohibition against cruel and/or unusual punishment to conform to United States Supreme Court interpretation of the Eighth Amendment" were affirmatively misleading. *See* 773 So.2d at 16–17. This Court explained that although the title offered the impression that "the amendment will promote the rights of Florida citizens through the rulings of the United States Supreme Court," the amendment actually restricted the rights of Floridians because the United States Constitution ban against "cruel *and* unusual" punishment provided fewer protections than the Florida Constitution ban on "cruel *or* unusual punishment." *Id.* at 17. Thus, the "or" carried special significance because it prohibited punishment that is *either* cruel *or* unusual, whereas under the United States Constitution, the punishment is prohibited only if it is both cruel *and* unusual.

However, the proposal in *Armstrong* is distinguishable from the proposed amendments that we review today. While the word "or" in the *Armstrong* proposal was used in conjunction with two adjectives, here the word "or" separates two clauses of a sentence which share the same negative verb; i.e., "shall not be drawn." This verb modifies both clauses, thereby indicating that *both* clauses impose a restrictive imperative, *each of which must be satisfied*. For example, if a statute provides that "one person shall not kill another *or* cause him/her grievous bodily harm," it is illogical to suggest that the statute prohibits one action *but not the other*. Rather, the "shall not" unquestionably applies to both actions—*both* killing *and* causing grievous bodily harm are prohibited. Similarly, the negative verb "shall not be drawn" in the proposed amendments modifies both clauses "with the intent or result of denying or abridging the equal opportunity of racial or language minorities to participate in the political process" and "to diminish their ability to elect representatives of their choice." Under this sentence, *both* effects are prohibited.[3] ....

Language Minorities—The Legislature's claim that this term is vague or ambiguous is not persuasive. The term "language minorities" is both legally and commonly understood to refer to any language other than English. *See, e.g.,* 42 U.S.C. § 1973b(f)(1)....

Elimination of Multi-Member Districts—Lastly, the Legislature contends that the summary of the legislative-boundary proposal is misleading because it fails to inform voters that it changes the Florida Constitution to no longer permit multi-member legislative districts and to mandate single-member legislative districts. The Florida Constitution currently mandates that legislative districts consist of either "contiguous, overlapping or identical territory." Art. III, § 16(a), Fla. Const. In 1972, we held that this language permits multi-member legislative districts:

> [T]he Constitution requires that there be one senator elected from each Senatorial district and one member of the House of Representatives elected from each representative district. This, standing alone, would require single-member districts. However, the Constitution further provides that districts may be "identical territory." This means that multi-members of the Senate or the House of Representatives may be elected from the identical territory if such territory were designated as constituting several districts. To require single-member districts would void the provision of Fla. Const., art. III, § 16(a) ... authorizing the creation of districts in "identical territory."
>
> ....
>
> Under the provisions of Fla. Const., art. III, § 1 and 16 ... multi-member districts are permissible and such multi-member districts may coexist with single-member districts in the same plan.

In re Apportionment Law Senate Joint Resolution No. 1305, 263 So.2d 797, 806–07 (Fla.1972).

The Legislature contends that adoption of the proposed legislative-boundary amendment—which includes a "contiguous" requirement but does not mention overlapping or identical districts—operates to repeal article III, section 16(a) of the Florida Consti-

---

3. [FN 2.] One legal dictionary has explained:
   "[O]r" has an inclusive sense as well as an exclusive sense. Hence:

   ....

   • The "inclusive or": A or B, or both
   • The "exclusive or": A or B, but not both.
   Bryan A. Garner, *A Dictionary of Modern Legal Usage* 624 (2d ed.1995).

tution. Under this rationale the Legislature argues that because identical districts are no longer permitted, the proposal amends the Florida Constitution to implement a single-member district requirement, and the ballot summary fails to inform voters of this significant change. *See Nonpartisan,* 926 So.2d at 1226 (noting that the "identical territory" provision in article III, section 16(a) permits the creation of multi-member districts).

We disagree that adoption of the legislative-boundary proposal will have the asserted effect. This Court has explained:

> A new constitutional provision prevails over prior provisions of the Constitution (a) if it specifically repeals them or (b) if it cannot be harmonized with them. Nevertheless, it is settled that *implied repeal of one constitutional provision by another is not favored,* and every reasonable effort will be made to give effect to both provisions. Unless the later amendment expressly repeals or purports to modify an existing provision, *the old and new should stand and operate together unless the clear intent of the later provision is thereby defeated.*

Jackson v. City of Jacksonville, 225 So.2d 497, 500–501 (Fla.1969) (emphasis supplied). Since the legislative-boundary proposal does *not* expressly repeal section 16(a), this constitutional provision will be considered repealed by implication *only if* it cannot be harmonized with the proposal.

We conclude that harmonization of these two provisions is possible and, therefore, "identical" multi-member districts in Florida will still be constitutionally permissible even if the legislative-boundary proposal is adopted. In 1982, this Court clarified that the word "contiguous" in article III, section 16(a) "means only that each district must be contiguous *within itself*" and does not refer "to the relationship of the districts to each other." *In re Apportionment Law Appearing as Senate Joint Resolution No. 1E,* 414 So.2d 1040, 1045, 1050 (Fla.1982) (emphasis supplied). Thus, under this Court's prior case law, the reference to "contiguous" in the proposed legislative-boundary amendment solely addresses the characteristics of an individual district—not its relationship with any other district....

III. CONCLUSION

In conclusion, we hold that the proposed amendments meet the legal requirements of article XI, section 3 of the Florida Constitution, and the ballot titles and summaries comply with section 101.161(1), Florida Statutes (2008). Accordingly, we approve the amendments for placement on the ballot.

It is so ordered.

* * *

Questions

1. Why did the sponsors of the Fair Districts amendments submit two separate initiative proposals instead of a single combined proposal?

2. How does the Court explain the single subject standard of Article XI, Section 3?

3. Has this evolved from the one announced in *Fine v. Firestone?*

Advisory Opinion to the Attorney General re: Voting Restoration Amendment

215 So. 3d 1202 (Fla. 2017)

LEWIS, J.

The Attorney General of Florida has requested this Court's opinion as to the validity of an initiative petition circulated pursuant to article XI, section 3 of the Florida Constitution. We have jurisdiction. *See* art. IV, § 10, art. V, § 3(b)(10), Fla. Const.

FACTS AND BACKGROUND

On October 4, 2016, the Attorney General petitioned this Court for an advisory opinion as to the validity of an initiative petition sponsored by Floridians for a Fair Democracy ("the Sponsor") and circulated, pursuant to article XI, section 3 of the Florida Constitution. The Sponsor submitted a brief supporting the validity of the initiative petition.

The full text of the proposed amendment to article VI, section 4 of the Florida Constitution states:

> Article VI, Section 4. Disqualifications.—
>
> (a) No person convicted of a felony, or adjudicated in this or any other state to be mentally incompetent, shall be qualified to vote or hold office until restoration of civil rights or removal of disability. <u>Except as provided in subsection (b) of this section, any disqualification from voting arising from a felony conviction shall terminate and voting rights shall be restored upon completion of all terms of sentence including parole or probation.</u>
>
> (b) <u>No person convicted of murder or a felony sexual offense shall be qualified to vote until restoration of civil rights.</u>
>
> * * *

The ballot title for the amendment is: "Voter Restoration Amendment." The ballot summary states:

> This amendment restores the voting rights of Floridians with felony convictions after they complete all terms of their sentence including parole or probation. The amendment would not apply to those convicted of murder or sexual offenses, who would continue to be permanently barred from voting unless the Governor and Cabinet vote to restore their voting rights on a case by case basis.

On October 28, 2016, the Financial Impact Estimating Conference forwarded to the Attorney General a financial impact statement on the initiative petition. On November 1, 2016, the Attorney General requested this Court's opinion as to whether the financial impact statement prepared by the Financial Impact Estimating Conference on the constitutional amendment is in accordance with section 100.371, Florida Statutes (2016). The financial impact statement regarding the Voter Restoration Amendment states:

The precise effect of this amendment on state and local government costs cannot be determined, but the operation of current voter registration laws, combined with an increased number of felons registering to vote, will produce higher overall costs relative to the processes in place today. The impact, if any, on state and local government revenues cannot be determined. The fiscal impact of any future legislation that implements a different process cannot be reasonably determined.

No briefs or comments were submitted to this Court in response to the financial impact statement.

ANALYSIS

Standard of Review

We have explained the standard of review for citizen initiative petitions as follows:

"This Court has traditionally applied a deferential standard of review to the validity of a citizen initiative petition and 'has been reluctant to interfere' with 'the right of self-determination for *all* Florida's citizens' to formulate 'their own organic law.'" [citations omitted] This Court does "not consider or address the merits or wisdom of the proposed amendment" and must "act with extreme care, caution, and restraint before it removes a constitutional amendment from the vote of the people." [citations omitted]

Advisory Op. to Att'y Gen. re Rights of Elec. Consumers Regarding Solar Energy Choice (*Solar Energy*), 188 So.3d 822, 827 (Fla. 2016).

When this Court renders an advisory opinion concerning a proposed constitutional amendment arising through the citizen initiative process, the Court limits its inquiry to two issues: (1) whether the amendment itself satisfies the single-subject requirement of article XI, section 3, Florida Constitution; and (2) whether the ballot title and summary satisfy the clarity requirements of section 101.161, Florida Statutes.

[citations omitted] Accordingly, we are obligated to uphold the proposal unless it is "clearly and conclusively defective." *Advisory Op. to Att'y Gen. re Fla.'s Amend. to Reduce Class Size*, 816 So. 2d 580, 582 (Fla. 2002).

Single-Subject Requirement

Article XI, section 3 of the Florida Constitution establishes the general requirement that a proposed citizen initiative amendment "shall embrace but one subject and matter directly connected therewith." Art. XI, § 3, Fla. Const. "In evaluating whether a proposed amendment violates the single-subject requirement, the Court must determine whether it has a logical and natural oneness of purpose." [*Advisory Op. to Att'y Gen. re Use of Marijuana for Debilitating Med. Conditions* (*Medical Marijuana II*)], 181 So.3d 471, 477 (Fla. 2015) (internal citations omitted). The single-subject requirement applies to the citizen initiative method of amending the Florida Constitution because the citizen initiative process does not afford the same opportunity for public

hearing and debate that accompanies other constitutional proposal and drafting processes. *See Advisory Op. to the Att'y Gen. re 1.35% Prop. Tax Cap,
Unless Voter Approved*, 2 So.3d 968, 972 (Fla. 2009).

* * *

Solar Energy, 188 So.3d at 827–28. This Court has further explained that "[a] proposal
that affects several branches of government will not automatically fail; rather, it is
when a proposal substantially alters or performs the functions of multiple branches
that it violates the single-subject test." *Advisory Op. to Att'y Gen. re Fish & Wildlife
Conservation Comm'n*, 705 So.2d 1351, 1353–54 (Fla. 1998).

   Here, the initiative has "a logical and natural oneness of purpose," specifically,
whether Floridians wish to include a provision in our state constitution permitting
the restoration of voting rights to Floridians with felony convictions, excluding those
with murder and felony sex offenses, once they have completed all of the terms of
their sentences. The proposed amendment's provision excluding persons with convictions for murder or felony sex offenses is directly connected with this purpose.
Furthermore, this exclusion removes a class of offenders from automatic voter
restoration eligibility based on the nature of their offenses, thus removing the possibility that voters be forced to "accept part of an initiative proposal which they
oppose in order to obtain a change in the constitution which they support." [citations
omitted] Therefore, the proposed amendment does not engage in impermissible
logrolling....

   Additionally, the proposed amendment does not substantially alter or perform
the functions of multiple branches. As it currently stands, the Governor, with the
approval of two members of the Florida Cabinet, may restore civil rights on a case-
by-case basis. *See* art. IV, §8, Fla. Const. If the proposed amendment passes, the
Governor and the Florida Cabinet would still review the restoration of civil rights
on a case-by-case basis, but only for those persons convicted of murder or felony
sexual offenses, rather than for all felony offenders, which would reduce their current
obligations in an insignificant way. "[I]t [is] difficult to conceive of a constitutional
amendment that would not affect other aspects of government to some extent." *Advisory Op. to Att'y Gen. re Ltd. Casinos*, 644 So.2d 71, 74 (Fla. 1994)....

   Accordingly, we conclude that the proposed amendment complies with the single-subject requirement of article XI, section 3 of the Florida Constitution.

Ballot Title and Summary

   Section 101.161(1) provides the following requirements for the ballot title and
summary:

> The ballot summary of the amendment or other public measure shall be an
> explanatory statement, not exceeding 75 words in length, of the chief purpose
> of that measure.... The ballot title shall consist of a caption, not exceeding 15
> words in length, by which the measure is commonly referred to or spoken of.

§101.161(1), Fla. Stat. (2016).

The purpose of these requirements is "to provide fair notice of the content of the proposed amendment so that the voter will not be misled as to its purpose, and can cast an intelligent and informed ballot." *Advisory Op. to Att'y Gen. re Term Limits Pledge*, 718 So.2d 798, 803 (Fla. 1998).

This Court's review of the validity of a ballot title and summary under section 101.161(1) involves two inquiries:

> First, the Court asks whether "the ballot title and summary ... fairly inform the voter of the chief purpose of the amendment." *Right to Treatment and Rehabilitation for Non-Violent Drug Offenses*, 818 So.2d [491, 497 (Fla. 2002).... Second, the Court asks "whether the language of the title and summary, as written, misleads the public." *Advisory Op. to Att'y Gen. re Right of Citizens to Choose Health Care Providers*, 705 So.2d 563, 566 (Fla. 1998).

... "While the ballot title and summary must state in clear and unambiguous language the chief purpose of the measure, they need not explain every detail or ramification of the proposed amendment." *Solar Energy*, 188 So.3d at 831 (quoting *Advisory Op. to Att'y Gen. re 1.35% Prop. Tax Cap*, 2 So.3d 968, 974 (Fla. 2016)).

Here, the ballot title and summary comply with the respective word limitations. The title is three words in length and the summary contains sixty-two words, which is within the word requirements of section 101.161(1).

Thus, the remaining issues are: (1) whether the ballot title and summary inform voters of the chief purpose of the proposed amendment; and (2) whether the ballot title and summary are misleading. We conclude that both issues are satisfied here.

First, the ballot title and summary clearly and unambiguously inform the voters of the chief purpose of the proposed amendment. Read together, the title and summary would reasonably lead voters to understand that the chief purpose of the amendment is to automatically restore voting rights to felony offenders, except those convicted of murder or felony sexual offenses, upon completion of all terms of their sentence.

Second, the ballot title and summary also do not mislead voters with regard to the actual content of the proposed amendment. Rather, together they recite the language of the amendment almost in full. [citations omitted]

Accordingly, for the reasons expressed above, we conclude that the ballot title and summary comply with the clarity requirements of section 101.161.

Financial Impact Statement

We have also detailed our obligation to review financial impact statements:

> We have an independent obligation to review the financial impact statement to ensure that it is clear and unambiguous and in compliance with Florida law. *See Adv. Op. to Atty. Gen. re Use of Marijuana for Certain Medical Conditions*, 132 So.3d [786, 809 (Fla. 2014)] (citing *Adv. Op. to Atty. Gen. re*

Referenda Required for Adoption & Amend. of Local Gov't Comprehensive Land Use Plans, 963 So. 2d 210, 214 (Fla. 2007)). Article XI, section 5(c), of the Florida Constitution provides, "The legislature shall provide by general law, prior to the holding of an election pursuant to this section, for the provision of a statement to the public regarding the probable financial impact of any amendment proposed by initiative pursuant to section 3." Additionally, section 100.371(5)(a), Florida Statutes (2015), provides that the financial impact statement must address "the estimated increase or decrease in any revenues or costs to state or local governments resulting from the proposed initiative." Section 100.371(5)(c) 2, Florida Statutes (2015), requires the financial impact statement to be "clear and unambiguous" and "no more than 75 words in length."

We have explained that our "review of financial impact statements is narrow." *Adv. Op. to Att'y Gen. re Water & Land Conservation*, 123 So.3d [47, 52 (Fla. 2013)]. We address only "whether the statement is clear, unambiguous, consists of no more than seventy-five words, and is limited to address the estimated increase or decrease in any revenues or costs to the state or local governments." *Advisory Op. to Att'y Gen. re Local Gov't Comprehensive Land Use Plans*, 963 So.2d [210, 214 (Fla. 2007)].

Medical Marijuana II, 181 So.3d at 479.

We conclude that the financial impact statement complies with the word limit and meets the other statutory requirements set forth in section 100.371(5), Florida Statutes (2016). The financial impact statement is seventy-four words in length, thus complying with the seventy-five-word limit, and is limited to the subject of the estimated increase or decrease in revenues or costs to state and local governments. Additionally, it clearly and unambiguously states that there are likely increased costs associated with the influx of felons registering to vote, but that the exact amount of cost increase cannot be determined. Moreover, the financial impact statement clearly and unambiguously explains that the Financial Impact Estimating Conference could not determine the impact on state and local government revenue. Therefore, we conclude that the financial impact statement complies with section 100.371(5)....

CONCLUSION

In conclusion, we hold that the proposed amendment meets the legal requirements of article XI, section 3 of the Florida Constitution, and that the ballot title and summary complies with section 101.161(1). Moreover, we conclude that the financial impact statement complies with section 100.371(5). Accordingly, we approve the amendment for placement on the ballot.

It is so ordered.

LABARGA, C.J., and PARIENTE, QUINCE, CANADY, POLSTON, and LAWSON, JJ., concur.

Advisory Opinion to the Attorney General re: Prohibits Possession of Defined Assault Weapons

296 So. 3d 376 (Fla. 2020)

PER CURIAM.

The Attorney General of Florida has requested this Court's opinion as to the validity of a citizen initiative petition circulated pursuant to article XI, section 3 of the Florida Constitution. We have jurisdiction. *See* art. IV, § 10, art. V, § 3(b)(10), Fla. Const. For the reasons explained below, we conclude that the proposed initiative, titled "Prohibits possession of defined assault weapons" (the "Initiative"), should not be placed on the ballot.

BACKGROUND

On July 26, 2019, the Attorney General petitioned this Court for an opinion as to the validity of the Initiative, which is sponsored by Ban Assault Weapons NOW. The sponsor submitted a brief supporting the validity of the Initiative, as did Brady and Team ENOUGH and the Municipalities. The Attorney General, the National Rifle Association, and the National Shooting Sports Foundation submitted briefs in opposition.

The Initiative would amend article I, section 8 of the Florida Constitution as follows:

ARTICLE I, SECTION 8. Right to Bear Arms.—

(a) The right of the people to keep and bear arms in defense of themselves and of the lawful authority of the state shall not be infringed, except that the manner of bearing arms may be regulated by law.

(b) There shall be a mandatory period of three days, excluding weekends and legal holidays, between the purchase and delivery at retail of any handgun. For the purposes of this section, "purchase" means the transfer of money or other valuable consideration to the retailer, and "handgun" means a firearm capable of being carried and used by one hand, such as a pistol or revolver. Holders of a concealed weapon permit as prescribed in Florida law shall not be subject to the provisions of this paragraph.

(c) The legislature shall enact legislation implementing subsection (b) of this section, effective no later than December 31, 1991, which shall provide that anyone violating the provisions of subsection (b) shall be guilty of a felony.

(d) This restriction shall not apply to a trade in of another handgun.

(e) The possession of an assault weapon, as that term is defined in this subsection, is prohibited in Florida except as provided in this subsection. This subsection shall be construed in conformity with the Second Amendment to the United States Constitution as interpreted by the United States Supreme Court.

1) Definitions—

a) Assault Weapons—For purposes of this subsection, any semiautomatic rifle or shotgun capable of holding more than ten (10) rounds of ammunition at once, either in a fixed or detachable magazine, or any other ammunition-feeding device. This subsection does not apply to handguns.

b) Semiautomatic — For purposes of this subsection, any weapon which fires a single projectile or a number of ball shots through a rifled or smooth bore for each single function of the trigger without further manual action required.

c) Ammunition-feeding device — For purposes of this subsection, any magazine, belt, drum, feed strip, or similar device for a firearm.

2) Limitations —

a) This subsection shall not apply to military or law enforcement use, or use by federal personnel, in conduct of their duties, or to an assault weapon being imported for sale and delivery to a federal, state or local governmental agency for use by employees of such agencies to perform official duties.

b) This subsection does not apply to any firearm that is not semi-automatic, as defined in this subsection.

c) This subsection does not apply to handguns, as defined in Article I, Section 8(b), Florida Constitution.

d) If a person had lawful possession of an assault weapon prior to the effective date of this subsection, the person's possession of that assault weapon is not unlawful (1) during the first year after the effective date of this subsection, or (2) after the person has registered with the Florida Department of Law Enforcement or a successor agency, within one year of the effective date of this subsection, by providing a sworn or attested statement, that the weapon was lawfully in his or her possession prior to the effective date of this subsection and by identifying the weapon by make, model, and serial number. The agency must provide and the person must retain proof of registration in order for possession to remain lawful under this subsection. Registration records shall be available on a permanent basis to local, state and federal law enforcement agencies for valid law enforcement purposes but shall otherwise be confidential.

3) Criminal Penalties — Violation of this subsection is a third-degree felony. The legislature may designate greater but not lesser, penalties for violations.

4) Self-executing — This provision shall be self-executing except where legislative action is authorized in subsection (3) to designate a more severe penalty for violation of this subsection. No legislative or administrative action may conflict with, diminish or delay the requirements of this subsection.

5) Severability — The provisions of this subsection are severable. If any clause, sentence, paragraph, section or subsection of this measure, or an ap-

plication thereof, is adjudged invalid by any court of competent jurisdiction, other provisions shall continue to be in effect to the fullest extent possible.

6) Effective date — The effective date of this amendment shall be thirty days after its passage by the voters.

The ballot title for the Initiative is "Prohibits possession of defined assault weapons," and the ballot summary reads as follows:

Prohibits possession of assault weapons, defined as semiautomatic rifles and shotguns capable of holding more than 10 rounds of ammunition at once, either in fixed or detachable magazine, or any other ammunition feeding device. Possession of handguns is not prohibited. Exempts military and law enforcement personnel in their official duties. Exempts and requires registration of assault weapons lawfully possessed prior to this provision's effective date. Creates criminal penalties for violations of this amendment.

* * *

ANALYSIS

While the parties have raised a number of issues for this Court's consideration, we address only one issue that is dispositive — the ballot summary affirmatively misleads voters regarding the exemption addressed in the next to last sentence of the ballot summary, which provides that the Initiative "[e]xempts and requires registration of assault weapons lawfully possessed prior to this provision's effective date." This misleading language violates section 101.161(1), Florida Statutes (2019), which sets forth the requirements for the ballot title and summary of an initiative petition and provides as follows:

[A] ballot summary of such amendment or other public measure shall be printed in clear and unambiguous language on the ballot.... The ballot summary of the amendment or other public measure shall be an explanatory statement, not exceeding 75 words in length, of the chief purpose of the measure.... The ballot title shall consist of a caption, not exceeding 15 words in length, by which the measure is commonly referred to or spoken of.

§ 101.161(1), Fla. Stat. (2019).

* * *

"Ballot language may be clearly and conclusively defective either in an affirmative sense, because it misleads the voters as to the material effects of the amendment, or in a negative sense by failing to inform the voters of those material effects." [citations omitted] Therefore, "the Court must consider two questions: '(1) whether the ballot title and summary ... fairly inform the voter of the chief purpose of the amendment; and (2) whether the language of the title and the summary, as written, misleads the public.'" [citations omitted]

Here, the ballot summary fails to satisfy the requirements of section 101.161(1) and is affirmatively misleading because the meaning of the text of the ballot summary does not accurately describe the meaning of the Initiative's text regarding the exemption.

Specifically, the next to last sentence of the ballot summary informs voters that the Initiative "[e]xempts and requires registration of *assault weapons* lawfully possessed prior to this provision's effective date" (emphasis added), when in fact the Initiative does no such thing. Contrary to the ballot summary, the Initiative's text exempts only "*the person's*," meaning the current owner's, possession of that assault weapon. The Initiative's text provides:

> If a person had lawful possession of an assault weapon prior to the effective date of this subsection, *the person's possession* of that assault weapon is not unlawful (1) during the first year after the effective date of this subsection, or (2) after the person has registered with the Florida Department of Law Enforcement or a successor agency, within one year of the effective date of this subsection, by providing a sworn or attested statement, that the weapon was lawfully in his or her possession prior to the effective date of this subsection and by identifying the weapon by make, model, and serial number.

(Emphasis added.) While the ballot summary purports to exempt registered assault weapons lawfully possessed prior to the Initiative's effective date, the Initiative does not categorically exempt the assault weapon, only the current owner's possession of that assault weapon. The ballot summary is therefore affirmatively misleading.

The Proponents argue that, notwithstanding this divergence in text and meaning, voters will understand that the registered assault weapon itself would not be exempt, just the current owner's possession of it. We reject this argument. The ballot summary informs voters that registered assault weapons lawfully possessed prior to the Initiative's effective date are exempt from the scope of the Initiative altogether, which misleads voters to believe that any lawfully possessed assault weapons will continue to remain lawful. However, the Initiative contemplates the eventual criminalization of the possession of assault weapons, even if the assault weapon itself was lawfully possessed and registered prior to the Initiative's effective date. As the Opponents argue, if an individual registers and attests to lawful possession of an assault weapon, and then lends, gifts, or leaves in a will that assault weapon to a family member or friend, then that family member or friend would be in criminal violation of the Initiative — a felony offense. The summary indicates the opposite, that once registered, the assault weapon will be exempt. Therefore, because the ballot summary is affirmatively misleading, it does not satisfy the requirements of section 101.161.

CONCLUSION

For the reasons stated, we conclude that the ballot summary is misleading and does not comply with section 101.161(1), Florida Statutes. Accordingly, this Initiative cannot be placed on the ballot.

It is so ordered.

* * *

LABARGA, J., dissenting.

Because I conclude that the ballot summary satisfies the requirements of section 101.161(1), Florida Statutes (2019), I believe the Initiative should appear on the ballot for voter consideration.

The ballot title clearly communicates the chief purpose of the Initiative, and the ballot summary clearly summarizes the content of the proposed amendment. The language with which the majority takes exception, "[e]xempts and requires registration of assault weapons lawfully possessed prior to this provision's effective date," is not affirmatively misleading. In fact, the language is accurate, and the majority simply concludes that the language is insufficiently narrow.

In applying the requirements of section 101.161(1), this Court must be mindful that the ballot summary is just that — a summary — consisting of no more than seventy-five words. As this Court has stated: "We recognize that the seventy-five word limit on ballot summaries prevents the summary from revealing all the details or ramifications of the proposed amendment. Accordingly, we have never required that the summary explain the complete details of a proposal at great and undue length, nor do we do so now." *Smith v. Am. Airlines, Inc.*, 606 So. 2d 618, 621 (Fla. 1992)....

"[V]oters are generally required to do their homework and educate themselves about the details of a proposal and about the pros and cons of adopting the proposal." *Smith*, 606 So. 2d at 621. The ballot title and summary provide fair notice and equip voters to educate themselves about the details of the Initiative. Consequently, the Initiative should be placed on the ballot.

I dissent to the majority's decision precluding the Initiative from voter consideration.

B. Article XI, Section 5(c) — Financial Impact Statements for Initiative Amendments

Advisory Opinion to the Attorney General re: Raising Florida's Minimum Wage

285 So. 3d 1273 (Fla. 2019)

PER CURIAM

[The Supreme Court found that this proposed initiative amendment complied with the single subject requirement and that the ballot title and summary were clear and unambiguous, and the Court approved the proposal. However, the Court then addressed the financial impact statement for the proposal.]

C. Financial Impact Statement

We previously concluded, in *Advisory Opinion to the Attorney General re Referenda Required for Adoption*, 963 So. 2d 210, 210 (Fla. 2007), that we have jurisdiction to review financial impact statements. We now conclude that this determination was clearly erroneous and, because we cannot exercise jurisdiction that the constitution does not provide, recede from it.

Our jurisdiction is defined in article V, section 3 of the Florida Constitution. The only provision of article V, section 3 that has been argued as providing jurisdiction to review financial impact statements is section 3(b)(10), which provides that this Court "[s]hall, when requested by the attorney general pursuant to the provisions of Section 10 of Article IV, render an advisory opinion of the justices, addressing issues as provided by general law." Because article V, section 3(b)(10) references the portion of the constitution that requires the Attorney General to seek our review of initiative petitions, art. IV, § 10, and that provision in turn references the provision of the constitution recognizing the right to file an initiative petition, art. XI, § 3, article V, section 3(b)(10) is best presented by beginning with the portion of the constitution addressing initiative petitions, proceeding to consider the portion of the constitution directing the Attorney General to seek our opinion on initiative petitions, and then reviewing the text of article V, section 3(b)(10).

Article XI, section 3 sets forth the power of the people to propose amendments to the constitution by initiative in these terms:

> The power to propose the revision or amendment of any portion or portions of this constitution by initiative is reserved to the people, provided that, any such revision or amendment, except for those limiting the power of government to raise revenue, shall embrace but one subject and matter directly connected therewith. It may be invoked by filing with the custodian of state records a petition containing a copy of the proposed revision or amendment, signed by a number of electors in each of one half of the congressional districts of the state, and of the state as a whole, equal to eight percent of the votes cast in each of such districts respectively and in the state as a whole in the last preceding election in which presidential electors were chosen.

Article IV, section 10 sets forth the Attorney General's duty to seek this Court's review of an initiative petition, as follows:

> The attorney general shall, as directed by general law, request the opinion of the justices of the supreme court as to the validity of any initiative petition circulated pursuant to Section 3 of Article XI. The justices shall, subject to their rules of procedure, permit interested persons to be heard on the questions presented and shall render their written opinion no later than April 1 of the year in which the initiative is to be submitted to the voters pursuant to Section 5 of Article XI.

As noted above, article V, section 3(b)(10) defines this Court's jurisdiction with respect to a request by the Attorney General under article IV, section 10, by stating that this Court "[s]hall, when requested by the attorney general pursuant to the provisions of Section 10 of Article IV, render an advisory opinion of the justices, addressing issues as provided by general law." Notably, none of the three quoted provisions mention financial impact statements.

Financial impact statements are addressed in a different provision of the constitution, article XI, section 5(c). Article XI, section 5(c) states, "The legislature shall provide by general law, prior to the holding of an election pursuant to this section, for the provision of a statement to the public regarding the probable financial impact of any amendment proposed by initiative pursuant to section 3 [of article XI]."

The Legislature has arranged for the provision of financial impact statements to the public within section 100.371(13). Section 100.371(13) creates the FIEC and requires it to analyze the financial impact of a proposed amendment and prepare a statement of that financial impact within a certain time frame of receipt of the proposed amendment from the Secretary of State. § 100.371(13)(a), (c). The statute contemplates that the financial impact statement will be placed on the ballot with the related proposed amendment unless it is not judicially approved. § 100.371(13)(a), (c) 3. The statute dictates the length and content of the financial impact statement and requires the FIEC to submit the financial impact statement to the Attorney General. § 100.371(13)(a), (c) 2. The statement must be "clear and unambiguous," no more than 150 words, and address "the estimated increase or decrease in any revenues or costs to state or local governments, estimated economic impact on the state and local economy, and the overall impact to the state budget resulting from the proposed initiative." § 100.371(13)(a), (c) 2.

In the scheme the Legislature enacted for the preparation and publication of financial impact statements, the Legislature expressly contemplated this Court's review of such statements. § 100.371(13)(c) 3, (e) 1, 2; *see also* § 16.061(3) ("Any fiscal impact statement that *the* court finds not to be in accordance with s. 100.371 shall be remanded solely to the Financial Impact Estimating Conference for redrafting." (emphasis added)).[4] However, that contemplation does not, in itself, give us jurisdiction. Although article V, section 3(b)(10) directs this Court to review issues provided by general law, that direction does not open the door for this Court to exercise original jurisdiction to review any issue provided by general law as to any subject. That direction pertains to issues concerning the validity of initiative petitions, as that alone is the subject matter of both article V, section (3)(b)(10) and article IV, section 10. Therefore, article V section 3(b)(10) does not grant this Court original jurisdiction to review issues pertaining to financial impact statements unless a financial impact statement is properly considered a part of an initiative petition.

* * *

Not only does the constitution not make a financial impact statement a part of an initiative petition, neither does current statutory law. The Attorney General properly concedes these points.

* * *

---

4. [FN 2.] It is not clear, however, that the Legislature contemplated that this Court's review authority be exclusive. See § 100.371(13)(c) 2. ("Any financial impact statement that *a* court finds not to be in accordance with this section shall be remanded solely to the Financial Impact Estimating Conference for redrafting." (emphasis added)).

As for statutory law, our review of the current statutes governing initiative petitions and financial impact statements confirms that the Legislature has not made the financial impact statement a part of an initiative petition. To implement article XI, section 5's directive to arrange for the provision of a financial impact statement to the public, the Legislature created a public entity, the FIEC, that is solely responsible for that task and has not required the person or group sponsoring an initiative petition to include that statement in the petition. *See* §§ 15.21(2), 100.371(13), 101.161(2), Fla. Stat. (2019); *see also Referenda Required for Adoption*, 963 So. 2d at 217 n.7 (Bell, J. dissenting) ("The financial impact statement is not prepared by the sponsor and is not signed by any electors."). The sponsor's responsibility in preparing an initiative petition is to establish the text of the proposed amendment and create a ballot summary and ballot title, which the sponsor submits to the Secretary of State for approval before circulating for signatures. §§ 15.21(2), 100.371(2), 101.161(2). In fact, the FIEC has no responsibility to prepare a financial impact statement until after the sponsor has filed the initiative petition with the Secretary of State and the Secretary of State has forwarded it to the FIEC. § 100.371(13)(a). Given that the initiative petition must be filed before the FIEC has any responsibility to create a financial impact statement, and that the sponsor of the initiative petition has no responsibilities with respect to the financial impact statement, the initiative petition and financial impact statement can only be considered separate documents.

Because a financial impact statement is not an initiative petition and does not constitute any part of an initiative petition under the Florida Constitution or under the system the Legislature has created for the preparation and publication of these separate documents, any issues pertaining to the financial impact statement fall outside the scope of direct review authorized by article V, section 3(b)(10). While those issues are "provided by general law," they are not within the subject matter addressed in article V, section 3(b)(10). For these reasons, we do not have original jurisdiction to review financial impact statements.

Having reached this conclusion based on the plain language of the constitution, and recognizing that this Court does not create its own jurisdiction, but rather exercises the jurisdiction provided by the constitution, we are not at liberty to adhere to our precedent....

CONCLUSION

For the foregoing reasons, we conclude that the initiative petition and proposed ballot title and summary for the proposed amendment "Raising Florida's Minimum Wage" meet the legal requirements of article XI, section 3 of the Florida Constitution and section 101.161(1). Accordingly, we approve the amendment for placement on the ballot. We express no opinion on the validity of the financial impact statement.

It is so ordered.

CANADY, C.J., and POLSTON, LABARGA, LAWSON, and MUÑIZ, JJ., concur.

Questions

1. Why does the Supreme Court decline to review the financial impact statement for the proposed initiative amendment?

2. Why does the Court say that the financial impact statement is not "part of any initiative petition"?

3. What method would be available to challenge a proposed financial impact statement?

C. Article XI, Section 1 — Proposal by Legislature

Armstrong v. Harris

773 So. 2d 7 (Fla. 2000)

SHAW, J.

We have on appeal a judgment certified by the district court to be of great public importance requiring immediate resolution by this Court. We have jurisdiction. Art. V, §3(b)(5), Fla. Const.

I. FACTS

The Florida Legislature filed with the Florida Secretary of State ("Secretary") a joint resolution (No. 3505) of the House of Representatives of the Florida Legislature proposing an amendment to article I, section 17, Florida Constitution, relating to excessive punishments (May 5, 1998). The proposed amendment was designated Amendment No. 2. Dr. Armstrong and other citizens filed a petition for writ of mandamus in this Court challenging the validity of the proposed amendment (October 9), but the Court by a four-to-three vote declined to exercise jurisdiction "without prejudice to Armstrong to file an appropriate action in circuit court" (October 19). Armstrong then filed a complaint in circuit court seeking mandamus, injunctive, and declaratory relief (October 20), and the court ruled thusly: It dismissed the claim for mandamus relief, denied injunctive relief, and withheld ruling on the claim for declaratory relief (October 26). Armstrong sought certiorari review in the district court (October 26); that court certified the issue to this Court (October 28). On the day preceding the general election, this Court unanimously dismissed the appeal for technical reasons, without prejudice (November 2). Voters at the general election approved the amendment (November 3).

Armstrong filed a motion in this Court asking the Court to remand the case to the district court (November 11). He then filed in circuit court the present amended petition claiming that the ballot title and summary are inaccurate and again seeking mandamus, injunctive, and declaratory relief (December 3). The Secretary filed an answer in circuit court conceding that this claim is justiciable in an action for injunctive or declaratory relief but asserting that the ballot title and summary are accurate (December 28). Armstrong sought summary judgment, contending that the ballot title and summary are misleading as a matter of law (January 4, 1999). The Secretary filed a cross-motion for summary judgment, arguing that the ballot title and summary are adequate (January 27). The circuit court's authority to decide the matter was not challenged or raised as an issue. This Court then issued an order formally remanding the case to the circuit court, without prejudice, to resolve the pending issues (February 2, 1999). The circuit court reviewed the respective arguments in the summary judgment motions and granted summary judgment in favor of the Secretary, concluding that the Secretary's legal argument was more persuasive (February 25). Armstrong appealed (March 15). The district court certified the case to this Court via "pass through" jurisdiction (March 31).

Armstrong contends that both the ballot title and summary to Amendment No. 2 are defective for several reasons: They fail to disclose that the current prohibition against "cruel *or* unusual punishment" would be changed to "cruel *and* unusual punishment"; they give the false impression that the death penalty is in danger of being abolished and needs to be "preserved"; and they fail to give notice that the amendment would alter the separation of powers between the branches of government by giving the Legislature unfettered discretion to establish both the method of execution and the crimes susceptible to the death penalty.

II. STANDING

In her answer brief before this Court, the Secretary argued—as she did below—that the ballot title and summary are accurate. She never argued or suggested that Armstrong lacks standing to pursue this action. Following oral argument before this Court, the Secretary submitted a supplemental brief in which she now contends that Armstrong cannot pursue this appeal because the general election already has taken place, the voters have approved the amendment, and Armstrong's action was dilatory. We disagree.

Article XI, section 5, Florida Constitution, contains a pre-election notice requirement which provides that a proposed constitutional amendment must be published in newspapers of general circulation throughout the state at both ten and six weeks prior to the election. The purpose of this requirement is to avoid a "November surprise" in which voters are taken unawares in the voting booth by a proposed amendment. If citizens are given adequate pre-election notice, those who object to the substance of an amendment can voice their views in the public forum, and those who object to the regularity of the ballot title and summary can challenge the amendment in court.

Assuming that Armstrong received constructive notice of the present amendment in conformity with article XI, section 5, his failure to file the initial petition until several weeks later (i.e., three and a half weeks before the election) does not appear dilatory. Nothing in the record reveals that, prior to obtaining constructive notice, Armstrong, et al., constituted a formal political apparatus or an established special interest group with clear pre-publication knowledge of the amendment. Rather, appellants appear to be an ad hoc group of concerned citizens who, upon receiving notice, required a reasonable period of time in which to exercise their electoral prerogative—i.e., to meet and discuss the matter; to organize; to chart a course of action; to fund their organization, if necessary; to employ counsel; to research the issues, and to file suit. Given the pre-election publication schedule set forth in article XI, section 5, appellants filed their petition within a reasonable time after receiving constructive notice of the proposed amendment.

III. THE ACCURACY REQUIREMENT

A court may declare a proposed constitutional amendment invalid only if the record shows that the proposal is clearly and conclusively defective; the standard of review for a pure question of law is de novo.... A proposed amendment ultimately must be submitted to the electors for approval at the next general election. Article XI, section 5, Florida Constitution, states:

SECTION 5. Amendment or revision election.—

(a) *A proposed amendment to or revision of this constitution, or any part of it, shall be submitted to the electors at the next general election* held more than ninety days after the joint resolution, initiative petition or report of revision commission, constitutional convention or taxation and budget reform commission proposing it is filed with the custodian of state records, unless, pursuant to law enacted by the affirmative vote of three-fourth of the membership of each house of the legislature and limited to a single amendment or revision, it is submitted at an earlier special election held more than ninety days after such filing.

Art. XI, § 5, Fla. Const. (emphasis added). Implicit in this provision is the requirement that the proposed amendment be *accurately* represented on the ballot; otherwise, voter approval would be a nullity. *See generally Askew* [*v. Firestone*], 421 So.2d at 155 [(Fla. 1982)] ("[T]he Constitution requires ... that the ballot be fair and advise the voter sufficiently to enable him intelligently to cast his ballot.")

This accuracy requirement, which applies to all proposed constitutional amendments, has been codified by the Legislature in chapter 101, Florida Statutes (1997). Because the text of a proposed amendment oftentimes is detailed and lengthy, section 101.161 provides that only a title and brief summary of the amendment's "chief purpose" may be listed on the ballot. The actual text of the amendment does not appear:

101.161 Referenda; ballots.—

(1) Whenever a constitutional amendment or other public measure is submitted to the vote of the people, *the substance of such amendment or other public measure shall be printed in clear and unambiguous language on the ballot* after the list of candidates, followed by the word "yes" and also by the word "no," and shall be styled in such a manner that a "yes" vote will indicate approval of the proposal and a "no" vote will indicate rejection. The wording of the substance of the amendment or other public measure and the ballot title to appear on the ballot shall be embodied in the joint resolution, constitutional revision commission proposal, constitutional convention proposal, taxation and budget reform commission proposal, or enabling resolution or ordinance. *The substance of the amendment or other public measure shall be*

an explanatory statement, not exceeding 75 words in length, of the chief purpose of the measure. The ballot title shall consist of a caption, not exceeding 15 words in length, by which the measure is commonly referred to or spoken of.

§ 101.161(1), Fla. Stat. (1997) (emphasis added). Significantly, both the ballot title and summary are prepared by the amendment's sponsor.

Because voters will not have the actual text of the amendment before them in the voting booth when they enter their votes, the accuracy requirement is of paramount importance for the ballot title and summary.... In practice, the accuracy requirement in article XI, section 5, functions as a kind of "truth in packaging" law for the ballot.

IV. LEGISLATIVELY PROPOSED AMENDMENTS

The Secretary in her supplemental brief argues that the Court should adopt a special standard for evaluating the validity of constitutional amendments proposed by the Legislature. She does not contend that all legislatively proposed amendments are automatically exempt from the accuracy requirement or that the courts have no authority to review such amendments. Rather, she claims that the accuracy requirement is applicable to legislatively proposed amendments only if a party can show conclusively that the Legislature engaged in fraud, deceit, or trickery. We disagree.

Article XI, section 1, Florida Constitution, sets forth the procedure for amending the constitution via legislative resolution:

Section 1. Proposal by legislature.—Amendment of a section or revision of one or more articles, or the whole, of this constitution may be proposed by joint resolution agreed to by three-fifths of the membership of each house of the legislature. The full text of the joint resolution and the vote of each member voting shall be entered on the journal of each house.

Art. XI, § 1, Fla. Const.

Although the constitution does not expressly authorize judicial review of amendments proposed by the Legislature, this Court long ago explained that the courts are the proper forum in which to litigate the validity of such amendments:

Under our system of constitutional government regulated by law, a determination of whether an amendment to the Constitution has been validly proposed and agreed to by the Legislature depends upon the fact of substantial compliance or noncompliance with the mandatory provisions of the existing Constitution as to how such amendments shall be proposed and agreed to, and *such determination is necessarily required to be in a judicial forum where the Constitution provides no other means of authoritatively determining such questions.*

Crawford v. Gilchrist, 64 Fla. 41, 50, 59 So. 963, 966 (1912) (emphasis added). This Court has reviewed legislatively proposed amendments throughout this century, and we have evaluated amendments' validity on various grounds, including ballot accuracy.

In conducting this review, we traditionally have accorded a measure of deference to the Legislature.... This deference, however, is not boundless, for the constitution imposes strict minimum requirements that apply across-the-board to all constitutional amendments, including those arising in the Legislature.

[T]he gist of the constitutional accuracy requirement is simple: A ballot title and summary cannot either "fly under false colors" or "hide the ball" as to the amendment's true effect. The applicability of this requirement also is simple: It applies across-the-board to all constitutional amendments, including those proposed by the Legislature.

V. THE PRESENT CASE

Pursuant to Florida's statutory scheme, the text of the proposed amendment in the present case did not appear on the ballot;[5] only the following language appeared:

NO. 2

CONSTITUTIONAL AMENDMENT

ARTICLE 1, SECTION 17

(LEGISLATIVE)

BALLOT TITLE: PRESERVATION OF THE DEATH PENALTY; UNITED STATES SUPREME COURT INTERPRETATION OF CRUEL AND UNUSUAL PUNISHMENT

BALLOT SUMMARY: Proposing an amendment to Section 17 of Article I of the State Constitution preserving the death penalty, and permitting any execution method unless prohibited by the Federal Constitution. Requires construction of the prohibition against cruel and/or unusual punishment to conform to United States Supreme Court interpretation of the Eighth Amendment. Prohibits reduction of a death sentence based on invalidity of execution method, and provides for continued force of sentence. Provides for retroactive applicability.

… This ballot title and summary are deficient under article XI, section 5, for several reasons.

---

5. [FN 25.] The full text of the proposed amendment as it appears in Joint Resolution No. 3505 reads as follows:

FULL TEXT OF PROPOSED AMENDMENT:

SECTION 17. Excessive punishments. — Excessive fines, cruel and ~~or~~ unusual punishment, attainder, forfeiture of estate, indefinite imprisonment, and unreasonable detention of witnesses are forbidden. <u>The death penalty is an authorized punishment for capital crimes designated by the Legislature. The prohibition against cruel or unusual punishment, and the prohibition against cruel and unusual punishment, shall be construed in conformity with decisions of the United States Supreme Court which interpret the prohibition against cruel and unusual punishment provided in the Eighth Amendment to the United States Constitution. Any method of execution shall be allowed, unless prohibited by the United States Constitution. Methods of execution may be designated by the Legislature, and a change in any method of execution may be applied retroactively. A sentence of death shall not be reduced on the basis that a method of execution is invalid. In any case in which an execution method is declared invalid, the death sentence shall remain in force until the sentence can be lawfully executed by any valid method. This section shall apply retroactively.</u>

H.J.Res. 3505, Regular Session (Fla.1998) (words stricken are deletions; words underlined are additions).

A. *"Flying Under False Colors"*

The ballot title and summary are misleading because the latter portion of the title ("UNITED STATES SUPREME COURT INTERPRETATION OF CRUEL AND UNUSUAL PUNISHMENT") and the second sentence in the summary ("Requires construction of the prohibition against cruel and/or unusual punishment to conform to United States Supreme Court interpretation of the Eighth Amendment.") imply that the amendment will promote the rights of Florida citizens through the rulings of the United States Supreme Court.

Florida's Cruel or Unusual Punishment Clause was adopted in 1838 by the Founding Fathers at the first constitutional convention in Port St. Joe and provided as follows:

> That the great and essential principles of liberty and free government, may be recognized and established, we declare:
>
> . . . .
>
> 12. That excessive bail shall in no case be required; nor shall excessive fines be imposed; *nor shall cruel or unusual punishments be inflicted.*

Art. 1, § 12, Fla. Const. of 1838 (emphasis added). The Clause has remained an integral part of our state constitution ever since and today provides:

> Excessive punishments. — Excessive fines, *cruel or unusual punishment,* attainder, forfeiture of estate, indefinite imprisonment, and unreasonable detention of witnesses *are forbidden.*

Art. 1, § 17, Fla. Const. Use of the word "or" instead of "and" in the Clause indicates that the framers intended that both alternatives (i.e., "cruel" and "unusual") were to be embraced individually and disjunctively within the Clause's proscription.

This Court in *Traylor v. State,* 596 So.2d 957 (Fla.1992), explained that our system of constitutional government in Florida is grounded on a principle of "robust individualism" and that our state constitutional rights thus provide greater freedom from government intrusion into the lives of citizens than do their federal counterparts.... In short: "[T]he federal Constitution ... represents the floor for basic freedoms; the state constitution, the ceiling." *Id.*

In the present case, by changing the wording of the Cruel or Unusual Punishment Clause to become "Cruel *and* Unusual" and by requiring that our state Clause be interpreted in conformity with its federal counterpart, the proposed amendment effectively strikes the state Clause from the constitutional scheme. Under such a scenario, the organic law governing either cruel or unusual punishments in Florida would consist of a floor (i.e., the federal constitution) and nothing more. The Court in *Traylor* addressed precisely this scenario:

> Under the federalist principles expressed above, *where a proposed constitutional revision results in the loss or restriction of an independent fundamental state right, the loss must be made known to each participating voter at the time of the general election. Cf. People Against Tax Revenue Mismanagement v.*

County of Leon, 583 So.2d 1373, 1376 (Fla.1991) (*"This is especially true if the ballot language gives the appearance of creating new rights or protections, when the actual effect is to reduce or eliminate rights* or protections already in existence.").

Traylor at 962–63 n. 5 (emphasis added). In the present case, a citizen could well have voted in favor of the proposed amendment thinking that he or she was protecting state constitutional rights when in fact the citizen was doing *the exact opposite*—i.e., he or she was voting to nullify those rights.

B. *"Hiding The Ball"*

To conform to section 101.161(1), a ballot summary must state "the chief purpose" of the proposed amendment. In evaluating an amendment's chief purpose, a court must look not to subjective criteria espoused by the amendment's sponsor but to objective criteria inherent in the amendment itself, such as the amendment's main effect. In the present case, as explained above, the main effect of the amendment is simple, clear-cut, and beyond dispute: The amendment will nullify the Cruel or Unusual Punishment Clause. This effect far outstrips the stated purpose (i.e., to "preserve" the death penalty), for the amendment will nullify a longstanding constitutional provision that applies to *all* criminal punishments, not just the death penalty.

VI. POST-ELECTION INVALIDATION

The Secretary in her supplemental brief claims that Armstrong cannot proceed with this suit because the election already has taken place and voters have approved the amendment. The favorable vote of the electors, she contends, cleansed the amendment of any defect. We disagree.

Where a proposed constitutional amendment contains a defect in form, a vote of approval by the electorate may in some cases cleanse the amendment of the defect. This Court in *Sylvester v. Tindall,* 154 Fla. 663, 18 So.2d 892 (1944), stated the general rule:

> [O]nce an amendment is duly proposed and is actually published and submitted to a vote of the people and by them adopted without any question having been raised prior to the election as to the method by which the amendment gets before them, the effect of a favorable vote by the people is to cure defects in the form of the submission.

Sylvester, 154 Fla. at 669, 18 So.2d at 895. This rule, however, is subject to a caveat: The defect in form must be technical and minor, which was the case in *Sylvester*[.] Where the defect goes to the heart of the amendment, on the other hand, the flaw may be fatal.

* * *

[T]he ballot language in the present case is defective for what it does *not* say: It does not tell voters the "chief purpose" of the amendment. The present case, however, is even more compelling.... First, ... the challenge here was initiated nearly a month before the election took place, rather than after the election. Second, ... the text of the present amendment did not appear on the ballot, and the title and summary—which did appear—were misleading because they implied that the amendment would promote the rights of Florida citizens and they contained several factual inaccuracies.

* * *

Accordingly, we reaffirm our holding ... that a favorable popular vote standing alone does not confer automatic validity on a defective amendment. When a defect goes to the very heart of the amendment, ... it is impossible to say with any certainty what the vote of the electorate would have been "if the voting public had been given the whole truth." *Wadhams,* 567 So.2d at 417. In such a case, the popular vote was based not on the whole truth but on part-truth.

VII. CONCLUSION

Although this Court traditionally has accorded a measure of deference to constitutional amendments proposed by the Legislature, our discretion is limited by the constitution itself. The accuracy requirement in article XI, section 5, imposes a strict minimum standard for ballot clarity. This requirement plays no favorites—it applies across-the-board to *all* constitutional amendments, including those proposed by the Legislature. The purpose of this requirement is above reproach—it is to ensure that each voter will cast a ballot based on the *full* truth. To function effectively—and to remain viable—a constitutional democracy must require no less.

* * *

Under our constitutional form of government in Florida, the Legislature is authorized to enact statutory laws and the courts can define the common law, but only the people—by direct vote—can delineate the organic law. The constitution is the one abiding voice of the body politic and encompasses the collective wisdom and counsel of our forebears, recorded verbatim throughout the ages. While any successive legislature is free to question the wisdom of the Founding Fathers and propose the striking of the Cruel or Unusual Punishment Clause, the Due Process Clause, the Right to Bear Arms Clause, the Freedom of Speech Clause, the Freedom of Religion Clause, or any other basic right enumerated in the Declaration of Rights, that legislature must do so plainly, in clear and certain terms. When Florida citizens are being called upon to nullify an original act of the Founding Fathers, each citizen is entitled—indeed, each is duty-bound—to cast a ballot with eyes wide open.

Based on the foregoing, we hold that proposed Amendment No. 2 clearly and conclusively violates the accuracy requirement in article XI, section 5, Florida Constitution. The ballot title and summary "fly under false colors" and "hide the ball" as to the amendment's true effect. Most important, voters were not told on the ballot that the amendment will nullify the Cruel or Unusual Punishment Clause, an integral part of the Declaration of Rights since our state's birth. Voters thus were not permitted to cast a ballot with eyes wide open on this issue. Because the validity of the electoral process was fundamentally compromised, we conclude that proposed Amendment No. 2 must be stricken.

It is so ordered.

WELLS, C.J., dissenting.

I have a fundamental difference with the majority concerning whether the Florida Constitution grants this Court the power to strike from the Constitution a constitutional amendment that the Legislature proposed and the voters approved based on a conclusion that the amendment's ballot title and summary were misleading. This amendment was proposed in accord with the procedures set forth in article XI, section 1. There is no assertion that those procedures were not followed when both houses of the Legislature voted unanimously to propose the amendment. The proposed amendment was placed on the ballot pursuant to article XI, section 5. There is no assertion that procedures for submitting the amendment to the voters were not followed. The amendment was approved by well in excess of a majority of the electorate: 72.8 percent voted in favor of the amendment. I read no basis in the Constitution under these circumstances to find that this Court has the power to strike this amendment.

In order to find that it has this extraordinary power, the majority writes into article XI, section 5, an "accuracy requirement" and then holds that the judicially-created requirement provides a basis for this Court to review legislatively-proposed amendments to the Constitution. Language to support this is simply nonexistent in the express language of article XI, section 5. Next, relying upon the created language, the majority finds that this judicially-grafted requirement is breached by coming to the subjective conclusion that the ballot summary (also unmentioned in article XI, section 5) does not meet this requirement.

[T]his Court in *Smathers v. Smith*, 338 So.2d 825 (Fla.1976), had denied a request for such an exercise of power in respect to a legislatively proposed amendment. In *Smith*, this Court determined in an opinion written by Justice England that the Court had limited power of review in respect to a legislatively proposed amendment. The broad attack upon the proposed amendment rejected in *Smith* was similar to the attack the majority approves in this case:

> Smith asserts several reasons why the proposed amendment is improper. *He suggests that its language is unclear, its meaning obscure and its purpose too vague; that the Legislature lacks power to propose as a constitutional amendment a revision of governmental powers as sweeping and broad as he contends this amendment contains;* that the amendment would violate the "one person — one vote" guarantee of the Fourteenth Amendment of the United States Constitution; *that the notice of the contents of the amendment which would appear on the ballot violates Section 101.161, Florida Statutes (1975);* and that the amendment is inadequate to inform the public of the substantial shift in governmental power which it would effect. Smith also contends that the amendment in reality alters the separation of powers guaranteed in Article II, Section 3 of the Florida Constitution, in that it gives to the Legislature authority to exercise an interpretive power previously reposed exclusively in the judiciary.

... [We] approach the subject matter of the case mindful of our limited role in reviewing constitutional proposals which have been adopted by the Legislature for direct submission to the people.

> Another thing we should keep in mind is that we are dealing with a constitutional democracy in which sovereignty resides in the people. It is their Constitution that we are construing. They have a right to change, abrogate or modify it in any manner they see fit so long as they keep within the confines of the Federal Constitution. The legislature which approved and submitted the proposed amendment took the same oath to protect and defend the Constitution that we did and our first duty is to uphold their action if there is any reasonable theory under which it can be done....

[Gray v. Golden, 89 So.2d 785, 790 (Fla.1956).] It is in that framework that we limit our discussion to the critical issue which is here presented by the parties, and we rest our decision solely on the question of whether the amendment was proposed by the Legislature in conformity with Article XI, Section 1 of the Constitution.... Because there is doubt as to whether the Legislature has violated what appear to be strictures on their amendatory powers, we are compelled to sustain this legislative action.

Smith, 338 So.2d at 826–27 (footnote omitted) (emphasis added).... In *Collier [v. Gray*, 116 Fla. 845, 157 So. 40 (1934)], this Court specifically stated:

> While the procedure prescribed by the Constitution for proposals to amend the Constitution must be duly followed and none of the requisite steps may be omitted, *yet unless the courts are satisfied that the Constitution has been violated in the submission of a proposed amendment they should uphold it.*

116 Fla. at 857–58, 157 So. at 45 (emphasis added). Although the majority here first refers to article I, section 5, as having an "implicit accuracy requirement," the majority basically justifies its power to strike the constitutional amendment on the basis that the Legislature's ballot title and summary are misleading, in violation of section 101.161, Florida Statutes. I believe it is illogical and contradictory for the Court to conclude that a legislatively proposed amendment fails because it violates a statute. Obviously, a legislatively proposed amendment would supersede a prior legislative enactment with which it did not comply....

If the Legislature misled the voters, I conclude that the remedy is at the ballot box—not in the Court. There is simply no constitutional authority for a judicial veto of a legislatively proposed amendment, just as there is no gubernatorial veto. I believe it is crucial to always keep in mind that the very first sentence of article 1, section 1, of the Florida Constitution is, "All political power is inherent in the people." I do not find in article V, which is the article of the Constitution which provides to the Court its power, any basis to conclude that the people have given to the Court the power to intercede between the people and their elected representatives when the Legislature proposes amending the Constitution by the constitutionally required supermajority.

* * *

My view is further bolstered by the express provision in the Constitution for this Court to review citizens' initiatives. The Constitution in article XI provides five methods of amending the Constitution: (1) proposal by Legislature, section 1; (2) revision commission, section 2; (3) initiative, section 3; (4) constitutional convention, section 4; and (5) taxation and budget reform commission, section 6. Only in respect to citizens' initiatives does the Constitution give to this Court express power to review amendments. Article V, section 3(b)(10), does provide, in respect to this method of amending the Constitution, that this Court

> Shall, when requested by the attorney general pursuant to the provisions of section 10 of Article IV, render an advisory opinion of the justices, addressing issues as provided by general law.

Article IV, section 10, provides:

> The attorney general shall, as directed by general law, request the opinion of the justices of the supreme court as to the validity of any initiative petition circulated pursuant to Section 3 of Article XI. The justices shall, subject to their rules of procedure, permit interested persons to be heard on the questions presented and shall render their written opinion expeditiously.

Article XI, section 3, pertains to citizen initiatives. In respect to amendments proposed by a constitutional revision commission or a constitutional convention or by the Legislature, the Constitution is silent as to any power given to the Court for review. Since the Constitution does not expressly give the Court this power, I must conclude that the Court should not assume it by implication.... I agree with respondent that the exception to this would only be if there was evidence of fraud, which is clearly not present in this case.

* * *

I recognize that petitioners sought to have this matter canceled from the ballot by a late filing just prior to the election. However, the fact is that this attempt did not succeed. The voters approved the amendment by 72.8 percent of those voting. The majority's post-election analysis as to why the amendment so overwhelmingly succeeded is merely speculation and conjecture....

* * *

Finally, though in my view we do not reach the issue, I do not agree with the subjective conclusion of the majority that a unanimous Legislature "clearly and conclusively" misled Florida voters. Rather, I agree with the subjective conclusion of the trial judge that respondent's argument is more persuasive. I conclude that the ballot title and summary do inform that the state constitutional provision against cruel or unusual punishment is to be construed in accord with decisions of the United States Constitution.... Also, respondent is correct that it has never been determined that there is a material difference between the phrases "cruel or unusual" and "cruel and unusual" for purposes of the application of capital punishment. I find it to be a particularly strained interpretation where the majority construes that "legislative designation" eliminates a veto by the Governor. "Designated by the Legislature" is already in article X, section 17(b) of the Constitution without controversy. I believe it is significant that the record in this case contains nothing in the way of factual evidence to support the majority's subjective conclusion that misleading language misled the voters. Thus, even if I found in the Constitution the power to review legislatively-proposed amendments, I would not, on the basis of the present record, join in striking from the Constitution what the Legislature and the people themselves have put into the Constitution by such substantial votes.

For the foregoing reasons, the decision of the circuit court should be affirmed and the petitions denied.

Commentary and Questions

The Legislature responded to the Supreme Court's decision in *Armstrong v. Harris* by amending Section 101.161, Florida Statutes to remove the 75-word limit for ballot summaries only for amendments proposed by legislative joint resolution. The Legislature then re-submitted the same amendment to the voters, but with the entire text of the amendment to Article I, Section 17 contained in the ballot summary. Several county supervisors of elections challenged the proposed amendment claiming that the summary was still not clear, but the district court allowed the proposal to appear on the ballot. *See Sancho v. Smith*, 830 So. 2d 856, 861-62 (1st DCA), *rev. denied*, 828 So. 2d 389 (Fla. 2002) (finding that placing the entire text of the amendment within the summary "accurately describes" the proposal). Florida voters then approved the re-submitted amendment to Article I, Section 17.

As we look at *Armstrong v. Harris*,

1. When is the Supreme Court willing to invalidate an amendment after the voters have approved it? What standard does the Court use to remove an amendment?

2. How does the Court evaluate the change from "cruel or unusual punishments" to "cruel and unusual punishments" in the amendment? Why did the Court find the summary to be defective?

3. Why did Chief Justice Wells dissent with the majority's view of the Court's authority to review legislative amendment proposals?

Florida Department of State v. Florida State Conference of NAACP Branches

43 So. 3d 662 (Fla. 2010)

PER CURIAM.

The Florida Department of State, Dawn K. Roberts in her official capacity as the Secretary of State, the Florida Senate, and the Florida House of Representatives ("Roberts and the Legislature"), appealed to the First District Court of Appeal from a July 12, 2010, judgment of the circuit court striking a legislatively proposed constitutional amendment from the November 2010 general election ballot. The First District certified to this Court that the judgment is of great public importance and that the appeal requires immediate resolution by this Court under our jurisdiction set forth in article

V, section 3(b)(5), of the Florida Constitution. We agreed and granted expedited review to decide the question of great public importance—whether proposed Amendment 7, amending article III of the Florida Constitution, meets the requirements of Florida law for inclusion on the November 2010 ballot. As further explained below, we affirm the judgment of the circuit court striking proposed Amendment 7 from the ballot because the ballot language fails to inform the voter of the chief purpose and effect the amendment will have on existing, mandatory constitutional provisions in article III.

1. FACTS

On May 18, 2010, the Florida Legislature filed with the Florida Secretary of State a joint legislative resolution, Fla. H.J. Res. 7231 (2010) (HJR 7231), proposing an amendment to article III of the Florida Constitution.

* * *

Section 101.161, Florida Statutes (2009), provides that whenever a constitutional amendment is proposed for submission to a vote of the people, the substance of the amendment shall be printed in clear and unambiguous language on the ballot. *See* § 101.161(1), Fla. Stat. (2009). We have held that "[t]he purpose of section 101.161(1) is to assure that the electorate is advised of the true meaning, and ramifications, of an amendment." *Askew v. Firestone,* 421 So.2d 151, 156 (Fla.1982). In HJR 7231, the Legislature adopted the following statement, which essentially mirrors the language contained in proposed Amendment 7, and resolved that it be placed on the ballot as follows:

BE IT FURTHER RESOLVED that the following statement be placed on the ballot:

CONSTITUTIONAL AMENDMENT

ARTICLE III, SECTION 20

STANDARDS FOR LEGISLATURE TO FOLLOW IN LEGISLATIVE AND CONGRESSIONAL REDISTRICTING.—In establishing congressional and legislative district boundaries or plans, the state shall apply federal requirements and balance and implement the standards in the State Constitution. The state shall take into consideration the ability of racial and language minorities to participate in the political process and elect candidates of their choice, and communities of common interest other than political parties may be respected and promoted, both without subordination to any other provision of article III of the State Constitution. Districts and plans are valid if the balancing and implementation of standards is rationally related to the standards contained in the State Constitution and is consistent with federal law.

On May 21, 2010, a complaint for declaratory and injunctive relief was filed in the circuit court seeking to prevent placement of proposed Amendment 7 on the November ballot. The suit was filed against the Florida Department of State and Secretary of State Dawn K. Roberts by plaintiffs Florida State Conference of NAACP Branches; Adora Obi Nweze; The League of Women Voters of Florida, Inc.; Deirdre Macnab; Robert Milligan; Nathaniel P. Reed; Democracia Ahora; and Jorge Mursuli. After the complaint was filed, Governor Charlie Crist was allowed to intervene as amicus curiae in support of plaintiffs, and the Florida House of Representatives and the Florida Senate were allowed to intervene as defendants in the circuit court.

The complaint alleged, inter alia, that the ballot title and summary for Amendment 7 fail to inform the voters that the amendment (1) would limit the mandatory application of constitutional standards and allow the Legislature to subordinate existing standards in article III to permissive and vague standards in the amendment; (2) would allow the Legislature to consider but not implement specific protections for minority voters contained in proposed constitutional Amendments 5 and 6, also slated for the November ballot; (3) would allow the Legislature to "balance" standards in such a way as to create districts favoring or disfavoring incumbents; and (4) is intended to require validation of any district or plan that is related to nonmandatory standards in Amendment 7. The plaintiffs also alleged that the ballot title is misleading in that it purports to provide "standards" for redistricting while actually eliminating them.

The plaintiffs filed a motion for summary judgment seeking a judgment that the proposed amendment fails to advise voters of its chief purpose and true effect. Defendants Roberts and the Legislature filed cross motions for summary judgment. The parties agreed that there existed no disputed issues of material fact, and a final hearing was held on July 8, 2010. On July 12, 2010, the circuit court entered its order granting the plaintiffs' motion for summary final judgment and denying the defendants' motions for summary judgment. The circuit court's order found that the ballot language does not meet the requirements of section 101.161(1) in that it does not fairly advise the voters of the ramifications of the amendment. As a result, the circuit court enjoined the Department of State from placing Amendment 7 on the November 2010 ballot. In so ruling, the trial judge made the following pertinent findings:

> Apart from the number of districts to be drawn, the Florida Constitution currently contains only one requirement binding on the legislature when they meet every ten years to draw districts. That one mandatory requirement is that each district be contiguous. Amendment 7, if it were to pass, would make that one mandatory requirement aspirational only and would subordinate contiguity to the other aspirational goals or "standards" contained in Amendment 7.

> ....

> To be clear, there is nothing unlawful or improper about what the legislative proposal seeks to do. The wisdom of a proposed amendment is not a matter of concern for this Court. But to be legally entitled to a place on the ballot, the summary and title must be fair and must advise the voter sufficiently to enable the voter to intelligently vote for or against the amendment.... Requiring that all districts be contiguous is a valuable right afforded to all citizens of Florida. A citizen cannot, and should not, be asked to give up that right without being fully informed and making an intelligent decision to do so.

> Amendment 7, if passed, would allow this or any future legislature, if it chose to do so, to gerrymander districts guided by no mandatory requirements or standards and subject to no effective accountability so long as its

decisions were rationally related to, and balanced with, the aspirational goals set out in Amendment 7 and the subordinate goal of contiguity.

Thus, the primary basis on which the circuit court invalidated the ballot language was that it failed to inform the voters that article III of the Florida Constitution currently contains a mandatory contiguity requirement which, if Amendment 7 is adopted, could be subordinated to the other considerations set forth in proposed Amendment 7.

II. ANALYSIS

The standard of review of the validity of a proposed constitutional amendment is de novo. *Armstrong v. Harris,* 773 So.2d 7, 11 (Fla.2000). We are ever mindful that "[t]he Court must act with extreme care, caution, and restraint before it removes a constitutional amendment from the vote of the people." *Askew v. Firestone,* 421 So.2d 151, 156 (Fla.1982). "A court may declare a proposed constitutional amendment invalid only if the record shows that the proposal is clearly and conclusively defective...." *Armstrong,* 773 So.2d at 11 (citing *Askew,* 421 So.2d at 154).

A. Requirement that Ballot Language Inform Voters of Legal Effect and Ramifications of a Proposed Amendment

In reviewing the validity of ballot language submitted to the voters for a proposed constitutional amendment, we do not consider or review the substantive merits or the wisdom of the amendment.

* * *

To conform to section 101.161(1), the ballot language "must state 'the chief purpose' of the proposed amendment. In evaluating an amendment's chief purpose, a court must look not to subjective criteria espoused by the amendment's sponsor but to objective criteria inherent in the amendment itself, such as the amendment's main effect." *Armstrong,* 773 So.2d at 18 (footnote omitted). In this analysis, we consider two questions: "(1) whether the ballot title and summary, in clear and unambiguous language, fairly inform the voter of the chief purpose of the amendment; and (2) whether the language of the title and summary, as written, misleads the public." *Standards for Establishing Legislative District Boundaries,* 2 So.3d at 184 (quoting *Advisory Op. to Att'y Gen. re Prohibiting State Spending for Experimentation that Involves the Destruction of a Live Human Embryo,* 959 So.2d 210, 213–14 (Fla.2007)). This evaluation also includes consideration of the amendment's "true meaning, and ramifications." *Armstrong,* 773 So.2d at 16 (quoting *Askew,* 421 So.2d at 156)....

Moreover, we have consistently adhered to the principle "that lawmakers who are asked to consider constitutional changes, and the people who are asked to approve them, must be able to comprehend the sweep of each proposal from a fair notification in the proposition itself that it is neither less nor more extensive than it appears to be." *Smathers v. Smith,* 338 So.2d 825, 829 (Fla.1976). It is by these basic and longstanding principles that we must measure the ballot language presented to the voter for Amendment 7.

We do not ignore the fact that HJR 7231, proposing Amendment 7, was the product of a joint resolution passed by a three-fifths vote of the Legislature. While we traditionally accord a measure of deference to the Legislature, "[t]his deference ... is not boundless, for the constitution imposes strict minimum requirements that apply across-the-board to all constitutional amendments, including those arising in the Legislature." *Armstrong*, 773 So.2d at 14. We also recognize that section 101.161(1), which places strict requirements on ballot language presented for any constitutional amendment or other public measure, is also a legislative enactment entitled to this Court's deference.

B. The Ballot Language for Proposed Amendment 7

With these principles in mind, we turn to the question before the Court—whether the ballot language proposed for Amendment 7 comports with the requirements of section 101.161, the Florida Constitution, and our case law governing placement of proposed constitutional amendments on the ballot. The ballot language for proposed Amendment 7 states in pertinent part that in redistricting, "[t]he state shall take into consideration the ability of racial and language minorities to participate in the political process and elect candidates of their choice, and communities of common interest other than political parties may be respected and promoted, *both without subordination to any other provision of article III* of the State Constitution." *See* HJR 7231 (emphasis added).

In this case, the circuit court struck Amendment 7 from the ballot because the court concluded the ballot language did not inform the voters that the amendment would allow the existing mandatory constitutional requirement in article III, section 16(a), requiring that districts be contiguous to be subordinated to the discretionary standards contained in Amendment 7. We agree with this finding. Under the text of Amendment 7, if the discretionary considerations in Amendment 7 are not to be subordinated to any other provisions of article III, then it must follow that other provisions of article III may be subordinated to the discretionary considerations in the balancing process set forth in Amendment 7. This clearly alters the nature of the contiguity requirement currently contained in article III, section 16(a), of the constitution. Unfortunately, neither the text of the amendment nor the explanatory statement proposed by the Legislature makes this fact clear. Nowhere does the ballot language inform the voter that there is currently a mandatory contiguity requirement in article III, and nowhere does the language inform the voter that the contiguity requirement could be diluted by Amendment 7.

* * *

Although the circuit court did not reach the question of whether the ballot title is invalid as being misleading, we also find that the ballot title is misleading and precludes placement of Amendment 7 on the ballot. The ballot title states "Standards for Legislature to Follow in Legislative and Congressional Redistricting." While purporting to create and impose standards upon the Legislature in redistricting, the amendment actually eliminates actual standards and replaces them with discretionary considerations. Thus, we conclude that the title is misleading as to the true purpose and effect of the amendment.

III. CONCLUSION

Based upon the provisions of section 101.161(1), Florida Statutes, article XI, section 5, of the Florida Constitution, and our precedent, we hold that the ballot language setting forth the substance of Amendment 7 does not inform the voter of the true purpose and effect of the amendment on existing constitutional provisions and, further, is misleading. Accordingly, the judgment of the circuit court is affirmed and Amendment 7 may not be placed on the general election ballot for November 2010.

It is so ordered.

PARIENTE, LEWIS, QUINCE, LABARGA, and PERRY, JJ., concur.

CANADY, C.J., dissenting.

The basis for the majority's decision to preclude the people of Florida from voting on proposed amendment 7 is the assertion that the amendment is misleading because it fails to disclose that it would nullify the contiguity requirement currently in the Florida Constitution. But nothing about amendment 7 is misleading. The amendment, by its own plain terms, does not nullify the contiguity requirement but mandates the implementation of that requirement. I therefore dissent from the majority's ruling that the text of amendment 7 and its ballot title are defective and from the decision to remove the amendment from the ballot.

Article III, section 16(a) of the Florida Constitution provides that the Legislature "shall apportion the state ... into not less than thirty nor more than forty consecutively numbered senatorial districts of either contiguous, overlapping or identical territory, and into not less than eighty nor more than one hundred twenty consecutively numbered representative districts of either contiguous, overlapping or identical territory." Contrary to the majority's assertion, nothing in amendment 7 would nullify, dilute, or alter this provision of the Florida Constitution.

Amendment 7 provides that in establishing district boundaries or plans, "the state shall ... *balance and implement* the standards in this constitution." H.J. Res. 7231, 2010 Leg. (Fla.2010) (emphasis added). Amendment 7 further provides that "[t]he state shall take into consideration the ability of racial and language minorities to participate in the political process and elect candidates of their choice, and communities of common interest other than political parties may be respected and promoted, *both without subordination to any other provision of this article*." *Id.* (emphasis added). Finally, amendment 7 also states that "[d]istricts and plans are valid if the *balancing and implementation* of standards is rationally related to the standards contained in this constitution." *Id.* (emphasis added).

The majority's reading of the amendment fails to give full effect to these provisions. That reading is based on the inference that the references in the text of amendment 7 to "balance" and "balancing" and the "without subordination to" clause vest the Legislature with a wholly discretionary power to ignore the contiguity requirement of article III, section 16(a). But the inference relied on by the majority is rendered wholly untenable by the express requirement in the amendment that the State "balance *and implement* the standards in this constitution" and by the express provision that the "balancing *and implementation* of standards" must be "rationally related" to the constitutional standards. The majority's interpretation of amendment 7 effectively reads the words "*and implement*" together with "*and implementation*" out of the text of the amendment.

* * *

Contrary to the majority's suggestion, the standard at issue—contiguity—is not a standard that is subject to dilution.

> This Court has defined "contiguous" as "being in actual contact: touching along a boundary or at a point." A district lacks contiguity "when a part is isolated from the rest by the territory of another district" or when the lands "mutually touch only at a common corner or right angle."

In re Constitutionality of House Joint Resolution 1987, 817 So.2d 819, 827–28 (Fla.2002) (citation omitted) (quoting *In re Senate Joint Resolution 2G*, 597 So.2d 276, 279 (Fla.1992)). A district either meets the contiguity requirement or fails to meet that requirement. Contiguity is thus a determinate requirement and not a vague standard that may be applied in varying degrees. In this respect, contiguity is like the constitutional requirement that there be between thirty and forty senatorial districts and between eighty and 120 representative districts.

The direction to "balance and implement" standards does not—as the majority contends—grant discretion to not implement the contiguity standard. If the Legislature adopted a plan with districts that did not meet the contiguity requirement, the Legislature would have failed to "balance and implement the standards of the constitution" and the "balancing and implementation of standards" would not be "rationally related" to the standards of the constitution. Under amendment 7, the Legislature would have no more discretion to adopt a plan with districts not satisfying the contiguity requirement than it would have to adopt a plan with fifty senatorial districts and 150 representative districts. In short, the majority's reading of amendment 7 cannot be reconciled with the plain meaning of "implement."

Nor does the "without subordination to" clause justify the majority's conclusion that amendment 7 would nullify, dilute, or alter the contiguity requirement. Based on that clause, the majority reasons that the other requirements of the constitution "may be subordinated to the discretionary considerations in the balancing process set forth in Amendment 7." Majority op. at 668. The majority equates "without subordination to" with "superior to" or "without regard to." *Id.* In the full context of amendment 7, this interpretation is not plausible. The clause must be understood in conjunction with the provision that all of the constitutional standards must be implemented. H.J. Res. 7231, 2010 Leg. (Fla.2010). In context, "without subordination to" can only mean "not inferior to." It cannot be understood to suggest that the Legislature can fail to implement the other constitutional standards of article III.

* * *

But even if disbelief could be suspended and the ambiguity could be found, the majority's position would nonetheless founder on the rule that "[a] construction that nullifies a specific clause will not be given to a constitution unless absolutely required by the context." *Gray v. Bryant,* 125 So.2d 846, 858 (Fla.1960). Since amendment 7 does not expressly repeal the contiguity requirement now in the constitution, any ambiguity in amendment 7 should be resolved to harmonize the amendment with the existing contiguity provision. *See Jackson v. Consol. Gov't of Jacksonville,* 225 So.2d 497, 500–01 (Fla.1969). The majority's analysis simply fails to take into account this cardinal rule of constitutional interpretation.

The chief purpose of amendment 7 is clearly articulated and presented to the voters in the ballot summary, which sets forth verbatim the operative text of the amendment. The text of the amendment speaks for itself, and it conceals nothing from the voters. There is nothing about the ballot title or the ballot summary that is inaccurate or misleading. Instead, the inaccuracy lies in the majority's unwarranted interpretation of amendment 7, an interpretation which cannot be reconciled with the amendment's plain meaning and which violates fundamental principles of constitutional interpretation. The people are thus denied the right to vote on amendment 7 based on an interpretation of the amendment which cannot withstand scrutiny.

* * *

POLSTON, J., concurs.

Commentary

The legislative proposal considered by the Supreme Court in *Florida Department of State v. Florida State Conference of NAACP Branches,* was intended to govern how the Fair Districts initiative amendments would be applied during the legislative reapportionment process. However, that intent was not relevant to the Court's evaluation of the ballot title and summary. Thus, the Court, in considering the phrase "both without subordination to any other provision of Article III" looked only to the single existing contiguity requirement already contained in Article III. The Court did not consider the impact of the amendment on the multiple criteria for reapportionment that were proposed by the Fair Districts amendments—criteria which would also be subordinated to this amendment's discretionary standards.

D. Article XI, Section 2 — Constitution Revision Commission

This provision requires the assembly of a special commission to review the Florida Constitution and propose amendments or revisions. It is composed of 37 members, of whom the Attorney General is member ex officio, plus fifteen members selected by the Governor, nine by the Speaker of the House of Representatives, nine by the President of the Senate, and three by the Chief Justice of the Florida Supreme Court, who must make her choices "with the advice of the justices." The CRC first assembled in 1977–78, and afterwards met in 1997–98 and 2017–18. Article XI, Section 2(c) provides that the CRC convenes at the call of its chair (appointed by the Governor) and adopts its own rules of procedure.

As the case below shows, although the CRC files its proposals directly with the Secretary of State for placement on the ballot, these proposals remain subject to challenge for failure to comply with ballot and summary requirements.

Detzner v. League of Women Voters of Florida

256 So. 3d 803 (Fla. 2018)

PER CURIAM.

Appellant, Kenneth Detzner, Secretary of the Florida Department of State, seeks review of *League of Women Voters of Florida, Inc. v. Detzner*, No. 2018-CA-001523 (Fla. 2d Cir. Aug. 20, 2018). The circuit court granted summary judgment in favor of the League of Women Voters (LWV) and enjoined Detzner from placing Revision 8 on the ballot for the November 2018 general election. Detzner appealed the decision to the First District Court of Appeal, which certified to this Court that the judgment is of great public importance and requires immediate resolution by this Court. We have jurisdiction. *See* art. V, §3(b)(5), Fla. Const.

This Court considered this cause at oral argument on September 5, 2018, and on September 7, 2018, issued an order affirming the decision of the circuit court. This opinion provides the reasons for our decision.

Background

Article XI, section 2, of the Florida Constitution establishes the Constitution Revision Commission (CRC) to convene every twenty years to propose revisions to the Florida Constitution. *See* Art. XI, §2, Fla. Const. Then, the proposed constitutional amendment must be "submitted to the electors at the next general election." Art. XI, §5(a), Fla. Const.

On March 21, 2018, the Constitution Revision Commission (CRC), approved Proposal 71, which would have made the following revision to Article IX, Section 4(b):

> (b) The school board shall operate, control, and supervise all free public schools <u>established by</u> ~~within~~ the school district and determine the rate of school district taxes within the limits prescribed herein. Two or more school districts may operate and finance joint educational programs.

The sponsor of the proposal stated during debate that the revision was intended to overrule *Duval County School Board v. State Board of Education*, 998 So.2d 641 (Fla. 1st DCA 2008), and to allow the power to authorize new charter schools to be assigned to any of a variety of potential public or private entities.

The CRC combined Proposal 71 with Proposal 43 and Proposal 10, which also included changes to Article IX of the Florida Constitution. Later, the language was revised to read:

(b) The school board shall operate, control, and supervise all free public schools <u>established by the district school board</u> within the school district and determine the rate of school district taxes within the limits prescribed herein. Two or more school districts may operate and finance joint educational programs.

A motion to unbundle the three proposals was unsuccessful.

The CRC drafted and approved the following title and summary for inclusion on the ballot:

CONSTITUTIONAL AMENDMENT

ARTICLE IX, SECTION 4, NEW SECTION

ARTICLE XII, NEW SECTION

SCHOOL BOARD TERM LIMITS AND DUTIES; PUBLIC SCHOOLS.— Creates a term limit of eight consecutive years for school board members and requires the legislature to provide for the promotion of civic literacy in public schools. Currently, district school boards have a constitutional duty to operate, control, and supervise all public schools. The amendment maintains a school board's duties to public schools it establishes, but permits the state to operate, control, and supervise public schools not established by the school board.

On July 12, 2018, LWV filed a complaint seeking to enjoin Detzner, in his capacity as Secretary of State, from placing Revision 8 to the Florida Constitution on the November 2018 general election ballot. LWV argued that the revision could not be lawfully submitted to Florida voters because the ballot title and summary fail to inform voters of the chief purpose of the revision and are affirmatively misleading as to the true purpose and effect of the revision. The parties agreed to an expedited procedure through cross-motions for summary judgment, the trial court heard arguments on August 17, 2018, and, on August 20, 2018, granted summary judgment in favor of LWV and denied Detzner's motion.

In its order granting summary judgment to LWV, the circuit court determined that the ballot summary "invents a category of school . . . undefined in Florida law." Therefore, the court reasoned, "both the text and the summary are entirely unclear as to which schools will be affected by the revision." "The failure to use the term voters would understand, 'charter schools,' as well as the use of a phrase that has no established meaning under Florida law, fails to inform voters of the chief purpose and effect of this proposal." The court found that the deficiencies here were similar to those discussed in *Florida Department of State v. Florida State Conference of NAACP Branches*, 43 So.3d 662 (Fla. 2010), stating, "[N]owhere does the ballot summary inform the voter of the essential role school boards play in authorizing new schools, and nowhere does the language inform the voter that this role is intended to be diluted by Revision 8."

Additionally, the circuit court determined that the title was misleading through omission, stating that "the vague reference to 'school board . . . duties' is presumably intended to allude to Proposal 71 [but] a voter could easily believe . . . that it consists solely of a proposal to limit the term limits for school boards." The circuit court also found the ballot summary affirmatively misleading, stating that it "is conspicuously silent about who or what would undertake these responsibilities for schools not established by the school board." In conclusion, the circuit court found:

> Because the ballot summary for Revision 8 clearly and conclusively fails to adequately inform the voter of the chief purposes and effects of the revision, and is affirmatively misleading, placement of Revision 8 on the ballot would violate Article XI, Section 5, Florida Constitution, and Section 101.161(1), Florida Statutes.

On August 20, 2018, Detzner filed a notice of appeal with the First District Court of Appeal. On August 22, 2018, the First District certified the case for pass-through jurisdiction, finding that the appeal involves a question of great public importance that requires immediate resolution by this Court.

Standard of Review

Section 101.161(1), Florida Statutes (2018), is a "codification of the accuracy requirement implicit in article XI, section 5 of the Florida Constitution." *Advisory Op. to Att'y Gen. re Referenda Required for Adoption & Amendment Local Gov't Comprehensive Land Use Plans*, 902 So.2d 763, 770 (Fla. 2005)....

"Implicit in this provision is the requirement that the proposed amendment be *accurately* represented on the ballot; otherwise, voter approval would be a nullity." *Armstrong v. Harris*, 773 So.2d 7, 12 (Fla. 2000).... The purpose of section 101.161 is to ensure that voters are advised of the amendment's true meaning. *Advisory Op. to Att'y Gen. re Indep. Nonpartisan Comm'n to Apportion Legislative & Cong. Dists. Which Replaces Apportionment by Legislature*, 926 So.2d 1218, 1228 (Fla. 2006).

> A court may declare a proposed constitutional amendment invalid only if the record shows that the proposal is clearly and conclusively defective; the standard of review [in such cases] is de novo. Proposed amendments to the Florida Constitution may originate in any of several sources, including the Legislature, revision commission, citizen initiative, or constitutional convention. Regardless of source, a proposed amendment ultimately must be submitted to the electors for approval at the next general election.

Armstrong, 773 So.2d at 11 (footnotes omitted).

> The accuracy requirement in article XI, section 5, imposes a strict minimum standard for ballot clarity. This requirement plays no favorites—it applies across-the-board to *all* constitutional amendments.... The purpose of this requirement is above reproach—it is to ensure that each voter will cast a ballot based on the *full* truth. To function effectively—and to remain viable—a constitutional democracy must require no less.

Id. at 21.

We have stressed that a proposed amendment "must stand on its own merits and not be disguised as something else." *Askew*, 421 So.2d at 156. "A ballot title and summary cannot either 'fly under false colors' or 'hide the ball' as to the amendment's true effect." *Armstrong*, 773 So.2d at 16. In assessing the ballot title and summary for compliance with section 101.161(1), the reviewing court should ask two questions: first, whether the ballot title and summary "fairly inform the voter of the chief purpose of the amendment," and second, "whether the language of the title and summary, as written, misleads the public." *Advisory Op. to Atty. Gen. re Fla. Marriage Protection Amendment*, 926 So.2d 1229, 1236 (Fla. 2006). However, this Court does not consider the substantive merit of the proposed amendment. *Dep't of State v. Slough*, 992 So.2d 142, 147 (Fla. 2008).

* * *

Analysis

This case presents two issues for our consideration: (1) whether Revision 8's ballot title and summary is clearly and conclusively defective because it fails to inform voters of its effect and (2) whether the ballot title and summary are misleading. We conclude that because the ballot summary fails to include a clear statement of the chief purpose of the revision and fails to inform voters of its true meaning and ramifications, the ballot language is defective. That the ballot summary is unclear is best demonstrated by the proponents of the proposed revision, who each give different meaning to the language of the revision, its title, and its summary. We therefore affirm the decision of the circuit court.

Since 1998, the Florida Constitution has provided, "Adequate provision shall be made by law for a uniform, efficient, safe, secure, and high quality system of free public schools that allows students to obtain a high quality education...." Art. IX, § 1(a), Fla. Const. Also since then, section 4 has provided:

SECTION 4. School districts; school boards.—

(a) Each county shall constitute a school district; provided, two or more contiguous counties, upon vote of the electors of each county pursuant to law, may be combined into one school district. In each school district there shall be a school board composed of five or more members chosen by vote of the electors in a nonpartisan election for appropriately staggered terms of four years, as provided by law.

(b) The school board shall operate, control and supervise all free public schools within the school district and determine the rate of school district taxes within the limits prescribed herein. Two or more school districts may operate and finance joint educational programs.

In relevant part, the most recent CRC proposed the following revision to section 4(b) to be included on the ballot in the November 2018 general election:

(b) The school board shall operate, control, and supervise all free public schools established by the district school board within the school district and determine the rate of school district taxes within the limits prescribed herein. Two or more school districts may operate and finance joint educational programs.

Because section 101.161(1) requires a ballot summary to state "the chief purpose" of the proposed amendment, we look to objective criteria, like the amendments' main effect to determine whether a ballot summary complies with the statute. *Armstrong*, 773 So.2d at 18. Here, the ballot summary provides, "Currently, district school boards have a constitutional duty to operate, control, and supervise all public schools. The amendment maintains a school board's duties to public schools it establishes, but permits the state to operate, control, and supervise public schools not established by the school board."

While the ballot summary informs voters that district school boards will no longer have the authority to operate, control, and supervise public schools that they do not establish, the summary fails to explain who or what, other than district school boards, currently has the authority to establish public schools, which categories of public schools will be affected, and who or what will have the authority to establish future public schools if voters approve the revision. Failure to explain this key component of the revision is exacerbated by the fact that the phrase "established by" is not one that is consistently used in Florida Statutes, when addressing public schools....

Further, the ballot summary fails to explain which public schools or categories of schools will be affected. Currently, in addition to the general provision for K-12 education in section 1003.02, Florida Statutes (2018), providing that schools boards "must establish, organize, and operate their public K-12 schools and educational programs," the Florida Statutes provide for five additional public schools or categories of public schools. It is entirely unclear from both the text of the amendment and the ballot language which of these public schools, or categories of public schools, would be affected. Therefore, the problem "lies not with what the summary says, but, rather, with what it does not say." *Askew*, 421 So.2d at 156. Because voters will simply not be able to understand the true meaning and ramifications of the revision, the ballot language is clearly and conclusively defective.

That the voters will not be informed as to the true meaning and ramifications of the revision is evinced by the varying explanations offered by the proponents....

Because proponents of the proposed revision each give different meaning to the "clear and unambiguous" language of the revision, its title, and its summary, logic dictates that the language is neither clear nor unambiguous. Accordingly, the voters cannot be said to have fair and sufficient notice to intelligently cast his or her vote.

* * *

As demonstrated by the arguments of the Revision 8 proponents, this language either does nothing or changes everything. Considered within the context of the Constitution as a whole, which provides for a State Board of Education that regulates public education at the state level, and the Florida Statutes, which provide five distinct types of public schools, the ballot title and summary to Revision 8 do not ensure that the "electorate is advised of the true meaning, and ramifications, of [the] amendment." *Advisory Opinion to the Attorney Gen. re Tax Limitation*, 644 So.2d at 490 (quoting *Askew*, 421 So.2d at 156).

Conclusion

For the foregoing reasons, we previously affirmed the judgment of the circuit court enjoining Detzner from placing Revision 8 on the ballot for the November 2018 general election. No motion for rehearing will be entertained.

It is so ordered.

LEWIS, J., concurring.

I concur with the majority that Revision 8 should not be placed on the ballot for the November 2018 general election because it fails to clearly state the chief purpose of the revision and it fails to inform voters of its true meaning and ramifications. I also write separately because I believe that there is an additional reason Revision 8 must be stricken — namely, the proposed revision bundles multiple issues into one amendment, which causes confusion and ambiguity as to the chief purpose of the proposal.

Revision 8 attempts to bundle three issues affecting the Florida public school system: (1) school board member term limits, (2) the Legislature's promotion of civic literacy in public schools, and (3) the State's ability to operate, control, and supervise public schools not established by the district school boards — i.e., charter schools, *see* per curiam op. at 809. While all three of these matters concern the public school system on a general level, each targets and affects very specific — and very different — issues within that public school system, which only serves to confuse and distract the public as to the revision's true purpose and effect. In fact, at the March 20, 2018, Constitution Revision Commission (CRC) Session, Revision 8's sponsor, Commissioner Gaetz, explicitly acknowledged that the bundling would "help some of those other education issues pass. I don't think you are going to get too many people in the state of Florida who are going to look at a ballot that says our children ought to be civically literate and say we are sure as heck against that." However, bundling controversial issues into an amendment containing a widely popular issue to trick the voters is precisely the type of misleading language expressly forbidden under section 101.161(1), Florida Statutes (2018).

This Court has from time immemorial warned against bundling multiple issues into one constitutional amendment due to the inherently misleading nature of combining multiple subjects and the problematic choice it requires voters to make. *See City of Coral Gables v. Gray*, 154 Fla. 881, 19 So.2d 318, 322 (1944) ("Yet, if required to vote upon the proposed amendment as presently framed the electors will be put to it to accept, or reject, all subject matters contained therein, in toto, without the opportunity for discrimination. . . . [T]he elector would be put in the position where, in order to aid in carrying a proposition which he considered good or wise, he would be obliged to vote for another which he would otherwise reject as bad or foolish. It would sanction the practice of combining meritorious and vicious legislation in one proposal, so that the former could not be secured without submitting to the latter."); *see also Antuono v. City of Tampa*, 87 Fla. 82, 99 So. 324, 326 (1924). Nevertheless, the constitutional scheme under which the Court operated when announcing these warnings was vastly different than the one under which the Court today operates.

Currently, the Florida Constitution describes four procedures through which the Constitution can be amended or revised: (1) a joint resolution by the Legislature, Art. XI, § 1, Fla. Const., (2) a proposal by a constitution revision commission, Art. XI, § 2, Fla. Const., (3) a citizens' initiative process, Art. XI, § 3, Fla. Const., and (4) the establishment of a constitutional convention, Art. XI, § 4, Fla. Const. Out of these four procedures, only the citizens' initiative contains the restriction that a proposed amendment be limited to one subject. Art. XI, § 3, Fla. Const....

The safeguards we announced allowing public input in the drafting of a constitutional amendment pursuant to sections 1, 2, and 4, however, do not foreclose the possibility that a proposed revision under one of these "safer" constitutional sections might nonetheless impermissibly bundle multiple unrelated issues into one general amendment. Within the context of article XI, section 2, the inquiry turns on whether the bundling of multiple issues within one amendment results in a misleading ballot summary and title. *Cty. of Volusia v. Detzner*, 253 So.3d 507, 512, 2018 WL 4272435 (Fla. Sept. 7, 2018) ("It follows that the bundling of measures creates a defect only if the measures are presented on the ballot in a misleading way."). As discussed by the majority at length, Revision 8's ballot summary language is defective, misleading, and unclear. *See* per curiam op. at 808. In addition to the already-ambiguous language contained within the ballot summary with regard to charter schools, muddling multiple subjects in this proposed revision makes it very difficult—if not impossible—for a voter to fully understand the chief purpose of the measure, as required by section 101.161(1).

A voter cannot intelligently cast his or her ballot if multiple issues of varying complexity and clarity are lumped together under one general amendment—especially when presented through defective ballot summary language....

CANADY, C.J., dissenting.

Because I conclude that the appellees have failed to show that the ballot summary for Revision 8 is clearly and conclusively defective, I dissent from the majority's decision to strike this proposal from the ballot. The majority goes astray by invalidating the proposal on the basis of supposed deficiencies in the text of the proposed amendment itself. Under the standards required by our decisions, the ballot summary here correctly identifies the chief purpose of the proposed amendment. And the summary in no way either affirmatively misleads or misleads by omission. The people of Florida should have the opportunity to vote on this proposal to amend the Constitution.

The challenged portion of the ballot summary, which the majority declares to be defective, relates to a proposed change in article IX, section 4(b) regarding the scope of the duty (and concomitant authority) of school boards to "operate, control, and supervise" free public schools. This constitutional provision currently provides that each school board "shall operate, control and supervise all free public schools within the school district." The proposed amendment limits the scope of this provision to schools "established by the district school board." So under the proposed amendment, each "school board shall operate, control, and supervise all free public schools *established by the district school board* within the school district." (Emphasis added.)

From this proposed change in the text of article IX, section 4(b), five unmistakable and interrelated points emerge. (1) Under the proposed amendment, constitutional room will exist not only for school-board-established schools but also for a category of free public schools that are *not* "established by the district school board." (2) The existing constitutional duty of school boards to "operate, control and supervise" all free public schools will be curtailed by the proposed amendment. (3) Under the proposed amendment, school boards will have the constitutional duty (and concomitant authority) to "operate, control, and supervise" the schools they establish. (4) School boards will not, however, have any such constitutional duty (and authority) regarding schools they do not establish. (5) Understood in the context of the "paramount duty of the state" regarding public education established in article IX, section 1, the "operat[ion], control, and supervis[ion]" of public schools not established by a school board will necessarily be under the purview of the state. Anyone who understands these five points will necessarily understand the chief purpose of this proposed amendment and will not be misled concerning its effect. And anyone who reads the text of the summary will readily be led to an understanding of each basic point.

The summary contains three basic elements regarding this proposed change in the Constitution. These three elements in combination elegantly explain what the amendment does. In the first element, the summary discloses the crucial fact regarding the existing constitutional provision: "Currently, district school boards have a constitutional duty to operate, control, and supervise all public schools." This disclosure of the constitutional status quo provides the necessary basis for understanding the effect of the proposed amendment in curtailing the scope of school board duties. The second and third elements are contained in a single sentence that sets up a contrast: "The amendment *maintains* a school board's duties to public schools it establishes, *but permits* the state to operate, control, and supervise public schools not established by the school board." (Emphasis added.) Thus, the second element of the summary points out that the proposed amendment "*maintains* a school board's duties to public *schools it establishes*." (Emphasis added.) Third, the summary—having identified the scope of the duties of school boards that are maintained—specifies what the proposal changes by stating that the amendment "permits the state to operate, control, and supervise public schools not established by the school board."

The five points that emerge from the text of the amendment are all made evident by these disclosures contained in the summary. The summary brings home the distinction made in the text of the amendment between school-board-established schools and non-school-board-established schools. In doing so, the summary makes clear both that the duty of school boards to "operate, control, and supervise" currently extends to all public schools and that the duty of school boards will be curtailed by the proposed amendment. Explaining the effect of the amendment, the summary identifies the category of school-board-established schools as falling within the scope of the school board's duty to "operate, control, and supervise." It similarly identifies the category of non-school-board-established schools as falling outside the scope of the school board duty to "operate, control, and supervise." And it recognizes the authority of the State regarding the operation, control, and supervision of public schools not established by a school board that necessarily follows from the elimination of the school board duty to "operate, control, and supervise" such schools.

* * *

The majority cites the trial court's conclusion that "both the *text* and the summary are entirely unclear as to which schools will be affected by the revision." Majority op. at 806 (emphasis added). The majority also repeats the trial court's criticism that the ballot summary fails to "inform the voter of the essential role school boards play in authorizing new schools." *Id.* The majority also refers to the trial court's conclusion that the summary is misleading because it "is conspicuously silent about who or what would undertake the[] responsibilities [to operate, control, and supervise] for schools not established by the school board." Majority op. at 806.

Although the majority acknowledges that "we look to objective criteria" in evaluating the sufficiency of a ballot summary, majority op. at 809, it nonetheless focuses on subjective matters by asserting that the deficiency of the summary "is best demonstrated by the proponents of the proposed revision, who each give different meaning to the language of the revision, its title, and its summary." Majority op. at 809. Such subjective matters concerning what various proponents have said about a proposal are beside the point. The majority's line of analysis flies in the face of the principle established in our case law—to which the majority thoughtfully and meaninglessly tips its hat—that in determining whether a summary accurately describes a proposed amendment, "a court must look not to subjective criteria espoused by the amendment's sponsor but to *objective criteria inherent in the amendment itself.*" *Armstrong v. Harris,* 773 So.2d 7, 18 (Fla. 2000) (emphasis added).

* * *

[I]t is clear that the majority is condemning the summary because the text of the amendment leaves open certain questions. The summary thus is rejected because of what the text of the amendment "does not say." Majority op. at 810 (quoting *Askew,* 421 So.2d at 156). There is no requirement that a constitutional amendment resolve all questions concerning its implementation. And it is obvious that a proposed constitutional amendment is not bound by existing statutory terms. Here, as in the case of many constitutional provisions, space is established for the Legislature—which promulgates state policy through laws consistent with the Constitution—to make various policy choices related to implementation of the amendment. As the summary discloses, the amendment clearly affects schools not established by a school board. The policy choices related to such schools are properly left by the amendment to the Legislature. To conclude otherwise—as the majority does—is to attack the substance of the amendment itself.

* * *

In sum, the majority has failed to identify any defect in the summary.[6] The people should not be prevented from making their own decision concerning the merits of the proposed amendment. I strongly dissent from the decision to remove this proposed amendment from the ballot.

POLSTON and LAWSON, JJ., concur.

E. Article XI, Section 6 —
Taxation and Budget Reform Commission

Another intermittent review commission created by Article XI is the Taxation & Budget Reform Commission. This body likewise meets every 20 years, and has since 1987–88. It is likewise created by appointment, including eleven by the Governor, seven by the Speaker of the House, and seven by the President of the Senate. None of these appointees may be members of the Legislature. The Speaker and Senate President each appoint two ex officio members among sitting members of their respective houses and including one member of the minority party.

Unlike the CRC, Article XI, Section 6(d) places a specific mandate on the scope of the Taxation & Budget Reform Commission. The following case explores the limits of this mandate and the possibility of the Commission examining other matters which may or may not relate to its constitutional mission.

Ford v. Browning
992 So. 2d 132 (Fla. 2008)

WELLS, J.

Appellants filed a complaint in the Circuit Court of the Second Judicial Circuit for Leon County, challenging two proposed constitutional amendments submitted by the Taxation and Budget Reform Commission (TBRC) on the ground that TBRC does not have the authority to propose constitutional revisions on these subjects. The first constitutional proposal would amend the freedom of religion provision found in article I, section 3 of the Florida Constitution by eliminating the restriction on state funds being used in aid of any religion and adding a provision that an individual or entity cannot be barred from participating in a public program based on

---

6. [FN 7.] I also reject the view expressed in the concurring opinions that Revision 8 is defective because it bundles three issues into one proposed amendment. The Court recently rejected a similar argument regarding "bundling" in *County of Volusia v. Detzner*, 253 So.3d 507 (Fla. Sept. 7, 2018). Here, as in County of Volusia, "there is no basis for concluding" either "that the relationship between the issues addressed in separate measures identified in the ballot summary results in deception of the voters" or that "the structure of the ballot summary misleads the voters concerning what the proposal will do." *Id.* at 513. The Constitution contains an anti-bundling provision — known as a single subject requirement — in article XI, section 3, which governs certain amendments proposed through the initiative process. No similar requirement is contained in article XI, section 2, which governs proposals advanced by the Constitution Revision Commission. In the absence of such a requirement in the text of section 2, we should not impose one under a different label.

religion. The second constitutional proposal would amend the public education provision found in article IX, section 1, by directing school districts to spend at least sixty-five percent of their funding on classroom instruction and providing that the duty to provide for public education is not exclusively limited to free public schools. The appellants further alleged in their complaint that the ballot title and summary language accompanying one of the proposals did not accurately inform voters as to the true effect of the proposed amendment. They sought an injunction barring the Secretary of State from placing Proposed Amendments 7 and 9 on the ballot for the November 2008 general election.[7] Appellants filed a motion for temporary injunction, which was treated as a motion for final summary judgment. Following briefing and oral argument, the circuit court denied the appellants' motion for summary judgment and granted the cross-motions filed by the appellees and the intervenors, finding that TBRC had the authority to propose the amendments and that the challenged ballot title and summary were not misleading. Appellants appealed the judgment to the First District Court of Appeal, which certified to this Court that this case presents a question of great public importance requiring immediate resolution by this Court in light of the upcoming election. We have jurisdiction under article V, section 3(b)(5), of the Florida Constitution.

ANALYSIS

As an initial matter, it is important to stress that the wisdom or merits of the proposed amendments are not issues before the Court. *See Advisory Op. to the Att'y Gen. re Fla. Marriage Protection Amendment,* 926 So.2d 1229, 1233 (Fla.2006). Rather, the question before the Court is to determine the extent of the authority provided to TBRC by article XI, section 6(e) of the Florida Constitution to propose constitutional amendments and whether the authority extends to Proposed Amendments 7 and 9. Our standard of review is *de novo. See Zingale v. Powell,* 885 So.2d 277, 280 (Fla.2004) ("[C]onstitutional interpretation, like statutory interpretation, is performed *de novo.*").

When reviewing constitutional provisions, this Court "follows principles parallel to those of statutory interpretation." *Zingale,* 885 So.2d at 282. Any question regarding the meaning of a constitutional provision must begin with examining that provision's

---

7. [FN 1.] The ballot title and summary for Proposed Amendment 7 state:
RELIGIOUS FREEDOM
Proposing an amendment to the State Constitution to provide that an individual or entity may not be barred from participating in any public program because of religion and to delete the prohibition against using revenues from the public treasury directly or indirectly in aid of any church, sect, or religious denomination or in aid of any sectarian institution.
The ballot title and summary for Proposed Amendment 9 state:
REQUIRING 65 PERCENT OF SCHOOL FUNDING FOR CLASSROOM INSTRUCTION; STATE'S DUTY FOR CHILDREN'S EDUCATION
Requires at least 65 percent of school funding received by school districts be spent on classroom instruction, rather than administration; allows for differences in administrative expenditures by district. Provides the constitutional requirement for the state to provide a "uniform, efficient, safe, secure, and high quality system of free public schools" is a minimum, nonexclusive duty. Reverses legal precedent prohibiting public funding of private school alternatives to public school programs without creating an entitlement.

explicit language. *See Fla. Soc'y of Ophthalmology v. Fla. Optometric Ass'n*, 489 So.2d 1118, 1119 (Fla.1986). If the constitutional language is clear, unambiguous, and addresses the matter at issue, it must be enforced as written, and courts do not turn to rules of constitutional construction. *Id.* If the explicit language is ambiguous or does not address the exact issue before the court, the court must endeavor to construe the constitutional provision in a manner consistent with the intent of the framers and the voters. *Crist v. Fla. Ass'n of Criminal Defense Lawyers, Inc.*, 978 So.2d 134, 140 (Fla.2008).

* * *

With these principles in mind, we turn to the language involved in the constitutional provision at issue. TBRC was created in 1988 via article XI, section 6, of the Florida Constitution. Subsection 6(d) sets forth TBRC's power to review and study matters; and subsection 6(e) sets forth TBRC's authority to act. Specifically, article XI, section 6(d)–(e), states as follows:

> (d) The commission shall examine the state budgetary process, the revenue needs and expenditure processes of the state, the appropriateness of the tax structure of the state, and governmental productivity and efficiency; review policy as it relates to the ability of state and local government to tax and adequately fund governmental operations and capital facilities required to meet the state's needs during the next twenty year period; determine methods favored by the citizens of the state to fund the needs of the state, including alternative methods for raising sufficient revenues for the needs of the state; determine measures that could be instituted to effectively gather funds from existing tax sources; examine constitutional limitations on taxation and expenditures at the state and local level; and review the state's comprehensive planning, budgeting and needs assessment processes to determine whether the resulting information adequately supports a strategic decisionmaking process.

> (e) The commission shall hold public hearings as it deems necessary to carry out its responsibilities under this section. The commission shall issue a report of the results of the review carried out, and propose to the legislature any recommended statutory changes related to the taxation or budgetary laws of the state. Not later than one hundred eighty days prior to the general election in the second year following the year in which the commission is established, *the commission shall file with the custodian of state records its proposal, if any, of a revision of this constitution or any part of it dealing with taxation or the state budgetary process.*

Art. XI, § 6(d)–(e), Fla. Const. (emphasis added).

The question to be resolved is the meaning of the limitation of TBRC's authority to propose constitutional amendments where that authority is limited to dealing with taxation or the state budgetary process. According to the appellees, TBRC's authority to propose constitutional revisions under subsection 6(e) must be read in conjunction with its powers to review and study matters under subsection 6(d). In support, the appellees point out that under section 6(d), TBRC is directed to "examine constitutional limitations on taxation and expenditures at the state and local level" and allege that it would be illogical for TBRC to examine this issue if it does not have the power to propose constitutional revisions to the voters in respect to both taxation and expenditures. The appellees do not contend that these proposed amendments deal with taxation, but according to the appellees, construing subsections 6(d) and 6(e) together, TBRC has the power to propose constitutional amendments regarding state revenue expenditures because expenditures are encompassed within the state budgetary process. The circuit court agreed and entered its judgment for the appellees.

We disagree. We find the appellees' and the circuit court's construction of section 6(e) to be contrary to the plain and unambiguous language of the constitutional provision. While we recognize that subsection 6(d) sets forth numerous subjects for TBRC to review and study, including "the state budgetary process, the revenue needs and expenditure processes of the state, the appropriateness of the tax structure of the state, *and* governmental productivity and efficiency," *see* art. XI, §6(d), Fla. Const. (emphasis added), we do not conclude that subsection 6(d) can be construed to authorize TBRC to propose constitutional amendments on these subjects. Rather, based on the review authorized by subsection 6(d), subsection 6(e) sets forth four duties that TBRC is authorized to perform: (1) holding public hearings as necessary; (2) issuing a report relative to results of its review; (3) proposing to the Legislature "recommended statutory changes related to the taxation or *budgetary laws of the state*"; and (4) filing proposed constitutional revisions "dealing with taxation or *the state budgetary process.*" Art. XI, §6(e), Fla. Const. (emphasis added). The review and study mandated by section 6(d) are for use in performing these four distinct duties.

In construing the authority given to the Commission in respect to its duties, it is important to recognize that subsection 6(e) expressly draws a distinction between TBRC's authority to propose to the Legislature recommendations of statutory changes related to "taxation or budgetary laws," which could include budgetary expenditures, and TBRC's authority to propose constitutional amendments, which is limited to dealing with "the state budgetary process." It is likewise important to note that subsection 6(e) does not use the phrase "deal with taxation or the state budget." We find that the phrase "the state budgetary process" has a meaning distinct from "budgetary laws of the state" and from "state budget." . . .

If this Court were to accept the appellee's view that the term "state budgetary process" includes any matter that addresses either raising revenue or any State expenditure, this definition would read out the word "process." The ordinary meaning of the word "process" is "a series of actions or operations conducing to an end." *Merriam Webster's Collegiate Dictionary* 929 (10th ed.1994). As this term is applied to "state budgetary process," it means the series of steps and actions that are necessary to producing a budget for the state. In other words, as the appellants suggest, it refers to "the structural and procedural aspects of developing and implementing the state budget." Additionally, if we were to accept the appellees' view that "state budgetary process" includes any matter that either raises revenue or involves any state expenditure, it would also render the term "taxation" superfluous since taxation is the raising of revenue.

We conclude that this construction is also consistent with TBRC's rule 1.005 (Functions and Duties), which provides in pertinent part:

> The "state budgetary process" means *the manner in which* every level of government in the state expends funds, incurs debt, assesses needs, acquires financial information, and administers its fiscal affairs, and includes the legislative appropriation process and the budgetary practices and principles of all agencies and subdivisions of the state involved in financial planning, determining, implementing, administering, and reviewing governmental programs and services.

See TBRC Rule 1.005 (2008) (emphasis added). The phrase "the manner in which" modifies the rest of TBRC's own definition of the term.

This plain meaning definition is also consistent with how "state budgeting process" is used in article III, section 19 of the Florida Constitution (entitled "State Budgeting, Planning and Appropriations Processes"), and Chapter 216, Florida Statutes, which sets forth various planning and budgeting processes.

* * *

TBRC is a constitutional body that has only those powers which were specifically designated to it. If certain powers are not explicitly provided to the Commission, this Court cannot add to the constitutional limitations by expanding its authority beyond the provisions stated. *See Southern Armored Serv., Inc. v. Mason,* 167 So.2d 848, 850 (Fla.1964) (holding that a commission is a body with special and limited power and "[i]t can only exercise the power expressly or impliedly granted to it and any reasonable doubt of existence of any power must be resolved against the exercise thereof").

We find that the plain reading of the term "state budgetary process" is clear and unambiguous—TBRC's jurisdiction to propose constitutional amendments does not extend to a subject solely because the State will expend funds on that subject or because it could affect the State's expenditures. TBRC's authority to propose constitutional amendments directly to the voters is constitutionally limited to two scenarios: if the proposal addresses taxation or the process by which the State's budget is procedurally composed and considered by the Legislature....

In the first challenged proposed amendment, Amendment 7 would amend article I, section 3, of the Florida Constitution, as follows:

> SECTION 3. Religious freedom.—There shall be no law respecting the establishment of religion or prohibiting or penalizing the free exercise thereof. Religious freedom shall not justify practices inconsistent with public morals, peace or safety. <u>An individual or entity may not be barred from participating in any public program because of religion.</u> ~~No revenue of the state or any~~

~~political subdivision or agency thereof shall ever be taken from the public treasury directly or indirectly in aid of any church, sect, or religious denomination or in aid of any sectarian institution.~~

(New language is indicated by underlining, and deleted language is struck through.) This proposal clearly does not address taxation or the state budgetary process as we have construed that provision.

In the next proposal, Amendment 9 would modify article IX, regarding education, by modifying article IX, section 1(a) to state as follows:

SECTION 1: Public <u>funding of</u> education.—

(a) The education of children is a fundamental value of the people of the State of Florida. It is, therefore, a paramount duty of the state to make adequate provision for the education of all children residing within its borders. <u>This duty shall be fulfilled, at a minimum and not exclusively, through adequate</u> ~~Adequate~~ provision ~~shall be made~~ by law for a uniform, efficient, safe, secure, and high quality system of free public schools that allows students to obtain a high quality education and for the establishment, maintenance, and operation of institutions of higher learning and other public education programs that the needs of the people may require. <u>Nothing in this subsection creates an entitlement to a publicly-financed private program.</u>

Proposed Amendment 9 would also add a new section 8 to article IX:

SECTION 8. Requiring sixty-five percent of school funding for classroom instruction.—At least sixty-five percent of the school funding received by school districts shall be spent on classroom instruction, rather than on administration. Classroom instruction and administration shall be defined by law. The legislature may also address differences in administrative expenditures by district for necessary services, such as transportation and food services. Funds for capital outlay shall not be included in the calculation required by this section.

Again, the appellees assert that TBRC has the authority to propose this constitutional amendment because it addresses a constitutional limitation on expenditures and is thus part of the state budgetary process since expenditures are a part of the process. For the reasons addressed above, as this amendment involves merely specific expenditures and not the budgetary process, we hold that TBRC exceeded its constitutional authority in proposing Amendment 9.

* * *

It is so ordered.

LEWIS, J., concurring.

I fully concur in the decision of the majority that TBRC lacked the authority to propose Amendments 7 and 9. I write separately to emphasize that, even if TBRC possessed the authority, proposed Amendment 9 is defective and would have been removed from the 2008 November general election ballot because of its misleading title. Section 101.161(1), Florida Statutes (2007), which governs the statutory requirements for ballot titles and summaries for constitutional amendments, states:

> Whenever a constitutional amendment or other public measure is submitted to the vote of the people, the substance of such amendment or other public measure shall be printed in *clear and unambiguous language* on the ballot.

(Emphasis supplied.)

As noted by the majority, the ballot title of Amendment 9 provides:

REQUIRING 65 PERCENT OF SCHOOL FUNDING FOR CLASSROOM INSTRUCTION; STATE'S DUTY FOR CHILDREN'S EDUCATION

This limited, narrow title clearly implies that Amendment 9 solely addresses the percentage of school funding which must be allocated to classroom instruction. The title completely fails to mention that proposed Amendment 9 eliminates existing Florida law that a statutory "voucher program" is contrary to the constitutionally-required "uniform, efficient, safe, secure, and high quality system of free public schools." Art. IX, § 1(a), Fla. Const.; *see Bush v. Holmes,* 919 So.2d 392, 412–13 (Fla.2006) (holding that statutorily created Opportunity Scholarship Program failed to comply with article IX, section 1(a) of the Florida Constitution). I recognize that the ballot summary mentions this effect of the proposed amendment. However, a limited, restrictive title which touts one effect of a proposed amendment, but totally fails to mention a very significant effect of that amendment, is inherently misleading. Voters who read the ballot title would be misinformed with regard to the full scope of proposed Amendment 9.

The complete failure to mention in the ballot title of proposed Amendment 9 the significant change it would produce in Florida law is not a matter of statutory word limits, nor is it a matter of creating a simple title by which the proposed Amendment shall be known. The highlighting of one significant change implemented by a proposed amendment in the ballot title, but to omit the second, equally or more significant change—by total omission from the title and, instead, relegating its sole reference to the last sentence in the ballot summary—constitutes nothing more than word play in an attempt to achieve passage of the proposed amendment. This is a classic example of "hiding the ball."

* * *

Florida law requires the use of straightforward and direct language in a ballot title and summary, not creative "wordsmithing" in an attempt to ensure passage.

ANSTEAD and PARIENTE, JJ., concur.

Questions

1. In *Ford v. Browning,* how does the Supreme Court describe the limits on the power of the Taxation and Budget Reform Commission to proposed constitutional amendments? Why did the Court reject the Commission's argument that this authority extended to amendments regarding state revenue expenditures?

2. What were the flaws in the Commission's two proposed amendments?

Index